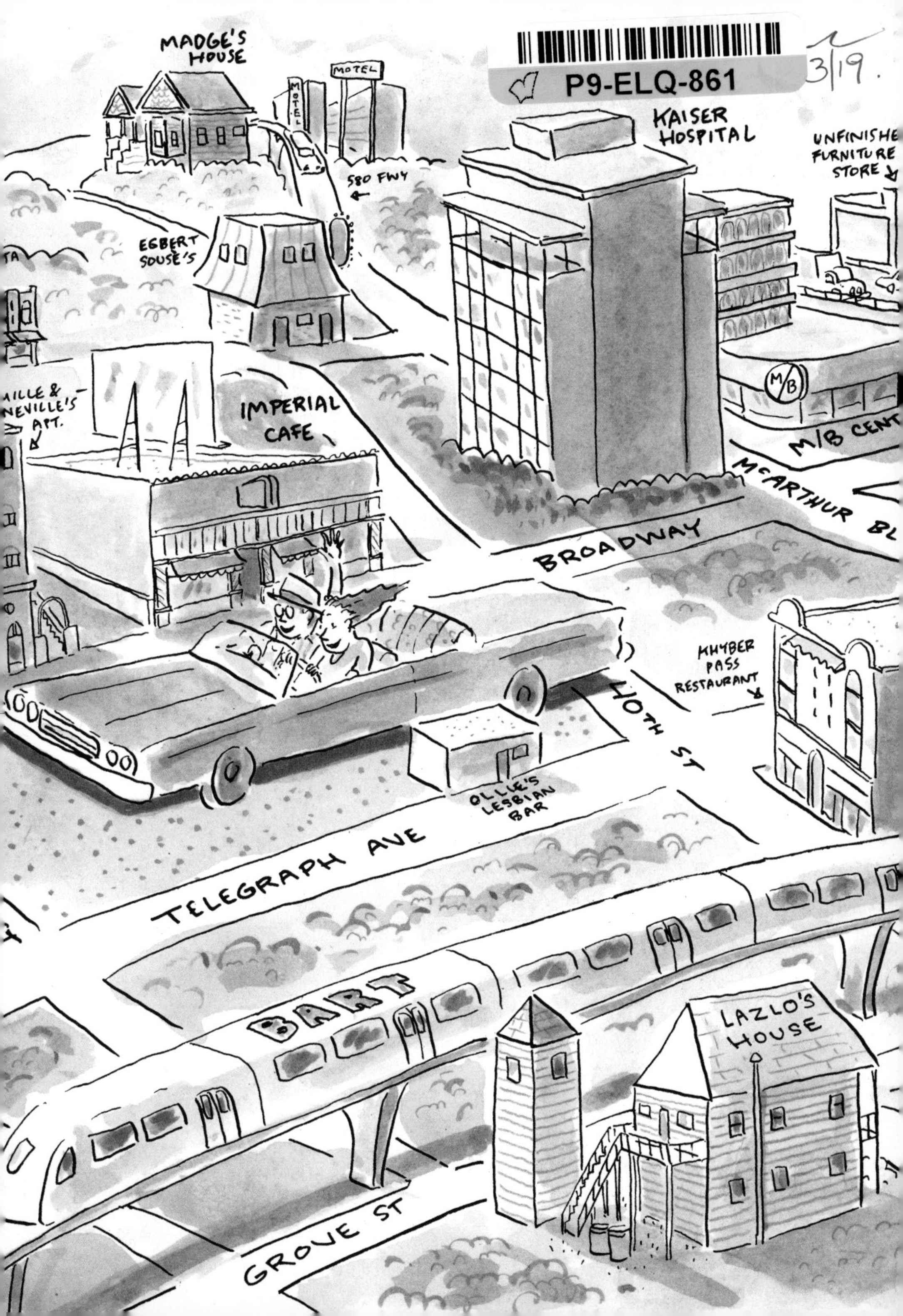
MADGE'S HOUSE
MOTEL
MOTEL
580 FWY
KAISER HOSPITAL
UNFINISHE FURNITURE STORE
EGBERT SOUSE'S
MILLE & NEVILLE'S APT.
IMPERIAL CAFE
M/B
M/B CENT
McARTHUR BL
BROADWAY
KHYBER PASS RESTAURANT
40TH ST
OLLIE'S LESBIAN BAR
TELEGRAPH AVE
BART
LAZLO'S HOUSE
GROVE ST

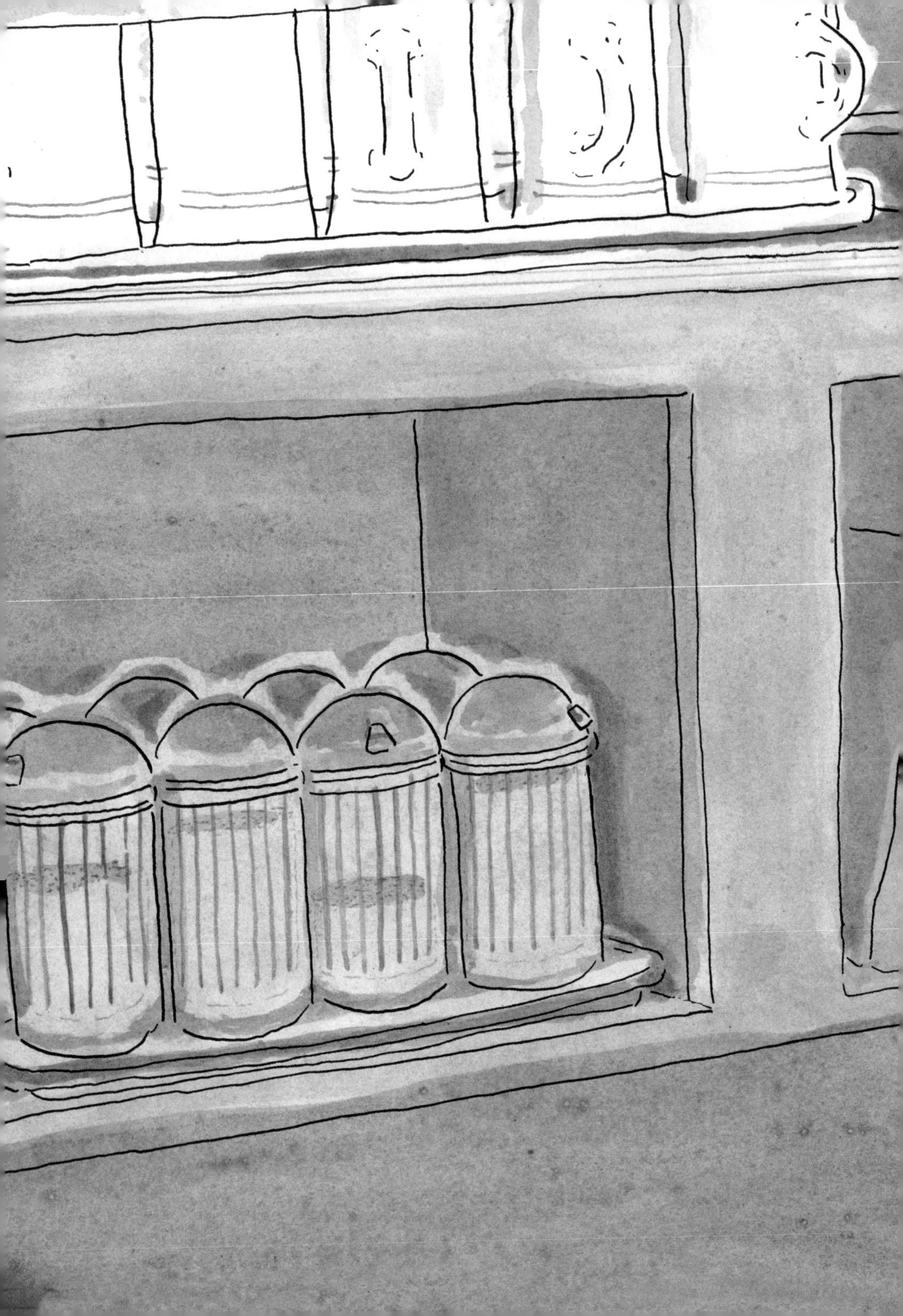

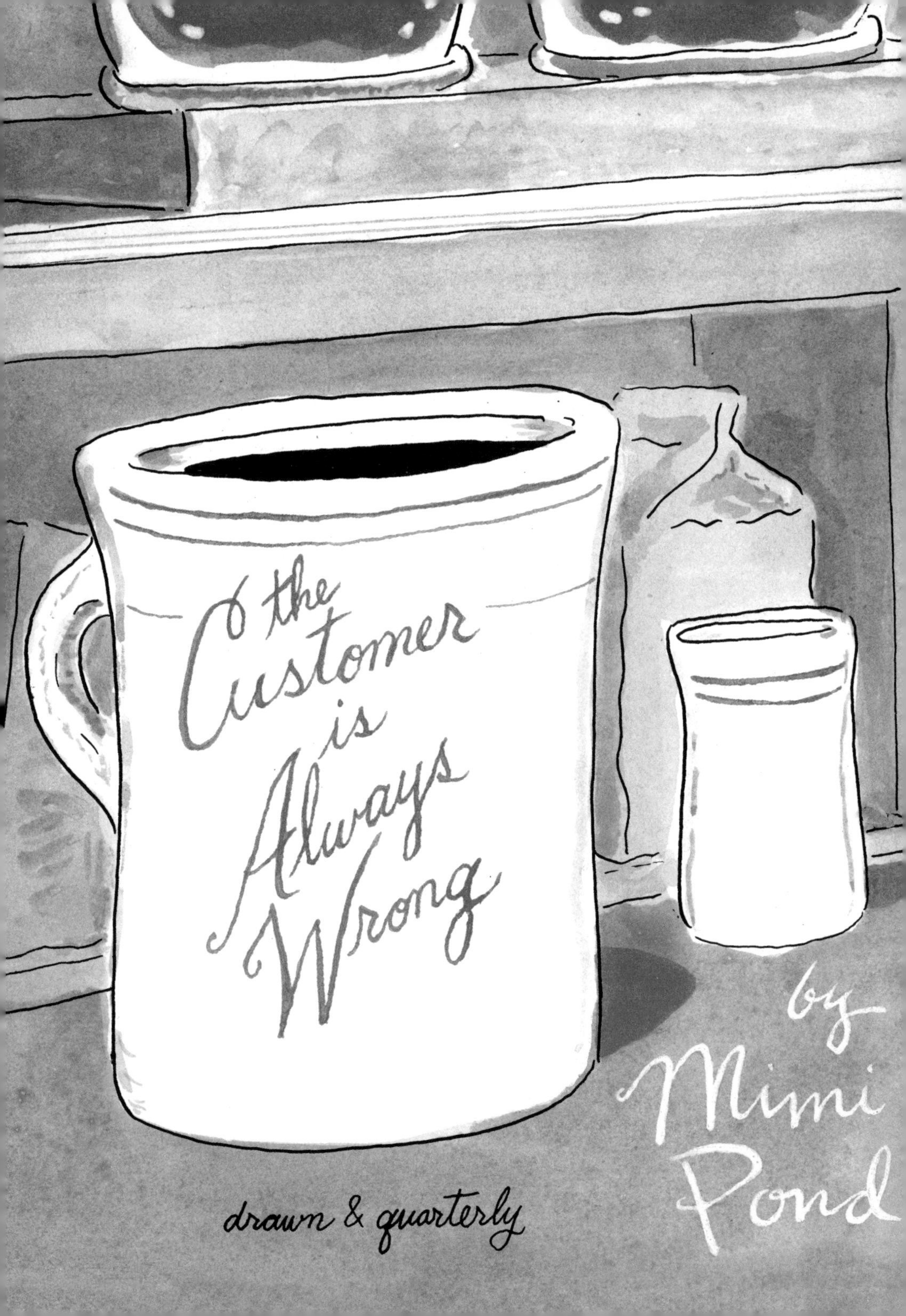
the Customer is Always Wrong
by Mimi Pond
drawn & quarterly

GRAPHIC
PON

DISCLAIMER

THIS GRAPHIC NOVEL IS A FICTIONALIZED MEMOIR BASED ON PERSONAL EXPERIENCES OF THE AUTHOR. THE NAMES HAVE BEEN CHANGED, AND CERTAIN CHARACTERS, PLACES, AND INCIDENTS HAVE BEEN MODIFIED IN SERVICE TO THE STORY.

DRAWNANDQUARTERLY.COM
MIMIPOND.COM

FIRST EDITION: AUGUST 2017
PRINTED IN CHINA
10 9 8 7 6 5 4 3 2 1

LIBRARY AND ARCHIVES CANADA CATALOGUING IN PUBLICATION
POND, MIMI, AUTHOR
          THE CUSTOMER IS ALWAYS WRONG / MIMI POND
ISBN 978-1-77046-282-3 (HARDBACK)
    1. GRAPHIC NOVELS.   I. TITLE.
PNG727. P66C87 2017   741.5'973   C2016-905190-0

PUBLISHED IN THE USA BY DRAWN & QUARTERLY,
A CLIENT PUBLISHER OF FARRAR, STRAUS AND GIROUX.
ORDERS: 888. 330. 8477

PUBLISHED IN CANADA BY DRAWN & QUARTERLY,
A CLIENT PUBLISHER OF RAINCOAST BOOKS.
ORDERS: 800. 663. 5714

PUBLISHED IN THE UNITED KINGDOM BY DRAWN & QUARTERLY,
A CLIENT PUBLISHER OF PUBLISHERS GROUP UK.
ORDERS: INFO @ PGUK. CO. UK

THANKS

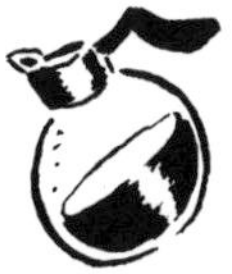

MY HUSBAND, **WAYNE WHITE**, THE UNDISPUTED GENIUS, THE GIANT, THE HARDEST WORKING MAN IN ART, HAS ALWAYS BEEN MY MOST STALWART CHEERLEADER, MY ROCK, MY ROLE MODEL, AND A HUNK OF BURNING LOVE. I CAN'T IMAGINE TRYING TO COMPLETE **THE CUSTOMER IS ALWAYS WRONG** OR **OVER EASY** WITHOUT HIM.

OUR CHILDREN, **WOODROW** AND **LULU WHITE**, ARE THE VERY CENTER OF MY LIFE AND HAVE ALWAYS GIVEN ME JOY, DELIGHT, STRENGTH, AND UNCONDITIONAL LOVE. THEIR ENDURING FAITH IN ME AND MY WORK HAS MEANT EVERYTHING. IF I HAVE LEARNED ANYTHING AS A MOTHER, IT IS THAT YOUR DREAMS ARE ALSO YOUR CHILDREN'S DREAMS. THEY NEED TO KNOW THAT YOUR HOPES AND YOUR DREAMS ARE ACHIEVABLE AND NOT TO BE SET ASIDE. IT'S LIKE THEY SAY: **IF MAMA AIN'T HAPPY, AIN'T NOBODY HAPPY.**

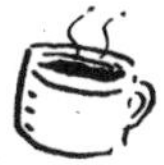

TOM DEVLIN, PEGGY BURNS, CHRIS OLIVEROS, JULIA POHL-MIRANDA, TRACY HURREN, ANN CUNNINGHAM, SAM TSE, AND EVERYONE ELSE AT DRAWN & QUARTERLY HAS BEEN AN AUTHOR'S DREAM OF WHAT A PUBLISHER SHOULD BE: COMPLETELY SUPPORTIVE, SMART, CRAFTY, SPECTACULARLY TALENTED AND DELIGHTFUL AT EVERY TURN, A RARE THING IN THIS CRAVEN WORLD. AND WITHOUT THE SAGE COUNSEL OF THE CANNY CHUCK VALAUSKAS, WHERE WOULD WE BE?

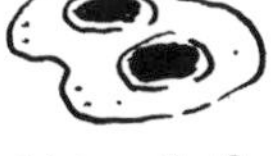

MANY OF THE DELIGHTFULLY MOTLEY CREW WITH WHOM I WORKED AT **MAMA'S ROYAL CAFE** IN OAKLAND, CALIFORNIA FROM 1978-1982 HAVE SHARED WITH ME THEIR UNFORGETTABLE STORIES, QUIPS, GOSSIP, AND LIFE LESSONS LEARNED. I WROTE THEM DOWN AND TRIED TO WEAVE THEM INTO A PLAUSIBLE METAPHOR FOR THE WAY WE LIVED THEN. I AM GRATEFUL TO THEM ALL.

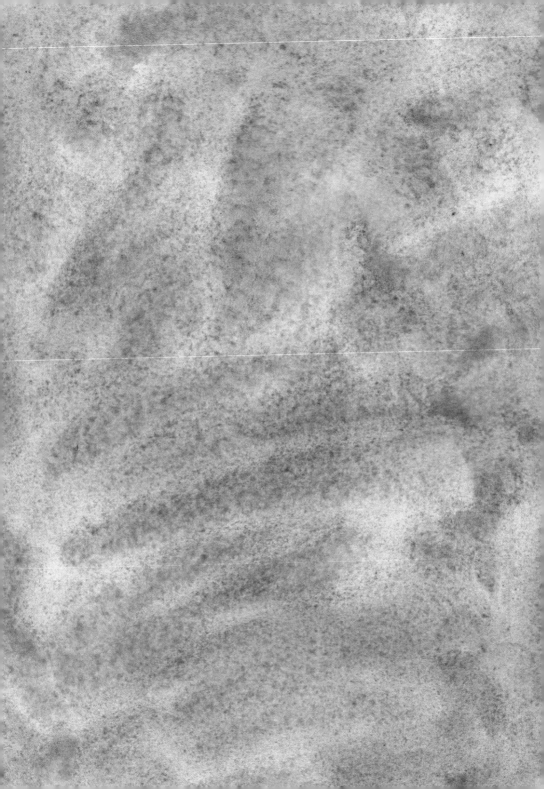

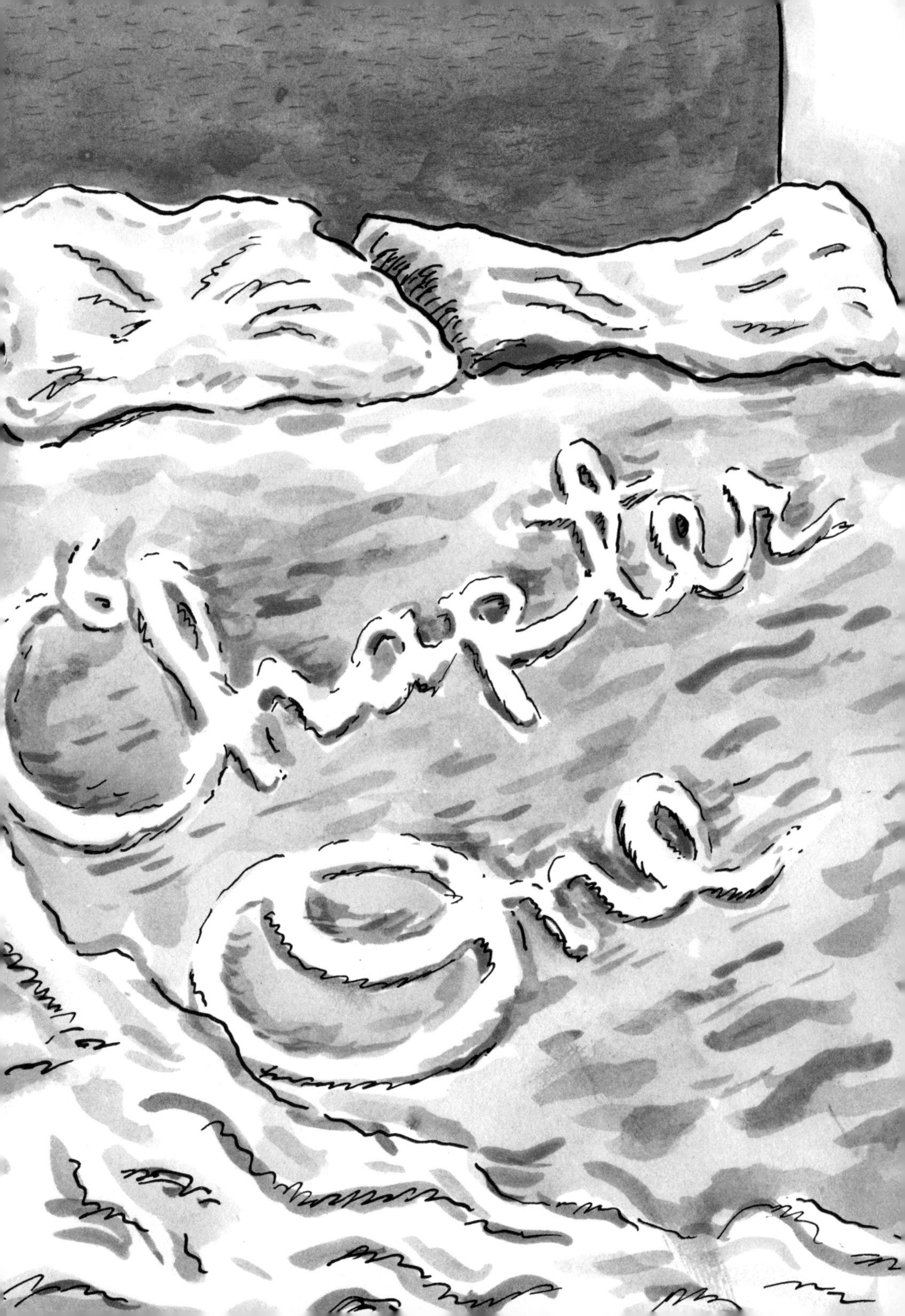
Chapter
One

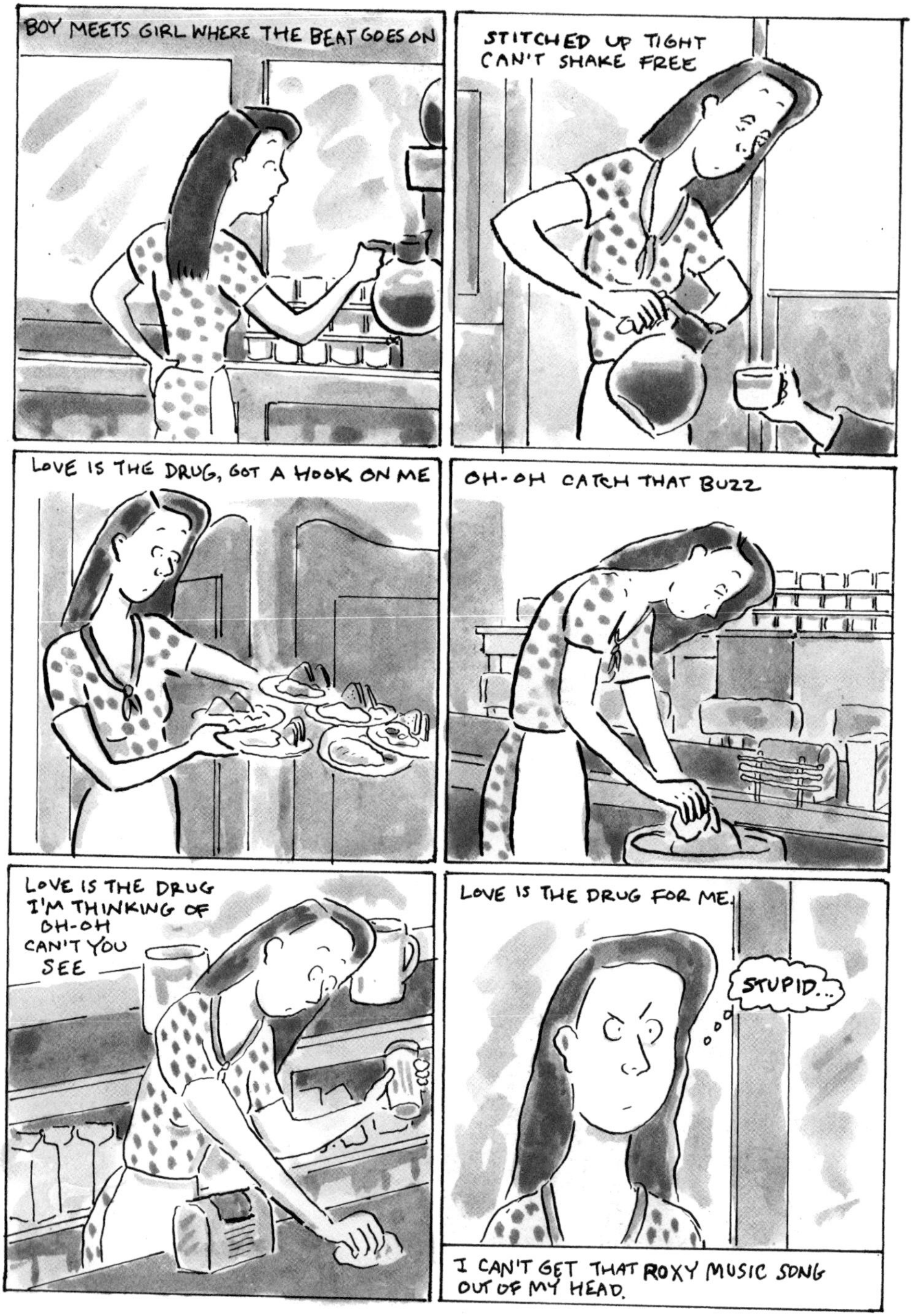
BOY MEETS GIRL WHERE THE BEAT GOES ON
STITCHED UP TIGHT
CAN'T SHAKE FREE
LOVE IS THE DRUG, GOT A HOOK ON ME
OH-OH CATCH THAT BUZZ
LOVE IS THE DRUG
I'M THINKING OF
OH-OH
CAN'T YOU
SEE
LOVE IS THE DRUG FOR ME.
STUPID...
I CAN'T GET THAT ROXY MUSIC SONG
OUT OF MY HEAD.

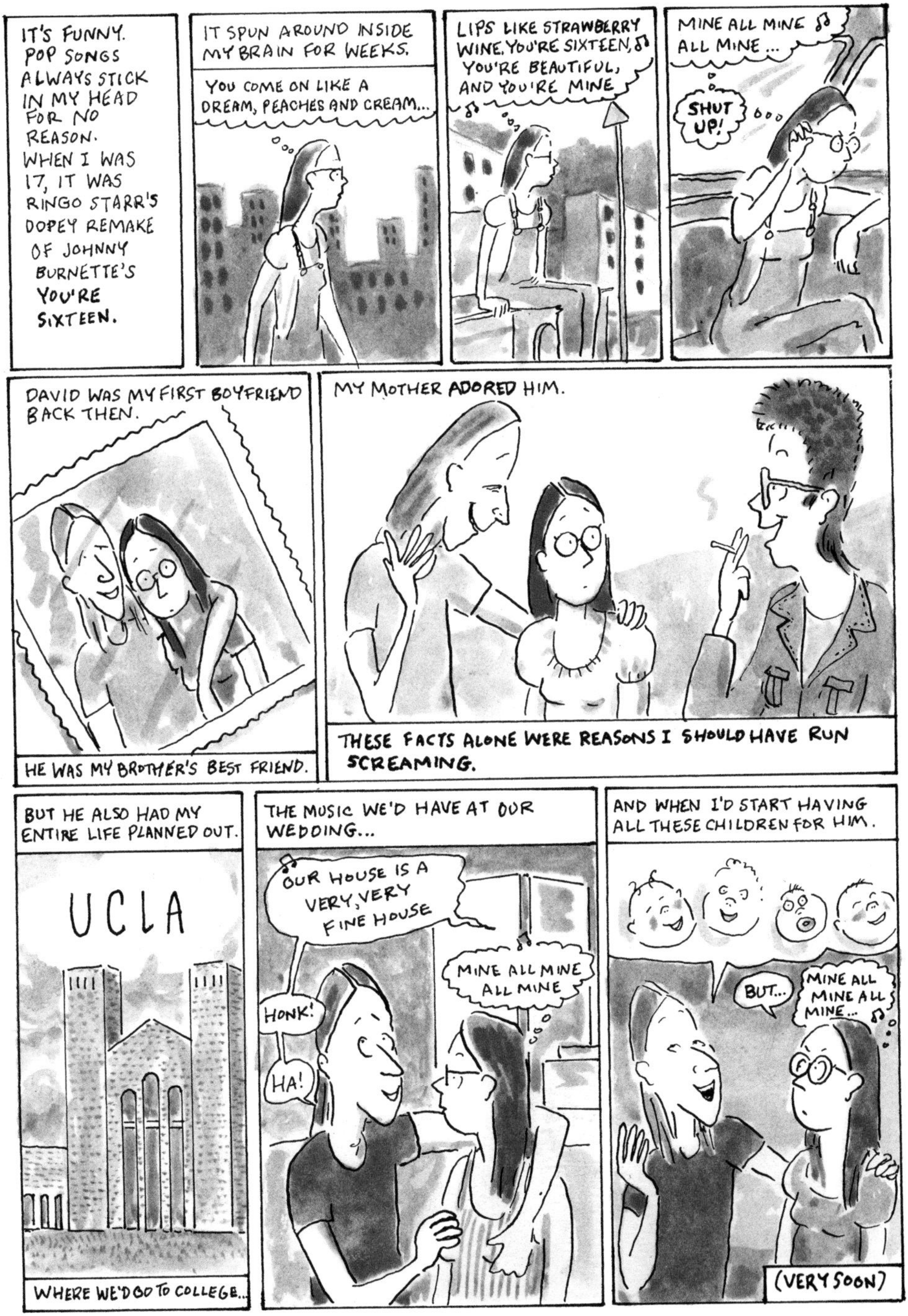
IT'S FUNNY. POP SONGS ALWAYS STICK IN MY HEAD FOR NO REASON. WHEN I WAS 17, IT WAS RINGO STARR'S DOPEY REMAKE OF JOHNNY BURNETTE'S YOU'RE SIXTEEN.
IT SPUN AROUND INSIDE MY BRAIN FOR WEEKS.
YOU COME ON LIKE A DREAM, PEACHES AND CREAM...
LIPS LIKE STRAWBERRY WINE, YOU'RE SIXTEEN, YOU'RE BEAUTIFUL, AND YOU'RE MINE
MINE ALL MINE ALL MINE...
SHUT UP!
DAVID WAS MY FIRST BOYFRIEND BACK THEN.
HE WAS MY BROTHER'S BEST FRIEND.
MY MOTHER ADORED HIM.
THESE FACTS ALONE WERE REASONS I SHOULD HAVE RUN SCREAMING.
BUT HE ALSO HAD MY ENTIRE LIFE PLANNED OUT.
UCLA
WHERE WE'D GO TO COLLEGE...
THE MUSIC WE'D HAVE AT OUR WEDDING...
OUR HOUSE IS A VERY, VERY FINE HOUSE
HONK!
HA!
MINE ALL MINE ALL MINE
AND WHEN I'D START HAVING ALL THESE CHILDREN FOR HIM.
BUT...
MINE ALL MINE ALL MINE...
(VERY SOON)

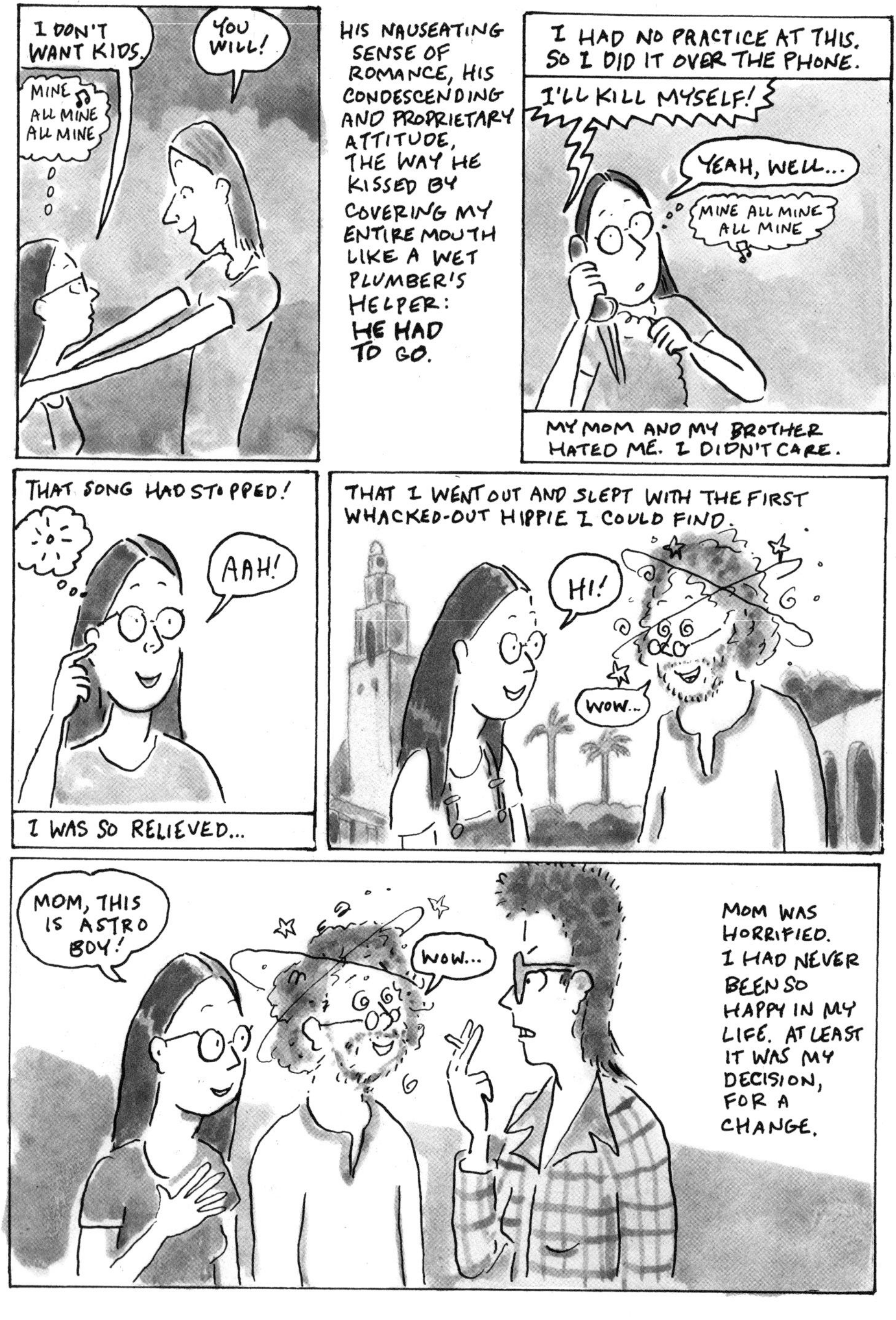
I DON'T WANT KIDS.
YOU WILL!
MINE ALL MINE ALL MINE
HIS NAUSEATING SENSE OF ROMANCE, HIS CONDESCENDING AND PROPRIETARY ATTITUDE, THE WAY HE KISSED BY COVERING MY ENTIRE MOUTH LIKE A WET PLUMBER'S HELPER: HE HAD TO GO.
I HAD NO PRACTICE AT THIS. SO I DID IT OVER THE PHONE.
I'LL KILL MYSELF!
YEAH, WELL...
MINE ALL MINE ALL MINE
MY MOM AND MY BROTHER HATED ME. I DIDN'T CARE.
THAT SONG HAD STOPPED!
AAH!
I WAS SO RELIEVED...
THAT I WENT OUT AND SLEPT WITH THE FIRST WHACKED-OUT HIPPIE I COULD FIND.
HI!
WOW...
MOM, THIS IS ASTRO BOY!
WOW...
MOM WAS HORRIFIED. I HAD NEVER BEEN SO HAPPY IN MY LIFE. AT LEAST IT WAS MY DECISION, FOR A CHANGE.

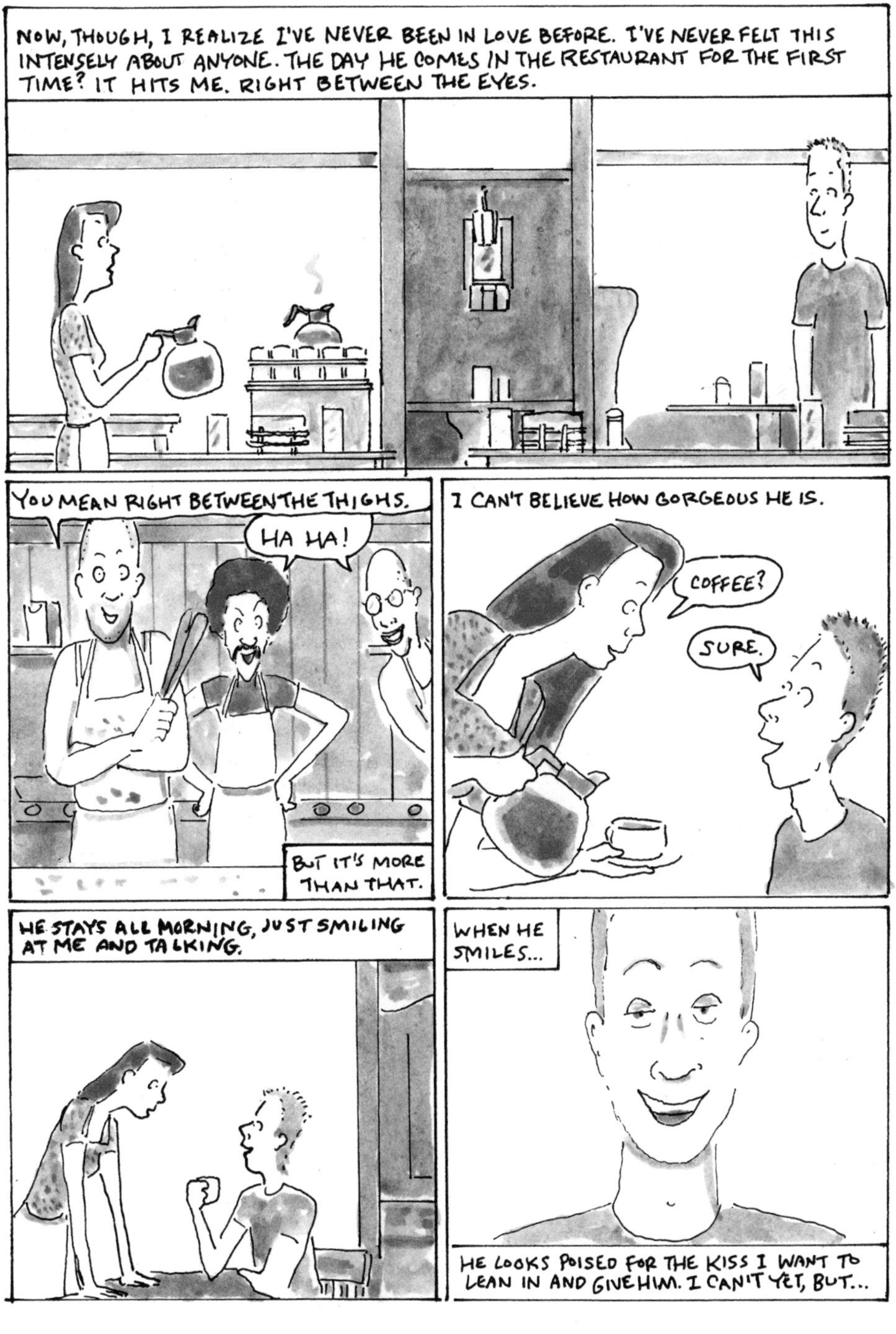
NOW, THOUGH, I REALIZE I'VE NEVER BEEN IN LOVE BEFORE. I'VE NEVER FELT THIS INTENSELY ABOUT ANYONE. THE DAY HE COMES IN THE RESTAURANT FOR THE FIRST TIME? IT HITS ME. RIGHT BETWEEN THE EYES.
YOU MEAN RIGHT BETWEEN THE THIGHS.
HA HA!
BUT IT'S MORE THAN THAT.
I CAN'T BELIEVE HOW GORGEOUS HE IS.
COFFEE?
SURE.
HE STAYS ALL MORNING, JUST SMILING AT ME AND TALKING.
WHEN HE SMILES...
HE LOOKS POISED FOR THE KISS I WANT TO LEAN IN AND GIVE HIM. I CAN'T YET, BUT...

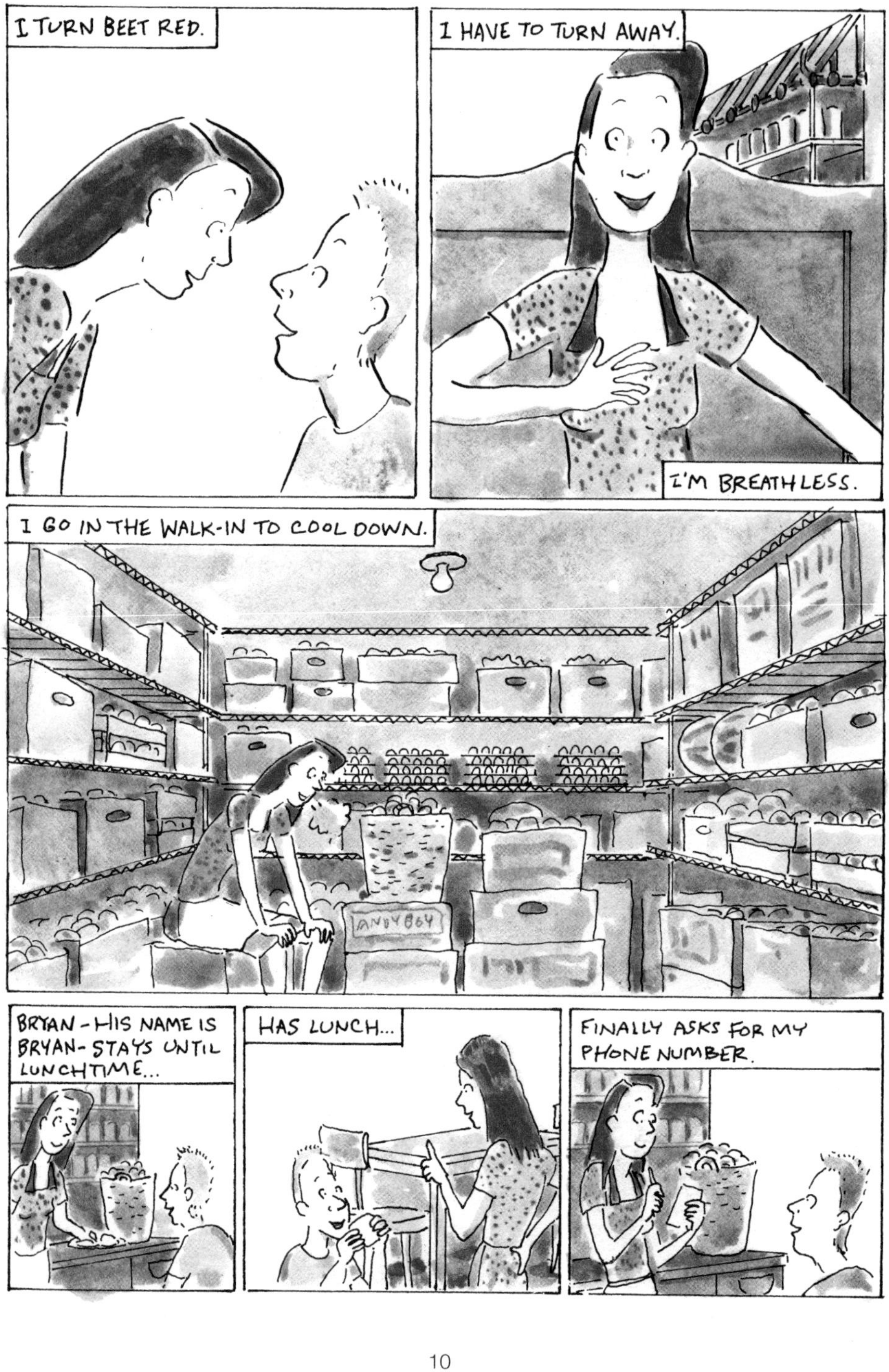
I TURN BEET RED.
I HAVE TO TURN AWAY.
I'M BREATHLESS.
I GO IN THE WALK-IN TO COOL DOWN.
BRYAN - HIS NAME IS BRYAN - STAYS UNTIL LUNCHTIME...
HAS LUNCH...
FINALLY ASKS FOR MY PHONE NUMBER.

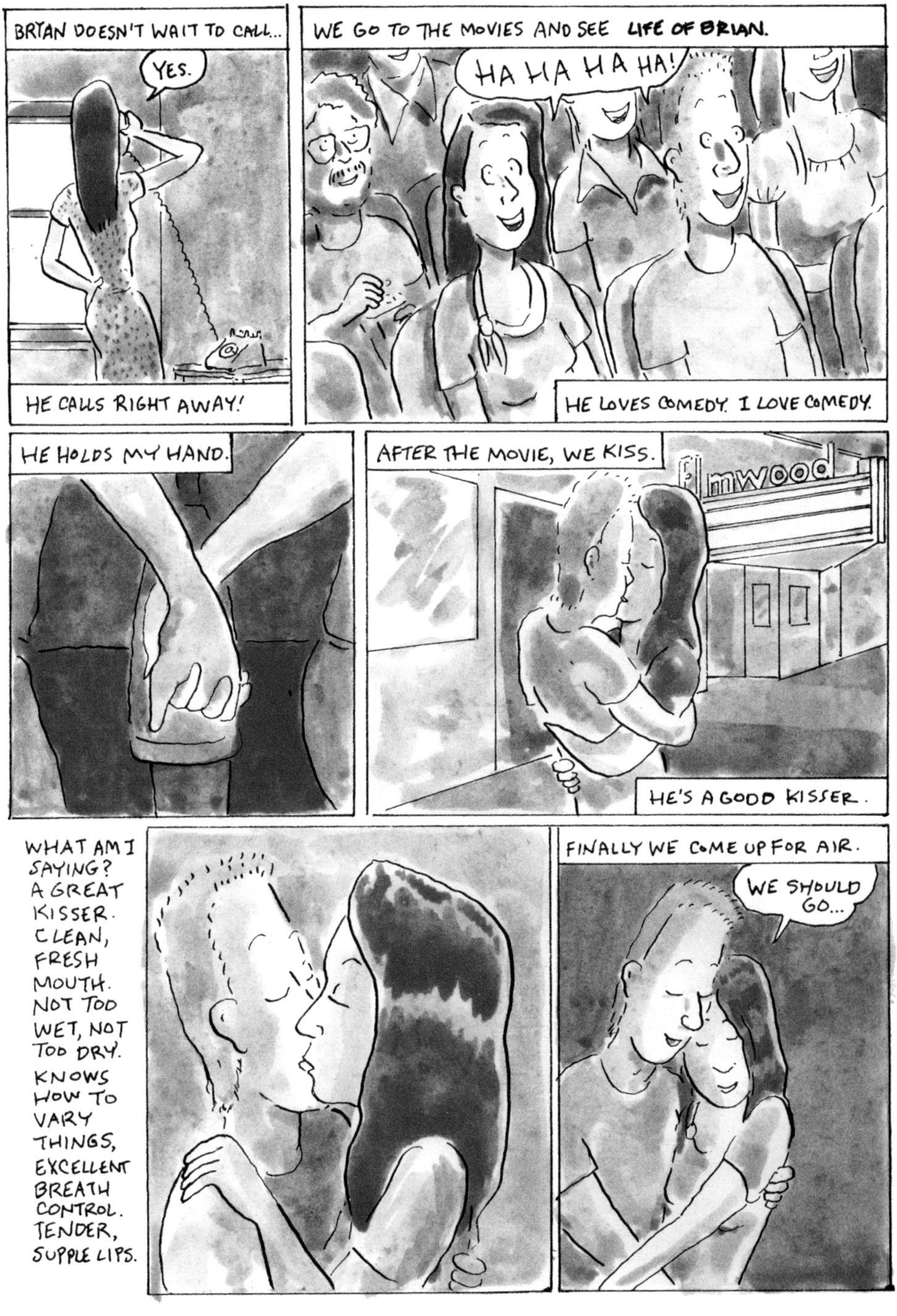
BRYAN DOESN'T WAIT TO CALL...
YES.
HE CALLS RIGHT AWAY!
WE GO TO THE MOVIES AND SEE LIFE OF BRIAN.
HA HA HA HA HA!
HE LOVES COMEDY. I LOVE COMEDY.
HE HOLDS MY HAND.
AFTER THE MOVIE, WE KISS.
Elmwood
HE'S A GOOD KISSER.
WHAT AM I SAYING? A GREAT KISSER. CLEAN, FRESH MOUTH. NOT TOO WET, NOT TOO DRY. KNOWS HOW TO VARY THINGS, EXCELLENT BREATH CONTROL. TENDER, SUPPLE LIPS.
FINALLY WE COME UP FOR AIR.
WE SHOULD GO...

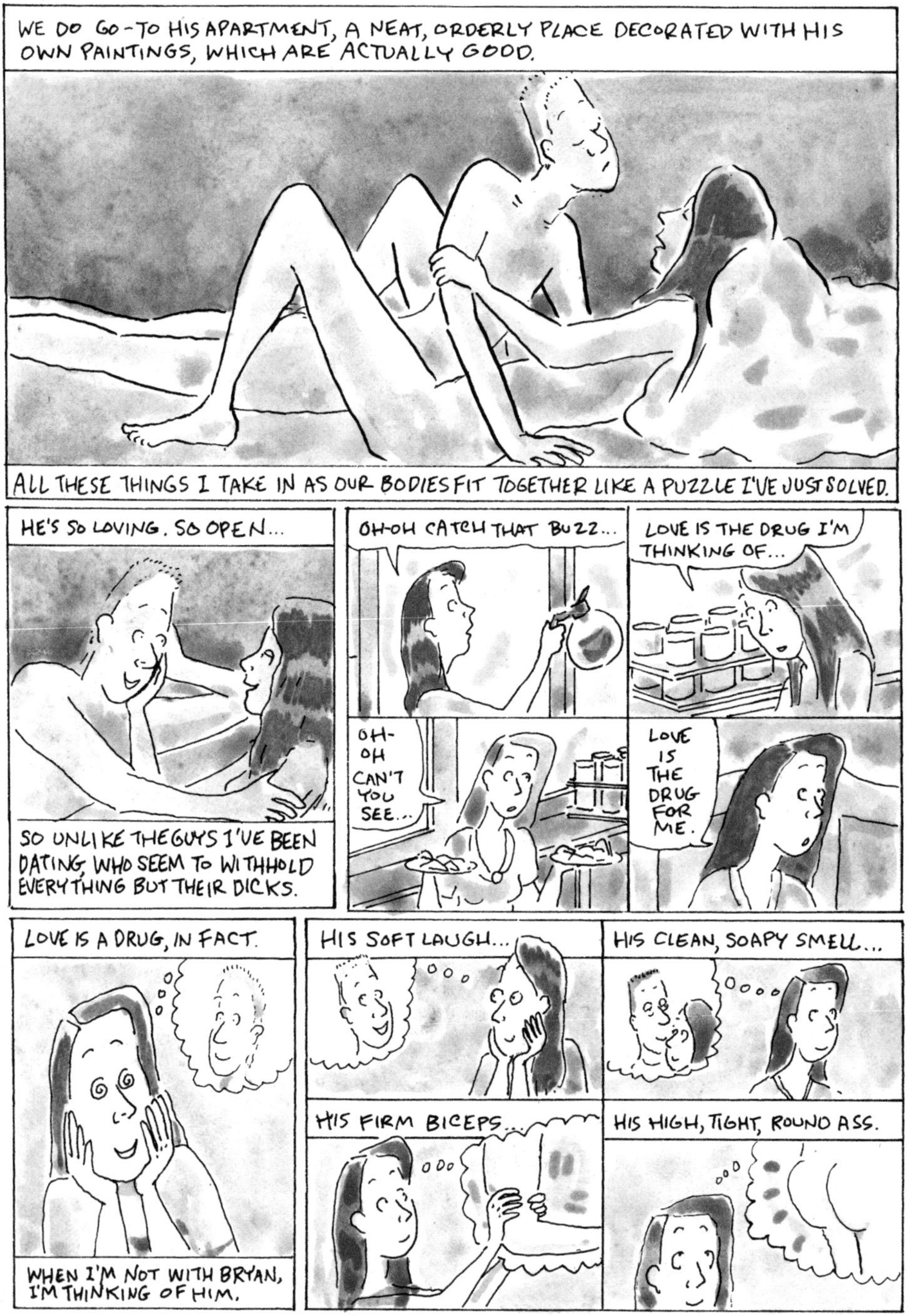
WE DO GO - TO HIS APARTMENT, A NEAT, ORDERLY PLACE DECORATED WITH HIS OWN PAINTINGS, WHICH ARE ACTUALLY GOOD.
ALL THESE THINGS I TAKE IN AS OUR BODIES FIT TOGETHER LIKE A PUZZLE I'VE JUST SOLVED.
HE'S SO LOVING. SO OPEN...
SO UNLIKE THE GUYS I'VE BEEN DATING, WHO SEEM TO WITHHOLD EVERYTHING BUT THEIR DICKS.
OH-OH CATCH THAT BUZZ...
LOVE IS THE DRUG I'M THINKING OF...
OH-OH CAN'T YOU SEE...
LOVE IS THE DRUG FOR ME.
LOVE IS A DRUG, IN FACT.
WHEN I'M NOT WITH BRYAN, I'M THINKING OF HIM.
HIS SOFT LAUGH...
HIS CLEAN, SOAPY SMELL...
HIS FIRM BICEPS...
HIS HIGH, TIGHT, ROUND ASS.

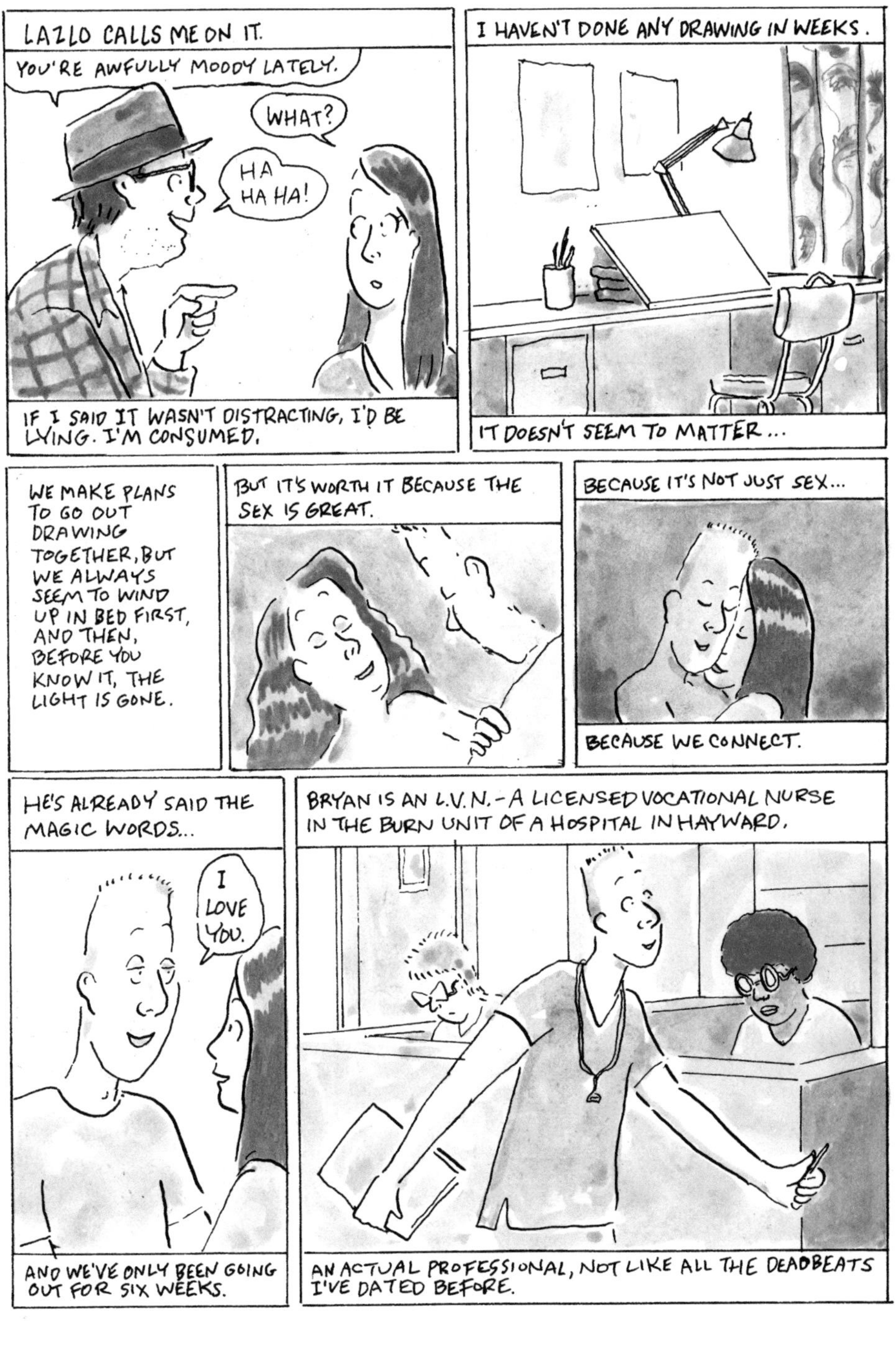
LAZLO CALLS ME ON IT.
YOU'RE AWFULLY MOODY LATELY.
WHAT?
HA HA HA!
IF I SAID IT WASN'T DISTRACTING, I'D BE LYING. I'M CONSUMED.
I HAVEN'T DONE ANY DRAWING IN WEEKS.
IT DOESN'T SEEM TO MATTER...
WE MAKE PLANS TO GO OUT DRAWING TOGETHER, BUT WE ALWAYS SEEM TO WIND UP IN BED FIRST, AND THEN, BEFORE YOU KNOW IT, THE LIGHT IS GONE.
BUT IT'S WORTH IT BECAUSE THE SEX IS GREAT.
BECAUSE IT'S NOT JUST SEX...
BECAUSE WE CONNECT.
HE'S ALREADY SAID THE MAGIC WORDS...
I LOVE YOU.
AND WE'VE ONLY BEEN GOING OUT FOR SIX WEEKS.
BRYAN IS AN L.V.N.-A LICENSED VOCATIONAL NURSE IN THE BURN UNIT OF A HOSPITAL IN HAYWARD.
AN ACTUAL PROFESSIONAL, NOT LIKE ALL THE DEADBEATS I'VE DATED BEFORE.

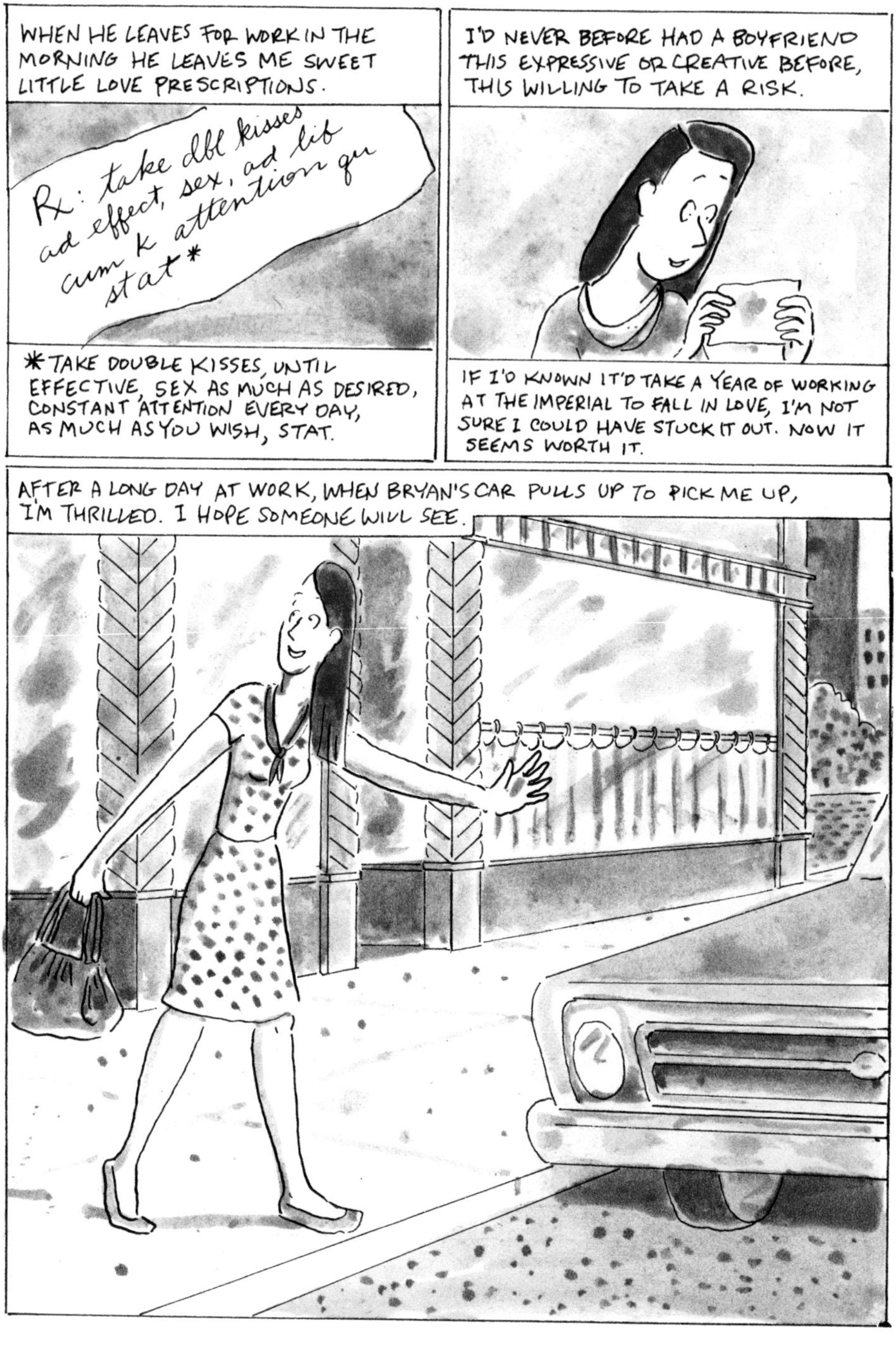
WHEN HE LEAVES FOR WORK IN THE MORNING HE LEAVES ME SWEET LITTLE LOVE PRESCRIPTIONS.
Rx: take dbl kisses ad effect, sex, ad lib cum k attention qu stat*
*TAKE DOUBLE KISSES, UNTIL EFFECTIVE, SEX AS MUCH AS DESIRED, CONSTANT ATTENTION EVERY DAY, AS MUCH AS YOU WISH, STAT.
I'D NEVER BEFORE HAD A BOYFRIEND THIS EXPRESSIVE OR CREATIVE BEFORE, THIS WILLING TO TAKE A RISK.
IF I'D KNOWN IT'D TAKE A YEAR OF WORKING AT THE IMPERIAL TO FALL IN LOVE, I'M NOT SURE I COULD HAVE STUCK IT OUT. NOW IT SEEMS WORTH IT.
AFTER A LONG DAY AT WORK, WHEN BRYAN'S CAR PULLS UP TO PICK ME UP, I'M THRILLED. I HOPE SOMEONE WILL SEE.

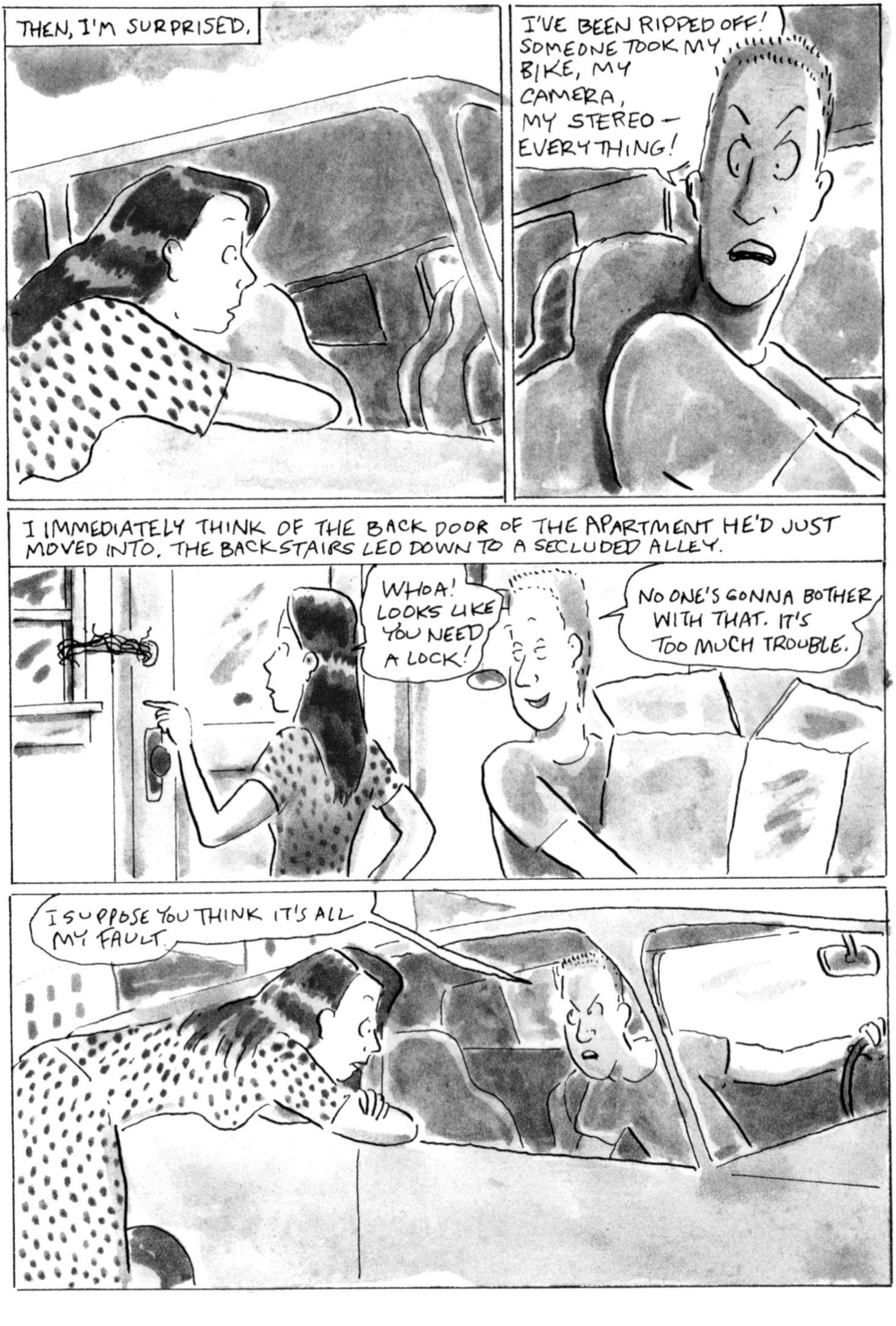
THEN, I'M SURPRISED.
I'VE BEEN RIPPED OFF! SOMEONE TOOK MY BIKE, MY CAMERA, MY STEREO — EVERYTHING!
I IMMEDIATELY THINK OF THE BACK DOOR OF THE APARTMENT HE'D JUST MOVED INTO. THE BACKSTAIRS LED DOWN TO A SECLUDED ALLEY.
WHOA! LOOKS LIKE YOU NEED A LOCK!
NO ONE'S GONNA BOTHER WITH THAT. IT'S TOO MUCH TROUBLE.
I SUPPOSE YOU THINK IT'S ALL MY FAULT.

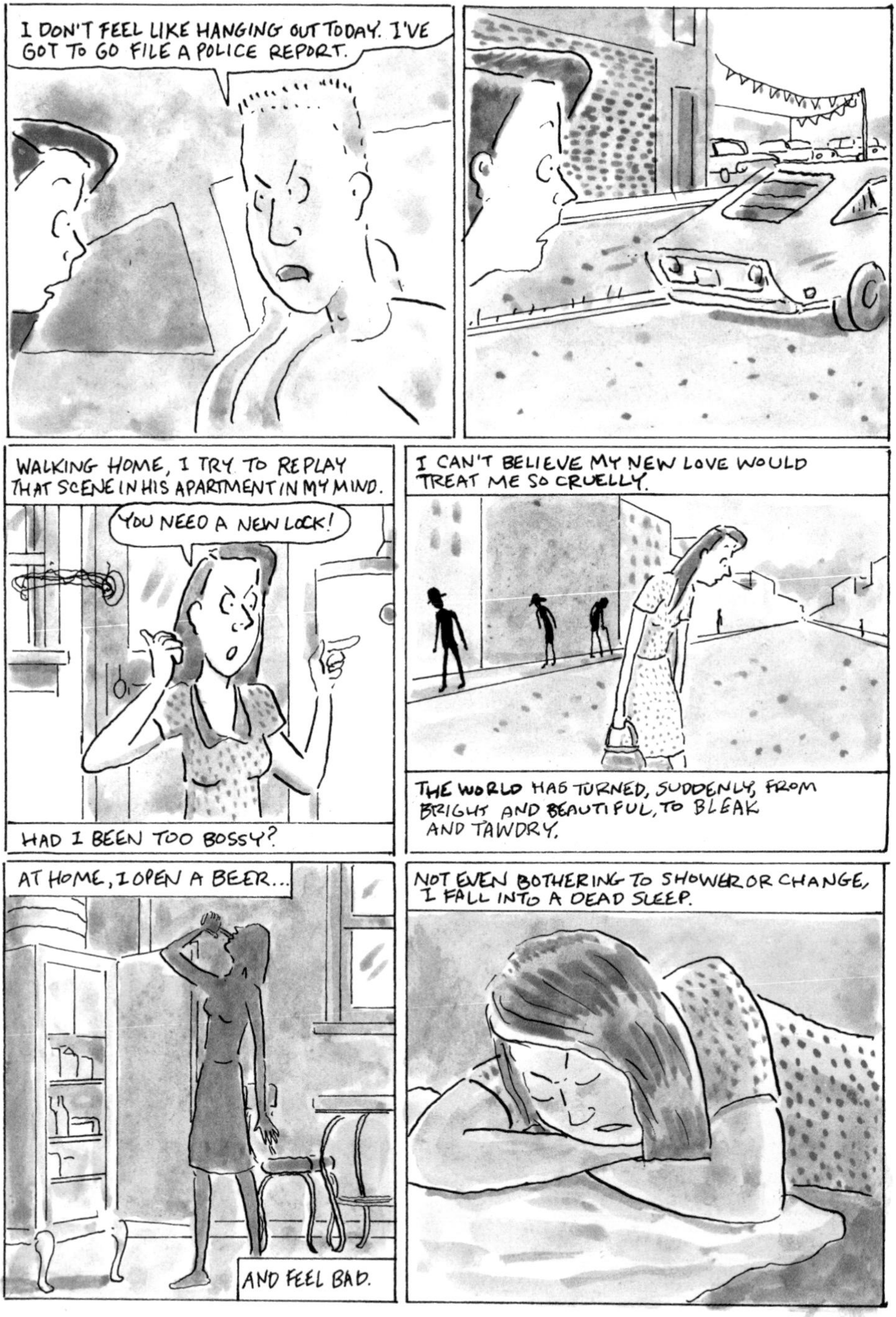
I DON'T FEEL LIKE HANGING OUT TODAY. I'VE GOT TO GO FILE A POLICE REPORT.
WALKING HOME, I TRY TO REPLAY THAT SCENE IN HIS APARTMENT IN MY MIND.
YOU NEED A NEW LOCK!
HAD I BEEN TOO BOSSY?
I CAN'T BELIEVE MY NEW LOVE WOULD TREAT ME SO CRUELLY.
THE WORLD HAS TURNED, SUDDENLY, FROM BRIGHT AND BEAUTIFUL, TO BLEAK AND TAWDRY.
AT HOME, I OPEN A BEER...
AND FEEL BAD.
NOT EVEN BOTHERING TO SHOWER OR CHANGE, I FALL INTO A DEAD SLEEP.

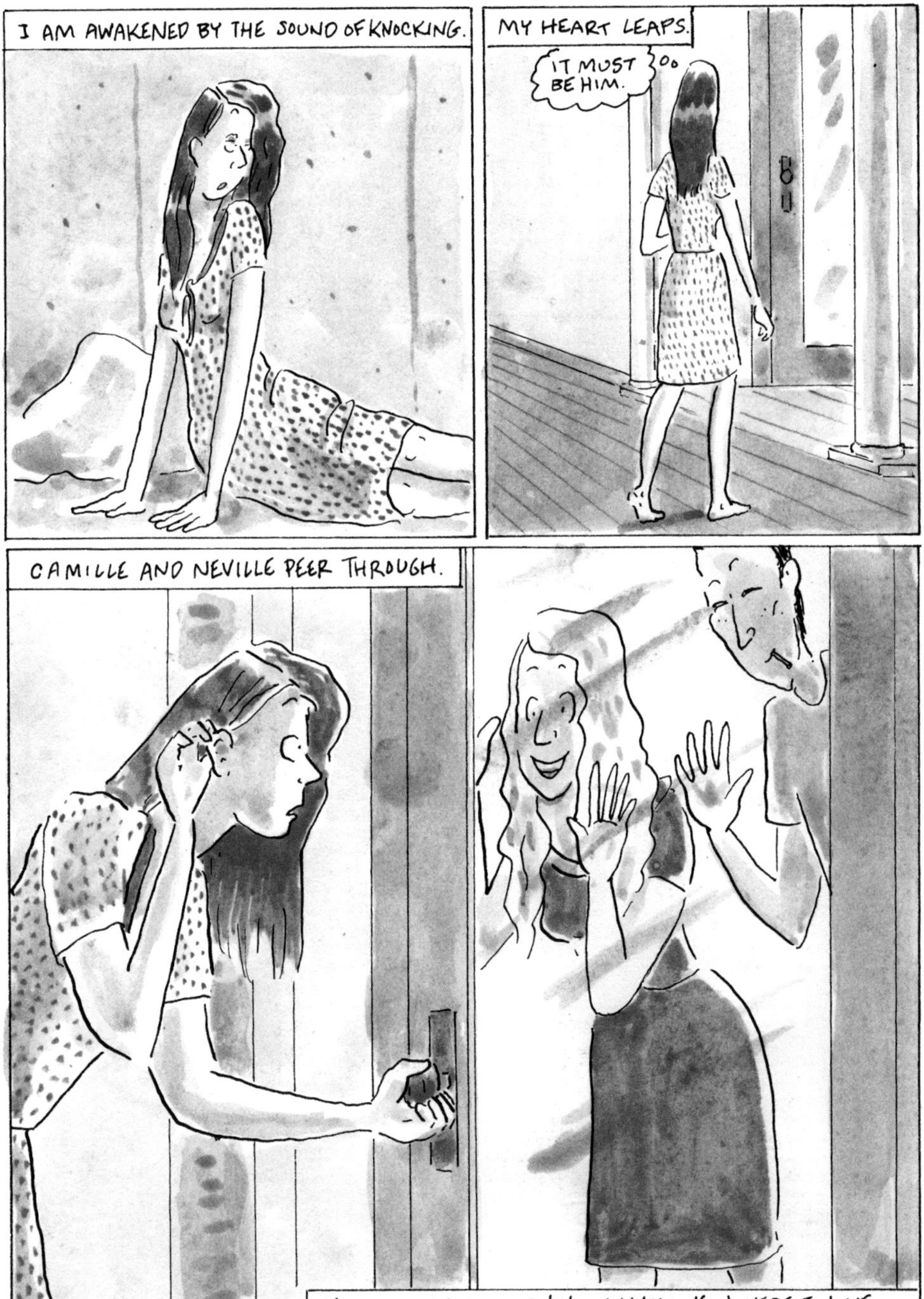
I AM AWAKENED BY THE SOUND OF KNOCKING.
MY HEART LEAPS.
IT MUST BE HIM.
CAMILLE AND NEVILLE PEER THROUGH.
I'M NOT SURE I WANT NEVILLE KNOWING WHERE I LIVE.

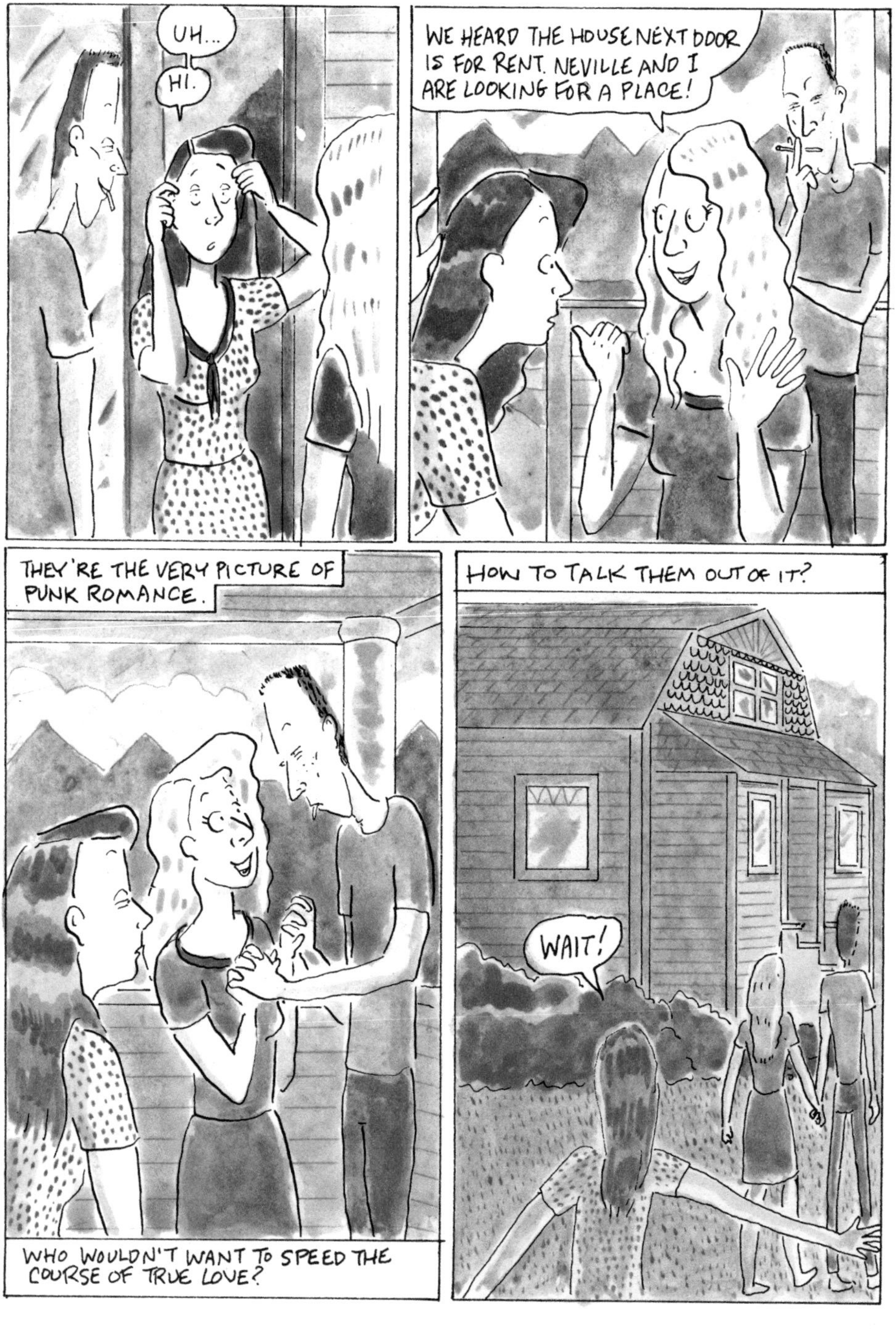
UH...
HI.
WE HEARD THE HOUSE NEXT DOOR IS FOR RENT. NEVILLE AND I ARE LOOKING FOR A PLACE!
THEY'RE THE VERY PICTURE OF PUNK ROMANCE.
WHO WOULDN'T WANT TO SPEED THE COURSE OF TRUE LOVE?
HOW TO TALK THEM OUT OF IT?
WAIT!

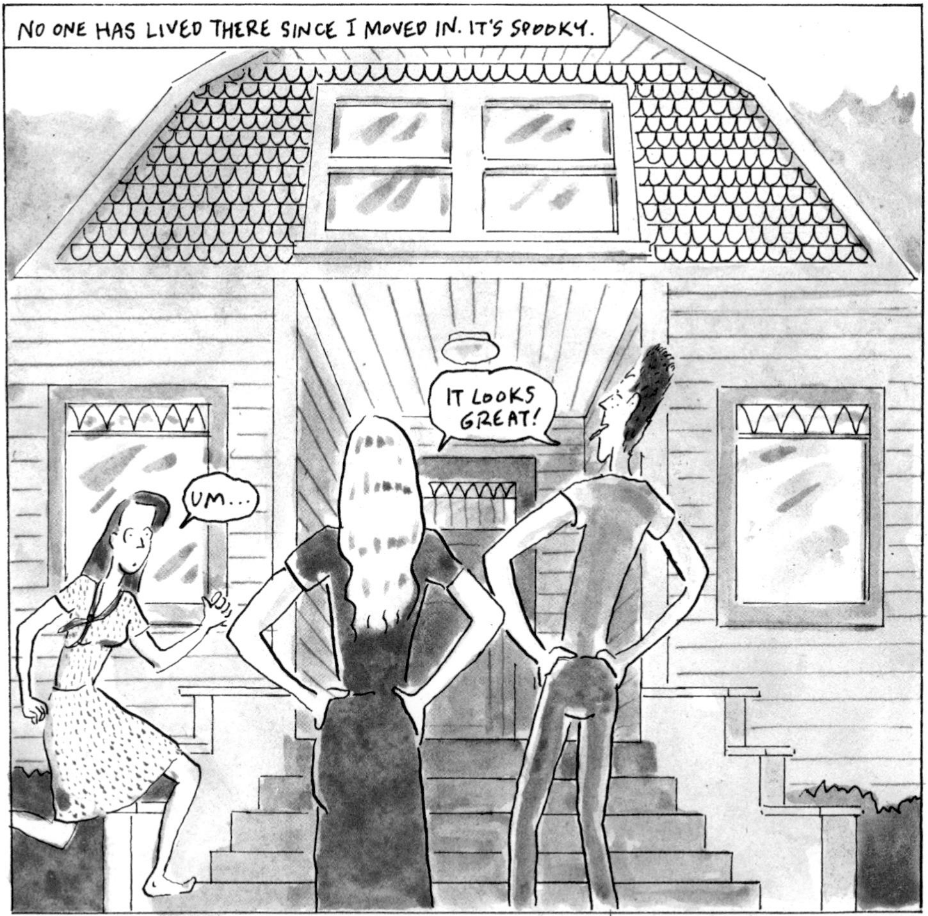
NO ONE HAS LIVED THERE SINCE I MOVED IN. IT'S SPOOKY.
UM...
IT LOOKS GREAT!

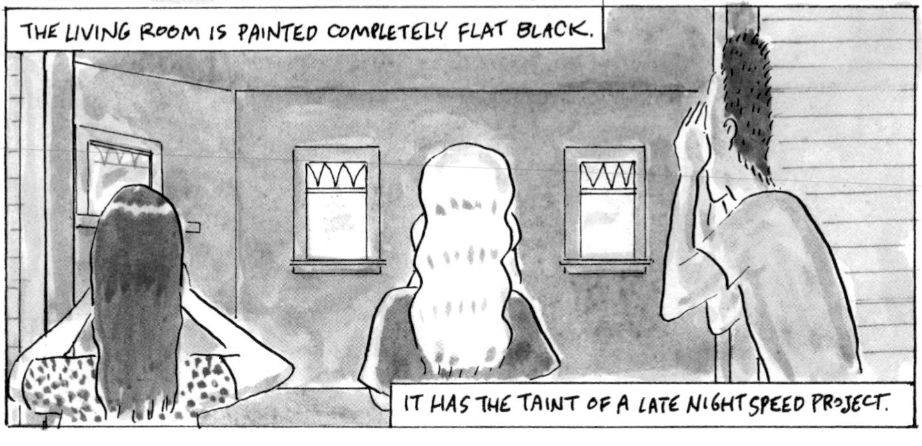
THE LIVING ROOM IS PAINTED COMPLETELY FLAT BLACK.
IT HAS THE TAINT OF A LATE NIGHT SPEED PROJECT.

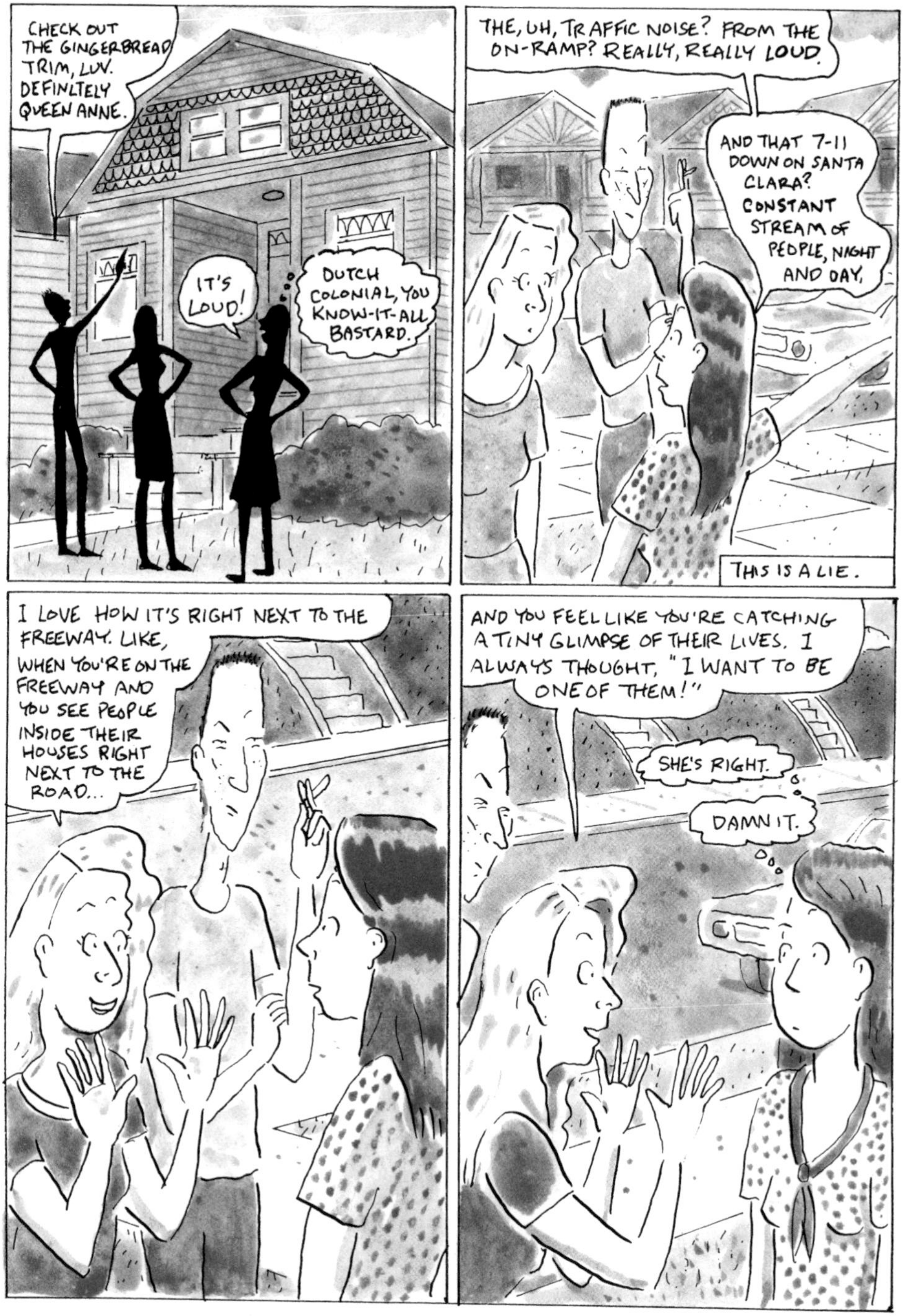
CHECK OUT THE GINGERBREAD TRIM, LUV. DEFINITELY QUEEN ANNE.
IT'S LOUD!
DUTCH COLONIAL, YOU KNOW-IT-ALL BASTARD.
THE, UH, TRAFFIC NOISE? FROM THE ON-RAMP? REALLY, REALLY LOUD.
AND THAT 7-11 DOWN ON SANTA CLARA? CONSTANT STREAM OF PEOPLE, NIGHT AND DAY.
THIS IS A LIE.
I LOVE HOW IT'S RIGHT NEXT TO THE FREEWAY. LIKE, WHEN YOU'RE ON THE FREEWAY AND YOU SEE PEOPLE INSIDE THEIR HOUSES RIGHT NEXT TO THE ROAD...
AND YOU FEEL LIKE YOU'RE CATCHING A TINY GLIMPSE OF THEIR LIVES. I ALWAYS THOUGHT, "I WANT TO BE ONE OF THEM!"
SHE'S RIGHT.
DAMN IT.

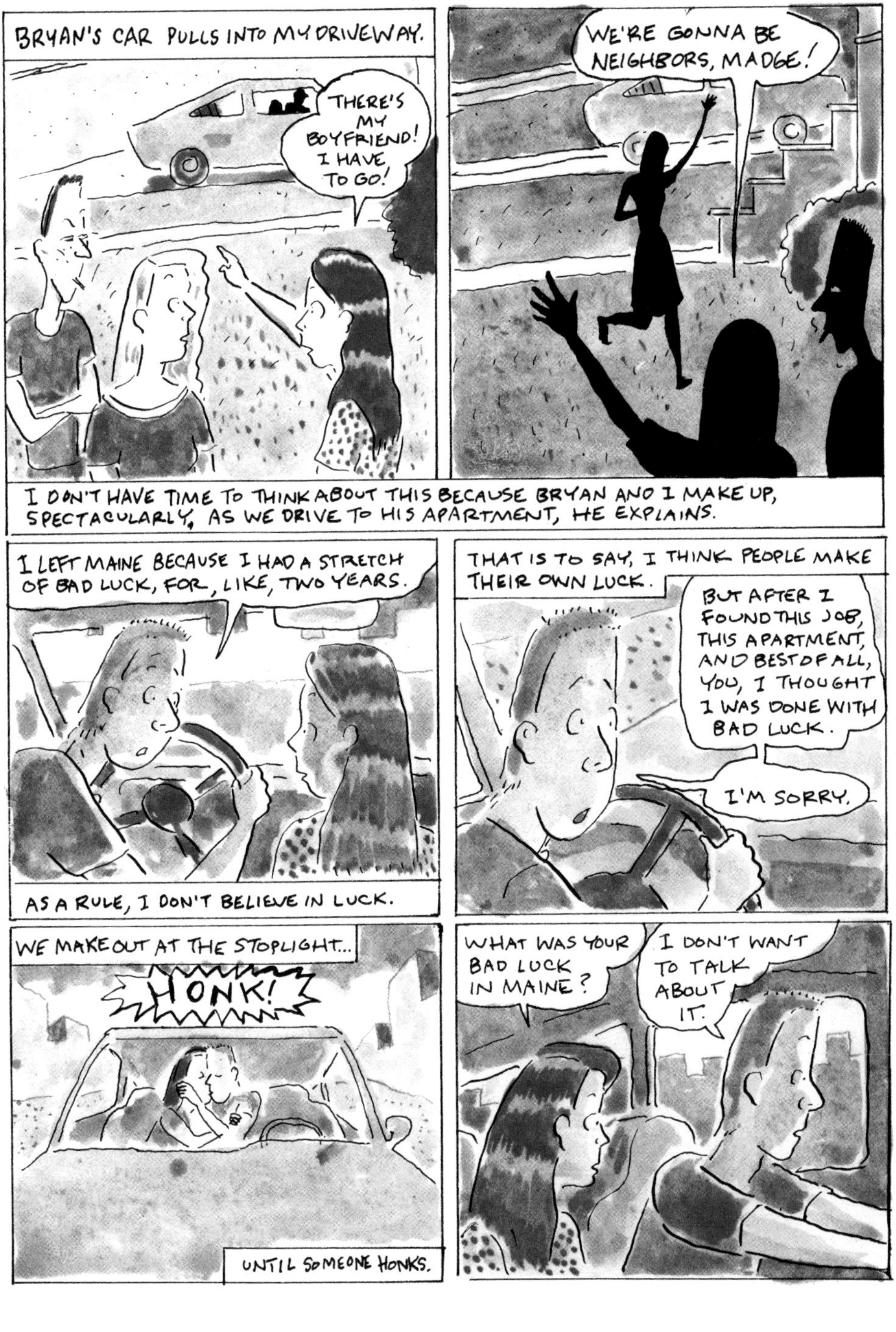
BRYAN'S CAR PULLS INTO MY DRIVEWAY.
THERE'S MY BOYFRIEND! I HAVE TO GO!
WE'RE GONNA BE NEIGHBORS, MADGE!
I DON'T HAVE TIME TO THINK ABOUT THIS BECAUSE BRYAN AND I MAKE UP, SPECTACULARLY, AS WE DRIVE TO HIS APARTMENT, HE EXPLAINS.
I LEFT MAINE BECAUSE I HAD A STRETCH OF BAD LUCK, FOR, LIKE, TWO YEARS.
AS A RULE, I DON'T BELIEVE IN LUCK.
THAT IS TO SAY, I THINK PEOPLE MAKE THEIR OWN LUCK.
BUT AFTER I FOUND THIS JOB, THIS APARTMENT, AND BEST OF ALL, YOU, I THOUGHT I WAS DONE WITH BAD LUCK.
I'M SORRY.
WE MAKE OUT AT THE STOPLIGHT...
HONK!
UNTIL SOMEONE HONKS.
WHAT WAS YOUR BAD LUCK IN MAINE?
I DON'T WANT TO TALK ABOUT IT.

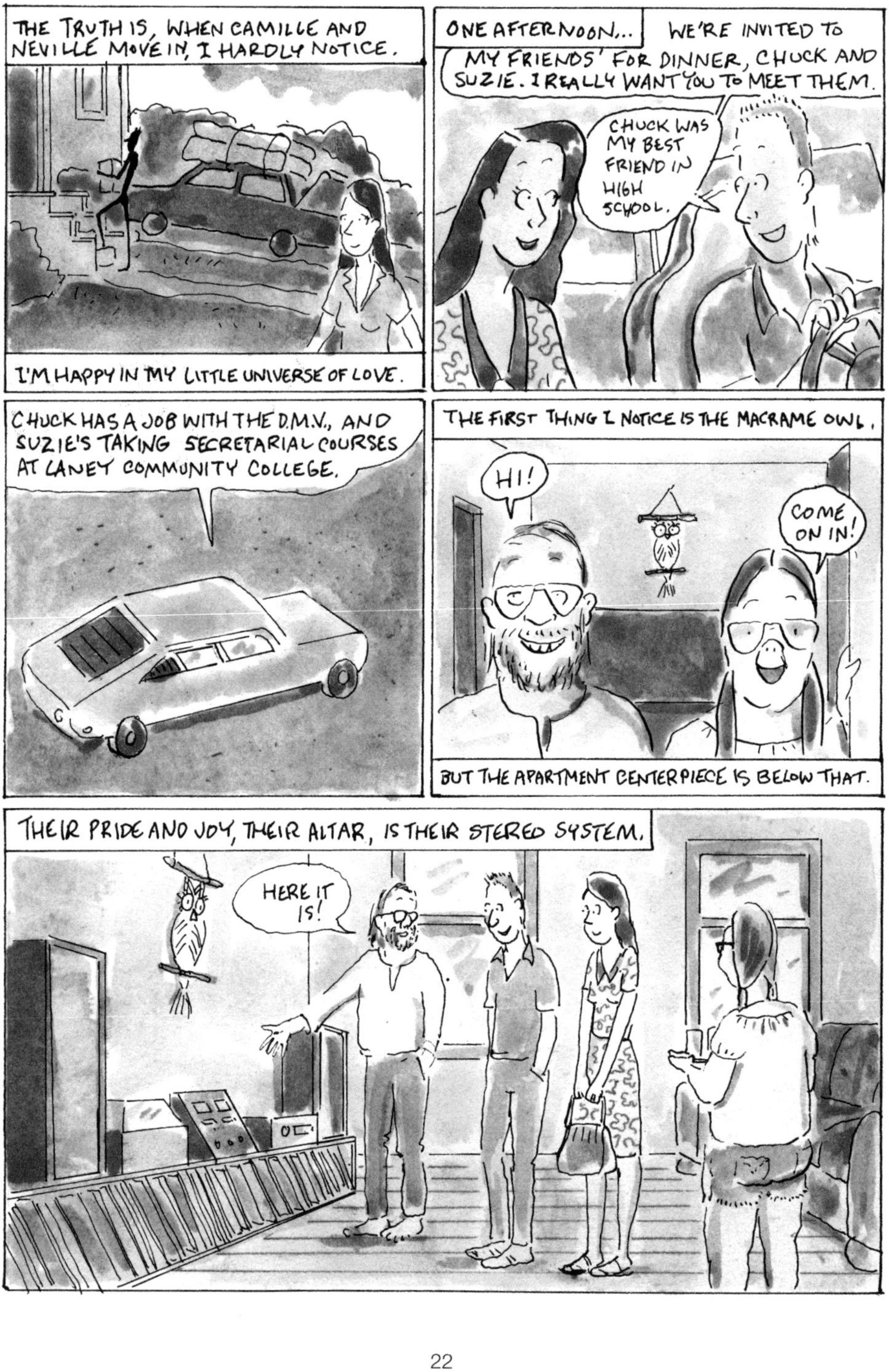
THE TRUTH IS, WHEN CAMILLE AND NEVILLE MOVE IN, I HARDLY NOTICE.
I'M HAPPY IN MY LITTLE UNIVERSE OF LOVE.
ONE AFTERNOON...
WE'RE INVITED TO MY FRIENDS' FOR DINNER, CHUCK AND SUZIE. I REALLY WANT YOU TO MEET THEM.
CHUCK WAS MY BEST FRIEND IN HIGH SCHOOL.
CHUCK HAS A JOB WITH THE D.M.V., AND SUZIE'S TAKING SECRETARIAL COURSES AT LANEY COMMUNITY COLLEGE.
THE FIRST THING I NOTICE IS THE MACRAME OWL.
HI!
COME ON IN!
BUT THE APARTMENT CENTERPIECE IS BELOW THAT.
THEIR PRIDE AND JOY, THEIR ALTAR, IS THEIR STEREO SYSTEM.
HERE IT IS!

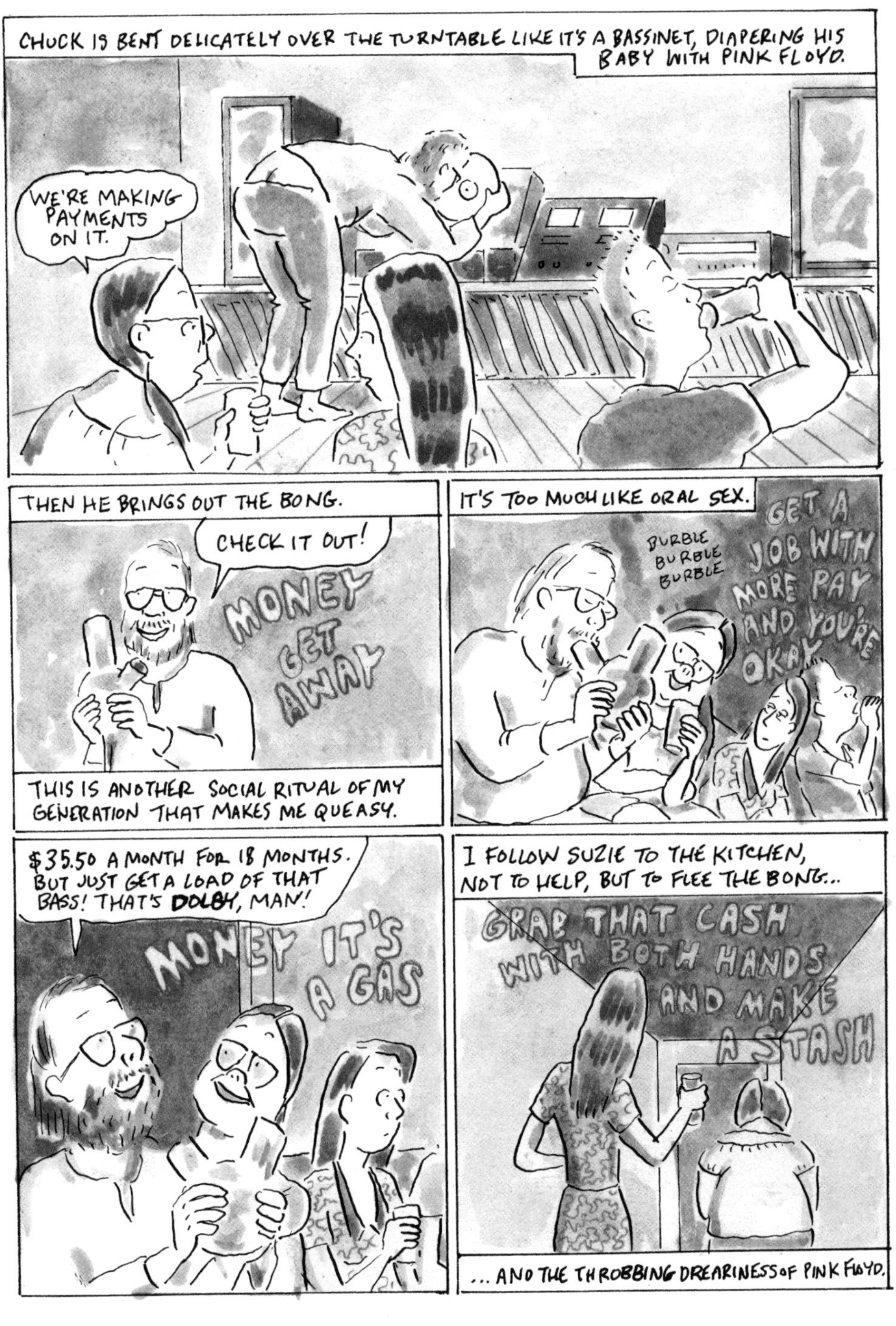
CHUCK IS BENT DELICATELY OVER THE TURNTABLE LIKE IT'S A BASSINET, DIAPERING HIS BABY WITH PINK FLOYD.
WE'RE MAKING PAYMENTS ON IT.
THEN HE BRINGS OUT THE BONG.
CHECK IT OUT!
MONEY GET AWAY
THIS IS ANOTHER SOCIAL RITUAL OF MY GENERATION THAT MAKES ME QUEASY.
IT'S TOO MUCH LIKE ORAL SEX.
BURBLE BURBLE BURBLE
GET A JOB WITH MORE PAY AND YOU'RE OKAY
$35.50 A MONTH FOR 18 MONTHS. BUT JUST GET A LOAD OF THAT BASS! THAT'S DOLBY, MAN!
MONEY IT'S A GAS
I FOLLOW SUZIE TO THE KITCHEN, NOT TO HELP, BUT TO FLEE THE BONG...
GRAB THAT CASH WITH BOTH HANDS AND MAKE A STASH
... AND THE THROBBING DREARINESS OF PINK FLOYD.

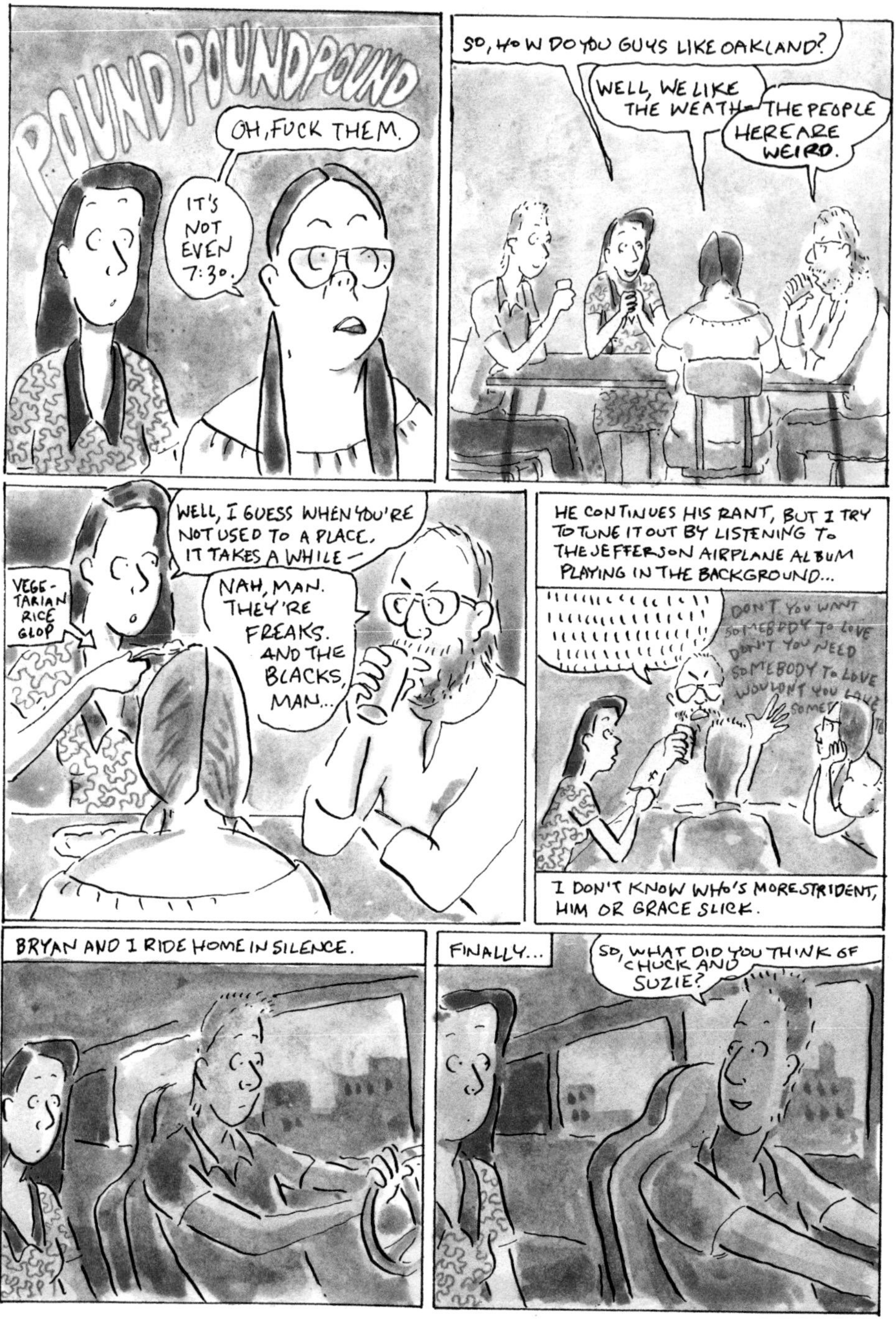
POUND POUND POUND
OH, FUCK THEM.
IT'S NOT EVEN 7:30.
SO, HOW DO YOU GUYS LIKE OAKLAND?
WELL, WE LIKE THE WEATH–
THE PEOPLE HERE ARE WEIRD.
WELL, I GUESS WHEN YOU'RE NOT USED TO A PLACE, IT TAKES A WHILE–
VEGETARIAN RICE GLOP
NAH, MAN. THEY'RE FREAKS. AND THE BLACKS, MAN...
HE CONTINUES HIS RANT, BUT I TRY TO TUNE IT OUT BY LISTENING TO THE JEFFERSON AIRPLANE ALBUM PLAYING IN THE BACKGROUND...
DON'T YOU WANT SOMEBODY TO LOVE
DON'T YOU NEED SOMEBODY TO LOVE
WOULDN'T YOU LOVE
I DON'T KNOW WHO'S MORE STRIDENT, HIM OR GRACE SLICK.
BRYAN AND I RIDE HOME IN SILENCE.
FINALLY...
SO, WHAT DID YOU THINK OF CHUCK AND SUZIE?

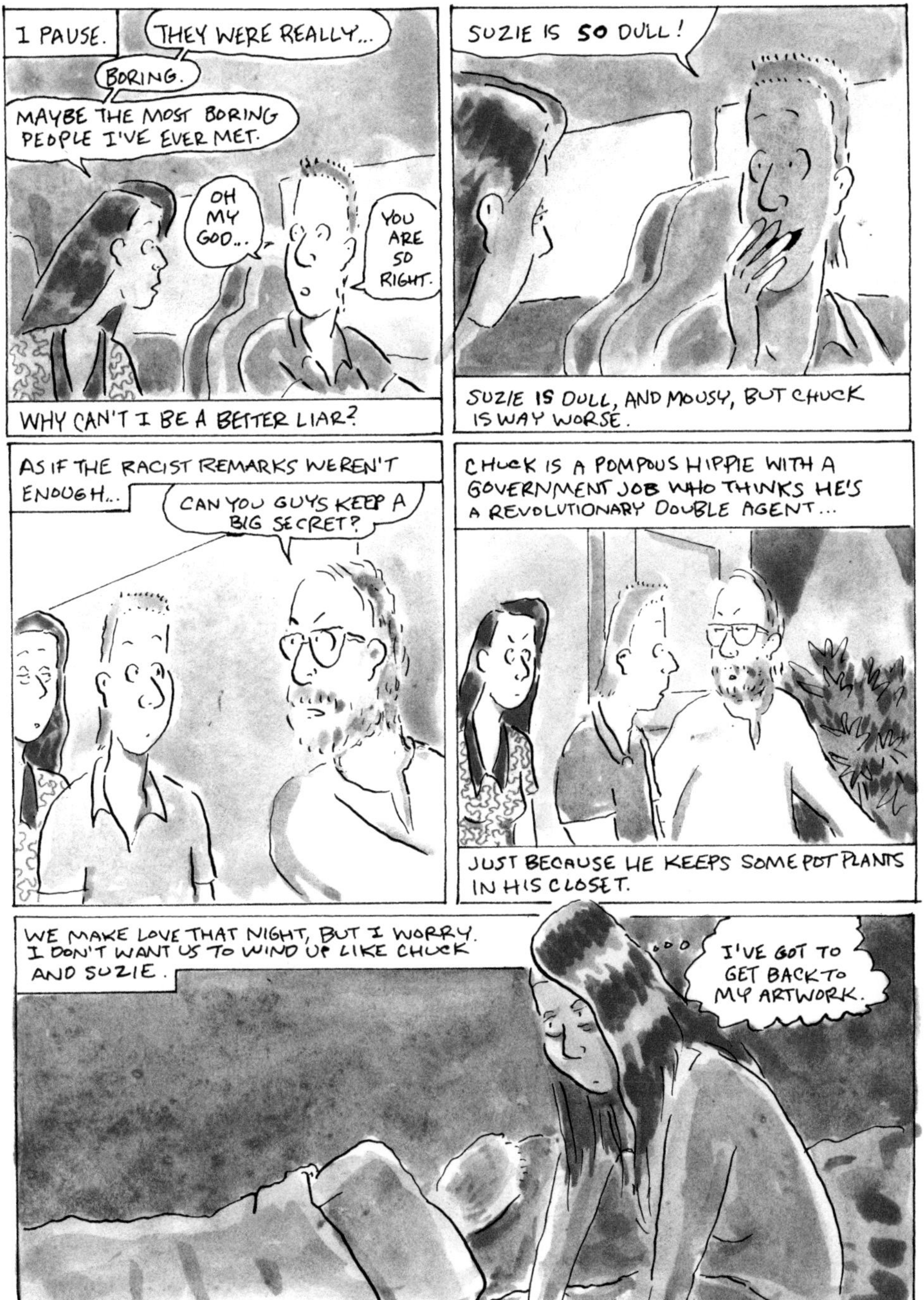
I PAUSE.
THEY WERE REALLY...
BORING.
MAYBE THE MOST BORING PEOPLE I'VE EVER MET.
OH MY GOD...
YOU ARE SO RIGHT.
WHY CAN'T I BE A BETTER LIAR?
SUZIE IS **SO** DULL!
SUZIE IS DULL, AND MOUSY, BUT CHUCK IS WAY WORSE.
AS IF THE RACIST REMARKS WEREN'T ENOUGH...
CAN YOU GUYS KEEP A BIG SECRET?
CHUCK IS A POMPOUS HIPPIE WITH A GOVERNMENT JOB WHO THINKS HE'S A REVOLUTIONARY DOUBLE AGENT...
JUST BECAUSE HE KEEPS SOME POT PLANTS IN HIS CLOSET.
WE MAKE LOVE THAT NIGHT, BUT I WORRY. I DON'T WANT US TO WIND UP LIKE CHUCK AND SUZIE.
I'VE GOT TO GET BACK TO MY ARTWORK.

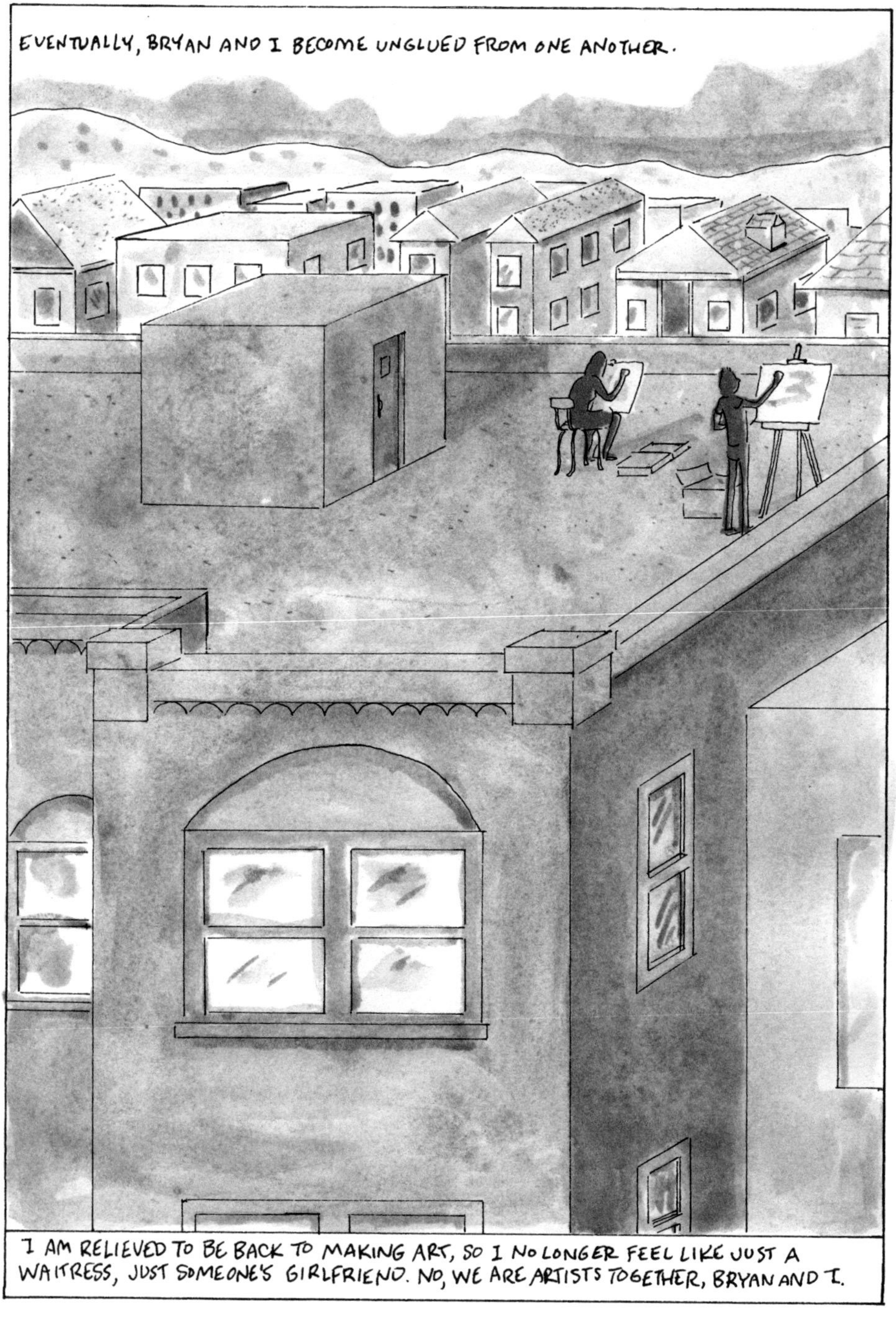
EVENTUALLY, BRYAN AND I BECOME UNGLUED FROM ONE ANOTHER.
I AM RELIEVED TO BE BACK TO MAKING ART, SO I NO LONGER FEEL LIKE JUST A WAITRESS, JUST SOMEONE'S GIRLFRIEND. NO, WE ARE ARTISTS TOGETHER, BRYAN AND I.

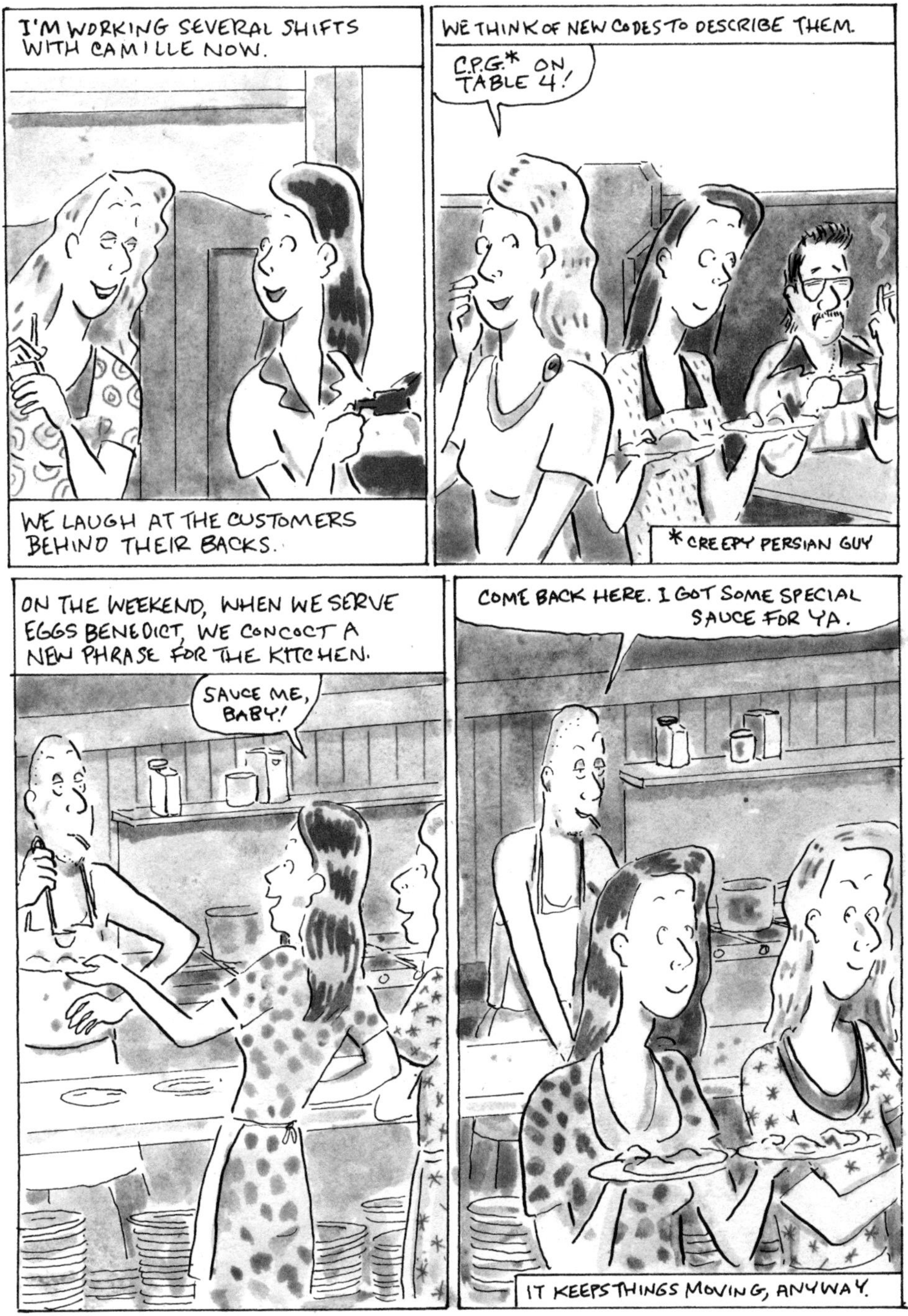
I'M WORKING SEVERAL SHIFTS WITH CAMILLE NOW.
WE LAUGH AT THE CUSTOMERS BEHIND THEIR BACKS.
WE THINK OF NEW CODES TO DESCRIBE THEM.
C.P.G.* ON TABLE 4!
*CREEPY PERSIAN GUY
ON THE WEEKEND, WHEN WE SERVE EGGS BENEDICT, WE CONCOCT A NEW PHRASE FOR THE KITCHEN.
SAUCE ME, BABY!
COME BACK HERE. I GOT SOME SPECIAL SAUCE FOR YA.
IT KEEPS THINGS MOVING, ANYWAY.

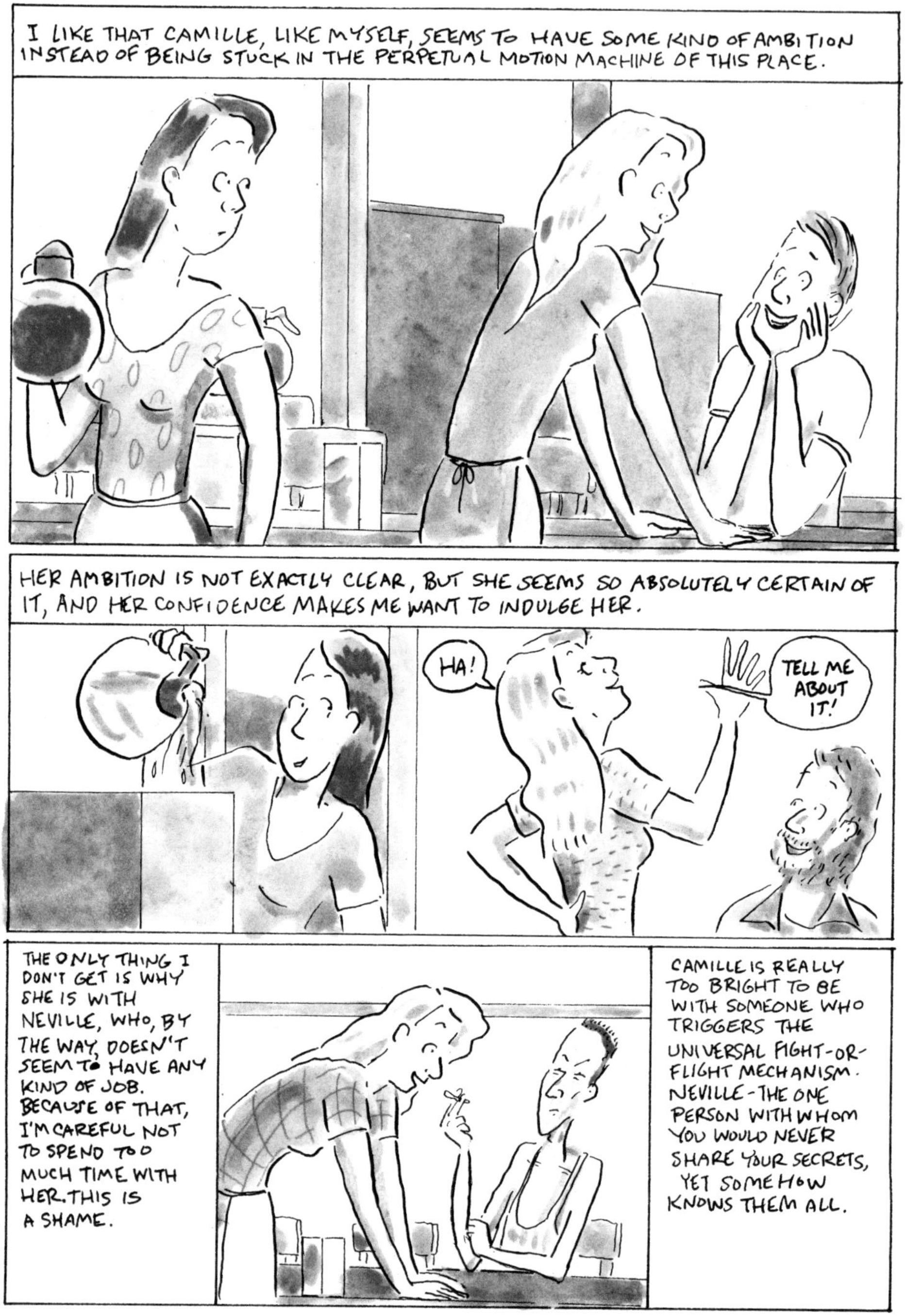
I LIKE THAT CAMILLE, LIKE MYSELF, SEEMS TO HAVE SOME KIND OF AMBITION INSTEAD OF BEING STUCK IN THE PERPETUAL MOTION MACHINE OF THIS PLACE.
HER AMBITION IS NOT EXACTLY CLEAR, BUT SHE SEEMS SO ABSOLUTELY CERTAIN OF IT, AND HER CONFIDENCE MAKES ME WANT TO INDULGE HER.
HA!
TELL ME ABOUT IT!
THE ONLY THING I DON'T GET IS WHY SHE IS WITH NEVILLE, WHO, BY THE WAY, DOESN'T SEEM TO HAVE ANY KIND OF JOB. BECAUSE OF THAT, I'M CAREFUL NOT TO SPEND TOO MUCH TIME WITH HER. THIS IS A SHAME.
CAMILLE IS REALLY TOO BRIGHT TO BE WITH SOMEONE WHO TRIGGERS THE UNIVERSAL FIGHT-OR-FLIGHT MECHANISM. NEVILLE - THE ONE PERSON WITH WHOM YOU WOULD NEVER SHARE YOUR SECRETS, YET SOMEHOW KNOWS THEM ALL.

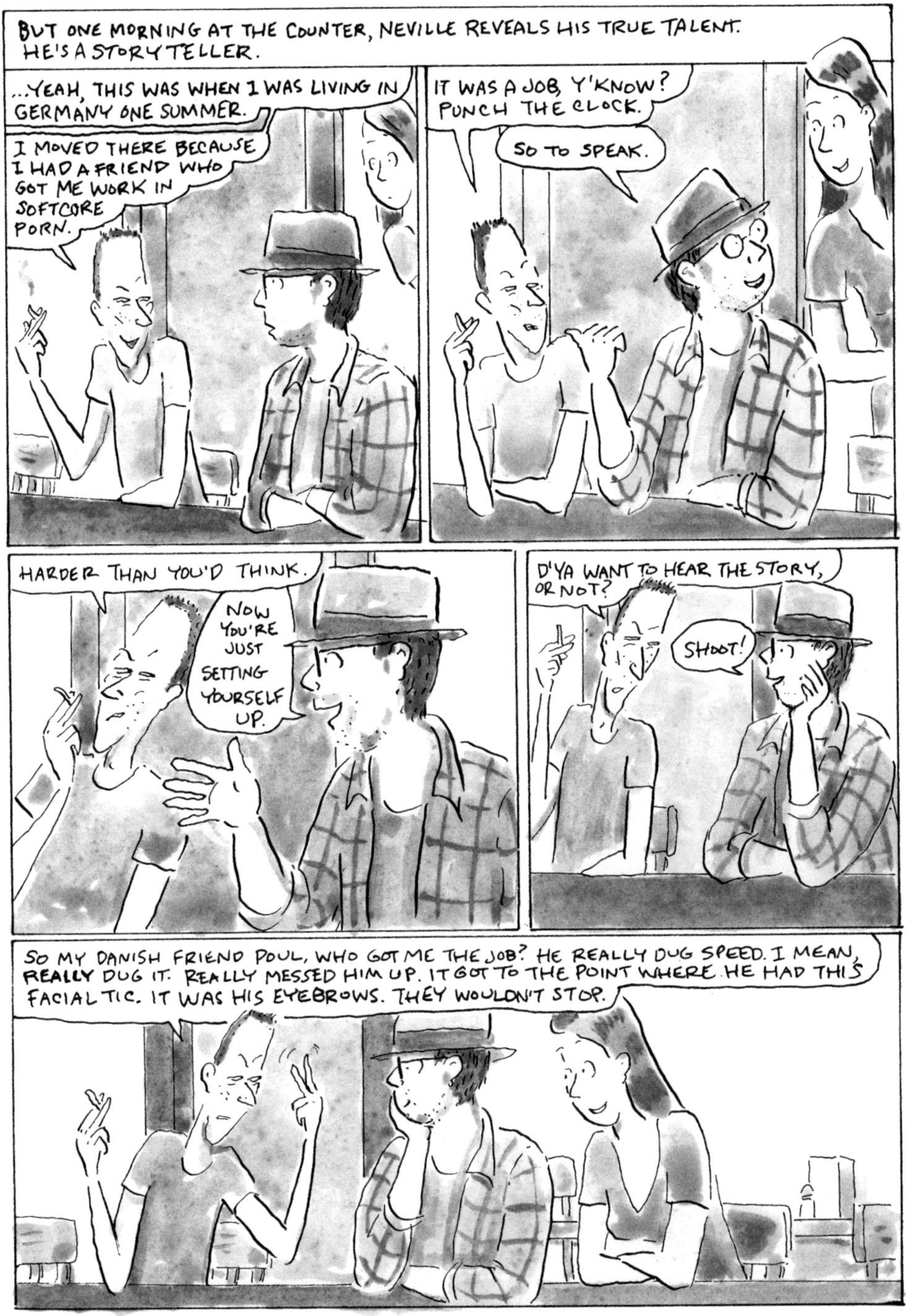
BUT ONE MORNING AT THE COUNTER, NEVILLE REVEALS HIS TRUE TALENT. HE'S A STORYTELLER.
...YEAH, THIS WAS WHEN I WAS LIVING IN GERMANY ONE SUMMER.
I MOVED THERE BECAUSE I HAD A FRIEND WHO GOT ME WORK IN SOFTCORE PORN.
IT WAS A JOB, Y'KNOW? PUNCH THE CLOCK.
SO TO SPEAK.
HARDER THAN YOU'D THINK.
NOW YOU'RE JUST SETTING YOURSELF UP.
D'YA WANT TO HEAR THE STORY, OR NOT?
SHOOT!
SO MY DANISH FRIEND POUL, WHO GOT ME THE JOB? HE REALLY DUG SPEED. I MEAN, REALLY DUG IT. REALLY MESSED HIM UP. IT GOT TO THE POINT WHERE HE HAD THIS FACIAL TIC. IT WAS HIS EYEBROWS. THEY WOULDN'T STOP.

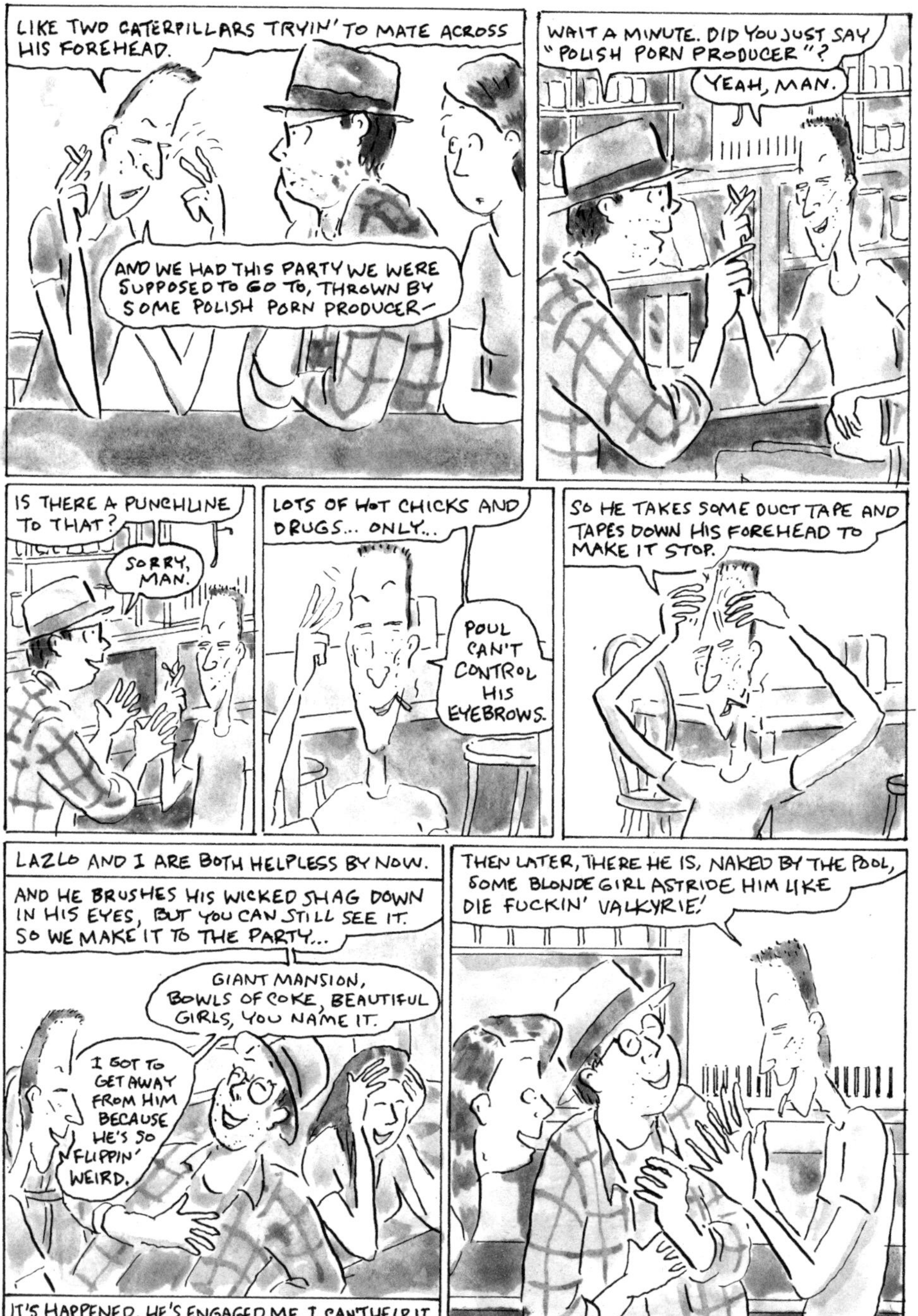
LIKE TWO CATERPILLARS TRYIN' TO MATE ACROSS HIS FOREHEAD.
AND WE HAD THIS PARTY WE WERE SUPPOSED TO GO TO, THROWN BY SOME POLISH PORN PRODUCER-
WAIT A MINUTE. DID YOU JUST SAY "POLISH PORN PRODUCER"?
YEAH, MAN.
IS THERE A PUNCHLINE TO THAT?
SORRY, MAN.
LOTS OF HOT CHICKS AND DRUGS... ONLY...
POUL CAN'T CONTROL HIS EYEBROWS.
SO HE TAKES SOME DUCT TAPE AND TAPES DOWN HIS FOREHEAD TO MAKE IT STOP.
LAZLO AND I ARE BOTH HELPLESS BY NOW.
AND HE BRUSHES HIS WICKED SHAG DOWN IN HIS EYES, BUT YOU CAN STILL SEE IT. SO WE MAKE IT TO THE PARTY...
GIANT MANSION, BOWLS OF COKE, BEAUTIFUL GIRLS, YOU NAME IT.
I GOT TO GET AWAY FROM HIM BECAUSE HE'S SO FLIPPIN' WEIRD.
IT'S HAPPENED. HE'S ENGAGED ME. I CAN'T HELP IT.
THEN LATER, THERE HE IS, NAKED BY THE POOL, SOME BLONDE GIRL ASTRIDE HIM LIKE DIE FUCKIN' VALKYRIE!

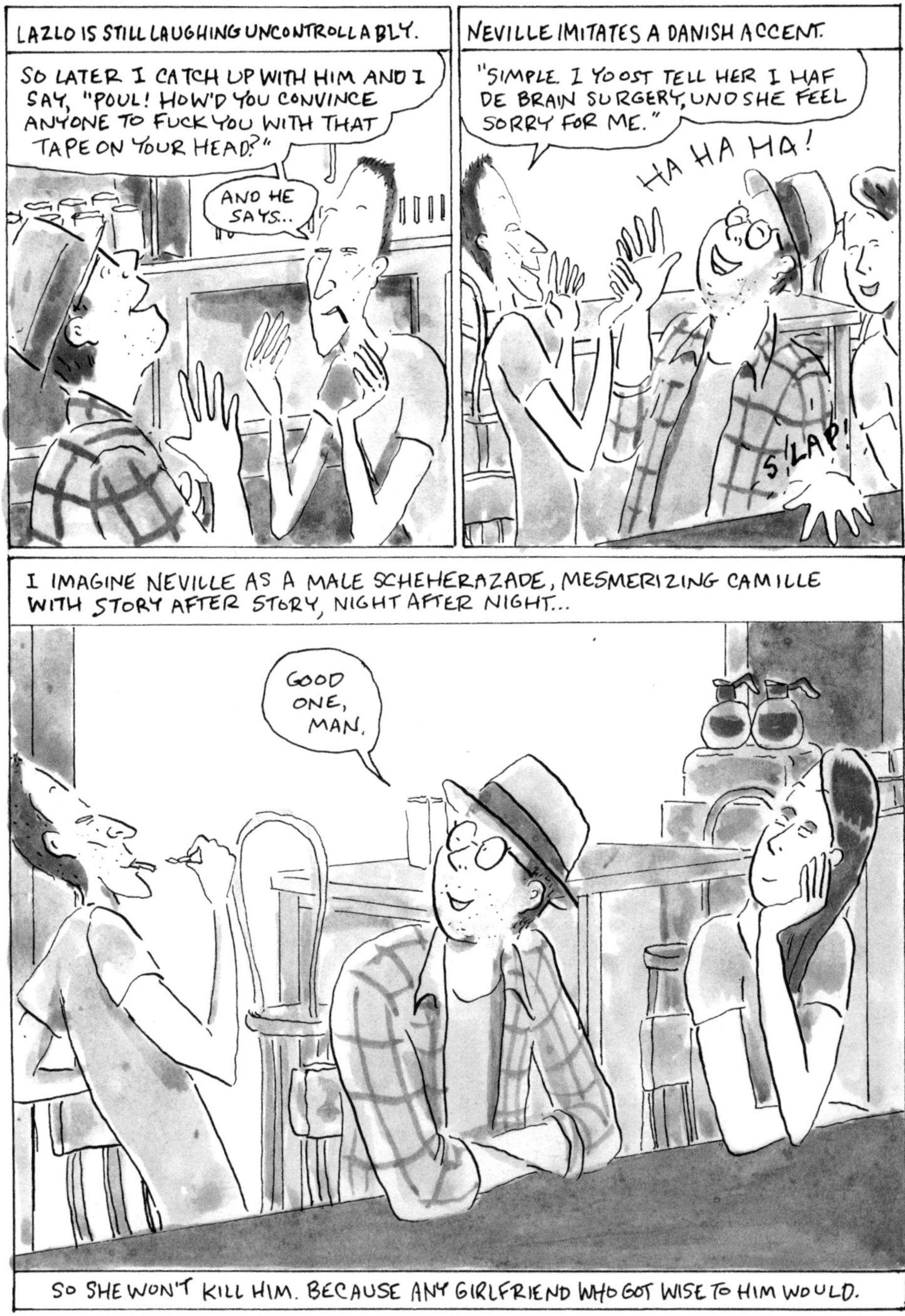
LAZLO IS STILL LAUGHING UNCONTROLLABLY.
SO LATER I CATCH UP WITH HIM AND I SAY, "POUL! HOW'D YOU CONVINCE ANYONE TO FUCK YOU WITH THAT TAPE ON YOUR HEAD?"
AND HE SAYS...
NEVILLE IMITATES A DANISH ACCENT.
"SIMPLE. I YOOST TELL HER I HAF DE BRAIN SURGERY, UND SHE FEEL SORRY FOR ME."
HA HA HA!
SLAP!
I IMAGINE NEVILLE AS A MALE SCHEHERAZADE, MESMERIZING CAMILLE WITH STORY AFTER STORY, NIGHT AFTER NIGHT...
GOOD ONE, MAN.
SO SHE WON'T KILL HIM. BECAUSE ANY GIRLFRIEND WHO GOT WISE TO HIM WOULD.

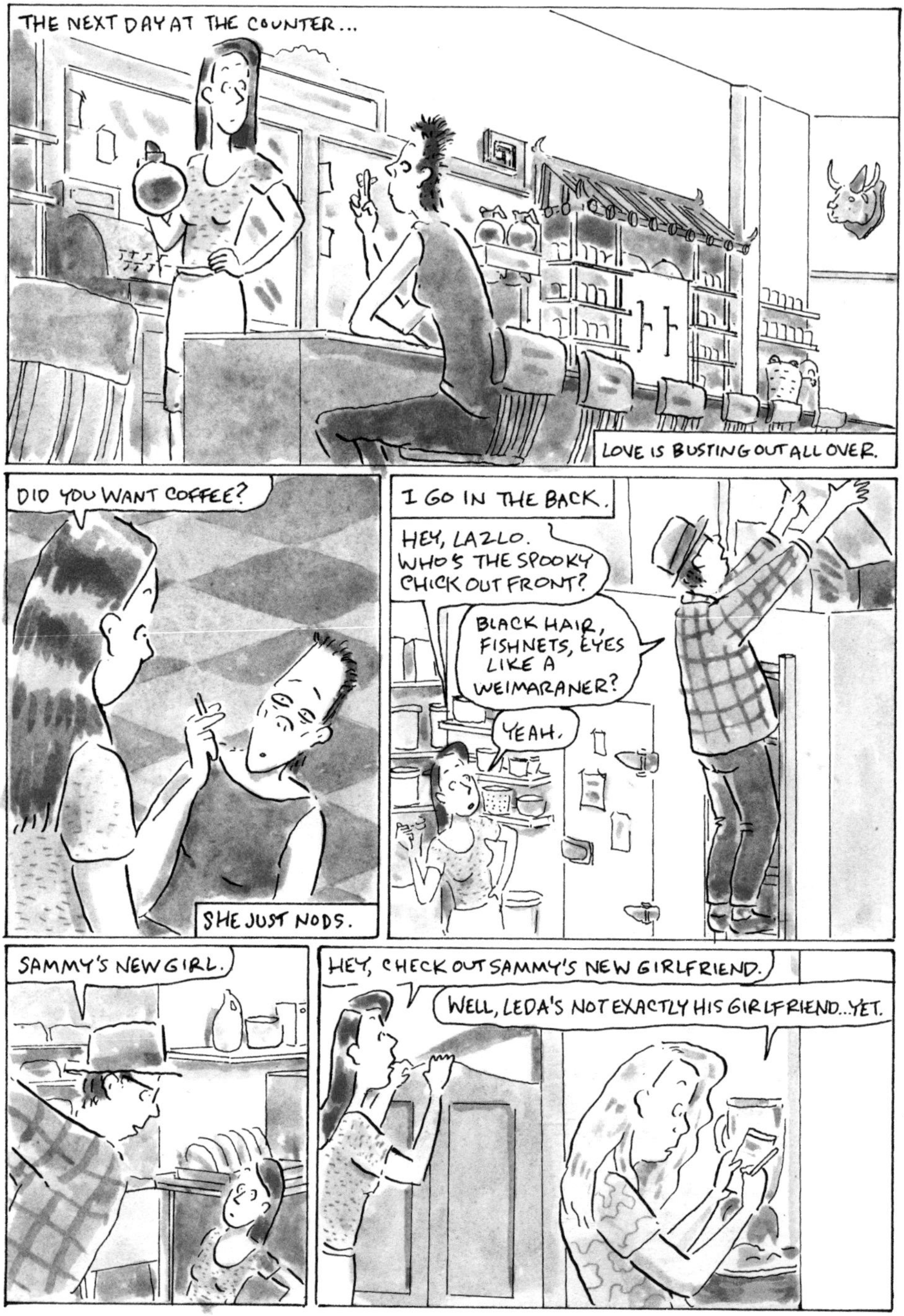
THE NEXT DAY AT THE COUNTER...
LOVE IS BUSTING OUT ALL OVER.
DID YOU WANT COFFEE?
SHE JUST NODS.
I GO IN THE BACK.
HEY, LAZLO. WHO'S THE SPOOKY CHICK OUT FRONT?
BLACK HAIR, FISHNETS, EYES LIKE A WEIMARANER?
YEAH.
SAMMY'S NEW GIRL.
HEY, CHECK OUT SAMMY'S NEW GIRLFRIEND.
WELL, LEDA'S NOT EXACTLY HIS GIRLFRIEND...YET.

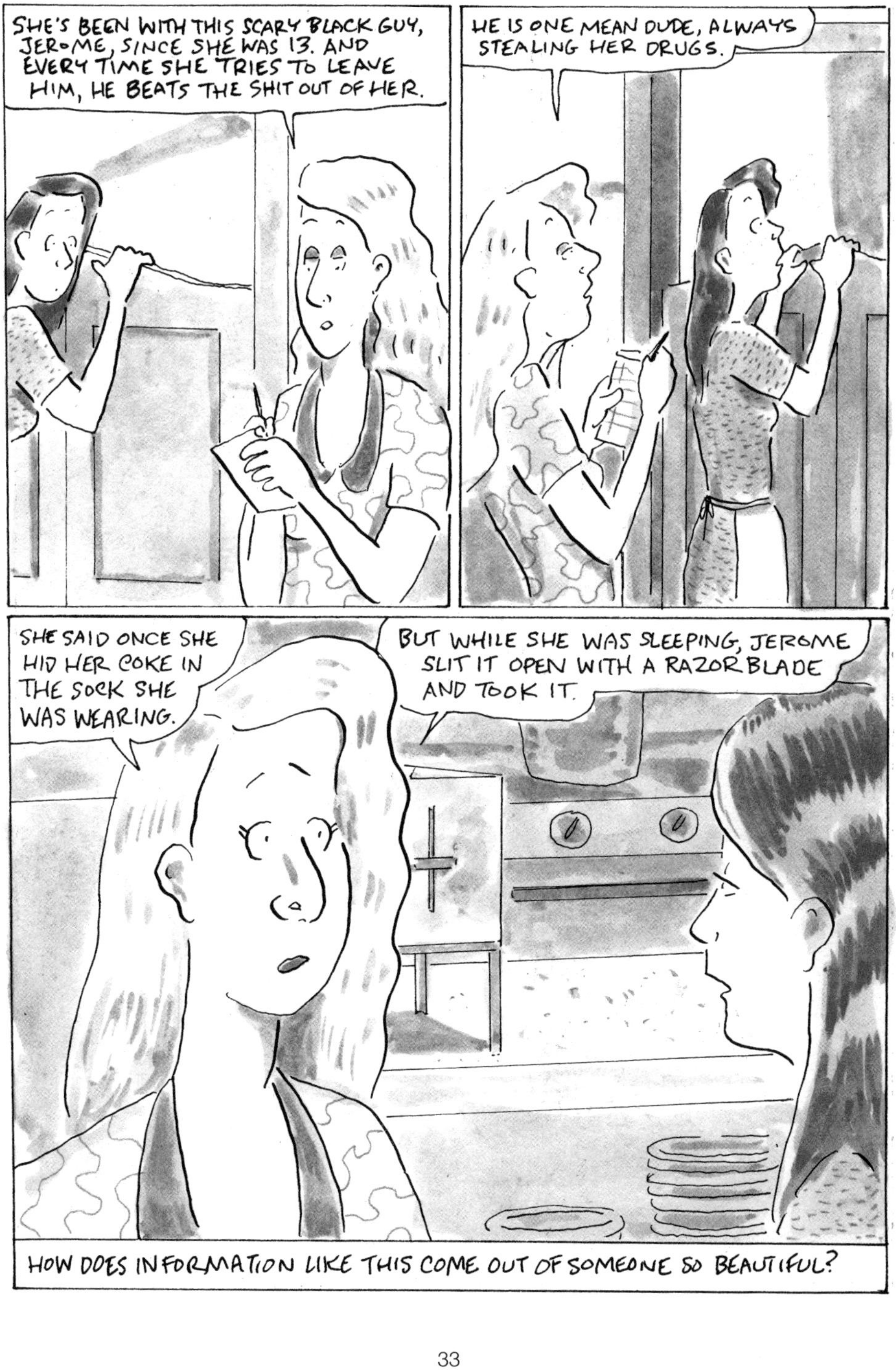
SHE'S BEEN WITH THIS SCARY BLACK GUY, JEROME, SINCE SHE WAS 13. AND EVERY TIME SHE TRIES TO LEAVE HIM, HE BEATS THE SHIT OUT OF HER.
HE IS ONE MEAN DUDE, ALWAYS STEALING HER DRUGS.
SHE SAID ONCE SHE HID HER COKE IN THE SOCK SHE WAS WEARING.
BUT WHILE SHE WAS SLEEPING, JEROME SLIT IT OPEN WITH A RAZOR BLADE AND TOOK IT.
HOW DOES INFORMATION LIKE THIS COME OUT OF SOMEONE SO BEAUTIFUL?

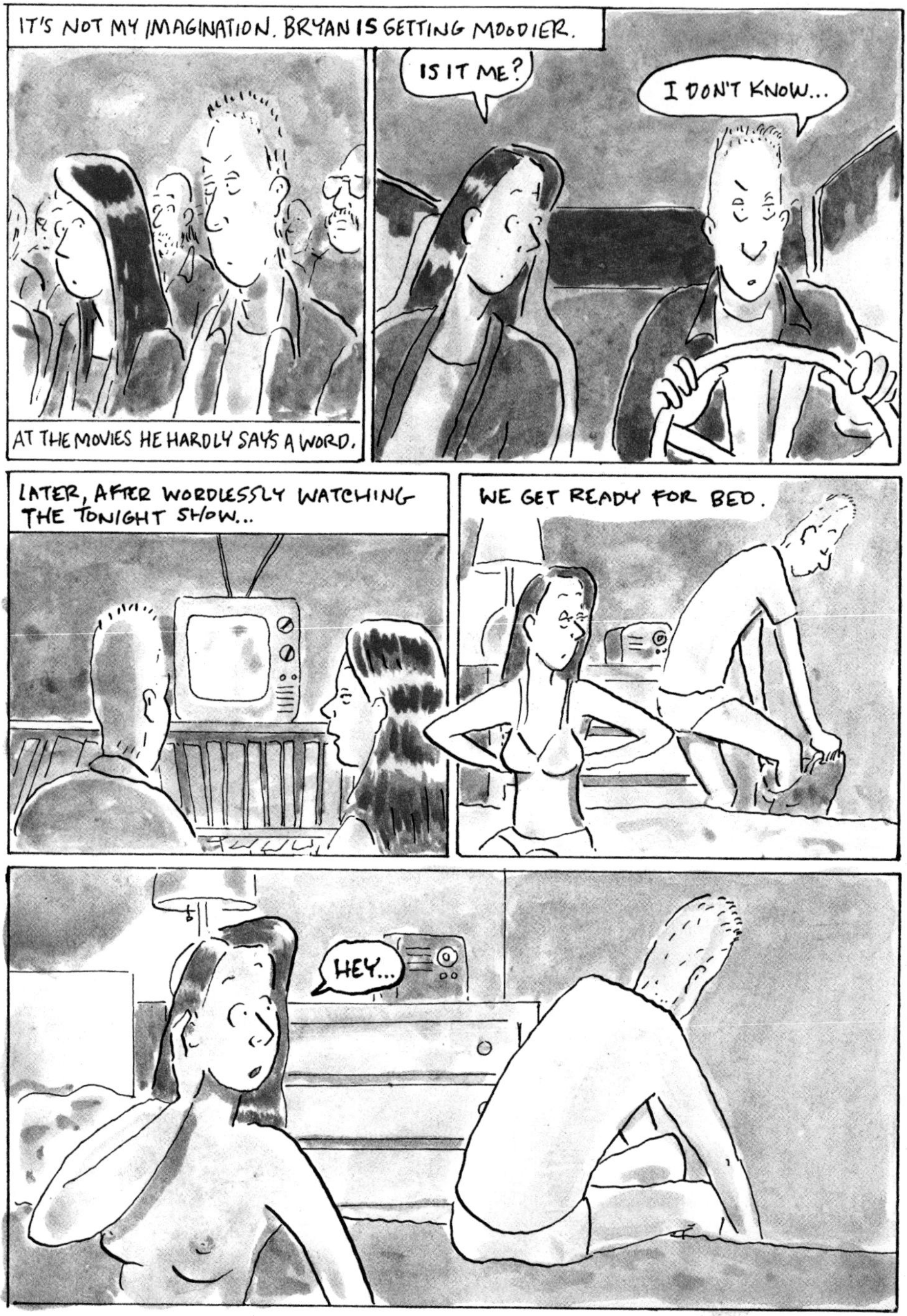
IT'S NOT MY IMAGINATION. BRYAN IS GETTING MOODIER.
AT THE MOVIES HE HARDLY SAYS A WORD.
IS IT ME?
I DON'T KNOW...
LATER, AFTER WORDLESSLY WATCHING THE TONIGHT SHOW...
WE GET READY FOR BED.
HEY...

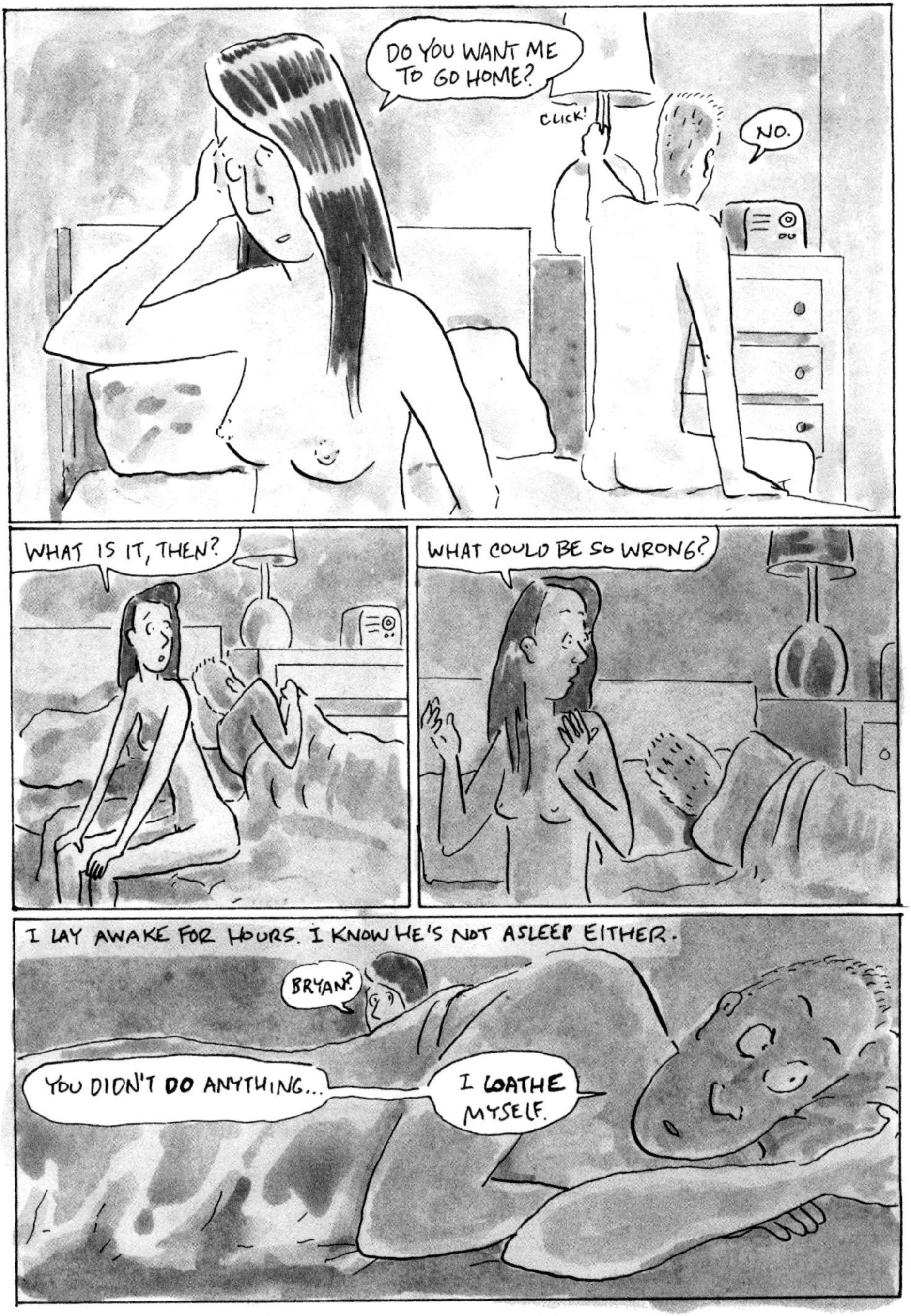
DO YOU WANT ME TO GO HOME?
CLICK!
NO.
WHAT IS IT, THEN?
WHAT COULD BE SO WRONG?
I LAY AWAKE FOR HOURS. I KNOW HE'S NOT ASLEEP EITHER.
BRYAN?
YOU DIDN'T DO ANYTHING...
I LOATHE MYSELF.

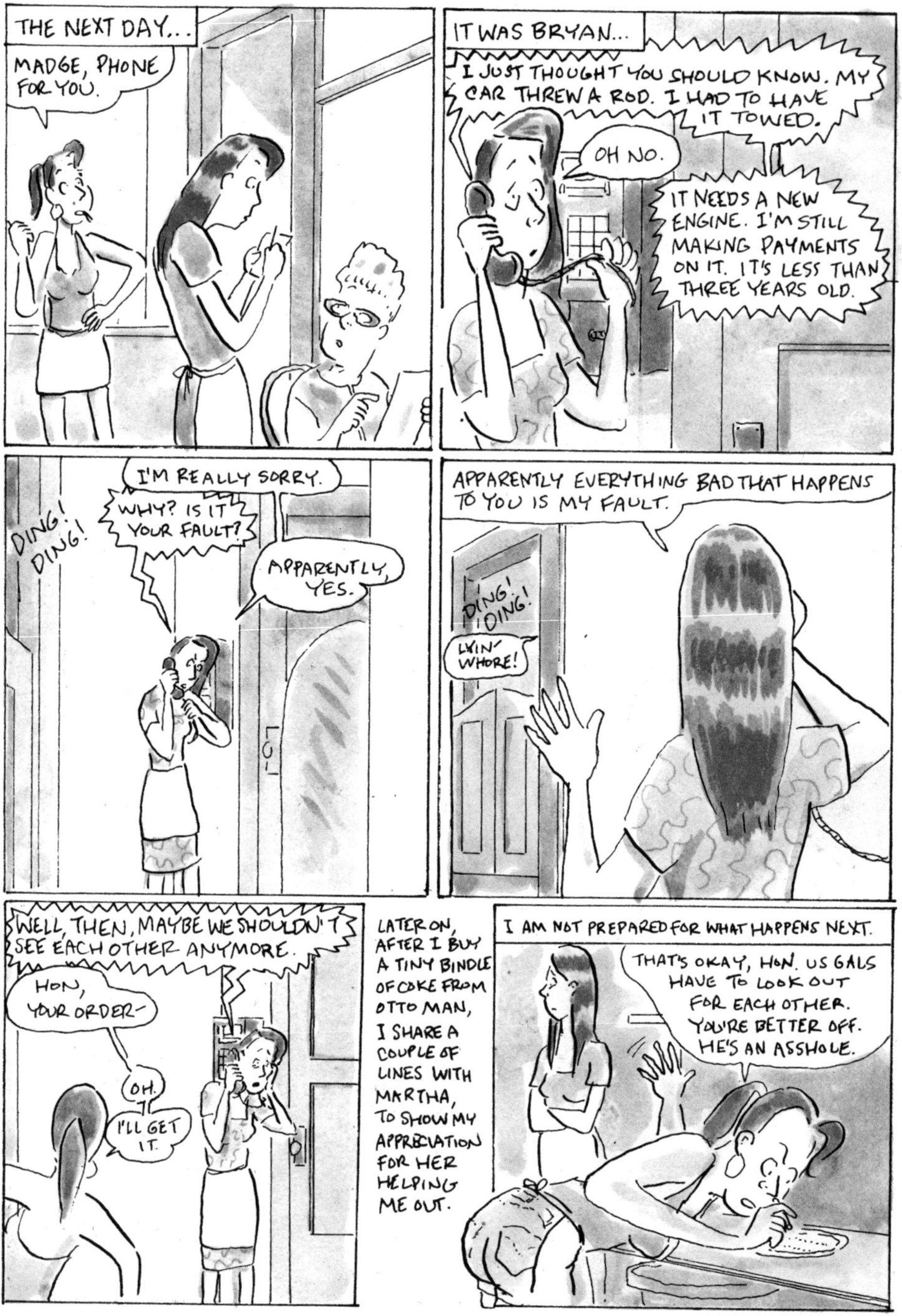
THE NEXT DAY...
MADGE, PHONE FOR YOU.
IT WAS BRYAN...
I JUST THOUGHT YOU SHOULD KNOW. MY CAR THREW A ROD. I HAD TO HAVE IT TOWED.
OH NO.
IT NEEDS A NEW ENGINE. I'M STILL MAKING PAYMENTS ON IT. IT'S LESS THAN THREE YEARS OLD.
I'M REALLY SORRY.
DING! DING!
WHY? IS IT YOUR FAULT?
APPARENTLY, YES.
APPARENTLY EVERYTHING BAD THAT HAPPENS TO YOU IS MY FAULT.
DING! DING!
LYIN' WHORE!
WELL, THEN, MAYBE WE SHOULDN'T SEE EACH OTHER ANYMORE.
HON, YOUR ORDER-
OH.
I'LL GET IT.
LATER ON, AFTER I BUY A TINY BINDLE OF COKE FROM OTTO MAN, I SHARE A COUPLE OF LINES WITH MARTHA, TO SHOW MY APPRECIATION FOR HER HELPING ME OUT.
I AM NOT PREPARED FOR WHAT HAPPENS NEXT.
THAT'S OKAY, HON. US GALS HAVE TO LOOK OUT FOR EACH OTHER. YOU'RE BETTER OFF. HE'S AN ASSHOLE.

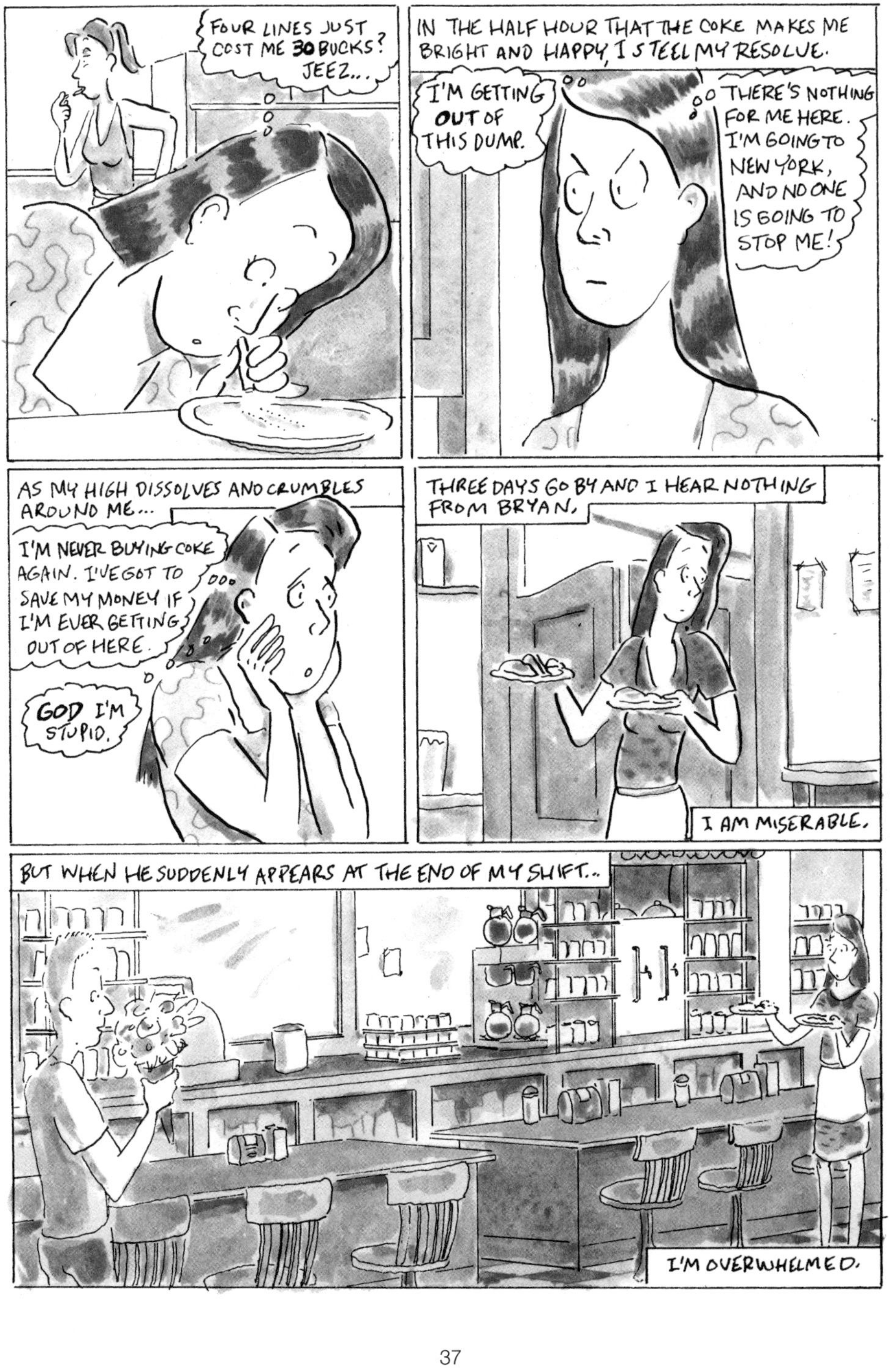
FOUR LINES JUST COST ME 30 BUCKS? JEEZ...
IN THE HALF HOUR THAT THE COKE MAKES ME BRIGHT AND HAPPY, I STEEL MY RESOLVE.
I'M GETTING OUT OF THIS DUMP.
THERE'S NOTHING FOR ME HERE. I'M GOING TO NEW YORK, AND NO ONE IS GOING TO STOP ME!
AS MY HIGH DISSOLVES AND CRUMBLES AROUND ME...
I'M NEVER BUYING COKE AGAIN. I'VE GOT TO SAVE MY MONEY IF I'M EVER GETTING OUT OF HERE.
GOD I'M STUPID.
THREE DAYS GO BY AND I HEAR NOTHING FROM BRYAN.
I AM MISERABLE.
BUT WHEN HE SUDDENLY APPEARS AT THE END OF MY SHIFT...
I'M OVERWHELMED.

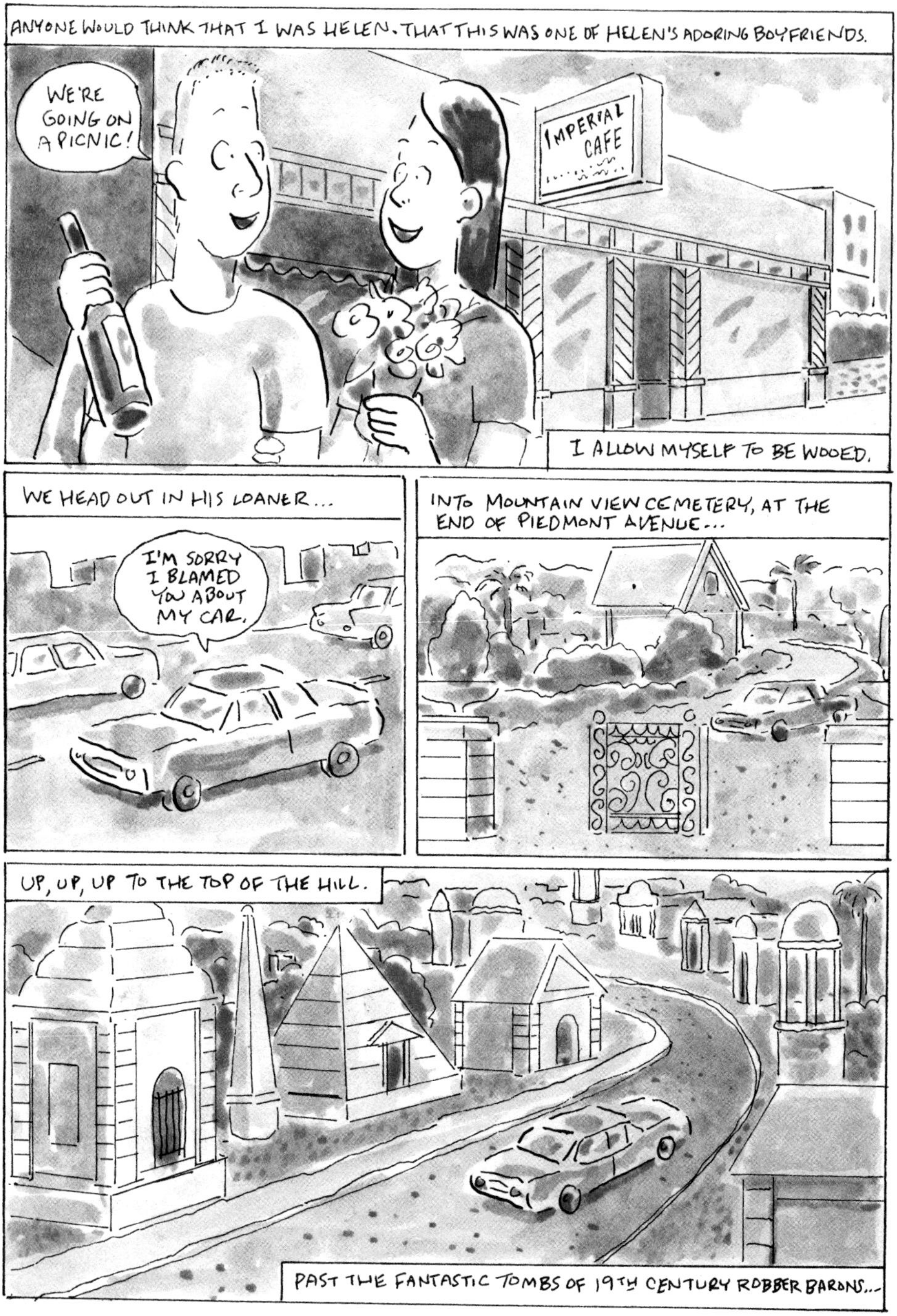
ANYONE WOULD THINK THAT I WAS HELEN. THAT THIS WAS ONE OF HELEN'S ADORING BOYFRIENDS.
WE'RE GOING ON A PICNIC!
IMPERIAL CAFE
I ALLOW MYSELF TO BE WOOED.
WE HEAD OUT IN HIS LOANER...
I'M SORRY I BLAMED YOU ABOUT MY CAR.
INTO MOUNTAIN VIEW CEMETERY, AT THE END OF PIEDMONT AVENUE...
UP, UP, UP TO THE TOP OF THE HILL.
PAST THE FANTASTIC TOMBS OF 19TH CENTURY ROBBER BARONS...

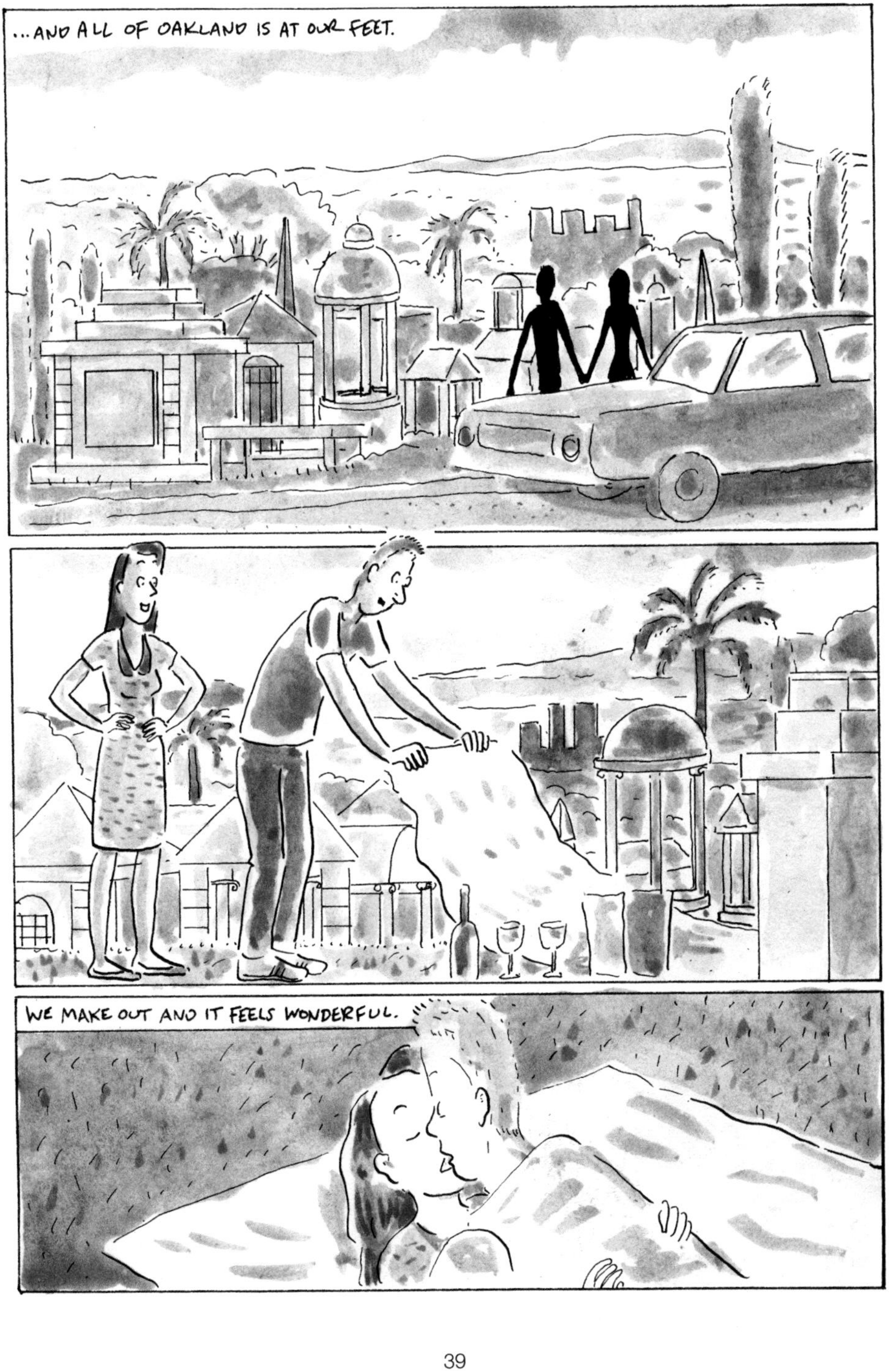
...AND ALL OF OAKLAND IS AT OUR FEET.
WE MAKE OUT AND IT FEELS WONDERFUL.

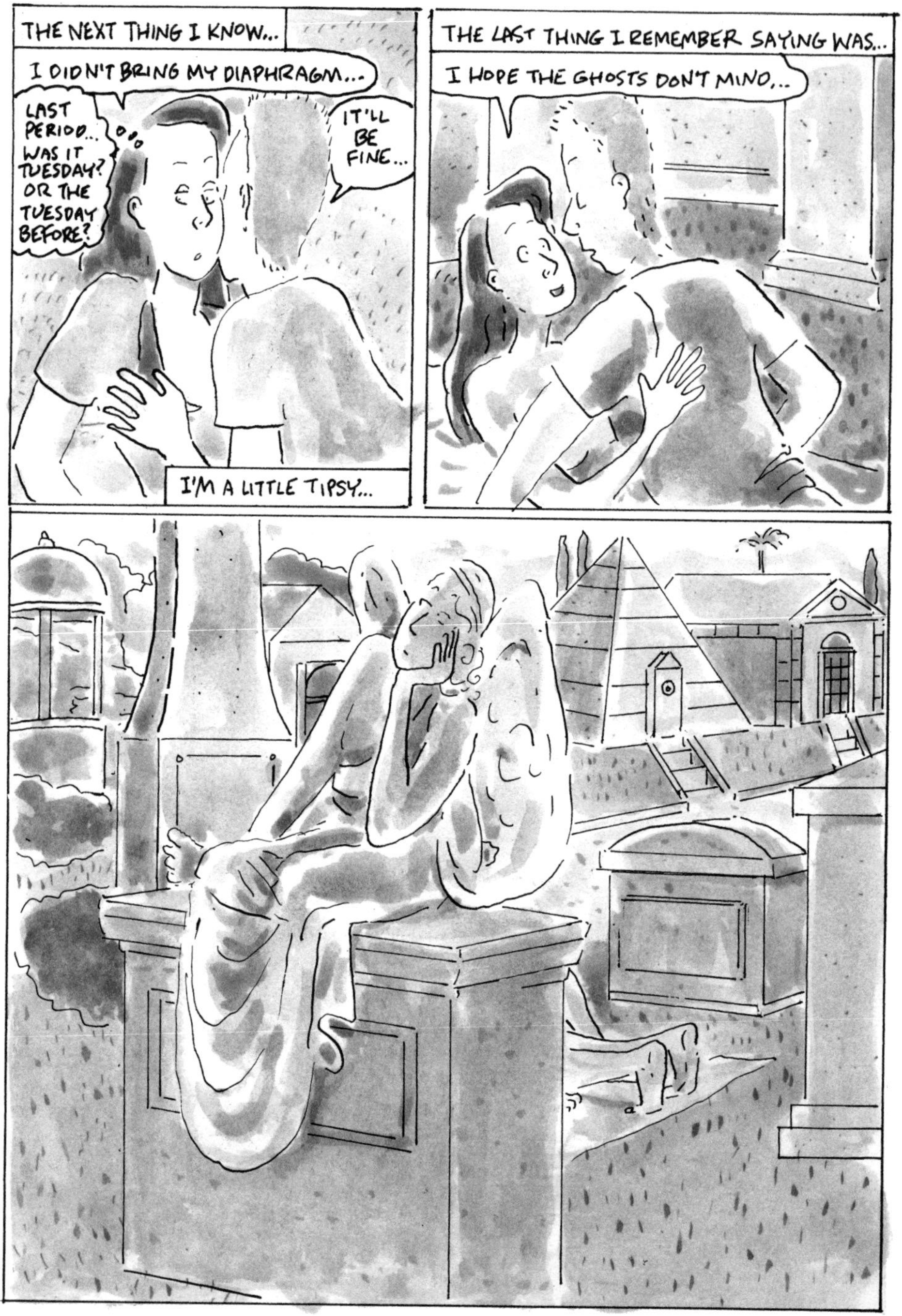
THE NEXT THING I KNOW...
I DIDN'T BRING MY DIAPHRAGM...
LAST PERIOD... WAS IT TUESDAY? OR THE TUESDAY BEFORE?
IT'LL BE FINE...
I'M A LITTLE TIPSY...
THE LAST THING I REMEMBER SAYING WAS...
I HOPE THE GHOSTS DON'T MIND...

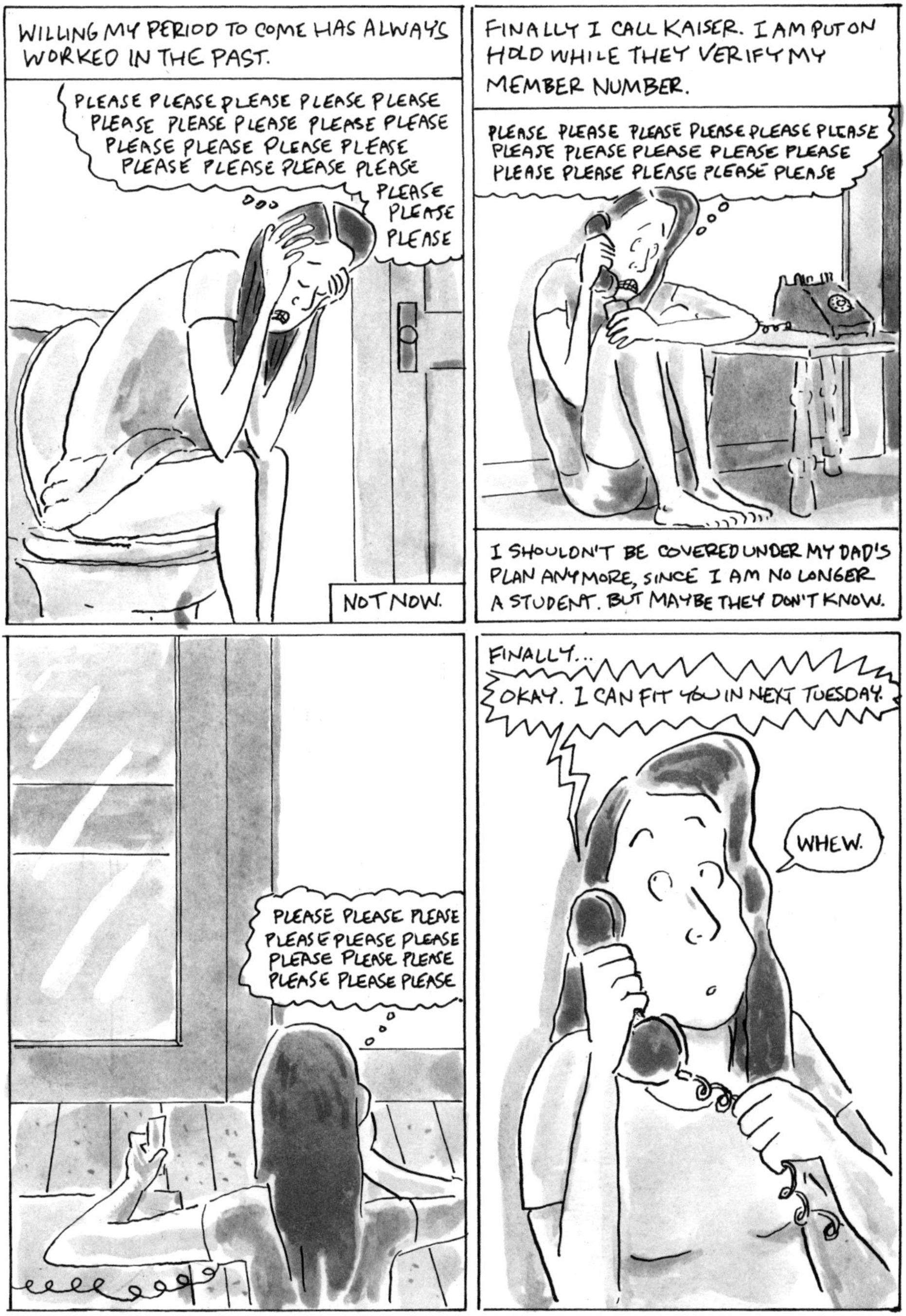
WILLING MY PERIOD TO COME HAS ALWAYS WORKED IN THE PAST.
PLEASE PLEASE
NOT NOW.
FINALLY I CALL KAISER. I AM PUT ON HOLD WHILE THEY VERIFY MY MEMBER NUMBER.
PLEASE PLEASE PLEASE PLEASE PLEASE PLEASE PLEASE PLEASE PLEASE PLEASE PLEASE PLEASE PLEASE PLEASE PLEASE PLEASE
I SHOULDN'T BE COVERED UNDER MY DAD'S PLAN ANYMORE, SINCE I AM NO LONGER A STUDENT. BUT MAYBE THEY DON'T KNOW.
PLEASE PLEASE PLEASE PLEASE PLEASE PLEASE PLEASE PLEASE PLEASE PLEASE PLEASE PLEASE
FINALLY...
OKAY. I CAN FIT YOU IN NEXT TUESDAY.
WHEW.

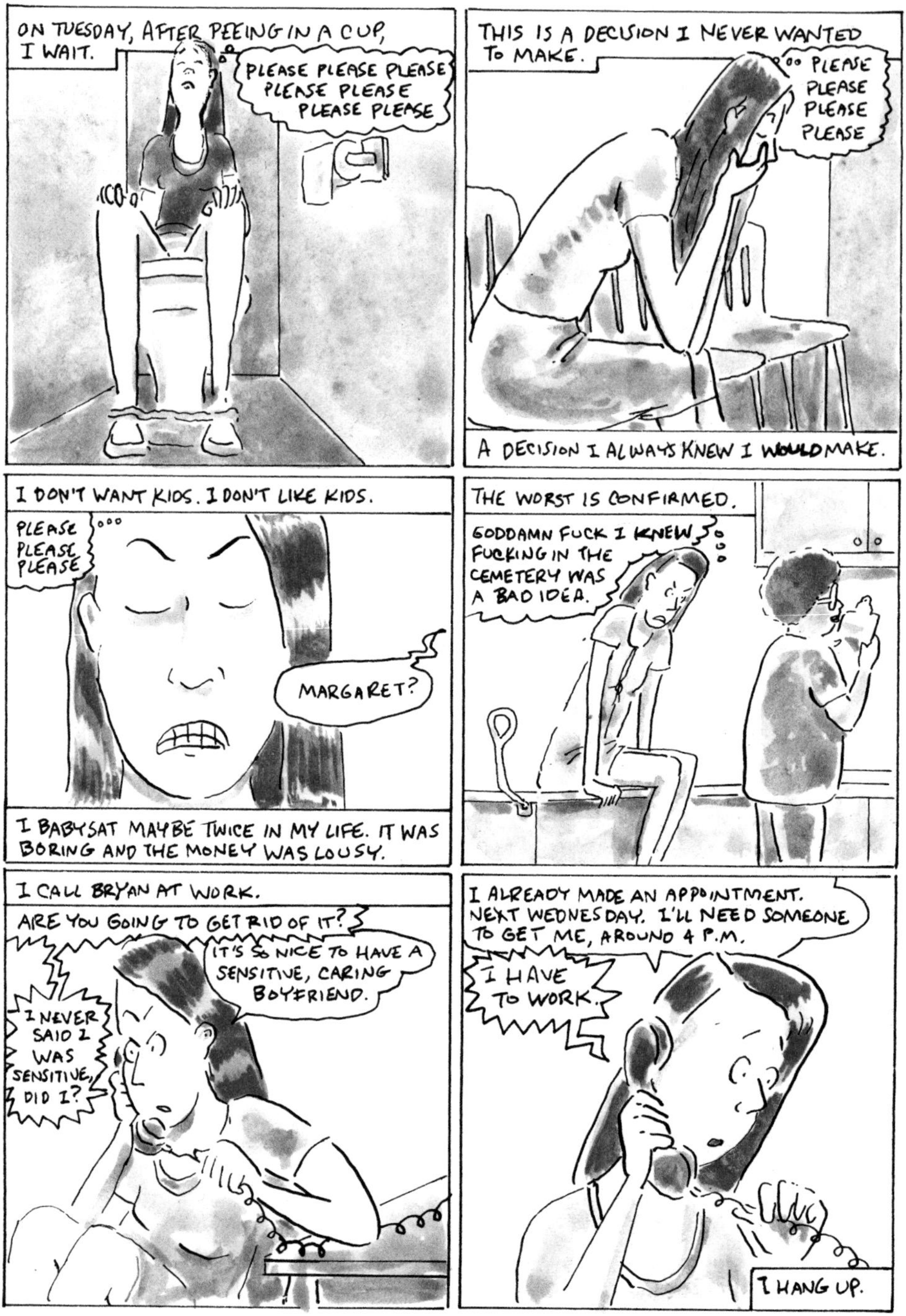
ON TUESDAY, AFTER PEEING IN A CUP, I WAIT.
PLEASE PLEASE PLEASE PLEASE PLEASE PLEASE PLEASE
THIS IS A DECISION I NEVER WANTED TO MAKE.
PLEASE PLEASE PLEASE PLEASE
A DECISION I ALWAYS KNEW I WOULD MAKE.
I DON'T WANT KIDS. I DON'T LIKE KIDS.
PLEASE PLEASE PLEASE
MARGARET?
I BABYSAT MAYBE TWICE IN MY LIFE. IT WAS BORING AND THE MONEY WAS LOUSY.
THE WORST IS CONFIRMED.
GODDAMN FUCK I KNEW FUCKING IN THE CEMETERY WAS A BAD IDEA.
I CALL BRYAN AT WORK.
ARE YOU GOING TO GET RID OF IT?
IT'S SO NICE TO HAVE A SENSITIVE, CARING BOYFRIEND.
I NEVER SAID I WAS SENSITIVE, DID I?
I ALREADY MADE AN APPOINTMENT. NEXT WEDNESDAY. I'LL NEED SOMEONE TO GET ME, AROUND 4 P.M.
I HAVE TO WORK.
I HANG UP.

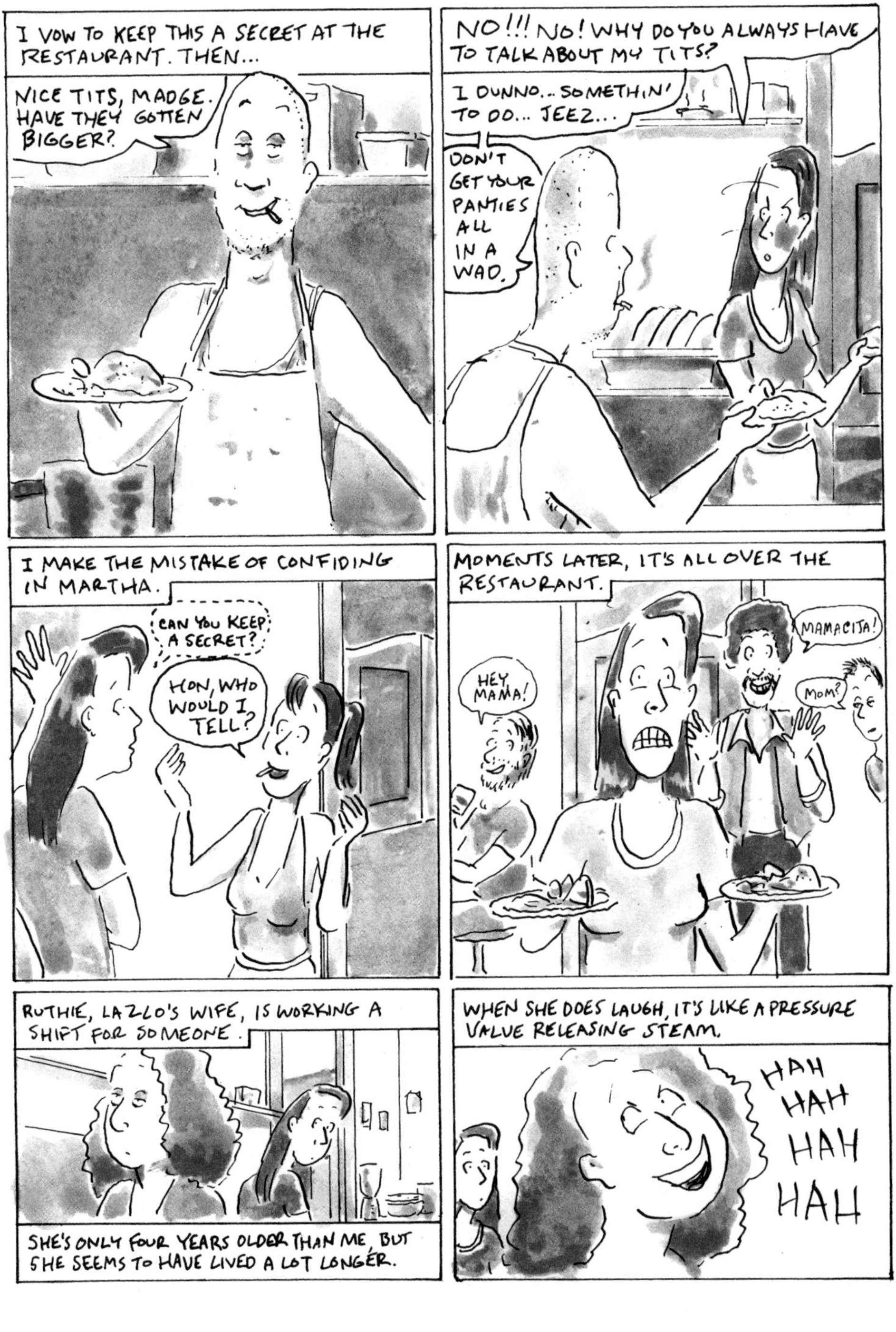
I VOW TO KEEP THIS A SECRET AT THE RESTAURANT. THEN...
NICE TITS, MADGE. HAVE THEY GOTTEN BIGGER?
NO!!! NO! WHY DO YOU ALWAYS HAVE TO TALK ABOUT MY TITS?
I DUNNO... SOMETHIN' TO DO... JEEZ...
DON'T GET YOUR PANTIES ALL IN A WAD.
I MAKE THE MISTAKE OF CONFIDING IN MARTHA.
CAN YOU KEEP A SECRET?
HON, WHO WOULD I TELL?
MOMENTS LATER, IT'S ALL OVER THE RESTAURANT.
HEY MAMA!
MAMACITA!
MOM?
RUTHIE, LAZLO'S WIFE, IS WORKING A SHIFT FOR SOMEONE.
SHE'S ONLY FOUR YEARS OLDER THAN ME, BUT SHE SEEMS TO HAVE LIVED A LOT LONGER.
WHEN SHE DOES LAUGH, IT'S LIKE A PRESSURE VALVE RELEASING STEAM.
HAH HAH HAH HAH

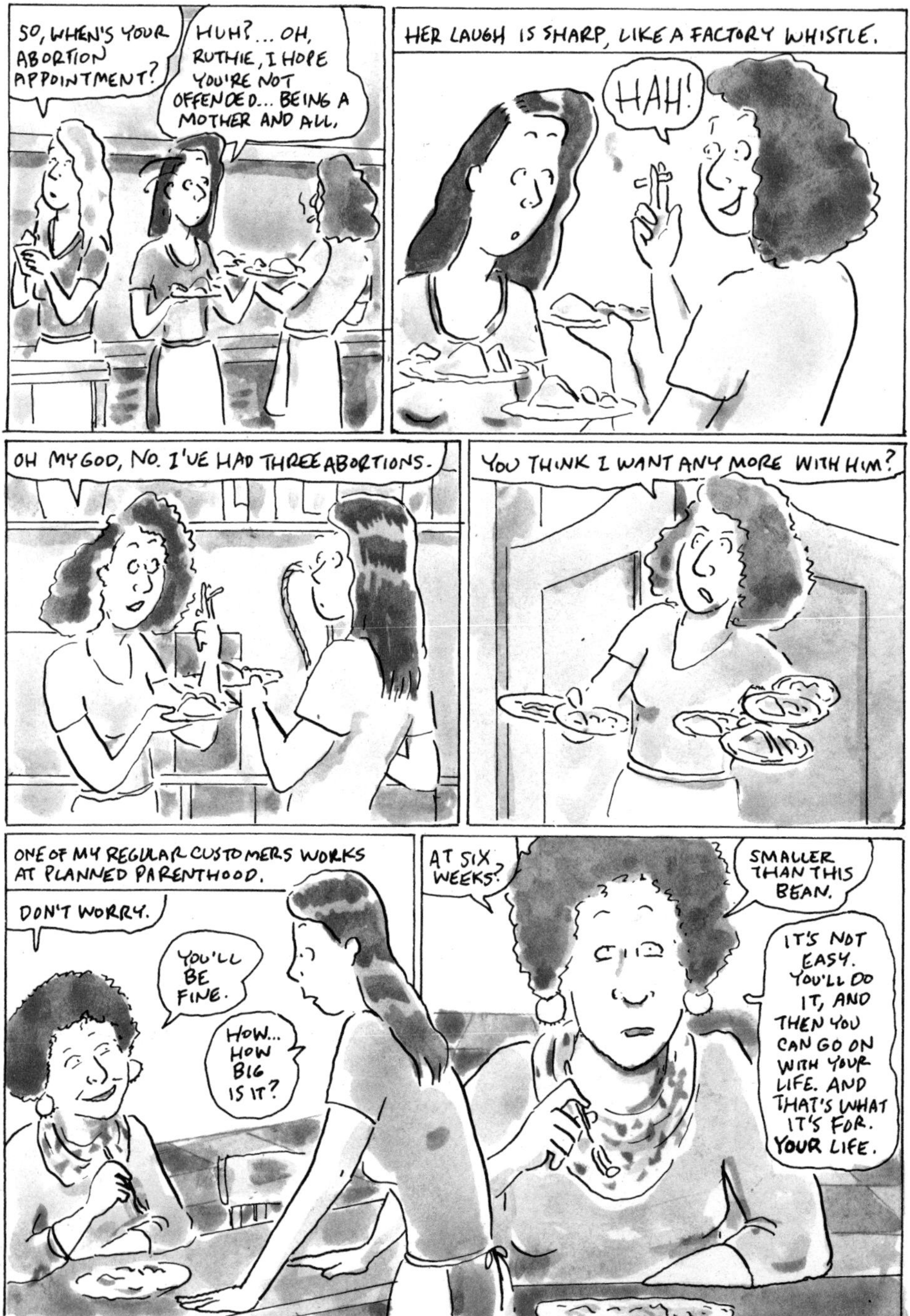
SO, WHEN'S YOUR ABORTION APPOINTMENT?
HUH?... OH, RUTHIE, I HOPE YOU'RE NOT OFFENDED... BEING A MOTHER AND ALL.
HER LAUGH IS SHARP, LIKE A FACTORY WHISTLE.
HAH!
OH MY GOD, NO. I'VE HAD THREE ABORTIONS.
YOU THINK I WANT ANY MORE WITH HIM?
ONE OF MY REGULAR CUSTOMERS WORKS AT PLANNED PARENTHOOD.
DON'T WORRY.
YOU'LL BE FINE.
HOW... HOW BIG IS IT?
AT SIX WEEKS?
SMALLER THAN THIS BEAN.
IT'S NOT EASY. YOU'LL DO IT, AND THEN YOU CAN GO ON WITH YOUR LIFE. AND THAT'S WHAT IT'S FOR. **YOUR** LIFE.

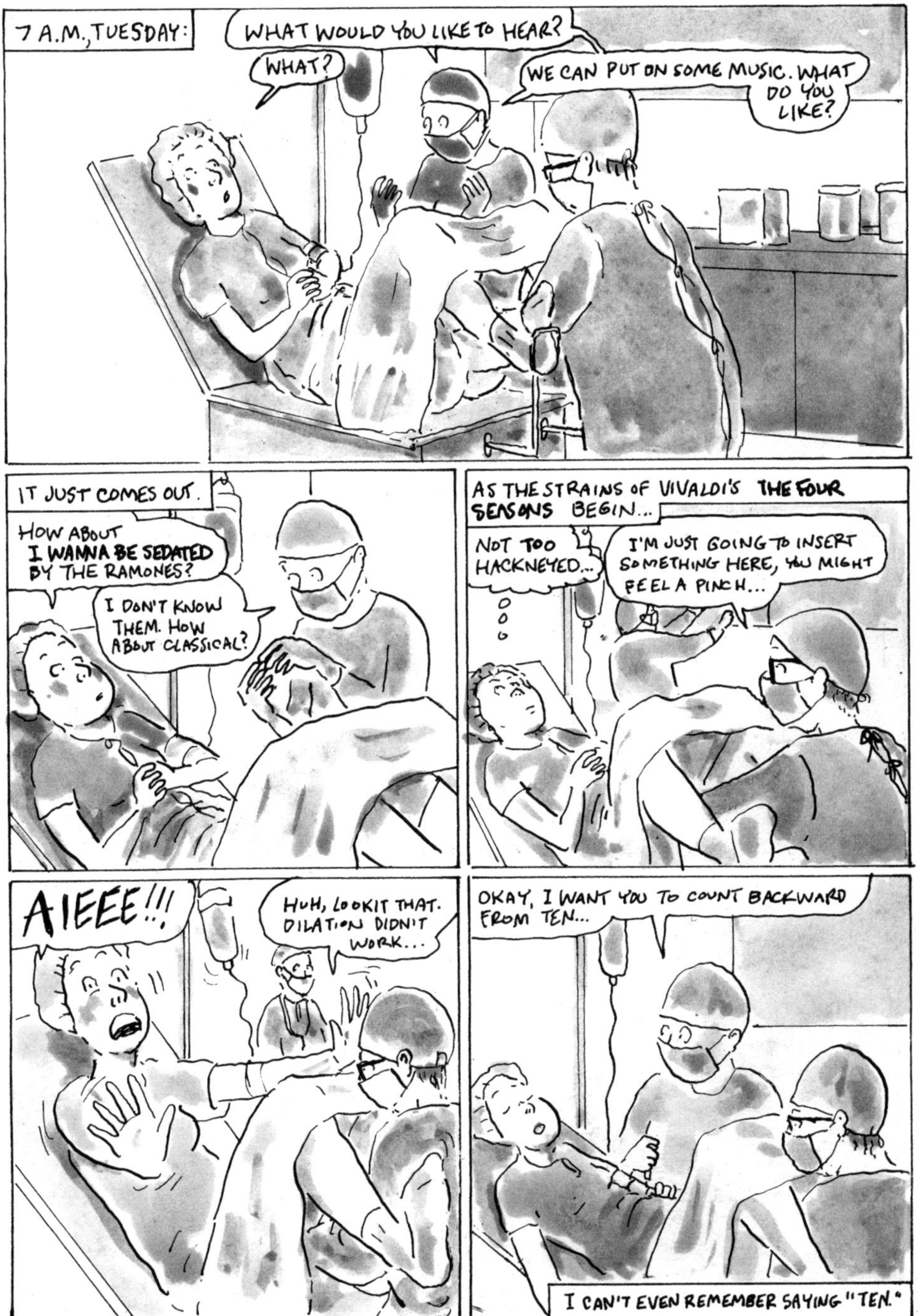
7 A.M., TUESDAY:
WHAT WOULD YOU LIKE TO HEAR?
WHAT?
WE CAN PUT ON SOME MUSIC. WHAT DO YOU LIKE?
IT JUST COMES OUT.
HOW ABOUT I WANNA BE SEDATED BY THE RAMONES?
I DON'T KNOW THEM. HOW ABOUT CLASSICAL?
AS THE STRAINS OF VIVALDI'S THE FOUR SEASONS BEGIN...
NOT TOO HACKNEYED...
I'M JUST GOING TO INSERT SOMETHING HERE, YOU MIGHT FEEL A PINCH...
AIEEE!!!
HUH, LOOKIT THAT. DILATION DIDN'T WORK...
OKAY, I WANT YOU TO COUNT BACKWARD FROM TEN...
I CAN'T EVEN REMEMBER SAYING "TEN."

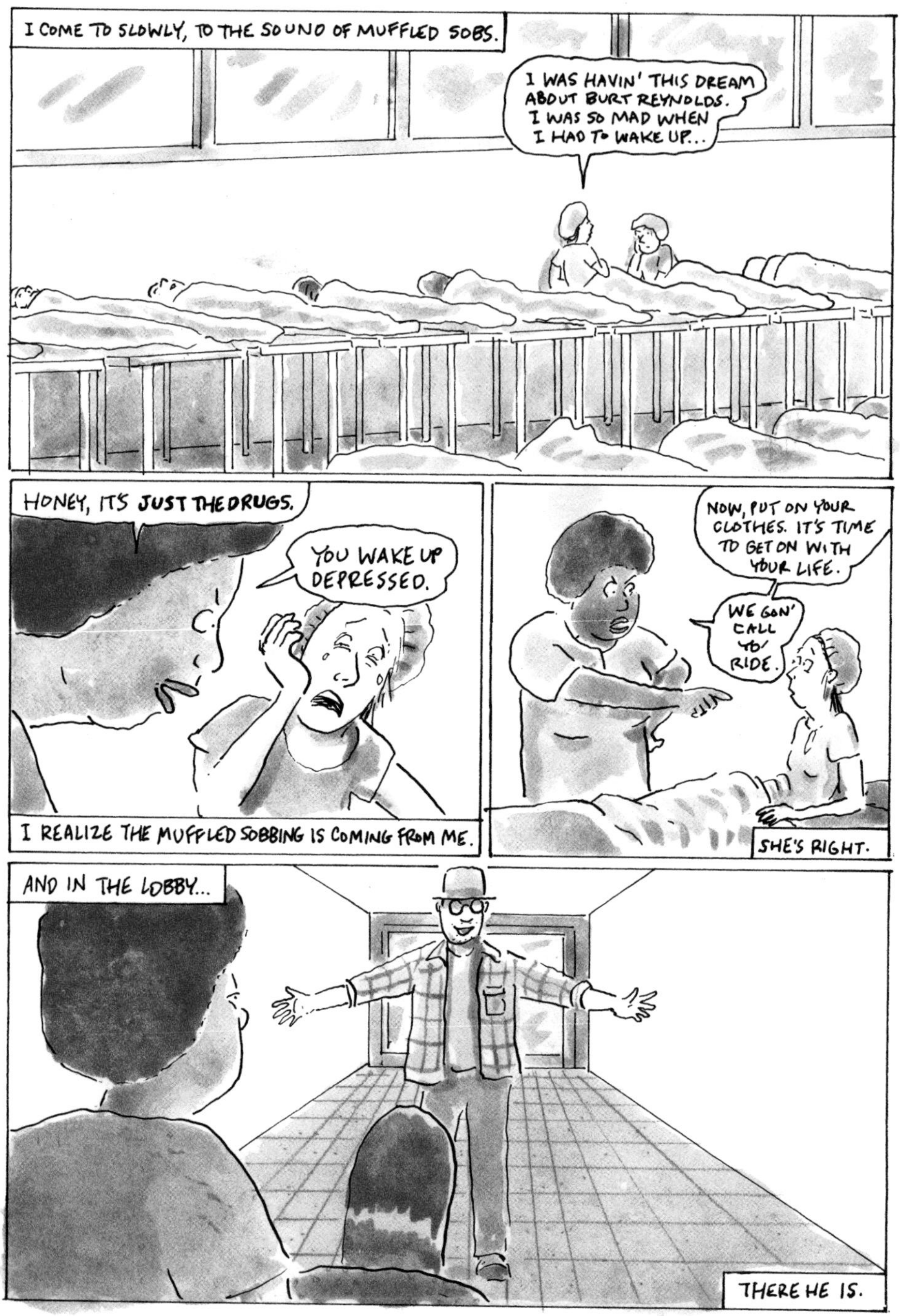
I COME TO SLOWLY, TO THE SOUND OF MUFFLED SOBS.
I WAS HAVIN' THIS DREAM ABOUT BURT REYNOLDS. I WAS SO MAD WHEN I HAD TO WAKE UP...
HONEY, IT'S JUST THE DRUGS.
YOU WAKE UP DEPRESSED.
I REALIZE THE MUFFLED SOBBING IS COMING FROM ME.
NOW, PUT ON YOUR CLOTHES. IT'S TIME TO GET ON WITH YOUR LIFE.
WE GON' CALL YO' RIDE.
SHE'S RIGHT.
AND IN THE LOBBY...
THERE HE IS.

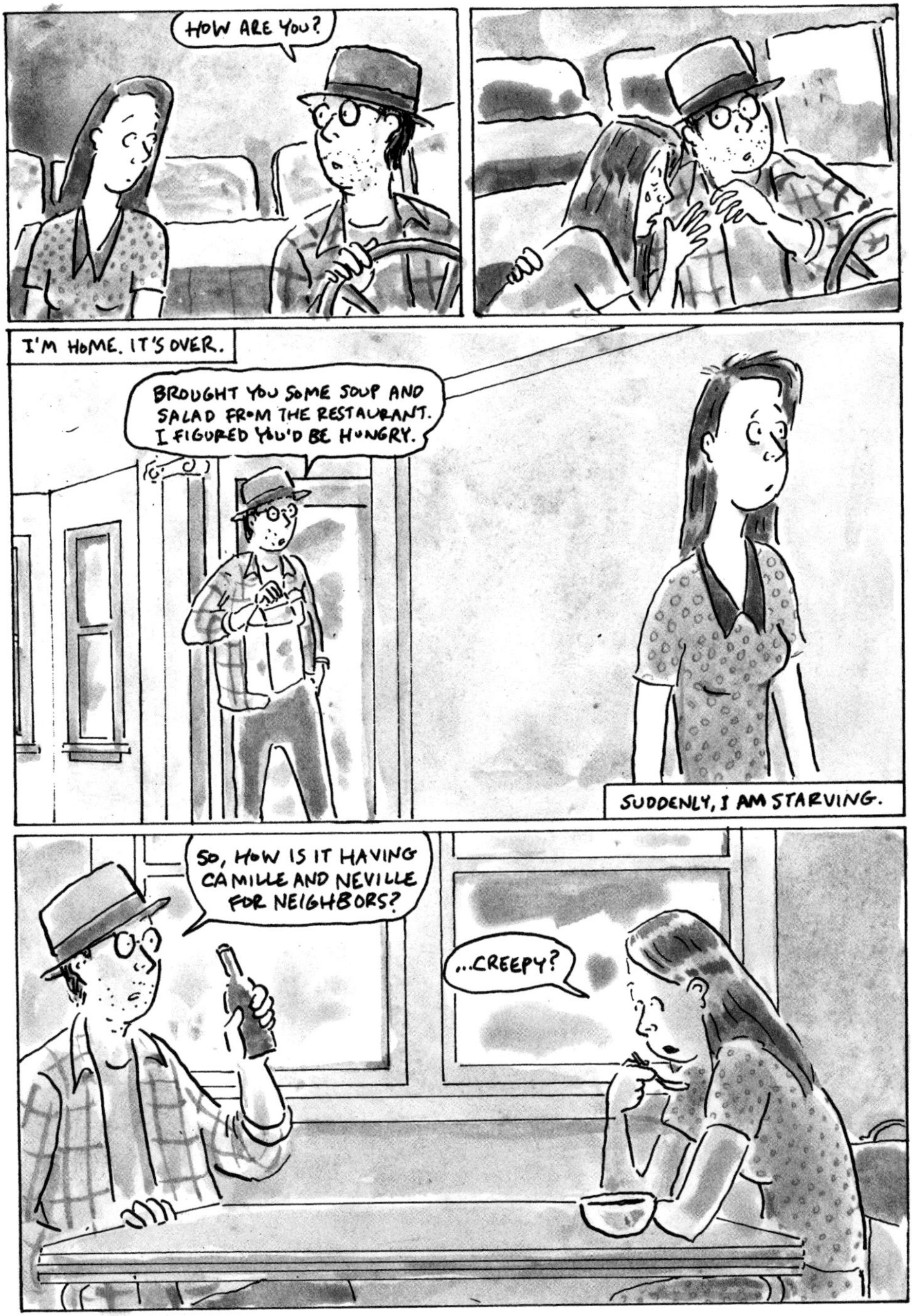
HOW ARE YOU?
I'M HOME. IT'S OVER.
BROUGHT YOU SOME SOUP AND SALAD FROM THE RESTAURANT. I FIGURED YOU'D BE HUNGRY.
SUDDENLY, I AM STARVING.
SO, HOW IS IT HAVING CAMILLE AND NEVILLE FOR NEIGHBORS?
...CREEPY?

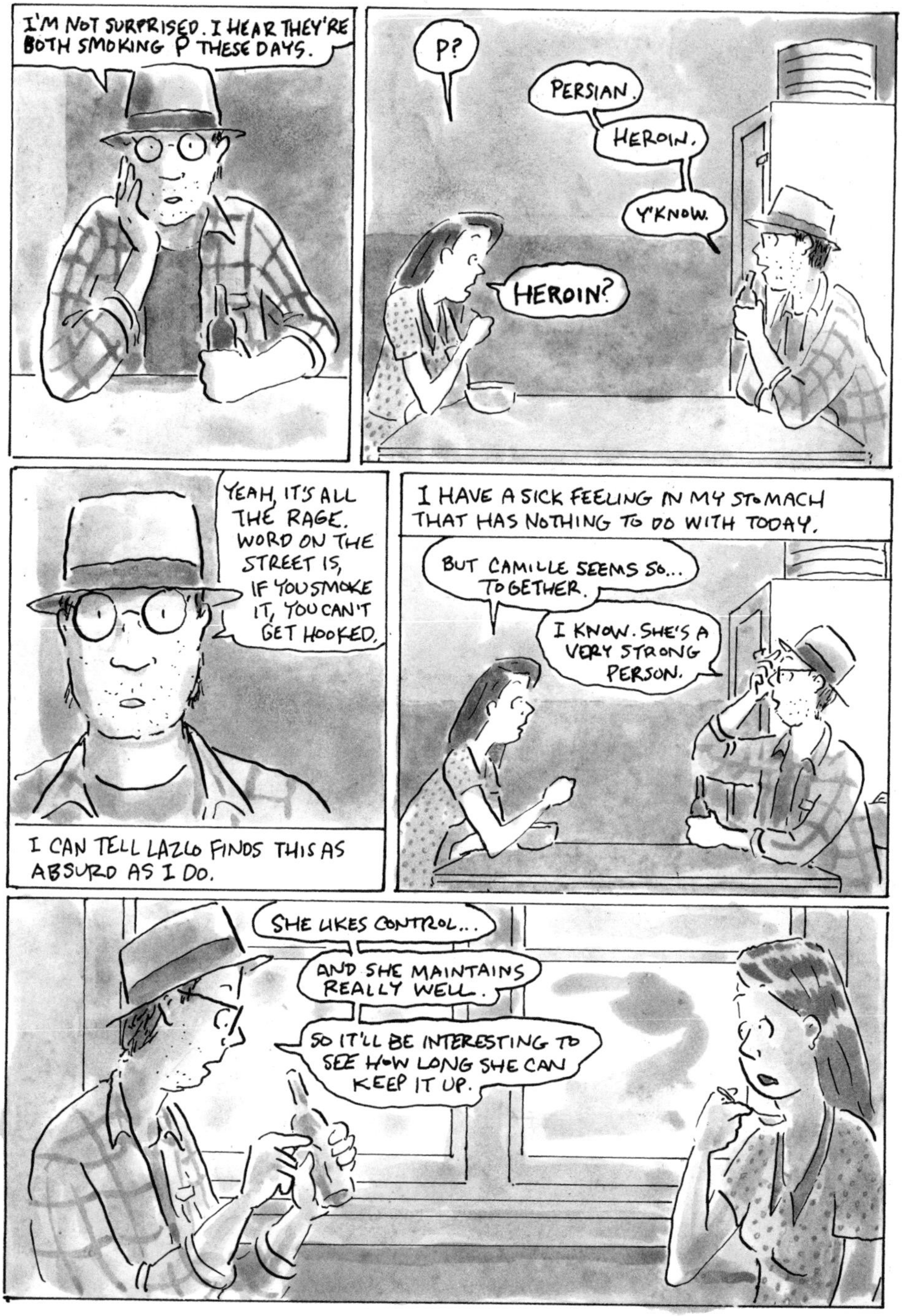
I'M NOT SURPRISED. I HEAR THEY'RE BOTH SMOKING P THESE DAYS.
P?
PERSIAN.
HEROIN.
Y'KNOW.
HEROIN?
YEAH, IT'S ALL THE RAGE. WORD ON THE STREET IS, IF YOU SMOKE IT, YOU CAN'T GET HOOKED.
I CAN TELL LAZLO FINDS THIS AS ABSURD AS I DO.
I HAVE A SICK FEELING IN MY STOMACH THAT HAS NOTHING TO DO WITH TODAY.
BUT CAMILLE SEEMS SO... TOGETHER.
I KNOW. SHE'S A VERY STRONG PERSON.
SHE LIKES CONTROL...
AND SHE MAINTAINS REALLY WELL.
SO IT'LL BE INTERESTING TO SEE HOW LONG SHE CAN KEEP IT UP.

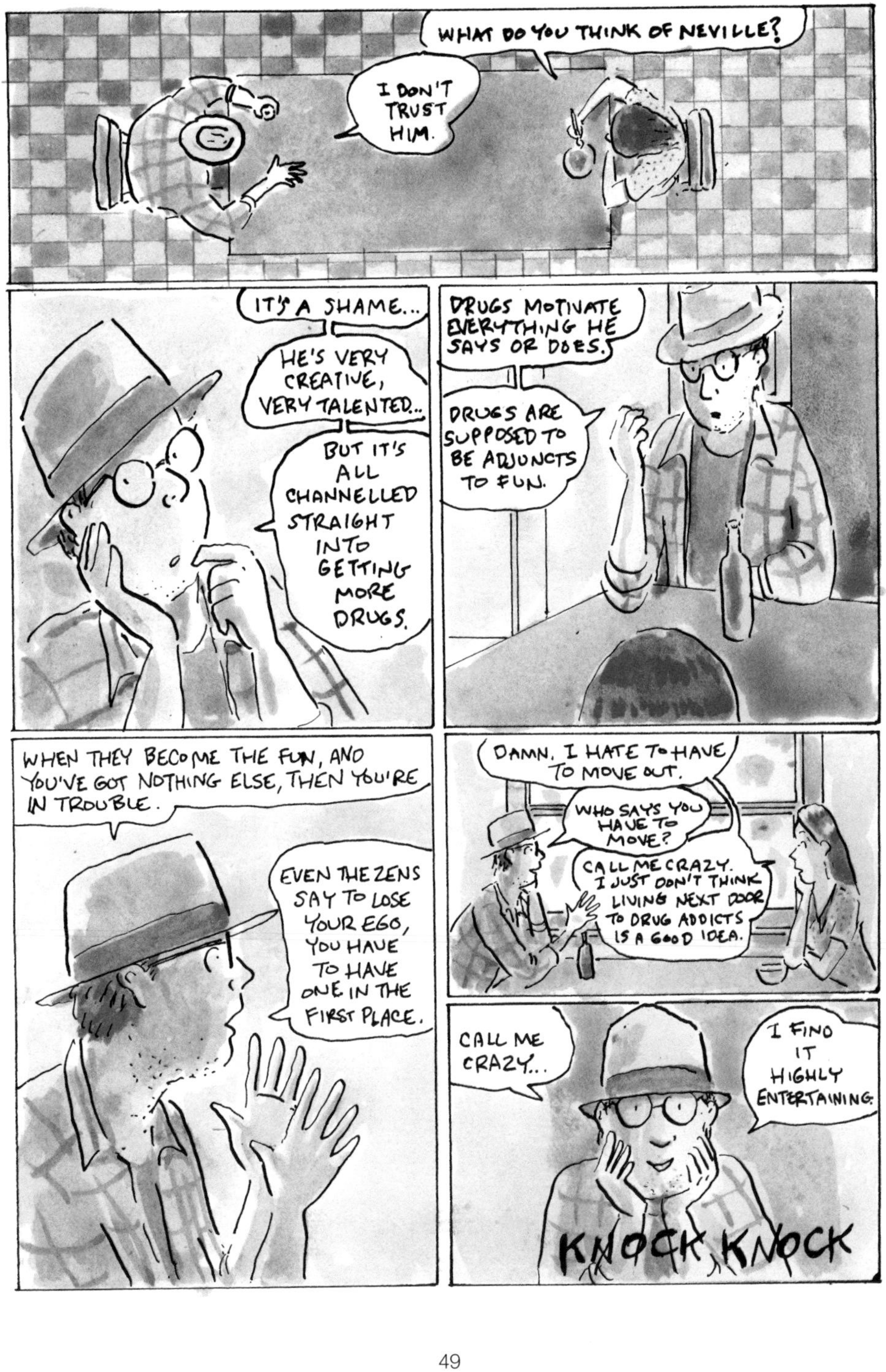
WHAT DO YOU THINK OF NEVILLE?
I DON'T TRUST HIM.
IT'S A SHAME...
HE'S VERY CREATIVE, VERY TALENTED...
BUT IT'S ALL CHANNELLED STRAIGHT INTO GETTING MORE DRUGS.
DRUGS MOTIVATE EVERYTHING HE SAYS OR DOES.
DRUGS ARE SUPPOSED TO BE ADJUNCTS TO FUN.
WHEN THEY BECOME THE FUN, AND YOU'VE GOT NOTHING ELSE, THEN YOU'RE IN TROUBLE.
EVEN THE ZENS SAY TO LOSE YOUR EGO, YOU HAVE TO HAVE ONE IN THE FIRST PLACE.
DAMN. I HATE TO HAVE TO MOVE OUT.
WHO SAYS YOU HAVE TO MOVE?
CALL ME CRAZY. I JUST DON'T THINK LIVING NEXT DOOR TO DRUG ADDICTS IS A GOOD IDEA.
CALL ME CRAZY...
I FIND IT HIGHLY ENTERTAINING.
KNOCK KNOCK

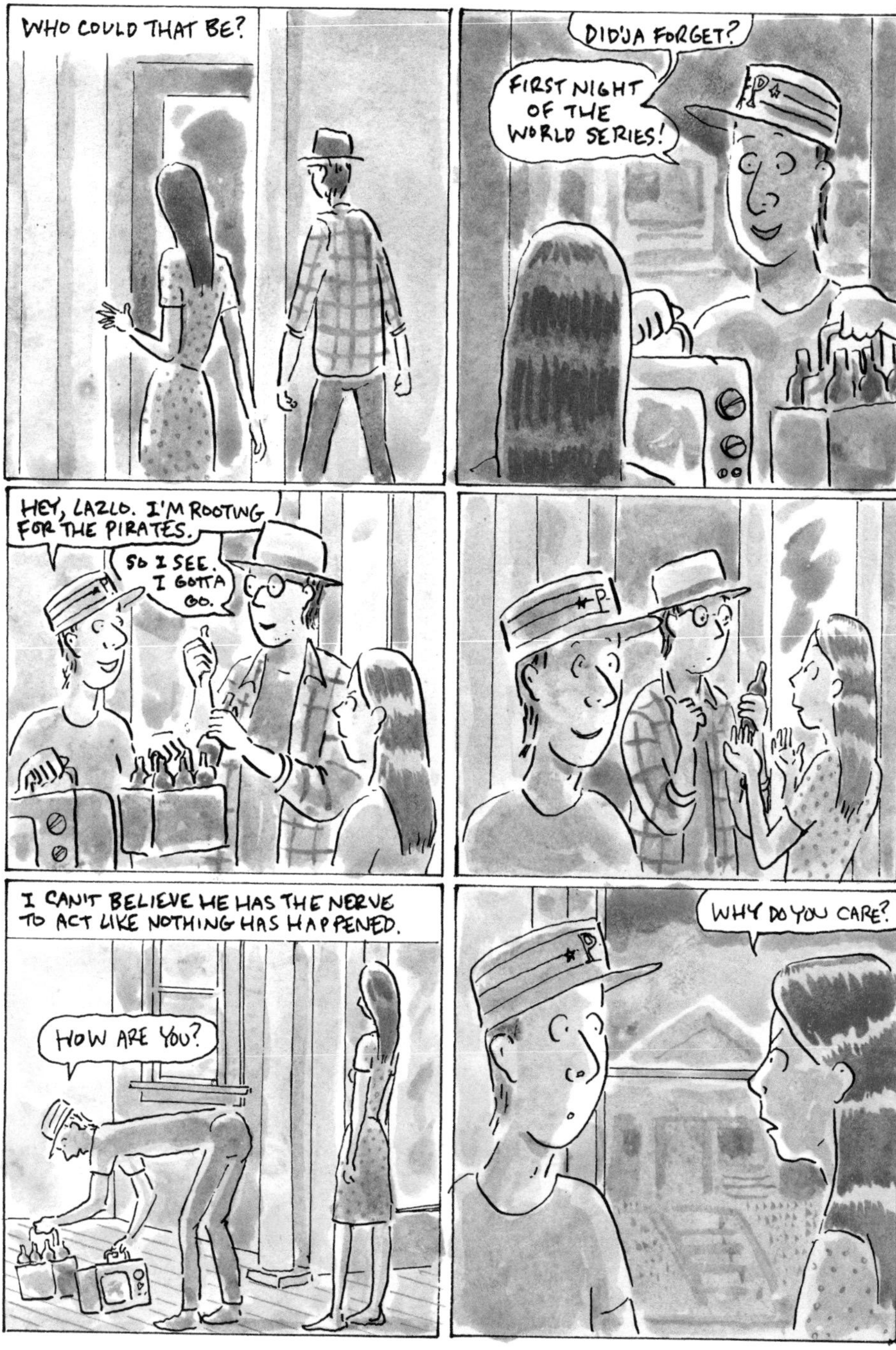
WHO COULD THAT BE?
DID'JA FORGET?
FIRST NIGHT OF THE WORLD SERIES!
HEY, LAZLO. I'M ROOTING FOR THE PIRATES.
SO I SEE. I GOTTA GO.
I CAN'T BELIEVE HE HAS THE NERVE TO ACT LIKE NOTHING HAS HAPPENED.
HOW ARE YOU?
WHY DO YOU CARE?

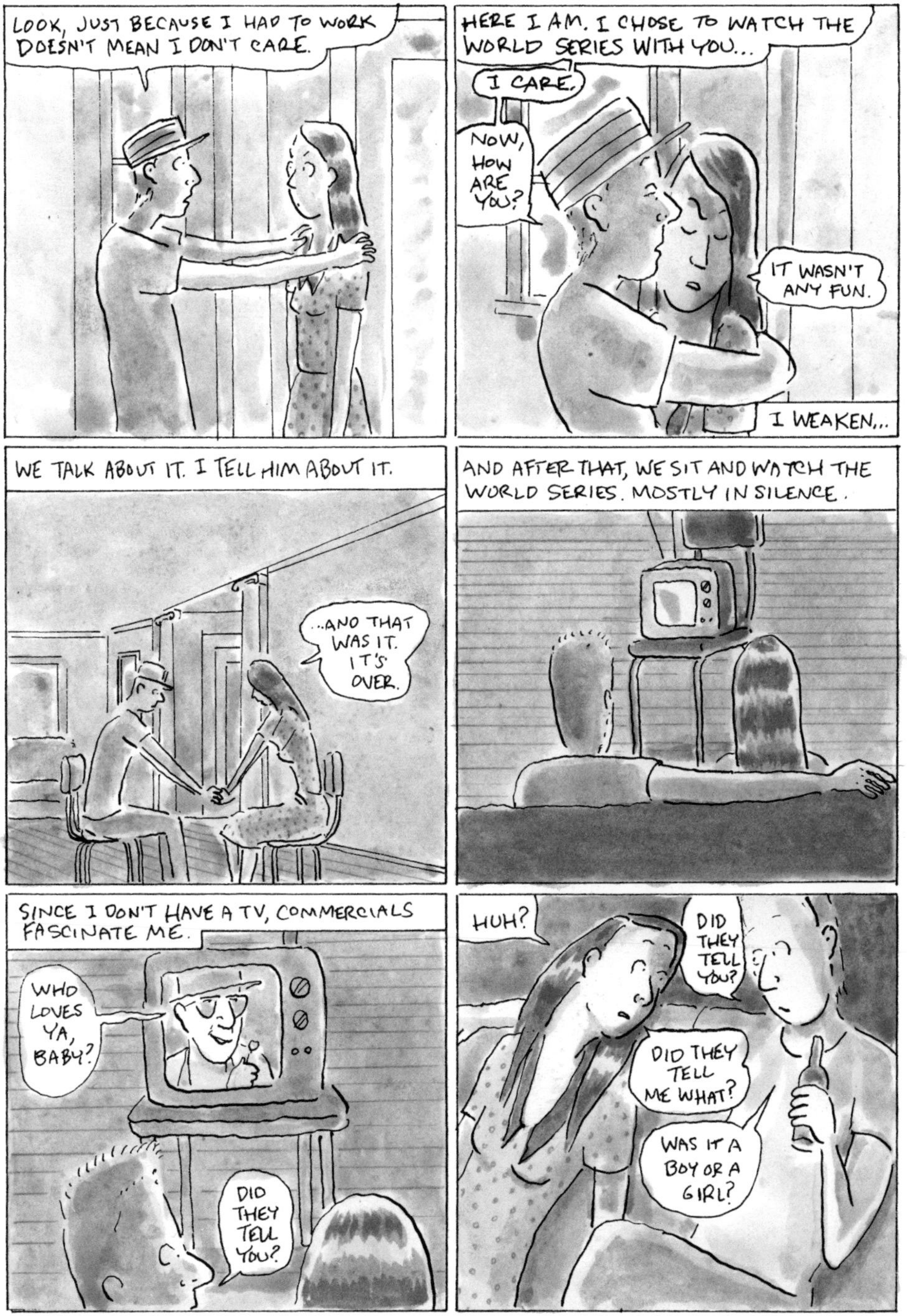
LOOK, JUST BECAUSE I HAD TO WORK DOESN'T MEAN I DON'T CARE.
HERE I AM. I CHOSE TO WATCH THE WORLD SERIES WITH YOU...
I CARE.
NOW, HOW ARE YOU?
IT WASN'T ANY FUN.
I WEAKEN...
WE TALK ABOUT IT. I TELL HIM ABOUT IT.
...AND THAT WAS IT. IT'S OVER.
AND AFTER THAT, WE SIT AND WATCH THE WORLD SERIES. MOSTLY IN SILENCE.
SINCE I DON'T HAVE A TV, COMMERCIALS FASCINATE ME.
WHO LOVES YA, BABY?
DID THEY TELL YOU?
HUH?
DID THEY TELL YOU?
DID THEY TELL ME WHAT?
WAS IT A BOY OR A GIRL?

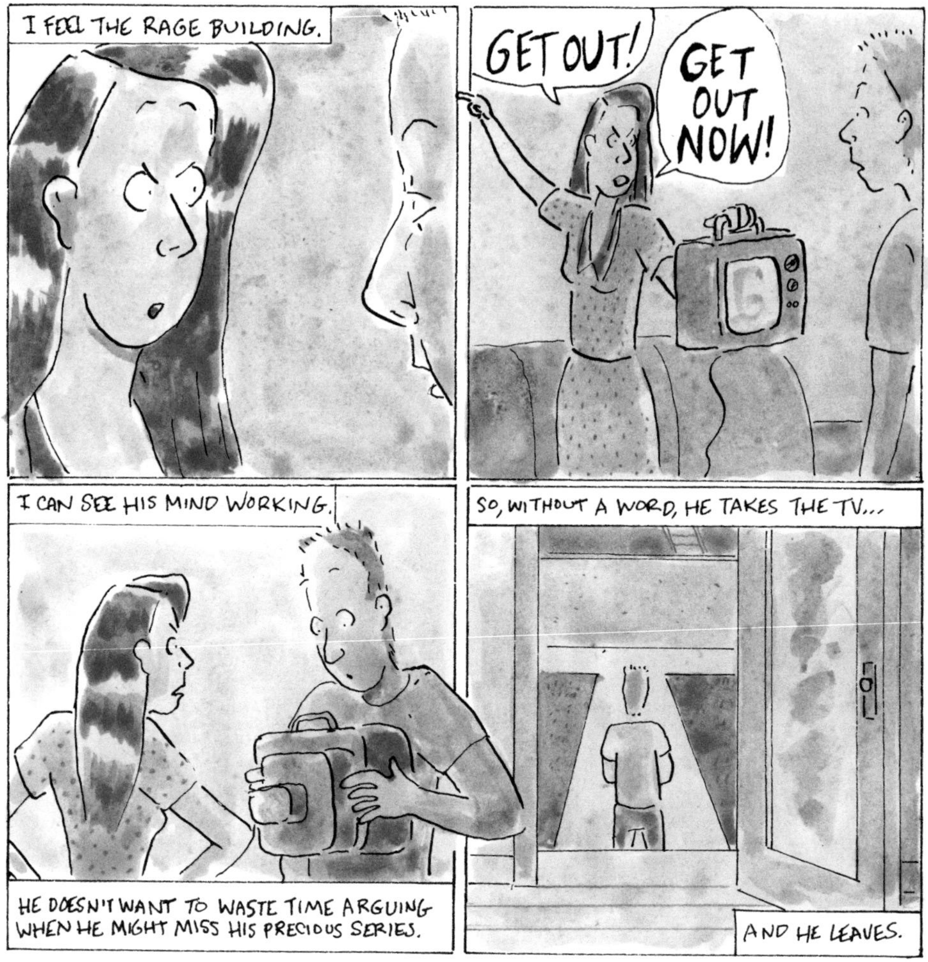
I FEEL THE RAGE BUILDING.
GET OUT!
GET OUT NOW!
I CAN SEE HIS MIND WORKING.
HE DOESN'T WANT TO WASTE TIME ARGUING WHEN HE MIGHT MISS HIS PRECIOUS SERIES.
SO, WITHOUT A WORD, HE TAKES THE TV...
AND HE LEAVES.

LATER, THAT'S WHAT I **WISHED** HAD HAPPENED.

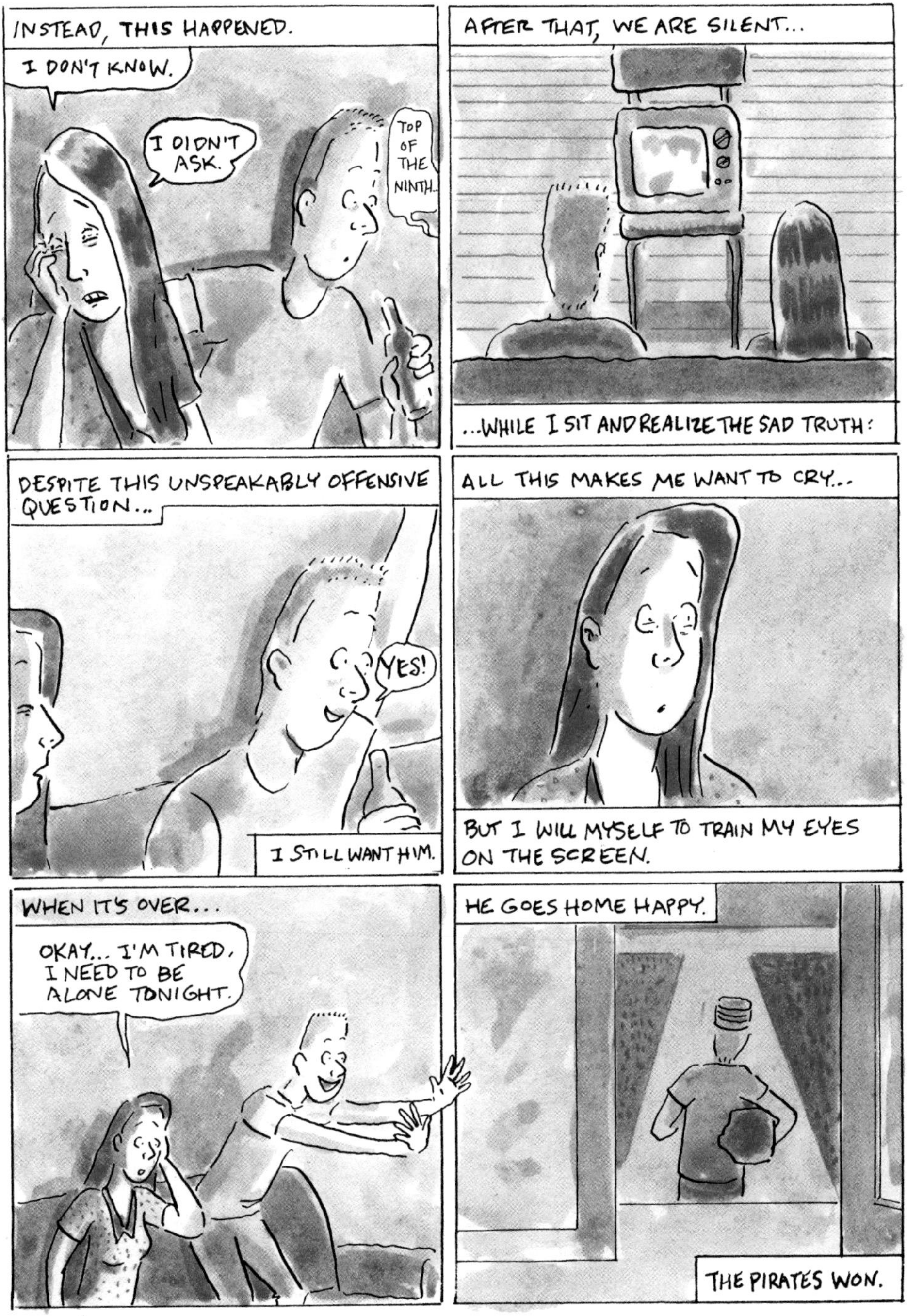

INSTEAD, THIS HAPPENED.
I DON'T KNOW.
I DIDN'T ASK.
TOP OF THE NINTH...
AFTER THAT, WE ARE SILENT...
...WHILE I SIT AND REALIZE THE SAD TRUTH:
DESPITE THIS UNSPEAKABLY OFFENSIVE QUESTION...
YES!
I STILL WANT HIM.
ALL THIS MAKES ME WANT TO CRY...
BUT I WILL MYSELF TO TRAIN MY EYES ON THE SCREEN.
WHEN IT'S OVER...
OKAY... I'M TIRED. I NEED TO BE ALONE TONIGHT.
HE GOES HOME HAPPY.
THE PIRATES WON.

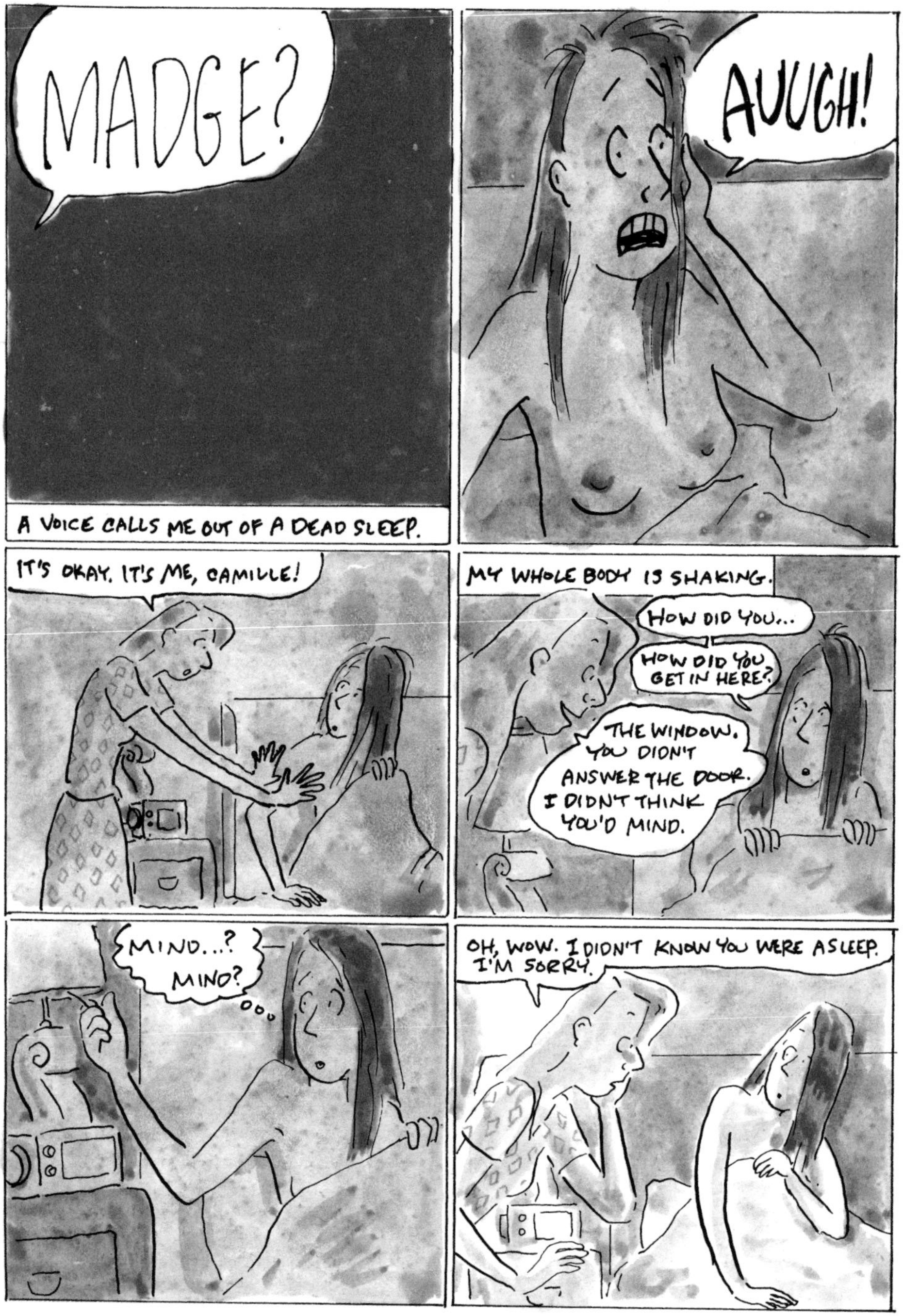
MADGE?
A VOICE CALLS ME OUT OF A DEAD SLEEP.
AUUGH!
IT'S OKAY. IT'S ME, CAMILLE!
MY WHOLE BODY IS SHAKING.
HOW DID YOU...
HOW DID YOU GET IN HERE?
THE WINDOW. YOU DIDN'T ANSWER THE DOOR. I DIDN'T THINK YOU'D MIND.
MIND...? MIND?
OH, WOW. I DIDN'T KNOW YOU WERE ASLEEP. I'M SORRY.

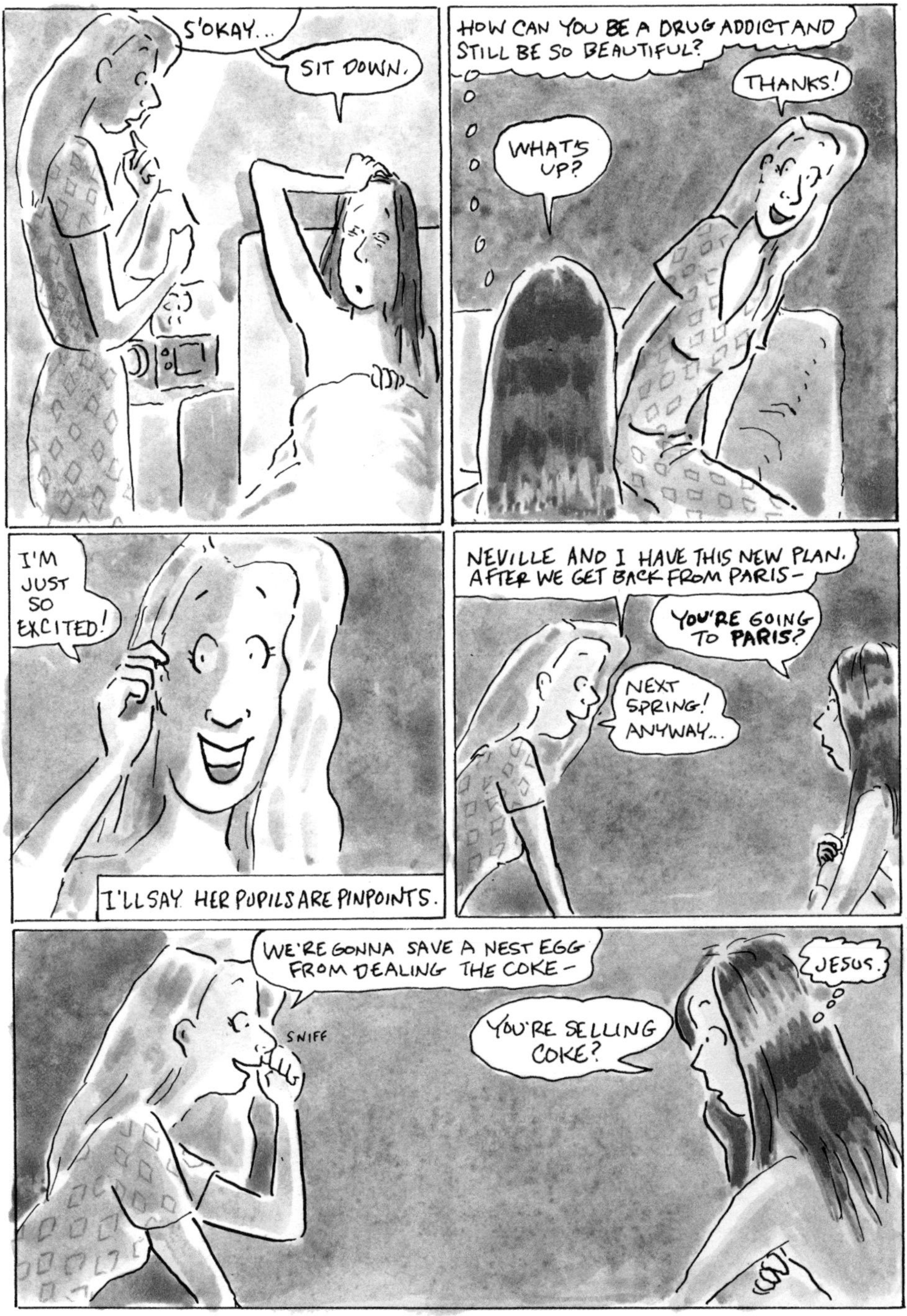
S'OKAY...
SIT DOWN.
HOW CAN YOU BE A DRUG ADDICT AND STILL BE SO BEAUTIFUL?
WHAT'S UP?
THANKS!
I'M JUST SO EXCITED!
I'LL SAY. HER PUPILS ARE PINPOINTS.
NEVILLE AND I HAVE THIS NEW PLAN. AFTER WE GET BACK FROM PARIS-
YOU'RE GOING TO PARIS?
NEXT SPRING! ANYWAY...
WE'RE GONNA SAVE A NEST EGG FROM DEALING THE COKE-
SNIFF
YOU'RE SELLING COKE?
JESUS.

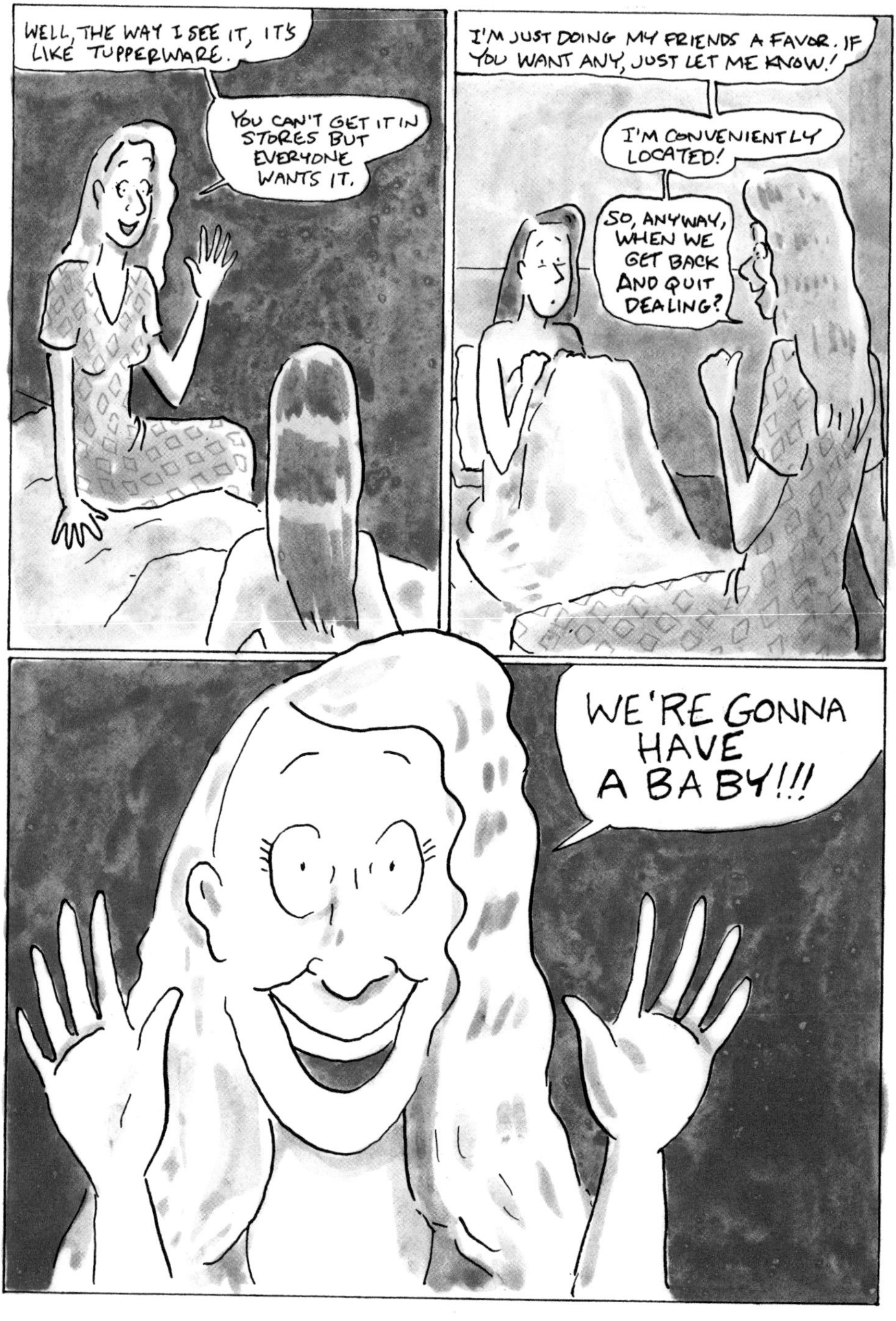
WELL, THE WAY I SEE IT, IT'S LIKE TUPPERWARE.
YOU CAN'T GET IT IN STORES BUT EVERYONE WANTS IT.
I'M JUST DOING MY FRIENDS A FAVOR. IF YOU WANT ANY, JUST LET ME KNOW!
I'M CONVENIENTLY LOCATED!
SO, ANYWAY, WHEN WE GET BACK AND QUIT DEALING?
WE'RE GONNA HAVE A BABY!!!

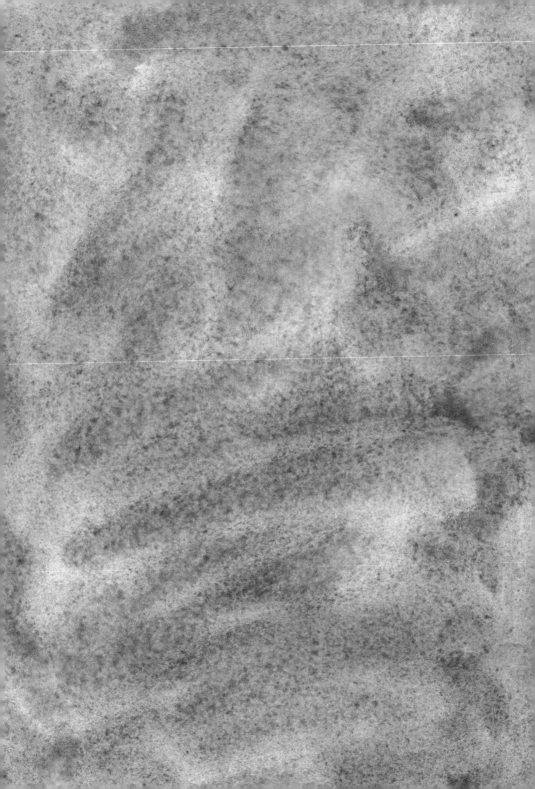

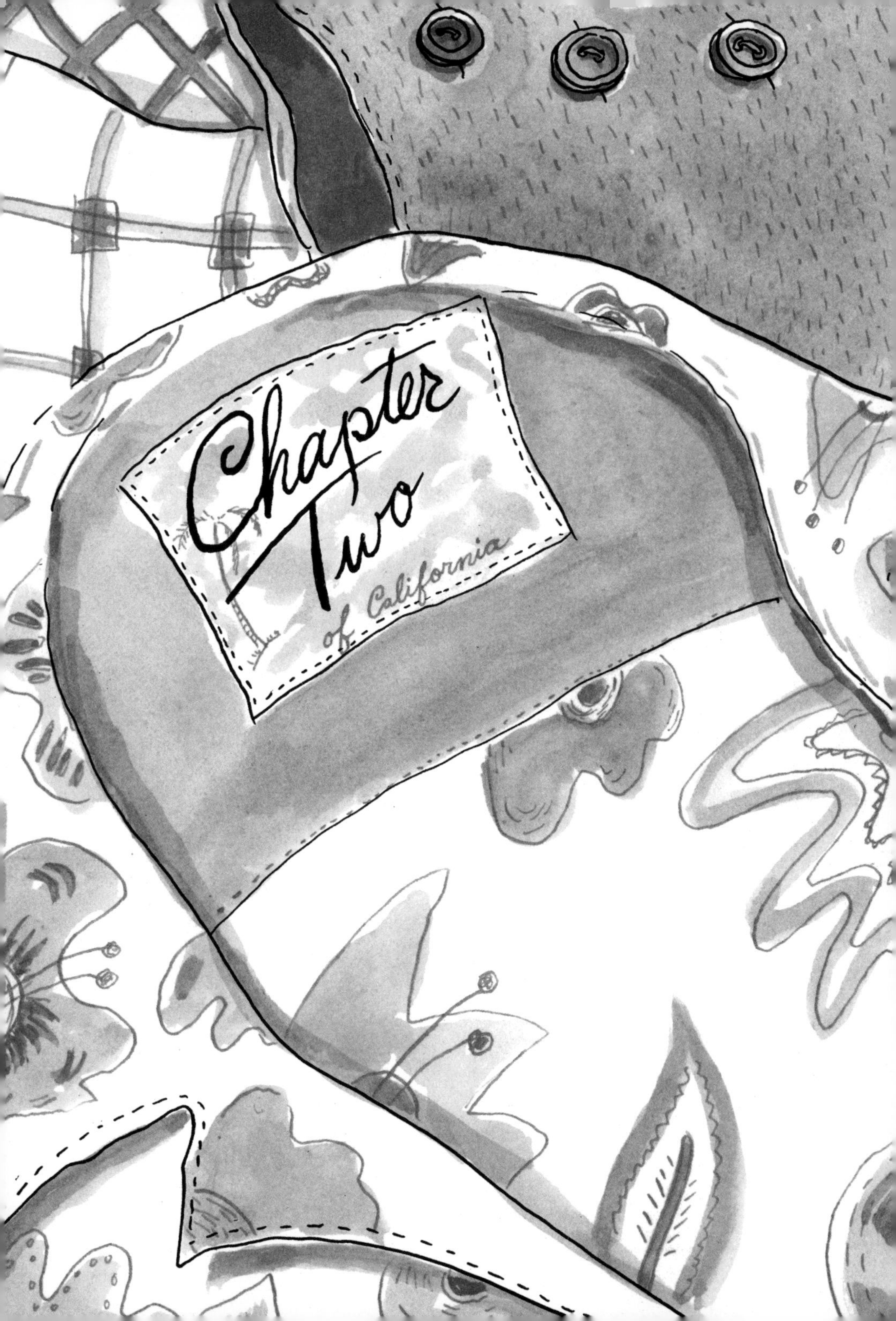
Chapter Two
of California

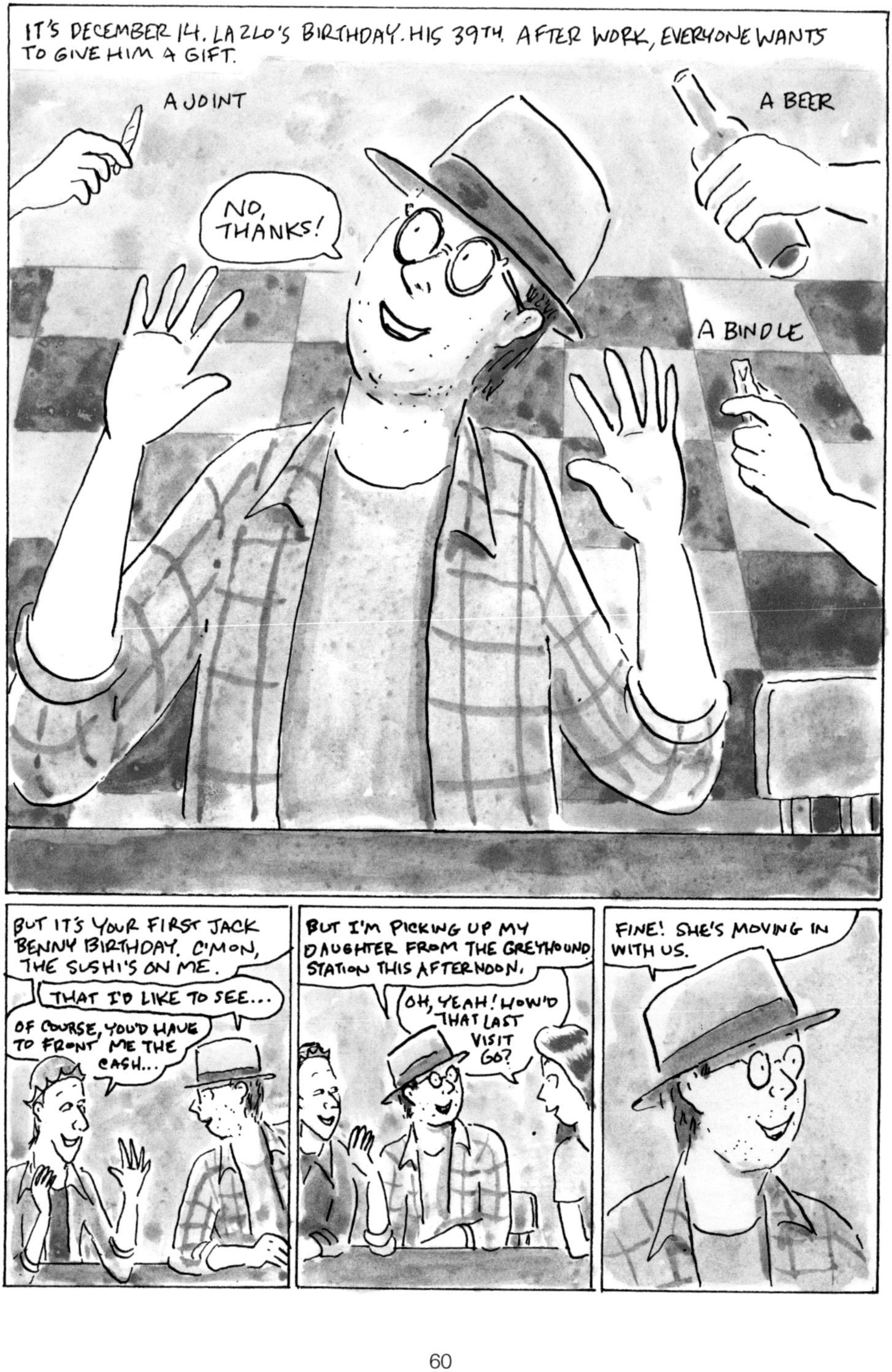
IT'S DECEMBER 14. LAZLO'S BIRTHDAY. HIS 39TH. AFTER WORK, EVERYONE WANTS TO GIVE HIM A GIFT.
A JOINT
A BEER
NO, THANKS!
A BINDLE
BUT IT'S YOUR FIRST JACK BENNY BIRTHDAY. C'MON, THE SUSHI'S ON ME.
THAT I'D LIKE TO SEE...
OF COURSE, YOU'D HAVE TO FRONT ME THE CASH...
BUT I'M PICKING UP MY DAUGHTER FROM THE GREYHOUND STATION THIS AFTERNOON.
OH, YEAH! HOW'D THAT LAST VISIT GO?
FINE! SHE'S MOVING IN WITH US.

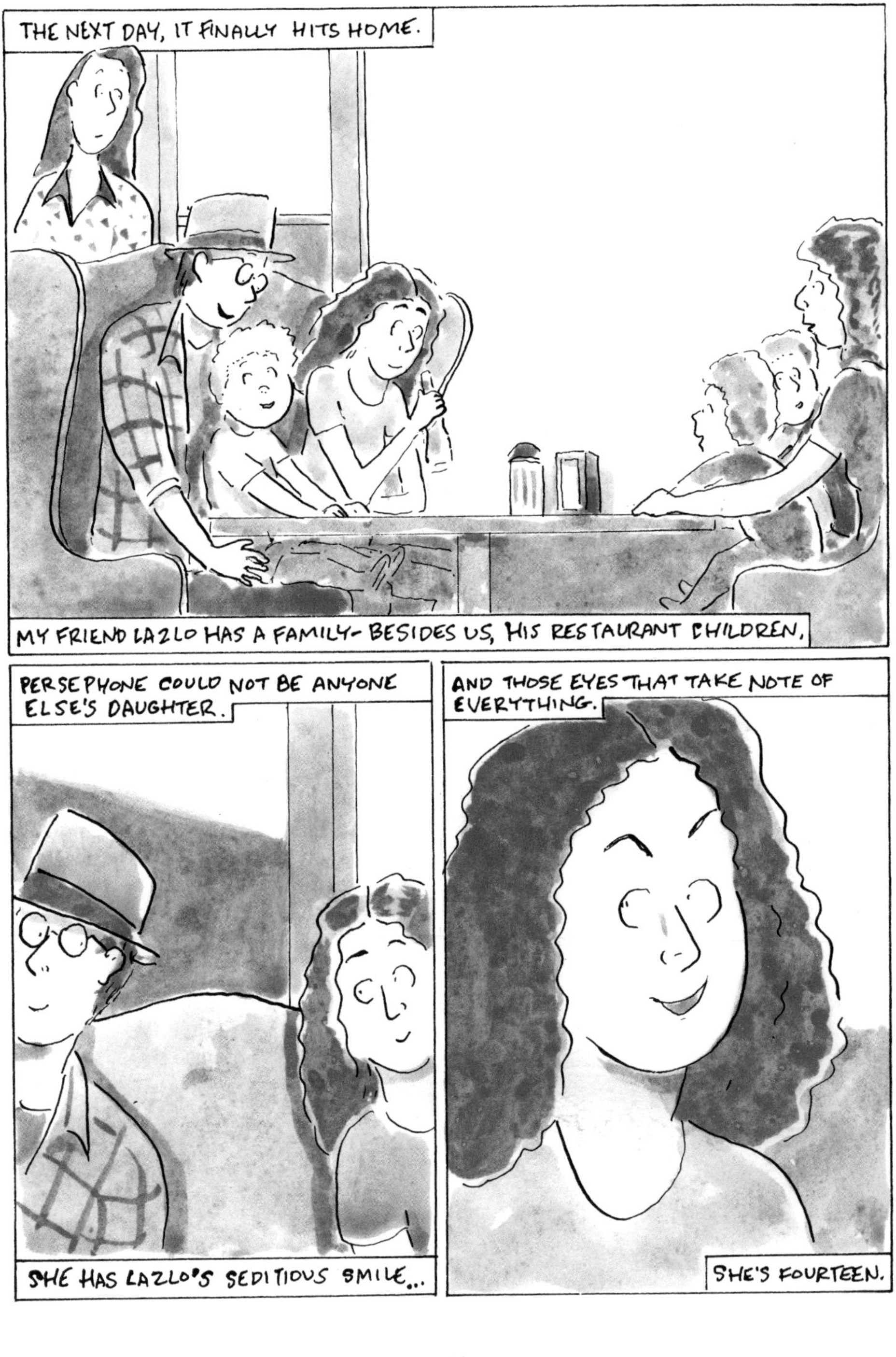
THE NEXT DAY, IT FINALLY HITS HOME.
MY FRIEND LAZLO HAS A FAMILY- BESIDES US, HIS RESTAURANT CHILDREN.
PERSEPHONE COULD NOT BE ANYONE ELSE'S DAUGHTER.
SHE HAS LAZLO'S SEDITIOUS SMILE...
AND THOSE EYES THAT TAKE NOTE OF EVERYTHING.
SHE'S FOURTEEN.

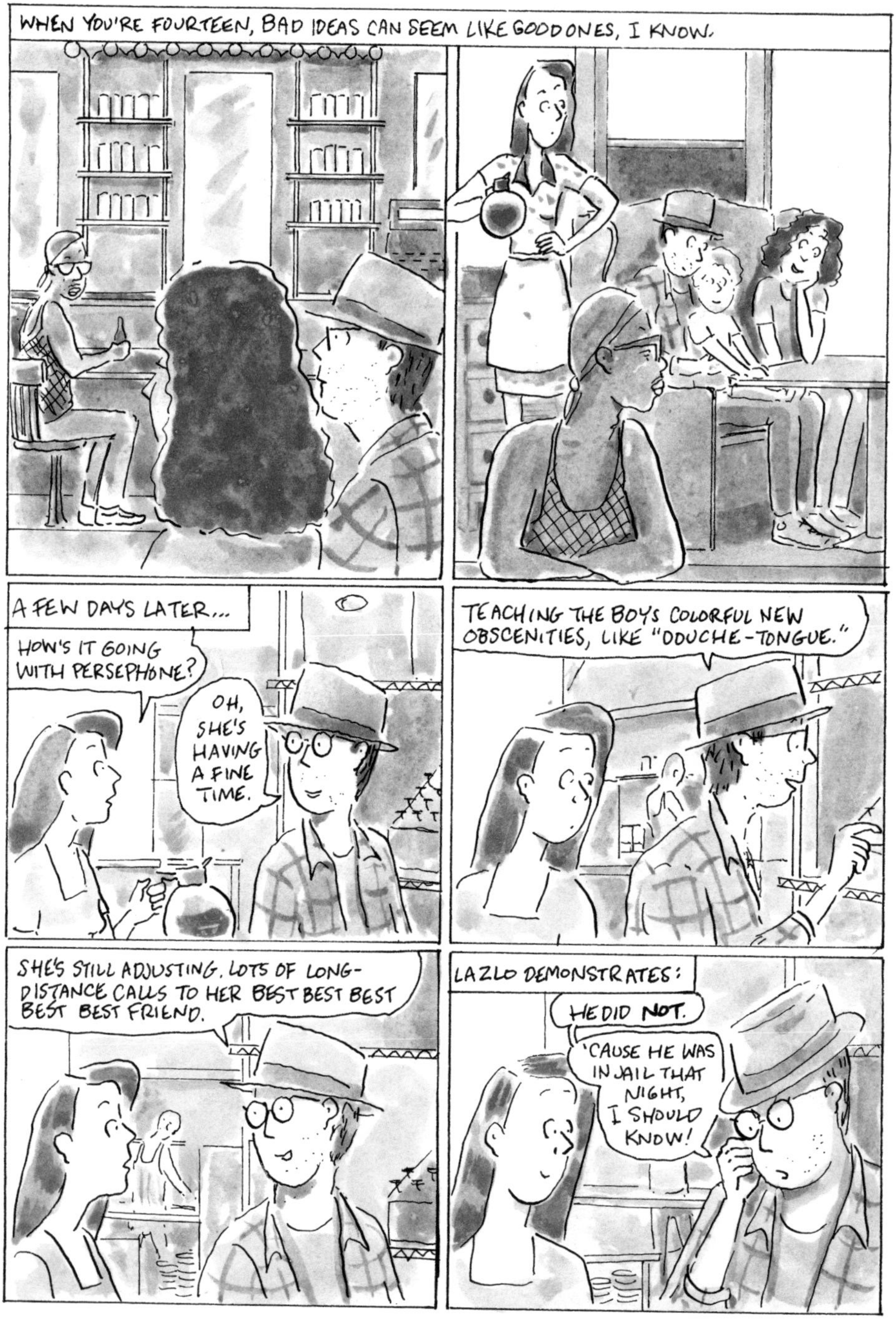
WHEN YOU'RE FOURTEEN, BAD IDEAS CAN SEEM LIKE GOOD ONES, I KNOW.
A FEW DAYS LATER...
HOW'S IT GOING WITH PERSEPHONE?
OH, SHE'S HAVING A FINE TIME.
TEACHING THE BOYS COLORFUL NEW OBSCENITIES, LIKE "DOUCHE-TONGUE."
SHE'S STILL ADJUSTING. LOTS OF LONG-DISTANCE CALLS TO HER BEST BEST BEST BEST BEST FRIEND.
LAZLO DEMONSTRATES:
HE DID NOT.
'CAUSE HE WAS IN JAIL THAT NIGHT, I SHOULD KNOW!

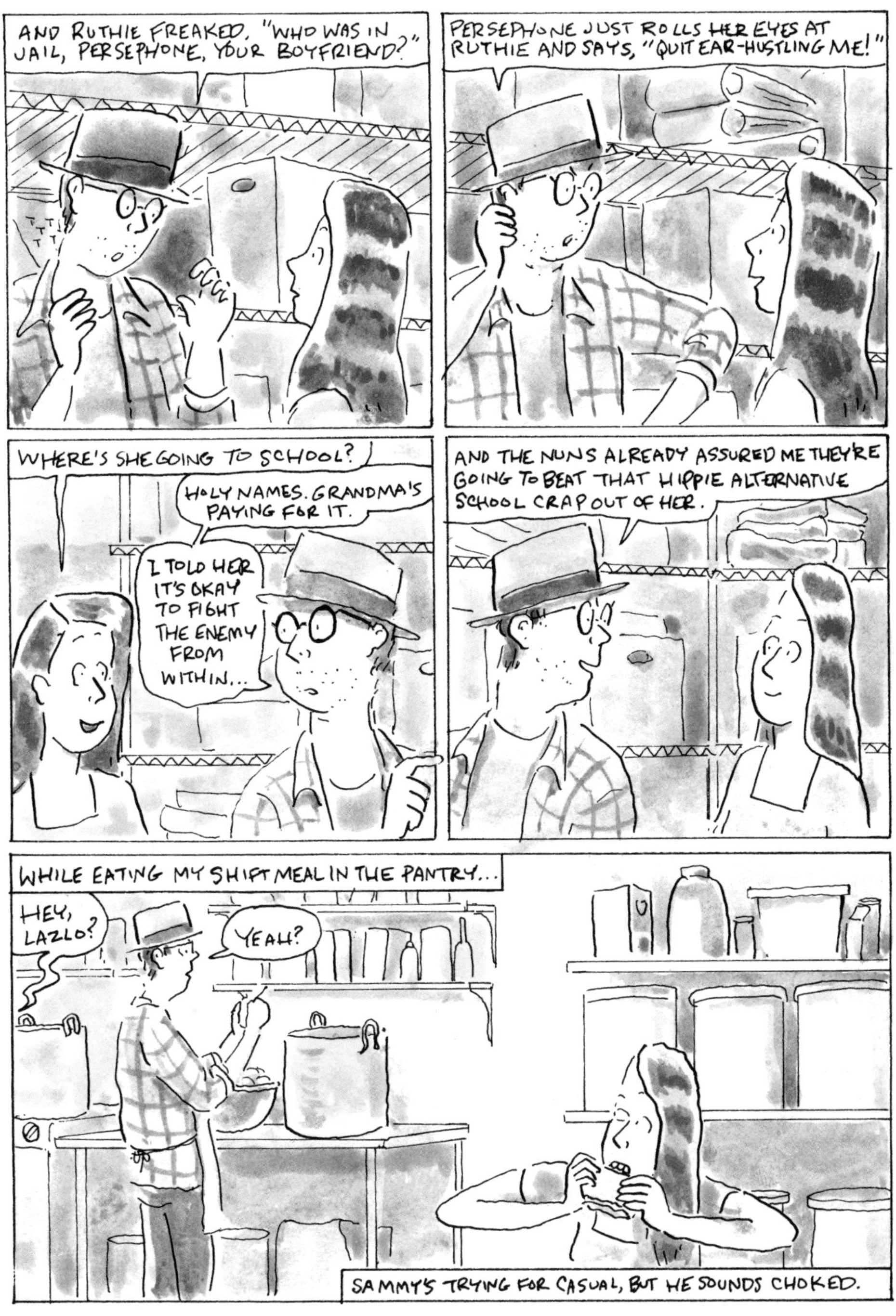
AND RUTHIE FREAKED, "WHO WAS IN JAIL, PERSEPHONE, YOUR BOYFRIEND?"
PERSEPHONE JUST ROLLS HER EYES AT RUTHIE AND SAYS, "QUIT EAR-HUSTLING ME!"
WHERE'S SHE GOING TO SCHOOL?
HOLY NAMES. GRANDMA'S PAYING FOR IT.
I TOLD HER IT'S OKAY TO FIGHT THE ENEMY FROM WITHIN...
AND THE NUNS ALREADY ASSURED ME THEY'RE GOING TO BEAT THAT HIPPIE ALTERNATIVE SCHOOL CRAP OUT OF HER.
WHILE EATING MY SHIFT MEAL IN THE PANTRY...
HEY, LAZLO?
YEAH?
SAMMY'S TRYING FOR CASUAL, BUT HE SOUNDS CHOKED.

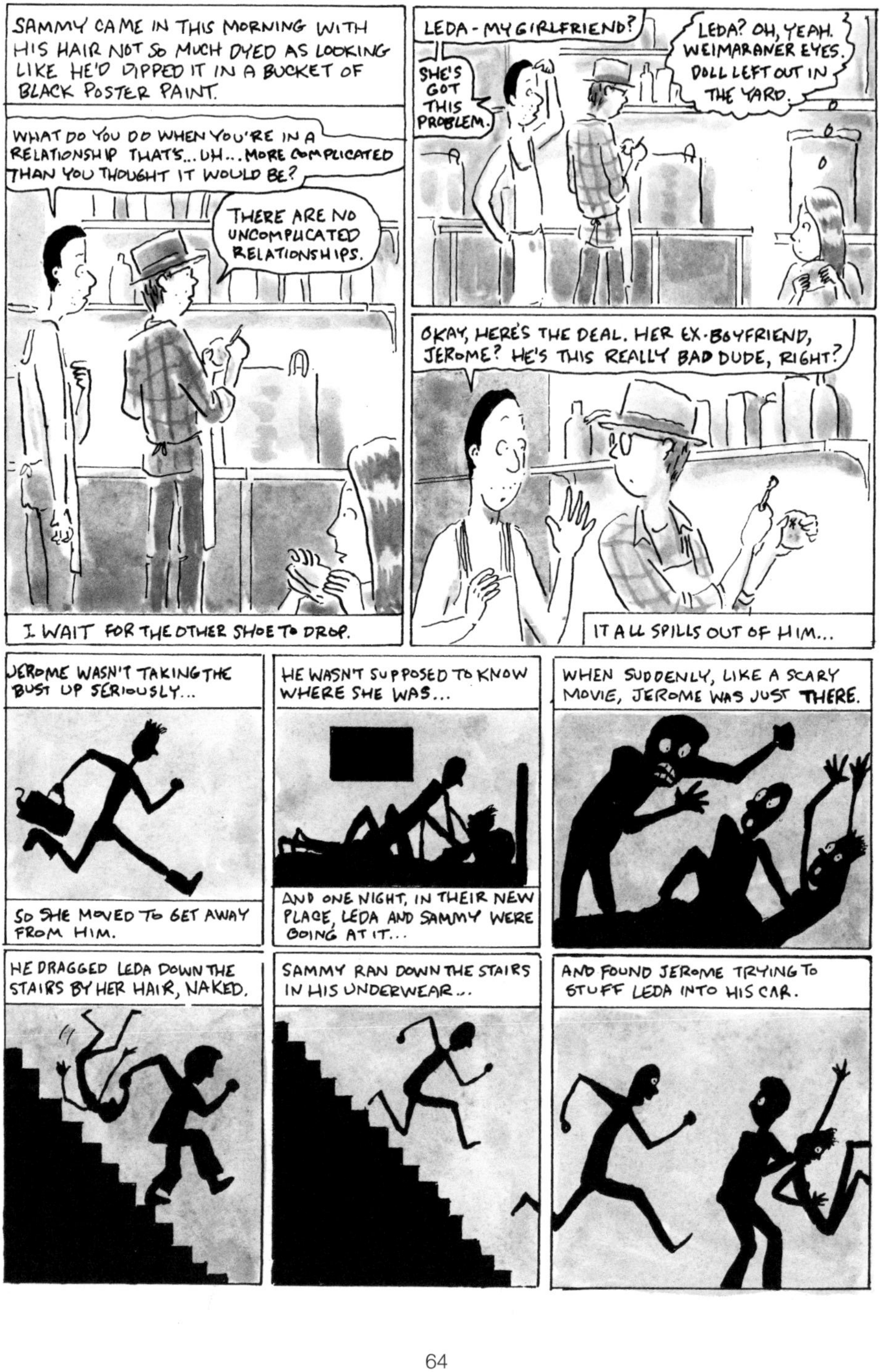
SAMMY CAME IN THIS MORNING WITH HIS HAIR NOT SO MUCH DYED AS LOOKING LIKE HE'D DIPPED IT IN A BUCKET OF BLACK POSTER PAINT.
WHAT DO YOU DO WHEN YOU'RE IN A RELATIONSHIP THAT'S... UH... MORE COMPLICATED THAN YOU THOUGHT IT WOULD BE?
THERE ARE NO UNCOMPLICATED RELATIONSHIPS.
I WAIT FOR THE OTHER SHOE TO DROP.
LEDA - MY GIRLFRIEND?
SHE'S GOT THIS PROBLEM.
LEDA? OH, YEAH. WEIMARANER EYES. DOLL LEFT OUT IN THE YARD.
OKAY, HERE'S THE DEAL. HER EX-BOYFRIEND, JEROME? HE'S THIS REALLY BAD DUDE, RIGHT?
IT ALL SPILLS OUT OF HIM...
JEROME WASN'T TAKING THE BUST UP SERIOUSLY...
SO SHE MOVED TO GET AWAY FROM HIM.
HE WASN'T SUPPOSED TO KNOW WHERE SHE WAS...
AND ONE NIGHT, IN THEIR NEW PLACE, LEDA AND SAMMY WERE GOING AT IT...
WHEN SUDDENLY, LIKE A SCARY MOVIE, JEROME WAS JUST THERE.
HE DRAGGED LEDA DOWN THE STAIRS BY HER HAIR, NAKED.
SAMMY RAN DOWN THE STAIRS IN HIS UNDERWEAR...
AND FOUND JEROME TRYING TO STUFF LEDA INTO HIS CAR.

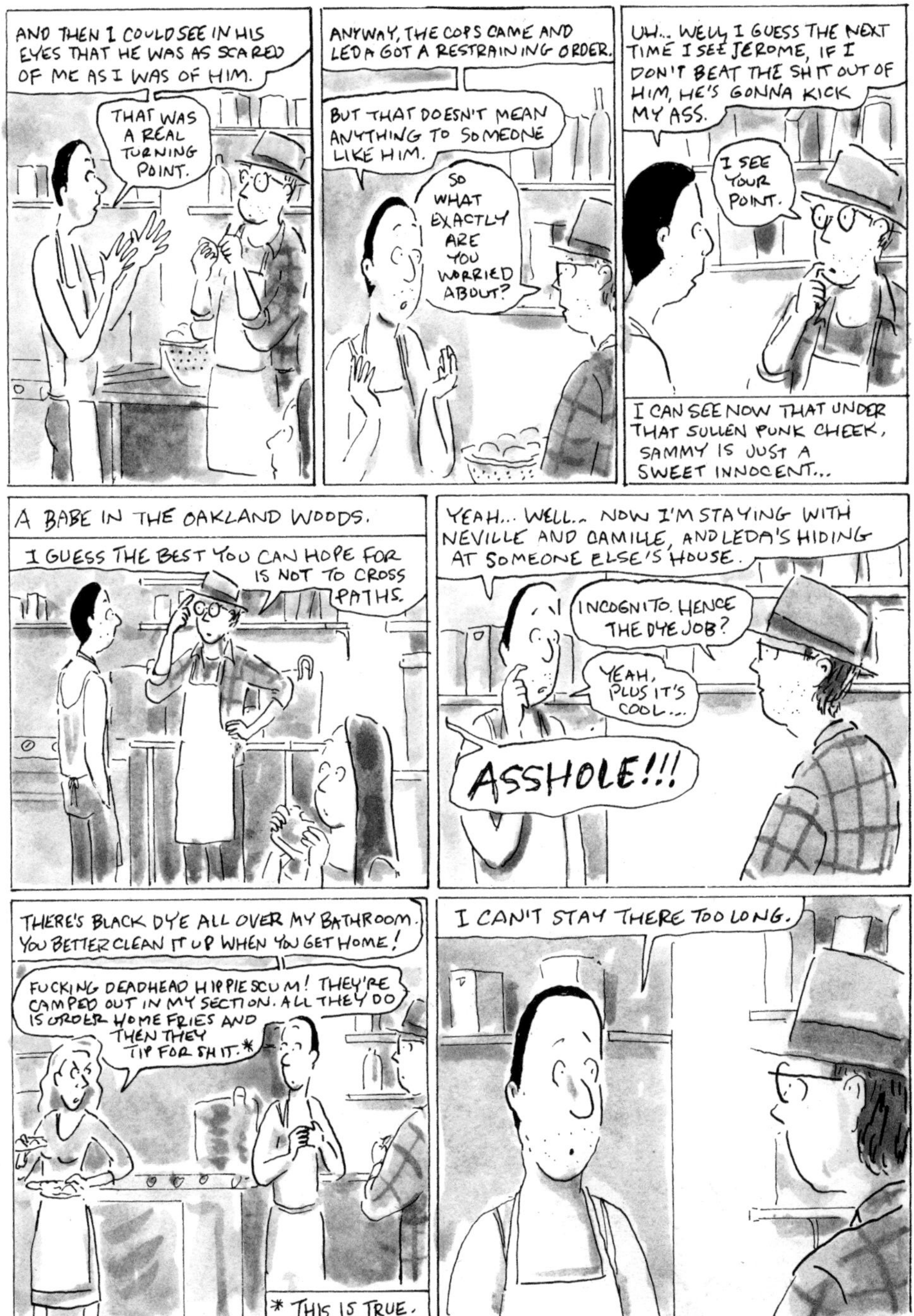
AND THEN I COULD SEE IN HIS EYES THAT HE WAS AS SCARED OF ME AS I WAS OF HIM.
THAT WAS A REAL TURNING POINT.
ANYWAY, THE COPS CAME AND LEDA GOT A RESTRAINING ORDER.
BUT THAT DOESN'T MEAN ANYTHING TO SOMEONE LIKE HIM.
SO WHAT EXACTLY ARE YOU WORRIED ABOUT?
UH... WELL, I GUESS THE NEXT TIME I SEE JEROME, IF I DON'T BEAT THE SHIT OUT OF HIM, HE'S GONNA KICK MY ASS.
I SEE YOUR POINT.
I CAN SEE NOW THAT UNDER THAT SULLEN PUNK CHEEK, SAMMY IS JUST A SWEET INNOCENT...
A BABE IN THE OAKLAND WOODS.
I GUESS THE BEST YOU CAN HOPE FOR IS NOT TO CROSS PATHS.
YEAH... WELL... NOW I'M STAYING WITH NEVILLE AND CAMILLE, AND LEDA'S HIDING AT SOMEONE ELSE'S HOUSE.
INCOGNITO. HENCE THE DYE JOB?
YEAH, PLUS IT'S COOL...
ASSHOLE!!!
THERE'S BLACK DYE ALL OVER MY BATHROOM. YOU BETTER CLEAN IT UP WHEN YOU GET HOME!
FUCKING DEADHEAD HIPPIESCUM! THEY'RE CAMPED OUT IN MY SECTION. ALL THEY DO IS ORDER HOME FRIES AND THEN THEY TIP FOR SHIT.*
* THIS IS TRUE.
I CAN'T STAY THERE TOO LONG.

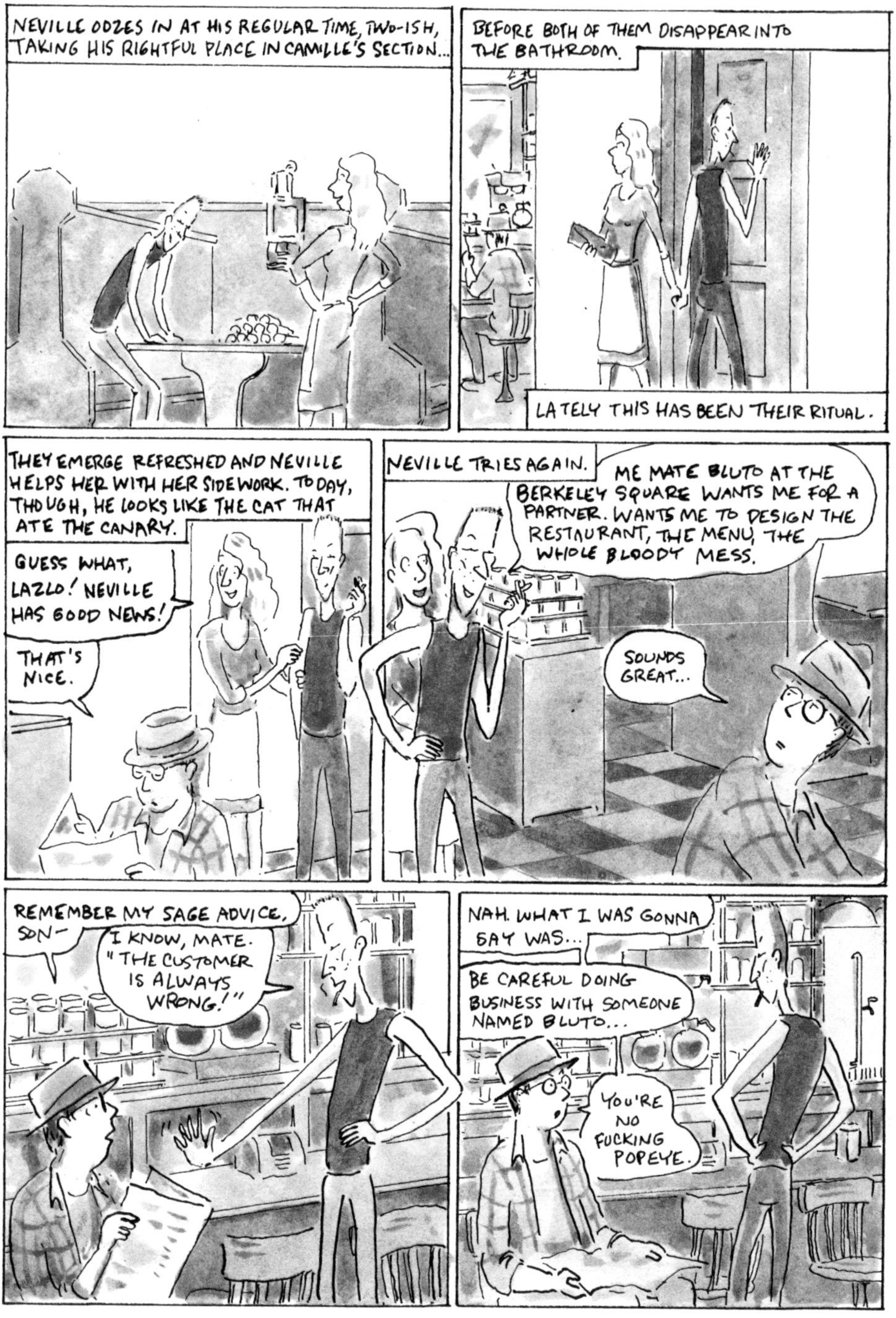
NEVILLE OOZES IN AT HIS REGULAR TIME, TWO-ISH, TAKING HIS RIGHTFUL PLACE IN CAMILLE'S SECTION...
BEFORE BOTH OF THEM DISAPPEAR INTO THE BATHROOM.
LATELY THIS HAS BEEN THEIR RITUAL.
THEY EMERGE REFRESHED AND NEVILLE HELPS HER WITH HER SIDEWORK. TODAY, THOUGH, HE LOOKS LIKE THE CAT THAT ATE THE CANARY.
GUESS WHAT, LAZLO! NEVILLE HAS GOOD NEWS!
THAT'S NICE.
NEVILLE TRIES AGAIN.
ME MATE BLUTO AT THE BERKELEY SQUARE WANTS ME FOR A PARTNER. WANTS ME TO DESIGN THE RESTAURANT, THE MENU, THE WHOLE BLOODY MESS.
SOUNDS GREAT...
REMEMBER MY SAGE ADVICE, SON-
I KNOW, MATE. "THE CUSTOMER IS ALWAYS WRONG!"
NAH. WHAT I WAS GONNA SAY WAS...
BE CAREFUL DOING BUSINESS WITH SOMEONE NAMED BLUTO...
YOU'RE NO FUCKING POPEYE.

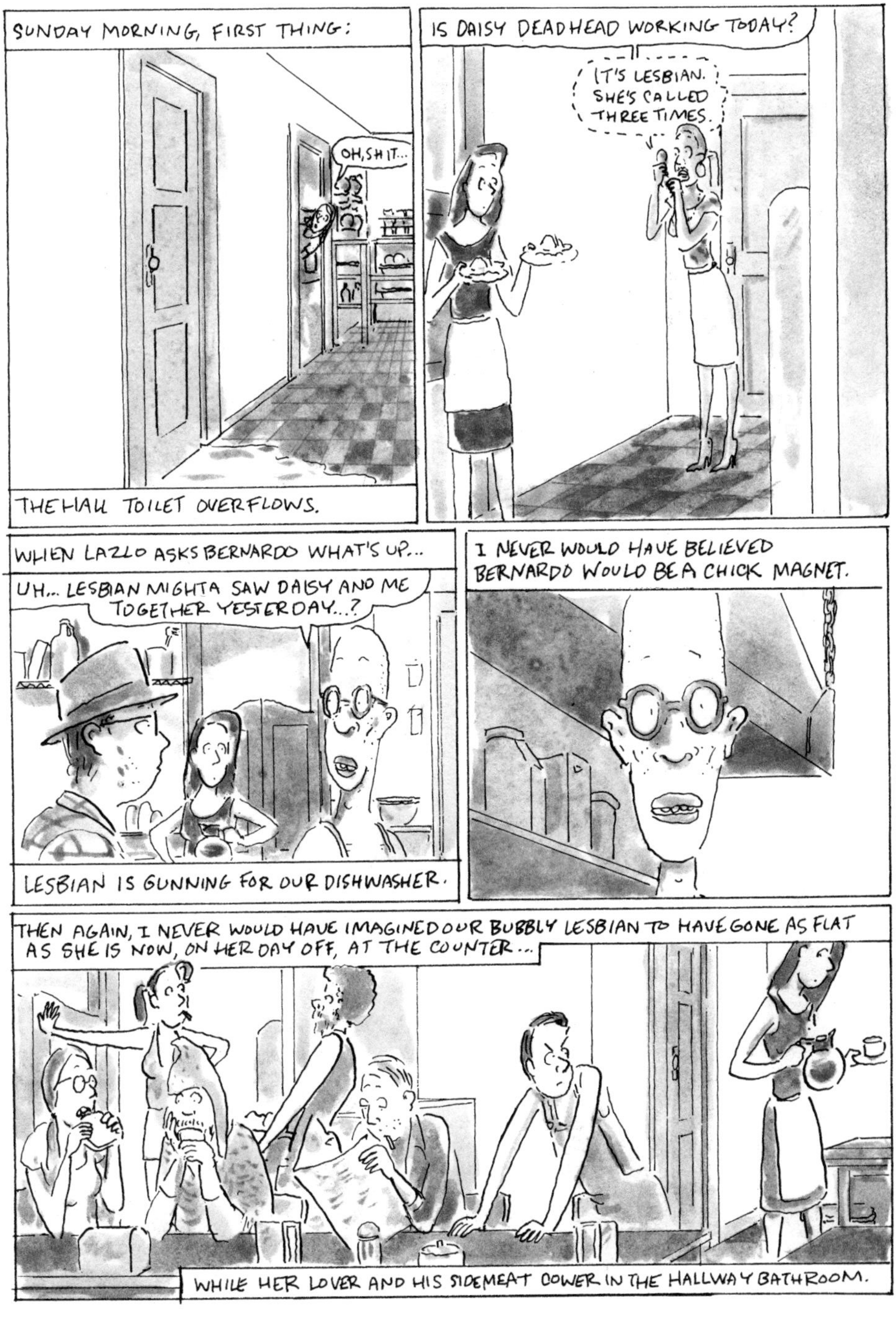

SUNDAY MORNING, FIRST THING:
OH, SHIT...
THE HALL TOILET OVERFLOWS.
IS DAISY DEADHEAD WORKING TODAY?
IT'S LESBIAN. SHE'S CALLED THREE TIMES.
WHEN LAZLO ASKS BERNARDO WHAT'S UP...
UH... LESBIAN MIGHTA SAW DAISY AND ME TOGETHER YESTERDAY...?
LESBIAN IS GUNNING FOR OUR DISHWASHER.
I NEVER WOULD HAVE BELIEVED BERNARDO WOULD BE A CHICK MAGNET.
THEN AGAIN, I NEVER WOULD HAVE IMAGINED OUR BUBBLY LESBIAN TO HAVE GONE AS FLAT AS SHE IS NOW, ON HER DAY OFF, AT THE COUNTER...
WHILE HER LOVER AND HIS SIDEMEAT COWER IN THE HALLWAY BATHROOM.

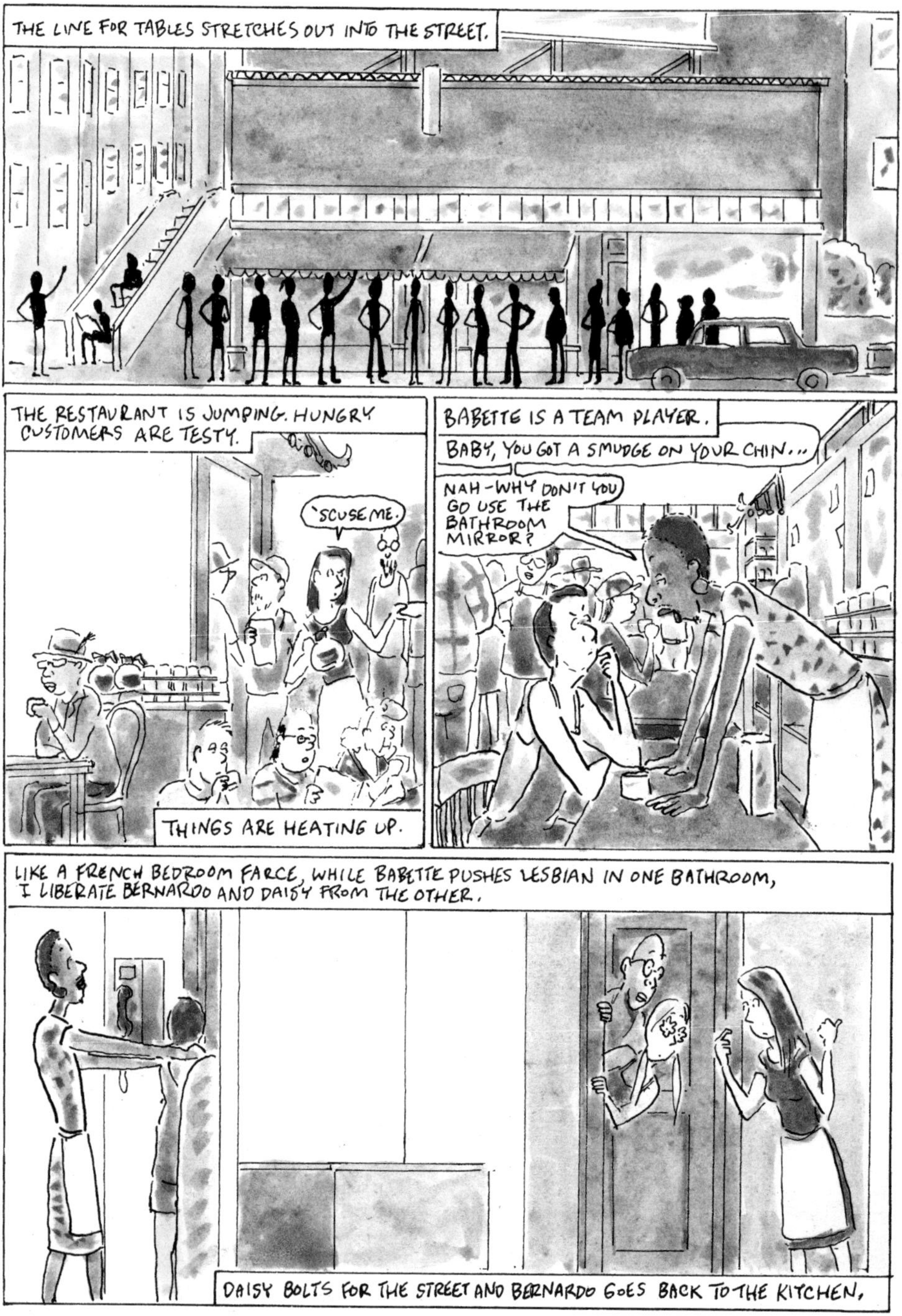
THE LINE FOR TABLES STRETCHES OUT INTO THE STREET.
THE RESTAURANT IS JUMPING. HUNGRY CUSTOMERS ARE TESTY.
'SCUSE ME.
THINGS ARE HEATING UP.
BABETTE IS A TEAM PLAYER.
BABY, YOU GOT A SMUDGE ON YOUR CHIN...
NAH-WHY DON'T YOU GO USE THE BATHROOM MIRROR?
LIKE A FRENCH BEDROOM FARCE, WHILE BABETTE PUSHES LESBIAN IN ONE BATHROOM, I LIBERATE BERNARDO AND DAISY FROM THE OTHER.
DAISY BOLTS FOR THE STREET AND BERNARDO GOES BACK TO THE KITCHEN.

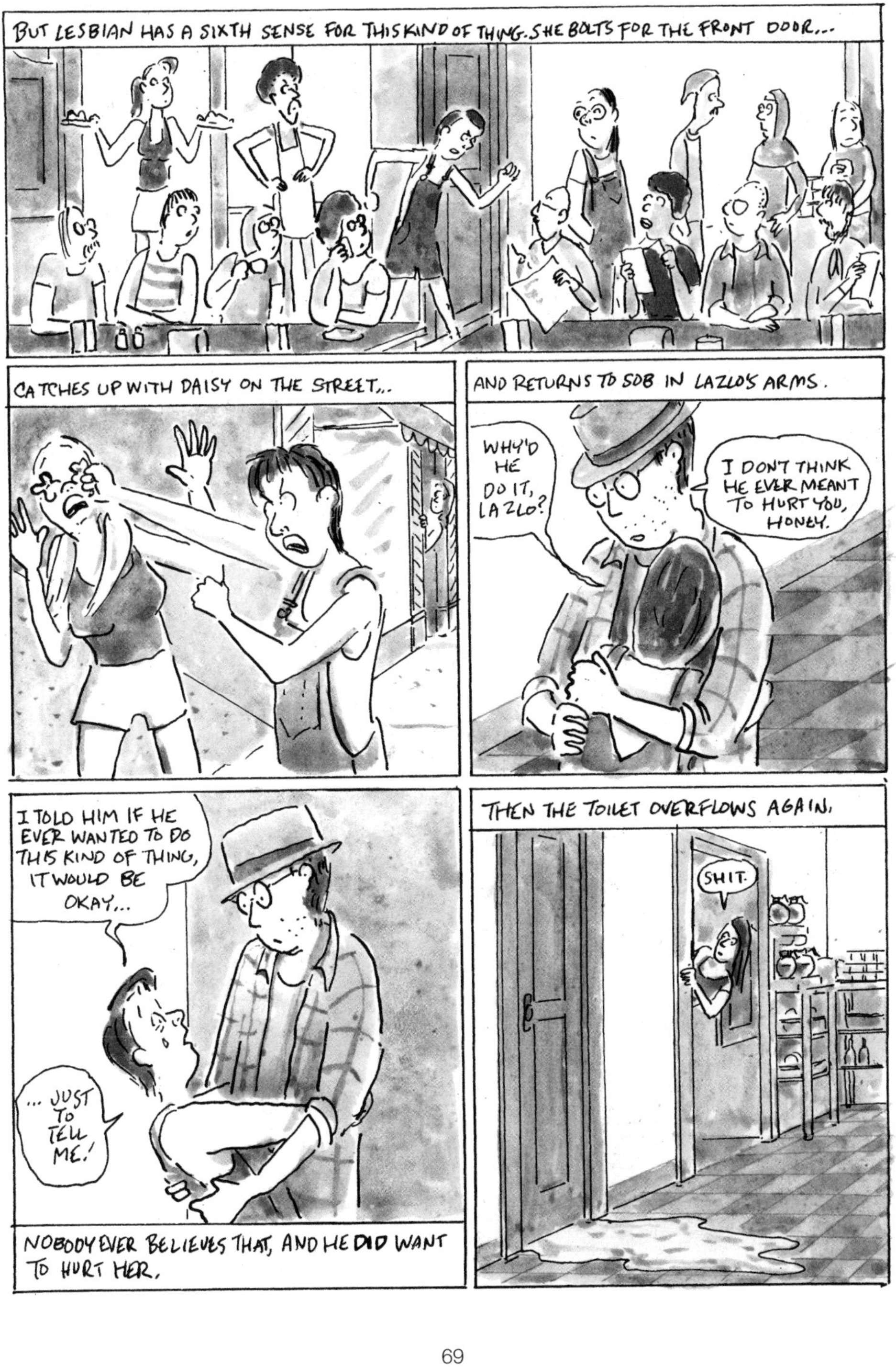
BUT LESBIAN HAS A SIXTH SENSE FOR THIS KIND OF THING. SHE BOLTS FOR THE FRONT DOOR...
CATCHES UP WITH DAISY ON THE STREET...
AND RETURNS TO SOB IN LAZLO'S ARMS.
WHY'D HE DO IT, LAZLO?
I DON'T THINK HE EVER MEANT TO HURT YOU, HONEY.
I TOLD HIM IF HE EVER WANTED TO DO THIS KIND OF THING, IT WOULD BE OKAY...
... JUST TO TELL ME!
NOBODY EVER BELIEVES THAT, AND HE DID WANT TO HURT HER.
THEN THE TOILET OVERFLOWS AGAIN.
SHIT.

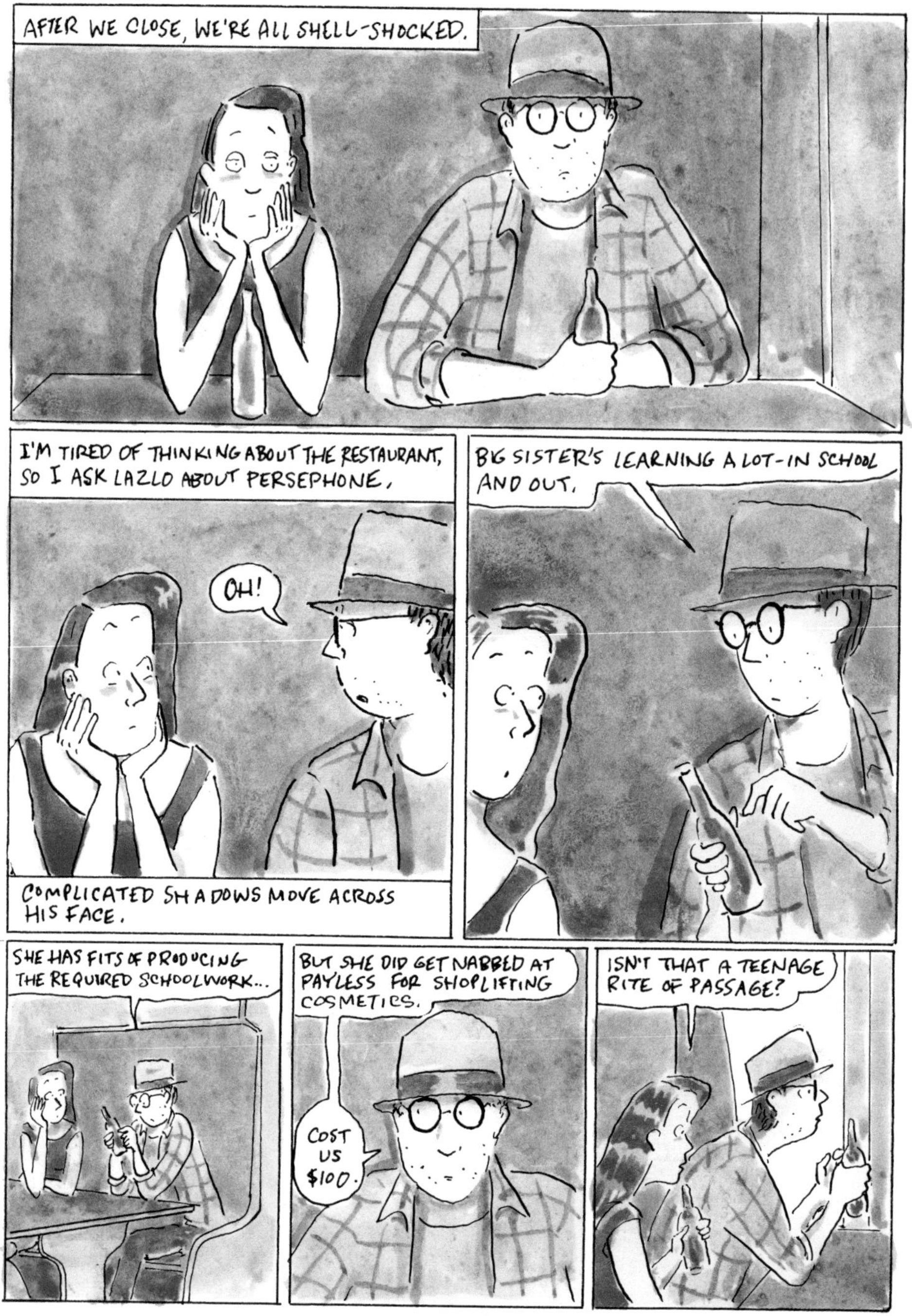
AFTER WE CLOSE, WE'RE ALL SHELL-SHOCKED.
I'M TIRED OF THINKING ABOUT THE RESTAURANT, SO I ASK LAZLO ABOUT PERSEPHONE.
OH!
COMPLICATED SHADOWS MOVE ACROSS HIS FACE.
BIG SISTER'S LEARNING A LOT-IN SCHOOL AND OUT.
SHE HAS FITS OF PRODUCING THE REQUIRED SCHOOLWORK...
BUT SHE DID GET NABBED AT PAYLESS FOR SHOPLIFTING COSMETICS.
COST US $100.
ISN'T THAT A TEENAGE RITE OF PASSAGE?

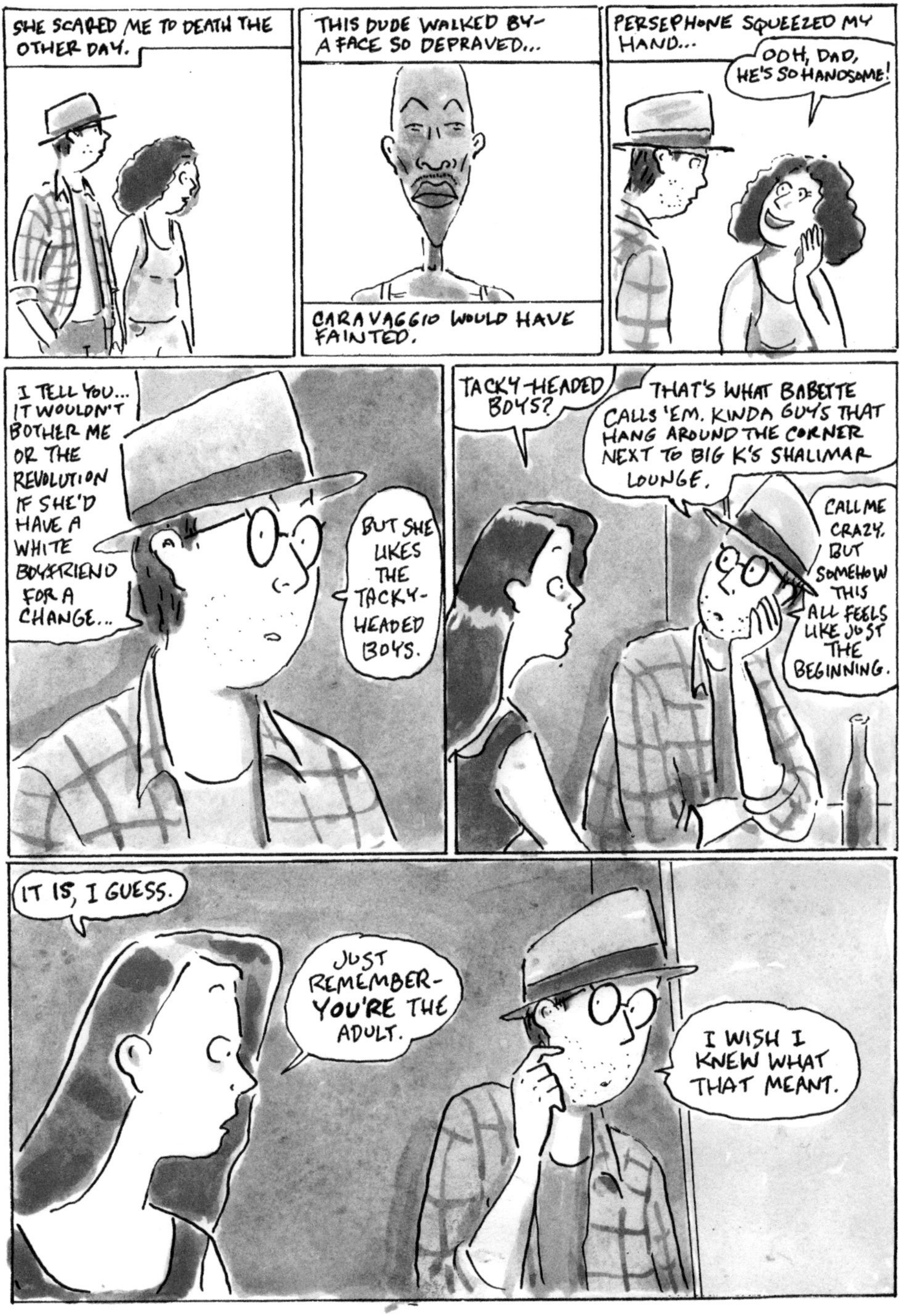
SHE SCARED ME TO DEATH THE OTHER DAY.
THIS DUDE WALKED BY- A FACE SO DEPRAVED...
CARAVAGGIO WOULD HAVE FAINTED.
PERSEPHONE SQUEEZED MY HAND...
OOH, DAD, HE'S SO HANDSOME!
I TELL YOU... IT WOULDN'T BOTHER ME OR THE REVOLUTION IF SHE'D HAVE A WHITE BOYFRIEND FOR A CHANGE...
BUT SHE LIKES THE TACKY-HEADED BOYS.
TACKY-HEADED BOYS?
THAT'S WHAT BABETTE CALLS 'EM. KINDA GUYS THAT HANG AROUND THE CORNER NEXT TO BIG K'S SHALIMAR LOUNGE.
CALL ME CRAZY, BUT SOMEHOW THIS ALL FEELS LIKE JUST THE BEGINNING.
IT IS, I GUESS.
JUST REMEMBER- YOU'RE THE ADULT.
I WISH I KNEW WHAT THAT MEANT.

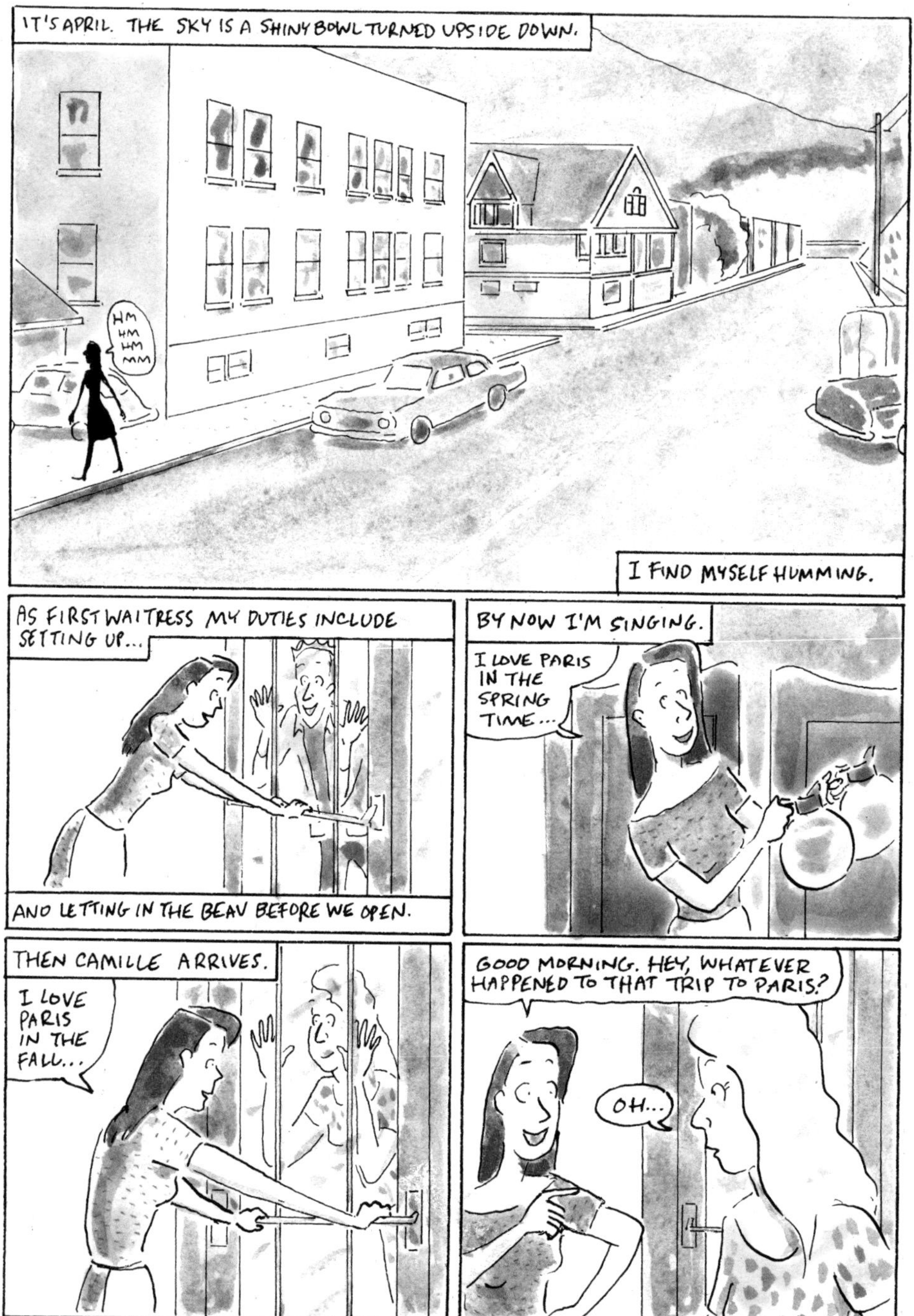
IT'S APRIL. THE SKY IS A SHINY BOWL TURNED UPSIDE DOWN.
HM HM HM MM
I FIND MYSELF HUMMING.
AS FIRST WAITRESS MY DUTIES INCLUDE SETTING UP...
AND LETTING IN THE BEAV BEFORE WE OPEN.
BY NOW I'M SINGING.
I LOVE PARIS IN THE SPRING TIME...
THEN CAMILLE ARRIVES.
I LOVE PARIS IN THE FALL...
GOOD MORNING. HEY, WHATEVER HAPPENED TO THAT TRIP TO PARIS?
OH...

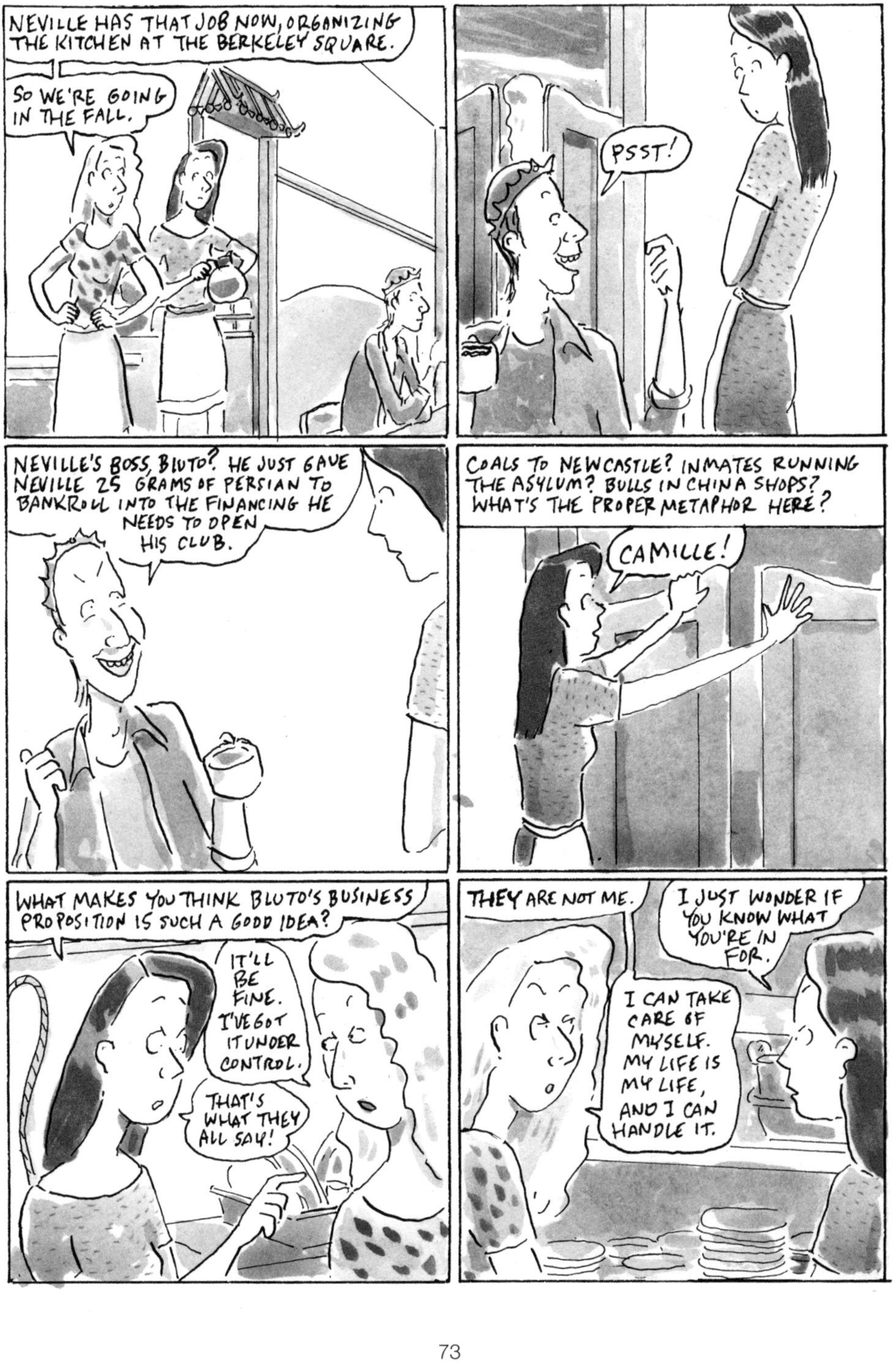
NEVILLE HAS THAT JOB NOW, ORGANIZING THE KITCHEN AT THE BERKELEY SQUARE.
SO WE'RE GOING IN THE FALL.
PSST!
NEVILLE'S BOSS, BLUTO? HE JUST GAVE NEVILLE 25 GRAMS OF PERSIAN TO BANKROLL INTO THE FINANCING HE NEEDS TO OPEN HIS CLUB.
COALS TO NEWCASTLE? INMATES RUNNING THE ASYLUM? BULLS IN CHINA SHOPS? WHAT'S THE PROPER METAPHOR HERE?
CAMILLE!
WHAT MAKES YOU THINK BLUTO'S BUSINESS PROPOSITION IS SUCH A GOOD IDEA?
IT'LL BE FINE. I'VE GOT IT UNDER CONTROL.
THAT'S WHAT THEY ALL SAY!
THEY ARE NOT ME.
I JUST WONDER IF YOU KNOW WHAT YOU'RE IN FOR.
I CAN TAKE CARE OF MYSELF. MY LIFE IS MY LIFE, AND I CAN HANDLE IT.

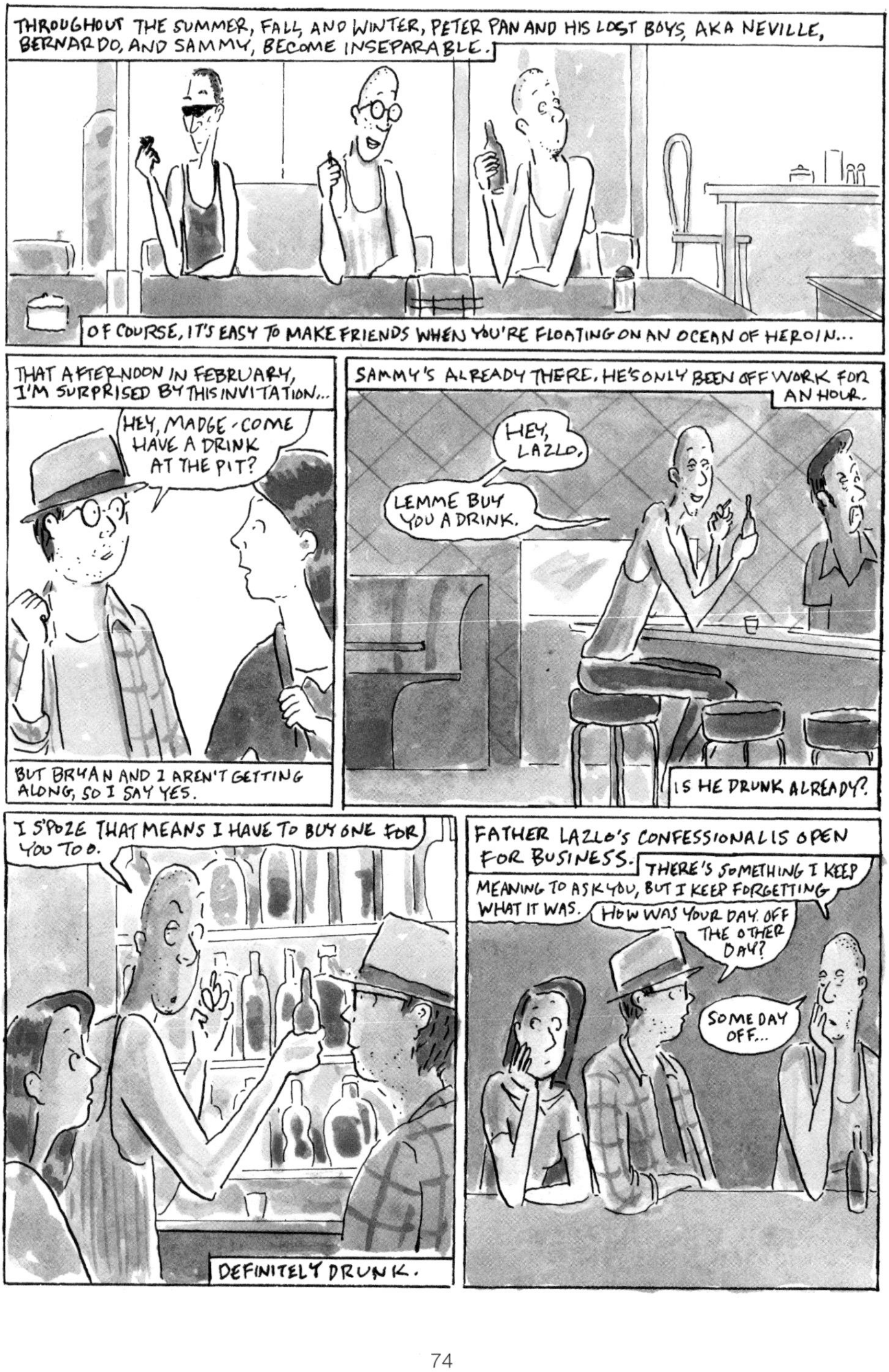
THROUGHOUT THE SUMMER, FALL, AND WINTER, PETER PAN AND HIS LOST BOYS, AKA NEVILLE, BERNARDO, AND SAMMY, BECOME INSEPARABLE.
OF COURSE, IT'S EASY TO MAKE FRIENDS WHEN YOU'RE FLOATING ON AN OCEAN OF HEROIN...
THAT AFTERNOON IN FEBRUARY, I'M SURPRISED BY THIS INVITATION...
HEY, MADGE - COME HAVE A DRINK AT THE PIT?
BUT BRYAN AND I AREN'T GETTING ALONG, SO I SAY YES.
SAMMY'S ALREADY THERE. HE'S ONLY BEEN OFF WORK FOR AN HOUR.
HEY, LAZLO,
LEMME BUY YOU A DRINK.
IS HE DRUNK ALREADY?
I S'POZE THAT MEANS I HAVE TO BUY ONE FOR YOU TOO.
DEFINITELY DRUNK.
FATHER LAZLO'S CONFESSIONAL IS OPEN FOR BUSINESS.
THERE'S SOMETHING I KEEP MEANING TO ASK YOU, BUT I KEEP FORGETTING WHAT IT WAS.
HOW WAS YOUR DAY OFF THE OTHER DAY?
SOME DAY OFF...

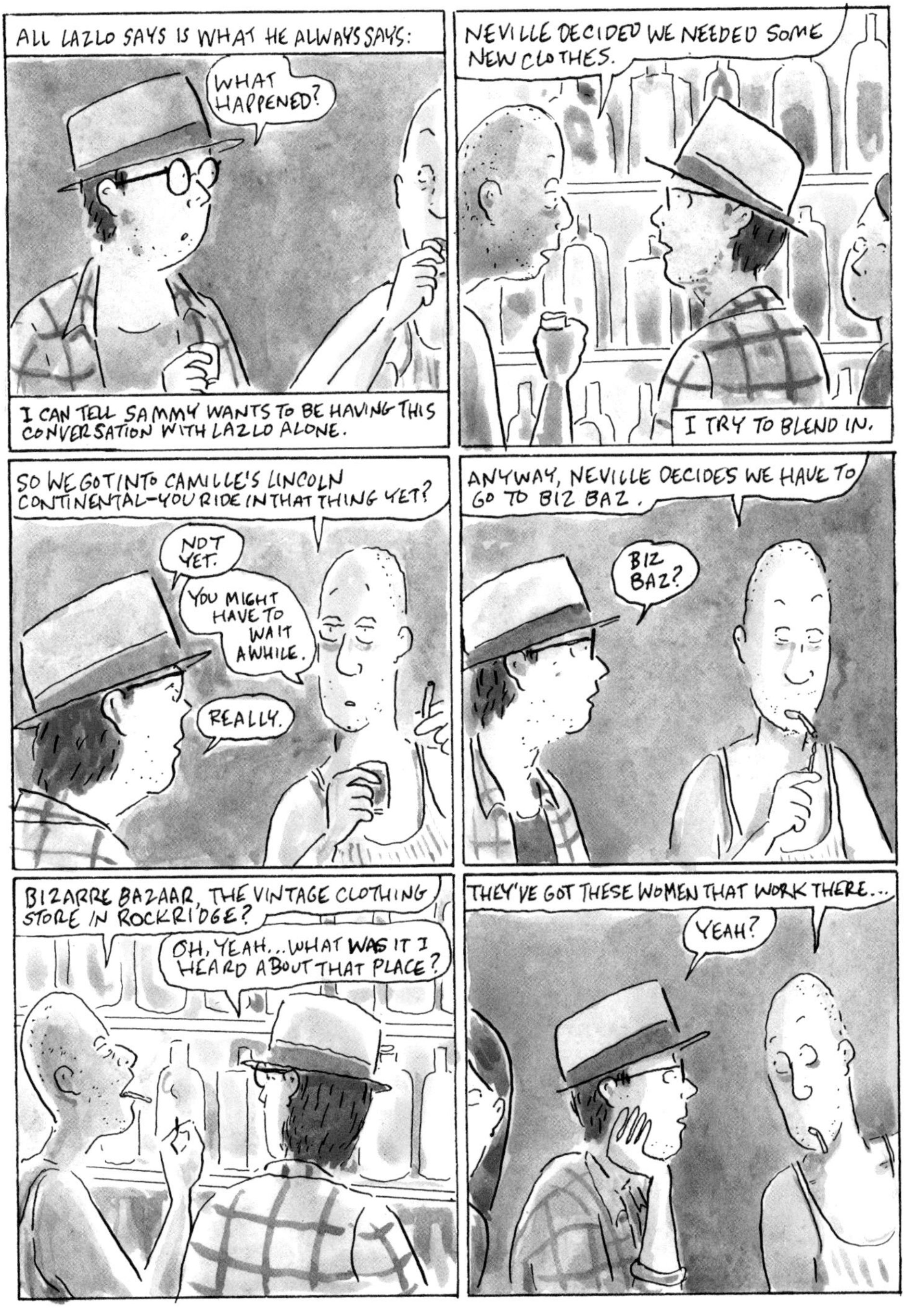
ALL LAZLO SAYS IS WHAT HE ALWAYS SAYS:
WHAT HAPPENED?
I CAN TELL SAMMY WANTS TO BE HAVING THIS CONVERSATION WITH LAZLO ALONE.
NEVILLE DECIDED WE NEEDED SOME NEW CLOTHES.
I TRY TO BLEND IN.
SO WE GOT INTO CAMILLE'S LINCOLN CONTINENTAL—YOU RIDE IN THAT THING YET?
NOT YET.
YOU MIGHT HAVE TO WAIT AWHILE.
REALLY.
ANYWAY, NEVILLE DECIDES WE HAVE TO GO TO BIZ BAZ.
BIZ BAZ?
BIZARRE BAZAAR, THE VINTAGE CLOTHING STORE IN ROCKRIDGE?
OH, YEAH... WHAT WAS IT I HEARD ABOUT THAT PLACE?
THEY'VE GOT THESE WOMEN THAT WORK THERE...
YEAH?

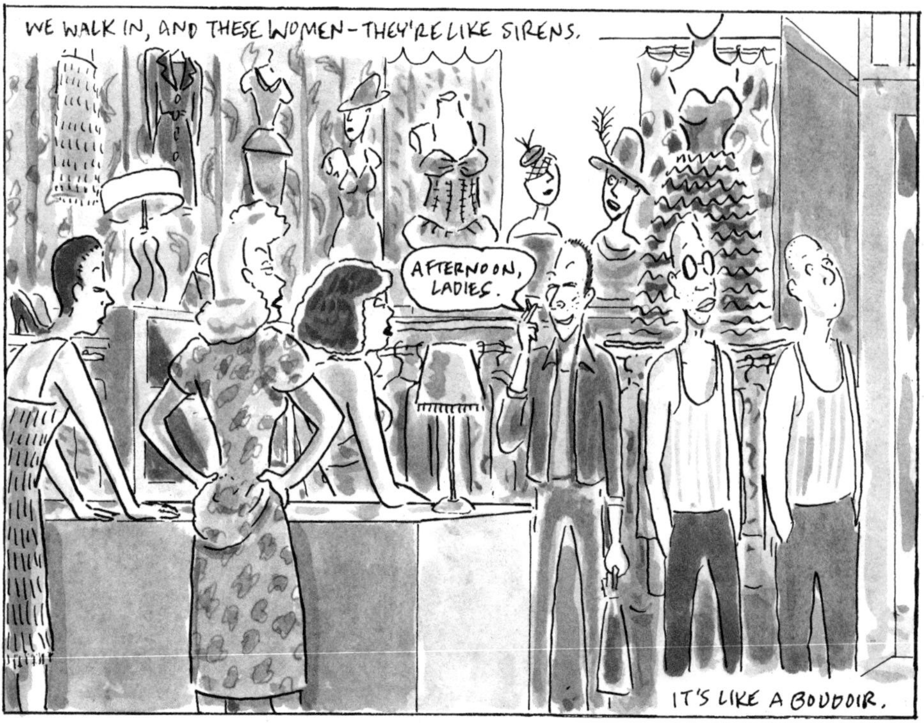
WE WALK IN, AND THESE WOMEN - THEY'RE LIKE SIRENS.
AFTERNOON, LADIES.
IT'S LIKE A BOUDOIR.

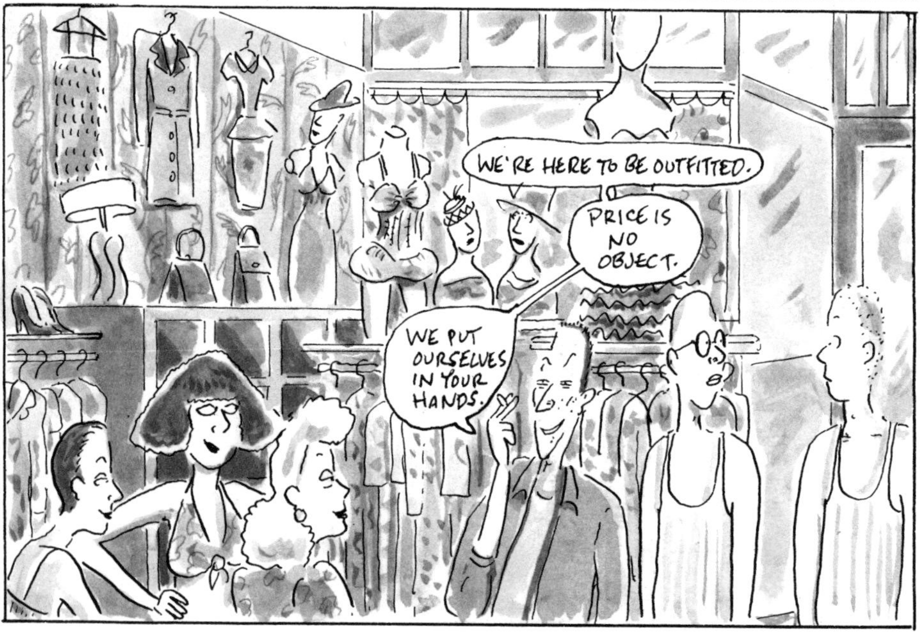
WE'RE HERE TO BE OUTFITTED.
PRICE IS NO OBJECT.
WE PUT OURSELVES IN YOUR HANDS.

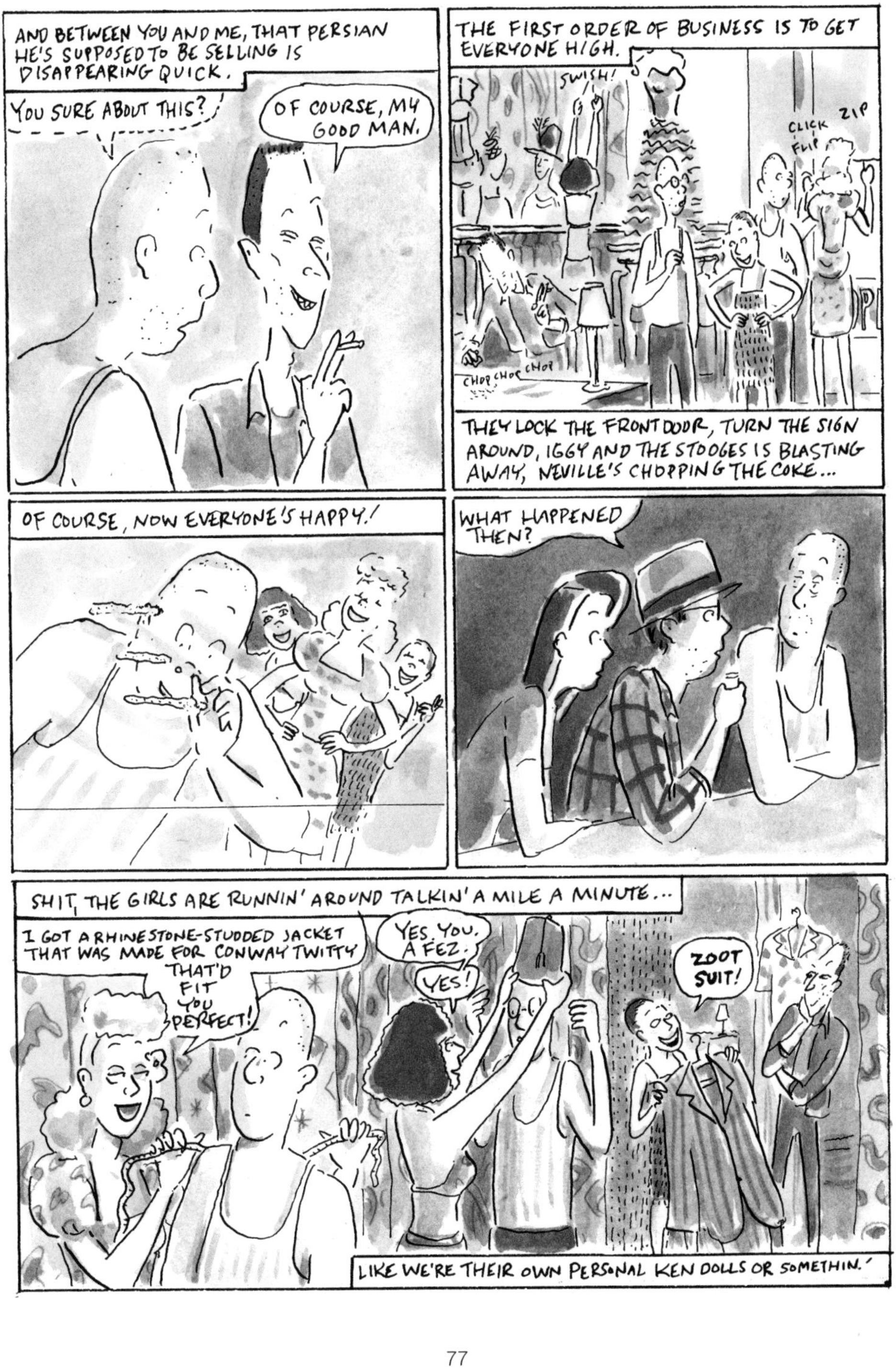
AND BETWEEN YOU AND ME, THAT PERSIAN HE'S SUPPOSED TO BE SELLING IS DISAPPEARING QUICK.
YOU SURE ABOUT THIS?
OF COURSE, MY GOOD MAN.
THE FIRST ORDER OF BUSINESS IS TO GET EVERYONE HIGH.
SWISH!
CLICK
FLIP
ZIP
CHOP CHOP CHOP
THEY LOCK THE FRONT DOOR, TURN THE SIGN AROUND, IGGY AND THE STOOGES IS BLASTING AWAY, NEVILLE'S CHOPPING THE COKE...
OF COURSE, NOW EVERYONE'S HAPPY!
WHAT HAPPENED THEN?
SHIT, THE GIRLS ARE RUNNIN' AROUND TALKIN' A MILE A MINUTE...
I GOT A RHINESTONE-STUDDED JACKET THAT WAS MADE FOR CONWAY TWITTY THAT'D FIT YOU PERFECT!
YES. YOU. A FEZ.
YES!
ZOOT SUIT!
LIKE WE'RE THEIR OWN PERSONAL KEN DOLLS OR SOMETHIN.'

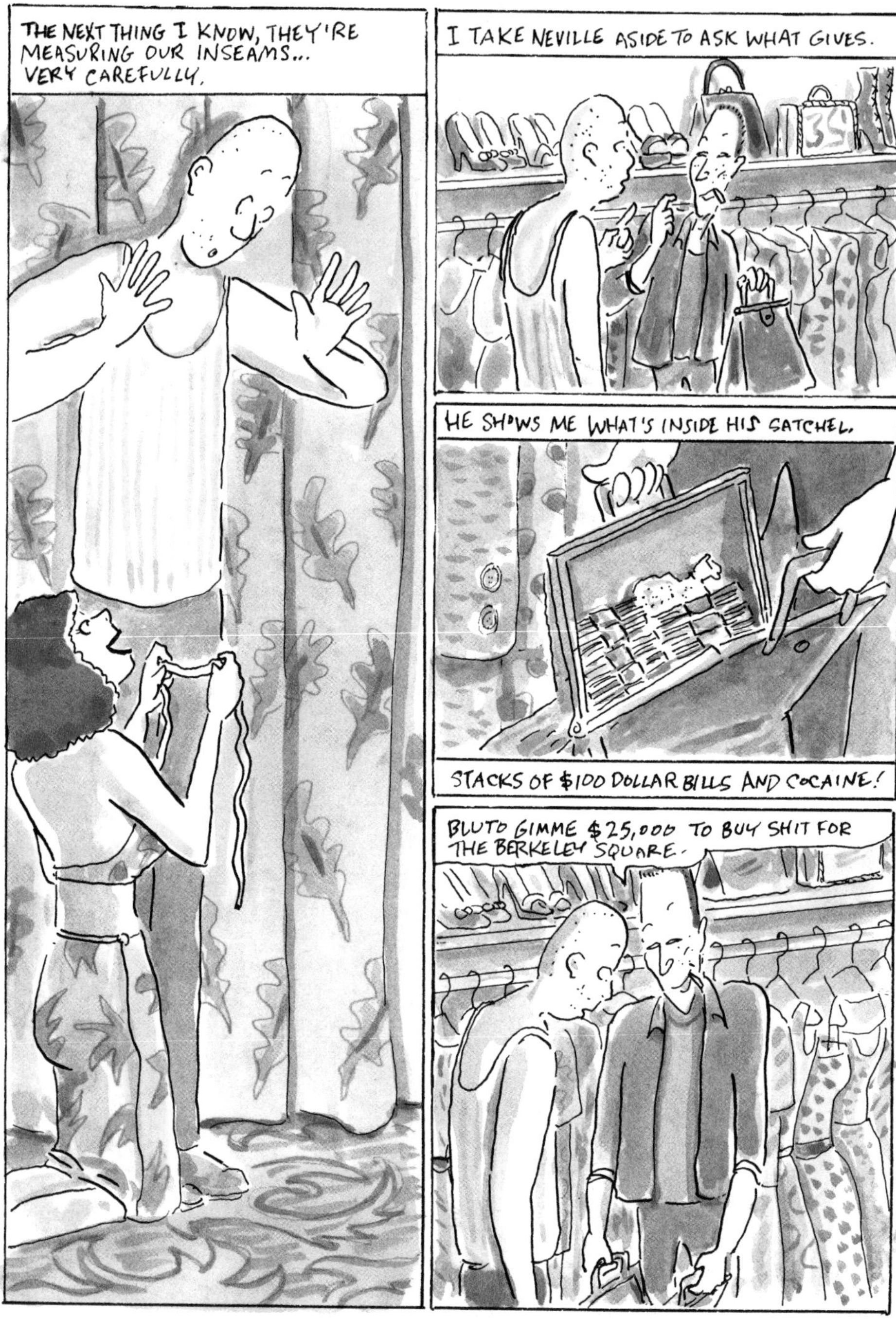
THE NEXT THING I KNOW, THEY'RE MEASURING OUR INSEAMS... VERY CAREFULLY.
I TAKE NEVILLE ASIDE TO ASK WHAT GIVES.
HE SHOWS ME WHAT'S INSIDE HIS SATCHEL.
STACKS OF $100 DOLLAR BILLS AND COCAINE!
BLUTO GIMME $25,000 TO BUY SHIT FOR THE BERKELEY SQUARE.

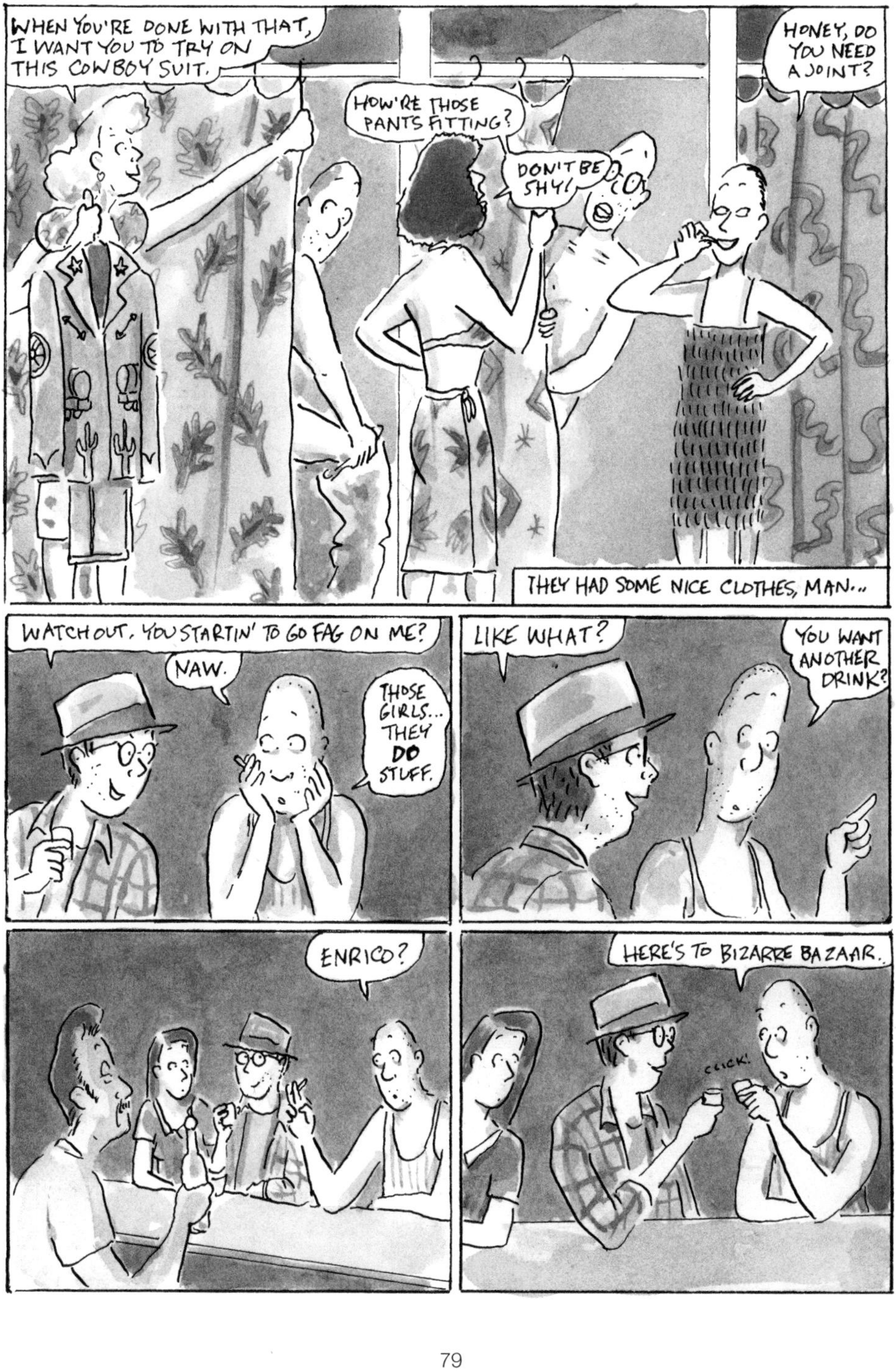
WHEN YOU'RE DONE WITH THAT, I WANT YOU TO TRY ON THIS COWBOY SUIT.
HOW'RE THOSE PANTS FITTING?
DON'T BE SHY!
HONEY, DO YOU NEED A JOINT?
THEY HAD SOME NICE CLOTHES, MAN...
WATCH OUT. YOU STARTIN' TO GO FAG ON ME?
NAW.
THOSE GIRLS... THEY **DO** STUFF.
LIKE WHAT?
YOU WANT ANOTHER DRINK?
ENRICO?
HERE'S TO BIZARRE BAZAAR.
CLICK!

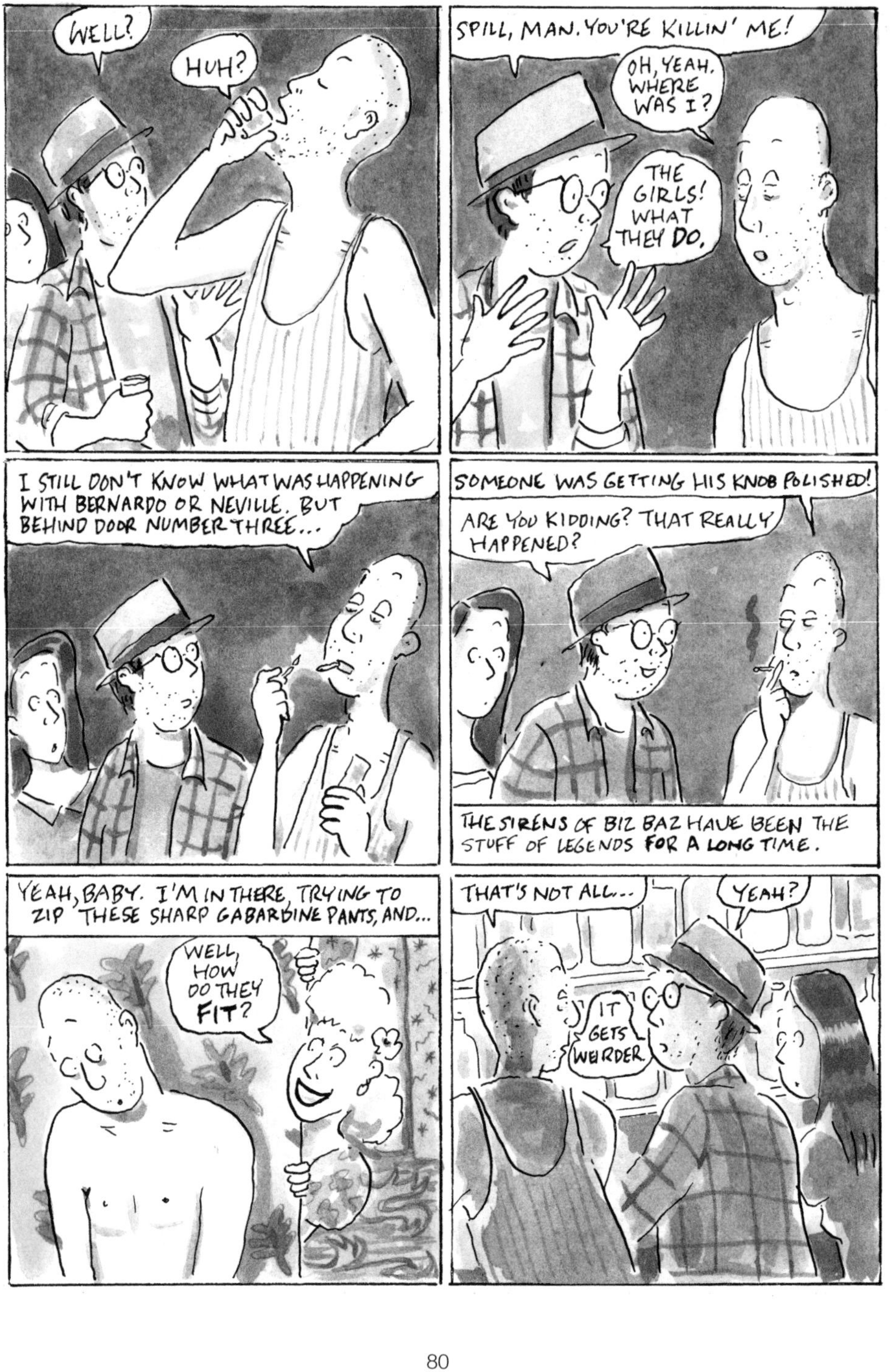
WELL?
HUH?
SPILL, MAN. YOU'RE KILLIN' ME!
OH, YEAH. WHERE WAS I?
THE GIRLS! WHAT THEY **DO.**
I STILL DON'T KNOW WHAT WAS HAPPENING WITH BERNARDO OR NEVILLE. BUT BEHIND DOOR NUMBER THREE...
SOMEONE WAS GETTING HIS KNOB POLISHED!
ARE YOU KIDDING? THAT REALLY HAPPENED?
THE SIRENS OF BIZ BAZ HAVE BEEN THE STUFF OF LEGENDS **FOR A LONG TIME.**
YEAH, BABY. I'M IN THERE, TRYING TO ZIP THESE SHARP GABARDINE PANTS, AND...
WELL, HOW DO THEY **FIT**?
THAT'S NOT ALL...
YEAH?
IT GETS WEIRDER.

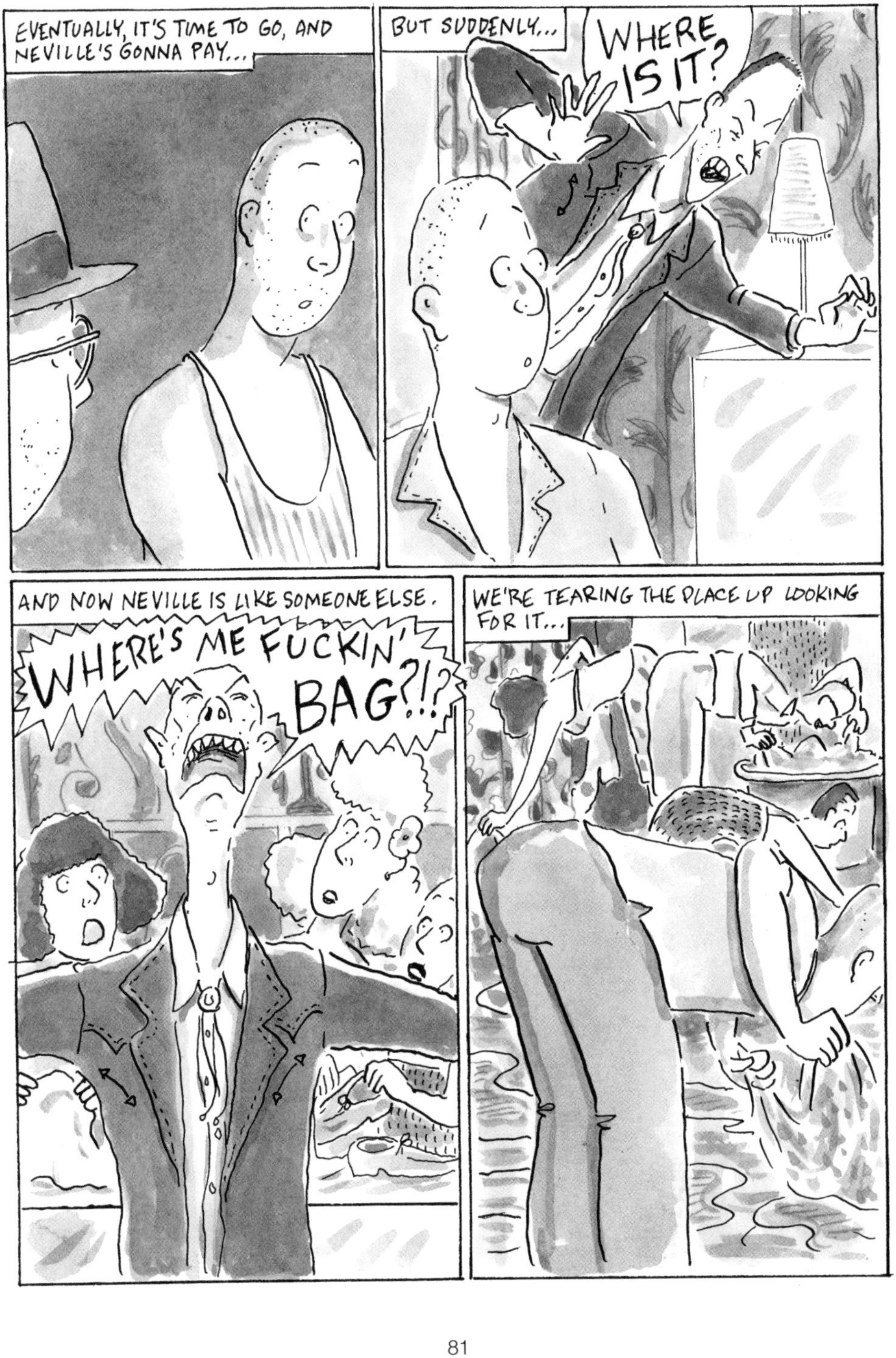
EVENTUALLY, IT'S TIME TO GO, AND NEVILLE'S GONNA PAY...
BUT SUDDENLY...
WHERE IS IT?
AND NOW NEVILLE IS LIKE SOMEONE ELSE.
WHERE'S ME FUCKIN' BAG?!?
WE'RE TEARING THE PLACE UP LOOKING FOR IT...

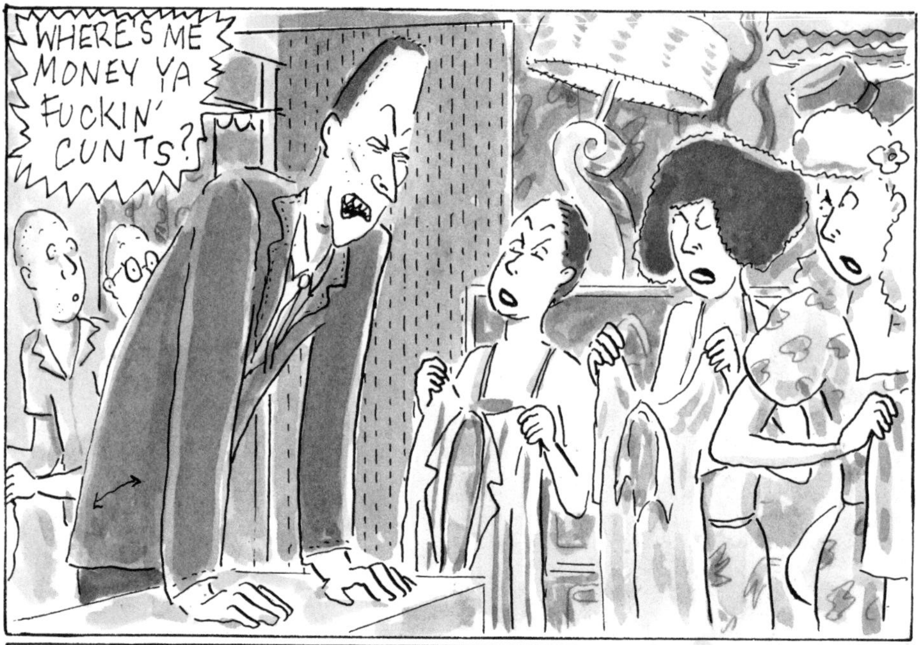
WHERE'S ME MONEY YA FUCKIN' CUNTS?

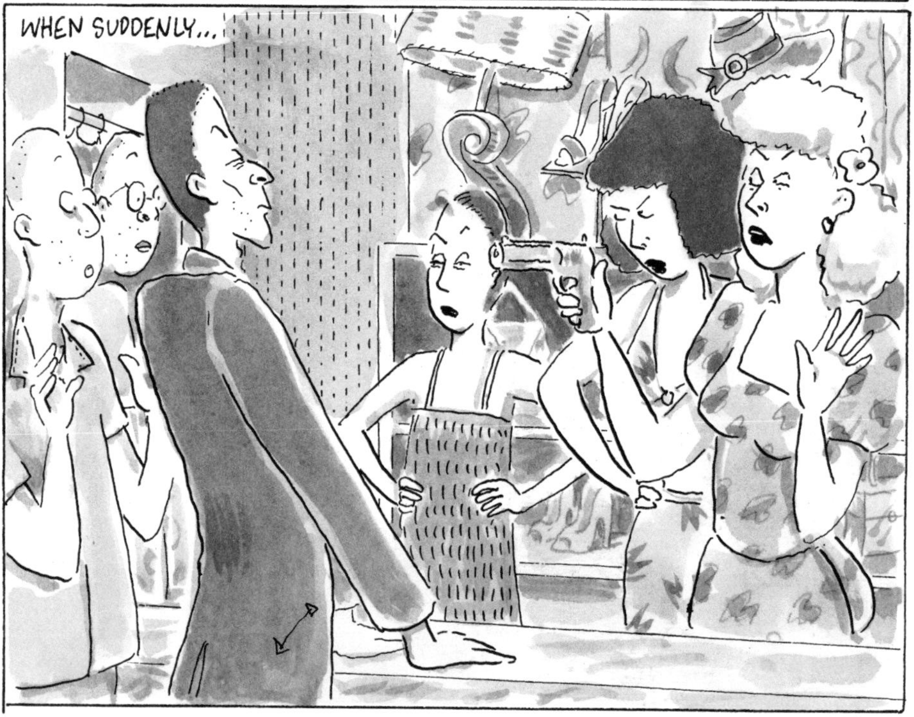
WHEN SUDDENLY...

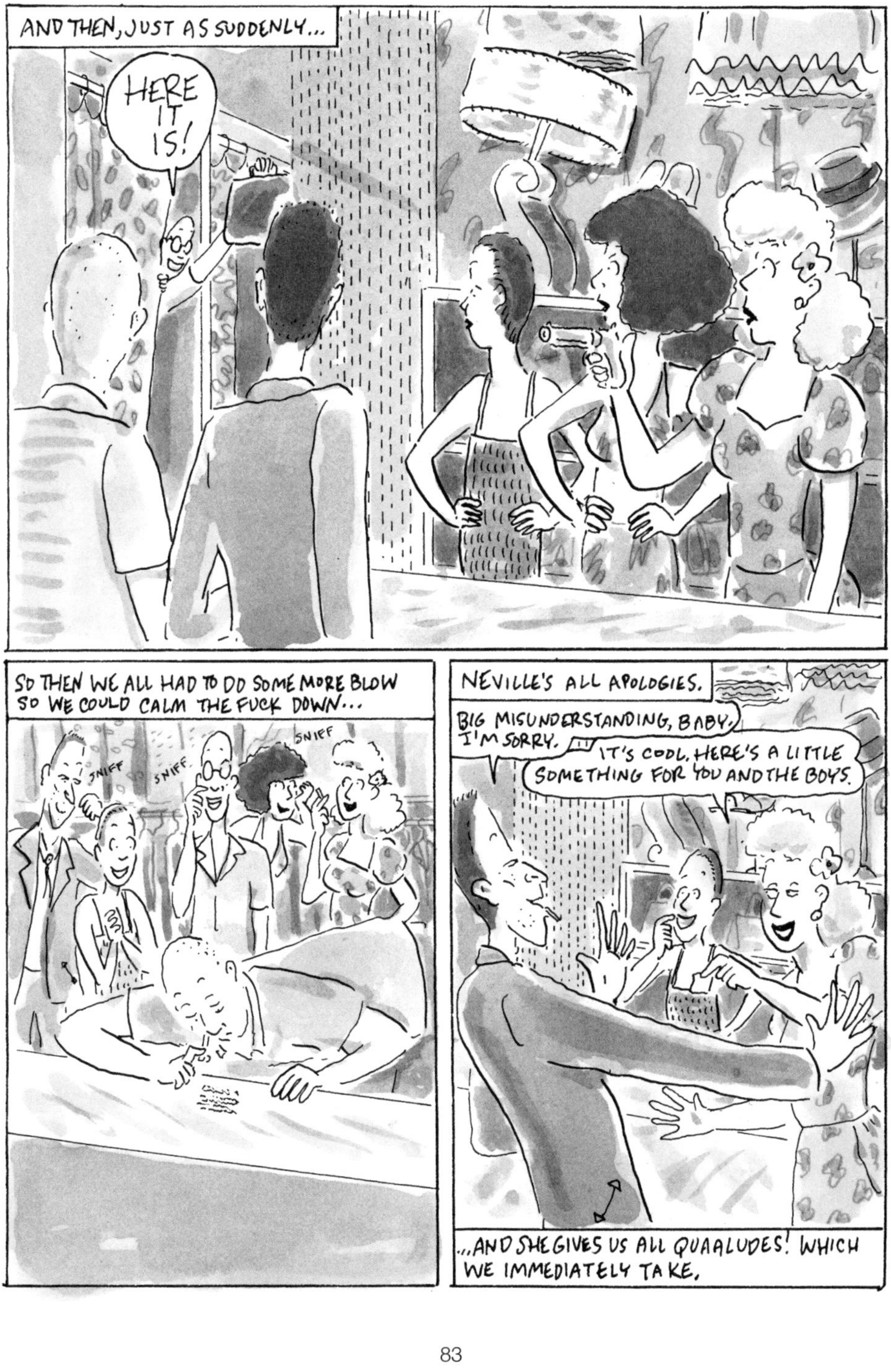
AND THEN, JUST AS SUDDENLY...
HERE IT IS!
SO THEN WE ALL HAD TO DO SOME MORE BLOW SO WE COULD CALM THE FUCK DOWN...
SNIFF
SNIFF
SNIFF
NEVILLE'S ALL APOLOGIES.
BIG MISUNDERSTANDING, BABY. I'M SORRY.
IT'S COOL. HERE'S A LITTLE SOMETHING FOR YOU AND THE BOYS.
...AND SHE GIVES US ALL QUAALUDES! WHICH WE IMMEDIATELY TAKE.

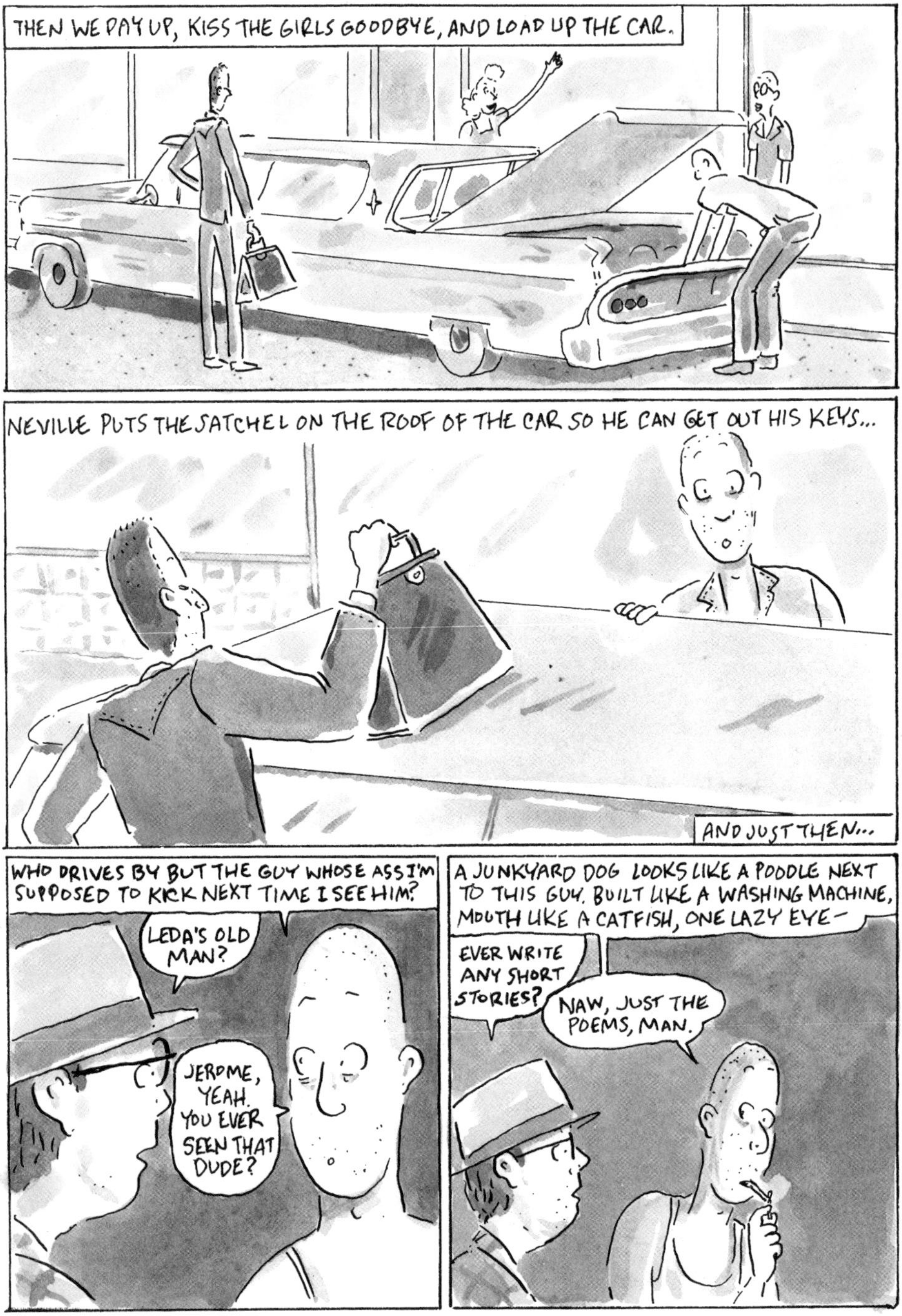
THEN WE PAY UP, KISS THE GIRLS GOODBYE, AND LOAD UP THE CAR.
NEVILLE PUTS THE SATCHEL ON THE ROOF OF THE CAR SO HE CAN GET OUT HIS KEYS...
AND JUST THEN...
WHO DRIVES BY BUT THE GUY WHOSE ASS I'M SUPPOSED TO KICK NEXT TIME I SEE HIM?
LEDA'S OLD MAN?
JEROME, YEAH. YOU EVER SEEN THAT DUDE?
A JUNKYARD DOG LOOKS LIKE A POODLE NEXT TO THIS GUY. BUILT LIKE A WASHING MACHINE, MOUTH LIKE A CATFISH, ONE LAZY EYE—
EVER WRITE ANY SHORT STORIES?
NAW, JUST THE POEMS, MAN.

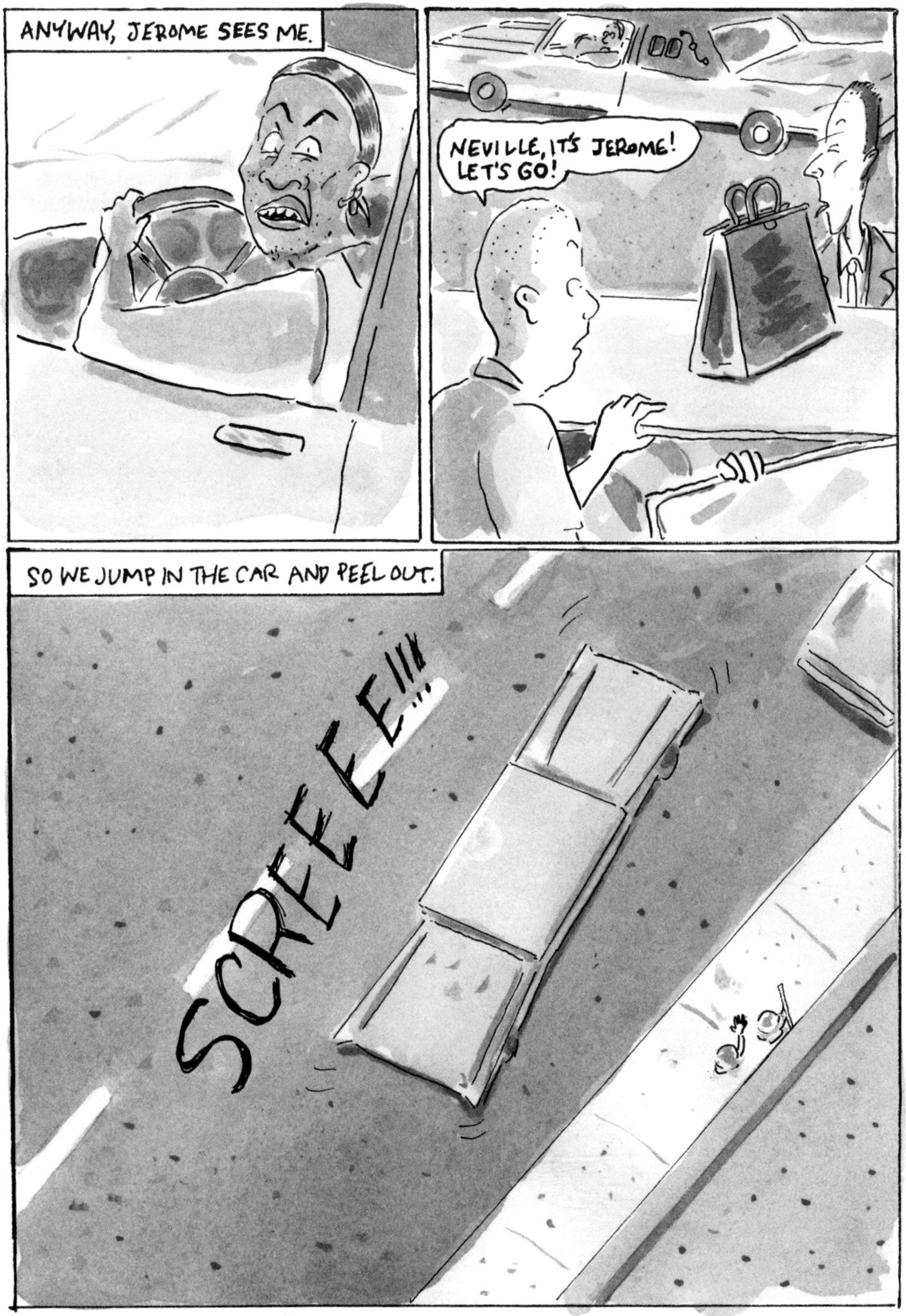
ANYWAY, JEROME SEES ME.
NEVILLE, IT'S JEROME! LET'S GO!
SO WE JUMP IN THE CAR AND PEEL OUT.
SCREEEE!!!

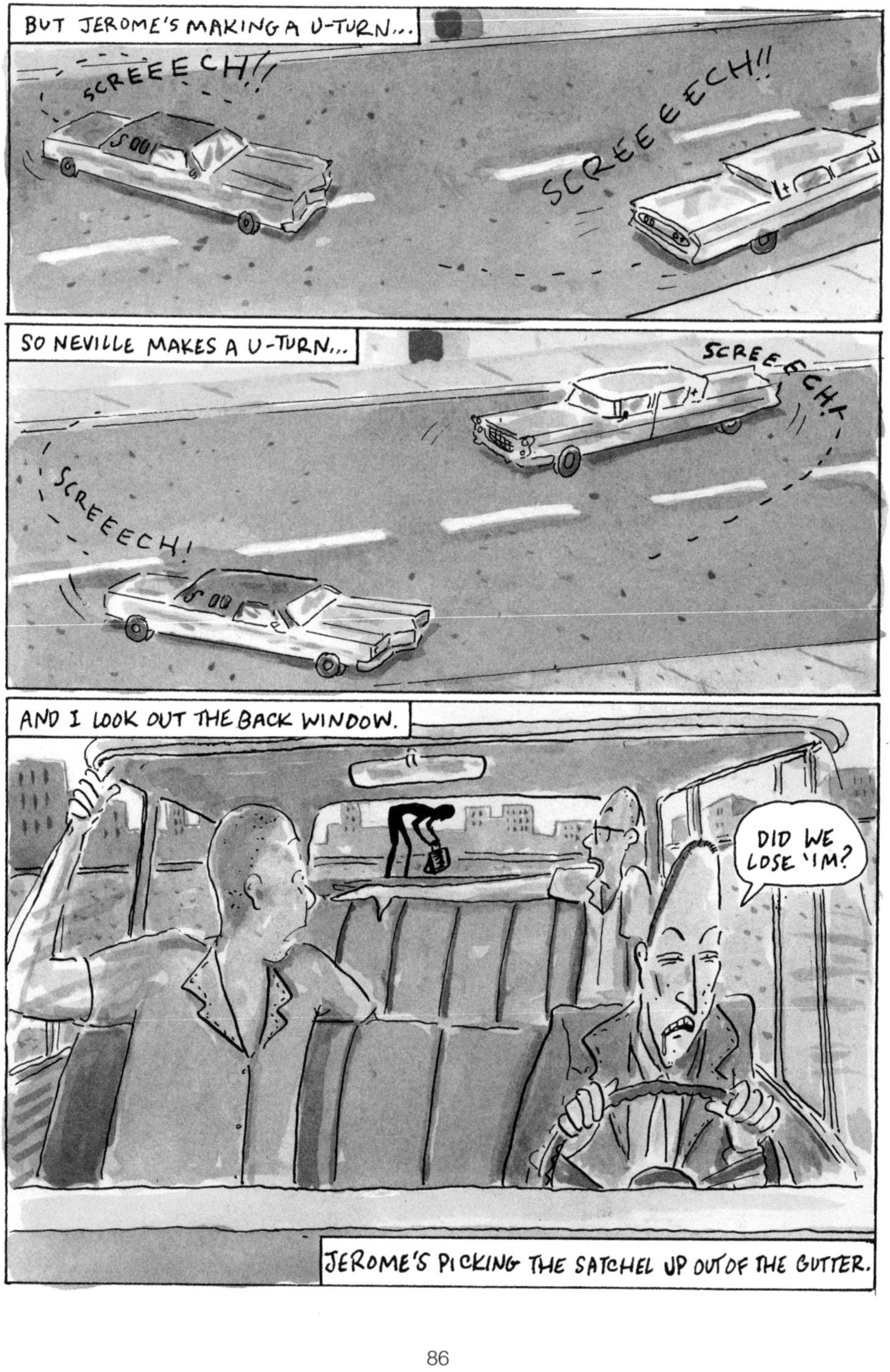
BUT JEROME'S MAKING A U-TURN...
SCREEECH!!
SCREEEECH!!
SO NEVILLE MAKES A U-TURN...
SCREEECH!
SCREEEECH!
AND I LOOK OUT THE BACK WINDOW.
DID WE LOSE 'IM?
JEROME'S PICKING THE SATCHEL UP OUT OF THE GUTTER.

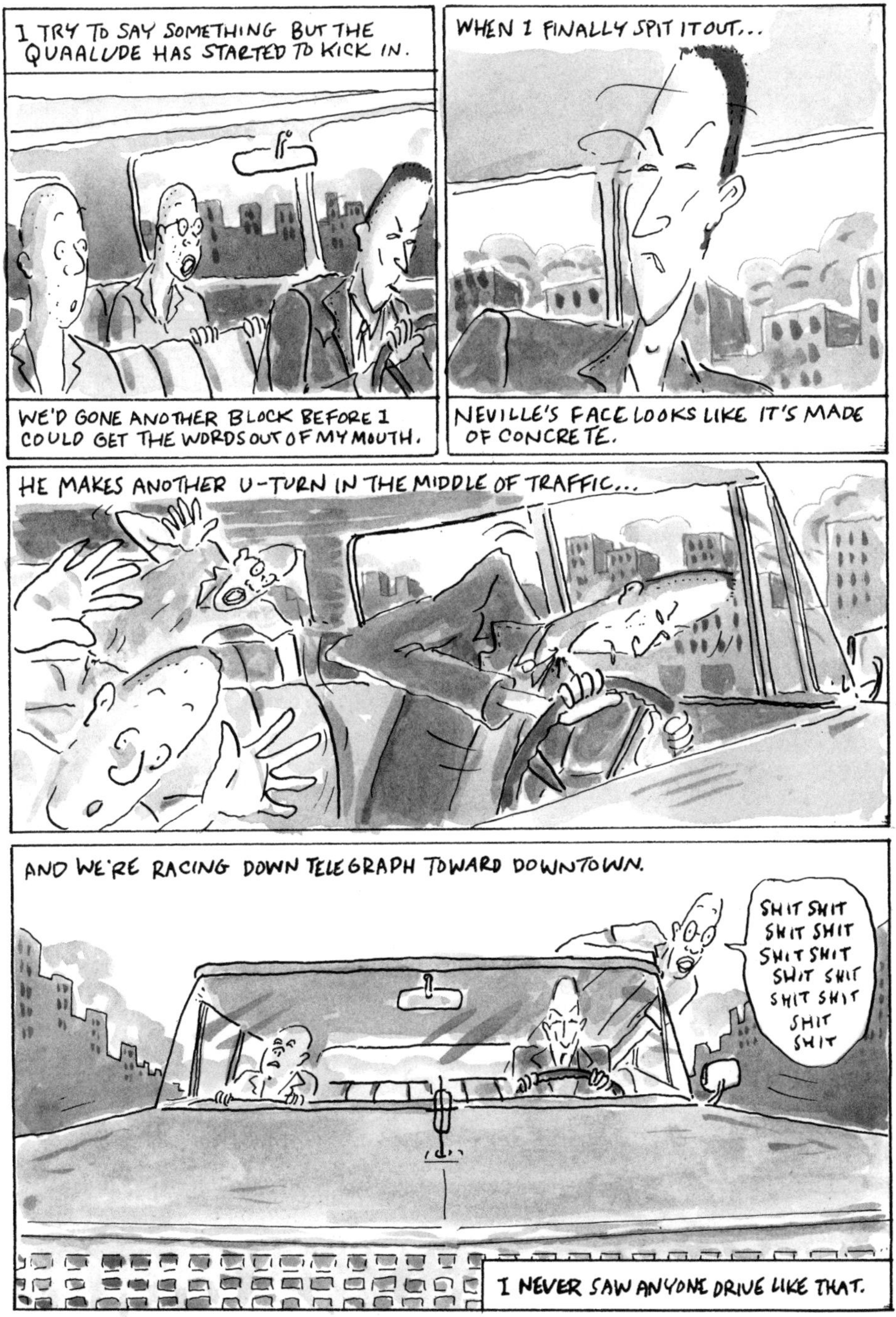
I TRY TO SAY SOMETHING BUT THE QUAALUDE HAS STARTED TO KICK IN.
WE'D GONE ANOTHER BLOCK BEFORE I COULD GET THE WORDS OUT OF MY MOUTH.
WHEN I FINALLY SPIT IT OUT...
NEVILLE'S FACE LOOKS LIKE IT'S MADE OF CONCRETE.
HE MAKES ANOTHER U-TURN IN THE MIDDLE OF TRAFFIC...
AND WE'RE RACING DOWN TELEGRAPH TOWARD DOWNTOWN.
SHIT SHIT SHIT SHIT SHIT SHIT SHIT SHIT SHIT SHIT SHIT SHIT
I NEVER SAW ANYONE DRIVE LIKE THAT.

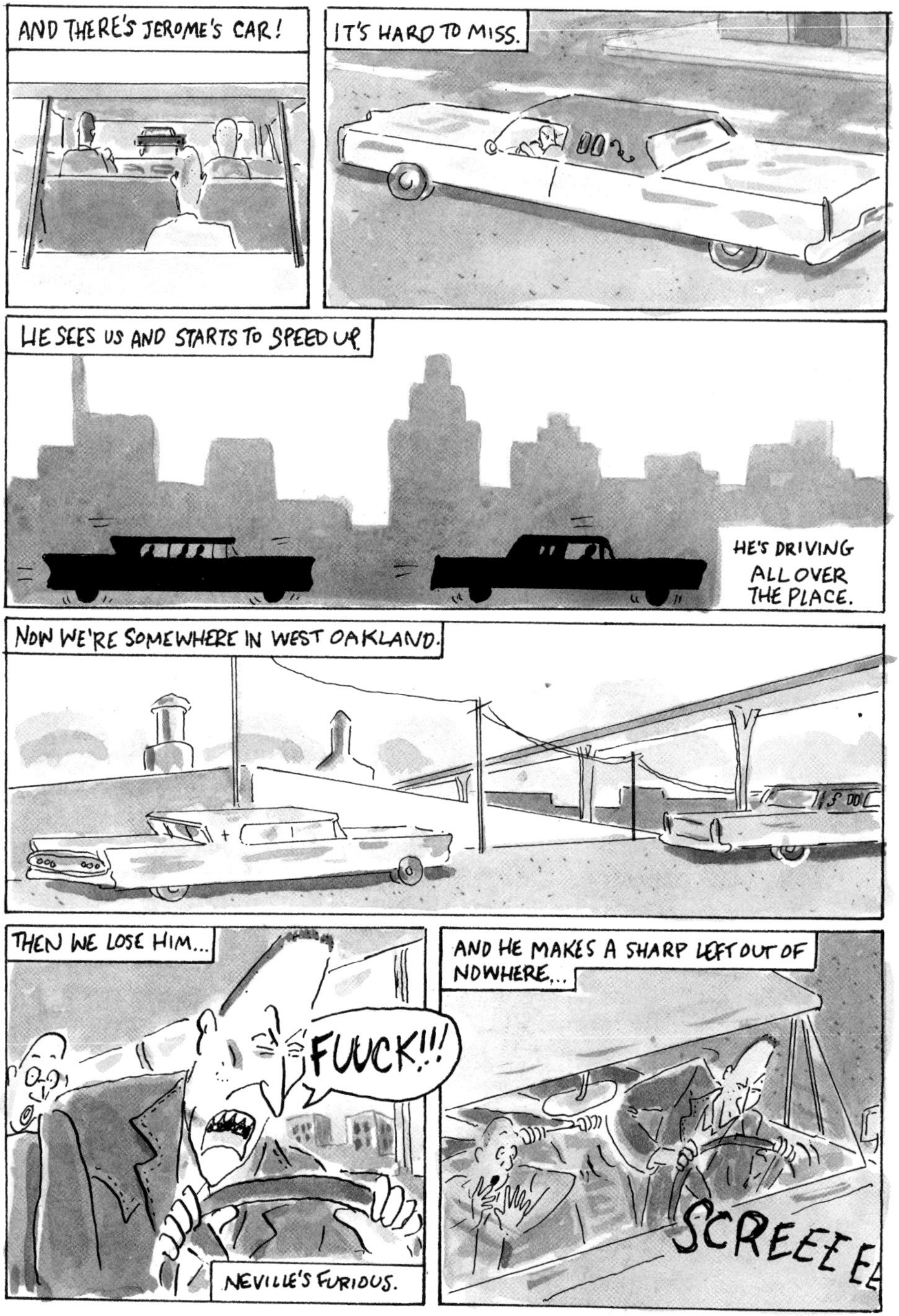
AND THERE'S JEROME'S CAR!
IT'S HARD TO MISS.
HE SEES US AND STARTS TO SPEED UP.
HE'S DRIVING ALL OVER THE PLACE.
NOW WE'RE SOMEWHERE IN WEST OAKLAND.
THEN WE LOSE HIM...
FUUCK!!!
NEVILLE'S FURIOUS.
AND HE MAKES A SHARP LEFT OUT OF NOWHERE...
SCREEEE

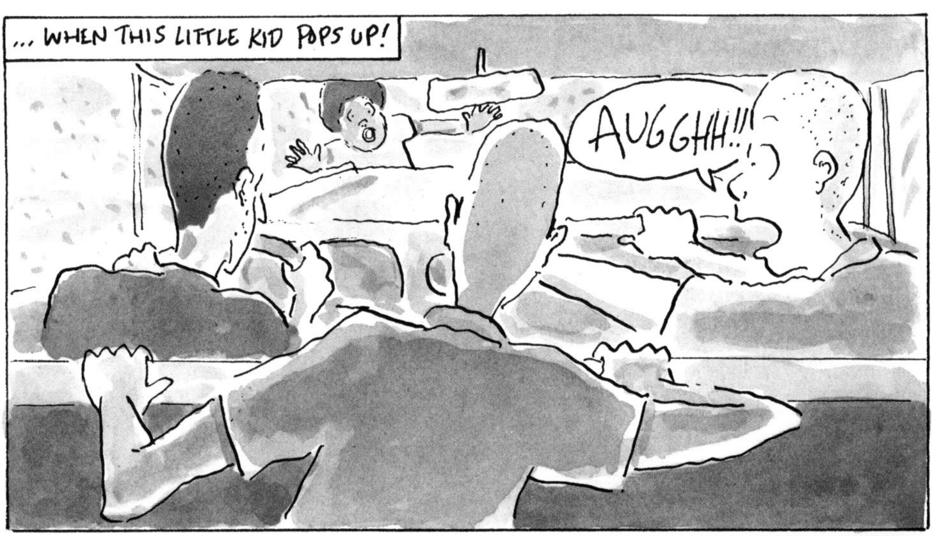
... WHEN THIS LITTLE KID POPS UP!
AUGGHH!!!

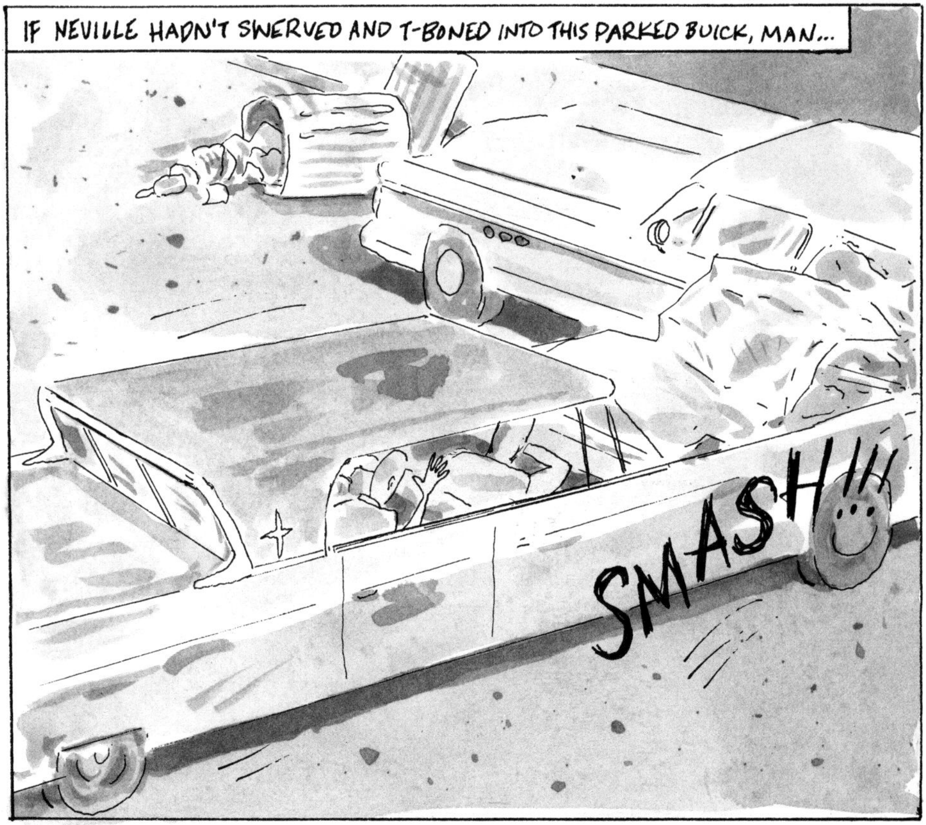
IF NEVILLE HADN'T SWERVED AND T-BONED INTO THIS PARKED BUICK, MAN...
SMASH!!!

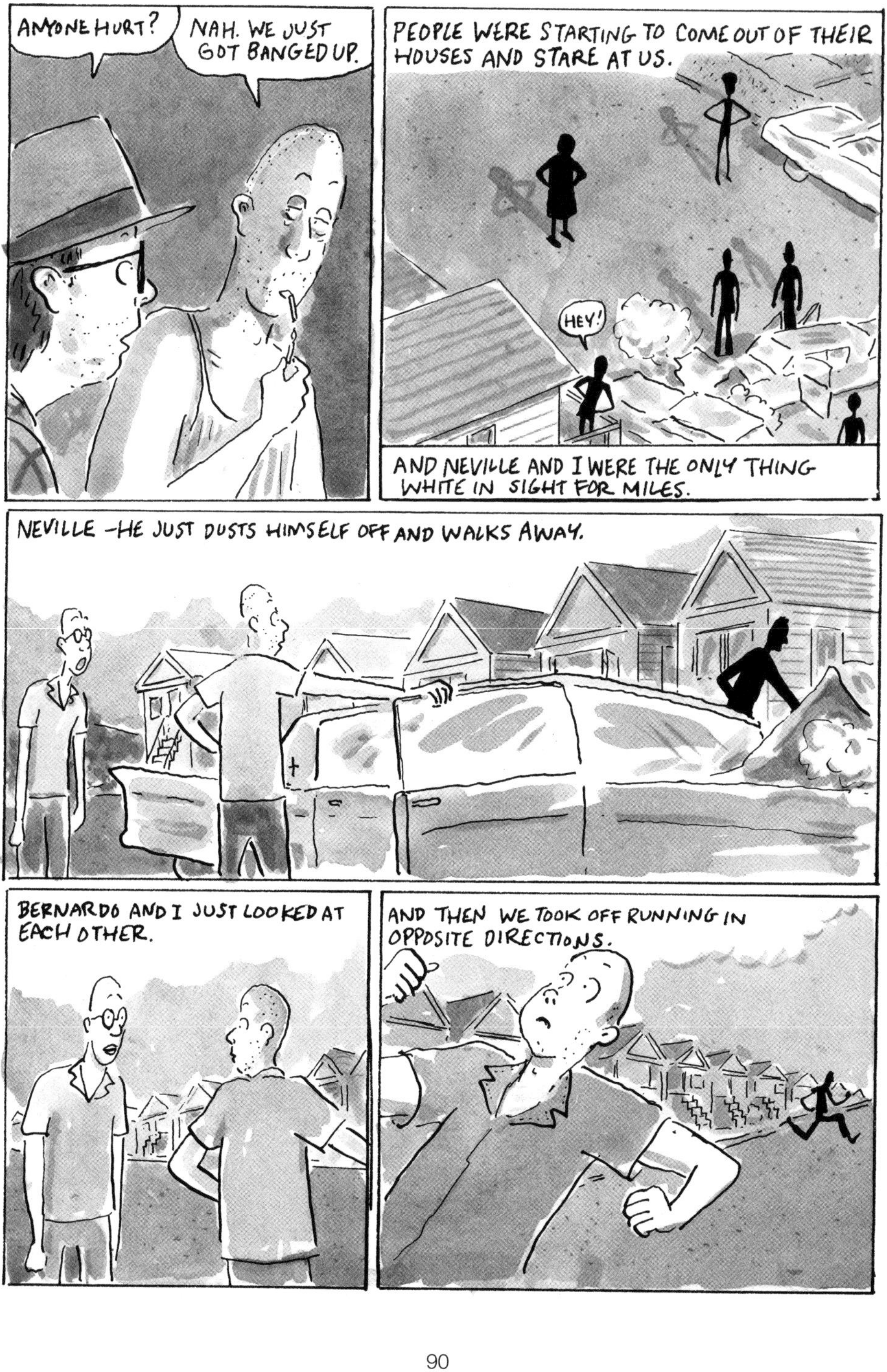
ANYONE HURT?
NAH. WE JUST GOT BANGED UP.
PEOPLE WERE STARTING TO COME OUT OF THEIR HOUSES AND STARE AT US.
HEY!
AND NEVILLE AND I WERE THE ONLY THING WHITE IN SIGHT FOR MILES.
NEVILLE –HE JUST DUSTS HIMSELF OFF AND WALKS AWAY.
BERNARDO AND I JUST LOOKED AT EACH OTHER.
AND THEN WE TOOK OFF RUNNING IN OPPOSITE DIRECTIONS.

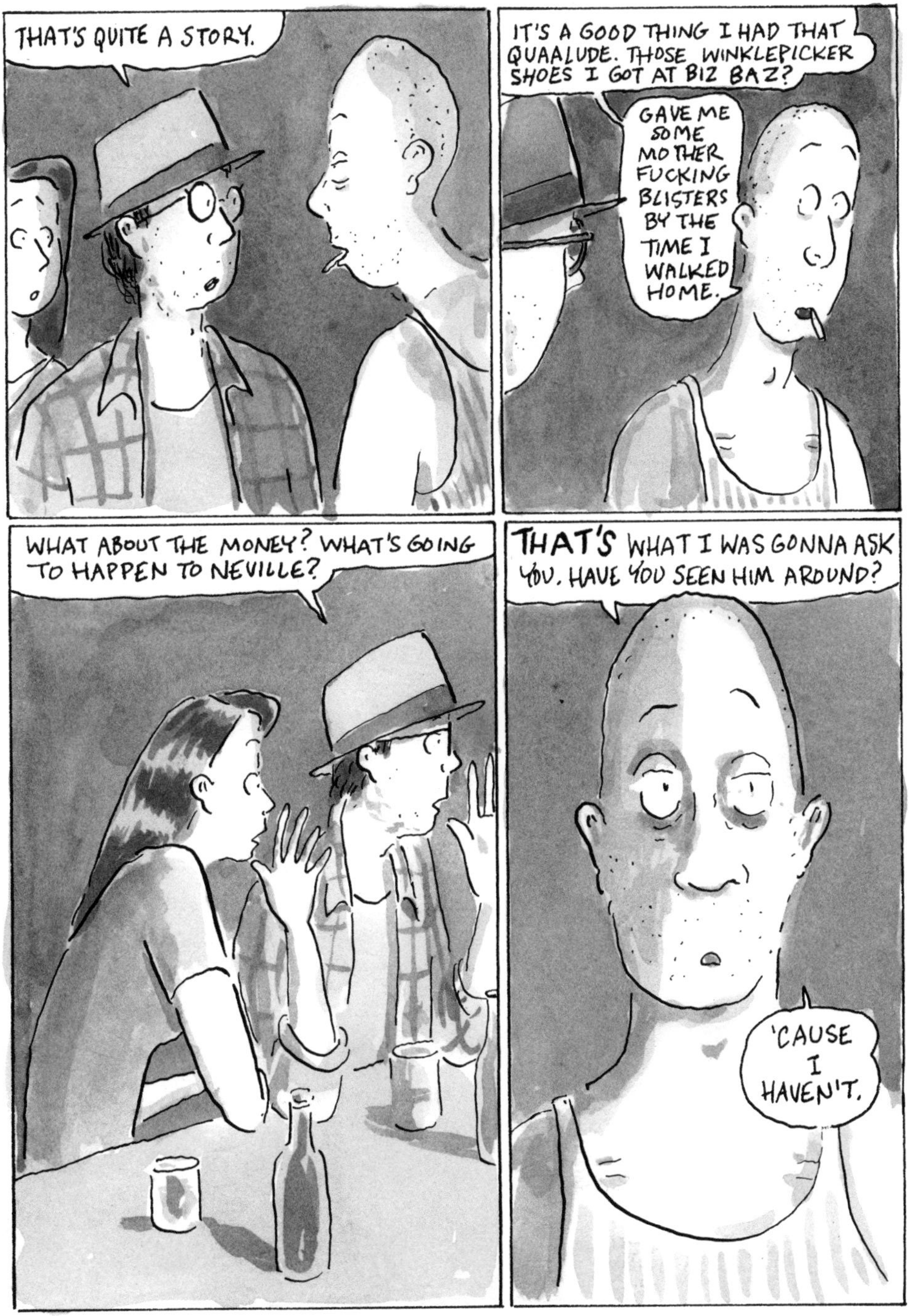
THAT'S QUITE A STORY.
IT'S A GOOD THING I HAD THAT QUAALUDE. THOSE WINKLEPICKER SHOES I GOT AT BIZ BAZ?
GAVE ME SOME MOTHER FUCKING BLISTERS BY THE TIME I WALKED HOME.
WHAT ABOUT THE MONEY? WHAT'S GOING TO HAPPEN TO NEVILLE?
THAT'S WHAT I WAS GONNA ASK YOU. HAVE YOU SEEN HIM AROUND?
'CAUSE I HAVEN'T.

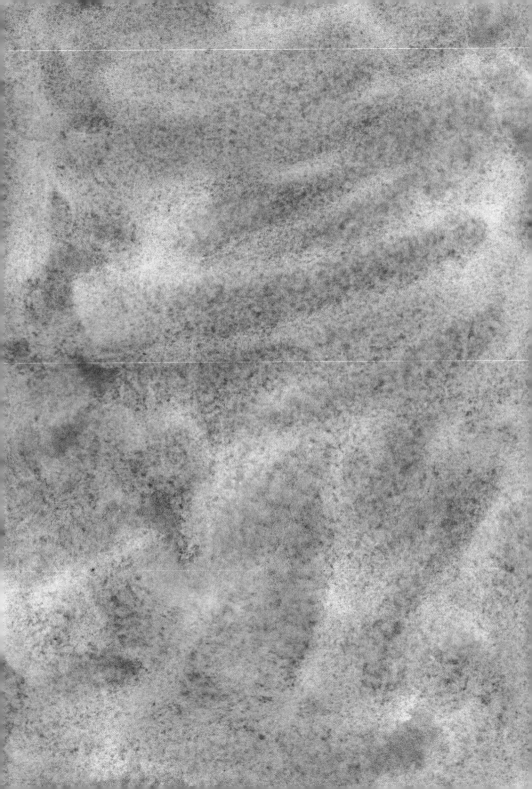

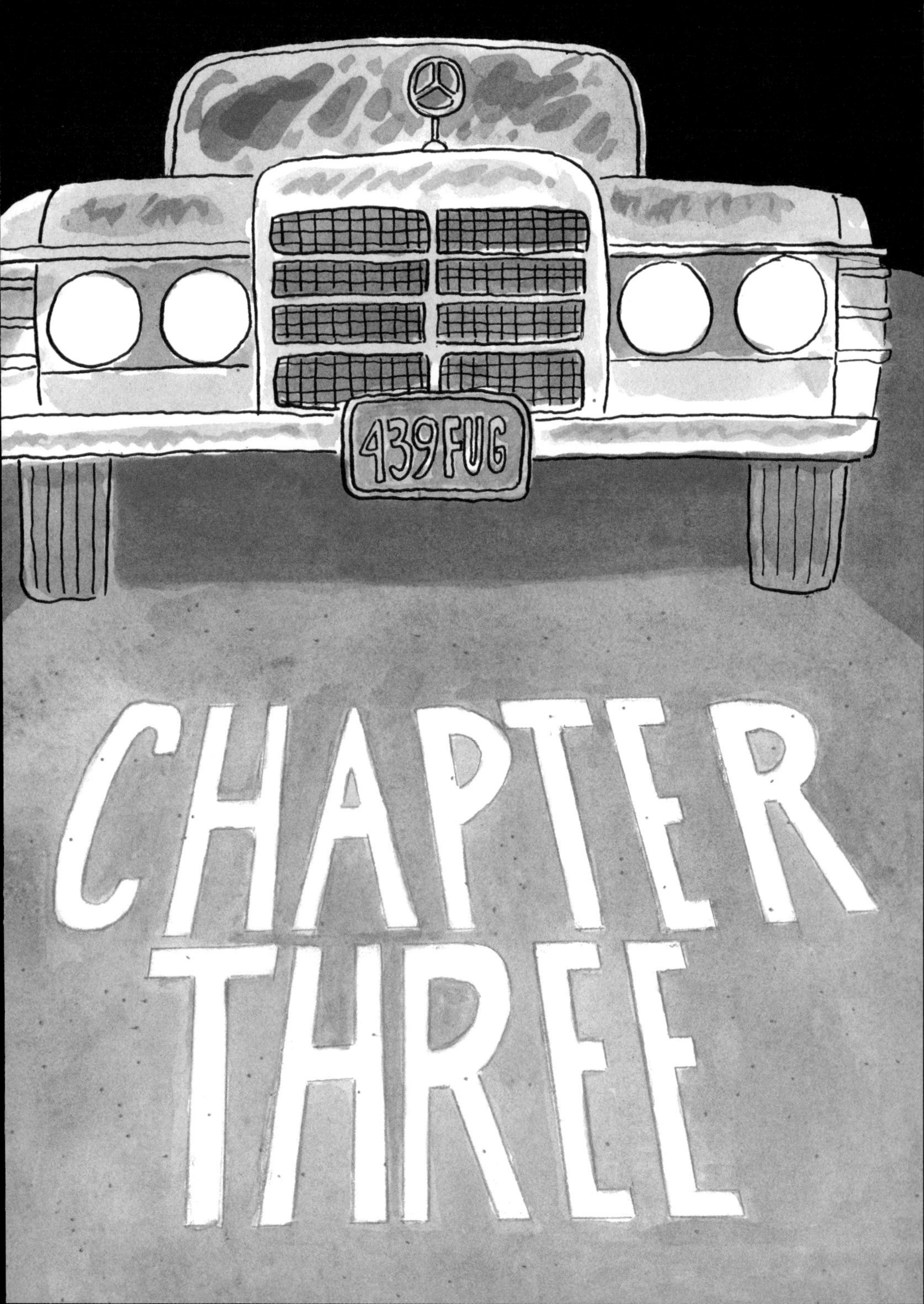
439FUG
CHAPTER
THREE

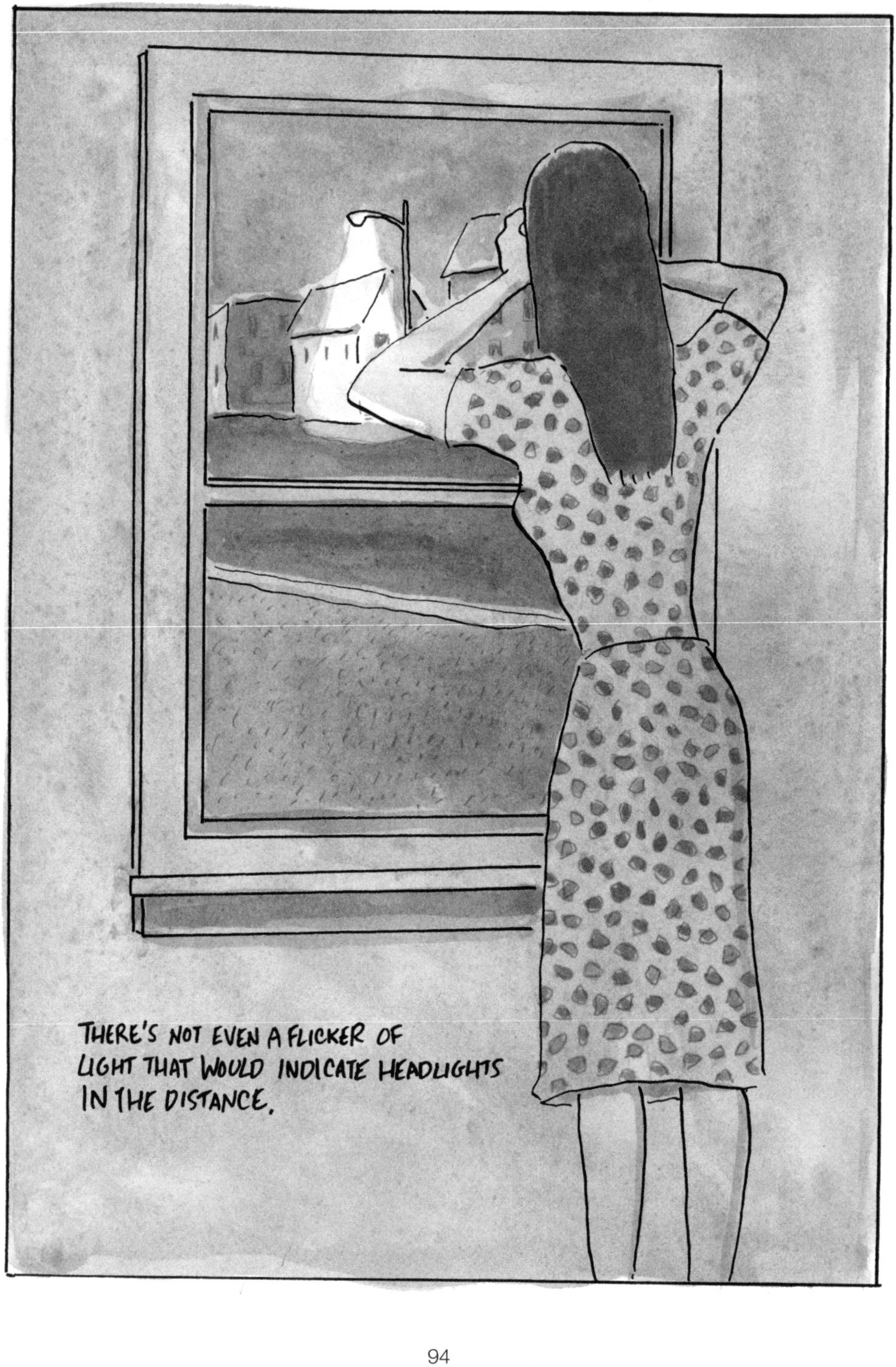
THERE'S NOT EVEN A FLICKER OF LIGHT THAT WOULD INDICATE HEADLIGHTS IN THE DISTANCE.

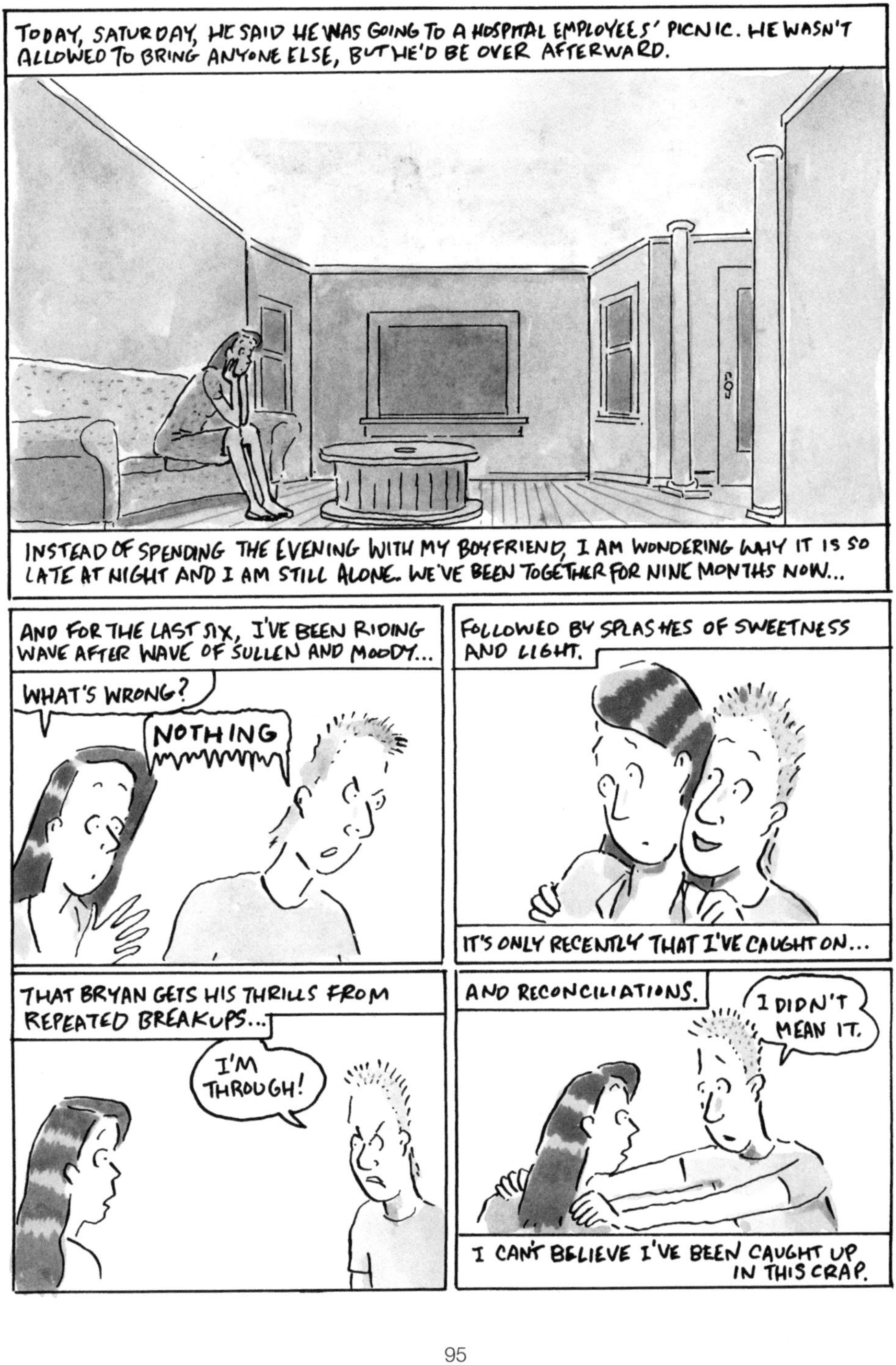
TODAY, SATURDAY, HE SAID HE WAS GOING TO A HOSPITAL EMPLOYEES' PICNIC. HE WASN'T ALLOWED TO BRING ANYONE ELSE, BUT HE'D BE OVER AFTERWARD.
INSTEAD OF SPENDING THE EVENING WITH MY BOYFRIEND, I AM WONDERING WHY IT IS SO LATE AT NIGHT AND I AM STILL ALONE. WE'VE BEEN TOGETHER FOR NINE MONTHS NOW...
AND FOR THE LAST SIX, I'VE BEEN RIDING WAVE AFTER WAVE OF SULLEN AND MOODY...
WHAT'S WRONG?
NOTHING
FOLLOWED BY SPLASHES OF SWEETNESS AND LIGHT.
IT'S ONLY RECENTLY THAT I'VE CAUGHT ON...
THAT BRYAN GETS HIS THRILLS FROM REPEATED BREAKUPS...
I'M THROUGH!
AND RECONCILIATIONS.
I DIDN'T MEAN IT.
I CAN'T BELIEVE I'VE BEEN CAUGHT UP IN THIS CRAP.

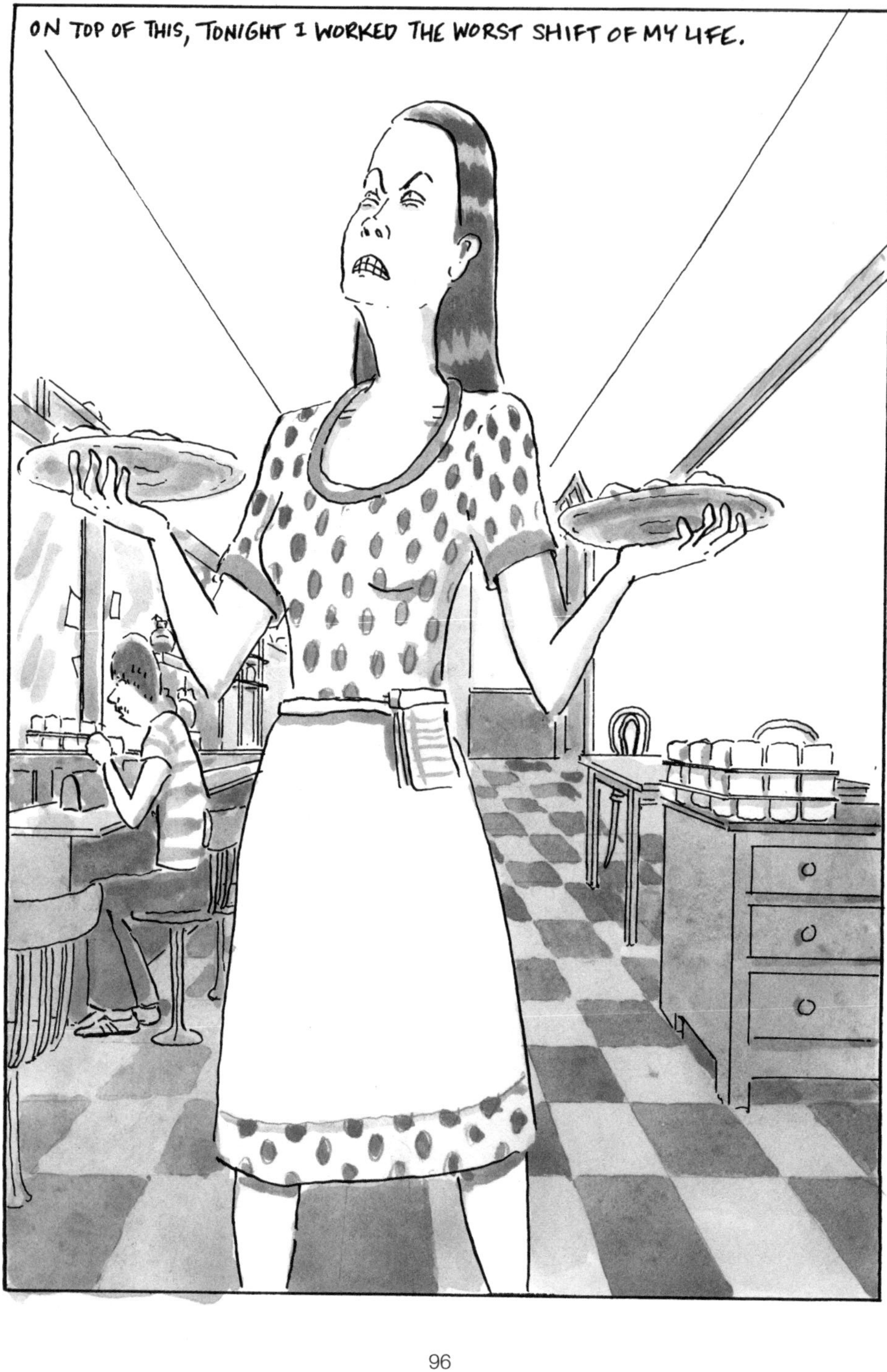
ON TOP OF THIS, TONIGHT I WORKED THE WORST SHIFT OF MY LIFE.

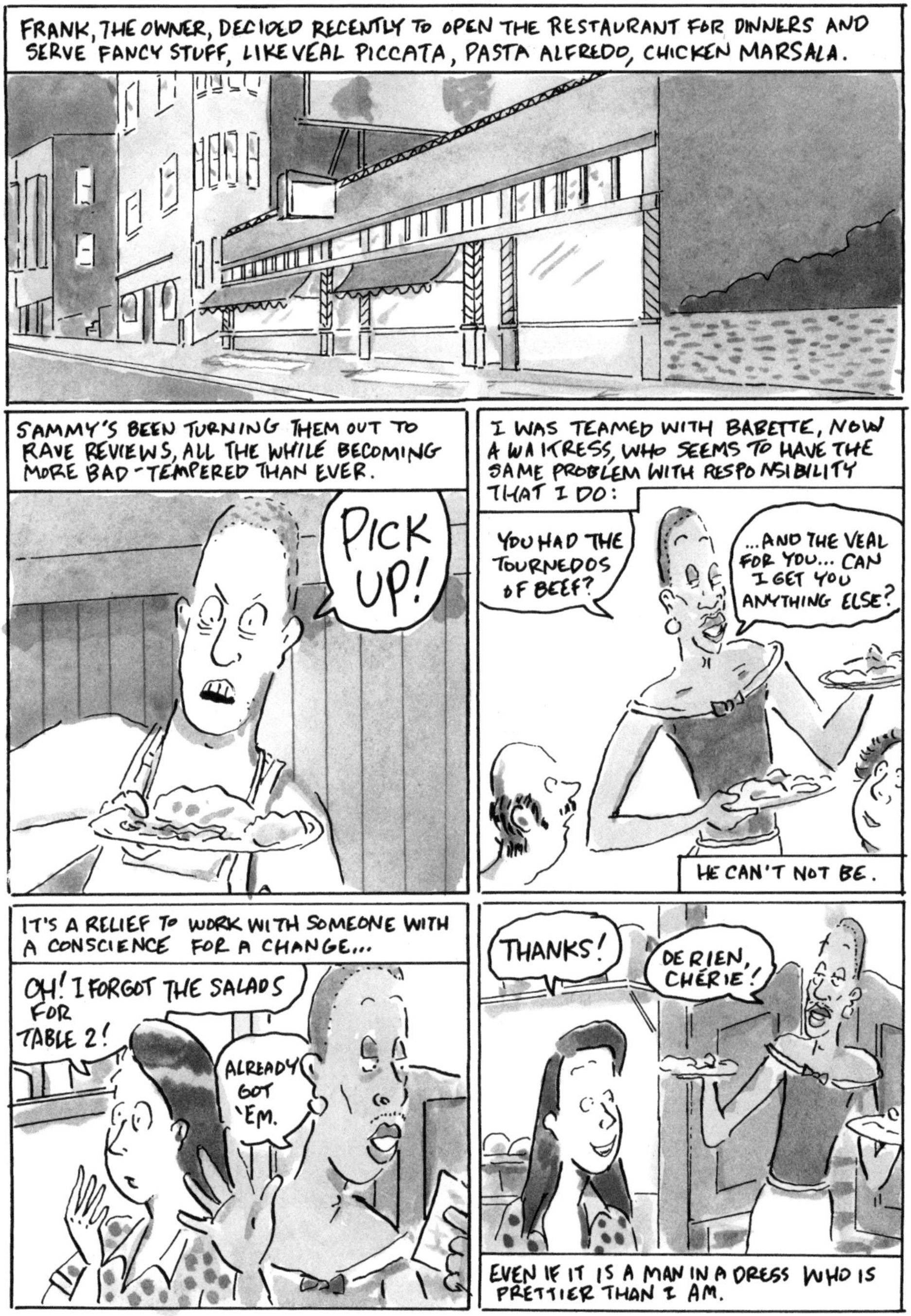
FRANK, THE OWNER, DECIDED RECENTLY TO OPEN THE RESTAURANT FOR DINNERS AND SERVE FANCY STUFF, LIKE VEAL PICCATA, PASTA ALFREDO, CHICKEN MARSALA.
SAMMY'S BEEN TURNING THEM OUT TO RAVE REVIEWS, ALL THE WHILE BECOMING MORE BAD-TEMPERED THAN EVER.
PICK UP!
I WAS TEAMED WITH BABETTE, NOW A WAITRESS, WHO SEEMS TO HAVE THE SAME PROBLEM WITH RESPONSIBILITY THAT I DO:
YOU HAD THE TOURNEDOS OF BEEF?
...AND THE VEAL FOR YOU... CAN I GET YOU ANYTHING ELSE?
HE CAN'T NOT BE.
IT'S A RELIEF TO WORK WITH SOMEONE WITH A CONSCIENCE FOR A CHANGE...
OH! I FORGOT THE SALADS FOR TABLE 2!
ALREADY GOT 'EM.
THANKS!
DE RIEN, CHÉRIE!
EVEN IF IT IS A MAN IN A DRESS WHO IS PRETTIER THAN I AM.

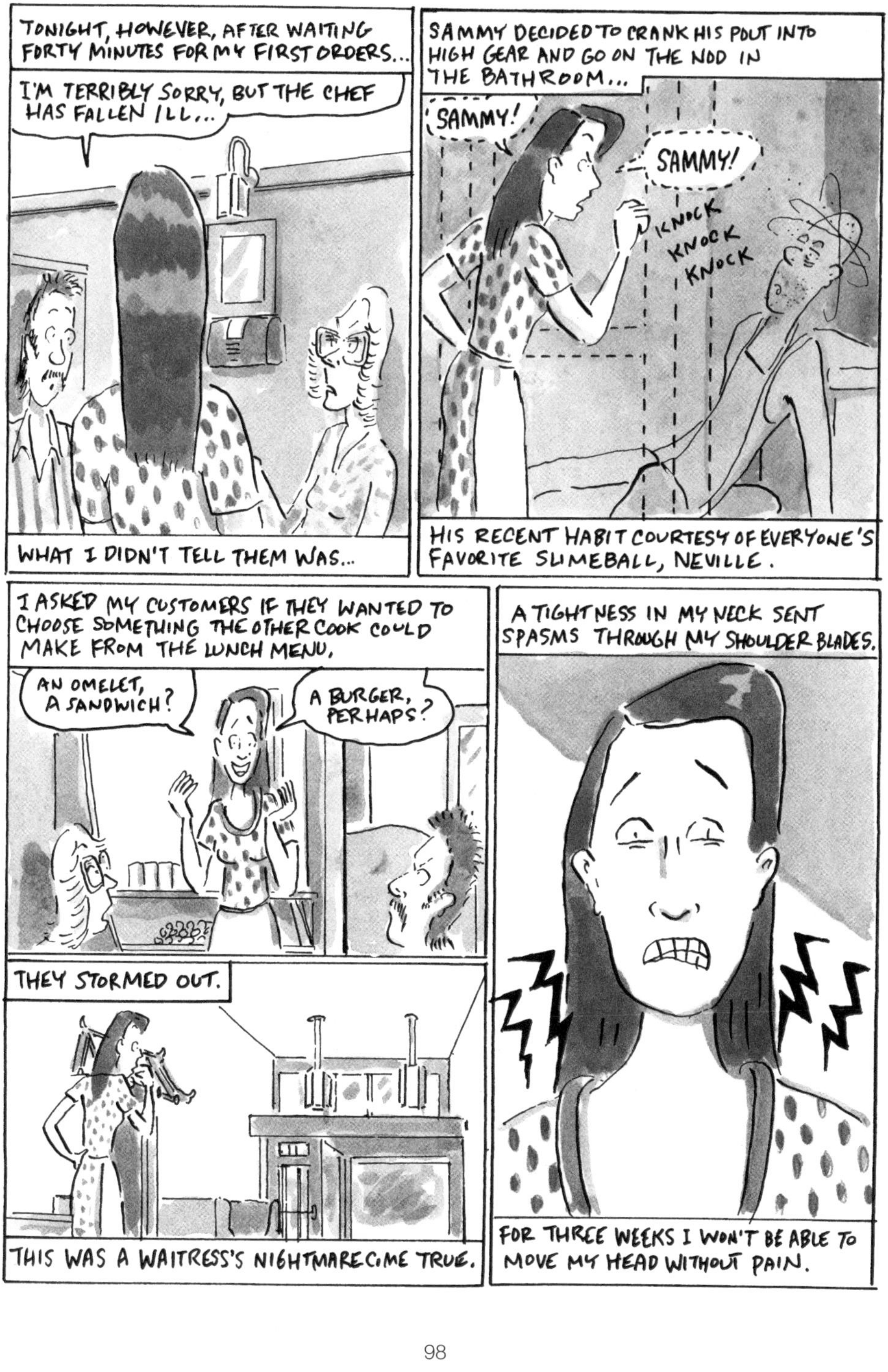
TONIGHT, HOWEVER, AFTER WAITING FORTY MINUTES FOR MY FIRST ORDERS...
I'M TERRIBLY SORRY, BUT THE CHEF HAS FALLEN ILL...
WHAT I DIDN'T TELL THEM WAS...
SAMMY DECIDED TO CRANK HIS POUT INTO HIGH GEAR AND GO ON THE NOD IN THE BATHROOM...
SAMMY!
SAMMY!
KNOCK KNOCK KNOCK
HIS RECENT HABIT COURTESY OF EVERYONE'S FAVORITE SLIMEBALL, NEVILLE.
I ASKED MY CUSTOMERS IF THEY WANTED TO CHOOSE SOMETHING THE OTHER COOK COULD MAKE FROM THE LUNCH MENU.
AN OMELET, A SANDWICH?
A BURGER, PERHAPS?
THEY STORMED OUT.
THIS WAS A WAITRESS'S NIGHTMARE COME TRUE.
A TIGHTNESS IN MY NECK SENT SPASMS THROUGH MY SHOULDER BLADES.
FOR THREE WEEKS I WON'T BE ABLE TO MOVE MY HEAD WITHOUT PAIN.

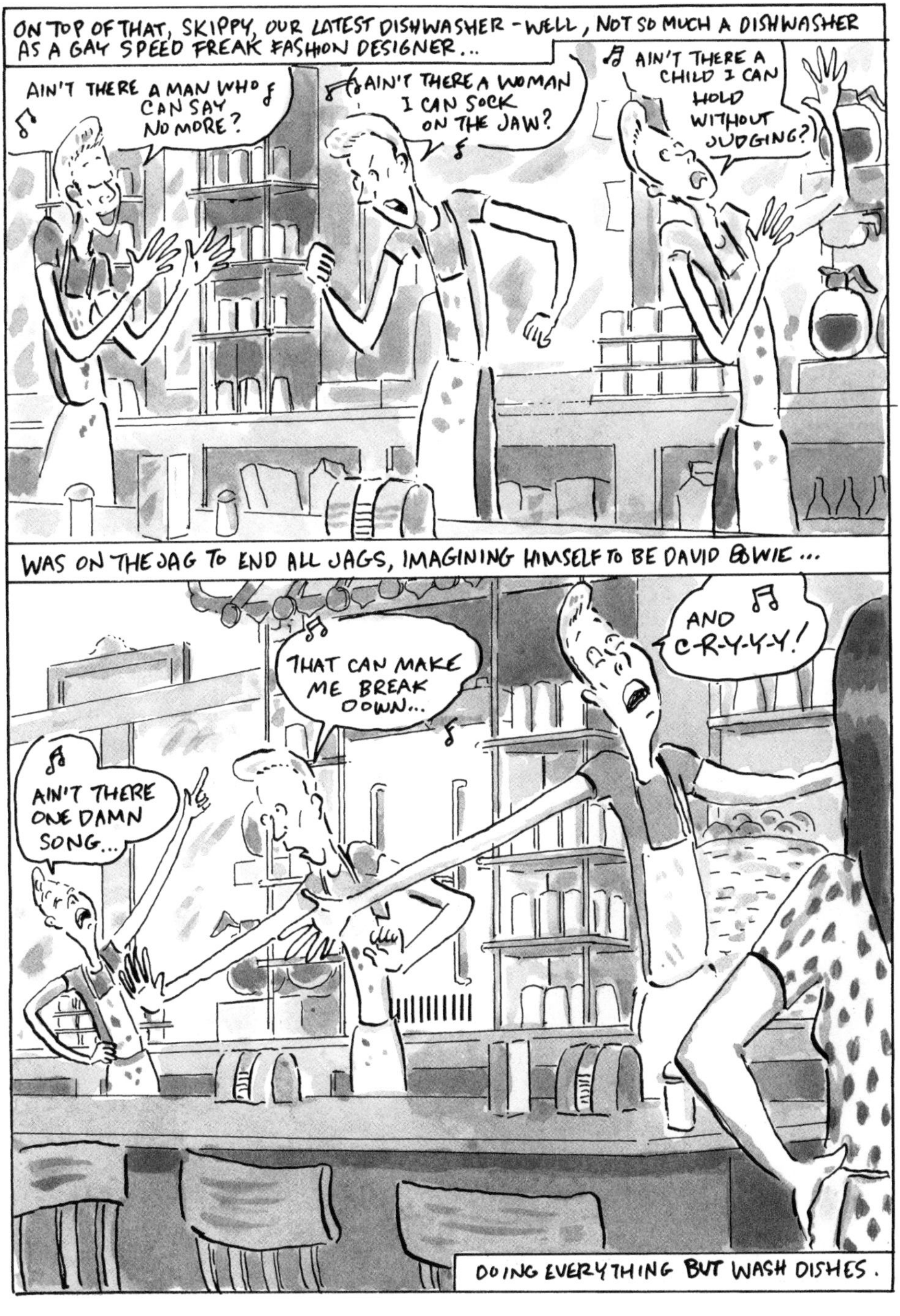
ON TOP OF THAT, SKIPPY, OUR LATEST DISHWASHER - WELL, NOT SO MUCH A DISHWASHER AS A GAY SPEED FREAK FASHION DESIGNER...
AIN'T THERE A MAN WHO CAN SAY NO MORE?
AIN'T THERE A WOMAN I CAN SOCK ON THE JAW?
AIN'T THERE A CHILD I CAN HOLD WITHOUT JUDGING?
WAS ON THE JAG TO END ALL JAGS, IMAGINING HIMSELF TO BE DAVID BOWIE...
AIN'T THERE ONE DAMN SONG...
THAT CAN MAKE ME BREAK DOWN...
AND C-R-Y-Y-Y!
DOING EVERYTHING BUT WASH DISHES.

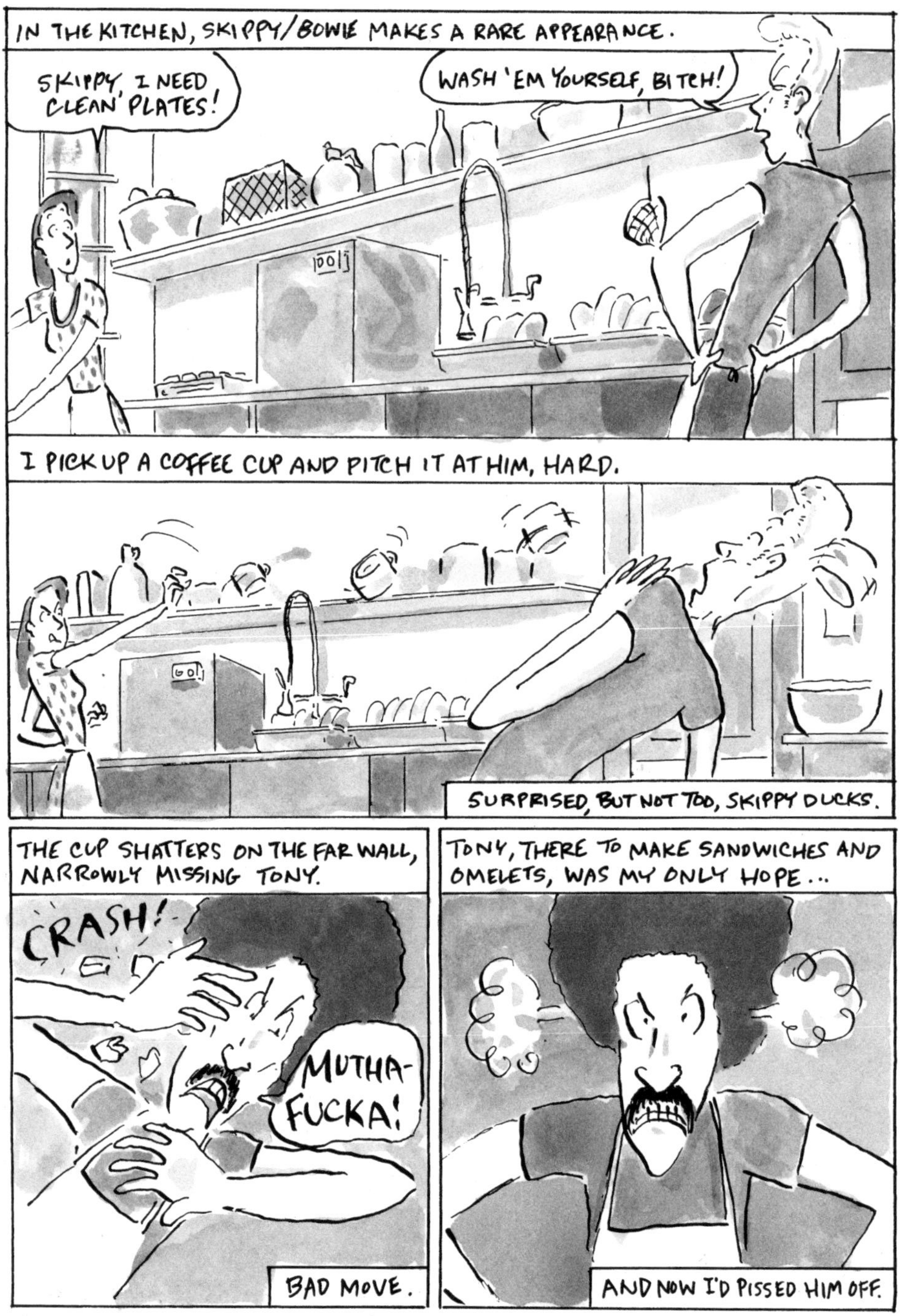
IN THE KITCHEN, SKIPPY/BOWIE MAKES A RARE APPEARANCE.
SKIPPY, I NEED CLEAN PLATES!
WASH 'EM YOURSELF, BITCH!
I PICK UP A COFFEE CUP AND PITCH IT AT HIM, HARD.
SURPRISED, BUT NOT TOO, SKIPPY DUCKS.
THE CUP SHATTERS ON THE FAR WALL, NARROWLY MISSING TONY.
CRASH!
MUTHA-FUCKA!
BAD MOVE.
TONY, THERE TO MAKE SANDWICHES AND OMELETS, WAS MY ONLY HOPE...
AND NOW I'D PISSED HIM OFF.

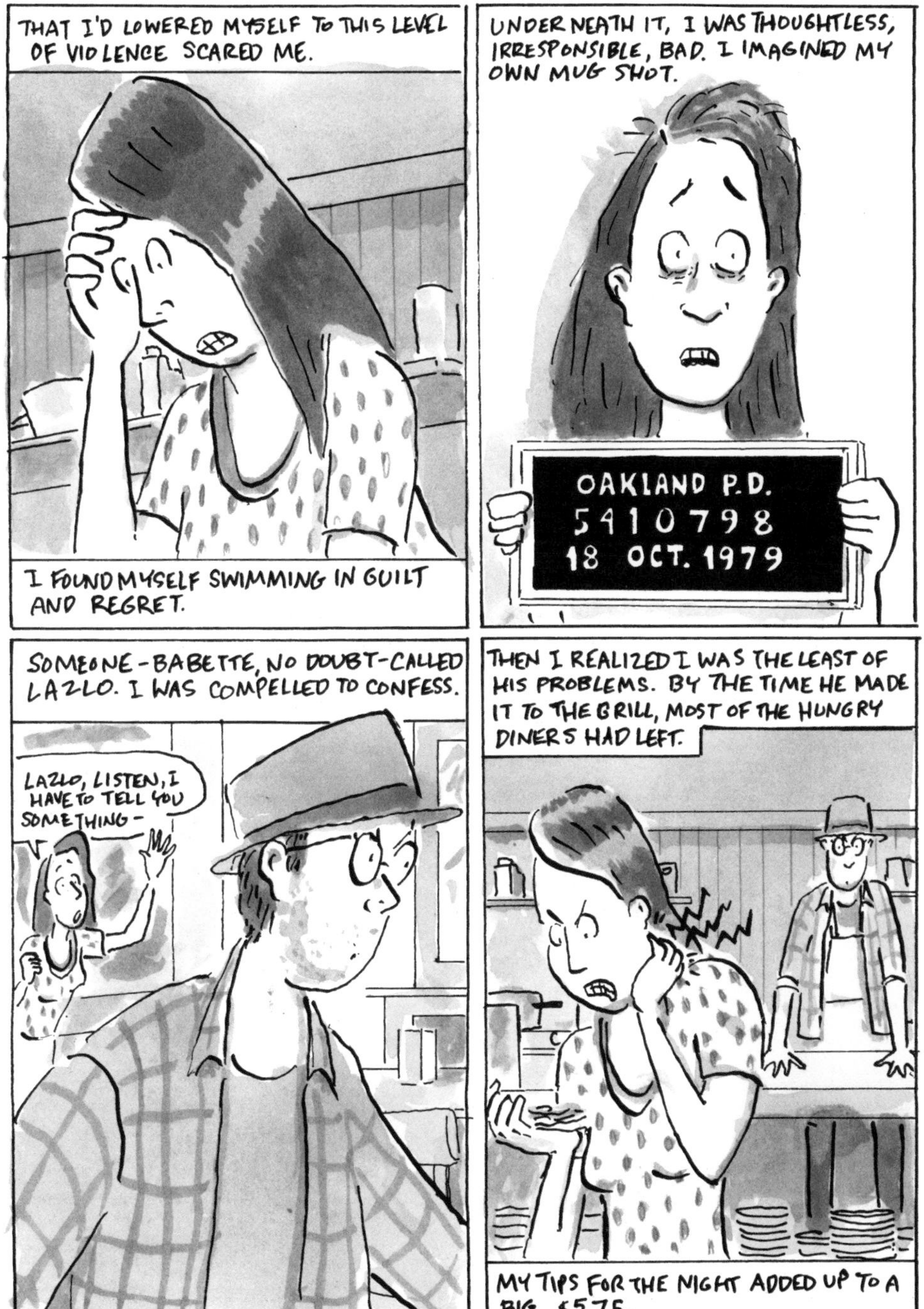
THAT I'D LOWERED MYSELF TO THIS LEVEL OF VIOLENCE SCARED ME.
I FOUND MYSELF SWIMMING IN GUILT AND REGRET.
UNDERNEATH IT, I WAS THOUGHTLESS, IRRESPONSIBLE, BAD. I IMAGINED MY OWN MUG SHOT.
OAKLAND P.D.
5410798
18 OCT. 1979
SOMEONE-BABETTE, NO DOUBT-CALLED LAZLO. I WAS COMPELLED TO CONFESS.
LAZLO, LISTEN, I HAVE TO TELL YOU SOMETHING-
THEN I REALIZED I WAS THE LEAST OF HIS PROBLEMS. BY THE TIME HE MADE IT TO THE GRILL, MOST OF THE HUNGRY DINERS HAD LEFT.
MY TIPS FOR THE NIGHT ADDED UP TO A BIG $5.75.

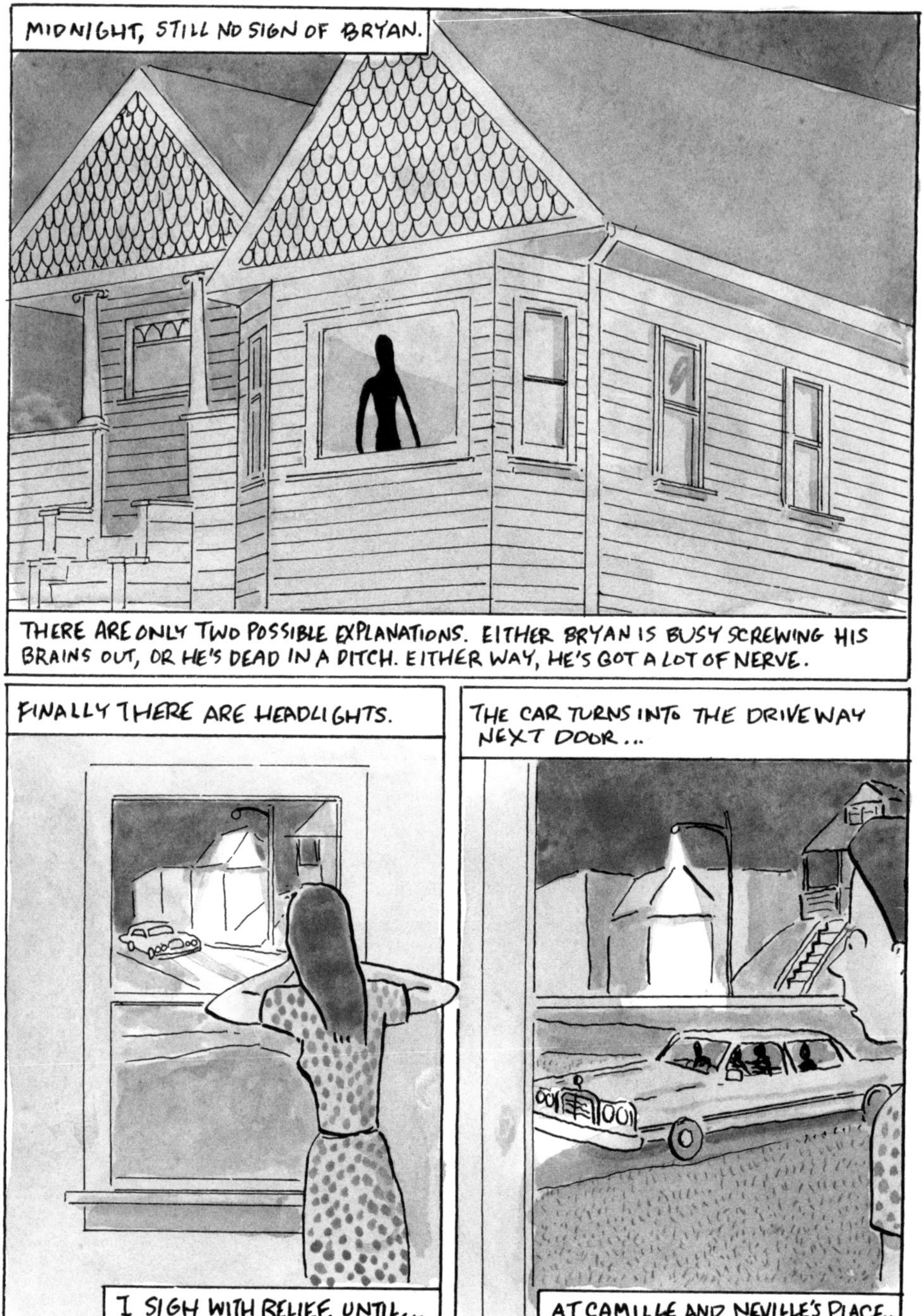
MIDNIGHT, STILL NO SIGN OF BRYAN.
THERE ARE ONLY TWO POSSIBLE EXPLANATIONS. EITHER BRYAN IS BUSY SCREWING HIS BRAINS OUT, OR HE'S DEAD IN A DITCH. EITHER WAY, HE'S GOT A LOT OF NERVE.
FINALLY THERE ARE HEADLIGHTS.
I SIGH WITH RELIEF, UNTIL...
THE CAR TURNS INTO THE DRIVEWAY NEXT DOOR...
AT CAMILLE AND NEVILLE'S PLACE.

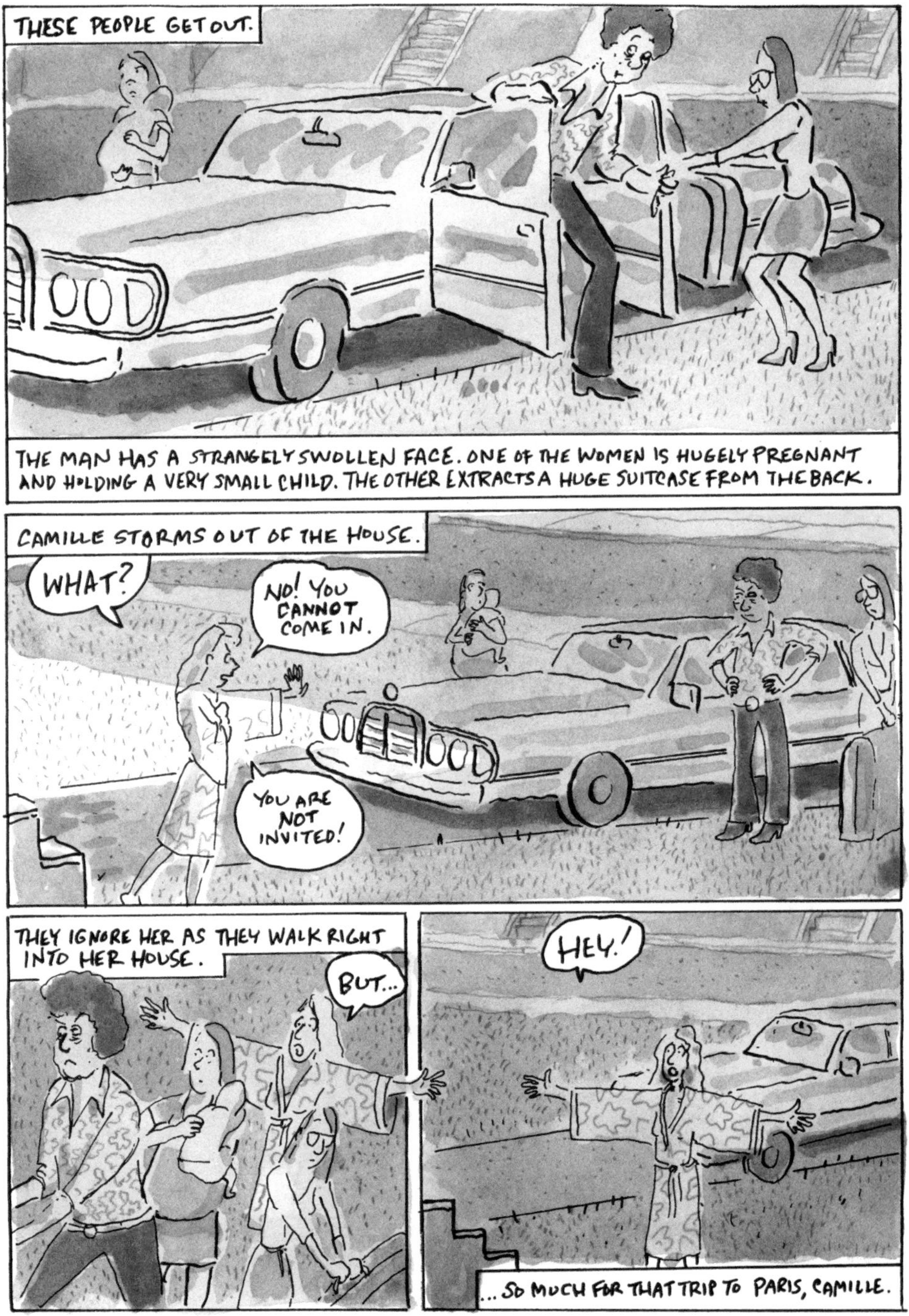
THESE PEOPLE GET OUT.
THE MAN HAS A STRANGELY SWOLLEN FACE. ONE OF THE WOMEN IS HUGELY PREGNANT AND HOLDING A VERY SMALL CHILD. THE OTHER EXTRACTS A HUGE SUITCASE FROM THE BACK.
CAMILLE STORMS OUT OF THE HOUSE.
WHAT?
NO! YOU CANNOT COME IN.
YOU ARE NOT INVITED!
THEY IGNORE HER AS THEY WALK RIGHT INTO HER HOUSE.
BUT...
HEY!
...SO MUCH FOR THAT TRIP TO PARIS, CAMILLE.

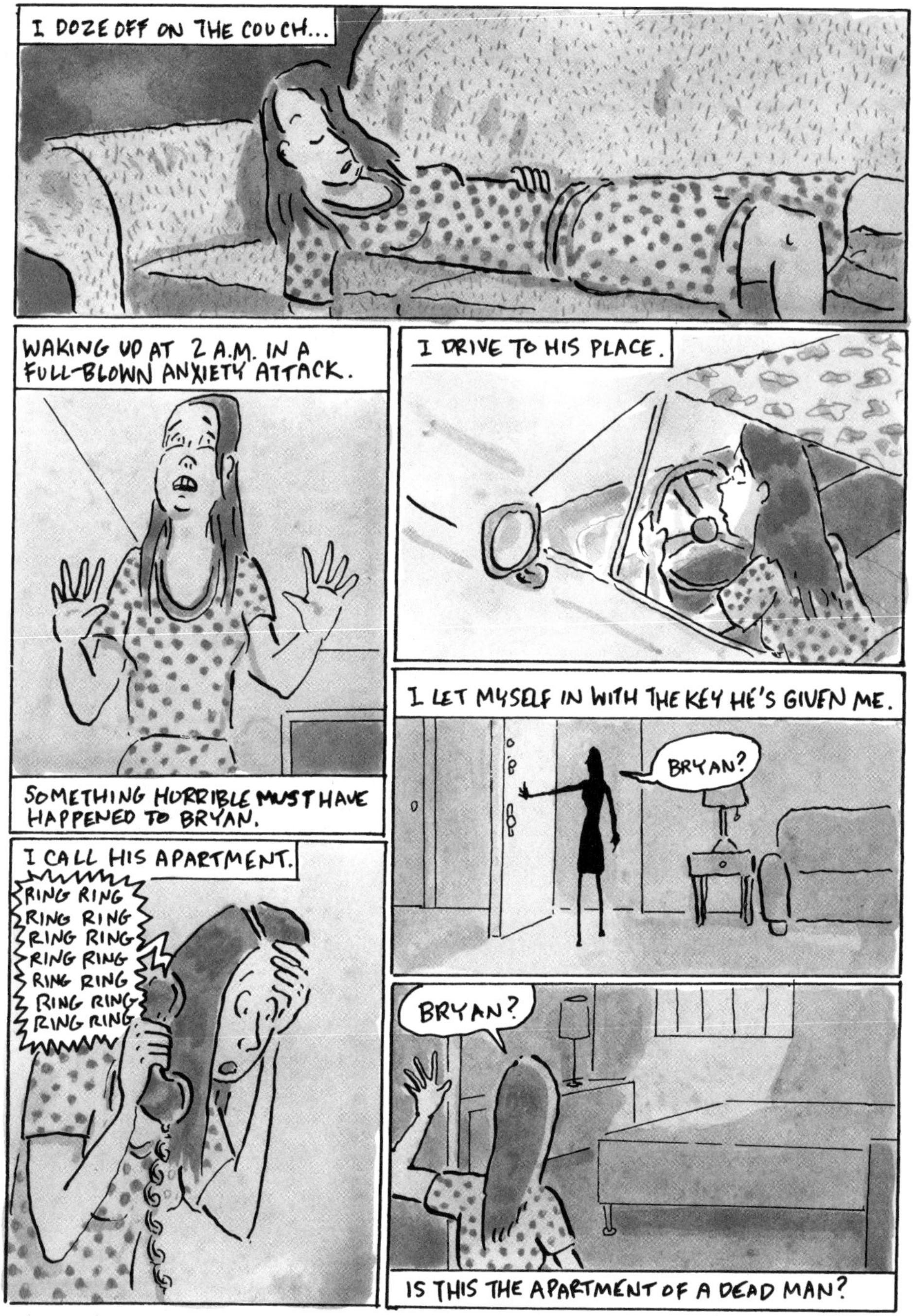
I DOZE OFF ON THE COUCH...
WAKING UP AT 2 A.M. IN A FULL-BLOWN ANXIETY ATTACK.
SOMETHING HORRIBLE MUST HAVE HAPPENED TO BRYAN.
I DRIVE TO HIS PLACE.
I CALL HIS APARTMENT.
RING RING RING RING RING RING RING RING RING RING RING RING RING RING
I LET MYSELF IN WITH THE KEY HE'S GIVEN ME.
BRYAN?
BRYAN?
IS THIS THE APARTMENT OF A DEAD MAN?

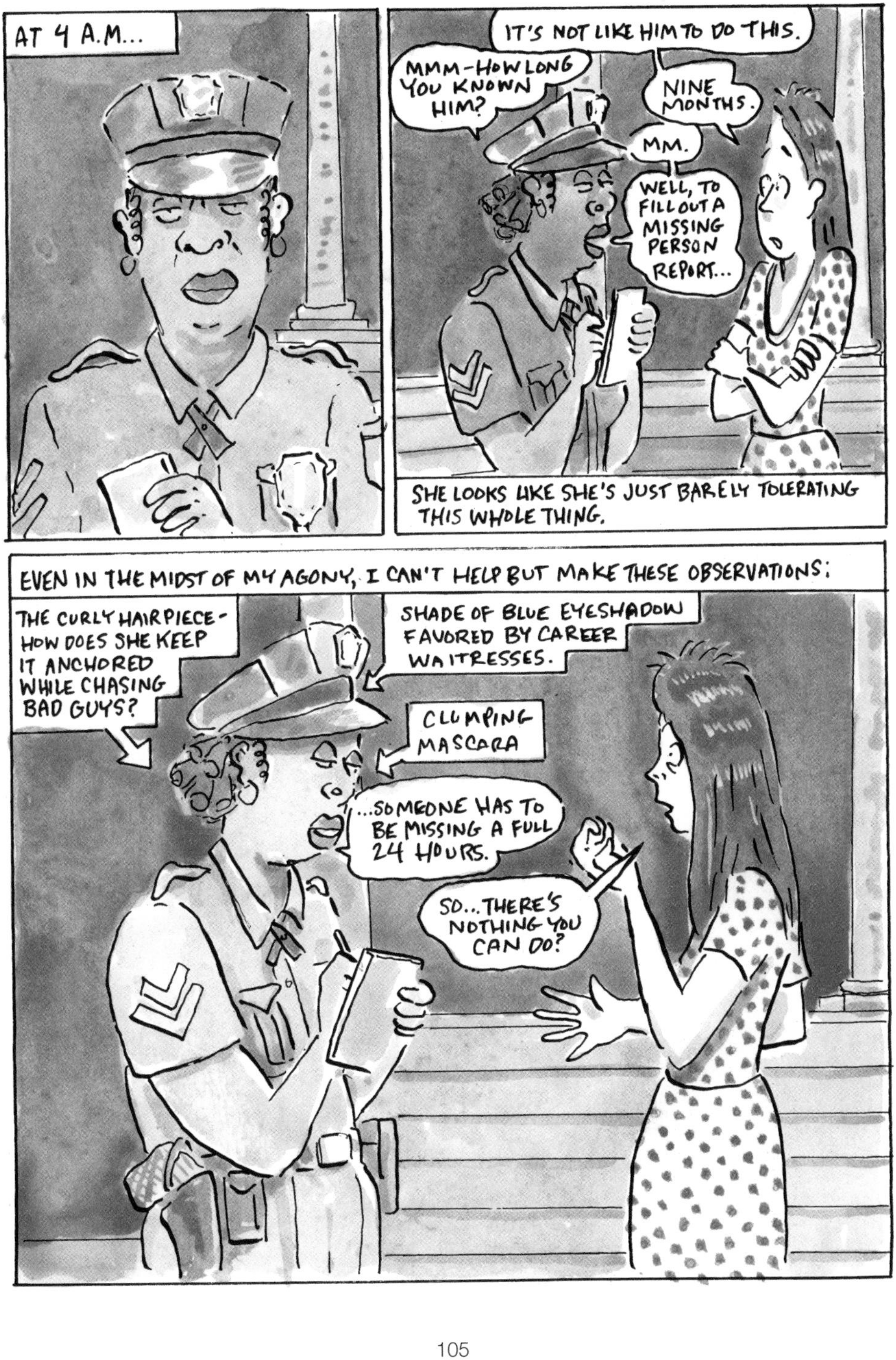
AT 4 A.M...
IT'S NOT LIKE HIM TO DO THIS.
MMM-HOW LONG YOU KNOWN HIM?
NINE MONTHS.
MM.
WELL, TO FILL OUT A MISSING PERSON REPORT...
SHE LOOKS LIKE SHE'S JUST BARELY TOLERATING THIS WHOLE THING.
EVEN IN THE MIDST OF MY AGONY, I CAN'T HELP BUT MAKE THESE OBSERVATIONS:
THE CURLY HAIRPIECE- HOW DOES SHE KEEP IT ANCHORED WHILE CHASING BAD GUYS?
SHADE OF BLUE EYESHADOW FAVORED BY CAREER WAITRESSES.
CLUMPING MASCARA
...SOMEONE HAS TO BE MISSING A FULL 24 HOURS.
SO... THERE'S NOTHING YOU CAN DO?

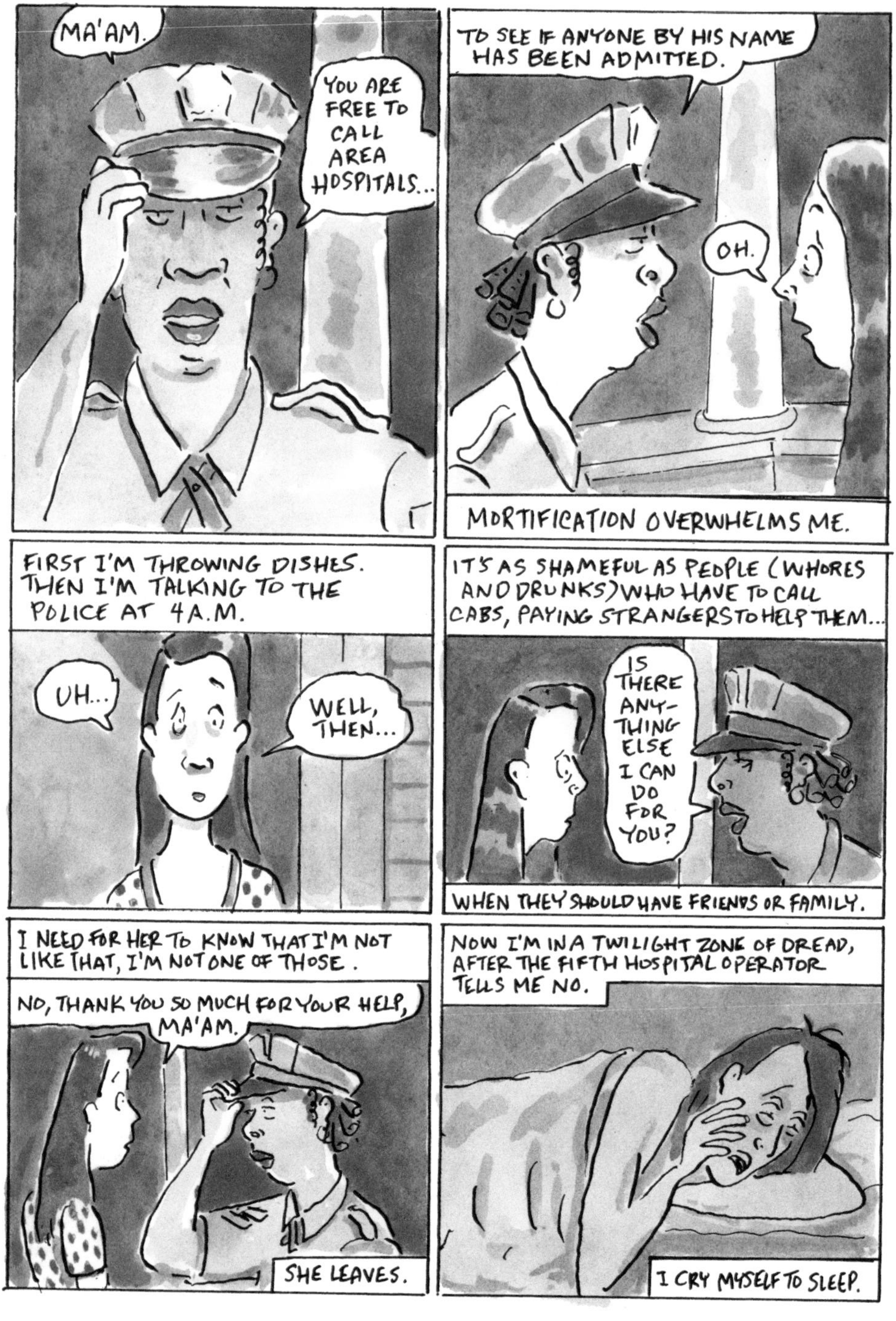
MA'AM.
YOU ARE FREE TO CALL AREA HOSPITALS...
TO SEE IF ANYONE BY HIS NAME HAS BEEN ADMITTED.
OH.
MORTIFICATION OVERWHELMS ME.
FIRST I'M THROWING DISHES. THEN I'M TALKING TO THE POLICE AT 4 A.M.
UH...
WELL, THEN...
IT'S AS SHAMEFUL AS PEOPLE (WHORES AND DRUNKS) WHO HAVE TO CALL CABS, PAYING STRANGERS TO HELP THEM...
IS THERE ANY-THING ELSE I CAN DO FOR YOU?
WHEN THEY SHOULD HAVE FRIENDS OR FAMILY.
I NEED FOR HER TO KNOW THAT I'M NOT LIKE THAT, I'M NOT ONE OF THOSE.
NO, THANK YOU SO MUCH FOR YOUR HELP, MA'AM.
SHE LEAVES.
NOW I'M IN A TWILIGHT ZONE OF DREAD, AFTER THE FIFTH HOSPITAL OPERATOR TELLS ME NO.
I CRY MYSELF TO SLEEP.

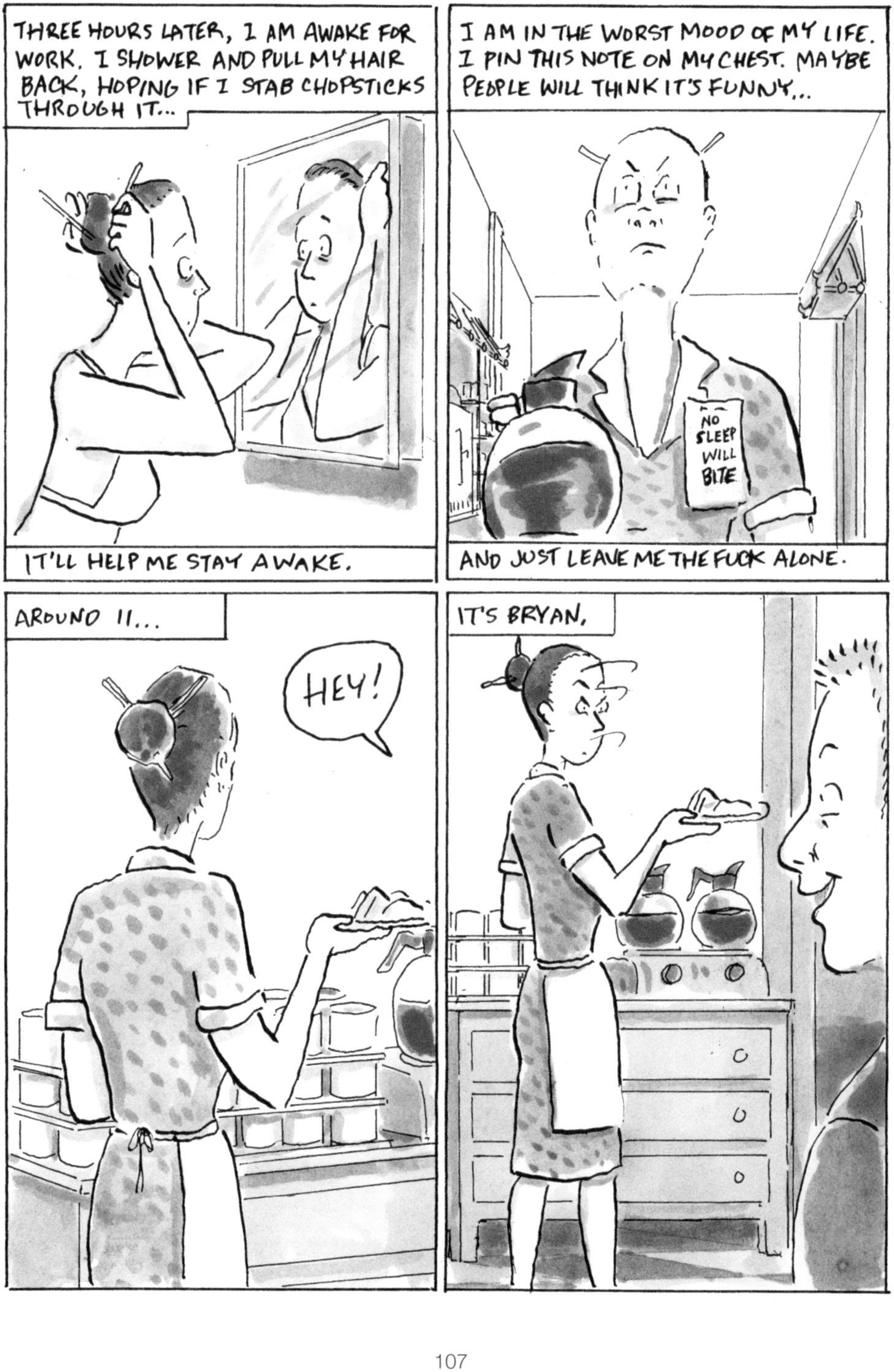
THREE HOURS LATER, I AM AWAKE FOR WORK. I SHOWER AND PULL MY HAIR BACK, HOPING IF I STAB CHOPSTICKS THROUGH IT...
IT'LL HELP ME STAY AWAKE.
I AM IN THE WORST MOOD OF MY LIFE. I PIN THIS NOTE ON MY CHEST. MAYBE PEOPLE WILL THINK IT'S FUNNY...
NO SLEEP WILL BITE
AND JUST LEAVE ME THE FUCK ALONE.
AROUND 11...
HEY!
IT'S BRYAN.

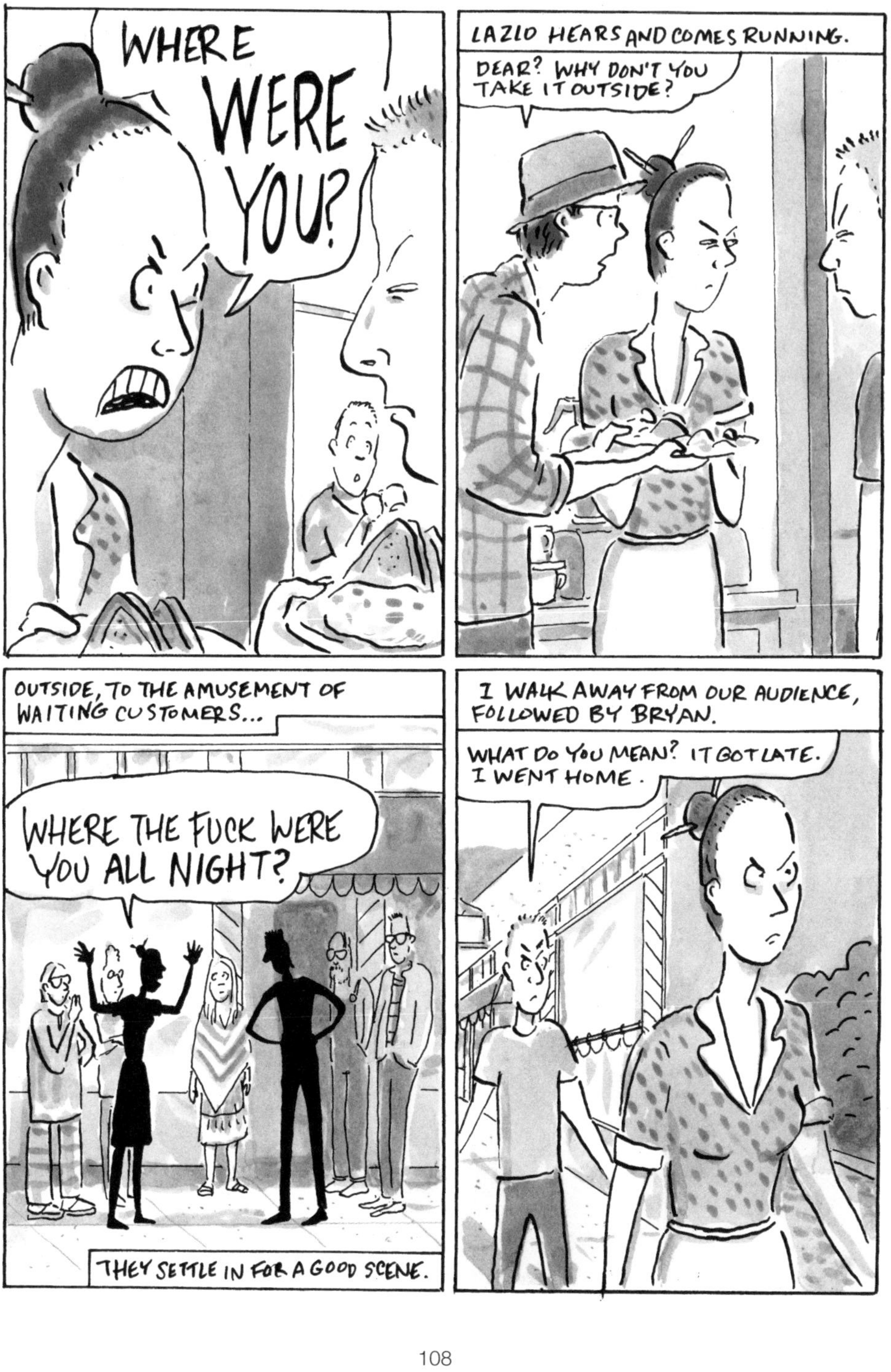
WHERE WERE YOU?
LAZLO HEARS AND COMES RUNNING.
DEAR? WHY DON'T YOU TAKE IT OUTSIDE?
OUTSIDE, TO THE AMUSEMENT OF WAITING CUSTOMERS...
WHERE THE FUCK WERE YOU ALL NIGHT?
THEY SETTLE IN FOR A GOOD SCENE.
I WALK AWAY FROM OUR AUDIENCE, FOLLOWED BY BRYAN.
WHAT DO YOU MEAN? IT GOT LATE. I WENT HOME.

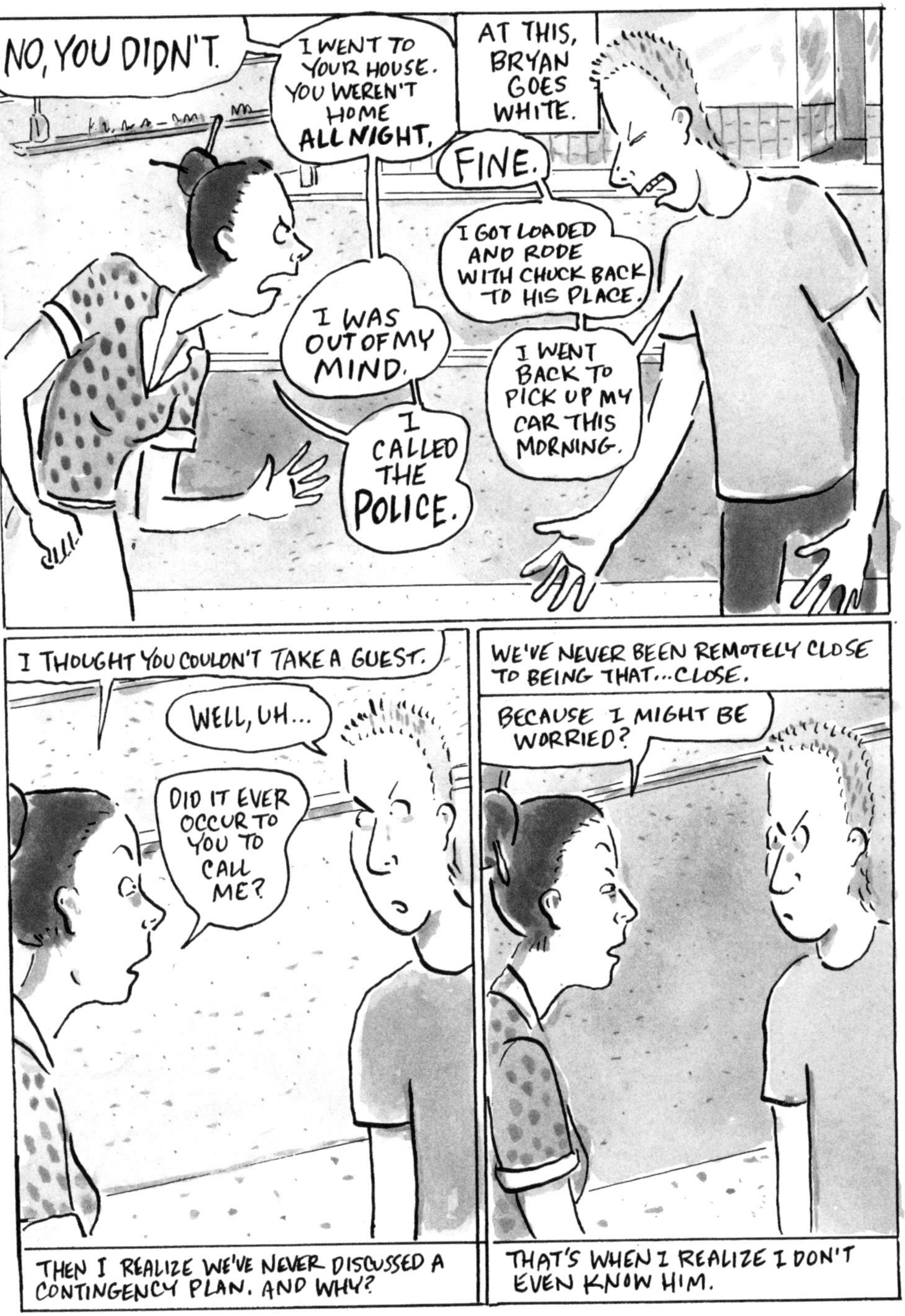
NO, YOU DIDN'T.
I WENT TO YOUR HOUSE. YOU WEREN'T HOME ALL NIGHT.
I WAS OUT OF MY MIND.
I CALLED THE POLICE.
AT THIS, BRYAN GOES WHITE.
FINE.
I GOT LOADED AND RODE WITH CHUCK BACK TO HIS PLACE.
I WENT BACK TO PICK UP MY CAR THIS MORNING.
I THOUGHT YOU COULDN'T TAKE A GUEST.
WELL, UH...
DID IT EVER OCCUR TO YOU TO CALL ME?
THEN I REALIZE WE'VE NEVER DISCUSSED A CONTINGENCY PLAN. AND WHY?
WE'VE NEVER BEEN REMOTELY CLOSE TO BEING THAT...CLOSE.
BECAUSE I MIGHT BE WORRIED?
THAT'S WHEN I REALIZE I DON'T EVEN KNOW HIM.

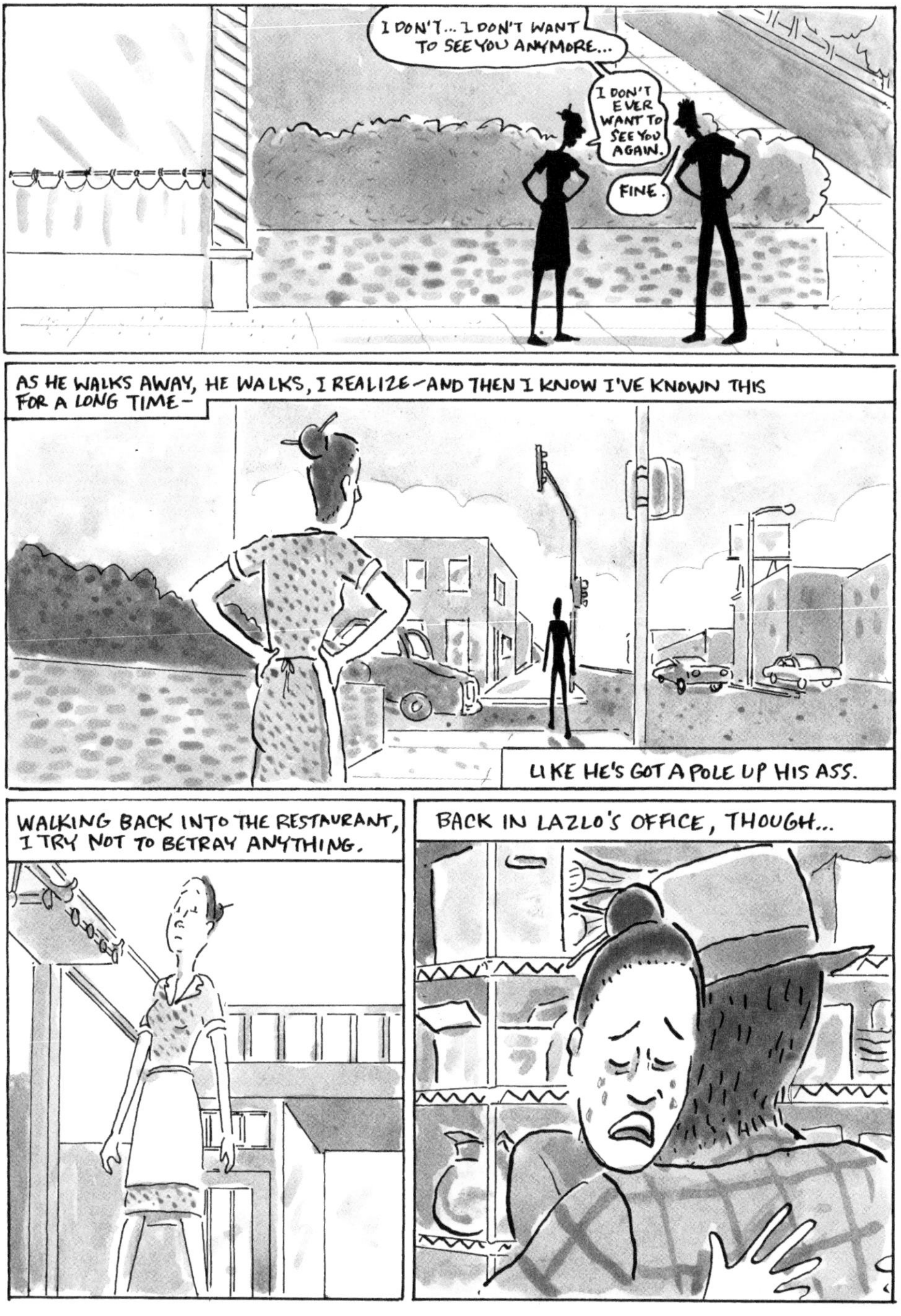

I DON'T... I DON'T WANT TO SEE YOU ANYMORE...
I DON'T EVER WANT TO SEE YOU AGAIN.
FINE.
AS HE WALKS AWAY, HE WALKS, I REALIZE—AND THEN I KNOW I'VE KNOWN THIS FOR A LONG TIME—
LIKE HE'S GOT A POLE UP HIS ASS.
WALKING BACK INTO THE RESTAURANT, I TRY NOT TO BETRAY ANYTHING.
BACK IN LAZLO'S OFFICE, THOUGH...

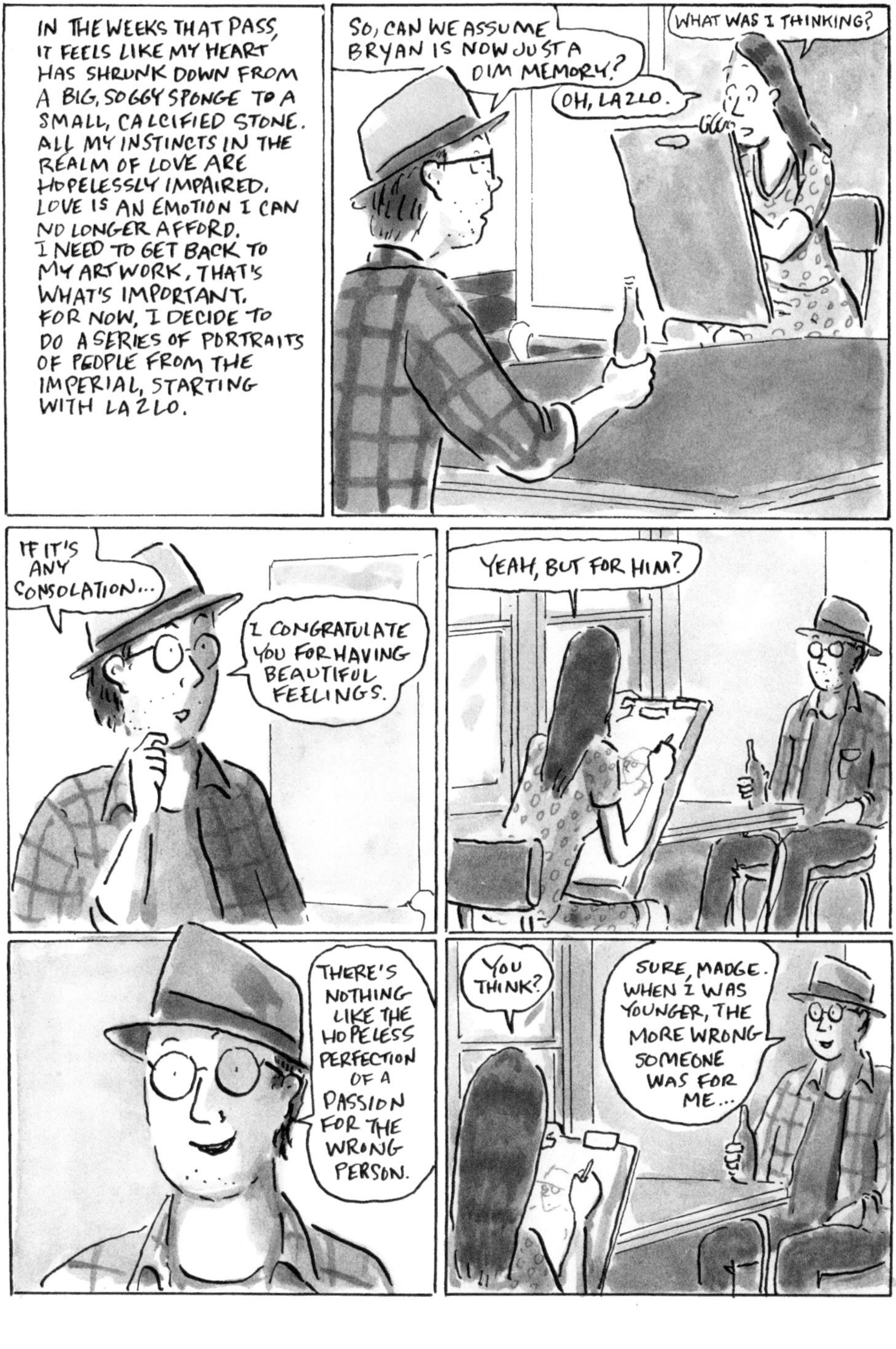
IN THE WEEKS THAT PASS, IT FEELS LIKE MY HEART HAS SHRUNK DOWN FROM A BIG, SOGGY SPONGE TO A SMALL, CALCIFIED STONE. ALL MY INSTINCTS IN THE REALM OF LOVE ARE HOPELESSLY IMPAIRED. LOVE IS AN EMOTION I CAN NO LONGER AFFORD. I NEED TO GET BACK TO MY ARTWORK, THAT'S WHAT'S IMPORTANT. FOR NOW, I DECIDE TO DO A SERIES OF PORTRAITS OF PEOPLE FROM THE IMPERIAL, STARTING WITH LAZLO.
SO, CAN WE ASSUME BRYAN IS NOW JUST A DIM MEMORY?
WHAT WAS I THINKING?
OH, LAZLO.
IF IT'S ANY CONSOLATION...
I CONGRATULATE YOU FOR HAVING BEAUTIFUL FEELINGS.
YEAH, BUT FOR HIM?
THERE'S NOTHING LIKE THE HOPELESS PERFECTION OF A PASSION FOR THE WRONG PERSON.
YOU THINK?
SURE, MADGE. WHEN I WAS YOUNGER, THE MORE WRONG SOMEONE WAS FOR ME...

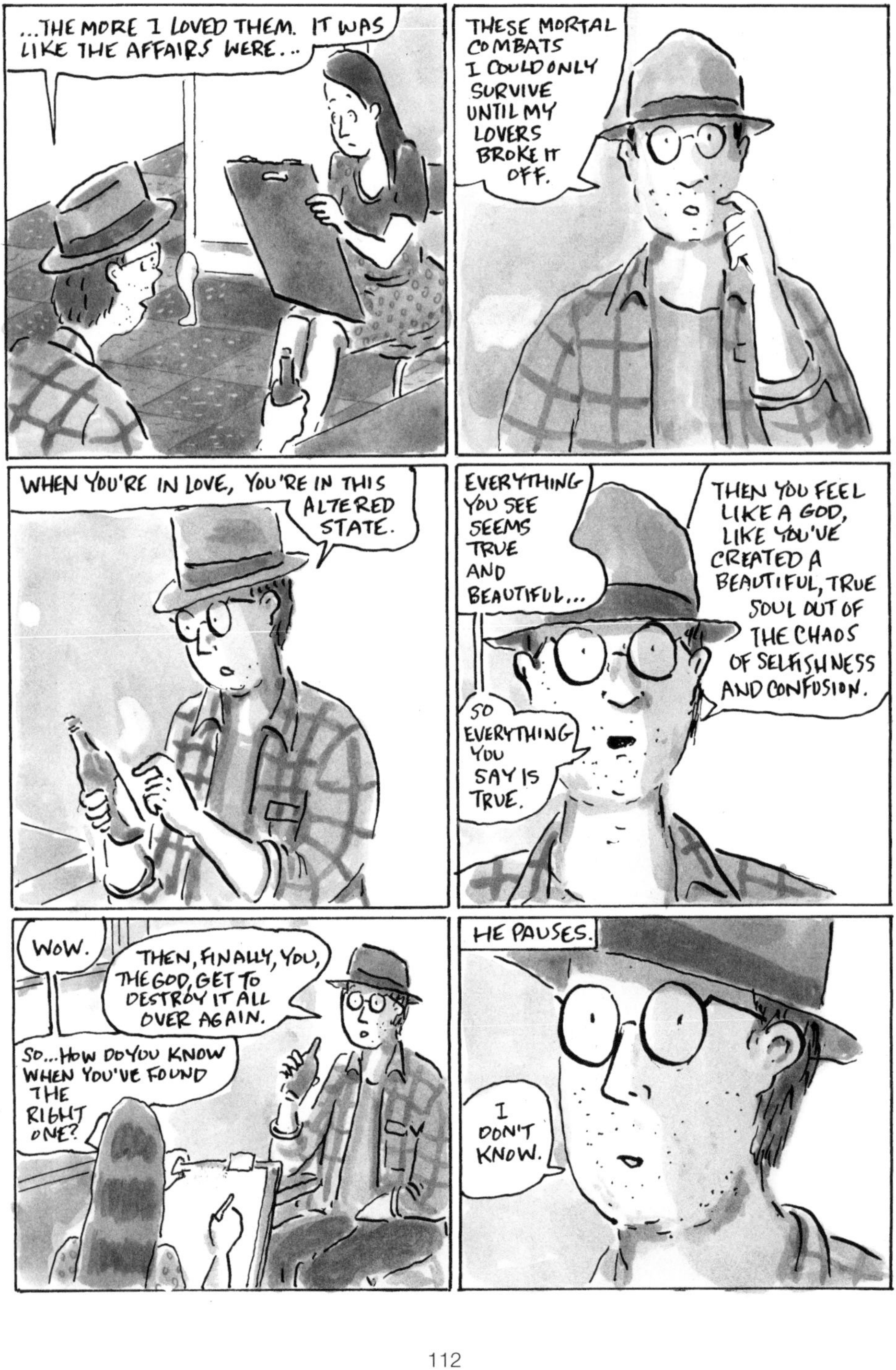

...THE MORE I LOVED THEM. IT WAS LIKE THE AFFAIRS WERE...
THESE MORTAL COMBATS I COULD ONLY SURVIVE UNTIL MY LOVERS BROKE IT OFF.
WHEN YOU'RE IN LOVE, YOU'RE IN THIS ALTERED STATE.
EVERYTHING YOU SEE SEEMS TRUE AND BEAUTIFUL...
THEN YOU FEEL LIKE A GOD, LIKE YOU'VE CREATED A BEAUTIFUL, TRUE SOUL OUT OF THE CHAOS OF SELFISHNESS AND CONFUSION.
SO EVERYTHING YOU SAY IS TRUE.
WOW.
THEN, FINALLY, YOU, THE GOD, GET TO DESTROY IT ALL OVER AGAIN.
SO...HOW DO YOU KNOW WHEN YOU'VE FOUND THE RIGHT ONE?
HE PAUSES.
I DON'T KNOW.

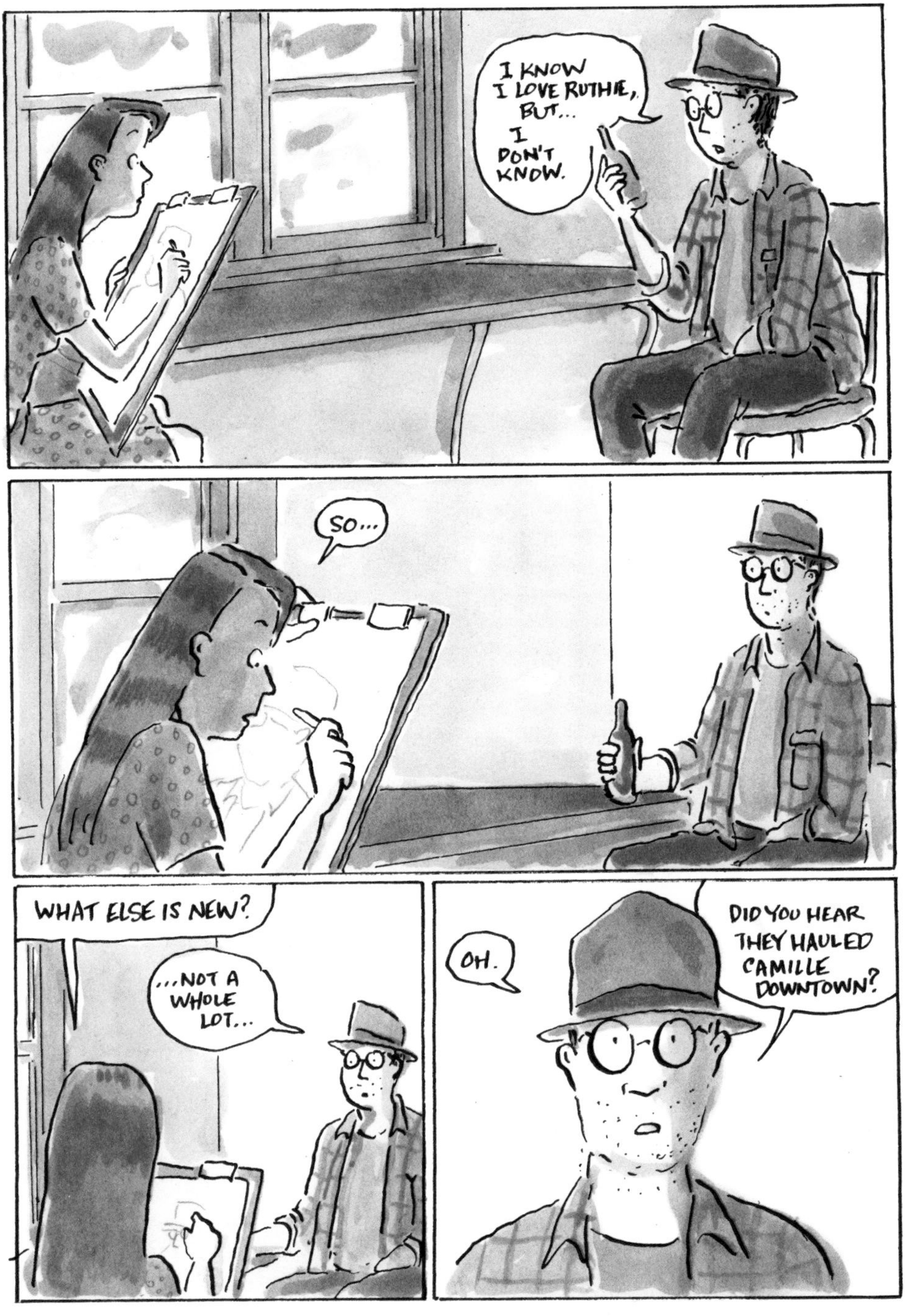
I KNOW I LOVE RUTHIE, BUT... I DON'T KNOW.
SO...
WHAT ELSE IS NEW?
...NOT A WHOLE LOT...
OH.
DID YOU HEAR THEY HAULED CAMILLE DOWNTOWN?

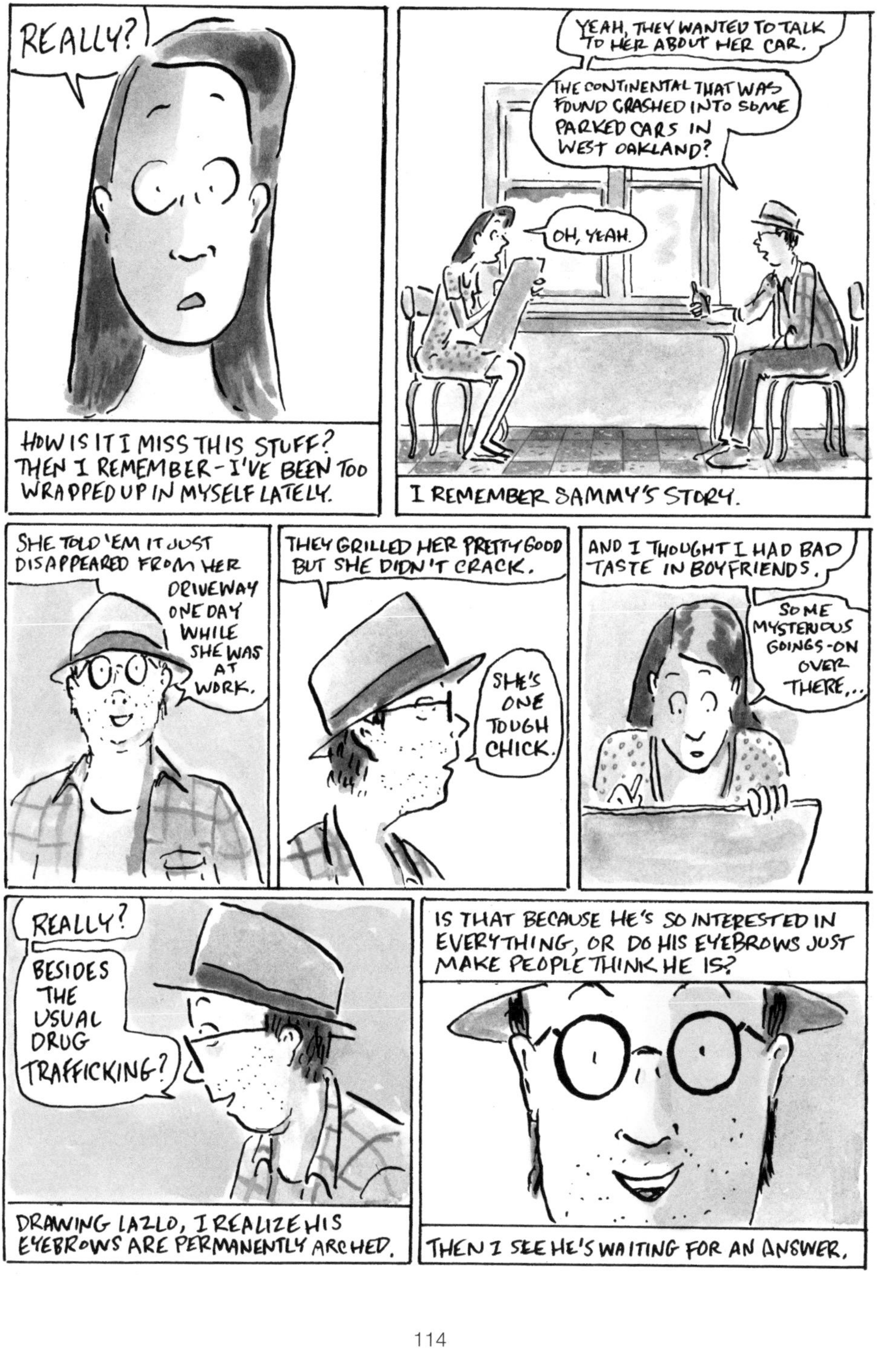
REALLY?
HOW IS IT I MISS THIS STUFF? THEN I REMEMBER - I'VE BEEN TOO WRAPPED UP IN MYSELF LATELY.
YEAH, THEY WANTED TO TALK TO HER ABOUT HER CAR.
THE CONTINENTAL THAT WAS FOUND CRASHED INTO SOME PARKED CARS IN WEST OAKLAND?
OH, YEAH.
I REMEMBER SAMMY'S STORY.
SHE TOLD 'EM IT JUST DISAPPEARED FROM HER DRIVEWAY ONE DAY WHILE SHE WAS AT WORK.
THEY GRILLED HER PRETTY GOOD BUT SHE DIDN'T CRACK.
SHE'S ONE TOUGH CHICK.
AND I THOUGHT I HAD BAD TASTE IN BOYFRIENDS.
SOME MYSTERIOUS GOINGS-ON OVER THERE,...
REALLY?
BESIDES THE USUAL DRUG TRAFFICKING?
DRAWING LAZLO, I REALIZE HIS EYEBROWS ARE PERMANENTLY ARCHED.
IS THAT BECAUSE HE'S SO INTERESTED IN EVERYTHING, OR DO HIS EYEBROWS JUST MAKE PEOPLE THINK HE IS?
THEN I SEE HE'S WAITING FOR AN ANSWER.

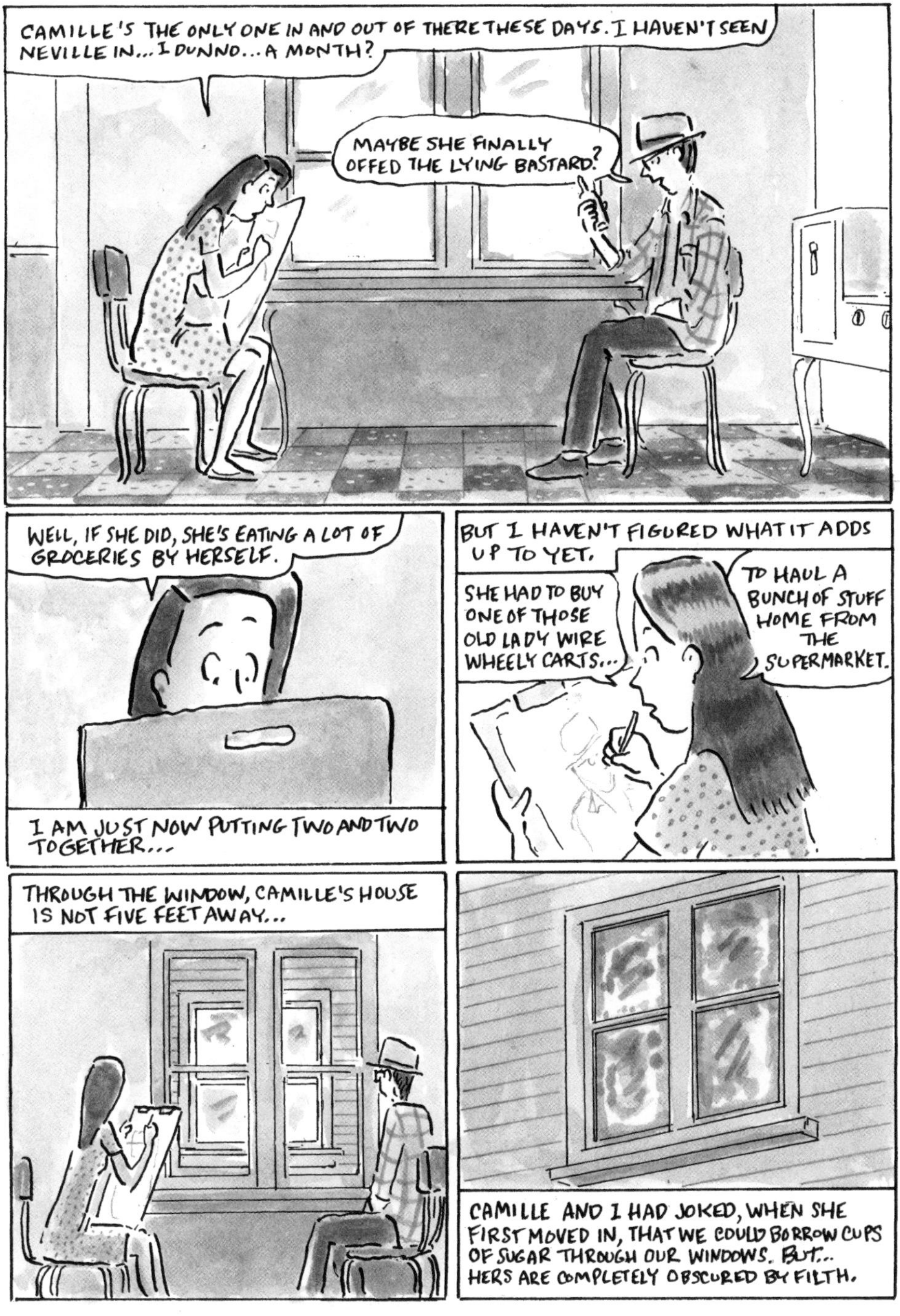
CAMILLE'S THE ONLY ONE IN AND OUT OF THERE THESE DAYS. I HAVEN'T SEEN NEVILLE IN... I DUNNO... A MONTH?
MAYBE SHE FINALLY OFFED THE LYING BASTARD?
WELL, IF SHE DID, SHE'S EATING A LOT OF GROCERIES BY HERSELF.
I AM JUST NOW PUTTING TWO AND TWO TOGETHER...
BUT I HAVEN'T FIGURED WHAT IT ADDS UP TO YET.
SHE HAD TO BUY ONE OF THOSE OLD LADY WIRE WHEELY CARTS...
TO HAUL A BUNCH OF STUFF HOME FROM THE SUPERMARKET.
THROUGH THE WINDOW, CAMILLE'S HOUSE IS NOT FIVE FEET AWAY...
CAMILLE AND I HAD JOKED, WHEN SHE FIRST MOVED IN, THAT WE COULD BORROW CUPS OF SUGAR THROUGH OUR WINDOWS. BUT... HERS ARE COMPLETELY OBSCURED BY FILTH.

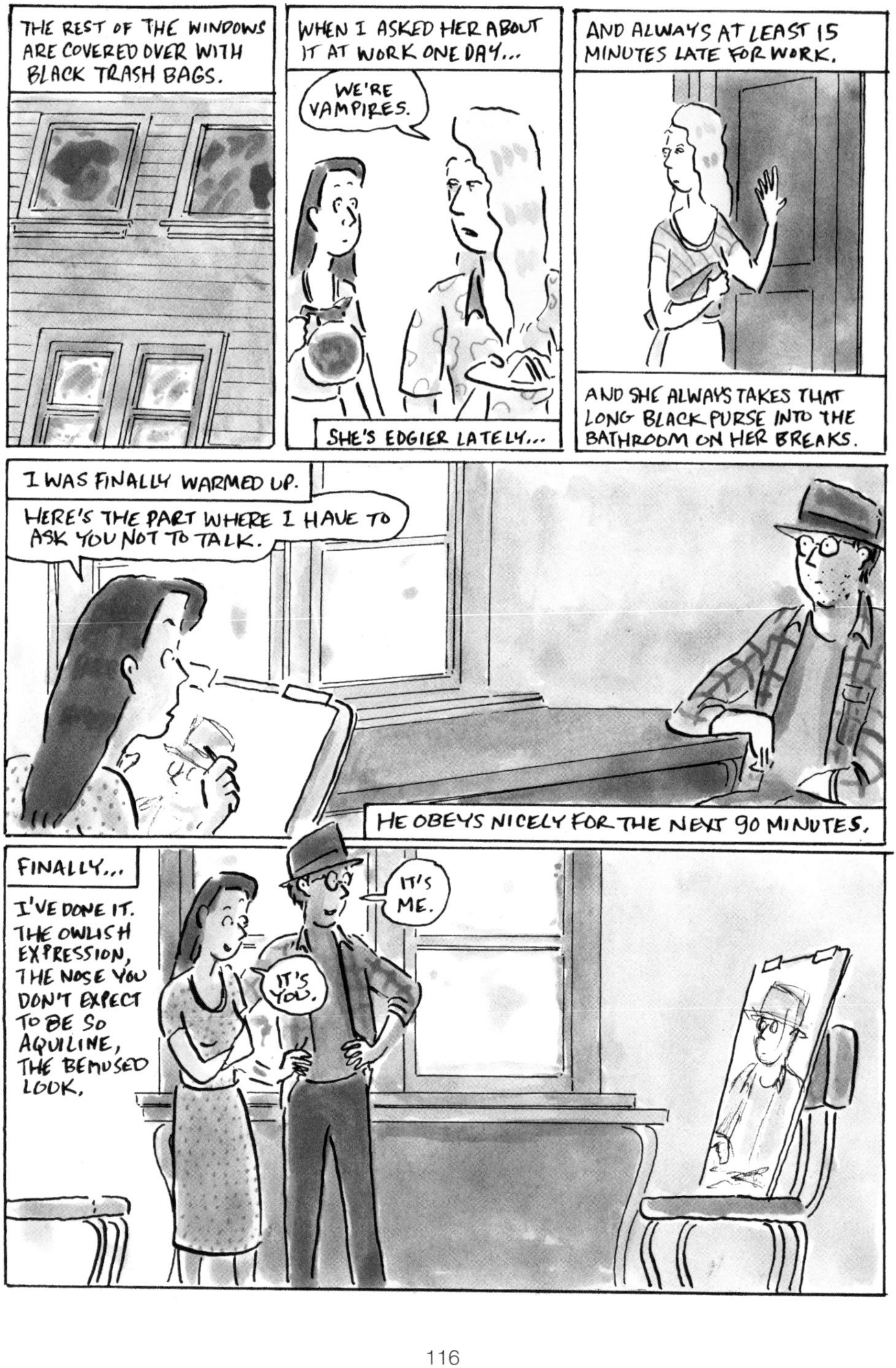
THE REST OF THE WINDOWS ARE COVERED OVER WITH BLACK TRASH BAGS.
WHEN I ASKED HER ABOUT IT AT WORK ONE DAY...
WE'RE VAMPIRES.
SHE'S EDGIER LATELY...
AND ALWAYS AT LEAST 15 MINUTES LATE FOR WORK.
AND SHE ALWAYS TAKES THAT LONG BLACK PURSE INTO THE BATHROOM ON HER BREAKS.
I WAS FINALLY WARMED UP.
HERE'S THE PART WHERE I HAVE TO ASK YOU NOT TO TALK.
HE OBEYS NICELY FOR THE NEXT 90 MINUTES.
FINALLY...
I'VE DONE IT. THE OWLISH EXPRESSION, THE NOSE YOU DON'T EXPECT TO BE SO AQUILINE, THE BEMUSED LOOK.
IT'S ME.
IT'S YOU.

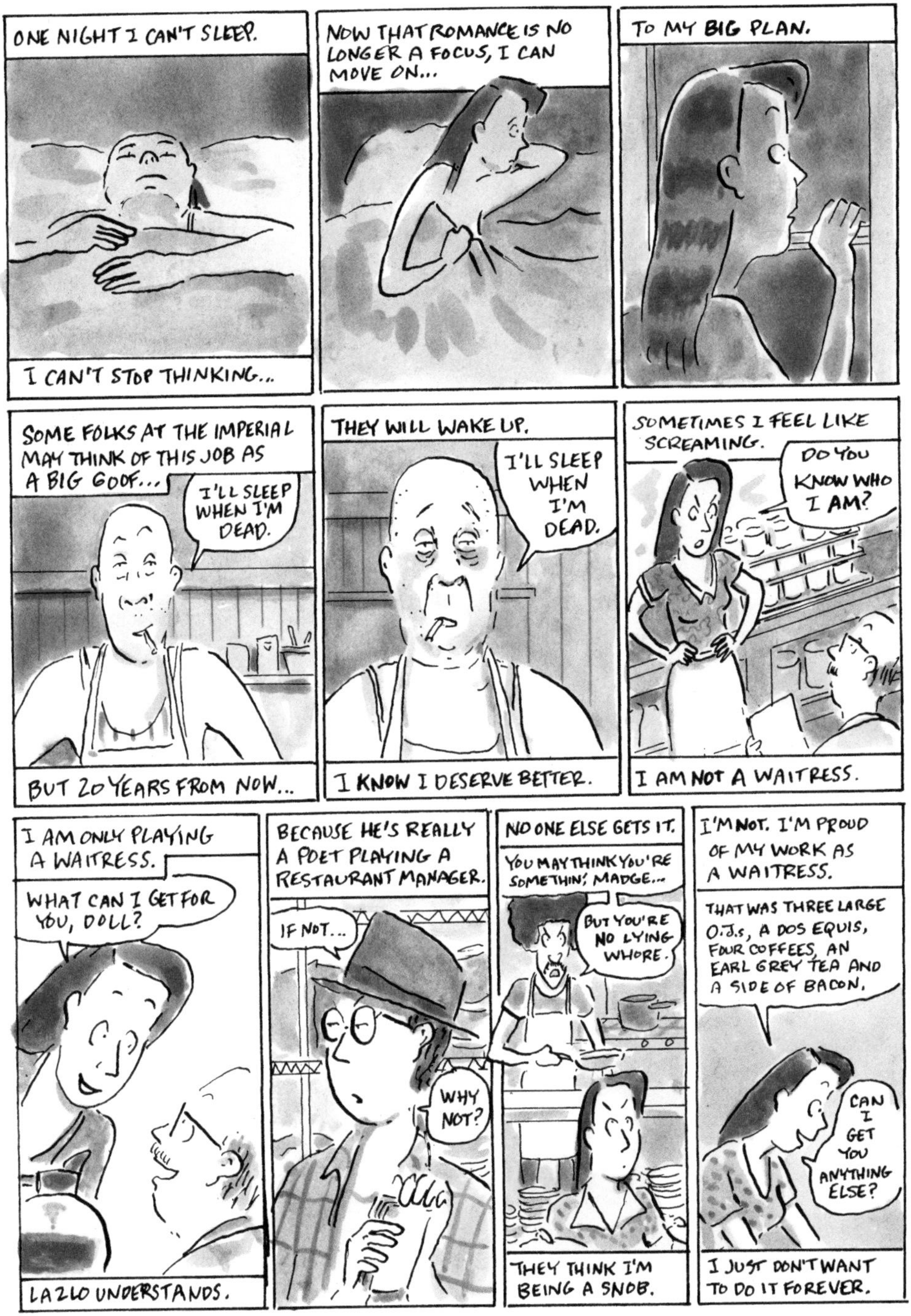

ONE NIGHT I CAN'T SLEEP.
I CAN'T STOP THINKING...
NOW THAT ROMANCE IS NO LONGER A FOCUS, I CAN MOVE ON...
TO MY BIG PLAN.
SOME FOLKS AT THE IMPERIAL MAY THINK OF THIS JOB AS A BIG GOOF...
I'LL SLEEP WHEN I'M DEAD.
BUT 20 YEARS FROM NOW...
THEY WILL WAKE UP.
I'LL SLEEP WHEN I'M DEAD.
I KNOW I DESERVE BETTER.
SOMETIMES I FEEL LIKE SCREAMING.
DO YOU KNOW WHO I AM?
I AM NOT A WAITRESS.
I AM ONLY PLAYING A WAITRESS.
WHAT CAN I GET FOR YOU, DOLL?
LAZLO UNDERSTANDS.
BECAUSE HE'S REALLY A POET PLAYING A RESTAURANT MANAGER.
IF NOT...
WHY NOT?
NO ONE ELSE GETS IT.
YOU MAY THINK YOU'RE SOMETHIN', MADGE...
BUT YOU'RE NO LYING WHORE.
THEY THINK I'M BEING A SNOB.
I'M NOT. I'M PROUD OF MY WORK AS A WAITRESS.
THAT WAS THREE LARGE O.J.s, A DOS EQUIS, FOUR COFFEES, AN EARL GREY TEA AND A SIDE OF BACON.
CAN I GET YOU ANYTHING ELSE?
I JUST DON'T WANT TO DO IT FOREVER.

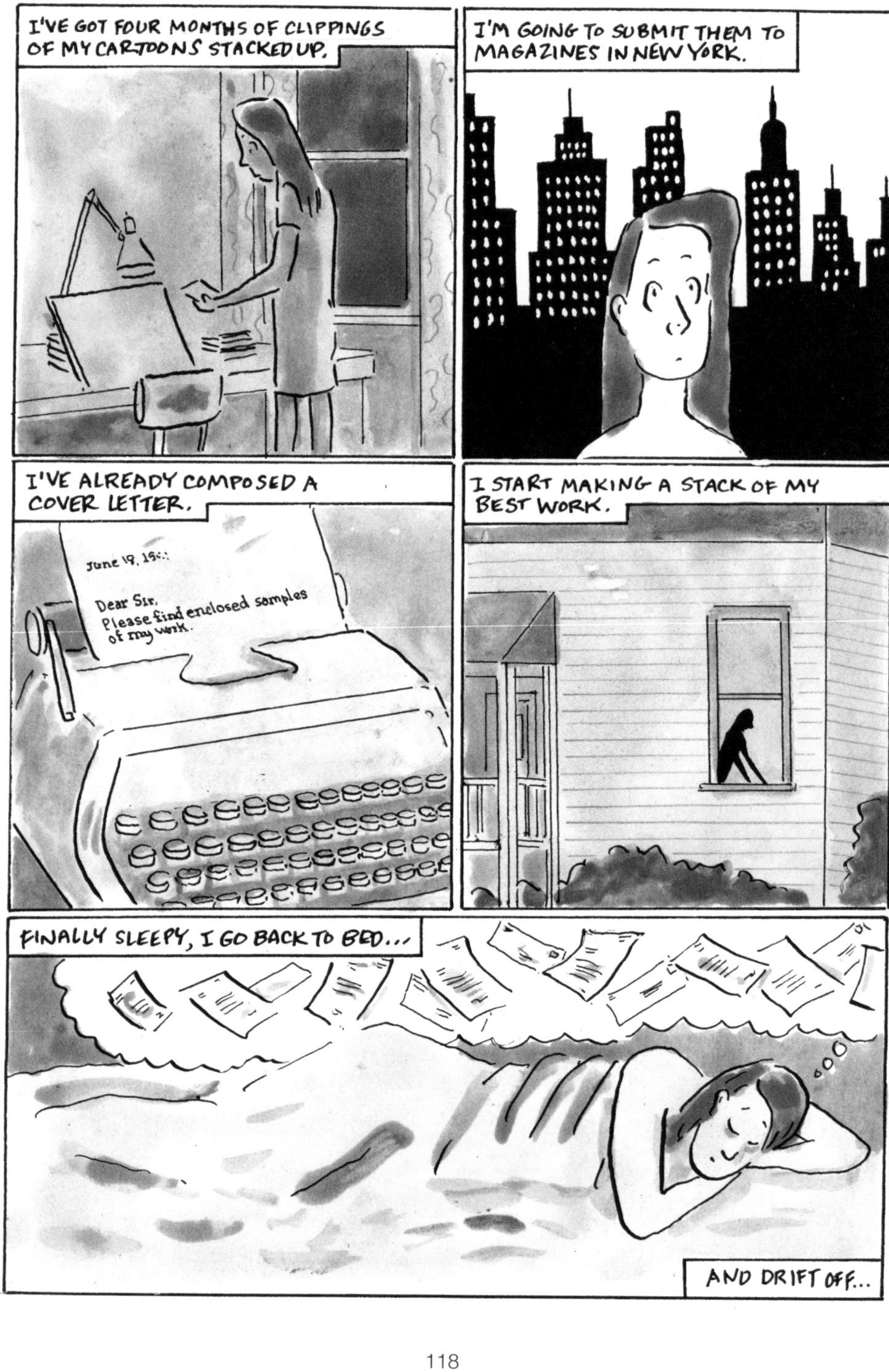
I'VE GOT FOUR MONTHS OF CLIPPINGS OF MY CARTOONS STACKED UP.
I'M GOING TO SUBMIT THEM TO MAGAZINES IN NEW YORK.
I'VE ALREADY COMPOSED A COVER LETTER.
Dear Sir,
Please find enclosed samples of my work.
I START MAKING A STACK OF MY BEST WORK.
FINALLY SLEEPY, I GO BACK TO BED...
AND DRIFT OFF...

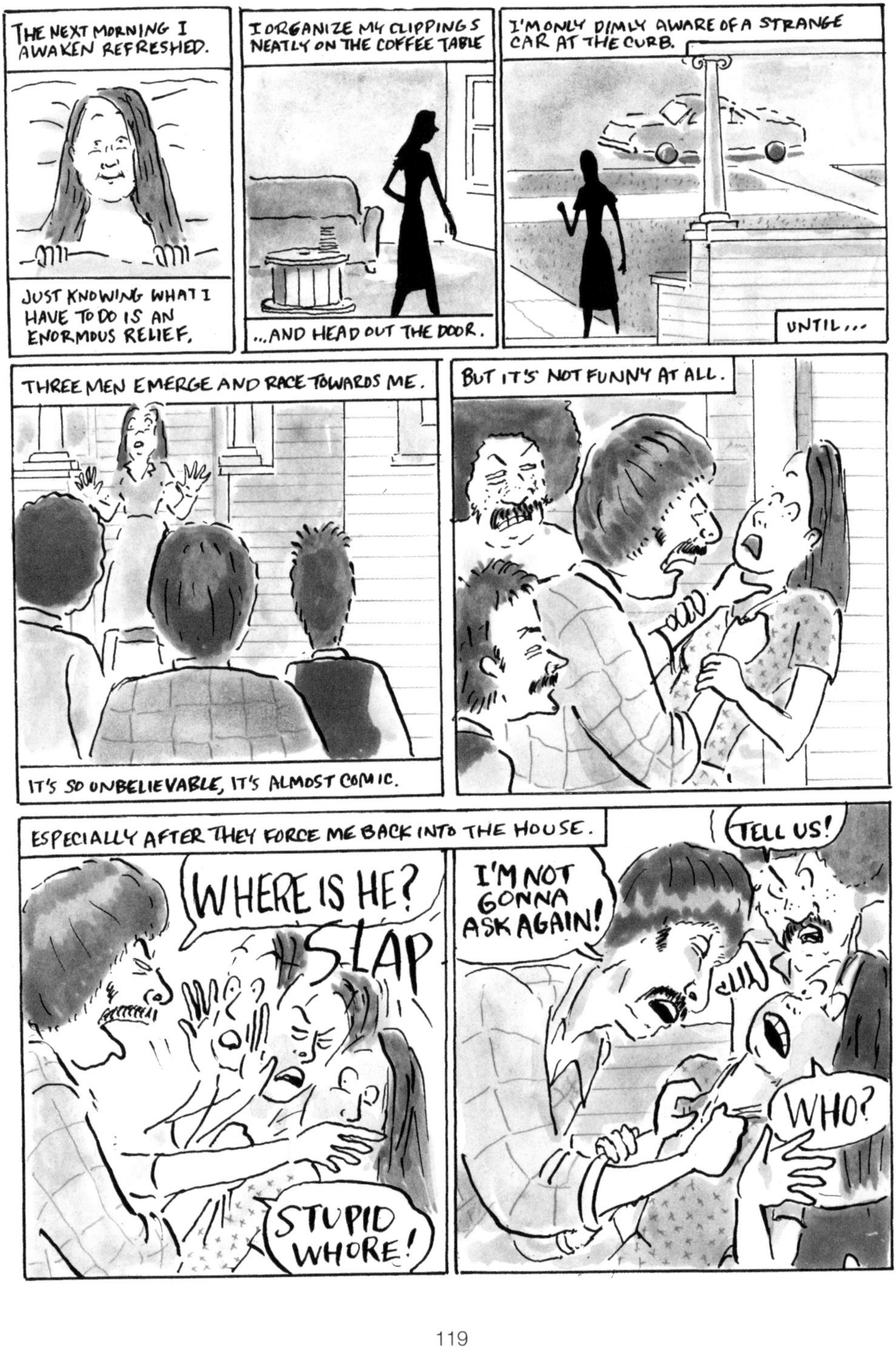
THE NEXT MORNING I AWAKEN REFRESHED.
JUST KNOWING WHAT I HAVE TO DO IS AN ENORMOUS RELIEF.
I ORGANIZE MY CLIPPINGS NEATLY ON THE COFFEE TABLE
...AND HEAD OUT THE DOOR.
I'M ONLY DIMLY AWARE OF A STRANGE CAR AT THE CURB.
UNTIL...
THREE MEN EMERGE AND RACE TOWARDS ME.
IT'S SO UNBELIEVABLE, IT'S ALMOST COMIC.
BUT IT'S NOT FUNNY AT ALL.
ESPECIALLY AFTER THEY FORCE ME BACK INTO THE HOUSE.
WHERE IS HE?
SLAP
STUPID WHORE!
TELL US!
I'M NOT GONNA ASK AGAIN!
WHO?

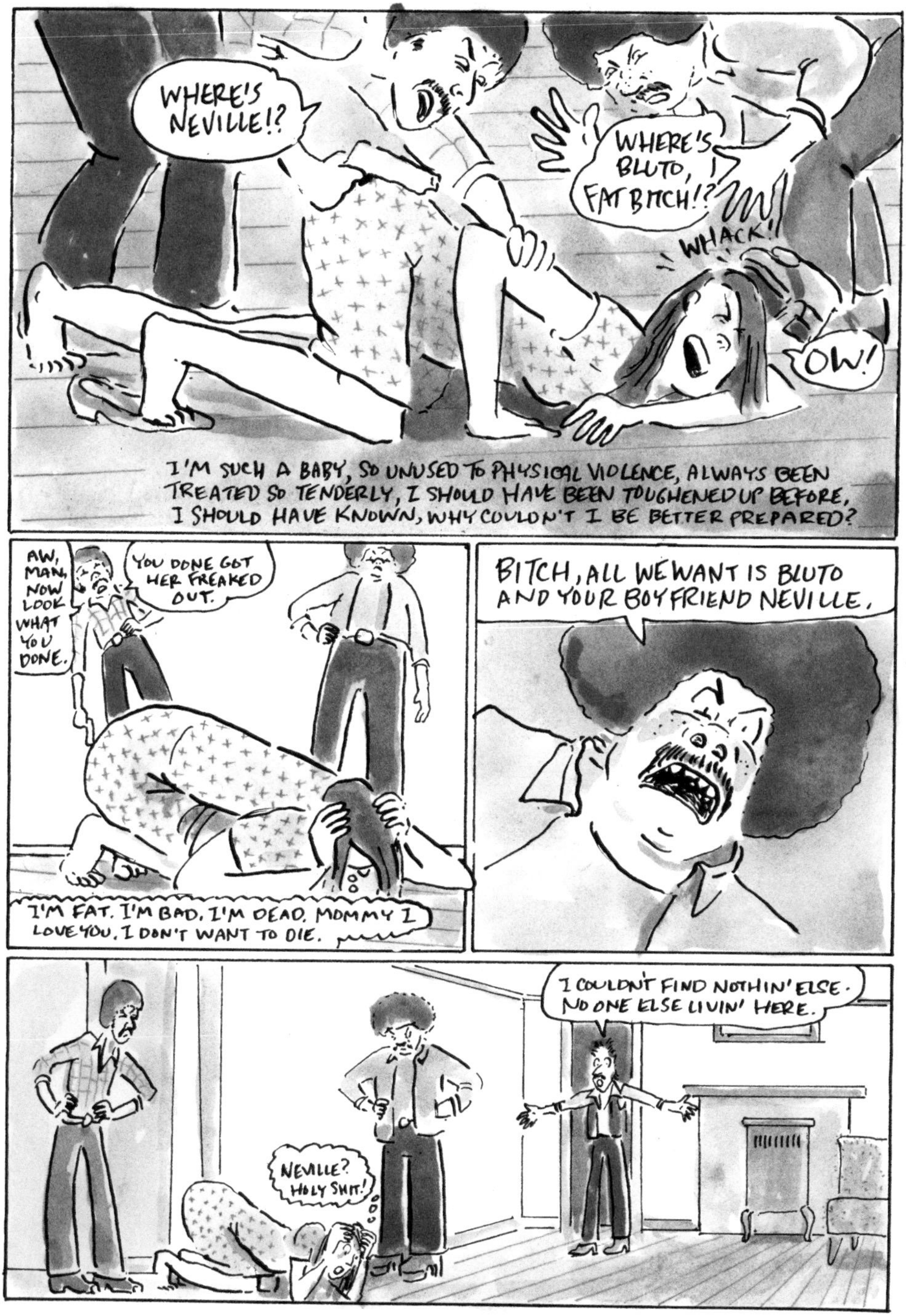
WHERE'S NEVILLE!?
WHERE'S BLUTO, FAT BITCH!?
WHACK!
OW!
I'M SUCH A BABY, SO UNUSED TO PHYSICAL VIOLENCE, ALWAYS BEEN TREATED SO TENDERLY, I SHOULD HAVE BEEN TOUGHENED UP BEFORE, I SHOULD HAVE KNOWN, WHY COULDN'T I BE BETTER PREPARED?
AW, MAN, NOW LOOK WHAT YOU DONE.
YOU DONE GOT HER FREAKED OUT.
I'M FAT. I'M BAD. I'M DEAD. MOMMY I LOVE YOU. I DON'T WANT TO DIE.
BITCH, ALL WE WANT IS BLUTO AND YOUR BOYFRIEND NEVILLE.
I COULDN'T FIND NOTHIN' ELSE. NO ONE ELSE LIVIN' HERE.
NEVILLE? HOLY SHIT!

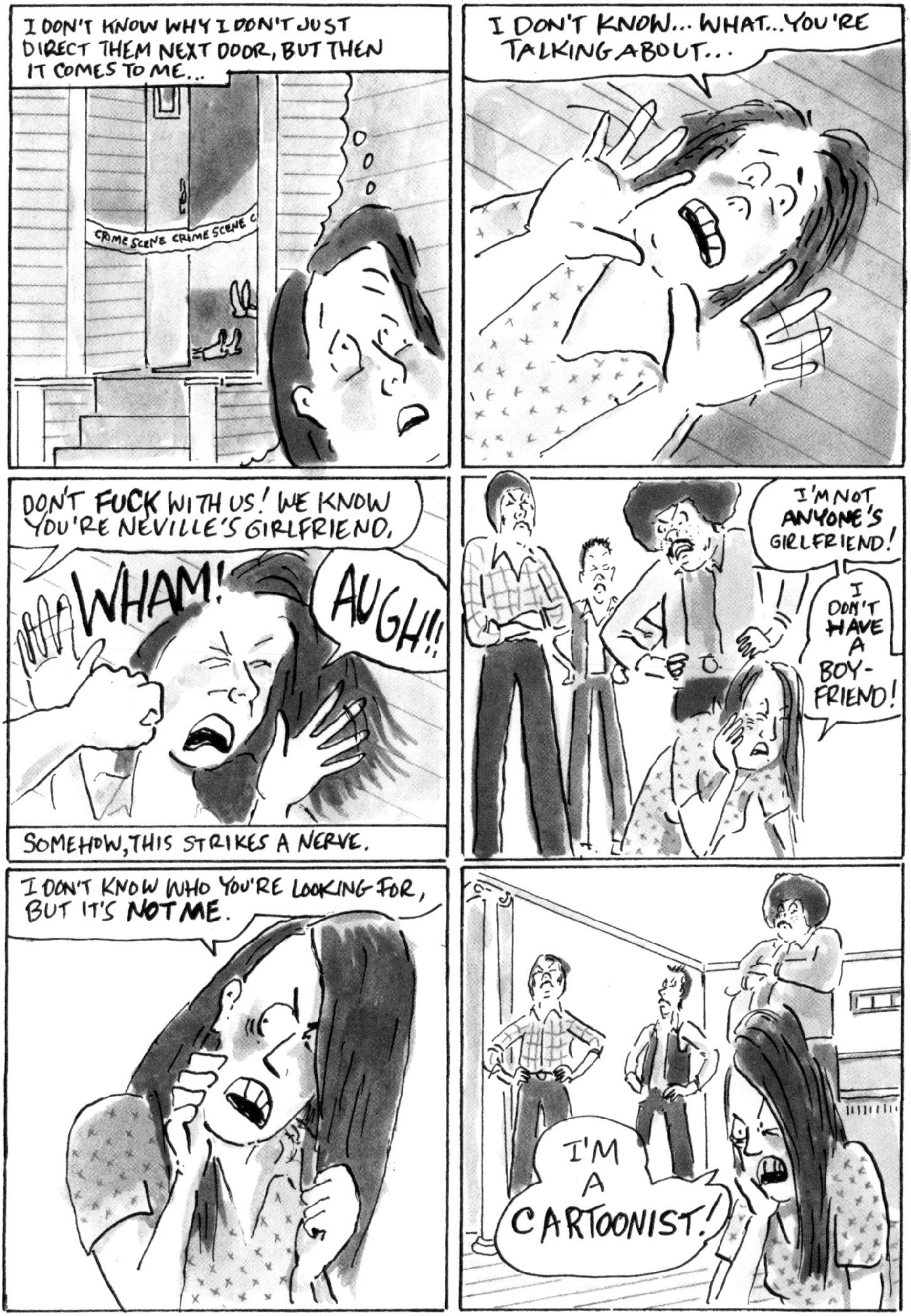
I DON'T KNOW WHY I DON'T JUST DIRECT THEM NEXT DOOR, BUT THEN IT COMES TO ME...
CRIME SCENE CRIME SCENE C
I DON'T KNOW... WHAT... YOU'RE TALKING ABOUT...
DON'T FUCK WITH US! WE KNOW YOU'RE NEVILLE'S GIRLFRIEND.
WHAM!
AUGH!!
SOMEHOW, THIS STRIKES A NERVE.
I'M NOT ANYONE'S GIRLFRIEND!
I DON'T HAVE A BOY-FRIEND!
I DON'T KNOW WHO YOU'RE LOOKING FOR, BUT IT'S NOT ME.
I'M A CARTOONIST!

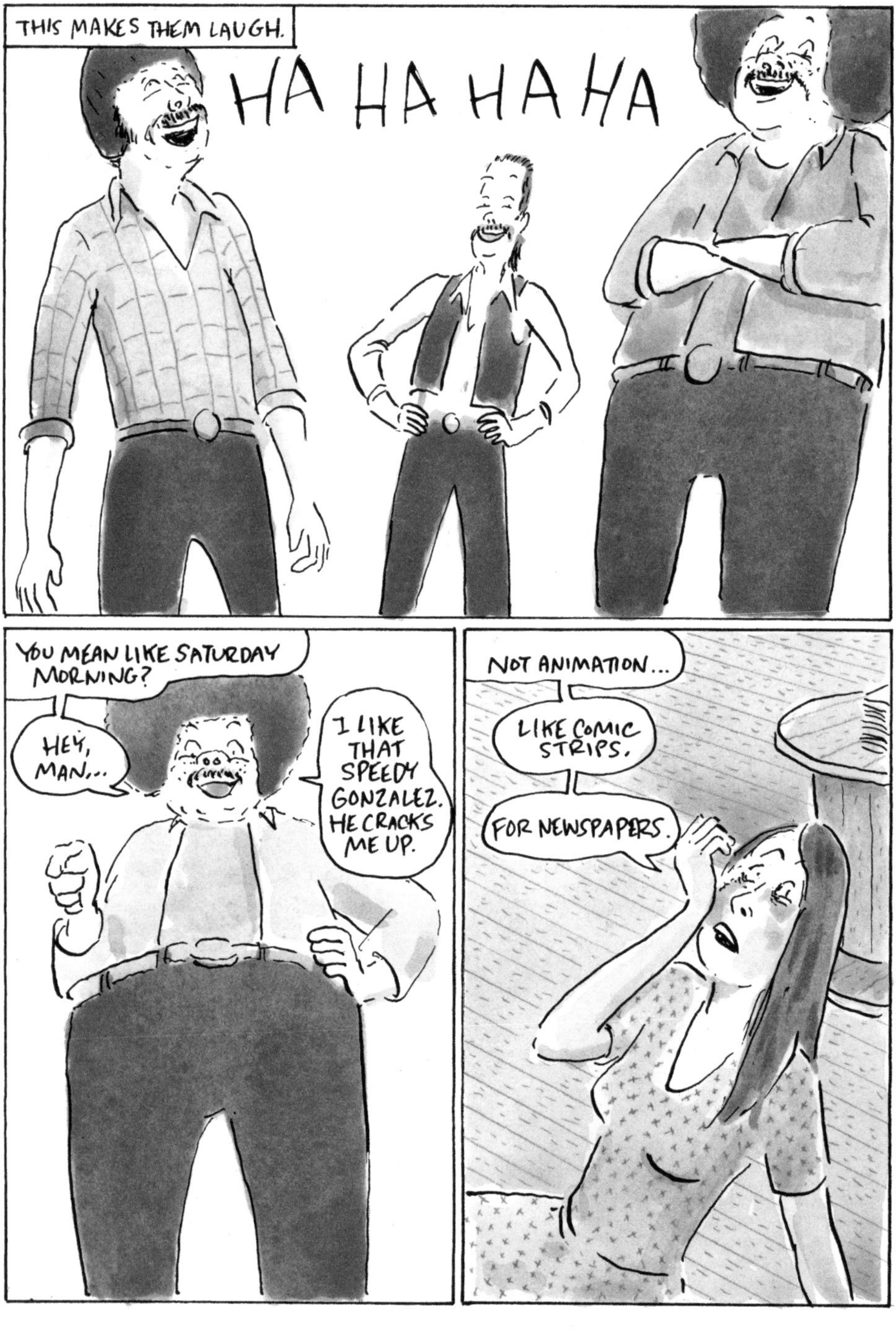
THIS MAKES THEM LAUGH.
HA HA HA HA HA
YOU MEAN LIKE SATURDAY MORNING?
HEY, MAN...
I LIKE THAT SPEEDY GONZALEZ. HE CRACKS ME UP.
NOT ANIMATION...
LIKE COMIC STRIPS.
FOR NEWSPAPERS.

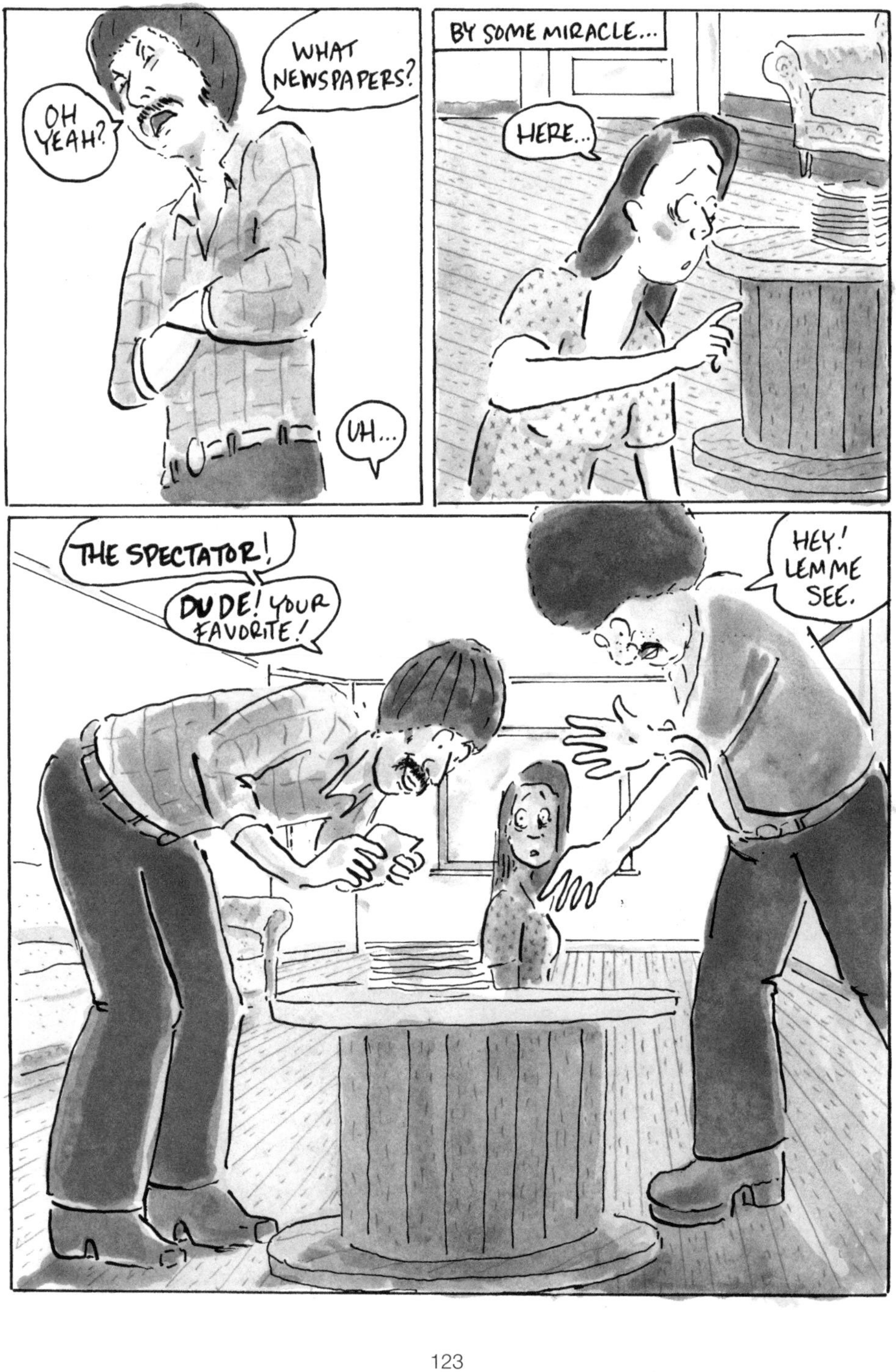
WHAT NEWSPAPERS?
OH YEAH?
UH...
BY SOME MIRACLE...
HERE...
THE SPECTATOR!
DUDE! YOUR FAVORITE!
HEY! LEMME SEE.

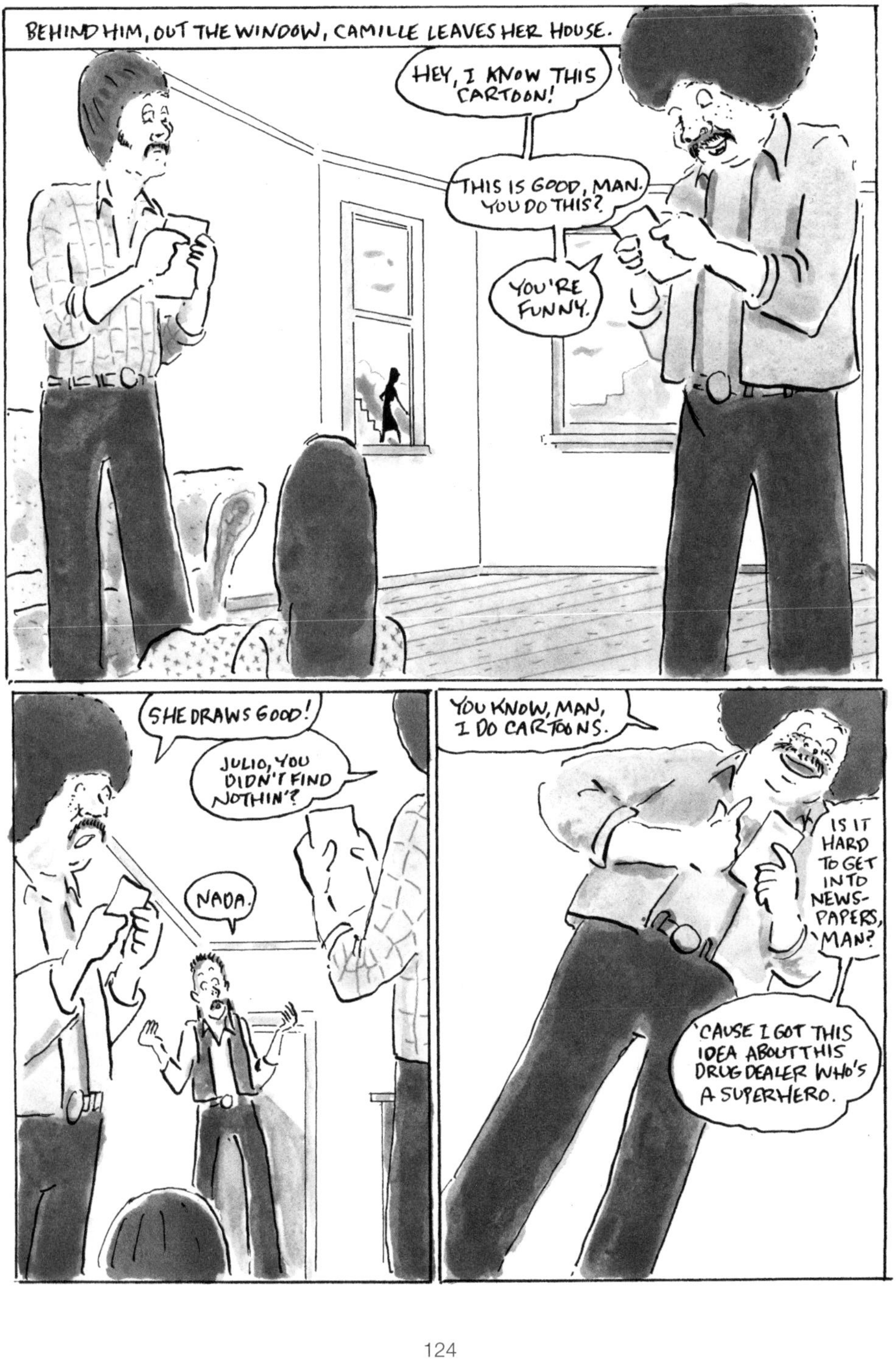
BEHIND HIM, OUT THE WINDOW, CAMILLE LEAVES HER HOUSE.
HEY, I KNOW THIS CARTOON!
THIS IS GOOD, MAN. YOU DO THIS?
YOU'RE FUNNY.
SHE DRAWS GOOD!
JULIO, YOU DIDN'T FIND NOTHIN'?
NADA.
YOU KNOW, MAN, I DO CARTOONS.
IS IT HARD TO GET INTO NEWS-PAPERS, MAN?
'CAUSE I GOT THIS IDEA ABOUT THIS DRUG DEALER WHO'S A SUPERHERO.

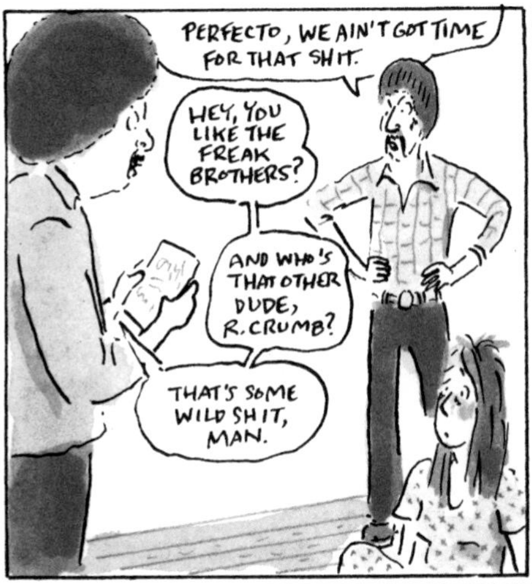
PERFECTO, WE AIN'T GOT TIME FOR THAT SHIT.
HEY, YOU LIKE THE FREAK BROTHERS?
AND WHO'S THAT OTHER DUDE, R. CRUMB?
THAT'S SOME WILD SHIT, MAN.

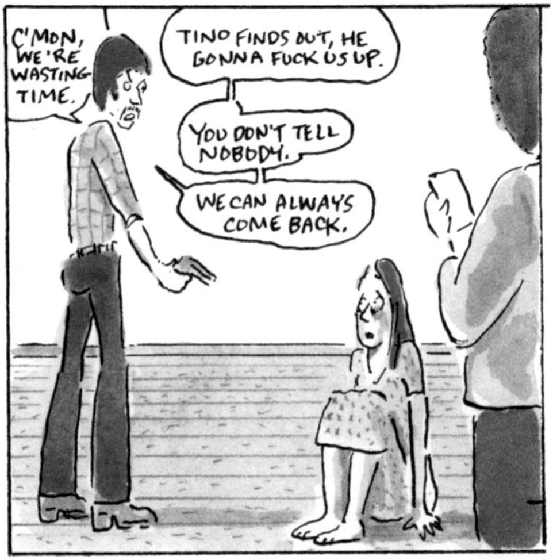
C'MON, WE'RE WASTING TIME.
TINO FINDS OUT, HE GONNA FUCK US UP.
YOU DON'T TELL NOBODY.
WE CAN ALWAYS COME BACK.

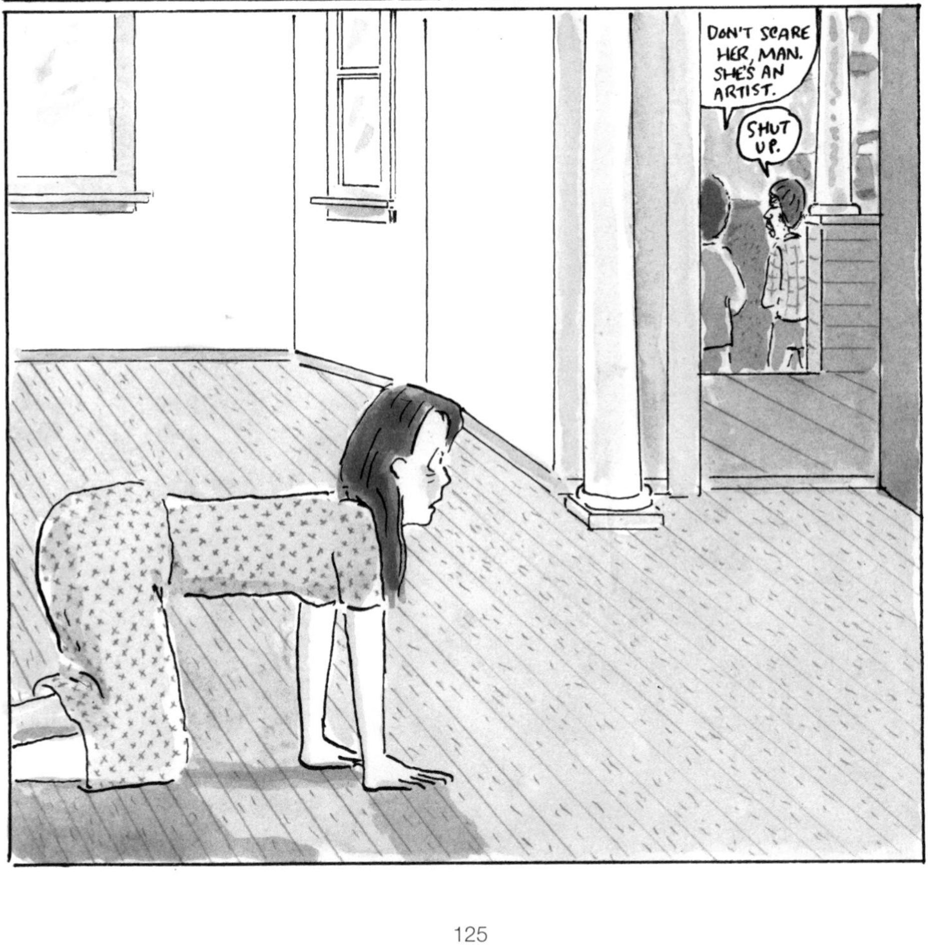
DON'T SCARE HER, MAN. SHE'S AN ARTIST.
SHUT UP.

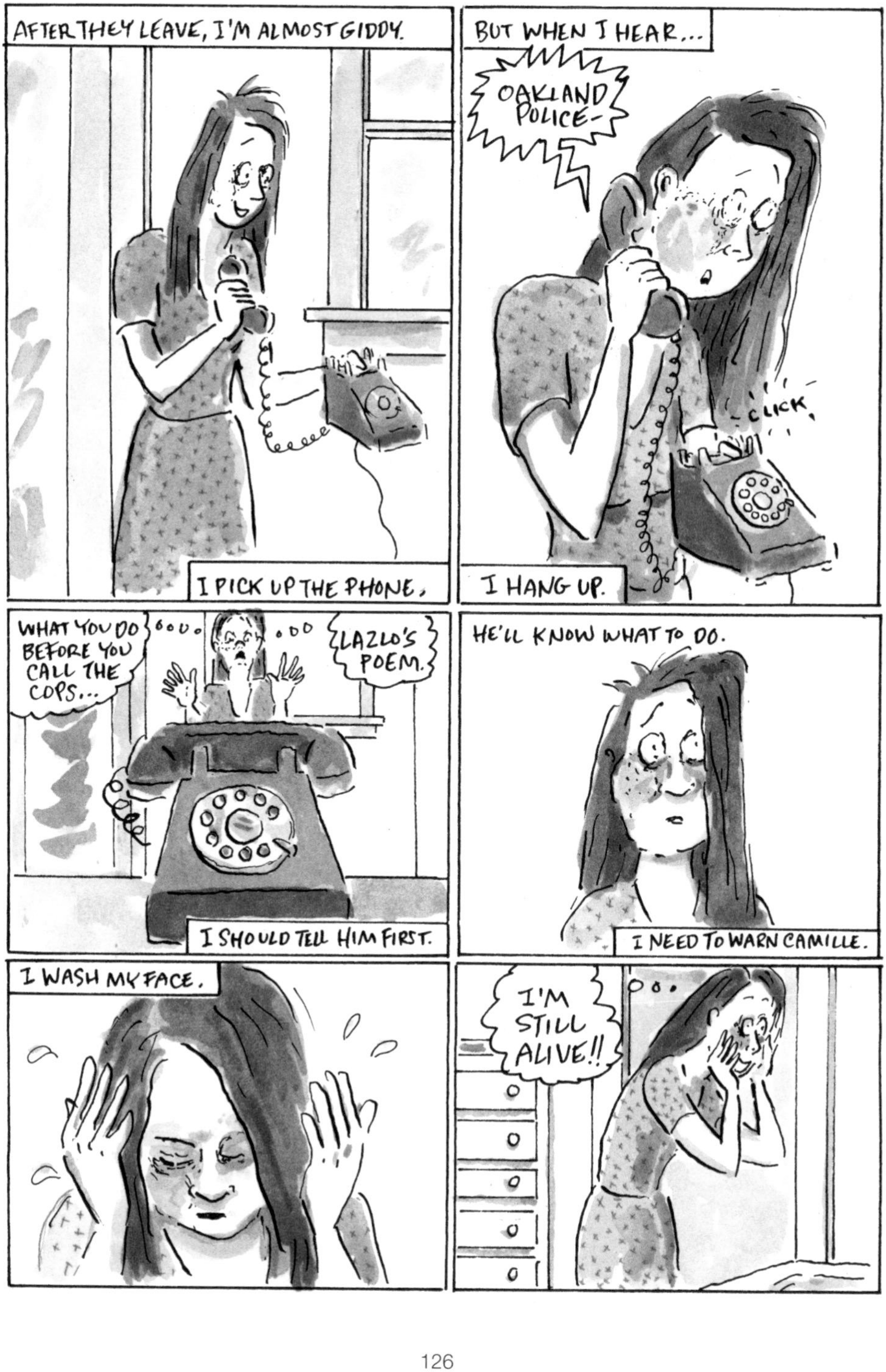
AFTER THEY LEAVE, I'M ALMOST GIDDY.
I PICK UP THE PHONE.
BUT WHEN I HEAR...
OAKLAND POLICE-
CLICK
I HANG UP.
WHAT YOU DO BEFORE YOU CALL THE COPS...
LAZLO'S POEM.
I SHOULD TELL HIM FIRST.
HE'LL KNOW WHAT TO DO.
I NEED TO WARN CAMILLE.
I WASH MY FACE.
I'M STILL ALIVE!!

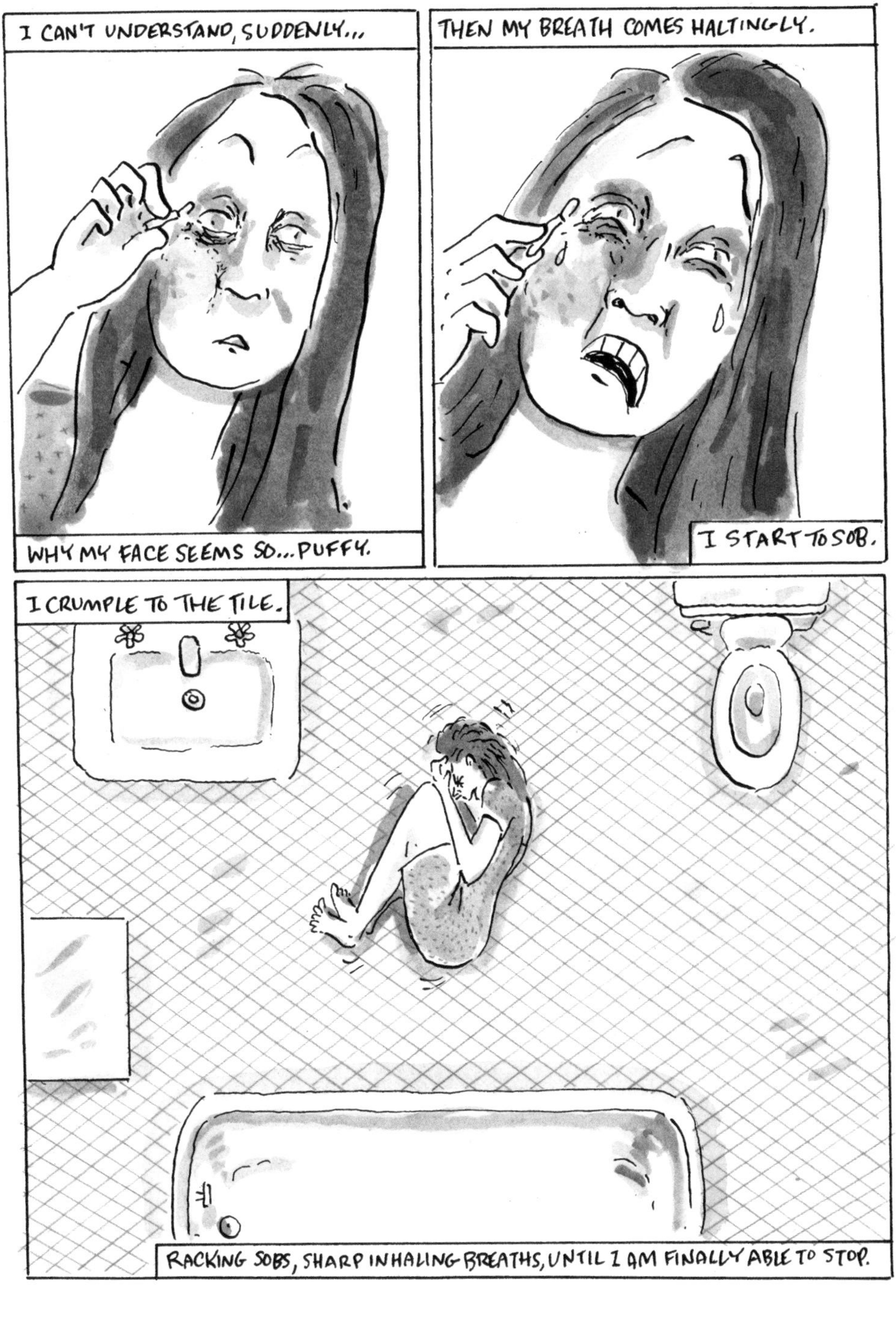
I CAN'T UNDERSTAND, SUDDENLY...
WHY MY FACE SEEMS SO... PUFFY.
THEN MY BREATH COMES HALTINGLY.
I START TO SOB.
I CRUMPLE TO THE TILE.
RACKING SOBS, SHARP INHALING BREATHS, UNTIL I AM FINALLY ABLE TO STOP.

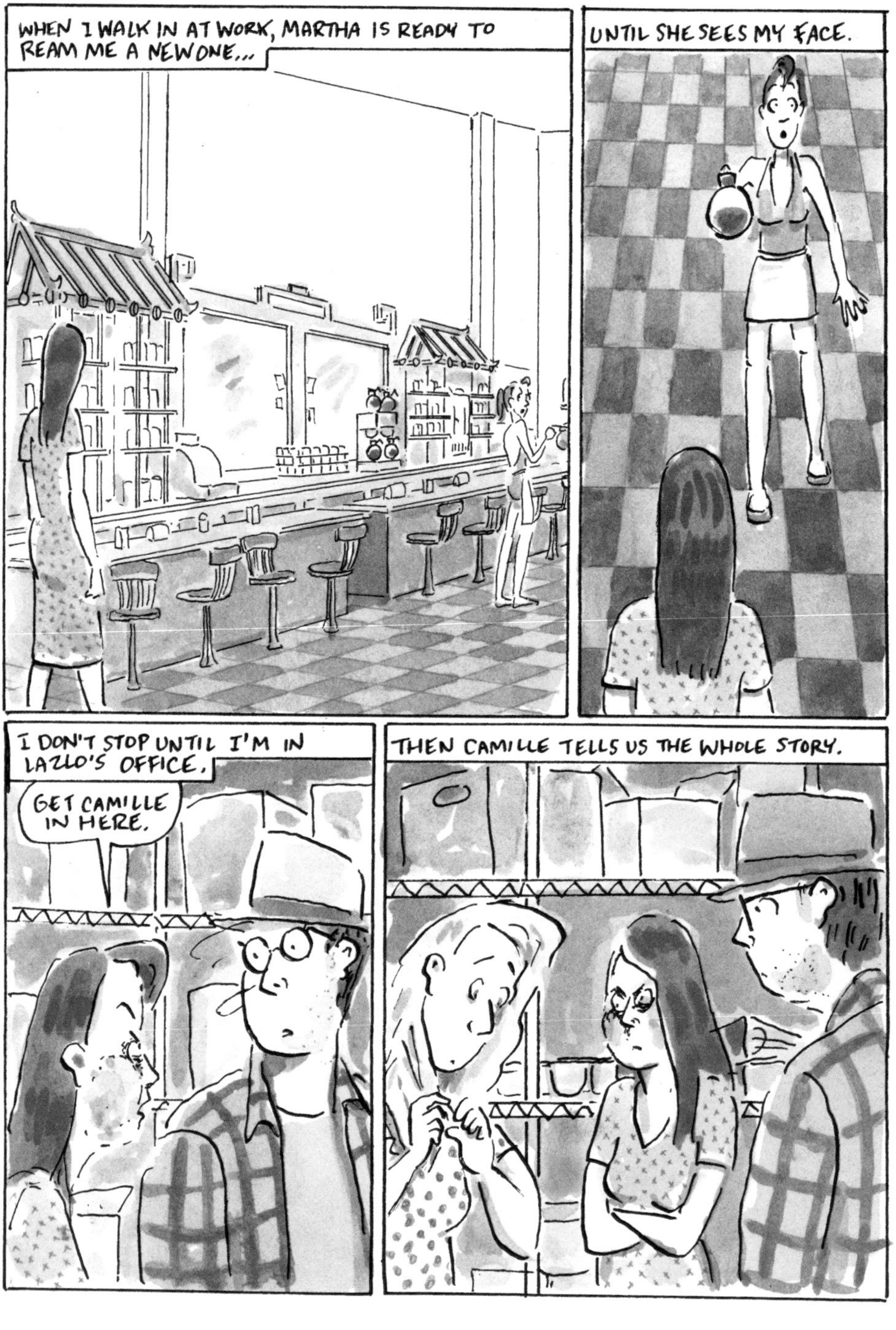
WHEN I WALK IN AT WORK, MARTHA IS READY TO REAM ME A NEW ONE...
UNTIL SHE SEES MY FACE.
I DON'T STOP UNTIL I'M IN LAZLO'S OFFICE.
GET CAMILLE IN HERE.
THEN CAMILLE TELLS US THE WHOLE STORY.

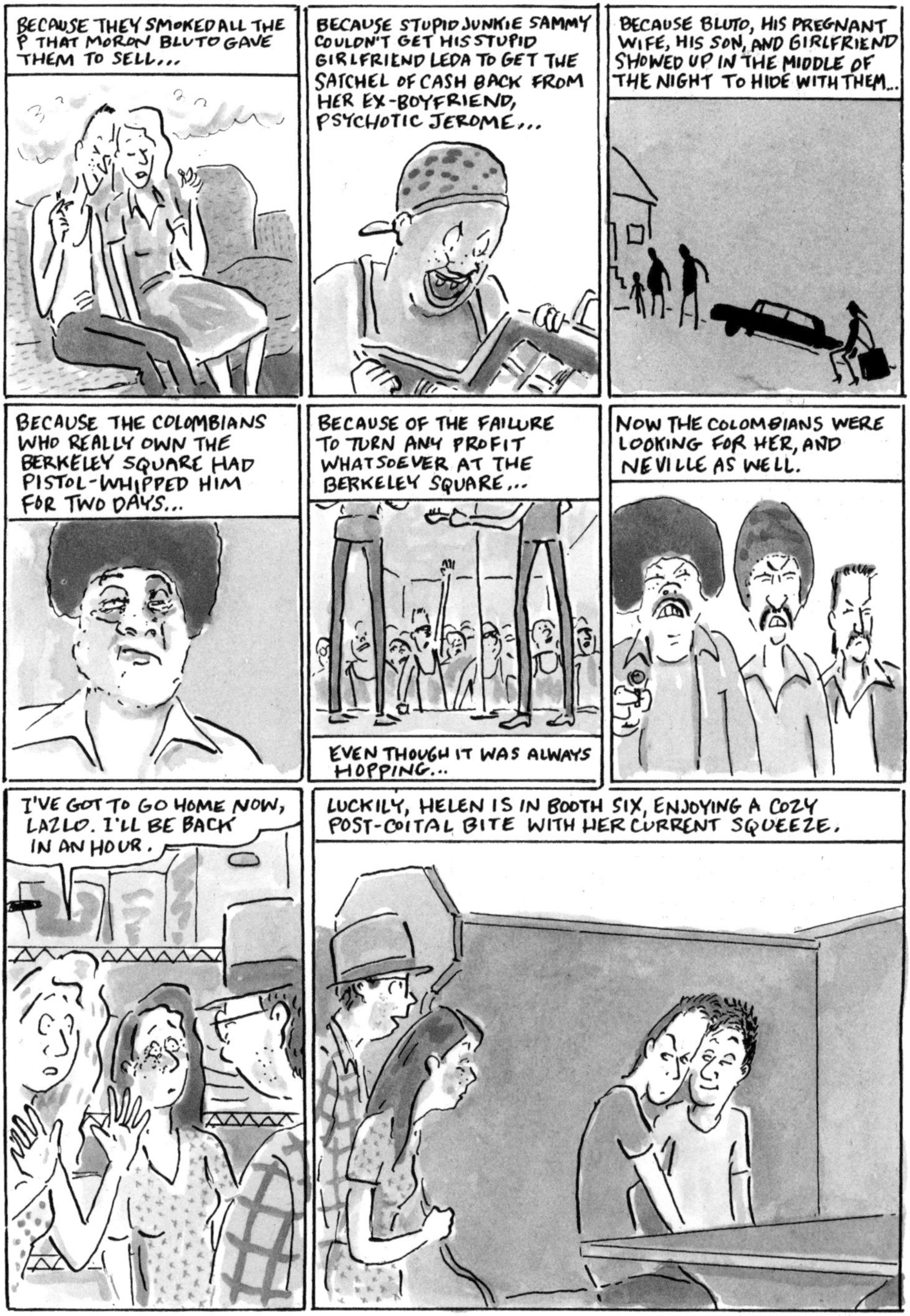
BECAUSE THEY SMOKED ALL THE P THAT MORON BLUTO GAVE THEM TO SELL...
BECAUSE STUPID JUNKIE SAMMY COULDN'T GET HIS STUPID GIRLFRIEND LEDA TO GET THE SATCHEL OF CASH BACK FROM HER EX-BOYFRIEND, PSYCHOTIC JEROME...
BECAUSE BLUTO, HIS PREGNANT WIFE, HIS SON, AND GIRLFRIEND SHOWED UP IN THE MIDDLE OF THE NIGHT TO HIDE WITH THEM...
BECAUSE THE COLOMBIANS WHO REALLY OWN THE BERKELEY SQUARE HAD PISTOL-WHIPPED HIM FOR TWO DAYS...
BECAUSE OF THE FAILURE TO TURN ANY PROFIT WHATSOEVER AT THE BERKELEY SQUARE...
EVEN THOUGH IT WAS ALWAYS HOPPING...
NOW THE COLOMBIANS WERE LOOKING FOR HER, AND NEVILLE AS WELL.
I'VE GOT TO GO HOME NOW, LAZLO. I'LL BE BACK IN AN HOUR.
LUCKILY, HELEN IS IN BOOTH SIX, ENJOYING A COZY POST-COITAL BITE WITH HER CURRENT SQUEEZE.

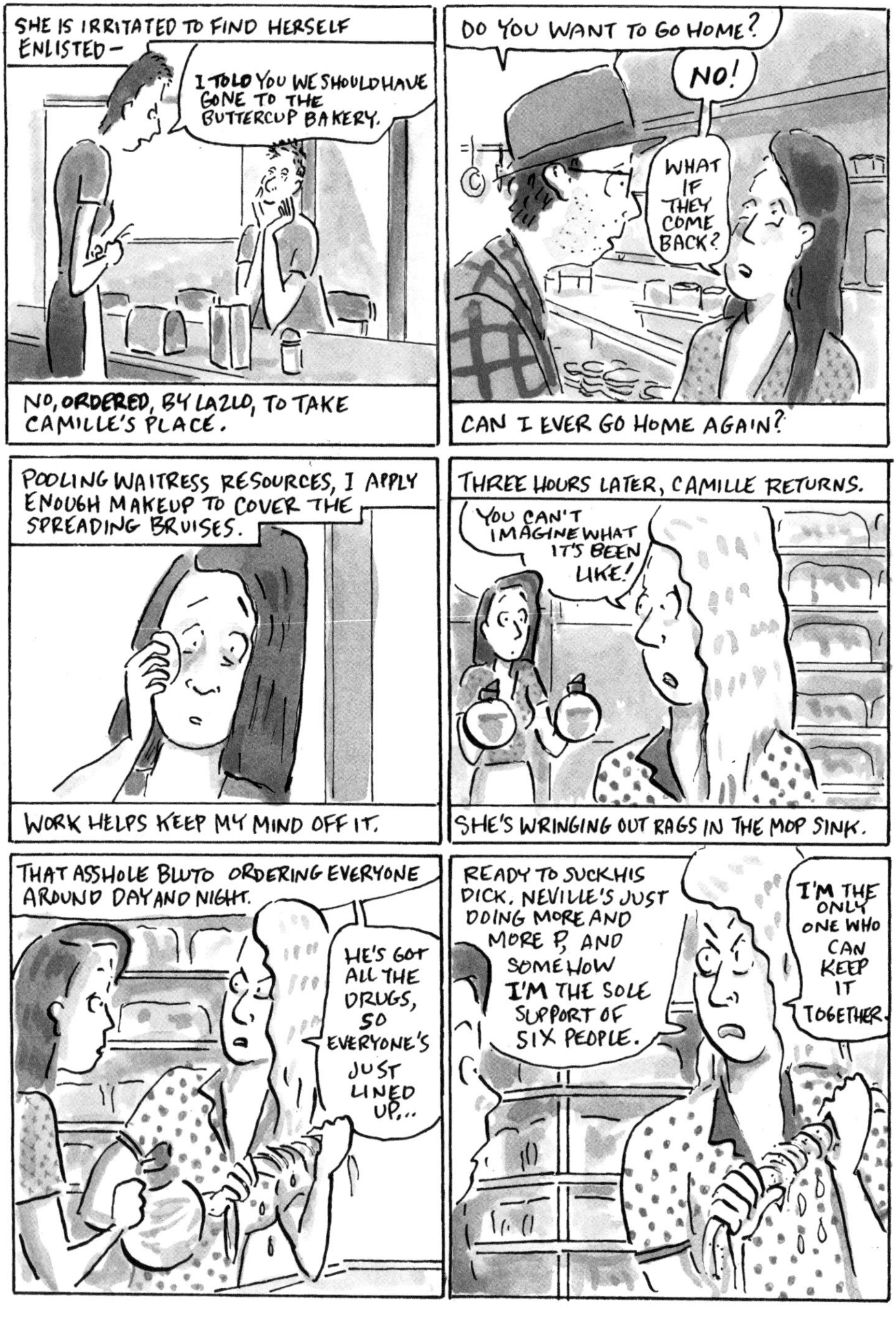
SHE IS IRRITATED TO FIND HERSELF ENLISTED—
I TOLD YOU WE SHOULD HAVE GONE TO THE BUTTERCUP BAKERY.
NO, ORDERED, BY LAZLO, TO TAKE CAMILLE'S PLACE.
DO YOU WANT TO GO HOME?
NO!
WHAT IF THEY COME BACK?
CAN I EVER GO HOME AGAIN?
POOLING WAITRESS RESOURCES, I APPLY ENOUGH MAKEUP TO COVER THE SPREADING BRUISES.
WORK HELPS KEEP MY MIND OFF IT.
THREE HOURS LATER, CAMILLE RETURNS.
YOU CAN'T IMAGINE WHAT IT'S BEEN LIKE!
SHE'S WRINGING OUT RAGS IN THE MOP SINK.
THAT ASSHOLE BLUTO ORDERING EVERYONE AROUND DAY AND NIGHT.
HE'S GOT ALL THE DRUGS, SO EVERYONE'S JUST LINED UP...
READY TO SUCK HIS DICK. NEVILLE'S JUST DOING MORE AND MORE P, AND SOMEHOW I'M THE SOLE SUPPORT OF SIX PEOPLE.
I'M THE ONLY ONE WHO CAN KEEP IT TOGETHER.

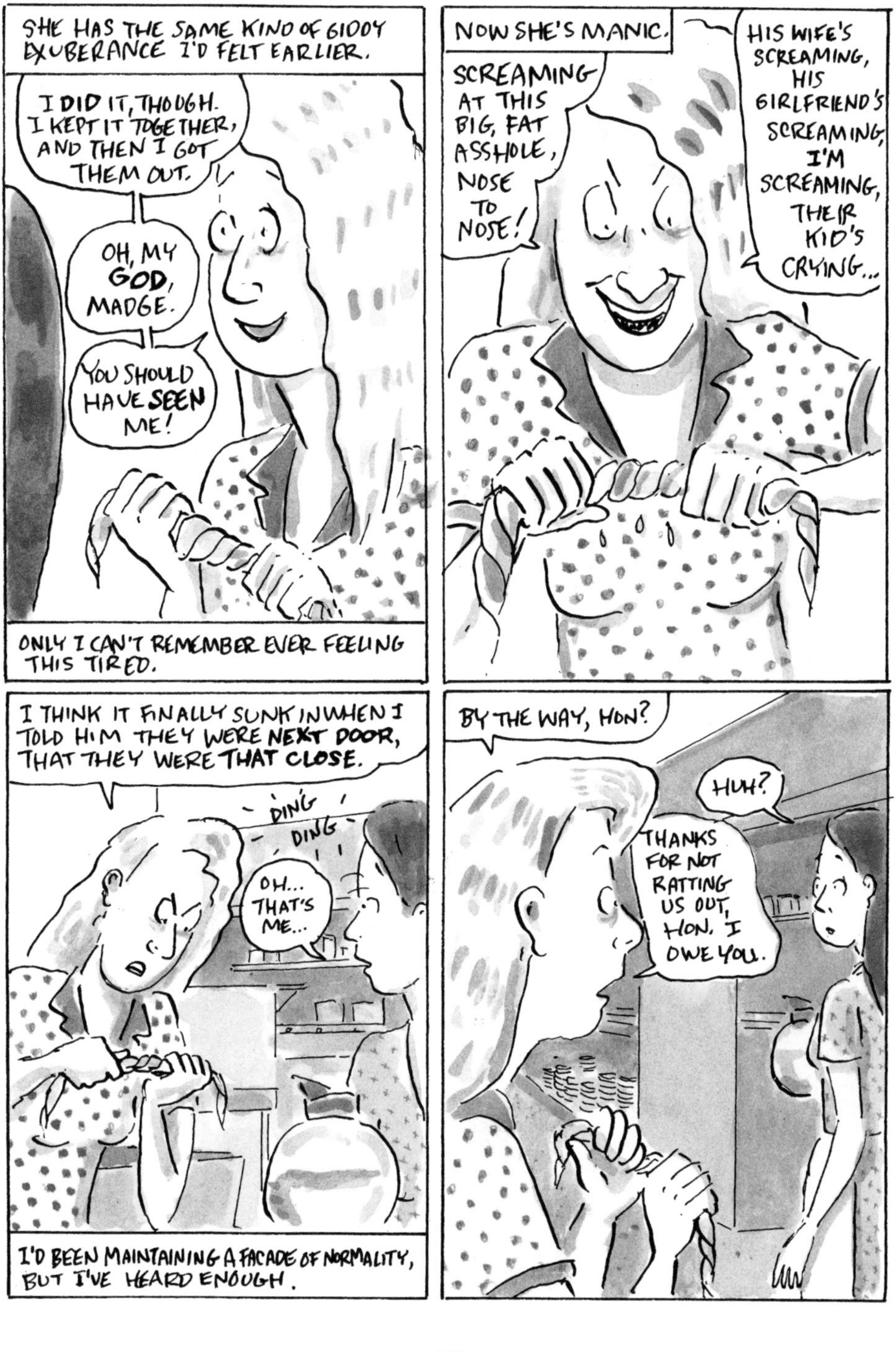
SHE HAS THE SAME KIND OF GIDDY EXUBERANCE I'D FELT EARLIER.
I DID IT, THOUGH. I KEPT IT TOGETHER, AND THEN I GOT THEM OUT.
OH, MY GOD, MADGE.
YOU SHOULD HAVE SEEN ME!
ONLY I CAN'T REMEMBER EVER FEELING THIS TIRED.
NOW SHE'S MANIC.
SCREAMING AT THIS BIG, FAT ASSHOLE, NOSE TO NOSE!
HIS WIFE'S SCREAMING, HIS GIRLFRIEND'S SCREAMING, I'M SCREAMING, THEIR KID'S CRYING...
I THINK IT FINALLY SUNK IN WHEN I TOLD HIM THEY WERE NEXT DOOR, THAT THEY WERE THAT CLOSE.
DING
DING
OH... THAT'S ME...
I'D BEEN MAINTAINING A FACADE OF NORMALITY, BUT I'VE HEARD ENOUGH.
BY THE WAY, HON?
HUH?
THANKS FOR NOT RATTING US OUT, HON. I OWE YOU.

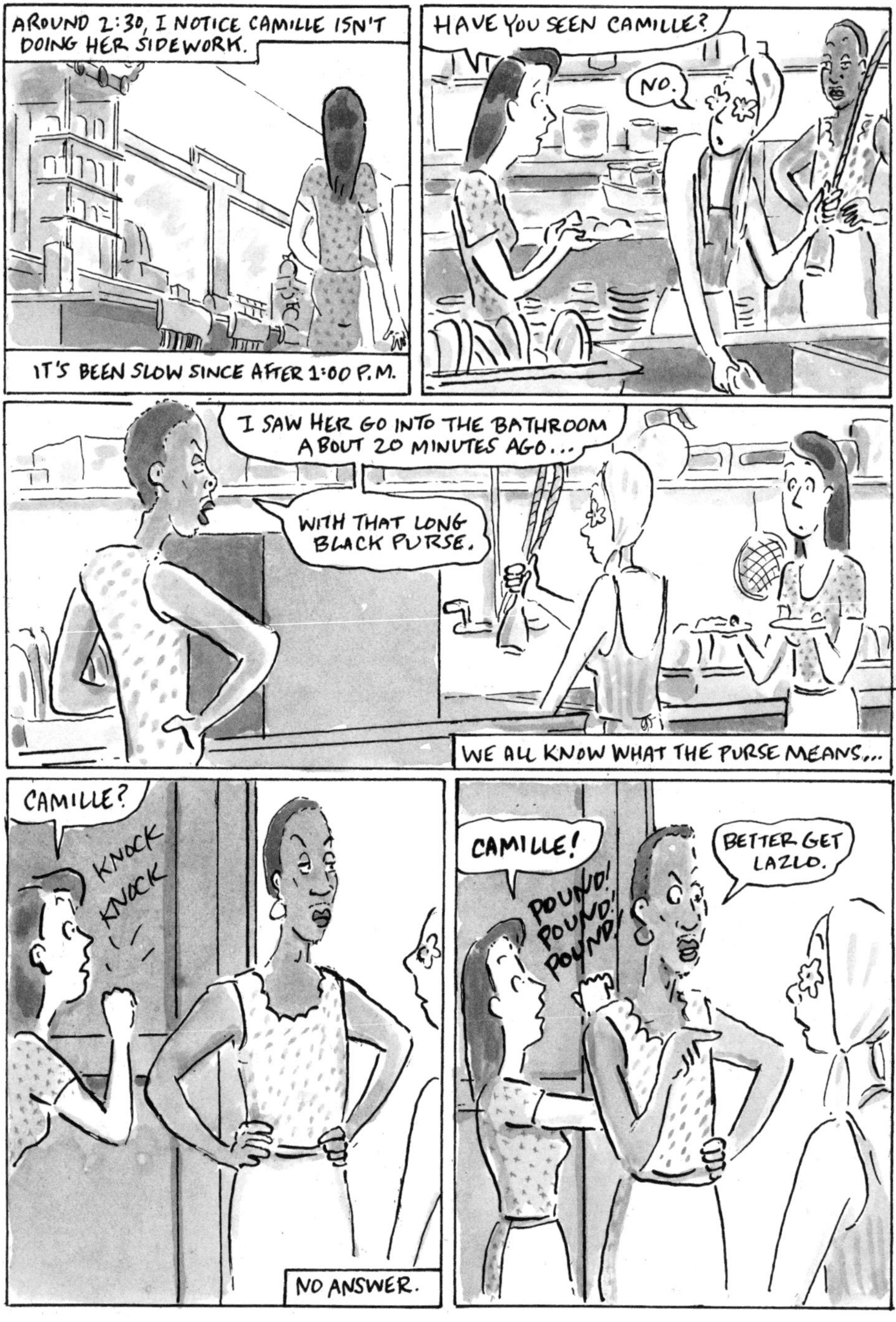

AROUND 2:30, I NOTICE CAMILLE ISN'T DOING HER SIDEWORK.
IT'S BEEN SLOW SINCE AFTER 1:00 P.M.
HAVE YOU SEEN CAMILLE?
NO.
I SAW HER GO INTO THE BATHROOM ABOUT 20 MINUTES AGO...
WITH THAT LONG BLACK PURSE.
WE ALL KNOW WHAT THE PURSE MEANS...
CAMILLE?
KNOCK KNOCK
NO ANSWER.
CAMILLE!
POUND! POUND! POUND!
BETTER GET LAZLO.

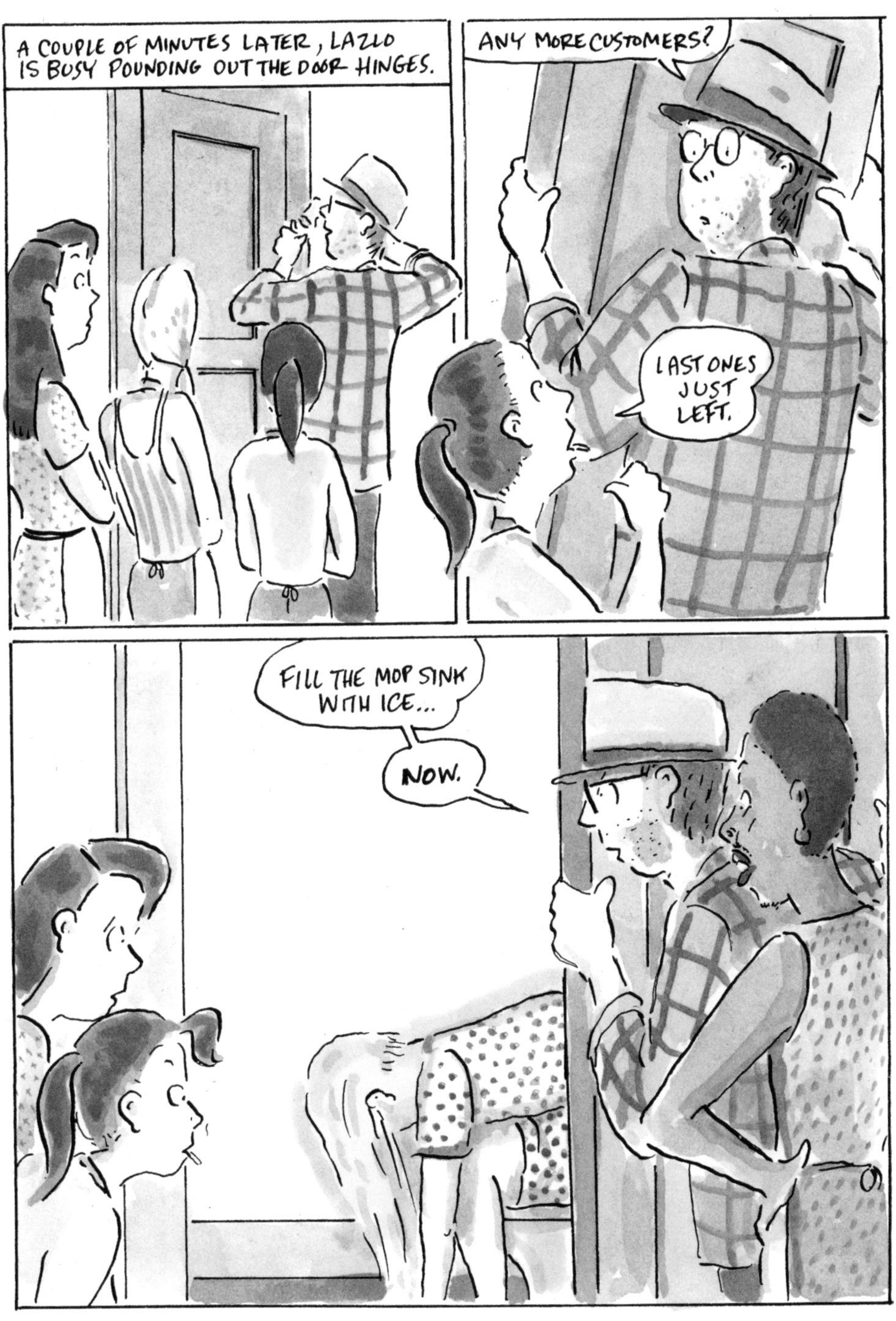
A COUPLE OF MINUTES LATER, LAZLO IS BUSY POUNDING OUT THE DOOR HINGES.
ANY MORE CUSTOMERS?
LAST ONES JUST LEFT.
FILL THE MOP SINK WITH ICE...
NOW.

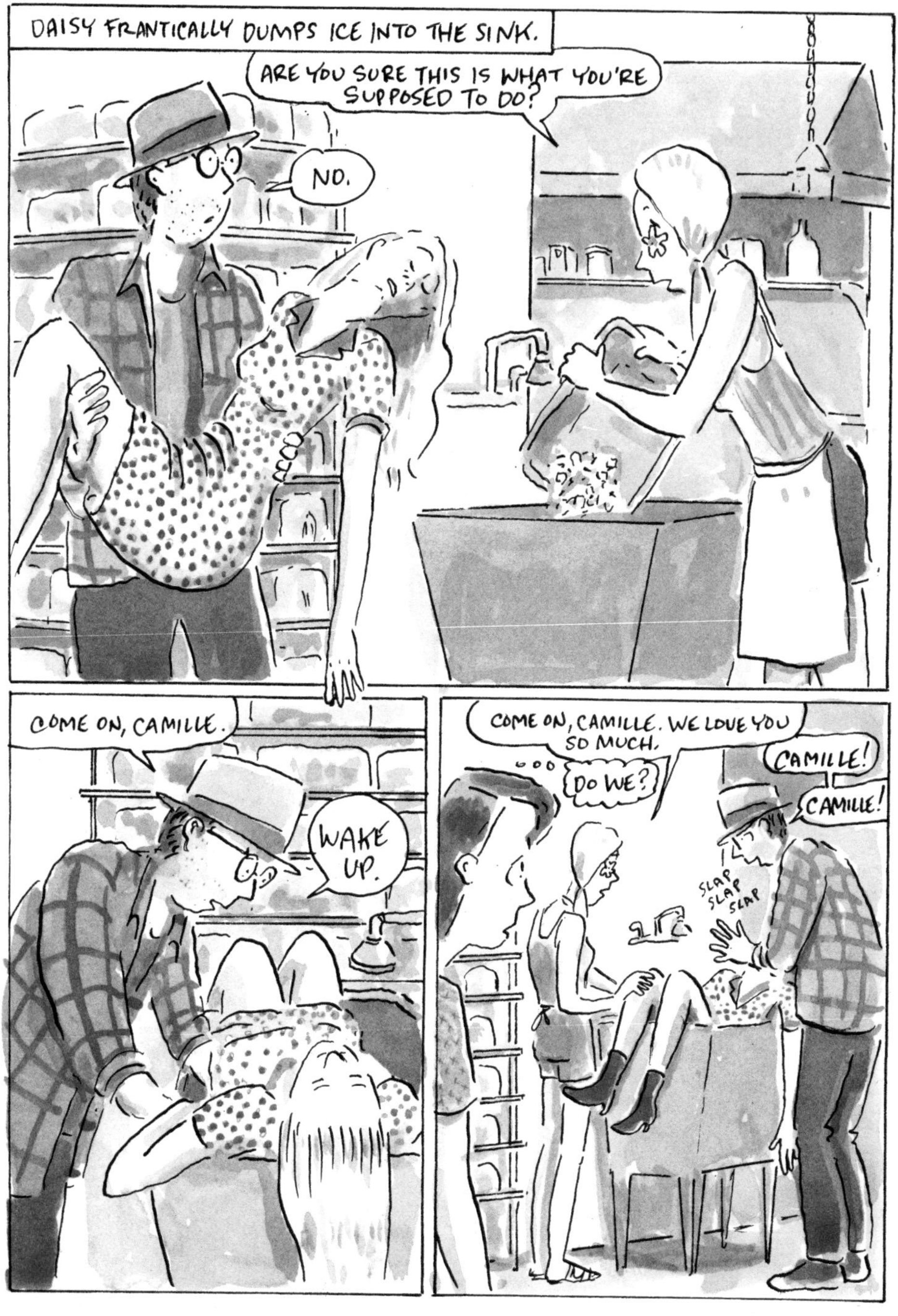
DAISY FRANTICALLY DUMPS ICE INTO THE SINK.
ARE YOU SURE THIS IS WHAT YOU'RE SUPPOSED TO DO?
NO.
COME ON, CAMILLE.
WAKE UP.
COME ON, CAMILLE. WE LOVE YOU SO MUCH.
DO WE?
CAMILLE!
CAMILLE!
SLAP SLAP SLAP

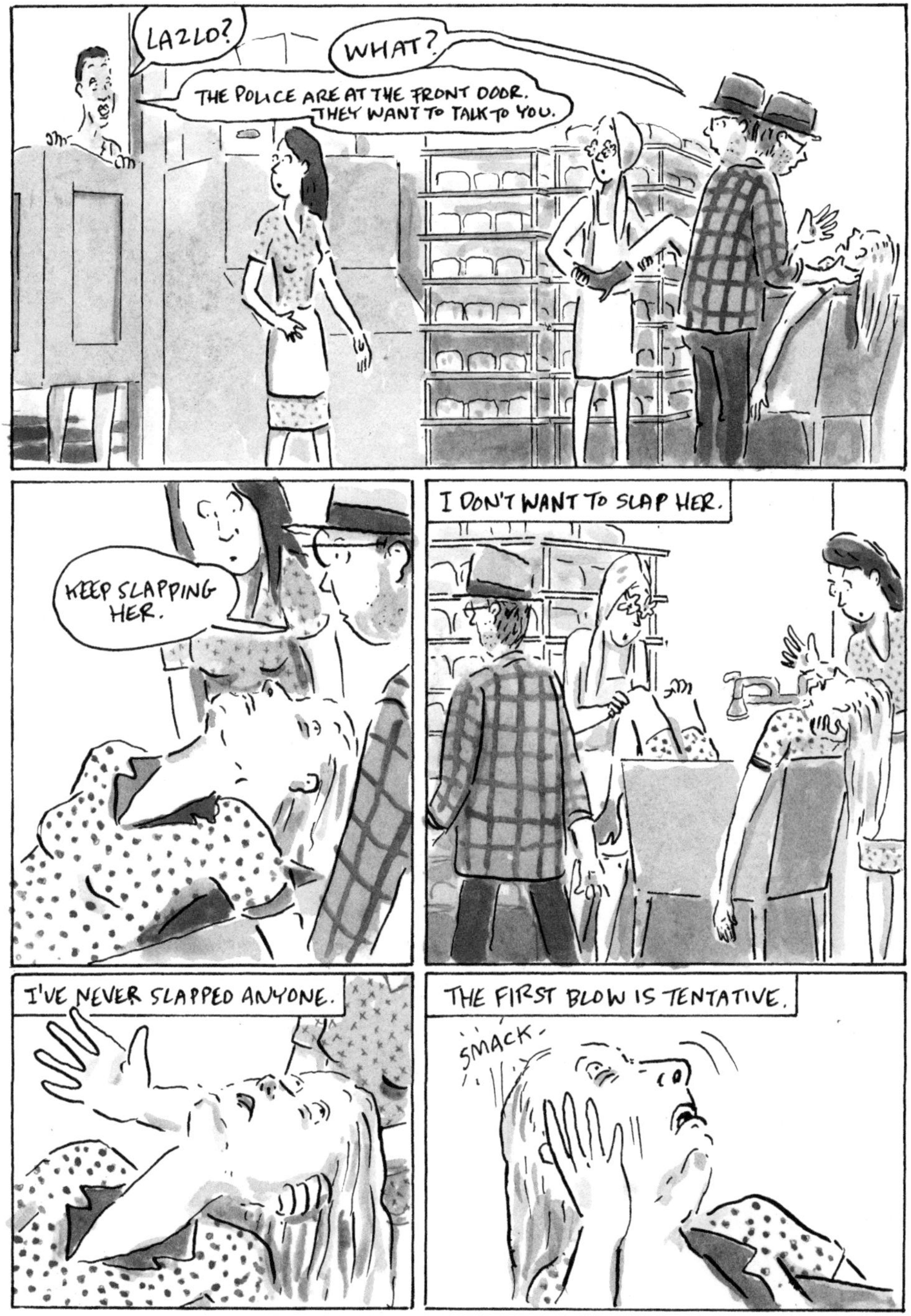
LAZLO?
WHAT?
THE POLICE ARE AT THE FRONT DOOR. THEY WANT TO TALK TO YOU.
KEEP SLAPPING HER.
I DON'T WANT TO SLAP HER.
I'VE NEVER SLAPPED ANYONE.
THE FIRST BLOW IS TENTATIVE.
SMACK

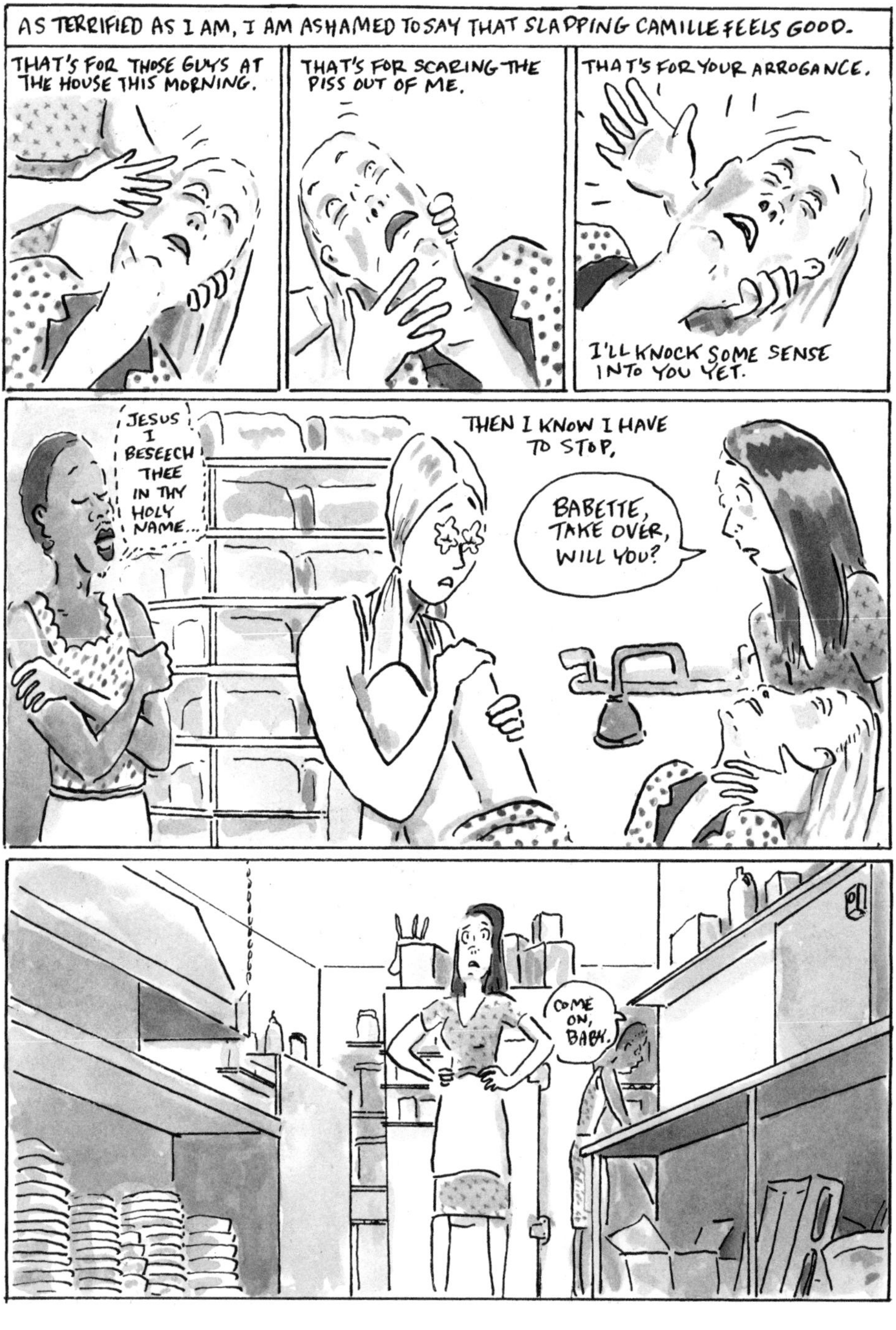
AS TERRIFIED AS I AM, I AM ASHAMED TO SAY THAT SLAPPING CAMILLE FEELS GOOD.
THAT'S FOR THOSE GUYS AT THE HOUSE THIS MORNING.
THAT'S FOR SCARING THE PISS OUT OF ME.
THAT'S FOR YOUR ARROGANCE.
I'LL KNOCK SOME SENSE INTO YOU YET.
JESUS I BESEECH THEE IN THY HOLY NAME...
THEN I KNOW I HAVE TO STOP,
BABETTE, TAKE OVER, WILL YOU?
COME ON, BABY.

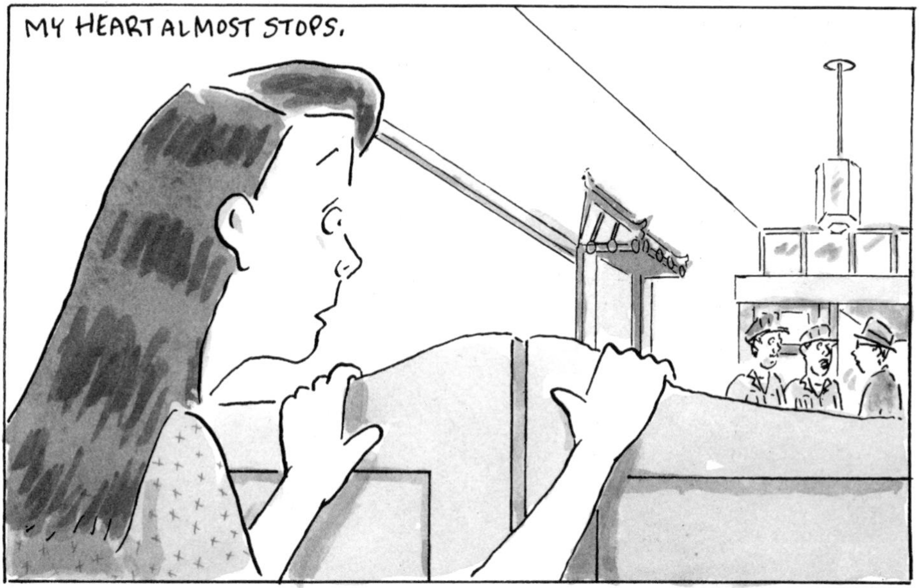
MY HEART ALMOST STOPS.

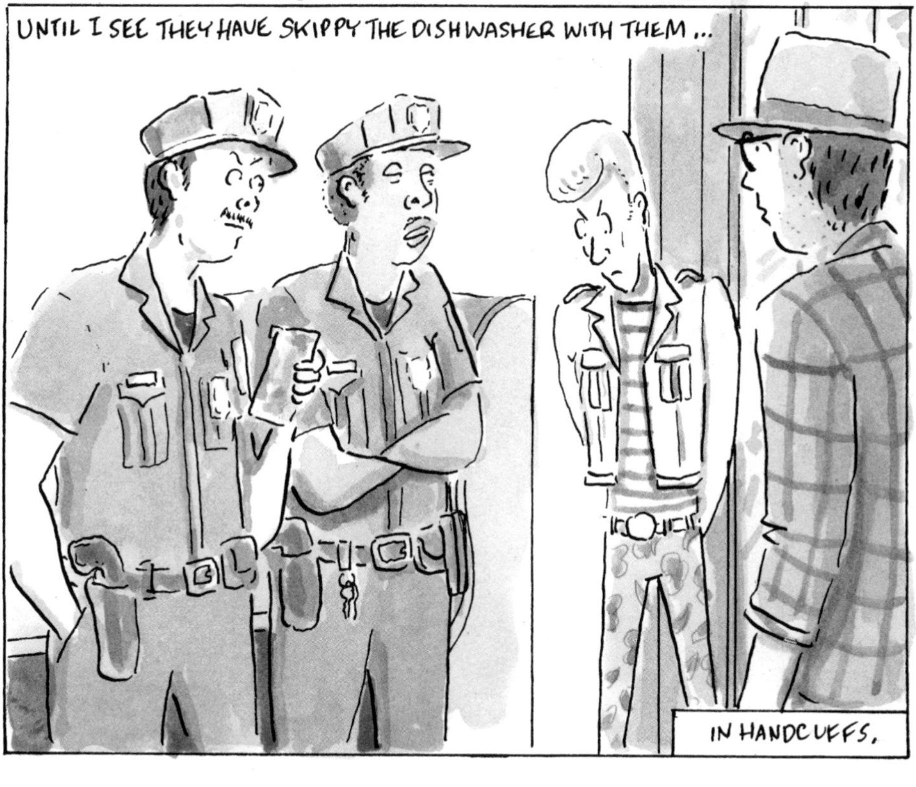
UNTIL I SEE THEY HAVE SKIPPY THE DISHWASHER WITH THEM...
IN HANDCUFFS.

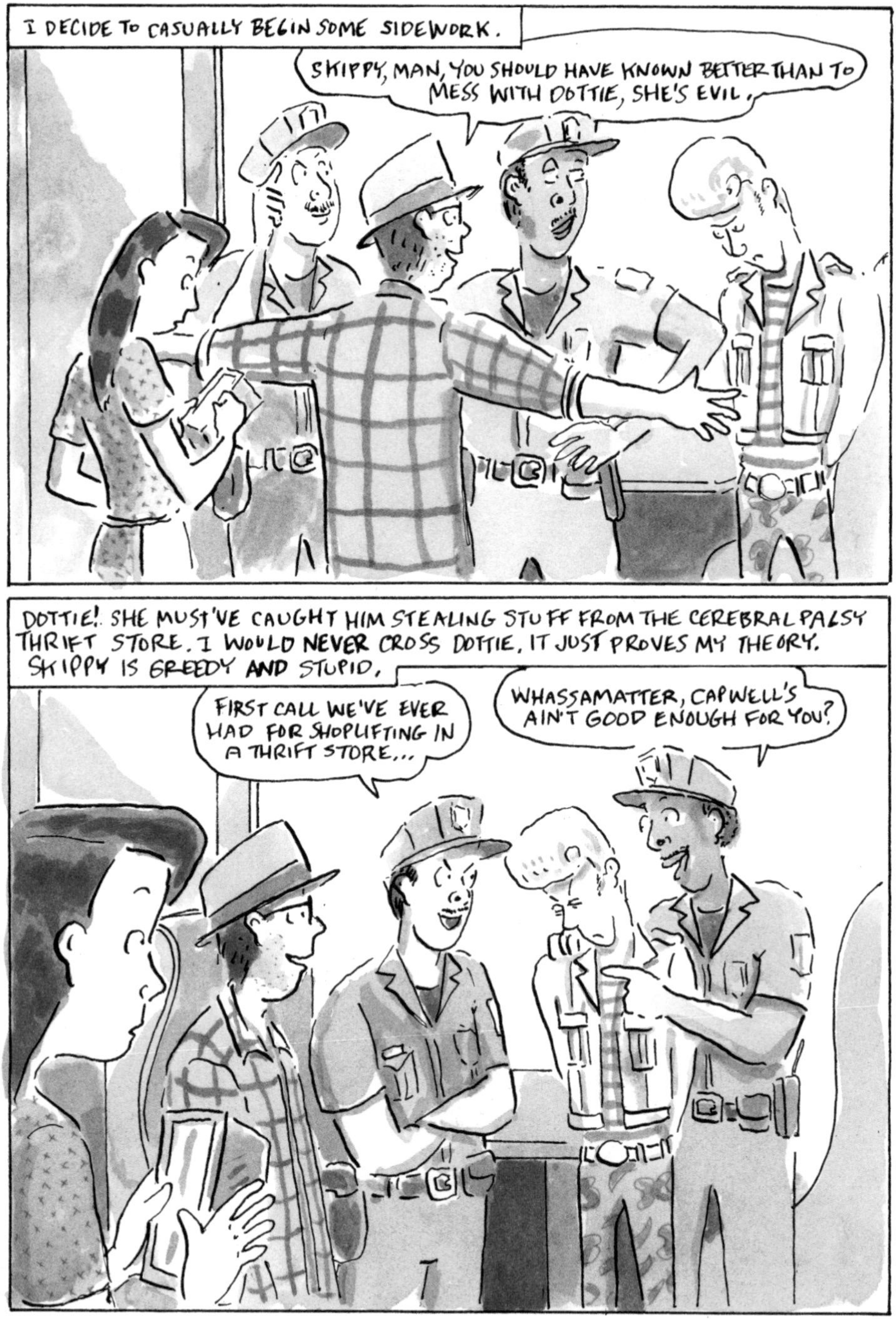
I DECIDE TO CASUALLY BEGIN SOME SIDEWORK.
SKIPPY, MAN, YOU SHOULD HAVE KNOWN BETTER THAN TO MESS WITH DOTTIE, SHE'S EVIL.
DOTTIE! SHE MUST'VE CAUGHT HIM STEALING STUFF FROM THE CEREBRAL PALSY THRIFT STORE. I WOULD **NEVER** CROSS DOTTIE. IT JUST PROVES MY THEORY. SKIPPY IS GREEDY **AND** STUPID.
FIRST CALL WE'VE EVER HAD FOR SHOPLIFTING IN A THRIFT STORE...
WHASSAMATTER, CAPWELL'S AIN'T GOOD ENOUGH FOR YOU?

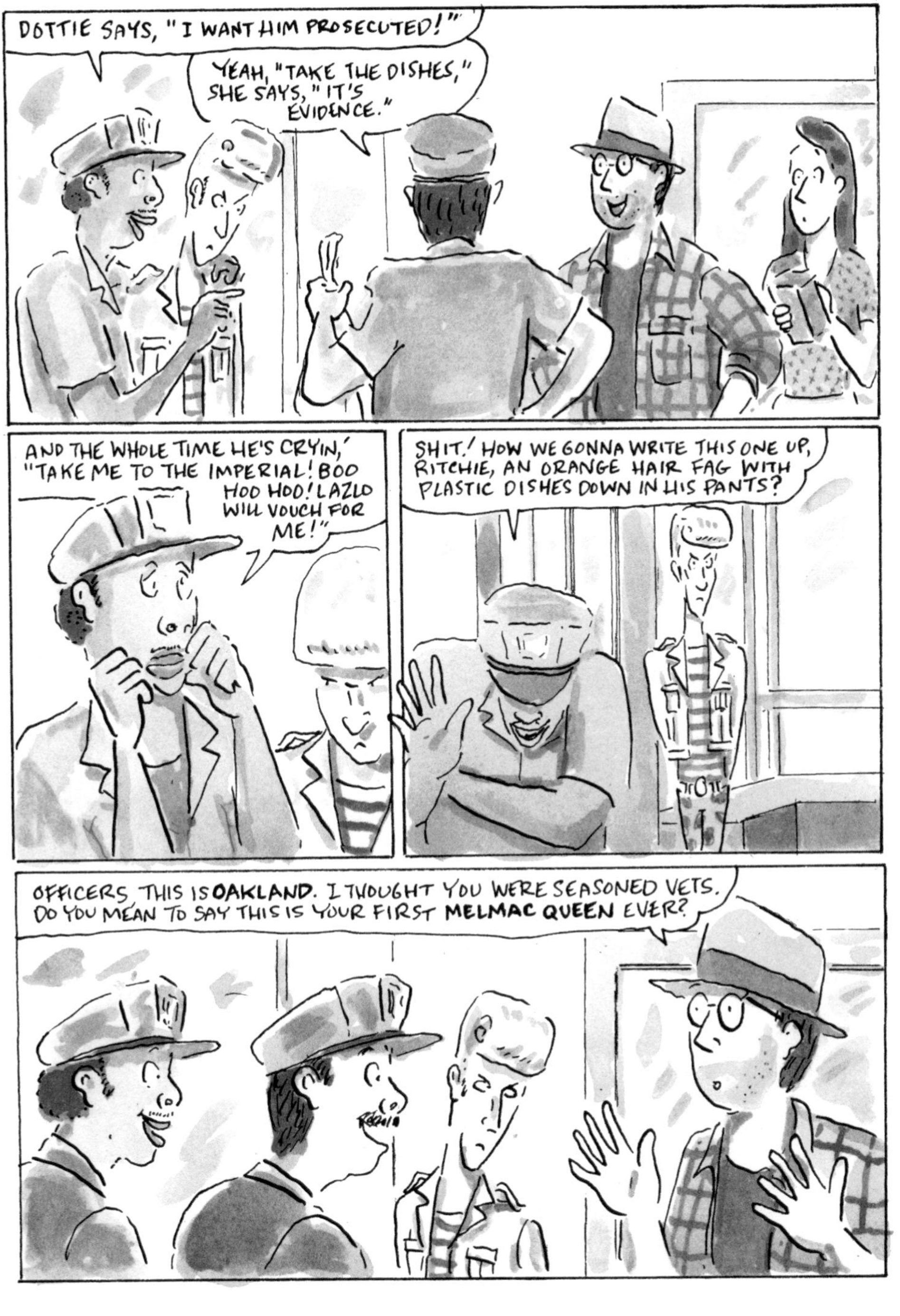
DOTTIE SAYS, "I WANT HIM PROSECUTED!"
YEAH, "TAKE THE DISHES," SHE SAYS, "IT'S EVIDENCE."
AND THE WHOLE TIME HE'S CRYIN,' "TAKE ME TO THE IMPERIAL! BOO HOO HOO! LAZLO WILL VOUCH FOR ME!"
SHIT! HOW WE GONNA WRITE THIS ONE UP, RITCHIE, AN ORANGE HAIR FAG WITH PLASTIC DISHES DOWN IN HIS PANTS?
OFFICERS THIS IS **OAKLAND**. I THOUGHT YOU WERE SEASONED VETS. DO YOU MEAN TO SAY THIS IS YOUR FIRST **MELMAC QUEEN** EVER?

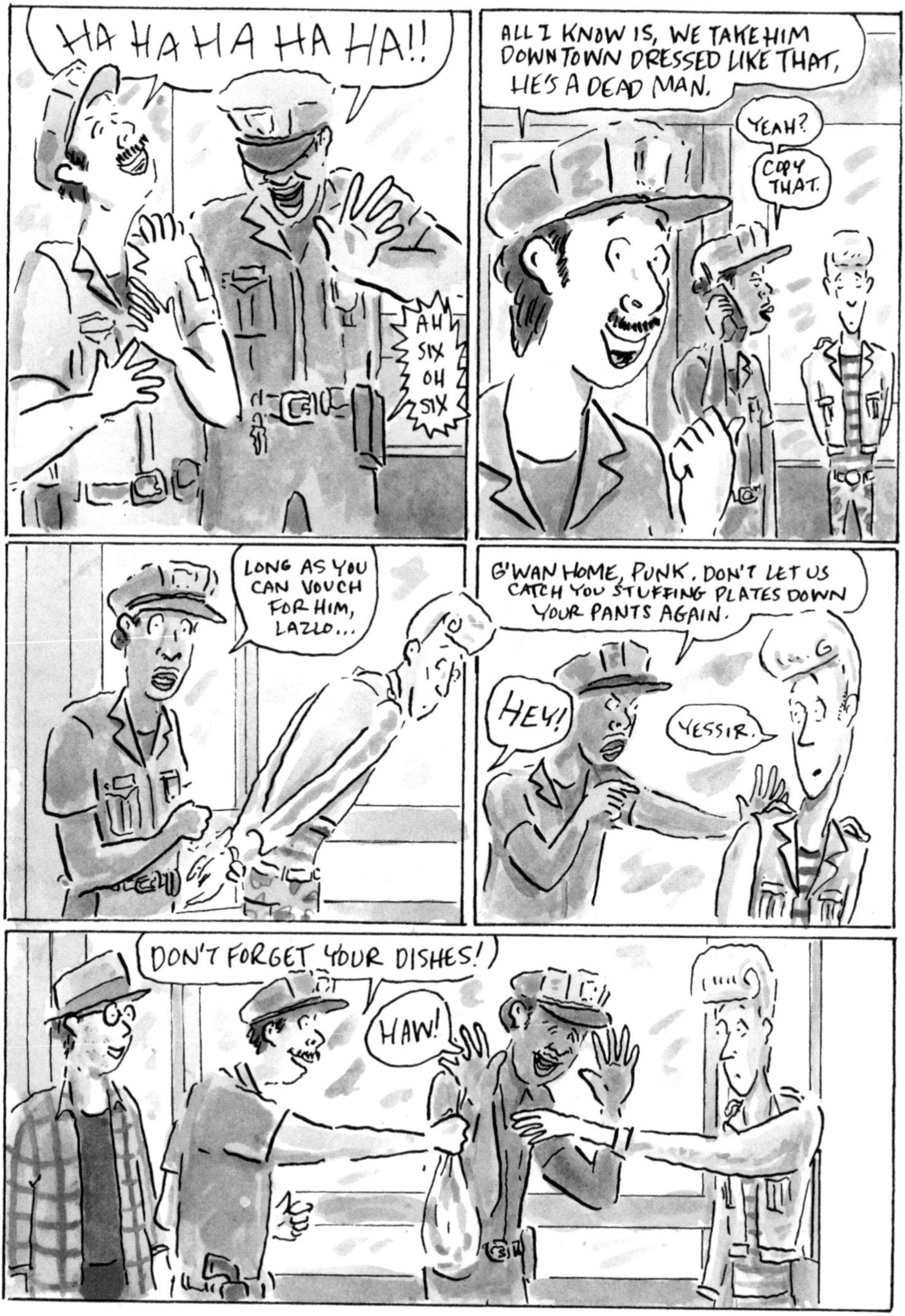
HA HA HA HA HA HA!!
AH SIX OH SIX
ALL I KNOW IS, WE TAKE HIM DOWNTOWN DRESSED LIKE THAT, HE'S A DEAD MAN.
YEAH?
COPY THAT.
LONG AS YOU CAN VOUCH FOR HIM, LAZLO...
G'WAN HOME, PUNK. DON'T LET US CATCH YOU STUFFING PLATES DOWN YOUR PANTS AGAIN.
HEY!
YESSIR.
DON'T FORGET YOUR DISHES!
HAW!

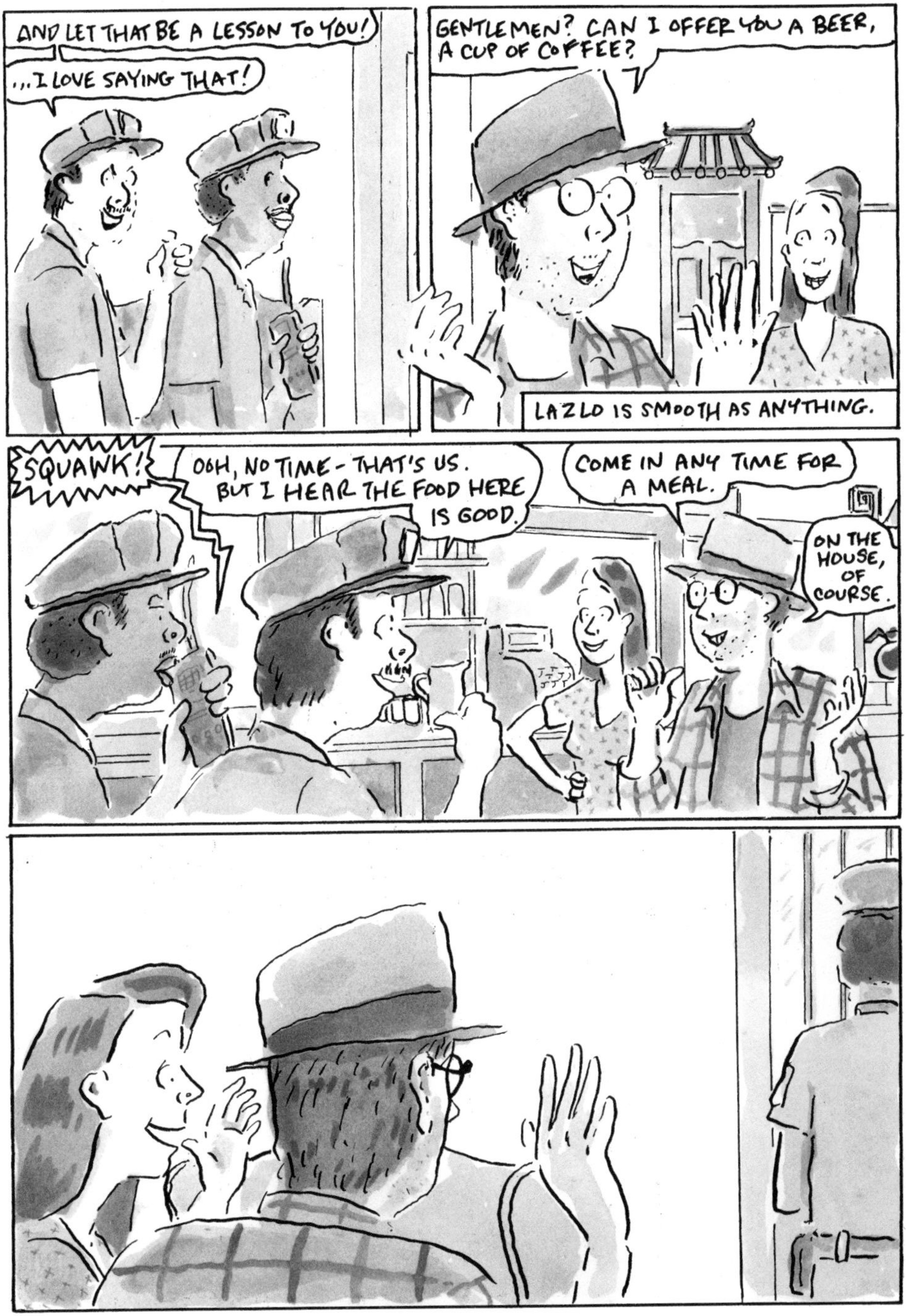
AND LET THAT BE A LESSON TO YOU!
...I LOVE SAYING THAT!
GENTLEMEN? CAN I OFFER YOU A BEER, A CUP OF COFFEE?
LAZLO IS SMOOTH AS ANYTHING.
SQUAWK!
OOH, NO TIME - THAT'S US. BUT I HEAR THE FOOD HERE IS GOOD.
COME IN ANY TIME FOR A MEAL.
ON THE HOUSE, OF COURSE.

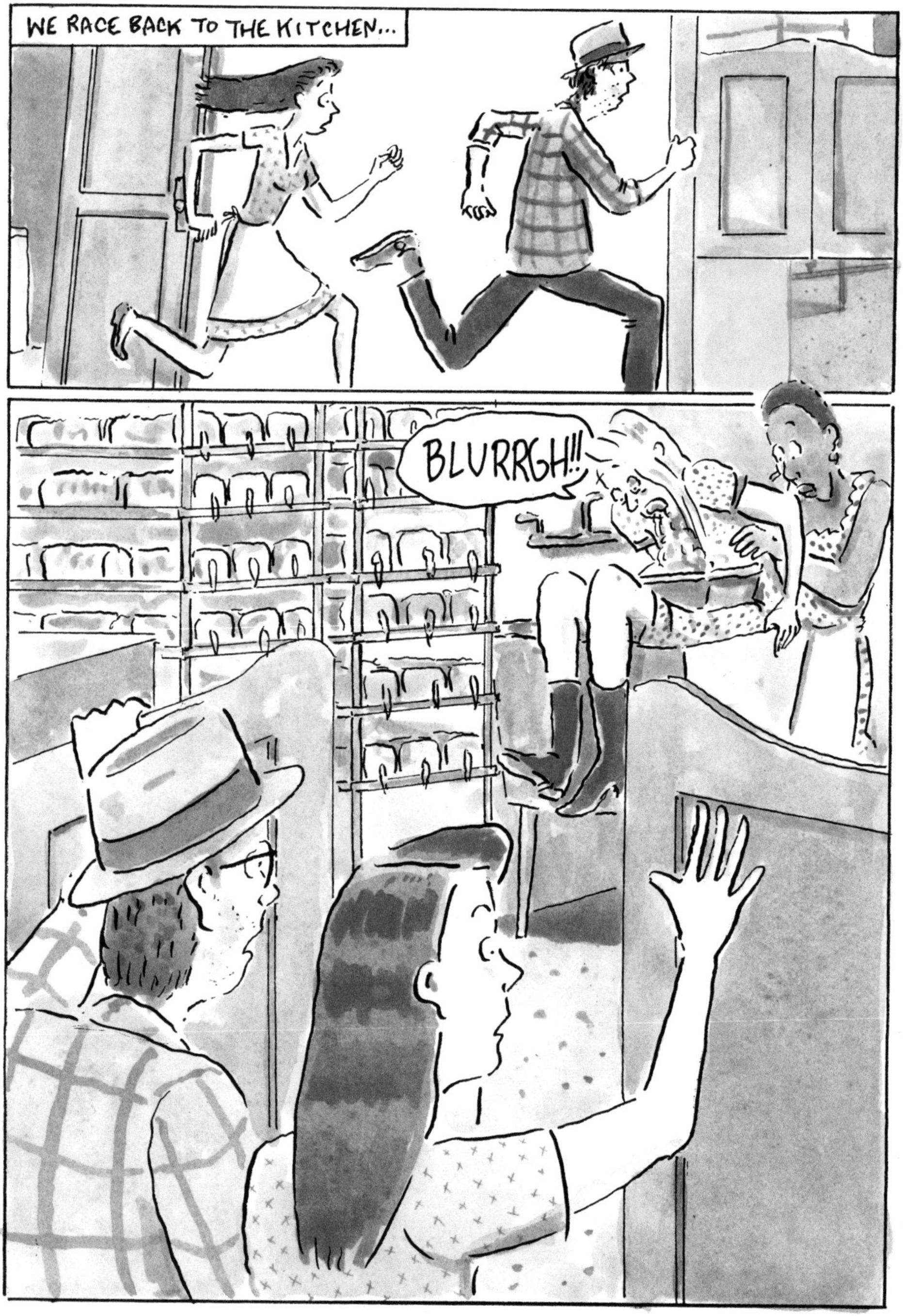
WE RACE BACK TO THE KITCHEN...
BLURRGH!!

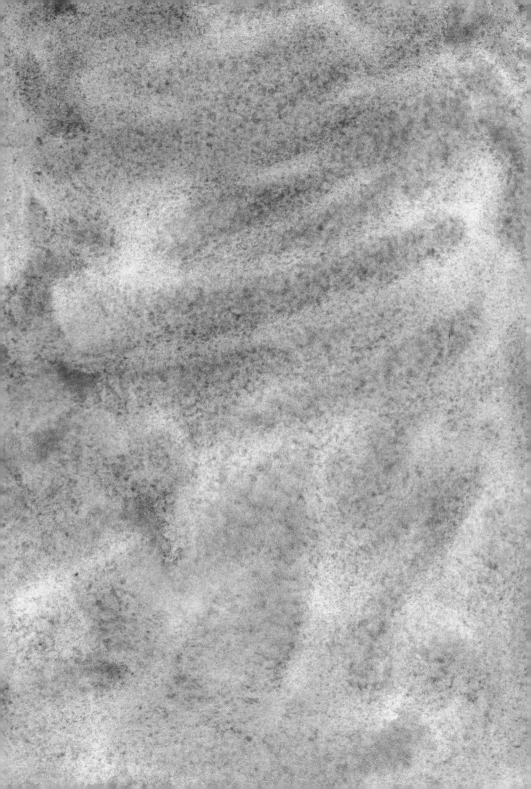

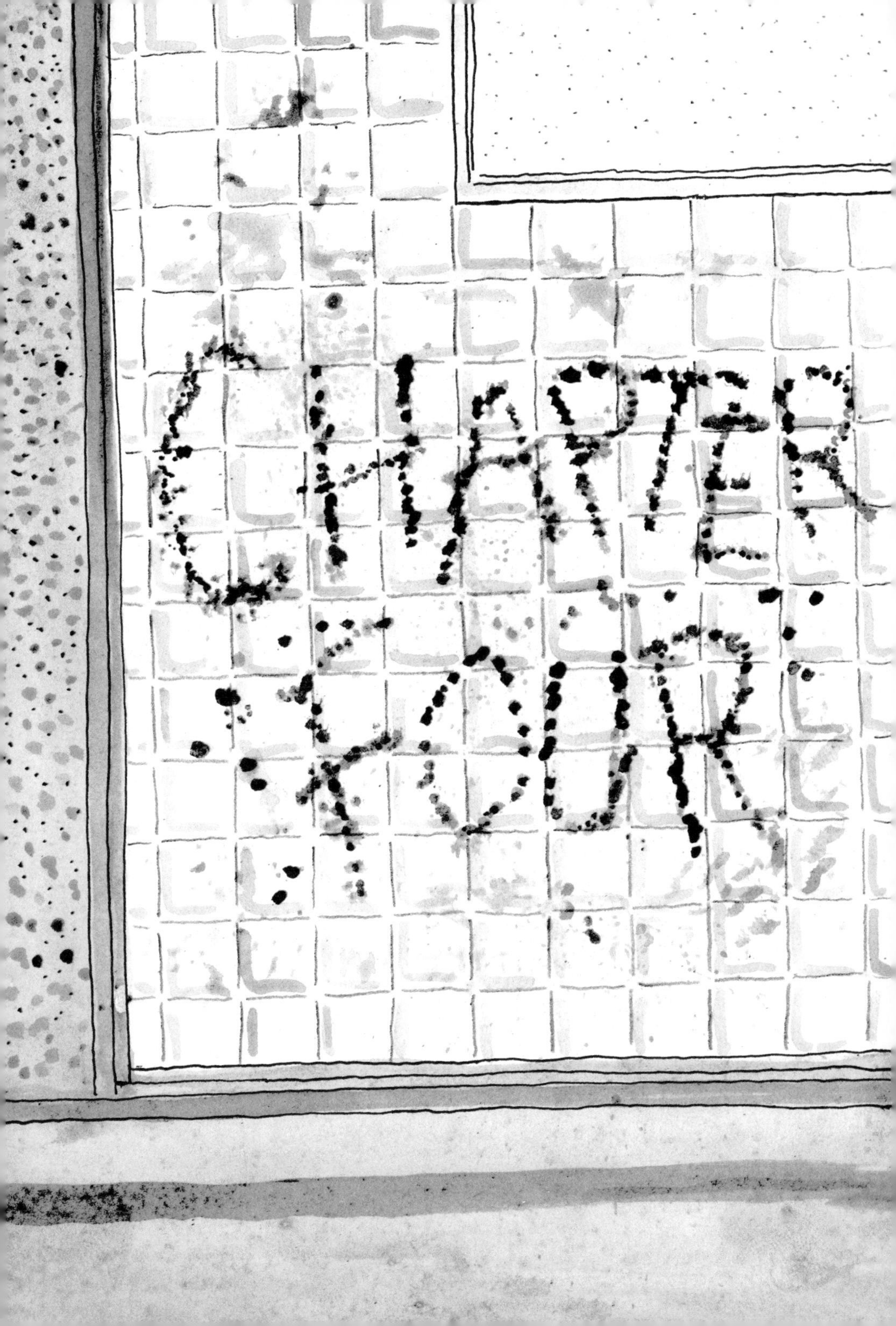
CHAPTER FOUR

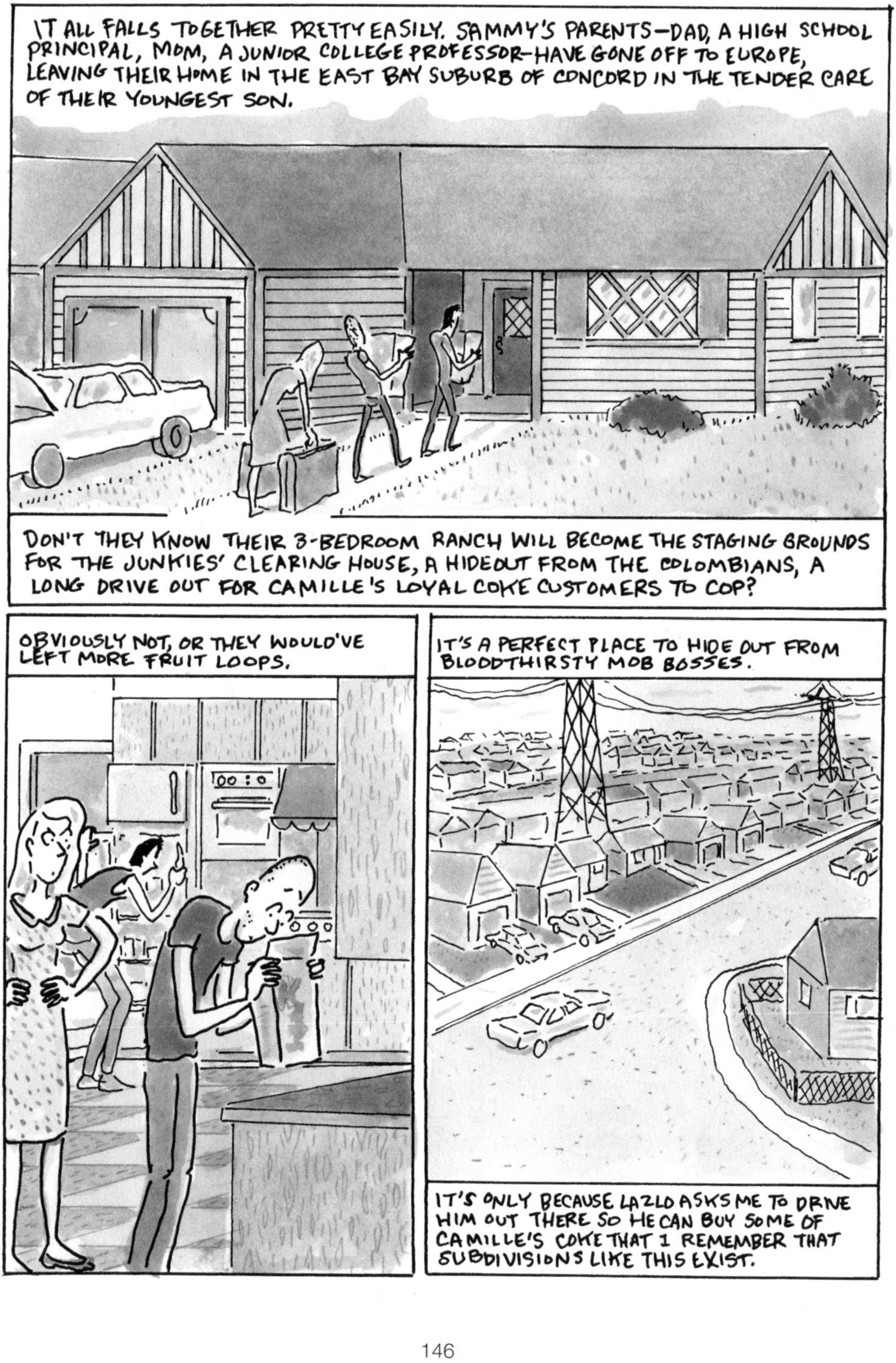
IT ALL FALLS TOGETHER PRETTY EASILY. SAMMY'S PARENTS—DAD, A HIGH SCHOOL PRINCIPAL, MOM, A JUNIOR COLLEGE PROFESSOR—HAVE GONE OFF TO EUROPE, LEAVING THEIR HOME IN THE EAST BAY SUBURB OF CONCORD IN THE TENDER CARE OF THEIR YOUNGEST SON.
DON'T THEY KNOW THEIR 3-BEDROOM RANCH WILL BECOME THE STAGING GROUNDS FOR THE JUNKIES' CLEARING HOUSE, A HIDEOUT FROM THE COLOMBIANS, A LONG DRIVE OUT FOR CAMILLE'S LOYAL COKE CUSTOMERS TO COP?
OBVIOUSLY NOT, OR THEY WOULD'VE LEFT MORE FRUIT LOOPS.
IT'S A PERFECT PLACE TO HIDE OUT FROM BLOODTHIRSTY MOB BOSSES.
IT'S ONLY BECAUSE LAZLO ASKS ME TO DRIVE HIM OUT THERE SO HE CAN BUY SOME OF CAMILLE'S COKE THAT I REMEMBER THAT SUBDIVISIONS LIKE THIS EXIST.

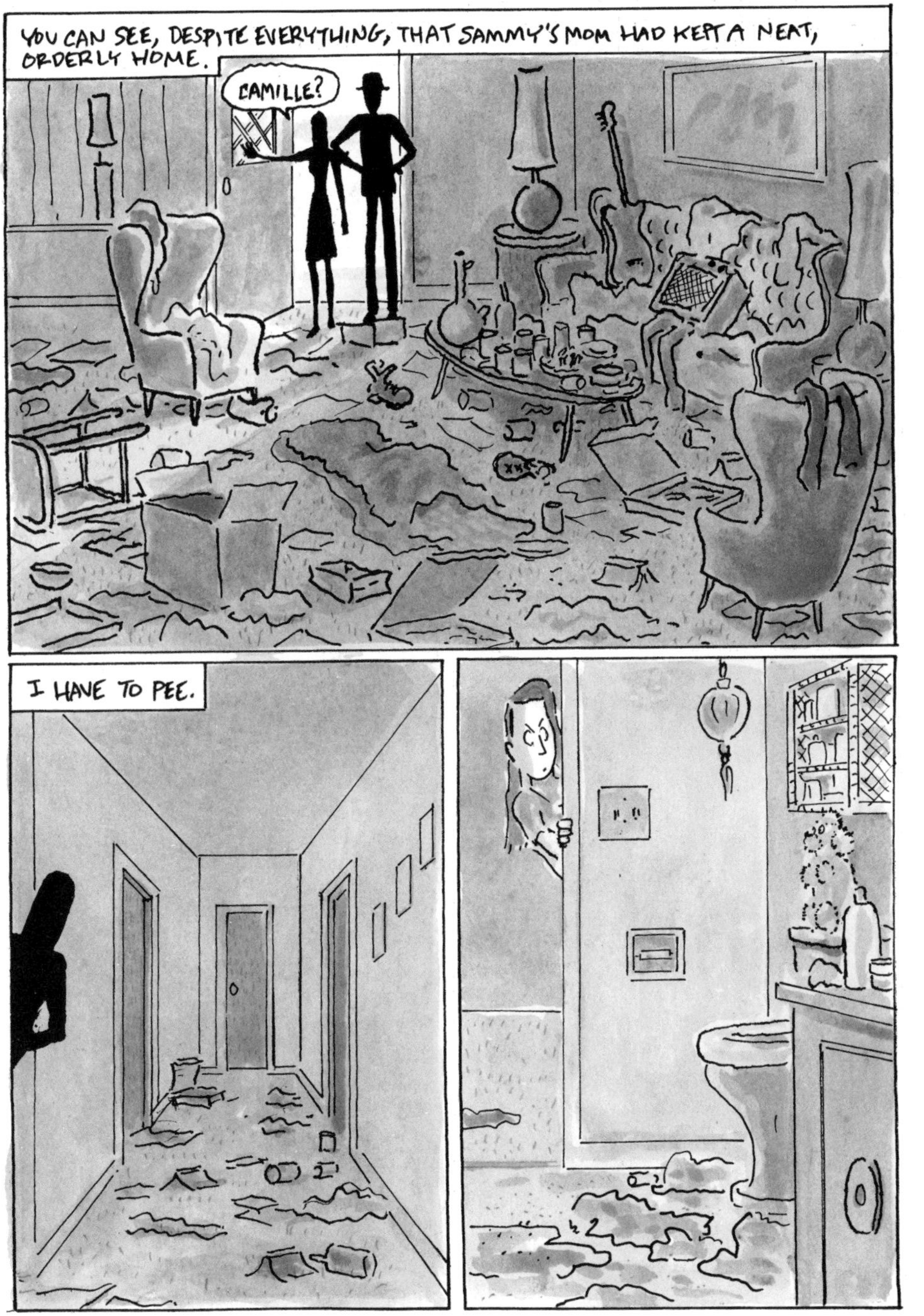
YOU CAN SEE, DESPITE EVERYTHING, THAT SAMMY'S MOM HAD KEPT A NEAT, ORDERLY HOME.
CAMILLE?
I HAVE TO PEE.

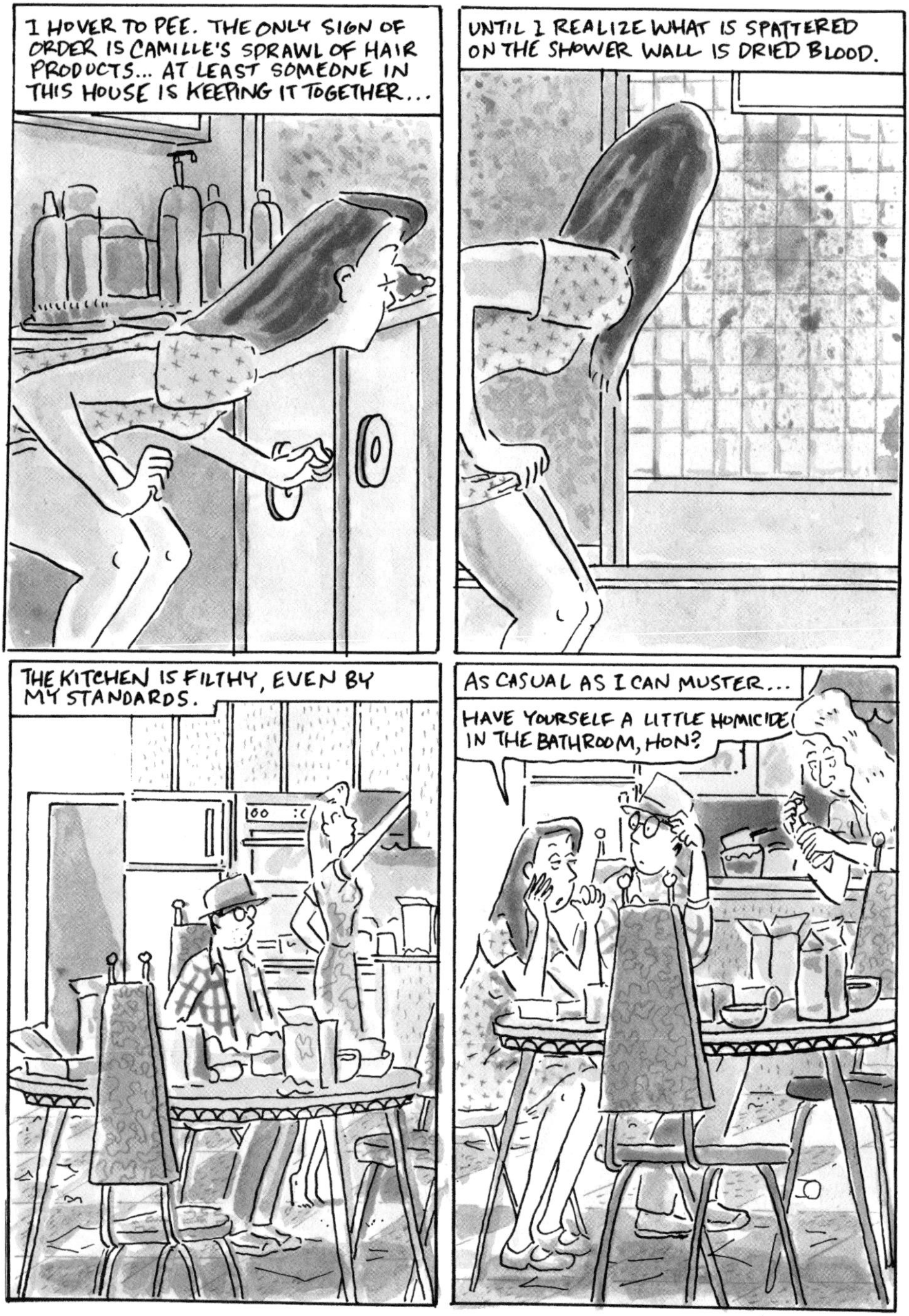
I HOVER TO PEE. THE ONLY SIGN OF ORDER IS CAMILLE'S SPRAWL OF HAIR PRODUCTS... AT LEAST SOMEONE IN THIS HOUSE IS KEEPING IT TOGETHER...
UNTIL I REALIZE WHAT IS SPATTERED ON THE SHOWER WALL IS DRIED BLOOD.
THE KITCHEN IS FILTHY, EVEN BY MY STANDARDS.
AS CASUAL AS I CAN MUSTER...
HAVE YOURSELF A LITTLE HOMICIDE IN THE BATHROOM, HON?

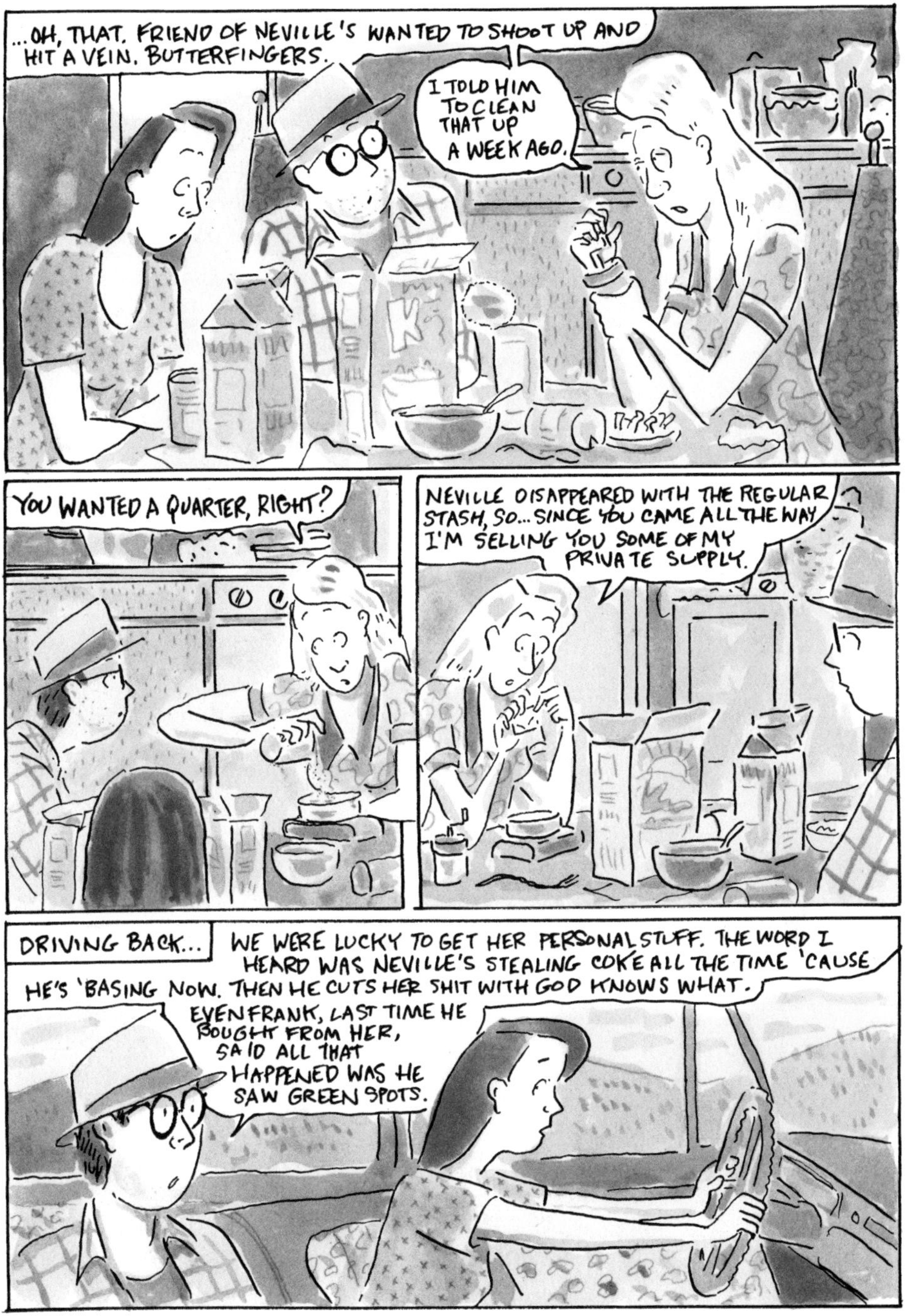
...OH, THAT. FRIEND OF NEVILLE'S WANTED TO SHOOT UP AND HIT A VEIN. BUTTERFINGERS.
I TOLD HIM TO CLEAN THAT UP A WEEK AGO.
YOU WANTED A QUARTER, RIGHT?
NEVILLE DISAPPEARED WITH THE REGULAR STASH, SO... SINCE YOU CAME ALL THE WAY I'M SELLING YOU SOME OF MY PRIVATE SUPPLY.
DRIVING BACK...
WE WERE LUCKY TO GET HER PERSONAL STUFF. THE WORD I HEARD WAS NEVILLE'S STEALING COKE ALL THE TIME 'CAUSE HE'S 'BASING NOW. THEN HE CUTS HER SHIT WITH GOD KNOWS WHAT.
EVEN FRANK, LAST TIME HE BOUGHT FROM HER, SAID ALL THAT HAPPENED WAS HE SAW GREEN SPOTS.

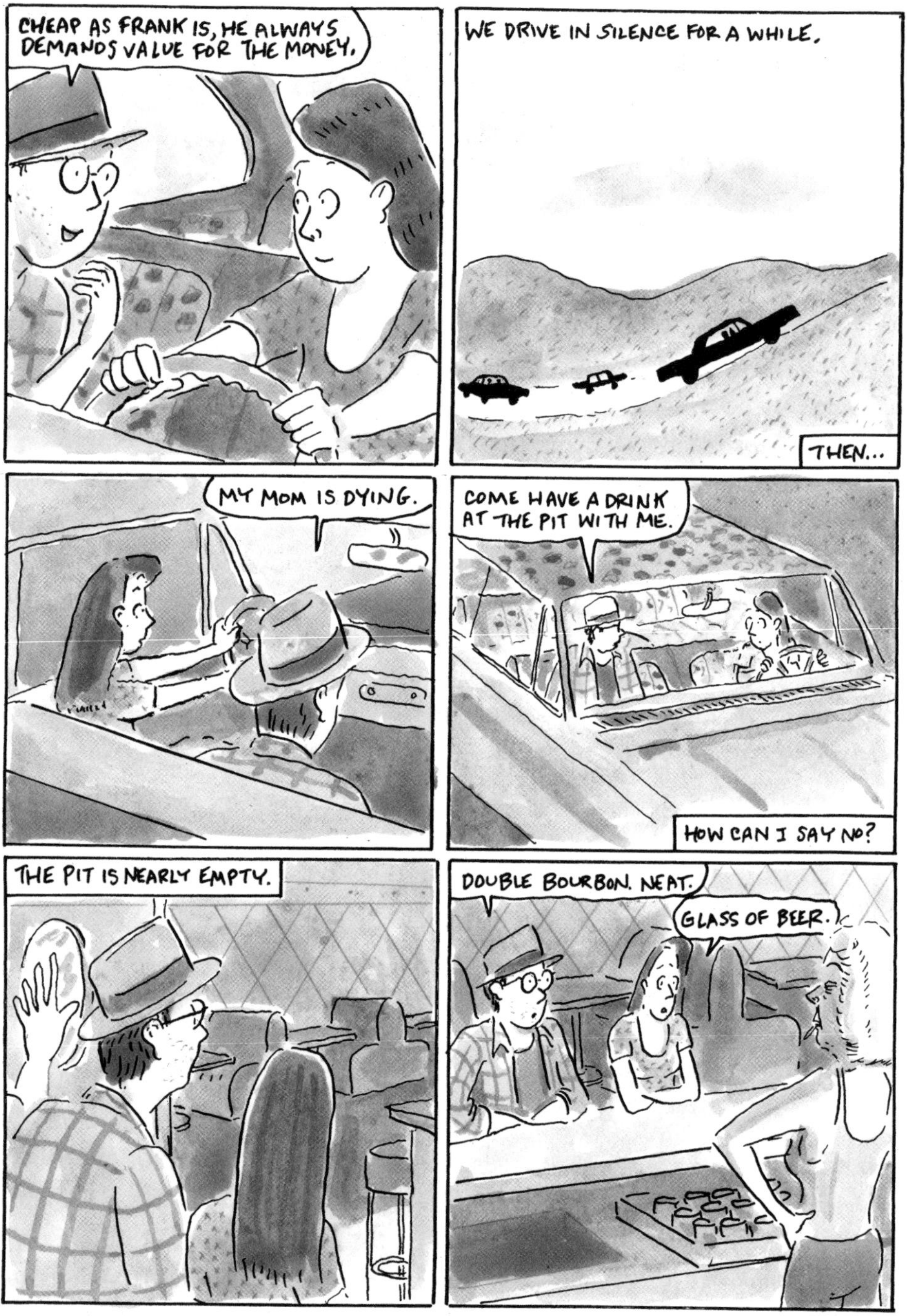
CHEAP AS FRANK IS, HE ALWAYS DEMANDS VALUE FOR THE MONEY.
WE DRIVE IN SILENCE FOR A WHILE.
THEN...
MY MOM IS DYING.
COME HAVE A DRINK AT THE PIT WITH ME.
HOW CAN I SAY NO?
THE PIT IS NEARLY EMPTY.
DOUBLE BOURBON. NEAT.
GLASS OF BEER.

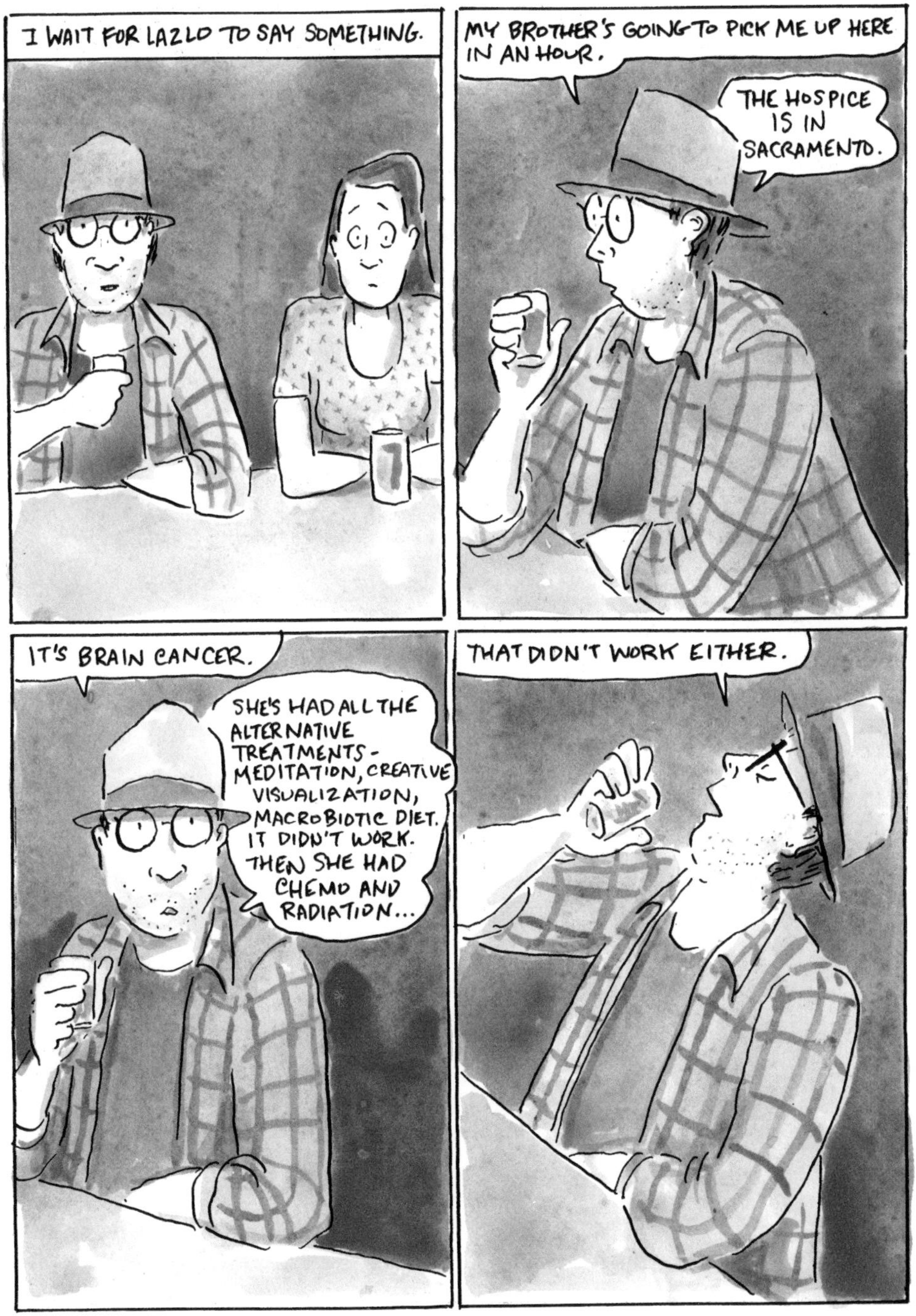
I WAIT FOR LAZLO TO SAY SOMETHING.
MY BROTHER'S GOING TO PICK ME UP HERE IN AN HOUR.
THE HOSPICE IS IN SACRAMENTO.
IT'S BRAIN CANCER.
SHE'S HAD ALL THE ALTERNATIVE TREATMENTS - MEDITATION, CREATIVE VISUALIZATION, MACROBIOTIC DIET. IT DIDN'T WORK. THEN SHE HAD CHEMO AND RADIATION...
THAT DIDN'T WORK EITHER.

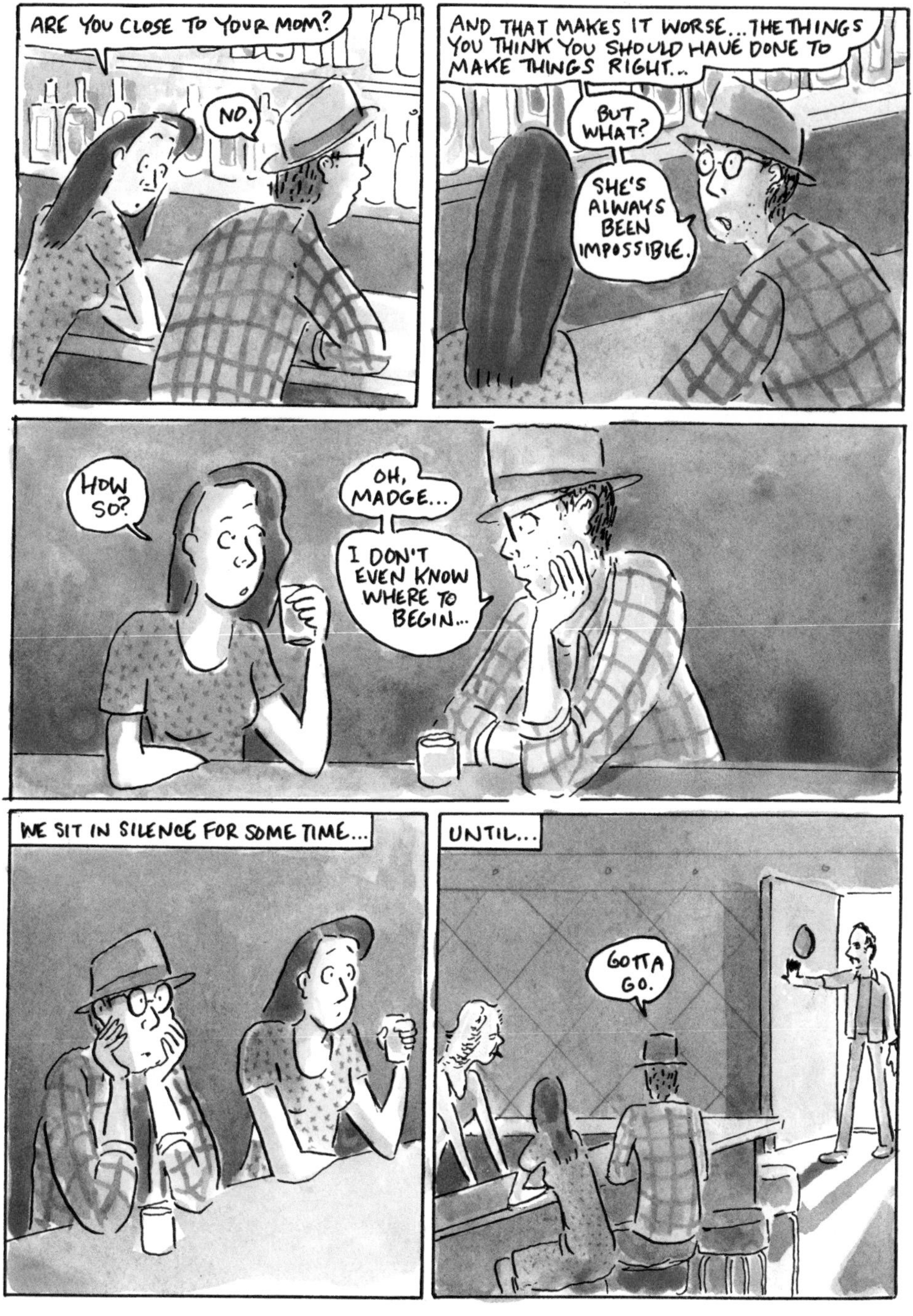
ARE YOU CLOSE TO YOUR MOM?
NO.
AND THAT MAKES IT WORSE... THE THINGS YOU THINK YOU SHOULD HAVE DONE TO MAKE THINGS RIGHT...
BUT WHAT?
SHE'S ALWAYS BEEN IMPOSSIBLE.
HOW SO?
OH, MADGE...
I DON'T EVEN KNOW WHERE TO BEGIN...
WE SIT IN SILENCE FOR SOME TIME...
UNTIL...
GOTTA GO.

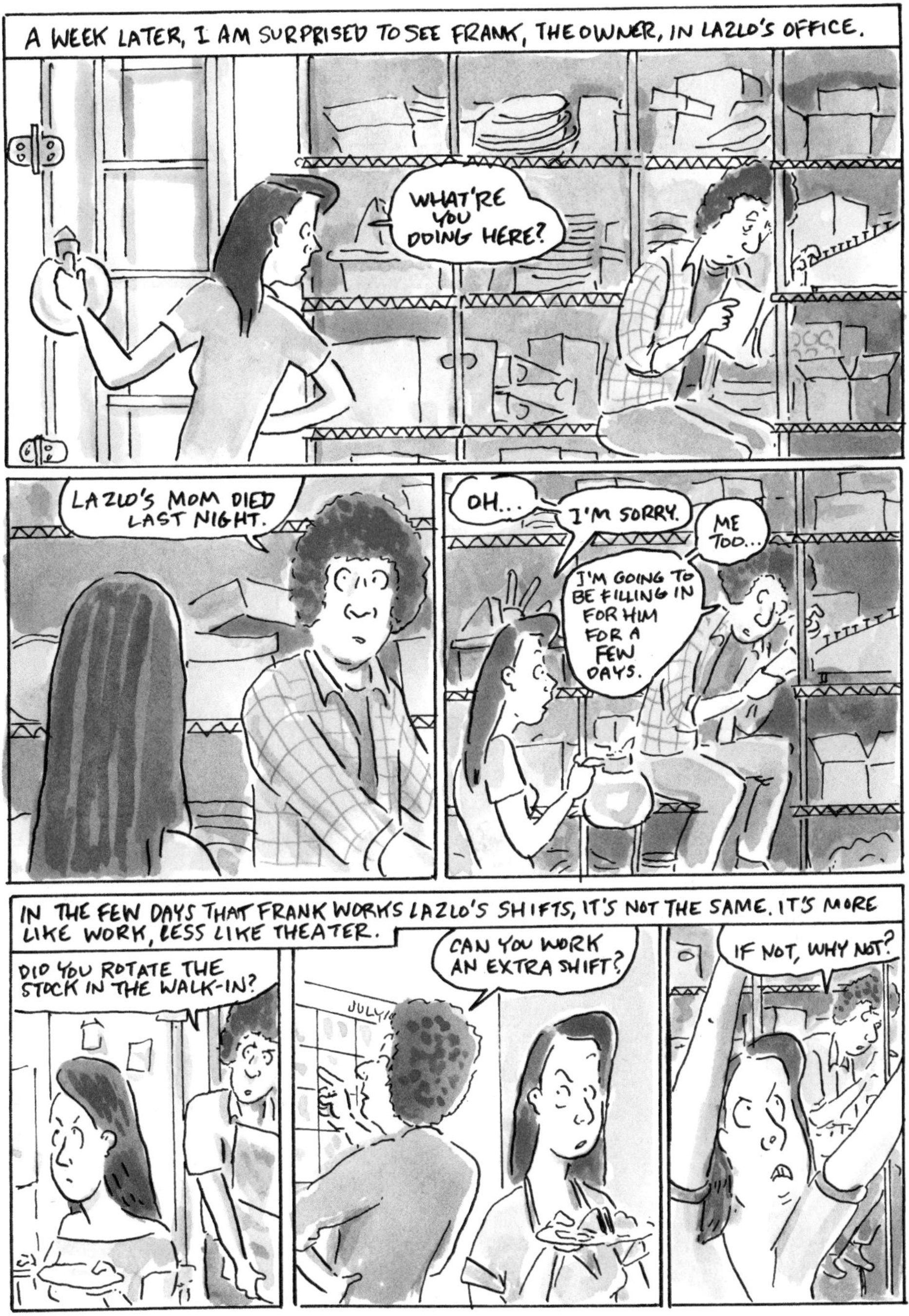
A WEEK LATER, I AM SURPRISED TO SEE FRANK, THE OWNER, IN LAZLO'S OFFICE.
WHAT'RE YOU DOING HERE?
LAZLO'S MOM DIED LAST NIGHT.
OH...
I'M SORRY.
ME TOO...
I'M GOING TO BE FILLING IN FOR HIM FOR A FEW DAYS.
IN THE FEW DAYS THAT FRANK WORKS LAZLO'S SHIFTS, IT'S NOT THE SAME. IT'S MORE LIKE WORK, LESS LIKE THEATER.
DID YOU ROTATE THE STOCK IN THE WALK-IN?
CAN YOU WORK AN EXTRA SHIFT?
IF NOT, WHY NOT?

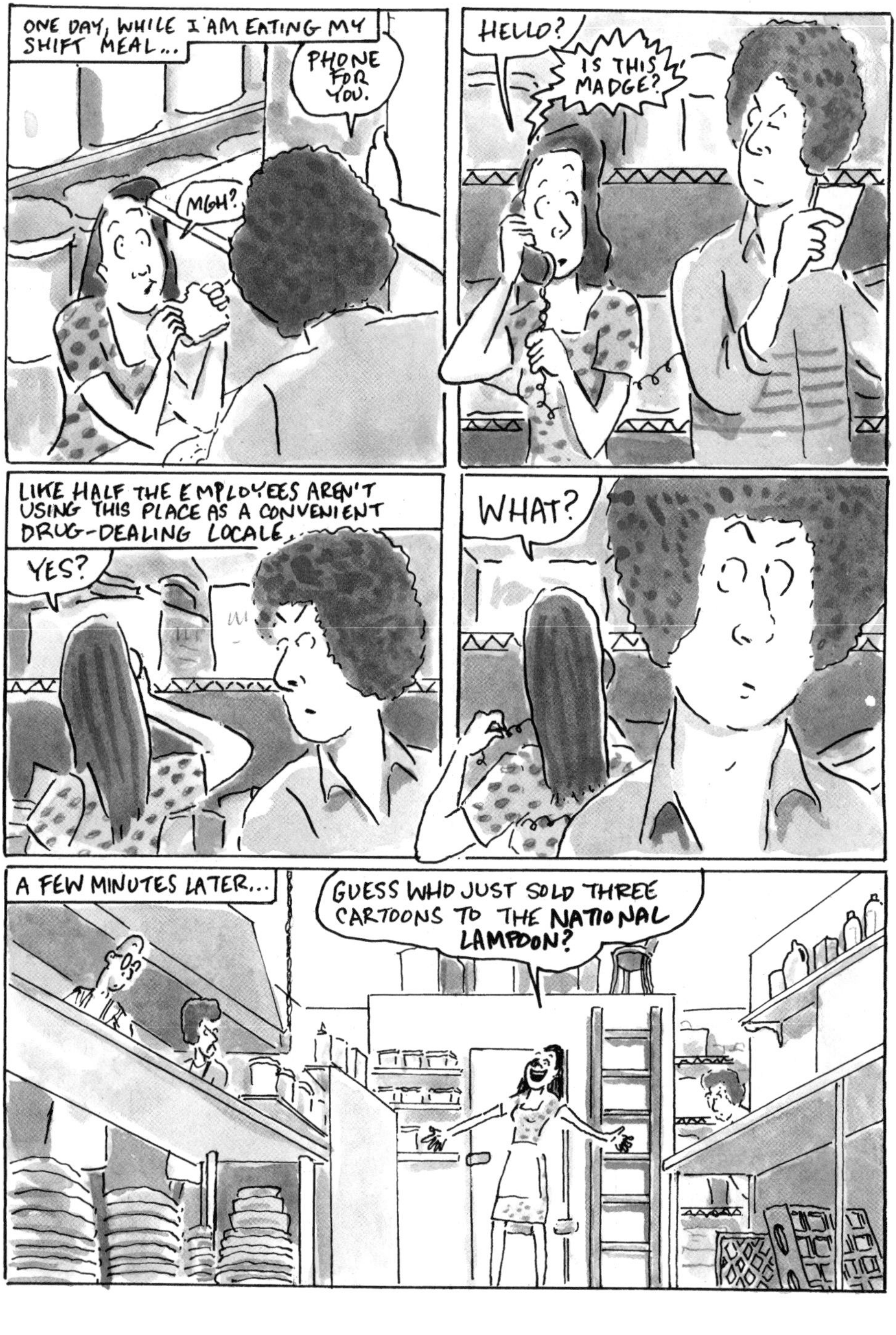
ONE DAY, WHILE I AM EATING MY SHIFT MEAL...
PHONE FOR YOU.
MGH?
HELLO?
IS THIS MADGE?
LIKE HALF THE EMPLOYEES AREN'T USING THIS PLACE AS A CONVENIENT DRUG-DEALING LOCALE...
YES?
WHAT?
A FEW MINUTES LATER...
GUESS WHO JUST SOLD THREE CARTOONS TO THE NATIONAL LAMPOON?

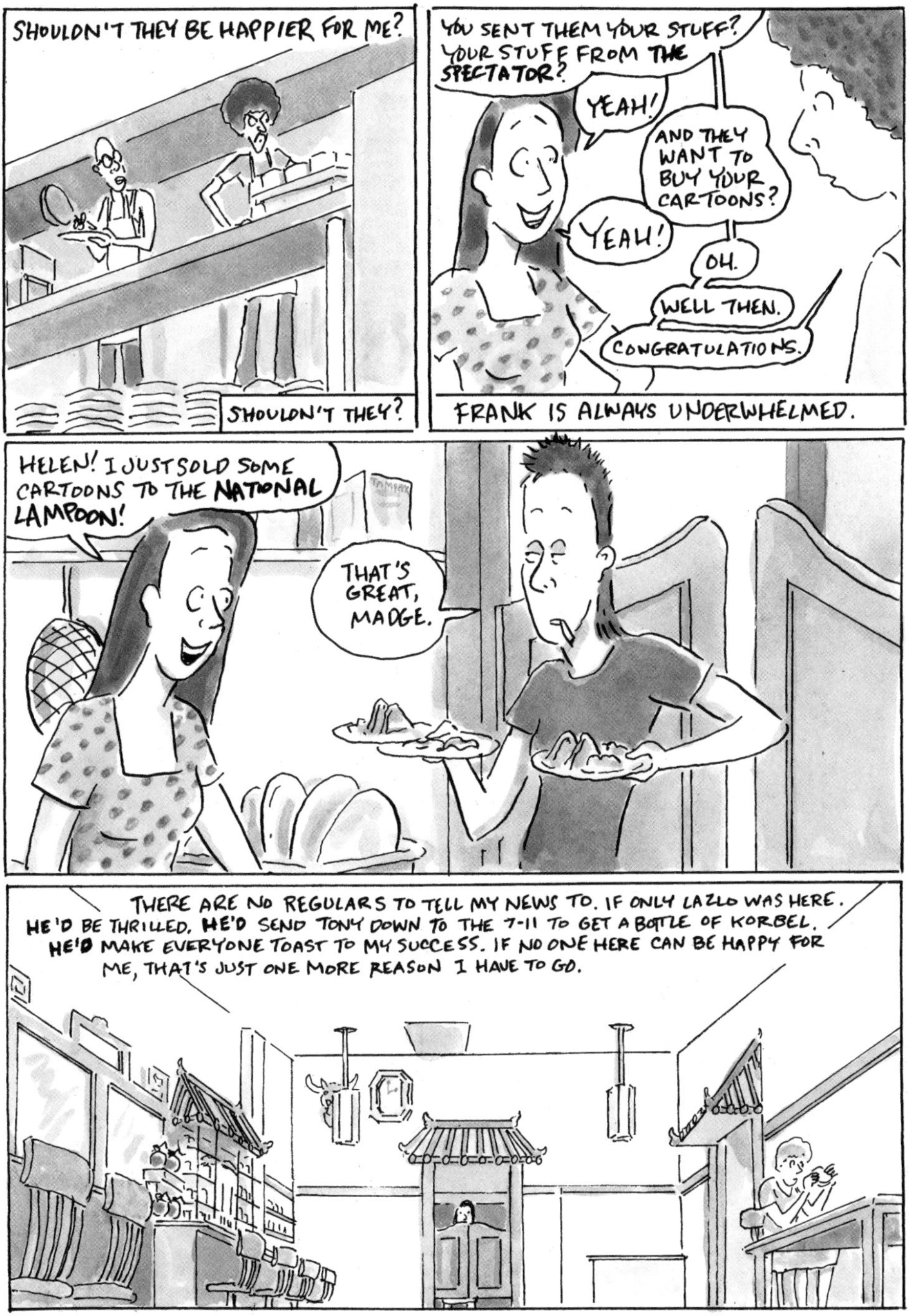
SHOULDN'T THEY BE HAPPIER FOR ME?
SHOULDN'T THEY?
YOU SENT THEM YOUR STUFF? YOUR STUFF FROM THE SPECTATOR?
YEAH!
AND THEY WANT TO BUY YOUR CARTOONS?
YEAH!
OH.
WELL THEN.
CONGRATULATIONS.
FRANK IS ALWAYS UNDERWHELMED.
HELEN! I JUST SOLD SOME CARTOONS TO THE NATIONAL LAMPOON!
THAT'S GREAT, MADGE.
THERE ARE NO REGULARS TO TELL MY NEWS TO. IF ONLY LAZLO WAS HERE. HE'D BE THRILLED. HE'D SEND TONY DOWN TO THE 7-11 TO GET A BOTTLE OF KORBEL. HE'D MAKE EVERYONE TOAST TO MY SUCCESS. IF NO ONE HERE CAN BE HAPPY FOR ME, THAT'S JUST ONE MORE REASON I HAVE TO GO.

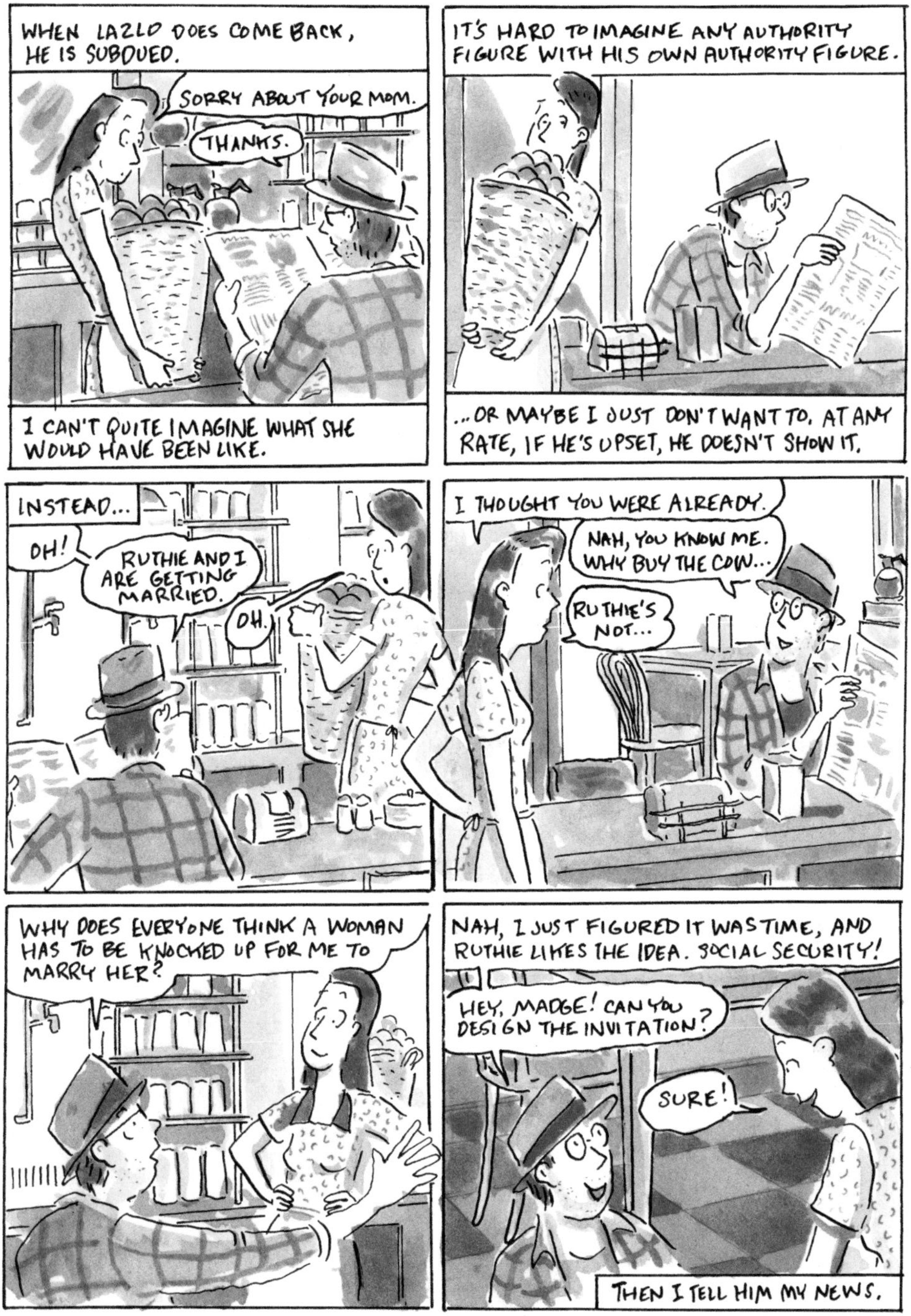
WHEN LAZLO DOES COME BACK, HE IS SUBDUED.
SORRY ABOUT YOUR MOM.
THANKS.
I CAN'T QUITE IMAGINE WHAT SHE WOULD HAVE BEEN LIKE.
IT'S HARD TO IMAGINE ANY AUTHORITY FIGURE WITH HIS OWN AUTHORITY FIGURE.
...OR MAYBE I JUST DON'T WANT TO. AT ANY RATE, IF HE'S UPSET, HE DOESN'T SHOW IT.
INSTEAD...
OH!
RUTHIE AND I ARE GETTING MARRIED.
OH.
I THOUGHT YOU WERE ALREADY.
NAH, YOU KNOW ME. WHY BUY THE COW...
RUTHIE'S NOT...
WHY DOES EVERYONE THINK A WOMAN HAS TO BE KNOCKED UP FOR ME TO MARRY HER?
NAH, I JUST FIGURED IT WAS TIME, AND RUTHIE LIKES THE IDEA. SOCIAL SECURITY!
HEY, MADGE! CAN YOU DESIGN THE INVITATION?
SURE!
THEN I TELL HIM MY NEWS.

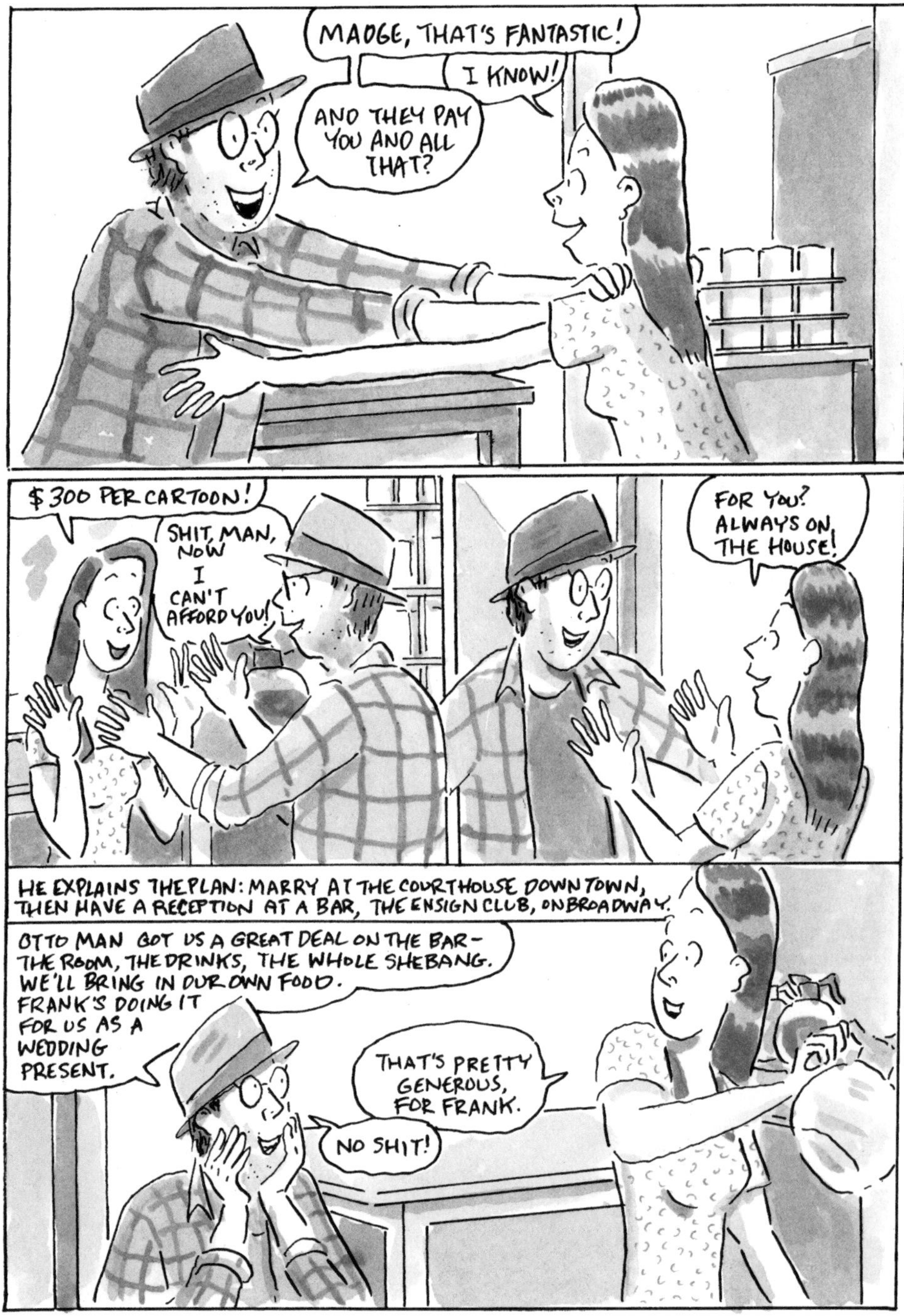
MADGE, THAT'S FANTASTIC!
AND THEY PAY YOU AND ALL THAT?
I KNOW!
$300 PER CARTOON!
SHIT, MAN, NOW I CAN'T AFFORD YOU!
FOR YOU? ALWAYS ON THE HOUSE!
HE EXPLAINS THE PLAN: MARRY AT THE COURTHOUSE DOWNTOWN, THEN HAVE A RECEPTION AT A BAR, THE ENSIGN CLUB, ON BROADWAY.
OTTO MAN GOT US A GREAT DEAL ON THE BAR - THE ROOM, THE DRINKS, THE WHOLE SHEBANG. WE'LL BRING IN OUR OWN FOOD. FRANK'S DOING IT FOR US AS A WEDDING PRESENT.
THAT'S PRETTY GENEROUS, FOR FRANK.
NO SHIT!

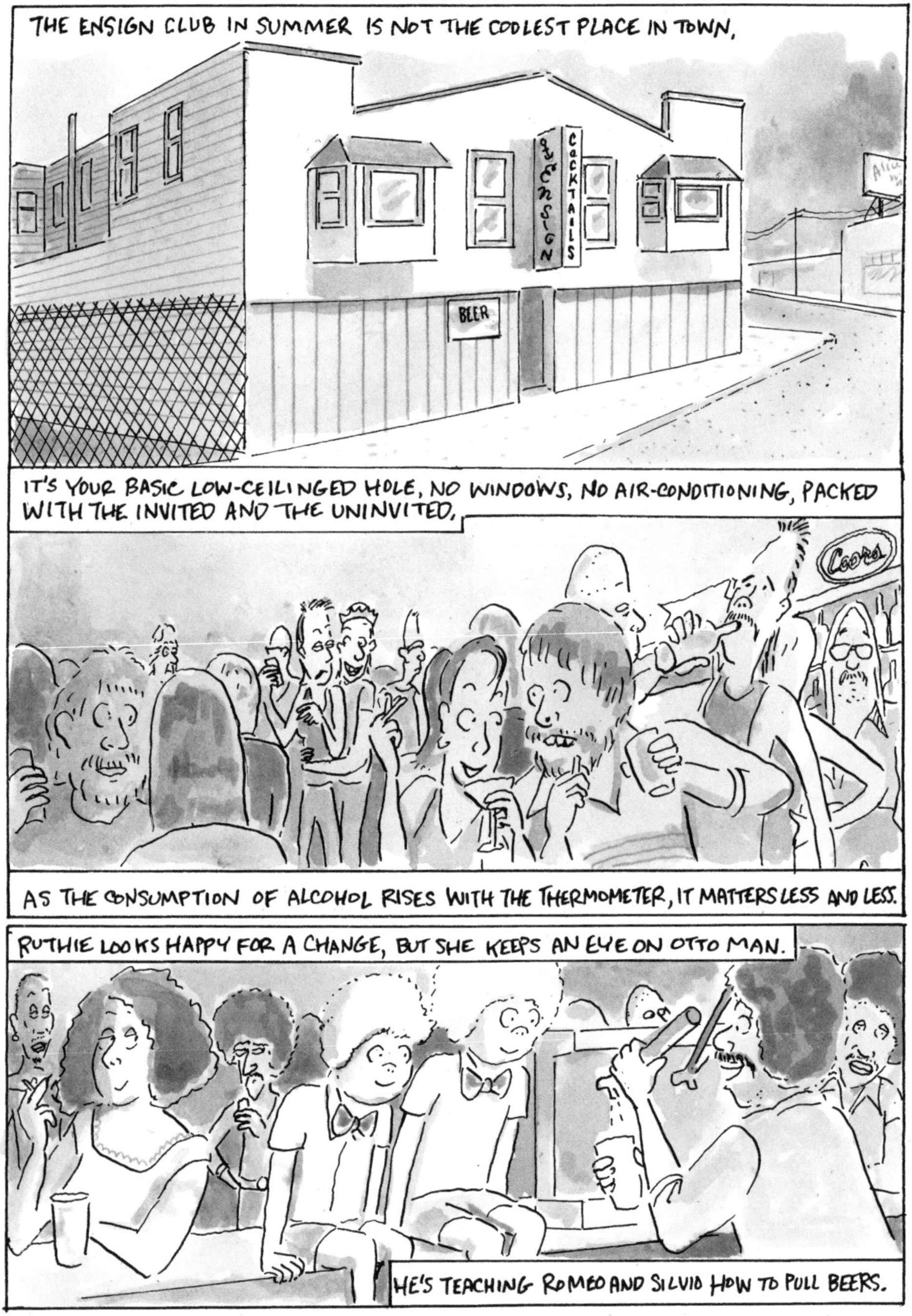
THE ENSIGN CLUB IN SUMMER IS NOT THE COOLEST PLACE IN TOWN,
ENSIGN
COCKTAILS
BEER
IT'S YOUR BASIC LOW-CEILINGED HOLE, NO WINDOWS, NO AIR-CONDITIONING, PACKED WITH THE INVITED AND THE UNINVITED,
Coors
AS THE CONSUMPTION OF ALCOHOL RISES WITH THE THERMOMETER, IT MATTERS LESS AND LESS.
RUTHIE LOOKS HAPPY FOR A CHANGE, BUT SHE KEEPS AN EYE ON OTTO MAN.
HE'S TEACHING ROMEO AND SILVIO HOW TO PULL BEERS.

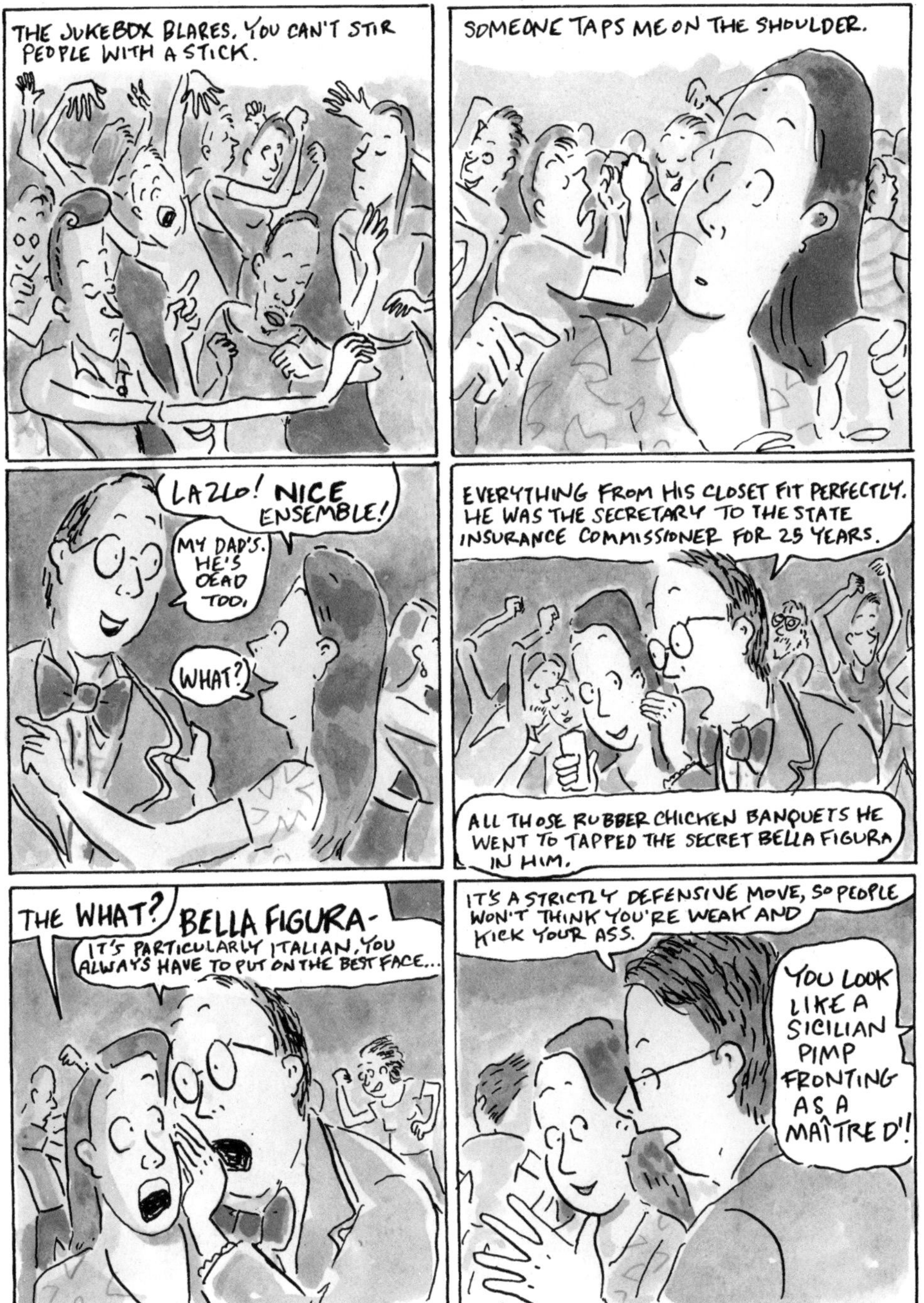
THE JUKEBOX BLARES. YOU CAN'T STIR PEOPLE WITH A STICK.
SOMEONE TAPS ME ON THE SHOULDER.
LAZLO! NICE ENSEMBLE!
MY DAD'S. HE'S DEAD TOO.
WHAT?
EVERYTHING FROM HIS CLOSET FIT PERFECTLY. HE WAS THE SECRETARY TO THE STATE INSURANCE COMMISSIONER FOR 25 YEARS.
ALL THOSE RUBBER CHICKEN BANQUETS HE WENT TO TAPPED THE SECRET BELLA FIGURA IN HIM.
THE WHAT?
BELLA FIGURA-
IT'S PARTICULARLY ITALIAN, YOU ALWAYS HAVE TO PUT ON THE BEST FACE...
IT'S A STRICTLY DEFENSIVE MOVE, SO PEOPLE WON'T THINK YOU'RE WEAK AND KICK YOUR ASS.
YOU LOOK LIKE A SICILIAN PIMP FRONTING AS A MAÎTRE D'!

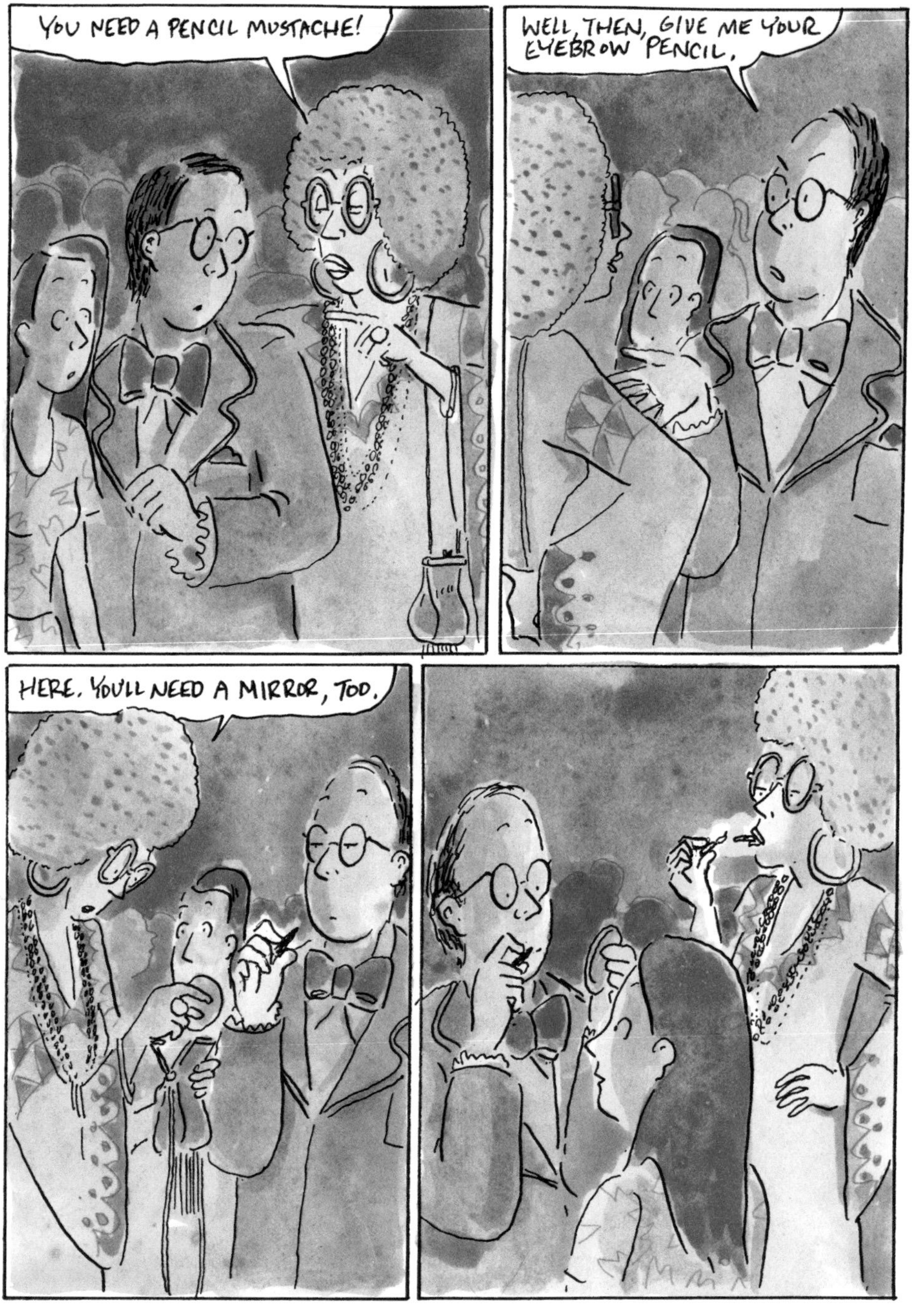
YOU NEED A PENCIL MUSTACHE!
WELL, THEN, GIVE ME YOUR EYEBROW PENCIL.
HERE. YOU'LL NEED A MIRROR, TOO.

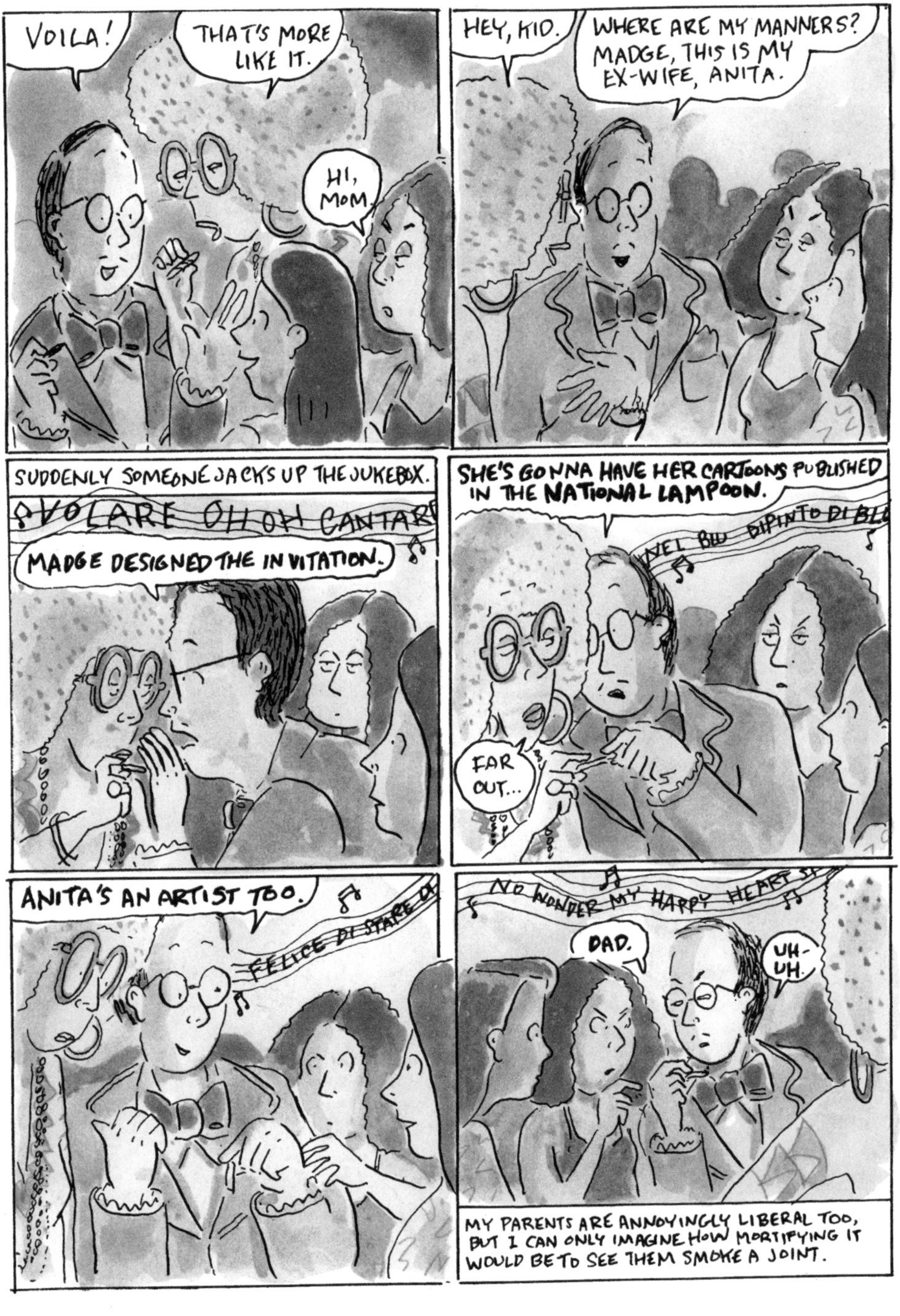
VOILA!
THAT'S MORE LIKE IT.
HI, MOM.
HEY, KID.
WHERE ARE MY MANNERS? MADGE, THIS IS MY EX-WIFE, ANITA.
SUDDENLY SOMEONE JACKS UP THE JUKEBOX.
VOLARE OH OH CANTAR
MADGE DESIGNED THE INVITATION.
SHE'S GONNA HAVE HER CARTOONS PUBLISHED IN THE NATIONAL LAMPOON.
NEL BLU DIPINTO DI BLU
FAR OUT...
ANITA'S AN ARTIST TOO.
FELICE DI STARE O
NO WONDER MY HAPPY HEART S
DAD.
UH-UH.
MY PARENTS ARE ANNOYINGLY LIBERAL TOO, BUT I CAN ONLY IMAGINE HOW MORTIFYING IT WOULD BE TO SEE THEM SMOKE A JOINT.

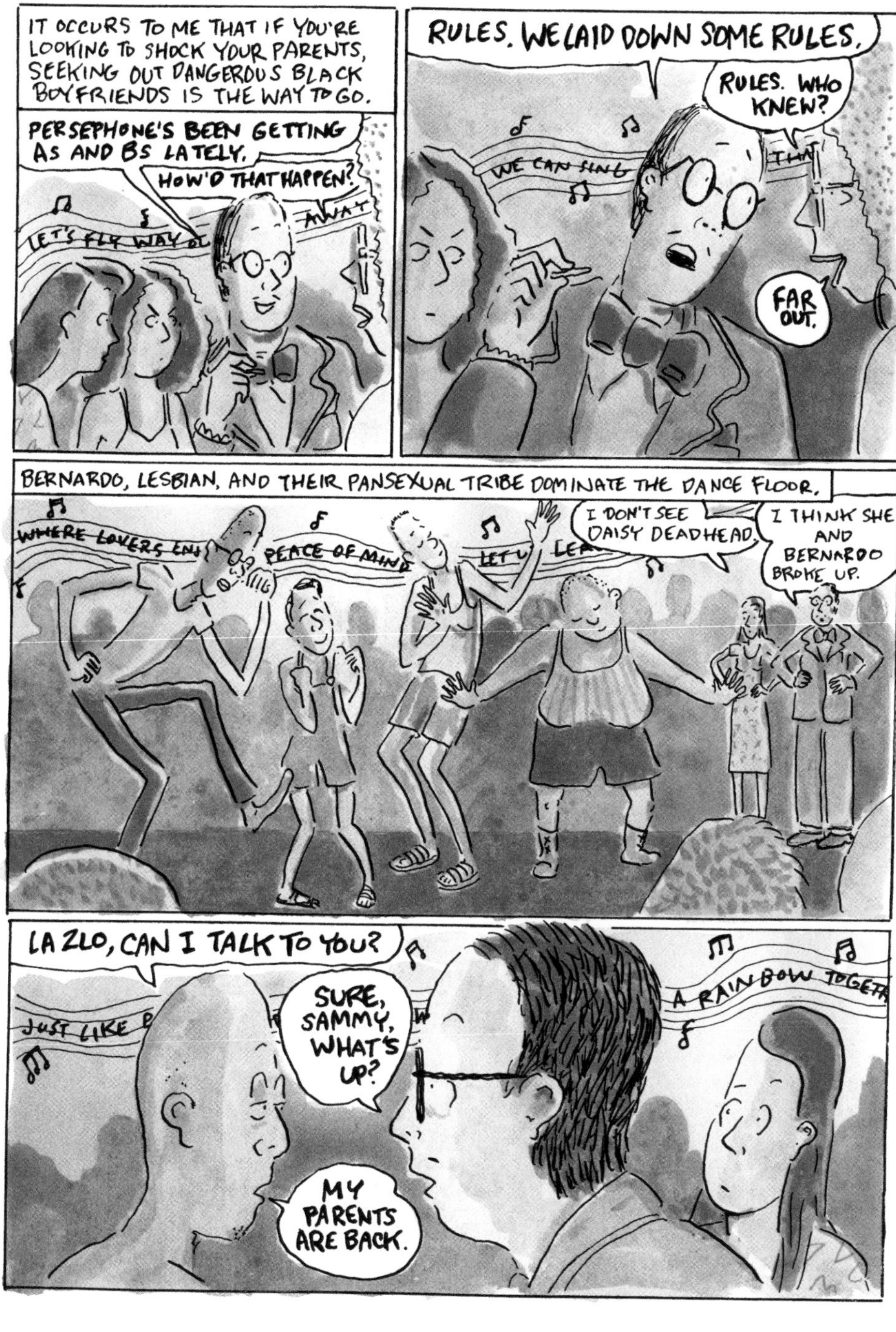
IT OCCURS TO ME THAT IF YOU'RE LOOKING TO SHOCK YOUR PARENTS, SEEKING OUT DANGEROUS BLACK BOYFRIENDS IS THE WAY TO GO.
PERSEPHONE'S BEEN GETTING AS AND BS LATELY.
HOW'D THAT HAPPEN?
LET'S FLY WAY
AWAY
RULES. WE LAID DOWN SOME RULES.
RULES. WHO KNEW?
WE CAN SING
FAR OUT.
BERNARDO, LESBIAN, AND THEIR PANSEXUAL TRIBE DOMINATE THE DANCE FLOOR.
PEACE OF MIND
I DON'T SEE DAISY DEADHEAD.
I THINK SHE AND BERNARDO BROKE UP.
LAZLO, CAN I TALK TO YOU?
SURE, SAMMY, WHAT'S UP?
A RAINBOW TOGETH
JUST LIKE
MY PARENTS ARE BACK.

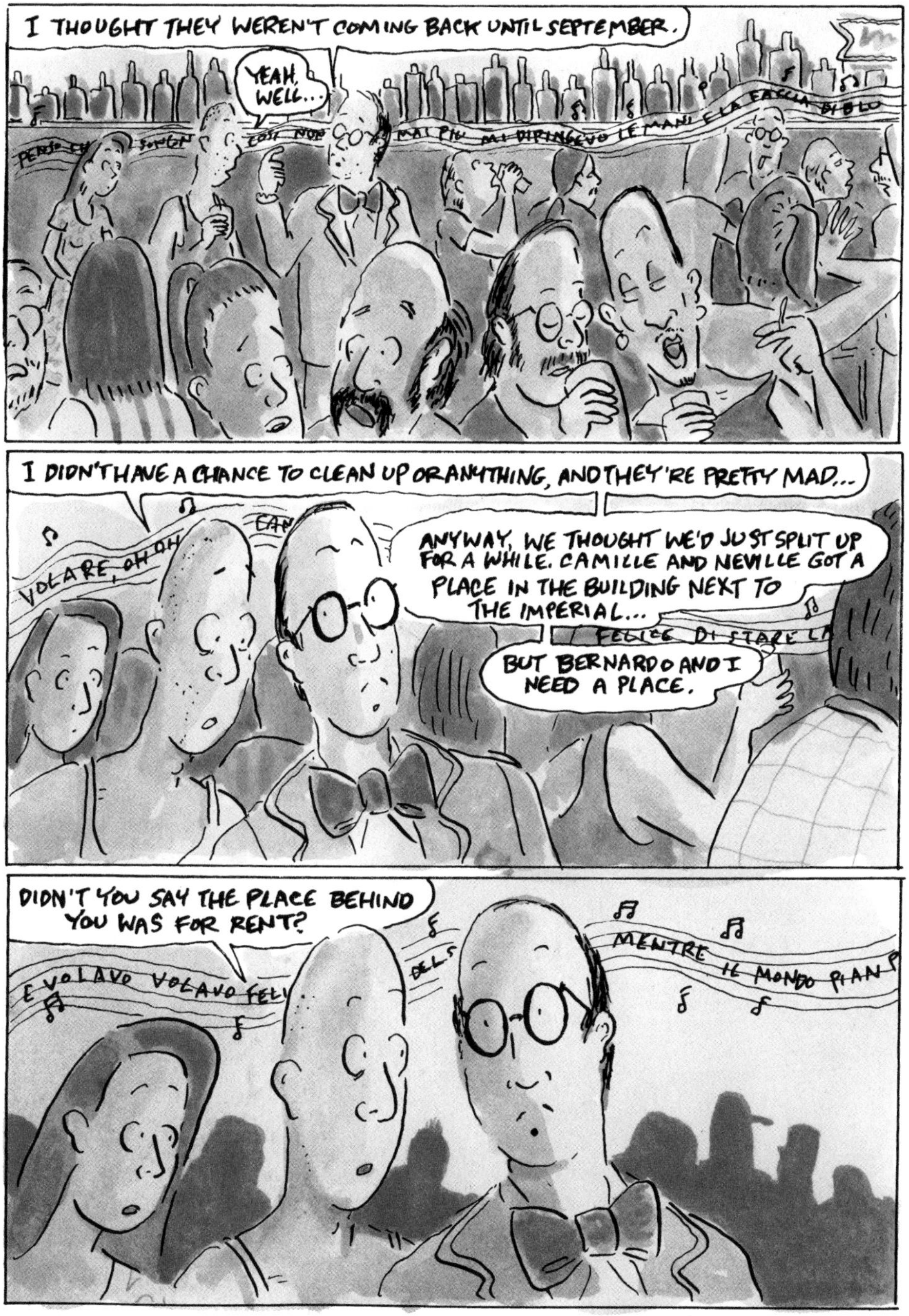
I THOUGHT THEY WEREN'T COMING BACK UNTIL SEPTEMBER.
YEAH, WELL...
I DIDN'T HAVE A CHANCE TO CLEAN UP OR ANYTHING, AND THEY'RE PRETTY MAD...
ANYWAY, WE THOUGHT WE'D JUST SPLIT UP FOR A WHILE. CAMILLE AND NEVILLE GOT A PLACE IN THE BUILDING NEXT TO THE IMPERIAL...
BUT BERNARDO AND I NEED A PLACE.
DIDN'T YOU SAY THE PLACE BEHIND YOU WAS FOR RENT?

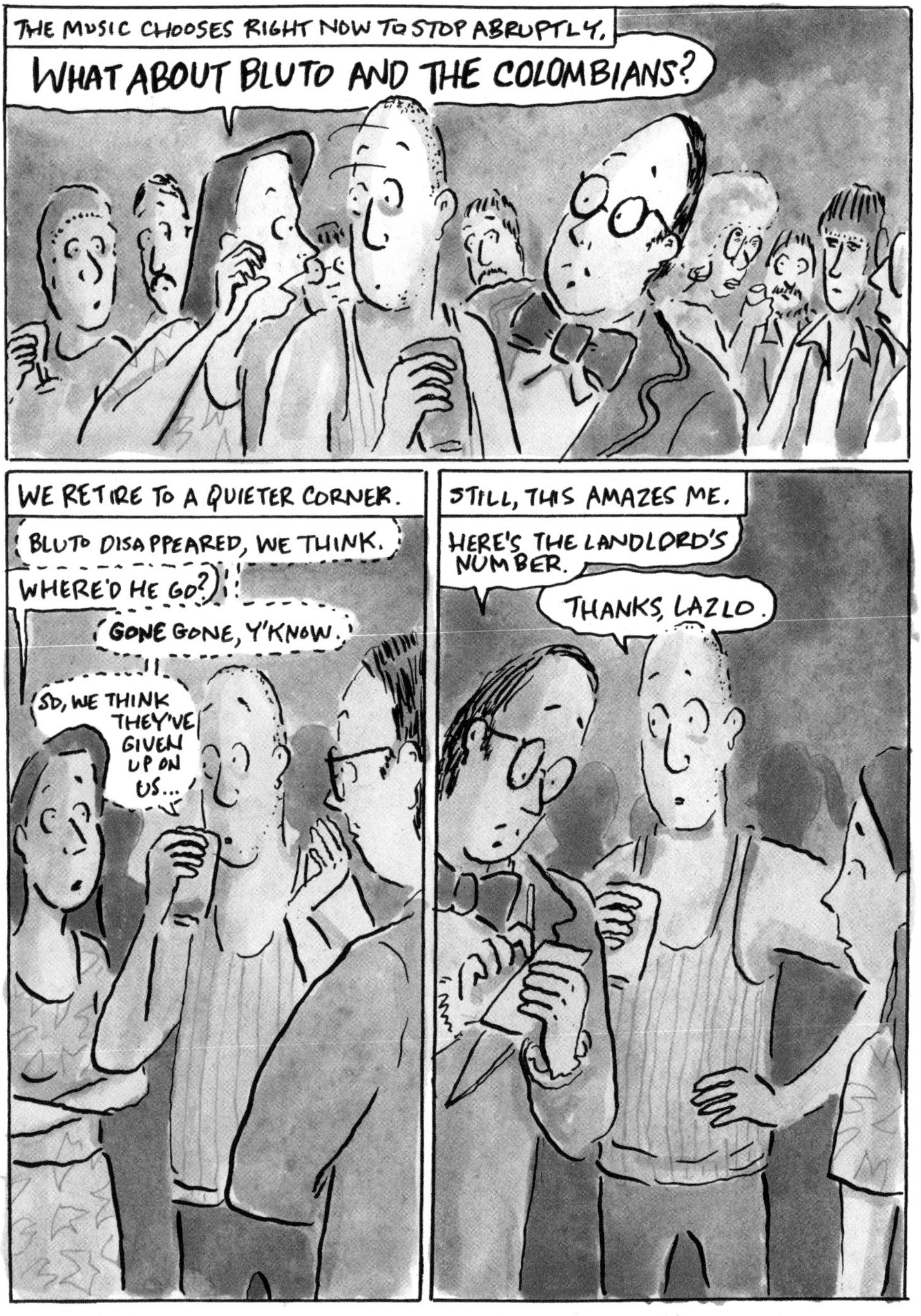
THE MUSIC CHOOSES RIGHT NOW TO STOP ABRUPTLY.
WHAT ABOUT BLUTO AND THE COLOMBIANS?
WE RETIRE TO A QUIETER CORNER.
BLUTO DISAPPEARED, WE THINK.
WHERE'D HE GO?
GONE GONE, Y'KNOW.
SO, WE THINK THEY'VE GIVEN UP ON US...
STILL, THIS AMAZES ME.
HERE'S THE LANDLORD'S NUMBER.
THANKS, LAZLO.

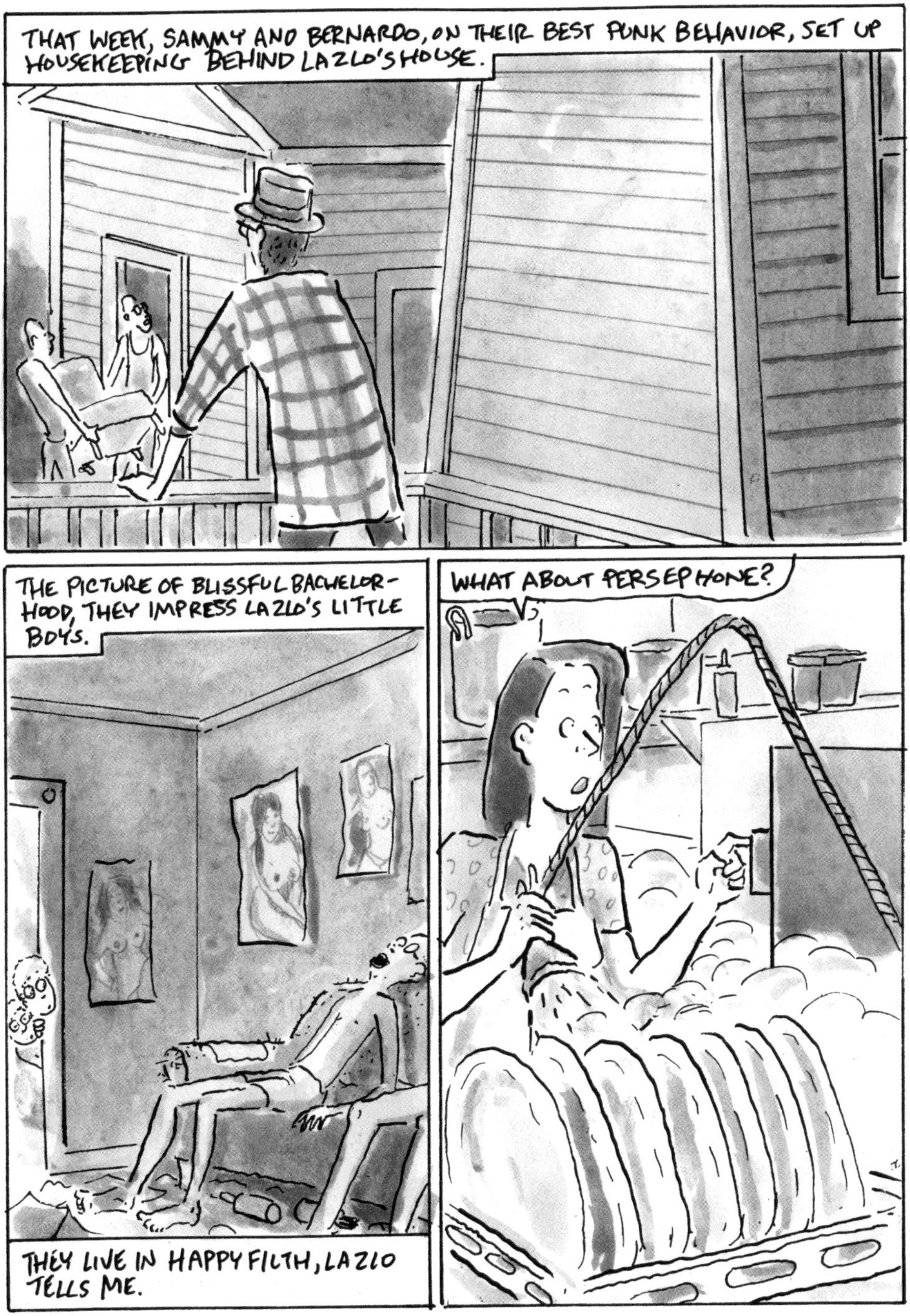
THAT WEEK, SAMMY AND BERNARDO, ON THEIR BEST PUNK BEHAVIOR, SET UP HOUSEKEEPING BEHIND LAZLO'S HOUSE.
THE PICTURE OF BLISSFUL BACHELOR-HOOD, THEY IMPRESS LAZLO'S LITTLE BOYS.
THEY LIVE IN HAPPY FILTH, LAZLO TELLS ME.
WHAT ABOUT PERSEPHONE?

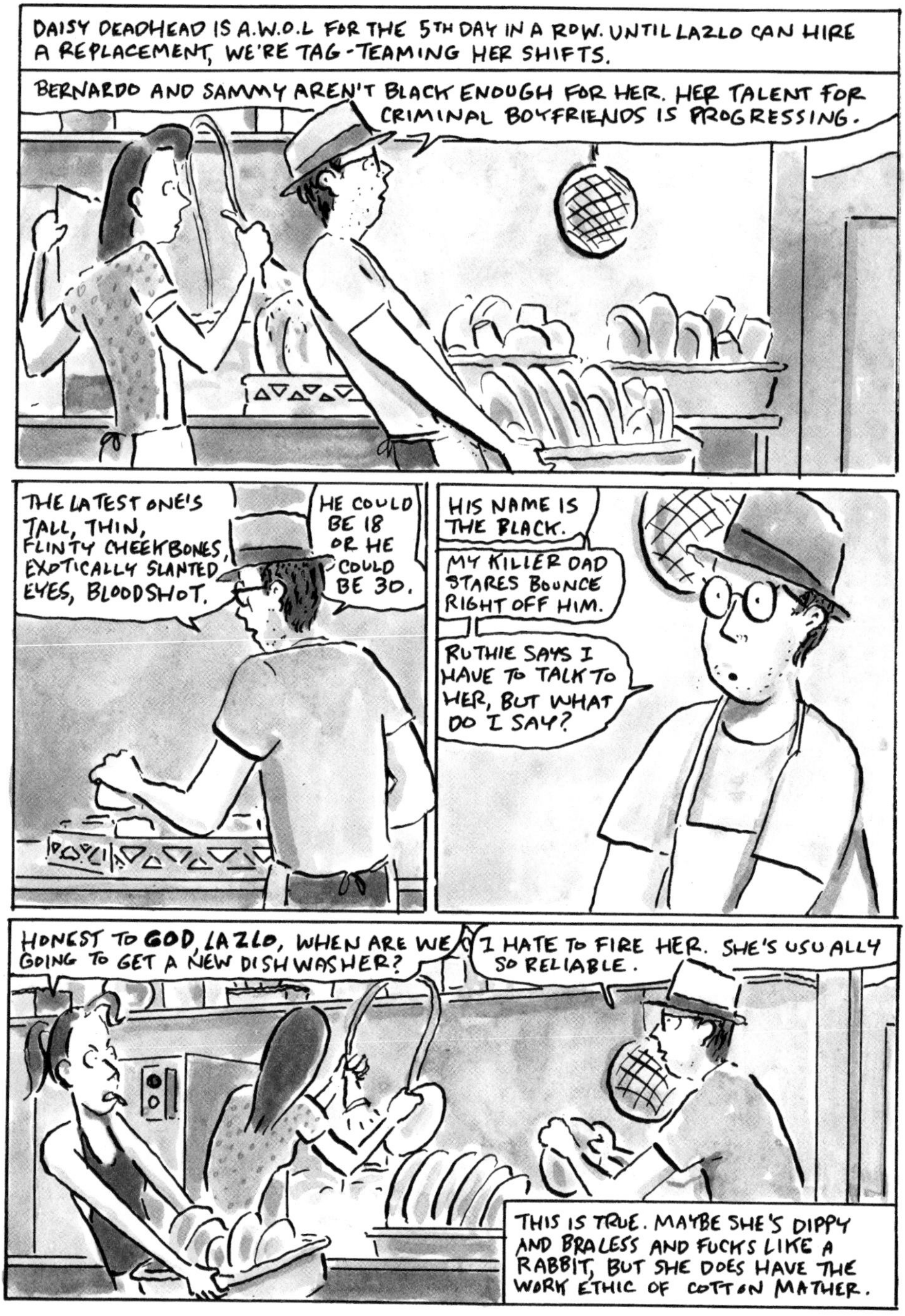
DAISY DEADHEAD IS A.W.O.L FOR THE 5TH DAY IN A ROW. UNTIL LAZLO CAN HIRE A REPLACEMENT, WE'RE TAG-TEAMING HER SHIFTS.
BERNARDO AND SAMMY AREN'T BLACK ENOUGH FOR HER. HER TALENT FOR CRIMINAL BOYFRIENDS IS PROGRESSING.
THE LATEST ONE'S TALL, THIN, FLINTY CHEEKBONES, EXOTICALLY SLANTED EYES, BLOODSHOT.
HE COULD BE 18 OR HE COULD BE 30.
HIS NAME IS THE BLACK.
MY KILLER DAD STARES BOUNCE RIGHT OFF HIM.
RUTHIE SAYS I HAVE TO TALK TO HER, BUT WHAT DO I SAY?
HONEST TO GOD, LAZLO, WHEN ARE WE GOING TO GET A NEW DISHWASHER?
I HATE TO FIRE HER. SHE'S USUALLY SO RELIABLE.
THIS IS TRUE. MAYBE SHE'S DIPPY AND BRALESS AND FUCKS LIKE A RABBIT, BUT SHE DOES HAVE THE WORK ETHIC OF COTTON MATHER.

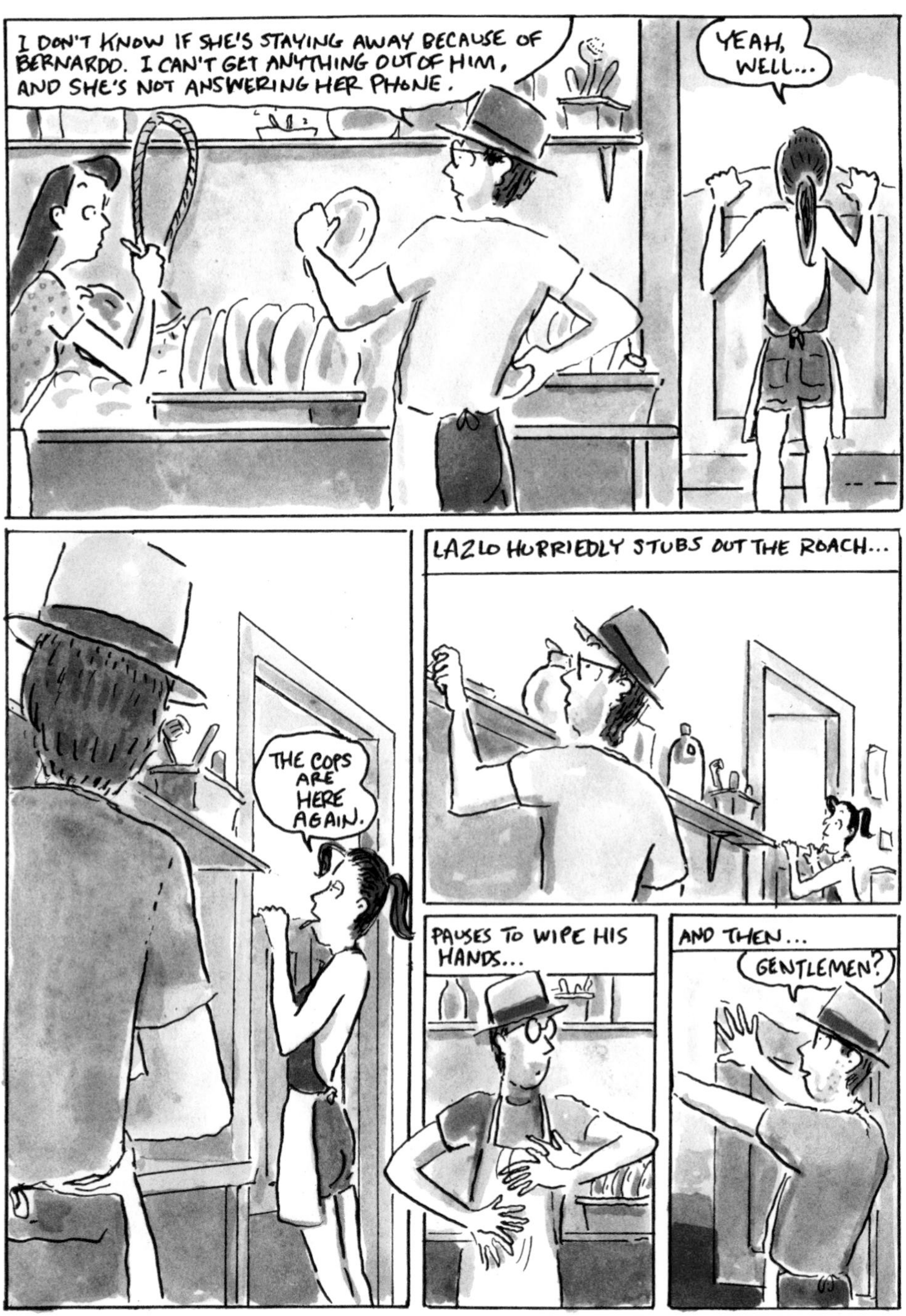

I DON'T KNOW IF SHE'S STAYING AWAY BECAUSE OF BERNARDO. I CAN'T GET ANYTHING OUT OF HIM, AND SHE'S NOT ANSWERING HER PHONE.
YEAH, WELL...
THE COPS ARE HERE AGAIN.
LAZLO HURRIEDLY STUBS OUT THE ROACH...
PAUSES TO WIPE HIS HANDS...
AND THEN...
GENTLEMEN?

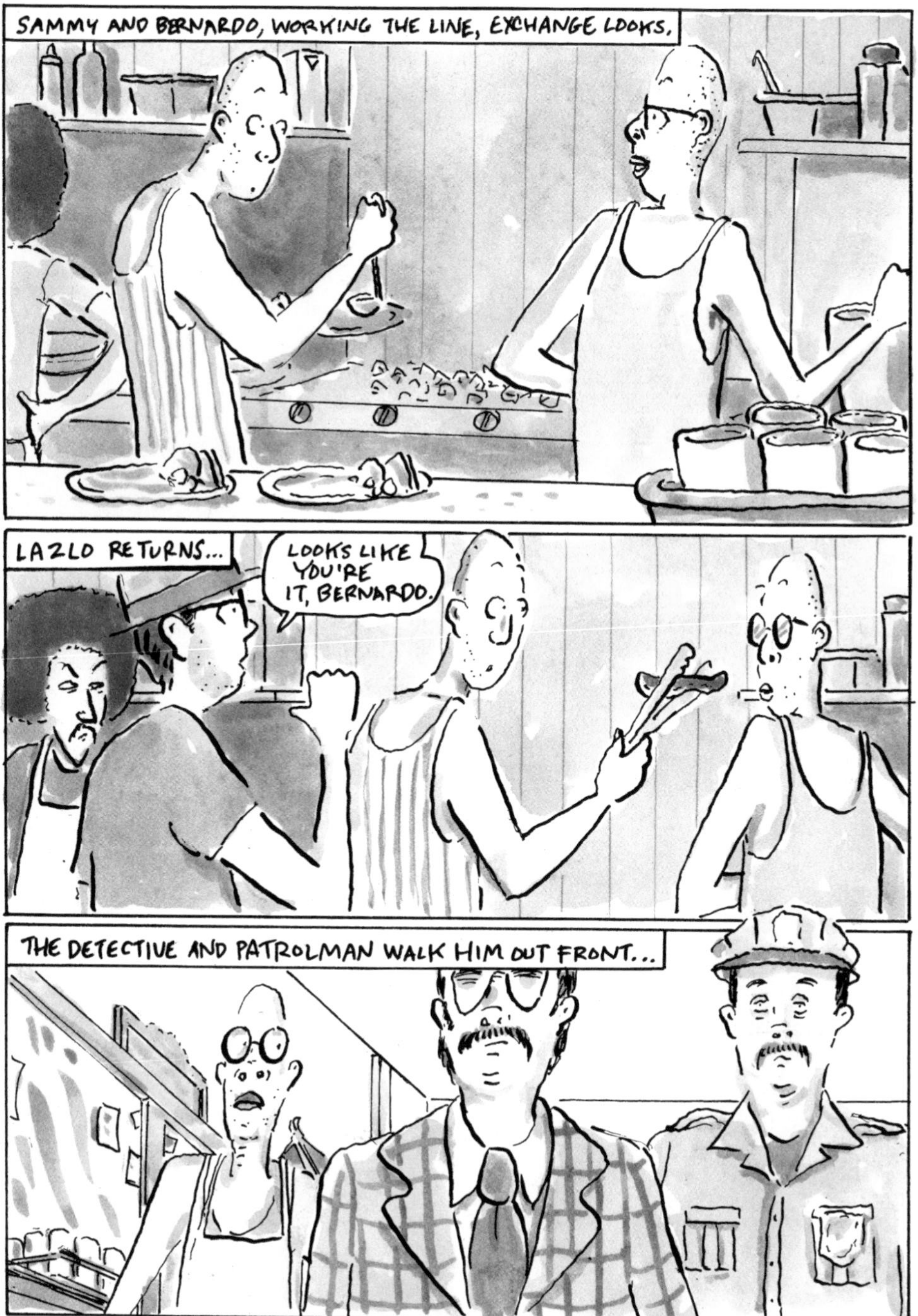
SAMMY AND BERNARDO, WORKING THE LINE, EXCHANGE LOOKS.
LAZLO RETURNS...
LOOKS LIKE YOU'RE IT, BERNARDO.
THE DETECTIVE AND PATROLMAN WALK HIM OUT FRONT...

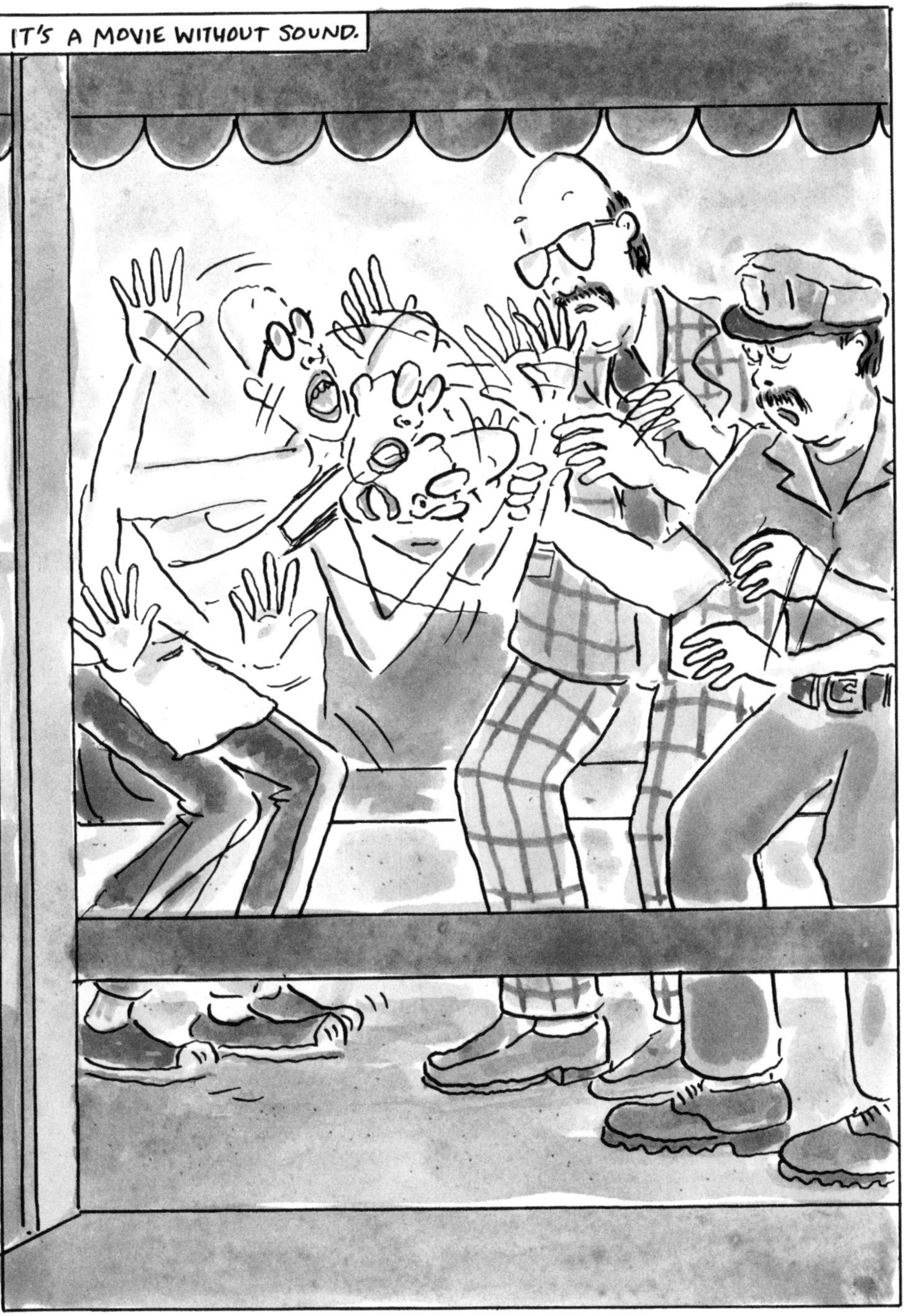
IT'S A MOVIE WITHOUT SOUND.

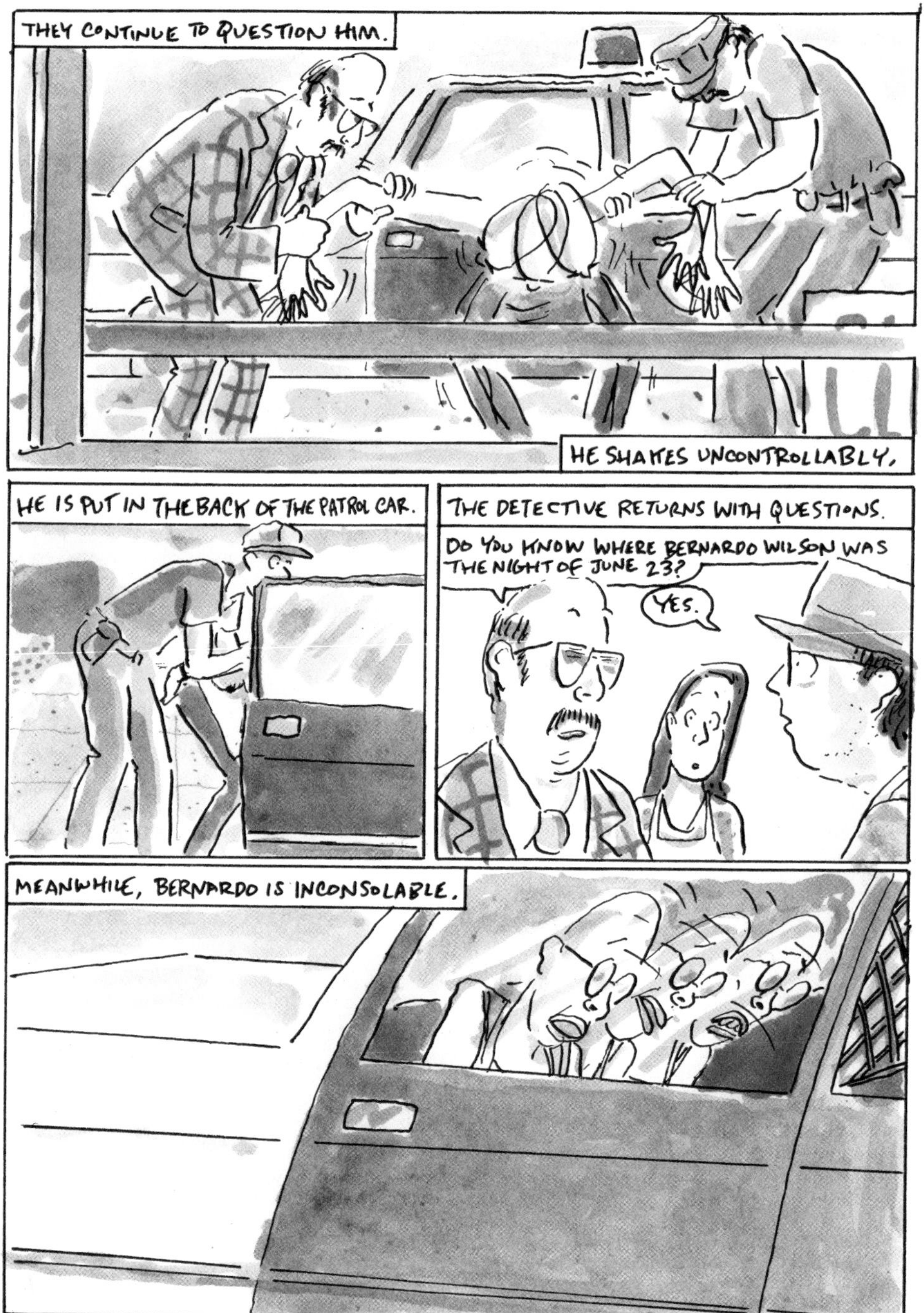
THEY CONTINUE TO QUESTION HIM.
HE SHAKES UNCONTROLLABLY.
HE IS PUT IN THE BACK OF THE PATROL CAR.
THE DETECTIVE RETURNS WITH QUESTIONS.
DO YOU KNOW WHERE BERNARDO WILSON WAS THE NIGHT OF JUNE 23?
YES.
MEANWHILE, BERNARDO IS INCONSOLABLE.

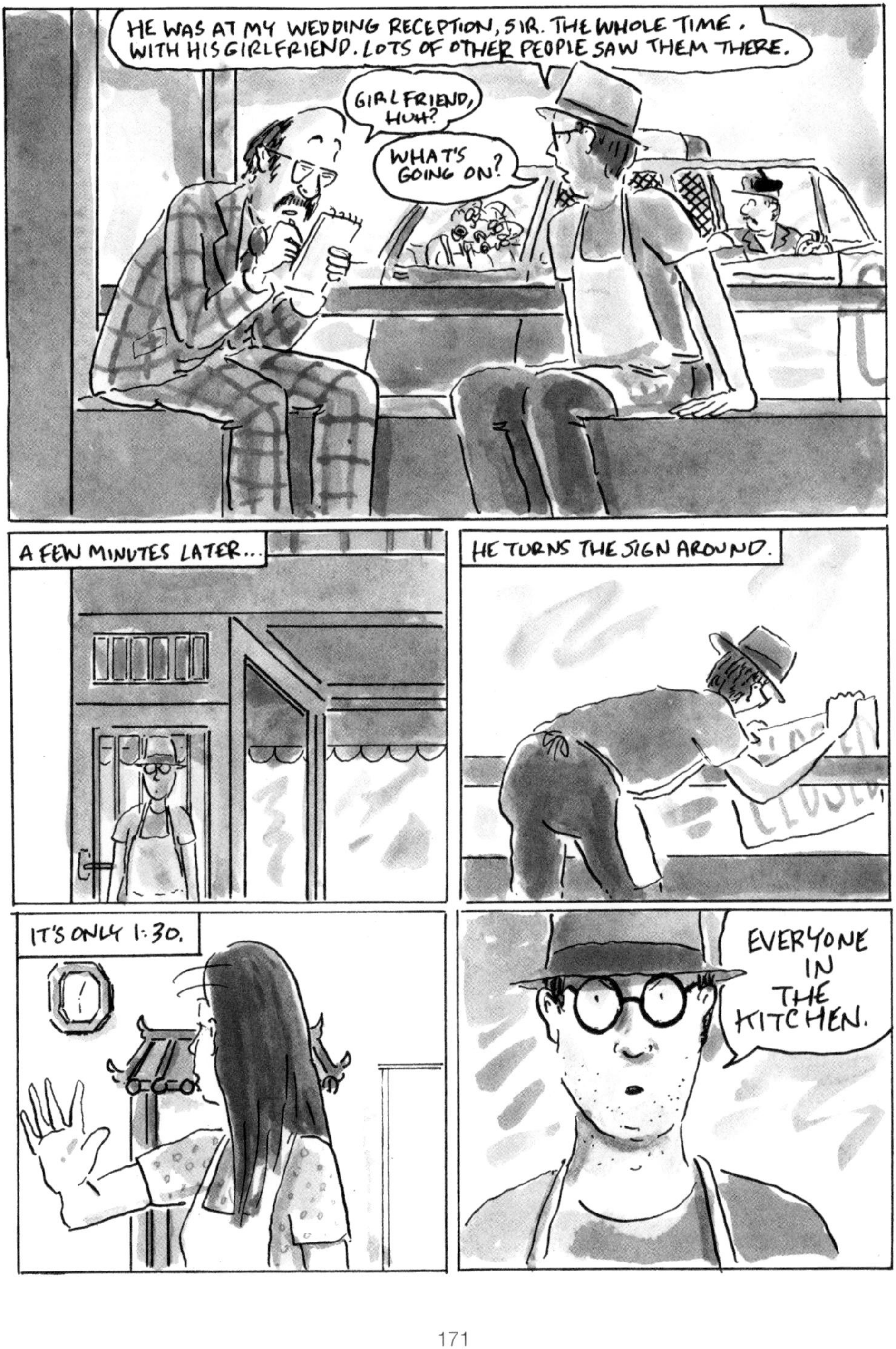
HE WAS AT MY WEDDING RECEPTION, SIR. THE WHOLE TIME. WITH HIS GIRLFRIEND. LOTS OF OTHER PEOPLE SAW THEM THERE.
GIRLFRIEND, HUH?
WHAT'S GOING ON?
A FEW MINUTES LATER...
HE TURNS THE SIGN AROUND.
CLOSED
IT'S ONLY 1:30.
EVERYONE IN THE KITCHEN.

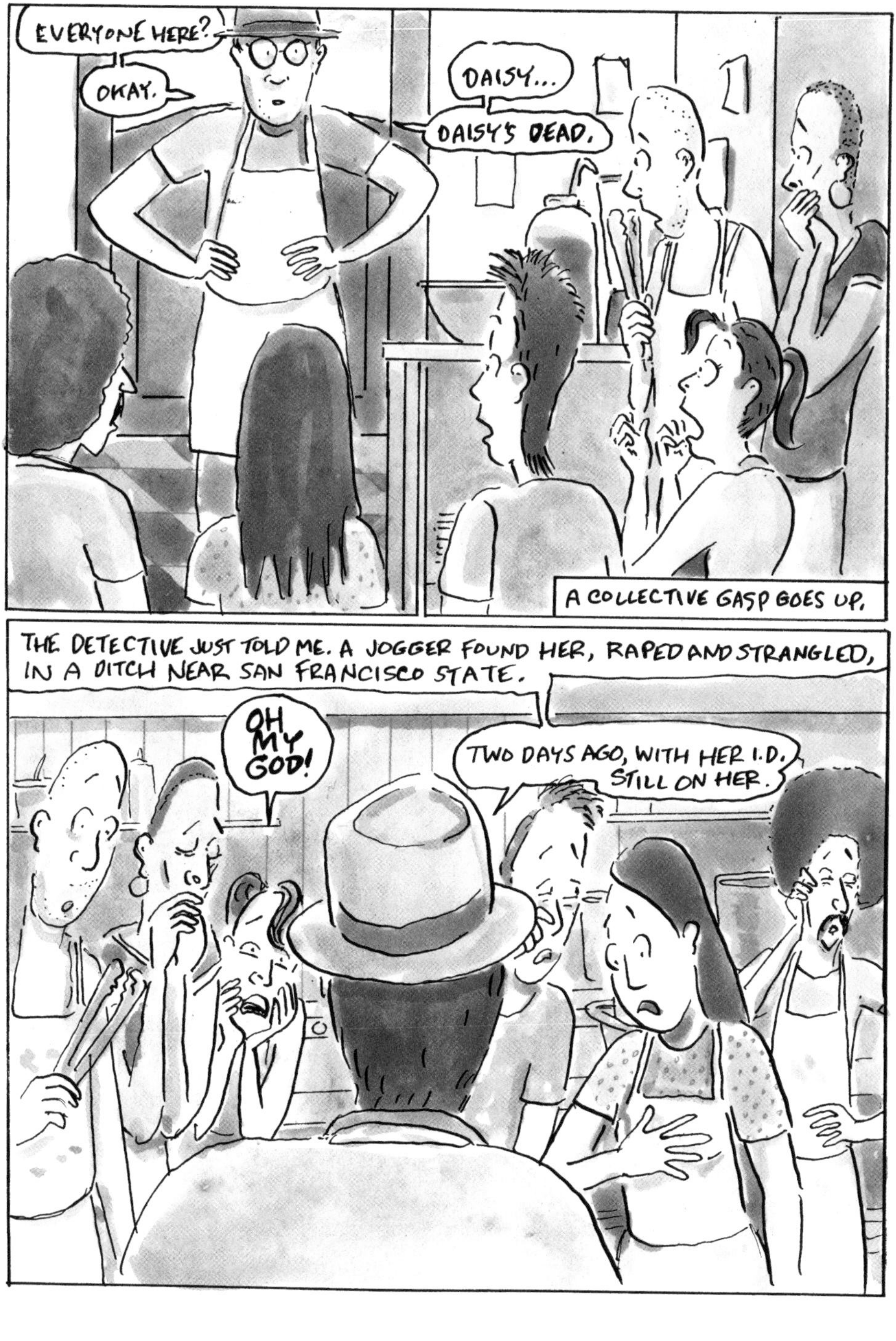
EVERYONE HERE?
OKAY.
DAISY...
DAISY'S DEAD.
A COLLECTIVE GASP GOES UP.
THE DETECTIVE JUST TOLD ME. A JOGGER FOUND HER, RAPED AND STRANGLED, IN A DITCH NEAR SAN FRANCISCO STATE.
OH MY GOD!
TWO DAYS AGO, WITH HER I.D. STILL ON HER.

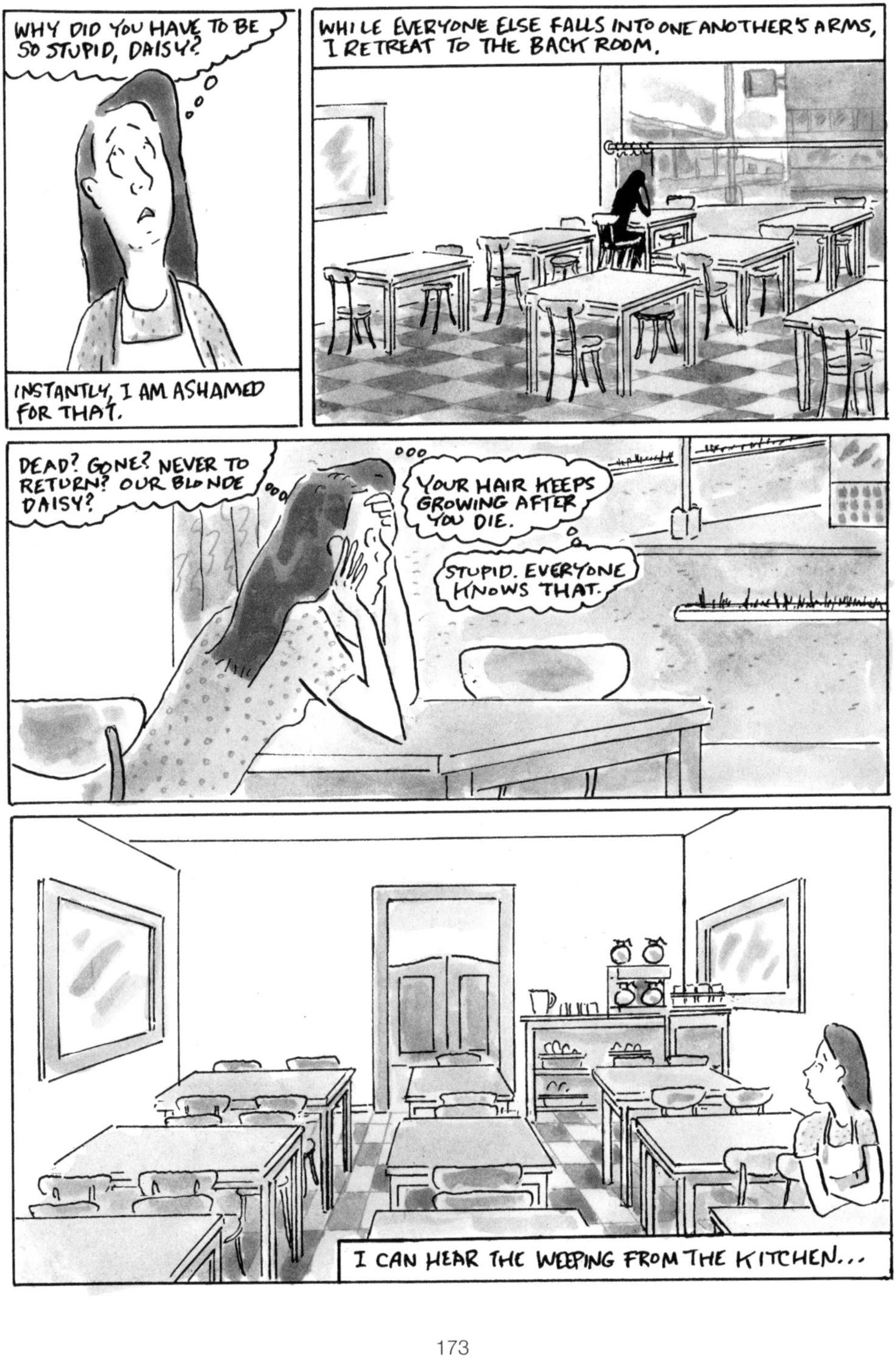
WHY DID YOU HAVE TO BE SO STUPID, DAISY?
INSTANTLY, I AM ASHAMED FOR THAT.
WHILE EVERYONE ELSE FALLS INTO ONE ANOTHER'S ARMS, I RETREAT TO THE BACK ROOM.
DEAD? GONE? NEVER TO RETURN? OUR BLONDE DAISY?
YOUR HAIR KEEPS GROWING AFTER YOU DIE.
STUPID. EVERYONE KNOWS THAT.
I CAN HEAR THE WEEPING FROM THE KITCHEN...

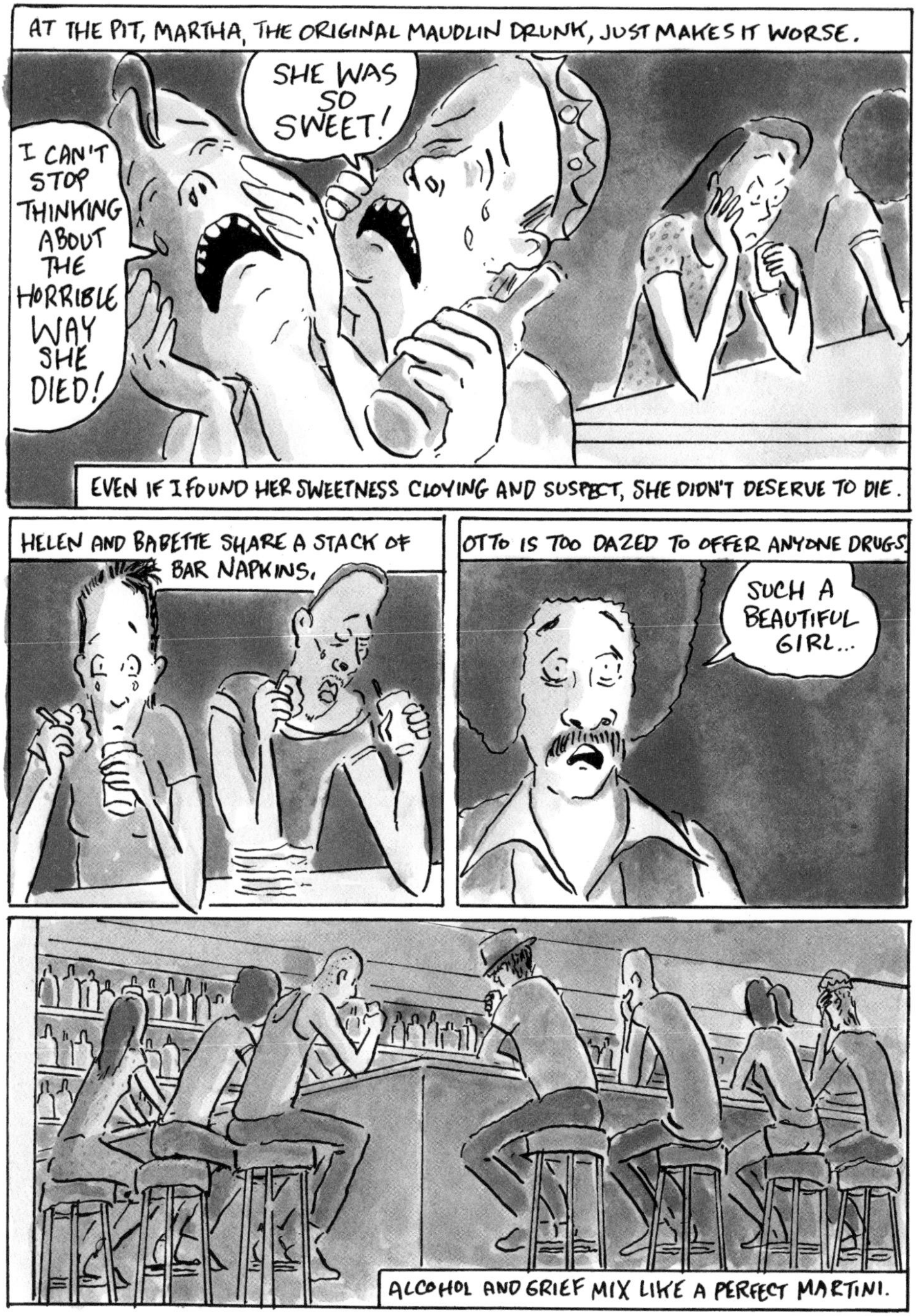
AT THE PIT, MARTHA, THE ORIGINAL MAUDLIN DRUNK, JUST MAKES IT WORSE.
I CAN'T STOP THINKING ABOUT THE HORRIBLE WAY SHE DIED!
SHE WAS SO SWEET!
EVEN IF I FOUND HER SWEETNESS CLOYING AND SUSPECT, SHE DIDN'T DESERVE TO DIE.
HELEN AND BABETTE SHARE A STACK OF BAR NAPKINS.
OTTO IS TOO DAZED TO OFFER ANYONE DRUGS.
SUCH A BEAUTIFUL GIRL...
ALCOHOL AND GRIEF MIX LIKE A PERFECT MARTINI.

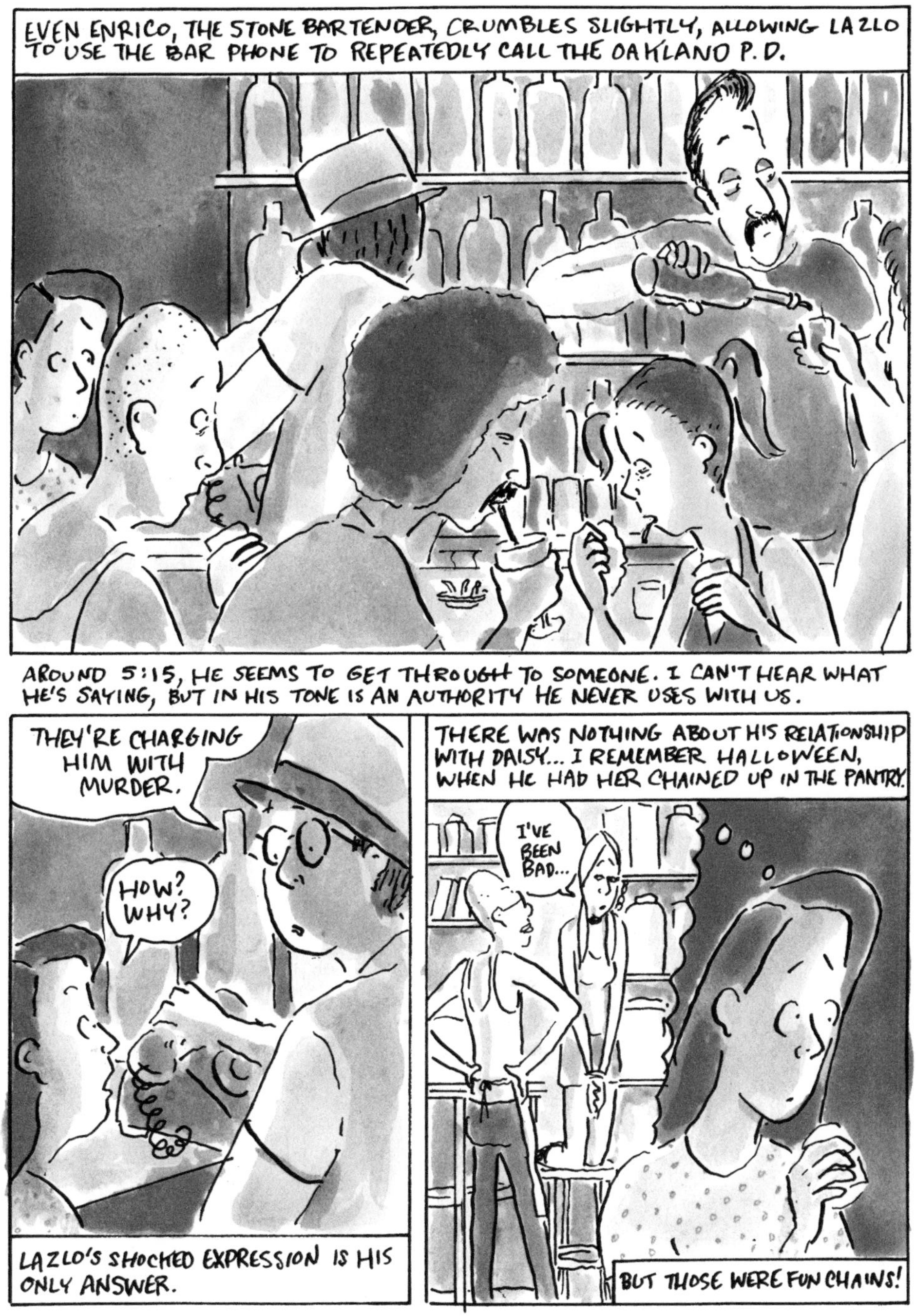
EVEN ENRICO, THE STONE BARTENDER, CRUMBLES SLIGHTLY, ALLOWING LAZLO TO USE THE BAR PHONE TO REPEATEDLY CALL THE OAKLAND P.D.
AROUND 5:15, HE SEEMS TO GET THROUGH TO SOMEONE. I CAN'T HEAR WHAT HE'S SAYING, BUT IN HIS TONE IS AN AUTHORITY HE NEVER USES WITH US.
THEY'RE CHARGING HIM WITH MURDER.
HOW? WHY?
LAZLO'S SHOCKED EXPRESSION IS HIS ONLY ANSWER.
THERE WAS NOTHING ABOUT HIS RELATIONSHIP WITH DAISY... I REMEMBER HALLOWEEN, WHEN HE HAD HER CHAINED UP IN THE PANTRY.
I'VE BEEN BAD...
BUT THOSE WERE FUN CHAINS!

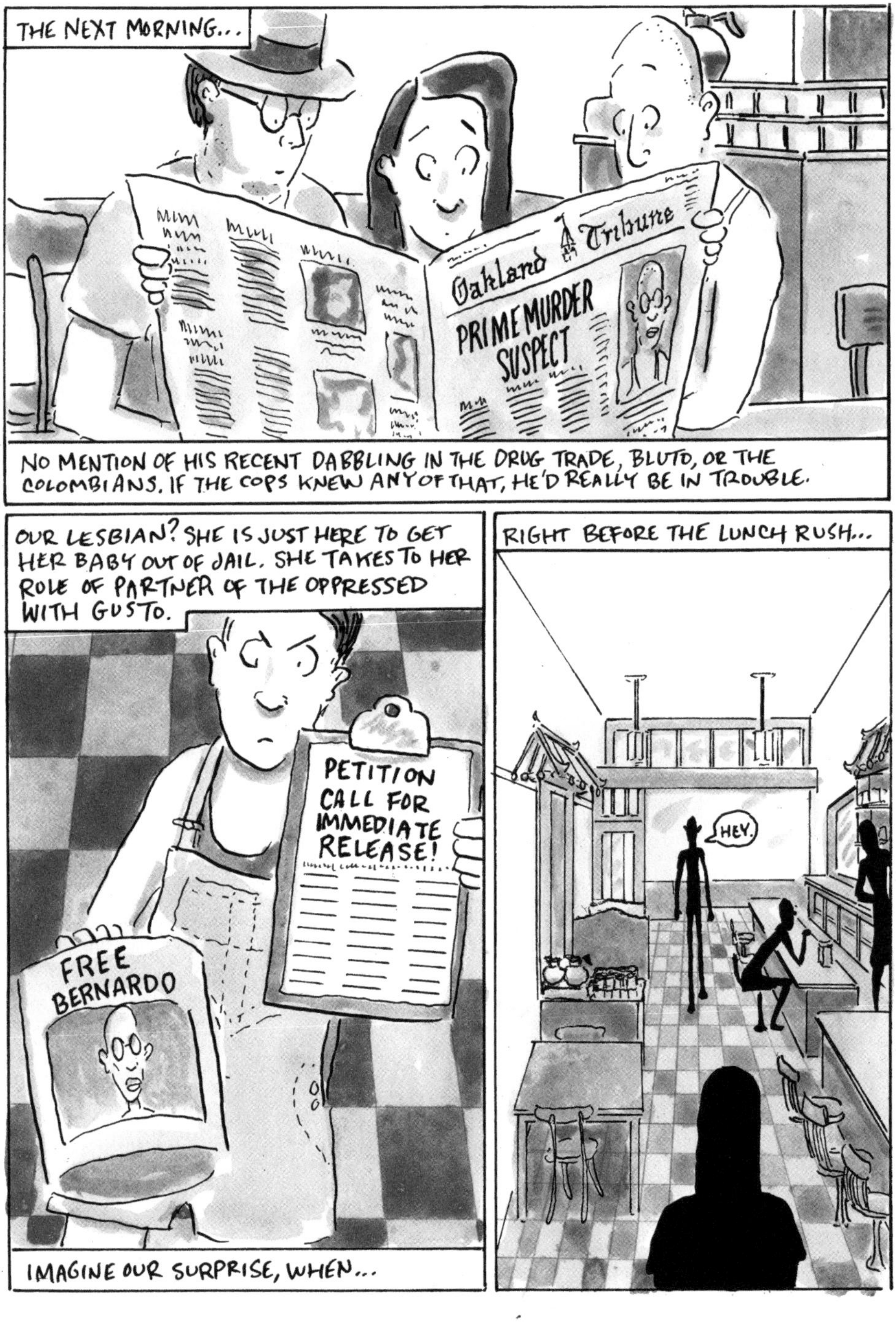
THE NEXT MORNING...
Oakland Tribune
PRIME MURDER SUSPECT
NO MENTION OF HIS RECENT DABBLING IN THE DRUG TRADE, BLUTO, OR THE COLOMBIANS. IF THE COPS KNEW ANY OF THAT, HE'D REALLY BE IN TROUBLE.
OUR LESBIAN? SHE IS JUST HERE TO GET HER BABY OUT OF JAIL. SHE TAKES TO HER ROLE OF PARTNER OF THE OPPRESSED WITH GUSTO.
PETITION CALL FOR IMMEDIATE RELEASE!
FREE BERNARDO
IMAGINE OUR SURPRISE, WHEN...
RIGHT BEFORE THE LUNCH RUSH...
HEY.

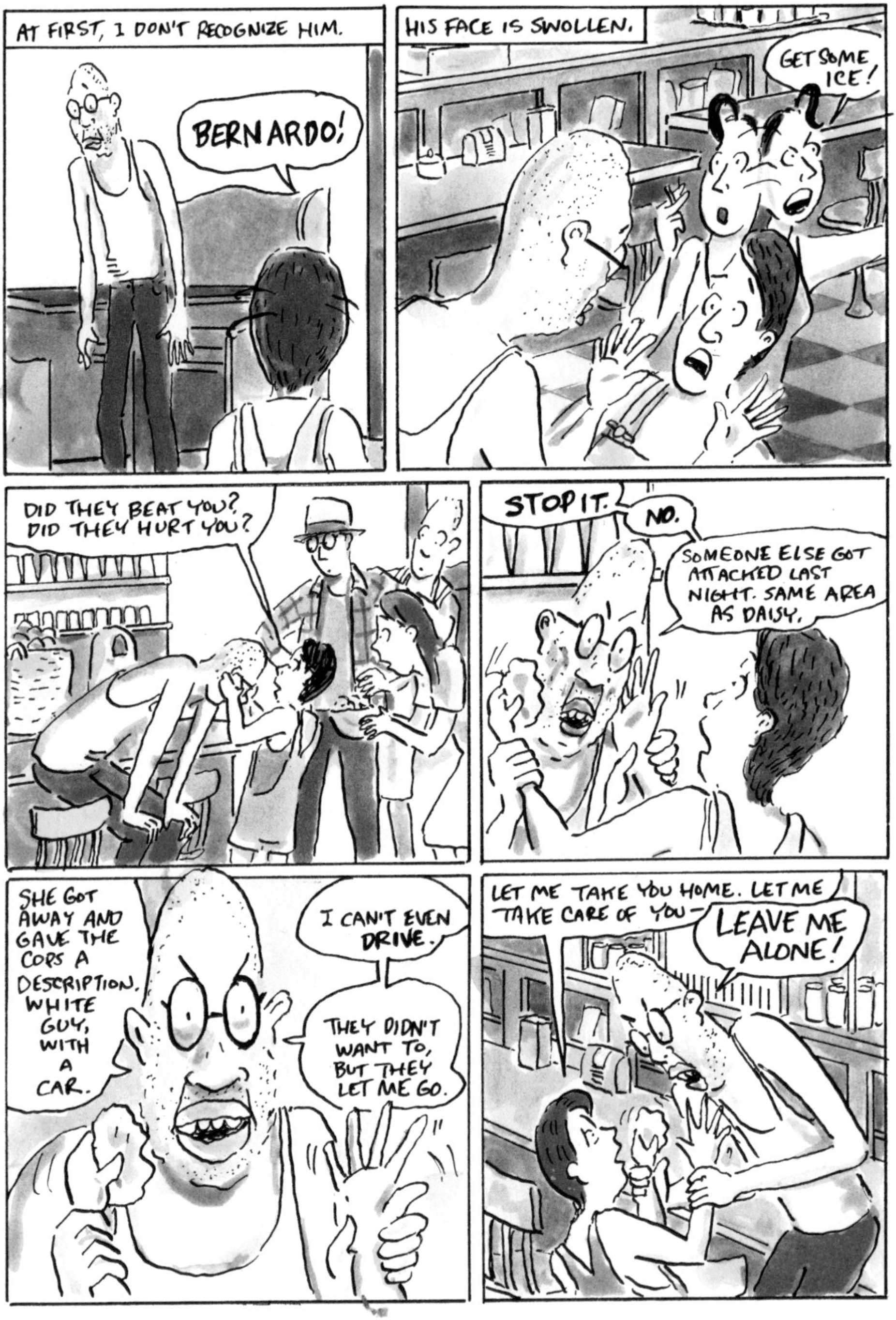
AT FIRST, I DON'T RECOGNIZE HIM.
BERNARDO!
HIS FACE IS SWOLLEN.
GET SOME ICE!
DID THEY BEAT YOU? DID THEY HURT YOU?
STOP IT.
NO.
SOMEONE ELSE GOT ATTACKED LAST NIGHT. SAME AREA AS DAISY.
SHE GOT AWAY AND GAVE THE COPS A DESCRIPTION. WHITE GUY, WITH A CAR.
I CAN'T EVEN DRIVE.
THEY DIDN'T WANT TO, BUT THEY LET ME GO.
LET ME TAKE YOU HOME. LET ME TAKE CARE OF YOU—
LEAVE ME ALONE!

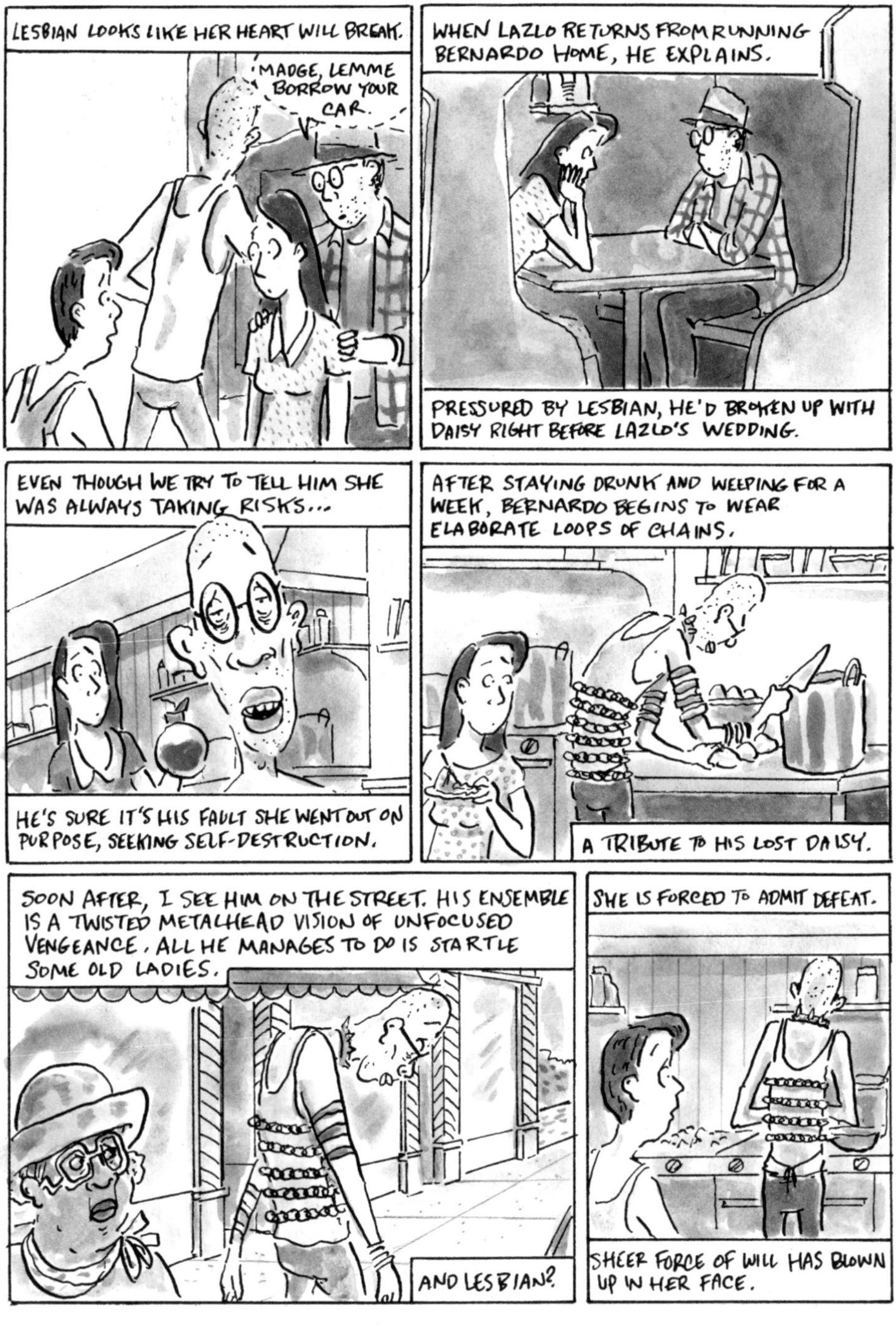
LESBIAN LOOKS LIKE HER HEART WILL BREAK.
MADGE, LEMME BORROW YOUR CAR.
WHEN LAZLO RETURNS FROM RUNNING BERNARDO HOME, HE EXPLAINS.
PRESSURED BY LESBIAN, HE'D BROKEN UP WITH DAISY RIGHT BEFORE LAZLO'S WEDDING.
EVEN THOUGH WE TRY TO TELL HIM SHE WAS ALWAYS TAKING RISKS...
HE'S SURE IT'S HIS FAULT SHE WENT OUT ON PURPOSE, SEEKING SELF-DESTRUCTION.
AFTER STAYING DRUNK AND WEEPING FOR A WEEK, BERNARDO BEGINS TO WEAR ELABORATE LOOPS OF CHAINS.
A TRIBUTE TO HIS LOST DAISY.
SOON AFTER, I SEE HIM ON THE STREET. HIS ENSEMBLE IS A TWISTED METALHEAD VISION OF UNFOCUSED VENGEANCE. ALL HE MANAGES TO DO IS STARTLE SOME OLD LADIES.
AND LESBIAN?
SHE IS FORCED TO ADMIT DEFEAT.
SHEER FORCE OF WILL HAS BLOWN UP IN HER FACE.

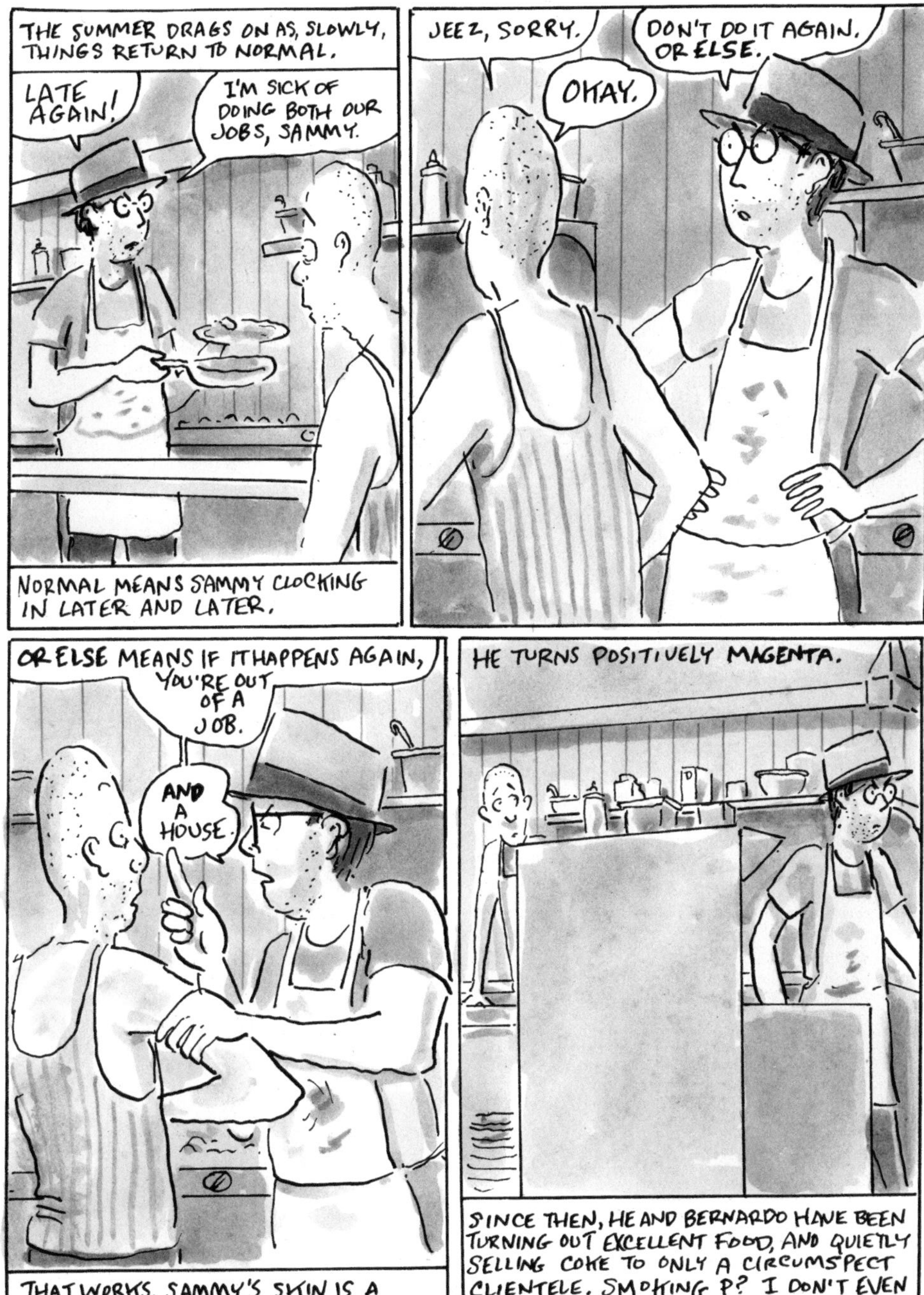

THE SUMMER DRAGS ON AS, SLOWLY, THINGS RETURN TO NORMAL.
LATE AGAIN!
I'M SICK OF DOING BOTH OUR JOBS, SAMMY.
NORMAL MEANS SAMMY CLOCKING IN LATER AND LATER.
JEEZ, SORRY.
DON'T DO IT AGAIN. OR ELSE.
OKAY.
OR ELSE MEANS IF IT HAPPENS AGAIN, YOU'RE OUT OF A JOB.
AND A HOUSE.
THAT WORKS. SAMMY'S SKIN IS A BAROMETER, ALWAYS BETRAYING HIM.
HE TURNS POSITIVELY MAGENTA.
SINCE THEN, HE AND BERNARDO HAVE BEEN TURNING OUT EXCELLENT FOOD, AND QUIETLY SELLING COKE TO ONLY A CIRCUMSPECT CLIENTELE. SMOKING P? I DON'T EVEN WANT TO KNOW.

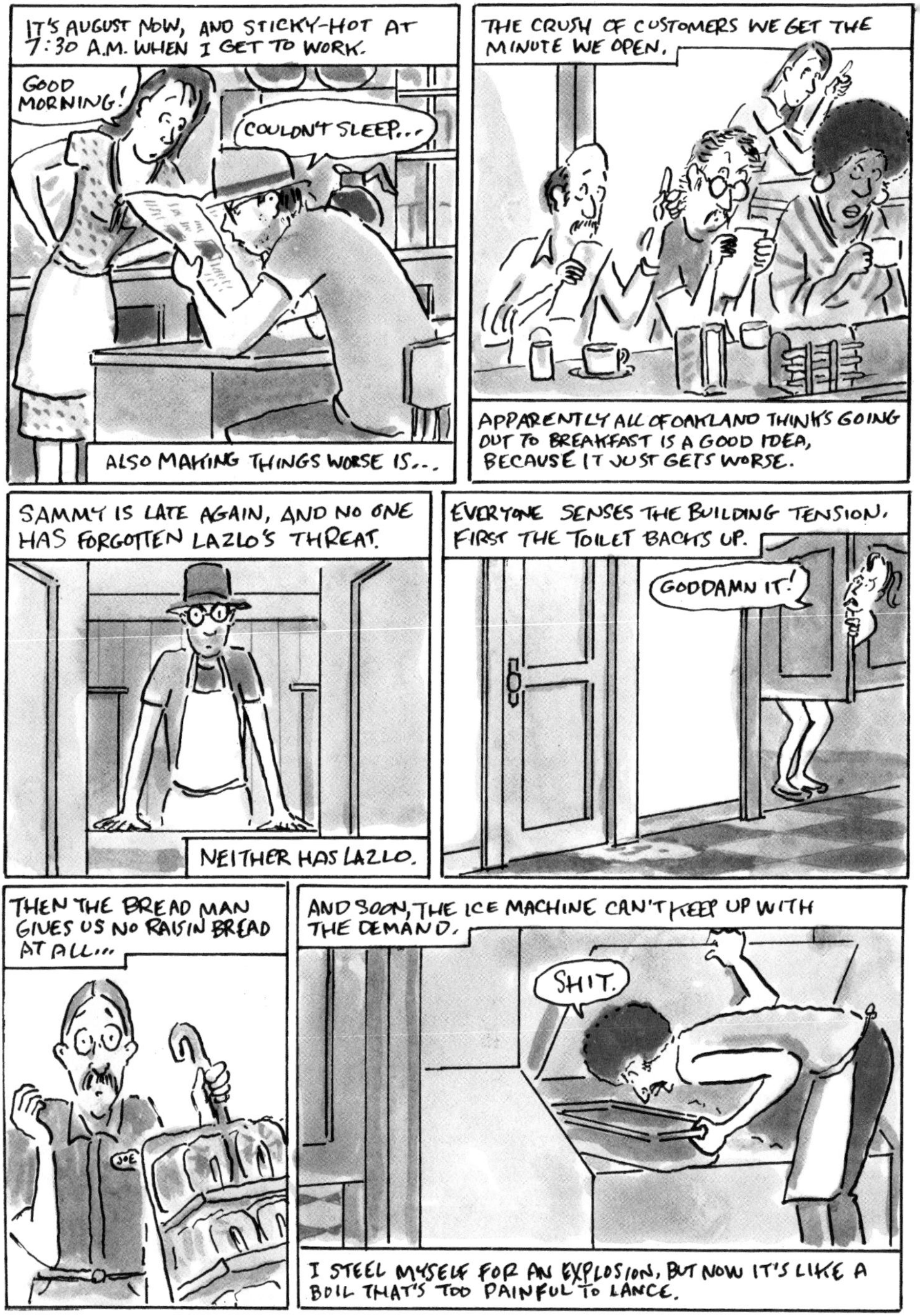
IT'S AUGUST NOW, AND STICKY-HOT AT 7:30 A.M. WHEN I GET TO WORK.
GOOD MORNING!
COULDN'T SLEEP...
ALSO MAKING THINGS WORSE IS...
THE CRUSH OF CUSTOMERS WE GET THE MINUTE WE OPEN.
APPARENTLY ALL OF OAKLAND THINKS GOING OUT TO BREAKFAST IS A GOOD IDEA, BECAUSE IT JUST GETS WORSE.
SAMMY IS LATE AGAIN, AND NO ONE HAS FORGOTTEN LAZLO'S THREAT.
NEITHER HAS LAZLO.
EVERYONE SENSES THE BUILDING TENSION. FIRST THE TOILET BACKS UP.
GODDAMN IT!
THEN THE BREAD MAN GIVES US NO RAISIN BREAD AT ALL...
JOE
AND SOON, THE ICE MACHINE CAN'T KEEP UP WITH THE DEMAND.
SHIT.
I STEEL MYSELF FOR AN EXPLOSION, BUT NOW IT'S LIKE A BOIL THAT'S TOO PAINFUL TO LANCE.

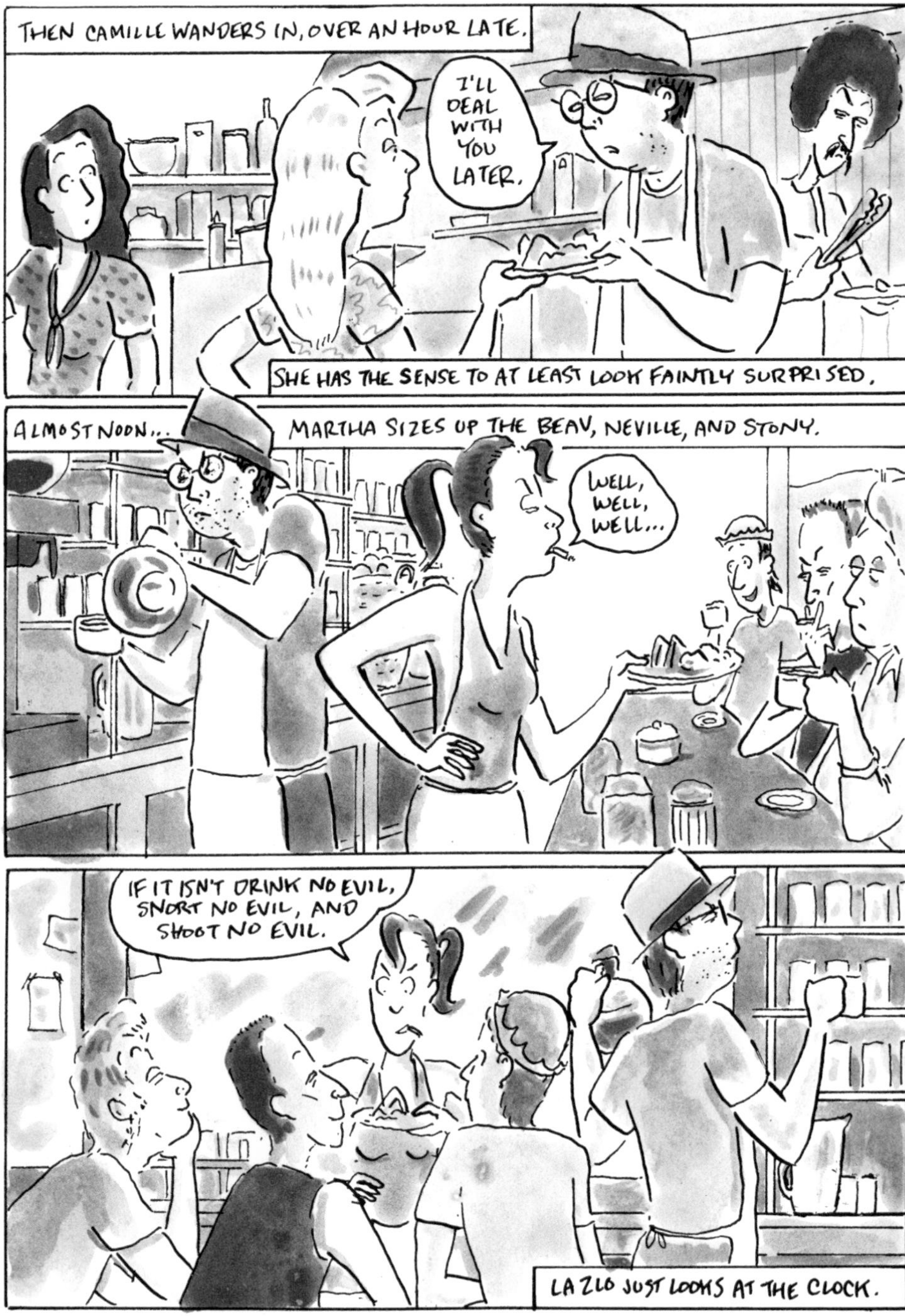
THEN CAMILLE WANDERS IN, OVER AN HOUR LATE.
I'LL DEAL WITH YOU LATER.
SHE HAS THE SENSE TO AT LEAST LOOK FAINTLY SURPRISED.
ALMOST NOON...
MARTHA SIZES UP THE BEAV, NEVILLE, AND STONY.
WELL, WELL, WELL...
IF IT ISN'T DRINK NO EVIL, SNORT NO EVIL, AND SHOOT NO EVIL.
LAZLO JUST LOOKS AT THE CLOCK.

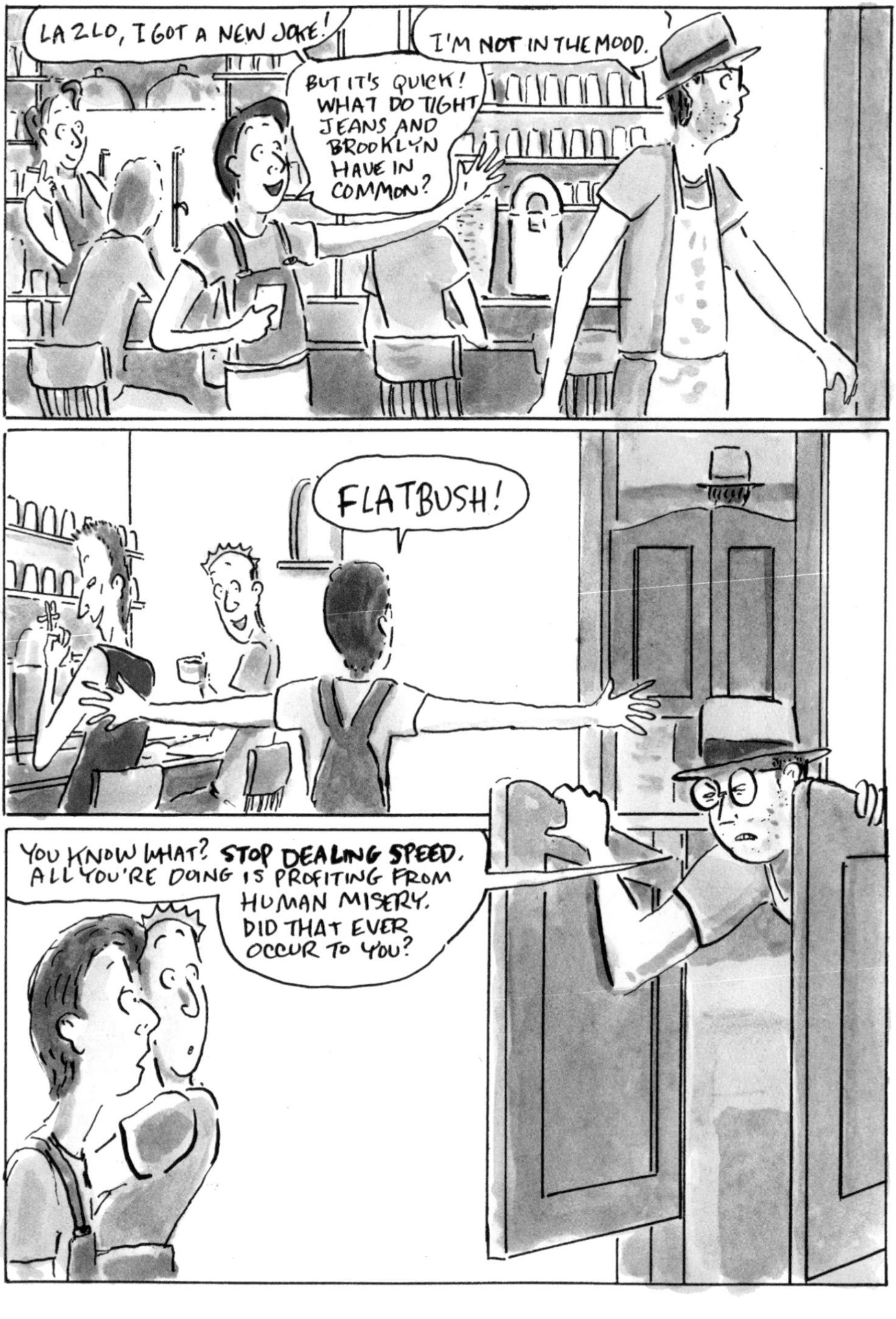
LAZLO, I GOT A NEW JOKE!
I'M NOT IN THE MOOD.
BUT IT'S QUICK! WHAT DO TIGHT JEANS AND BROOKLYN HAVE IN COMMON?
FLATBUSH!
YOU KNOW WHAT? STOP DEALING SPEED. ALL YOU'RE DOING IS PROFITING FROM HUMAN MISERY. DID THAT EVER OCCUR TO YOU?

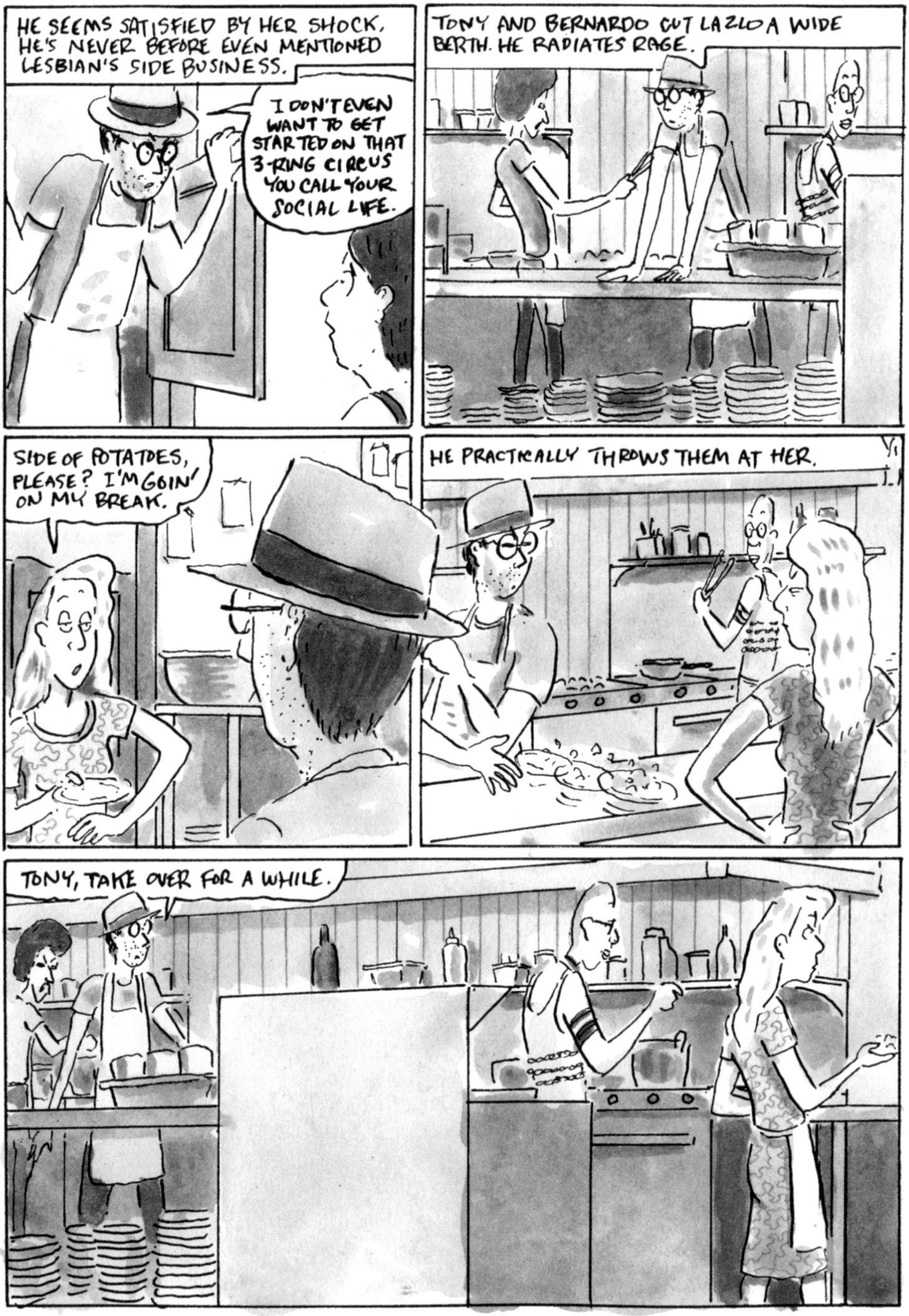
HE SEEMS SATISFIED BY HER SHOCK. HE'S NEVER BEFORE EVEN MENTIONED LESBIAN'S SIDE BUSINESS.
I DON'T EVEN WANT TO GET STARTED ON THAT 3-RING CIRCUS YOU CALL YOUR SOCIAL LIFE.
TONY AND BERNARDO CUT LAZLO A WIDE BERTH. HE RADIATES RAGE.
SIDE OF POTATOES, PLEASE? I'M GOIN' ON MY BREAK.
HE PRACTICALLY THROWS THEM AT HER.
TONY, TAKE OVER FOR A WHILE.

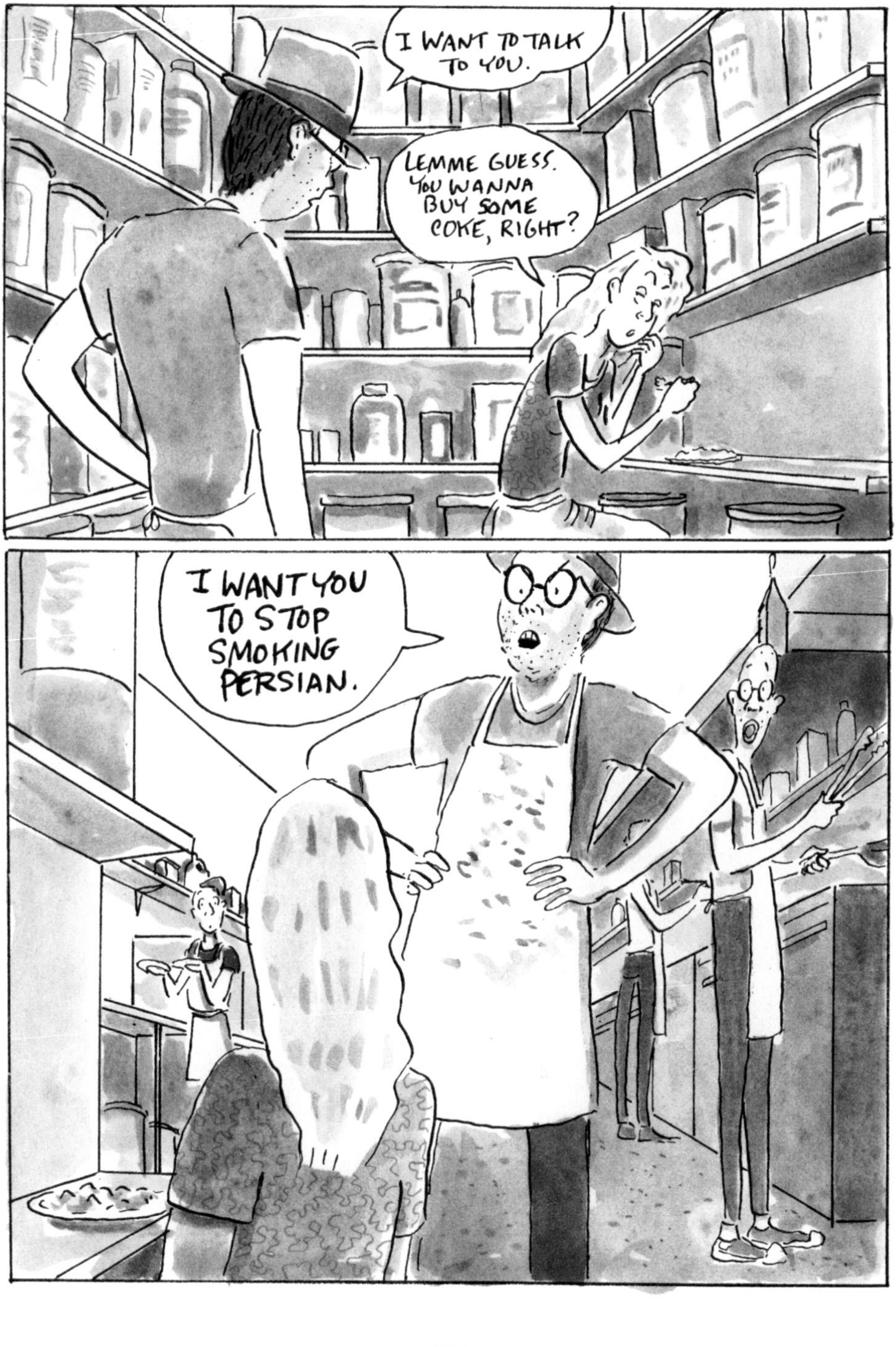
I WANT TO TALK TO YOU.
LEMME GUESS. YOU WANNA BUY SOME COKE, RIGHT?
I WANT YOU TO STOP SMOKING PERSIAN.

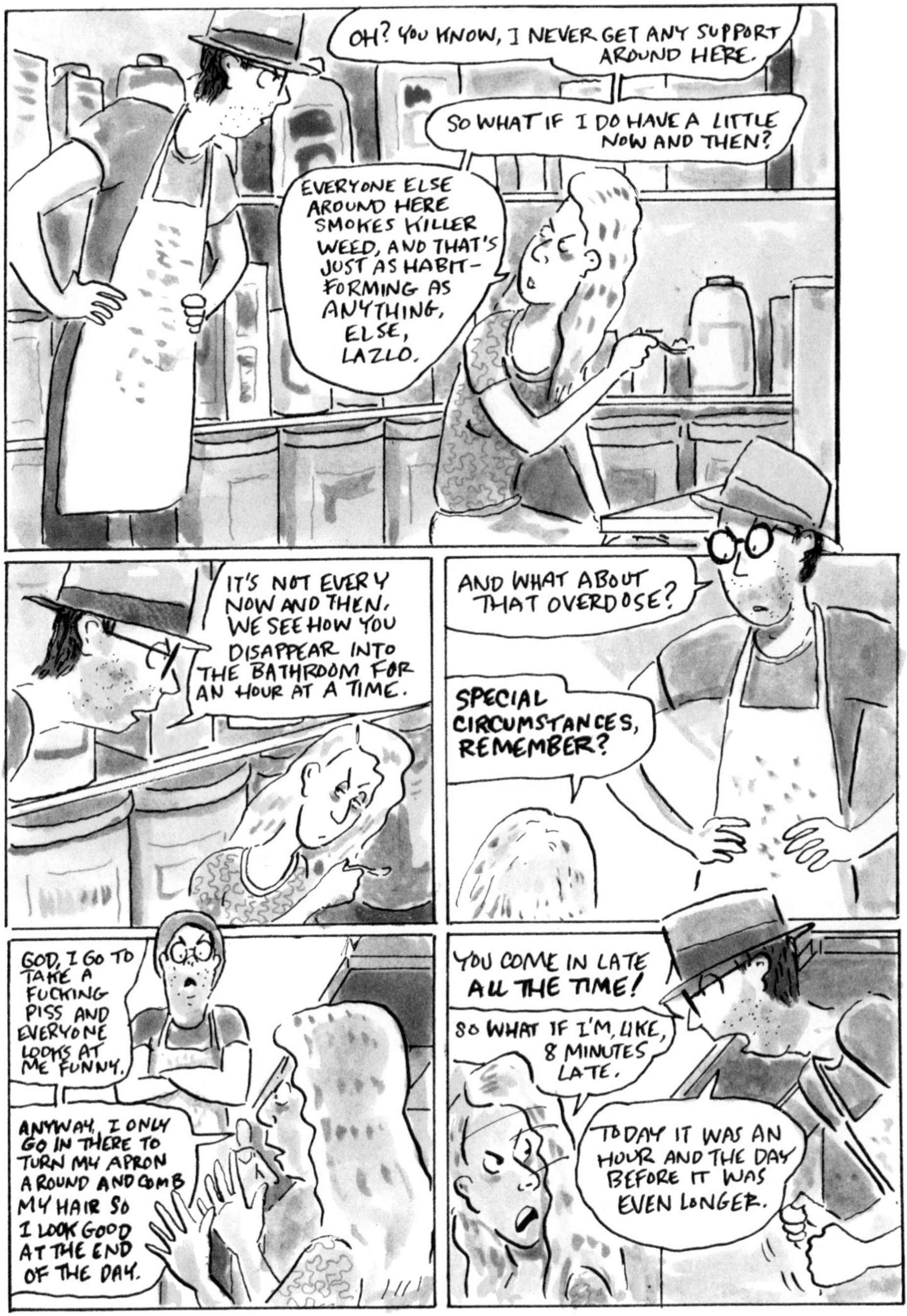
OH? YOU KNOW, I NEVER GET ANY SUPPORT AROUND HERE.
SO WHAT IF I DO HAVE A LITTLE NOW AND THEN?
EVERYONE ELSE AROUND HERE SMOKES KILLER WEED, AND THAT'S JUST AS HABIT-FORMING AS ANYTHING ELSE, LAZLO.
IT'S NOT EVERY NOW AND THEN. WE SEE HOW YOU DISAPPEAR INTO THE BATHROOM FOR AN HOUR AT A TIME.
AND WHAT ABOUT THAT OVERDOSE?
SPECIAL CIRCUMSTANCES, REMEMBER?
GOD, I GO TO TAKE A FUCKING PISS AND EVERYONE LOOKS AT ME FUNNY.
ANYWAY, I ONLY GO IN THERE TO TURN MY APRON AROUND AND COMB MY HAIR SO I LOOK GOOD AT THE END OF THE DAY.
YOU COME IN LATE ALL THE TIME!
SO WHAT IF I'M, LIKE, 8 MINUTES LATE.
TODAY IT WAS AN HOUR AND THE DAY BEFORE IT WAS EVEN LONGER.

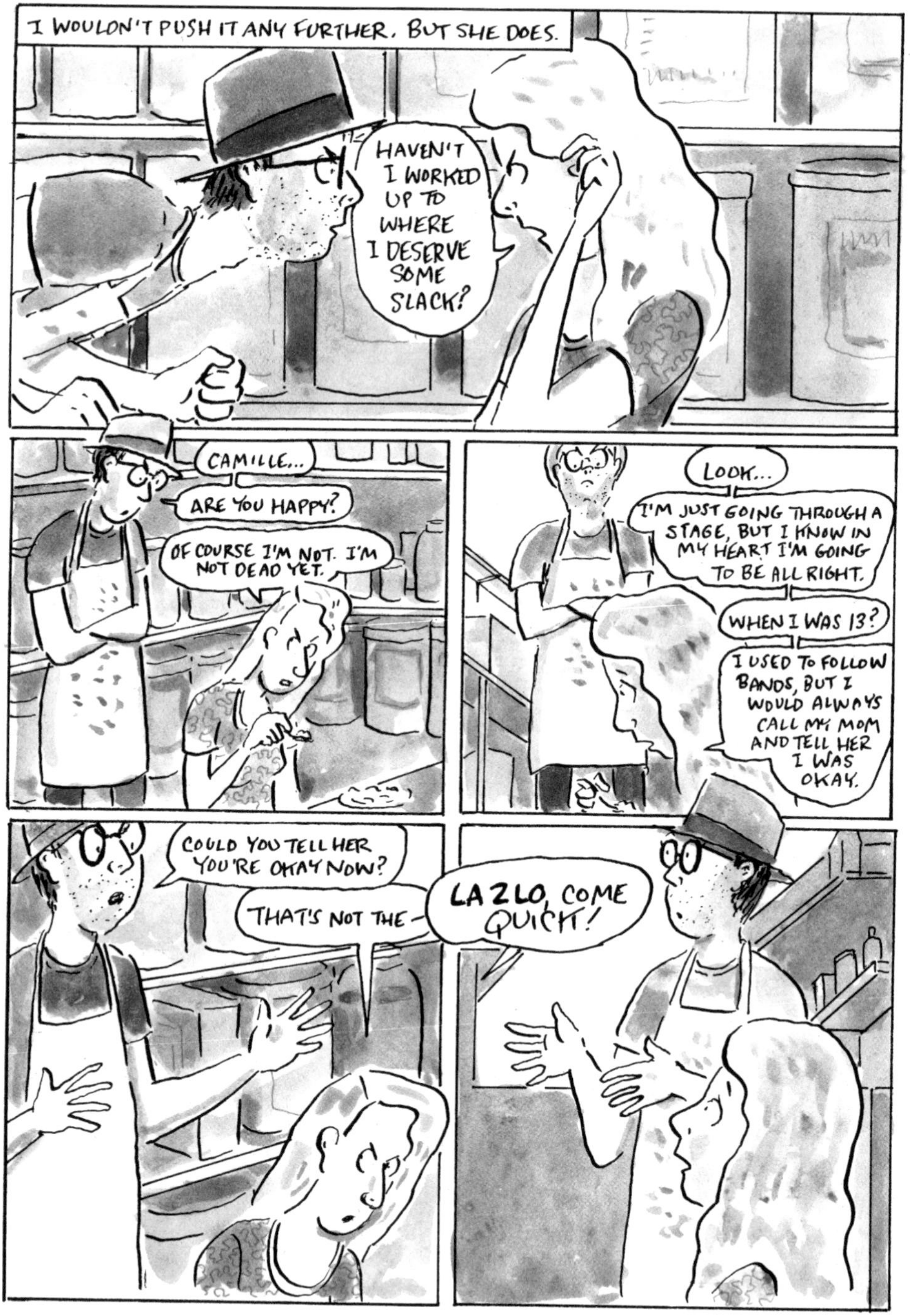
I WOULDN'T PUSH IT ANY FURTHER. BUT SHE DOES.
HAVEN'T I WORKED UP TO WHERE I DESERVE SOME SLACK?
CAMILLE...
ARE YOU HAPPY?
OF COURSE I'M NOT. I'M NOT DEAD YET.
LOOK...
I'M JUST GOING THROUGH A STAGE, BUT I KNOW IN MY HEART I'M GOING TO BE ALL RIGHT.
WHEN I WAS 13?
I USED TO FOLLOW BANDS, BUT I WOULD ALWAYS CALL MY MOM AND TELL HER I WAS OKAY.
COULD YOU TELL HER YOU'RE OKAY NOW?
THAT'S NOT THE—
LAZLO, COME QUICK!

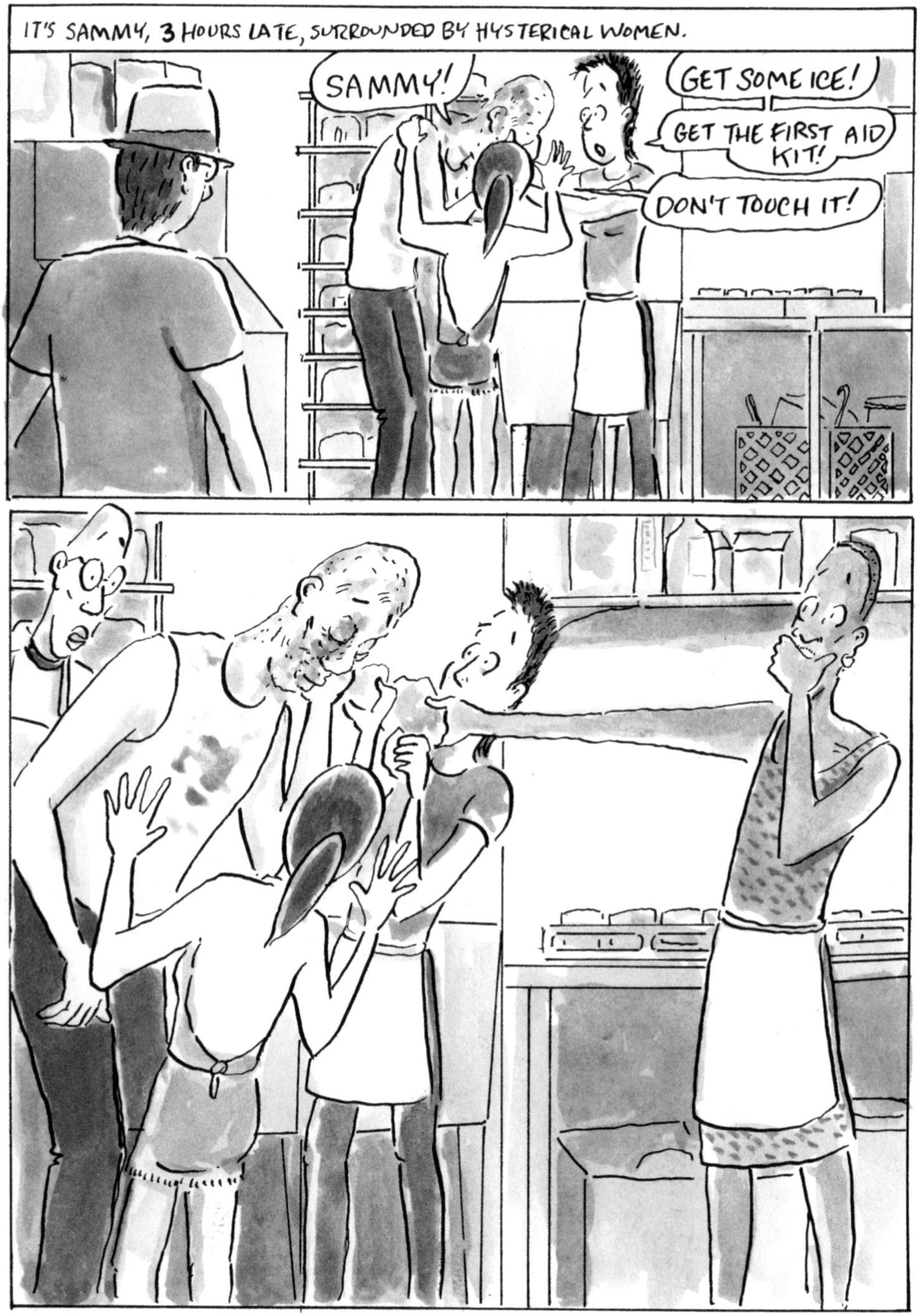
IT'S SAMMY, 3 HOURS LATE, SURROUNDED BY HYSTERICAL WOMEN.
SAMMY!
GET SOME ICE!
GET THE FIRST AID KIT!
DON'T TOUCH IT!

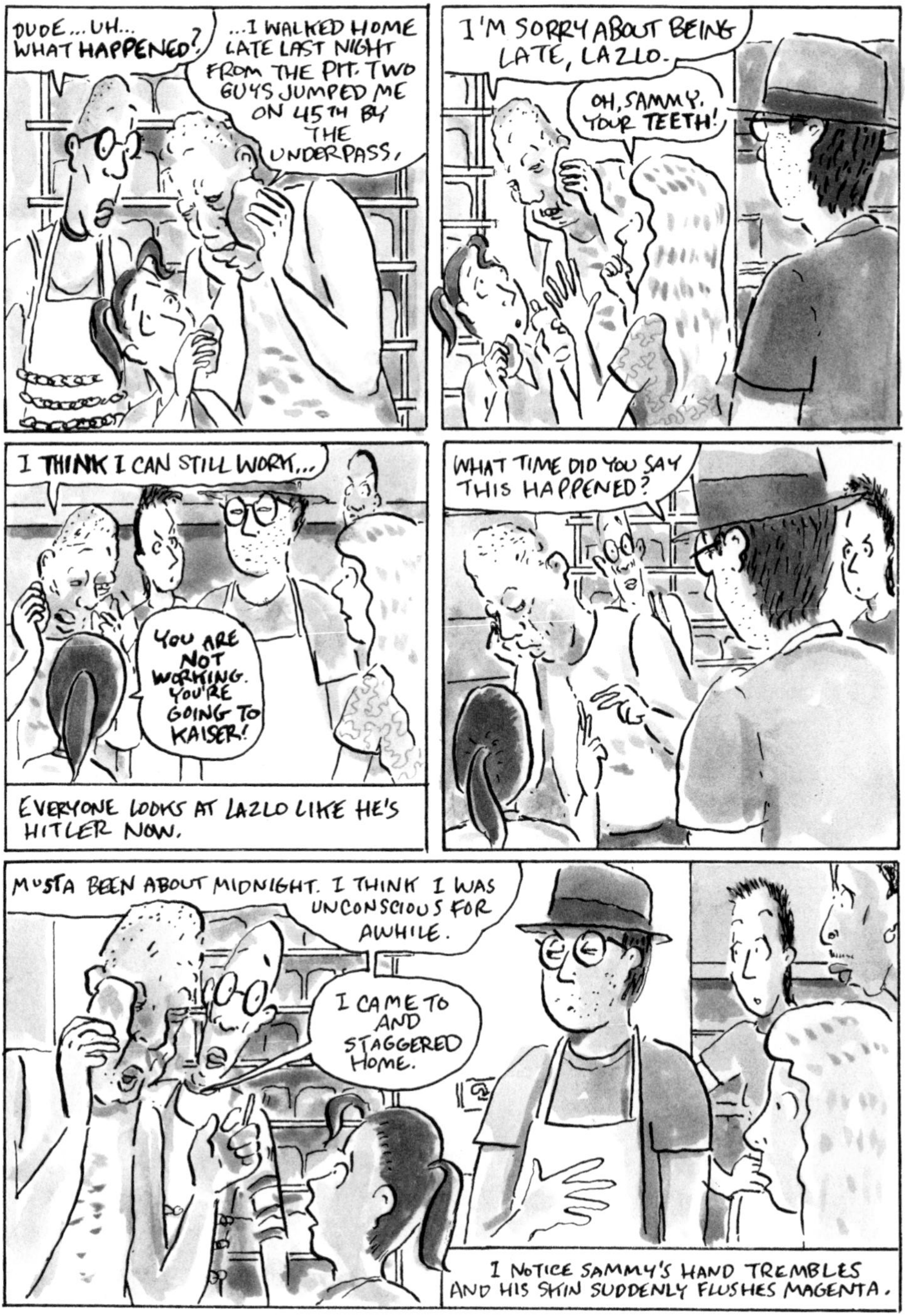
DUDE... UH... WHAT HAPPENED?
...I WALKED HOME LATE LAST NIGHT FROM THE PIT. TWO GUYS JUMPED ME ON 45TH BY THE UNDERPASS,
I'M SORRY ABOUT BEING LATE, LAZLO.
OH, SAMMY. YOUR TEETH!
I THINK I CAN STILL WORK...
YOU ARE NOT WORKING. YOU'RE GOING TO KAISER!
EVERYONE LOOKS AT LAZLO LIKE HE'S HITLER NOW.
WHAT TIME DID YOU SAY THIS HAPPENED?
MUSTA BEEN ABOUT MIDNIGHT. I THINK I WAS UNCONSCIOUS FOR AWHILE.
I CAME TO AND STAGGERED HOME.
I NOTICE SAMMY'S HAND TREMBLES AND HIS SKIN SUDDENLY FLUSHES MAGENTA.

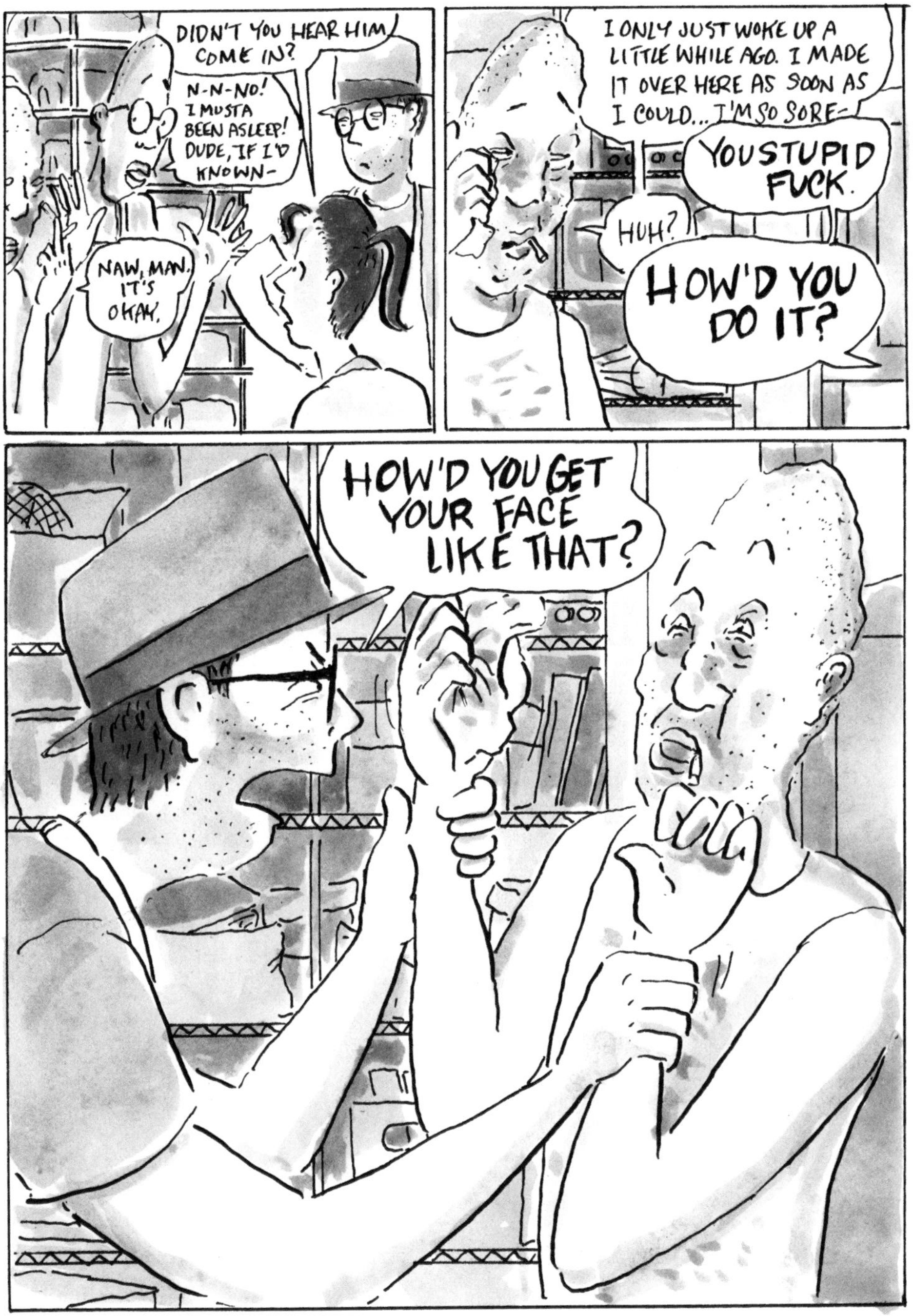
DIDN'T YOU HEAR HIM COME IN?
N-N-NO! I MUSTA BEEN ASLEEP! DUDE, IF I'D KNOWN-
NAW, MAN. IT'S OKAY.
I ONLY JUST WOKE UP A LITTLE WHILE AGO. I MADE IT OVER HERE AS SOON AS I COULD... I'M SO SORE-
YOU STUPID FUCK.
HUH?
HOW'D YOU DO IT?
HOW'D YOU GET YOUR FACE LIKE THAT?

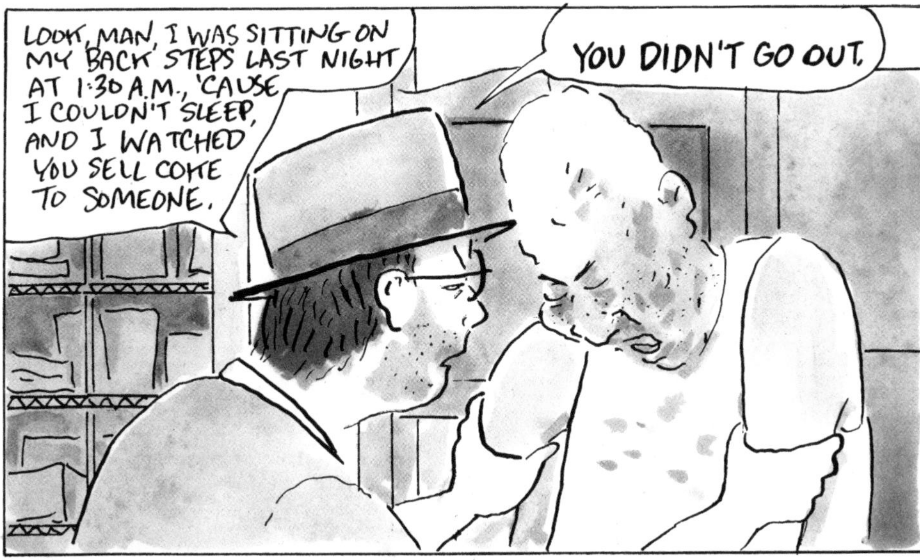
LOOK, MAN, I WAS SITTING ON MY BACK STEPS LAST NIGHT AT 1:30 A.M., 'CAUSE I COULDN'T SLEEP, AND I WATCHED YOU SELL COKE TO SOMEONE.
YOU DIDN'T GO OUT.

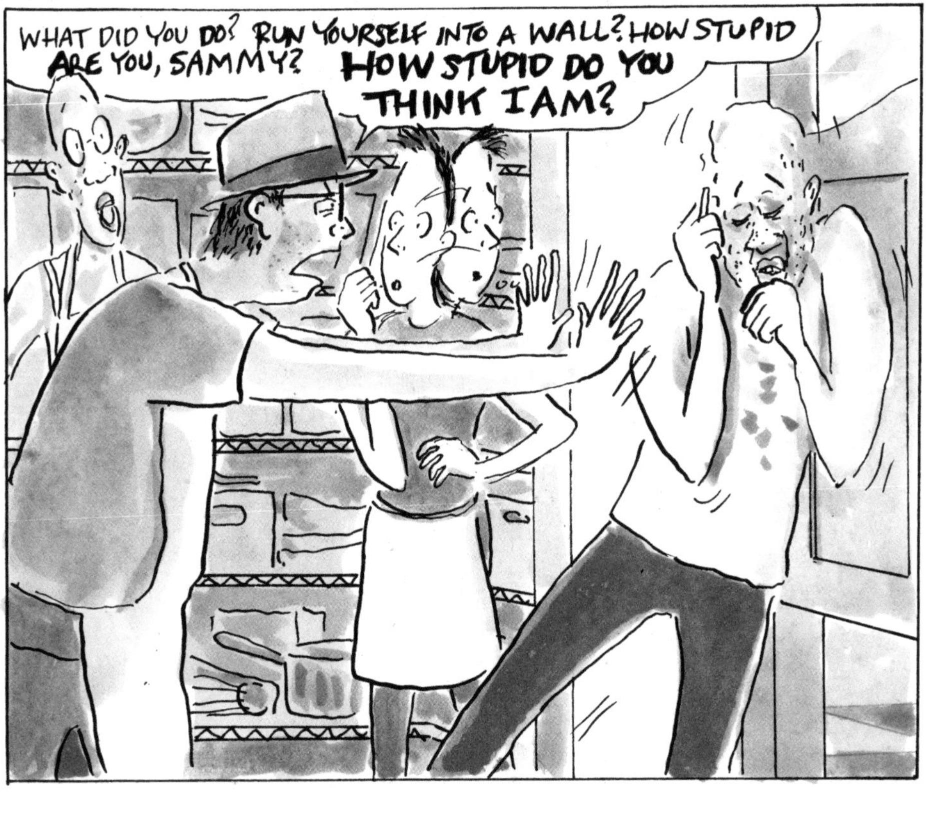
WHAT DID YOU DO? RUN YOURSELF INTO A WALL? HOW STUPID ARE YOU, SAMMY? HOW STUPID DO YOU THINK I AM?

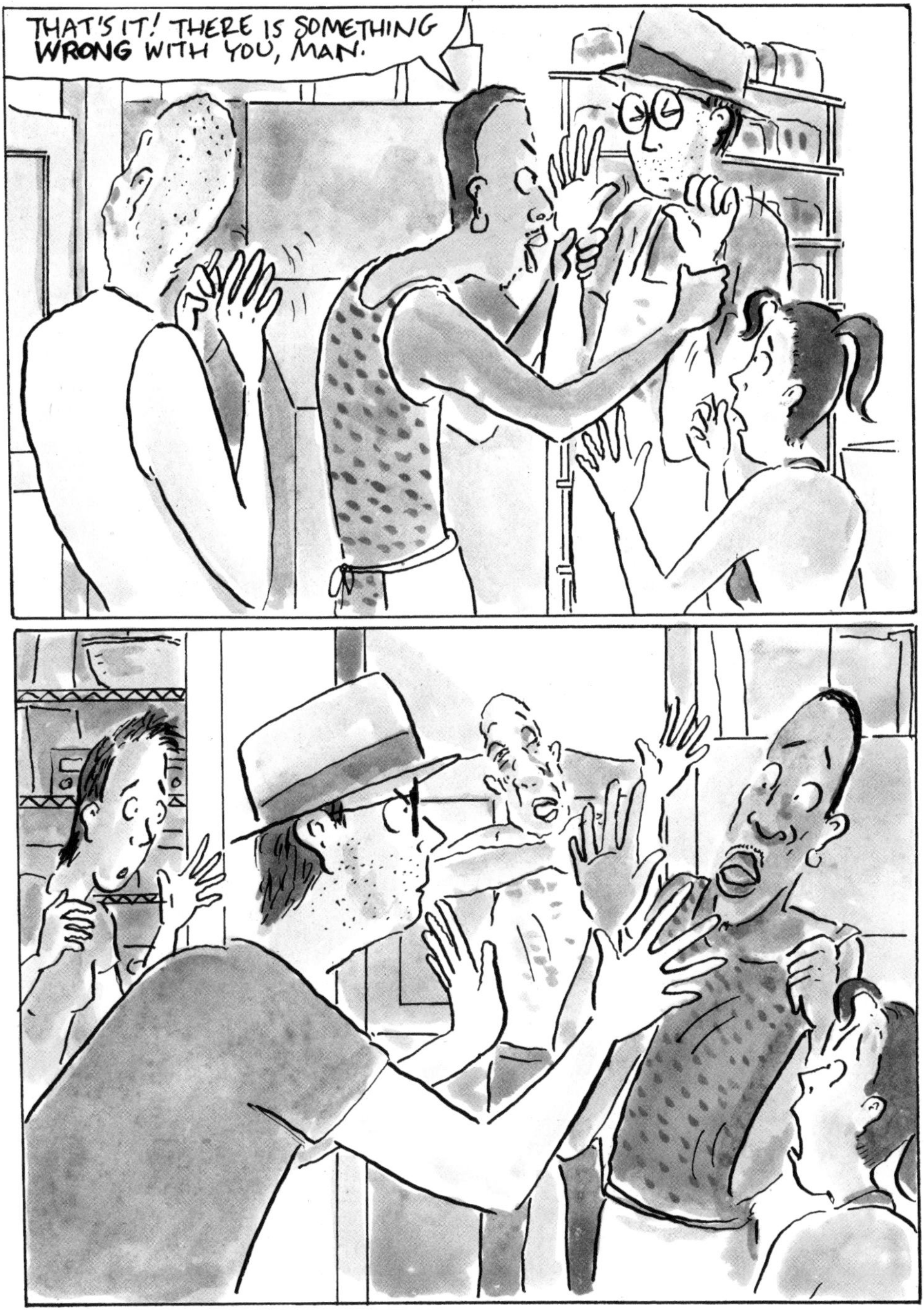
THAT'S IT! THERE IS SOMETHING WRONG WITH YOU, MAN.

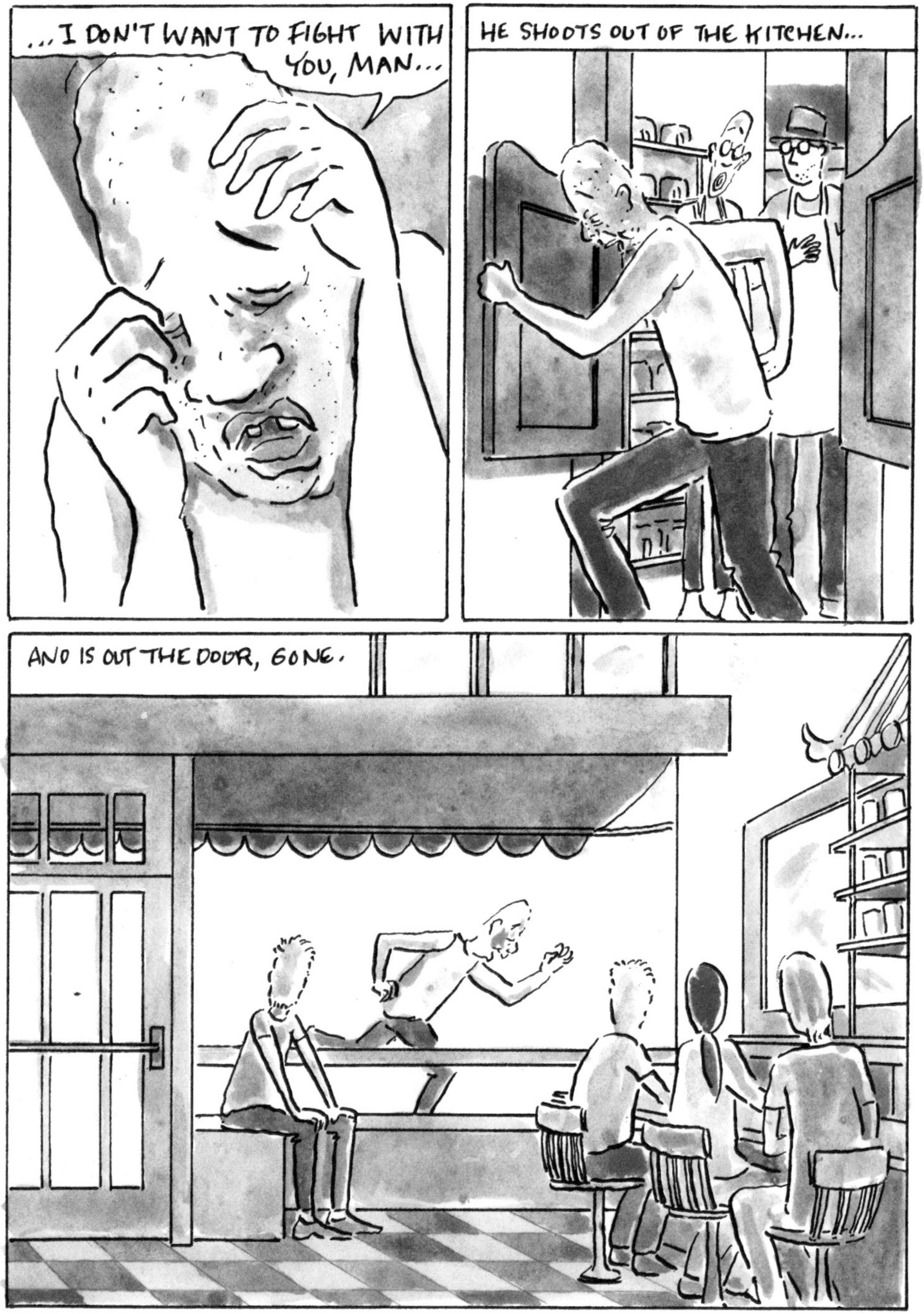
...I DON'T WANT TO FIGHT WITH YOU, MAN...
HE SHOOTS OUT OF THE KITCHEN...
AND IS OUT THE DOOR, GONE.

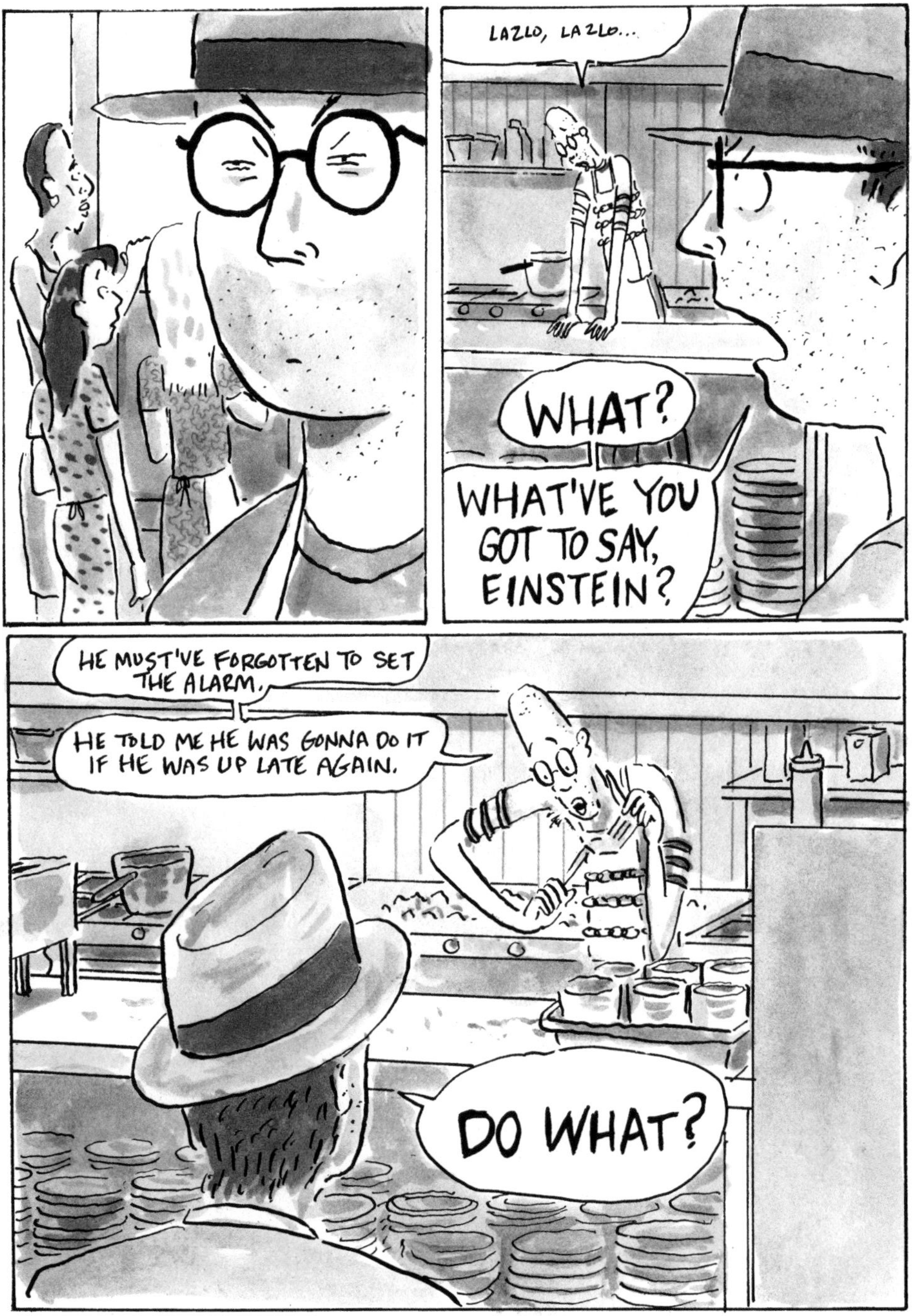
LAZLO, LAZLO...
WHAT?
WHAT'VE YOU GOT TO SAY, EINSTEIN?
HE MUST'VE FORGOTTEN TO SET THE ALARM.
HE TOLD ME HE WAS GONNA DO IT IF HE WAS UP LATE AGAIN.
DO WHAT?

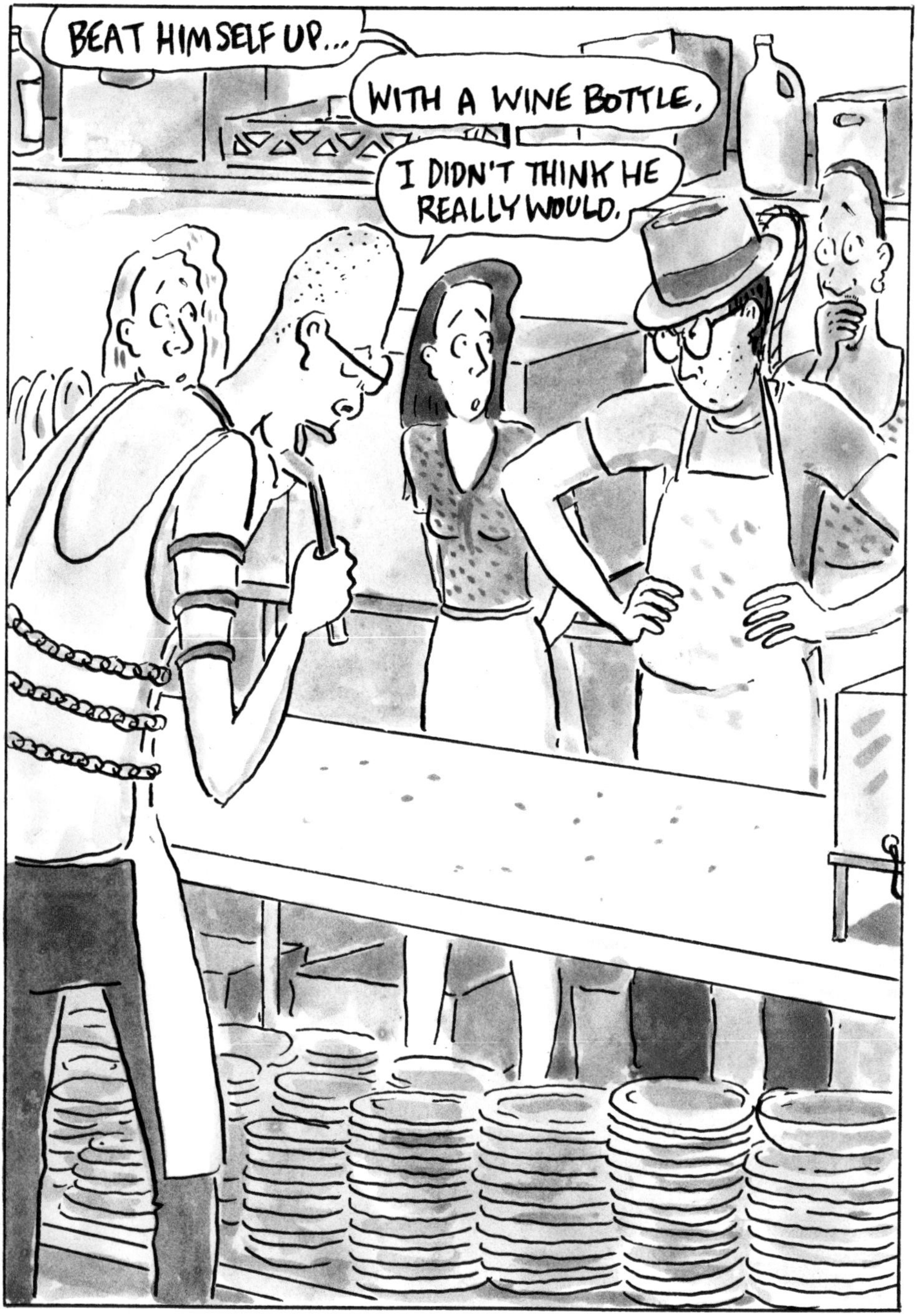

BEAT HIMSELF UP...
WITH A WINE BOTTLE.
I DIDN'T THINK HE REALLY WOULD.

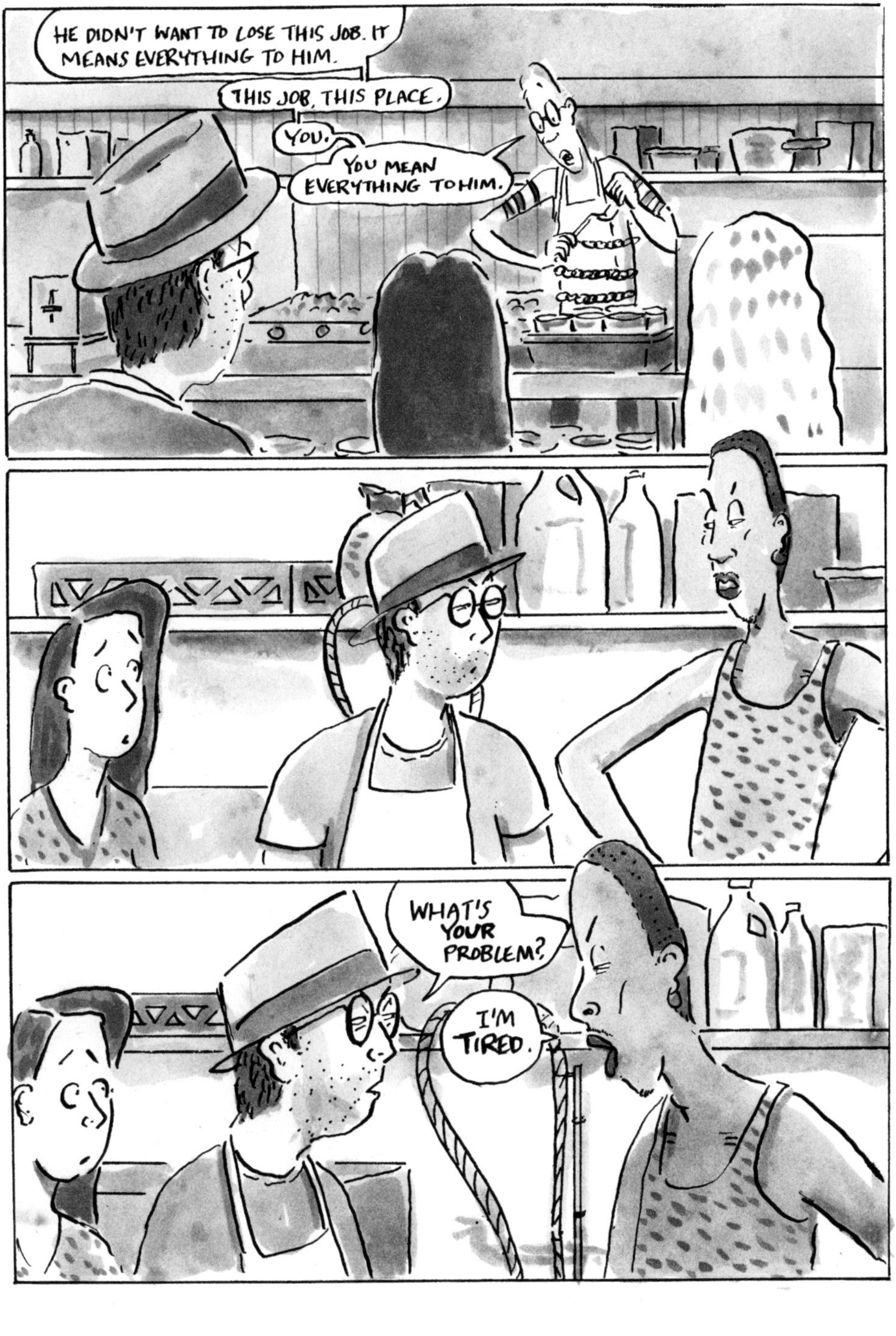
HE DIDN'T WANT TO LOSE THIS JOB. IT MEANS EVERYTHING TO HIM.
THIS JOB, THIS PLACE.
YOU.
YOU MEAN EVERYTHING TO HIM.
WHAT'S YOUR PROBLEM?
I'M TIRED.

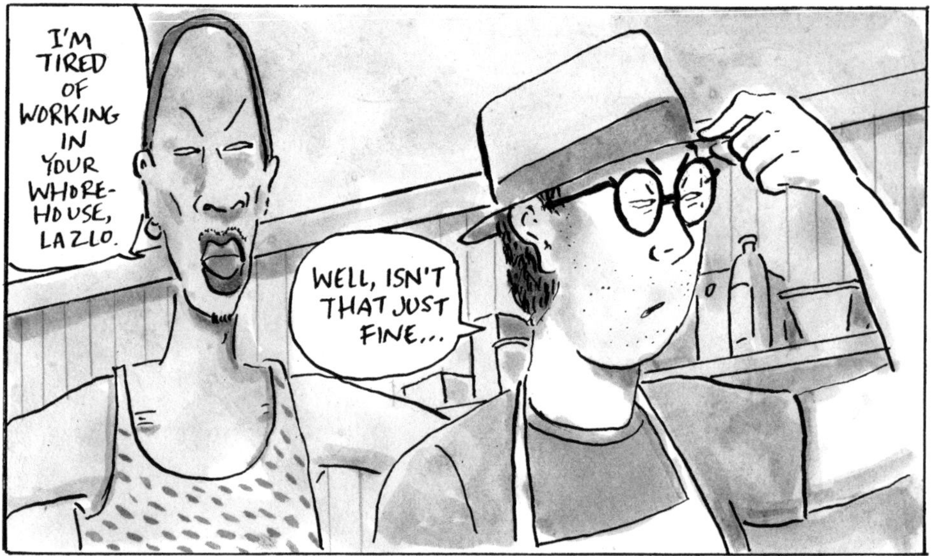
I'M TIRED OF WORKING IN YOUR WHORE-HOUSE, LAZLO.
WELL, ISN'T THAT JUST FINE...

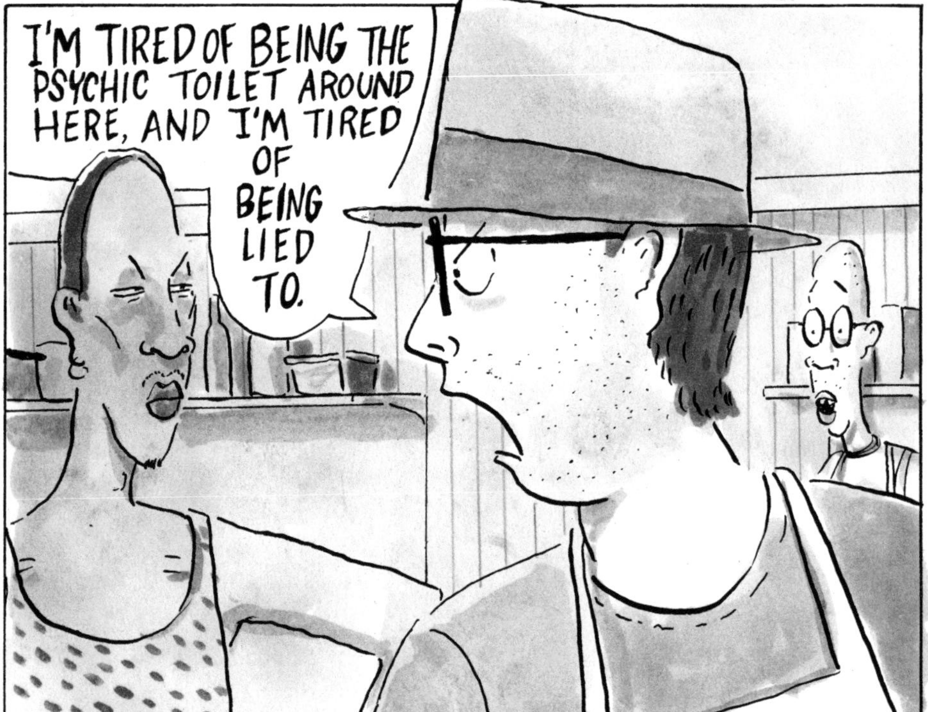
I'M TIRED OF BEING THE PSYCHIC TOILET AROUND HERE, AND I'M TIRED OF BEING LIED TO.

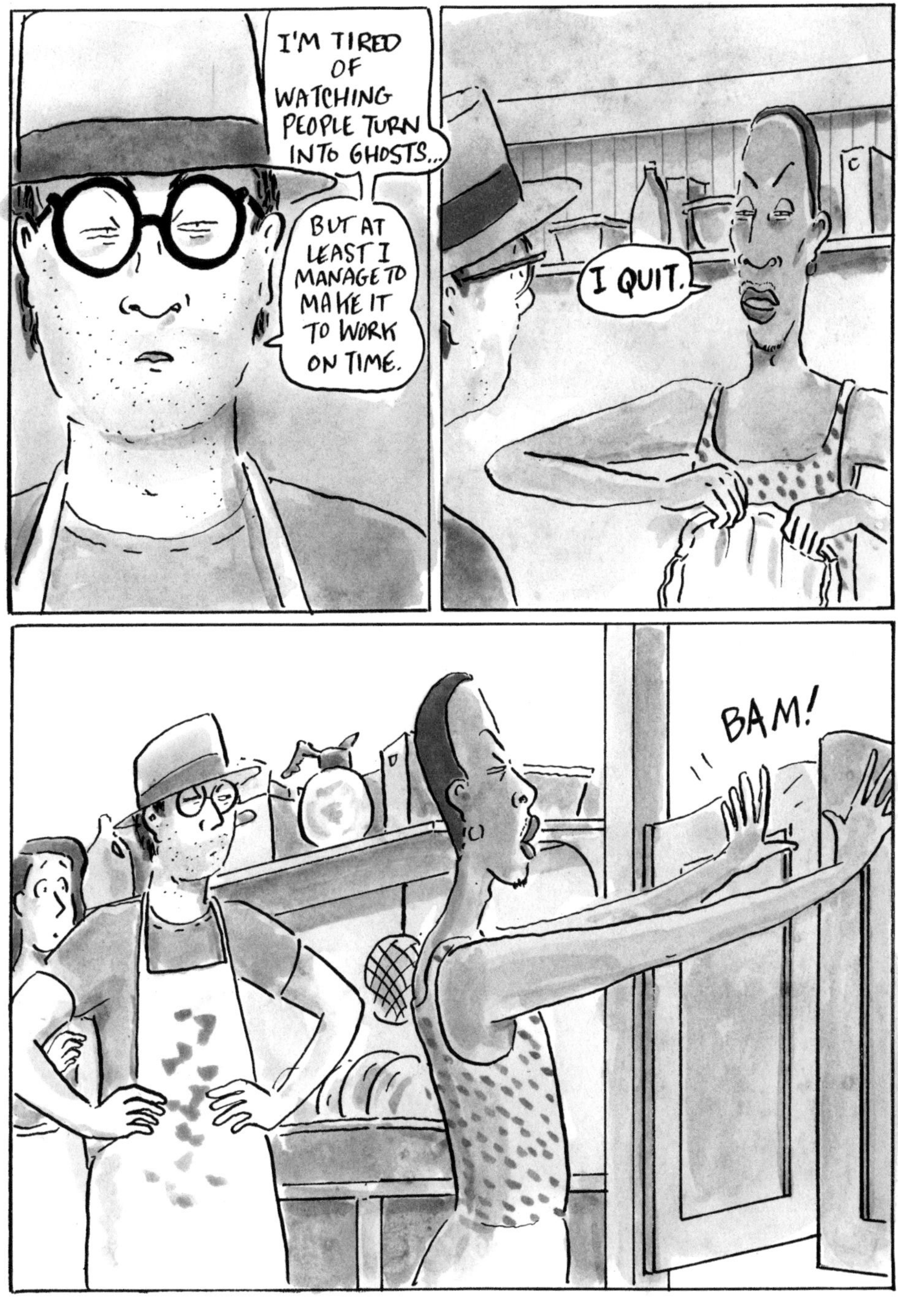
I'M TIRED OF WATCHING PEOPLE TURN INTO GHOSTS...
BUT AT LEAST I MANAGE TO MAKE IT TO WORK ON TIME.
I QUIT.
BAM!

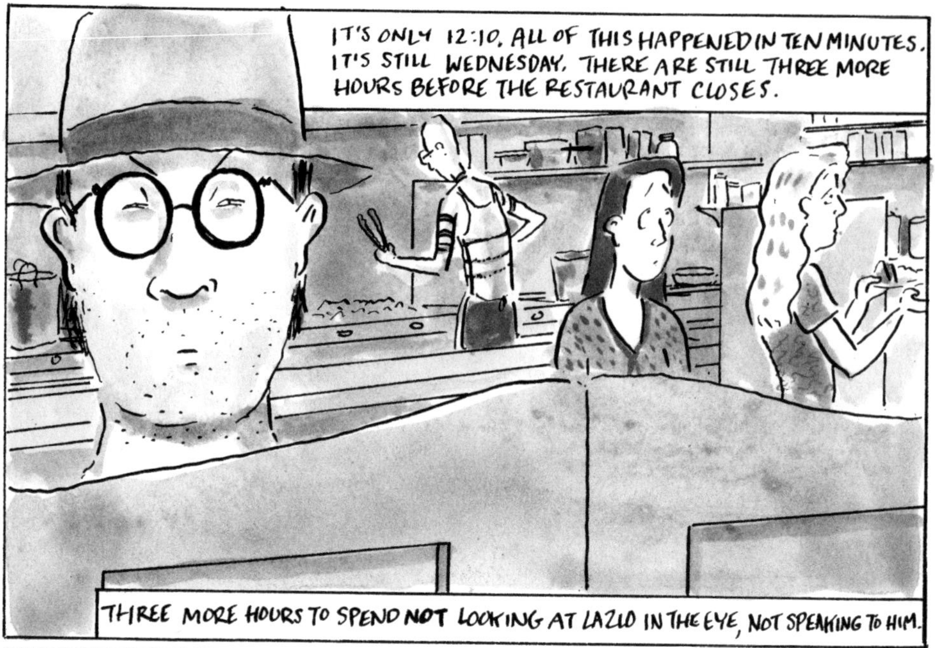
IT'S ONLY 12:10. ALL OF THIS HAPPENED IN TEN MINUTES. IT'S STILL WEDNESDAY. THERE ARE STILL THREE MORE HOURS BEFORE THE RESTAURANT CLOSES.
THREE MORE HOURS TO SPEND **NOT** LOOKING AT LAZLO IN THE EYE, NOT SPEAKING TO HIM.

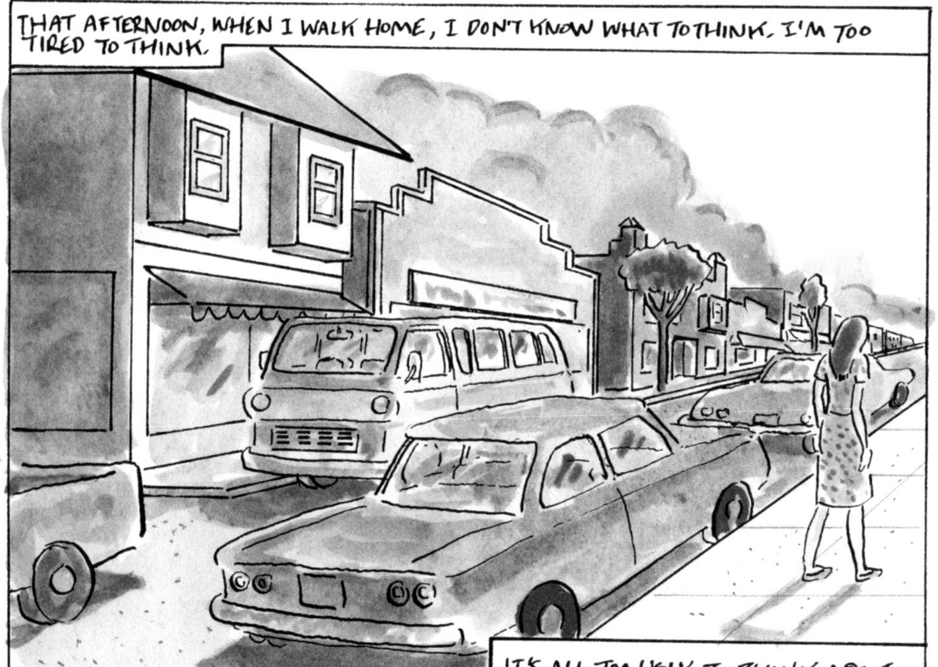
THAT AFTERNOON, WHEN I WALK HOME, I DON'T KNOW WHAT TO THINK. I'M TOO TIRED TO THINK.
IT'S ALL TOO UGLY TO THINK ABOUT.

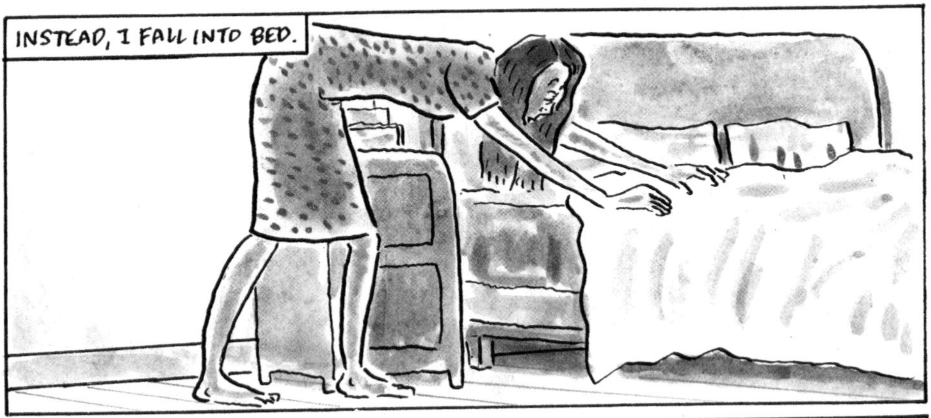
INSTEAD, I FALL INTO BED.

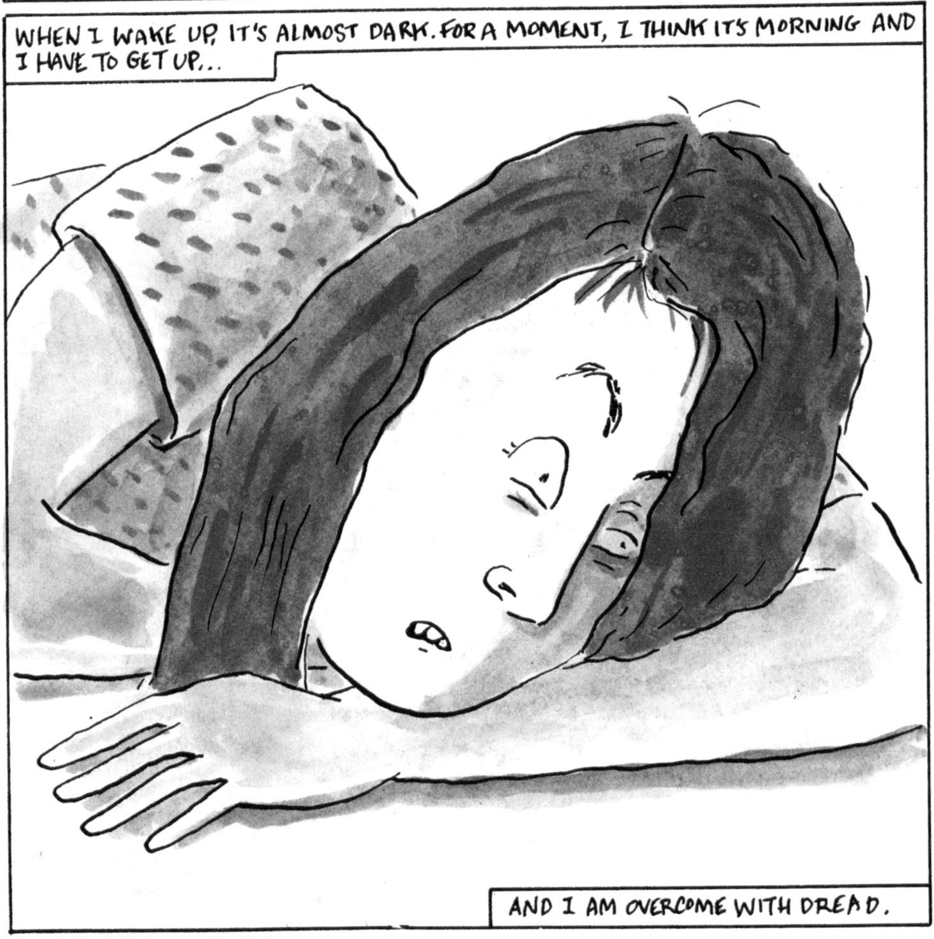
WHEN I WAKE UP, IT'S ALMOST DARK. FOR A MOMENT, I THINK IT'S MORNING AND I HAVE TO GET UP...
AND I AM OVERCOME WITH DREAD.

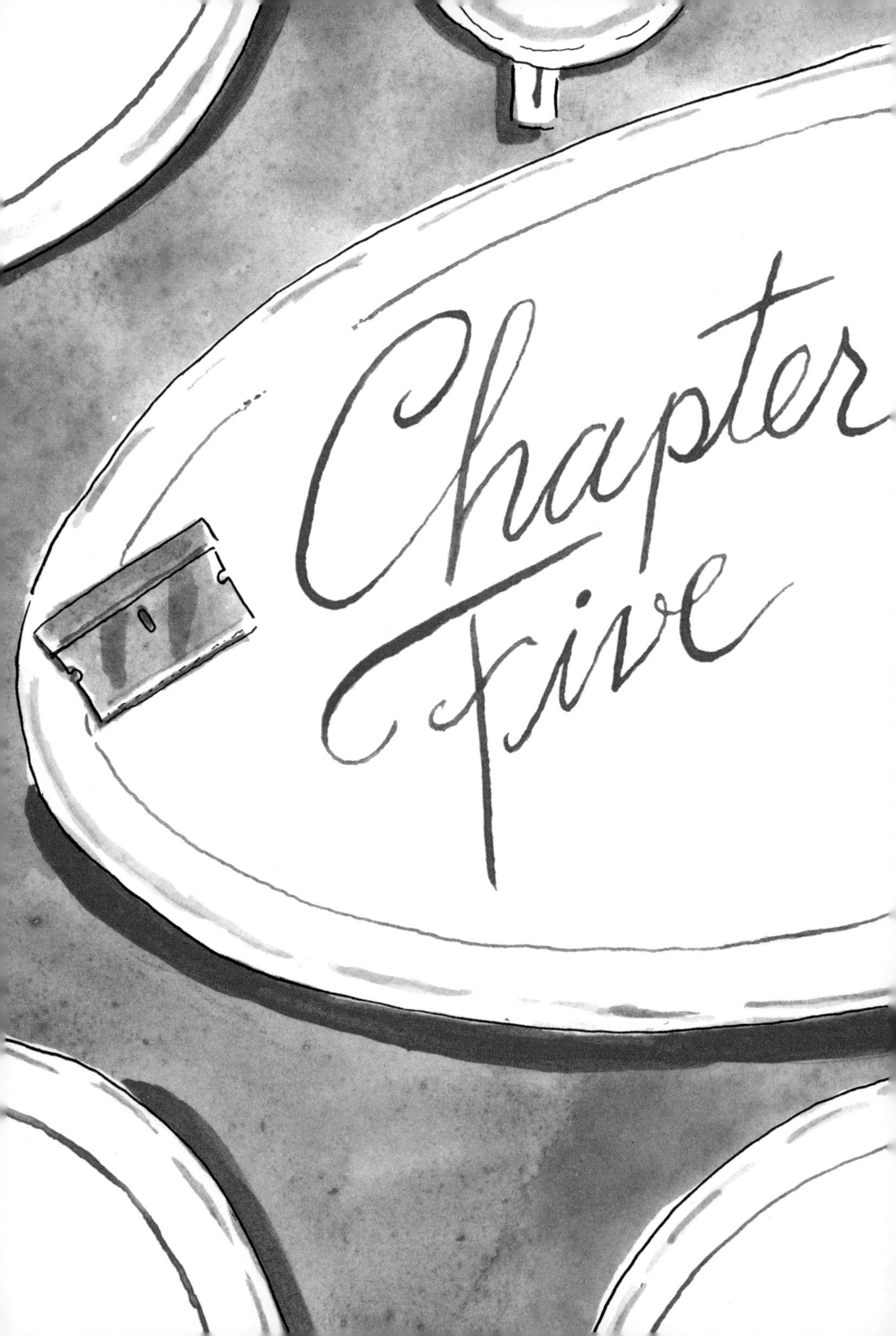
Chapter
Five

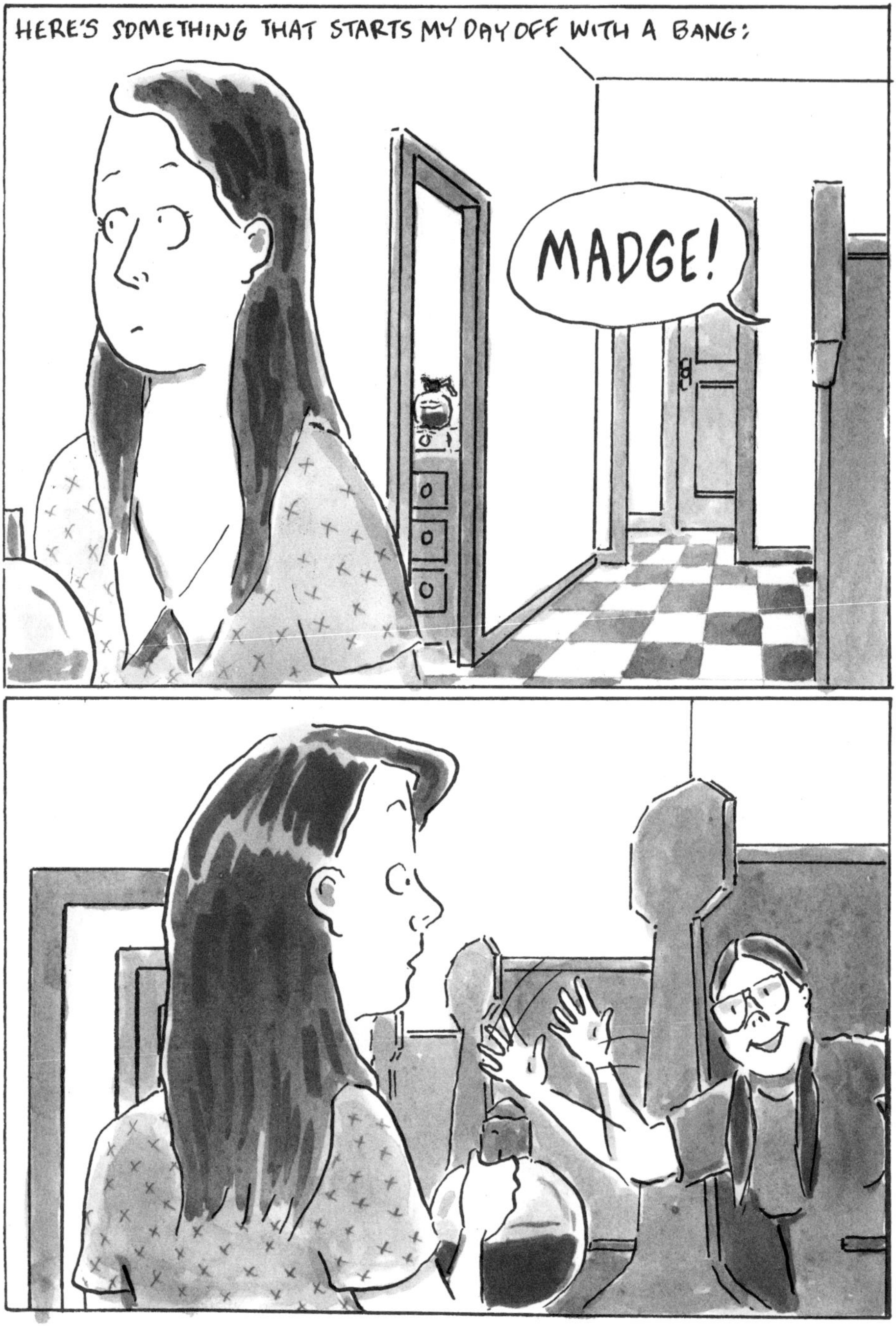
HERE'S SOMETHING THAT STARTS MY DAY OFF WITH A BANG:
MADGE!

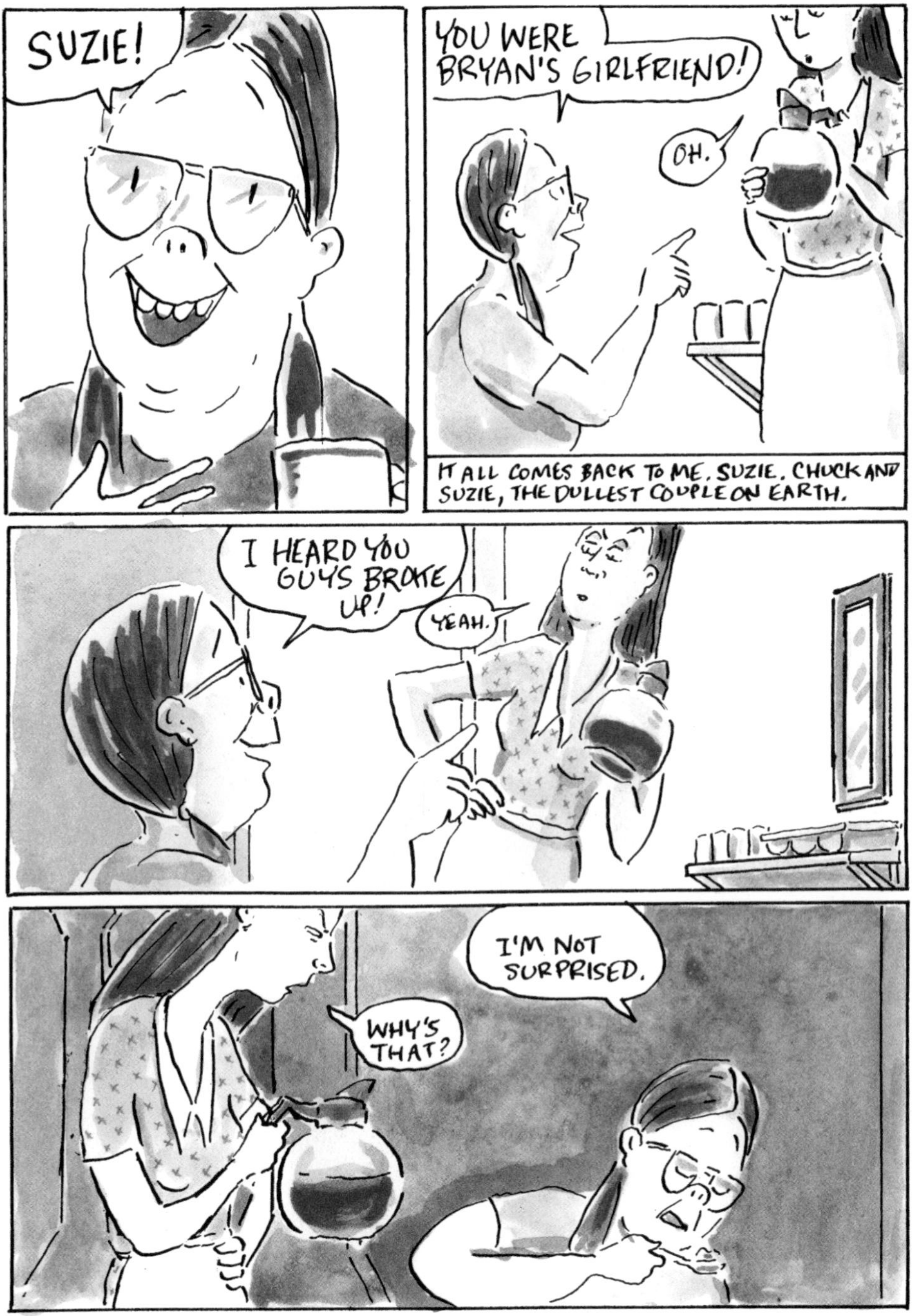
SUZIE!
YOU WERE BRYAN'S GIRLFRIEND!
OH.
IT ALL COMES BACK TO ME. SUZIE. CHUCK AND SUZIE, THE DULLEST COUPLE ON EARTH.
I HEARD YOU GUYS BROKE UP!
YEAH.
I'M NOT SURPRISED.
WHY'S THAT?

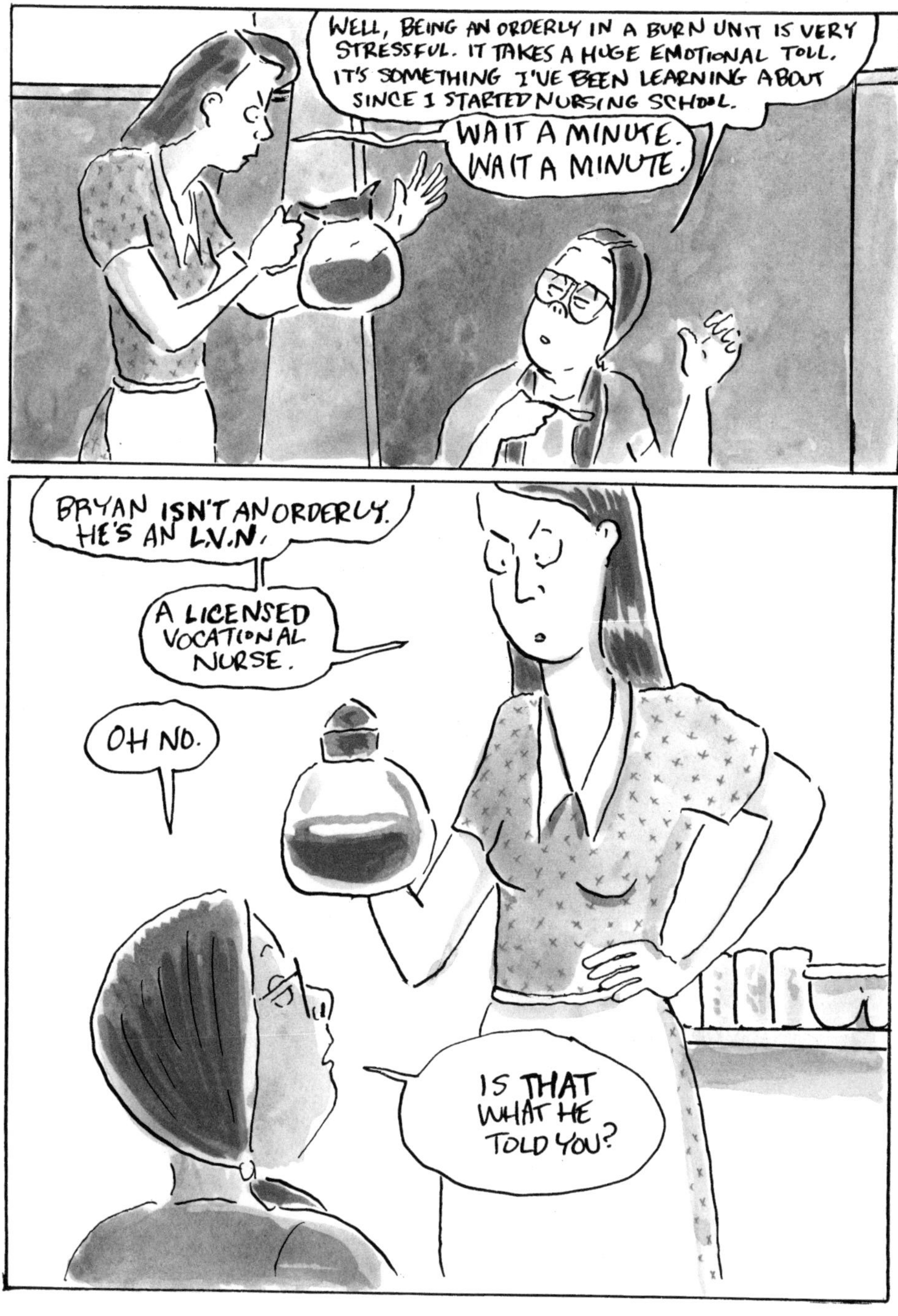
WELL, BEING AN ORDERLY IN A BURN UNIT IS VERY STRESSFUL. IT TAKES A HUGE EMOTIONAL TOLL. IT'S SOMETHING I'VE BEEN LEARNING ABOUT SINCE I STARTED NURSING SCHOOL.
WAIT A MINUTE. WAIT A MINUTE.
BRYAN ISN'T AN ORDERLY. HE'S AN L.V.N.
A LICENSED VOCATIONAL NURSE.
OH NO.
IS THAT WHAT HE TOLD YOU?

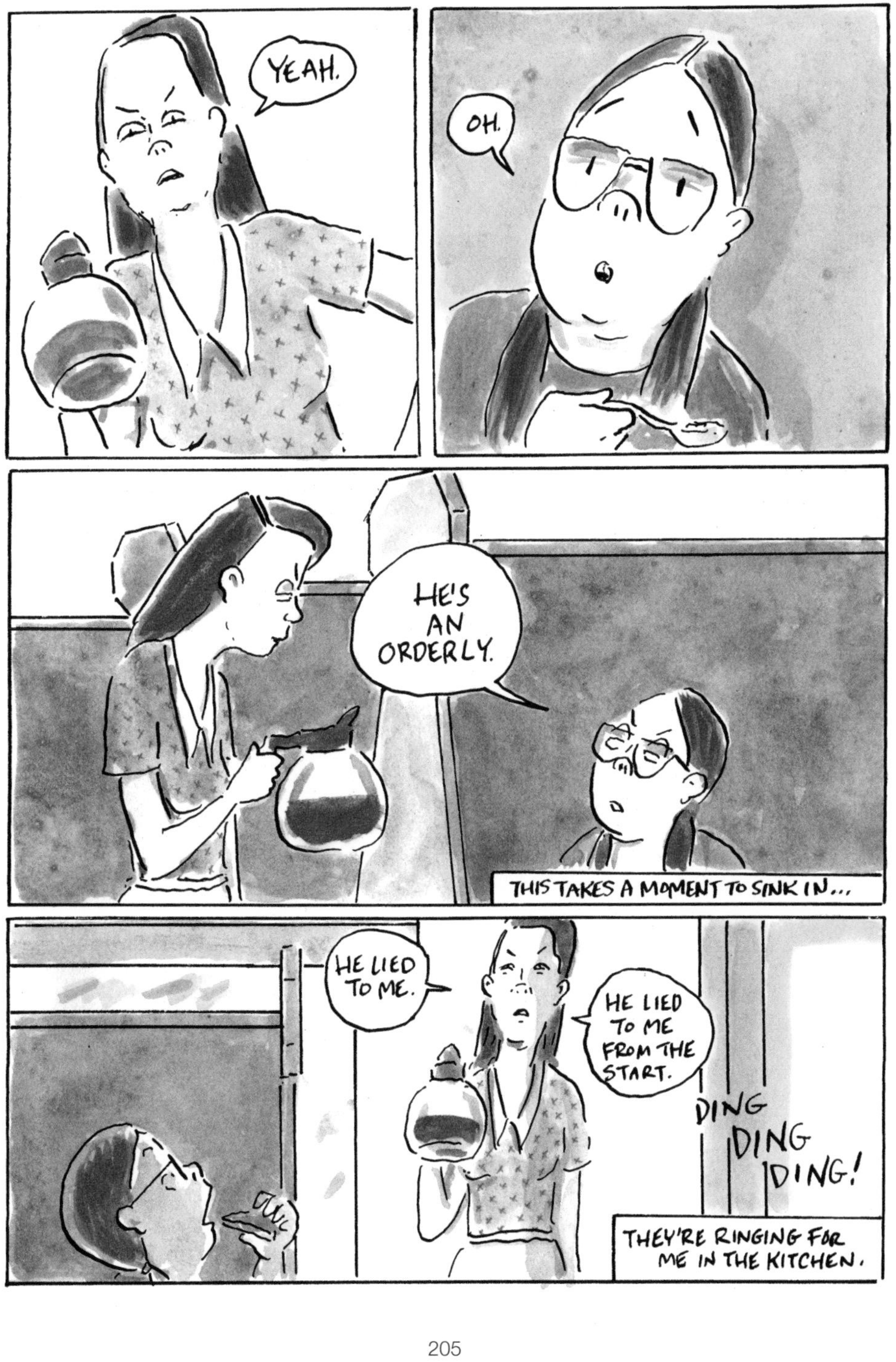
YEAH.
OH.
HE'S AN ORDERLY.
THIS TAKES A MOMENT TO SINK IN...
HE LIED TO ME.
HE LIED TO ME FROM THE START.
DING DING DING!
THEY'RE RINGING FOR ME IN THE KITCHEN.

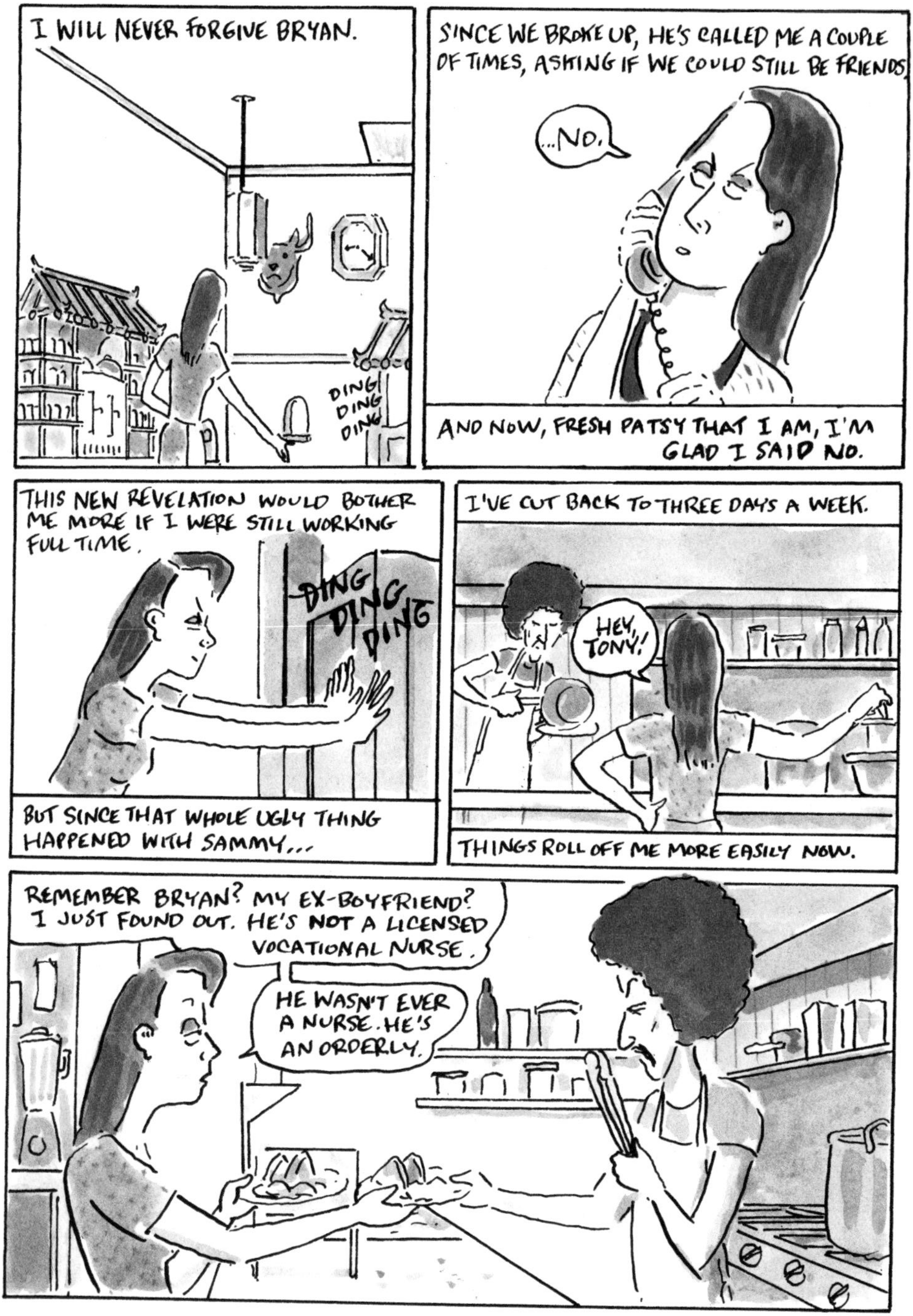

I WILL NEVER FORGIVE BRYAN.
DING DING DING
SINCE WE BROKE UP, HE'S CALLED ME A COUPLE OF TIMES, ASKING IF WE COULD STILL BE FRIENDS.
...NO.
AND NOW, FRESH PATSY THAT I AM, I'M GLAD I SAID NO.
THIS NEW REVELATION WOULD BOTHER ME MORE IF I WERE STILL WORKING FULL TIME.
DING DING DING
BUT SINCE THAT WHOLE UGLY THING HAPPENED WITH SAMMY...
I'VE CUT BACK TO THREE DAYS A WEEK.
HEY, TONY!
THINGS ROLL OFF ME MORE EASILY NOW.
REMEMBER BRYAN? MY EX-BOYFRIEND? I JUST FOUND OUT. HE'S NOT A LICENSED VOCATIONAL NURSE.
HE WASN'T EVER A NURSE. HE'S AN ORDERLY.

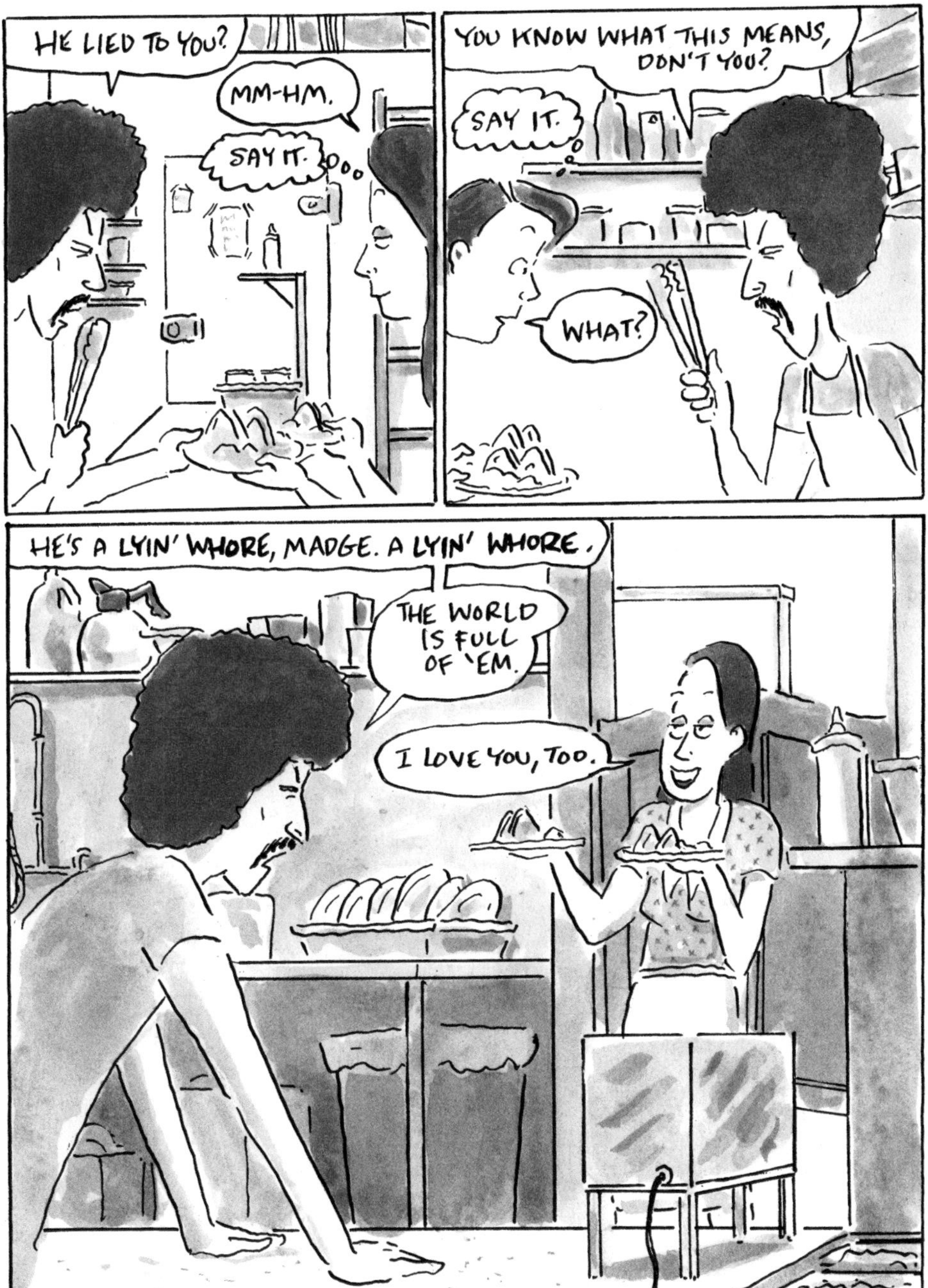
HE LIED TO YOU?
MM-HM.
SAY IT.
YOU KNOW WHAT THIS MEANS, DON'T YOU?
SAY IT.
WHAT?
HE'S A LYIN' WHORE, MADGE. A LYIN' WHORE.
THE WORLD IS FULL OF 'EM.
I LOVE YOU, TOO.

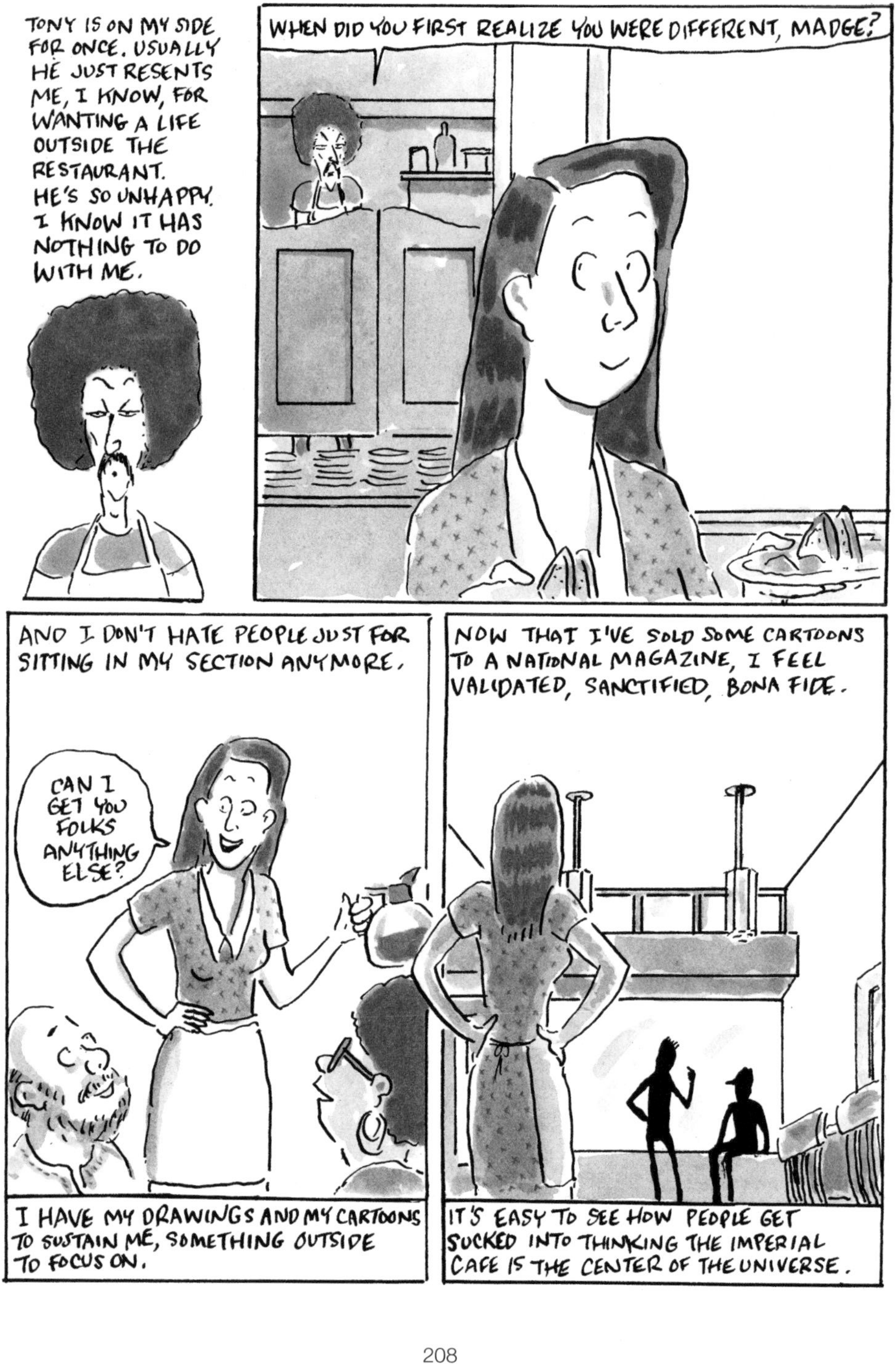
TONY IS ON MY SIDE FOR ONCE. USUALLY HE JUST RESENTS ME, I KNOW, FOR WANTING A LIFE OUTSIDE THE RESTAURANT. HE'S SO UNHAPPY. I KNOW IT HAS NOTHING TO DO WITH ME.
WHEN DID YOU FIRST REALIZE YOU WERE DIFFERENT, MADGE?
AND I DON'T HATE PEOPLE JUST FOR SITTING IN MY SECTION ANYMORE.
CAN I GET YOU FOLKS ANYTHING ELSE?
I HAVE MY DRAWINGS AND MY CARTOONS TO SUSTAIN ME, SOMETHING OUTSIDE TO FOCUS ON.
NOW THAT I'VE SOLD SOME CARTOONS TO A NATIONAL MAGAZINE, I FEEL VALIDATED, SANCTIFIED, BONA FIDE.
IT'S EASY TO SEE HOW PEOPLE GET SUCKED INTO THINKING THE IMPERIAL CAFE IS THE CENTER OF THE UNIVERSE.

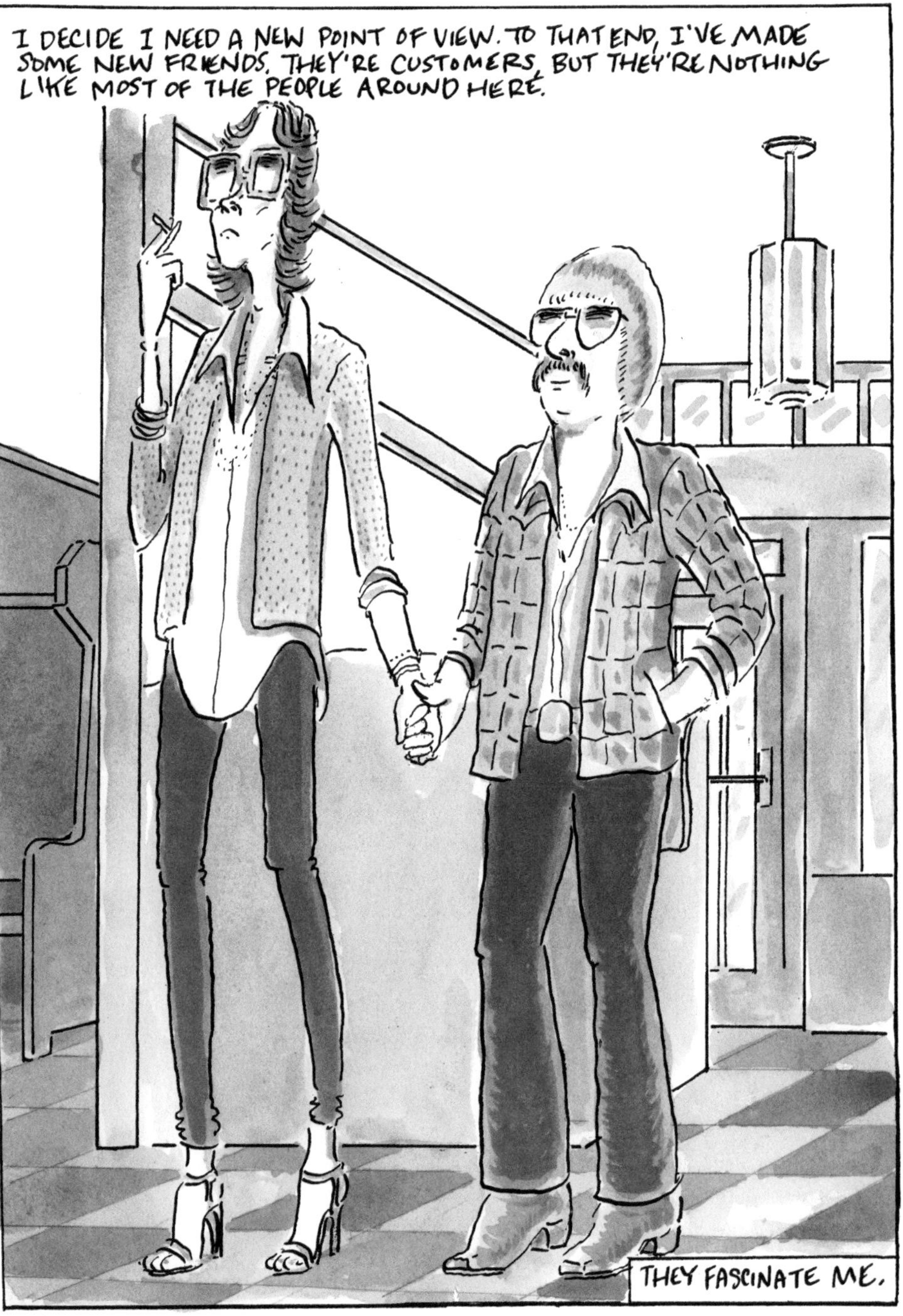
I DECIDE I NEED A NEW POINT OF VIEW. TO THAT END, I'VE MADE SOME NEW FRIENDS. THEY'RE CUSTOMERS, BUT THEY'RE NOTHING LIKE MOST OF THE PEOPLE AROUND HERE.
THEY FASCINATE ME.

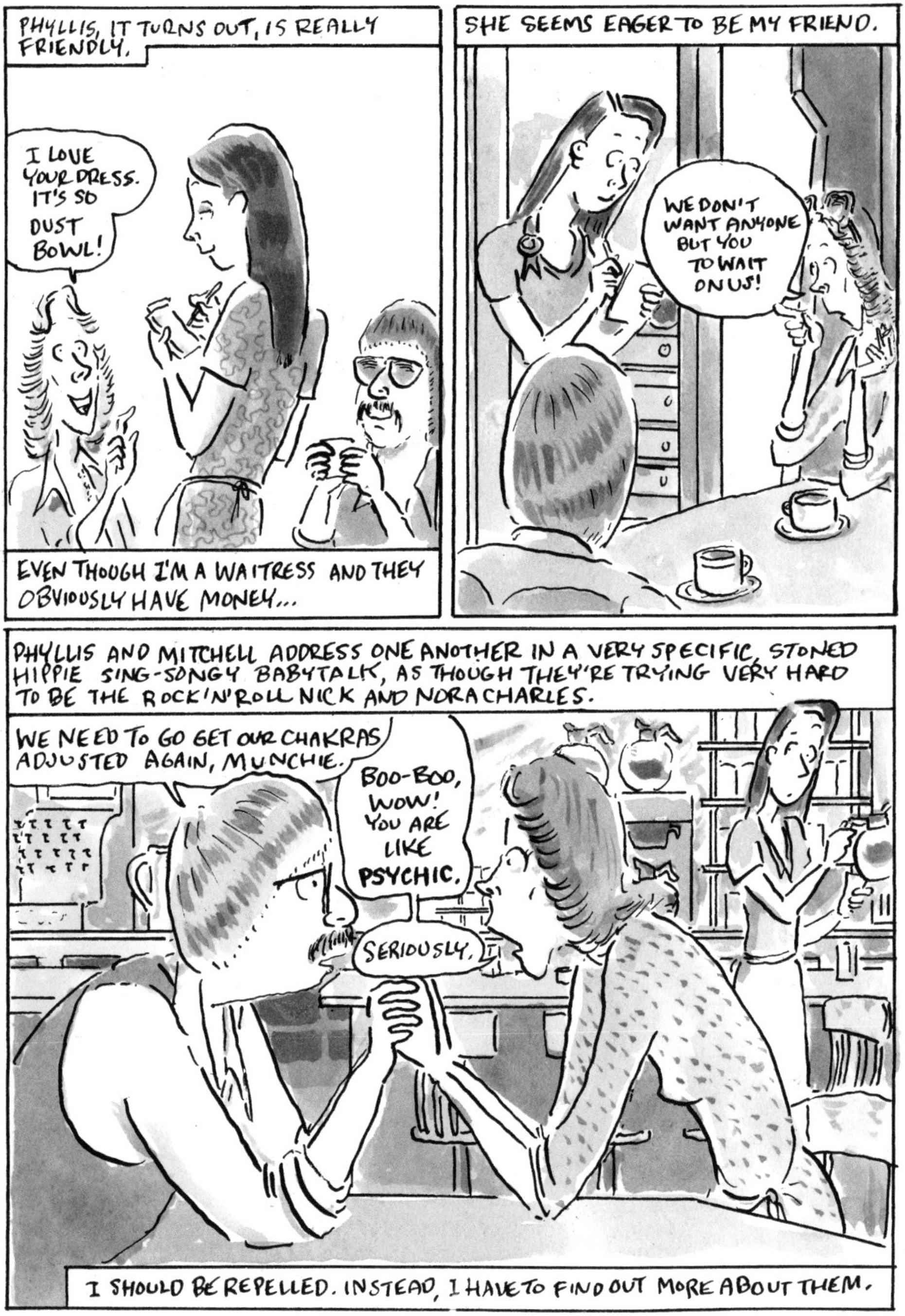

PHYLLIS, IT TURNS OUT, IS REALLY FRIENDLY.
I LOVE YOUR DRESS. IT'S SO DUST BOWL!
EVEN THOUGH I'M A WAITRESS AND THEY OBVIOUSLY HAVE MONEY...
SHE SEEMS EAGER TO BE MY FRIEND.
WE DON'T WANT ANYONE BUT YOU TO WAIT ON US!
PHYLLIS AND MITCHELL ADDRESS ONE ANOTHER IN A VERY SPECIFIC, STONED HIPPIE SING-SONGY BABYTALK, AS THOUGH THEY'RE TRYING VERY HARD TO BE THE ROCK'N'ROLL NICK AND NORA CHARLES.
WE NEED TO GO GET OUR CHAKRAS ADJUSTED AGAIN, MUNCHIE.
BOO-BOO, WOW! YOU ARE LIKE **PSYCHIC.**
SERIOUSLY.
I SHOULD BE REPELLED. INSTEAD, I HAVE TO FIND OUT MORE ABOUT THEM.

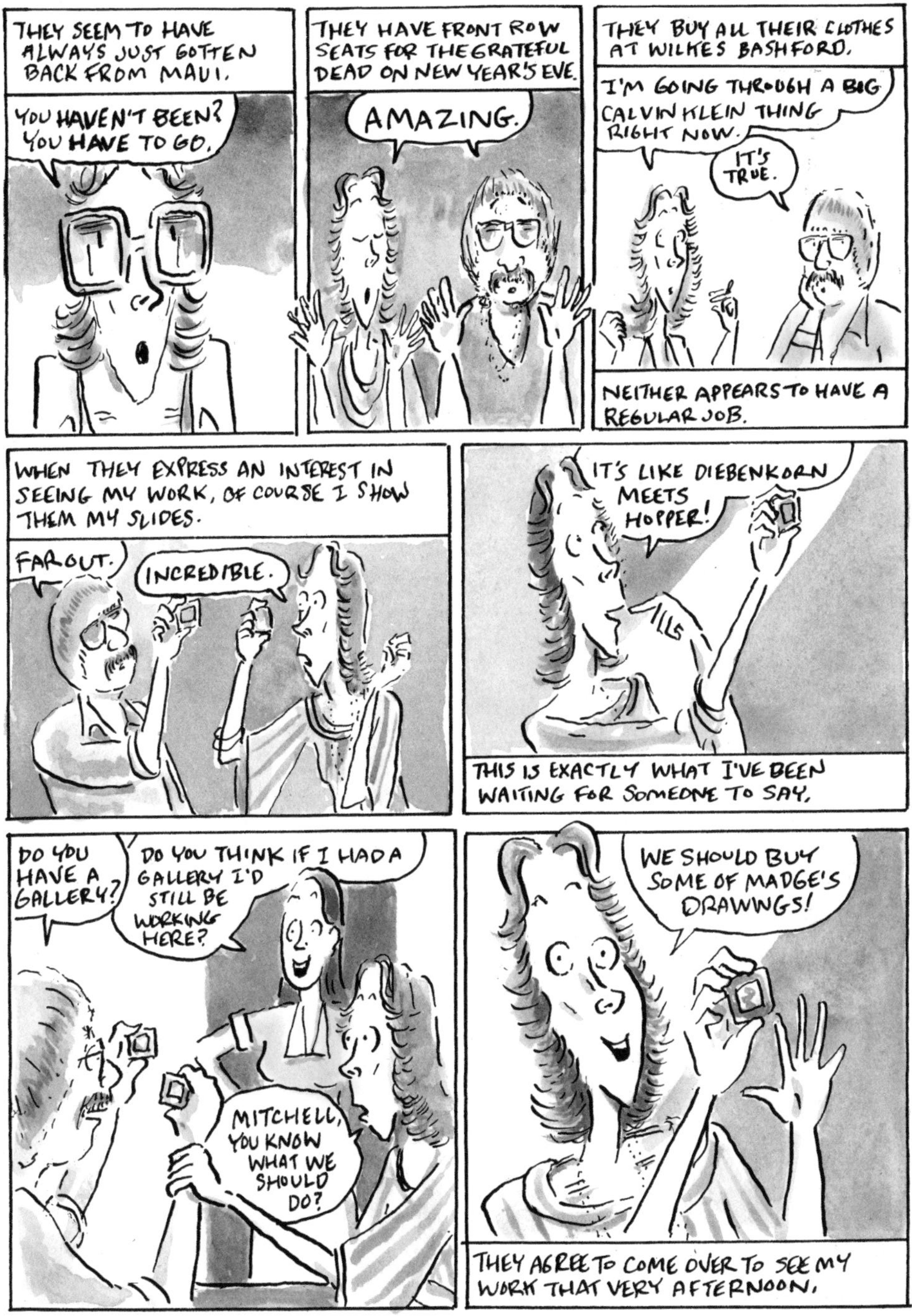
THEY SEEM TO HAVE ALWAYS JUST GOTTEN BACK FROM MAUI.
YOU HAVEN'T BEEN? YOU HAVE TO GO.
THEY HAVE FRONT ROW SEATS FOR THE GRATEFUL DEAD ON NEW YEAR'S EVE.
AMAZING.
THEY BUY ALL THEIR CLOTHES AT WILKES BASHFORD.
I'M GOING THROUGH A BIG CALVIN KLEIN THING RIGHT NOW.
IT'S TRUE.
NEITHER APPEARS TO HAVE A REGULAR JOB.
WHEN THEY EXPRESS AN INTEREST IN SEEING MY WORK, OF COURSE I SHOW THEM MY SLIDES.
FAR OUT.
INCREDIBLE.
IT'S LIKE DIEBENKORN MEETS HOPPER!
THIS IS EXACTLY WHAT I'VE BEEN WAITING FOR SOMEONE TO SAY.
DO YOU HAVE A GALLERY?
DO YOU THINK IF I HAD A GALLERY I'D STILL BE WORKING HERE?
MITCHELL, YOU KNOW WHAT WE SHOULD DO?
WE SHOULD BUY SOME OF MADGE'S DRAWINGS!
THEY AGREE TO COME OVER TO SEE MY WORK THAT VERY AFTERNOON.

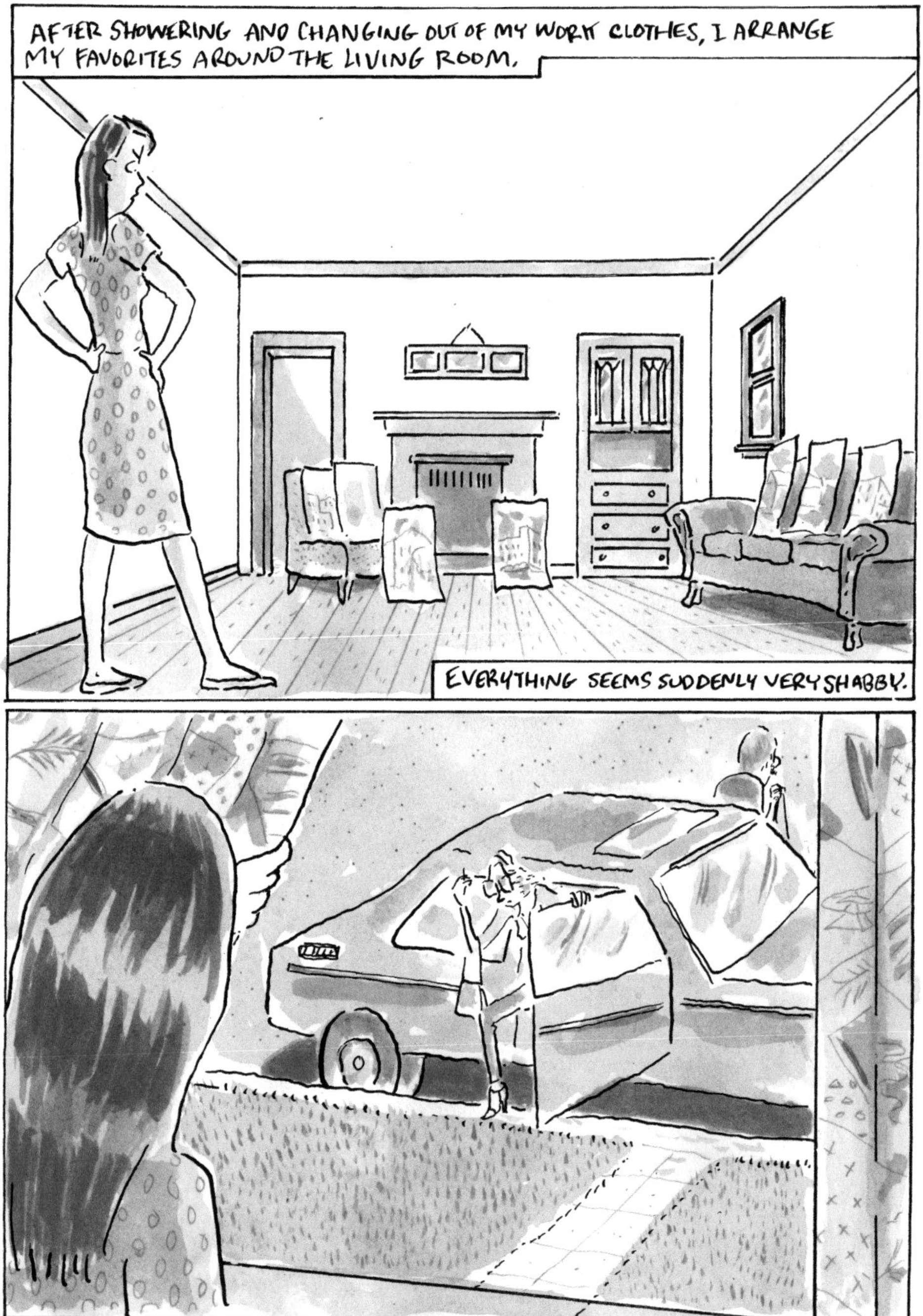
AFTER SHOWERING AND CHANGING OUT OF MY WORK CLOTHES, I ARRANGE MY FAVORITES AROUND THE LIVING ROOM.
EVERYTHING SEEMS SUDDENLY VERY SHABBY.

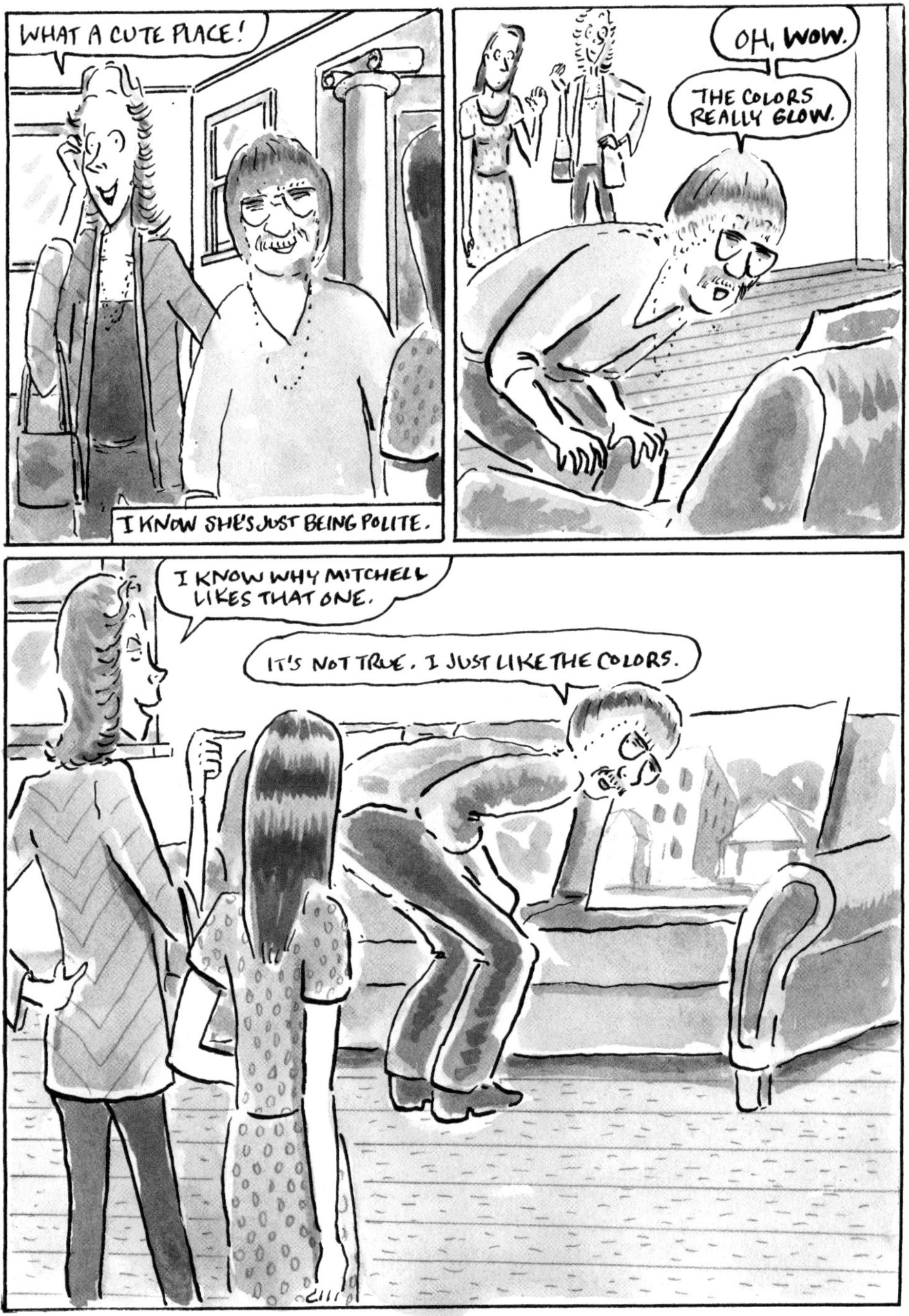
WHAT A CUTE PLACE!
I KNOW SHE'S JUST BEING POLITE.
OH, WOW.
THE COLORS REALLY GLOW.
I KNOW WHY MITCHELL LIKES THAT ONE.
IT'S NOT TRUE. I JUST LIKE THE COLORS.

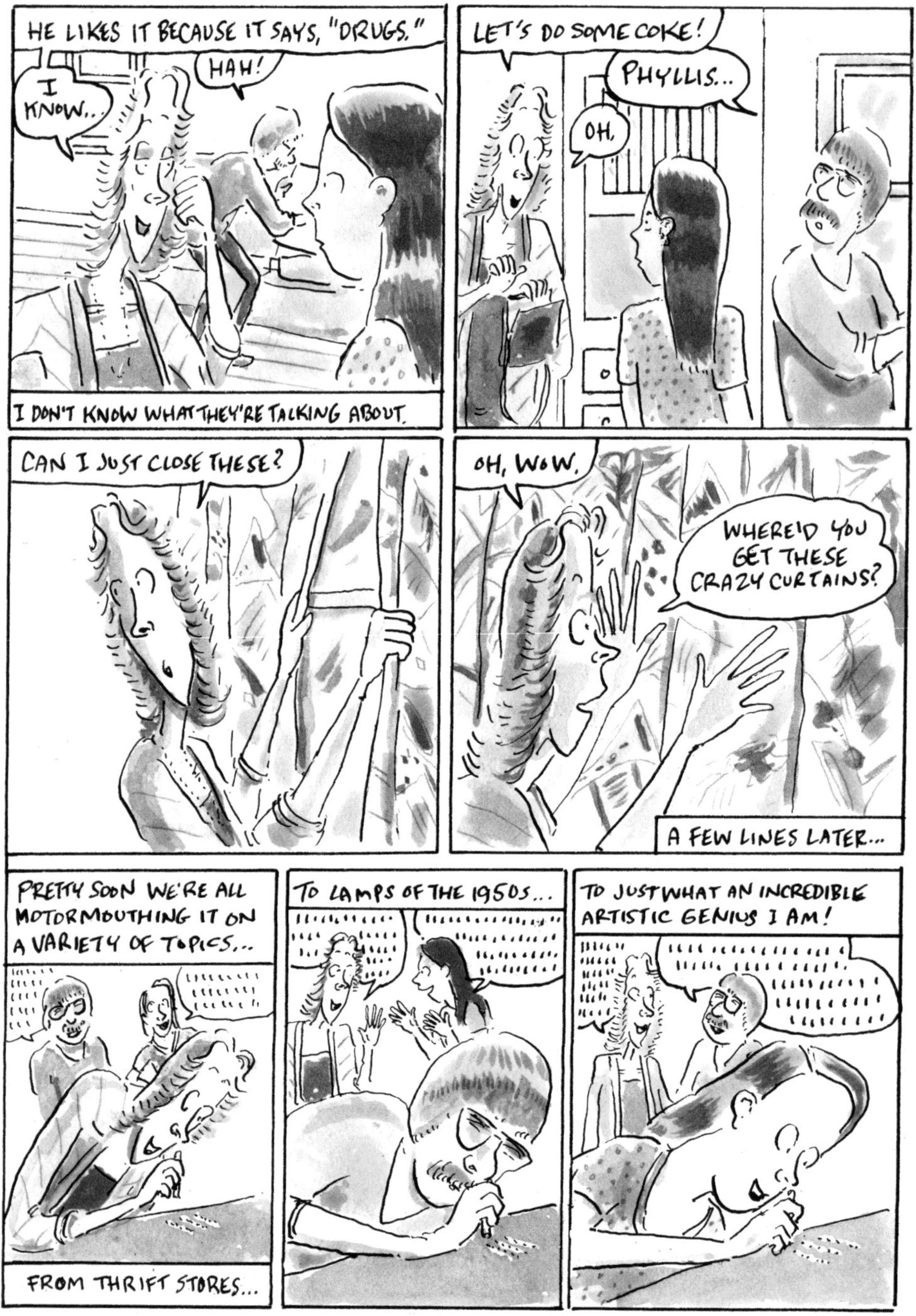
HE LIKES IT BECAUSE IT SAYS, "DRUGS."
I KNOW...
HAH!
I DON'T KNOW WHAT THEY'RE TALKING ABOUT.
LET'S DO SOME COKE!
PHYLLIS...
OH,
CAN I JUST CLOSE THESE?
OH, WOW.
WHERE'D YOU GET THESE CRAZY CURTAINS?
A FEW LINES LATER...
PRETTY SOON WE'RE ALL MOTORMOUTHING IT ON A VARIETY OF TOPICS...
FROM THRIFT STORES...
TO LAMPS OF THE 1950S...
TO JUST WHAT AN INCREDIBLE ARTISTIC GENIUS I AM!

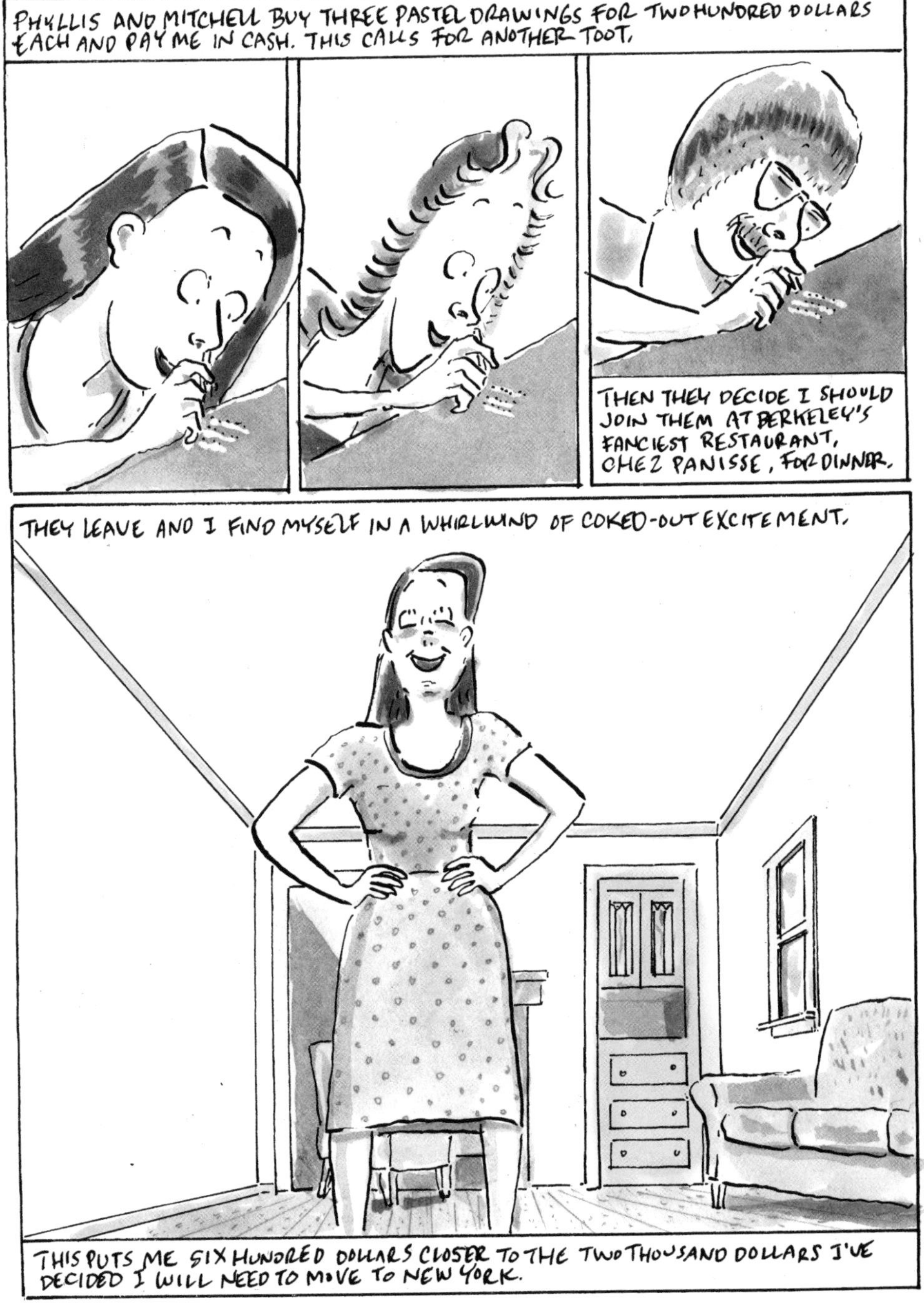
PHYLLIS AND MITCHELL BUY THREE PASTEL DRAWINGS FOR TWO HUNDRED DOLLARS EACH AND PAY ME IN CASH. THIS CALLS FOR ANOTHER TOOT.
THEN THEY DECIDE I SHOULD JOIN THEM AT BERKELEY'S FANCIEST RESTAURANT, CHEZ PANISSE, FOR DINNER.
THEY LEAVE AND I FIND MYSELF IN A WHIRLWIND OF COKED-OUT EXCITEMENT.
THIS PUTS ME SIX HUNDRED DOLLARS CLOSER TO THE TWO THOUSAND DOLLARS I'VE DECIDED I WILL NEED TO MOVE TO NEW YORK.

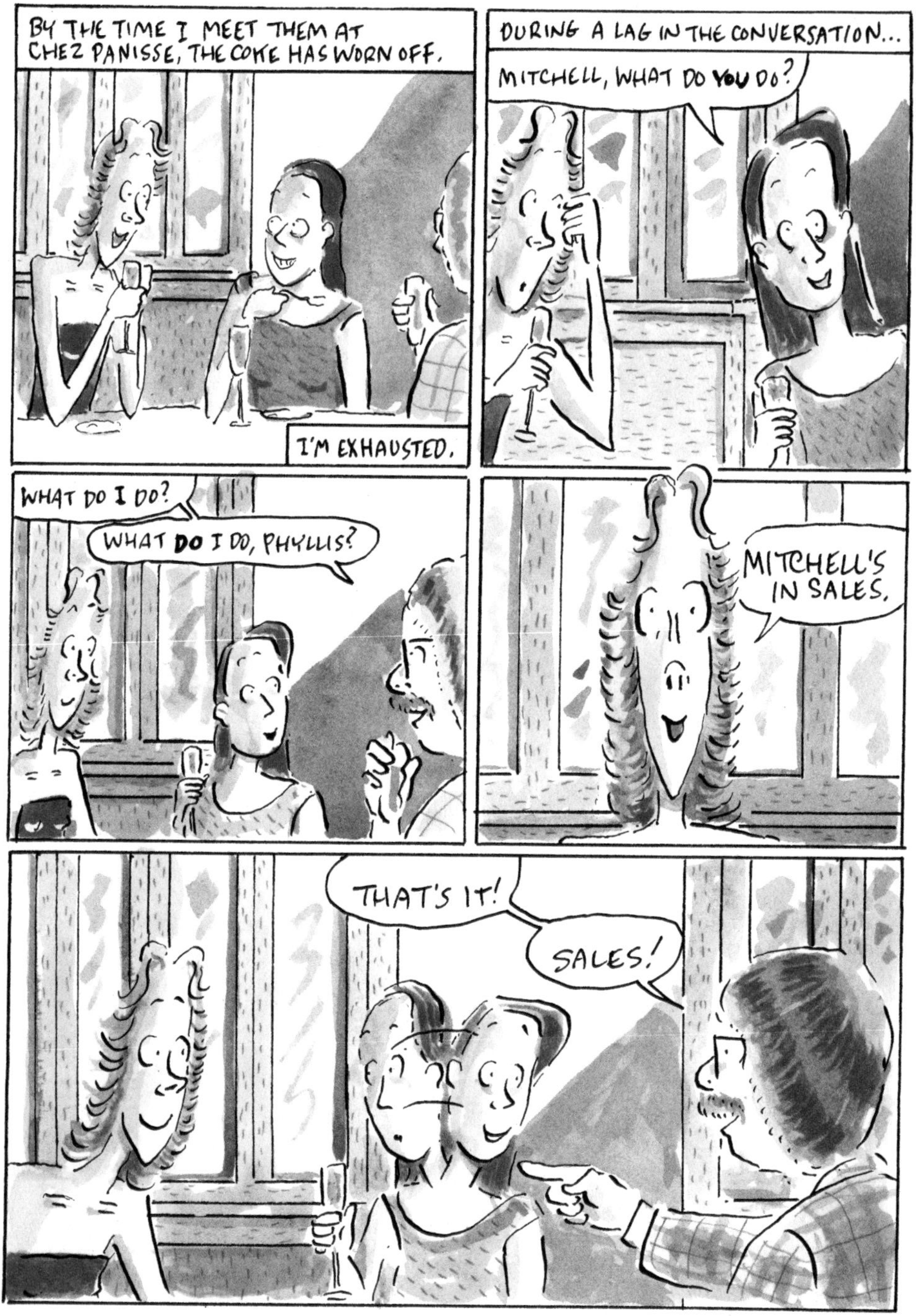
BY THE TIME I MEET THEM AT CHEZ PANISSE, THE COKE HAS WORN OFF.
I'M EXHAUSTED.
DURING A LAG IN THE CONVERSATION...
MITCHELL, WHAT DO YOU DO?
WHAT DO I DO?
WHAT DO I DO, PHYLLIS?
MITCHELL'S IN SALES.
THAT'S IT!
SALES!

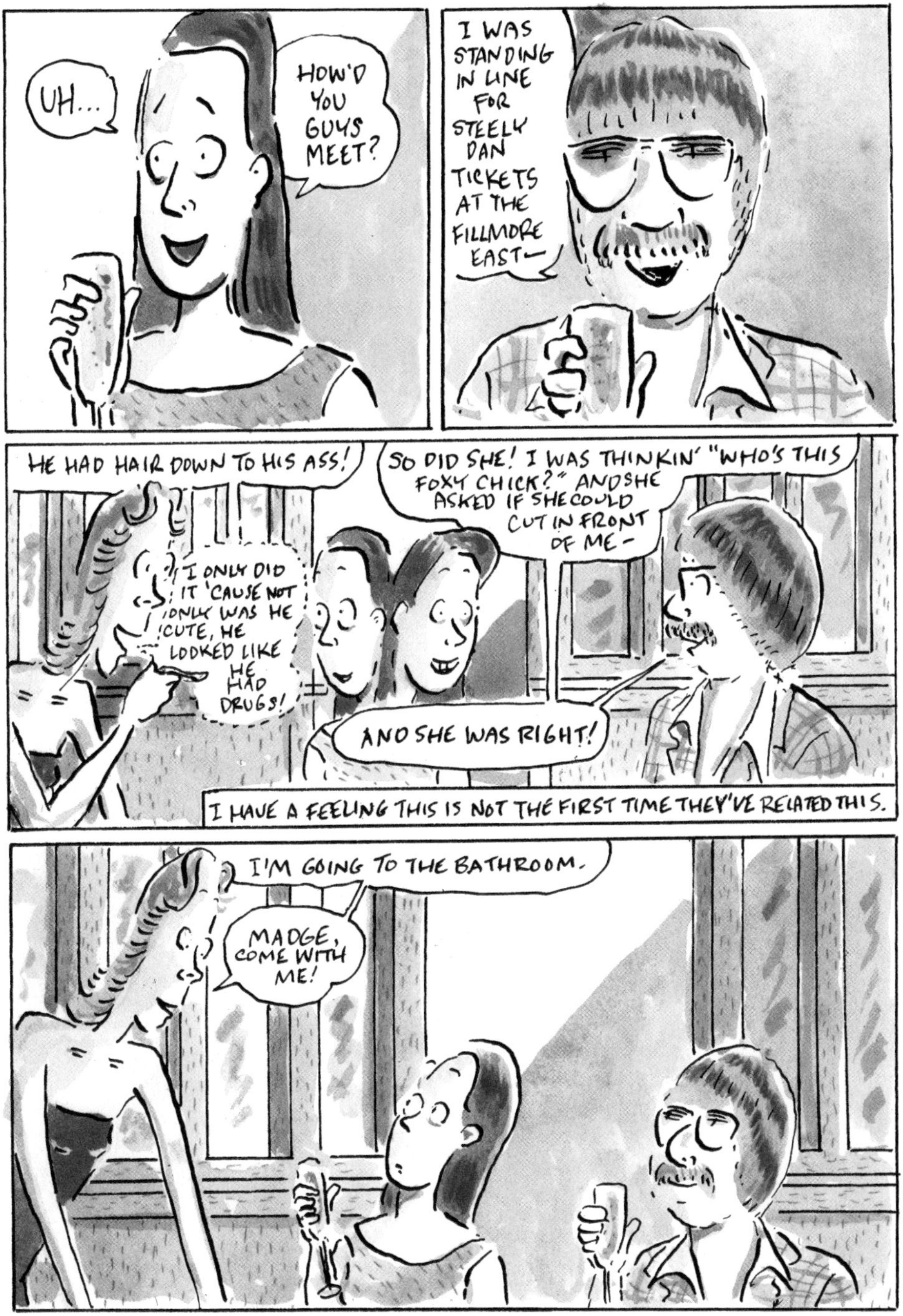
UH...
HOW'D YOU GUYS MEET?
I WAS STANDING IN LINE FOR STEELY DAN TICKETS AT THE FILLMORE EAST—
HE HAD HAIR DOWN TO HIS ASS!
SO DID SHE! I WAS THINKIN' "WHO'S THIS FOXY CHICK?" AND SHE ASKED IF SHE COULD CUT IN FRONT OF ME—
I ONLY DID IT 'CAUSE NOT ONLY WAS HE CUTE, HE LOOKED LIKE HE HAD DRUGS!
AND SHE WAS RIGHT!
I HAVE A FEELING THIS IS NOT THE FIRST TIME THEY'VE RELATED THIS.
I'M GOING TO THE BATHROOM.
MADGE, COME WITH ME!

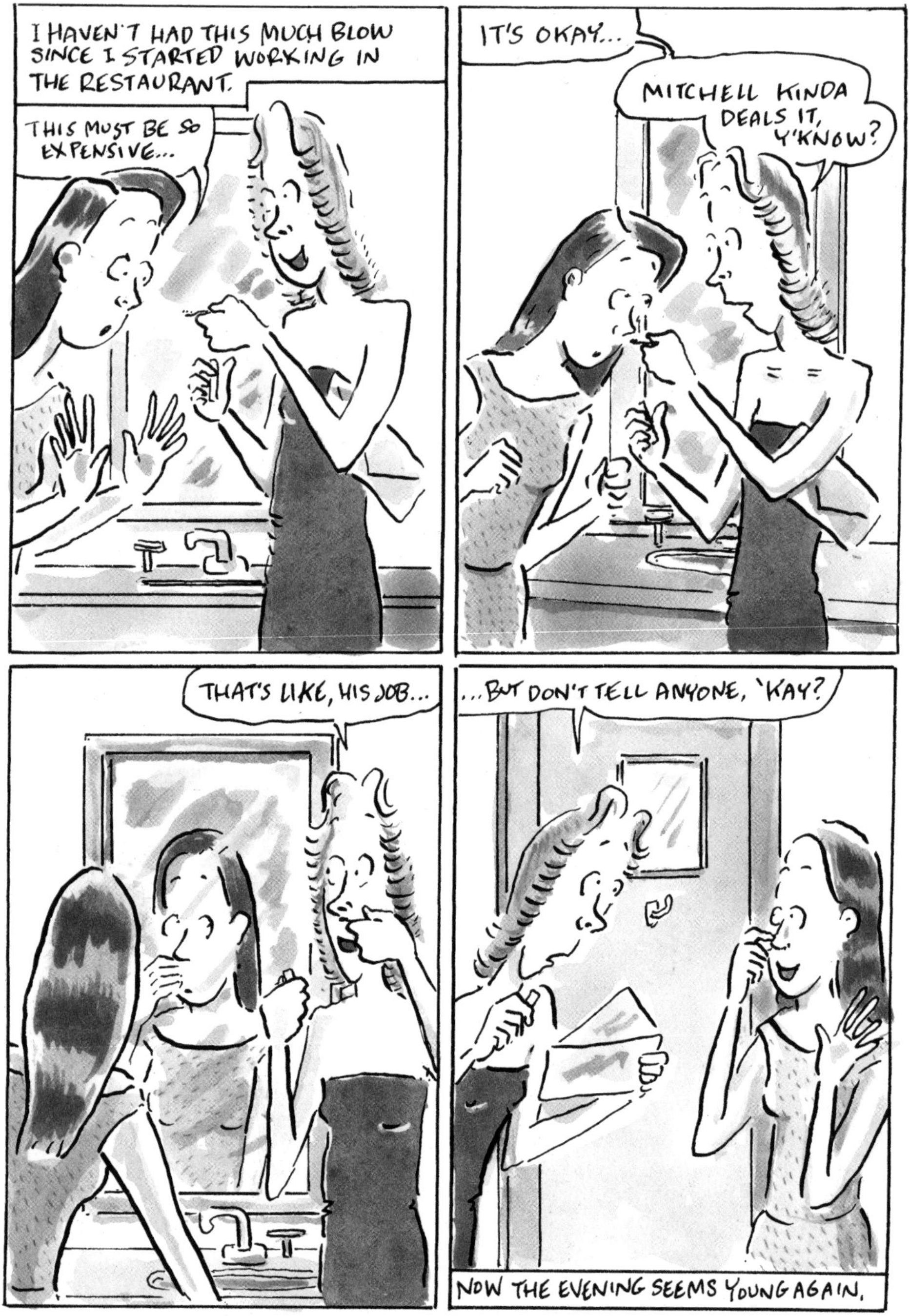
I HAVEN'T HAD THIS MUCH BLOW SINCE I STARTED WORKING IN THE RESTAURANT.
THIS MUST BE SO EXPENSIVE...
IT'S OKAY...
MITCHELL KINDA DEALS IT, Y'KNOW?
THAT'S LIKE, HIS JOB...
...BUT DON'T TELL ANYONE, 'KAY?
NOW THE EVENING SEEMS YOUNG AGAIN.

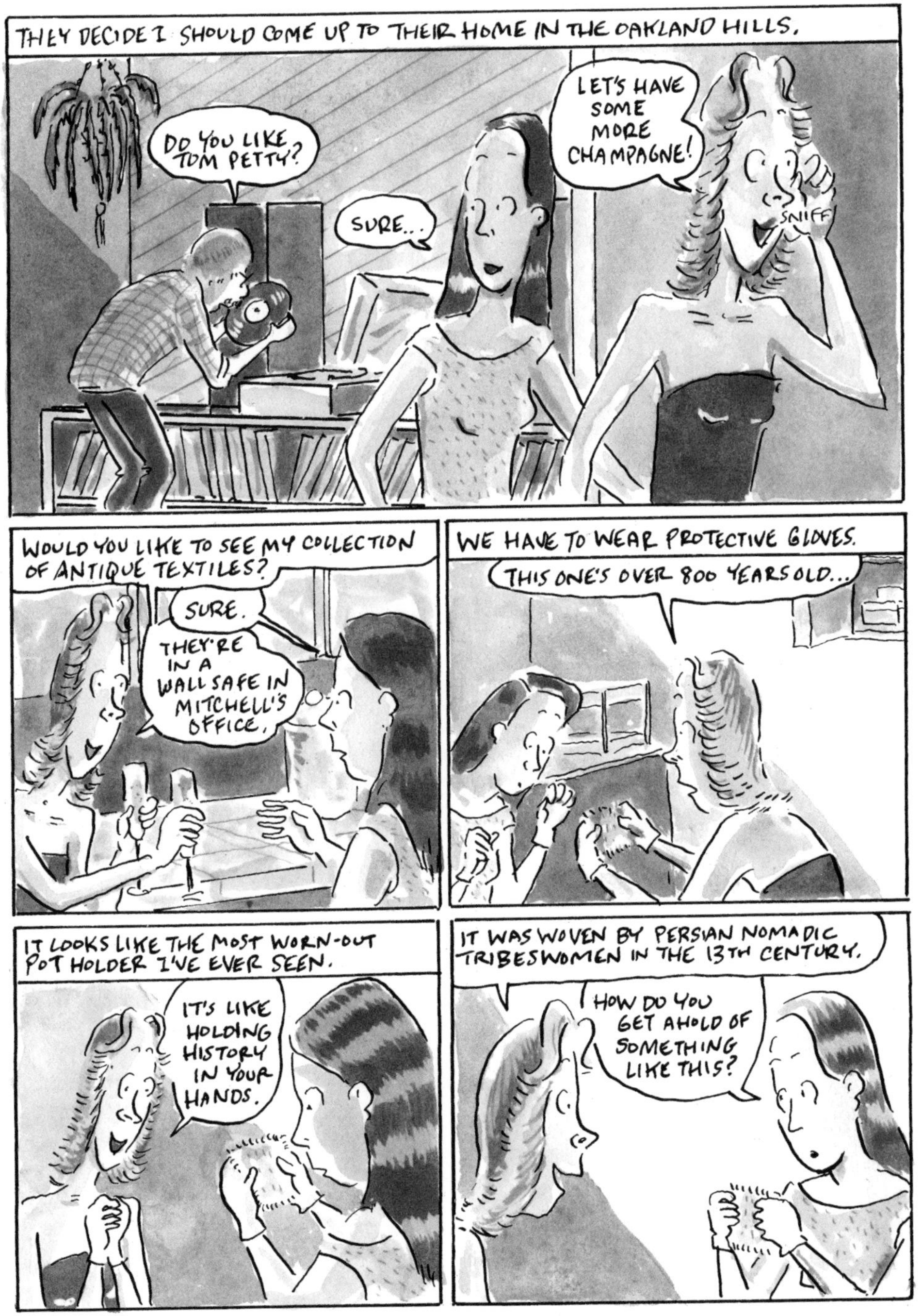

THEY DECIDE I SHOULD COME UP TO THEIR HOME IN THE OAKLAND HILLS.
DO YOU LIKE TOM PETTY?
SURE...
LET'S HAVE SOME MORE CHAMPAGNE!
SNIFF
WOULD YOU LIKE TO SEE MY COLLECTION OF ANTIQUE TEXTILES?
SURE.
THEY'RE IN A WALL SAFE IN MITCHELL'S OFFICE.
WE HAVE TO WEAR PROTECTIVE GLOVES.
THIS ONE'S OVER 800 YEARS OLD...
IT LOOKS LIKE THE MOST WORN-OUT POT HOLDER I'VE EVER SEEN.
IT'S LIKE HOLDING HISTORY IN YOUR HANDS.
IT WAS WOVEN BY PERSIAN NOMADIC TRIBESWOMEN IN THE 13TH CENTURY.
HOW DO YOU GET AHOLD OF SOMETHING LIKE THIS?

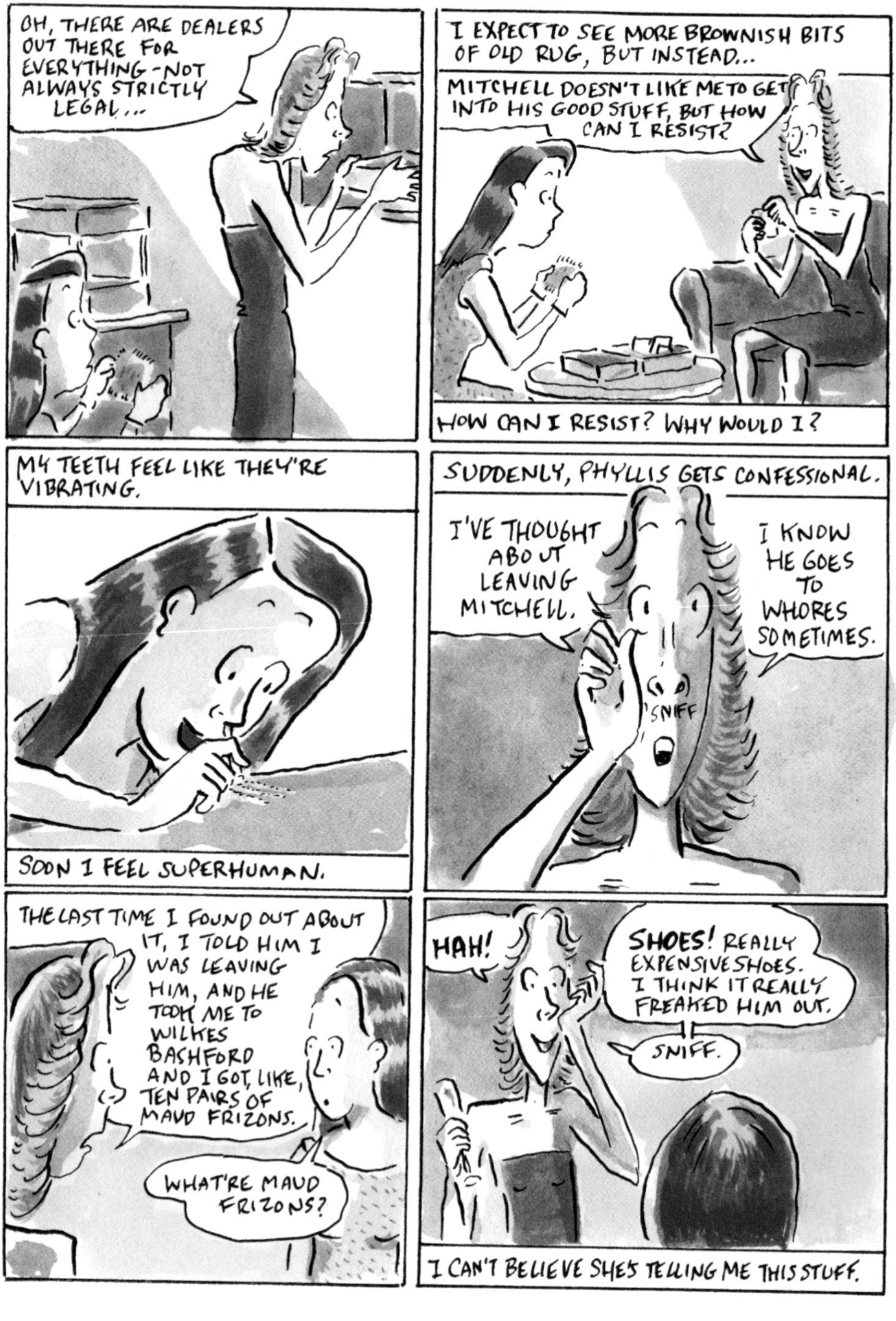
OH, THERE ARE DEALERS OUT THERE FOR EVERYTHING - NOT ALWAYS STRICTLY LEGAL...
I EXPECT TO SEE MORE BROWNISH BITS OF OLD RUG, BUT INSTEAD...
MITCHELL DOESN'T LIKE ME TO GET INTO HIS GOOD STUFF, BUT HOW CAN I RESIST?
HOW CAN I RESIST? WHY WOULD I?
MY TEETH FEEL LIKE THEY'RE VIBRATING.
SOON I FEEL SUPERHUMAN.
SUDDENLY, PHYLLIS GETS CONFESSIONAL.
I'VE THOUGHT ABOUT LEAVING MITCHELL.
I KNOW HE GOES TO WHORES SOMETIMES.
SNIFF
THE LAST TIME I FOUND OUT ABOUT IT, I TOLD HIM I WAS LEAVING HIM, AND HE TOOK ME TO WILKES BASHFORD AND I GOT, LIKE, TEN PAIRS OF MAUD FRIZONS.
WHAT'RE MAUD FRIZONS?
HAH!
SHOES! REALLY EXPENSIVE SHOES. I THINK IT REALLY FREAKED HIM OUT.
SNIFF.
I CAN'T BELIEVE SHE'S TELLING ME THIS STUFF.

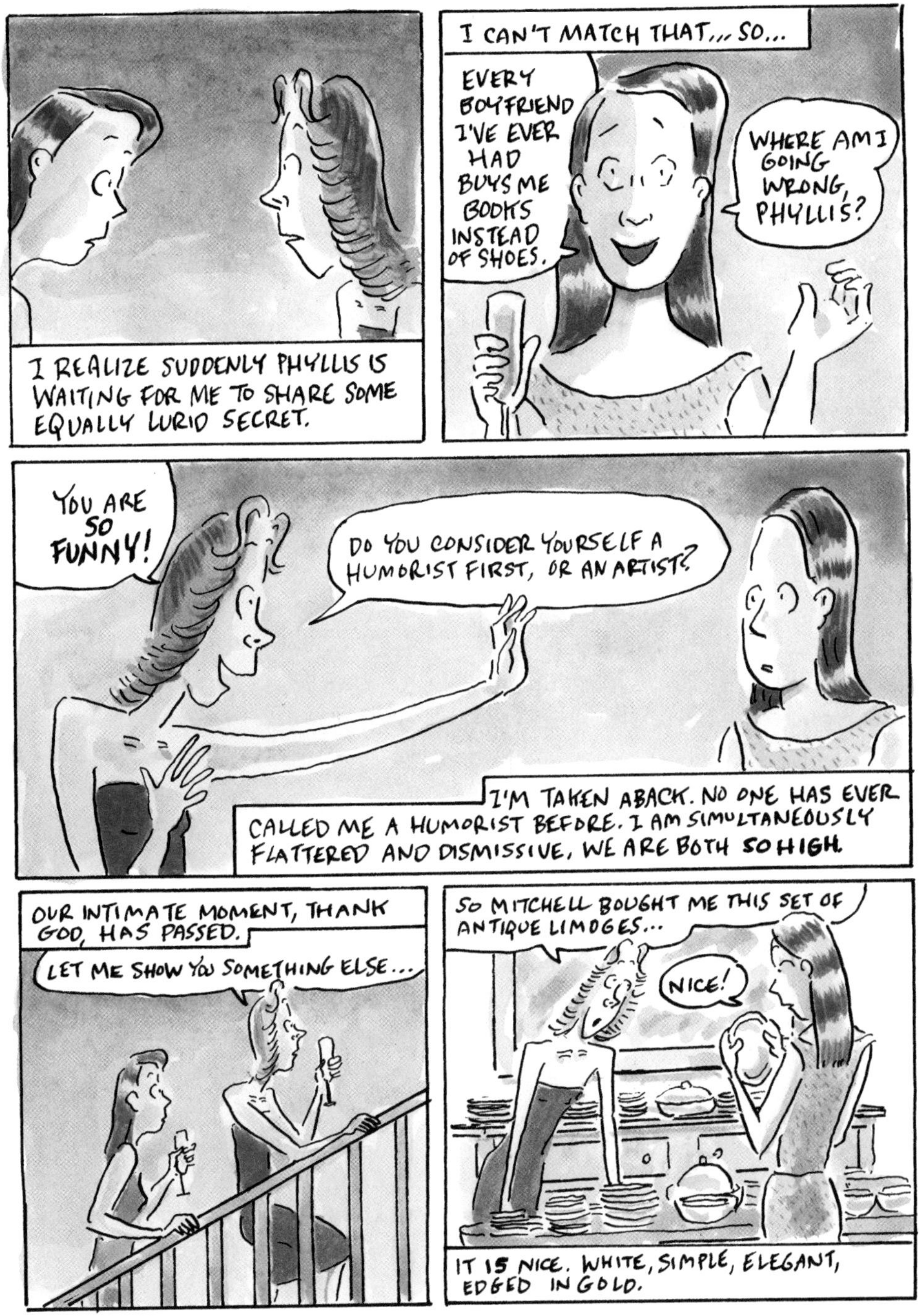
I REALIZE SUDDENLY PHYLLIS IS WAITING FOR ME TO SHARE SOME EQUALLY LURID SECRET.
I CAN'T MATCH THAT,,, SO...
EVERY BOYFRIEND I'VE EVER HAD BUYS ME BOOKS INSTEAD OF SHOES.
WHERE AM I GOING WRONG, PHYLLIS?
YOU ARE SO FUNNY!
DO YOU CONSIDER YOURSELF A HUMORIST FIRST, OR AN ARTIST?
I'M TAKEN ABACK. NO ONE HAS EVER CALLED ME A HUMORIST BEFORE. I AM SIMULTANEOUSLY FLATTERED AND DISMISSIVE, WE ARE BOTH SO HIGH.
OUR INTIMATE MOMENT, THANK GOD, HAS PASSED.
LET ME SHOW YOU SOMETHING ELSE...
SO MITCHELL BOUGHT ME THIS SET OF ANTIQUE LIMOGES...
NICE!
IT IS NICE. WHITE, SIMPLE, ELEGANT, EDGED IN GOLD.

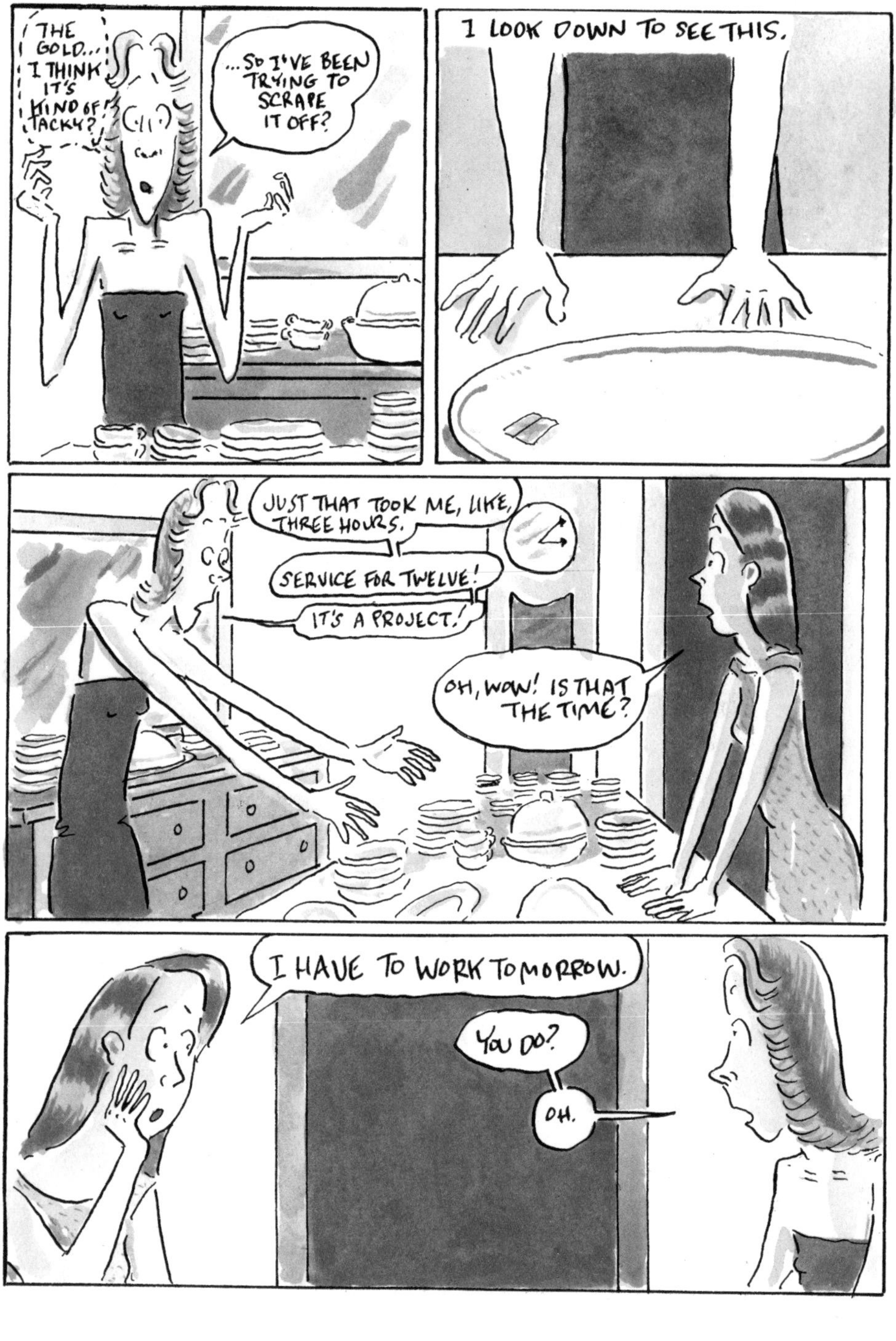
THE GOLD... I THINK IT'S KIND OF TACKY?
...SO I'VE BEEN TRYING TO SCRAPE IT OFF?
I LOOK DOWN TO SEE THIS.
JUST THAT TOOK ME, LIKE, THREE HOURS.
SERVICE FOR TWELVE!
IT'S A PROJECT!
OH, WOW! IS THAT THE TIME?
I HAVE TO WORK TOMORROW.
YOU DO?
OH.

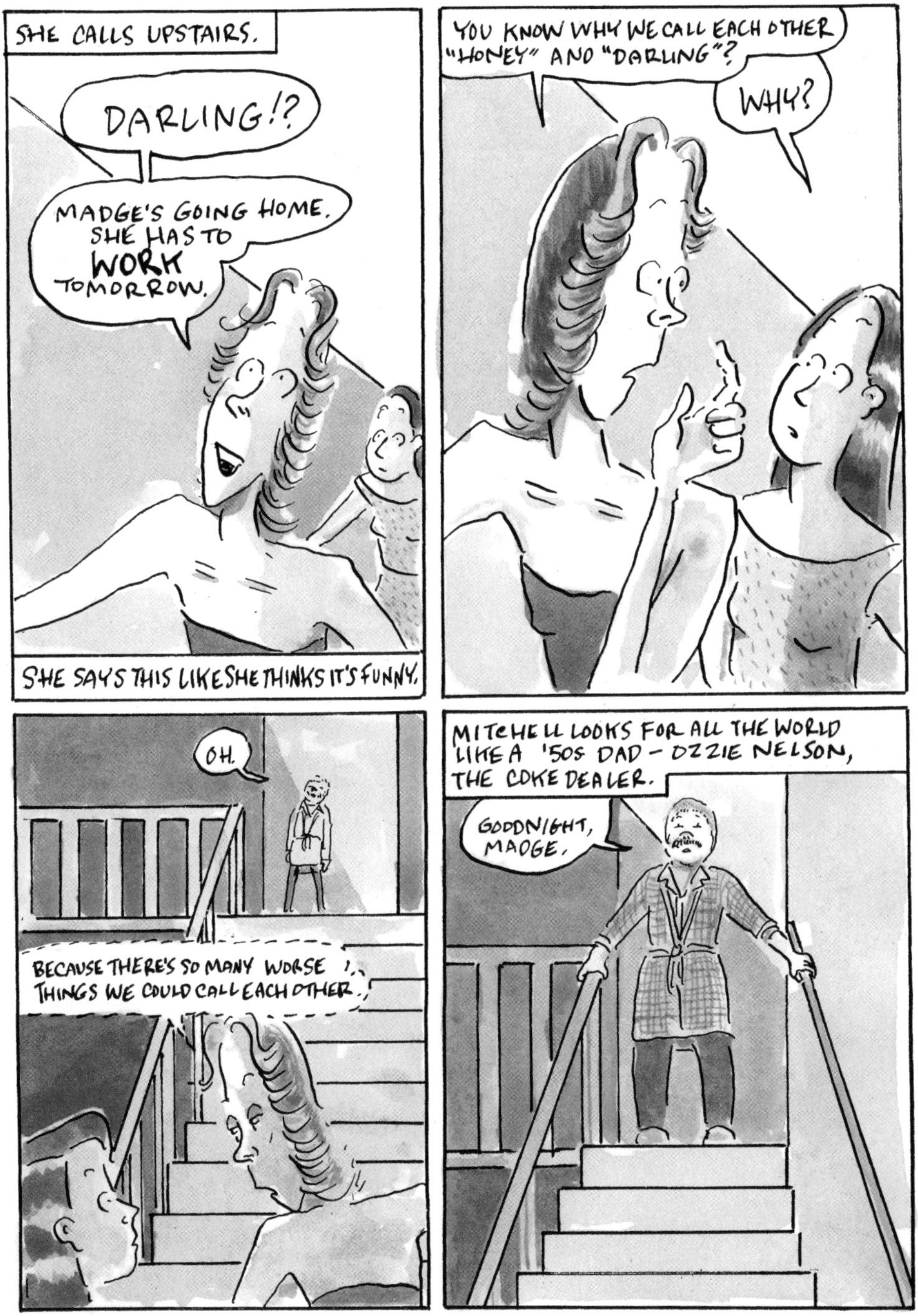
SHE CALLS UPSTAIRS.
DARLING!?
MADGE'S GOING HOME. SHE HAS TO WORK TOMORROW.
SHE SAYS THIS LIKE SHE THINKS IT'S FUNNY.
YOU KNOW WHY WE CALL EACH OTHER "HONEY" AND "DARLING"?
WHY?
OH.
BECAUSE THERE'S SO MANY WORSE THINGS WE COULD CALL EACH OTHER.
MITCHELL LOOKS FOR ALL THE WORLD LIKE A '50S DAD - OZZIE NELSON, THE COKE DEALER.
GOODNIGHT, MADGE.

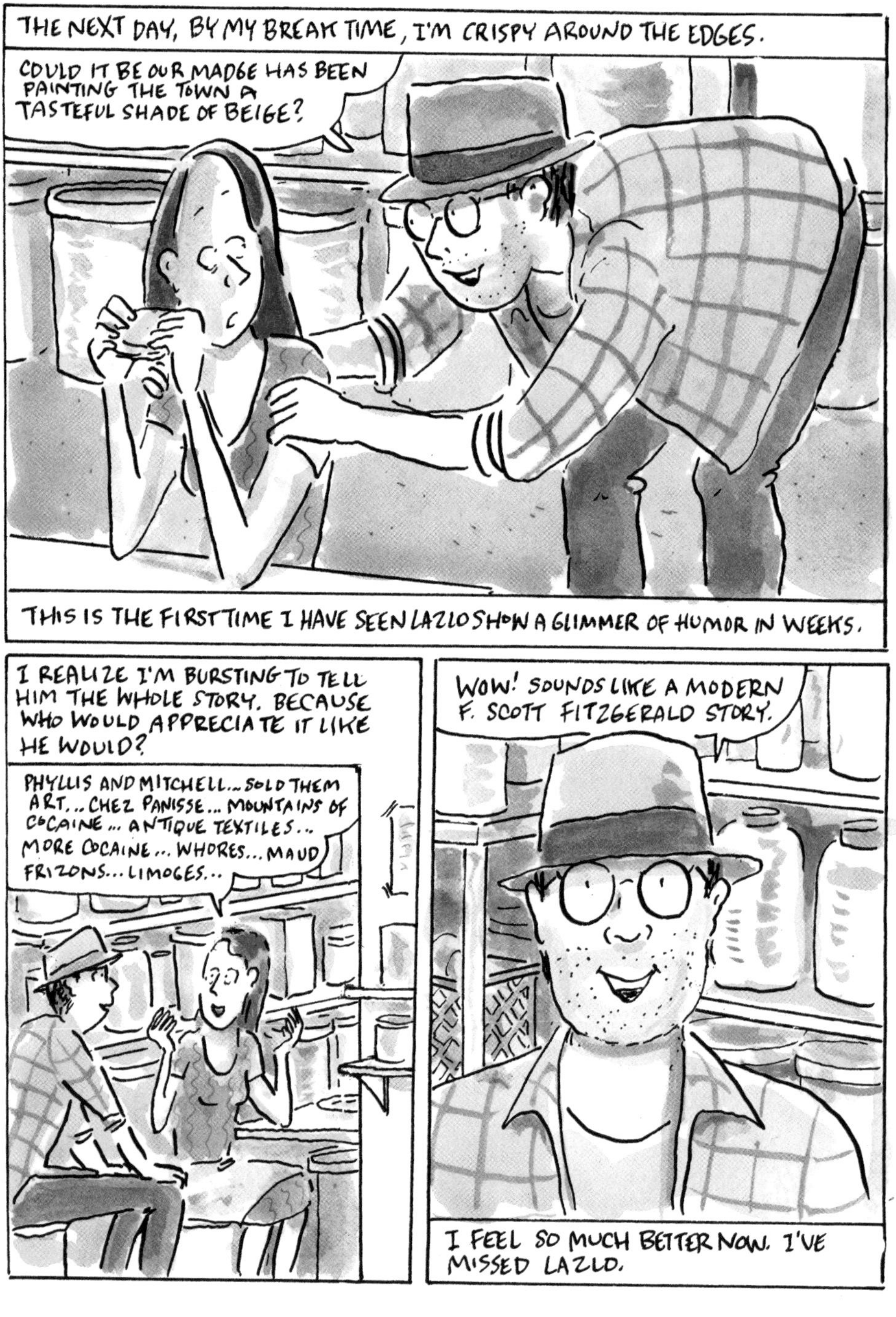
THE NEXT DAY, BY MY BREAK TIME, I'M CRISPY AROUND THE EDGES.
COULD IT BE OUR MADGE HAS BEEN PAINTING THE TOWN A TASTEFUL SHADE OF BEIGE?
THIS IS THE FIRST TIME I HAVE SEEN LAZLO SHOW A GLIMMER OF HUMOR IN WEEKS.
I REALIZE I'M BURSTING TO TELL HIM THE WHOLE STORY. BECAUSE WHO WOULD APPRECIATE IT LIKE HE WOULD?
PHYLLIS AND MITCHELL... SOLD THEM ART... CHEZ PANISSE... MOUNTAINS OF COCAINE... ANTIQUE TEXTILES... MORE COCAINE... WHORES... MAUD FRIZONS... LIMOGES...
WOW! SOUNDS LIKE A MODERN F. SCOTT FITZGERALD STORY.
I FEEL SO MUCH BETTER NOW. I'VE MISSED LAZLO.

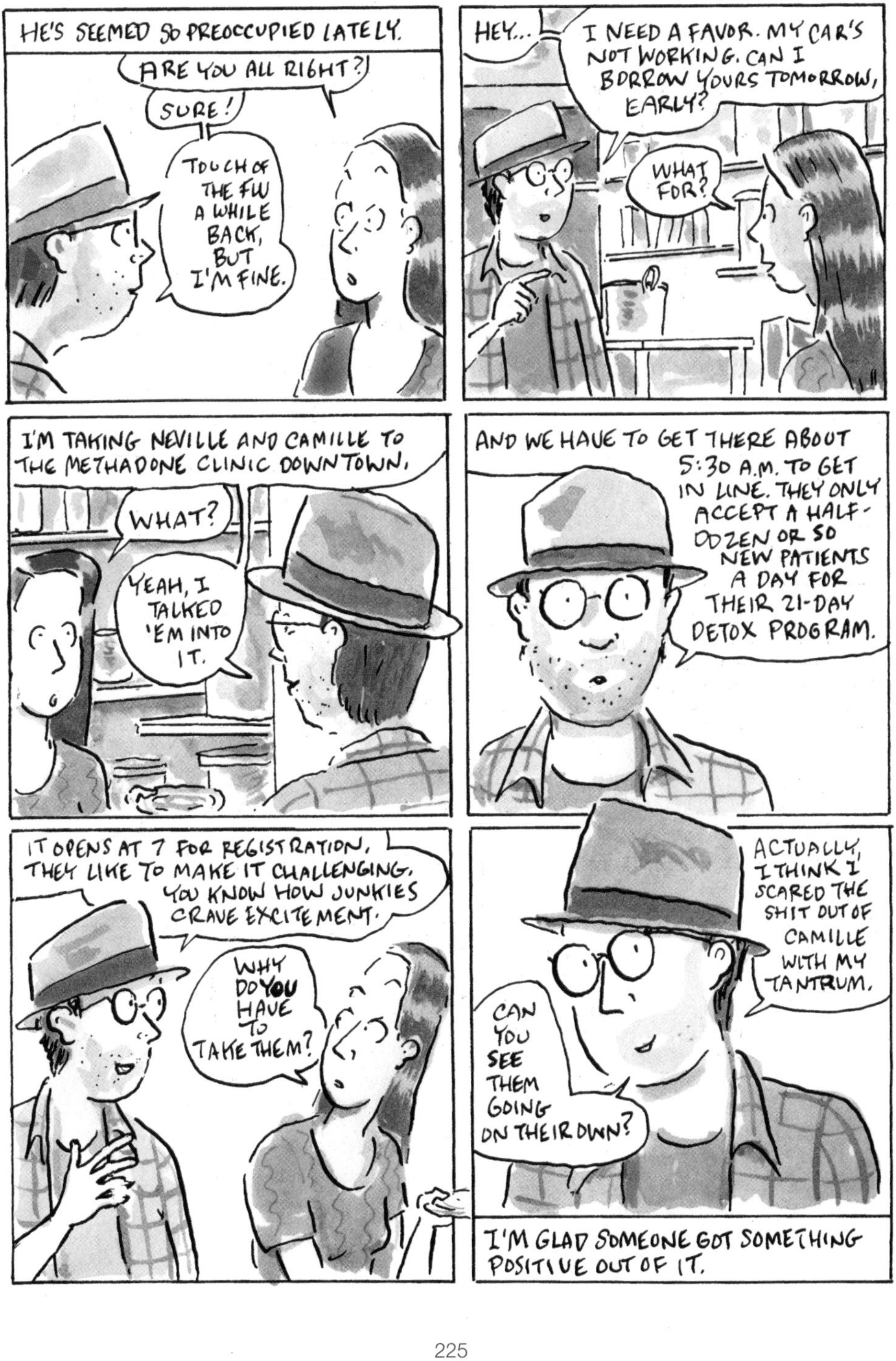
HE'S SEEMED SO PREOCCUPIED LATELY.
ARE YOU ALL RIGHT?
SURE!
TOUCH OF THE FLU A WHILE BACK, BUT I'M FINE.
HEY...
I NEED A FAVOR. MY CAR'S NOT WORKING. CAN I BORROW YOURS TOMORROW, EARLY?
WHAT FOR?
I'M TAKING NEVILLE AND CAMILLE TO THE METHADONE CLINIC DOWNTOWN.
WHAT?
YEAH, I TALKED 'EM INTO IT.
AND WE HAVE TO GET THERE ABOUT 5:30 A.M. TO GET IN LINE. THEY ONLY ACCEPT A HALF-DOZEN OR SO NEW PATIENTS A DAY FOR THEIR 21-DAY DETOX PROGRAM.
IT OPENS AT 7 FOR REGISTRATION. THEY LIKE TO MAKE IT CHALLENGING. YOU KNOW HOW JUNKIES CRAVE EXCITEMENT.
WHY DO **YOU** HAVE TO TAKE THEM?
ACTUALLY, I THINK I SCARED THE SHIT OUT OF CAMILLE WITH MY TANTRUM.
CAN YOU **SEE** THEM GOING ON THEIR OWN?
I'M GLAD SOMEONE GOT SOMETHING POSITIVE OUT OF IT.

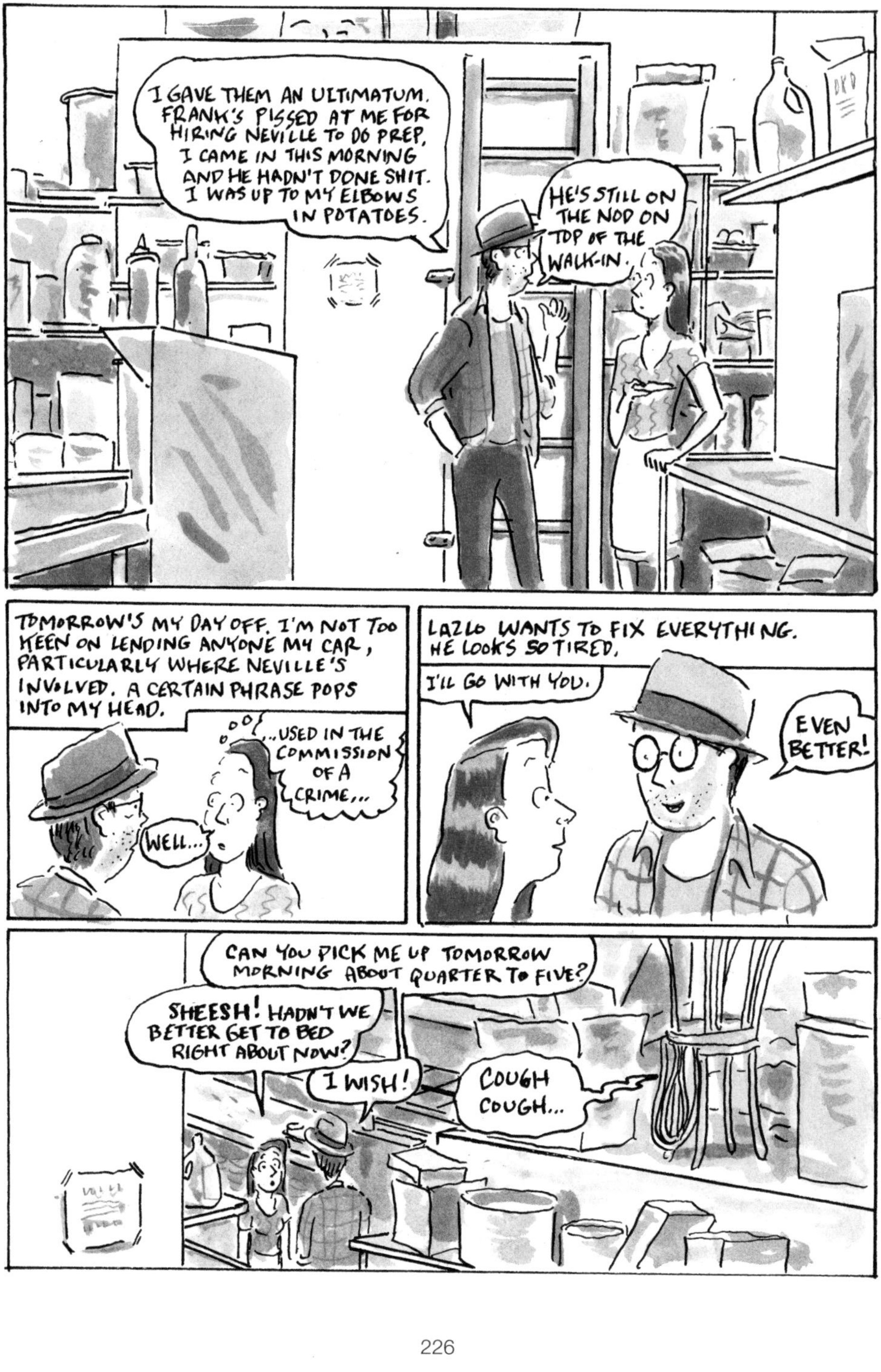
I GAVE THEM AN ULTIMATUM. FRANK'S PISSED AT ME FOR HIRING NEVILLE TO DO PREP, I CAME IN THIS MORNING AND HE HADN'T DONE SHIT. I WAS UP TO MY ELBOWS IN POTATOES.
HE'S STILL ON THE NOD ON TOP OF THE WALK-IN.
TOMORROW'S MY DAY OFF. I'M NOT TOO KEEN ON LENDING ANYONE MY CAR, PARTICULARLY WHERE NEVILLE'S INVOLVED. A CERTAIN PHRASE POPS INTO MY HEAD.
...USED IN THE COMMISSION OF A CRIME,...
WELL...
LAZLO WANTS TO FIX EVERYTHING. HE LOOKS SO TIRED.
I'LL GO WITH YOU.
EVEN BETTER!
CAN YOU PICK ME UP TOMORROW MORNING ABOUT QUARTER TO FIVE?
SHEESH! HADN'T WE BETTER GET TO BED RIGHT ABOUT NOW?
I WISH!
COUGH COUGH...

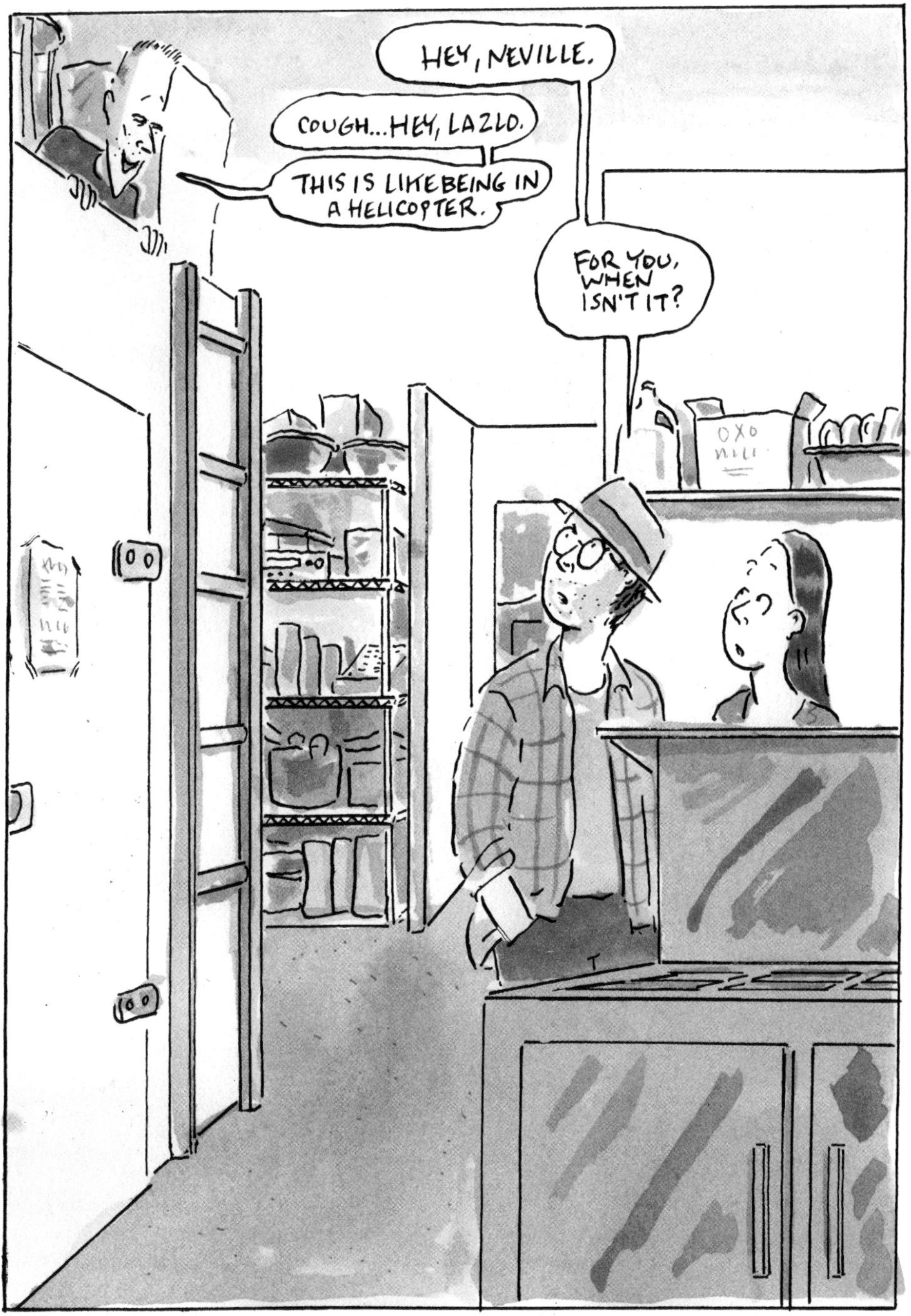
HEY, NEVILLE.
COUGH... HEY, LAZLO.
THIS IS LIKE BEING IN A HELICOPTER.
FOR YOU, WHEN ISN'T IT?

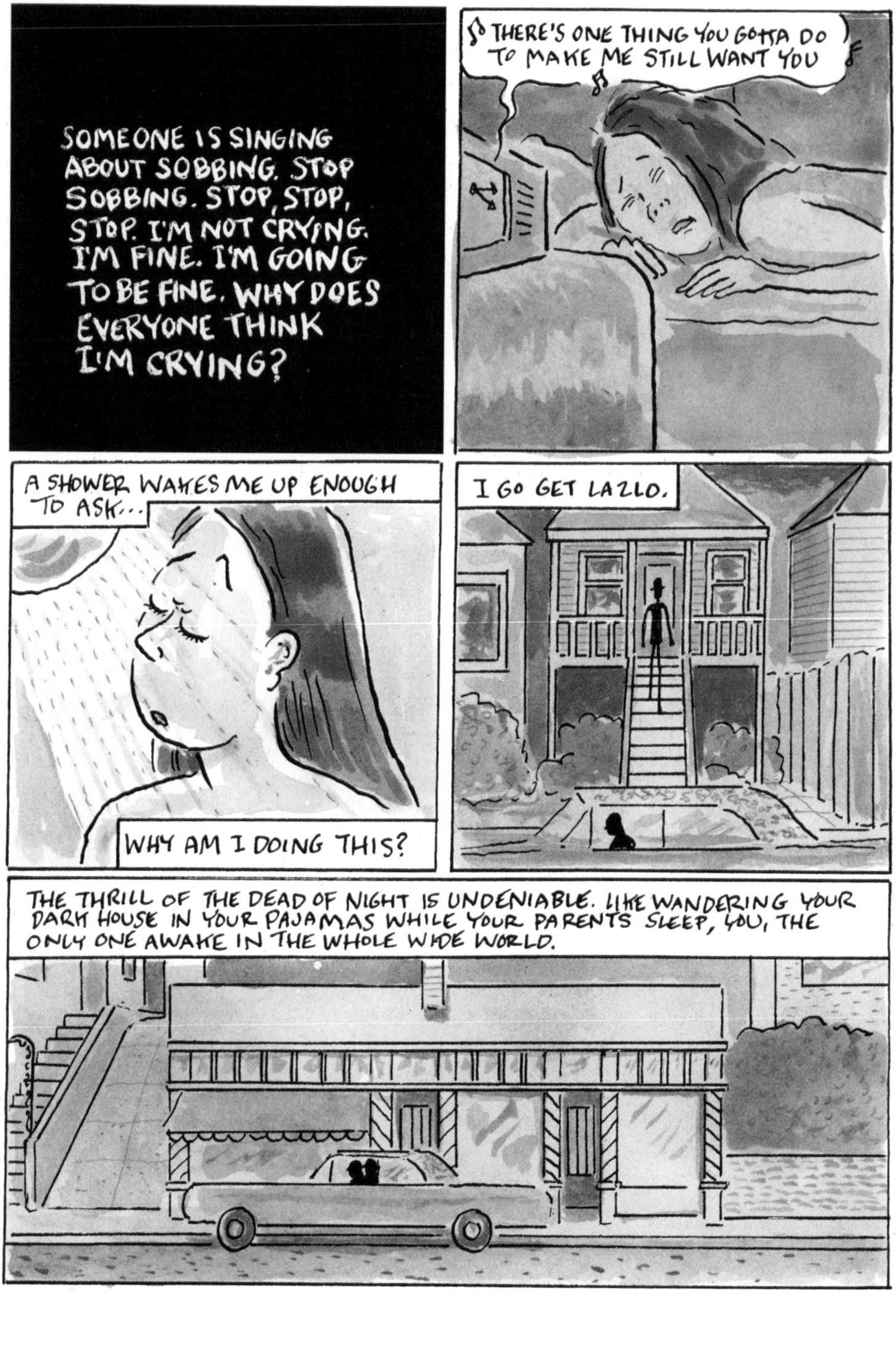
SOMEONE IS SINGING ABOUT SOBBING. STOP SOBBING. STOP, STOP, STOP. I'M NOT CRYING. I'M FINE. I'M GOING TO BE FINE. WHY DOES EVERYONE THINK I'M CRYING?
THERE'S ONE THING YOU GOTTA DO TO MAKE ME STILL WANT YOU
A SHOWER WAKES ME UP ENOUGH TO ASK...
WHY AM I DOING THIS?
I GO GET LAZLO.
THE THRILL OF THE DEAD OF NIGHT IS UNDENIABLE. LIKE WANDERING YOUR DARK HOUSE IN YOUR PAJAMAS WHILE YOUR PARENTS SLEEP, YOU, THE ONLY ONE AWAKE IN THE WHOLE WIDE WORLD.

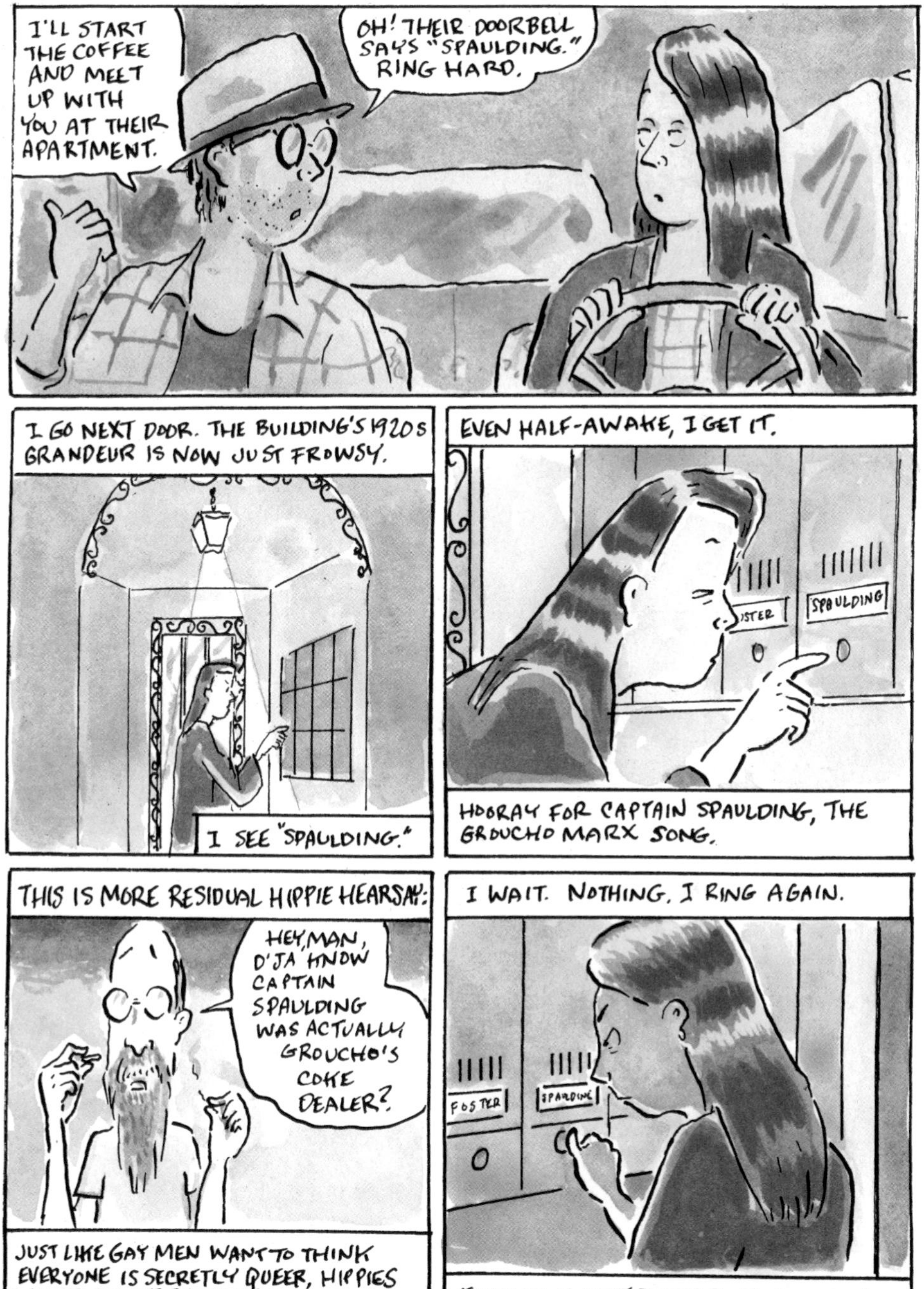
I'LL START THE COFFEE AND MEET UP WITH YOU AT THEIR APARTMENT.
OH! THEIR DOORBELL SAYS "SPAULDING." RING HARD.
I GO NEXT DOOR. THE BUILDING'S 1920s GRANDEUR IS NOW JUST FROWSY.
I SEE "SPAULDING."
EVEN HALF-AWAKE, I GET IT.
SPAULDING
HOORAY FOR CAPTAIN SPAULDING, THE GROUCHO MARX SONG.
THIS IS MORE RESIDUAL HIPPIE HEARSAY:
HEY, MAN, D'JA KNOW CAPTAIN SPAULDING WAS ACTUALLY GROUCHO'S COKE DEALER?
JUST LIKE GAY MEN WANT TO THINK EVERYONE IS SECRETLY QUEER, HIPPIES WANT TO BELIEVE EVERYONE IS ON DRUGS.
I WAIT. NOTHING. I RING AGAIN.
FOSTER
FINALLY, I JUST PRESS CONTINUOUSLY.

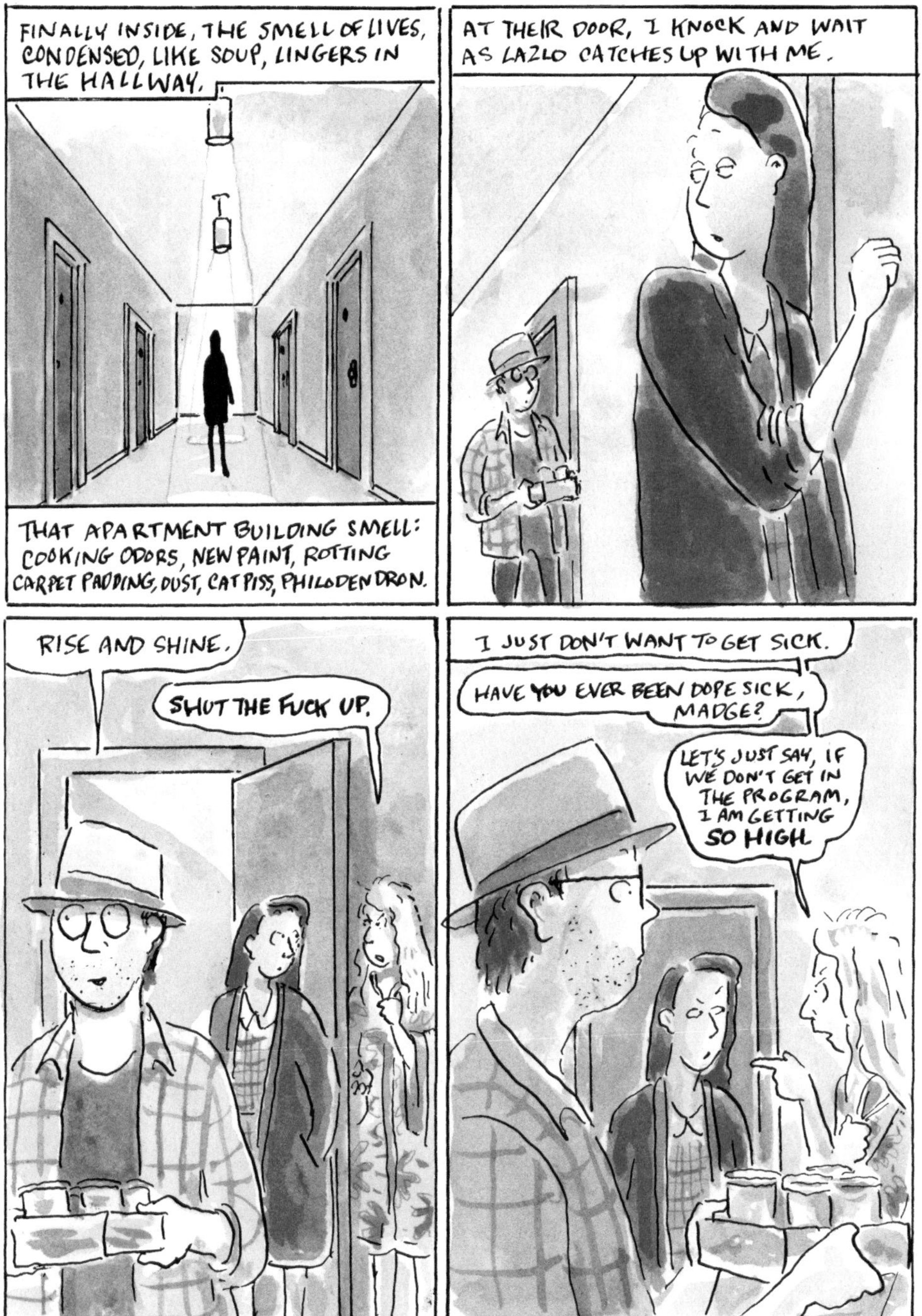
FINALLY INSIDE, THE SMELL OF LIVES, CONDENSED, LIKE SOUP, LINGERS IN THE HALLWAY.
THAT APARTMENT BUILDING SMELL: COOKING ODORS, NEW PAINT, ROTTING CARPET PADDING, DUST, CAT PISS, PHILODENDRON.
AT THEIR DOOR, I KNOCK AND WAIT AS LAZLO CATCHES UP WITH ME.
RISE AND SHINE.
SHUT THE FUCK UP.
I JUST DON'T WANT TO GET SICK.
HAVE YOU EVER BEEN DOPE SICK, MADGE?
LET'S JUST SAY, IF WE DON'T GET IN THE PROGRAM, I AM GETTING SO HIGH

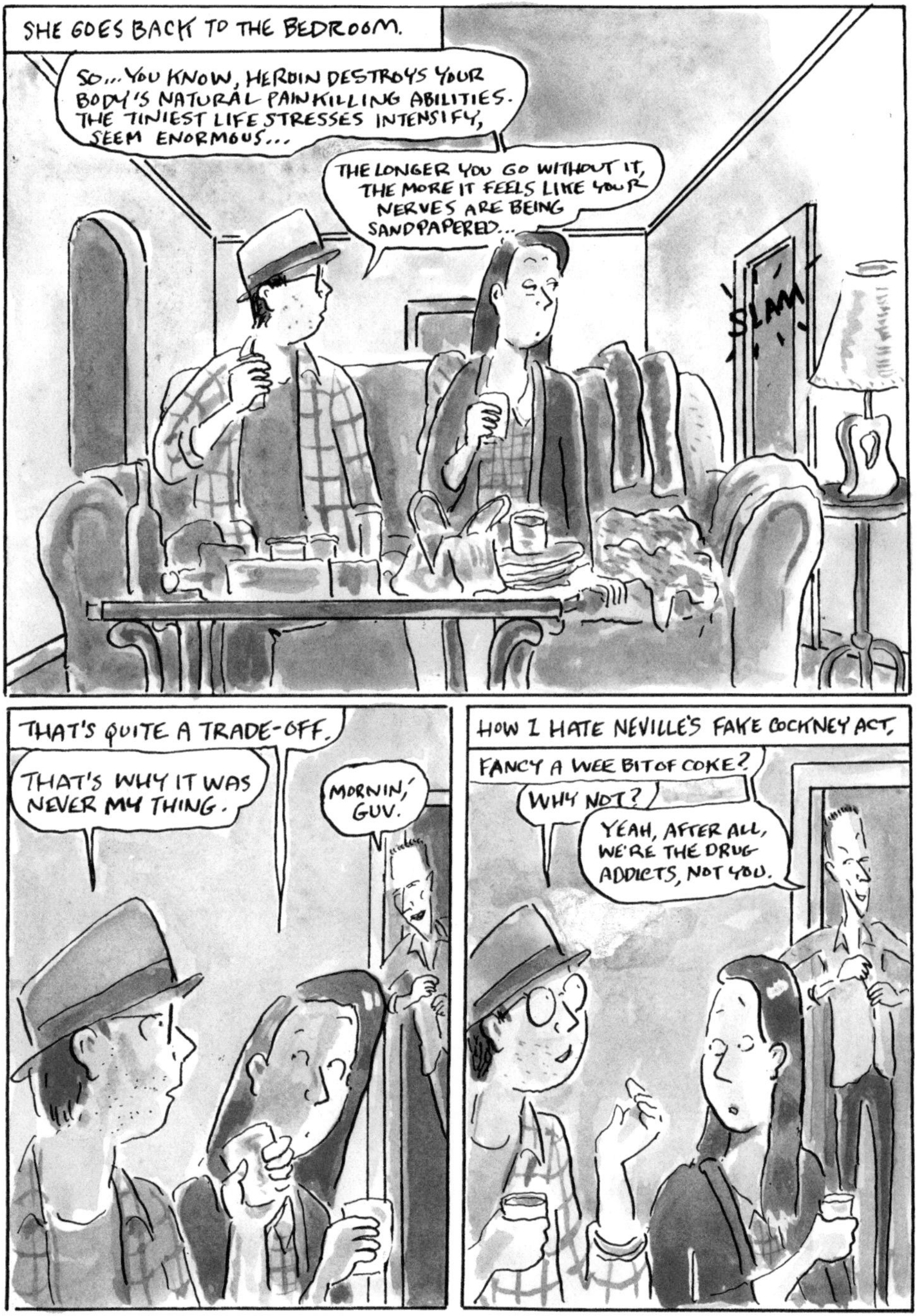
SHE GOES BACK TO THE BEDROOM.
SO... YOU KNOW, HEROIN DESTROYS YOUR BODY'S NATURAL PAINKILLING ABILITIES. THE TINIEST LIFE STRESSES INTENSIFY, SEEM ENORMOUS...
THE LONGER YOU GO WITHOUT IT, THE MORE IT FEELS LIKE YOUR NERVES ARE BEING SANDPAPERED...
SLAM
THAT'S QUITE A TRADE-OFF.
THAT'S WHY IT WAS NEVER MY THING.
MORNIN', GUV.
HOW I HATE NEVILLE'S FAKE COCKNEY ACT.
FANCY A WEE BIT OF COKE?
WHY NOT?
YEAH, AFTER ALL, WE'RE THE DRUG ADDICTS, NOT YOU.

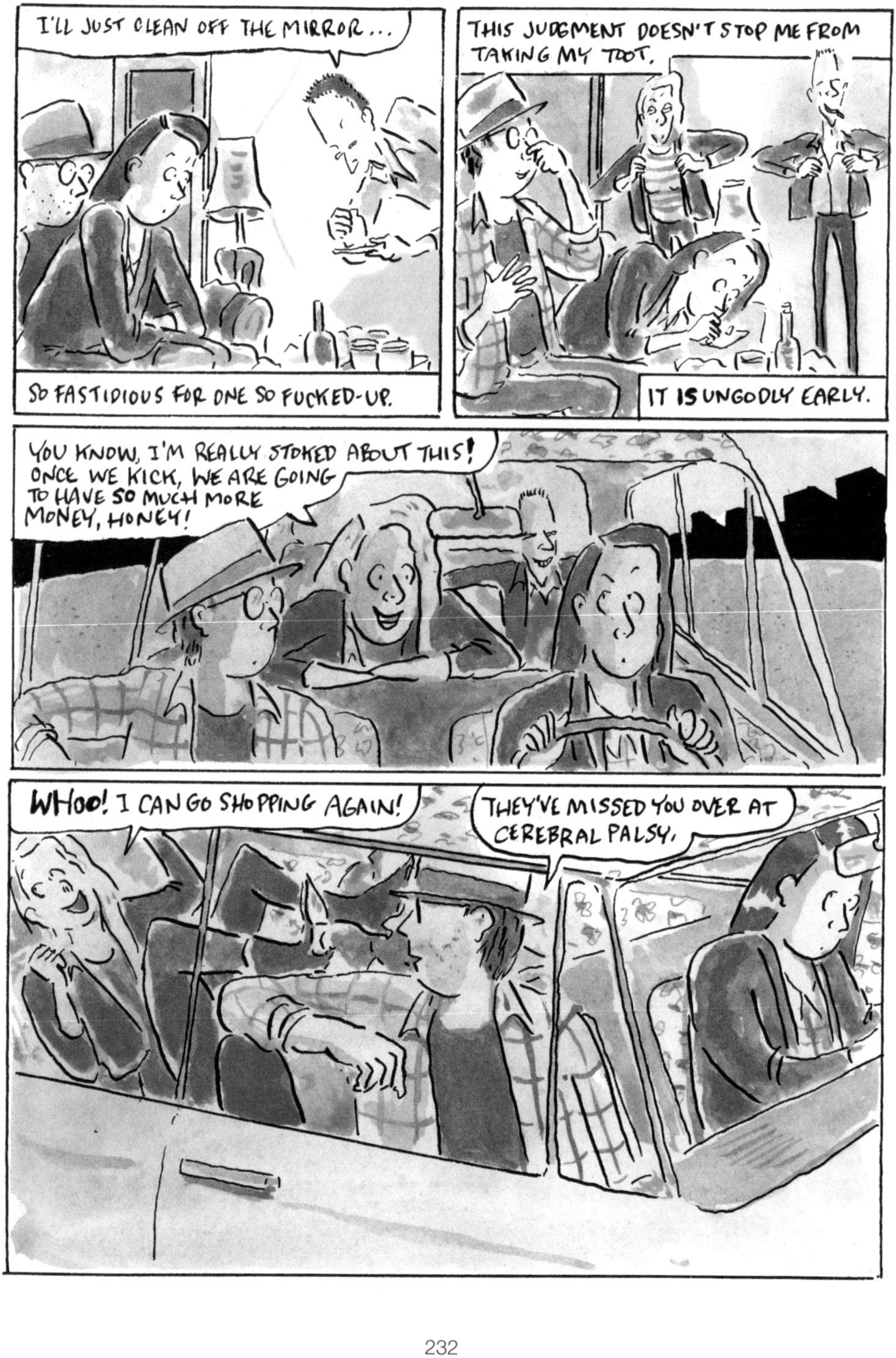
I'LL JUST CLEAN OFF THE MIRROR...
SO FASTIDIOUS FOR ONE SO FUCKED-UP.
THIS JUDGMENT DOESN'T STOP ME FROM TAKING MY TOOT.
IT IS UNGODLY EARLY.
YOU KNOW, I'M REALLY STOKED ABOUT THIS! ONCE WE KICK, WE ARE GOING TO HAVE SO MUCH MORE MONEY, HONEY!
WHOO! I CAN GO SHOPPING AGAIN!
THEY'VE MISSED YOU OVER AT CEREBRAL PALSY.

THE METHADONE CLINIC IS DEEP IN EAST OAKLAND.

HAH! FIRST IN LINE! WE'RE SUCH OVERACHIEVERS!

ALAMEDA-CONTR
HEALTH SERVIC

I TRY TO CONCENTRATE ON CAMILLE'S OPTIMISTIC CHATTER, ABOUT TAKING THAT TRIP TO EUROPE, ABOUT GETTING PREGNANT AGAIN. AFTER ALL, THE COOKS TOLD HER HOW GOOD SHE LOOKED JUST BEFORE HER LAST ABORTION.

LAZLO AND I WILL TRADE NOTES LATER, BUT NOW I FEEL LIKE I'M STRANDED ON A BOAT WITH CRAZY PEOPLE IN THE MIDDLE OF THE OCEAN.

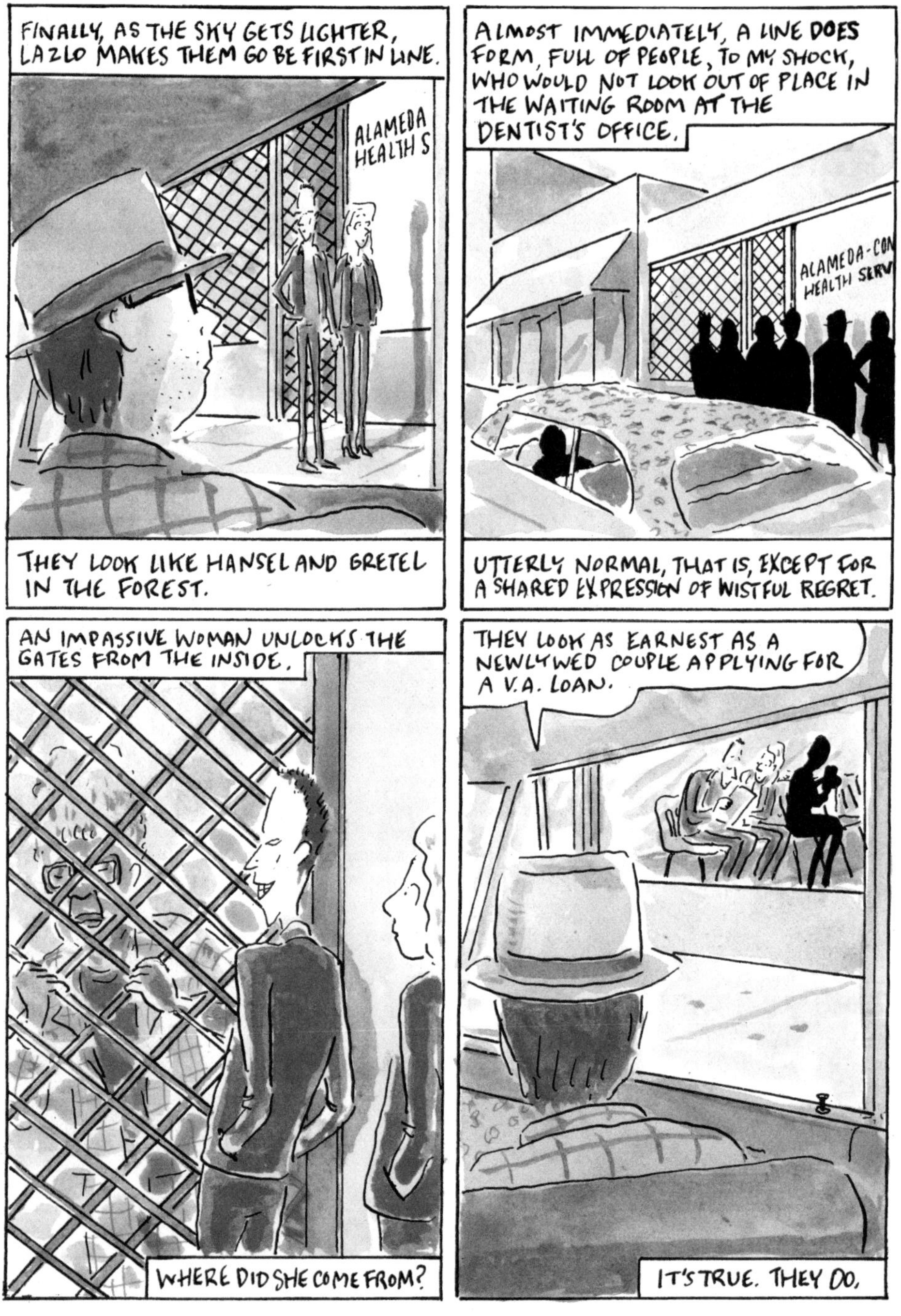
FINALLY, AS THE SKY GETS LIGHTER, LAZLO MAKES THEM GO BE FIRST IN LINE.
ALAMEDA HEALTH S
THEY LOOK LIKE HANSEL AND GRETEL IN THE FOREST.
ALMOST IMMEDIATELY, A LINE DOES FORM, FULL OF PEOPLE, TO MY SHOCK, WHO WOULD NOT LOOK OUT OF PLACE IN THE WAITING ROOM AT THE DENTIST'S OFFICE.
ALAMEDA-CO HEALTH SERV
UTTERLY NORMAL, THAT IS, EXCEPT FOR A SHARED EXPRESSION OF WISTFUL REGRET.
AN IMPASSIVE WOMAN UNLOCKS THE GATES FROM THE INSIDE.
WHERE DID SHE COME FROM?
THEY LOOK AS EARNEST AS A NEWLYWED COUPLE APPLYING FOR A V.A. LOAN.
IT'S TRUE. THEY DO.

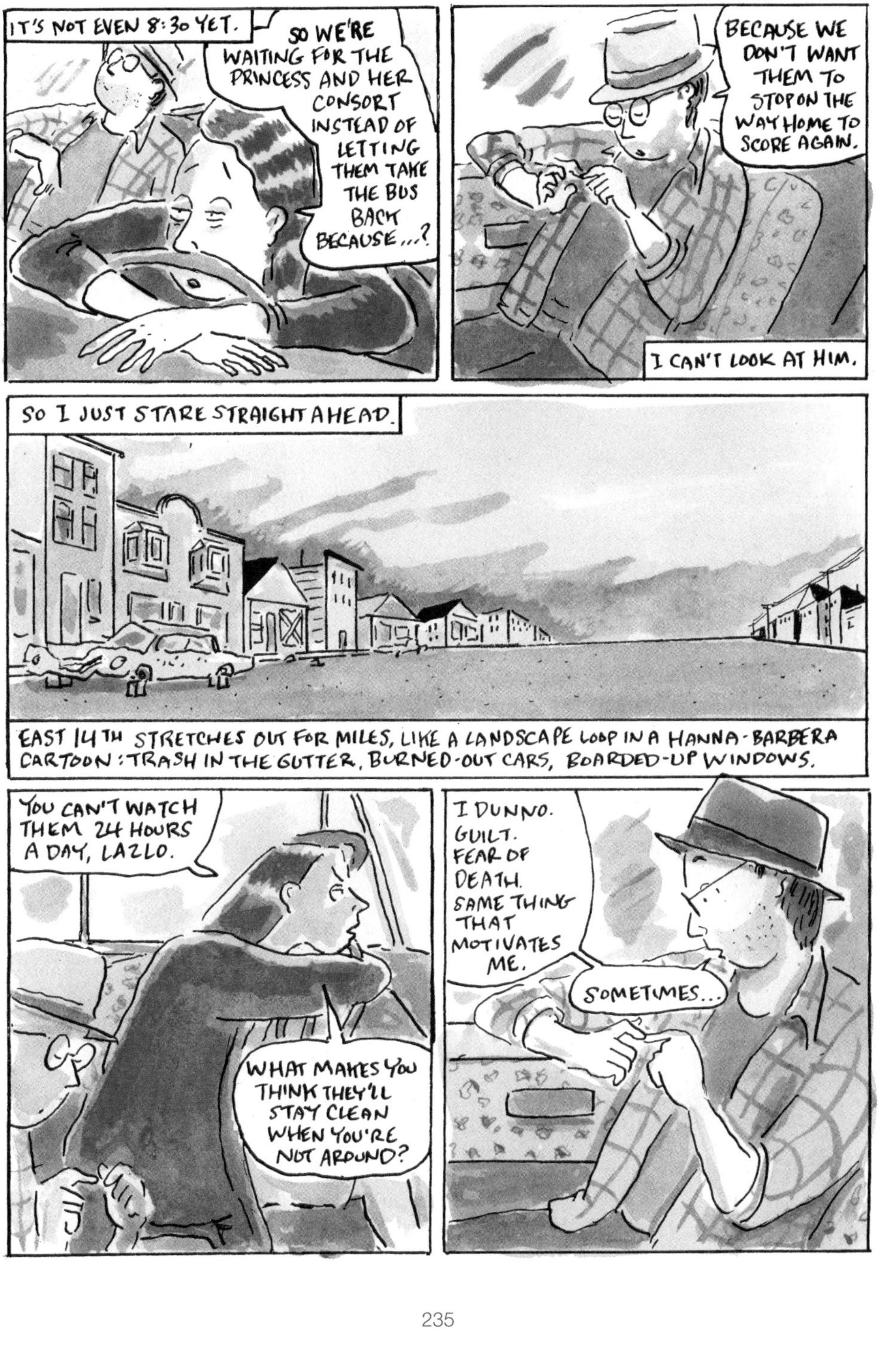
IT'S NOT EVEN 8:30 YET.
SO WE'RE WAITING FOR THE PRINCESS AND HER CONSORT INSTEAD OF LETTING THEM TAKE THE BUS BACK BECAUSE...?
BECAUSE WE DON'T WANT THEM TO STOP ON THE WAY HOME TO SCORE AGAIN.
I CAN'T LOOK AT HIM.
SO I JUST STARE STRAIGHT AHEAD.
EAST 14TH STRETCHES OUT FOR MILES, LIKE A LANDSCAPE LOOP IN A HANNA-BARBERA CARTOON: TRASH IN THE GUTTER, BURNED-OUT CARS, BOARDED-UP WINDOWS.
YOU CAN'T WATCH THEM 24 HOURS A DAY, LAZLO.
WHAT MAKES YOU THINK THEY'LL STAY CLEAN WHEN YOU'RE NOT AROUND?
I DUNNO. GUILT. FEAR OF DEATH. SAME THING THAT MOTIVATES ME.
SOMETIMES...

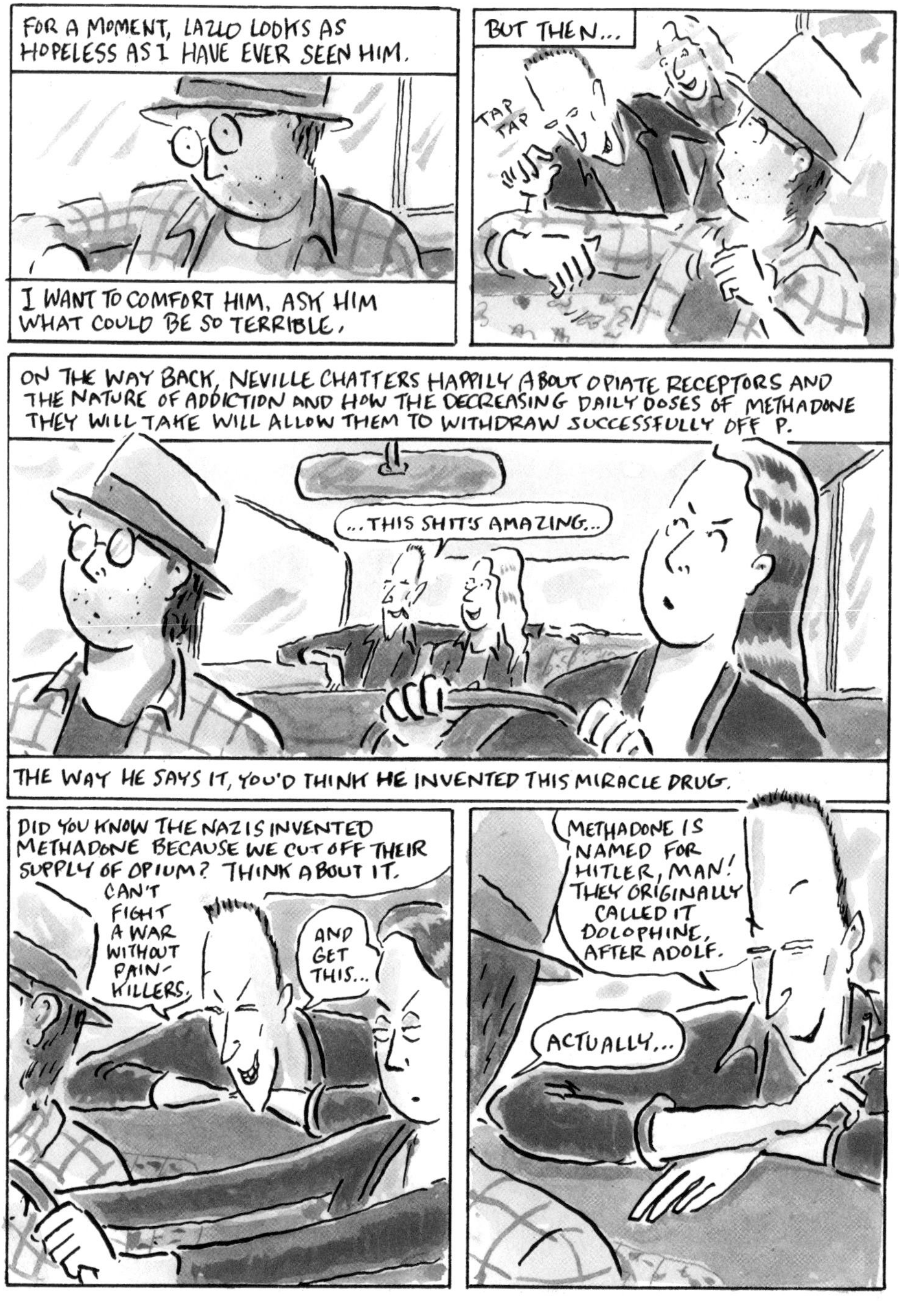

FOR A MOMENT, LAZLO LOOKS AS HOPELESS AS I HAVE EVER SEEN HIM.
I WANT TO COMFORT HIM, ASK HIM WHAT COULD BE SO TERRIBLE,
BUT THEN...
TAP TAP
ON THE WAY BACK, NEVILLE CHATTERS HAPPILY ABOUT OPIATE RECEPTORS AND THE NATURE OF ADDICTION AND HOW THE DECREASING DAILY DOSES OF METHADONE THEY WILL TAKE WILL ALLOW THEM TO WITHDRAW SUCCESSFULLY OFF P.
...THIS SHIT'S AMAZING...
THE WAY HE SAYS IT, YOU'D THINK HE INVENTED THIS MIRACLE DRUG.
DID YOU KNOW THE NAZIS INVENTED METHADONE BECAUSE WE CUT OFF THEIR SUPPLY OF OPIUM? THINK ABOUT IT.
CAN'T FIGHT A WAR WITHOUT PAIN-KILLERS.
AND GET THIS...
METHADONE IS NAMED FOR HITLER, MAN! THEY ORIGINALLY CALLED IT DOLOPHINE, AFTER ADOLF.
ACTUALLY...

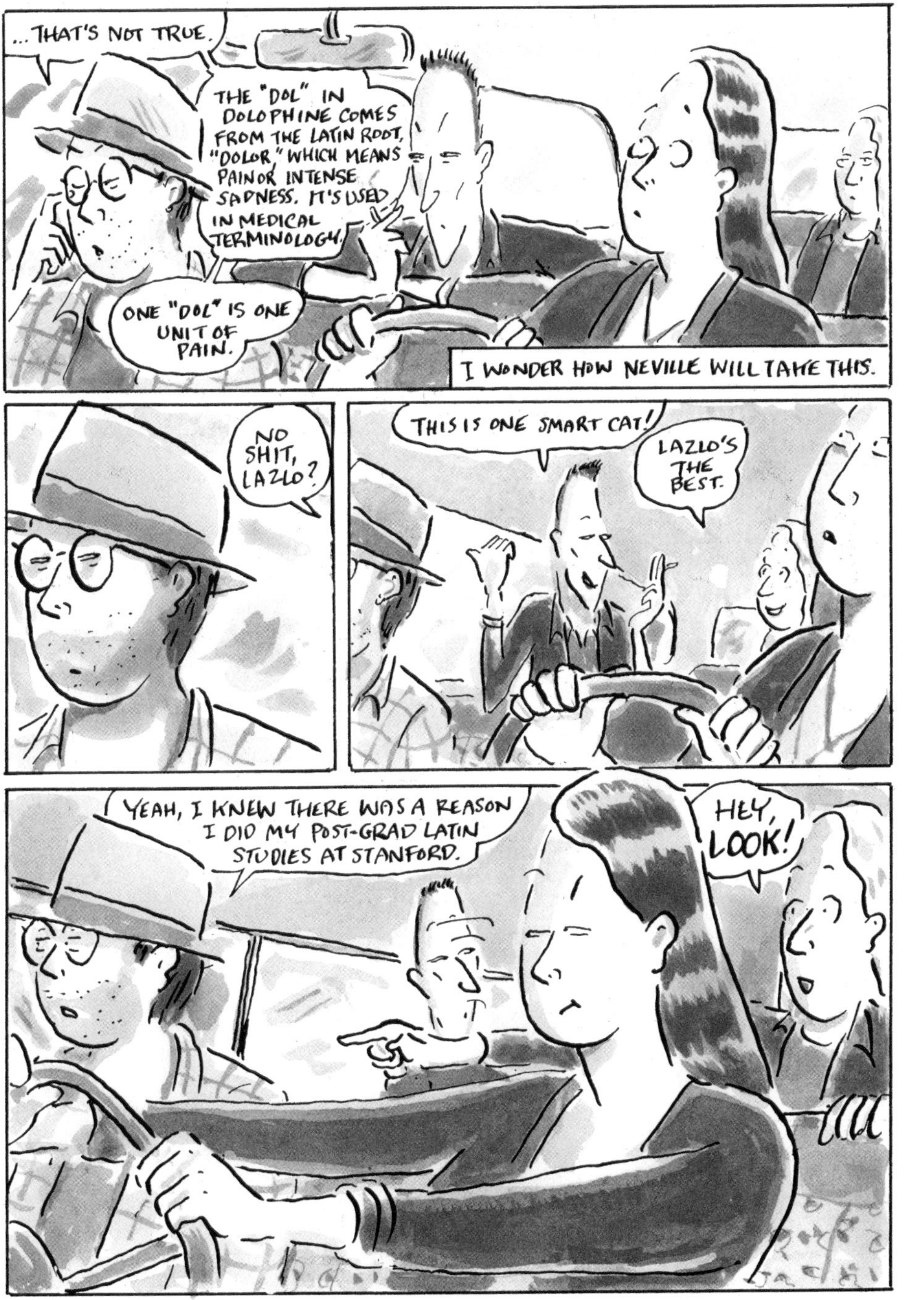
...THAT'S NOT TRUE.
THE "DOL" IN DOLOPHINE COMES FROM THE LATIN ROOT, "DOLOR," WHICH MEANS PAIN OR INTENSE SADNESS. IT'S USED IN MEDICAL TERMINOLOGY.
ONE "DOL" IS ONE UNIT OF PAIN.
I WONDER HOW NEVILLE WILL TAKE THIS.
NO SHIT, LAZLO?
THIS IS ONE SMART CAT!
LAZLO'S THE BEST.
YEAH, I KNEW THERE WAS A REASON I DID MY POST-GRAD LATIN STUDIES AT STANFORD.
HEY, LOOK!

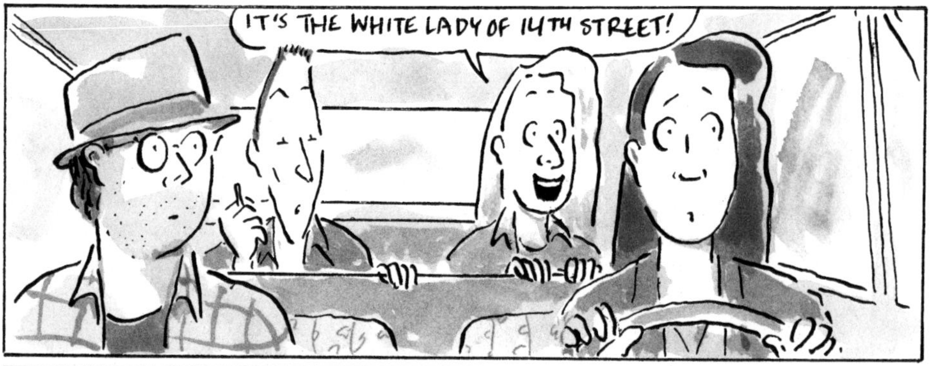
IT'S THE WHITE LADY OF 14TH STREET!

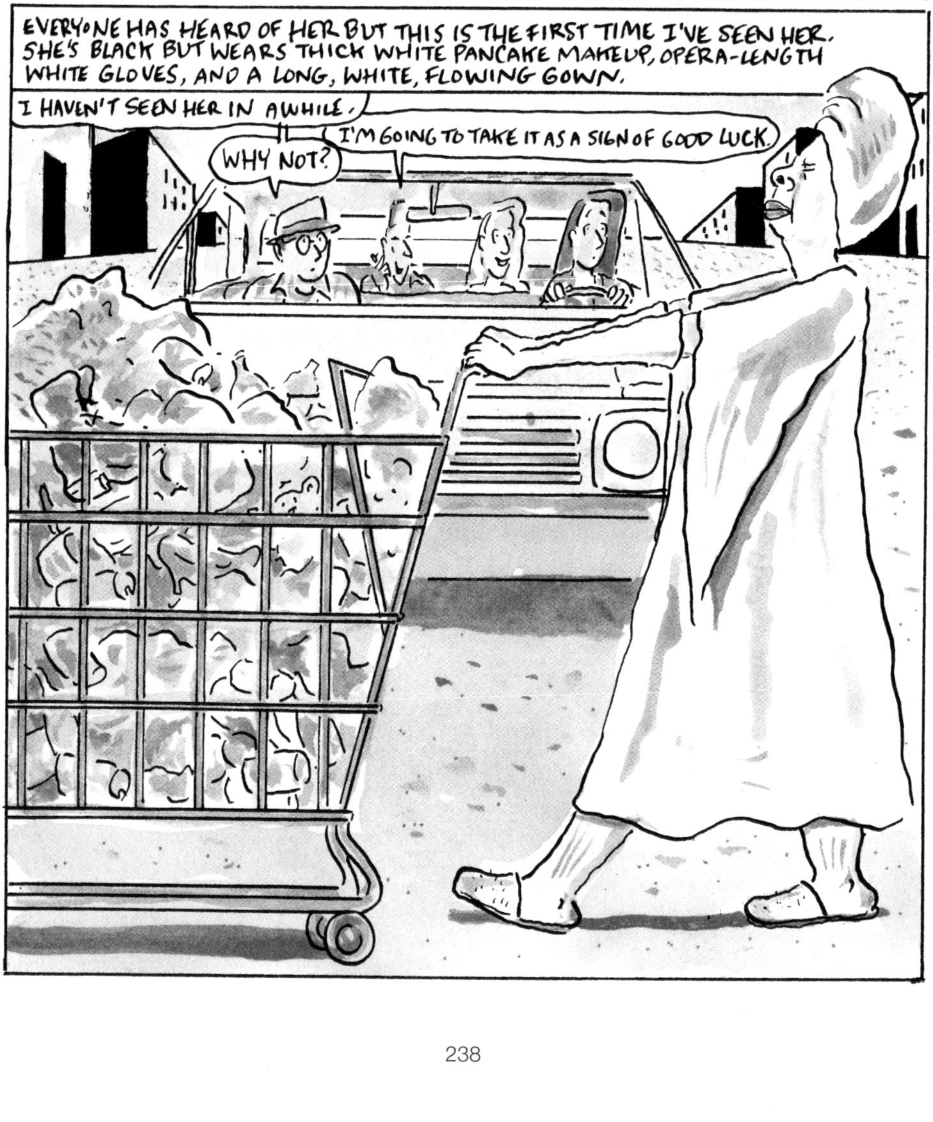
EVERYONE HAS HEARD OF HER BUT THIS IS THE FIRST TIME I'VE SEEN HER. SHE'S BLACK BUT WEARS THICK WHITE PANCAKE MAKEUP, OPERA-LENGTH WHITE GLOVES, AND A LONG, WHITE, FLOWING GOWN.
I HAVEN'T SEEN HER IN AWHILE.
WHY NOT?
I'M GOING TO TAKE IT AS A SIGN OF GOOD LUCK.

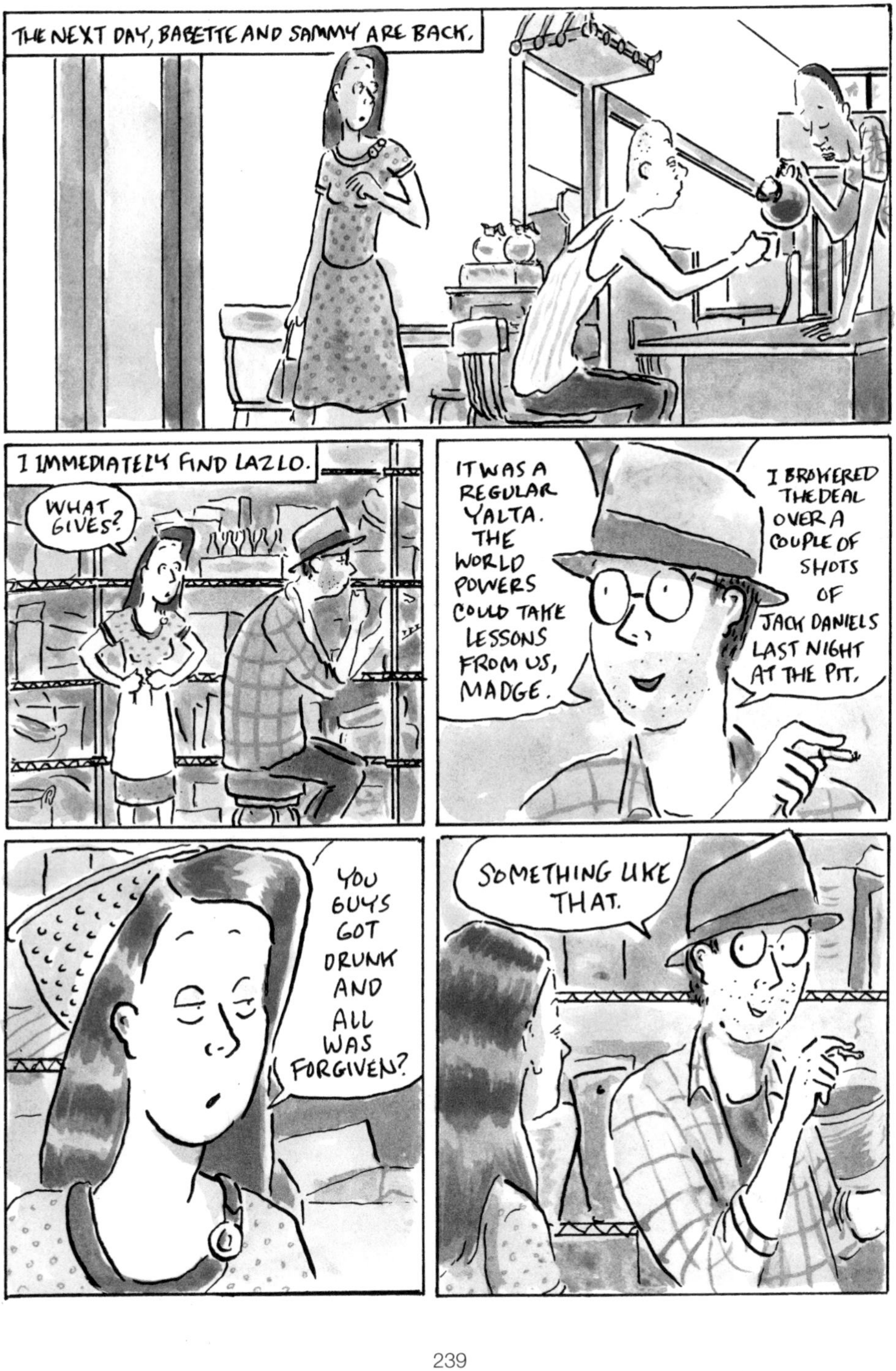
THE NEXT DAY, BABETTE AND SAMMY ARE BACK.
I IMMEDIATELY FIND LAZLO.
WHAT GIVES?
IT WAS A REGULAR YALTA. THE WORLD POWERS COULD TAKE LESSONS FROM US, MADGE.
I BROKERED THE DEAL OVER A COUPLE OF SHOTS OF JACK DANIELS LAST NIGHT AT THE PIT.
YOU GUYS GOT DRUNK AND ALL WAS FORGIVEN?
SOMETHING LIKE THAT.

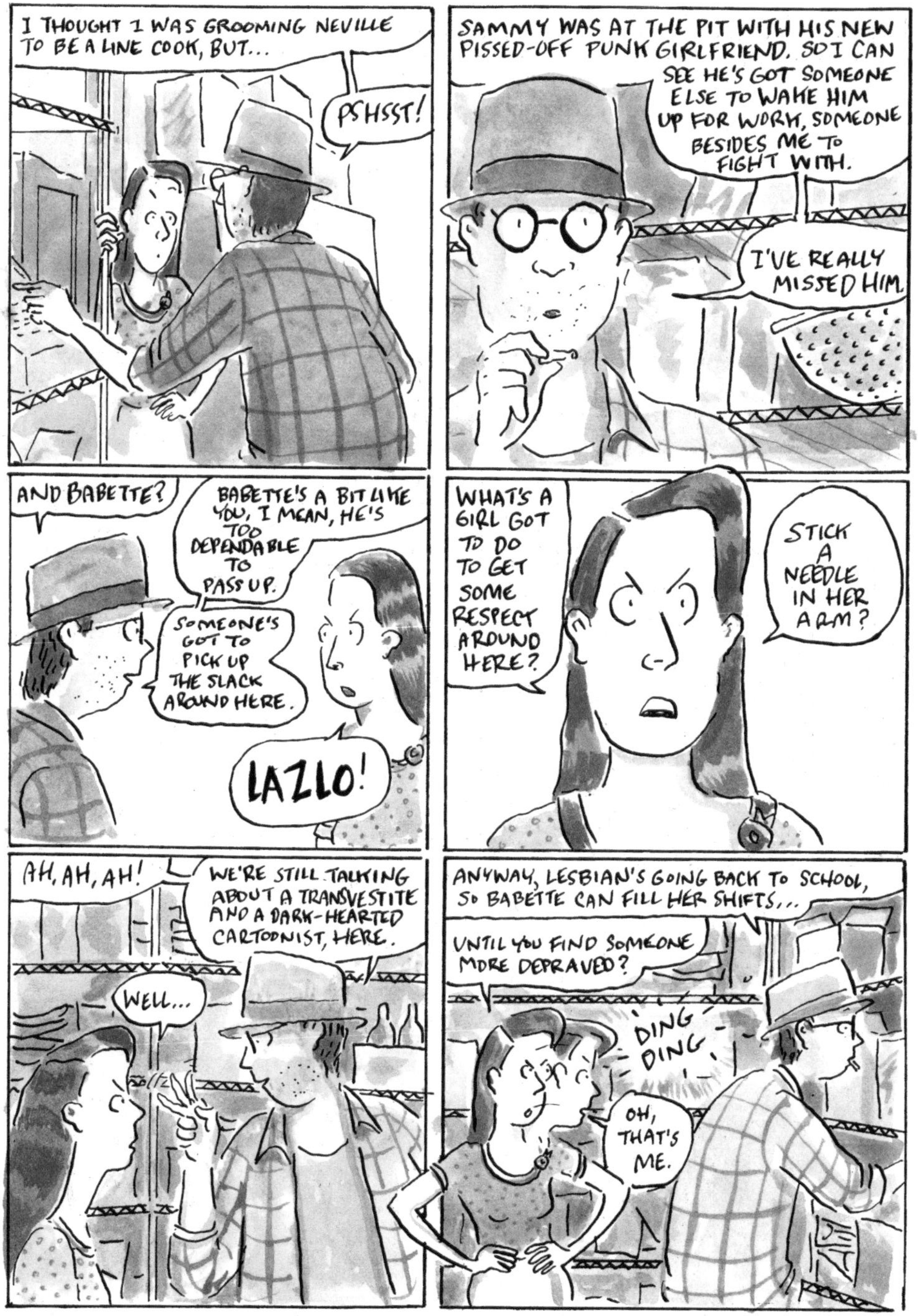
I THOUGHT I WAS GROOMING NEVILLE TO BE A LINE COOK, BUT...
PSHSST!
SAMMY WAS AT THE PIT WITH HIS NEW PISSED-OFF PUNK GIRLFRIEND. SO I CAN SEE HE'S GOT SOMEONE ELSE TO WAKE HIM UP FOR WORK, SOMEONE BESIDES ME TO FIGHT WITH.
I'VE REALLY MISSED HIM.
AND BABETTE?
BABETTE'S A BIT LIKE YOU, I MEAN, HE'S TOO DEPENDABLE TO PASS UP.
SOMEONE'S GOT TO PICK UP THE SLACK AROUND HERE.
LAZLO!
WHAT'S A GIRL GOT TO DO TO GET SOME RESPECT AROUND HERE?
STICK A NEEDLE IN HER ARM?
AH, AH, AH!
WE'RE STILL TALKING ABOUT A TRANSVESTITE AND A DARK-HEARTED CARTOONIST, HERE.
WELL...
ANYWAY, LESBIAN'S GOING BACK TO SCHOOL, SO BABETTE CAN FILL HER SHIFTS...
UNTIL YOU FIND SOMEONE MORE DEPRAVED?
DING DING
OH, THAT'S ME.

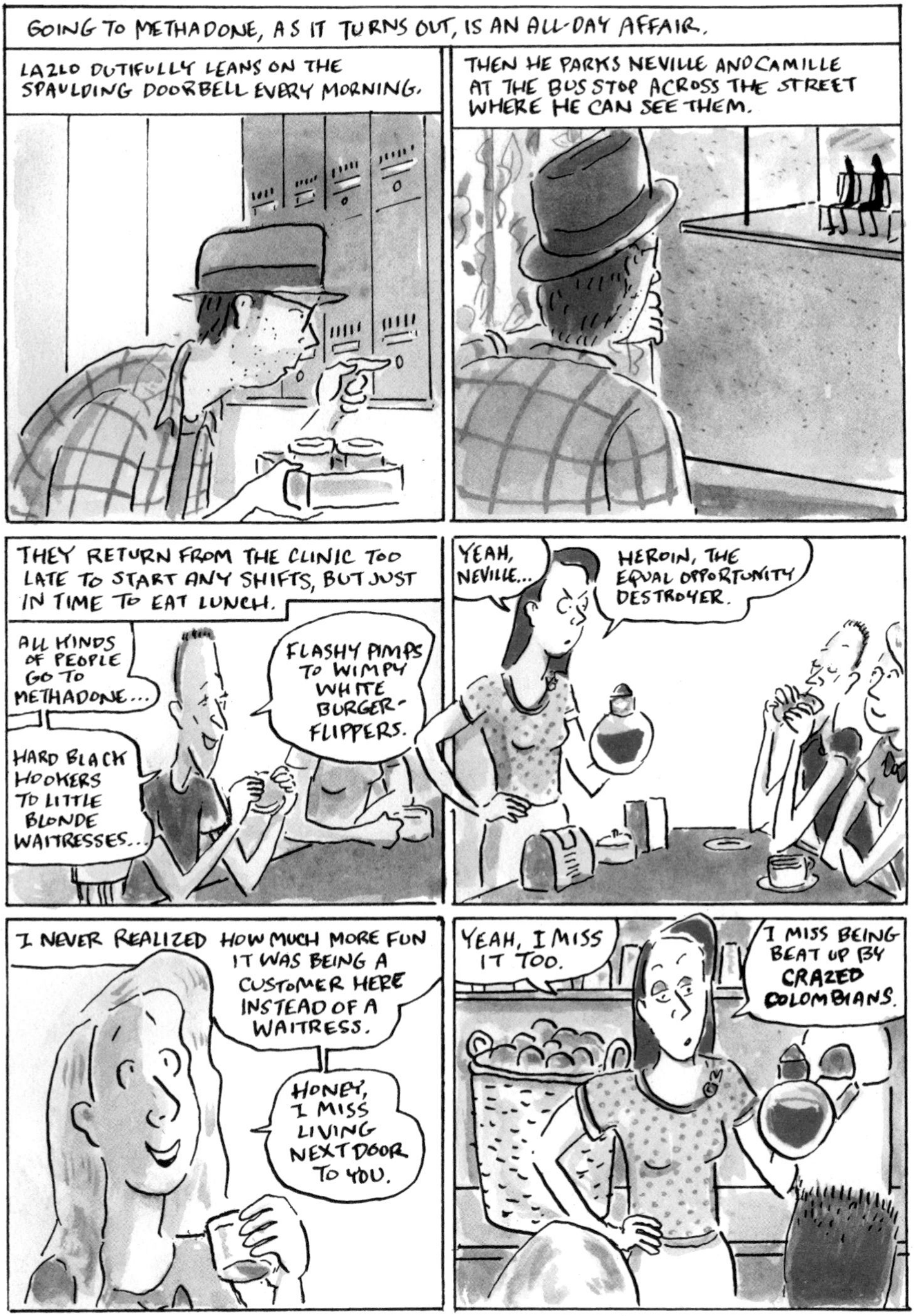

GOING TO METHADONE, AS IT TURNS OUT, IS AN ALL-DAY AFFAIR.
LAZLO DUTIFULLY LEANS ON THE SPAULDING DOORBELL EVERY MORNING.
THEN HE PARKS NEVILLE AND CAMILLE AT THE BUS STOP ACROSS THE STREET WHERE HE CAN SEE THEM.
THEY RETURN FROM THE CLINIC TOO LATE TO START ANY SHIFTS, BUT JUST IN TIME TO EAT LUNCH.
ALL KINDS OF PEOPLE GO TO METHADONE...
HARD BLACK HOOKERS TO LITTLE BLONDE WAITRESSES...
FLASHY PIMPS TO WIMPY WHITE BURGER-FLIPPERS.
YEAH, NEVILLE...
HEROIN, THE EQUAL OPPORTUNITY DESTROYER.
I NEVER REALIZED HOW MUCH MORE FUN IT WAS BEING A CUSTOMER HERE INSTEAD OF A WAITRESS.
HONEY, I MISS LIVING NEXT DOOR TO YOU.
YEAH, I MISS IT TOO.
I MISS BEING BEAT UP BY CRAZED COLOMBIANS.

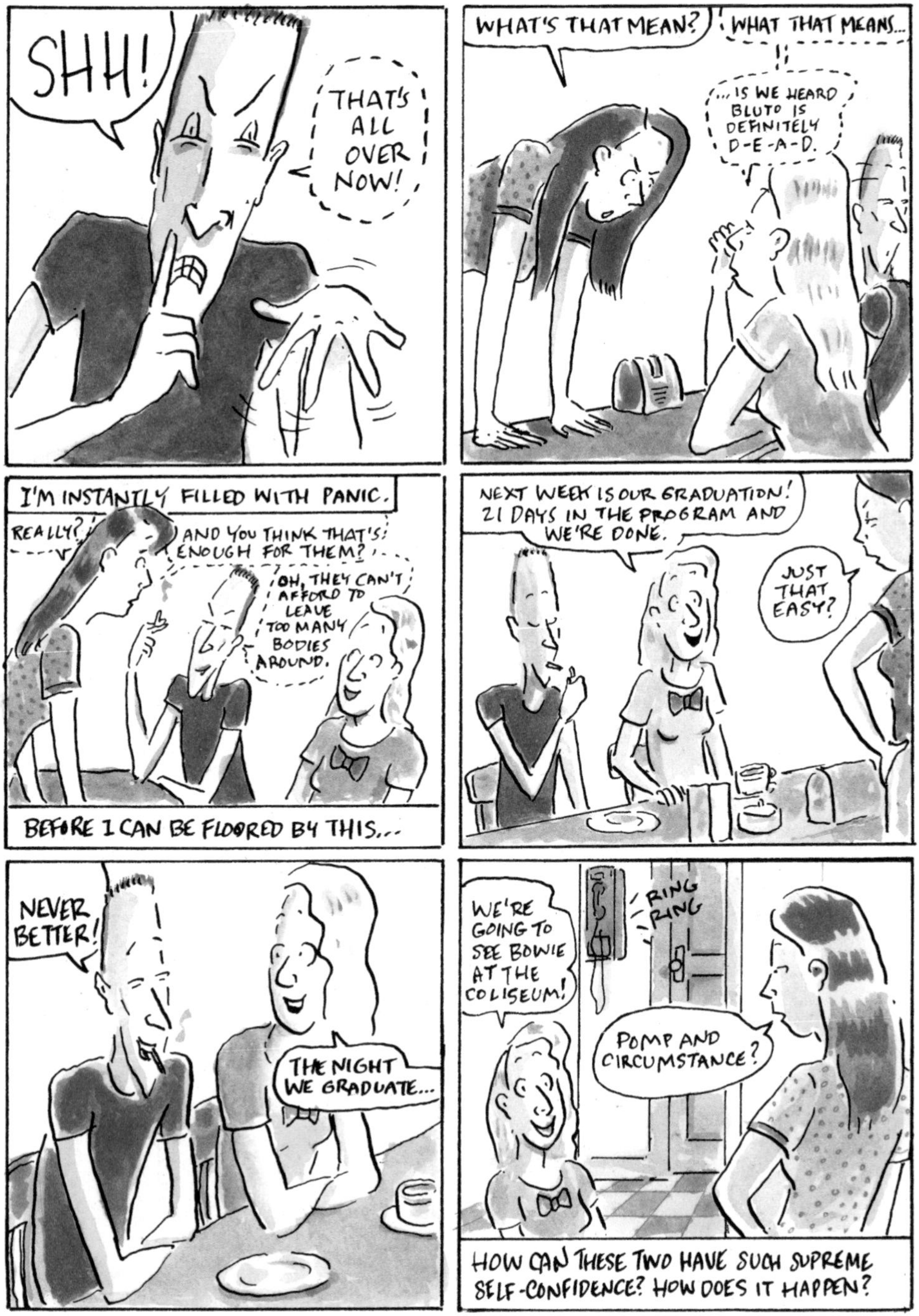
SHH!
THAT'S ALL OVER NOW!
WHAT'S THAT MEAN?
WHAT THAT MEANS...
...IS WE HEARD BLUTO IS DEFINITELY D-E-A-D.
I'M INSTANTLY FILLED WITH PANIC.
REALLY?
AND YOU THINK THAT'S ENOUGH FOR THEM?
OH, THEY CAN'T AFFORD TO LEAVE TOO MANY BODIES AROUND.
BEFORE I CAN BE FLOORED BY THIS...
NEXT WEEK IS OUR GRADUATION! 21 DAYS IN THE PROGRAM AND WE'RE DONE.
JUST THAT EASY?
NEVER BETTER!
THE NIGHT WE GRADUATE...
WE'RE GOING TO SEE BOWIE AT THE COLISEUM!
RING RING
POMP AND CIRCUMSTANCE?
HOW CAN THESE TWO HAVE SUCH SUPREME SELF-CONFIDENCE? HOW DOES IT HAPPEN?

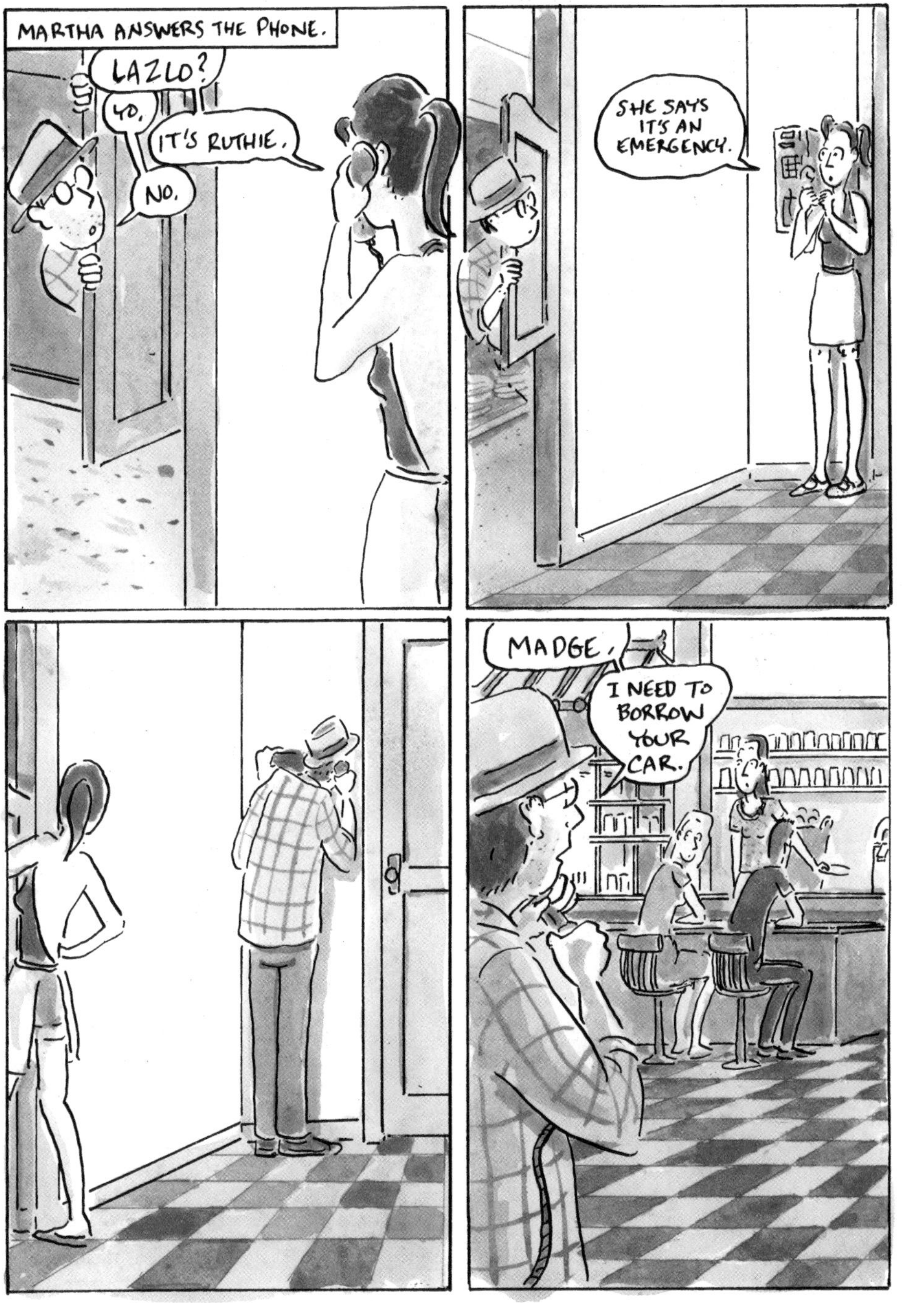
MARTHA ANSWERS THE PHONE.
LAZLO?
YO.
IT'S RUTHIE.
NO.
SHE SAYS IT'S AN EMERGENCY.
MADGE.
I NEED TO BORROW YOUR CAR.

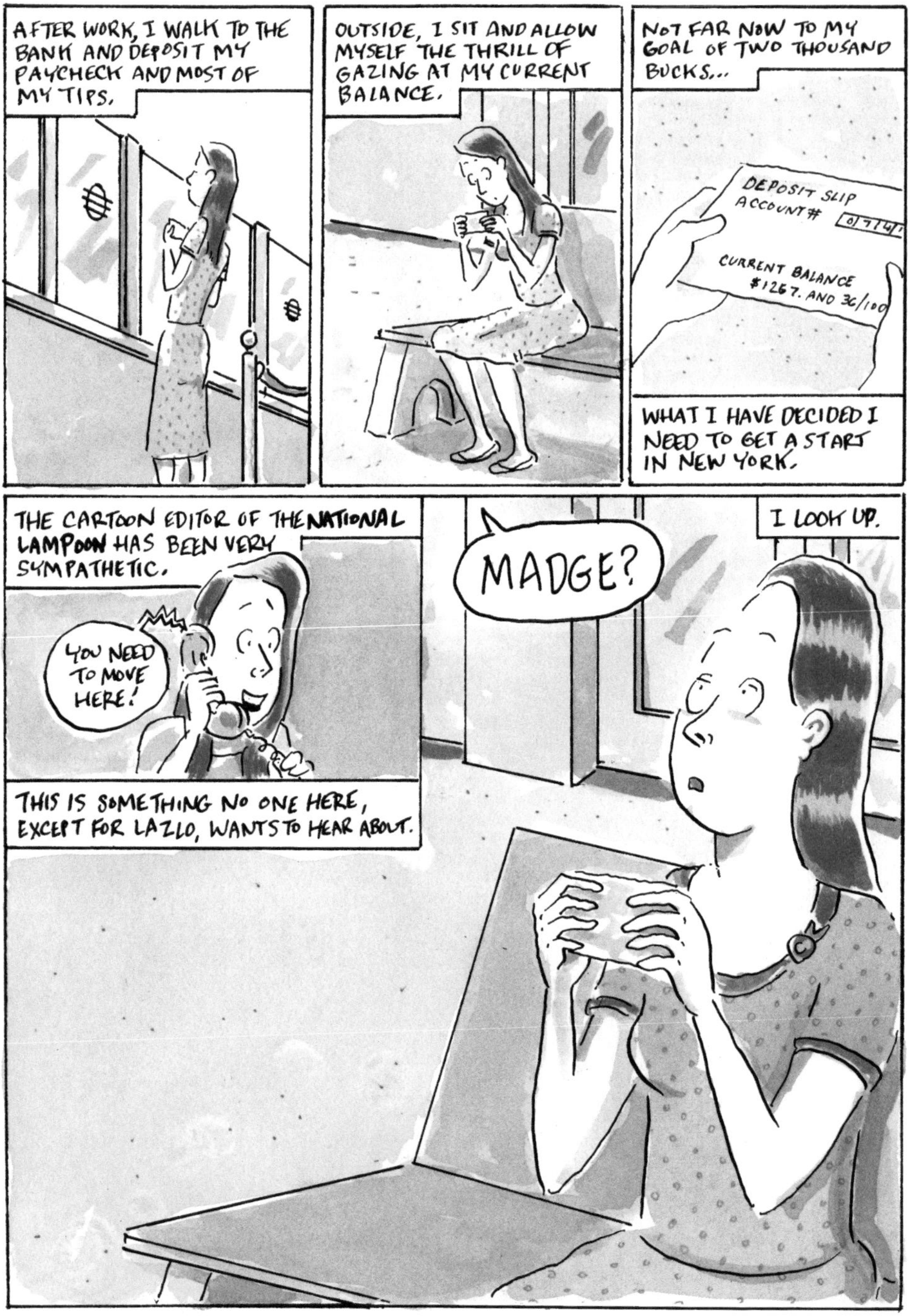
AFTER WORK, I WALK TO THE BANK AND DEPOSIT MY PAYCHECK AND MOST OF MY TIPS.
OUTSIDE, I SIT AND ALLOW MYSELF THE THRILL OF GAZING AT MY CURRENT BALANCE.
NOT FAR NOW TO MY GOAL OF TWO THOUSAND BUCKS...
DEPOSIT SLIP
ACCOUNT #
CURRENT BALANCE
$1267. AND 36/100
WHAT I HAVE DECIDED I NEED TO GET A START IN NEW YORK.
THE CARTOON EDITOR OF THE NATIONAL LAMPOON HAS BEEN VERY SYMPATHETIC.
YOU NEED TO MOVE HERE!
THIS IS SOMETHING NO ONE HERE, EXCEPT FOR LAZLO, WANTS TO HEAR ABOUT.
MADGE?
I LOOK UP.

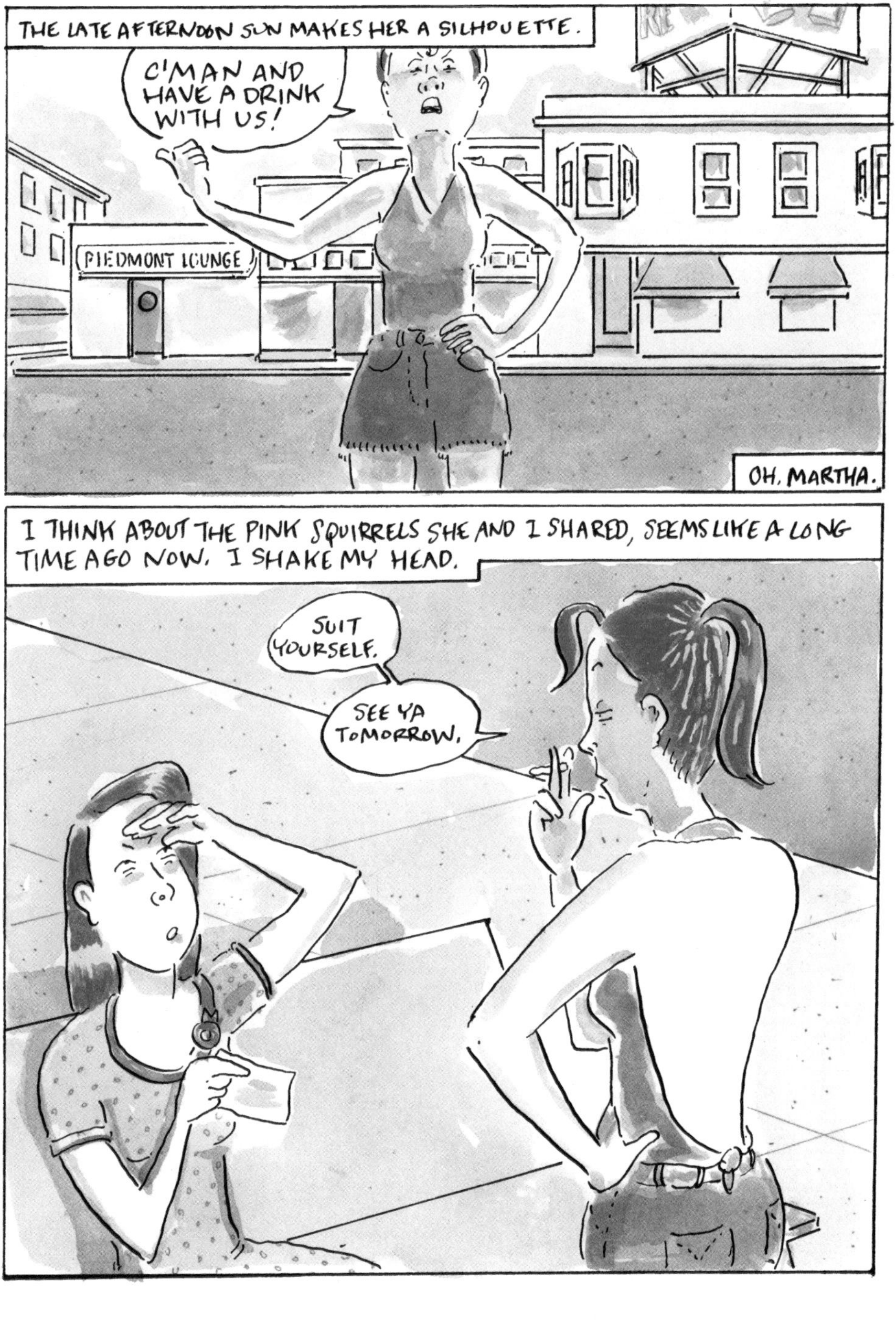
THE LATE AFTERNOON SUN MAKES HER A SILHOUETTE.
C'MAN AND HAVE A DRINK WITH US!
PIEDMONT LOUNGE
OH, MARTHA.
I THINK ABOUT THE PINK SQUIRRELS SHE AND I SHARED, SEEMS LIKE A LONG TIME AGO NOW. I SHAKE MY HEAD.
SUIT YOURSELF.
SEE YA TOMORROW.

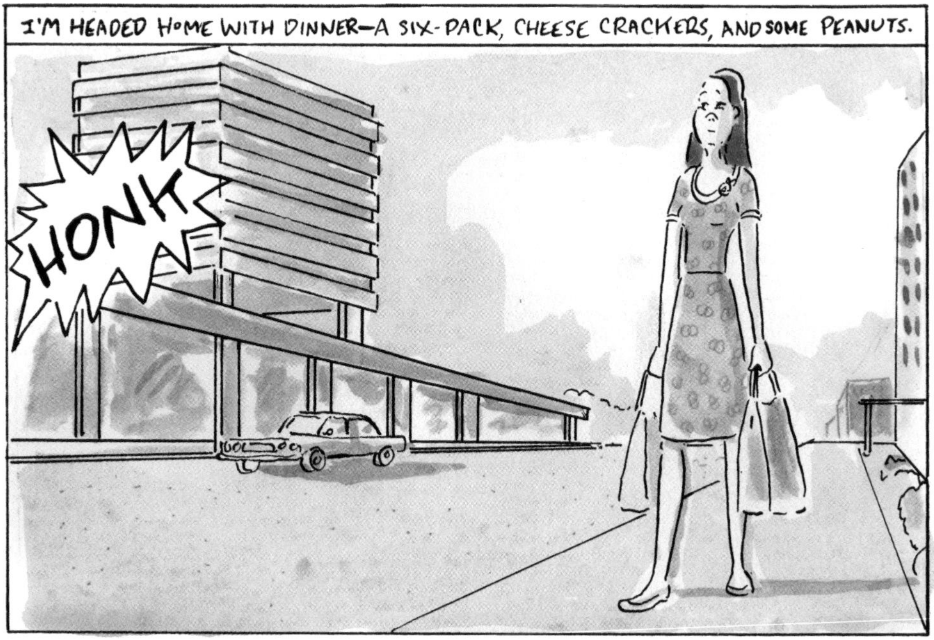
I'M HEADED HOME WITH DINNER—A SIX-PACK, CHEESE CRACKERS, AND SOME PEANUTS.
HONK

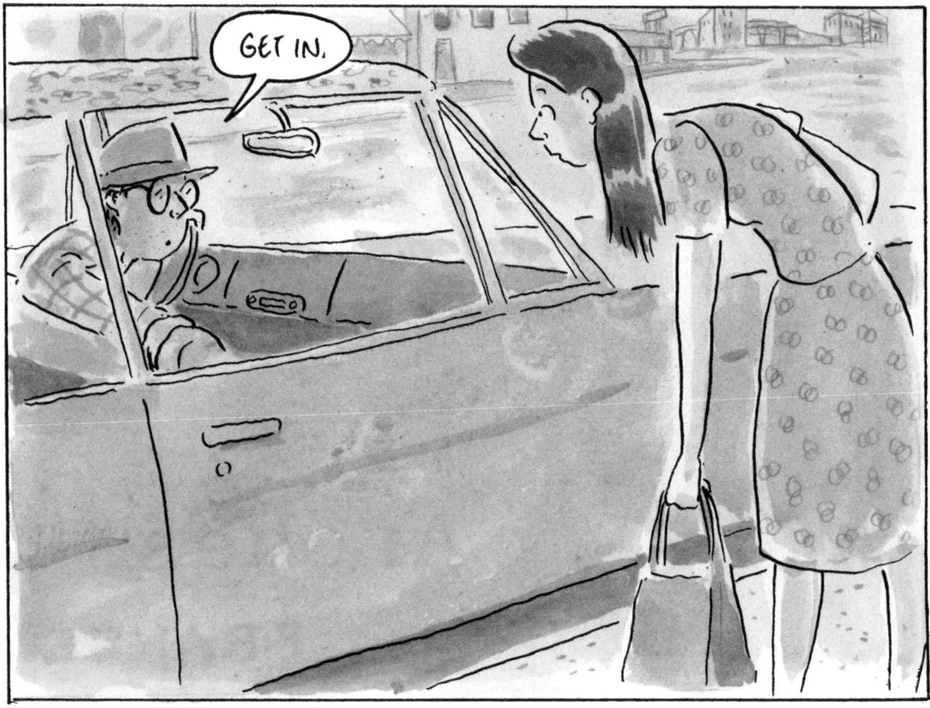
GET IN.

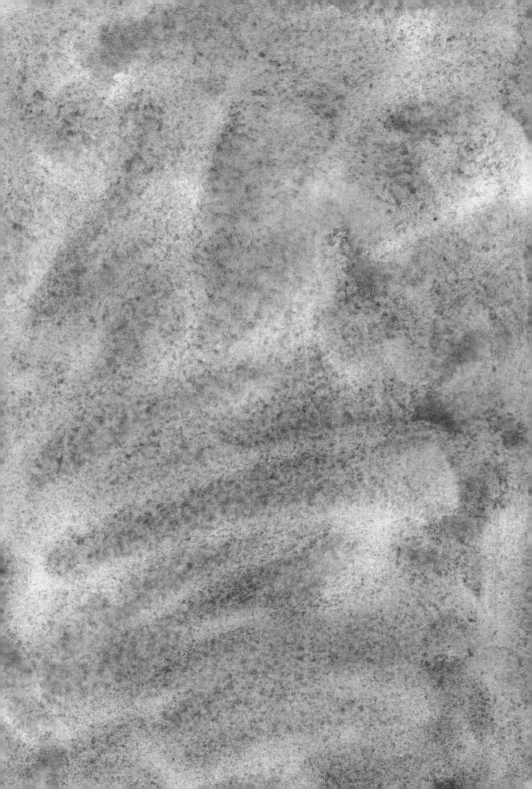

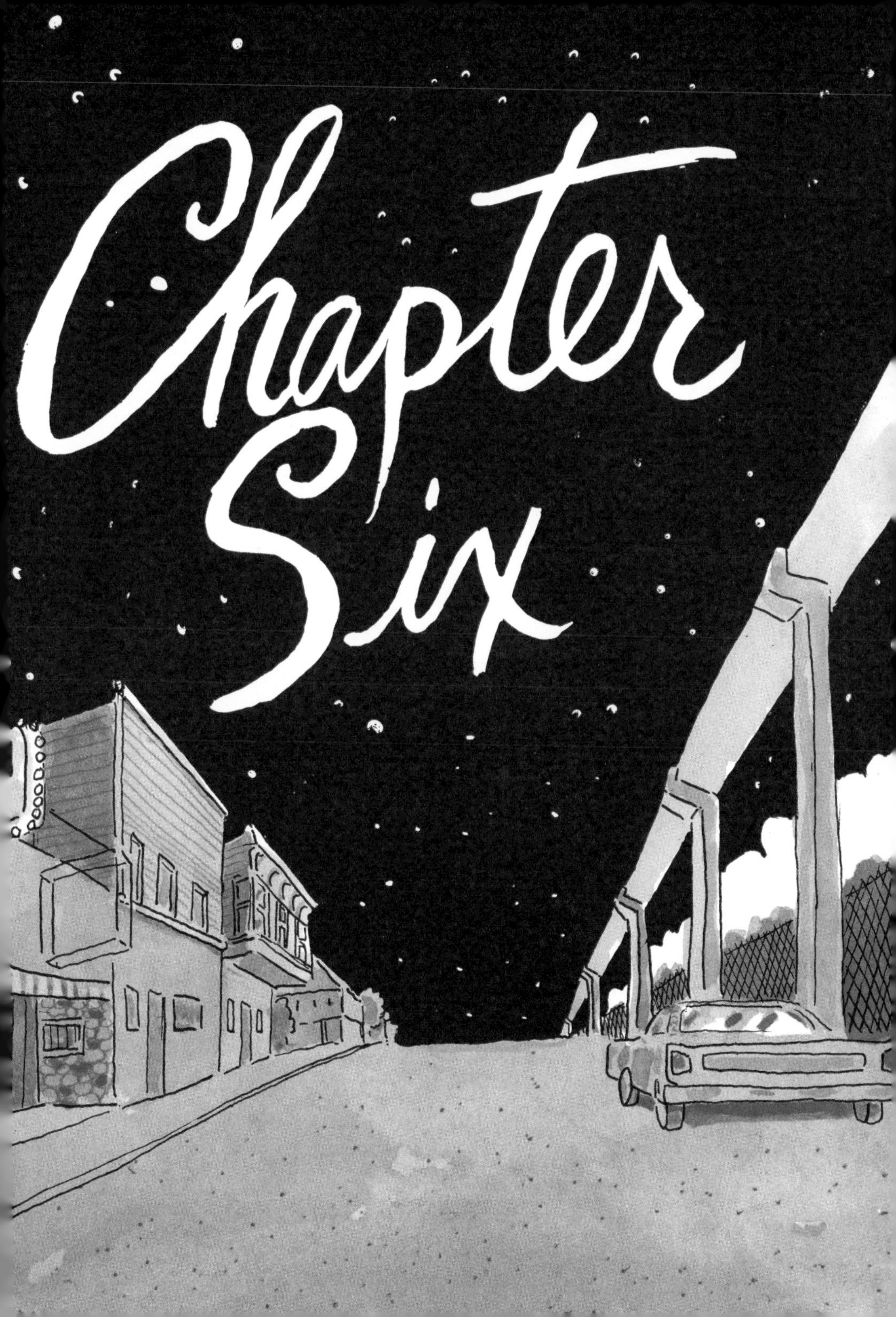
Chapter Six

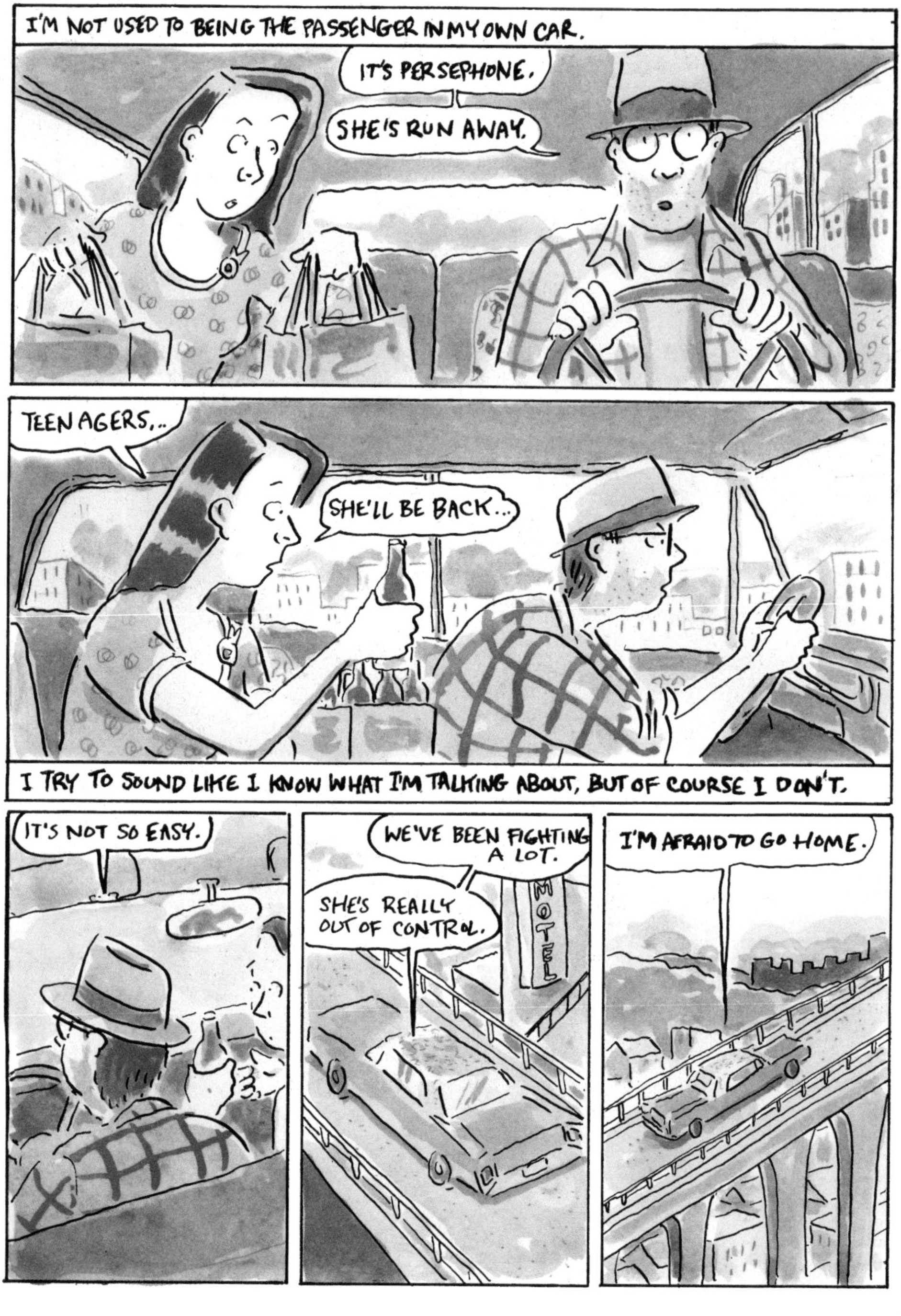
I'M NOT USED TO BEING THE PASSENGER IN MY OWN CAR.
IT'S PERSEPHONE.
SHE'S RUN AWAY.
TEENAGERS,..
SHE'LL BE BACK...
I TRY TO SOUND LIKE I KNOW WHAT I'M TALKING ABOUT, BUT OF COURSE I DON'T.
IT'S NOT SO EASY.
WE'VE BEEN FIGHTING A LOT.
SHE'S REALLY OUT OF CONTROL.
MOTEL
I'M AFRAID TO GO HOME.

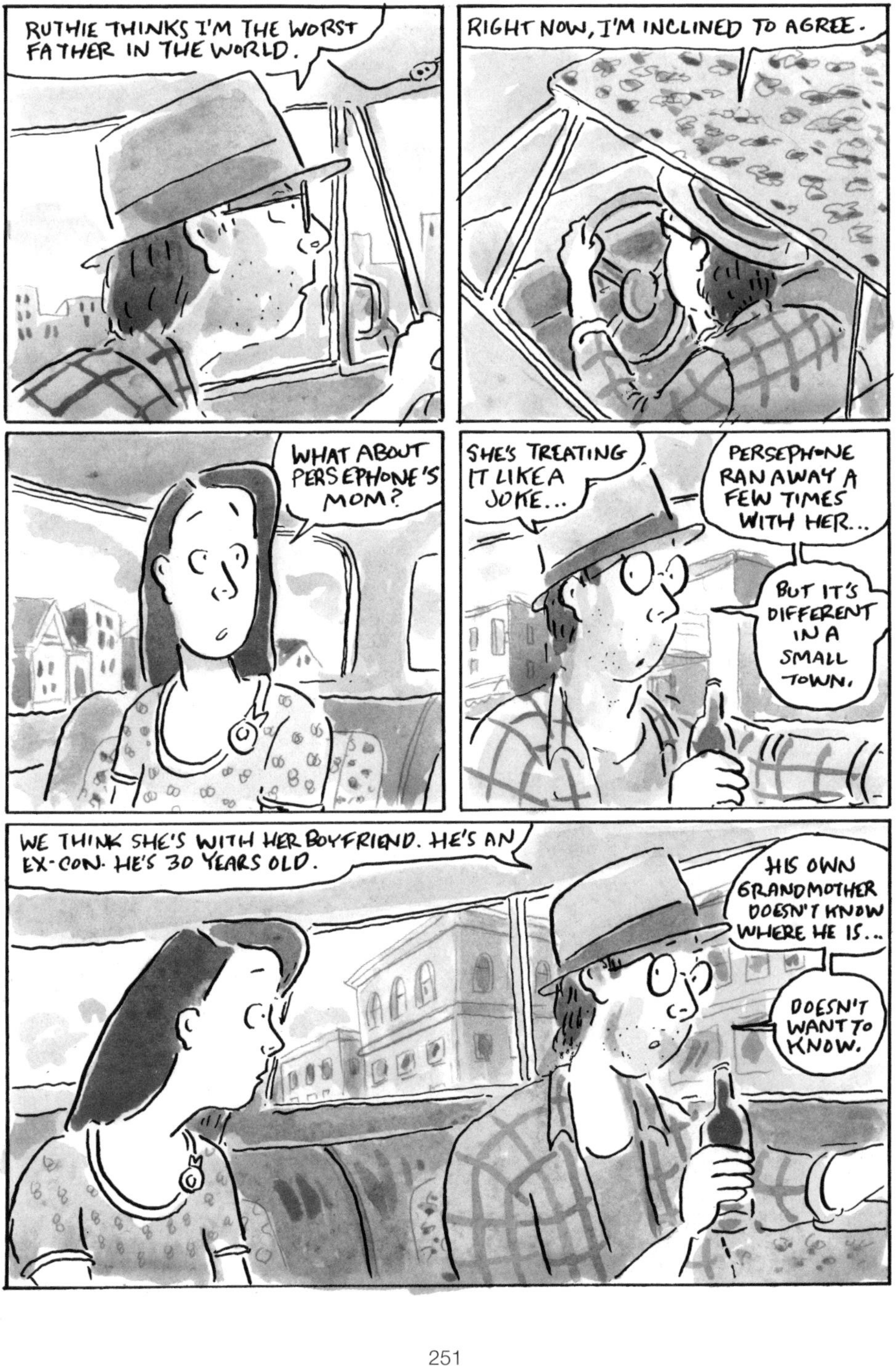
RUTHIE THINKS I'M THE WORST FATHER IN THE WORLD.
RIGHT NOW, I'M INCLINED TO AGREE.
WHAT ABOUT PERSEPHONE'S MOM?
SHE'S TREATING IT LIKE A JOKE...
PERSEPHONE RAN AWAY A FEW TIMES WITH HER...
BUT IT'S DIFFERENT IN A SMALL TOWN.
WE THINK SHE'S WITH HER BOYFRIEND. HE'S AN EX-CON. HE'S 30 YEARS OLD.
HIS OWN GRANDMOTHER DOESN'T KNOW WHERE HE IS...
DOESN'T WANT TO KNOW.

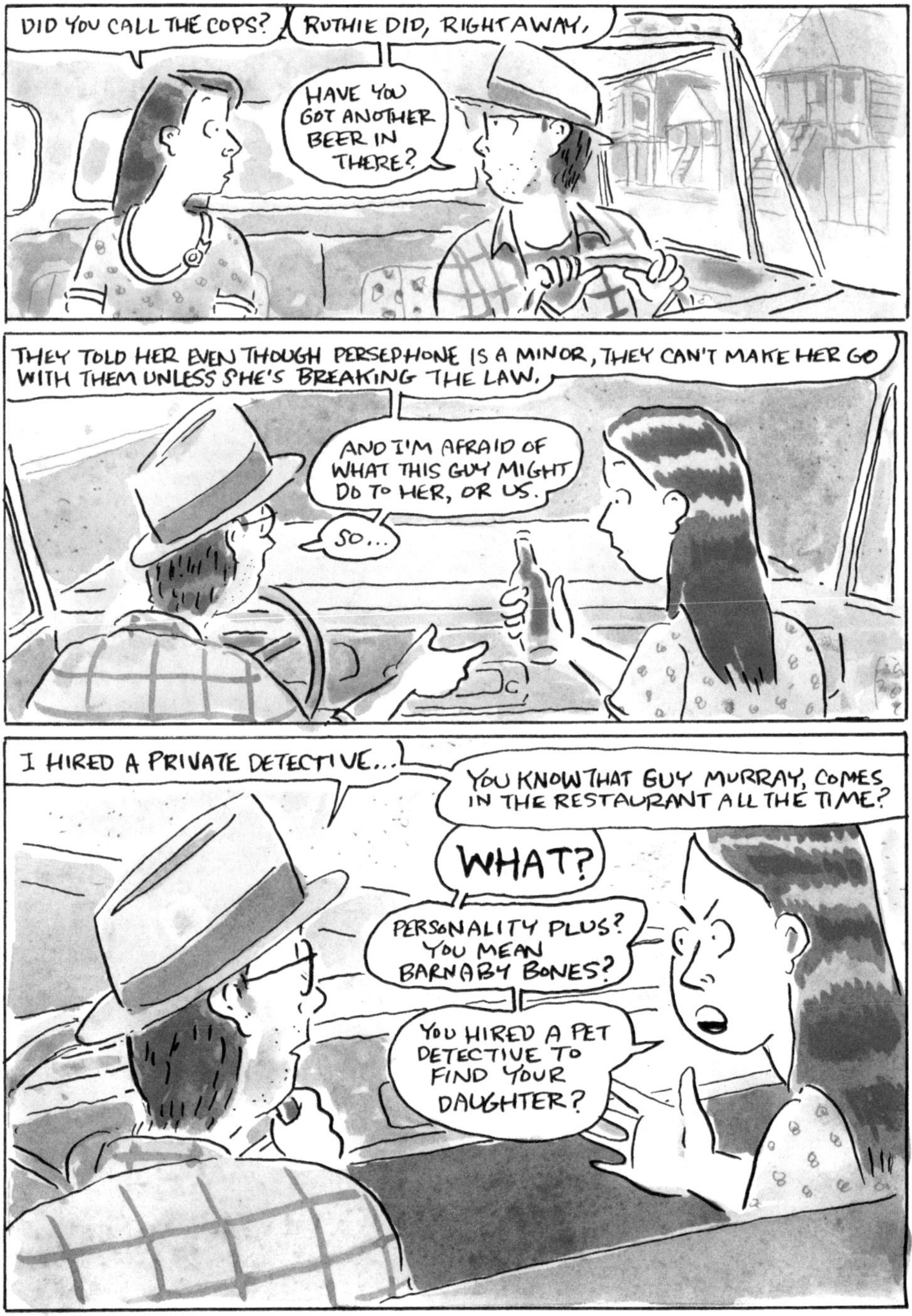
DID YOU CALL THE COPS?
RUTHIE DID, RIGHT AWAY,
HAVE YOU GOT ANOTHER BEER IN THERE?
THEY TOLD HER EVEN THOUGH PERSEPHONE IS A MINOR, THEY CAN'T MAKE HER GO WITH THEM UNLESS SHE'S BREAKING THE LAW.
AND I'M AFRAID OF WHAT THIS GUY MIGHT DO TO HER, OR US.
SO...
I HIRED A PRIVATE DETECTIVE...
YOU KNOW THAT GUY MURRAY, COMES IN THE RESTAURANT ALL THE TIME?
WHAT?
PERSONALITY PLUS? YOU MEAN BARNABY BONES?
YOU HIRED A PET DETECTIVE TO FIND YOUR DAUGHTER?

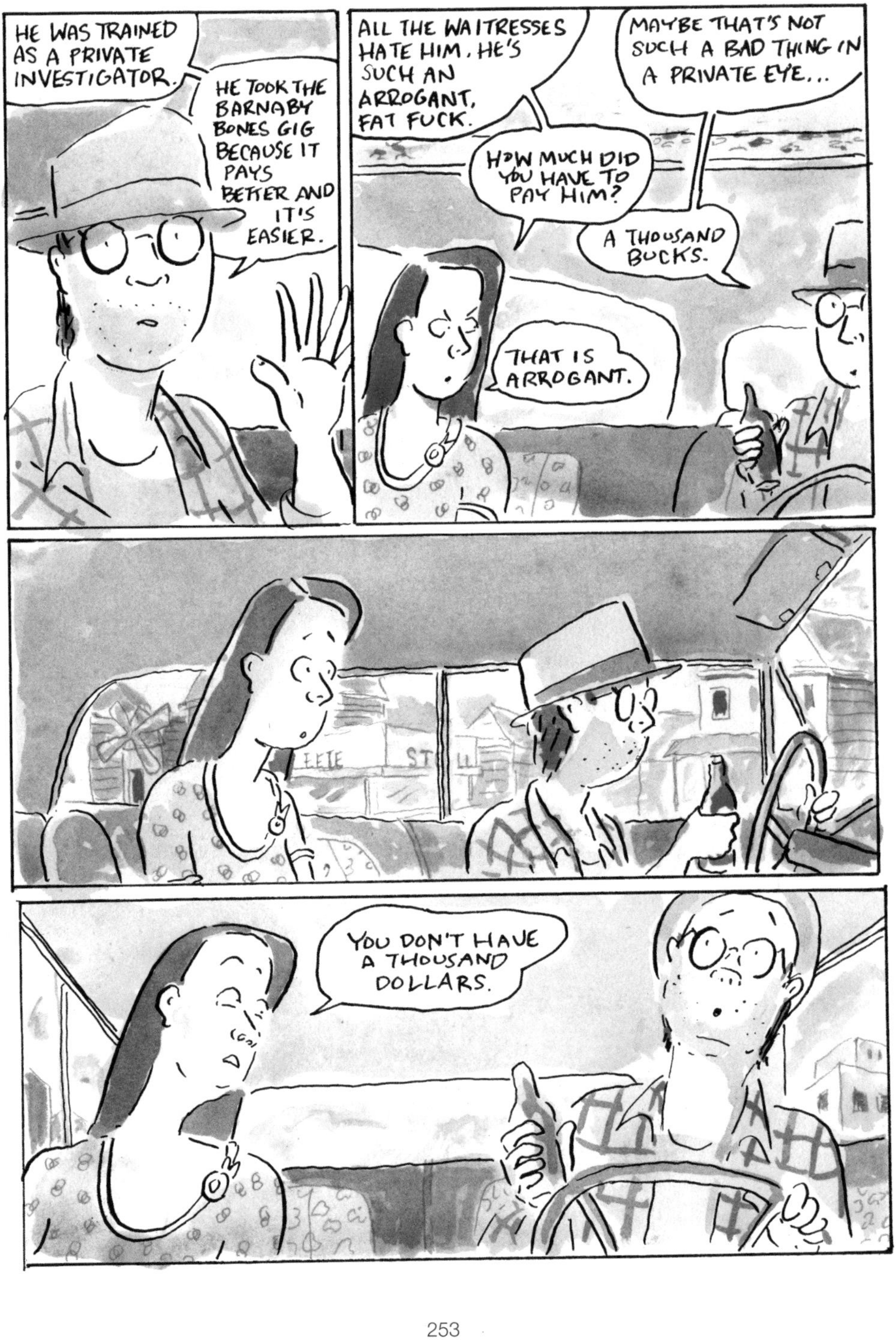
HE WAS TRAINED AS A PRIVATE INVESTIGATOR.
HE TOOK THE BARNABY BONES GIG BECAUSE IT PAYS BETTER AND IT'S EASIER.
ALL THE WAITRESSES HATE HIM. HE'S SUCH AN ARROGANT, FAT FUCK.
MAYBE THAT'S NOT SUCH A BAD THING IN A PRIVATE EYE...
HOW MUCH DID YOU HAVE TO PAY HIM?
A THOUSAND BUCKS.
THAT IS ARROGANT.
YOU DON'T HAVE A THOUSAND DOLLARS.

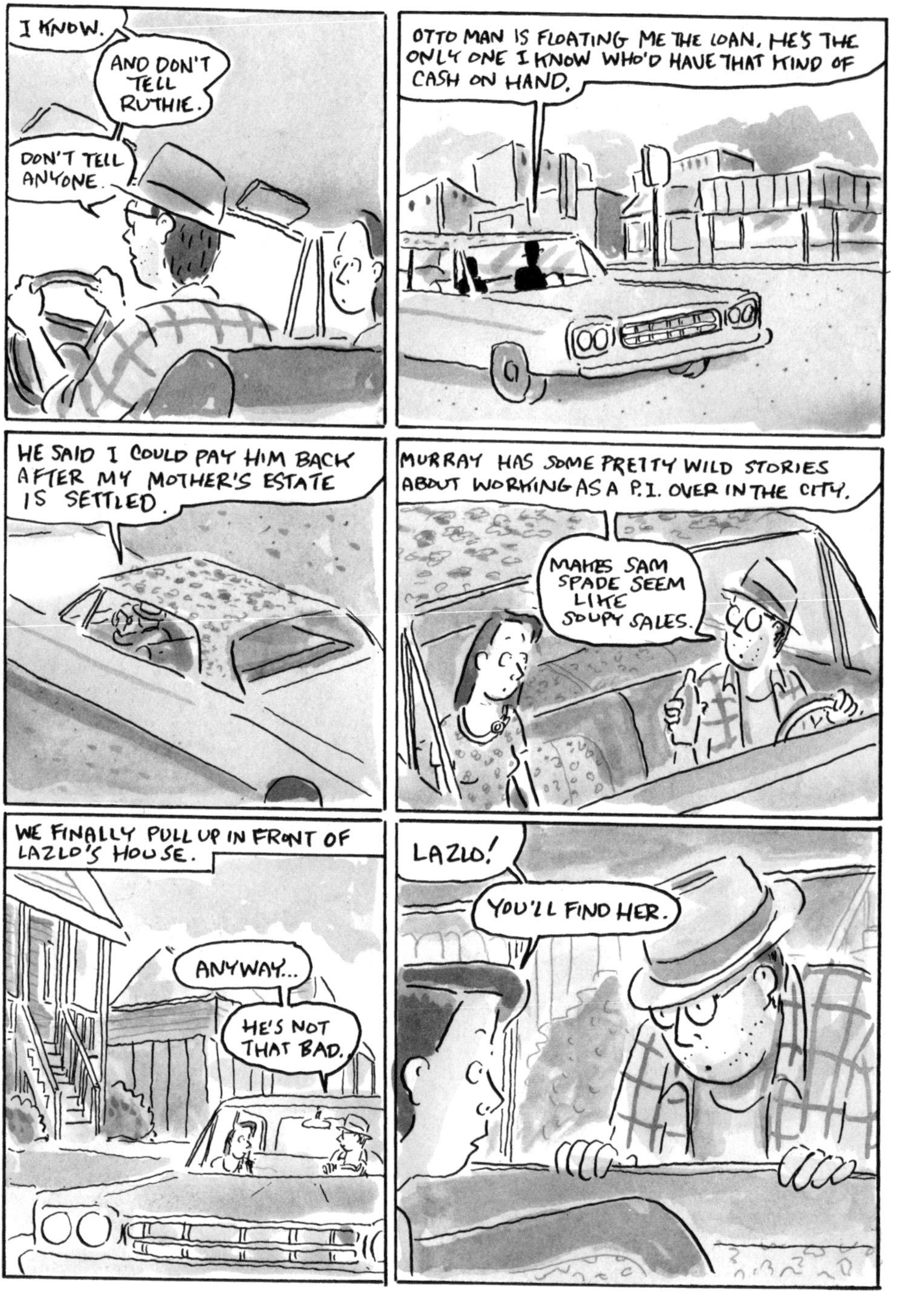
I KNOW.
AND DON'T TELL RUTHIE.
DON'T TELL ANYONE.
OTTO MAN IS FLOATING ME THE LOAN. HE'S THE ONLY ONE I KNOW WHO'D HAVE THAT KIND OF CASH ON HAND.
HE SAID I COULD PAY HIM BACK AFTER MY MOTHER'S ESTATE IS SETTLED.
MURRAY HAS SOME PRETTY WILD STORIES ABOUT WORKING AS A P.I. OVER IN THE CITY.
MAKES SAM SPADE SEEM LIKE SOUPY SALES.
WE FINALLY PULL UP IN FRONT OF LAZLO'S HOUSE.
ANYWAY...
HE'S NOT THAT BAD.
LAZLO!
YOU'LL FIND HER.

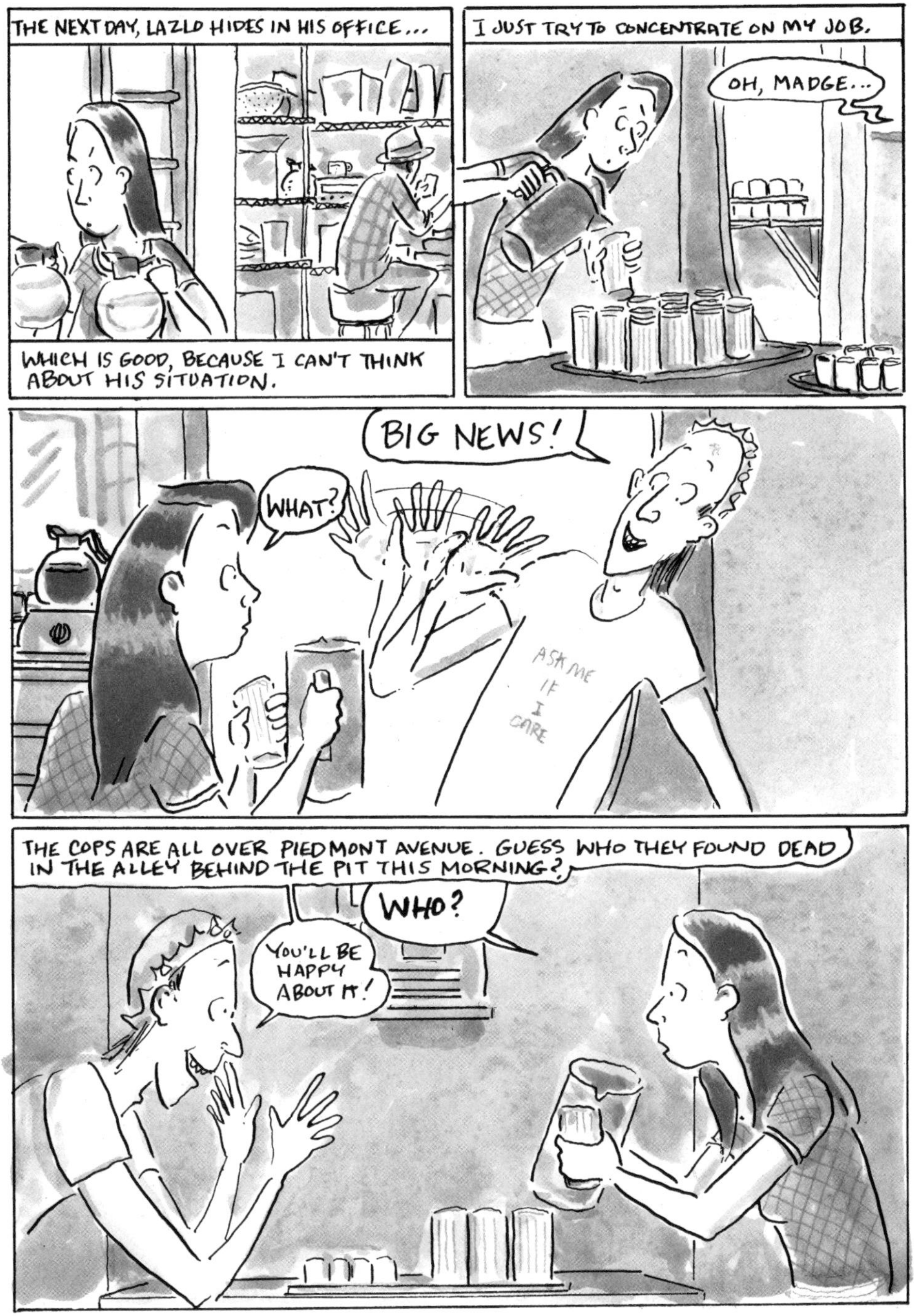
THE NEXT DAY, LAZLO HIDES IN HIS OFFICE...
WHICH IS GOOD, BECAUSE I CAN'T THINK ABOUT HIS SITUATION.
I JUST TRY TO CONCENTRATE ON MY JOB.
OH, MADGE...
BIG NEWS!
WHAT?
ASK ME IF I CARE
THE COPS ARE ALL OVER PIEDMONT AVENUE. GUESS WHO THEY FOUND DEAD IN THE ALLEY BEHIND THE PIT THIS MORNING?
WHO?
YOU'LL BE HAPPY ABOUT IT!

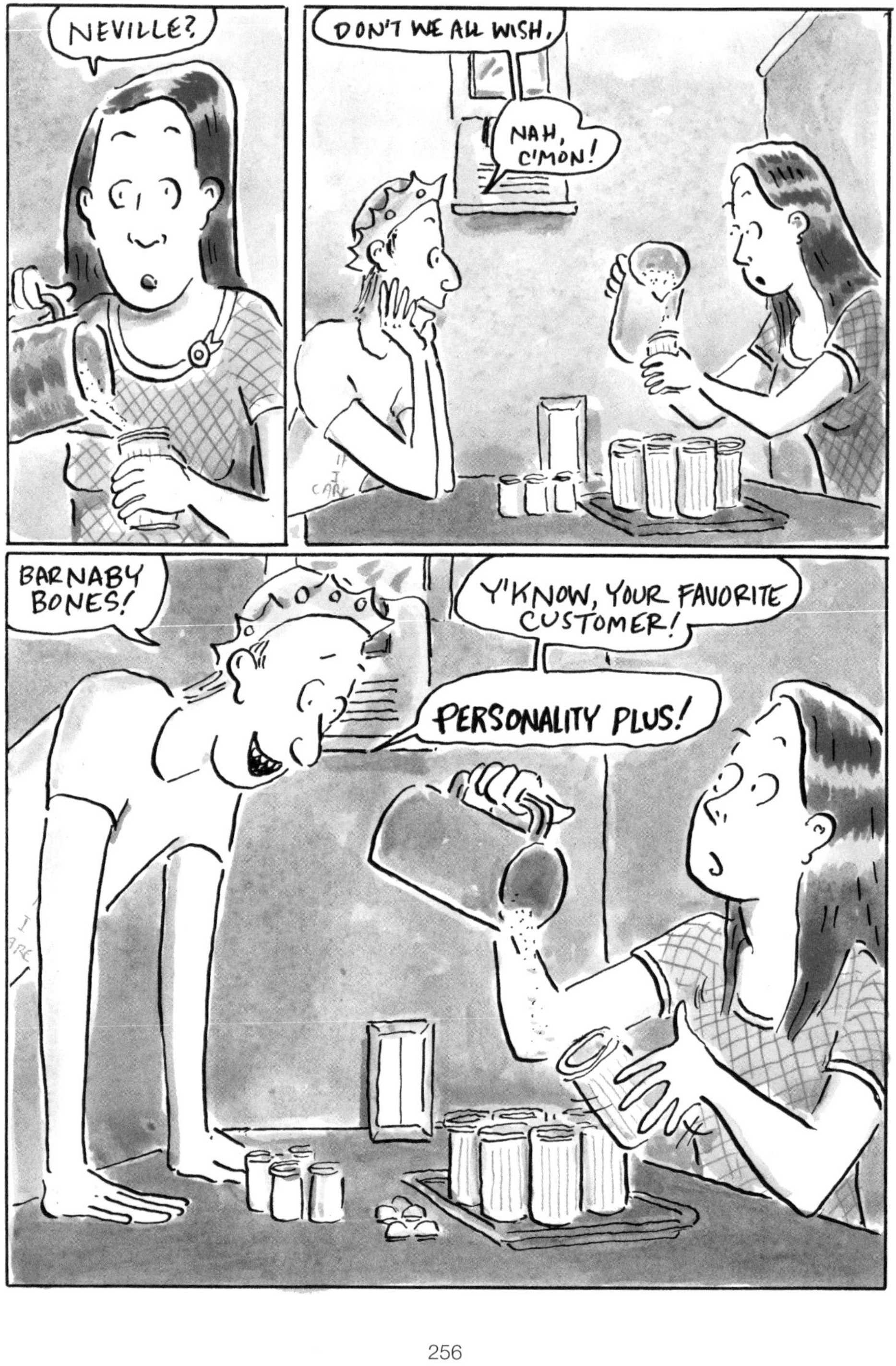
NEVILLE?
DON'T WE ALL WISH,
NAH, C'MON!
BARNABY BONES!
Y'KNOW, YOUR FAVORITE CUSTOMER!
PERSONALITY PLUS!

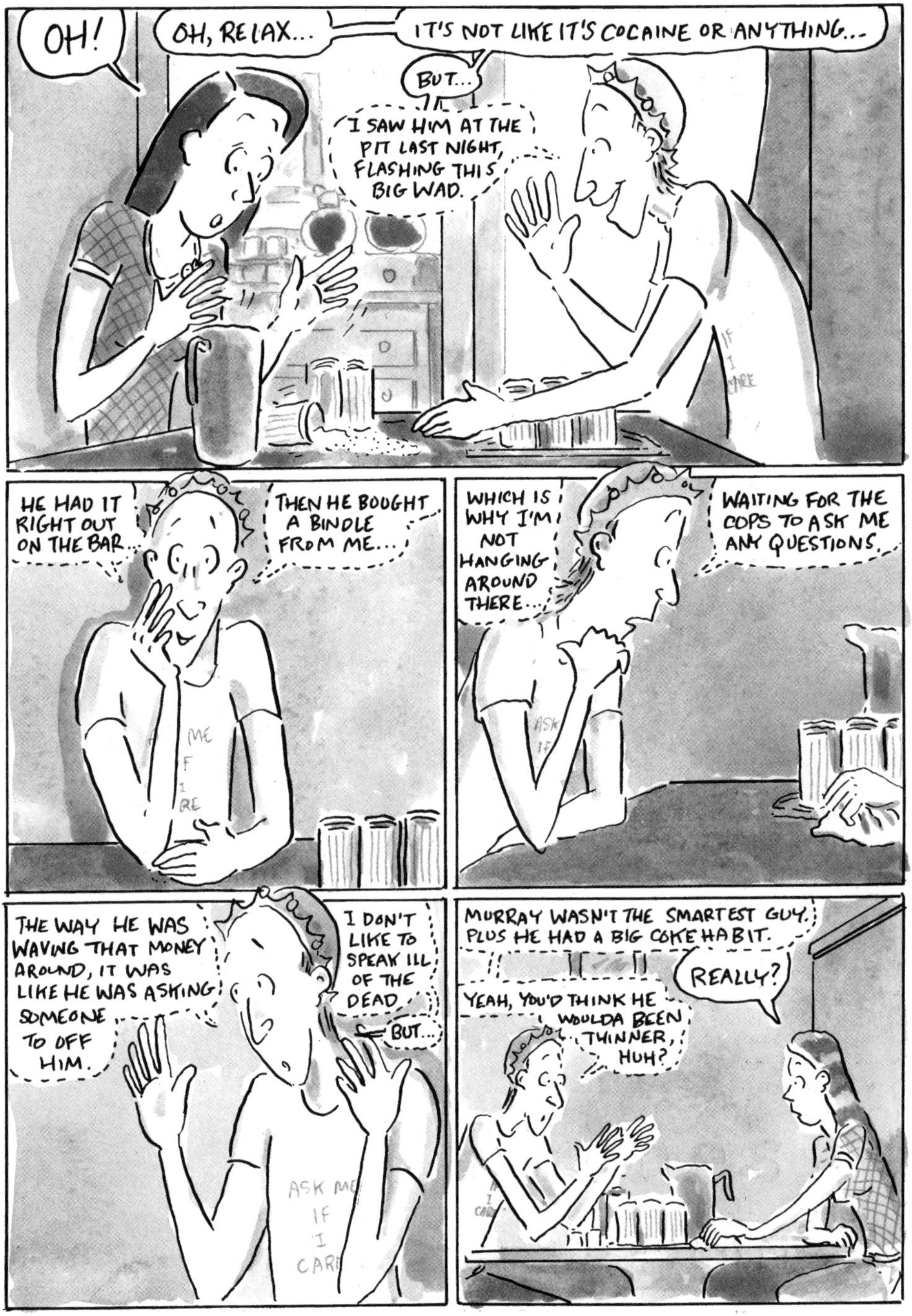
OH!
OH, RELAX...
IT'S NOT LIKE IT'S COCAINE OR ANYTHING...
BUT...
I SAW HIM AT THE PIT LAST NIGHT, FLASHING THIS BIG WAD.
HE HAD IT RIGHT OUT ON THE BAR...
THEN HE BOUGHT A BINDLE FROM ME...
WHICH IS WHY I'M NOT HANGING AROUND THERE...
WAITING FOR THE COPS TO ASK ME ANY QUESTIONS.
THE WAY HE WAS WAVING THAT MONEY AROUND, IT WAS LIKE HE WAS ASKING SOMEONE TO OFF HIM.
I DON'T LIKE TO SPEAK ILL OF THE DEAD
BUT...
MURRAY WASN'T THE SMARTEST GUY. PLUS HE HAD A BIG COKE HABIT.
REALLY?
YEAH, YOU'D THINK HE WOULDA BEEN THINNER, HUH?

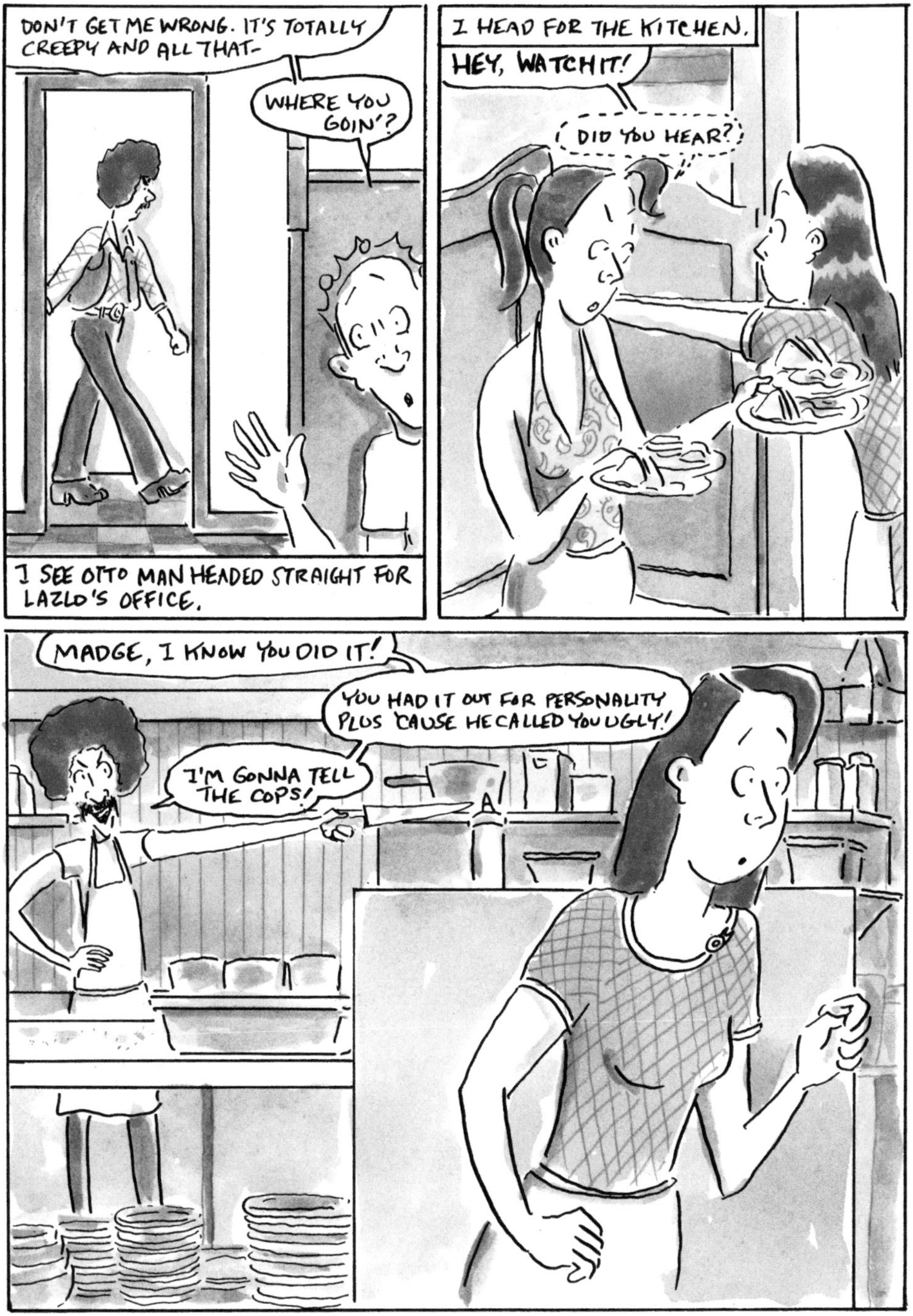
DON'T GET ME WRONG. IT'S TOTALLY CREEPY AND ALL THAT-
WHERE YOU GOIN'?
I SEE OTTO MAN HEADED STRAIGHT FOR LAZLO'S OFFICE.
I HEAD FOR THE KITCHEN.
HEY, WATCHIT!
DID YOU HEAR?
MADGE, I KNOW YOU DID IT!
YOU HAD IT OUT FOR PERSONALITY PLUS 'CAUSE HE CALLED YOU UGLY!
I'M GONNA TELL THE COPS!

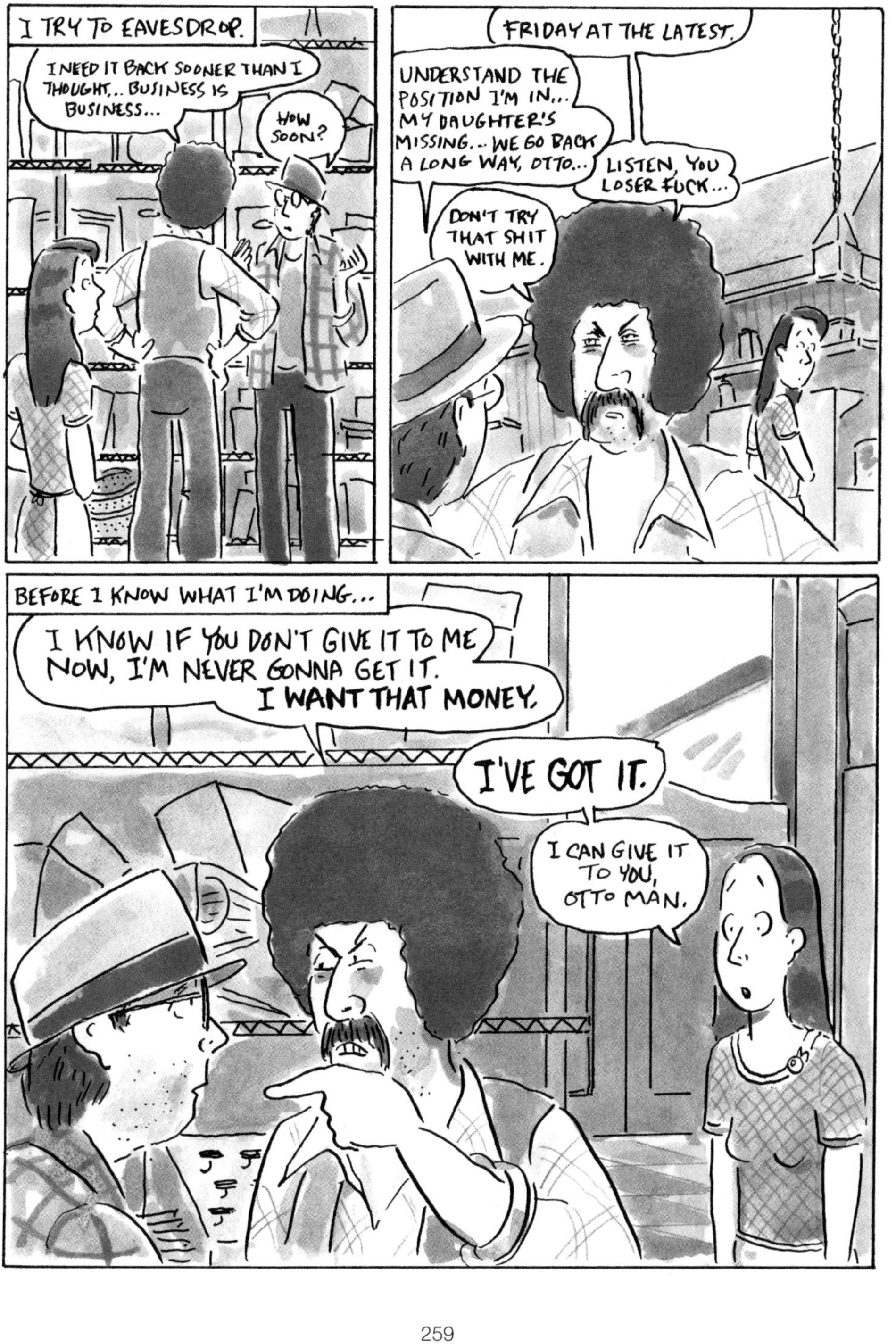
I TRY TO EAVESDROP.
I NEED IT BACK SOONER THAN I THOUGHT... BUSINESS IS BUSINESS...
HOW SOON?
FRIDAY AT THE LATEST.
UNDERSTAND THE POSITION I'M IN... MY DAUGHTER'S MISSING... WE GO BACK A LONG WAY, OTTO...
LISTEN, YOU LOSER FUCK...
DON'T TRY THAT SHIT WITH ME.
BEFORE I KNOW WHAT I'M DOING...
I KNOW IF YOU DON'T GIVE IT TO ME NOW, I'M NEVER GONNA GET IT. I WANT THAT MONEY.
I'VE GOT IT.
I CAN GIVE IT TO YOU, OTTO MAN.

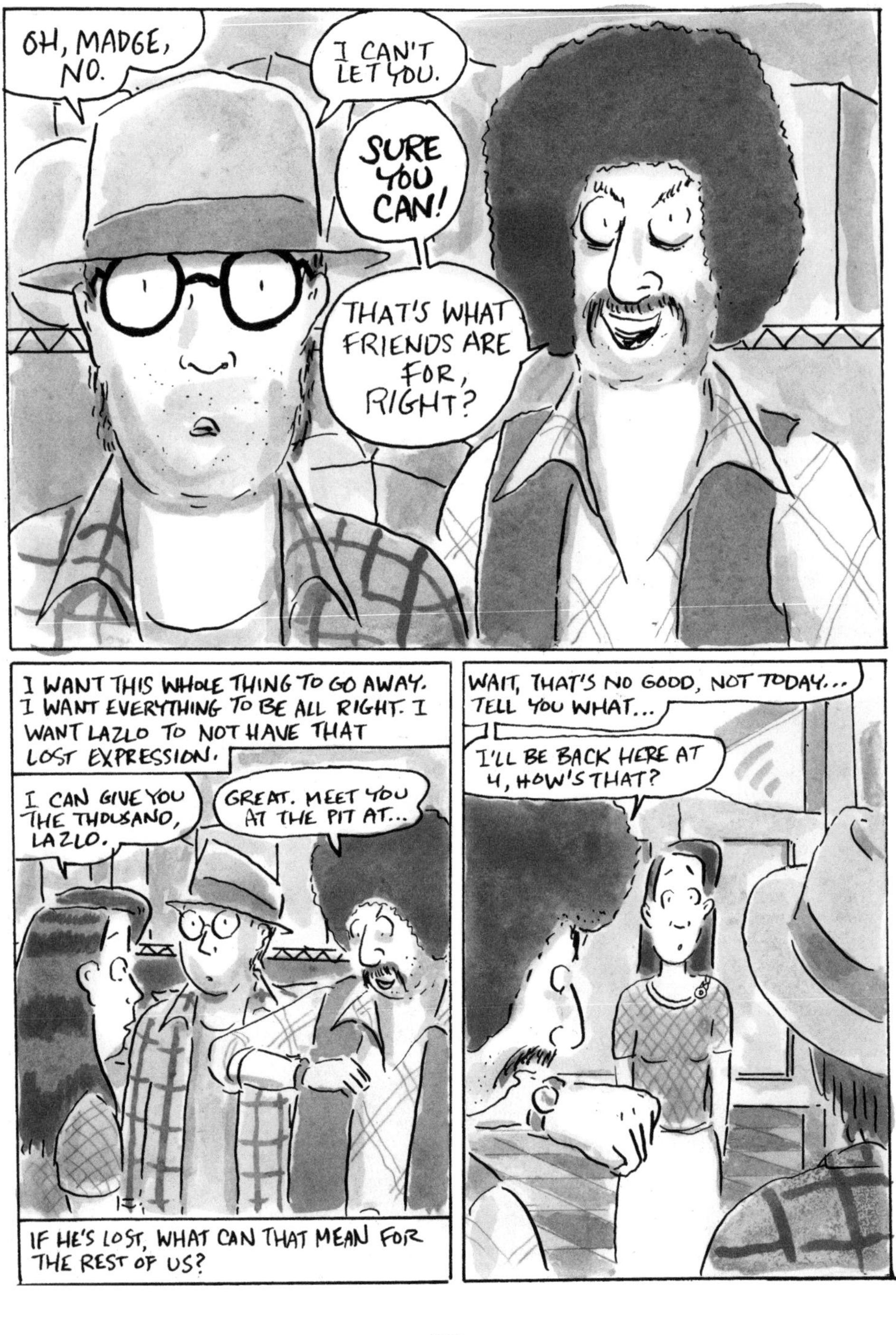
OH, MADGE, NO.
I CAN'T LET YOU.
SURE YOU CAN!
THAT'S WHAT FRIENDS ARE FOR, RIGHT?
I WANT THIS WHOLE THING TO GO AWAY. I WANT EVERYTHING TO BE ALL RIGHT. I WANT LAZLO TO NOT HAVE THAT LOST EXPRESSION.
I CAN GIVE YOU THE THOUSAND, LAZLO.
GREAT. MEET YOU AT THE PIT AT...
IF HE'S LOST, WHAT CAN THAT MEAN FOR THE REST OF US?
WAIT, THAT'S NO GOOD, NOT TODAY... TELL YOU WHAT...
I'LL BE BACK HERE AT 4, HOW'S THAT?

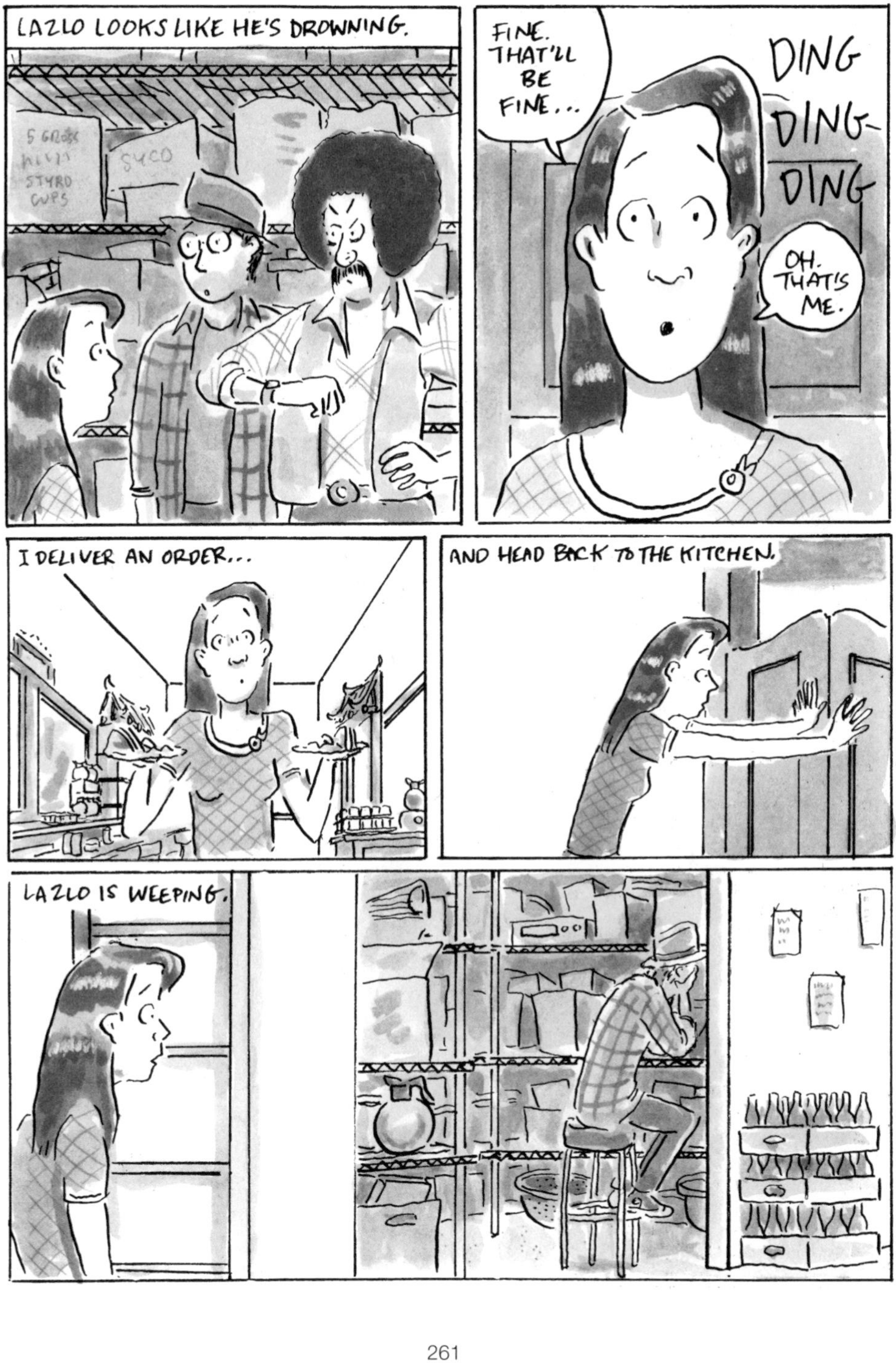
LAZLO LOOKS LIKE HE'S DROWNING.
5 GROSS
STYRO CUPS
SYCO
FINE. THAT'LL BE FINE...
DING
DING-
DING
OH. THAT'S ME.
I DELIVER AN ORDER...
AND HEAD BACK TO THE KITCHEN.
LAZLO IS WEEPING.

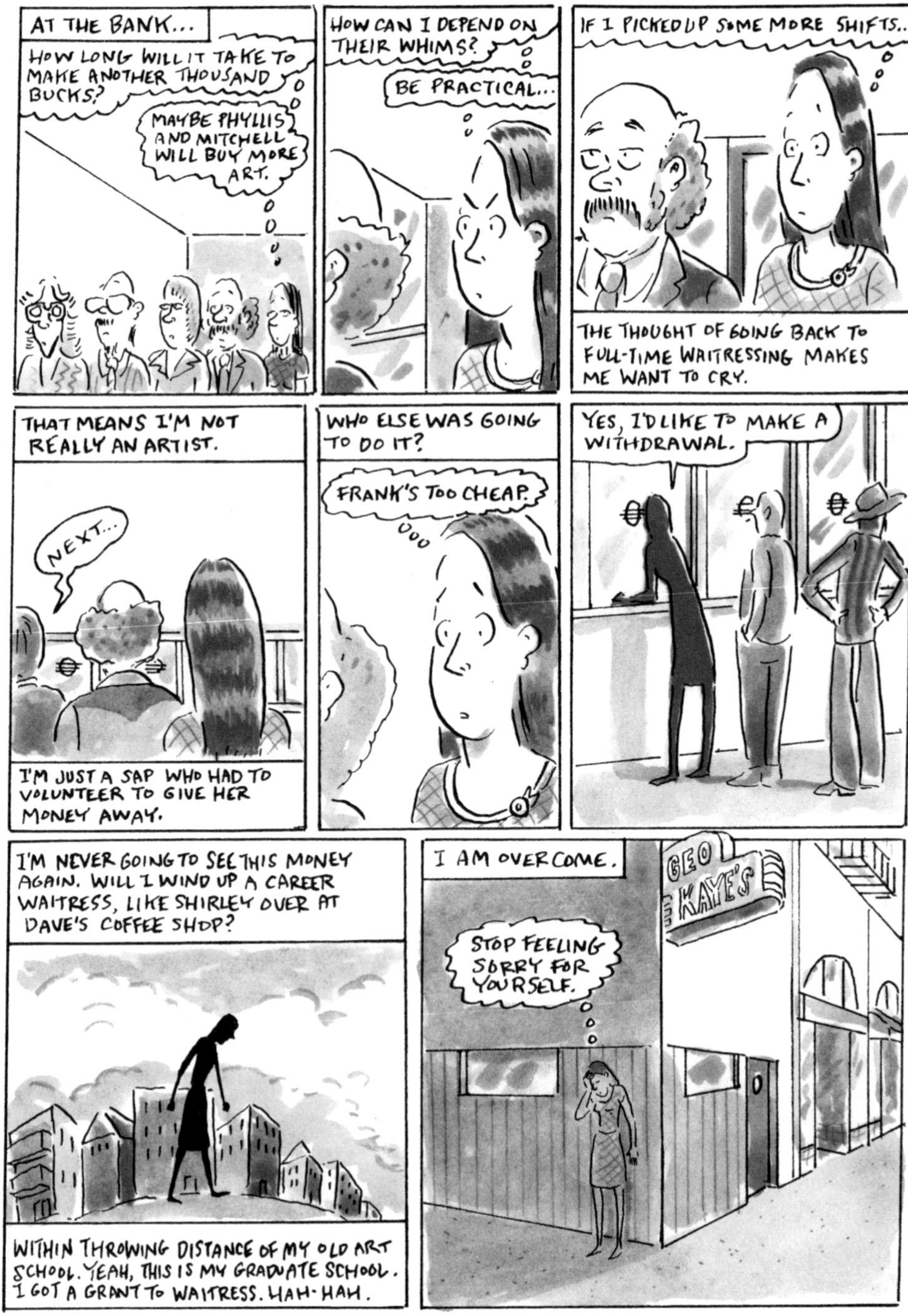
AT THE BANK...
HOW LONG WILL IT TAKE TO MAKE ANOTHER THOUSAND BUCKS?
MAYBE PHYLLIS AND MITCHELL WILL BUY MORE ART.
HOW CAN I DEPEND ON THEIR WHIMS?
BE PRACTICAL...
IF I PICKED UP SOME MORE SHIFTS...
THE THOUGHT OF GOING BACK TO FULL-TIME WAITRESSING MAKES ME WANT TO CRY.
THAT MEANS I'M NOT REALLY AN ARTIST.
NEXT...
I'M JUST A SAP WHO HAD TO VOLUNTEER TO GIVE HER MONEY AWAY.
WHO ELSE WAS GOING TO DO IT?
FRANK'S TOO CHEAP.
YES, I'D LIKE TO MAKE A WITHDRAWAL.
I'M NEVER GOING TO SEE THIS MONEY AGAIN. WILL I WIND UP A CAREER WAITRESS, LIKE SHIRLEY OVER AT DAVE'S COFFEE SHOP?
WITHIN THROWING DISTANCE OF MY OLD ART SCHOOL. YEAH, THIS IS MY GRADUATE SCHOOL. I GOT A GRANT TO WAITRESS. HAH-HAH.
I AM OVERCOME.
GEO KAYE'S
STOP FEELING SORRY FOR YOURSELF.

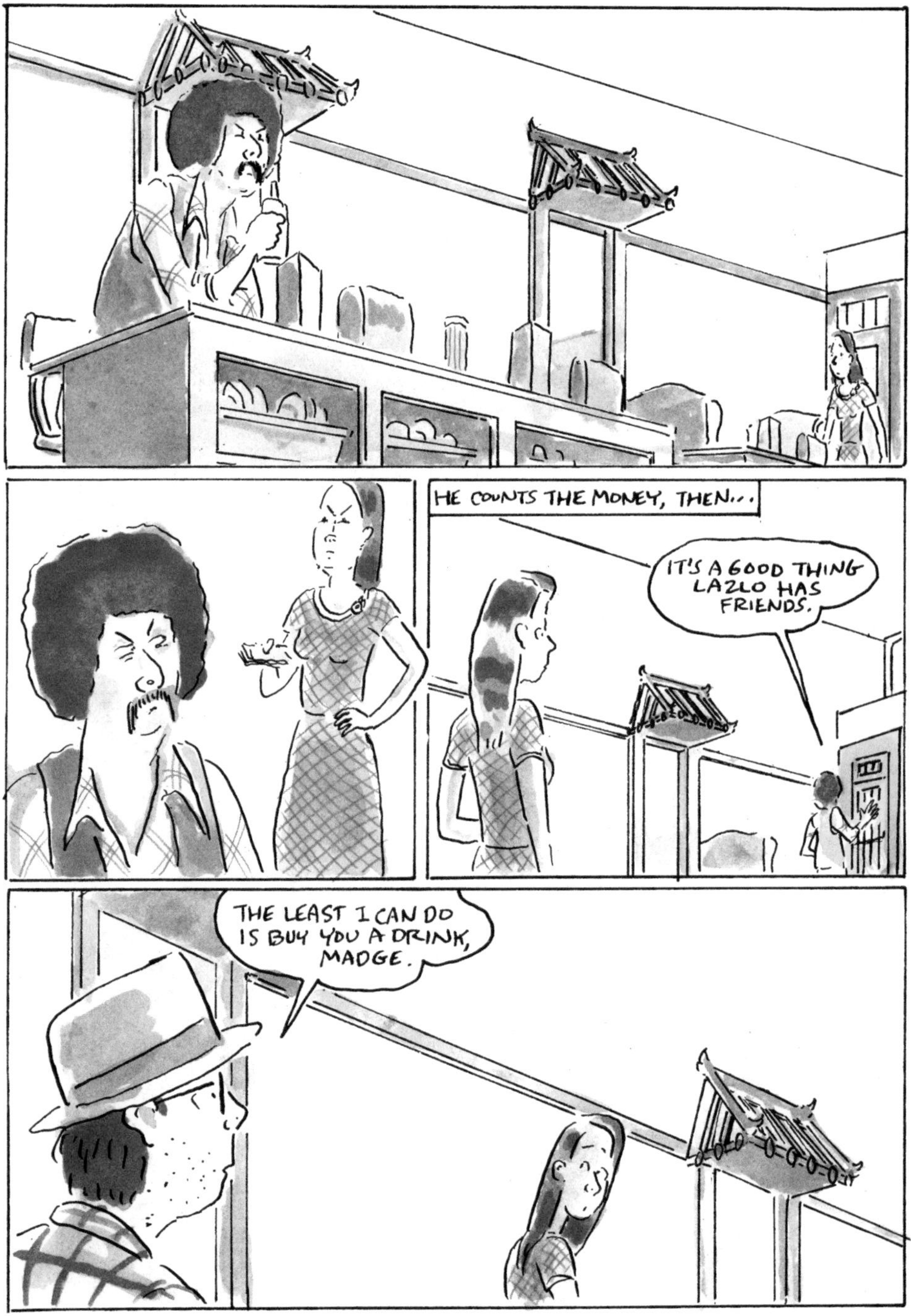
HE COUNTS THE MONEY, THEN...
IT'S A GOOD THING LAZLO HAS FRIENDS.
THE LEAST I CAN DO IS BUY YOU A DRINK, MADGE.

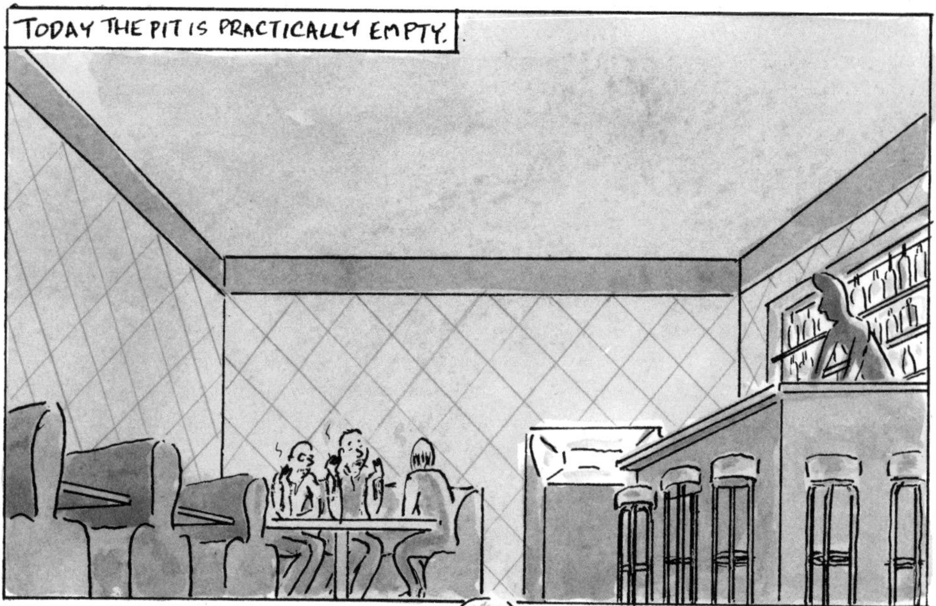
TODAY THE PIT IS PRACTICALLY EMPTY.

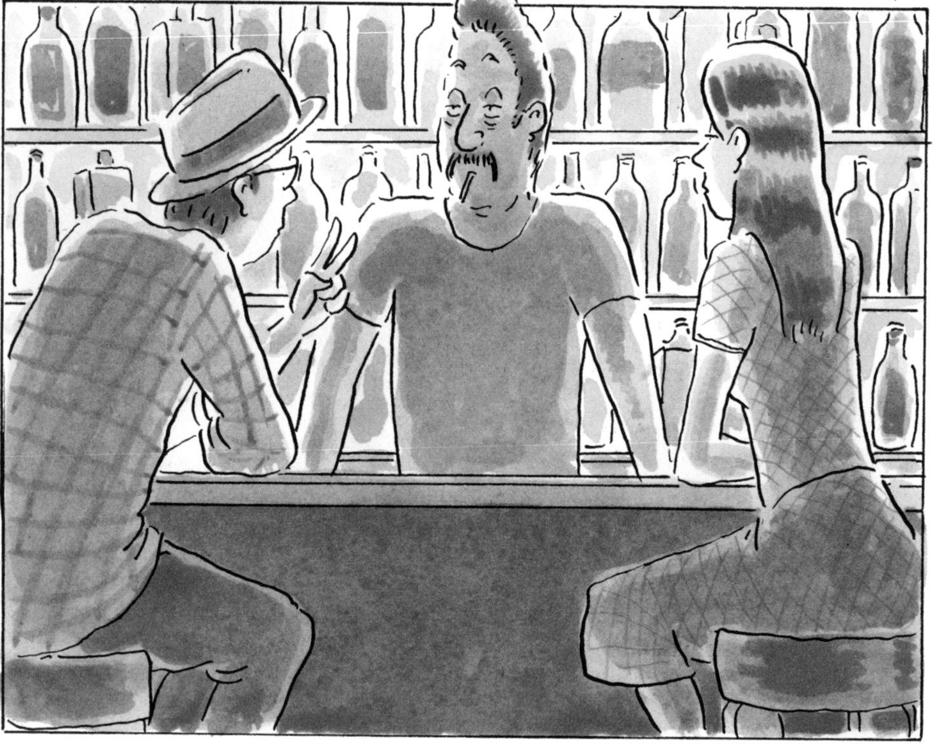

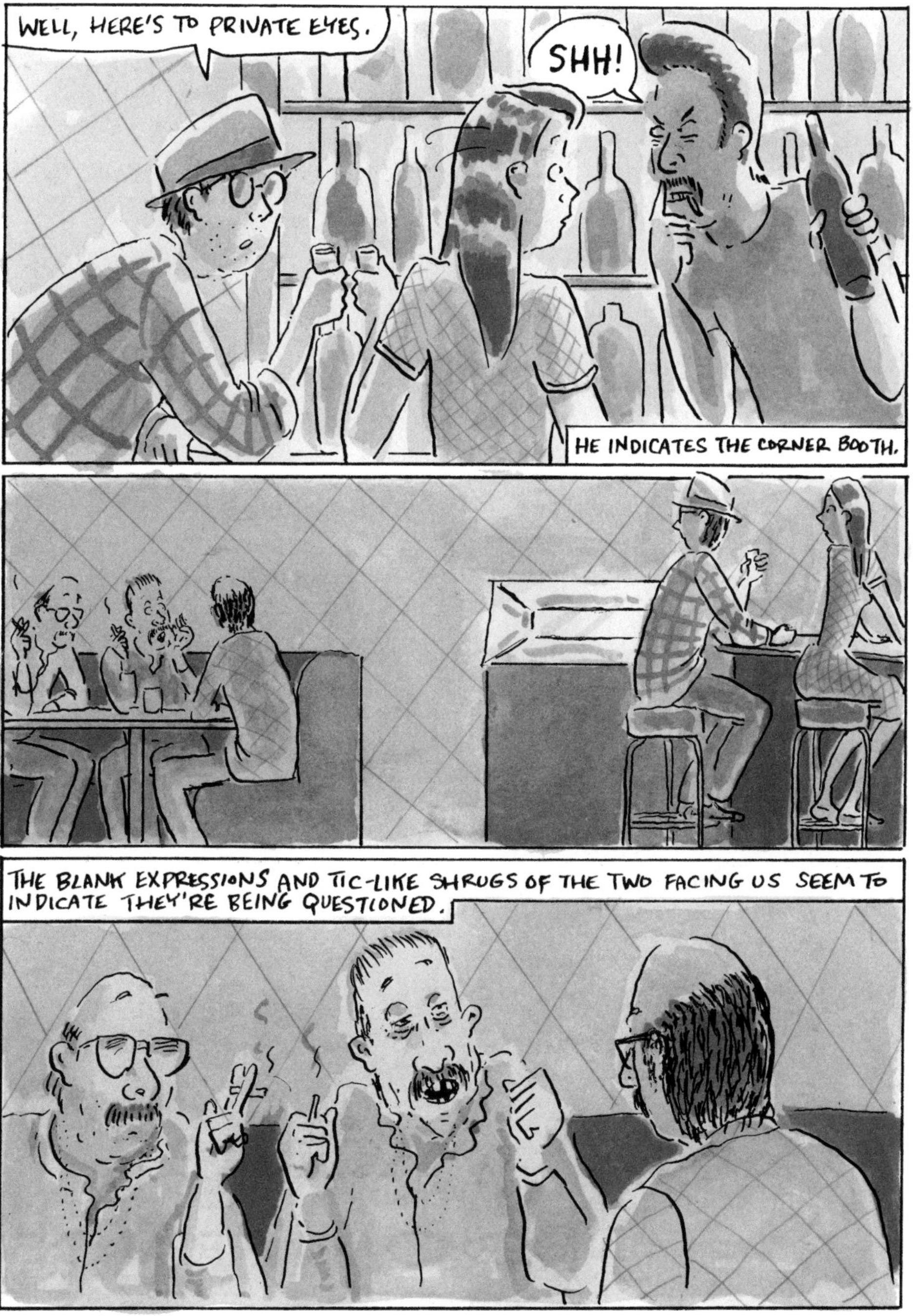
WELL, HERE'S TO PRIVATE EYES.
SHH!
HE INDICATES THE CORNER BOOTH.
THE BLANK EXPRESSIONS AND TIC-LIKE SHRUGS OF THE TWO FACING US SEEM TO INDICATE THEY'RE BEING QUESTIONED.

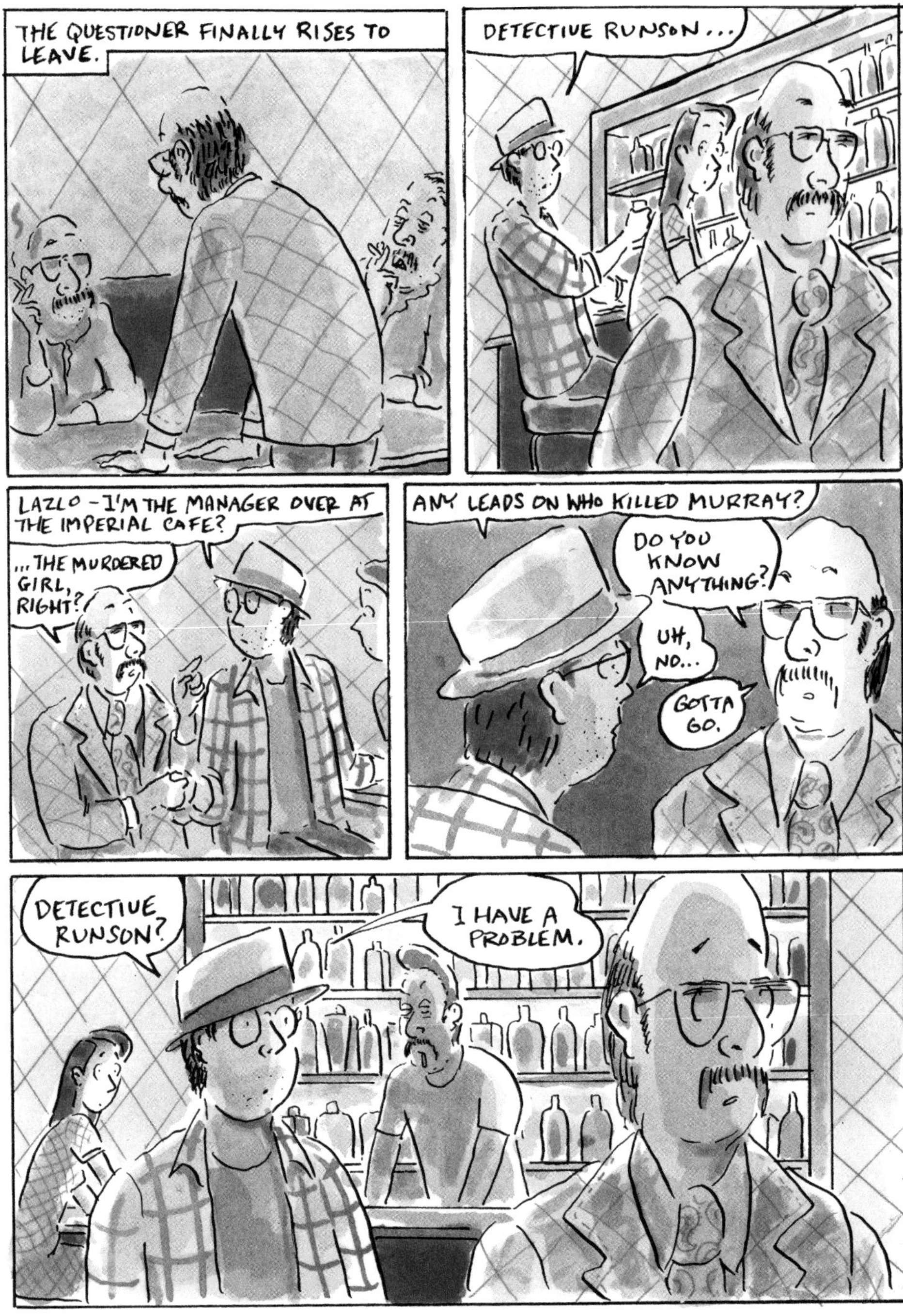
THE QUESTIONER FINALLY RISES TO LEAVE.
DETECTIVE RUNSON...
LAZLO - I'M THE MANAGER OVER AT THE IMPERIAL CAFE?
...THE MURDERED GIRL, RIGHT?
ANY LEADS ON WHO KILLED MURRAY?
DO YOU KNOW ANYTHING?
UH, NO...
GOTTA GO.
DETECTIVE RUNSON?
I HAVE A PROBLEM.

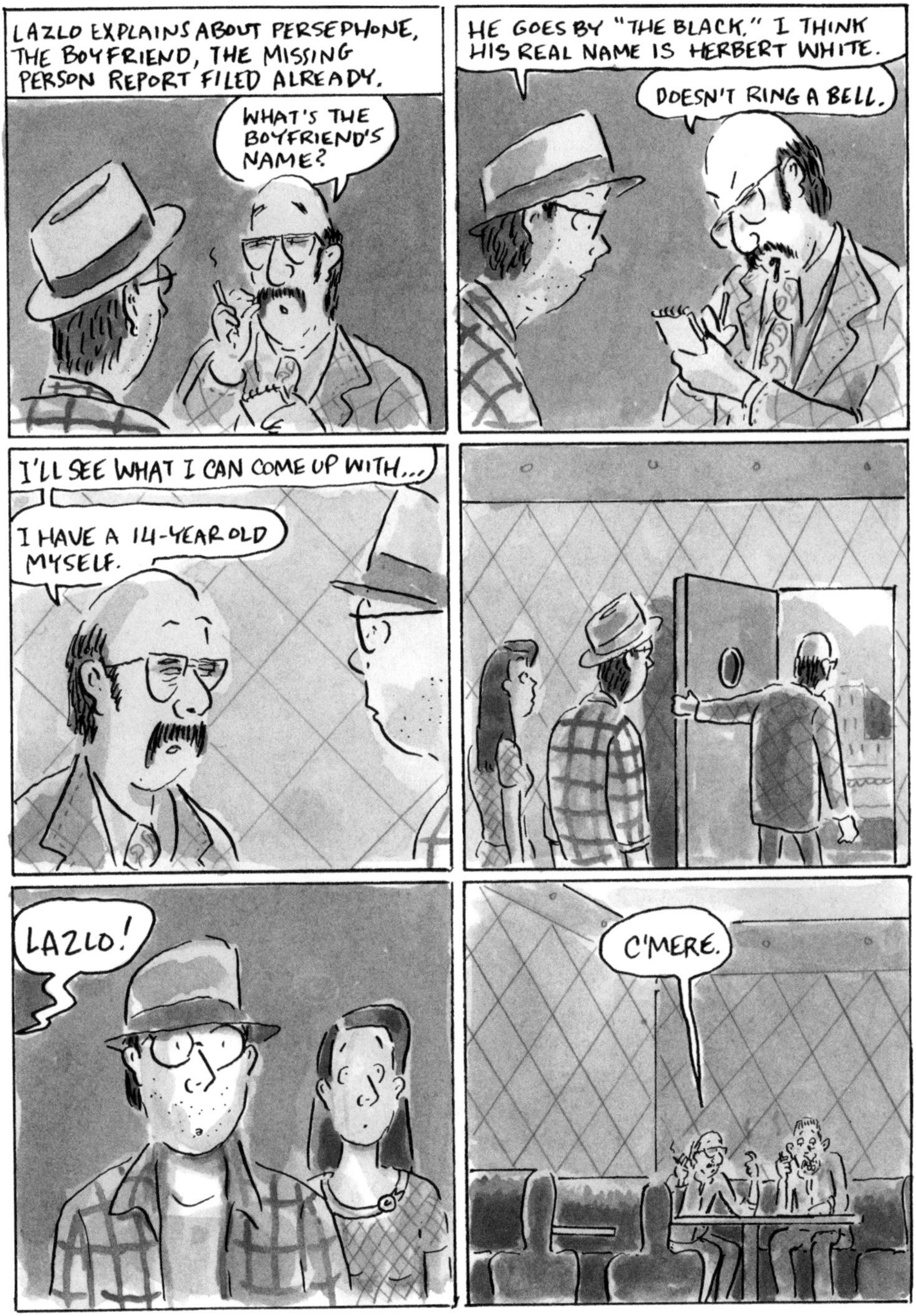
LAZLO EXPLAINS ABOUT PERSEPHONE, THE BOYFRIEND, THE MISSING PERSON REPORT FILED ALREADY.
WHAT'S THE BOYFRIEND'S NAME?
HE GOES BY "THE BLACK." I THINK HIS REAL NAME IS HERBERT WHITE.
DOESN'T RING A BELL.
I'LL SEE WHAT I CAN COME UP WITH...
I HAVE A 14-YEAR OLD MYSELF.
LAZLO!
C'MERE.

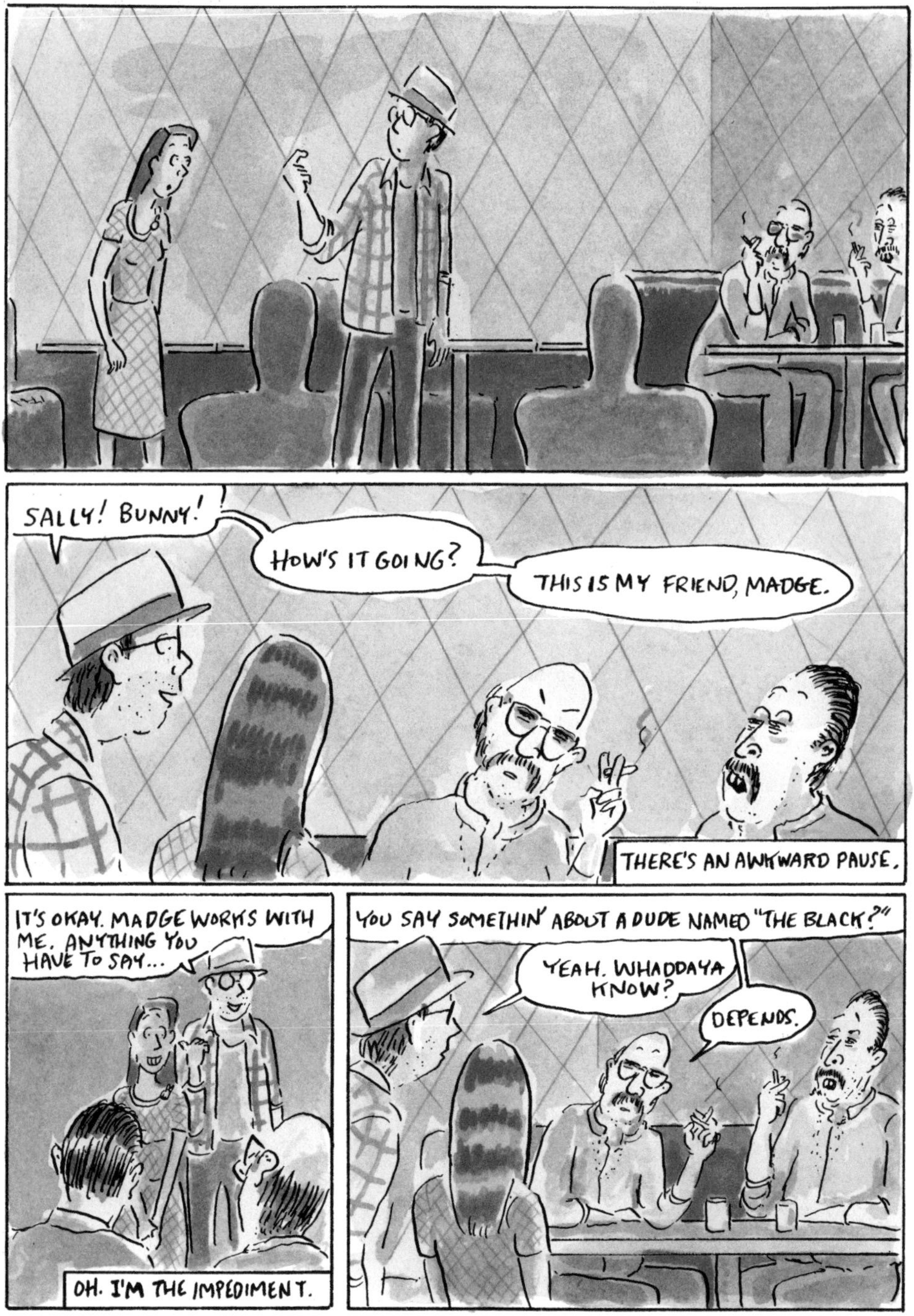
SALLY! BUNNY!
HOW'S IT GOING?
THIS IS MY FRIEND, MADGE.
THERE'S AN AWKWARD PAUSE.
IT'S OKAY. MADGE WORKS WITH ME. ANYTHING YOU HAVE TO SAY...
OH. I'M THE IMPEDIMENT.
YOU SAY SOMETHIN' ABOUT A DUDE NAMED "THE BLACK?"
YEAH. WHADDAYA KNOW?
DEPENDS.

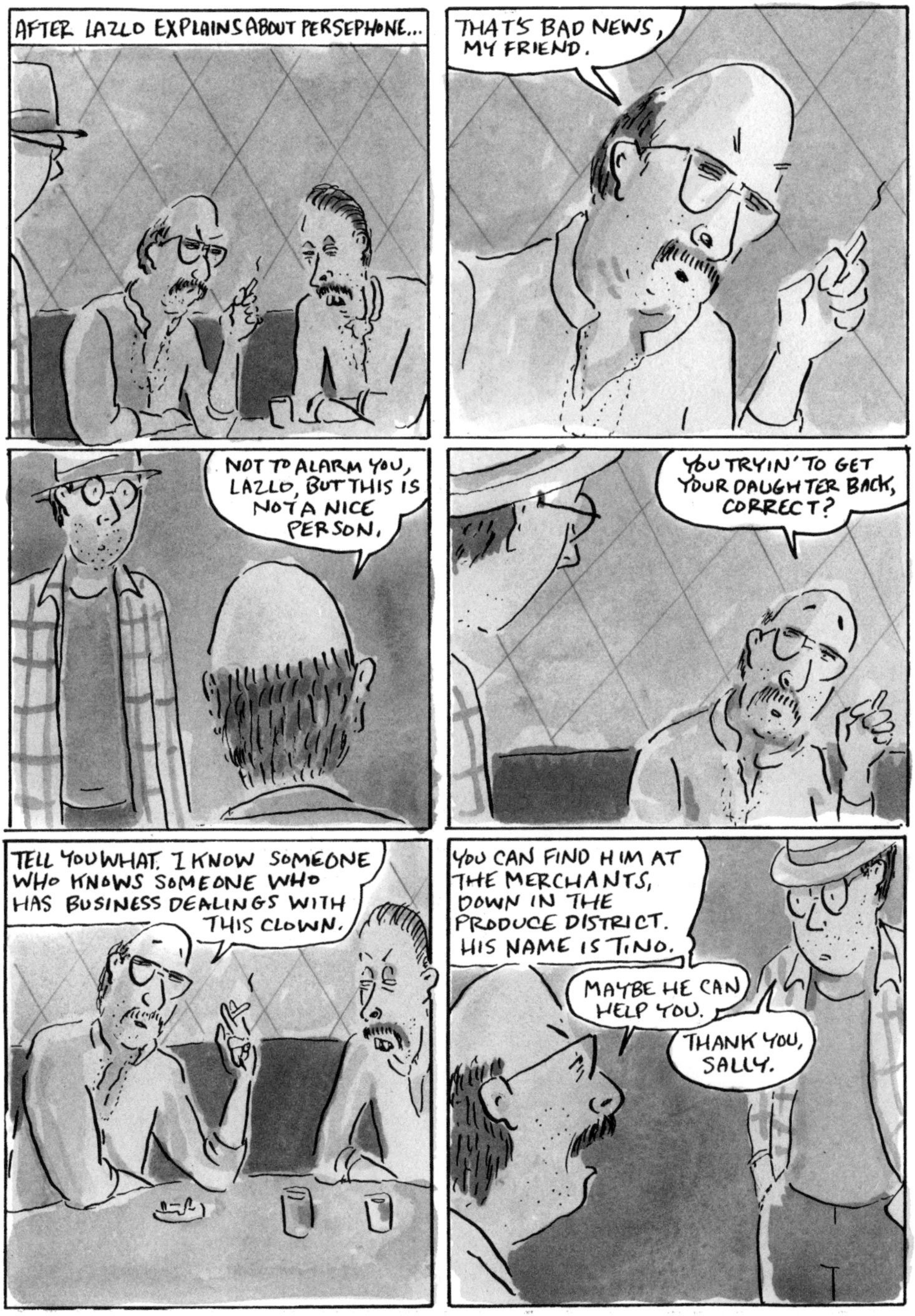
AFTER LAZLO EXPLAINS ABOUT PERSEPHONE...
THAT'S BAD NEWS, MY FRIEND.
NOT TO ALARM YOU, LAZLO, BUT THIS IS NOT A NICE PERSON.
YOU TRYIN' TO GET YOUR DAUGHTER BACK, CORRECT?
TELL YOU WHAT. I KNOW SOMEONE WHO KNOWS SOMEONE WHO HAS BUSINESS DEALINGS WITH THIS CLOWN.
YOU CAN FIND HIM AT THE MERCHANTS, DOWN IN THE PRODUCE DISTRICT. HIS NAME IS TINO.
MAYBE HE CAN HELP YOU.
THANK YOU, SALLY.

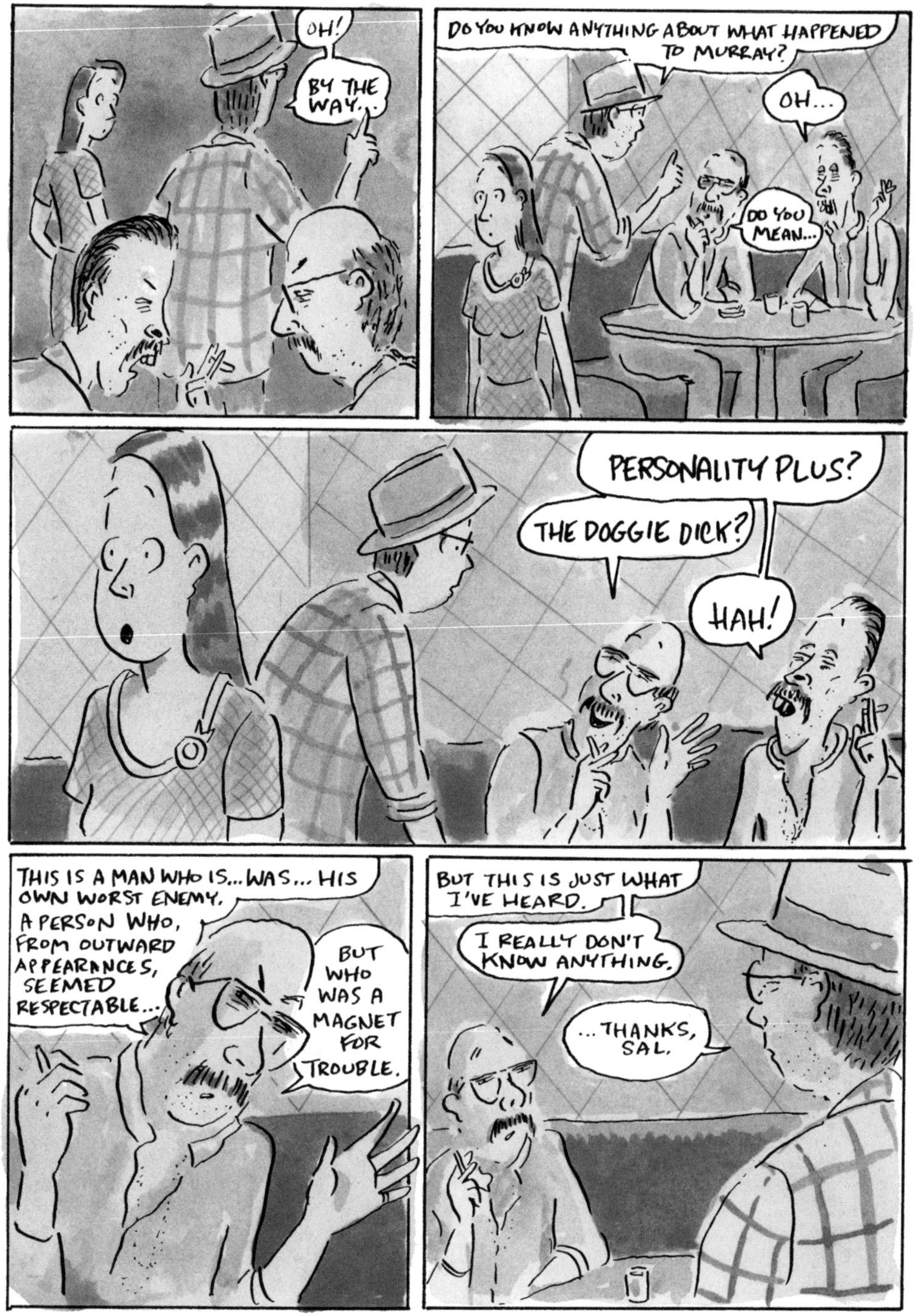
OH!
BY THE WAY...
DO YOU KNOW ANYTHING ABOUT WHAT HAPPENED TO MURRAY?
OH...
DO YOU MEAN...
PERSONALITY PLUS?
THE DOGGIE DICK?
HAH!
THIS IS A MAN WHO IS... WAS... HIS OWN WORST ENEMY.
A PERSON WHO, FROM OUTWARD APPEARANCES, SEEMED RESPECTABLE...
BUT WHO WAS A MAGNET FOR TROUBLE.
BUT THIS IS JUST WHAT I'VE HEARD.
I REALLY DON'T KNOW ANYTHING.
...THANKS, SAL.

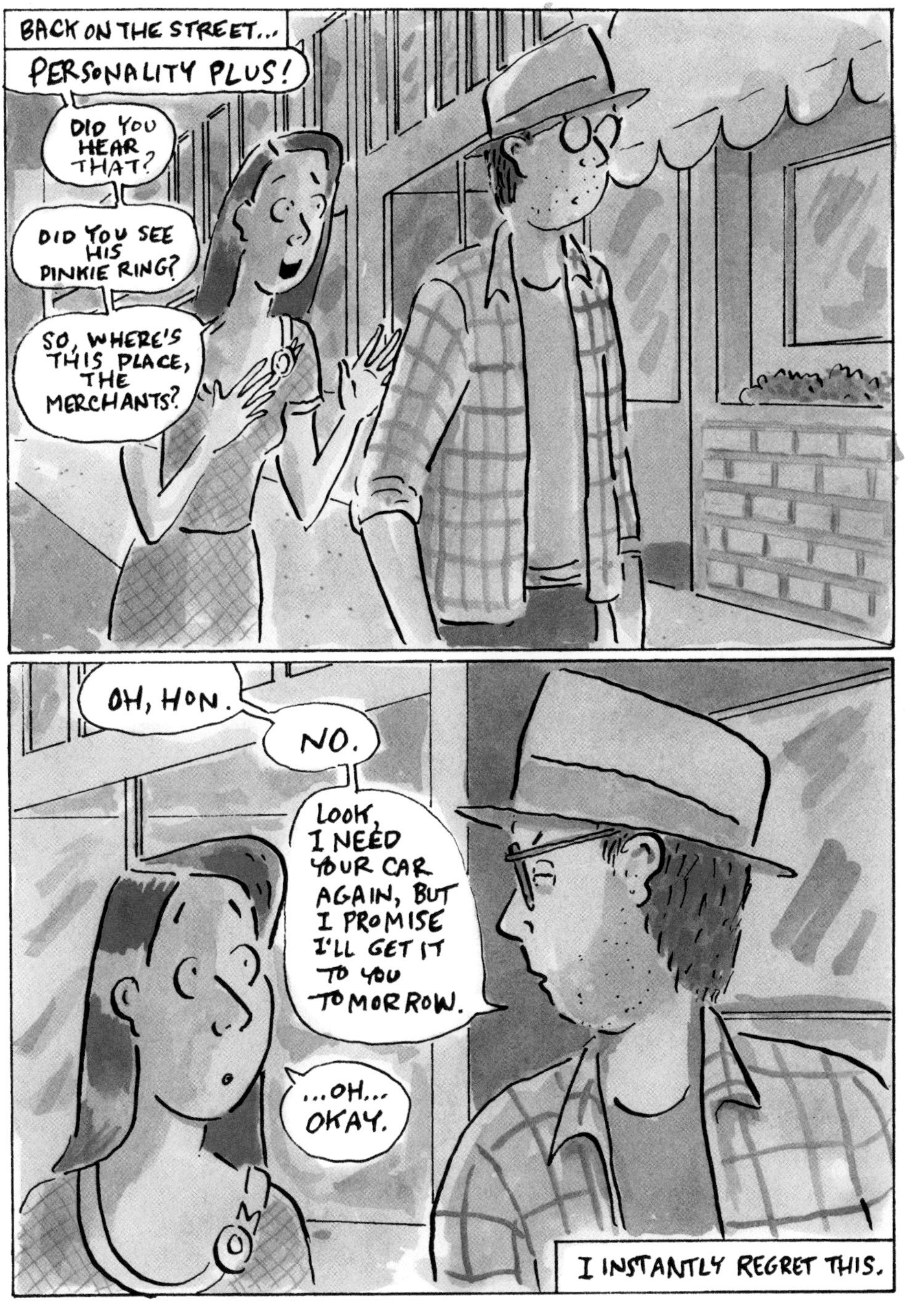
BACK ON THE STREET...
PERSONALITY PLUS!
DID YOU HEAR THAT?
DID YOU SEE HIS PINKIE RING?
SO, WHERE'S THIS PLACE, THE MERCHANTS?
OH, HON.
NO.
LOOK, I NEED YOUR CAR AGAIN, BUT I PROMISE I'LL GET IT TO YOU TOMORROW.
...OH... OKAY.
I INSTANTLY REGRET THIS.

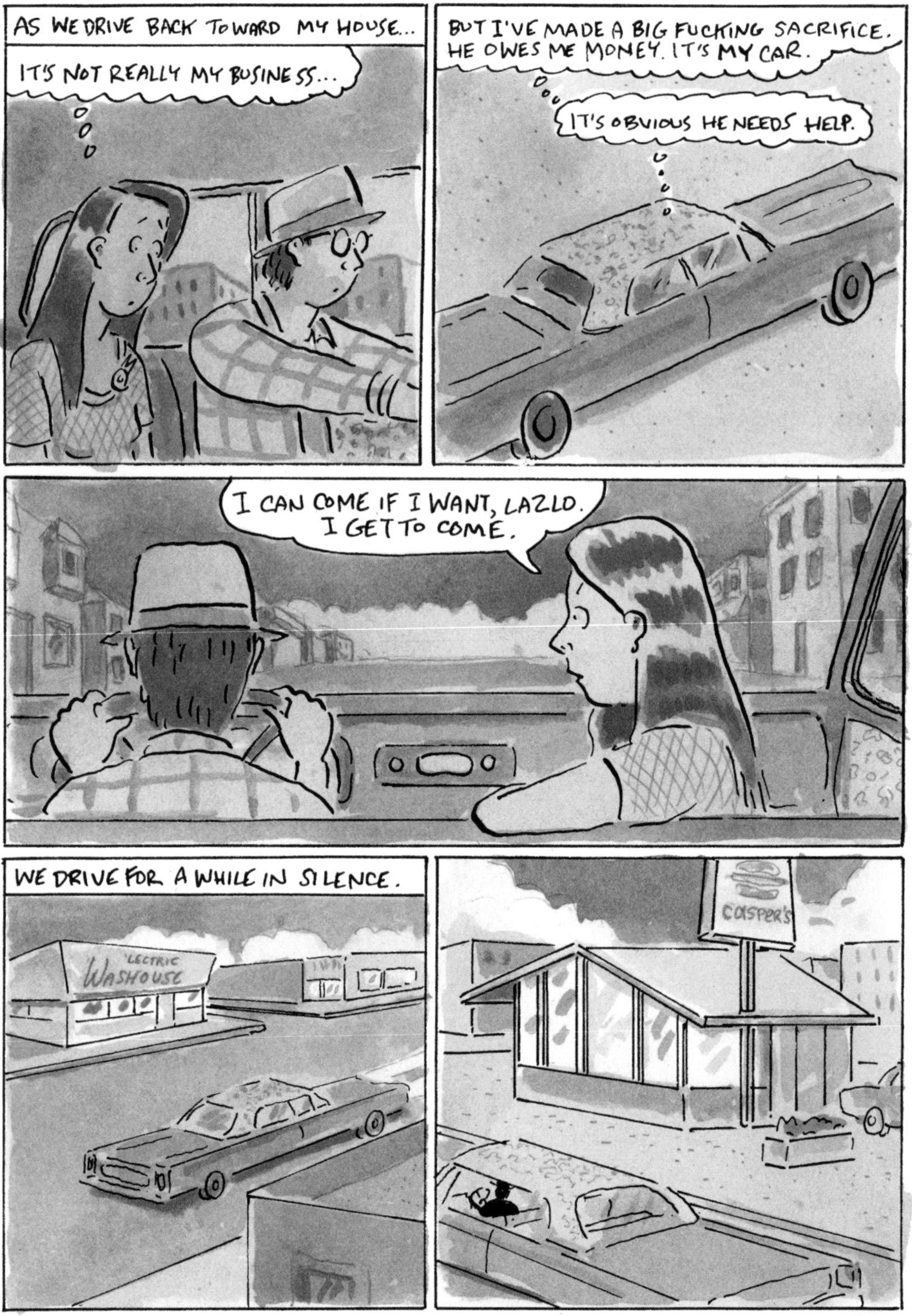
AS WE DRIVE BACK TOWARD MY HOUSE...
IT'S NOT REALLY MY BUSINESS...
BUT I'VE MADE A BIG FUCKING SACRIFICE. HE OWES ME MONEY. IT'S MY CAR.
IT'S OBVIOUS HE NEEDS HELP.
I CAN COME IF I WANT, LAZLO. I GET TO COME.
WE DRIVE FOR A WHILE IN SILENCE.
'LECTRIC WASHOUSE
CASPER'S

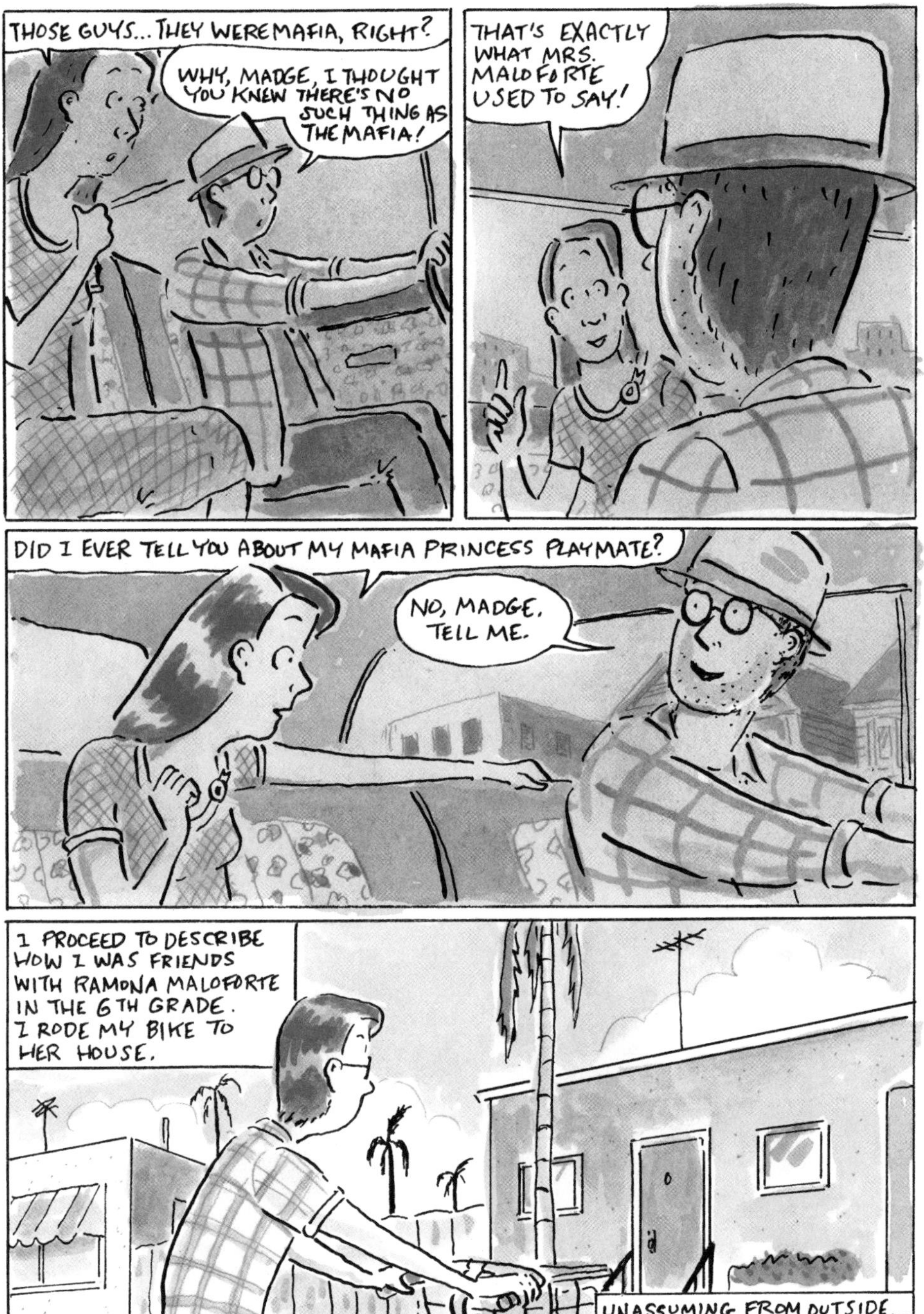

THOSE GUYS... THEY WERE MAFIA, RIGHT?
WHY, MADGE, I THOUGHT YOU KNEW THERE'S NO SUCH THING AS THE MAFIA!
THAT'S EXACTLY WHAT MRS. MALOFORTE USED TO SAY!
DID I EVER TELL YOU ABOUT MY MAFIA PRINCESS PLAYMATE?
NO, MADGE. TELL ME.
I PROCEED TO DESCRIBE HOW I WAS FRIENDS WITH RAMONA MALOFORTE IN THE 6TH GRADE. I RODE MY BIKE TO HER HOUSE.
UNASSUMING FROM OUTSIDE...

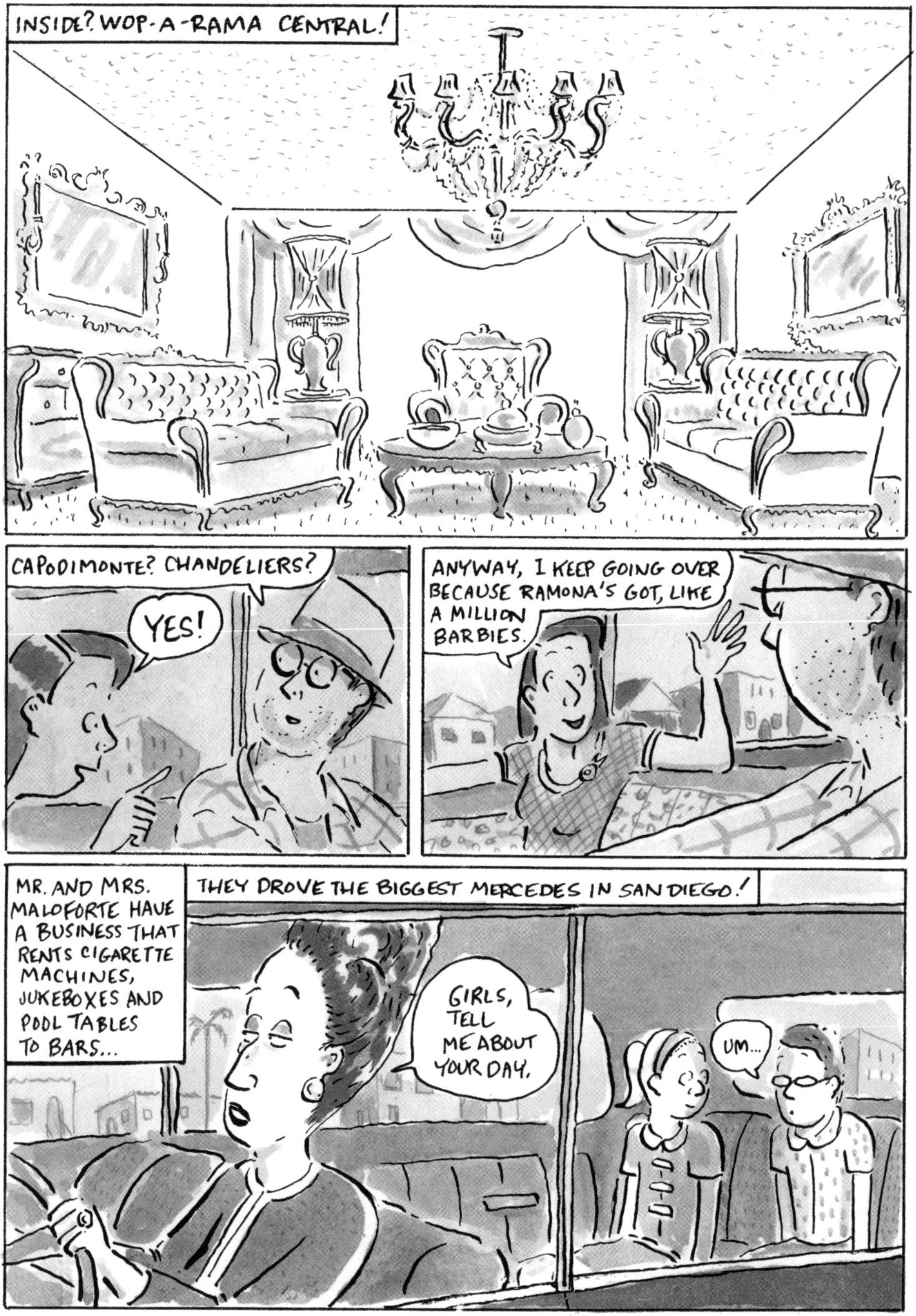
INSIDE? WOP-A-RAMA CENTRAL!
CAPODIMONTE? CHANDELIERS?
YES!
ANYWAY, I KEEP GOING OVER BECAUSE RAMONA'S GOT, LIKE A MILLION BARBIES.
MR. AND MRS. MALOFORTE HAVE A BUSINESS THAT RENTS CIGARETTE MACHINES, JUKEBOXES AND POOL TABLES TO BARS...
THEY DROVE THE BIGGEST MERCEDES IN SAN DIEGO!
GIRLS, TELL ME ABOUT YOUR DAY.
UM...

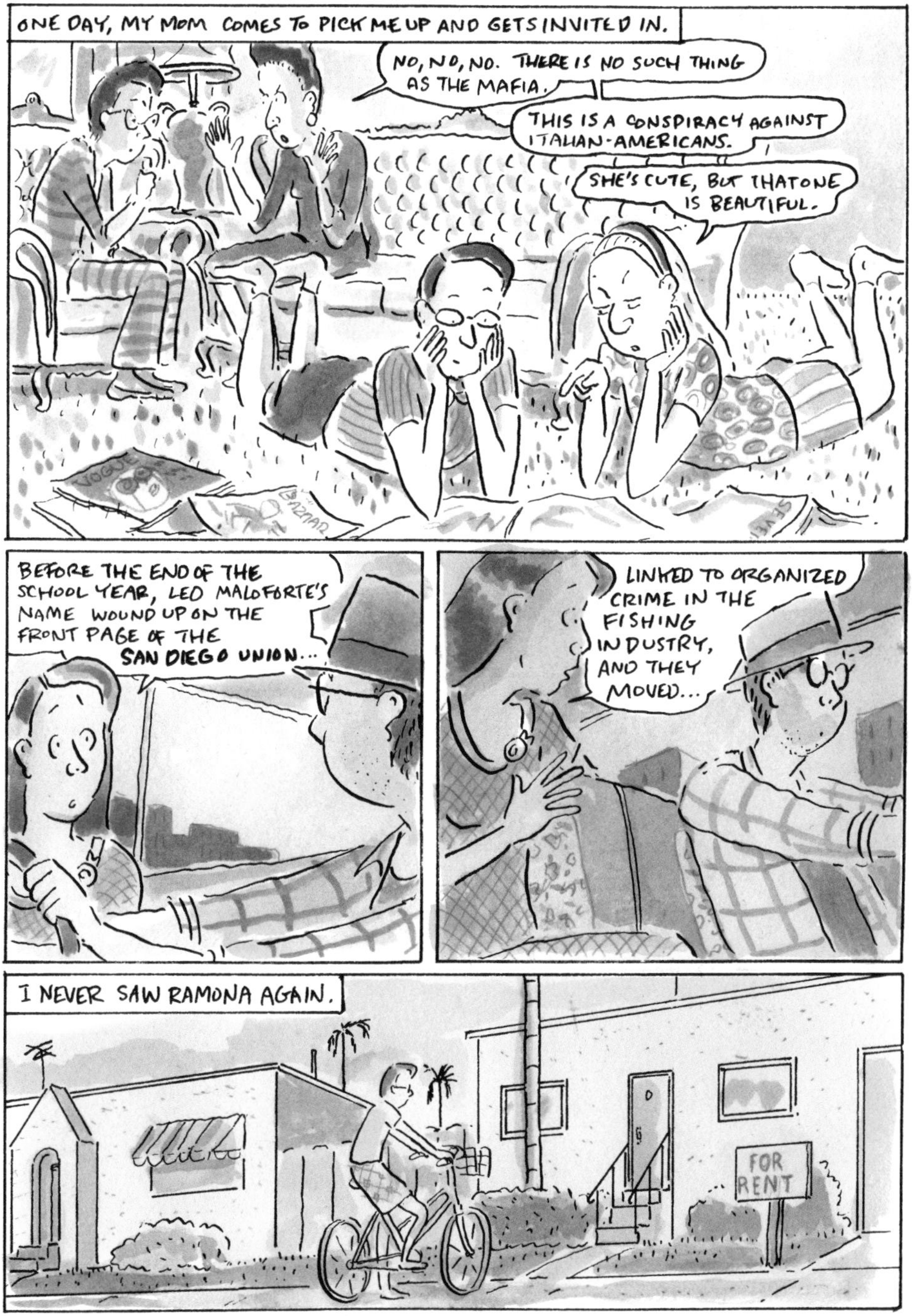
ONE DAY, MY MOM COMES TO PICK ME UP AND GETS INVITED IN.
NO, NO, NO. THERE IS NO SUCH THING AS THE MAFIA.
THIS IS A CONSPIRACY AGAINST ITALIAN-AMERICANS.
SHE'S CUTE, BUT THAT ONE IS BEAUTIFUL.
VOGUE
BAZAAR
BEFORE THE END OF THE SCHOOL YEAR, LEO MALOFORTE'S NAME WOUND UP ON THE FRONT PAGE OF THE SAN DIEGO UNION...
LINKED TO ORGANIZED CRIME IN THE FISHING INDUSTRY, AND THEY MOVED...
I NEVER SAW RAMONA AGAIN.
FOR RENT

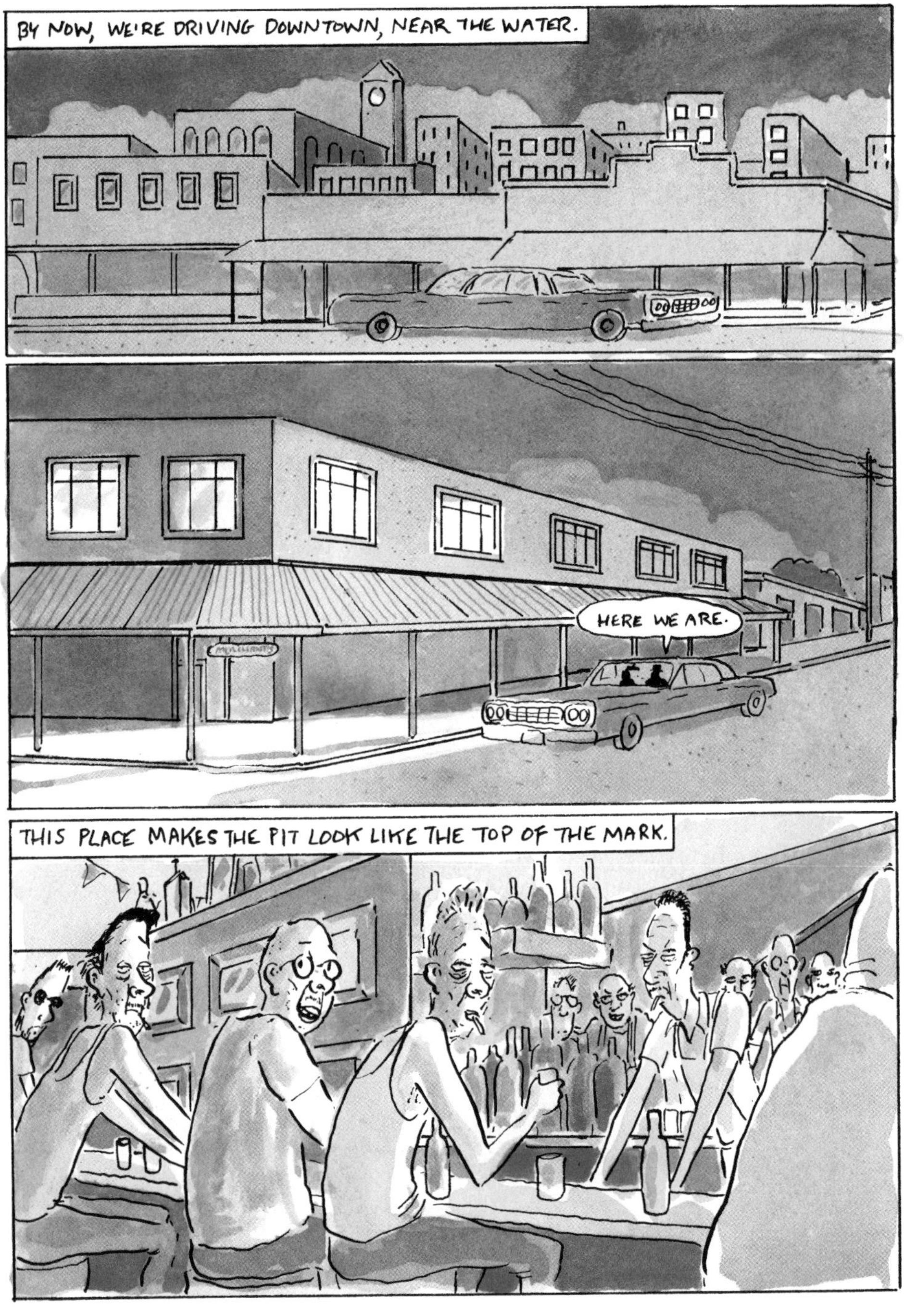
BY NOW, WE'RE DRIVING DOWNTOWN, NEAR THE WATER.
HERE WE ARE.
THIS PLACE MAKES THE PIT LOOK LIKE THE TOP OF THE MARK.

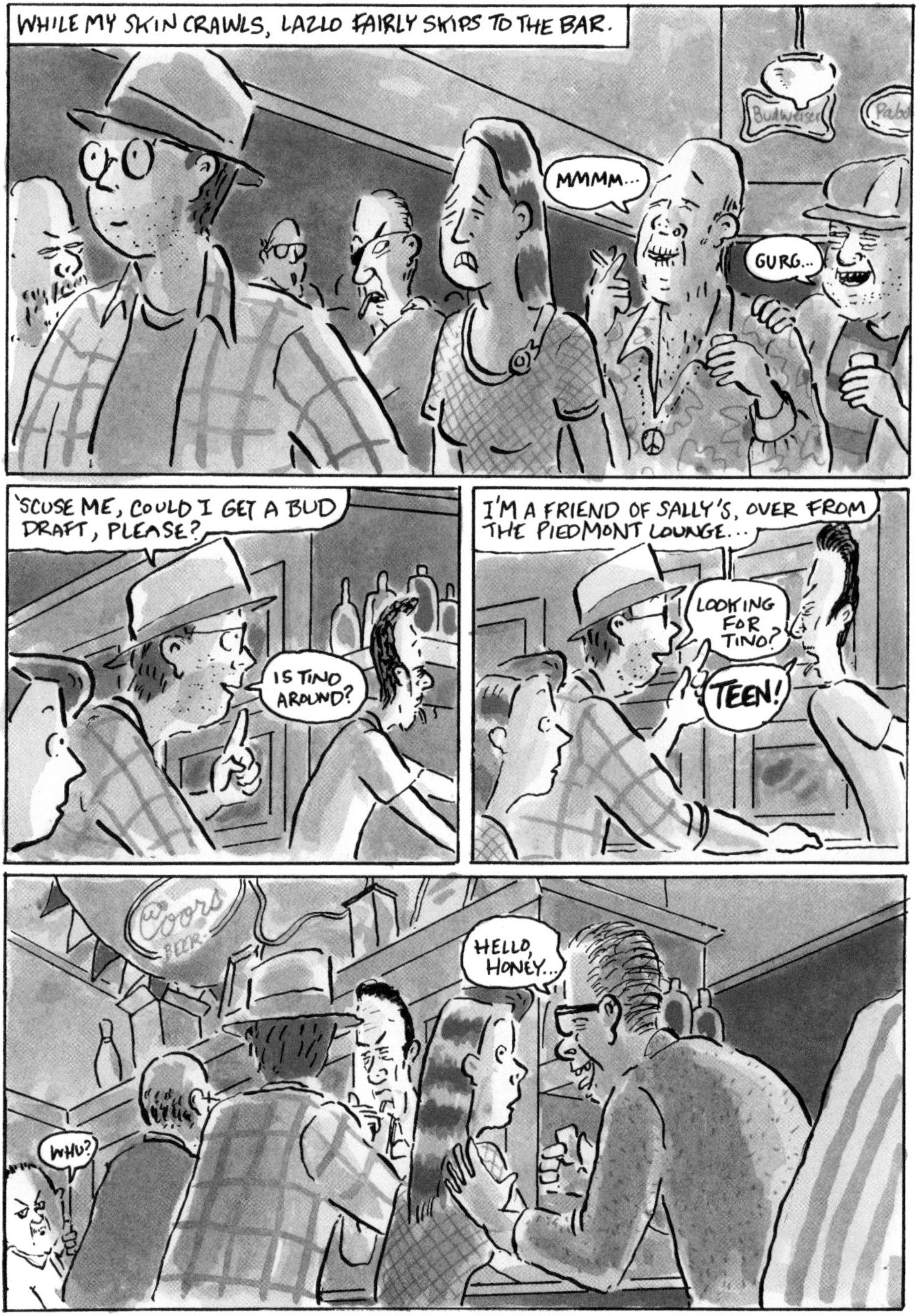
WHILE MY SKIN CRAWLS, LAZLO FAIRLY SKIPS TO THE BAR.
Budweiser
MMMM...
GURG...
'SCUSE ME, COULD I GET A BUD DRAFT, PLEASE?
IS TINO AROUND?
I'M A FRIEND OF SALLY'S, OVER FROM THE PIEDMONT LOUNGE...
LOOKING FOR TINO?
TEEN!
Coors BEER
HELLO, HONEY...
WHU?

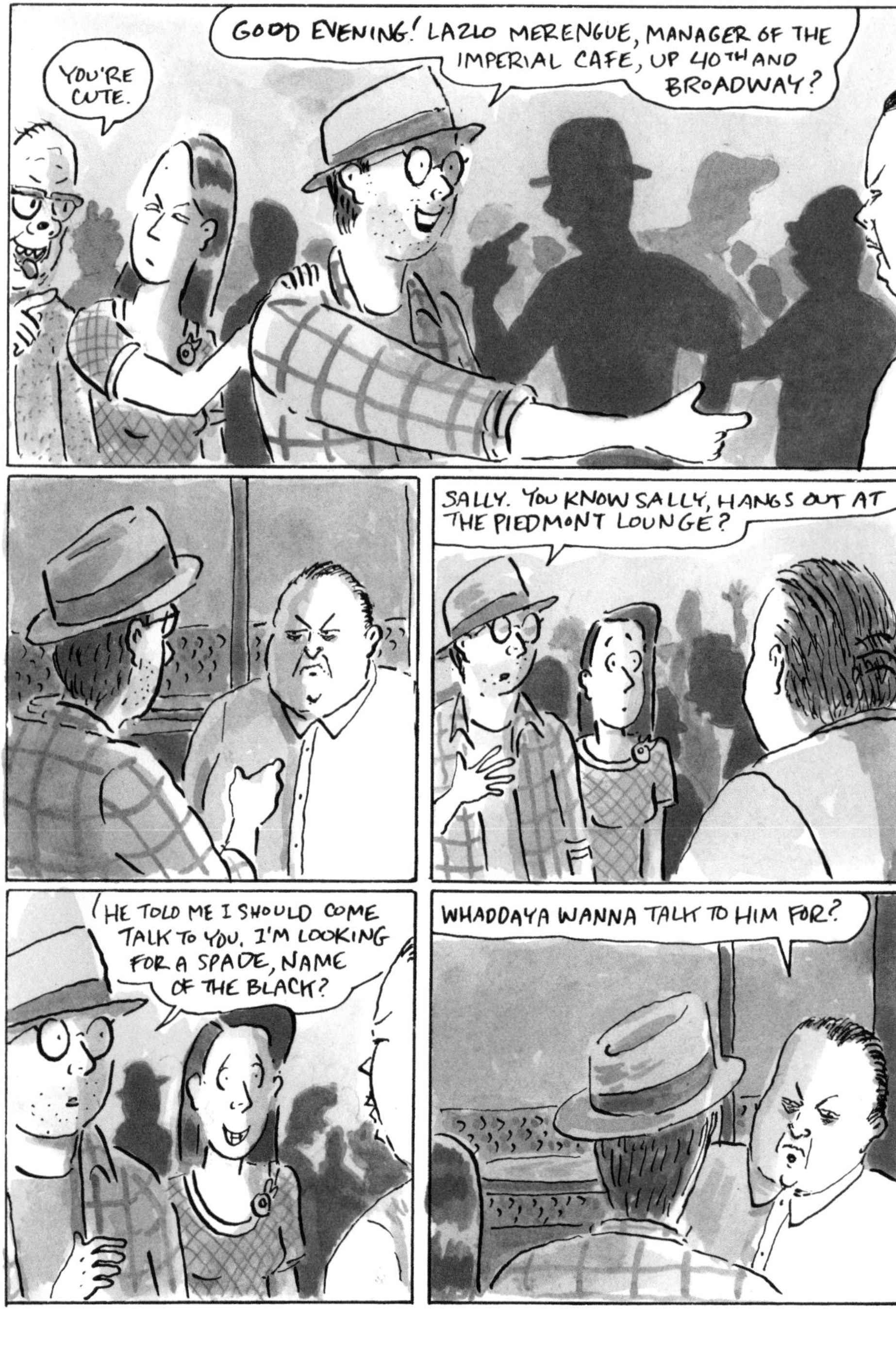
YOU'RE CUTE.
GOOD EVENING! LAZLO MERENGUE, MANAGER OF THE IMPERIAL CAFE, UP 40TH AND BROADWAY?
SALLY. YOU KNOW SALLY, HANGS OUT AT THE PIEDMONT LOUNGE?
HE TOLD ME I SHOULD COME TALK TO YOU. I'M LOOKING FOR A SPADE, NAME OF THE BLACK?
WHADDAYA WANNA TALK TO HIM FOR?

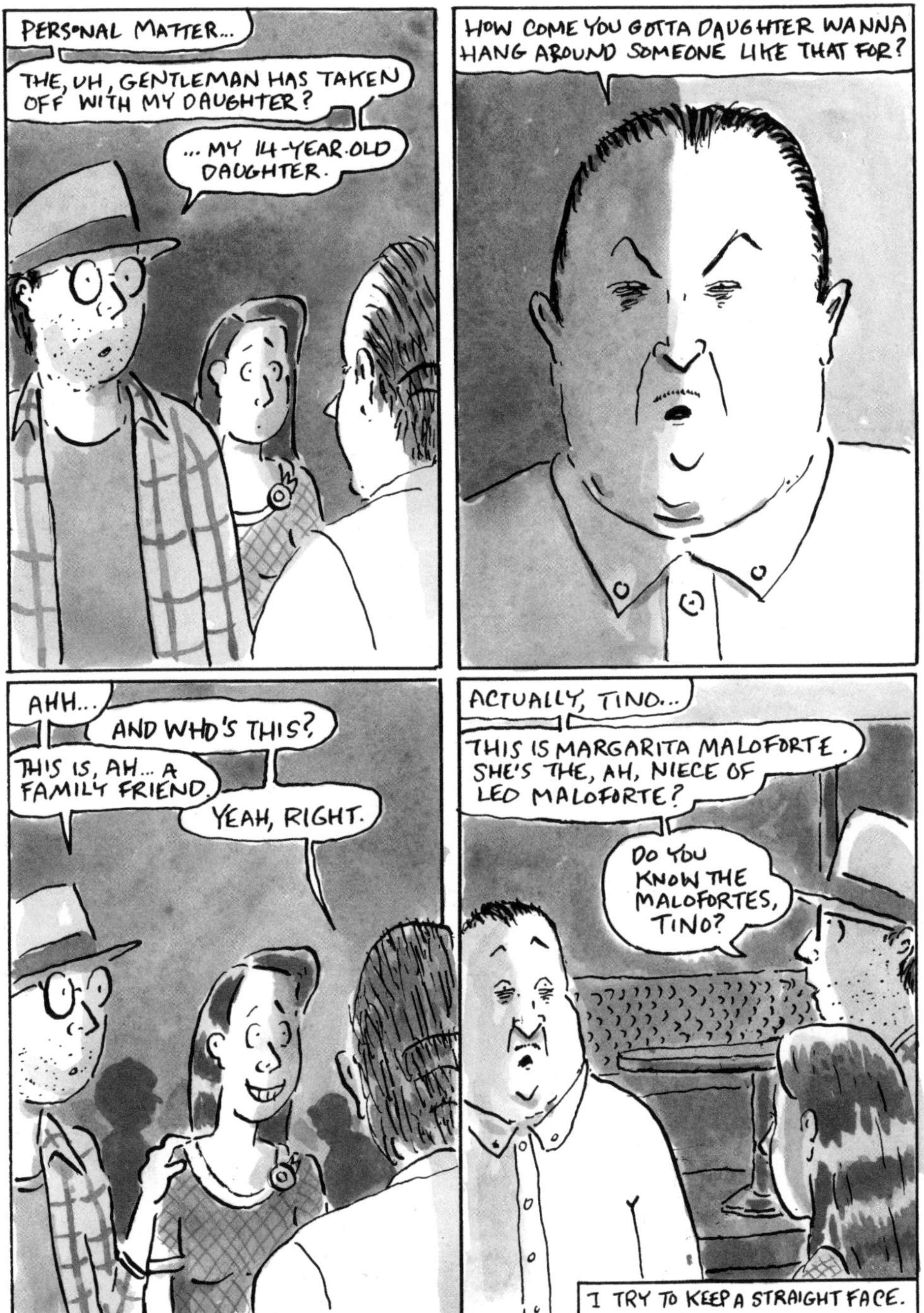
PERSONAL MATTER...
THE, UH, GENTLEMAN HAS TAKEN OFF WITH MY DAUGHTER?
... MY 14-YEAR-OLD DAUGHTER.
HOW COME YOU GOTTA DAUGHTER WANNA HANG AROUND SOMEONE LIKE THAT FOR?
AHH...
AND WHO'S THIS?
THIS IS, AH... A FAMILY FRIEND.
YEAH, RIGHT.
ACTUALLY, TINO...
THIS IS MARGARITA MALOFORTE. SHE'S THE, AH, NIECE OF LEO MALOFORTE?
DO YOU KNOW THE MALOFORTES, TINO?
I TRY TO KEEP A STRAIGHT FACE.

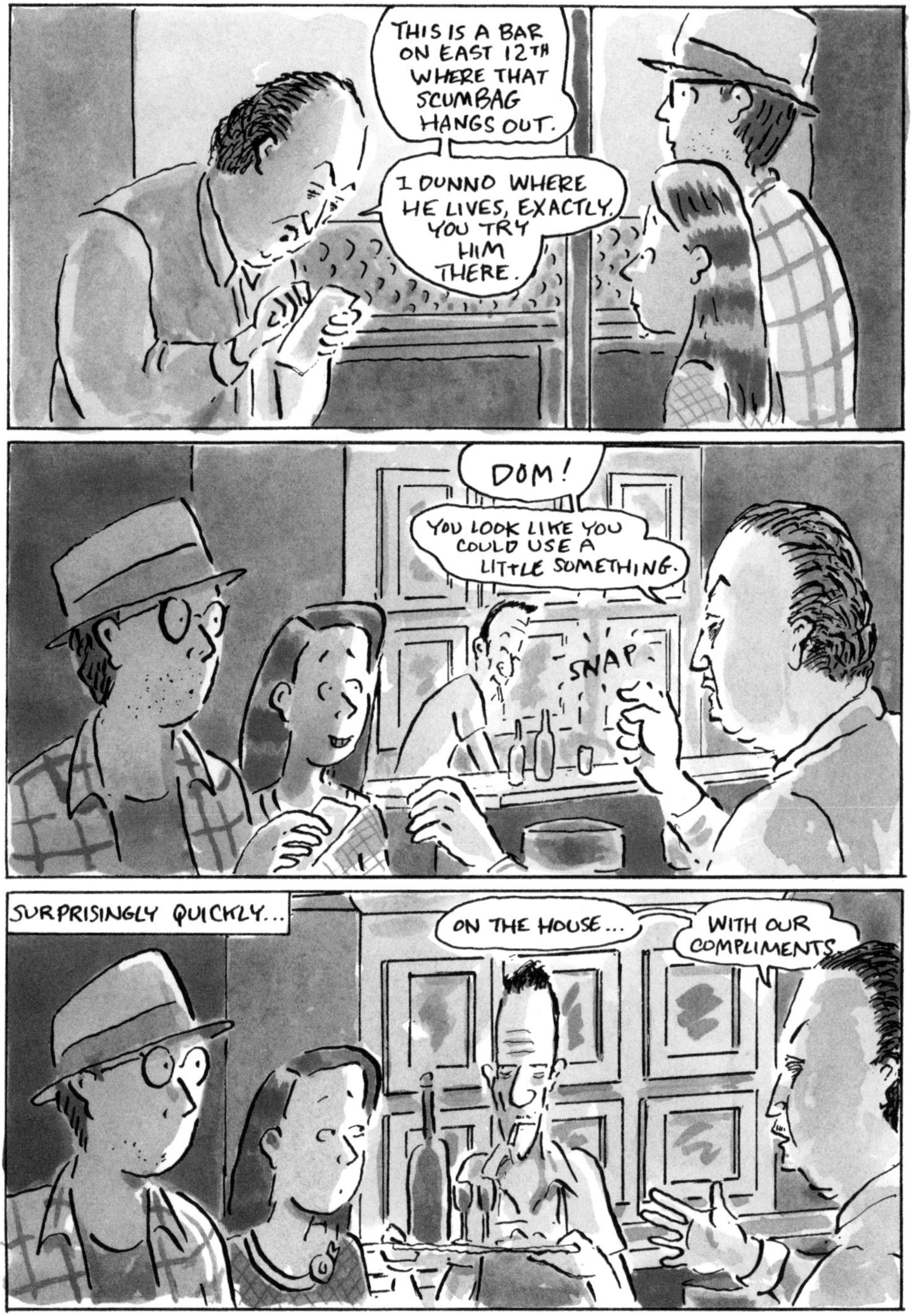
THIS IS A BAR ON EAST 12TH WHERE THAT SCUMBAG HANGS OUT.
I DUNNO WHERE HE LIVES, EXACTLY. YOU TRY HIM THERE.
DOM!
YOU LOOK LIKE YOU COULD USE A LITTLE SOMETHING.
SNAP
SURPRISINGLY QUICKLY...
ON THE HOUSE...
WITH OUR COMPLIMENTS.

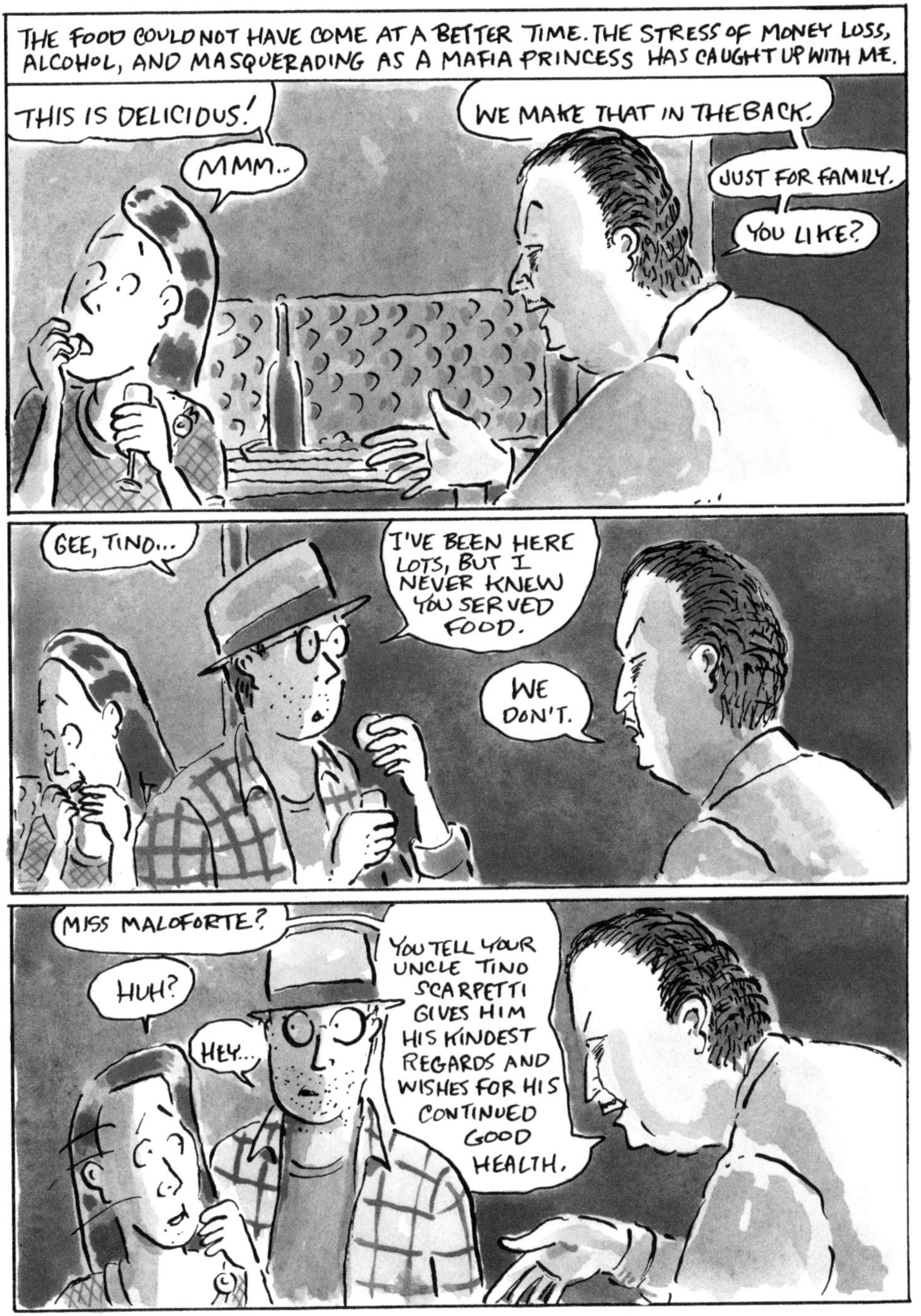
THE FOOD COULD NOT HAVE COME AT A BETTER TIME. THE STRESS OF MONEY LOSS, ALCOHOL, AND MASQUERADING AS A MAFIA PRINCESS HAS CAUGHT UP WITH ME.
THIS IS DELICIOUS!
MMM...
WE MAKE THAT IN THE BACK.
JUST FOR FAMILY.
YOU LIKE?
GEE, TINO...
I'VE BEEN HERE LOTS, BUT I NEVER KNEW YOU SERVED FOOD.
WE DON'T.
MISS MALOFORTE?
HUH?
HEY...
YOU TELL YOUR UNCLE TINO SCARPETTI GIVES HIM HIS KINDEST REGARDS AND WISHES FOR HIS CONTINUED GOOD HEALTH.

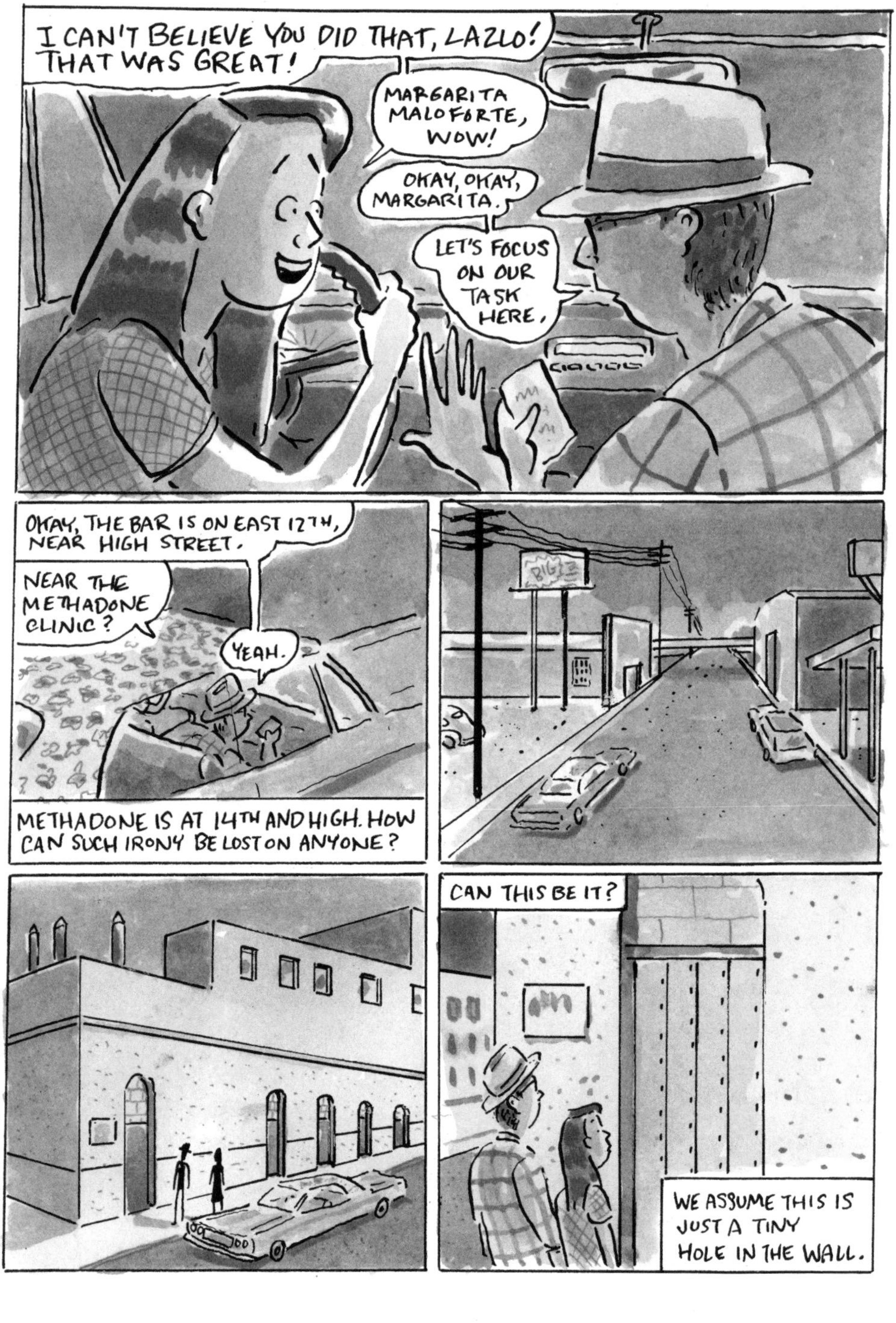
I CAN'T BELIEVE YOU DID THAT, LAZLO! THAT WAS GREAT!
MARGARITA MALOFORTE, WOW!
OKAY, OKAY, MARGARITA.
LET'S FOCUS ON OUR TASK HERE.
OKAY, THE BAR IS ON EAST 12TH, NEAR HIGH STREET.
NEAR THE METHADONE CLINIC?
YEAH.
METHADONE IS AT 14TH AND HIGH. HOW CAN SUCH IRONY BE LOST ON ANYONE?
BIG
CAN THIS BE IT?
WE ASSUME THIS IS JUST A TINY HOLE IN THE WALL.

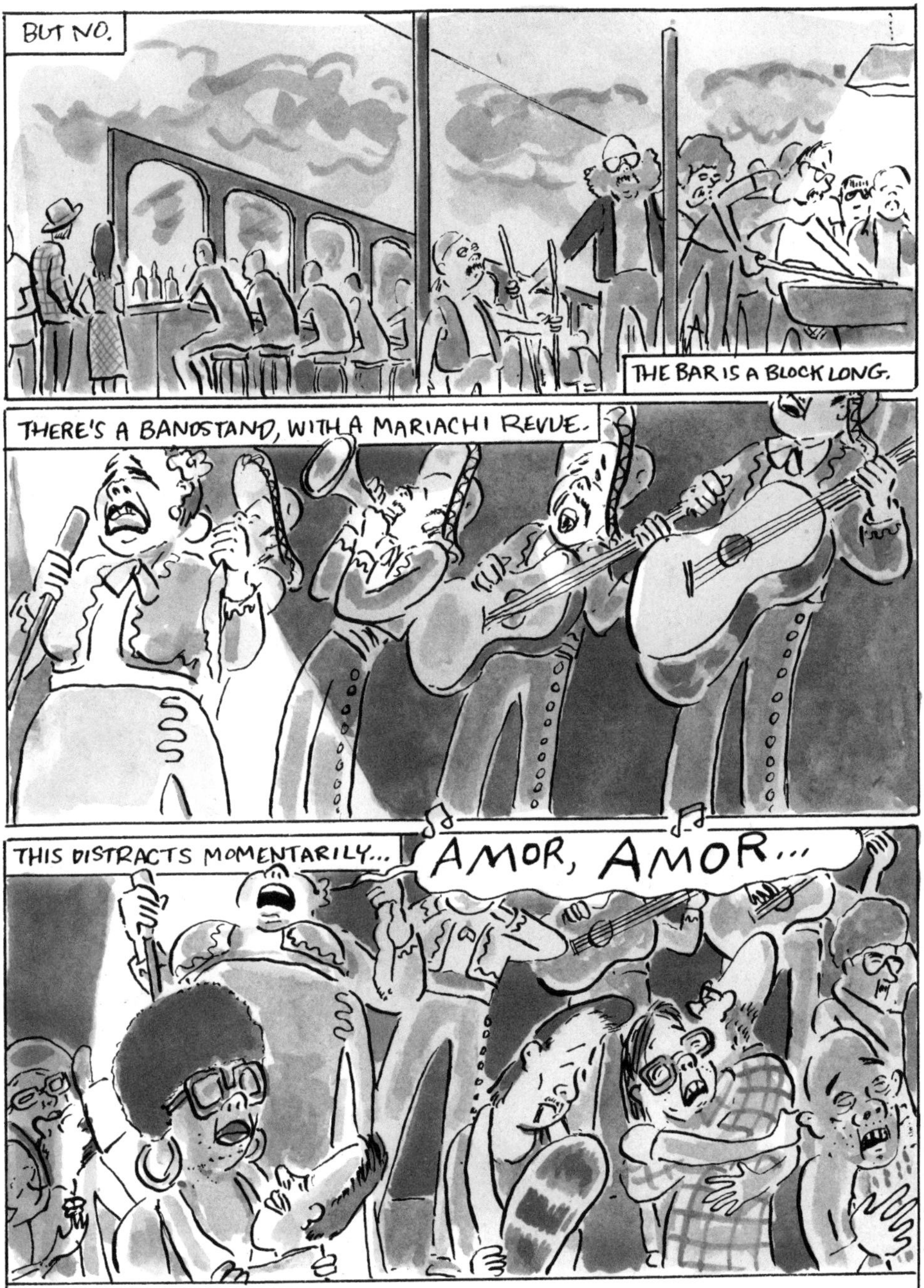

BUT NO.
THE BAR IS A BLOCK LONG.
THERE'S A BANDSTAND, WITH A MARIACHI REVUE.
THIS DISTRACTS MOMENTARILY...
AMOR, AMOR...
FROM THE CUSTOMERS, A MODEL U.N. FOR THE DISSOLUTE.

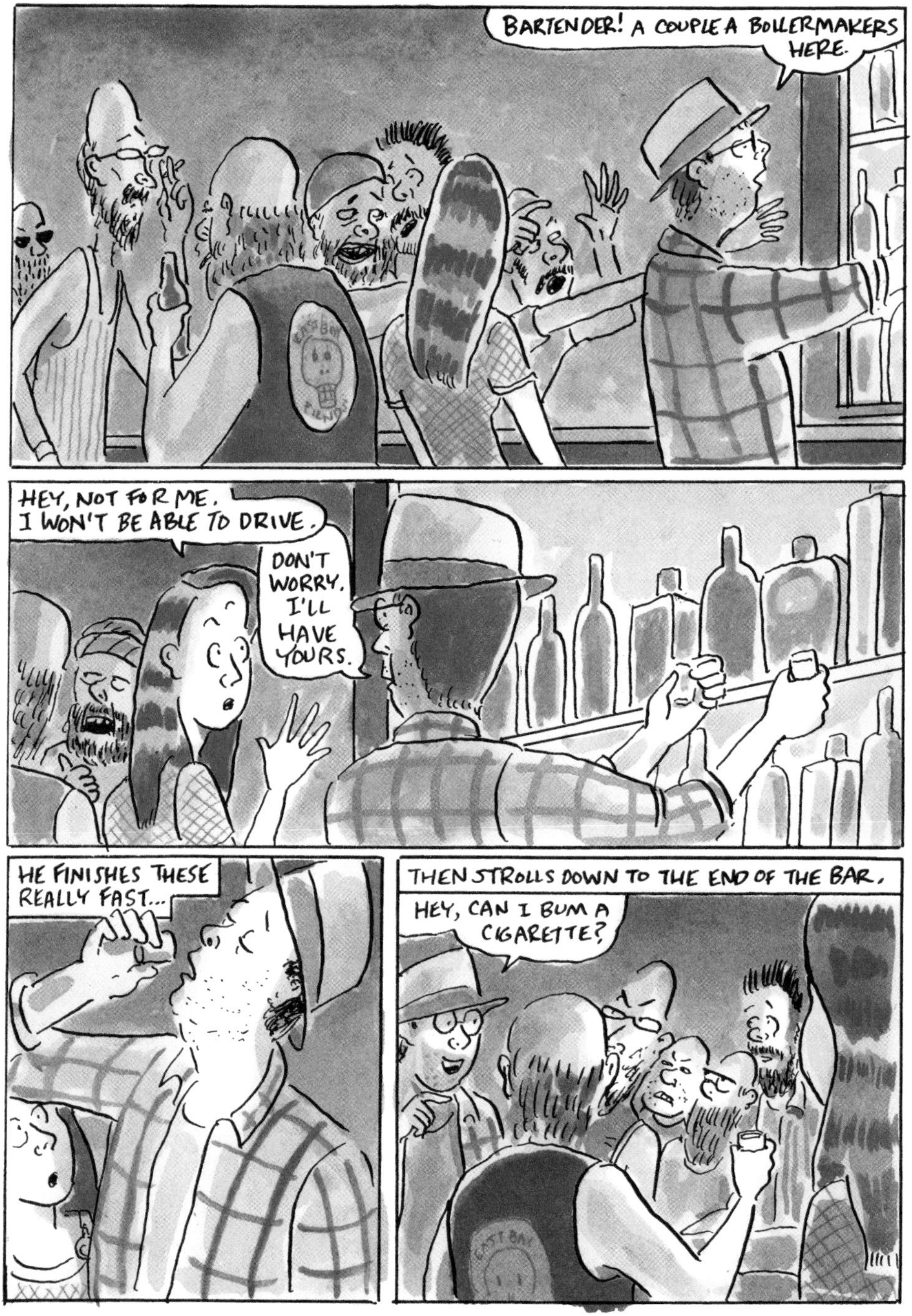
BARTENDER! A COUPLE A BOILERMAKERS HERE.
EAST BAY FIENDS
HEY, NOT FOR ME. I WON'T BE ABLE TO DRIVE.
DON'T WORRY. I'LL HAVE YOURS.
HE FINISHES THESE REALLY FAST...
THEN STROLLS DOWN TO THE END OF THE BAR.
HEY, CAN I BUM A CIGARETTE?
EAST BAY

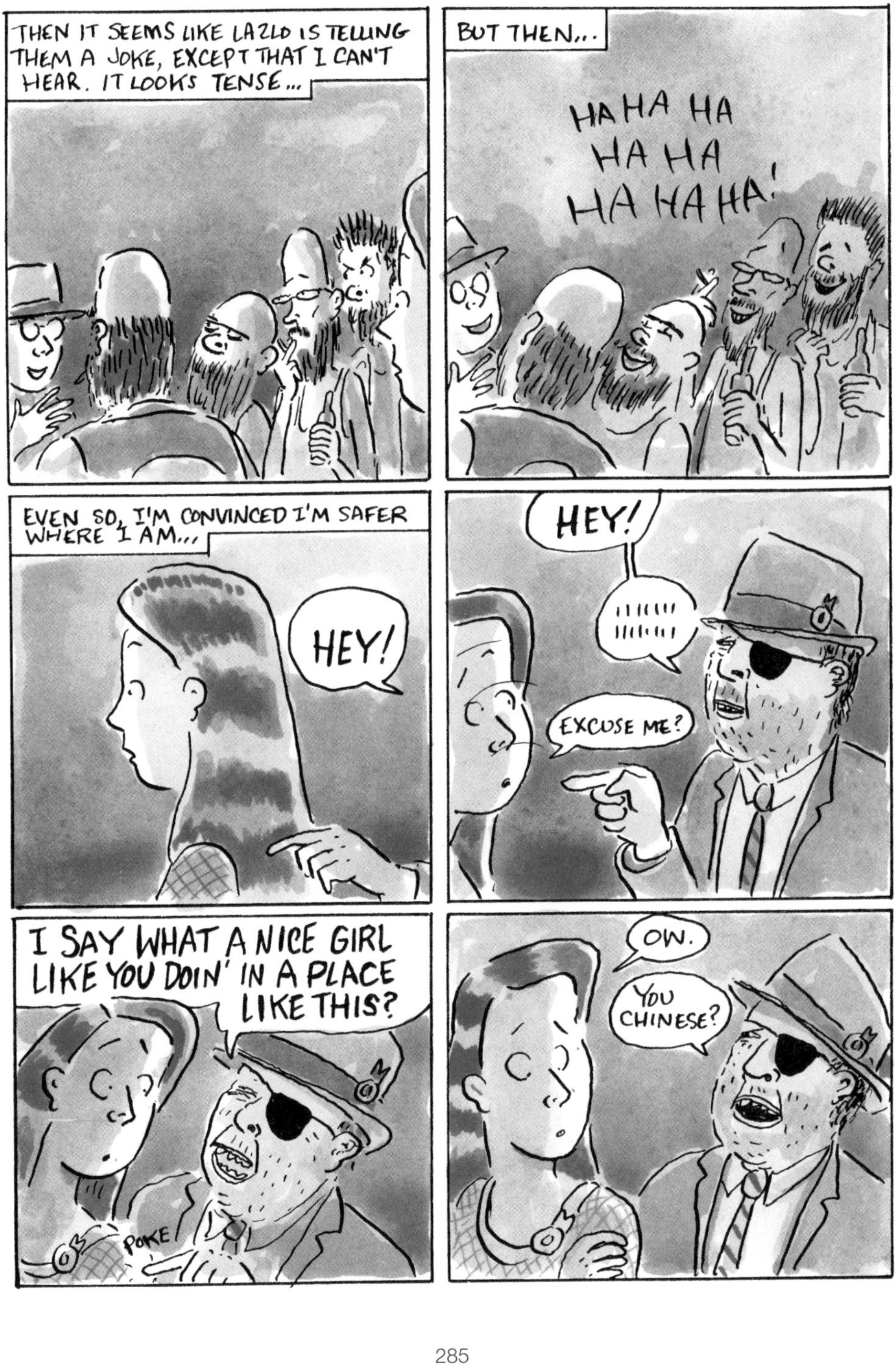
THEN IT SEEMS LIKE LAZLO IS TELLING THEM A JOKE, EXCEPT THAT I CAN'T HEAR. IT LOOKS TENSE...
BUT THEN...
HAHA HA HA HA HA HA HA!
EVEN SO, I'M CONVINCED I'M SAFER WHERE I AM...
HEY!
HEY!
EXCUSE ME?
I SAY WHAT A NICE GIRL LIKE YOU DOIN' IN A PLACE LIKE THIS?
POKE
OW.
YOU CHINESE?

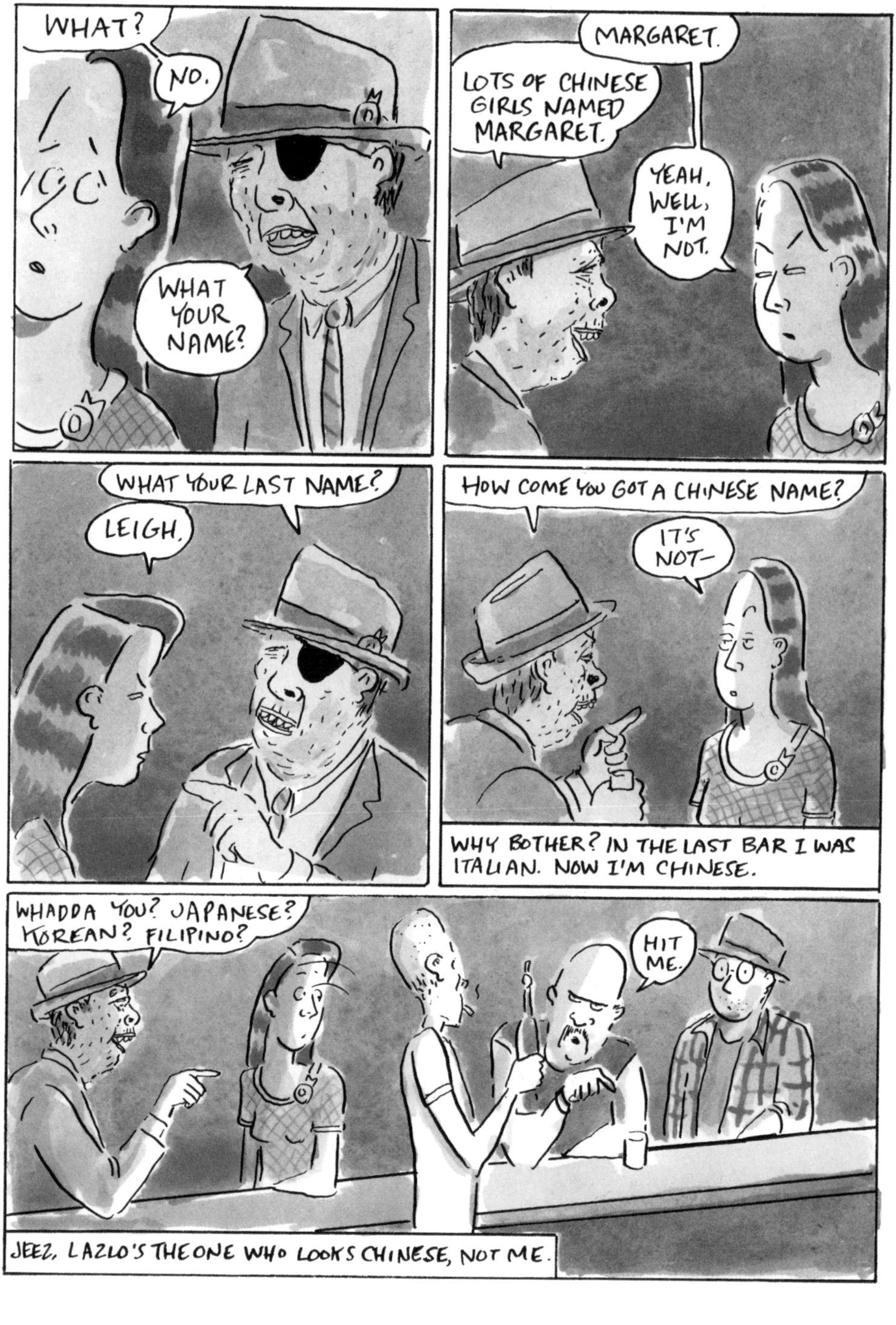
WHAT?
NO.
WHAT YOUR NAME?
MARGARET.
LOTS OF CHINESE GIRLS NAMED MARGARET.
YEAH, WELL, I'M NOT.
WHAT YOUR LAST NAME?
LEIGH.
HOW COME YOU GOT A CHINESE NAME?
IT'S NOT-
WHY BOTHER? IN THE LAST BAR I WAS ITALIAN. NOW I'M CHINESE.
WHADDA YOU? JAPANESE? KOREAN? FILIPINO?
HIT ME.
JEEZ, LAZLO'S THE ONE WHO LOOKS CHINESE, NOT ME.

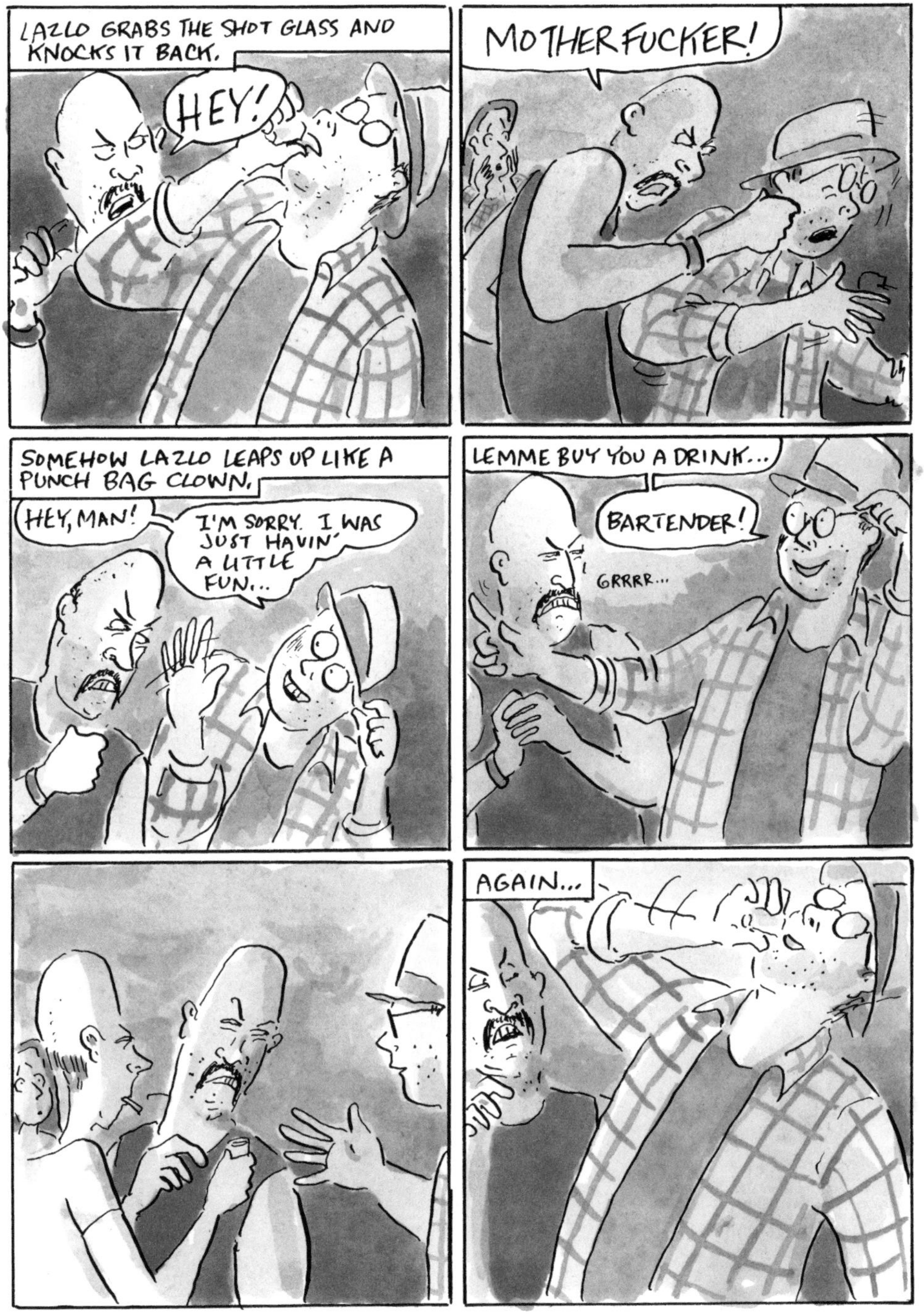
LAZLO GRABS THE SHOT GLASS AND KNOCKS IT BACK.
HEY!
MOTHERFUCKER!
SOMEHOW LAZLO LEAPS UP LIKE A PUNCH BAG CLOWN.
HEY, MAN!
I'M SORRY. I WAS JUST HAVIN' A LITTLE FUN...
LEMME BUY YOU A DRINK...
BARTENDER!
GRRRR...
AGAIN...

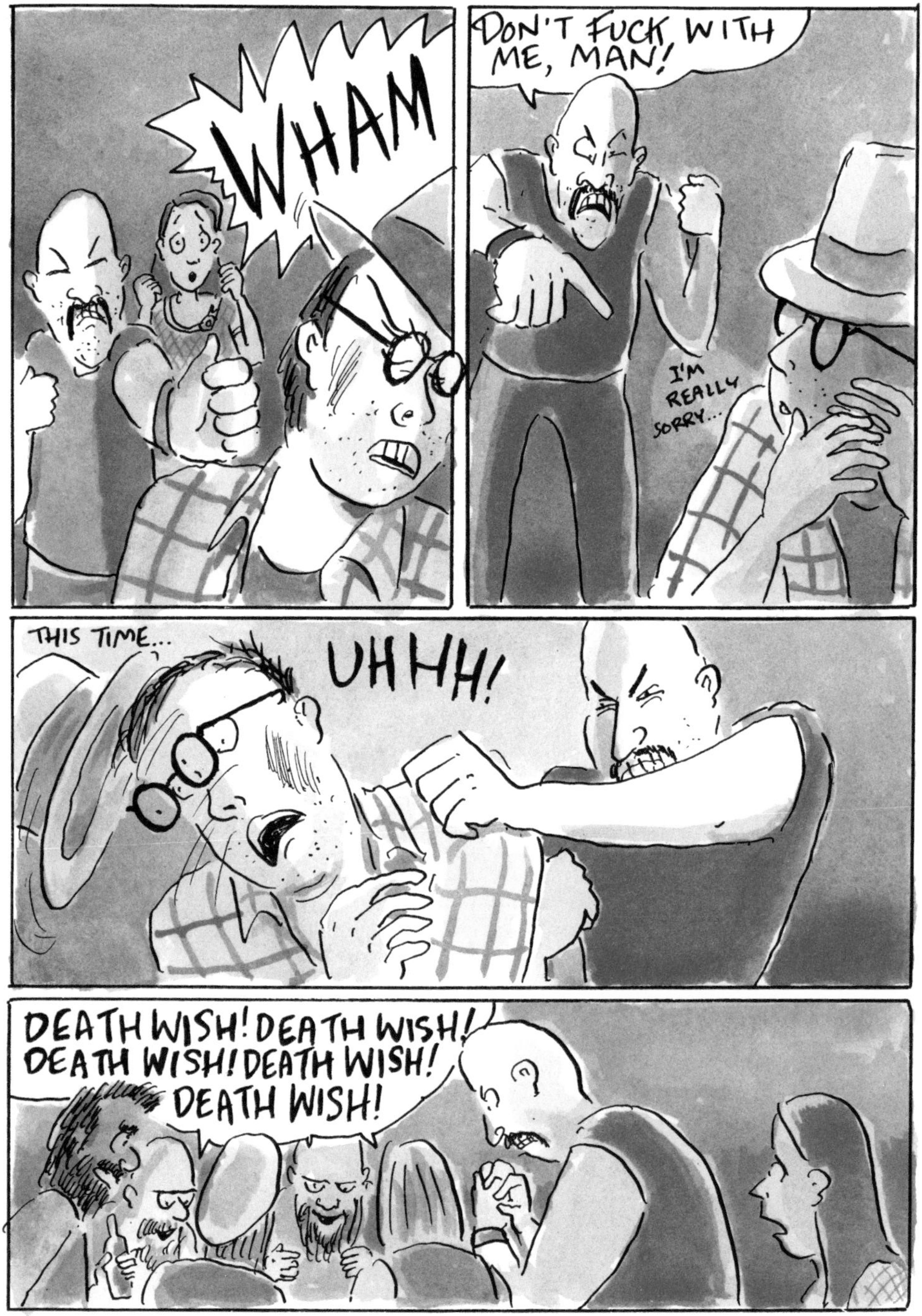
WHAM
DON'T FUCK WITH ME, MAN!
I'M REALLY SORRY...
THIS TIME...
UHHH!
DEATH WISH! DEATH WISH! DEATH WISH! DEATH WISH! DEATH WISH!

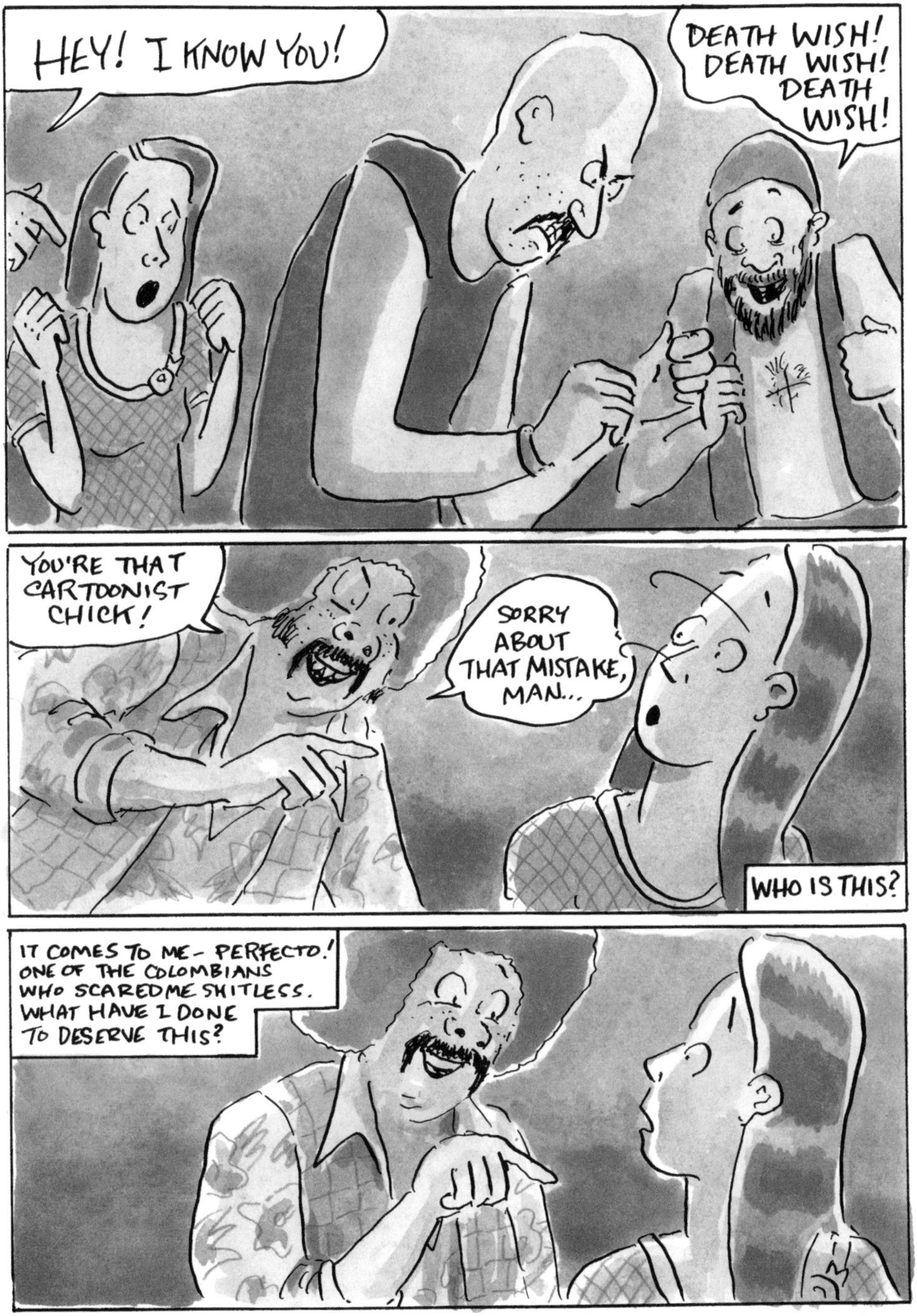
HEY! I KNOW YOU!
DEATH WISH! DEATH WISH! DEATH WISH!
YOU'RE THAT CARTOONIST CHICK!
SORRY ABOUT THAT MISTAKE, MAN...
WHO IS THIS?
IT COMES TO ME - PERFECTO! ONE OF THE COLOMBIANS WHO SCAREDME SHITLESS. WHAT HAVE I DONE TO DESERVE THIS?

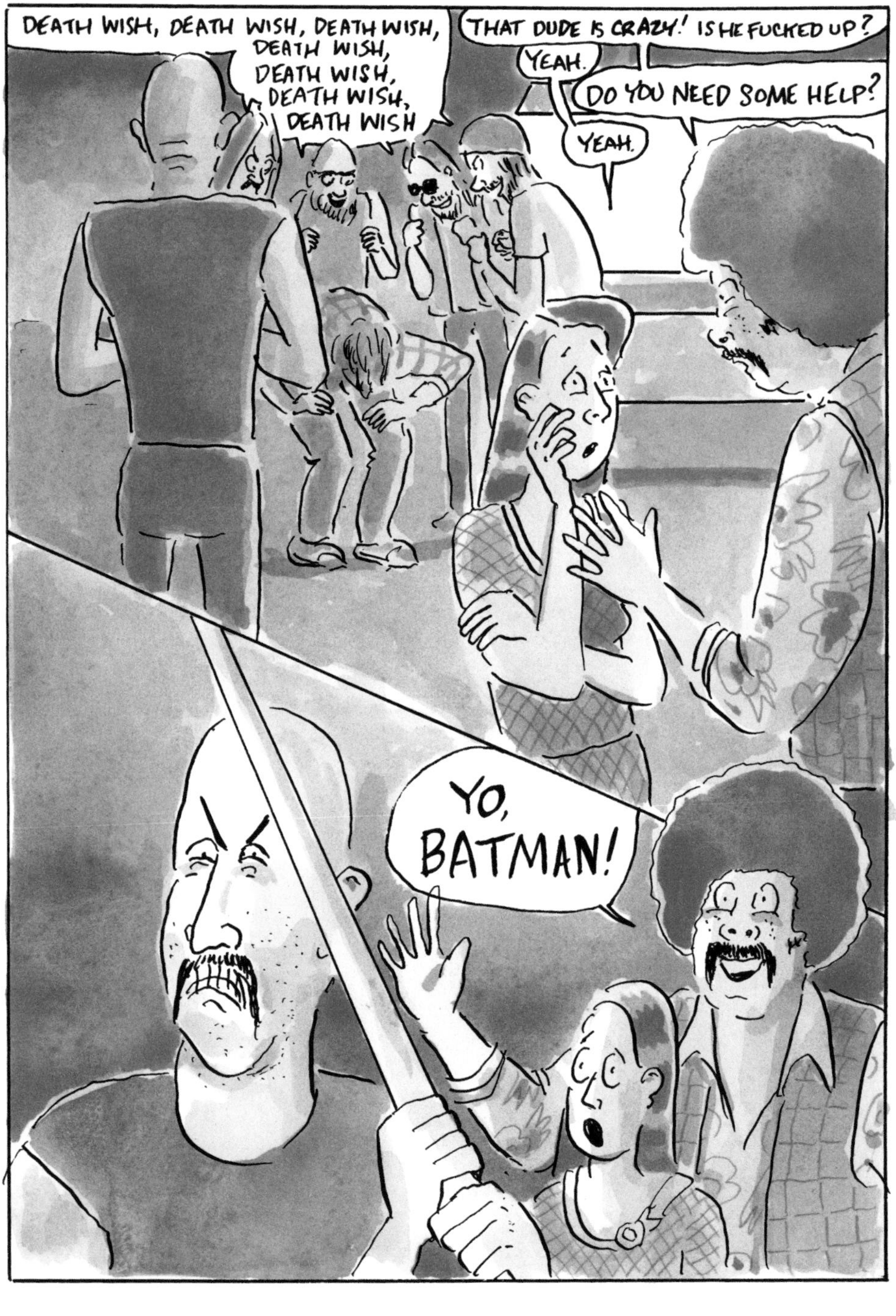
DEATH WISH, DEATH WISH, DEATH WISH, DEATH WISH, DEATH WISH, DEATH WISH, DEATH WISH
THAT DUDE IS CRAZY! IS HE FUCKED UP?
YEAH.
DO YOU NEED SOME HELP?
YEAH.
YO, BATMAN!

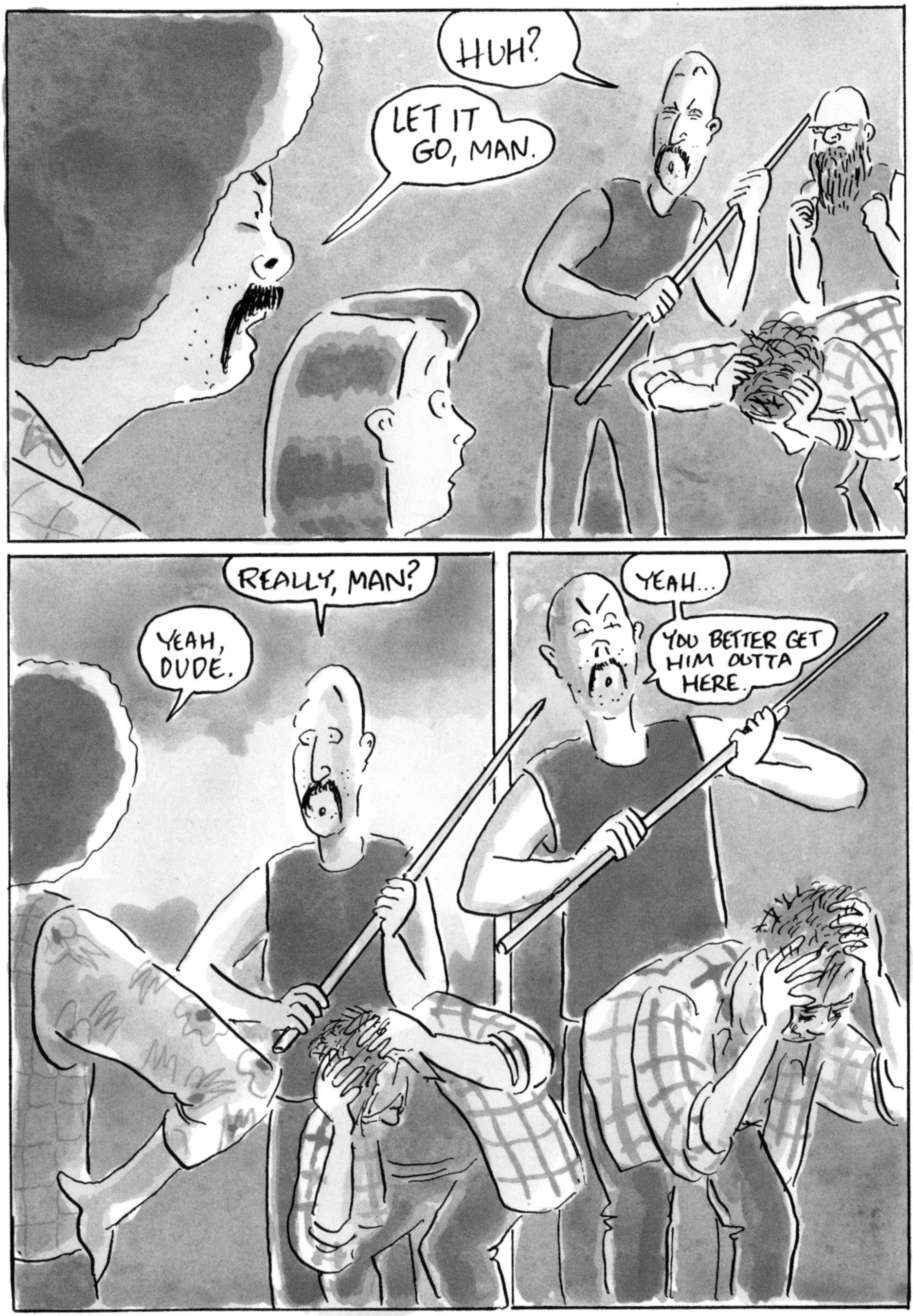
HUH?
LET IT GO, MAN.
REALLY, MAN?
YEAH, DUDE.
YEAH...
YOU BETTER GET HIM OUTTA HERE.

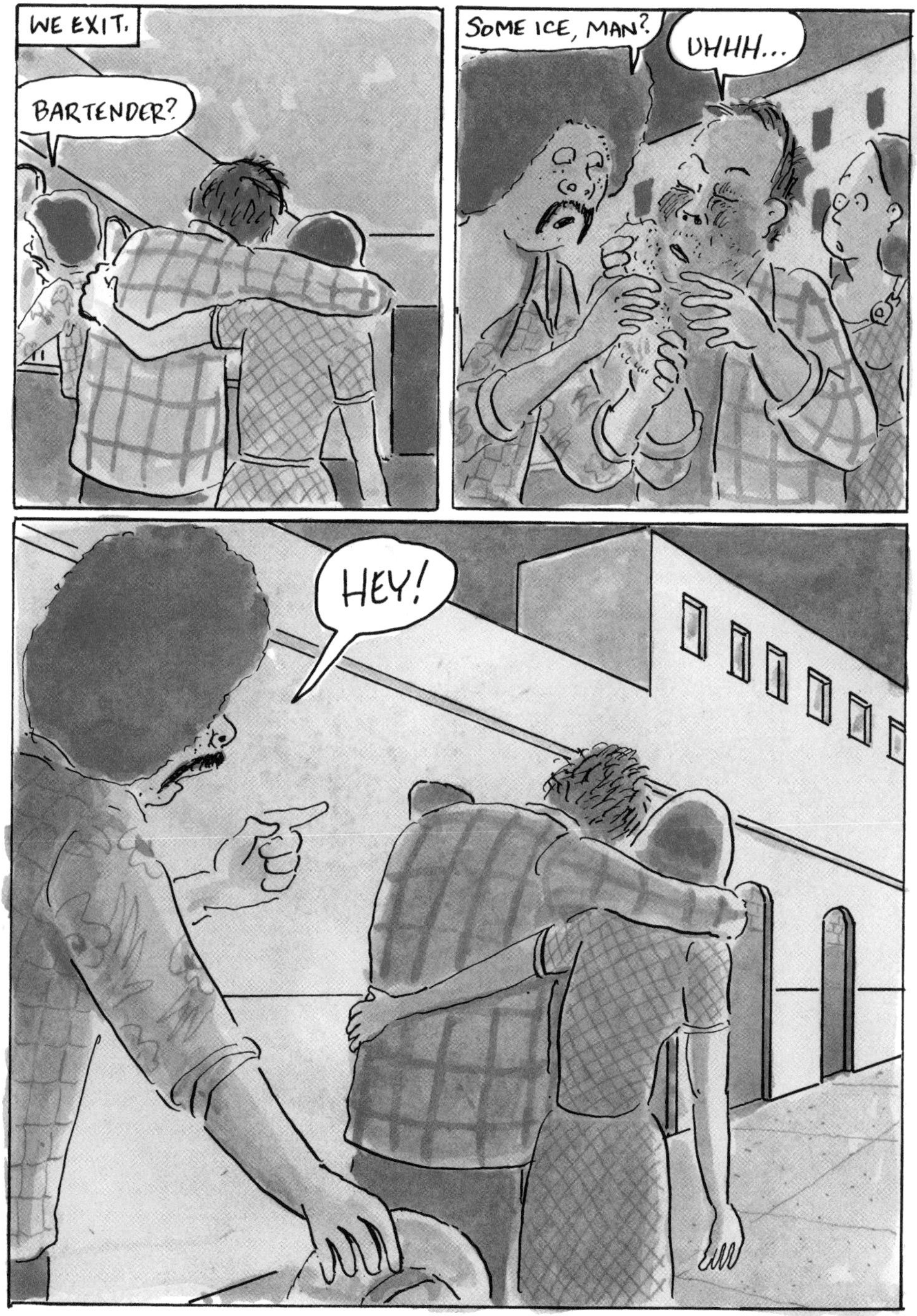
WE EXIT.
BARTENDER?
SOME ICE, MAN?
UHHH...
HEY!

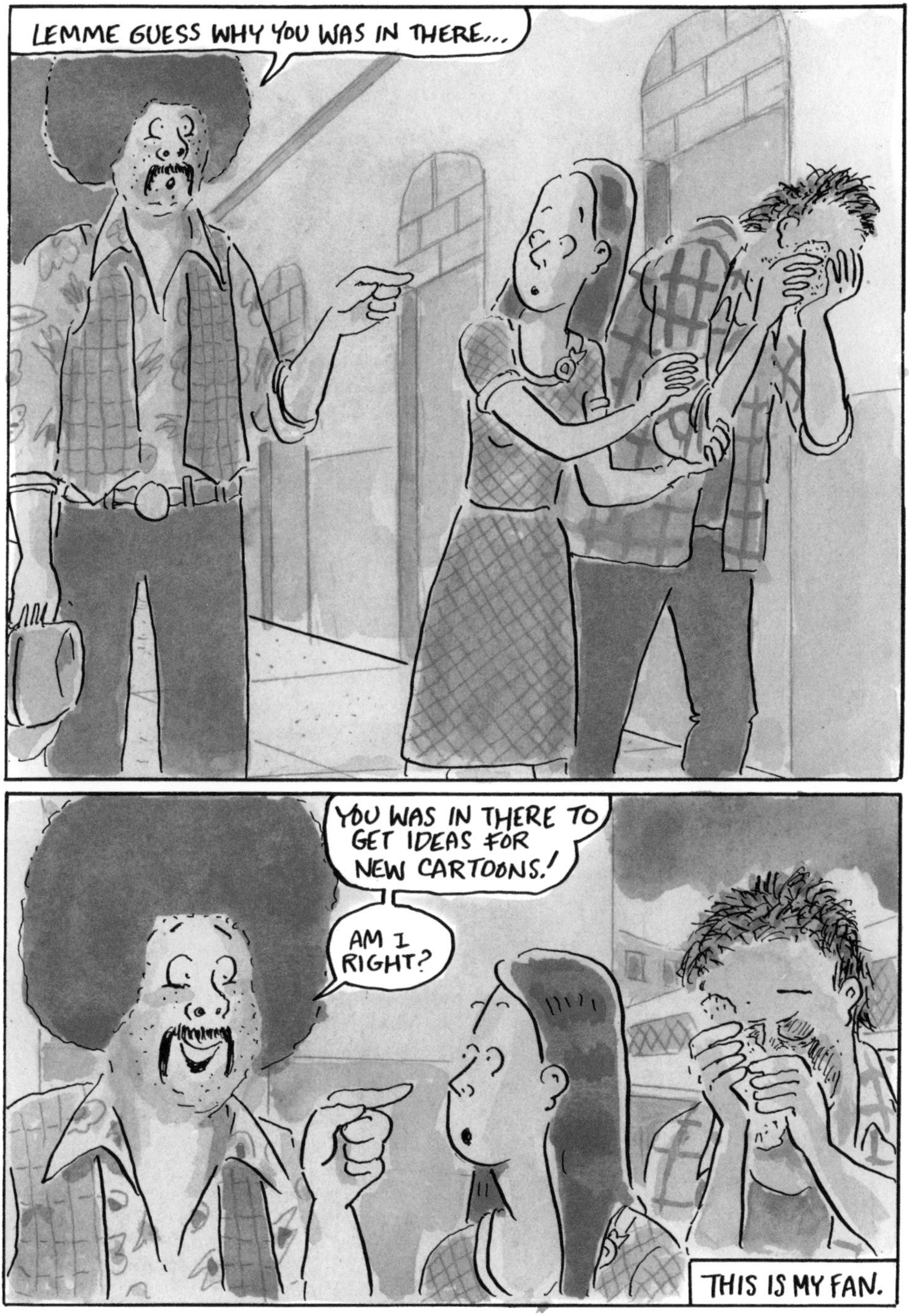
LEMME GUESS WHY YOU WAS IN THERE...
YOU WAS IN THERE TO GET IDEAS FOR NEW CARTOONS.!
AM I RIGHT?
THIS IS MY FAN.

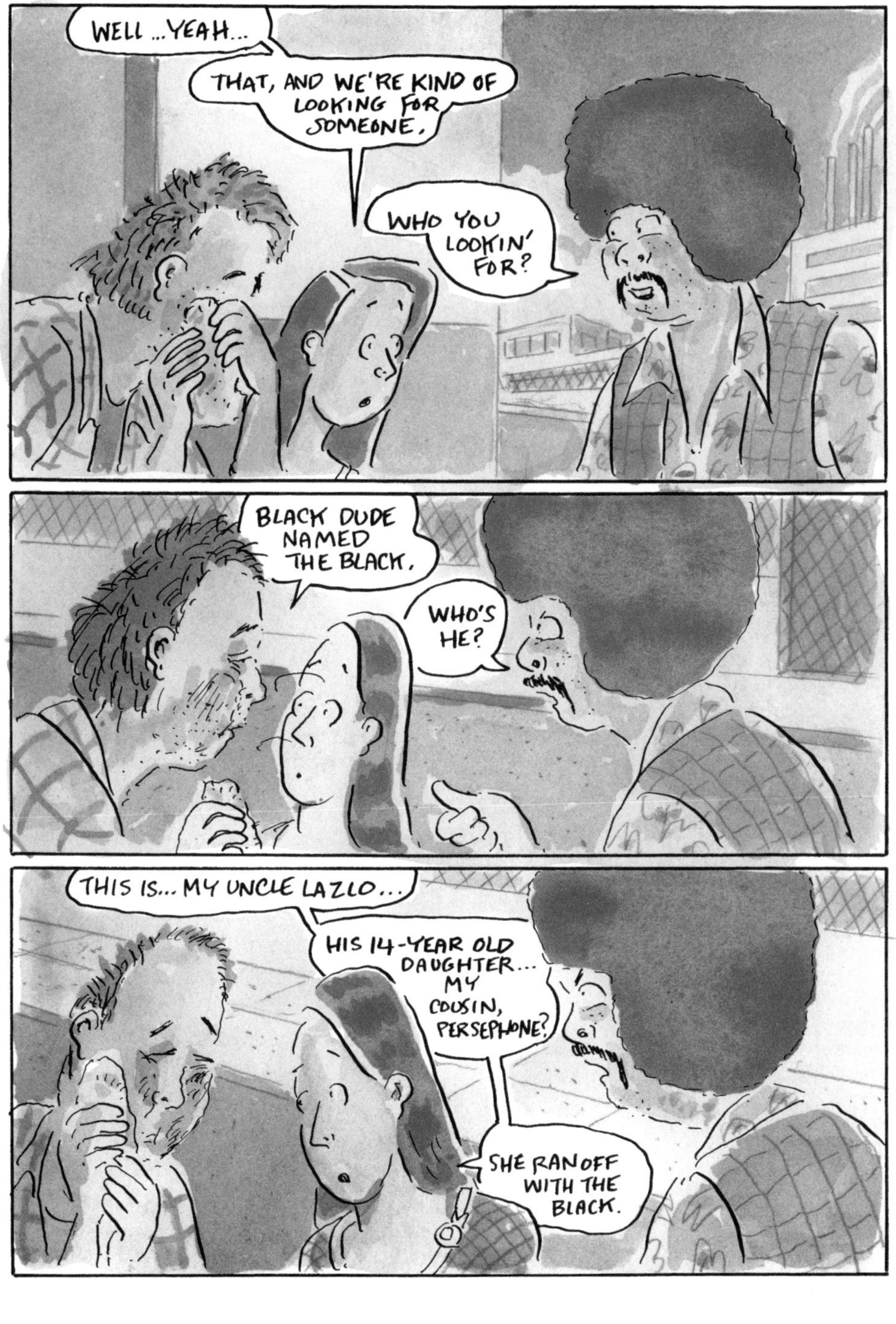
WELL ... YEAH ...
THAT, AND WE'RE KIND OF LOOKING FOR SOMEONE.
WHO YOU LOOKIN' FOR?
BLACK DUDE NAMED THE BLACK.
WHO'S HE?
THIS IS... MY UNCLE LAZLO...
HIS 14-YEAR OLD DAUGHTER... MY COUSIN, PERSEPHONE?
SHE RAN OFF WITH THE BLACK.

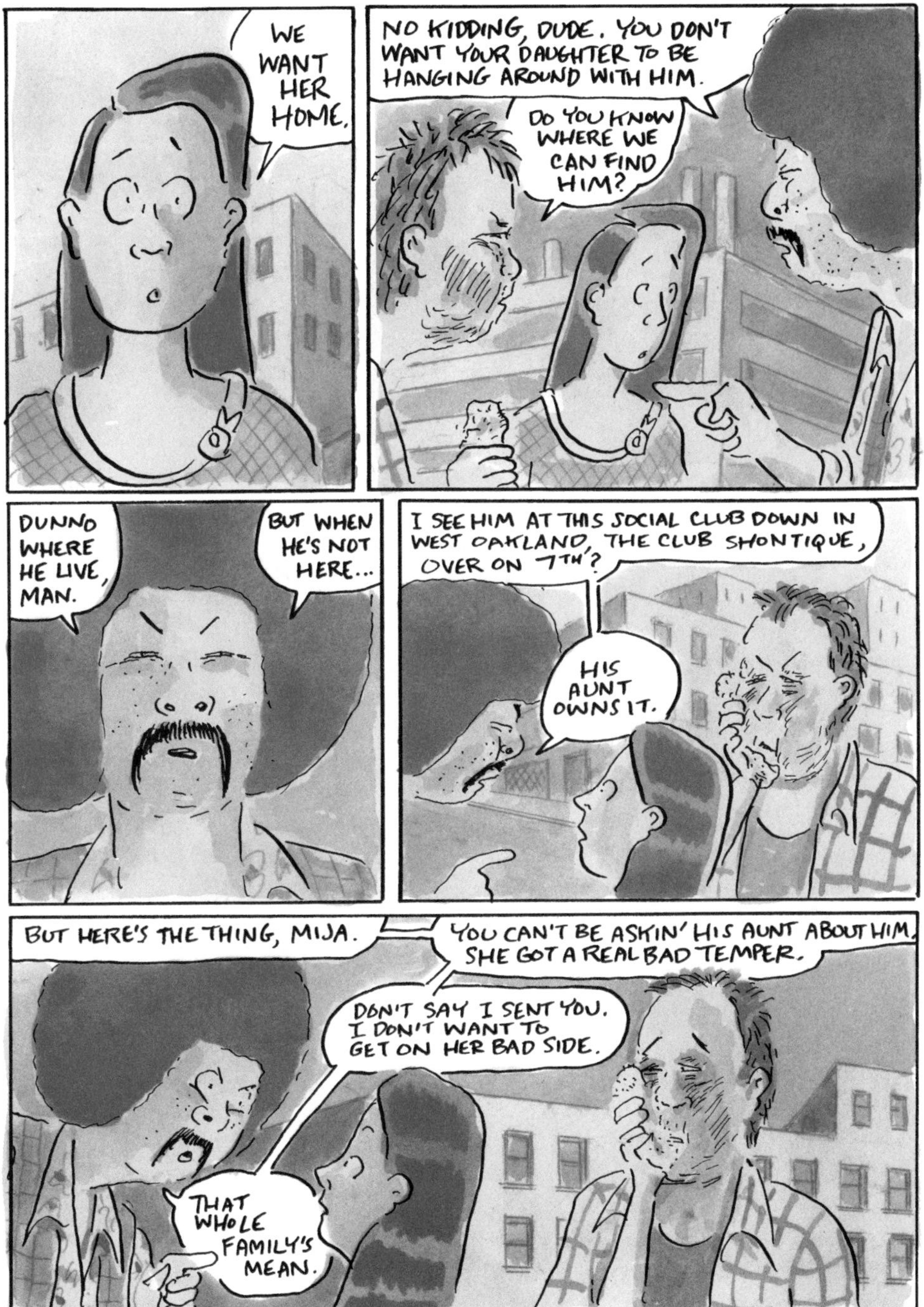
WE WANT HER HOME.
NO KIDDING, DUDE. YOU DON'T WANT YOUR DAUGHTER TO BE HANGING AROUND WITH HIM.
DO YOU KNOW WHERE WE CAN FIND HIM?
DUNNO WHERE HE LIVE, MAN.
BUT WHEN HE'S NOT HERE...
I SEE HIM AT THIS SOCIAL CLUB DOWN IN WEST OAKLAND, THE CLUB SHONTIQUE, OVER ON 7TH?
HIS AUNT OWNS IT.
BUT HERE'S THE THING, MIJA.
YOU CAN'T BE ASKIN' HIS AUNT ABOUT HIM. SHE GOT A REAL BAD TEMPER.
DON'T SAY I SENT YOU. I DON'T WANT TO GET ON HER BAD SIDE.
THAT WHOLE FAMILY'S MEAN.

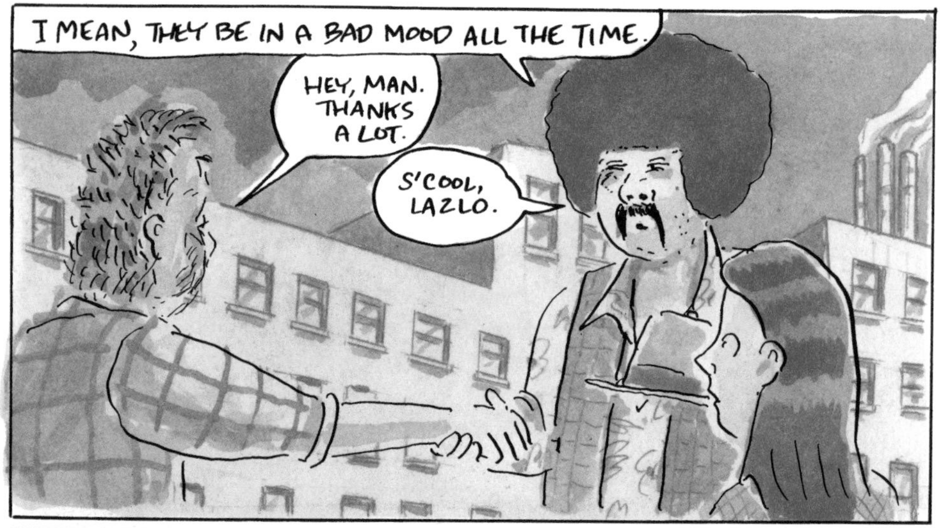
I MEAN, THEY BE IN A BAD MOOD ALL THE TIME.
HEY, MAN. THANKS A LOT.
S'COOL, LAZLO.

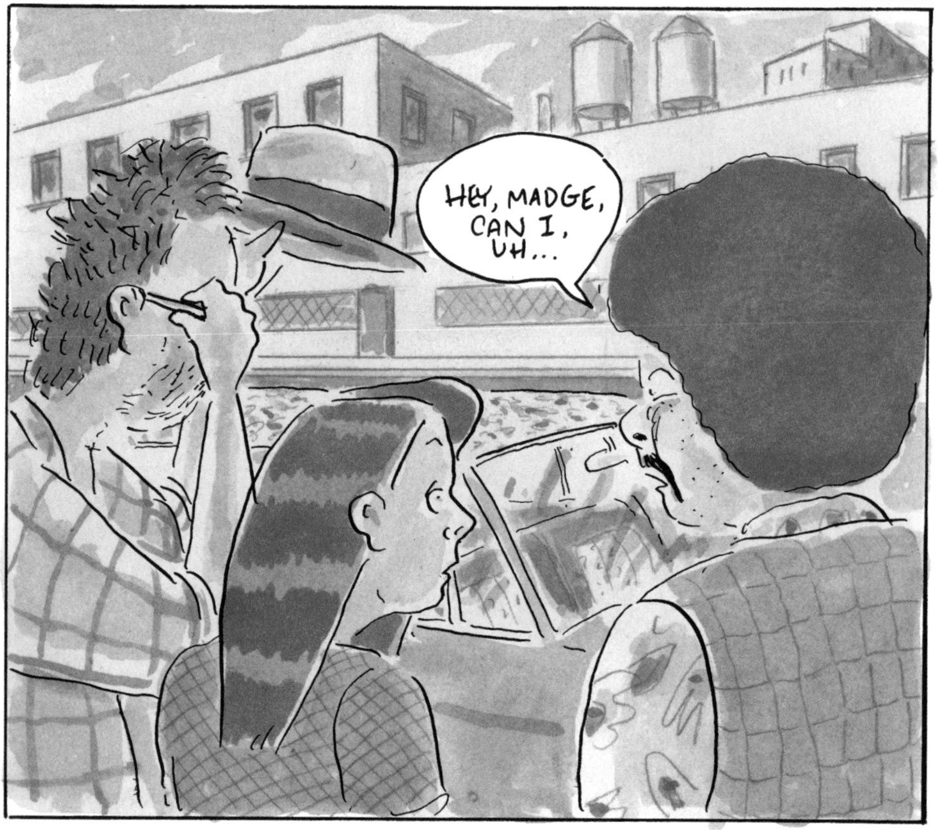
HEY, MADGE, CAN I, UH...

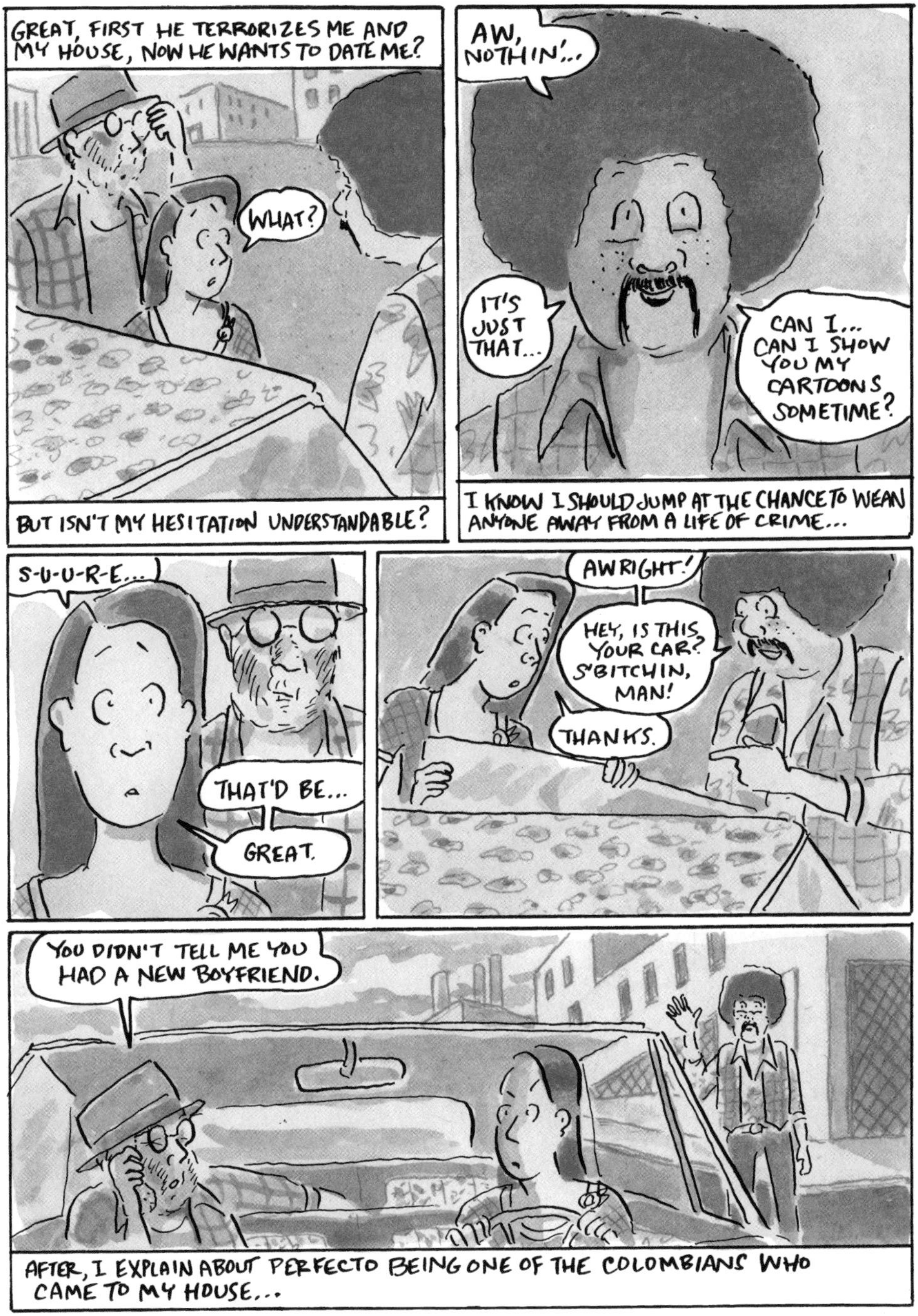
GREAT, FIRST HE TERRORIZES ME AND MY HOUSE, NOW HE WANTS TO DATE ME?
WHAT?
BUT ISN'T MY HESITATION UNDERSTANDABLE?
AW, NOTHIN'...
IT'S JUST THAT...
CAN I... CAN I SHOW YOU MY CARTOONS SOMETIME?
I KNOW I SHOULD JUMP AT THE CHANCE TO WEAN ANYONE AWAY FROM A LIFE OF CRIME...
S-U-U-R-E...
THAT'D BE...
GREAT.
AWRIGHT!
HEY, IS THIS YOUR CAR? S'BITCHIN, MAN!
THANKS.
YOU DIDN'T TELL ME YOU HAD A NEW BOYFRIEND.
AFTER, I EXPLAIN ABOUT PERFECTO BEING ONE OF THE COLOMBIANS WHO CAME TO MY HOUSE...

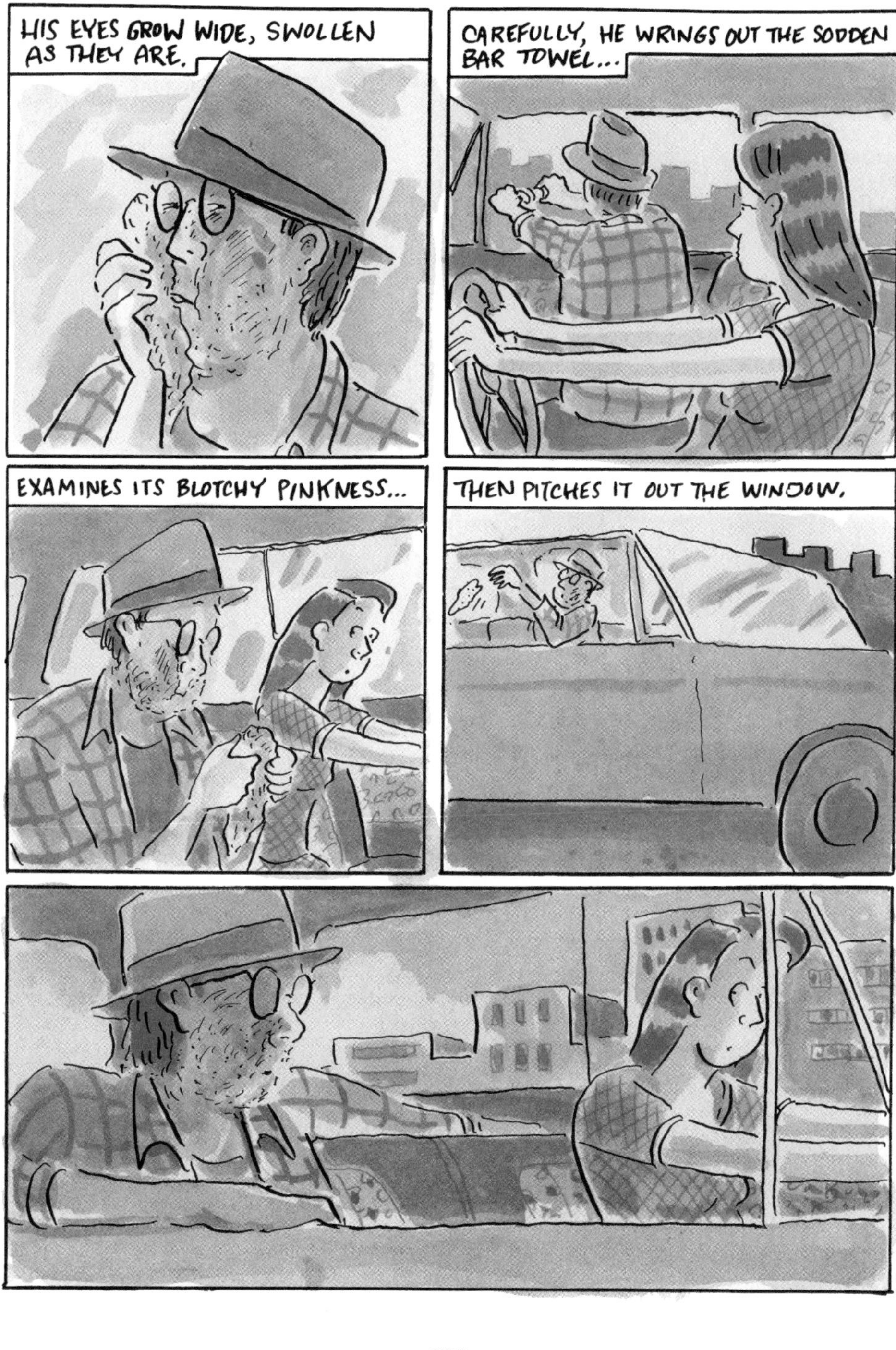
HIS EYES GROW WIDE, SWOLLEN AS THEY ARE.
CAREFULLY, HE WRINGS OUT THE SODDEN BAR TOWEL...
EXAMINES ITS BLOTCHY PINKNESS...
THEN PITCHES IT OUT THE WINDOW.

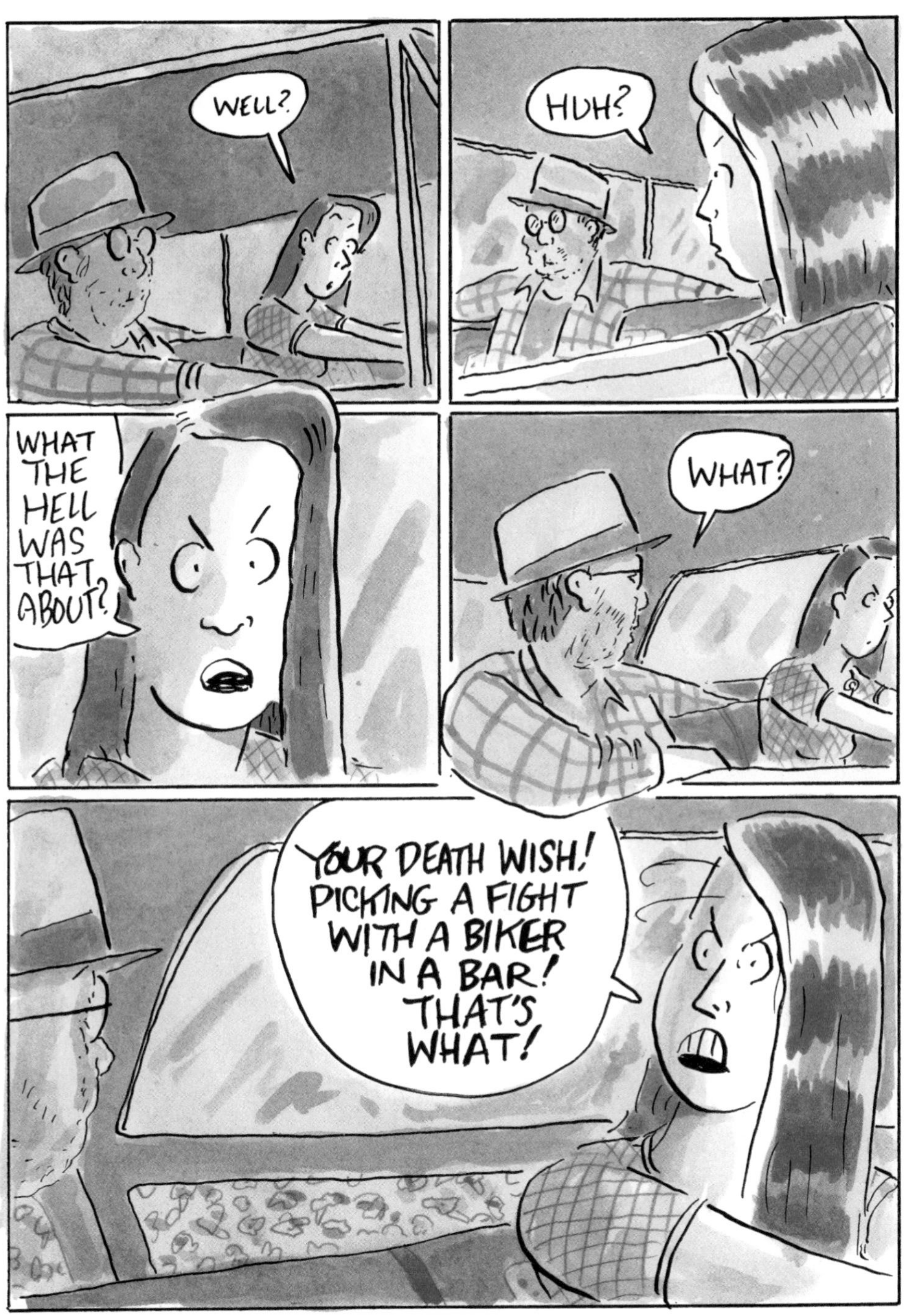
WELL?
HUH?
WHAT THE HELL WAS THAT ABOUT?
WHAT?
YOUR DEATH WISH! PICKING A FIGHT WITH A BIKER IN A BAR! THAT'S WHAT!

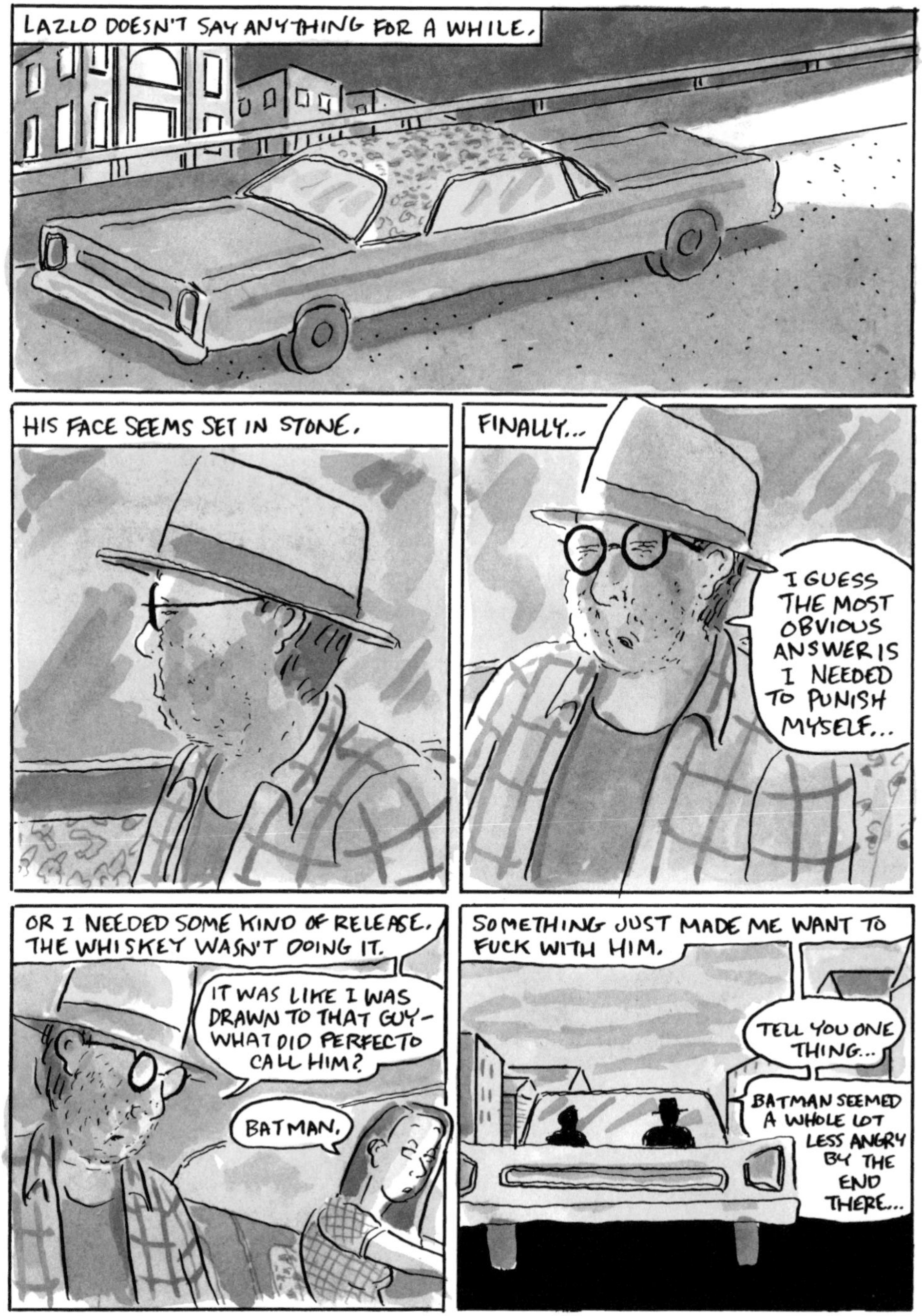
LAZLO DOESN'T SAY ANYTHING FOR A WHILE.
HIS FACE SEEMS SET IN STONE.
FINALLY...
I GUESS THE MOST OBVIOUS ANSWER IS I NEEDED TO PUNISH MYSELF...
OR I NEEDED SOME KIND OF RELEASE. THE WHISKEY WASN'T DOING IT.
IT WAS LIKE I WAS DRAWN TO THAT GUY- WHAT DID PERFECTO CALL HIM?
BATMAN.
SOMETHING JUST MADE ME WANT TO FUCK WITH HIM.
TELL YOU ONE THING...
BATMAN SEEMED A WHOLE LOT LESS ANGRY BY THE END THERE...

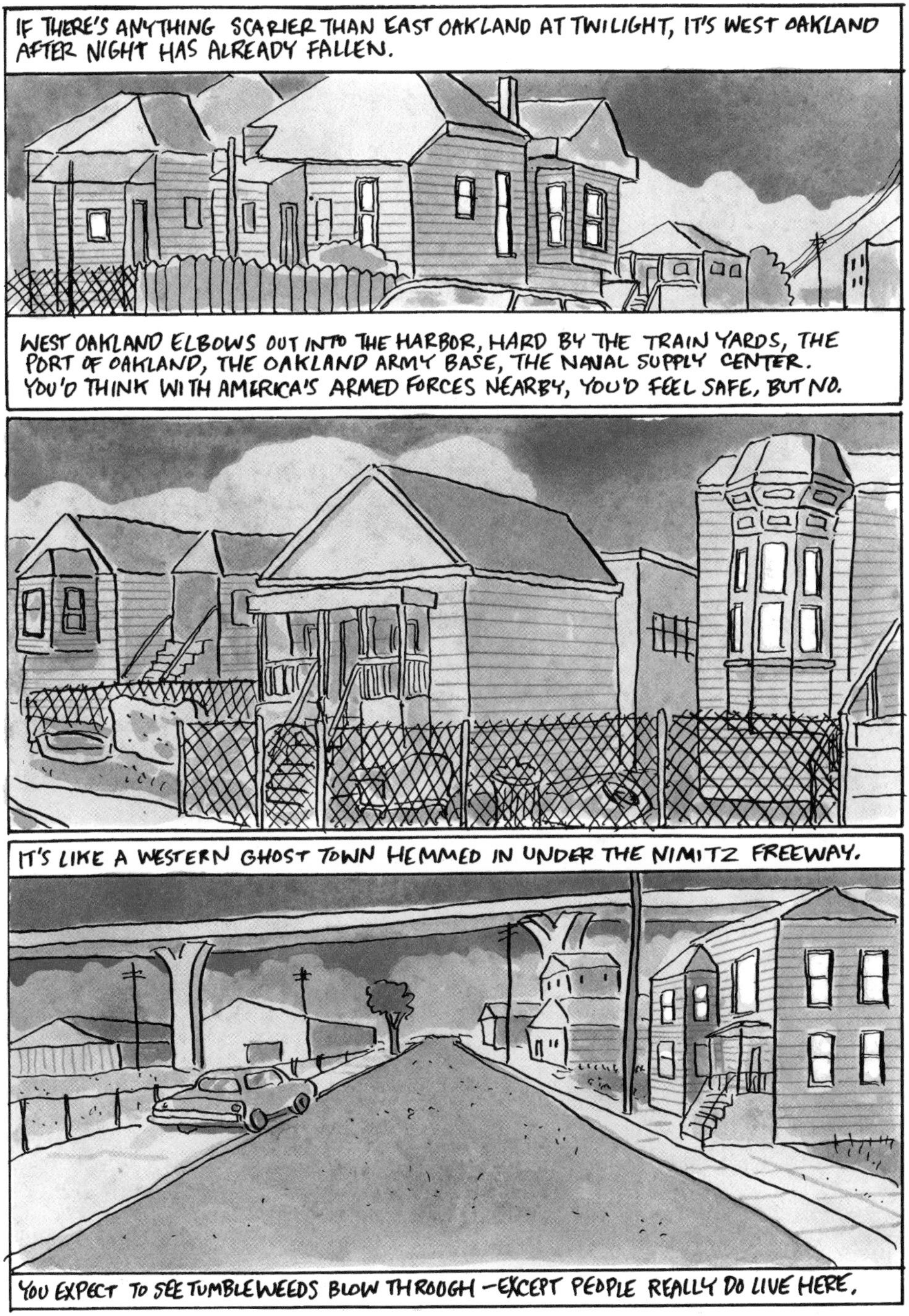
IF THERE'S ANYTHING SCARIER THAN EAST OAKLAND AT TWILIGHT, IT'S WEST OAKLAND AFTER NIGHT HAS ALREADY FALLEN.
WEST OAKLAND ELBOWS OUT INTO THE HARBOR, HARD BY THE TRAIN YARDS, THE PORT OF OAKLAND, THE OAKLAND ARMY BASE, THE NAVAL SUPPLY CENTER. YOU'D THINK WITH AMERICA'S ARMED FORCES NEARBY, YOU'D FEEL SAFE, BUT NO.
IT'S LIKE A WESTERN GHOST TOWN HEMMED IN UNDER THE NIMITZ FREEWAY.
YOU EXPECT TO SEE TUMBLEWEEDS BLOW THROUGH —EXCEPT PEOPLE REALLY DO LIVE HERE.

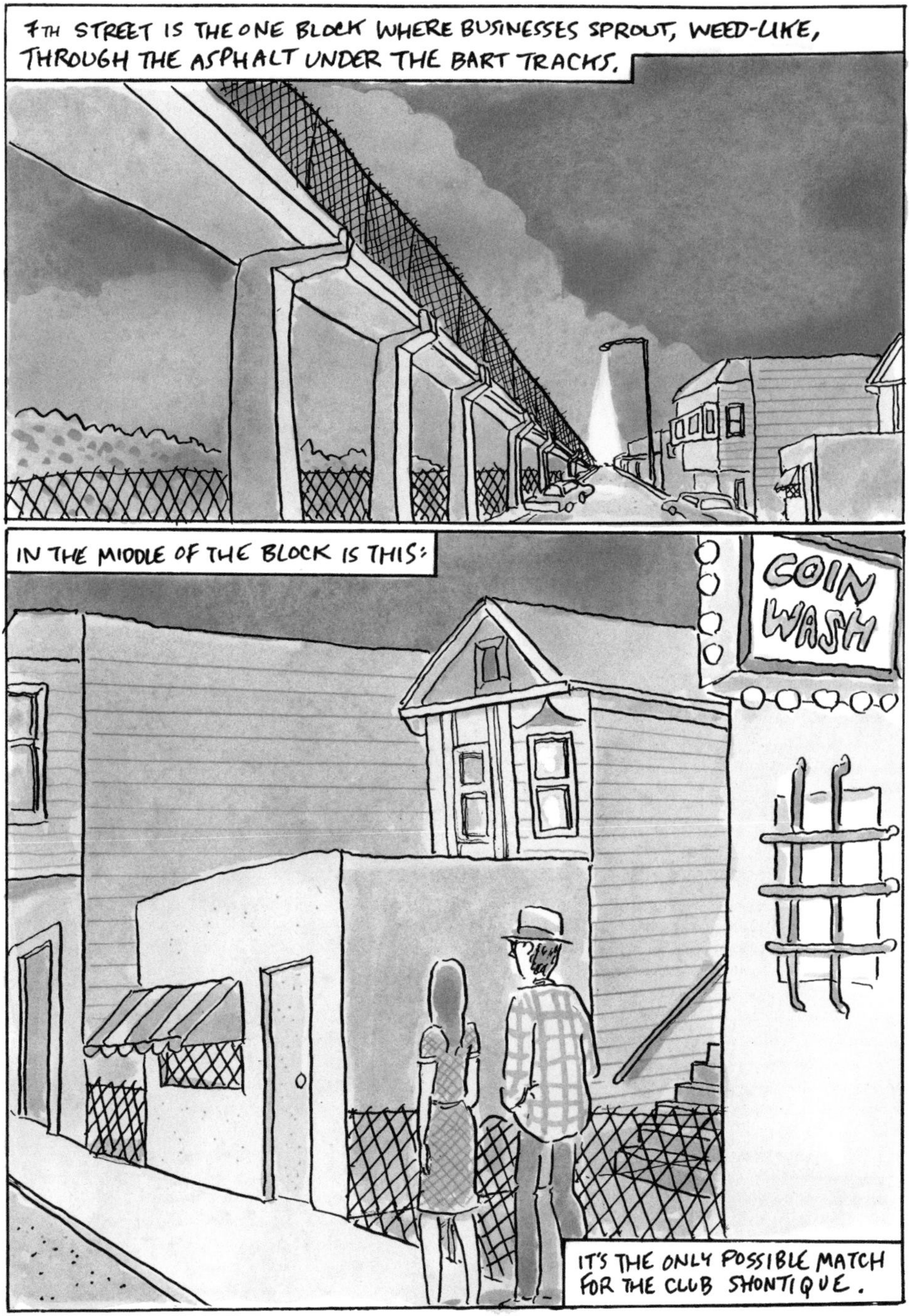
7TH STREET IS THE ONE BLOCK WHERE BUSINESSES SPROUT, WEED-LIKE, THROUGH THE ASPHALT UNDER THE BART TRACKS.
IN THE MIDDLE OF THE BLOCK IS THIS:
COIN WASH
IT'S THE ONLY POSSIBLE MATCH FOR THE CLUB SHONTIQUE.

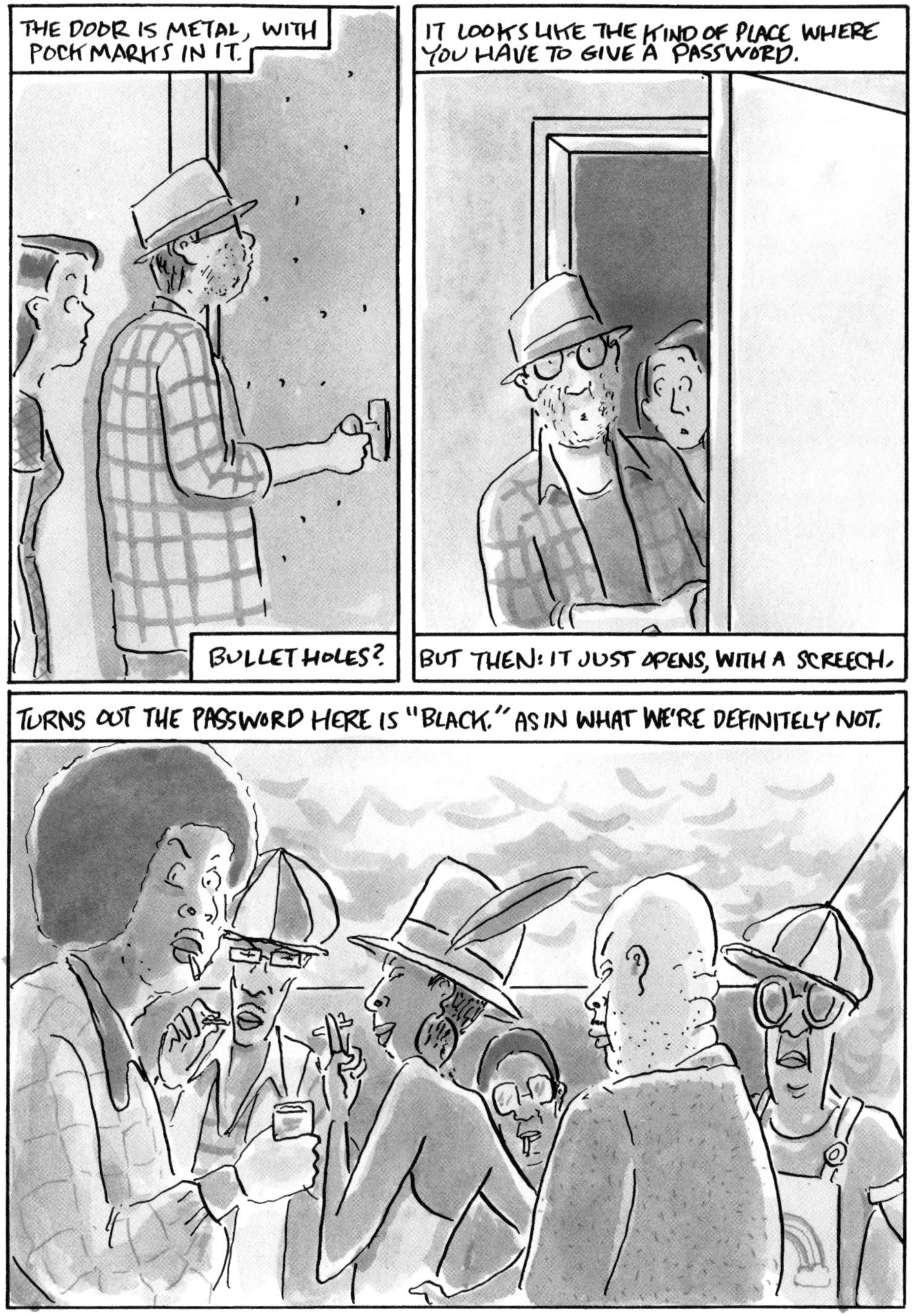
THE DOOR IS METAL, WITH POCKMARKS IN IT.
BULLET HOLES?
IT LOOKS LIKE THE KIND OF PLACE WHERE YOU HAVE TO GIVE A PASSWORD.
BUT THEN: IT JUST OPENS, WITH A SCREECH.
TURNS OUT THE PASSWORD HERE IS "BLACK." AS IN WHAT WE'RE DEFINITELY NOT.

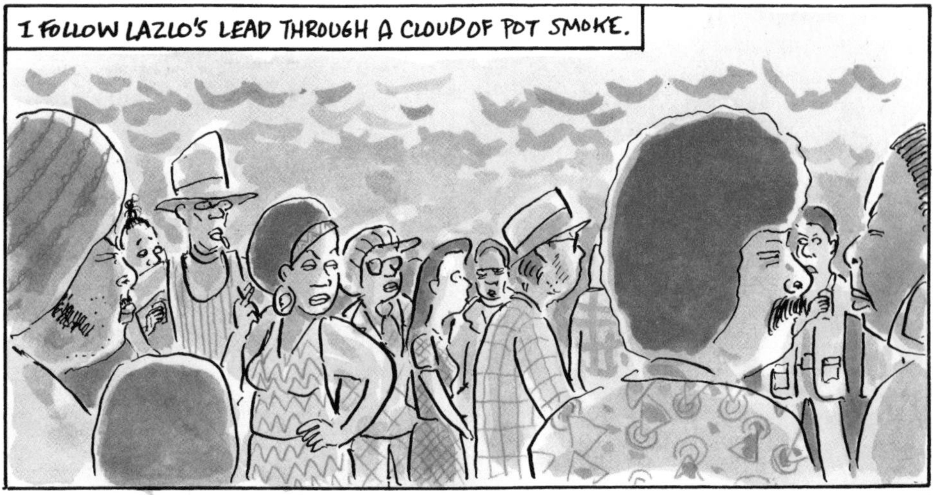
I FOLLOW LAZLO'S LEAD THROUGH A CLOUD OF POT SMOKE.

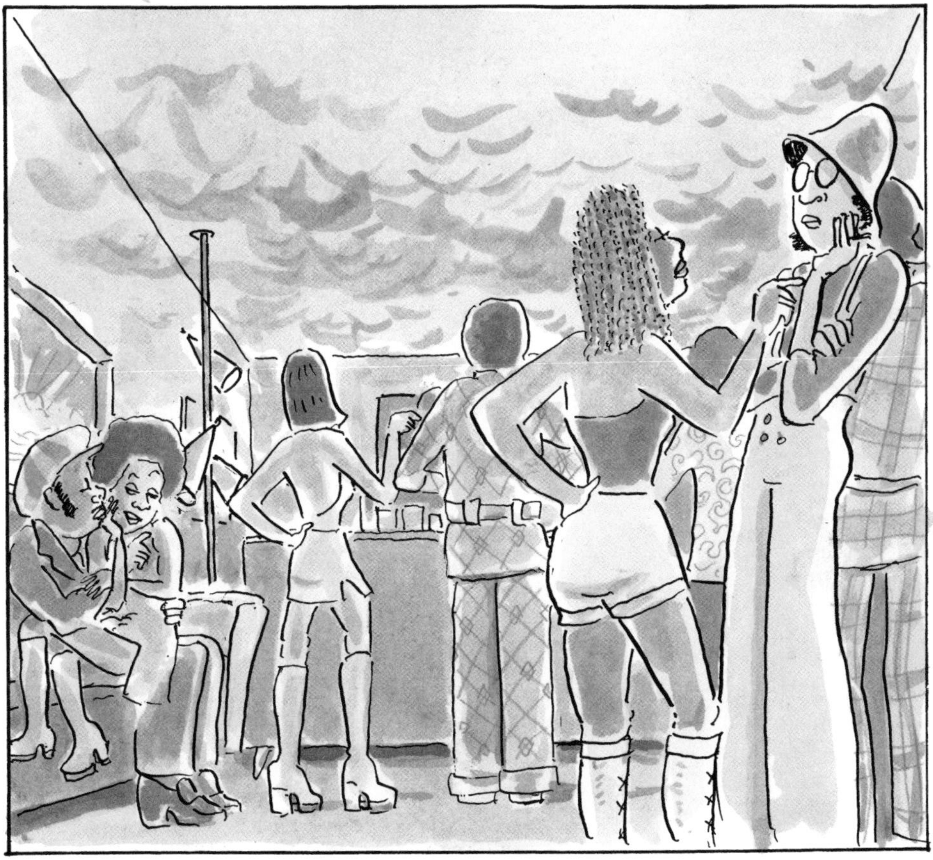

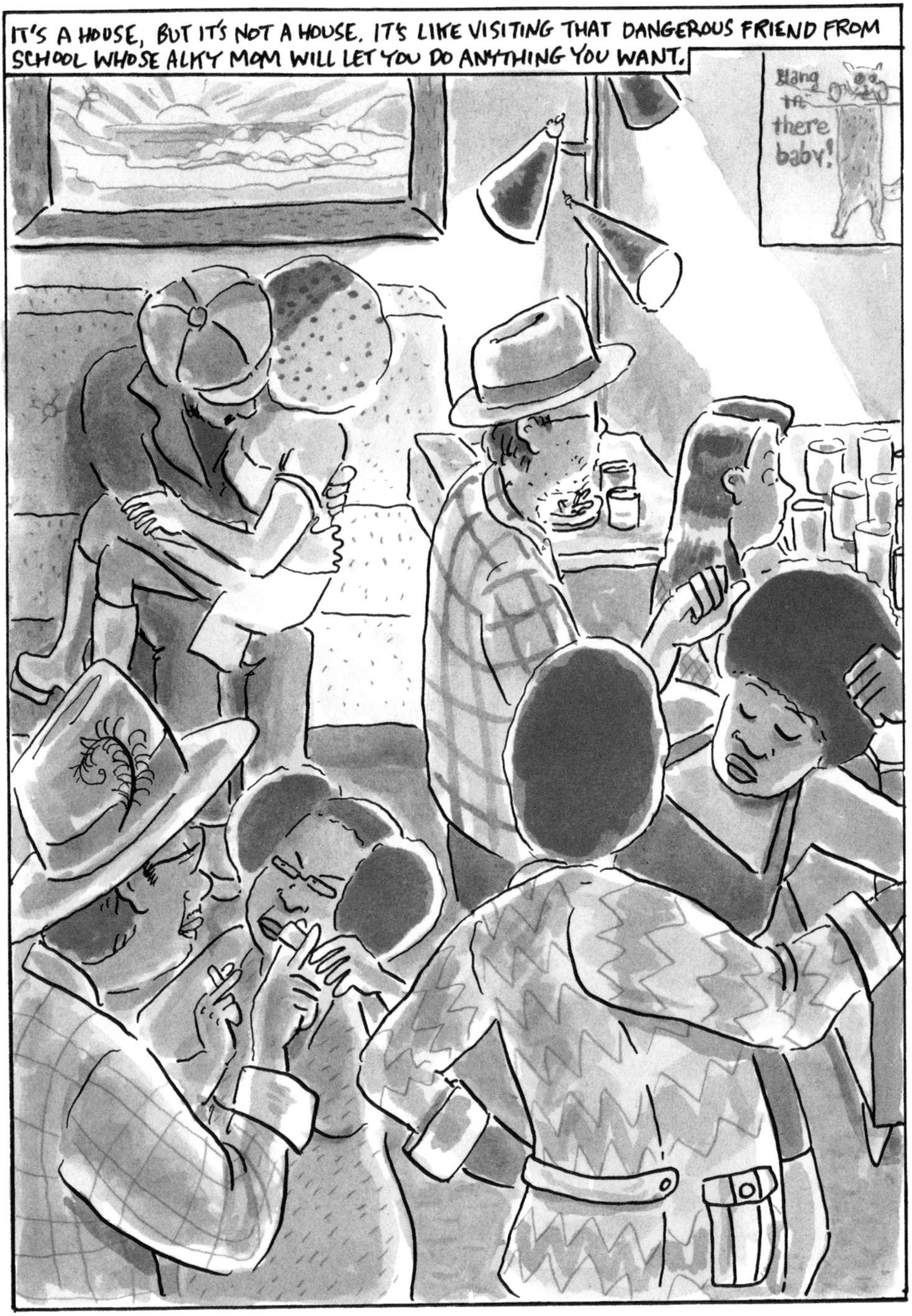
IT'S A HOUSE, BUT IT'S NOT A HOUSE. IT'S LIKE VISITING THAT DANGEROUS FRIEND FROM SCHOOL WHOSE ALKY MOM WILL LET YOU DO ANYTHING YOU WANT.
Hang in there baby!

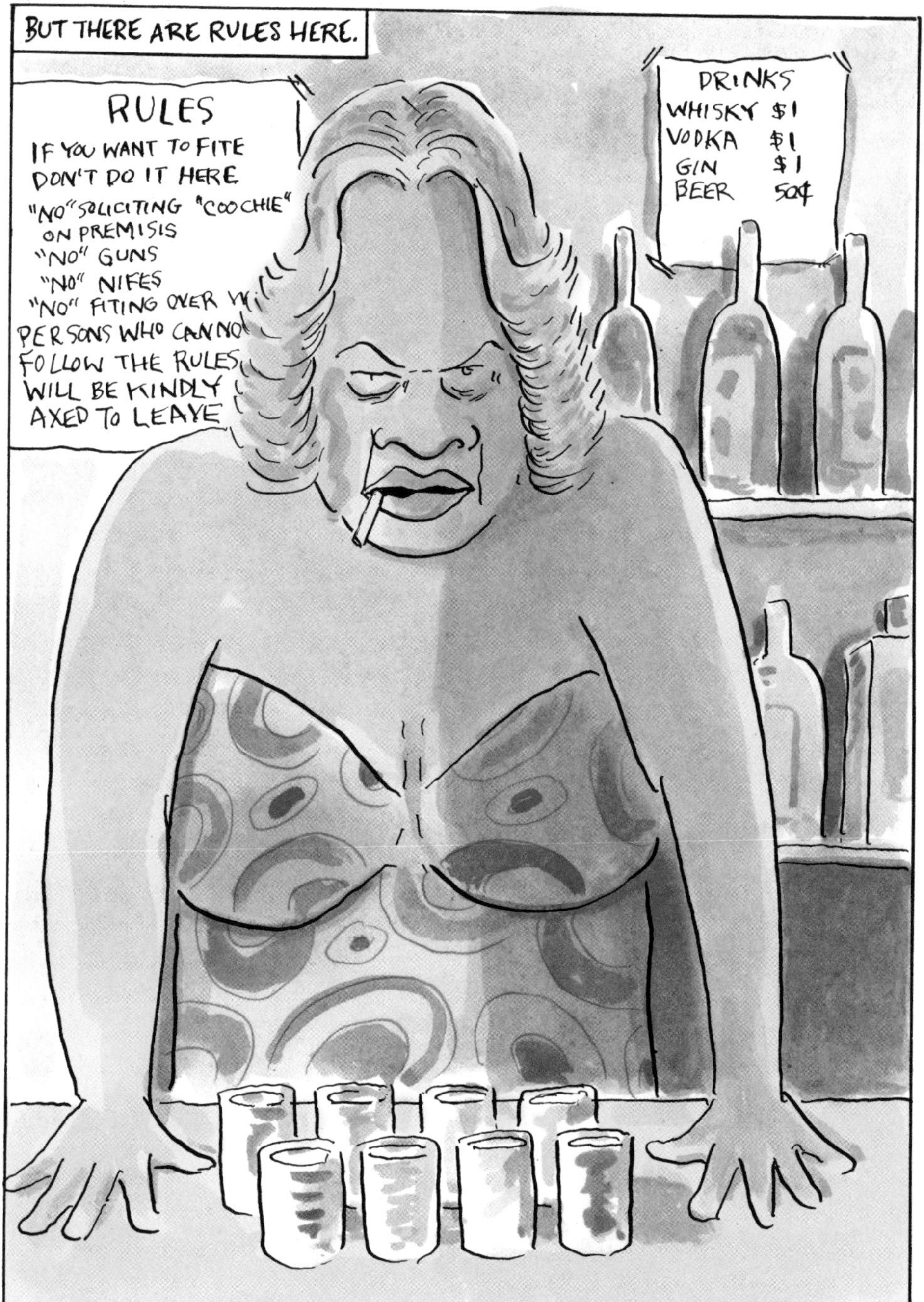
BUT THERE ARE RULES HERE.
RULES
IF YOU WANT TO FITE
DON'T DO IT HERE
"NO" SOLICITING "COOCHIE"
ON PREMISIS
"NO" GUNS
"NO" NIFES
"NO" FITING OVER
PERSONS WHO CANNO
FOLLOW THE RULES
WILL BE KINDLY
AXED TO LEAVE
DRINKS
WHISKY $1
VODKA $1
GIN $1
BEER 50¢

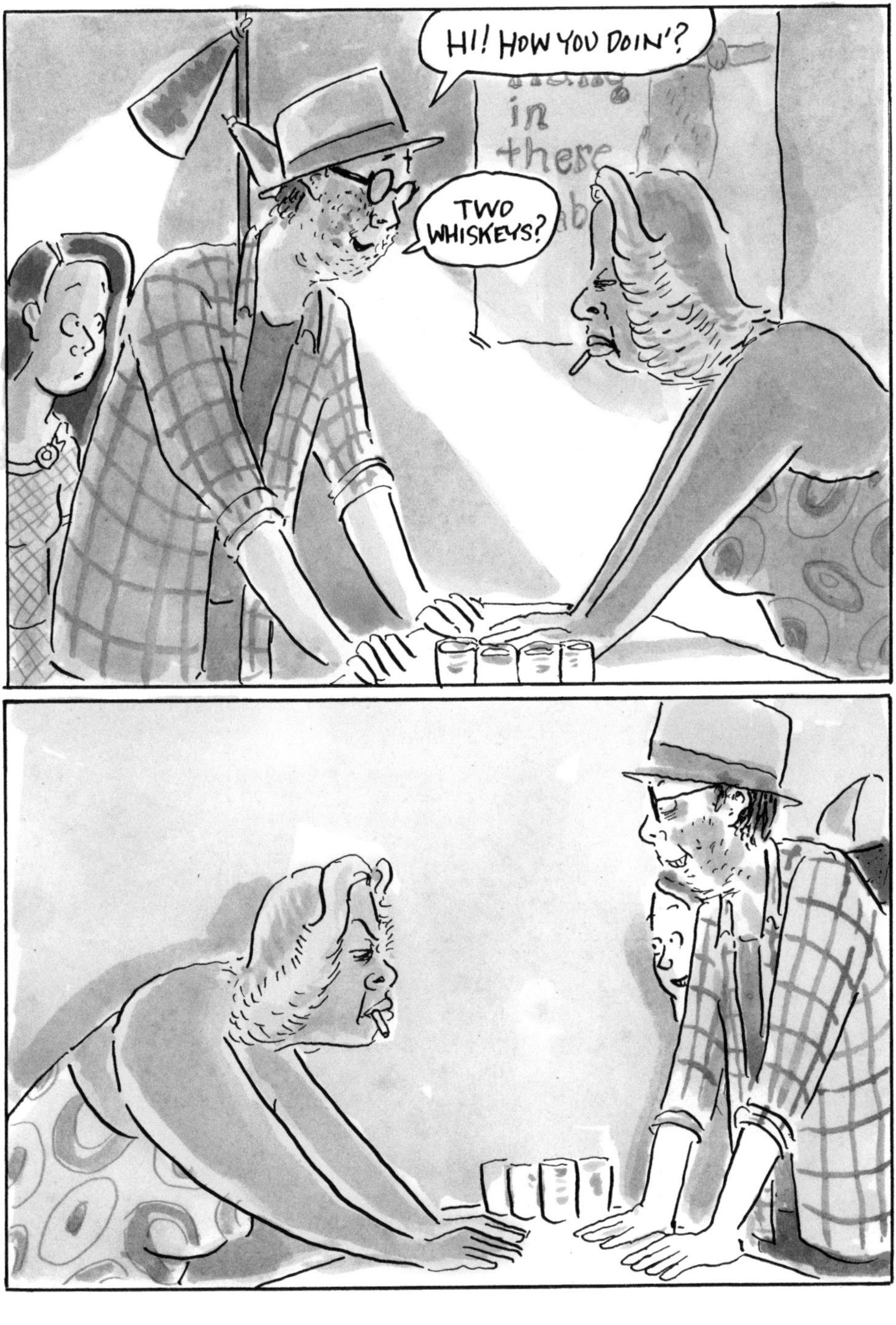
HI! HOW YOU DOIN'?
TWO WHISKEYS?

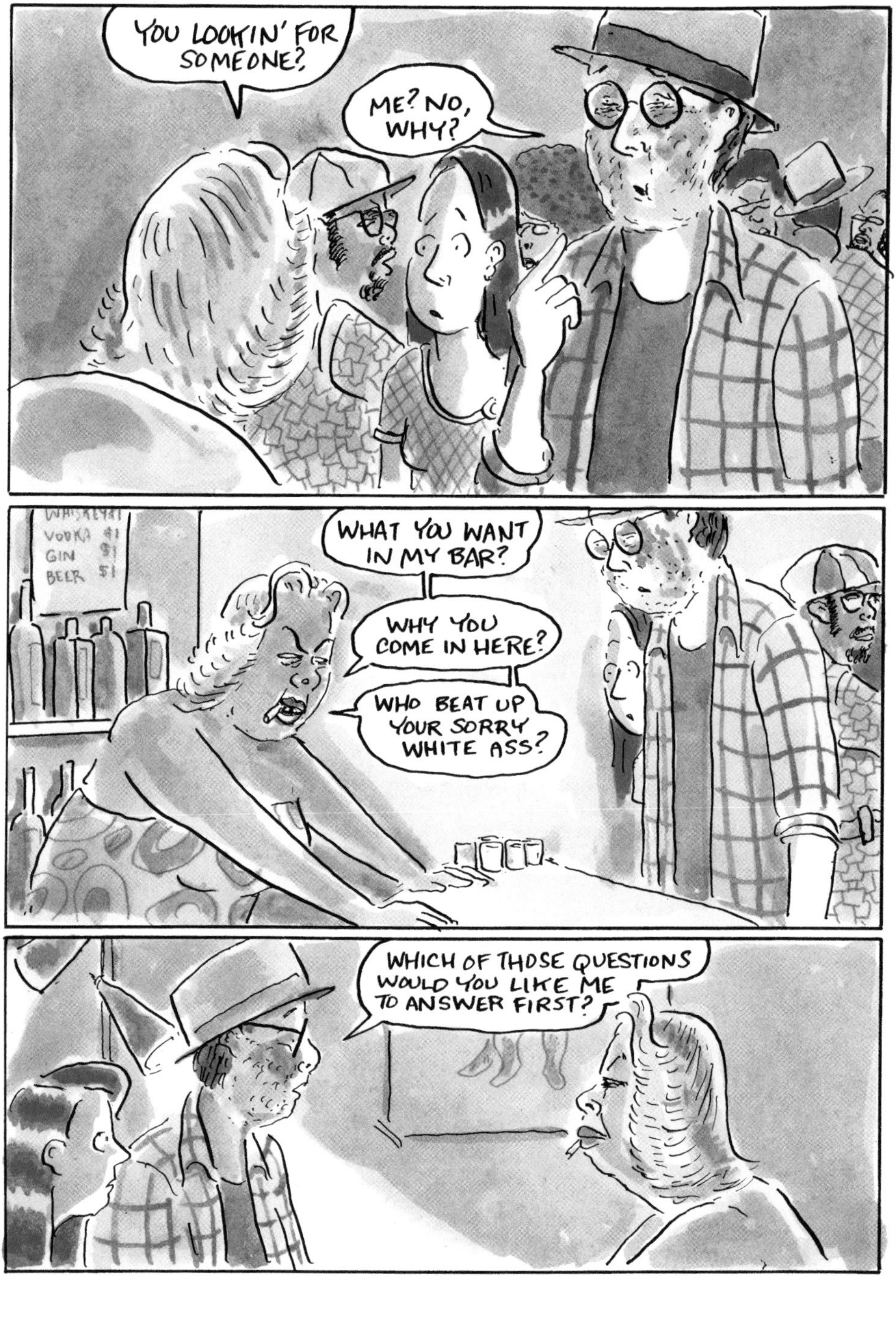
YOU LOOKIN' FOR SOMEONE?
ME? NO, WHY?
VODKA $1
GIN $1
BEER $1
WHAT YOU WANT IN MY BAR?
WHY YOU COME IN HERE?
WHO BEAT UP YOUR SORRY WHITE ASS?
WHICH OF THOSE QUESTIONS WOULD YOU LIKE ME TO ANSWER FIRST?

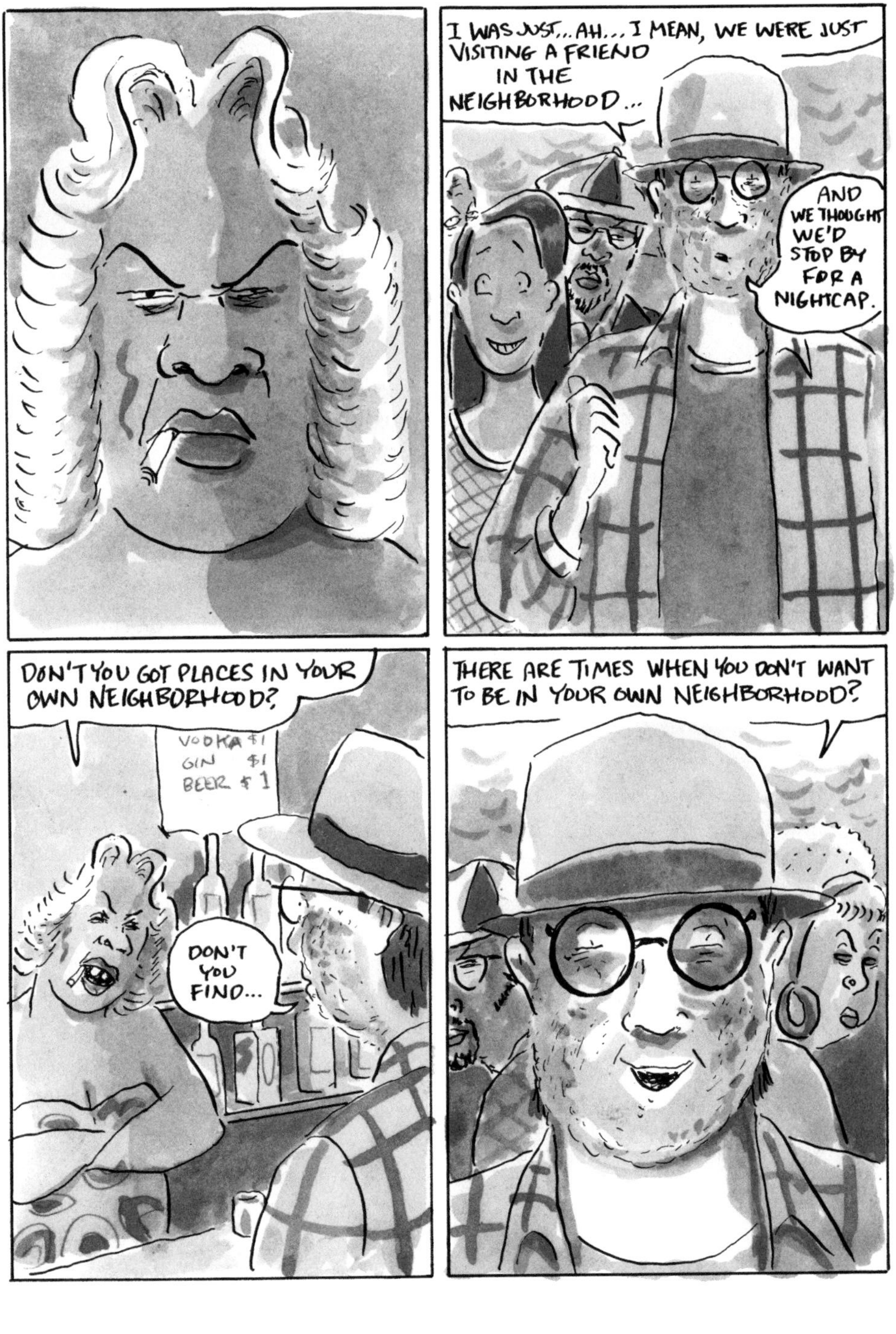
I WAS JUST... AH... I MEAN, WE WERE JUST VISITING A FRIEND IN THE NEIGHBORHOOD...
AND WE THOUGHT WE'D STOP BY FOR A NIGHTCAP.
DON'T YOU GOT PLACES IN YOUR OWN NEIGHBORHOOD?
VODKA $1
GIN $1
BEER $1
DON'T YOU FIND...
THERE ARE TIMES WHEN YOU DON'T WANT TO BE IN YOUR OWN NEIGHBORHOOD?

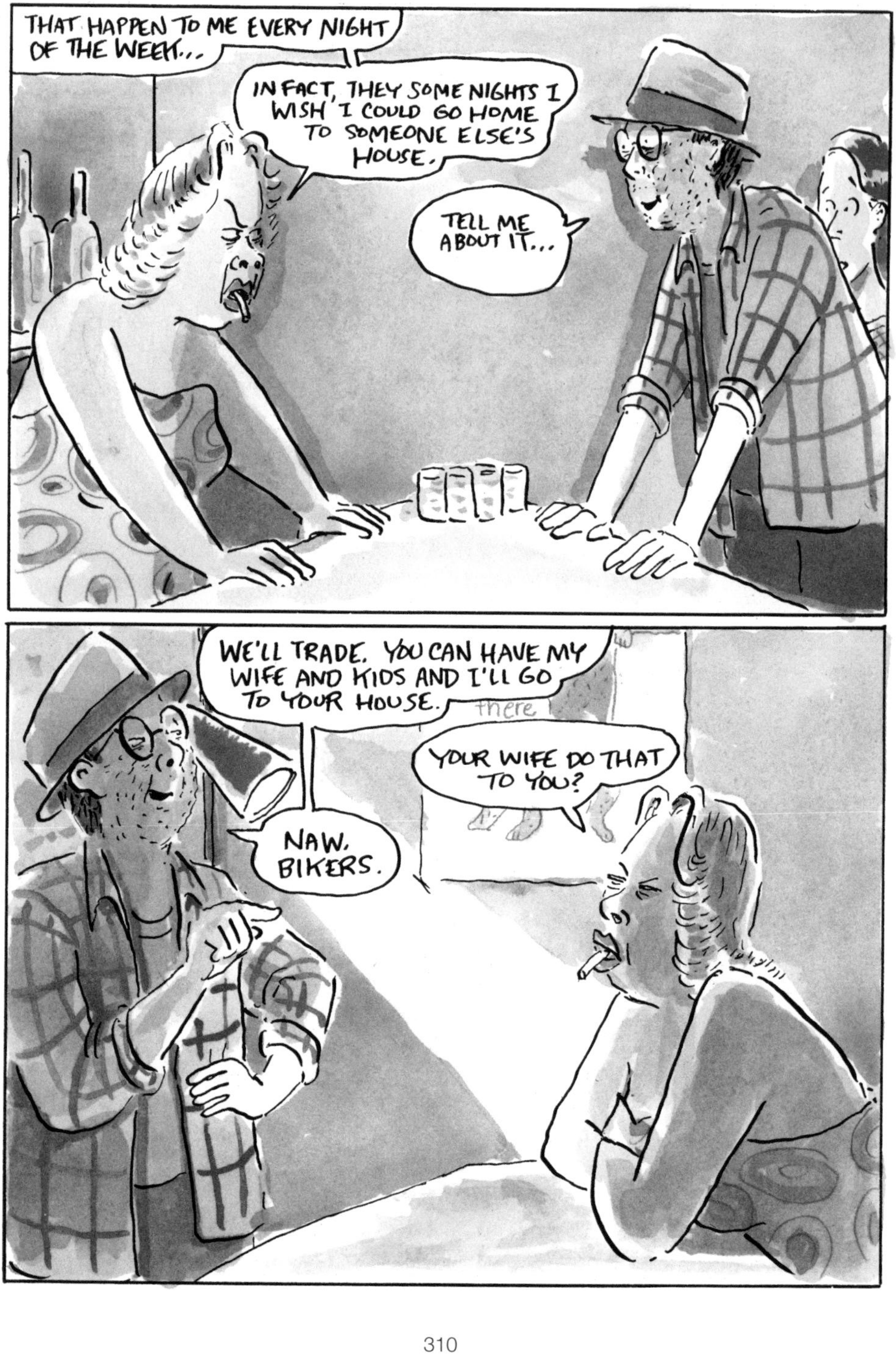
THAT HAPPEN TO ME EVERY NIGHT OF THE WEEK...
IN FACT, THEY SOME NIGHTS I WISH I COULD GO HOME TO SOMEONE ELSE'S HOUSE.
TELL ME ABOUT IT...
WE'LL TRADE. YOU CAN HAVE MY WIFE AND KIDS AND I'LL GO TO YOUR HOUSE.
there
YOUR WIFE DO THAT TO YOU?
NAW. BIKERS.

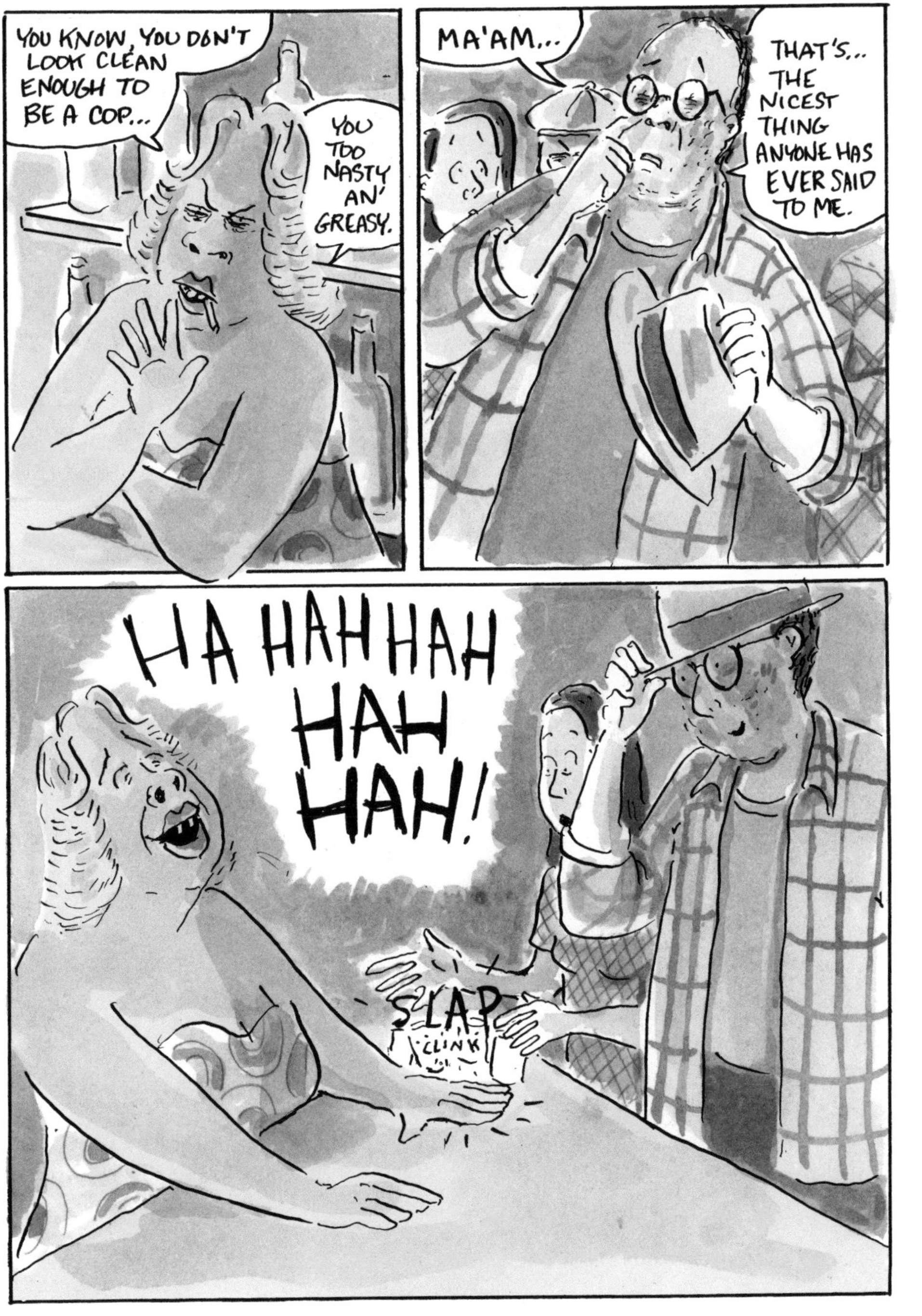
YOU KNOW, YOU DON'T LOOK CLEAN ENOUGH TO BE A COP...
YOU TOO NASTY AN' GREASY.
MA'AM...
THAT'S... THE NICEST THING ANYONE HAS EVER SAID TO ME.
HA HAHHAH HAH HAH!
SLAP
CLINK

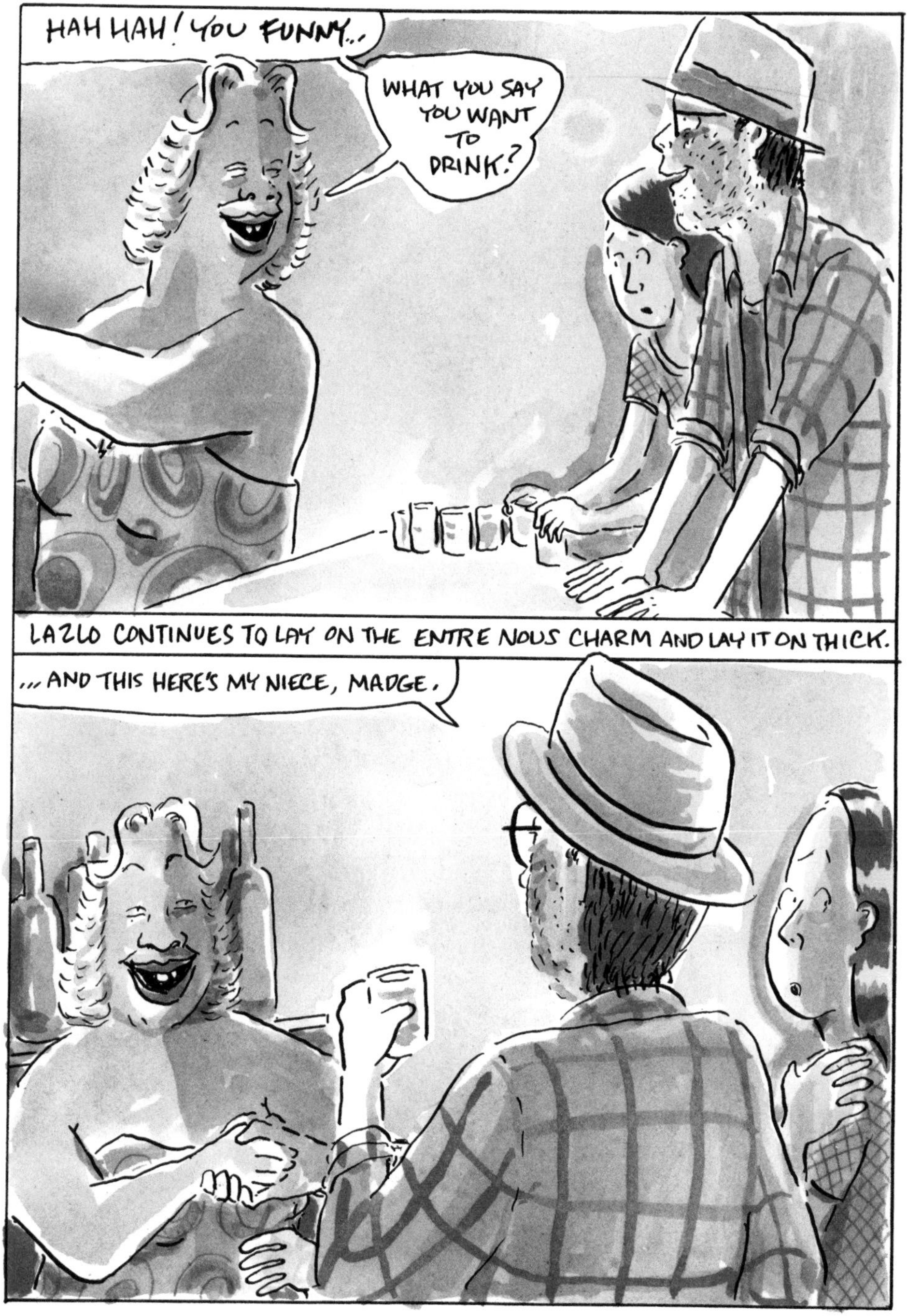
HAH HAH! YOU FUNNY..
WHAT YOU SAY YOU WANT TO DRINK?
LAZLO CONTINUES TO LAY ON THE ENTRE NOUS CHARM AND LAY IT ON THICK.
... AND THIS HERE'S MY NIECE, MADGE.

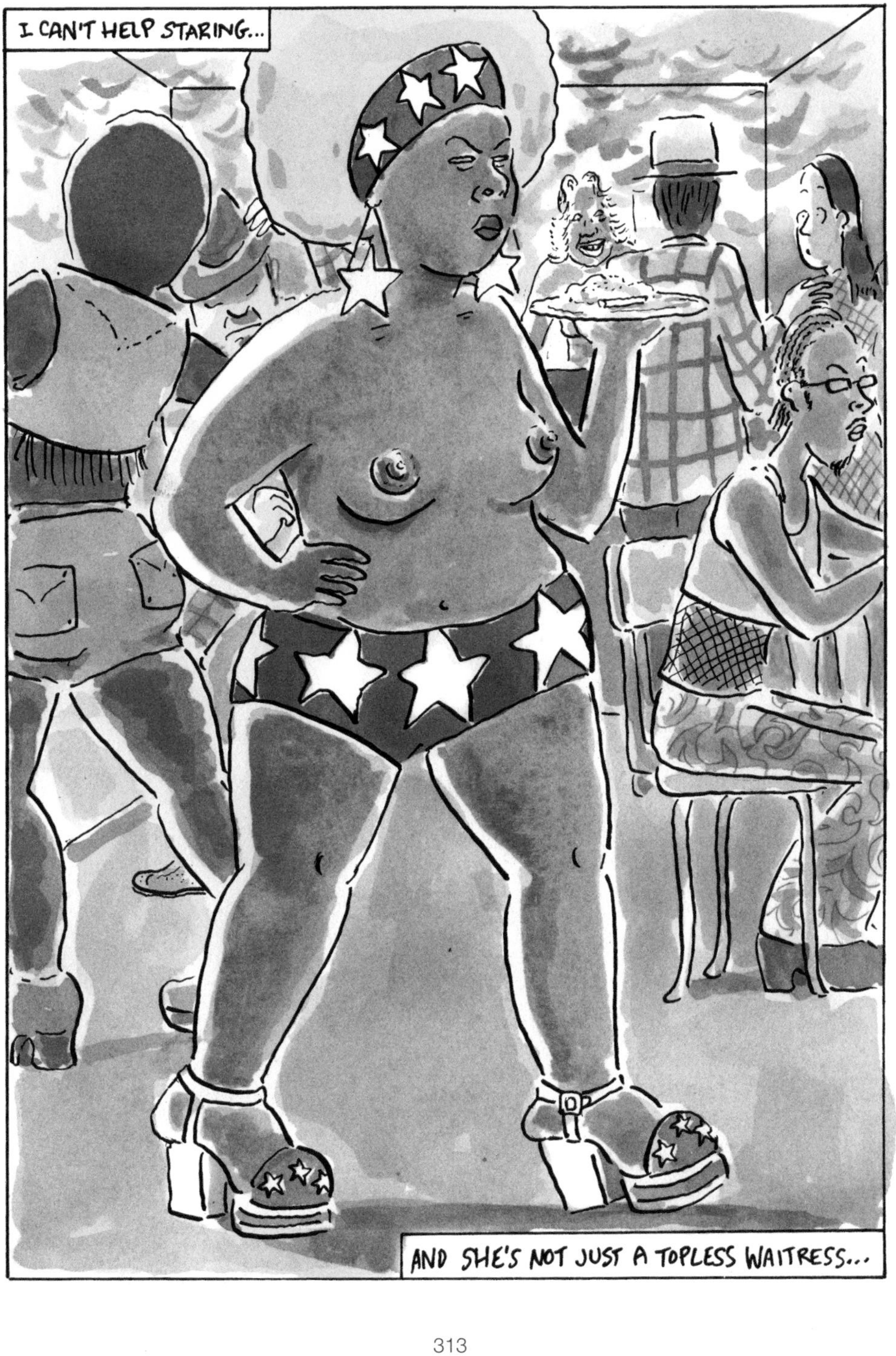
I CAN'T HELP STARING...
AND SHE'S NOT JUST A TOPLESS WAITRESS...

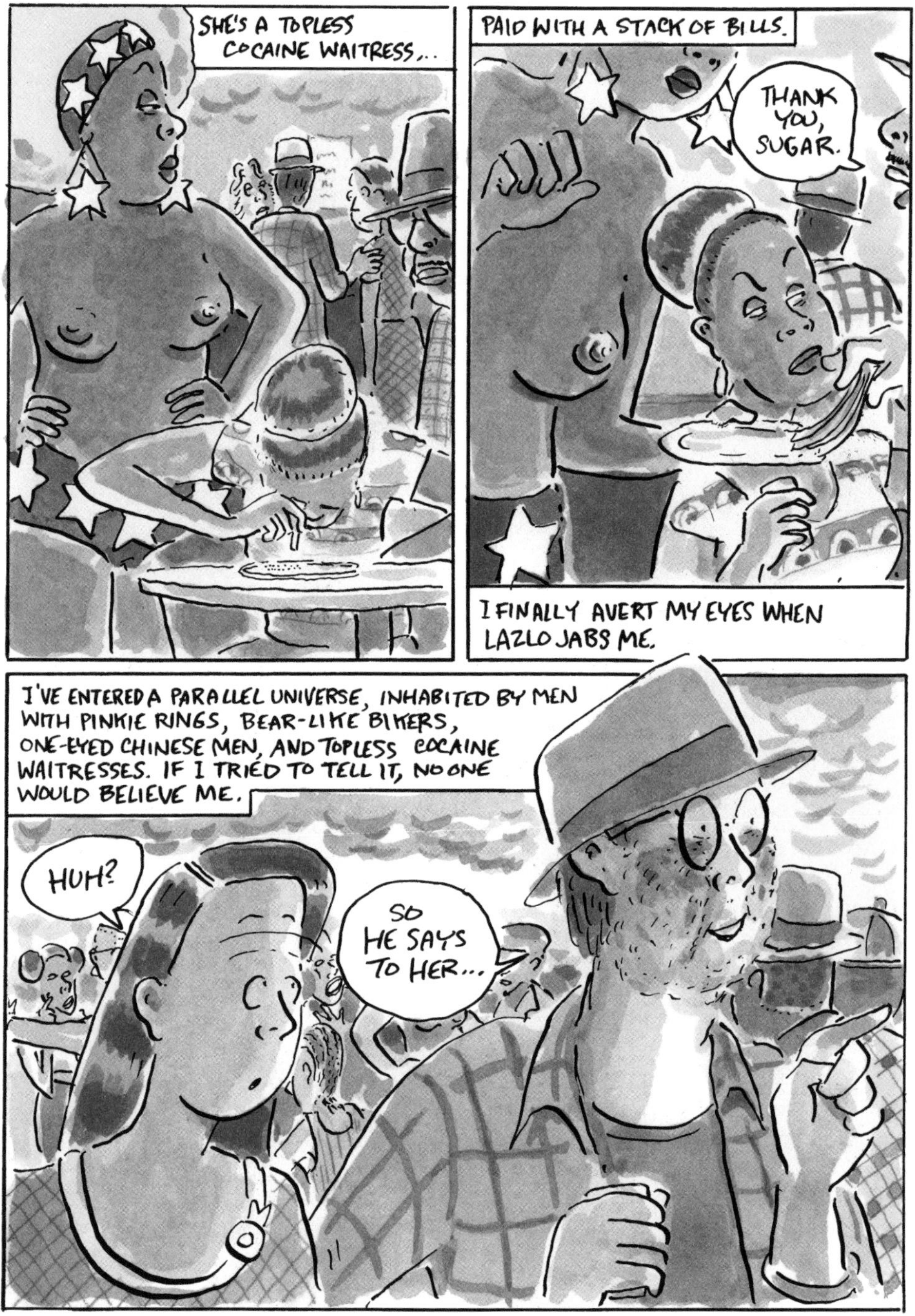
SHE'S A TOPLESS COCAINE WAITRESS...
PAID WITH A STACK OF BILLS.
THANK YOU, SUGAR.
I FINALLY AVERT MY EYES WHEN LAZLO JABS ME.
I'VE ENTERED A PARALLEL UNIVERSE, INHABITED BY MEN WITH PINKIE RINGS, BEAR-LIKE BIKERS, ONE-EYED CHINESE MEN, AND TOPLESS COCAINE WAITRESSES. IF I TRIED TO TELL IT, NO ONE WOULD BELIEVE ME.
HUH?
SO HE SAYS TO HER...

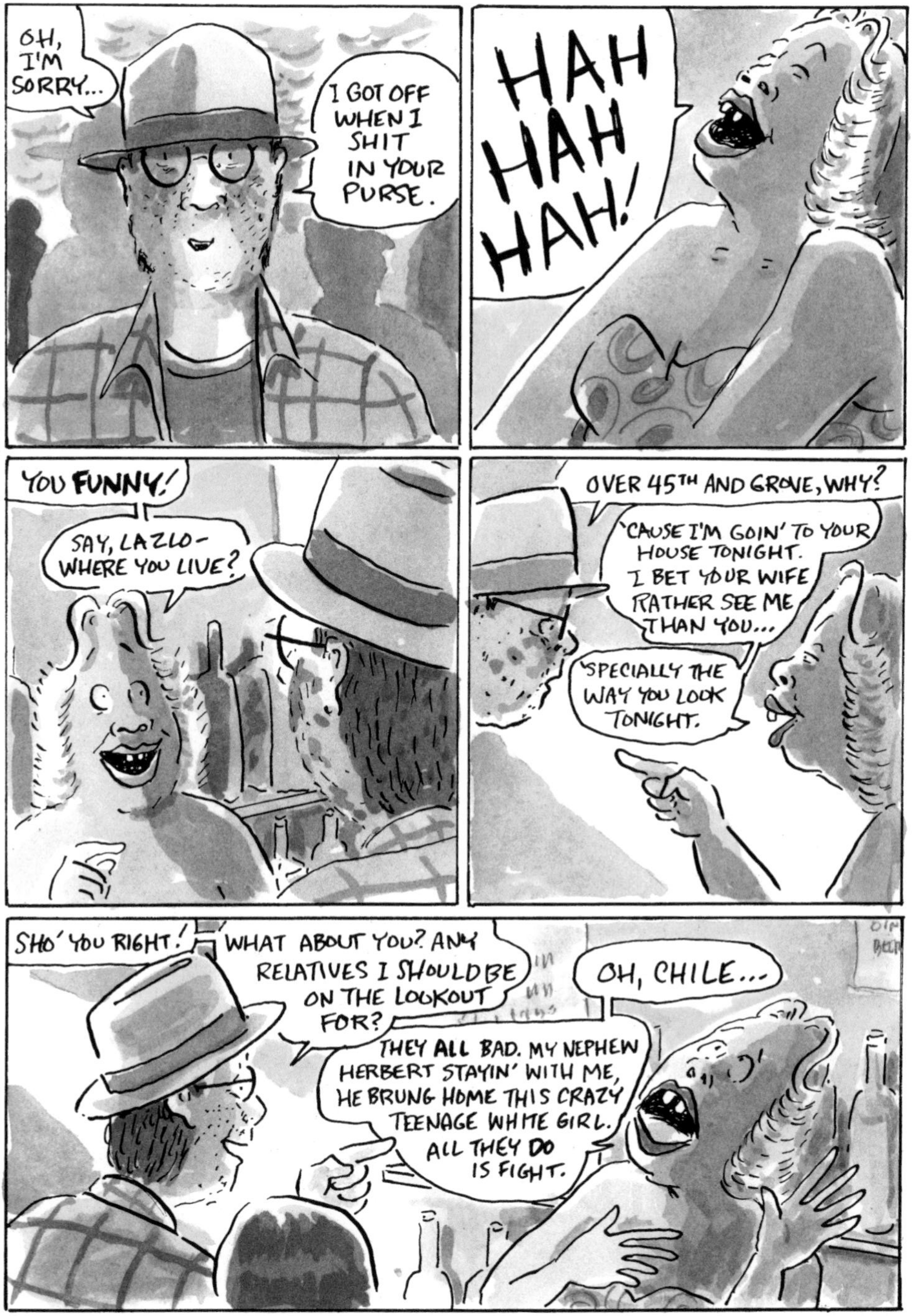
OH, I'M SORRY...
I GOT OFF WHEN I SHIT IN YOUR PURSE.
HAH HAH HAH!
YOU FUNNY!
SAY, LAZLO- WHERE YOU LIVE?
OVER 45TH AND GROVE, WHY?
'CAUSE I'M GOIN' TO YOUR HOUSE TONIGHT. I BET YOUR WIFE RATHER SEE ME THAN YOU...
'SPECIALLY THE WAY YOU LOOK TONIGHT.
SHO' YOU RIGHT!
WHAT ABOUT YOU? ANY RELATIVES I SHOULD BE ON THE LOOKOUT FOR?
OH, CHILE...
THEY ALL BAD. MY NEPHEW HERBERT STAYIN' WITH ME, HE BRUNG HOME THIS CRAZY TEENAGE WHITE GIRL. ALL THEY DO IS FIGHT.

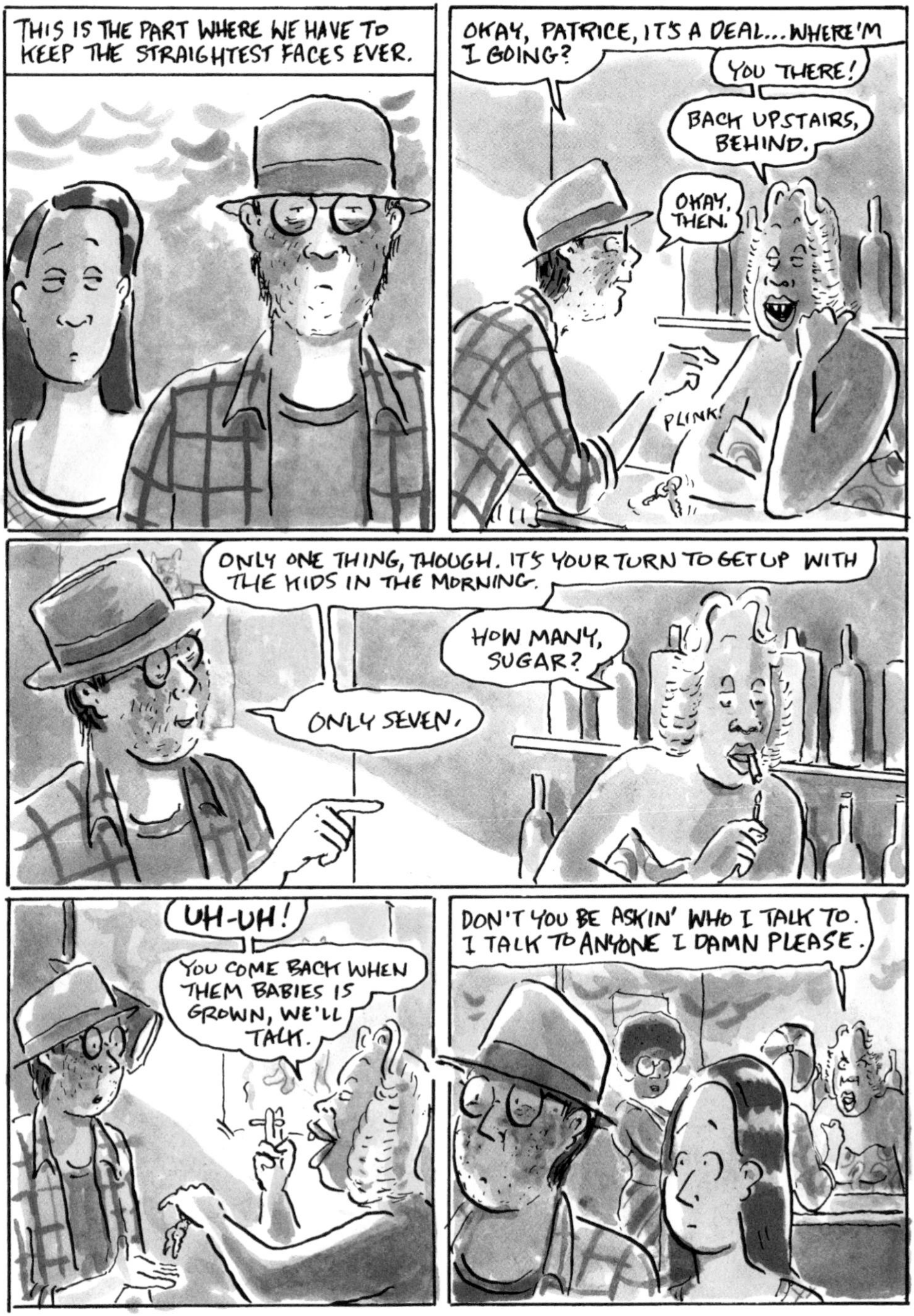
THIS IS THE PART WHERE WE HAVE TO KEEP THE STRAIGHTEST FACES EVER.
OKAY, PATRICE, IT'S A DEAL... WHERE'M I GOING?
YOU THERE!
BACK UPSTAIRS, BEHIND.
OKAY, THEN.
PLINK!
ONLY ONE THING, THOUGH. IT'S YOUR TURN TO GET UP WITH THE KIDS IN THE MORNING.
HOW MANY, SUGAR?
ONLY SEVEN.
UH-UH!
YOU COME BACK WHEN THEM BABIES IS GROWN, WE'LL TALK.
DON'T YOU BE ASKIN' WHO I TALK TO. I TALK TO ANYONE I DAMN PLEASE.

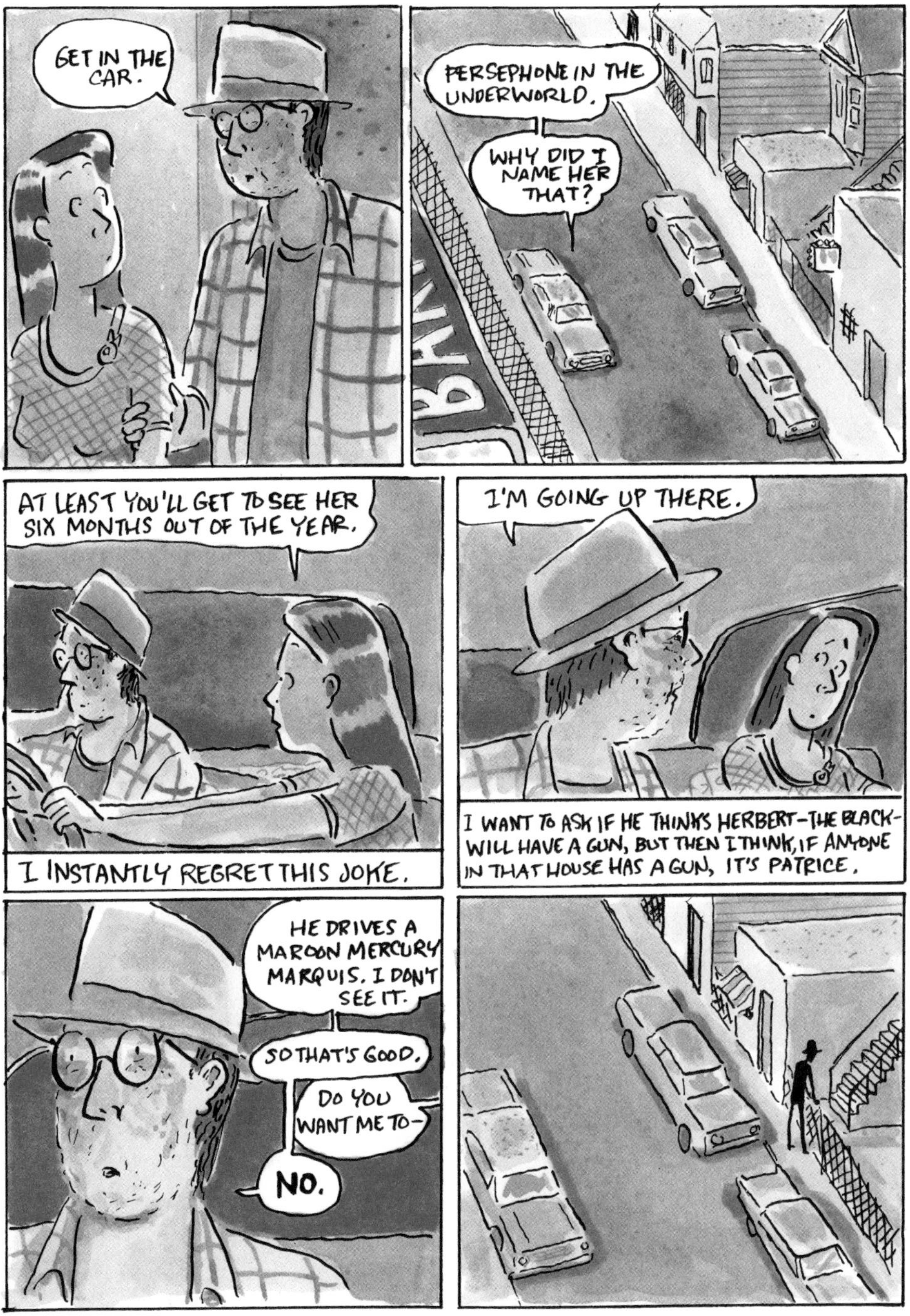
GET IN THE CAR.
PERSEPHONE IN THE UNDERWORLD.
WHY DID I NAME HER THAT?
AT LEAST YOU'LL GET TO SEE HER SIX MONTHS OUT OF THE YEAR.
I INSTANTLY REGRET THIS JOKE.
I'M GOING UP THERE.
I WANT TO ASK IF HE THINKS HERBERT—THE BLACK—WILL HAVE A GUN, BUT THEN I THINK, IF ANYONE IN THAT HOUSE HAS A GUN, IT'S PATRICE.
HE DRIVES A MAROON MERCURY MARQUIS. I DON'T SEE IT.
SO THAT'S GOOD.
DO YOU WANT ME TO—
NO.

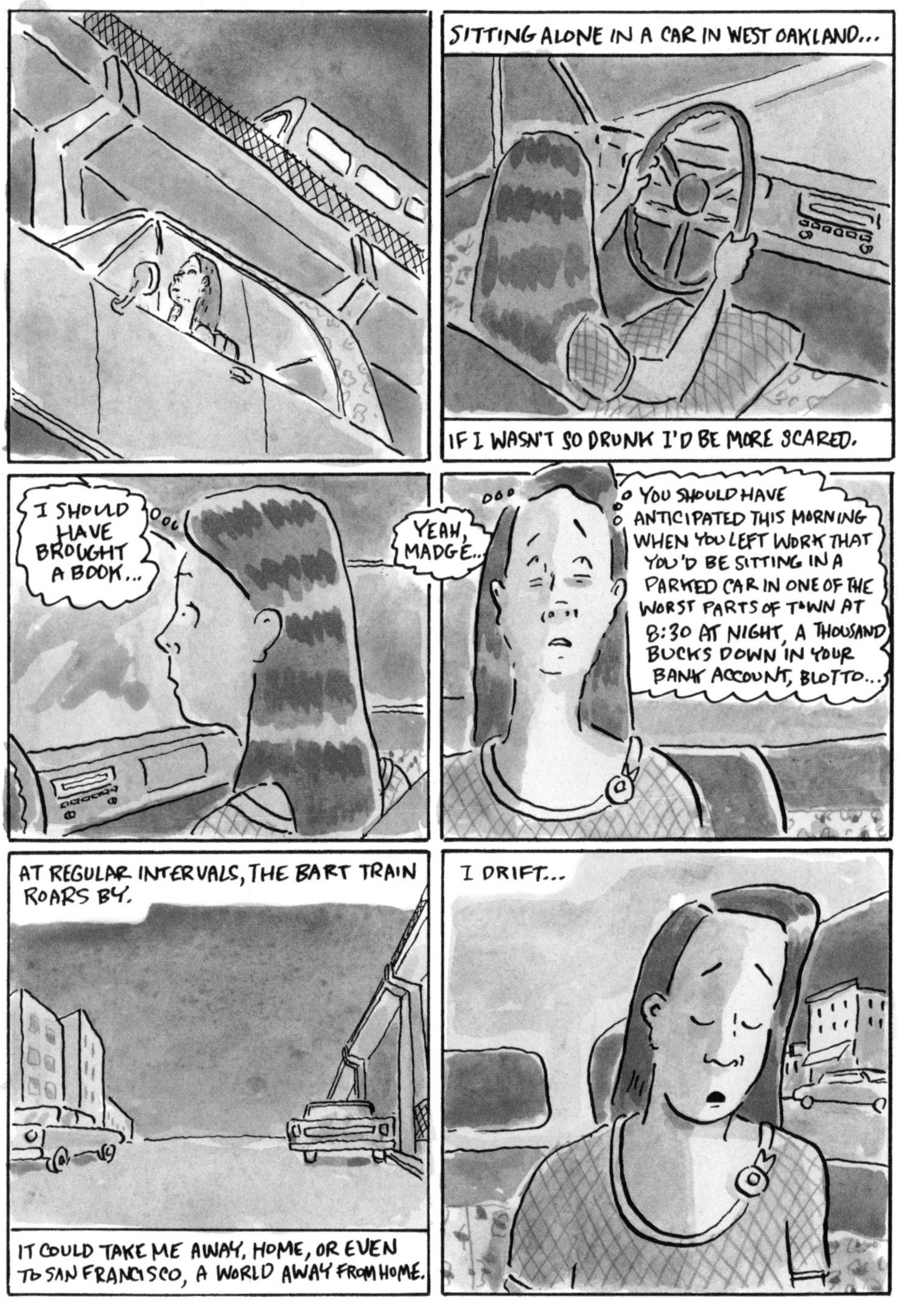
SITTING ALONE IN A CAR IN WEST OAKLAND...
IF I WASN'T SO DRUNK I'D BE MORE SCARED.
I SHOULD HAVE BROUGHT A BOOK...
YEAH, MADGE...
YOU SHOULD HAVE ANTICIPATED THIS MORNING WHEN YOU LEFT WORK THAT YOU'D BE SITTING IN A PARKED CAR IN ONE OF THE WORST PARTS OF TOWN AT 8:30 AT NIGHT, A THOUSAND BUCKS DOWN IN YOUR BANK ACCOUNT, BLOTTO...
AT REGULAR INTERVALS, THE BART TRAIN ROARS BY.
IT COULD TAKE ME AWAY, HOME, OR EVEN TO SAN FRANCISCO, A WORLD AWAY FROM HOME.
I DRIFT...

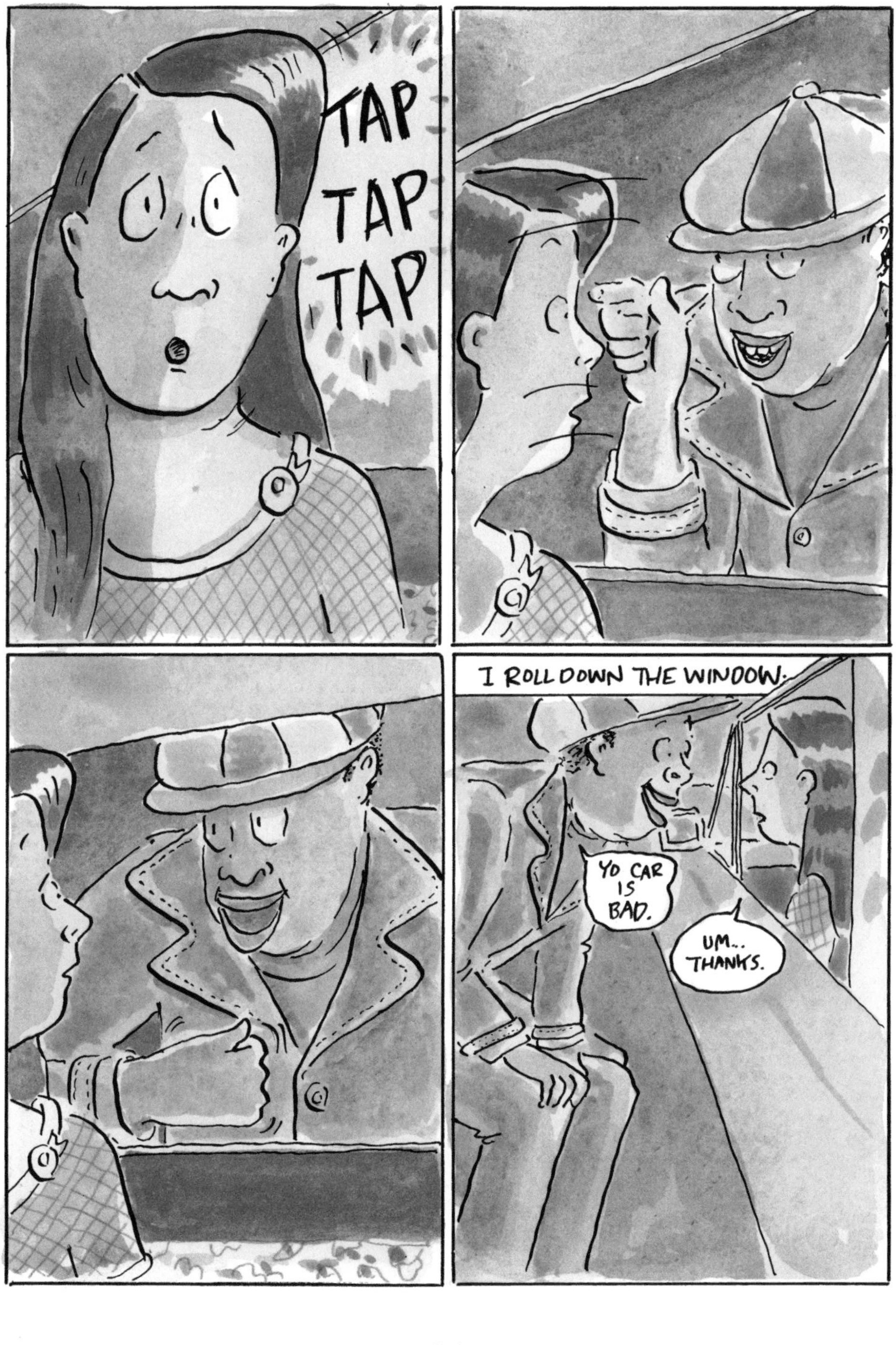
TAP
TAP
TAP
I ROLL DOWN THE WINDOW.
YO CAR IS BAD.
UM... THANKS.

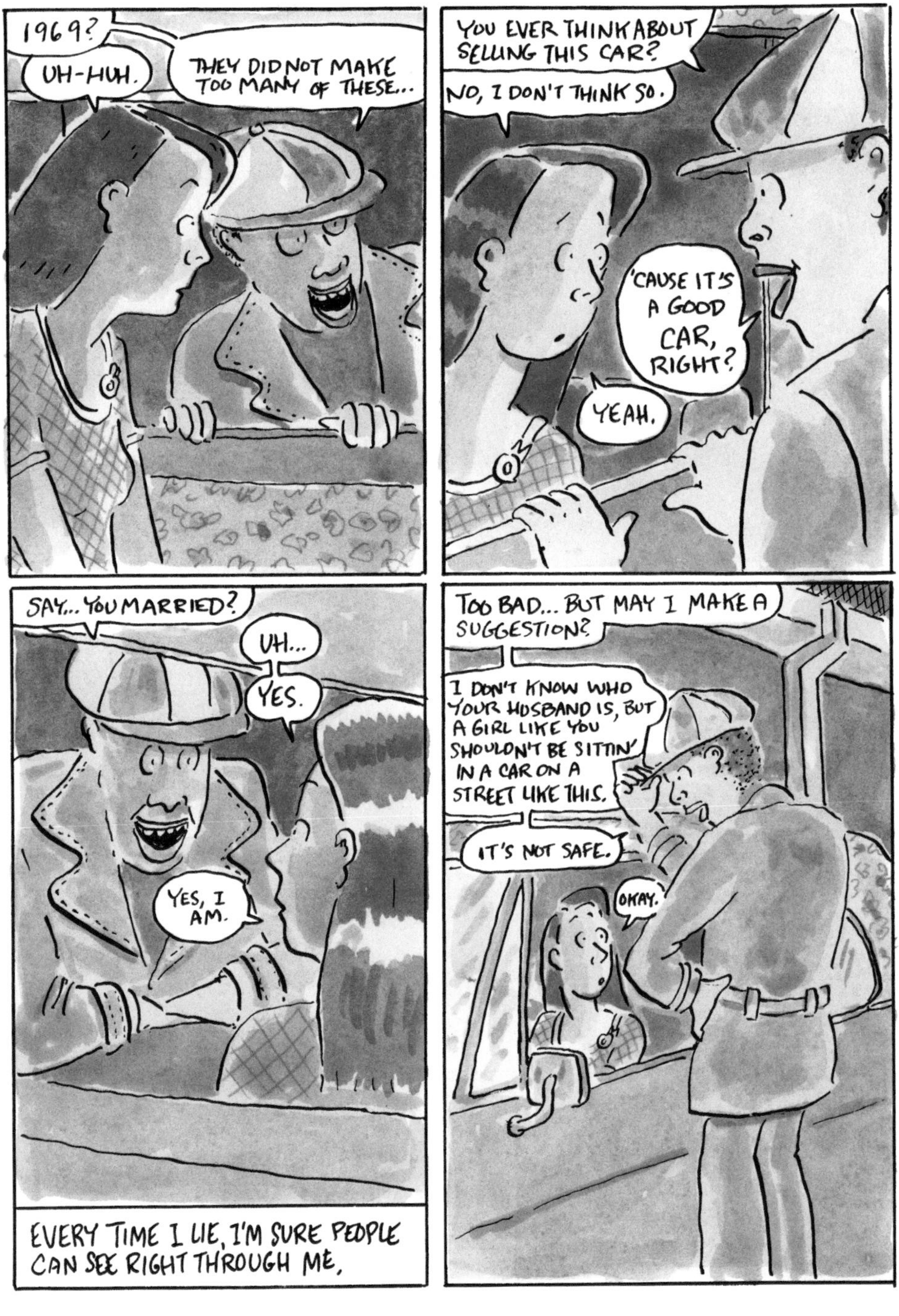
1969?
UH-HUH.
THEY DID NOT MAKE TOO MANY OF THESE...
YOU EVER THINK ABOUT SELLING THIS CAR?
NO, I DON'T THINK SO.
'CAUSE IT'S A GOOD CAR, RIGHT?
YEAH.
SAY... YOU MARRIED?
UH...
YES.
YES, I AM.
EVERY TIME I LIE, I'M SURE PEOPLE CAN SEE RIGHT THROUGH ME.
TOO BAD... BUT MAY I MAKE A SUGGESTION?
I DON'T KNOW WHO YOUR HUSBAND IS, BUT A GIRL LIKE YOU SHOULDN'T BE SITTIN' IN A CAR ON A STREET LIKE THIS.
IT'S NOT SAFE.
OKAY.

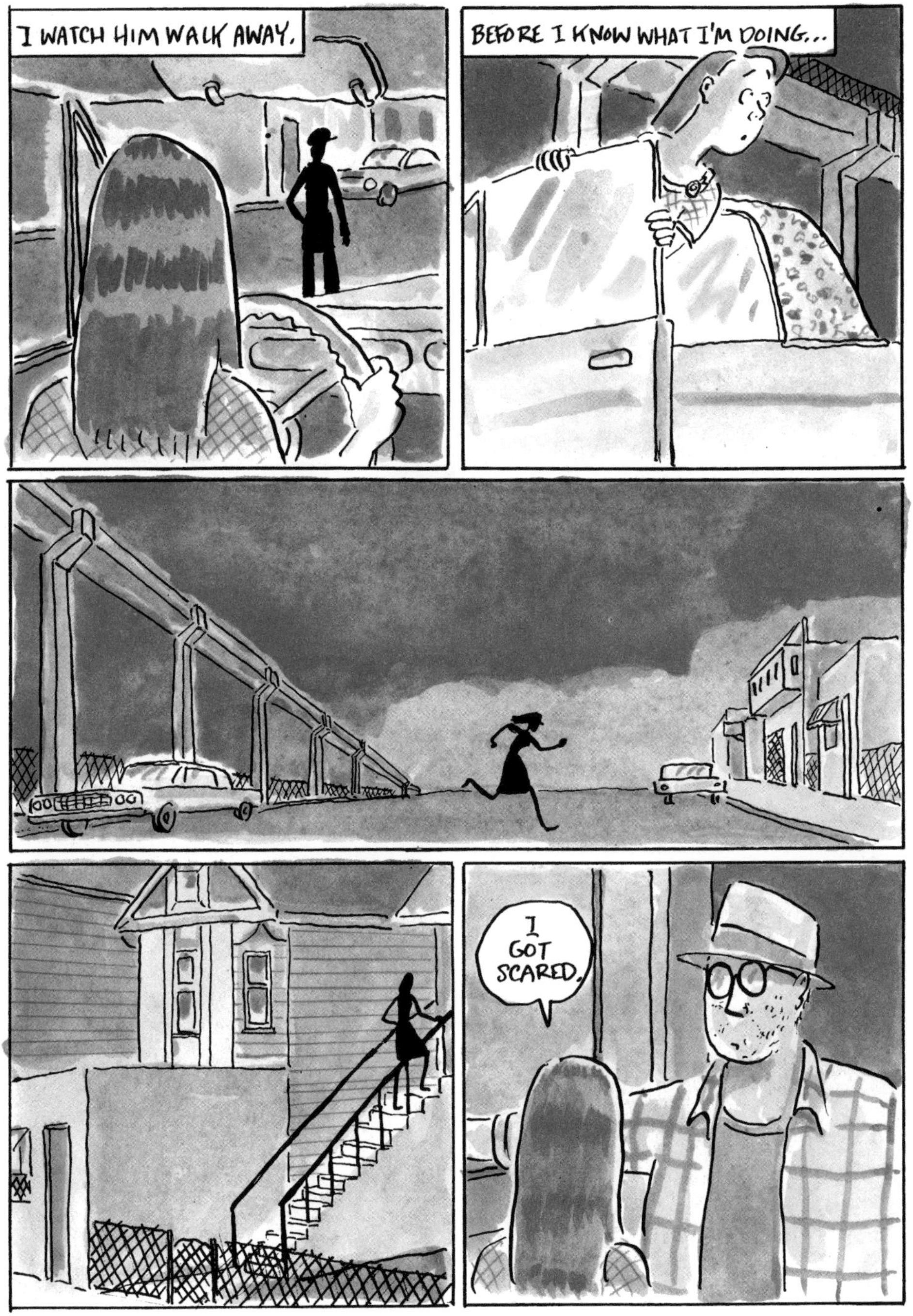
I WATCH HIM WALK AWAY.
BEFORE I KNOW WHAT I'M DOING...
I GOT SCARED.

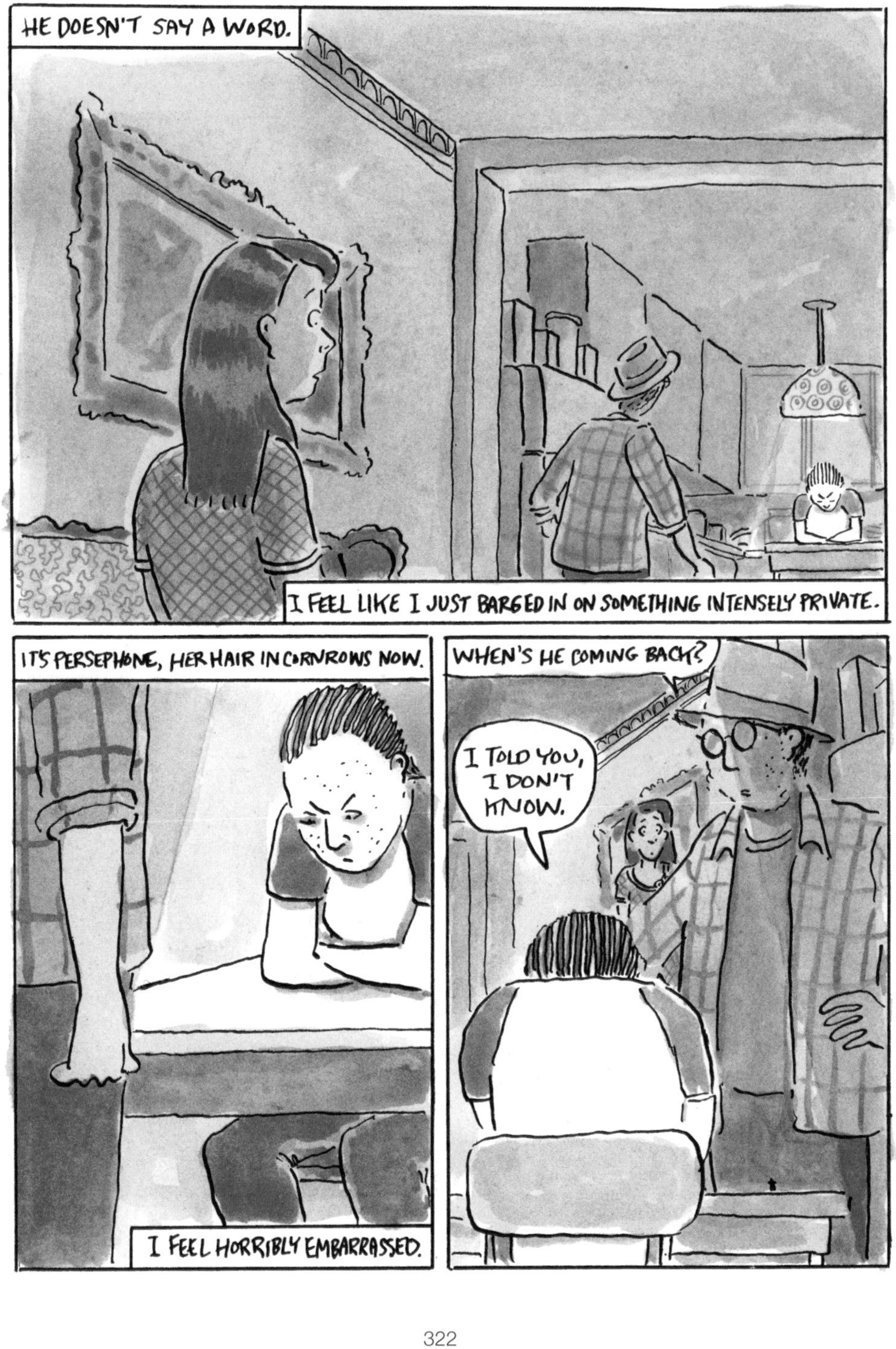
HE DOESN'T SAY A WORD.
I FEEL LIKE I JUST BARGED IN ON SOMETHING INTENSELY PRIVATE.
IT'S PERSEPHONE, HER HAIR IN CORNROWS NOW.
I FEEL HORRIBLY EMBARRASSED.
WHEN'S HE COMING BACK?
I TOLD YOU, I DON'T KNOW.

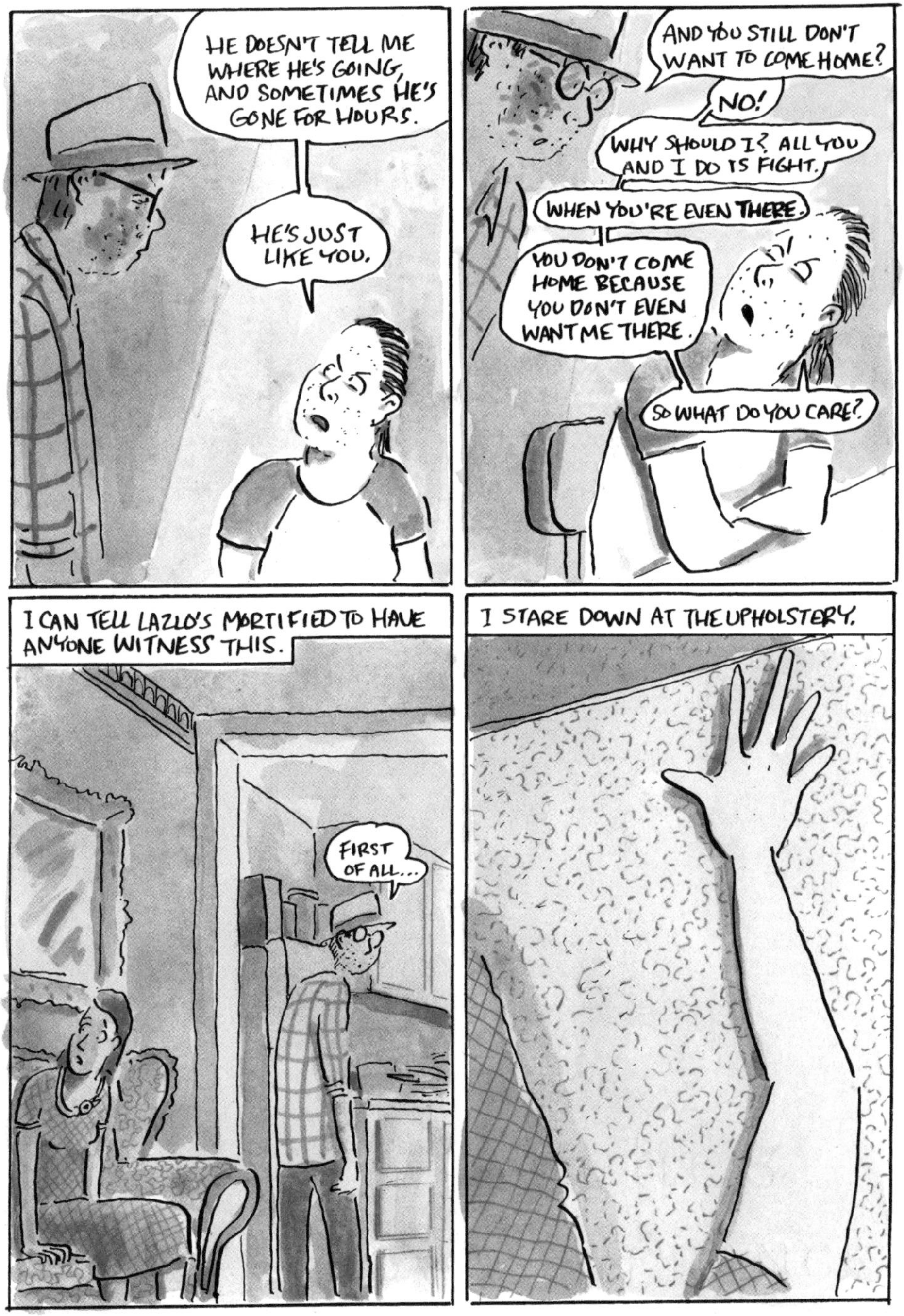
HE DOESN'T TELL ME WHERE HE'S GOING, AND SOMETIMES HE'S GONE FOR HOURS.
HE'S JUST LIKE YOU.
AND YOU STILL DON'T WANT TO COME HOME?
NO!
WHY SHOULD I? ALL YOU AND I DO IS FIGHT.
WHEN YOU'RE EVEN THERE.
YOU DON'T COME HOME BECAUSE YOU DON'T EVEN WANT ME THERE.
SO WHAT DO YOU CARE?
I CAN TELL LAZLO'S MORTIFIED TO HAVE ANYONE WITNESS THIS.
FIRST OF ALL...
I STARE DOWN AT THE UPHOLSTERY.

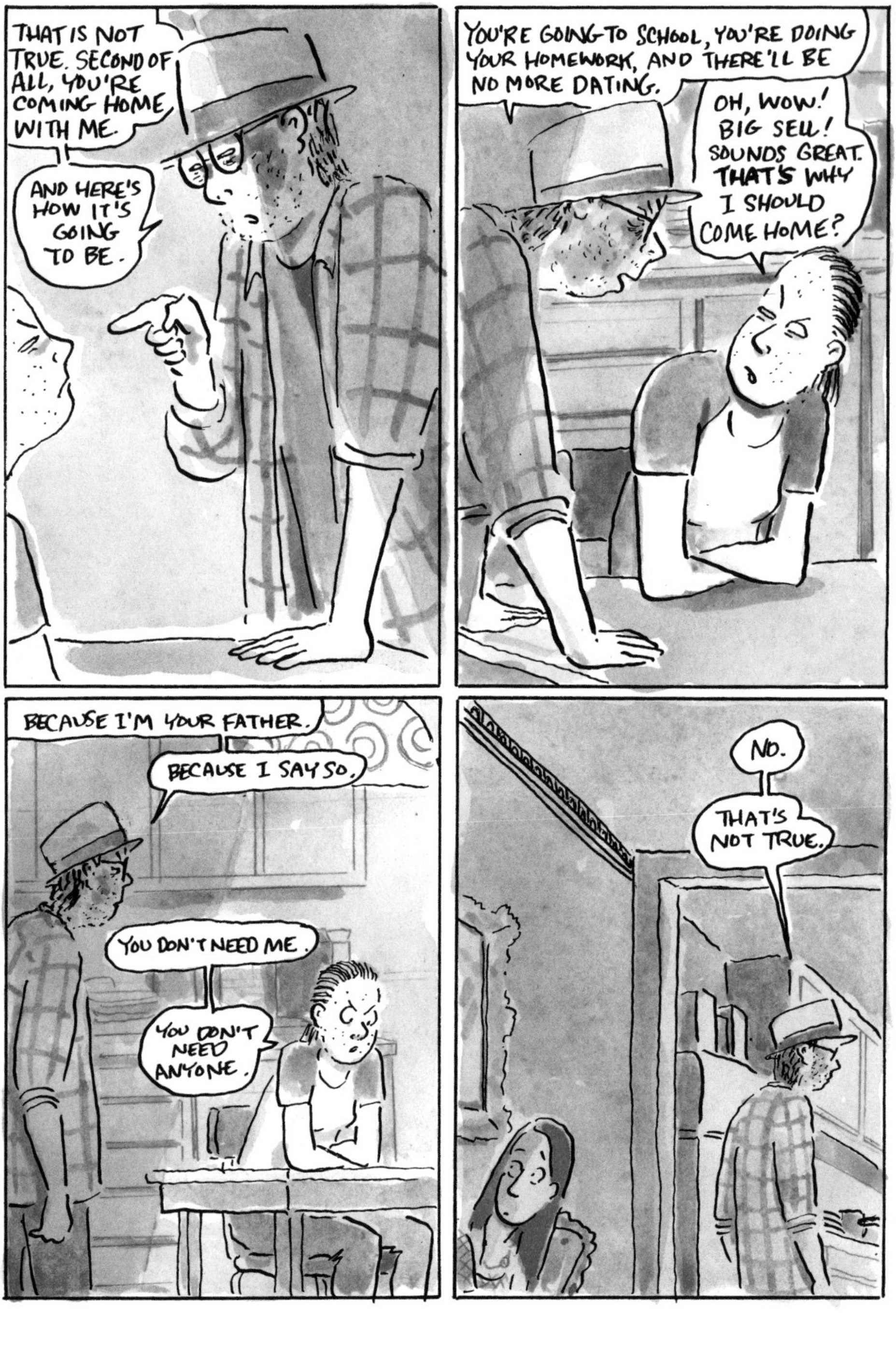
THAT IS NOT TRUE. SECOND OF ALL, YOU'RE COMING HOME WITH ME.
AND HERE'S HOW IT'S GOING TO BE.
YOU'RE GOING TO SCHOOL, YOU'RE DOING YOUR HOMEWORK, AND THERE'LL BE NO MORE DATING.
OH, WOW! BIG SELL! SOUNDS GREAT. THAT'S WHY I SHOULD COME HOME?
BECAUSE I'M YOUR FATHER.
BECAUSE I SAY SO.
YOU DON'T NEED ME.
YOU DON'T NEED ANYONE.
NO.
THAT'S NOT TRUE.

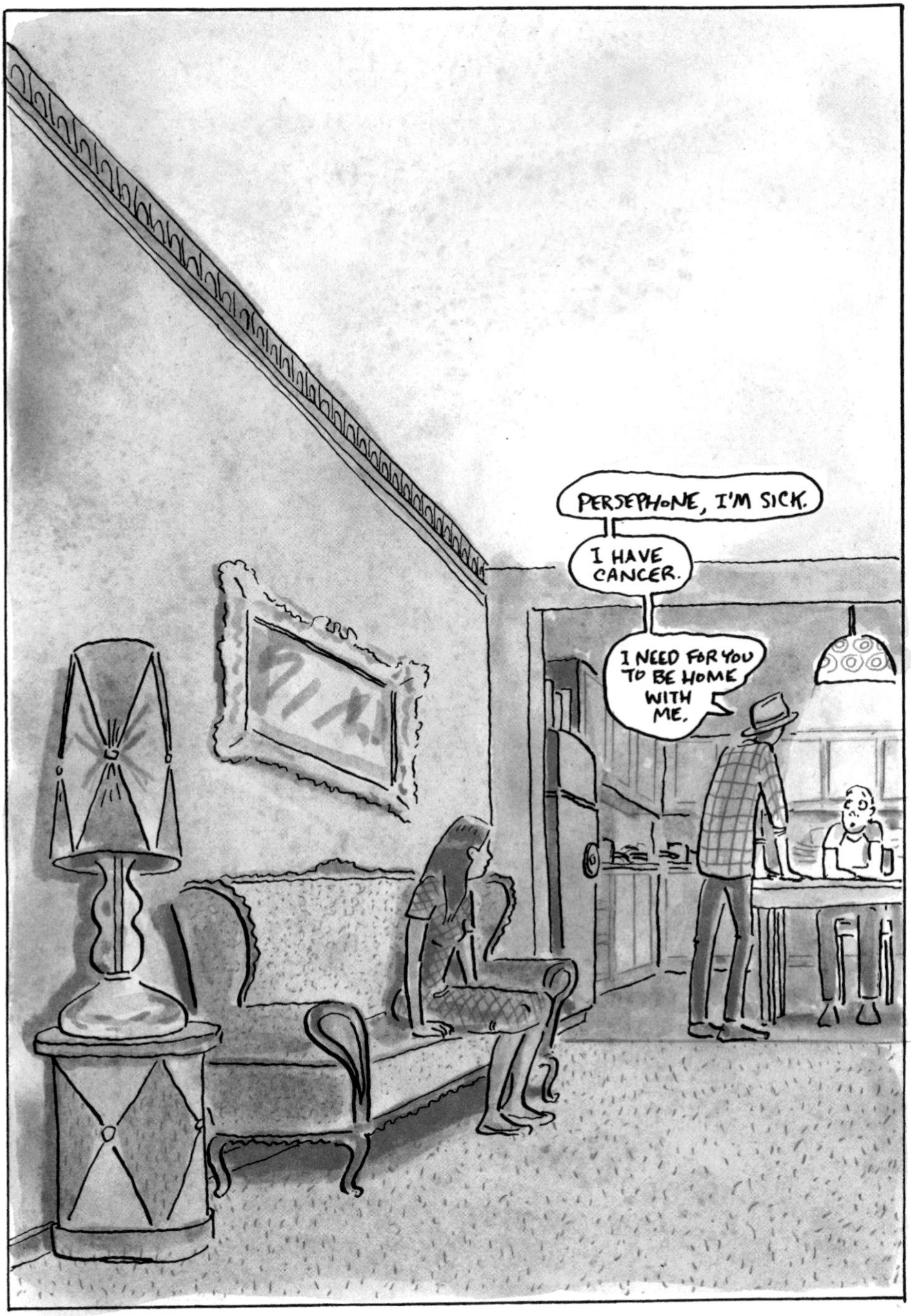
PERSEPHONE, I'M SICK.
I HAVE CANCER.
I NEED FOR YOU TO BE HOME WITH ME.

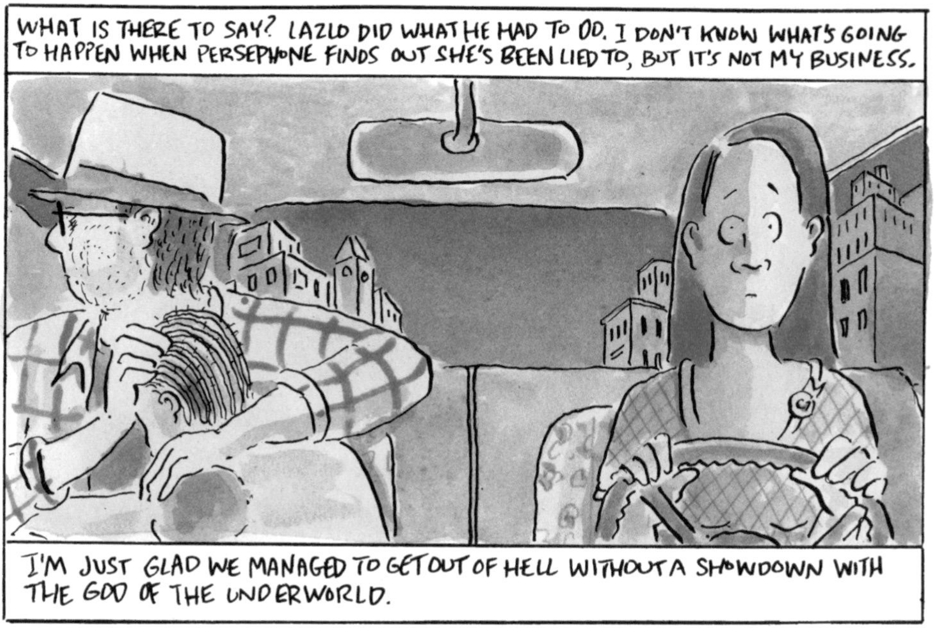
WHAT IS THERE TO SAY? LAZLO DID WHAT HE HAD TO DO. I DON'T KNOW WHAT'S GOING TO HAPPEN WHEN PERSEPHONE FINDS OUT SHE'S BEEN LIED TO, BUT IT'S NOT MY BUSINESS.
I'M JUST GLAD WE MANAGED TO GET OUT OF HELL WITHOUT A SHOWDOWN WITH THE GOD OF THE UNDERWORLD.

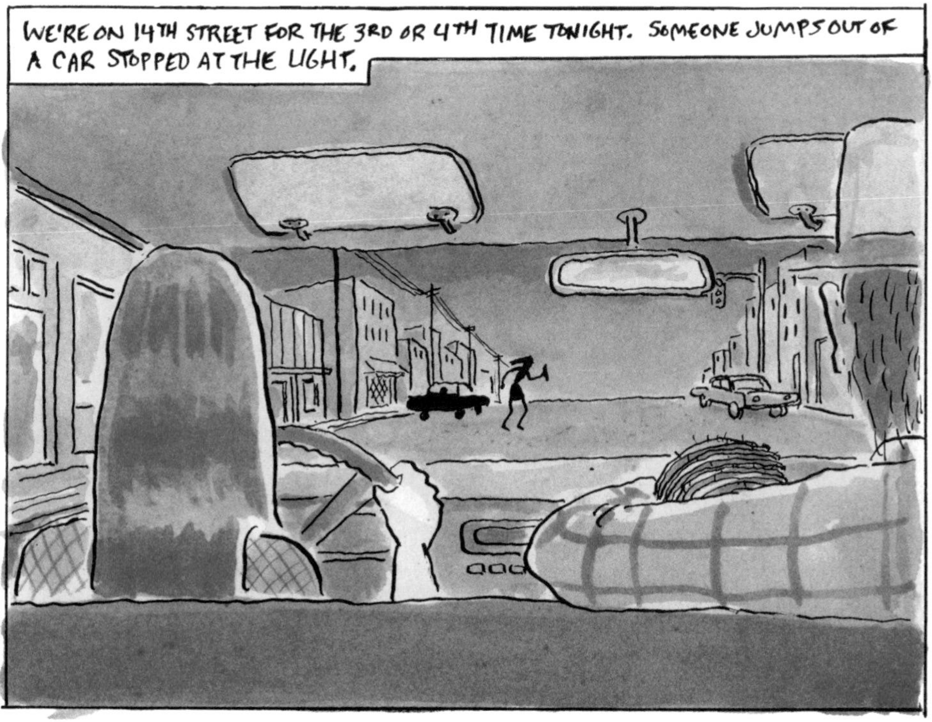
WE'RE ON 14TH STREET FOR THE 3RD OR 4TH TIME TONIGHT. SOMEONE JUMPS OUT OF A CAR STOPPED AT THE LIGHT.

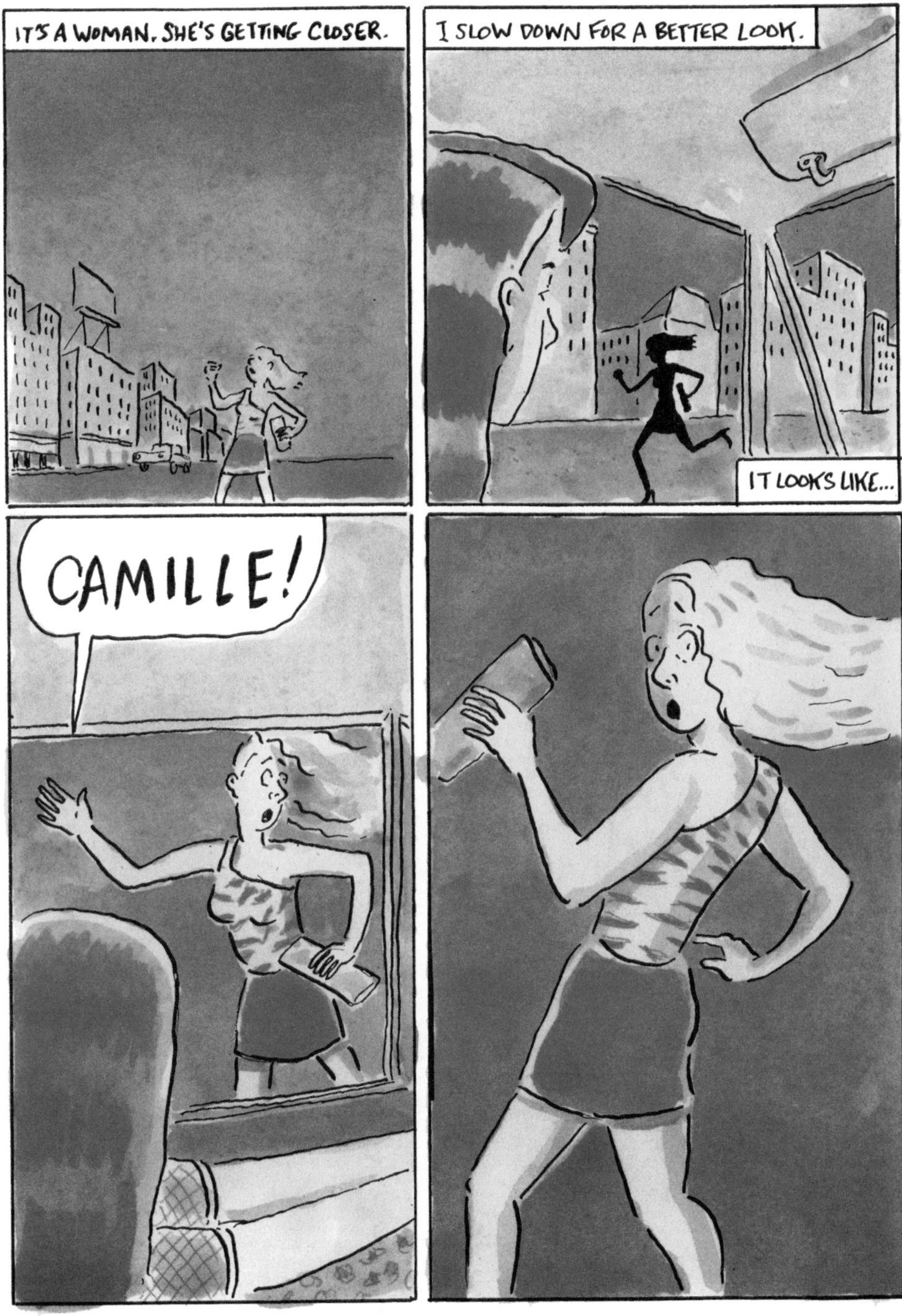
IT'S A WOMAN. SHE'S GETTING CLOSER.
I SLOW DOWN FOR A BETTER LOOK.
IT LOOKS LIKE...
CAMILLE!

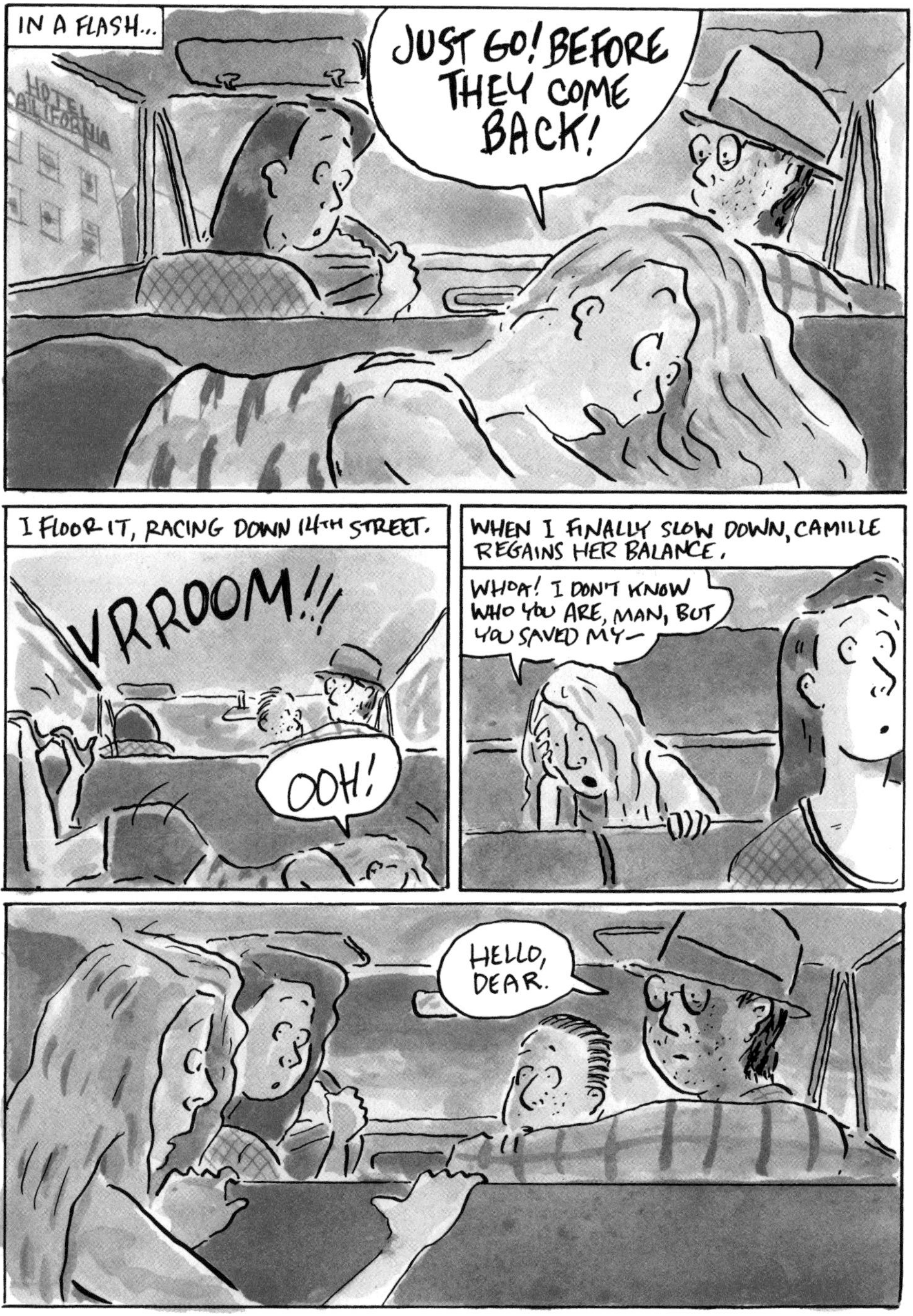
IN A FLASH...
HOTEL CALIFORNIA
JUST GO! BEFORE THEY COME BACK!
I FLOOR IT, RACING DOWN 14TH STREET.
VRROOM!!!
OOH!
WHEN I FINALLY SLOW DOWN, CAMILLE REGAINS HER BALANCE.
WHOA! I DON'T KNOW WHO YOU ARE, MAN, BUT YOU SAVED MY—
HELLO, DEAR.

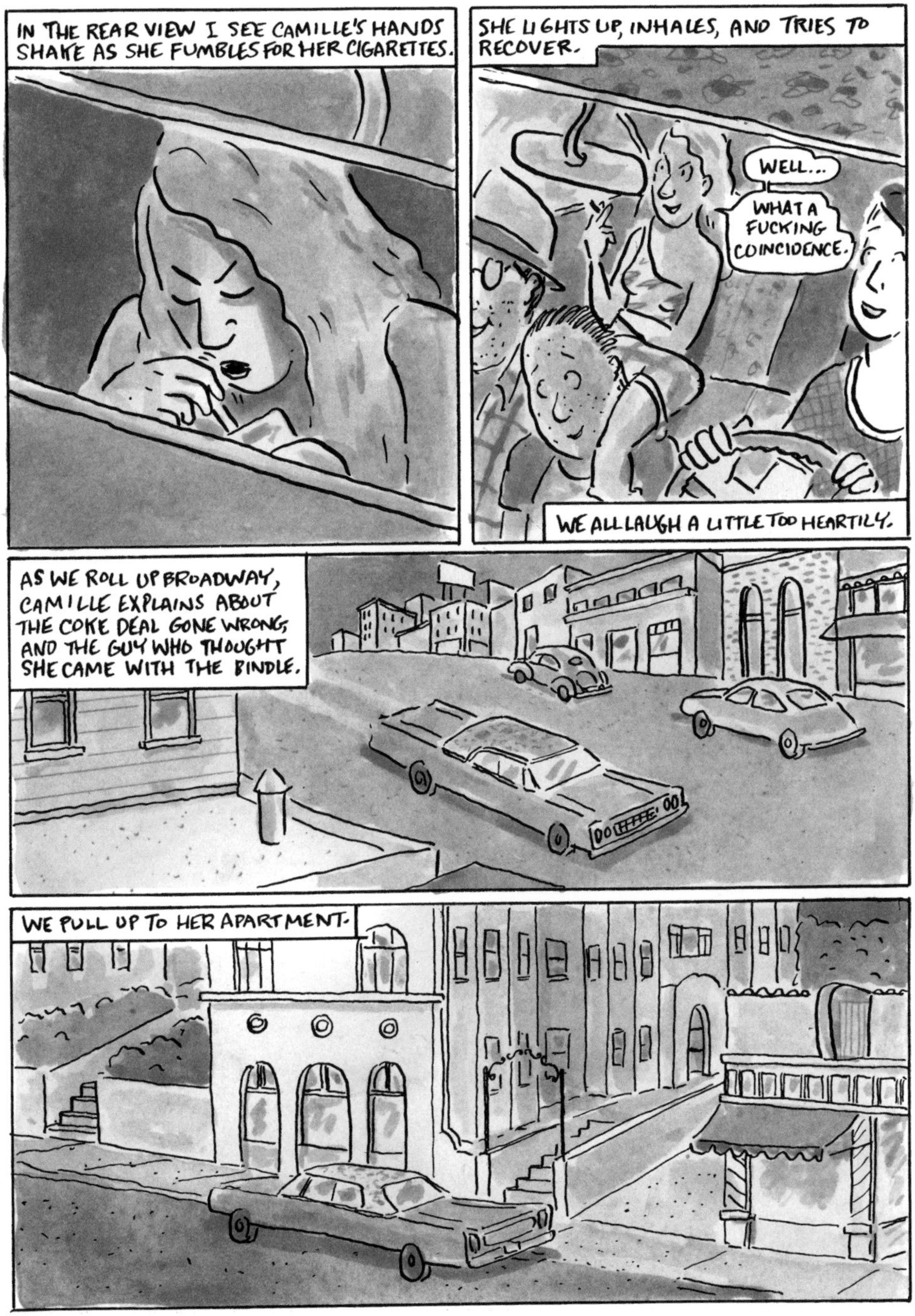
IN THE REAR VIEW I SEE CAMILLE'S HANDS SHAKE AS SHE FUMBLES FOR HER CIGARETTES.
SHE LIGHTS UP, INHALES, AND TRIES TO RECOVER.
WELL...
WHAT A FUCKING COINCIDENCE.
WE ALL LAUGH A LITTLE TOO HEARTILY.
AS WE ROLL UP BROADWAY, CAMILLE EXPLAINS ABOUT THE COKE DEAL GONE WRONG, AND THE GUY WHO THOUGHT SHE CAME WITH THE BINDLE.
WE PULL UP TO HER APARTMENT.

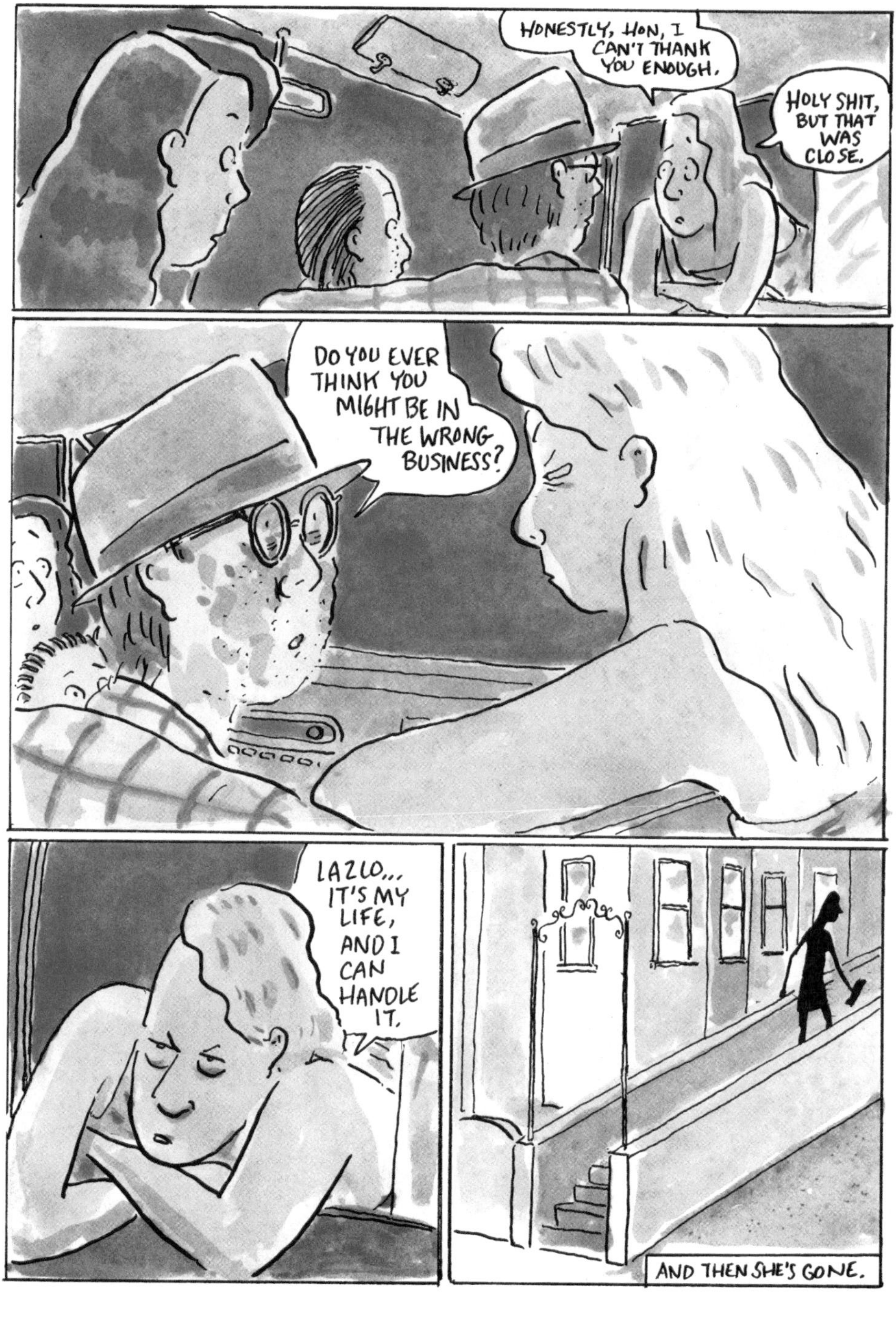
HONESTLY, HON, I CAN'T THANK YOU ENOUGH.
HOLY SHIT, BUT THAT WAS CLOSE.
DO YOU EVER THINK YOU MIGHT BE IN THE WRONG BUSINESS?
LAZLO... IT'S MY LIFE, AND I CAN HANDLE IT.
AND THEN SHE'S GONE.

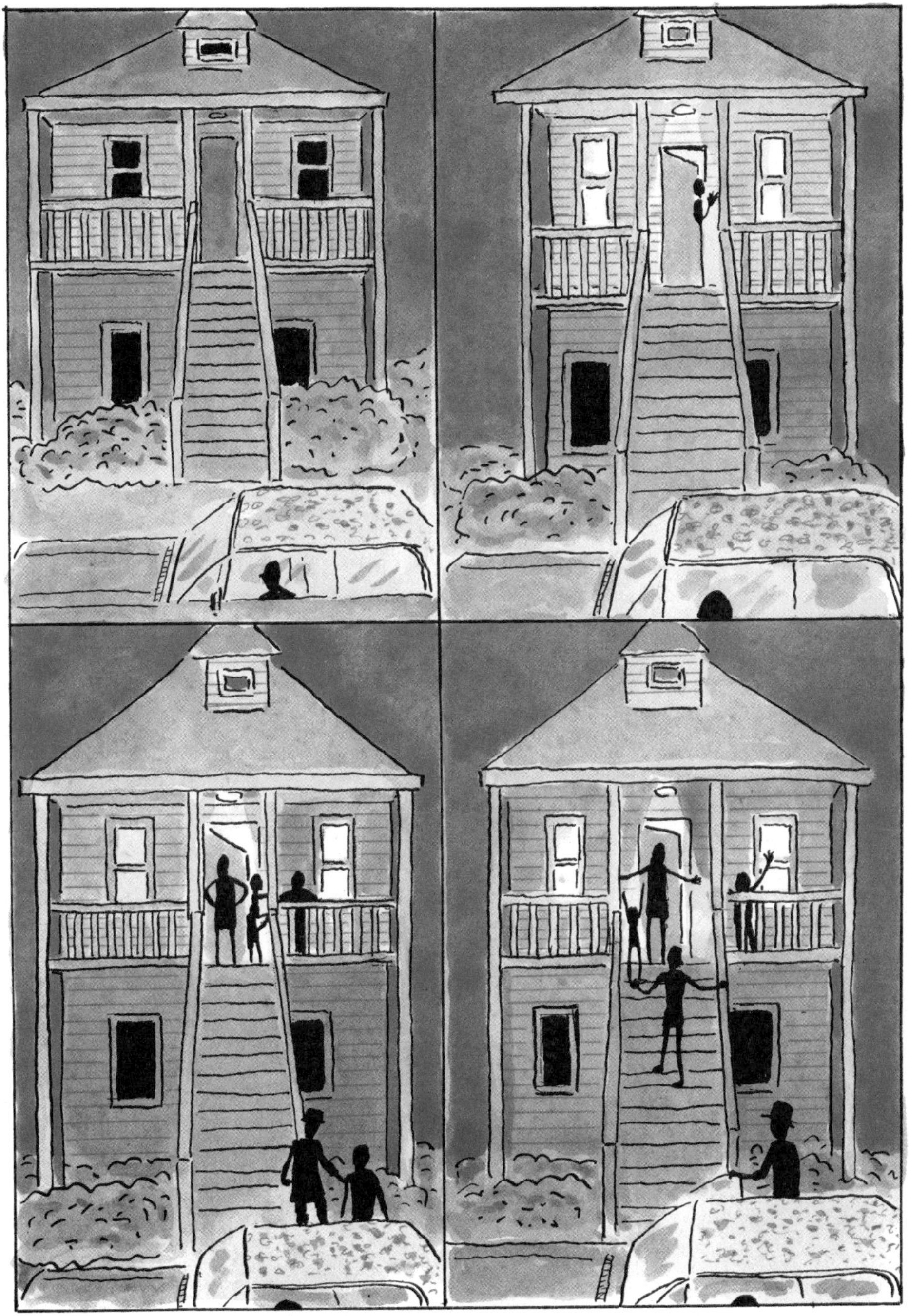

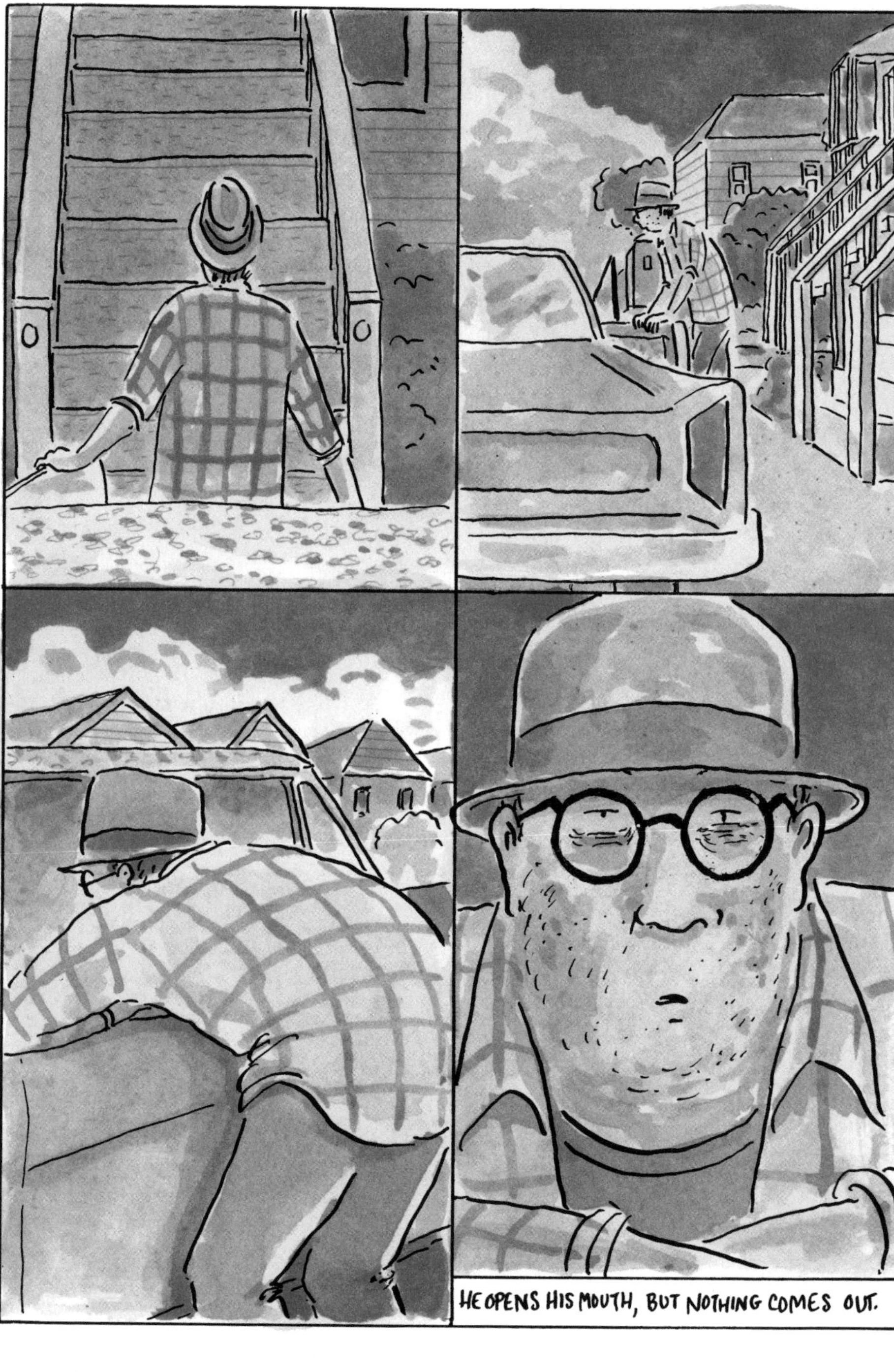
HE OPENS HIS MOUTH, BUT NOTHING COMES OUT.

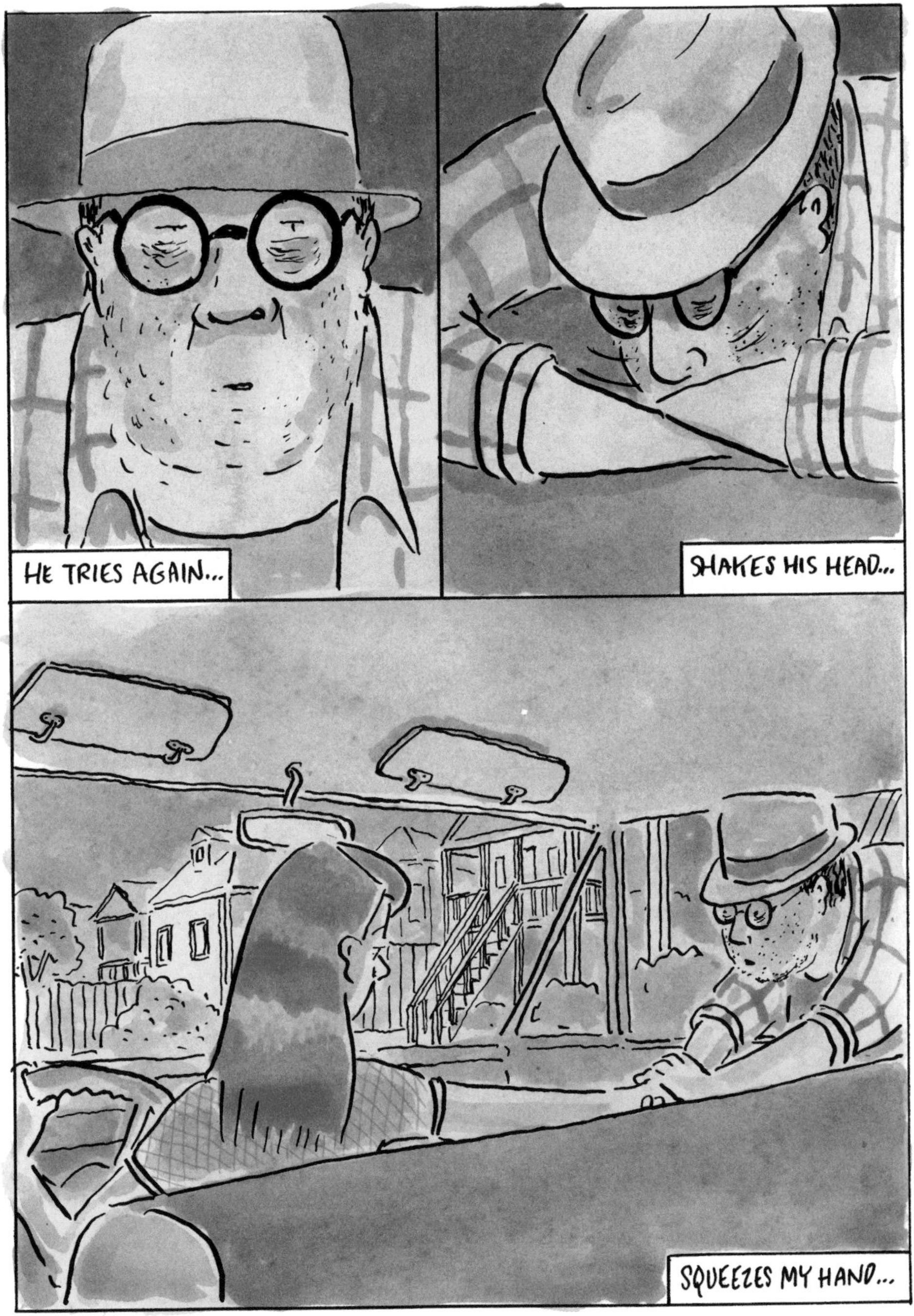
HE TRIES AGAIN...
SHAKES HIS HEAD...
SQUEEZES MY HAND...

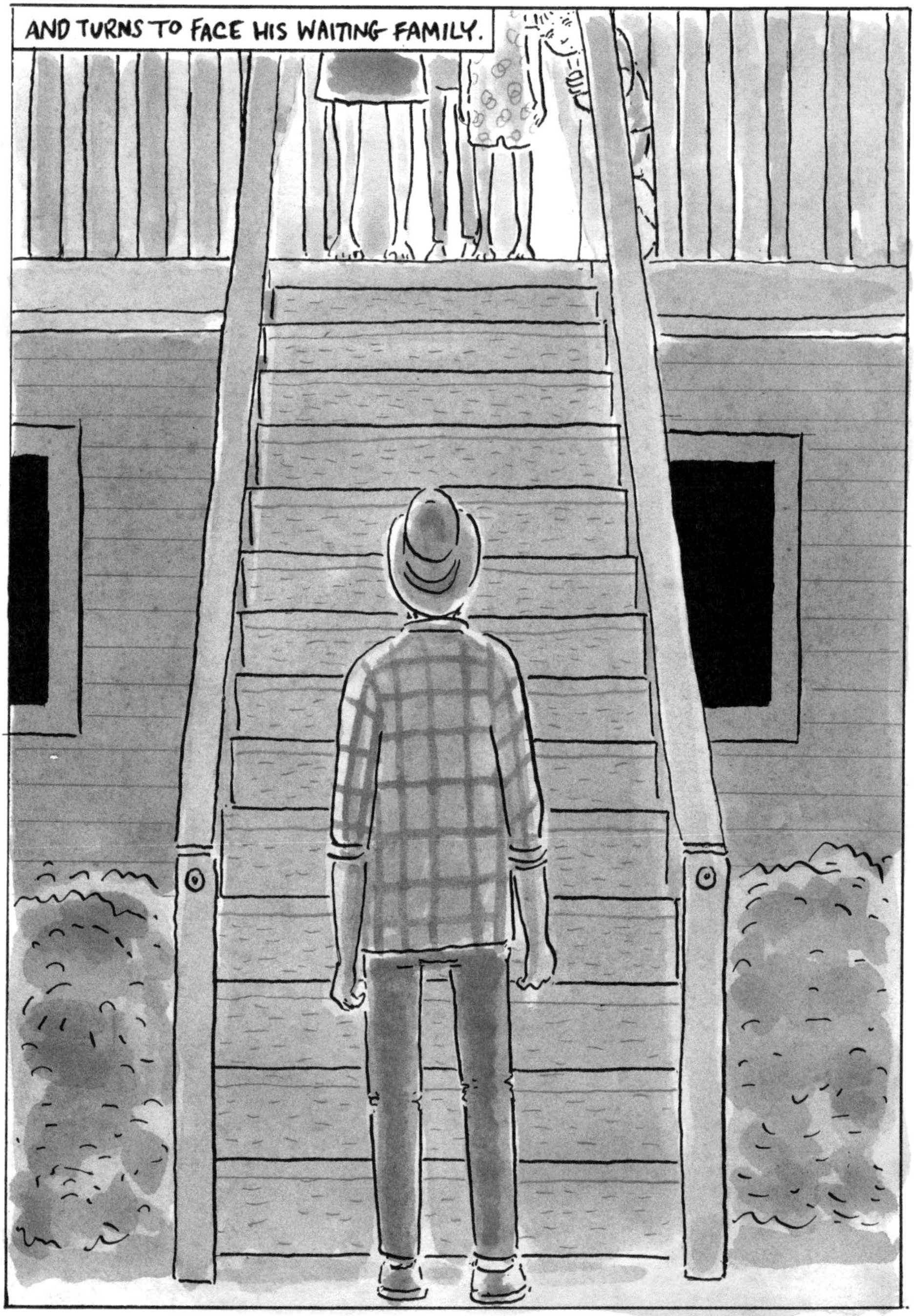
AND TURNS TO FACE HIS WAITING FAMILY.

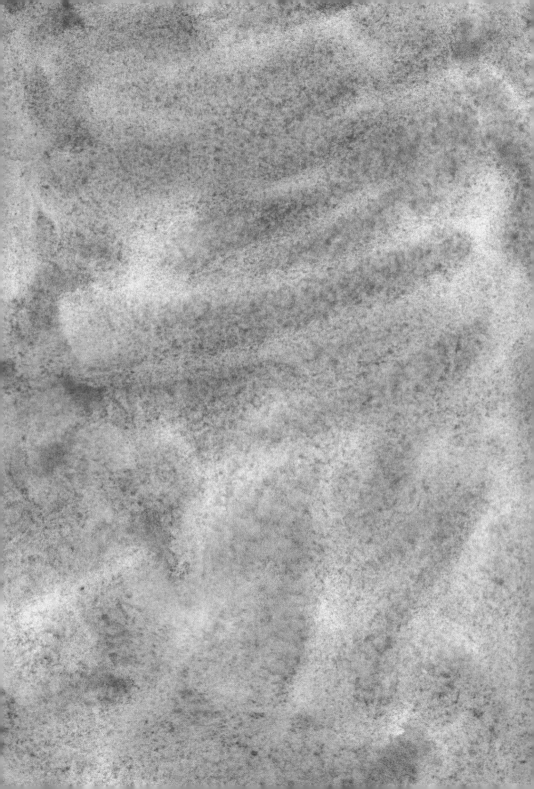

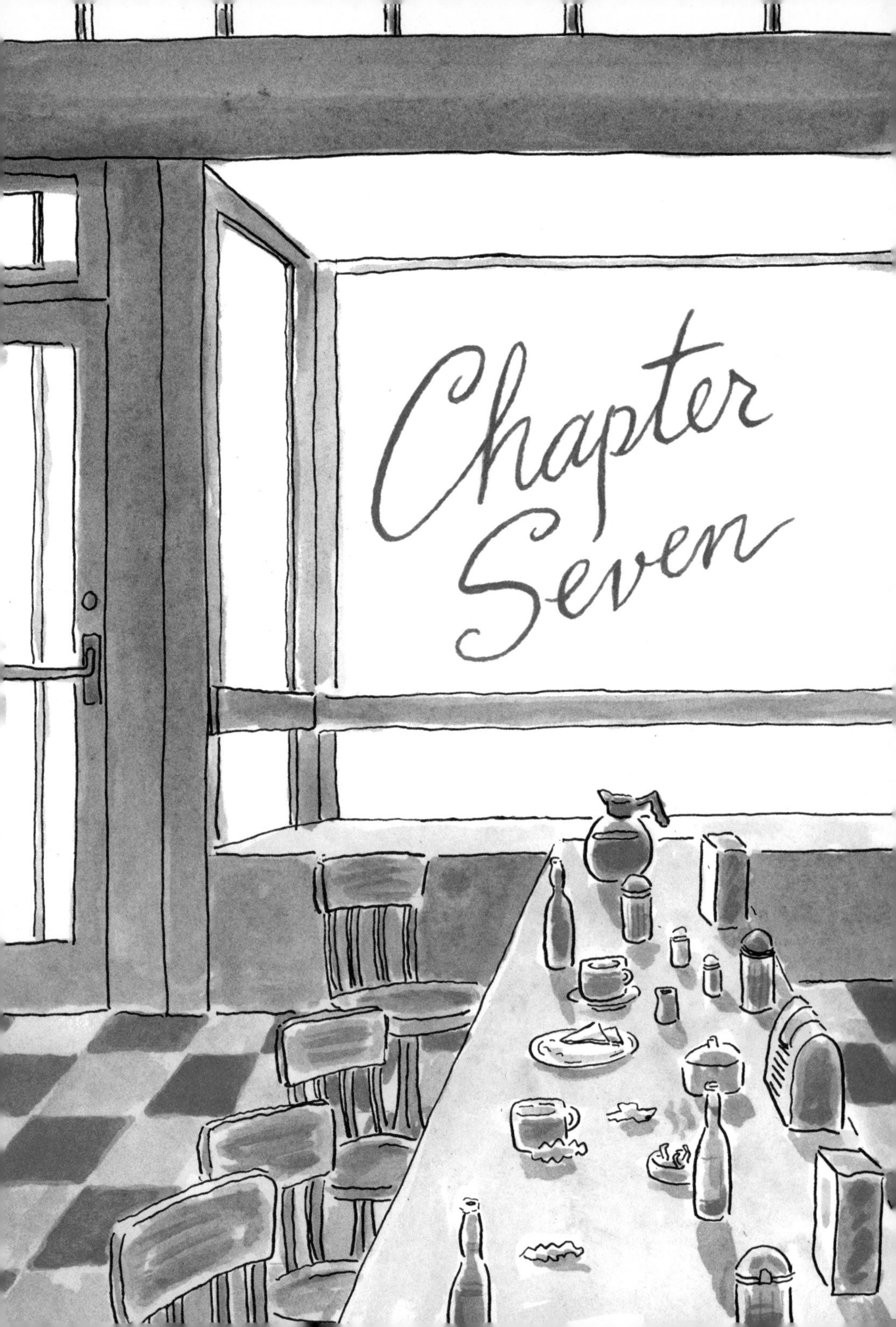
Chapter
Seven

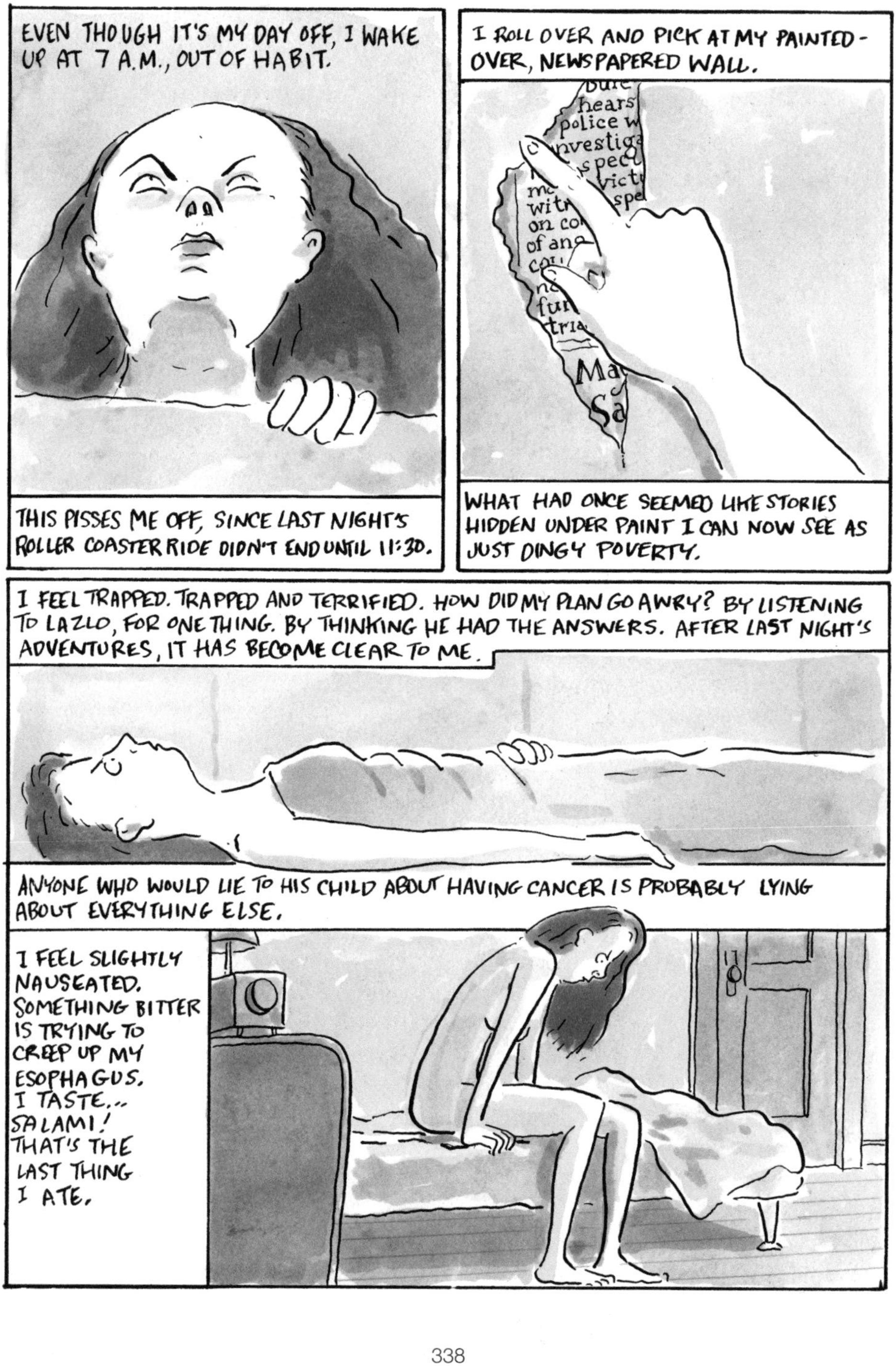

EVEN THOUGH IT'S MY DAY OFF, I WAKE UP AT 7 A.M., OUT OF HABIT.
THIS PISSES ME OFF, SINCE LAST NIGHT'S ROLLER COASTER RIDE DIDN'T END UNTIL 11:30.
I ROLL OVER AND PICK AT MY PAINTED-OVER, NEWSPAPERED WALL.
hears
police w
investiga
suspec
victi
witn
on co
of ana
fun
tria
WHAT HAD ONCE SEEMED LIKE STORIES HIDDEN UNDER PAINT I CAN NOW SEE AS JUST DINGY POVERTY.
I FEEL TRAPPED. TRAPPED AND TERRIFIED. HOW DID MY PLAN GO AWRY? BY LISTENING TO LAZLO, FOR ONE THING. BY THINKING HE HAD THE ANSWERS. AFTER LAST NIGHT'S ADVENTURES, IT HAS BECOME CLEAR TO ME.
ANYONE WHO WOULD LIE TO HIS CHILD ABOUT HAVING CANCER IS PROBABLY LYING ABOUT EVERYTHING ELSE.
I FEEL SLIGHTLY NAUSEATED. SOMETHING BITTER IS TRYING TO CREEP UP MY ESOPHAGUS. I TASTE... SALAMI! THAT'S THE LAST THING I ATE.

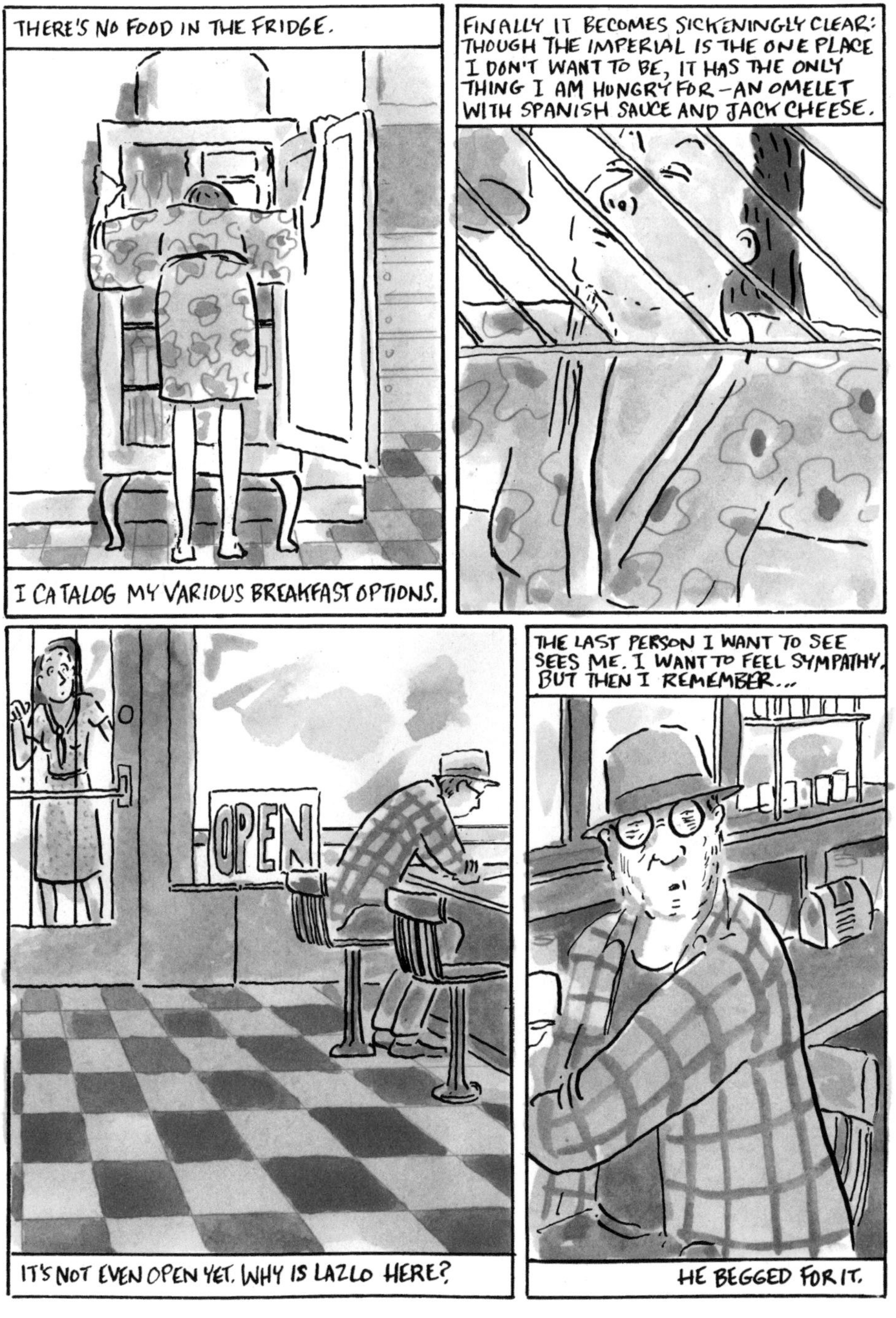
THERE'S NO FOOD IN THE FRIDGE.
I CATALOG MY VARIOUS BREAKFAST OPTIONS.
FINALLY IT BECOMES SICKENINGLY CLEAR: THOUGH THE IMPERIAL IS THE ONE PLACE I DON'T WANT TO BE, IT HAS THE ONLY THING I AM HUNGRY FOR—AN OMELET WITH SPANISH SAUCE AND JACK CHEESE.
OPEN
IT'S NOT EVEN OPEN YET. WHY IS LAZLO HERE?
THE LAST PERSON I WANT TO SEE SEES ME. I WANT TO FEEL SYMPATHY, BUT THEN I REMEMBER...
HE BEGGED FOR IT.

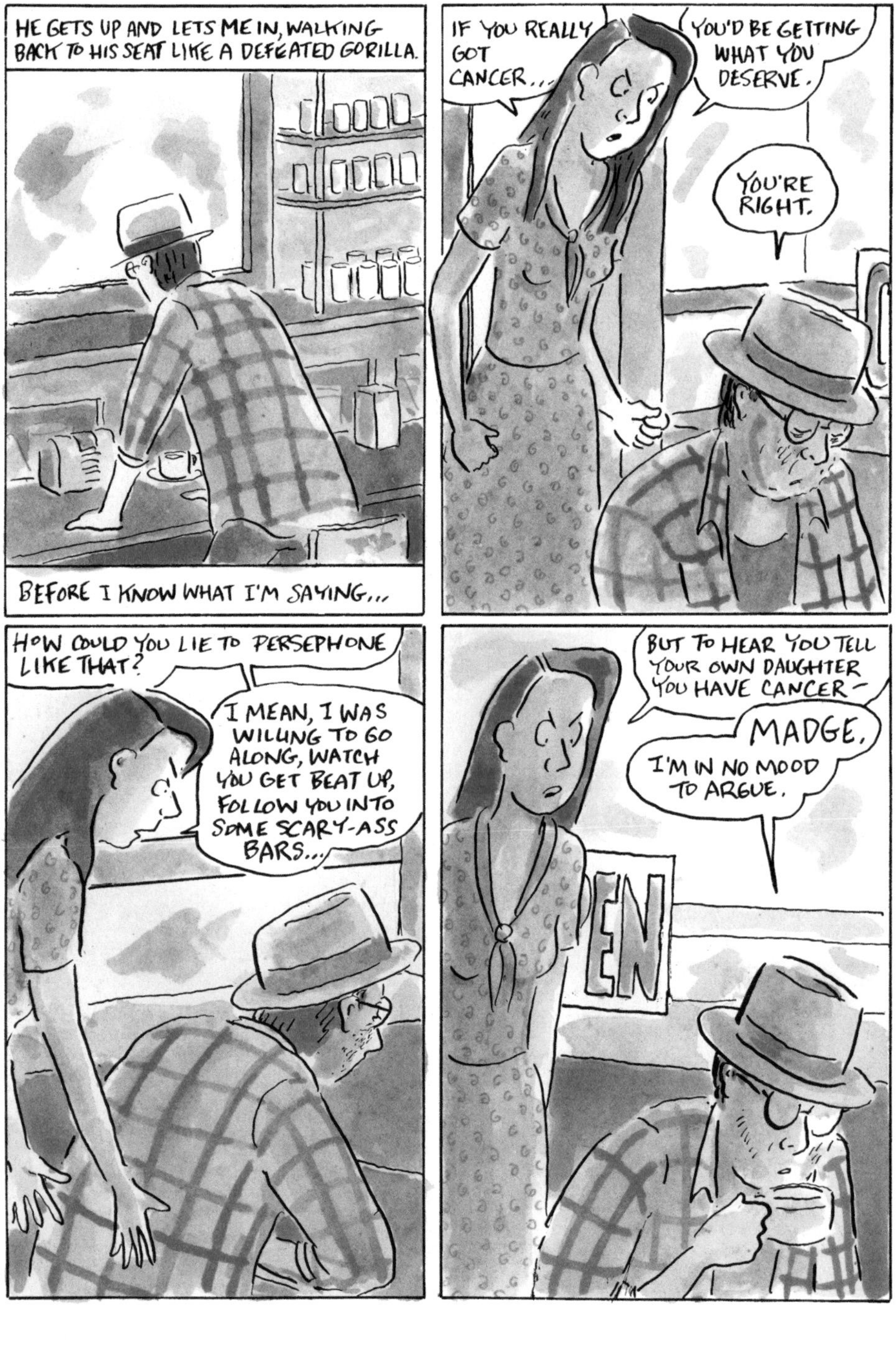
HE GETS UP AND LETS ME IN, WALKING BACK TO HIS SEAT LIKE A DEFEATED GORILLA.
BEFORE I KNOW WHAT I'M SAYING...
IF YOU REALLY GOT CANCER...
YOU'D BE GETTING WHAT YOU DESERVE.
YOU'RE RIGHT.
HOW COULD YOU LIE TO PERSEPHONE LIKE THAT?
I MEAN, I WAS WILLING TO GO ALONG, WATCH YOU GET BEAT UP, FOLLOW YOU INTO SOME SCARY-ASS BARS...
BUT TO HEAR YOU TELL YOUR OWN DAUGHTER YOU HAVE CANCER-
MADGE, I'M IN NO MOOD TO ARGUE.
EN

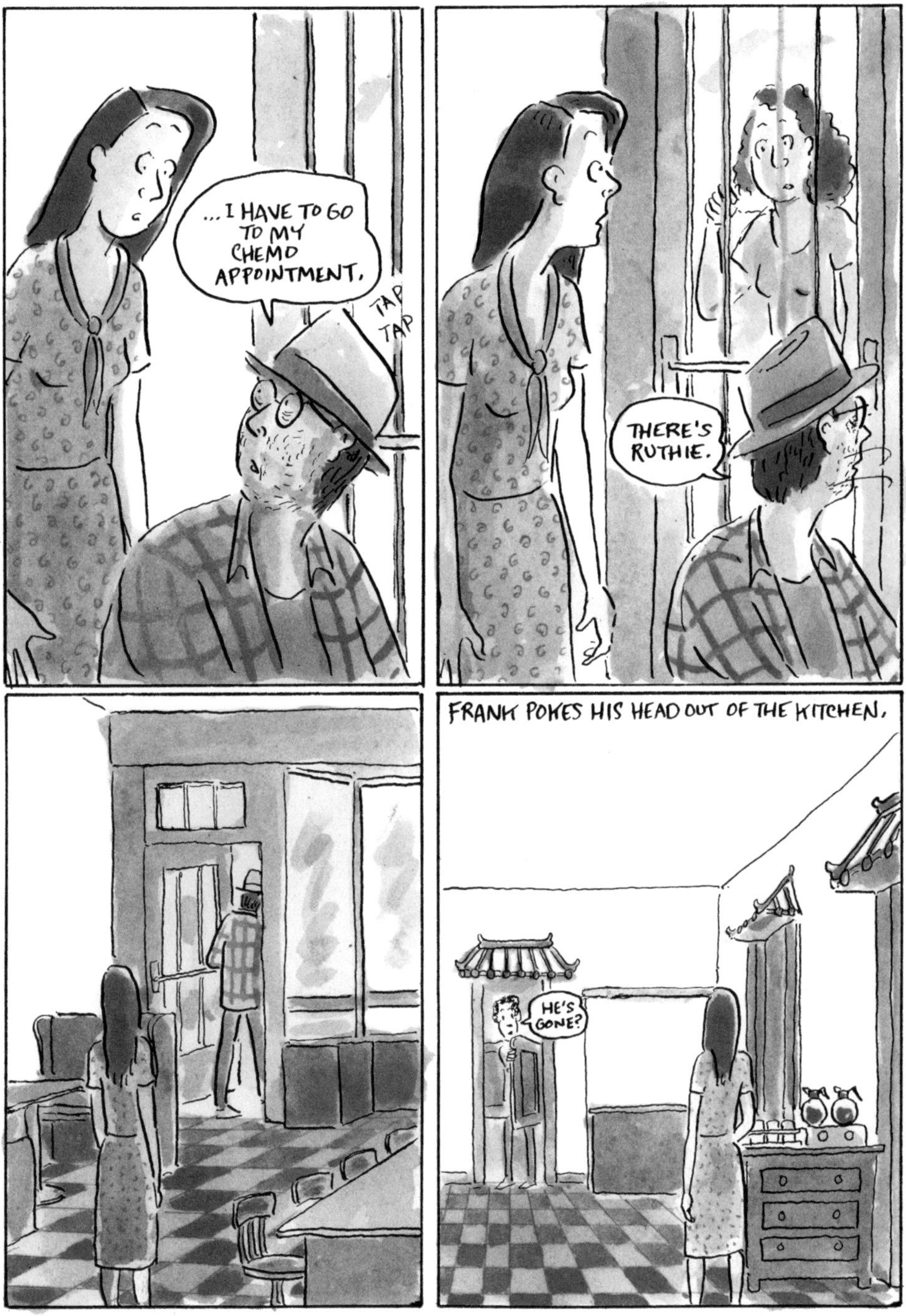
...I HAVE TO GO TO MY CHEMO APPOINTMENT.
TAP TAP
THERE'S RUTHIE.
FRANK POKES HIS HEAD OUT OF THE KITCHEN.
HE'S GONE?

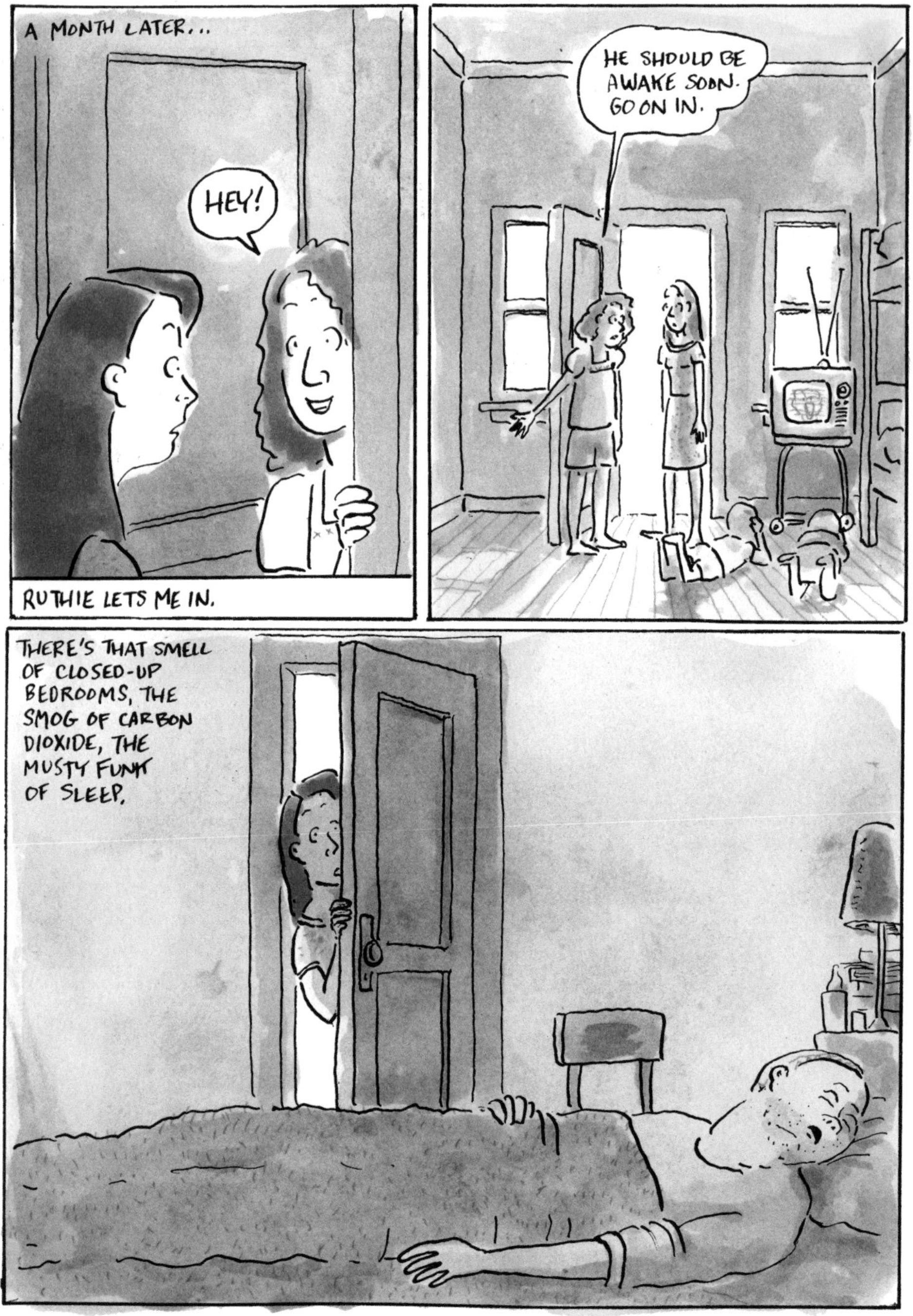
A MONTH LATER...
HEY!
RUTHIE LETS ME IN.
HE SHOULD BE AWAKE SOON. GO ON IN.
THERE'S THAT SMELL OF CLOSED-UP BEDROOMS, THE SMOG OF CARBON DIOXIDE, THE MUSTY FUNK OF SLEEP.

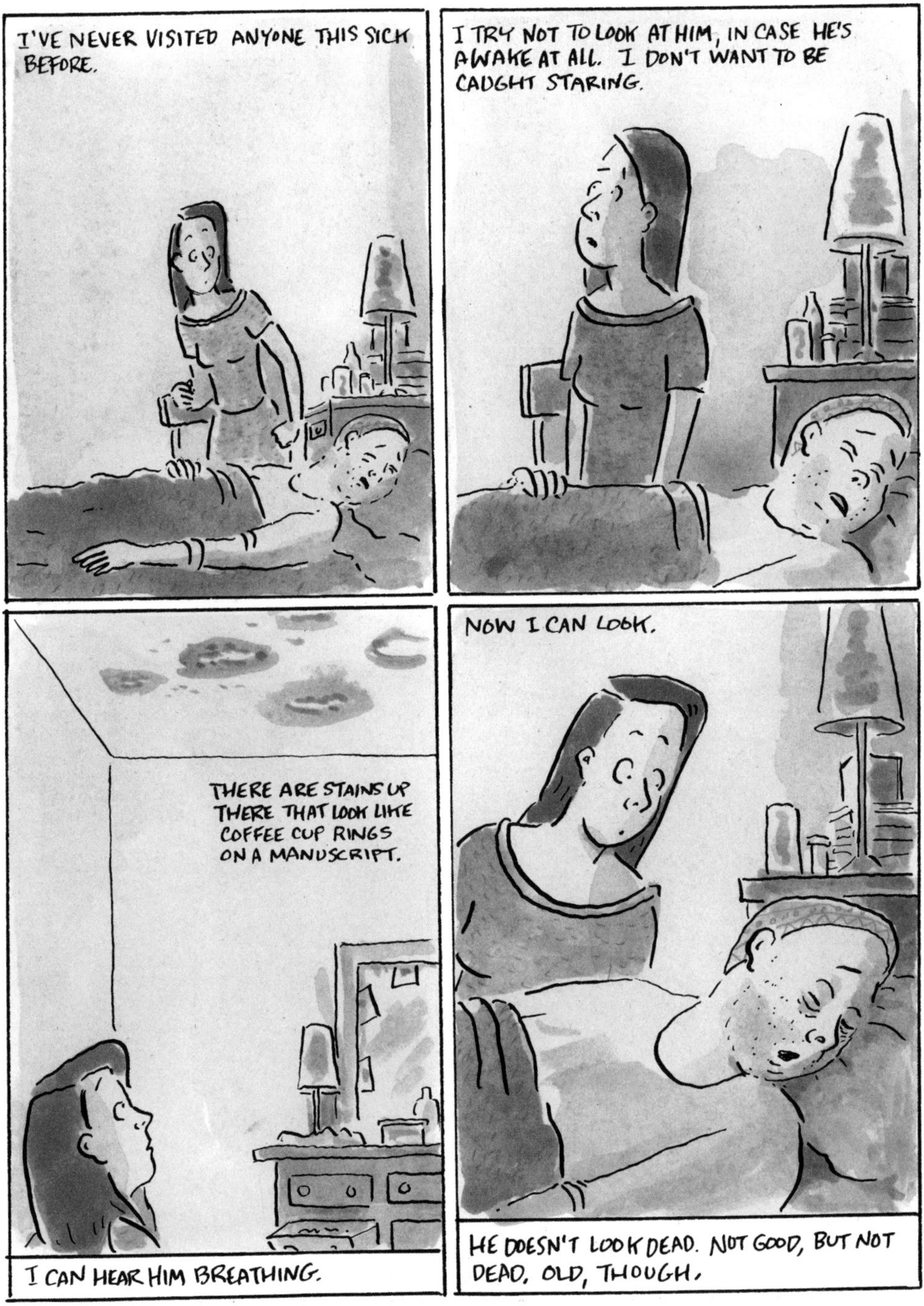
I'VE NEVER VISITED ANYONE THIS SICK BEFORE.
I TRY NOT TO LOOK AT HIM, IN CASE HE'S AWAKE AT ALL. I DON'T WANT TO BE CAUGHT STARING.
THERE ARE STAINS UP THERE THAT LOOK LIKE COFFEE CUP RINGS ON A MANUSCRIPT.
I CAN HEAR HIM BREATHING.
NOW I CAN LOOK.
HE DOESN'T LOOK DEAD. NOT GOOD, BUT NOT DEAD. OLD, THOUGH.

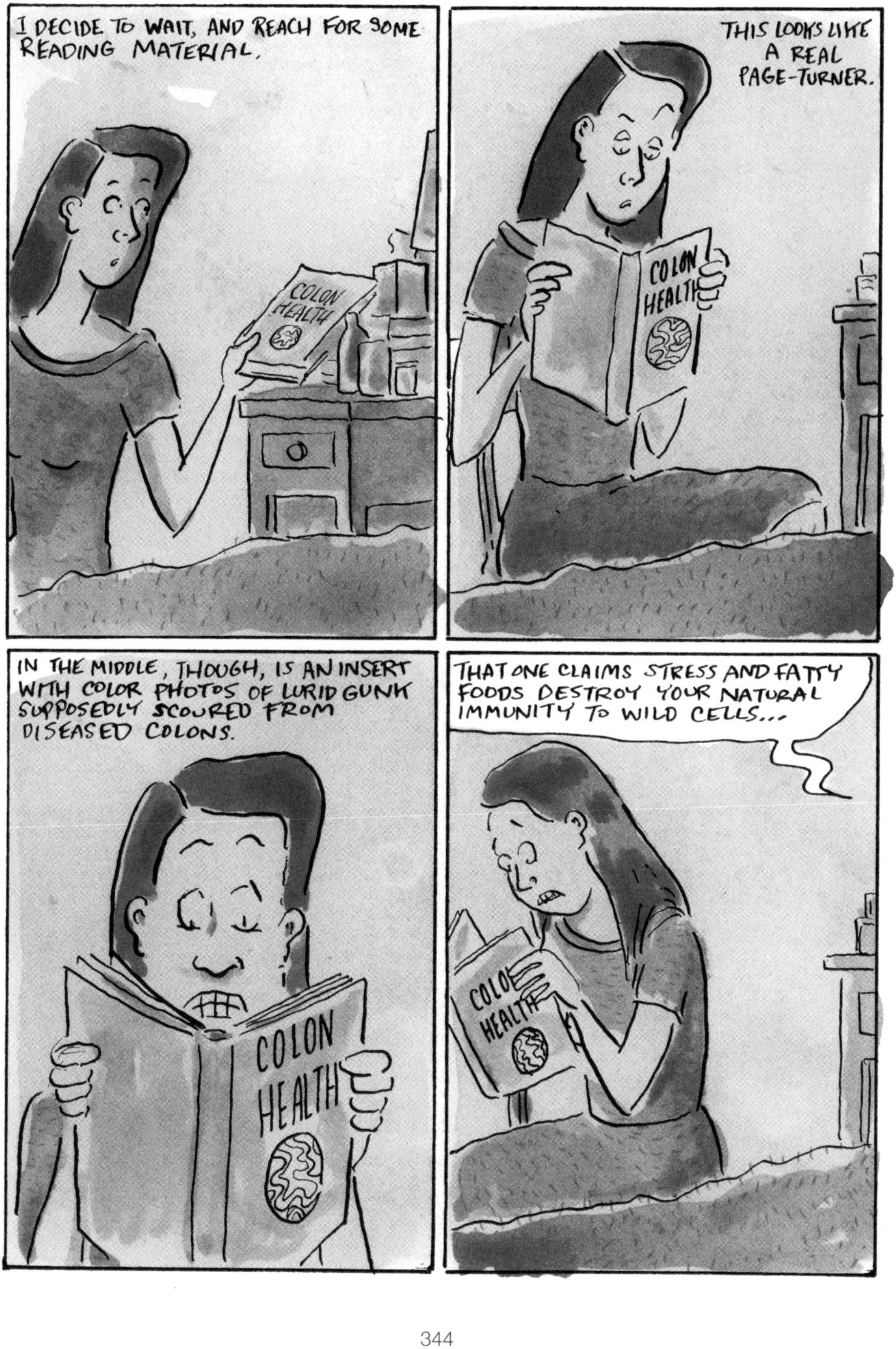
I DECIDE TO WAIT, AND REACH FOR SOME READING MATERIAL.
COLON HEALTH
THIS LOOKS LIKE A REAL PAGE-TURNER.
COLON HEALTH
IN THE MIDDLE, THOUGH, IS AN INSERT WITH COLOR PHOTOS OF LURID GUNK SUPPOSEDLY SCOURED FROM DISEASED COLONS.
COLON HEALTH
THAT ONE CLAIMS STRESS AND FATTY FOODS DESTROY YOUR NATURAL IMMUNITY TO WILD CELLS...
HEALTH

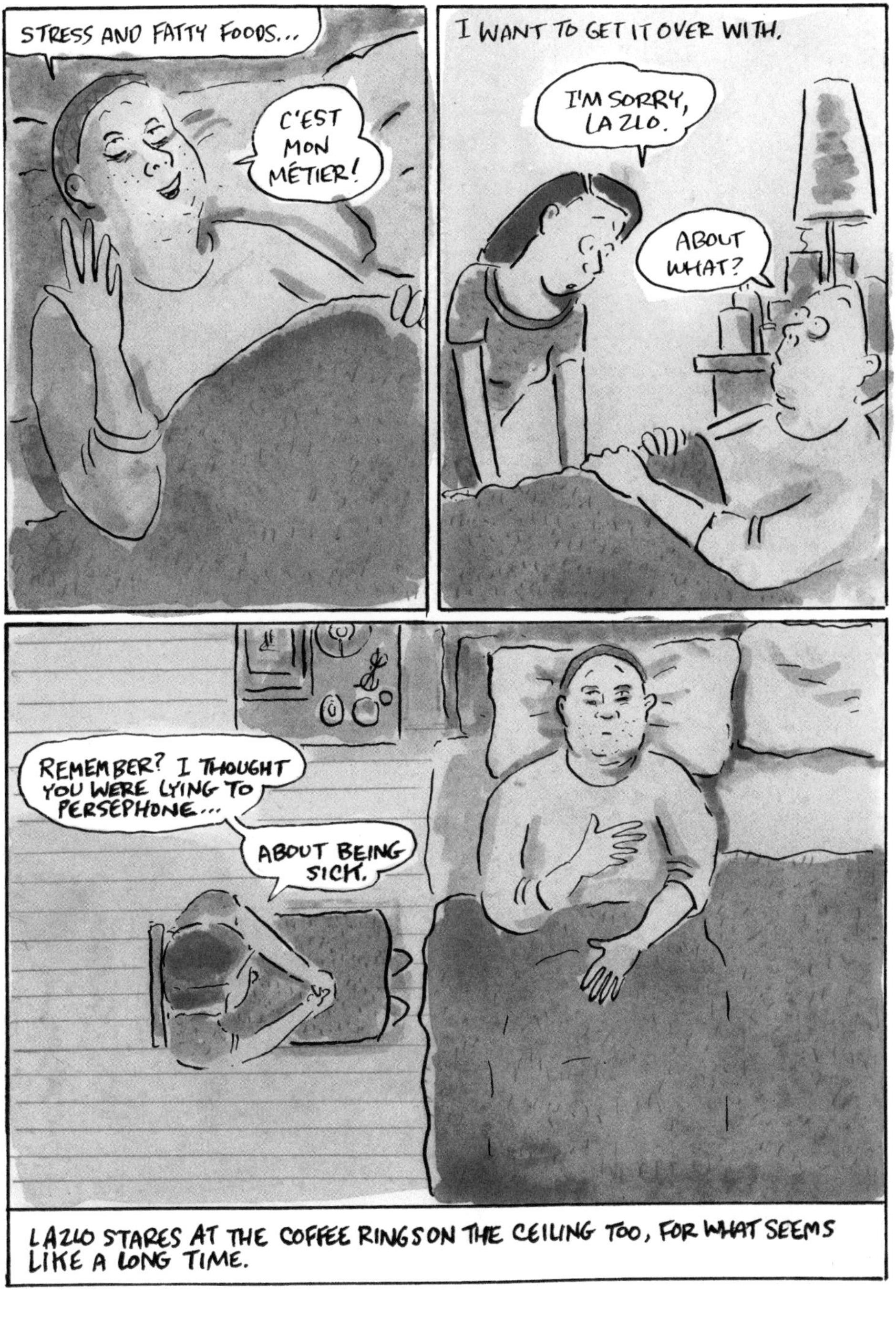
STRESS AND FATTY FOODS...
C'EST MON MÉTIER!
I WANT TO GET IT OVER WITH.
I'M SORRY, LAZLO.
ABOUT WHAT?
REMEMBER? I THOUGHT YOU WERE LYING TO PERSEPHONE...
ABOUT BEING SICK.
LAZLO STARES AT THE COFFEE RINGS ON THE CEILING TOO, FOR WHAT SEEMS LIKE A LONG TIME.

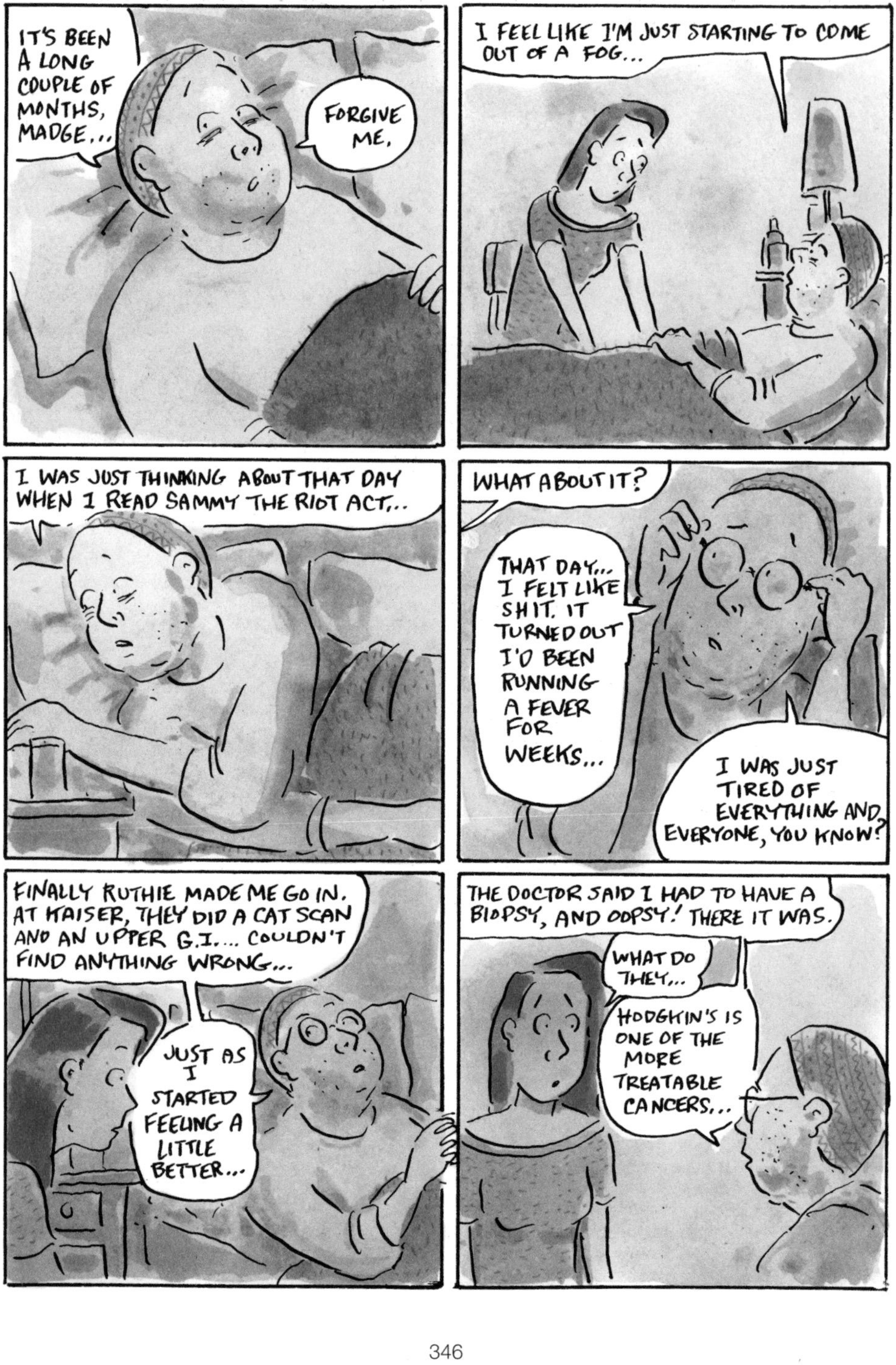
IT'S BEEN A LONG COUPLE OF MONTHS, MADGE...
FORGIVE ME.
I FEEL LIKE I'M JUST STARTING TO COME OUT OF A FOG...
I WAS JUST THINKING ABOUT THAT DAY WHEN I READ SAMMY THE RIOT ACT...
WHAT ABOUT IT?
THAT DAY... I FELT LIKE SHIT. IT TURNED OUT I'D BEEN RUNNING A FEVER FOR WEEKS...
I WAS JUST TIRED OF EVERYTHING AND EVERYONE, YOU KNOW?
FINALLY RUTHIE MADE ME GO IN. AT KAISER, THEY DID A CAT SCAN AND AN UPPER G.I.... COULDN'T FIND ANYTHING WRONG...
JUST AS I STARTED FEELING A LITTLE BETTER...
THE DOCTOR SAID I HAD TO HAVE A BIOPSY, AND OOPSY! THERE IT WAS.
WHAT DO THEY...
HODGKIN'S IS ONE OF THE MORE TREATABLE CANCERS...

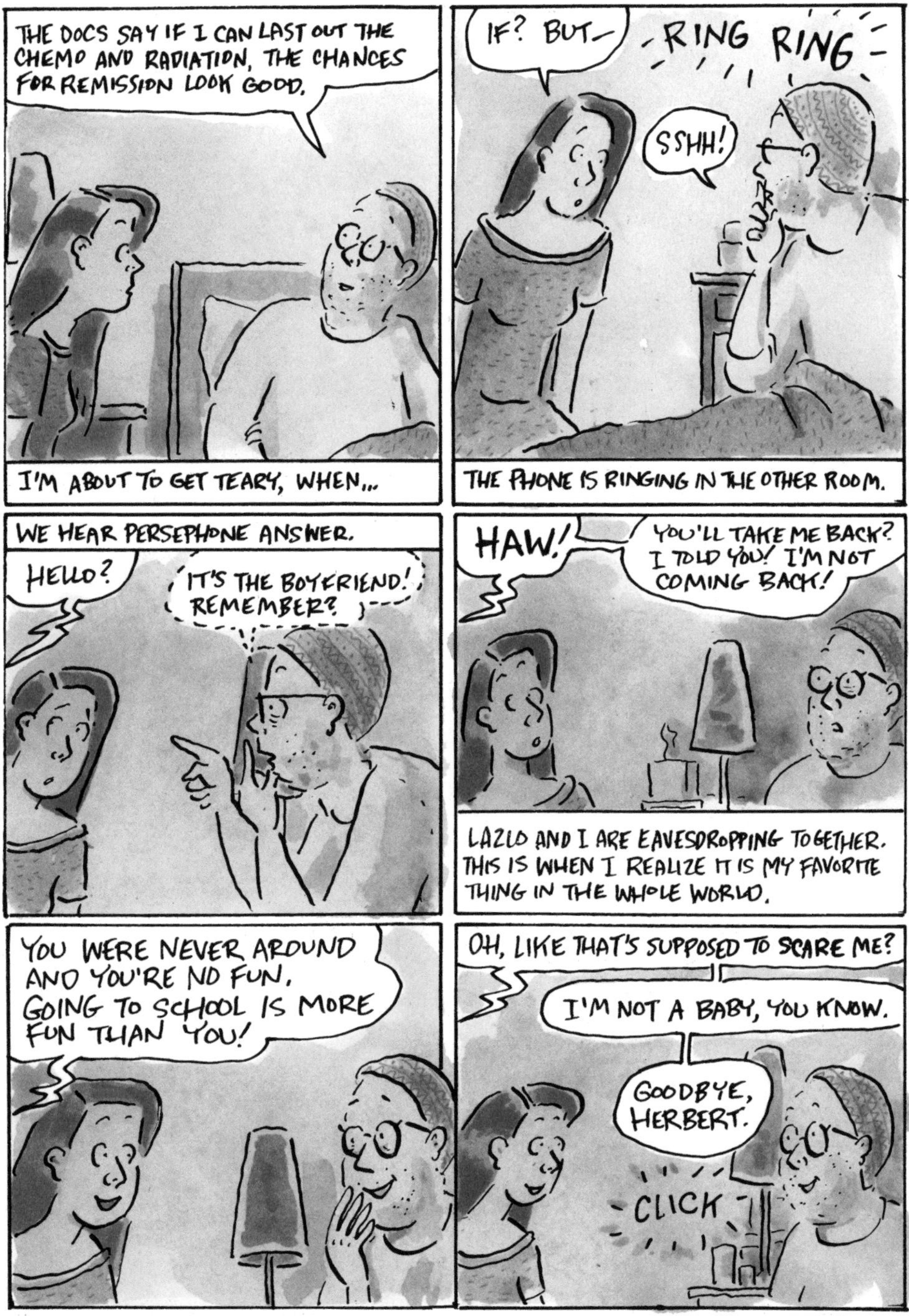
THE DOCS SAY IF I CAN LAST OUT THE CHEMO AND RADIATION, THE CHANCES FOR REMISSION LOOK GOOD.
I'M ABOUT TO GET TEARY, WHEN...
IF? BUT—
RING RING
SSHH!
THE PHONE IS RINGING IN THE OTHER ROOM.
WE HEAR PERSEPHONE ANSWER.
HELLO?
IT'S THE BOYFRIEND! REMEMBER?
HAW!
YOU'LL TAKE ME BACK? I TOLD YOU! I'M NOT COMING BACK!
LAZLO AND I ARE EAVESDROPPING TOGETHER. THIS IS WHEN I REALIZE IT IS MY FAVORITE THING IN THE WHOLE WORLD.
YOU WERE NEVER AROUND AND YOU'RE NO FUN. GOING TO SCHOOL IS MORE FUN THAN YOU!
OH, LIKE THAT'S SUPPOSED TO SCARE ME?
I'M NOT A BABY, YOU KNOW.
GOODBYE, HERBERT.
CLICK

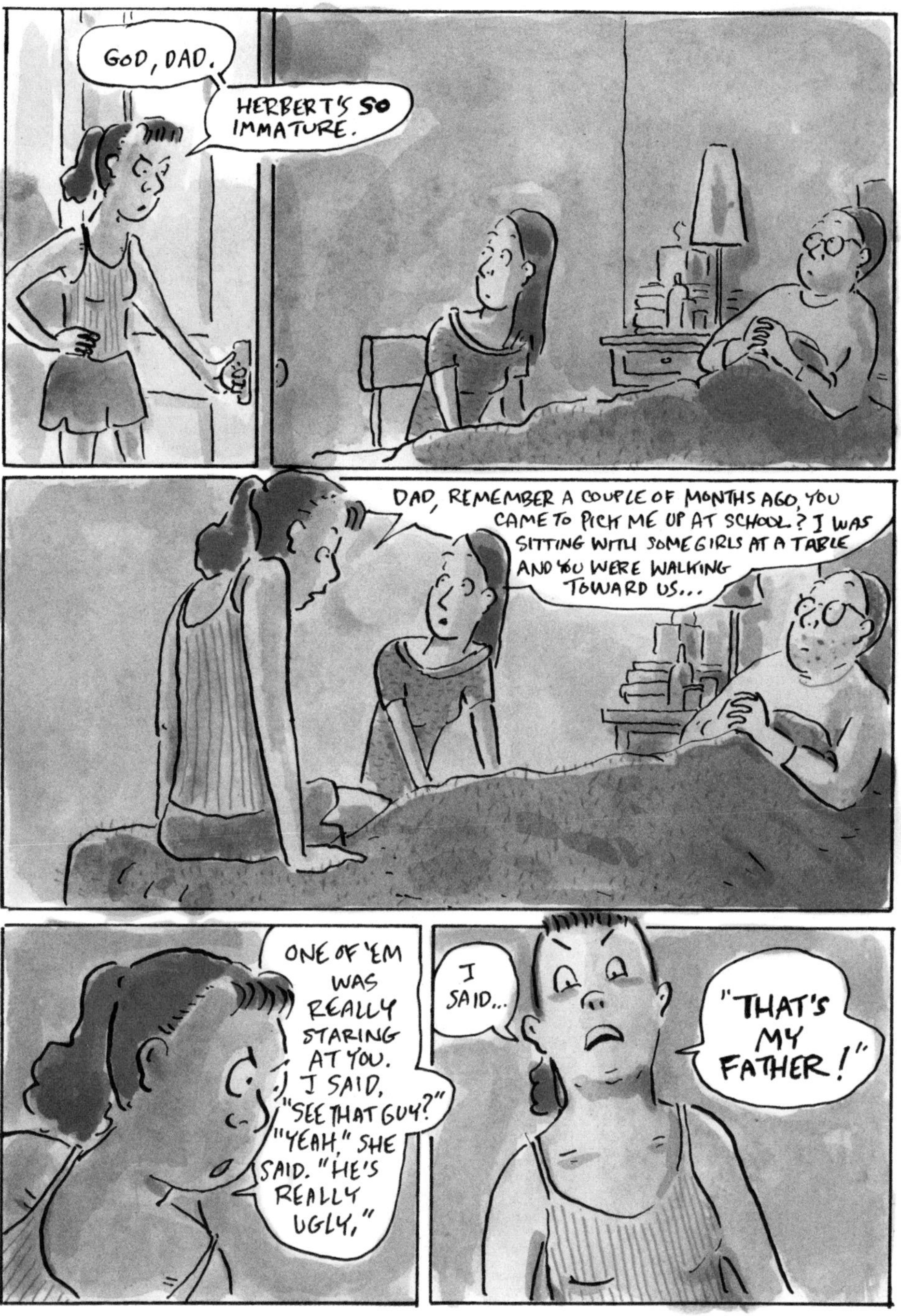
GOD, DAD.
HERBERT'S SO IMMATURE.
DAD, REMEMBER A COUPLE OF MONTHS AGO, YOU CAME TO PICK ME UP AT SCHOOL? I WAS SITTING WITH SOME GIRLS AT A TABLE AND YOU WERE WALKING TOWARD US...
ONE OF 'EM WAS REALLY STARING AT YOU. I SAID, "SEE THAT GUY?" "YEAH," SHE SAID. "HE'S REALLY UGLY,"
I SAID...
"THAT'S MY FATHER!"

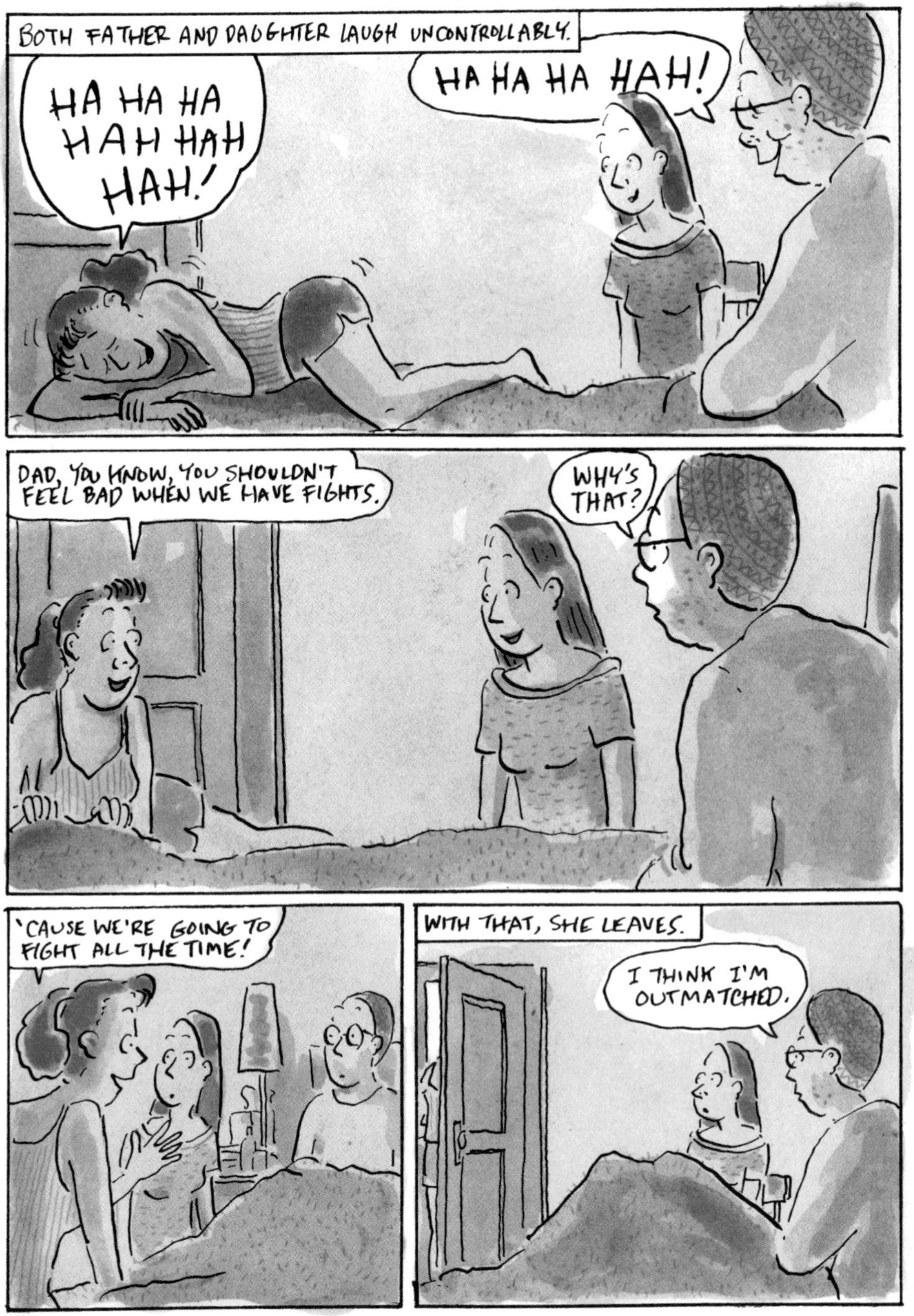
BOTH FATHER AND DAUGHTER LAUGH UNCONTROLLABLY.
HA HA HA HAH HAH HAH!
HA HA HA HAH!
DAD, YOU KNOW, YOU SHOULDN'T FEEL BAD WHEN WE HAVE FIGHTS.
WHY'S THAT?
'CAUSE WE'RE GOING TO FIGHT ALL THE TIME!
WITH THAT, SHE LEAVES.
I THINK I'M OUTMATCHED.

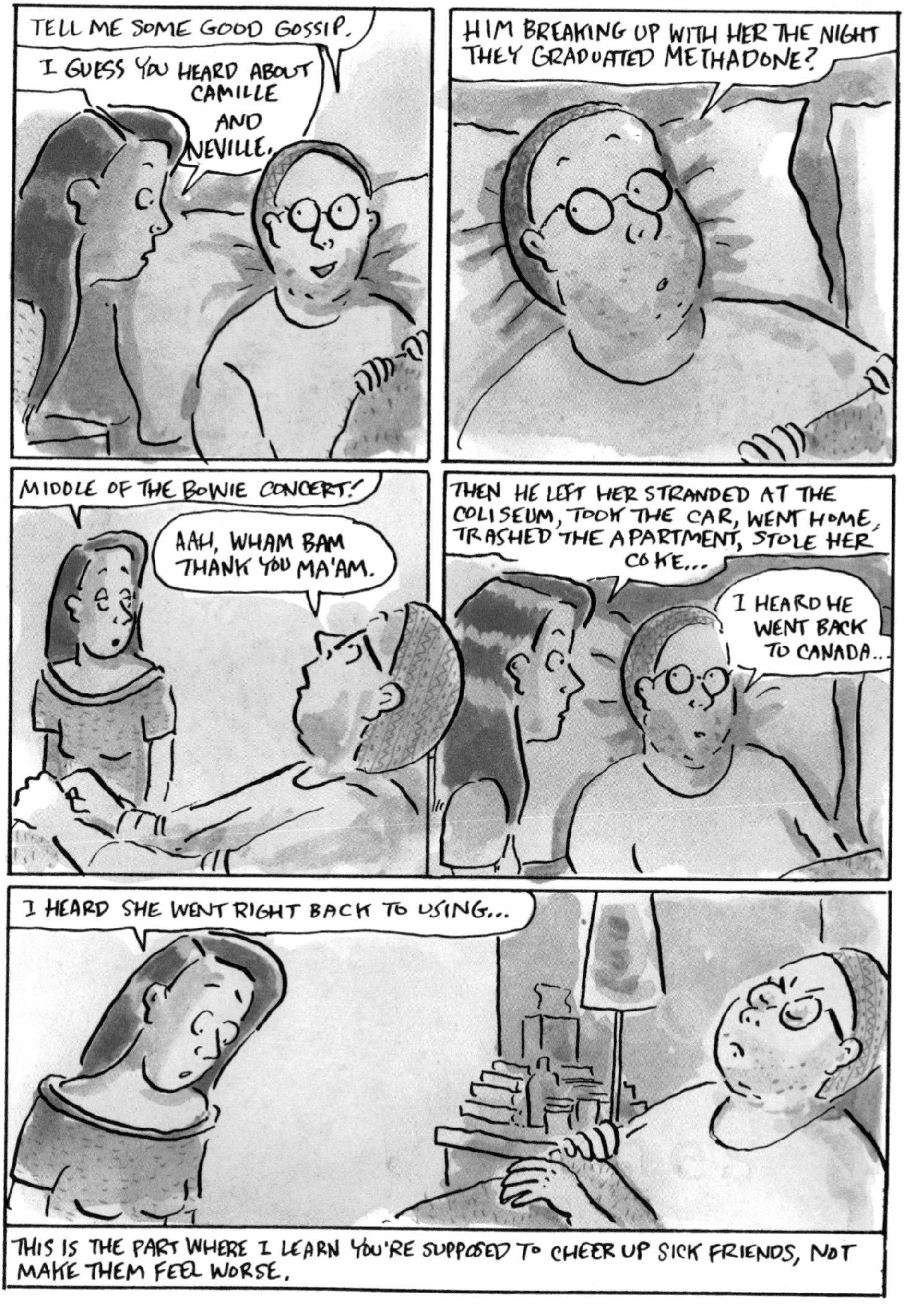
TELL ME SOME GOOD GOSSIP.
I GUESS YOU HEARD ABOUT CAMILLE AND NEVILLE.
HIM BREAKING UP WITH HER THE NIGHT THEY GRADUATED METHADONE?
MIDDLE OF THE BOWIE CONCERT!
AAH, WHAM BAM THANK YOU MA'AM.
THEN HE LEFT HER STRANDED AT THE COLISEUM, TOOK THE CAR, WENT HOME, TRASHED THE APARTMENT, STOLE HER COKE...
I HEARD HE WENT BACK TO CANADA...
I HEARD SHE WENT RIGHT BACK TO USING...
THIS IS THE PART WHERE I LEARN YOU'RE SUPPOSED TO CHEER UP SICK FRIENDS, NOT MAKE THEM FEEL WORSE.

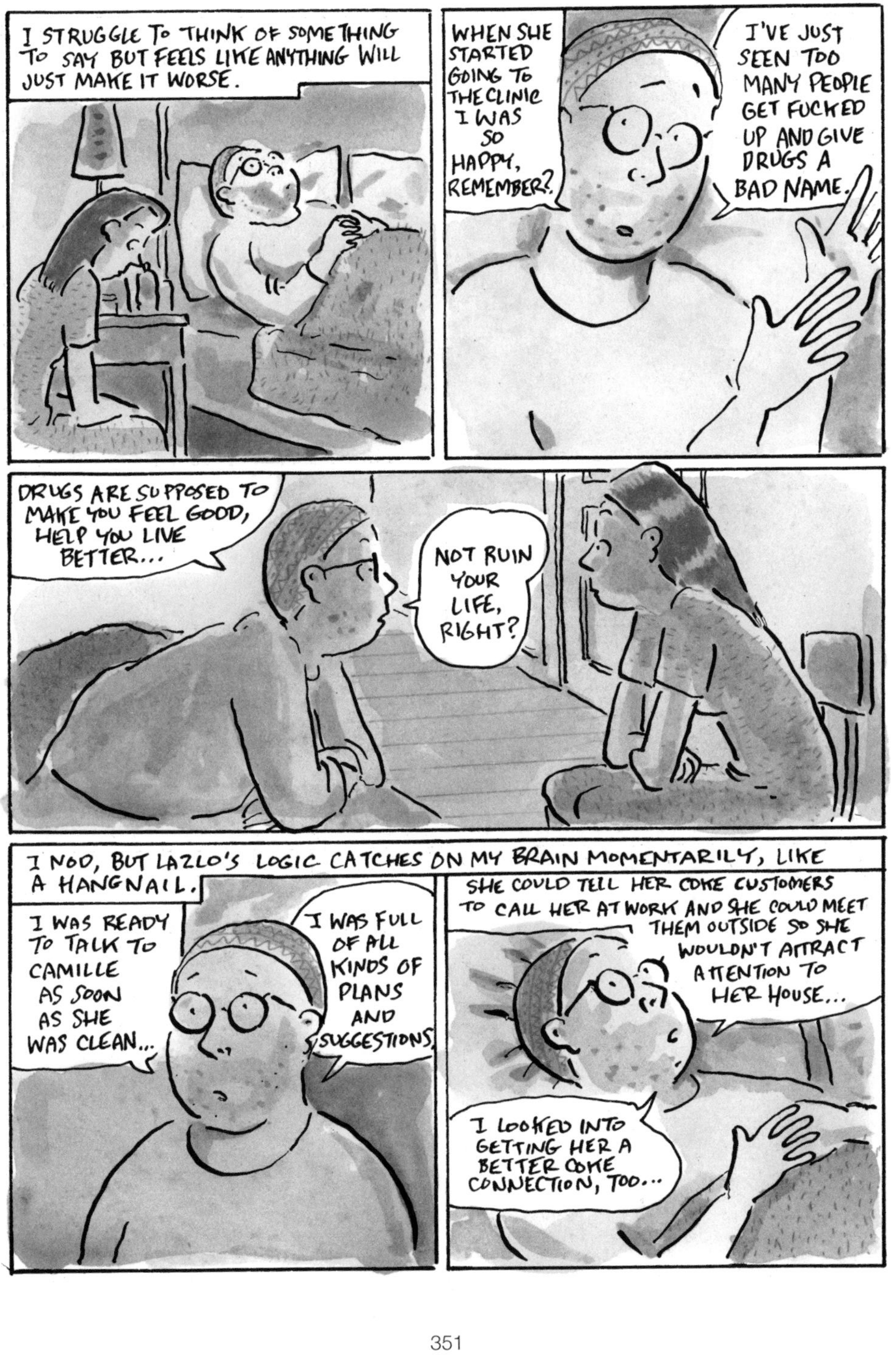
I STRUGGLE TO THINK OF SOMETHING TO SAY BUT FEELS LIKE ANYTHING WILL JUST MAKE IT WORSE.
WHEN SHE STARTED GOING TO THE CLINIC I WAS SO HAPPY, REMEMBER?
I'VE JUST SEEN TOO MANY PEOPLE GET FUCKED UP AND GIVE DRUGS A BAD NAME.
DRUGS ARE SUPPOSED TO MAKE YOU FEEL GOOD, HELP YOU LIVE BETTER...
NOT RUIN YOUR LIFE, RIGHT?
I NOD, BUT LAZLO'S LOGIC CATCHES ON MY BRAIN MOMENTARILY, LIKE A HANGNAIL.
I WAS READY TO TALK TO CAMILLE AS SOON AS SHE WAS CLEAN...
I WAS FULL OF ALL KINDS OF PLANS AND SUGGESTIONS.
SHE COULD TELL HER COKE CUSTOMERS TO CALL HER AT WORK AND SHE COULD MEET THEM OUTSIDE SO SHE WOULDN'T ATTRACT ATTENTION TO HER HOUSE...
I LOOKED INTO GETTING HER A BETTER COKE CONNECTION, TOO...

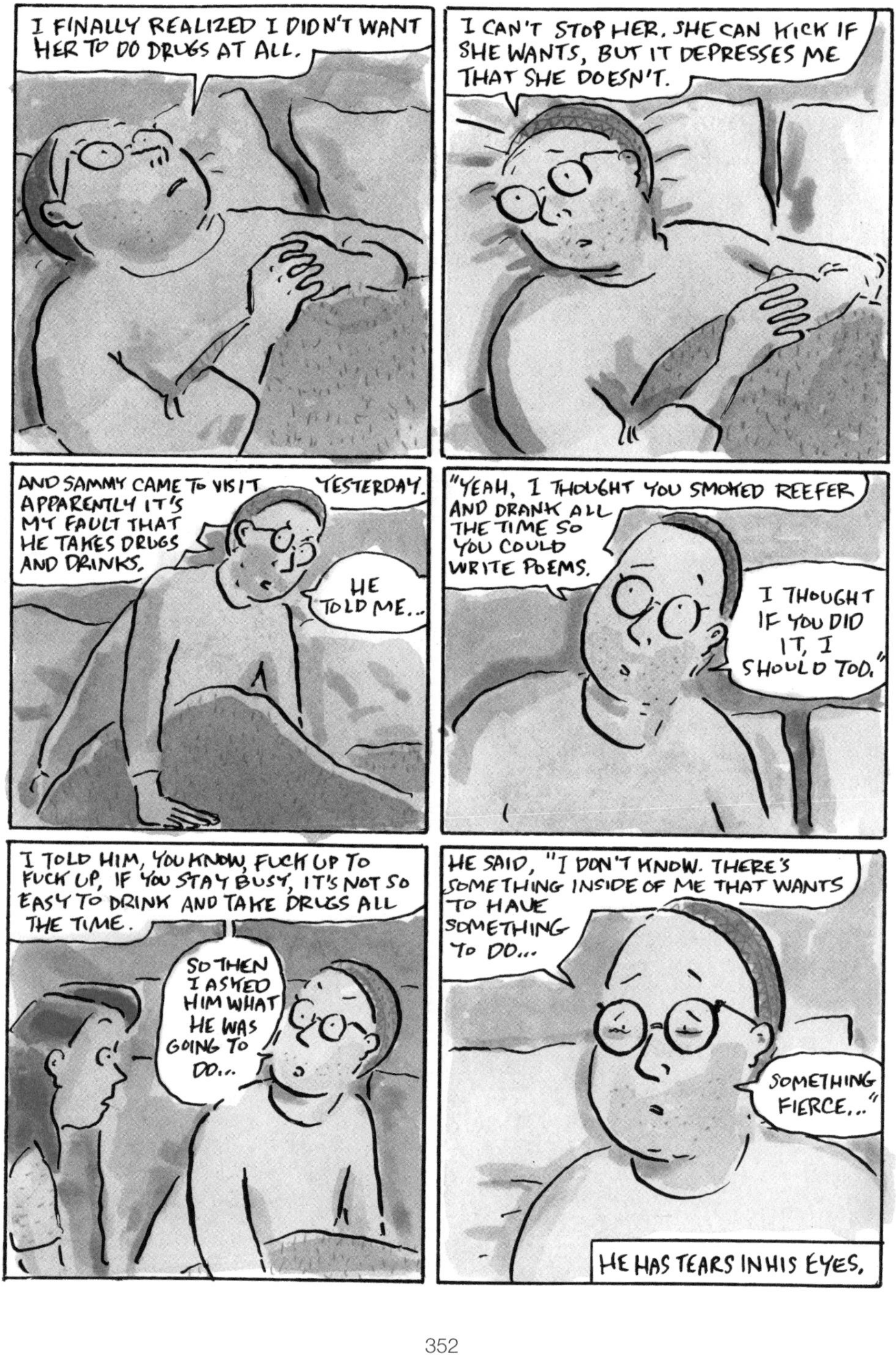
I FINALLY REALIZED I DIDN'T WANT HER TO DO DRUGS AT ALL.
I CAN'T STOP HER. SHE CAN KICK IF SHE WANTS, BUT IT DEPRESSES ME THAT SHE DOESN'T.
AND SAMMY CAME TO VISIT YESTERDAY. APPARENTLY IT'S MY FAULT THAT HE TAKES DRUGS AND DRINKS.
HE TOLD ME...
"YEAH, I THOUGHT YOU SMOKED REEFER AND DRANK ALL THE TIME SO YOU COULD WRITE POEMS.
I THOUGHT IF YOU DID IT, I SHOULD TOO."
I TOLD HIM, YOU KNOW, FUCK UP TO FUCK UP, IF YOU STAY BUSY, IT'S NOT SO EASY TO DRINK AND TAKE DRUGS ALL THE TIME.
SO THEN I ASKED HIM WHAT HE WAS GOING TO DO...
HE SAID, "I DON'T KNOW. THERE'S SOMETHING INSIDE OF ME THAT WANTS TO HAVE SOMETHING TO DO...
SOMETHING FIERCE..."
HE HAS TEARS IN HIS EYES.

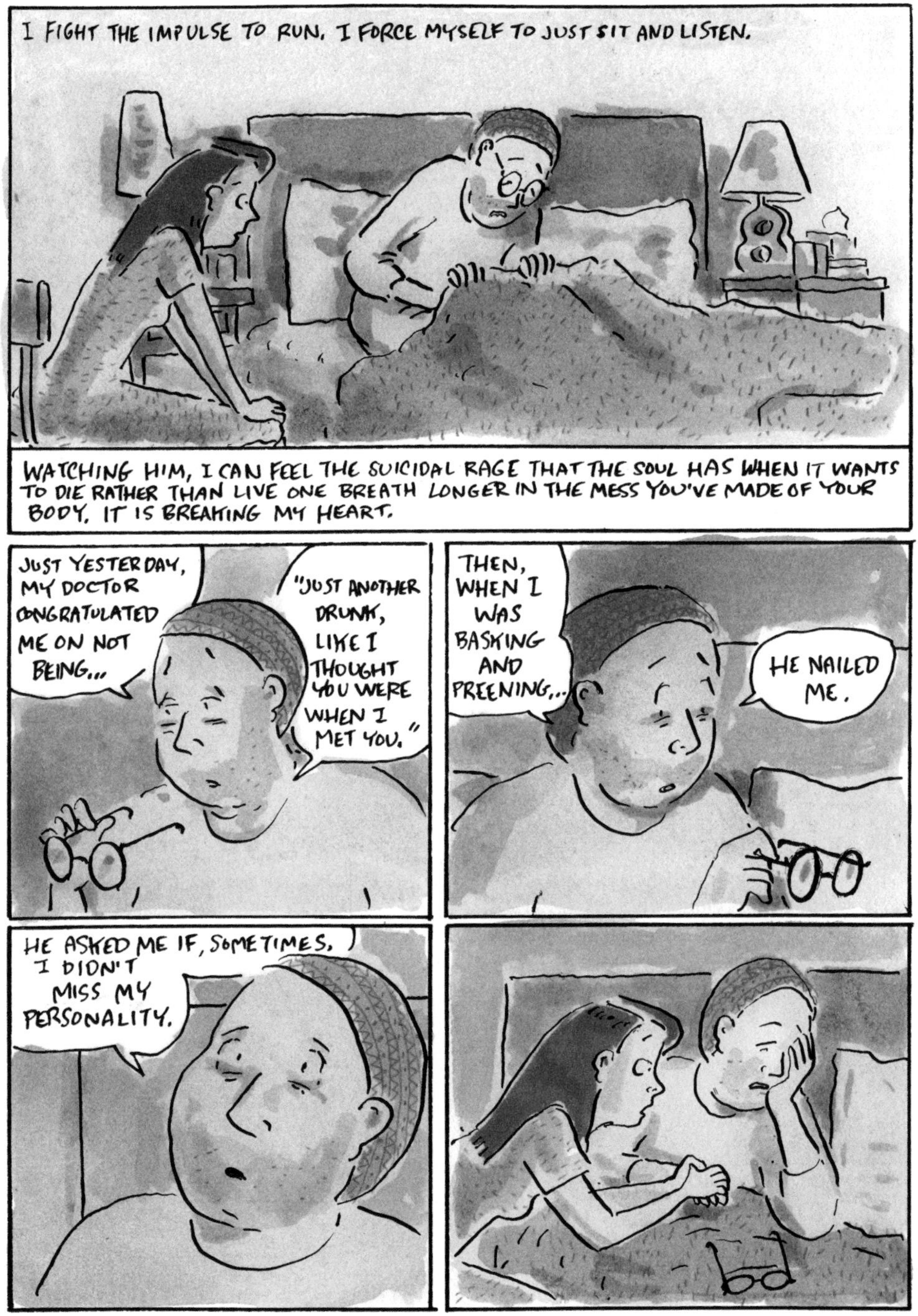
I FIGHT THE IMPULSE TO RUN. I FORCE MYSELF TO JUST SIT AND LISTEN.
WATCHING HIM, I CAN FEEL THE SUICIDAL RAGE THAT THE SOUL HAS WHEN IT WANTS TO DIE RATHER THAN LIVE ONE BREATH LONGER IN THE MESS YOU'VE MADE OF YOUR BODY. IT IS BREAKING MY HEART.
JUST YESTERDAY, MY DOCTOR CONGRATULATED ME ON NOT BEING...
"JUST ANOTHER DRUNK, LIKE I THOUGHT YOU WERE WHEN I MET YOU."
THEN, WHEN I WAS BASKING AND PREENING...
HE NAILED ME.
HE ASKED ME IF, SOMETIMES, I DIDN'T MISS MY PERSONALITY.

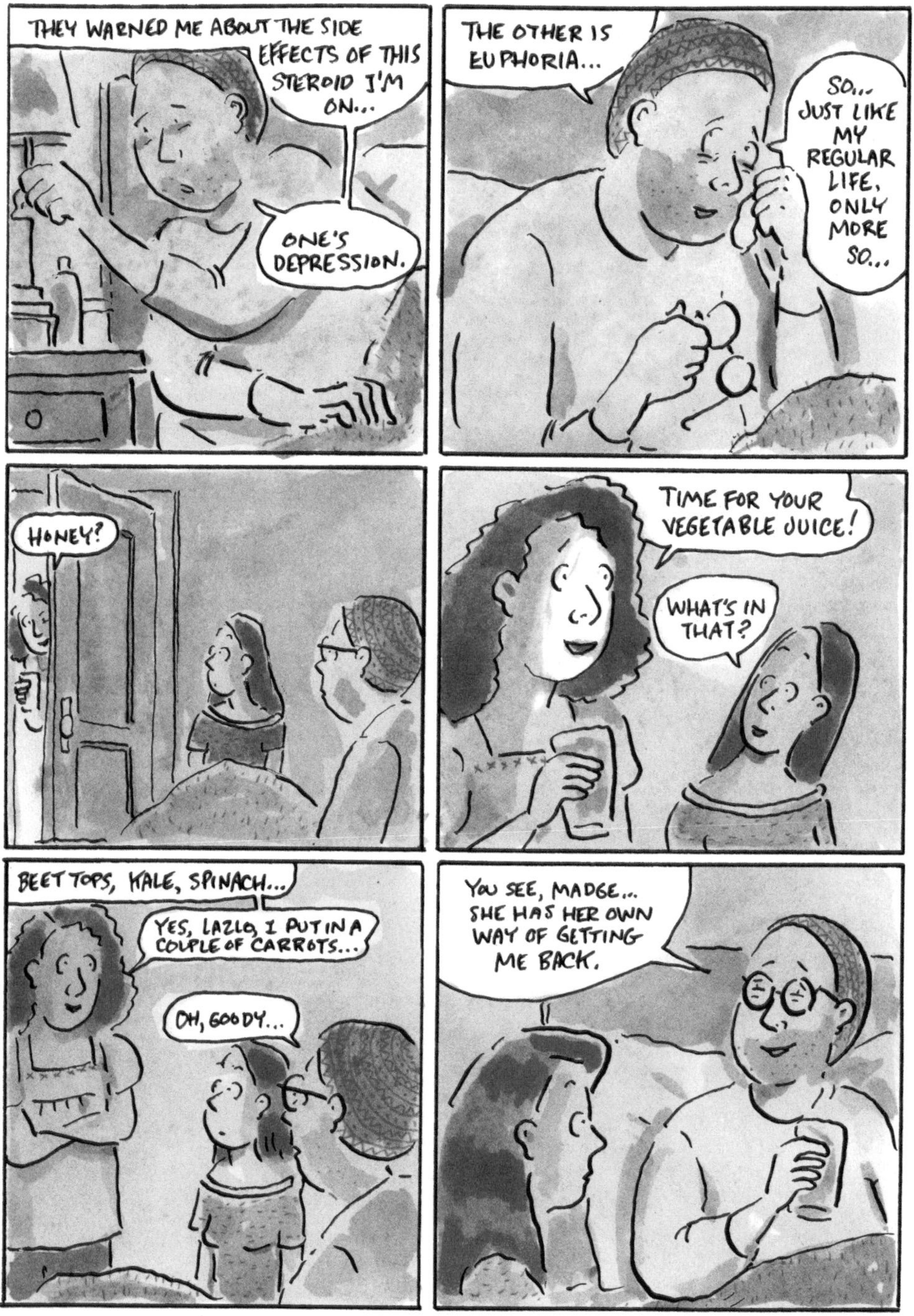
THEY WARNED ME ABOUT THE SIDE EFFECTS OF THIS STEROID I'M ON...
ONE'S DEPRESSION.
THE OTHER IS EUPHORIA...
SO... JUST LIKE MY REGULAR LIFE, ONLY MORE SO...
HONEY?
TIME FOR YOUR VEGETABLE JUICE!
WHAT'S IN THAT?
BEET TOPS, KALE, SPINACH...
YES, LAZLO, I PUT IN A COUPLE OF CARROTS...
OH, GOODY...
YOU SEE, MADGE... SHE HAS HER OWN WAY OF GETTING ME BACK.

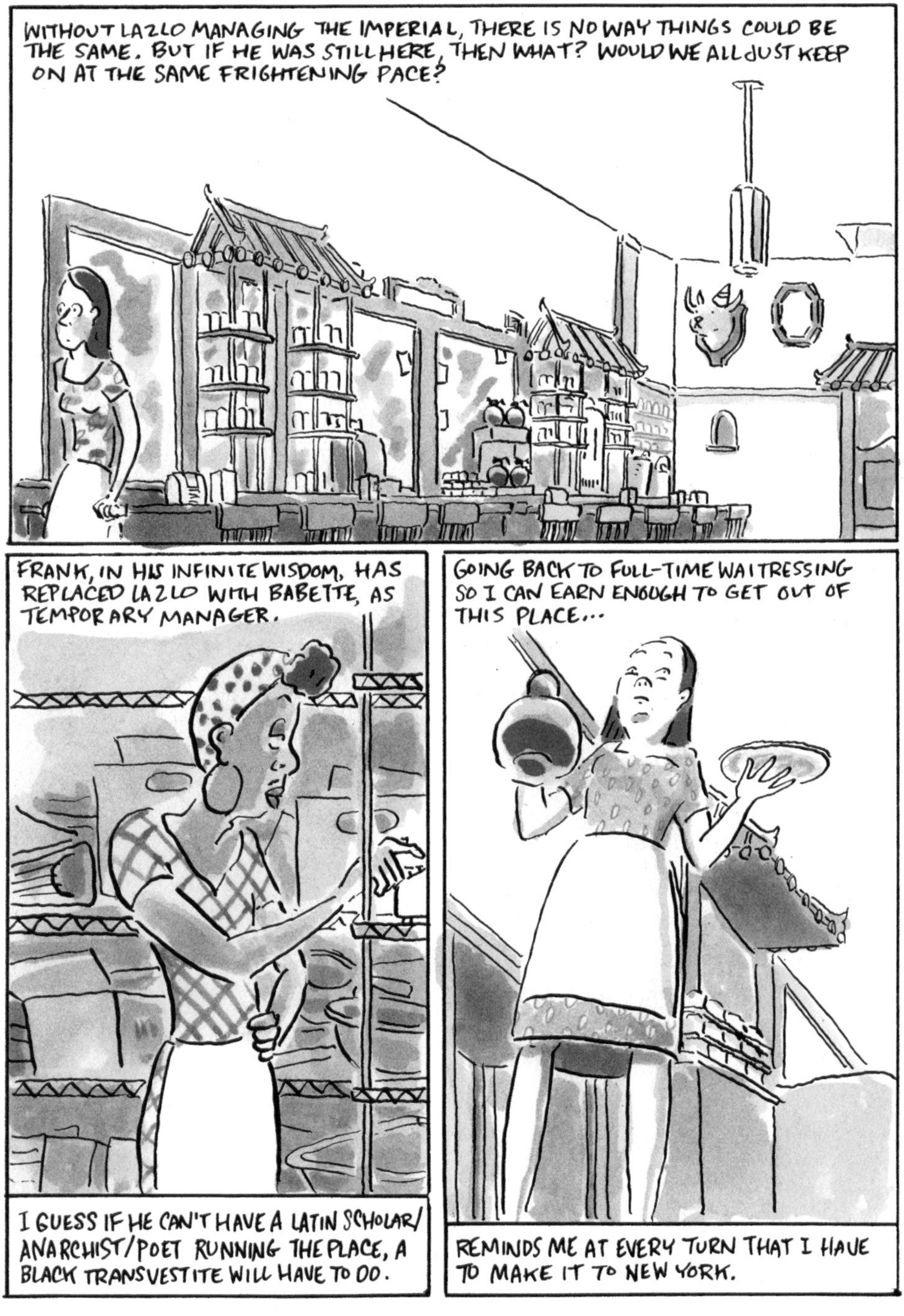
WITHOUT LAZLO MANAGING THE IMPERIAL, THERE IS NO WAY THINGS COULD BE THE SAME. BUT IF HE WAS STILL HERE, THEN WHAT? WOULD WE ALL JUST KEEP ON AT THE SAME FRIGHTENING PACE?
FRANK, IN HIS INFINITE WISDOM, HAS REPLACED LAZLO WITH BABETTE, AS TEMPORARY MANAGER.
I GUESS IF HE CAN'T HAVE A LATIN SCHOLAR/ ANARCHIST/POET RUNNING THE PLACE, A BLACK TRANSVESTITE WILL HAVE TO DO.
GOING BACK TO FULL-TIME WAITRESSING SO I CAN EARN ENOUGH TO GET OUT OF THIS PLACE...
REMINDS ME AT EVERY TURN THAT I HAVE TO MAKE IT TO NEW YORK.

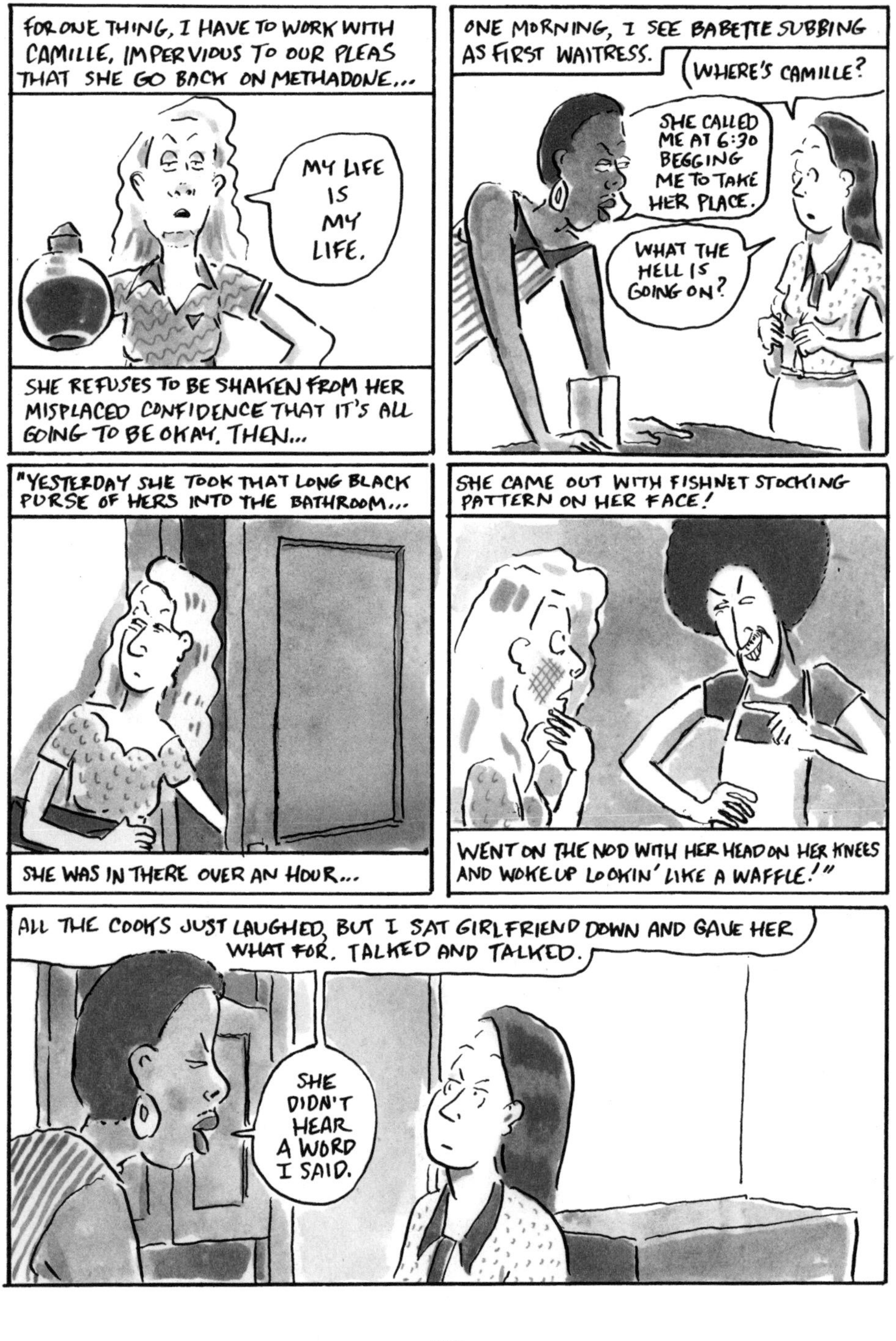
FOR ONE THING, I HAVE TO WORK WITH CAMILLE, IMPERVIOUS TO OUR PLEAS THAT SHE GO BACK ON METHADONE...
MY LIFE IS MY LIFE.
SHE REFUSES TO BE SHAKEN FROM HER MISPLACED CONFIDENCE THAT IT'S ALL GOING TO BE OKAY. THEN...
ONE MORNING, I SEE BABETTE SUBBING AS FIRST WAITRESS.
WHERE'S CAMILLE?
SHE CALLED ME AT 6:30 BEGGING ME TO TAKE HER PLACE.
WHAT THE HELL IS GOING ON?
"YESTERDAY SHE TOOK THAT LONG BLACK PURSE OF HERS INTO THE BATHROOM...
SHE WAS IN THERE OVER AN HOUR...
SHE CAME OUT WITH FISHNET STOCKING PATTERN ON HER FACE!
WENT ON THE NOD WITH HER HEAD ON HER KNEES AND WOKE UP LOOKIN' LIKE A WAFFLE!"
ALL THE COOKS JUST LAUGHED, BUT I SAT GIRLFRIEND DOWN AND GAVE HER WHAT FOR. TALKED AND TALKED.
SHE DIDN'T HEAR A WORD I SAID.

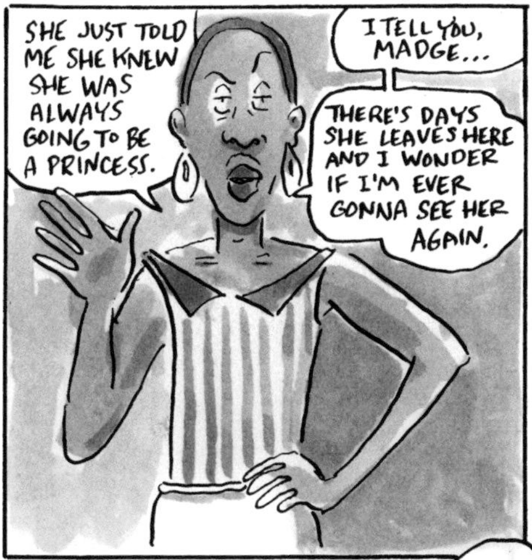
SHE JUST TOLD ME SHE KNEW SHE WAS ALWAYS GOING TO BE A PRINCESS.
I TELL YOU, MADGE...
THERE'S DAYS SHE LEAVES HERE AND I WONDER IF I'M EVER GONNA SEE HER AGAIN.

SHE COULDN'T WORK THAT DAY BECAUSE HER MOM CAME AND DRAGGED HER TO REHAB BACK EAST.

A MONTH LATER, CAMILLE CAME BACK TO OAKLAND AND WENT BACK ON METHADONE. THERE WERE NO SHIFTS OPEN, AND SHE HAD TO FIND SOMETHING. THEN HER FORMER DEALER, GINGER, OFFERED HER A GIG CLEANING HER HOUSE.

I KNOW. CLEANING THE HOUSE OF THE PERSON WHO USED TO SELL YOU HEROIN DOES NOT SOUND LIKE THE BEST IDEA... BUT WHEN YOU'RE A PRINCESS, YOU WON'T SETTLE FOR BEING JUST ANYONE'S MAID.

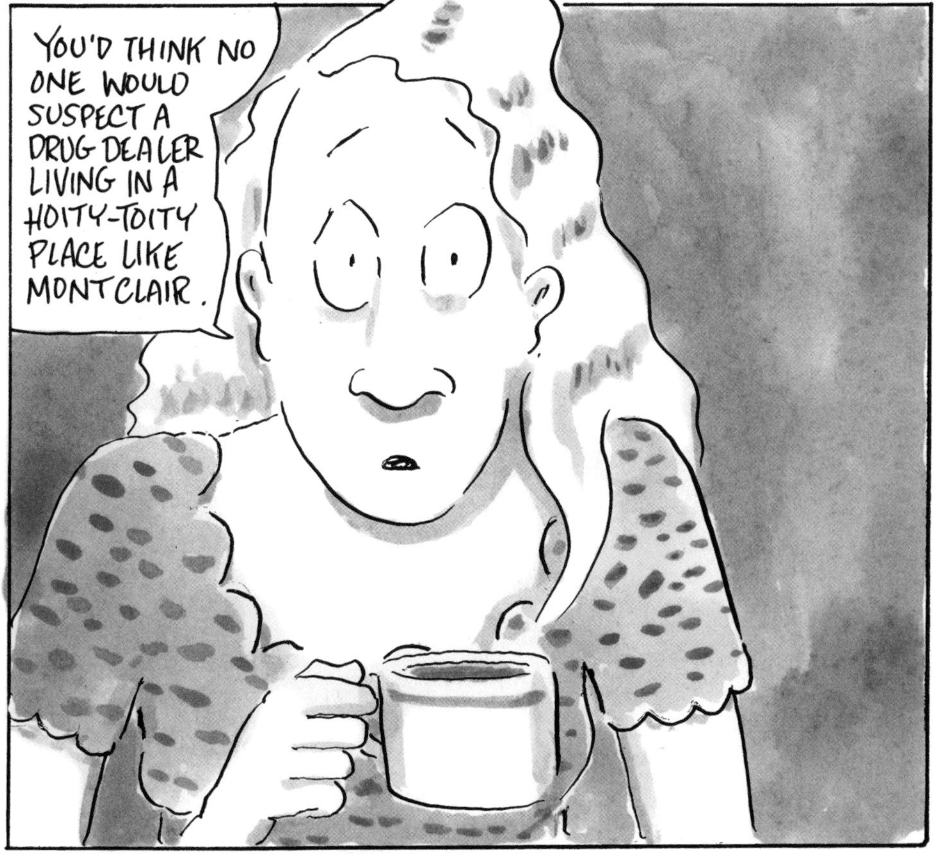
YOU'D THINK NO ONE WOULD SUSPECT A DRUG DEALER LIVING IN A HOITY-TOITY PLACE LIKE MONTCLAIR.

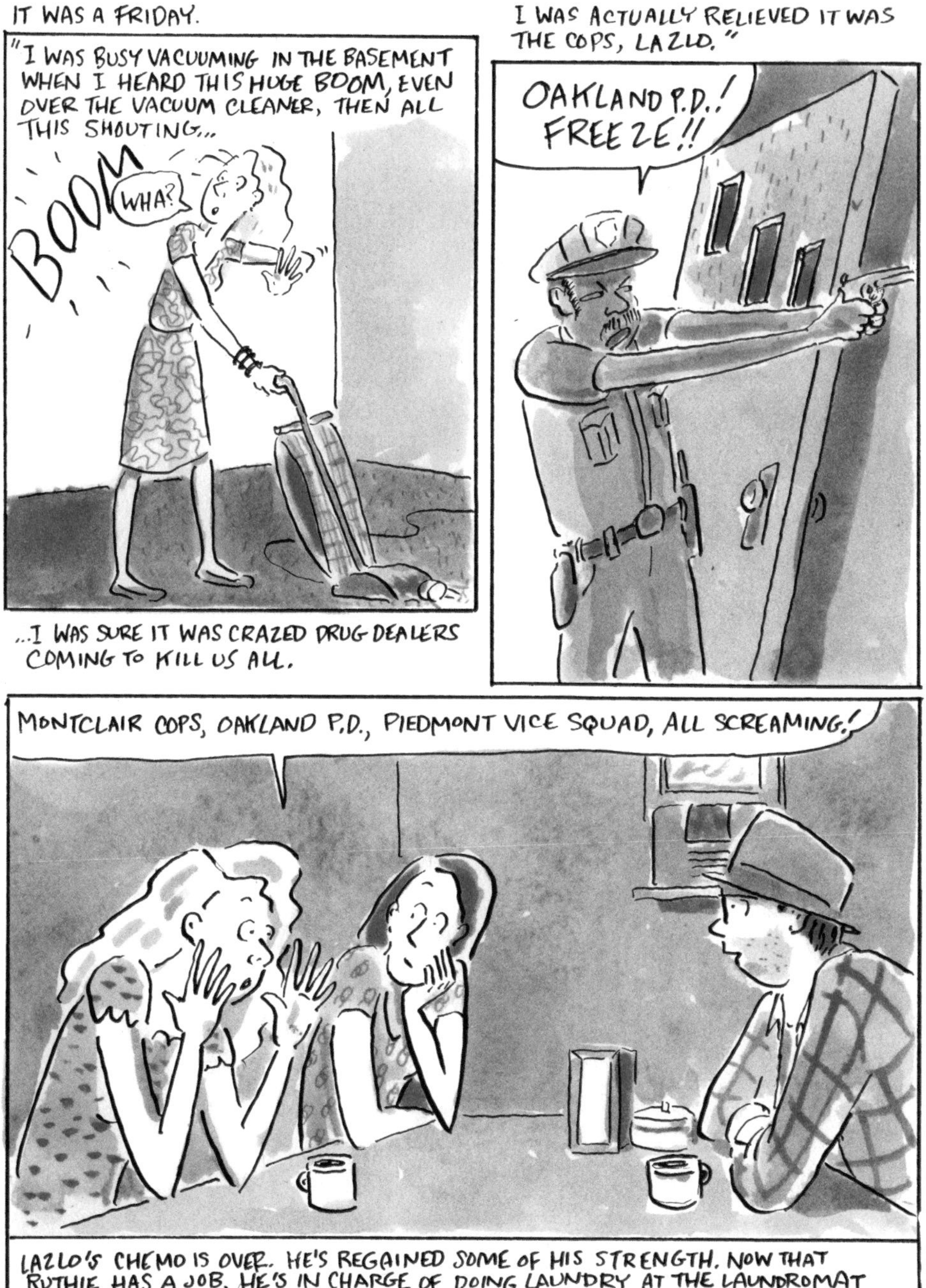
IT WAS A FRIDAY.
"I WAS BUSY VACUUMING IN THE BASEMENT WHEN I HEARD THIS HUGE BOOM, EVEN OVER THE VACUUM CLEANER, THEN ALL THIS SHOUTING...
BOOM
WHA?
...I WAS SURE IT WAS CRAZED DRUG DEALERS COMING TO KILL US ALL.
I WAS ACTUALLY RELIEVED IT WAS THE COPS, LAZLO."
OAKLAND P.D.! FREEZE!!
MONTCLAIR COPS, OAKLAND P.D., PIEDMONT VICE SQUAD, ALL SCREAMING!
LAZLO'S CHEMO IS OVER. HE'S REGAINED SOME OF HIS STRENGTH. NOW THAT RUTHIE HAS A JOB, HE'S IN CHARGE OF DOING LAUNDRY AT THE LAUNDROMAT DOWN THE STREET.

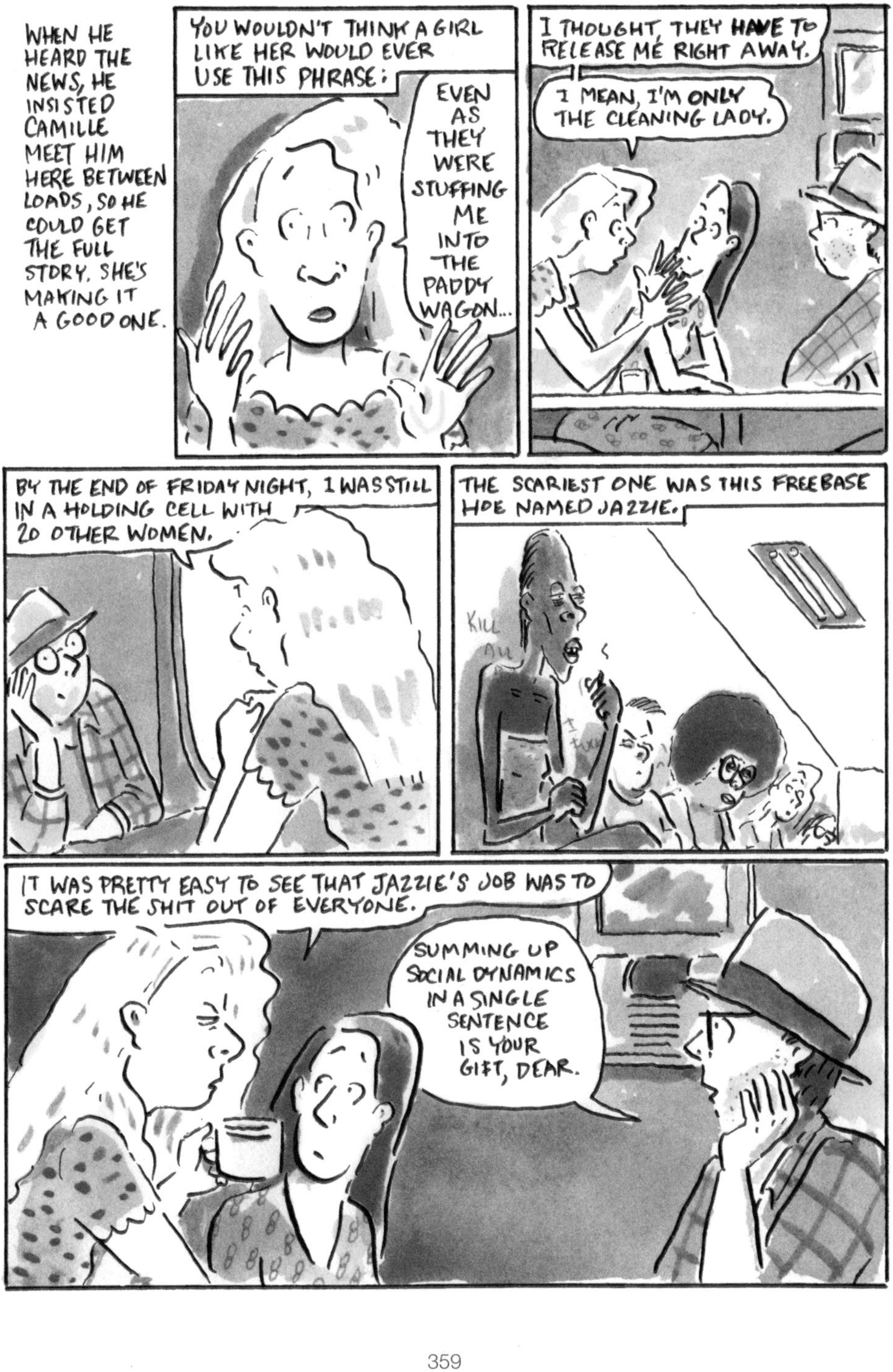
WHEN HE HEARD THE NEWS, HE INSISTED CAMILLE MEET HIM HERE BETWEEN LOADS, SO HE COULD GET THE FULL STORY. SHE'S MAKING IT A GOOD ONE.
YOU WOULDN'T THINK A GIRL LIKE HER WOULD EVER USE THIS PHRASE:
EVEN AS THEY WERE STUFFING ME INTO THE PADDY WAGON...
I THOUGHT, THEY HAVE TO RELEASE ME RIGHT AWAY.
I MEAN, I'M ONLY THE CLEANING LADY.
BY THE END OF FRIDAY NIGHT, I WAS STILL IN A HOLDING CELL WITH 20 OTHER WOMEN.
THE SCARIEST ONE WAS THIS FREEBASE HOE NAMED JAZZIE.
IT WAS PRETTY EASY TO SEE THAT JAZZIE'S JOB WAS TO SCARE THE SHIT OUT OF EVERYONE.
SUMMING UP SOCIAL DYNAMICS IN A SINGLE SENTENCE IS YOUR GIFT, DEAR.

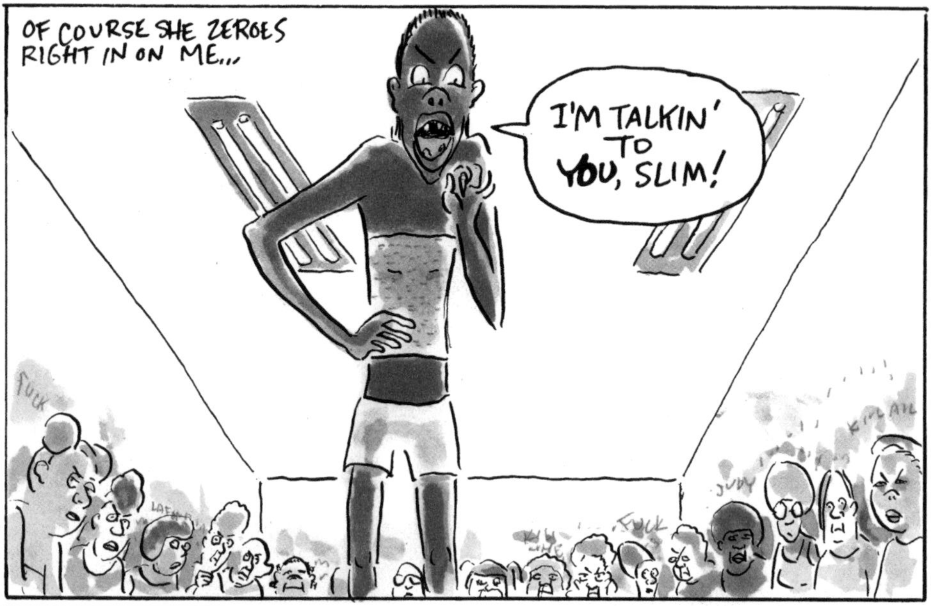
OF COURSE SHE ZEROES RIGHT IN ON ME...
I'M TALKIN' TO **YOU**, SLIM!

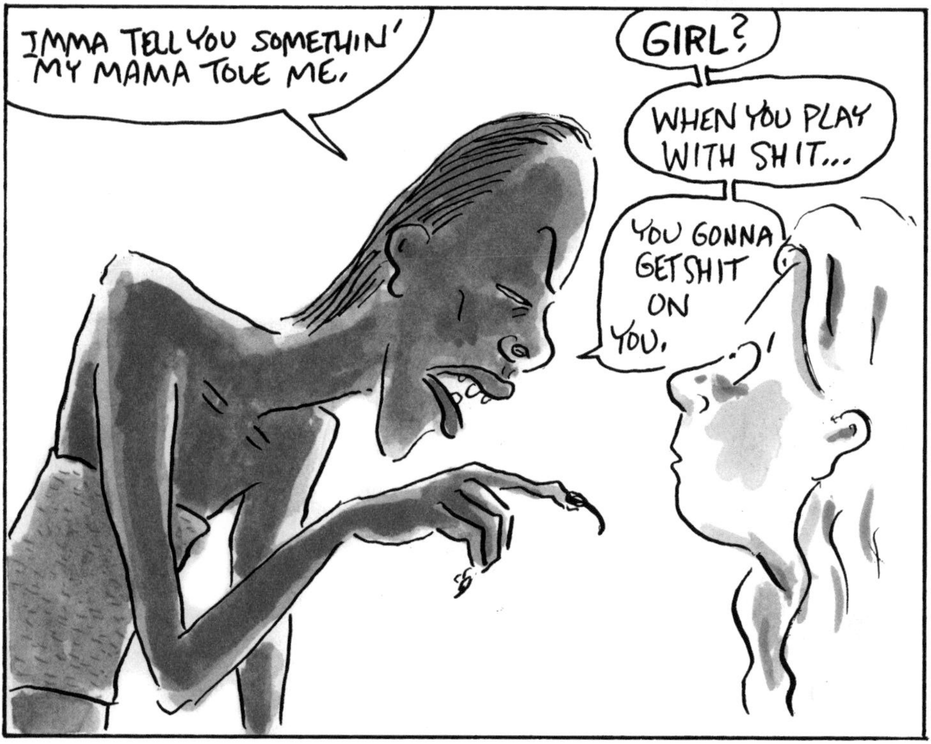
IMMA TELL YOU SOMETHIN' MY MAMA TOLE ME.
GIRL?
WHEN YOU PLAY WITH SHIT...
YOU GONNA GET SHIT ON YOU.

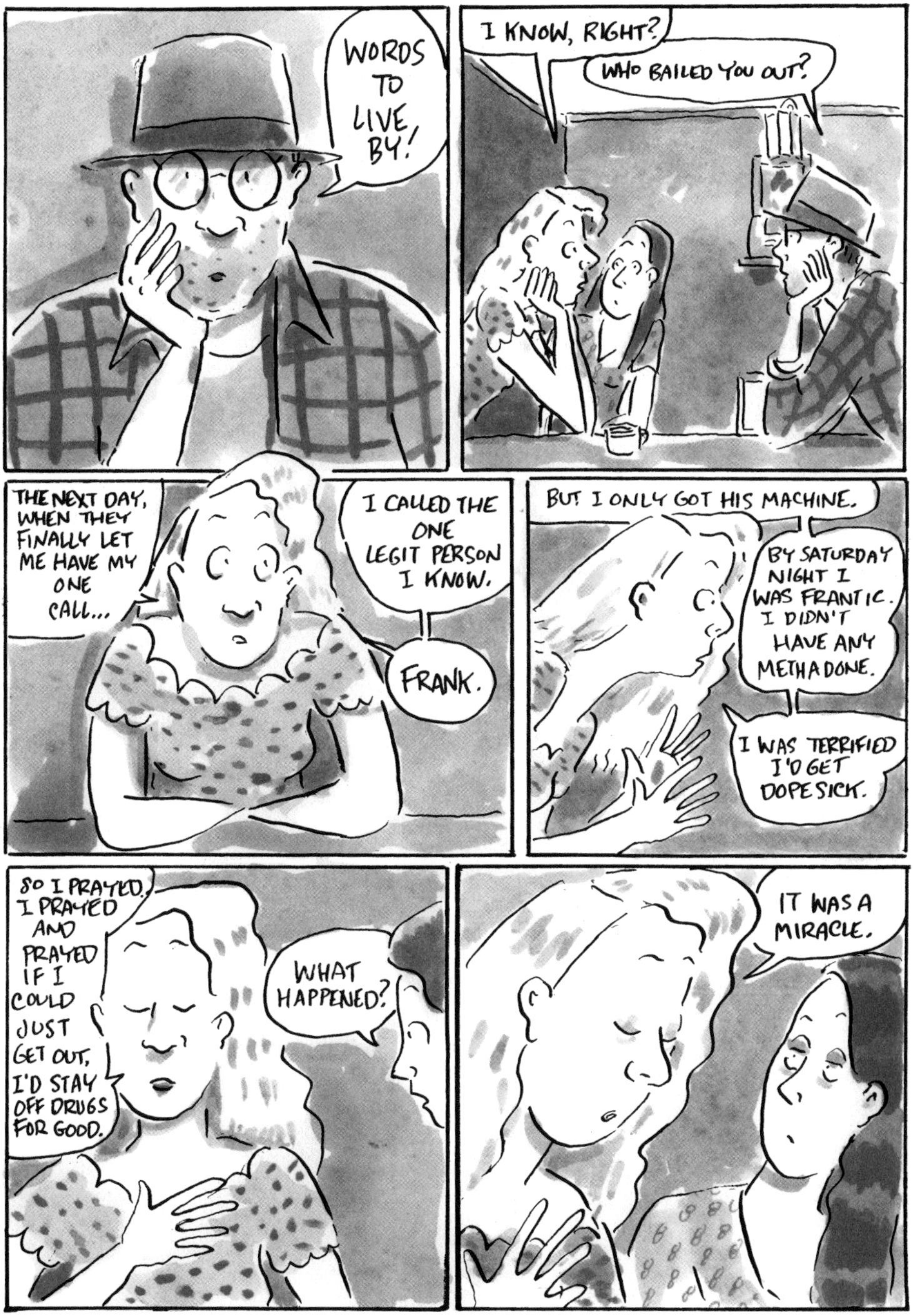
WORDS TO LIVE BY!
I KNOW, RIGHT?
WHO BAILED YOU OUT?
THE NEXT DAY, WHEN THEY FINALLY LET ME HAVE MY ONE CALL...
I CALLED THE ONE LEGIT PERSON I KNOW.
FRANK.
BUT I ONLY GOT HIS MACHINE.
BY SATURDAY NIGHT I WAS FRANTIC. I DIDN'T HAVE ANY METHADONE.
I WAS TERRIFIED I'D GET DOPESICK.
SO I PRAYED. I PRAYED AND PRAYED IF I COULD JUST GET OUT, I'D STAY OFF DRUGS FOR GOOD.
WHAT HAPPENED?
IT WAS A MIRACLE.

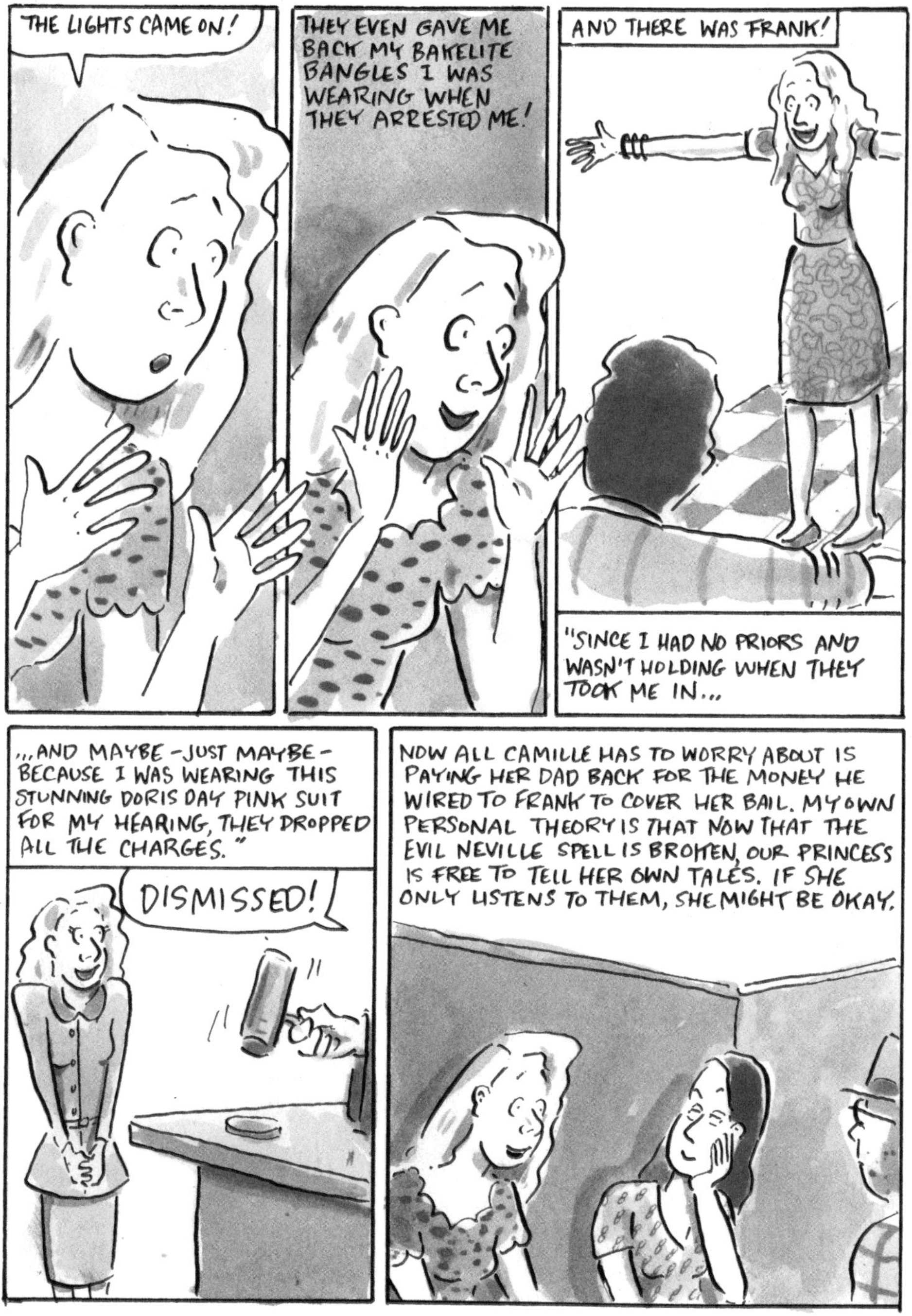
THE LIGHTS CAME ON!
THEY EVEN GAVE ME BACK MY BAKELITE BANGLES I WAS WEARING WHEN THEY ARRESTED ME!
AND THERE WAS FRANK!
"SINCE I HAD NO PRIORS AND WASN'T HOLDING WHEN THEY TOOK ME IN...
...AND MAYBE - JUST MAYBE - BECAUSE I WAS WEARING THIS STUNNING DORIS DAY PINK SUIT FOR MY HEARING, THEY DROPPED ALL THE CHARGES."
DISMISSED!
NOW ALL CAMILLE HAS TO WORRY ABOUT IS PAYING HER DAD BACK FOR THE MONEY HE WIRED TO FRANK TO COVER HER BAIL. MY OWN PERSONAL THEORY IS THAT NOW THAT THE EVIL NEVILLE SPELL IS BROKEN, OUR PRINCESS IS FREE TO TELL HER OWN TALES. IF SHE ONLY LISTENS TO THEM, SHE MIGHT BE OKAY.

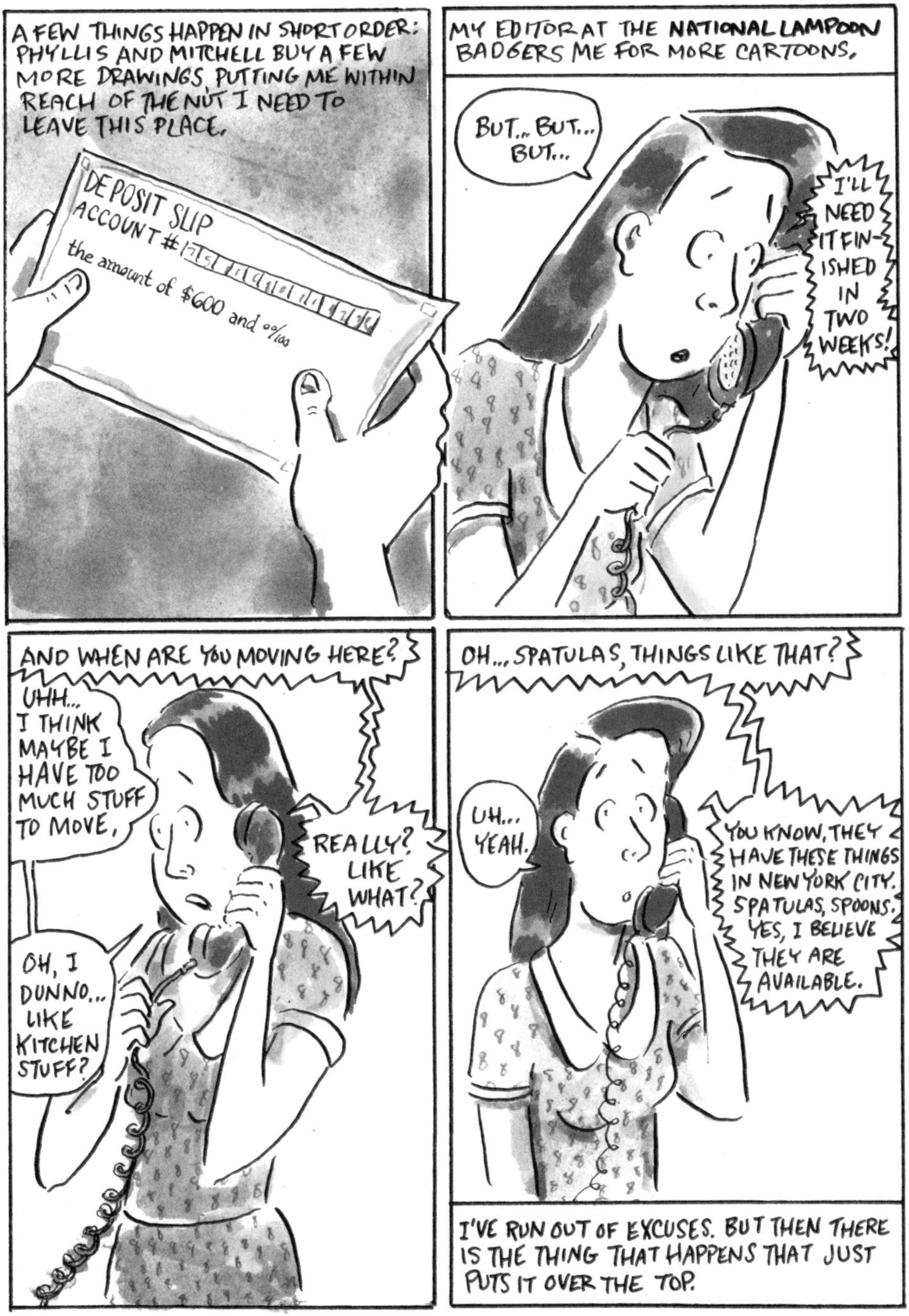
A FEW THINGS HAPPEN IN SHORT ORDER: PHYLLIS AND MITCHELL BUY A FEW MORE DRAWINGS, PUTTING ME WITHIN REACH OF THE NUT I NEED TO LEAVE THIS PLACE.
DEPOSIT SLIP
ACCOUNT #
the amount of $600 and 00/100
MY EDITOR AT THE NATIONAL LAMPOON BADGERS ME FOR MORE CARTOONS.
I'LL NEED IT FIN-ISHED IN TWO WEEKS!
BUT... BUT... BUT...
AND WHEN ARE YOU MOVING HERE?
UHH... I THINK MAYBE I HAVE TOO MUCH STUFF TO MOVE.
REALLY? LIKE WHAT?
OH, I DUNNO... LIKE KITCHEN STUFF?
OH... SPATULAS, THINGS LIKE THAT?
UH... YEAH.
YOU KNOW, THEY HAVE THESE THINGS IN NEW YORK CITY. SPATULAS, SPOONS. YES, I BELIEVE THEY ARE AVAILABLE.
I'VE RUN OUT OF EXCUSES. BUT THEN THERE IS THE THING THAT HAPPENS THAT JUST PUTS IT OVER THE TOP.

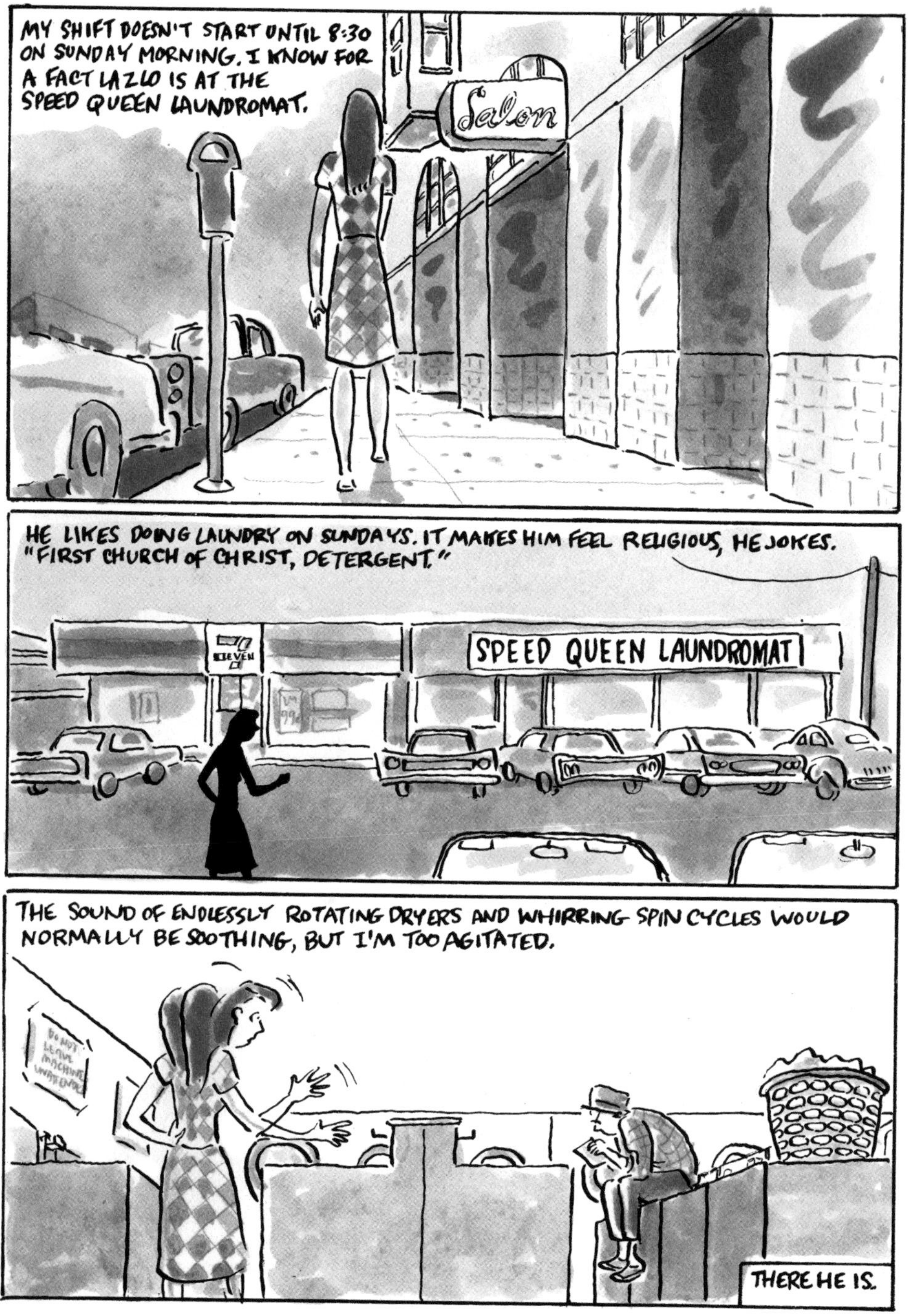
MY SHIFT DOESN'T START UNTIL 8:30 ON SUNDAY MORNING. I KNOW FOR A FACT LAZLO IS AT THE SPEED QUEEN LAUNDROMAT.
Salon
HE LIKES DOING LAUNDRY ON SUNDAYS. IT MAKES HIM FEEL RELIGIOUS, HE JOKES. "FIRST CHURCH OF CHRIST, DETERGENT."
SPEED QUEEN LAUNDROMAT
THE SOUND OF ENDLESSLY ROTATING DRYERS AND WHIRRING SPIN CYCLES WOULD NORMALLY BE SOOTHING, BUT I'M TOO AGITATED.
THERE HE IS.

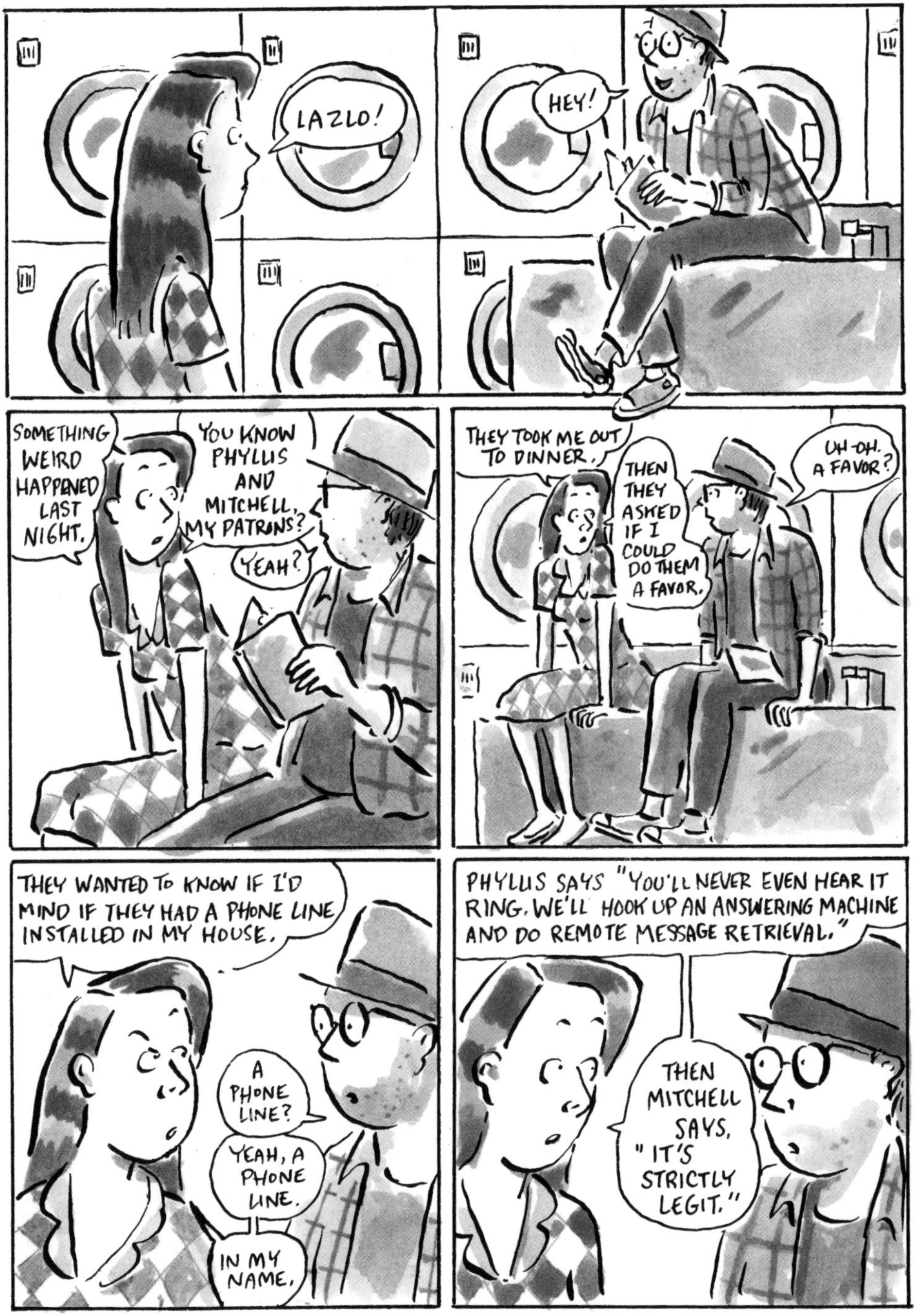
LAZLO!
HEY!
SOMETHING WEIRD HAPPENED LAST NIGHT.
YOU KNOW PHYLLIS AND MITCHELL, MY PATRONS?
YEAH?
THEY TOOK ME OUT TO DINNER.
THEN THEY ASKED IF I COULD DO THEM A FAVOR.
UH-OH. A FAVOR?
THEY WANTED TO KNOW IF I'D MIND IF THEY HAD A PHONE LINE INSTALLED IN MY HOUSE.
A PHONE LINE?
YEAH, A PHONE LINE.
IN MY NAME.
PHYLLIS SAYS "YOU'LL NEVER EVEN HEAR IT RING. WE'LL HOOK UP AN ANSWERING MACHINE AND DO REMOTE MESSAGE RETRIEVAL."
THEN MITCHELL SAYS, "IT'S STRICTLY LEGIT."

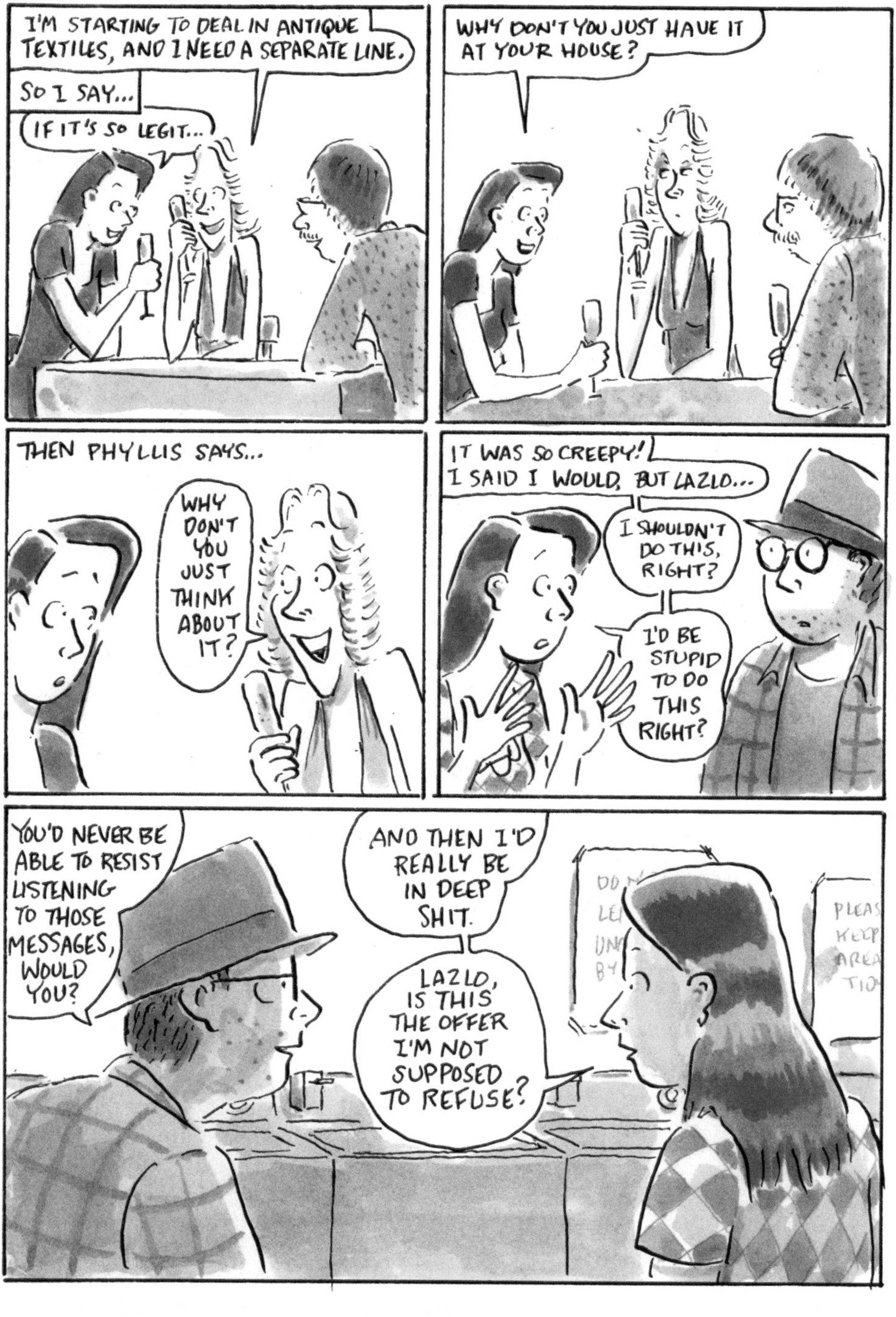
I'M STARTING TO DEAL IN ANTIQUE TEXTILES, AND I NEED A SEPARATE LINE.
SO I SAY...
IF IT'S SO LEGIT...
WHY DON'T YOU JUST HAVE IT AT YOUR HOUSE?
THEN PHYLLIS SAYS...
WHY DON'T YOU JUST THINK ABOUT IT?
IT WAS SO CREEPY! I SAID I WOULD, BUT LAZLO...
I SHOULDN'T DO THIS, RIGHT?
I'D BE STUPID TO DO THIS RIGHT?
YOU'D NEVER BE ABLE TO RESIST LISTENING TO THOSE MESSAGES, WOULD YOU?
AND THEN I'D REALLY BE IN DEEP SHIT.
LAZLO, IS THIS THE OFFER I'M NOT SUPPOSED TO REFUSE?

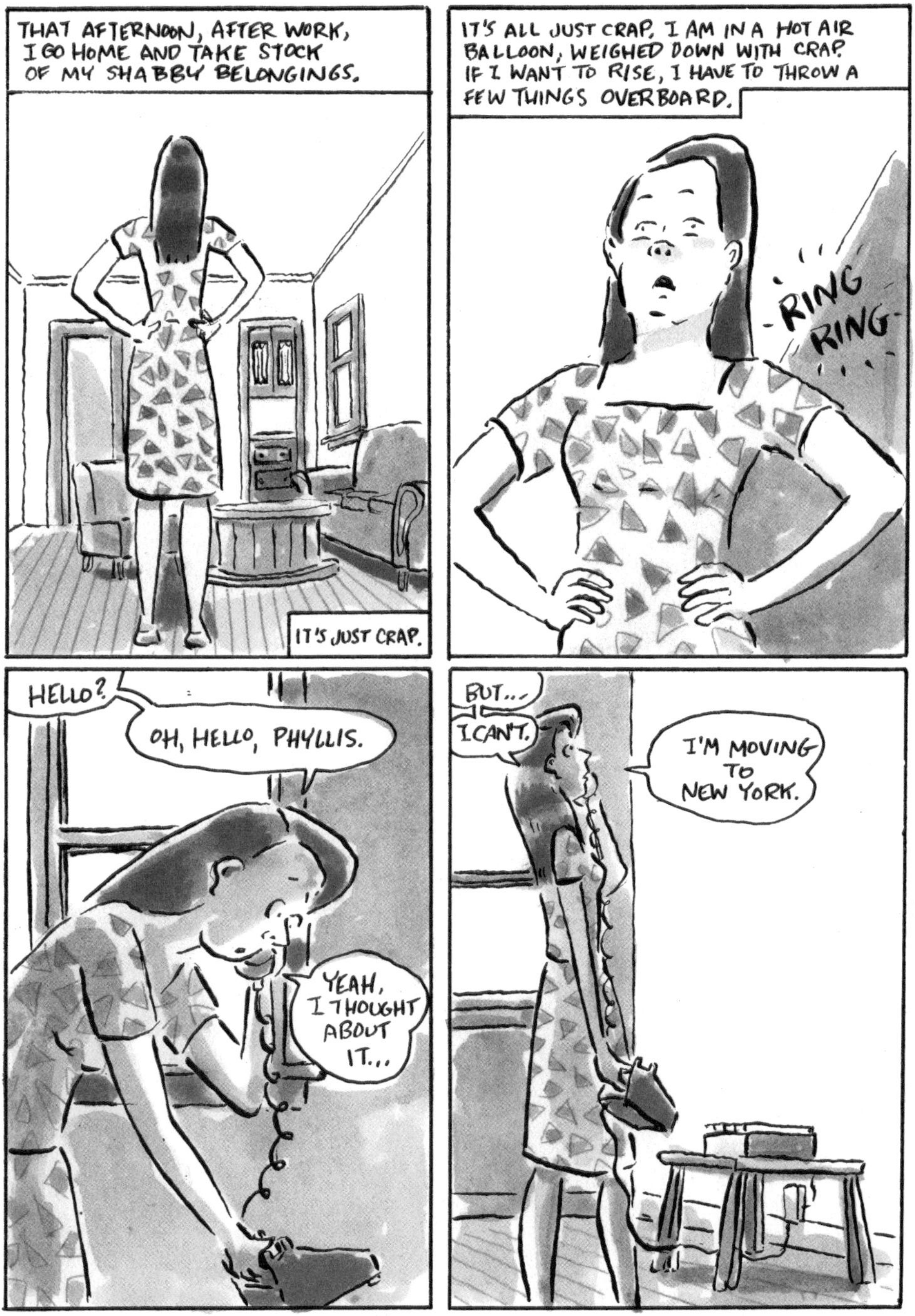

THAT AFTERNOON, AFTER WORK, I GO HOME AND TAKE STOCK OF MY SHABBY BELONGINGS.
IT'S JUST CRAP.
IT'S ALL JUST CRAP, I AM IN A HOT AIR BALLOON, WEIGHED DOWN WITH CRAP. IF I WANT TO RISE, I HAVE TO THROW A FEW THINGS OVERBOARD.
RING RING
HELLO?
OH, HELLO, PHYLLIS.
YEAH, I THOUGHT ABOUT IT...
BUT...
I CAN'T.
I'M MOVING TO NEW YORK.

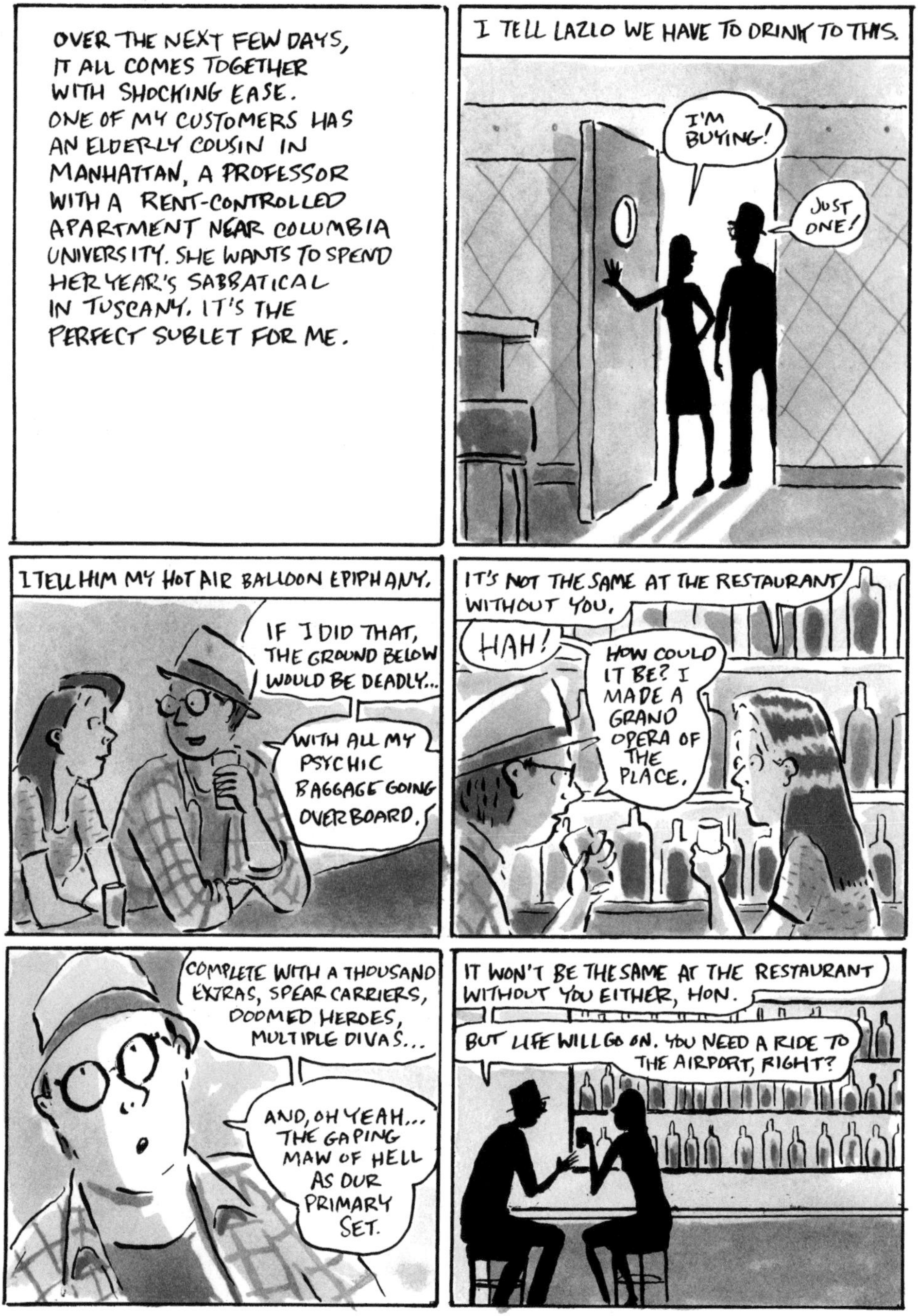
OVER THE NEXT FEW DAYS, IT ALL COMES TOGETHER WITH SHOCKING EASE. ONE OF MY CUSTOMERS HAS AN ELDERLY COUSIN IN MANHATTAN, A PROFESSOR WITH A RENT-CONTROLLED APARTMENT NEAR COLUMBIA UNIVERSITY. SHE WANTS TO SPEND HER YEAR'S SABBATICAL IN TUSCANY. IT'S THE PERFECT SUBLET FOR ME.
I TELL LAZLO WE HAVE TO DRINK TO THIS.
I'M BUYING!
JUST ONE!
I TELL HIM MY HOT AIR BALLOON EPIPHANY.
IF I DID THAT, THE GROUND BELOW WOULD BE DEADLY...
WITH ALL MY PSYCHIC BAGGAGE GOING OVERBOARD.
IT'S NOT THE SAME AT THE RESTAURANT WITHOUT YOU.
HAH!
HOW COULD IT BE? I MADE A GRAND OPERA OF THE PLACE.
COMPLETE WITH A THOUSAND EXTRAS, SPEAR CARRIERS, DOOMED HEROES, MULTIPLE DIVAS...
AND, OH YEAH... THE GAPING MAW OF HELL AS OUR PRIMARY SET.
IT WON'T BE THE SAME AT THE RESTAURANT WITHOUT YOU EITHER, HON.
BUT LIFE WILL GO ON. YOU NEED A RIDE TO THE AIRPORT, RIGHT?

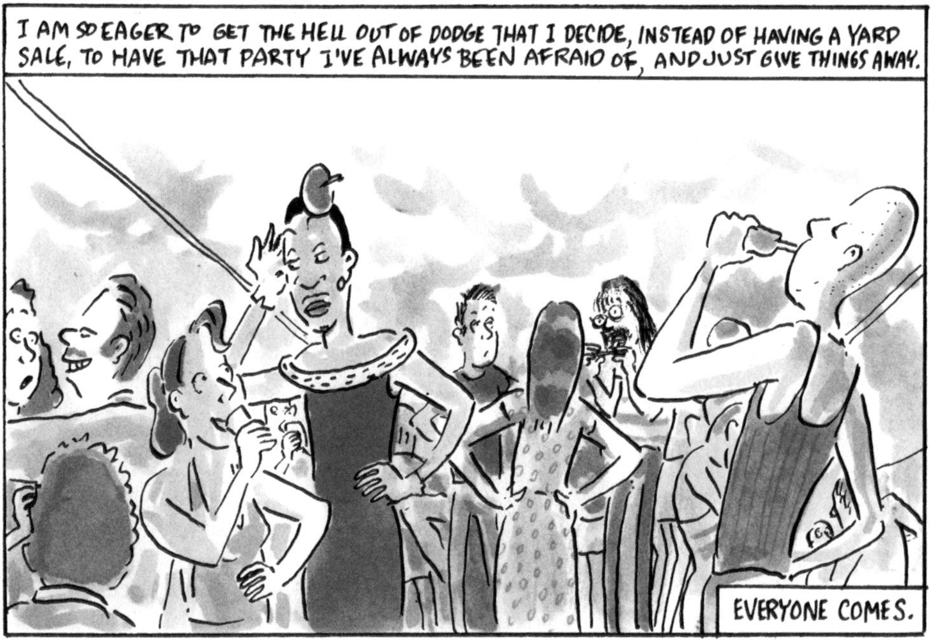
I AM SO EAGER TO GET THE HELL OUT OF DODGE THAT I DECIDE, INSTEAD OF HAVING A YARD SALE, TO HAVE THAT PARTY I'VE ALWAYS BEEN AFRAID OF, AND JUST GIVE THINGS AWAY.
EVERYONE COMES.

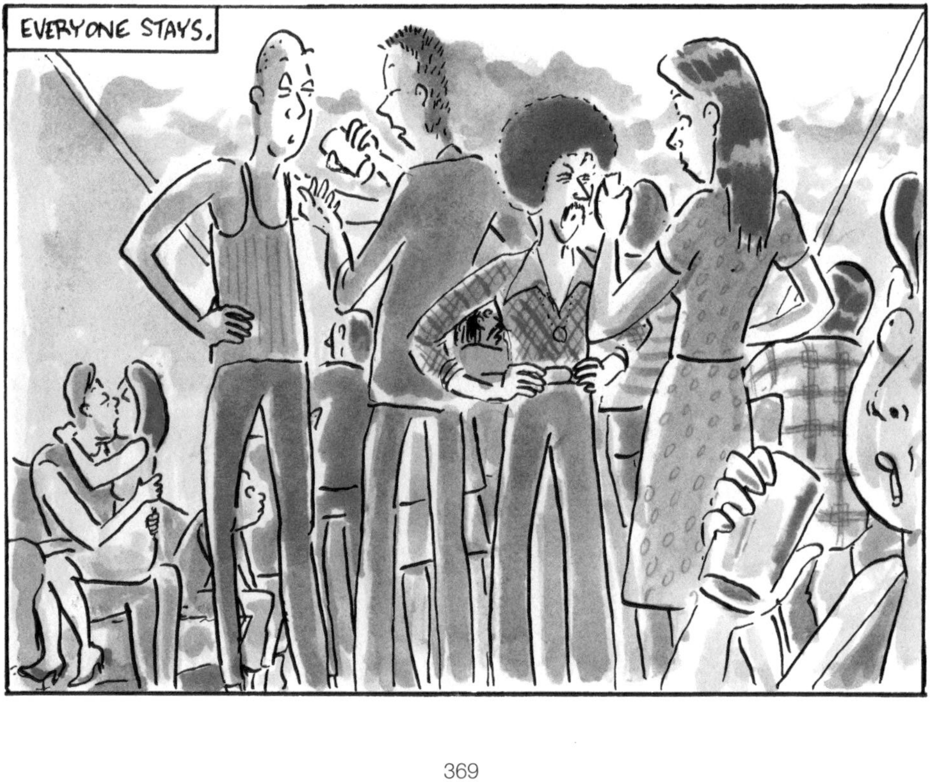
EVERYONE STAYS.

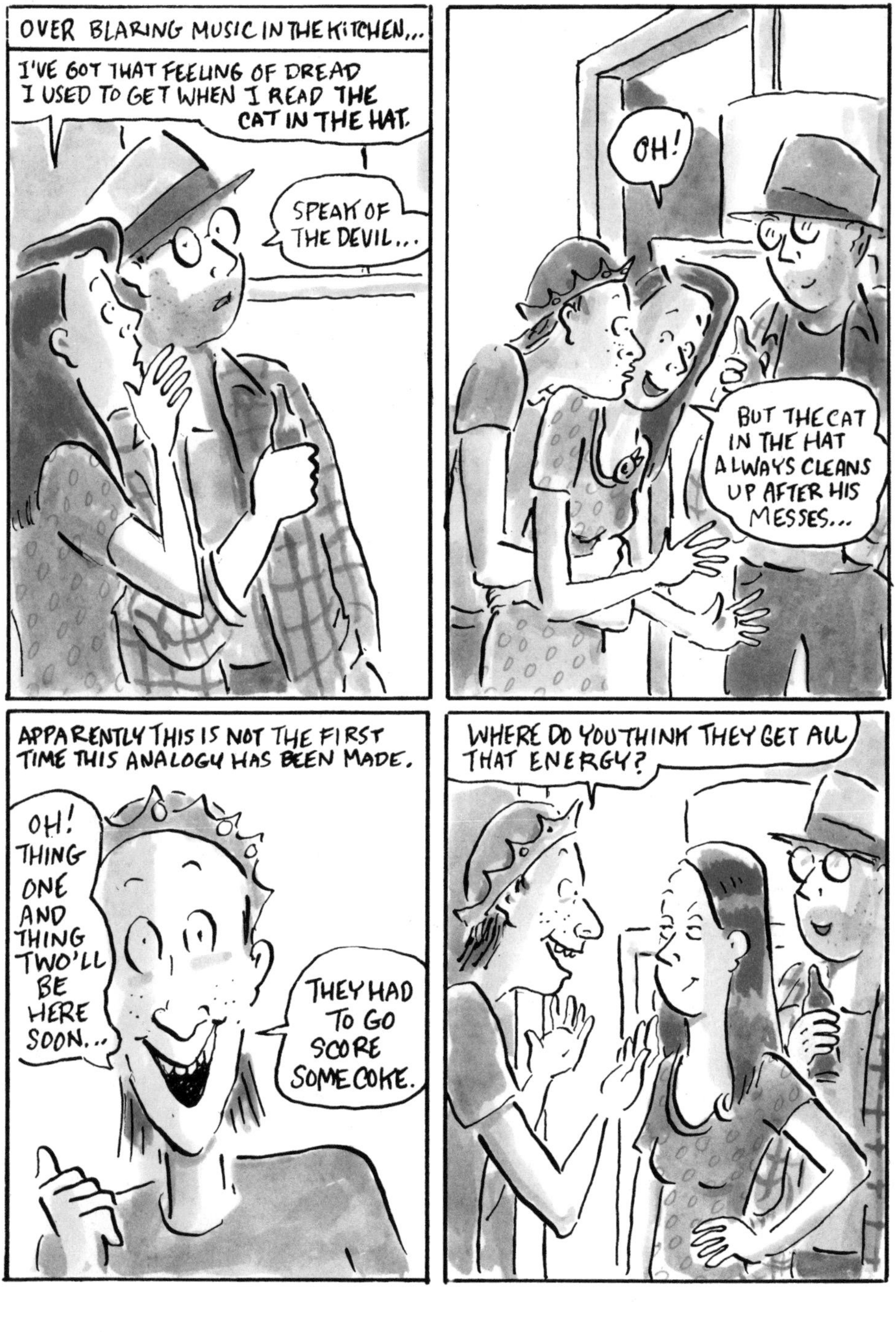
OVER BLARING MUSIC IN THE KITCHEN...
I'VE GOT THAT FEELING OF DREAD I USED TO GET WHEN I READ THE CAT IN THE HAT.
SPEAK OF THE DEVIL...
OH!
BUT THE CAT IN THE HAT ALWAYS CLEANS UP AFTER HIS MESSES...
APPARENTLY THIS IS NOT THE FIRST TIME THIS ANALOGY HAS BEEN MADE.
OH! THING ONE AND THING TWO'LL BE HERE SOON...
THEY HAD TO GO SCORE SOME COKE.
WHERE DO YOU THINK THEY GET ALL THAT ENERGY?

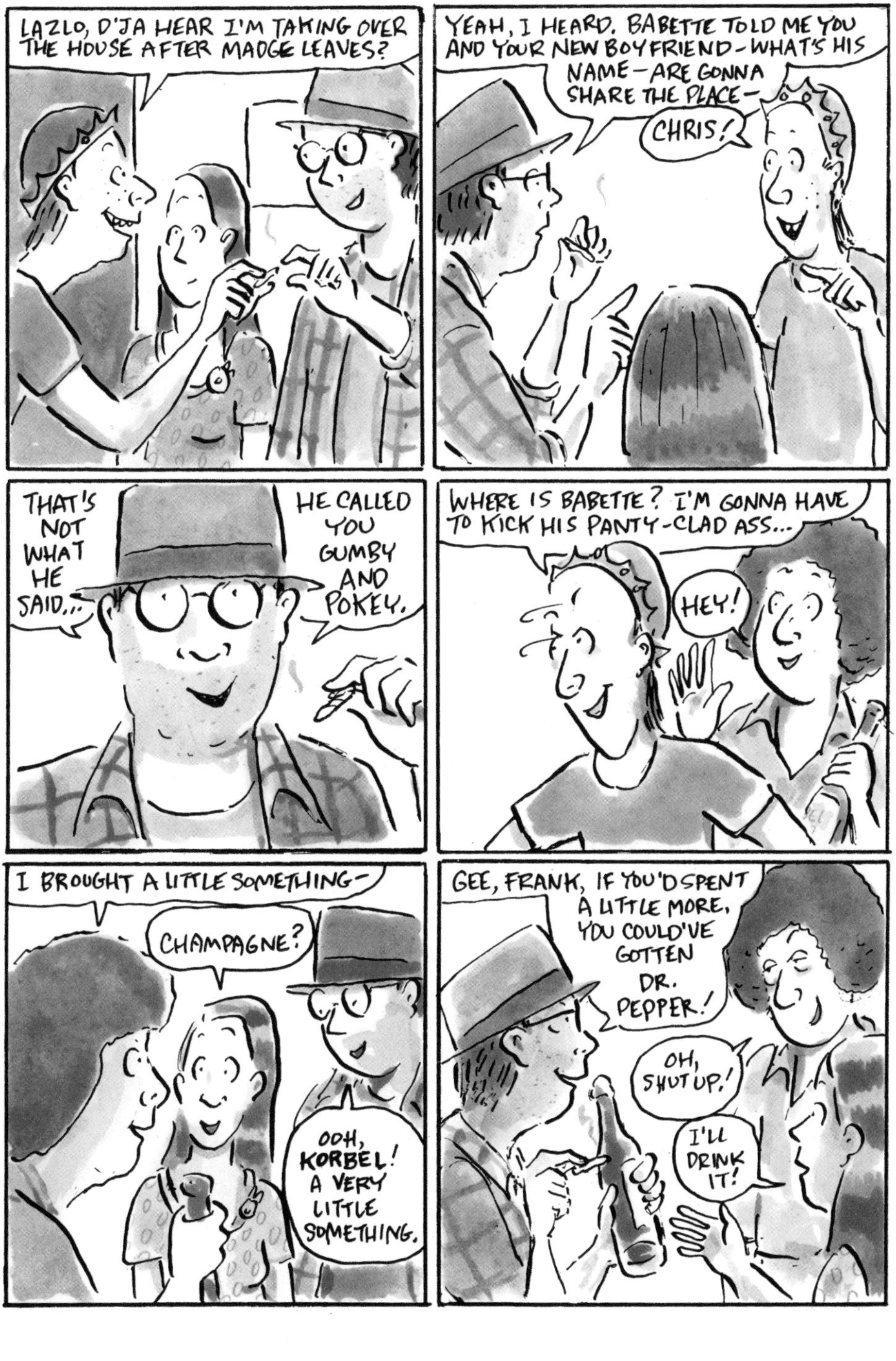
LAZLO, D'JA HEAR I'M TAKING OVER THE HOUSE AFTER MADGE LEAVES?
YEAH, I HEARD. BABETTE TOLD ME YOU AND YOUR NEW BOYFRIEND - WHAT'S HIS NAME - ARE GONNA SHARE THE PLACE -
CHRIS!
THAT'S NOT WHAT HE SAID...
HE CALLED YOU GUMBY AND POKEY.
WHERE IS BABETTE? I'M GONNA HAVE TO KICK HIS PANTY-CLAD ASS...
HEY!
I BROUGHT A LITTLE SOMETHING -
CHAMPAGNE?
OOH, KORBEL! A VERY LITTLE SOMETHING.
GEE, FRANK, IF YOU'D SPENT A LITTLE MORE, YOU COULD'VE GOTTEN DR. PEPPER!
OH, SHUT UP!
I'LL DRINK IT!

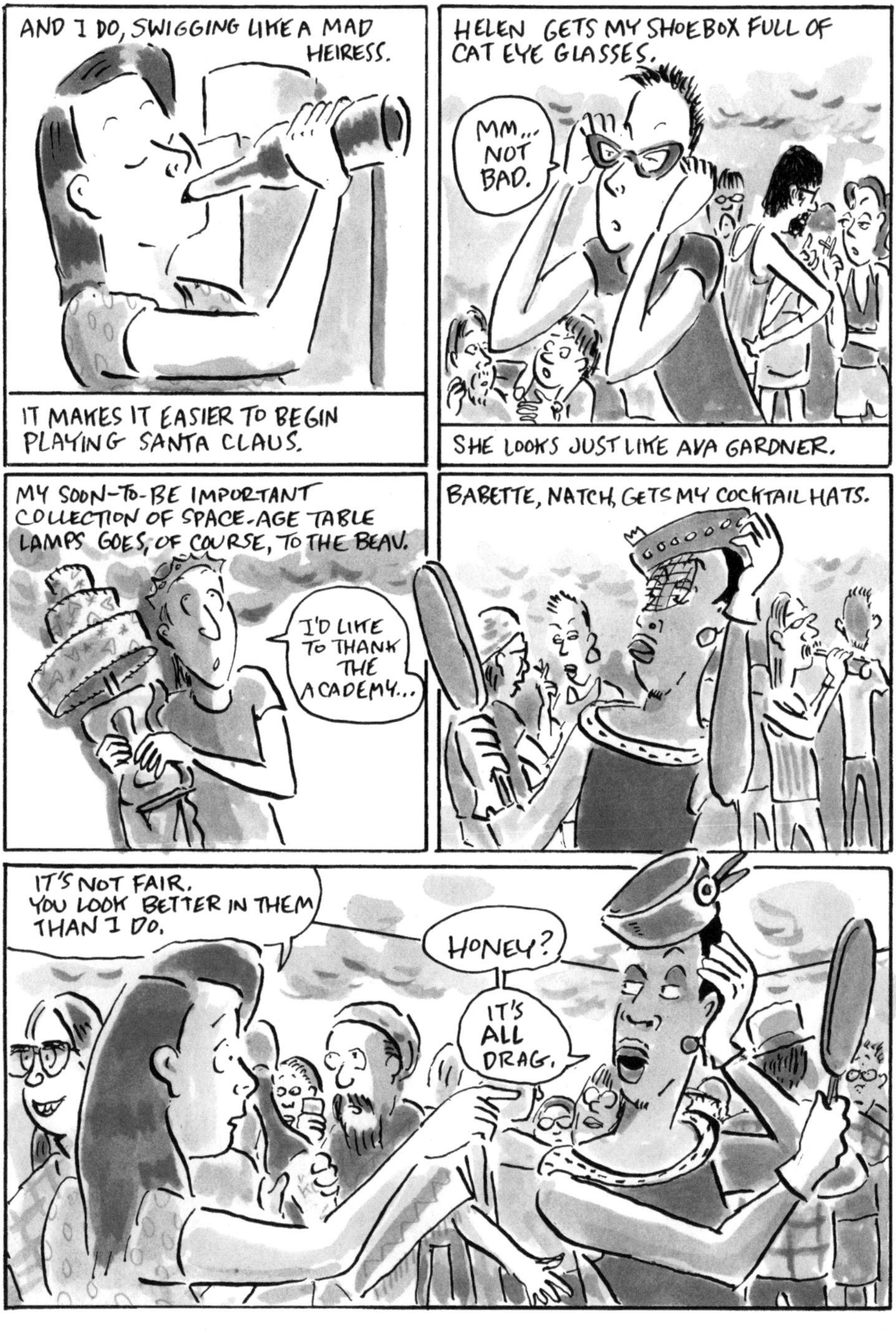
AND I DO, SWIGGING LIKE A MAD HEIRESS.
IT MAKES IT EASIER TO BEGIN PLAYING SANTA CLAUS.
HELEN GETS MY SHOEBOX FULL OF CAT EYE GLASSES.
MM... NOT BAD.
SHE LOOKS JUST LIKE AVA GARDNER.
MY SOON-TO-BE IMPORTANT COLLECTION OF SPACE-AGE TABLE LAMPS GOES, OF COURSE, TO THE BEAV.
I'D LIKE TO THANK THE ACADEMY...
BABETTE, NATCH, GETS MY COCKTAIL HATS.
IT'S NOT FAIR. YOU LOOK BETTER IN THEM THAN I DO.
HONEY?
IT'S ALL DRAG.

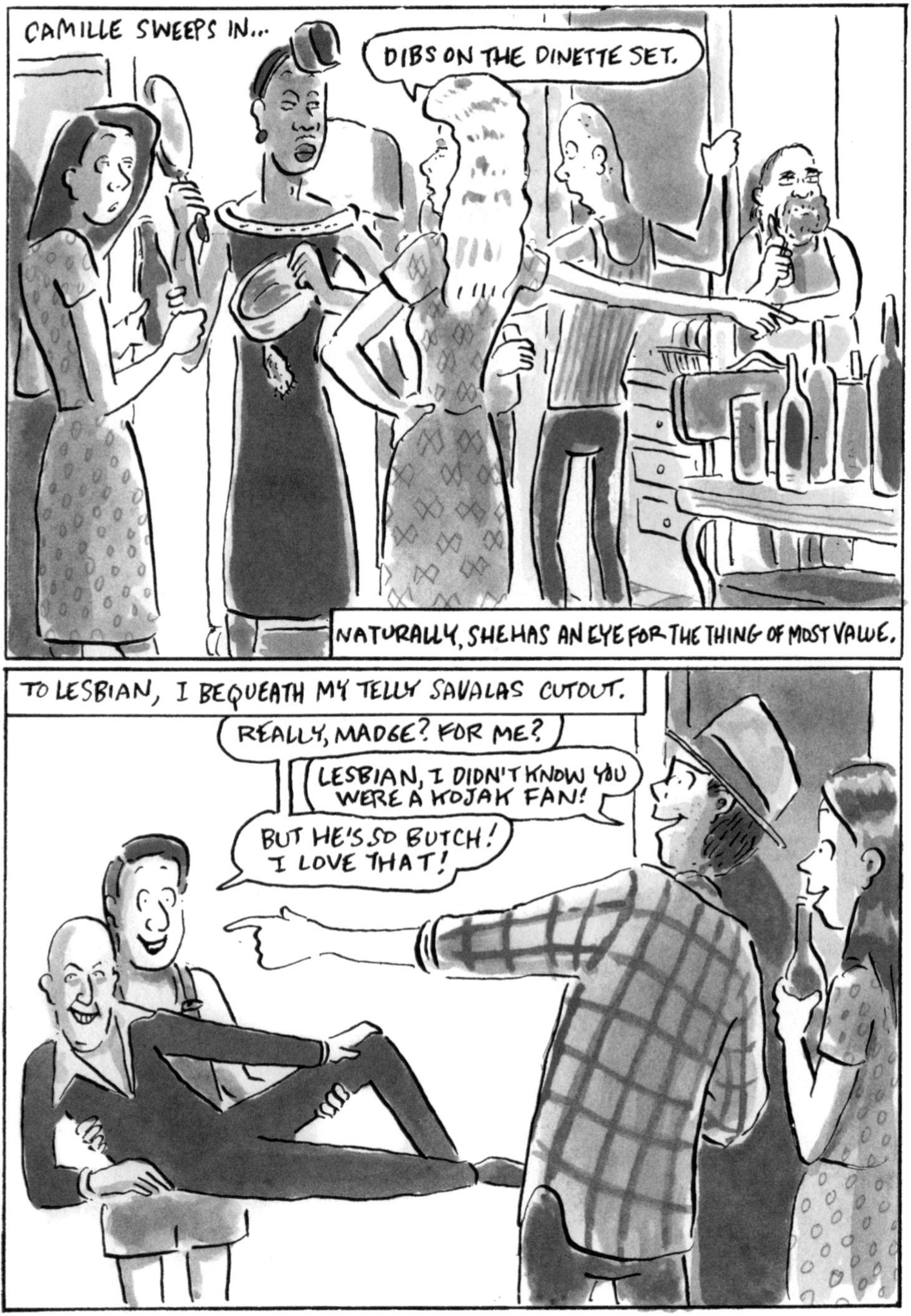
CAMILLE SWEEPS IN...
DIBS ON THE DINETTE SET.
NATURALLY, SHE HAS AN EYE FOR THE THING OF MOST VALUE.
TO LESBIAN, I BEQUEATH MY TELLY SAVALAS CUTOUT.
REALLY, MADGE? FOR ME?
LESBIAN, I DIDN'T KNOW YOU WERE A KOJAK FAN!
BUT HE'S SO BUTCH! I LOVE THAT!

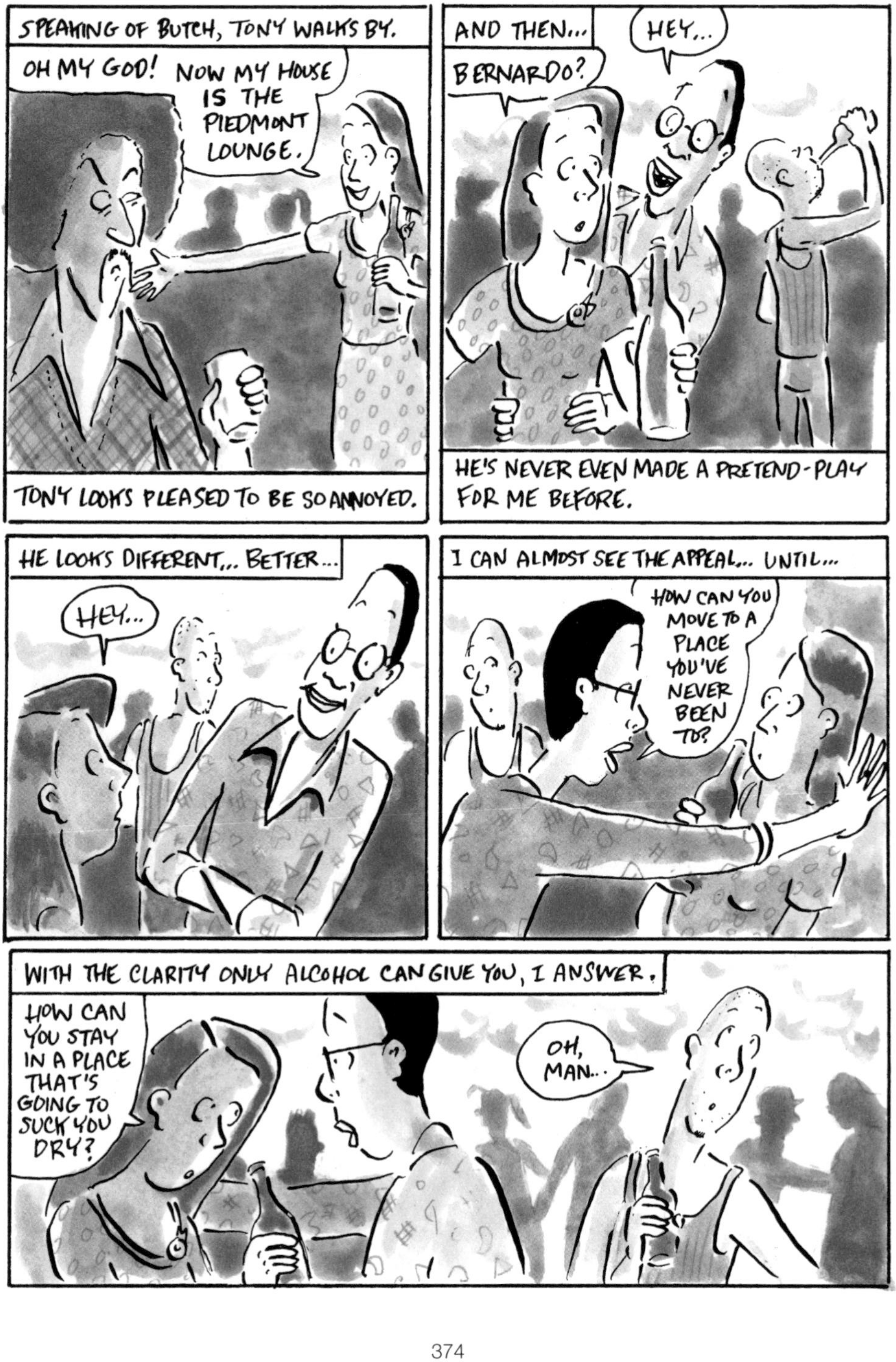

SPEAKING OF BUTCH, TONY WALKS BY.
OH MY GOD!
NOW MY HOUSE IS THE PIEDMONT LOUNGE.
TONY LOOKS PLEASED TO BE SO ANNOYED.
AND THEN...
BERNARDO?
HEY...
HE'S NEVER EVEN MADE A PRETEND-PLAY FOR ME BEFORE.
HE LOOKS DIFFERENT... BETTER...
HEY...
I CAN ALMOST SEE THE APPEAL... UNTIL...
HOW CAN YOU MOVE TO A PLACE YOU'VE NEVER BEEN TO?
WITH THE CLARITY ONLY ALCOHOL CAN GIVE YOU, I ANSWER.
HOW CAN YOU STAY IN A PLACE THAT'S GOING TO SUCK YOU DRY?
OH, MAN...

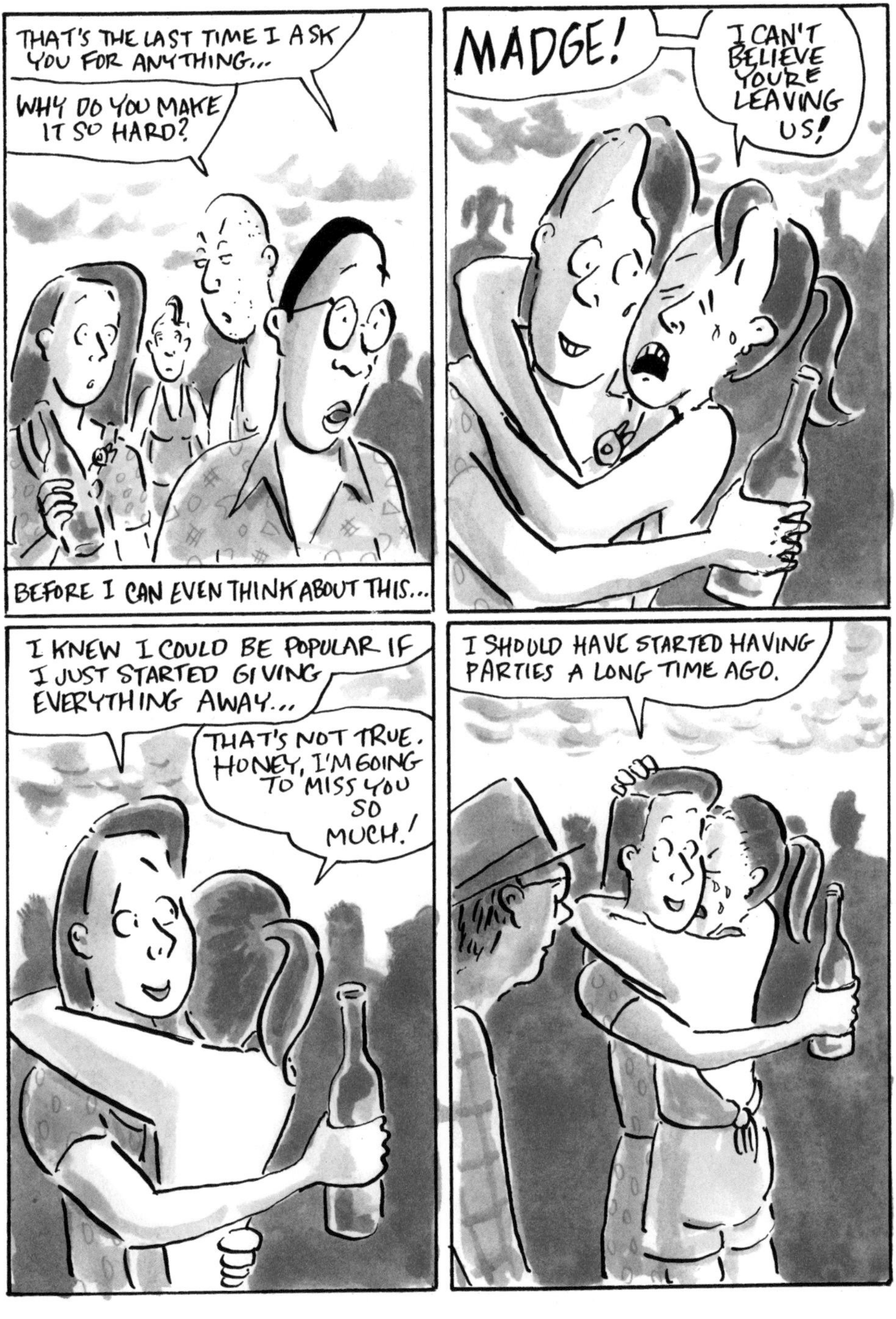
THAT'S THE LAST TIME I ASK YOU FOR ANYTHING...
WHY DO YOU MAKE IT SO HARD?
BEFORE I CAN EVEN THINK ABOUT THIS...
MADGE!
I CAN'T BELIEVE YOU'RE LEAVING US!
I KNEW I COULD BE POPULAR IF I JUST STARTED GIVING EVERYTHING AWAY...
THAT'S NOT TRUE. HONEY, I'M GOING TO MISS YOU SO MUCH!
I SHOULD HAVE STARTED HAVING PARTIES A LONG TIME AGO.

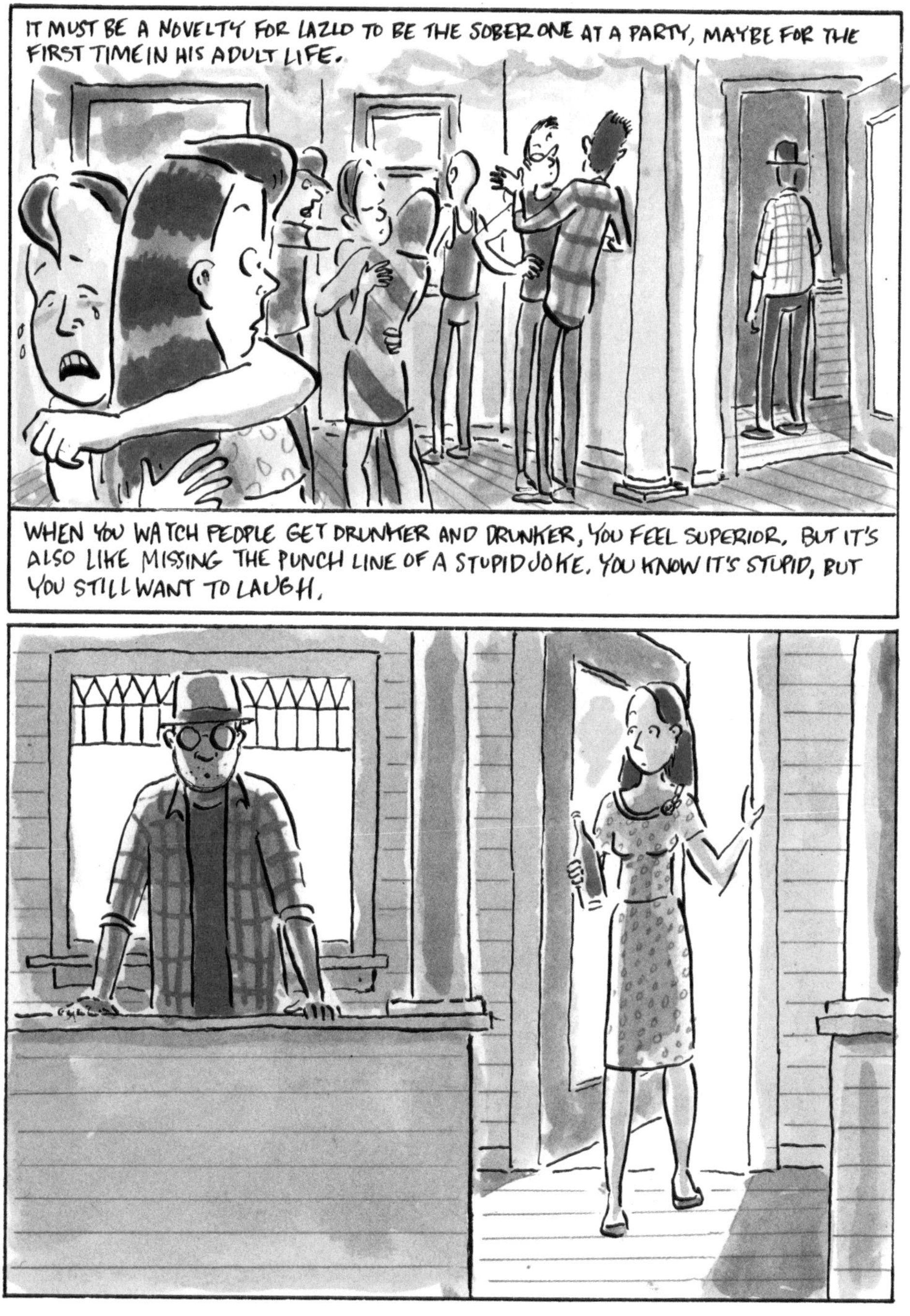
IT MUST BE A NOVELTY FOR LAZLO TO BE THE SOBER ONE AT A PARTY, MAYBE FOR THE FIRST TIME IN HIS ADULT LIFE.
WHEN YOU WATCH PEOPLE GET DRUNKER AND DRUNKER, YOU FEEL SUPERIOR. BUT IT'S ALSO LIKE MISSING THE PUNCH LINE OF A STUPID JOKE. YOU KNOW IT'S STUPID, BUT YOU STILL WANT TO LAUGH.

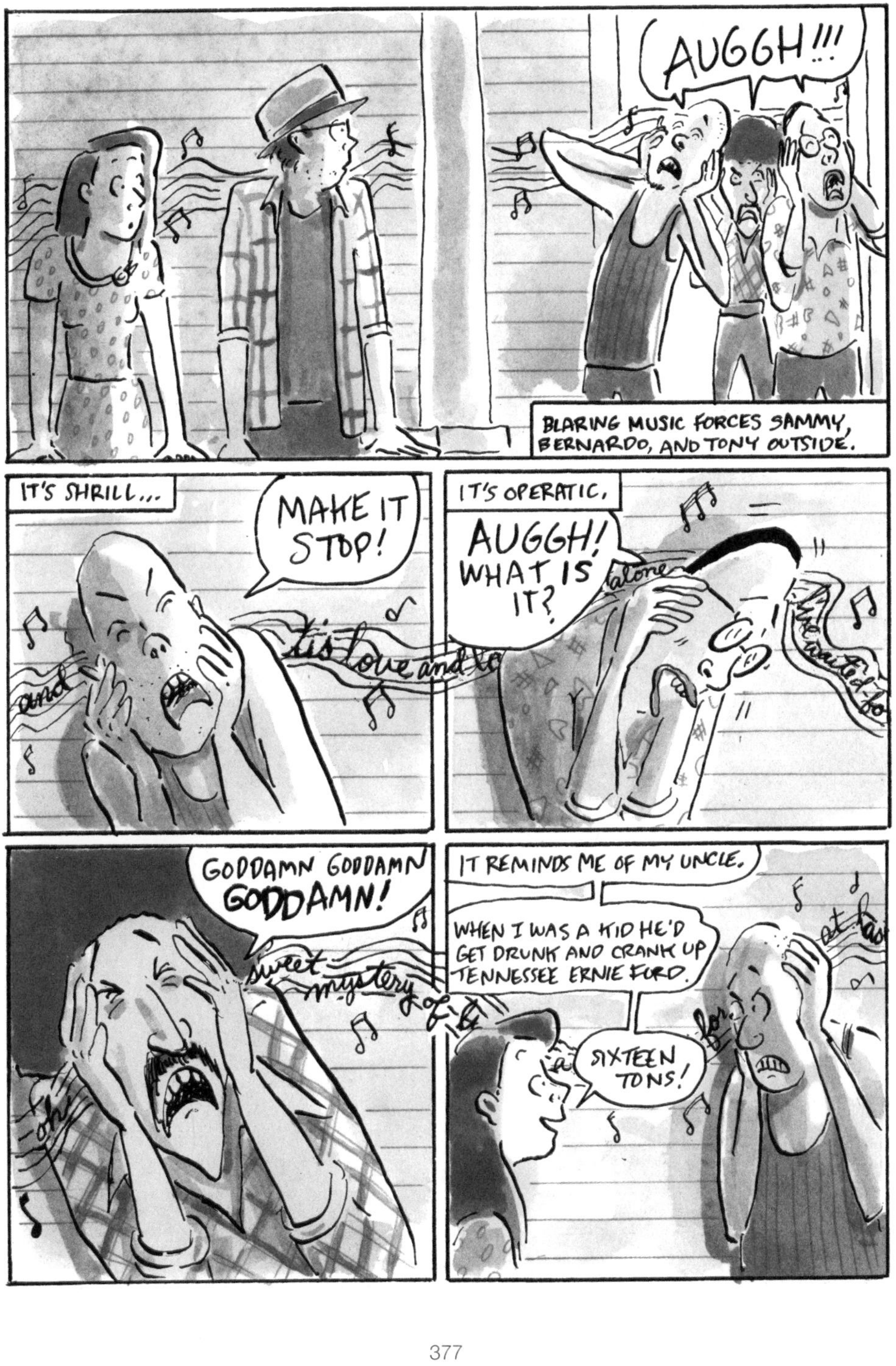
AUGGH!!!
BLARING MUSIC FORCES SAMMY, BERNARDO, AND TONY OUTSIDE.
IT'S SHRILL...
MAKE IT STOP!
IT'S OPERATIC,
AUGGH! WHAT IS IT?
GODDAMN GODDAMN GODDAMN!
sweet mystery of it
IT REMINDS ME OF MY UNCLE.
WHEN I WAS A KID HE'D GET DRUNK AND CRANK UP TENNESSEE ERNIE FORD.
SIXTEEN TONS!

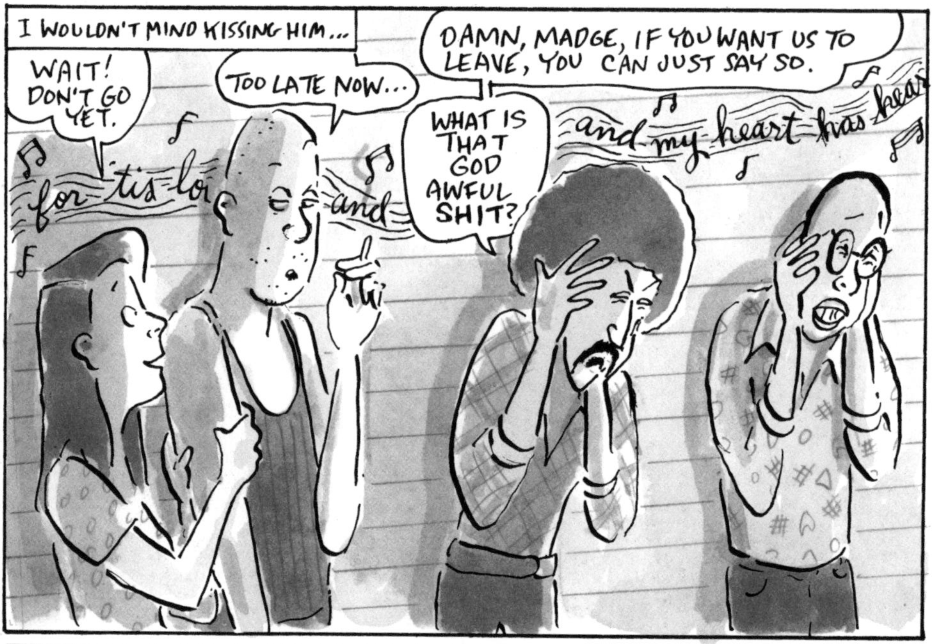
I WOULDN'T MIND KISSING HIM...
WAIT! DON'T GO YET.
TOO LATE NOW...
DAMN, MADGE, IF YOU WANT US TO LEAVE, YOU CAN JUST SAY SO.
WHAT IS THAT GOD AWFUL SHIT?
for tis
and
and my heart has

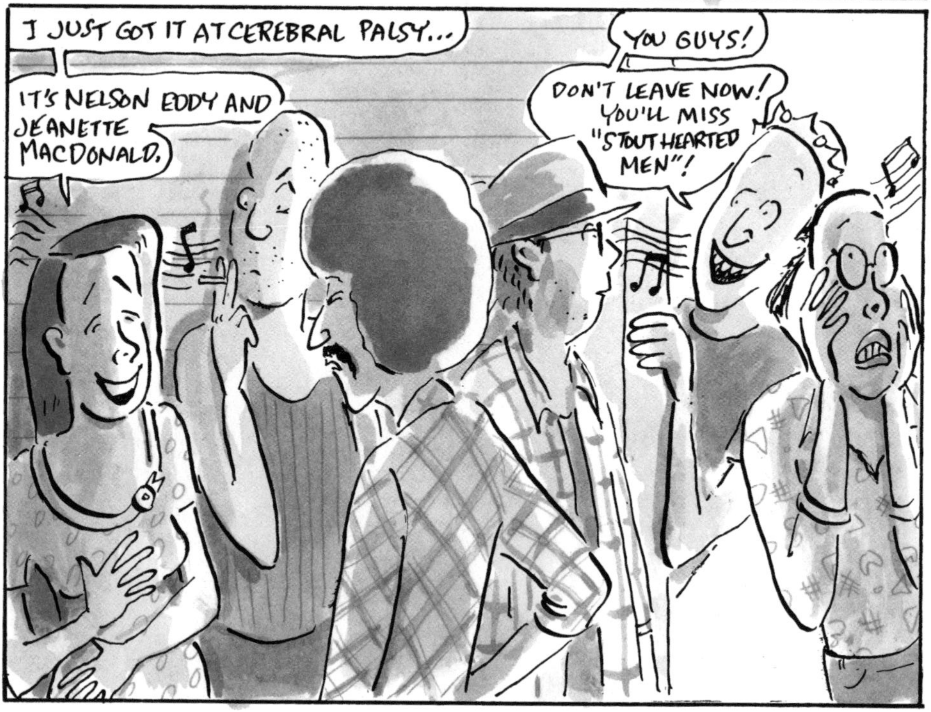
I JUST GOT IT AT CEREBRAL PALSY...
IT'S NELSON EDDY AND JEANETTE MACDONALD.
YOU GUYS!
DON'T LEAVE NOW! YOU'LL MISS "STOUTHEARTED MEN"!

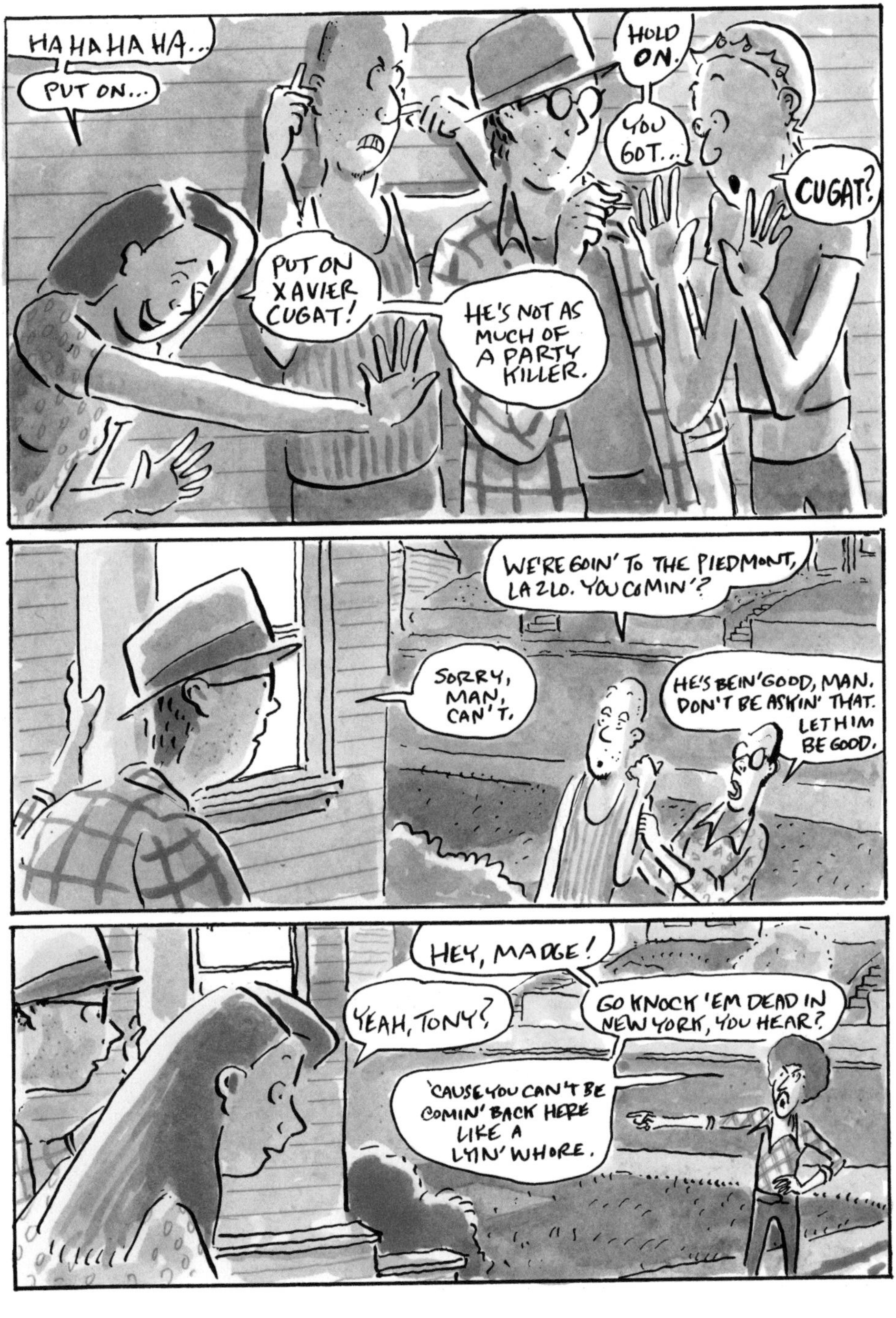
HA HA HA HA...
PUT ON...
HOLD ON.
YOU GOT...
CUGAT?
PUT ON XAVIER CUGAT!
HE'S NOT AS MUCH OF A PARTY KILLER.
WE'RE GOIN' TO THE PIEDMONT, LAZLO. YOU COMIN'?
SORRY, MAN, CAN'T.
HE'S BEIN' GOOD, MAN. DON'T BE ASKIN' THAT. LET HIM BE GOOD.
HEY, MADGE!
YEAH, TONY?
GO KNOCK 'EM DEAD IN NEW YORK, YOU HEAR?
'CAUSE YOU CAN'T BE COMIN' BACK HERE LIKE A LYIN' WHORE.

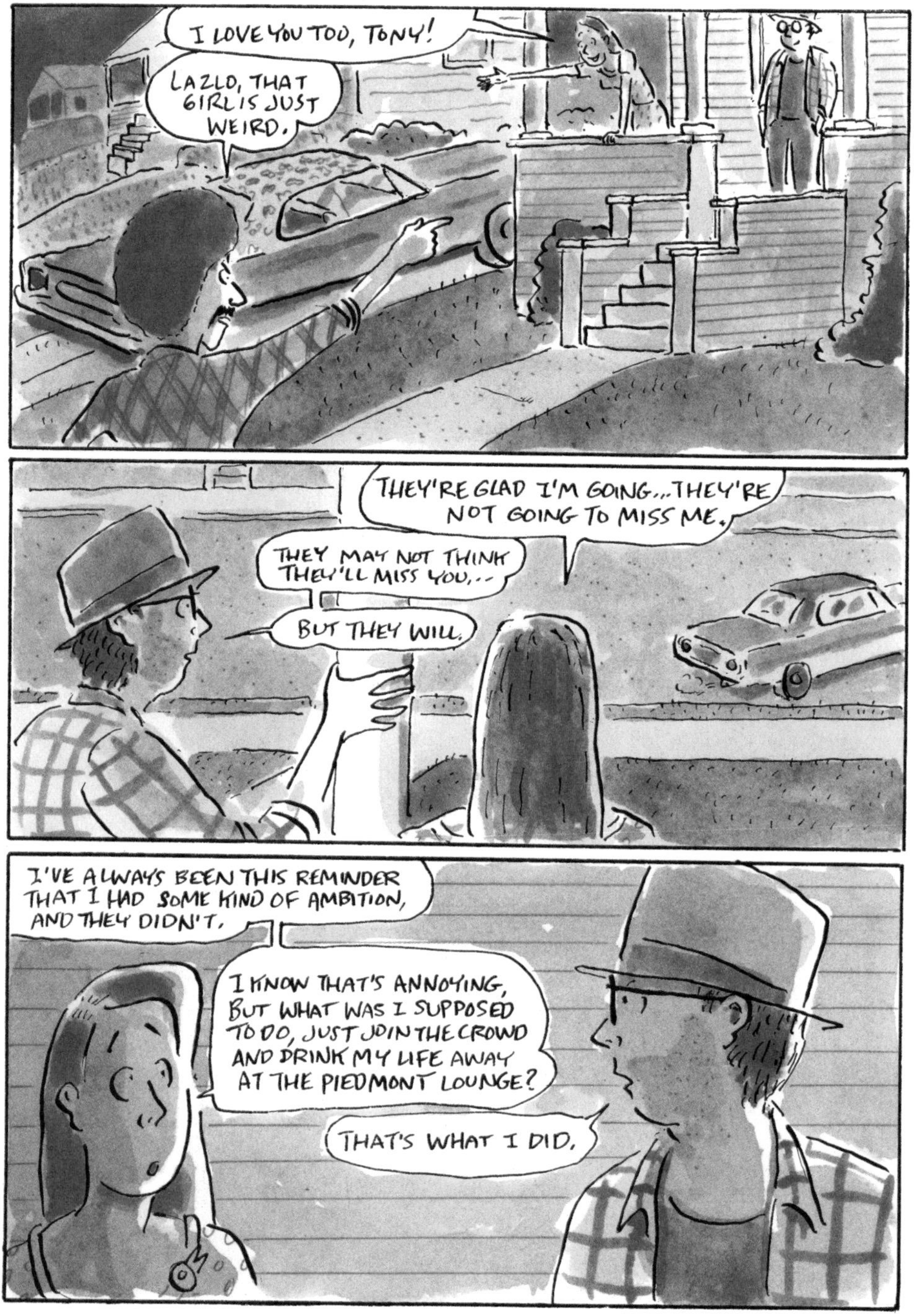
I LOVE YOU TOO, TONY!
LAZLO, THAT GIRL IS JUST WEIRD.
THEY'RE GLAD I'M GOING... THEY'RE NOT GOING TO MISS ME.
THEY MAY NOT THINK THEY'LL MISS YOU...
BUT THEY WILL.
I'VE ALWAYS BEEN THIS REMINDER THAT I HAD SOME KIND OF AMBITION, AND THEY DIDN'T.
I KNOW THAT'S ANNOYING, BUT WHAT WAS I SUPPOSED TO DO, JUST JOIN THE CROWD AND DRINK MY LIFE AWAY AT THE PIEDMONT LOUNGE?
THAT'S WHAT I DID.

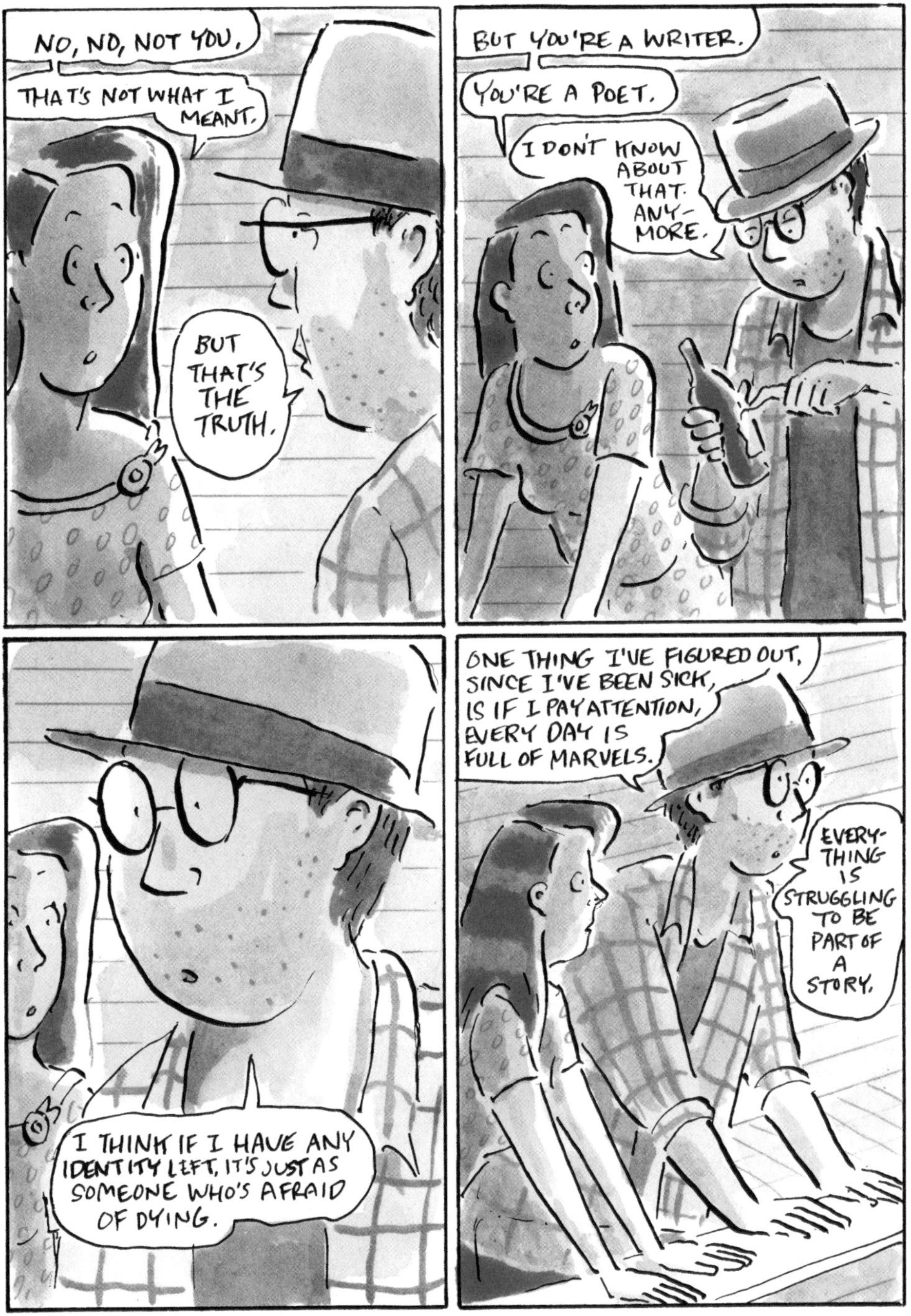
NO, NO, NOT YOU,
THAT'S NOT WHAT I MEANT.
BUT THAT'S THE TRUTH.
BUT YOU'RE A WRITER.
YOU'RE A POET.
I DON'T KNOW ABOUT THAT. ANY-MORE.
I THINK IF I HAVE ANY IDENTITY LEFT, IT'S JUST AS SOMEONE WHO'S AFRAID OF DYING.
ONE THING I'VE FIGURED OUT, SINCE I'VE BEEN SICK, IS IF I PAY ATTENTION, EVERY DAY IS FULL OF MARVELS.
EVERY-THING IS STRUGGLING TO BE PART OF A STORY.

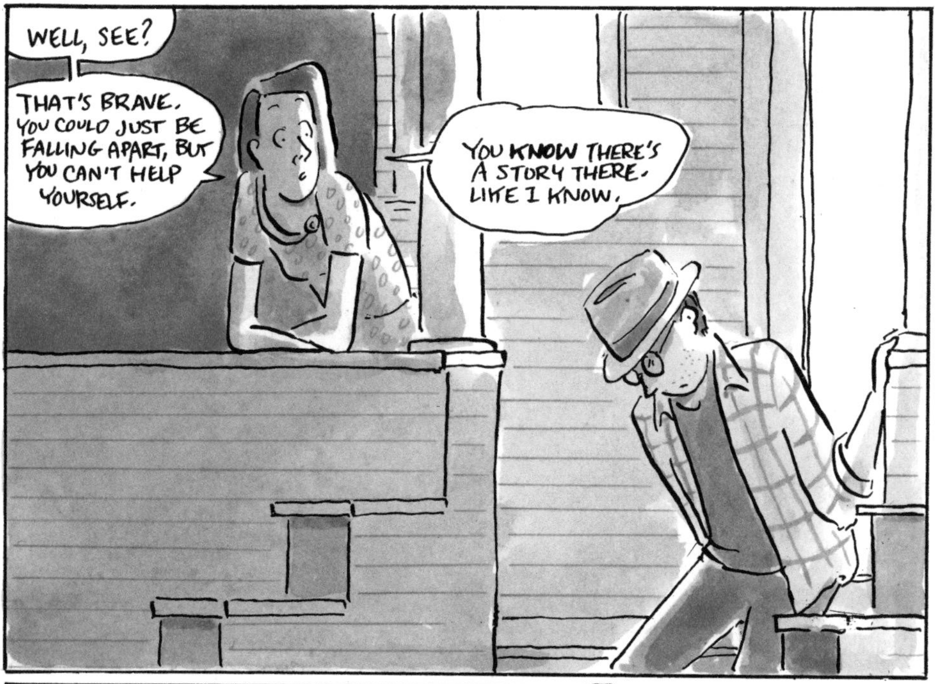
WELL, SEE?
THAT'S BRAVE. YOU COULD JUST BE FALLING APART, BUT YOU CAN'T HELP YOURSELF.
YOU KNOW THERE'S A STORY THERE. LIKE I KNOW.

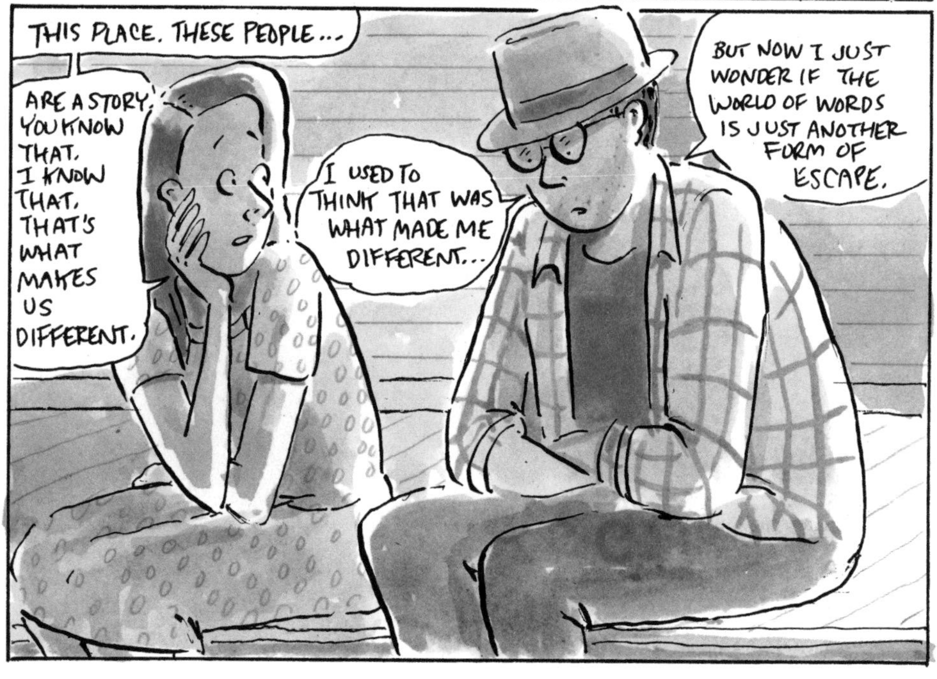
THIS PLACE. THESE PEOPLE...
ARE A STORY. YOU KNOW THAT. I KNOW THAT. THAT'S WHAT MAKES US DIFFERENT.
I USED TO THINK THAT WAS WHAT MADE ME DIFFERENT...
BUT NOW I JUST WONDER IF THE WORLD OF WORDS IS JUST ANOTHER FORM OF ESCAPE.

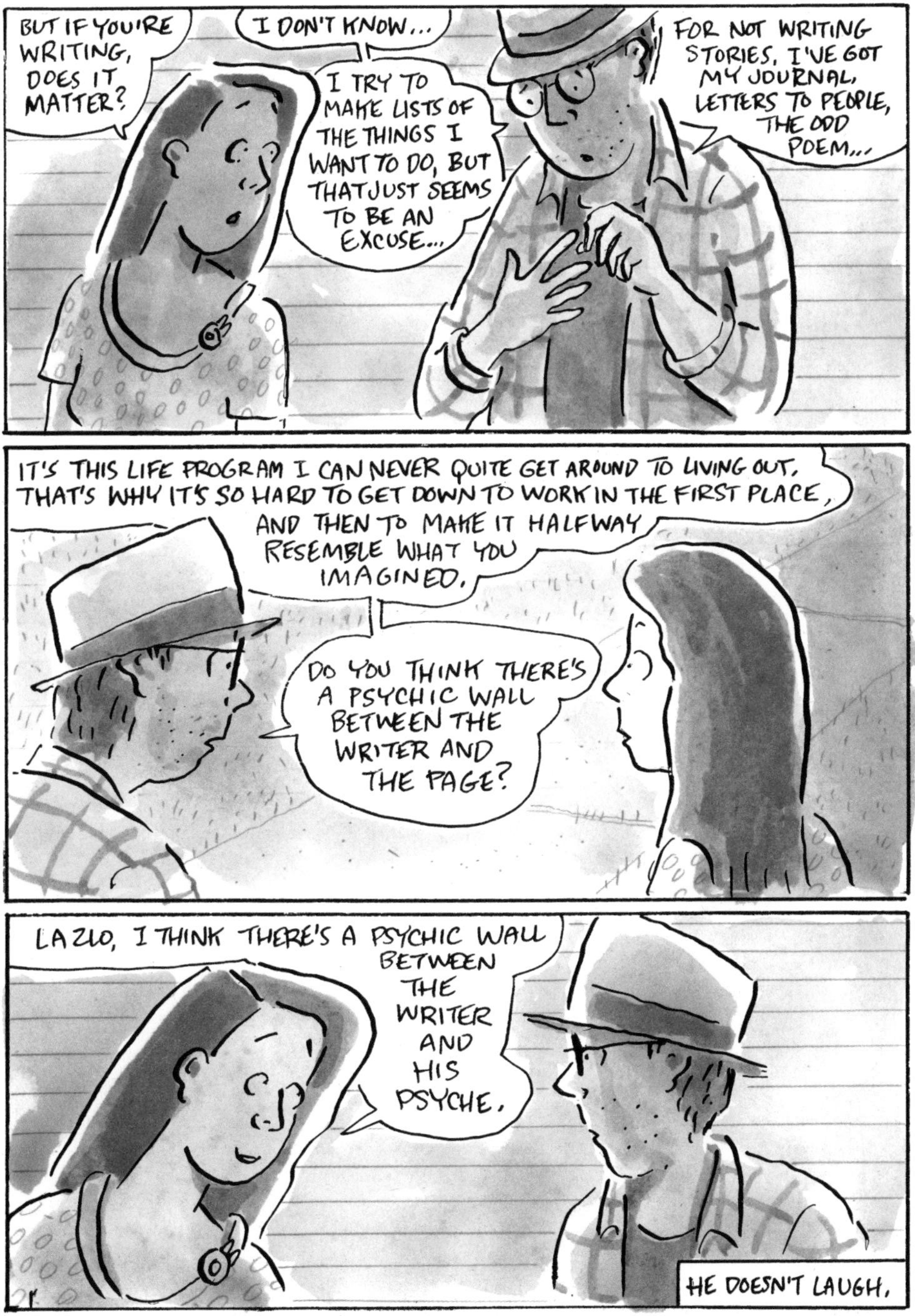

BUT IF YOU'RE WRITING, DOES IT MATTER?
I DON'T KNOW...
I TRY TO MAKE LISTS OF THE THINGS I WANT TO DO, BUT THAT JUST SEEMS TO BE AN EXCUSE...
FOR NOT WRITING STORIES, I'VE GOT MY JOURNAL, LETTERS TO PEOPLE, THE ODD POEM...
IT'S THIS LIFE PROGRAM I CAN NEVER QUITE GET AROUND TO LIVING OUT, THAT'S WHY IT'S SO HARD TO GET DOWN TO WORK IN THE FIRST PLACE,
AND THEN TO MAKE IT HALFWAY RESEMBLE WHAT YOU IMAGINED.
DO YOU THINK THERE'S A PSYCHIC WALL BETWEEN THE WRITER AND THE PAGE?
LAZLO, I THINK THERE'S A PSYCHIC WALL BETWEEN THE WRITER AND HIS PSYCHE.
HE DOESN'T LAUGH.

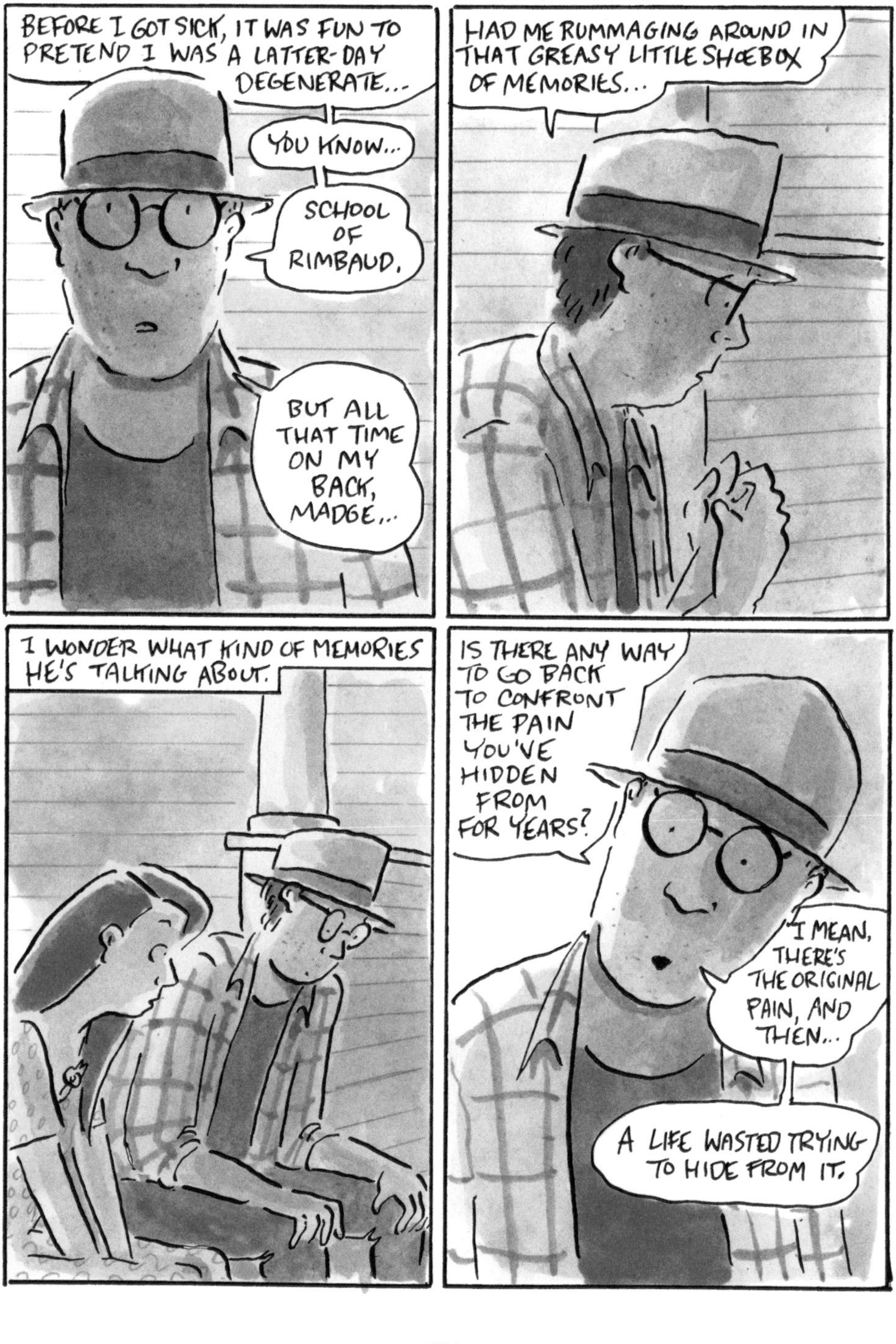
BEFORE I GOT SICK, IT WAS FUN TO PRETEND I WAS A LATTER-DAY DEGENERATE...
YOU KNOW...
SCHOOL OF RIMBAUD.
BUT ALL THAT TIME ON MY BACK, MADGE...
HAD ME RUMMAGING AROUND IN THAT GREASY LITTLE SHOEBOX OF MEMORIES...
I WONDER WHAT KIND OF MEMORIES HE'S TALKING ABOUT.
IS THERE ANY WAY TO GO BACK TO CONFRONT THE PAIN YOU'VE HIDDEN FROM FOR YEARS?
I MEAN, THERE'S THE ORIGINAL PAIN, AND THEN...
A LIFE WASTED TRYING TO HIDE FROM IT.

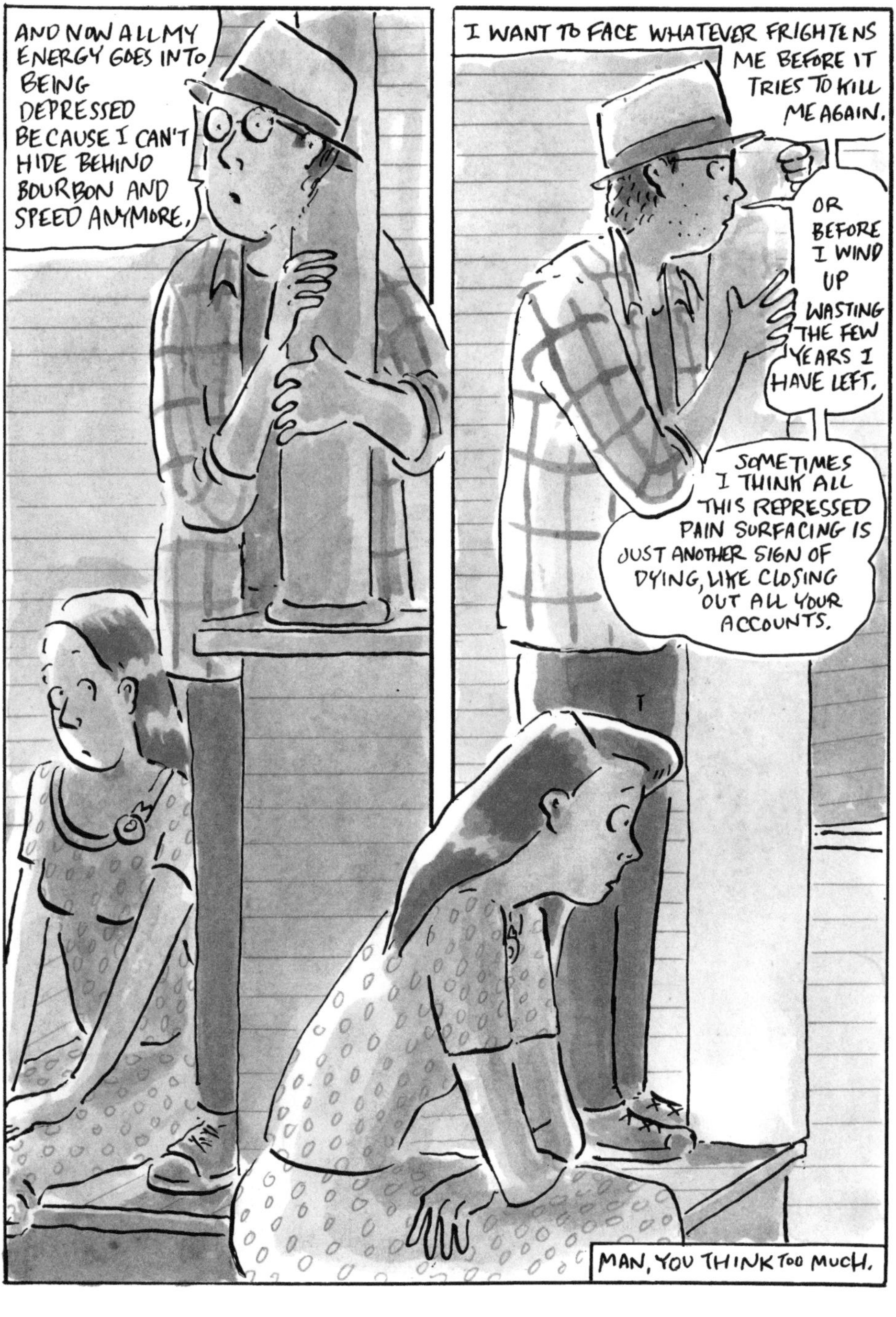
AND NOW ALL MY ENERGY GOES INTO BEING DEPRESSED BECAUSE I CAN'T HIDE BEHIND BOURBON AND SPEED ANYMORE,
I WANT TO FACE WHATEVER FRIGHTENS ME BEFORE IT TRIES TO KILL ME AGAIN.
OR BEFORE I WIND UP WASTING THE FEW YEARS I HAVE LEFT.
SOMETIMES I THINK ALL THIS REPRESSED PAIN SURFACING IS JUST ANOTHER SIGN OF DYING, LIKE CLOSING OUT ALL YOUR ACCOUNTS.
MAN, YOU THINK TOO MUCH.

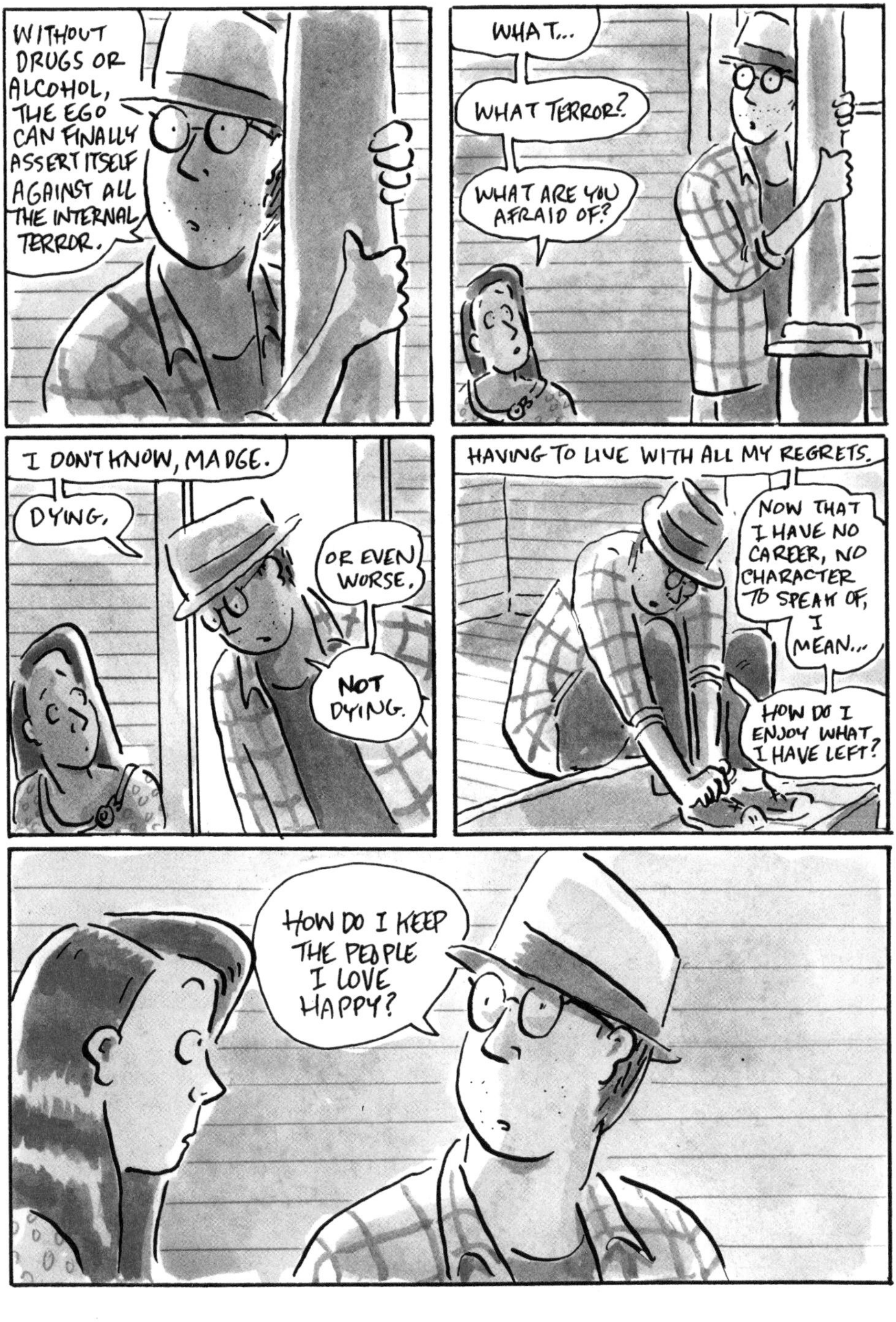
WITHOUT DRUGS OR ALCOHOL, THE EGO CAN FINALLY ASSERT ITSELF AGAINST ALL THE INTERNAL TERROR.
WHAT...
WHAT TERROR?
WHAT ARE YOU AFRAID OF?
I DON'T KNOW, MADGE.
DYING.
OR EVEN WORSE,
NOT DYING.
HAVING TO LIVE WITH ALL MY REGRETS.
NOW THAT I HAVE NO CAREER, NO CHARACTER TO SPEAK OF, I MEAN...
HOW DO I ENJOY WHAT I HAVE LEFT?
HOW DO I KEEP THE PEOPLE I LOVE HAPPY?

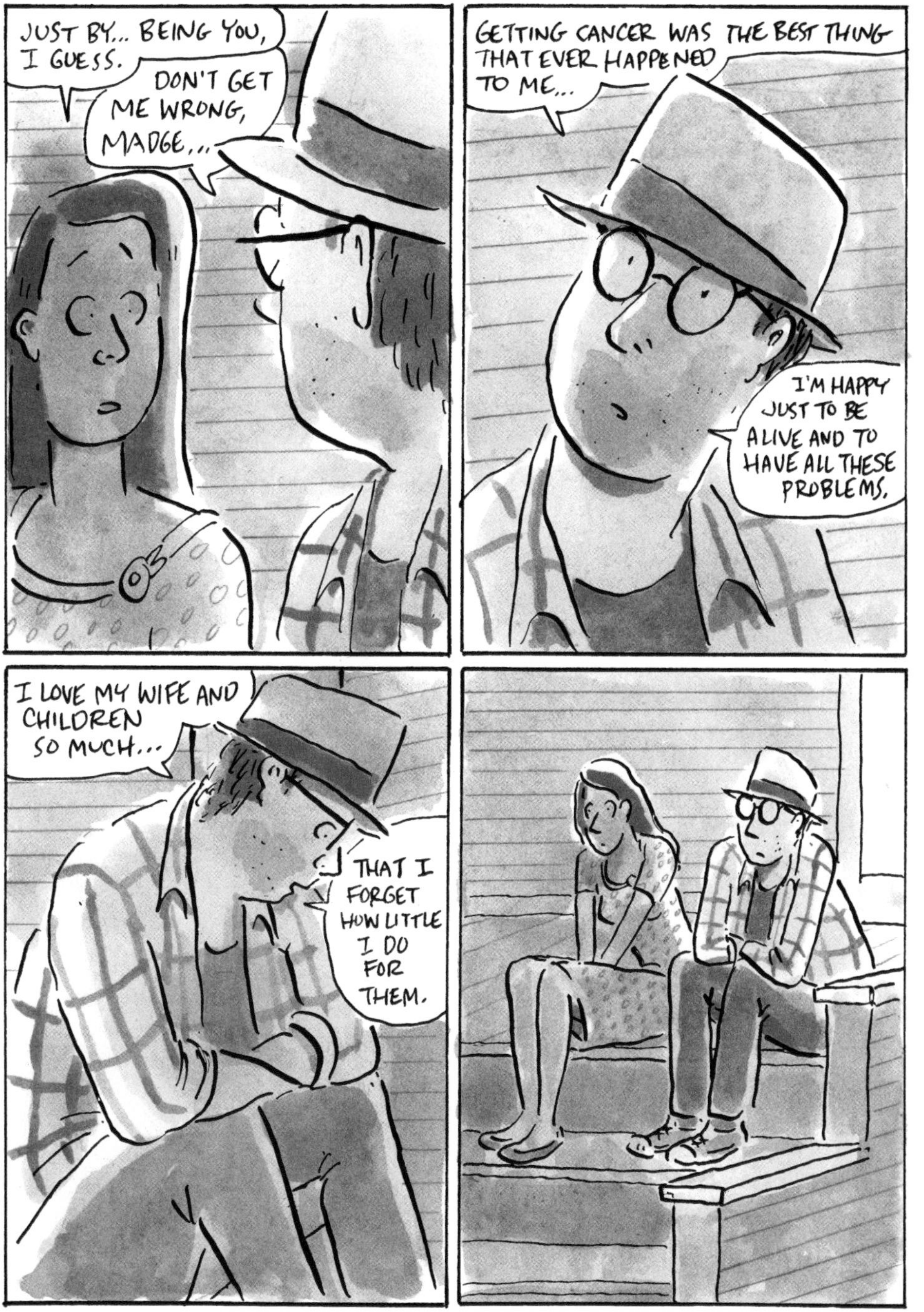
JUST BY... BEING YOU, I GUESS.
DON'T GET ME WRONG, MADGE...
GETTING CANCER WAS THE BEST THING THAT EVER HAPPENED TO ME...
I'M HAPPY JUST TO BE ALIVE AND TO HAVE ALL THESE PROBLEMS.
I LOVE MY WIFE AND CHILDREN SO MUCH...
THAT I FORGET HOW LITTLE I DO FOR THEM.

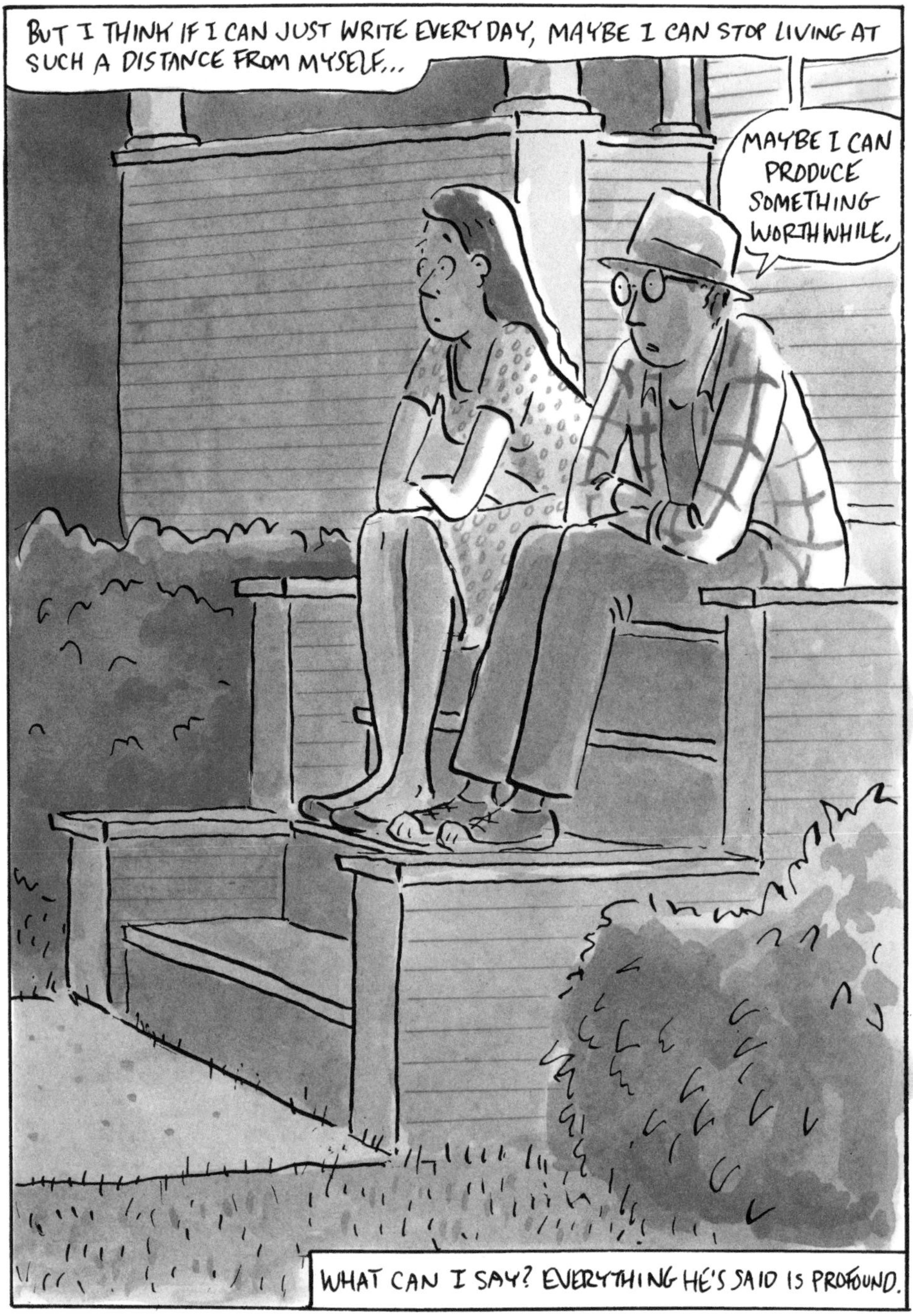
BUT I THINK IF I CAN JUST WRITE EVERY DAY, MAYBE I CAN STOP LIVING AT SUCH A DISTANCE FROM MYSELF...
MAYBE I CAN PRODUCE SOMETHING WORTHWHILE.
WHAT CAN I SAY? EVERYTHING HE'S SAID IS PROFOUND.

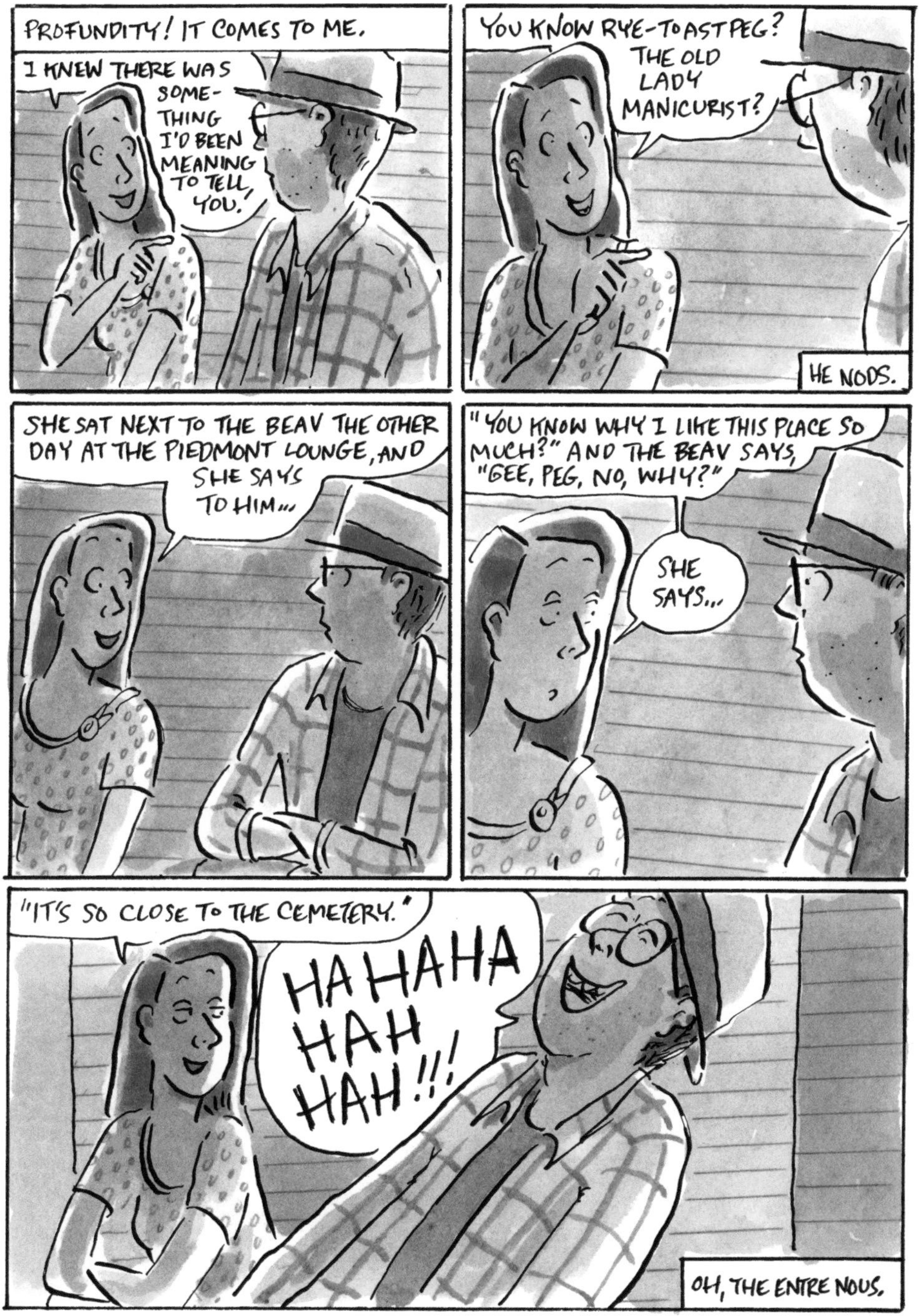
PROFUNDITY! IT COMES TO ME.
I KNEW THERE WAS SOMETHING I'D BEEN MEANING TO TELL YOU.
YOU KNOW RYE-TOAST PEG?
THE OLD LADY MANICURIST?
HE NODS.
SHE SAT NEXT TO THE BEAV THE OTHER DAY AT THE PIEDMONT LOUNGE, AND SHE SAYS TO HIM...
"YOU KNOW WHY I LIKE THIS PLACE SO MUCH?" AND THE BEAV SAYS, "GEE, PEG, NO, WHY?"
SHE SAYS...
"IT'S SO CLOSE TO THE CEMETERY."
HAHAHA HAH HAH!!!
OH, THE ENTRE NOUS.

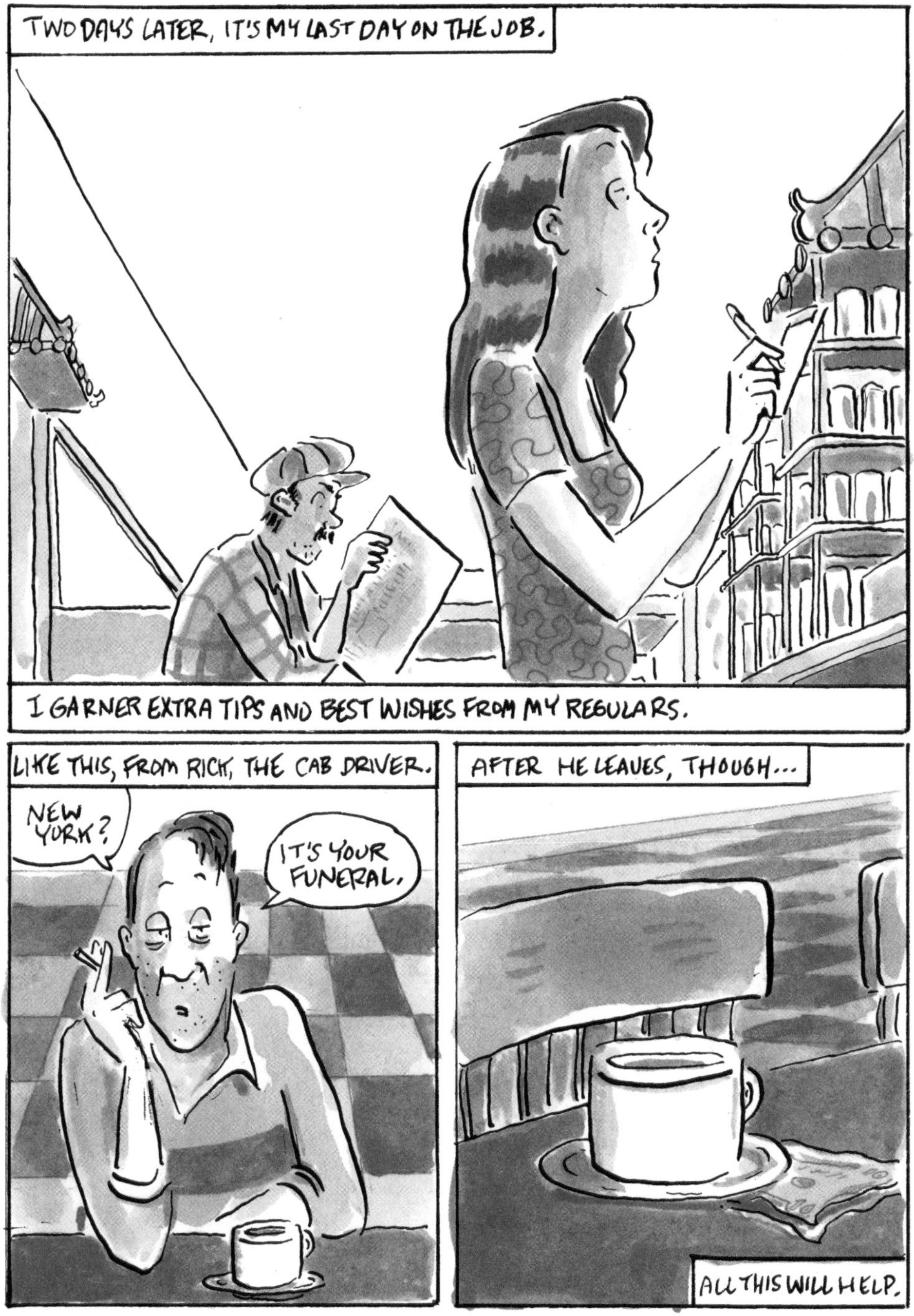
TWO DAYS LATER, IT'S MY LAST DAY ON THE JOB.
I GARNER EXTRA TIPS AND BEST WISHES FROM MY REGULARS.
LIKE THIS, FROM RICK, THE CAB DRIVER.
NEW YORK?
IT'S YOUR FUNERAL.
AFTER HE LEAVES, THOUGH...
ALL THIS WILL HELP.

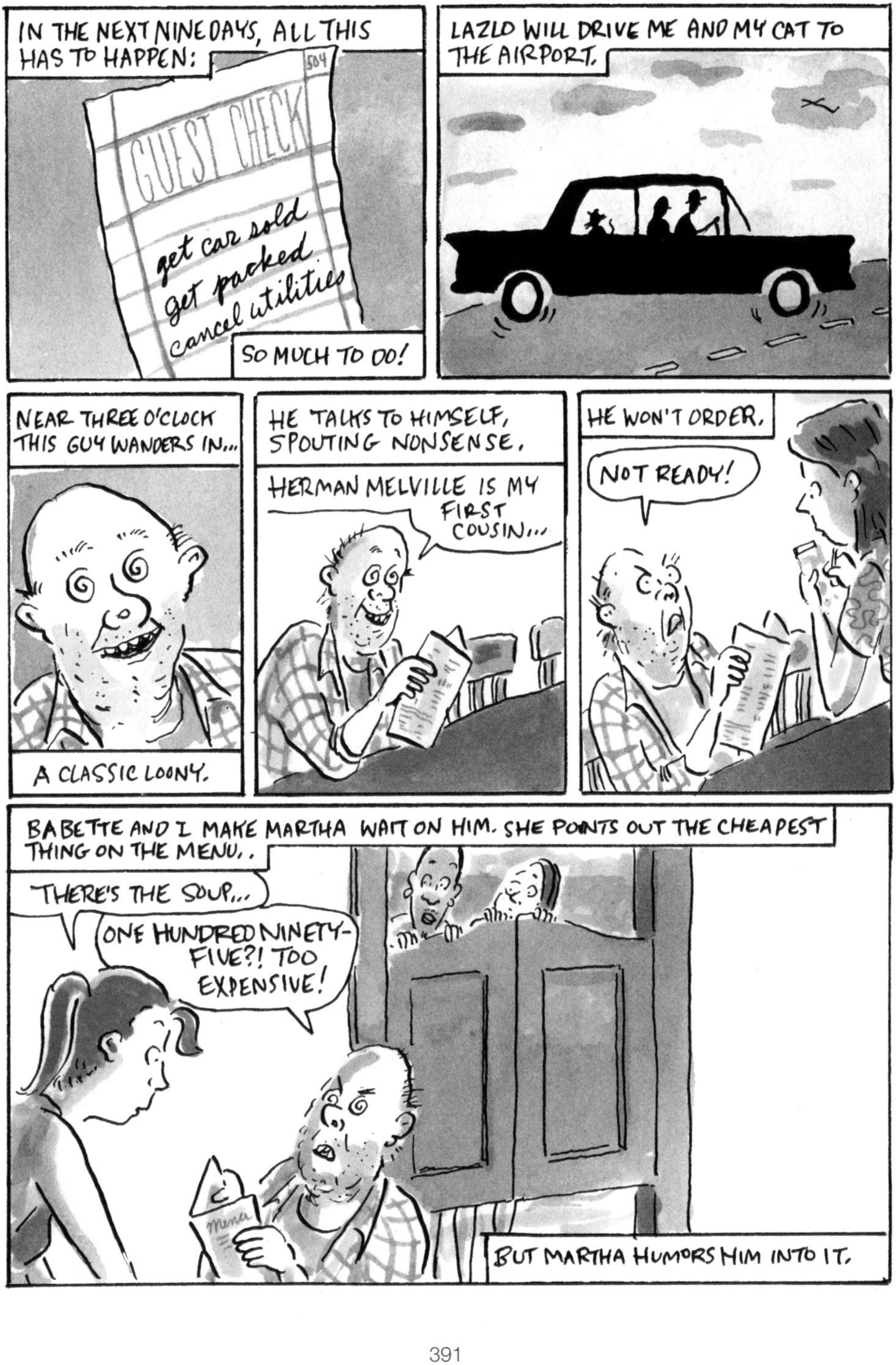
IN THE NEXT NINE DAYS, ALL THIS HAS TO HAPPEN:
GUEST CHECK
504
get car sold
get packed
cancel utilities
SO MUCH TO DO!
LAZLO WILL DRIVE ME AND MY CAT TO THE AIRPORT.
NEAR THREE O'CLOCK THIS GUY WANDERS IN...
A CLASSIC LOONY.
HE TALKS TO HIMSELF, SPOUTING NONSENSE.
HERMAN MELVILLE IS MY FIRST COUSIN...
HE WON'T ORDER.
NOT READY!
BABETTE AND I MAKE MARTHA WAIT ON HIM. SHE POINTS OUT THE CHEAPEST THING ON THE MENU..
THERE'S THE SOUP...
ONE HUNDRED NINETY-FIVE?! TOO EXPENSIVE!
Menu
BUT MARTHA HUMORS HIM INTO IT.

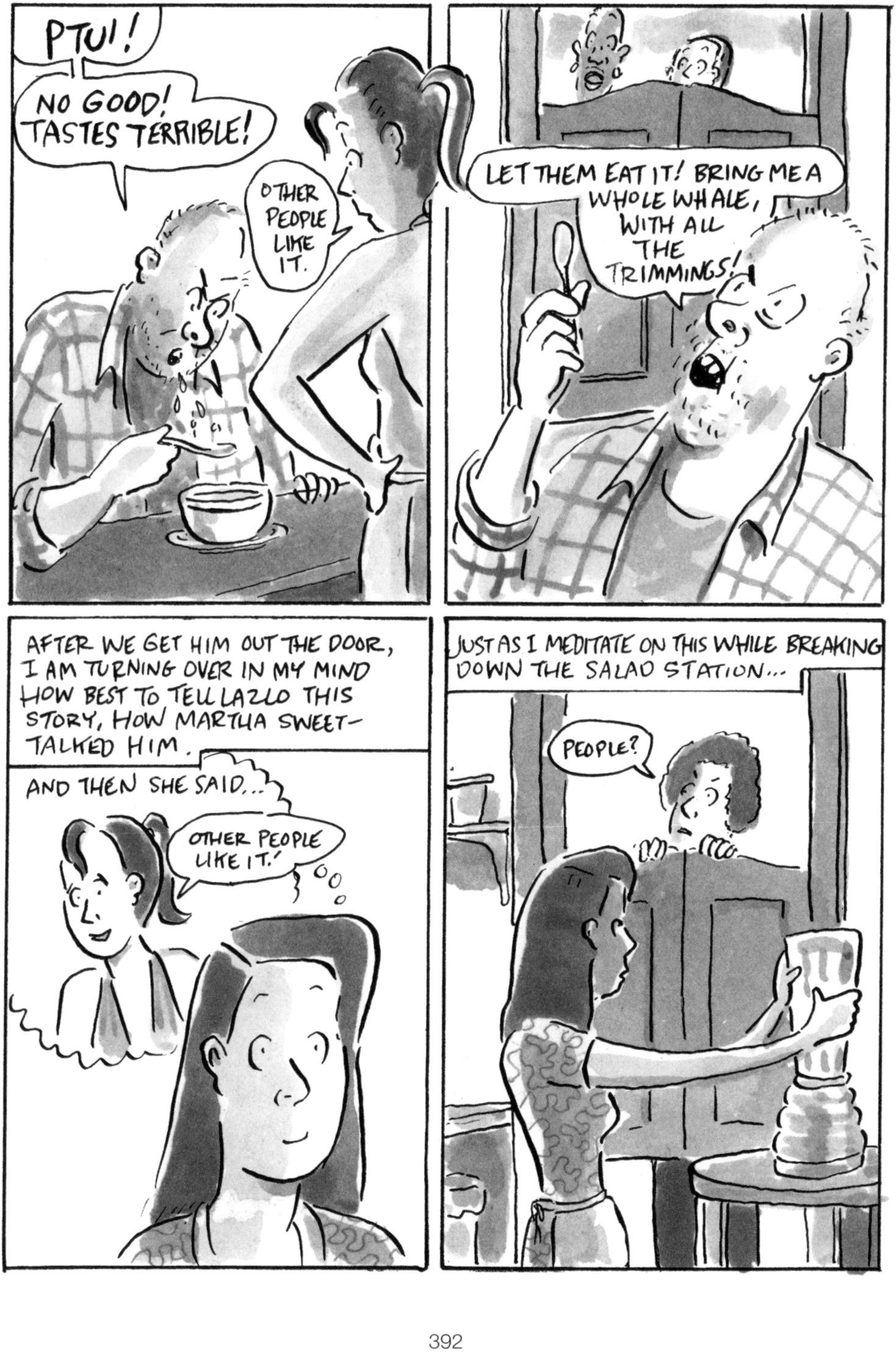
PTUI!
NO GOOD! TASTES TERRIBLE!
OTHER PEOPLE LIKE IT.
LET THEM EAT IT! BRING ME A WHOLE WHALE, WITH ALL THE TRIMMINGS!
AFTER WE GET HIM OUT THE DOOR, I AM TURNING OVER IN MY MIND HOW BEST TO TELL LAZLO THIS STORY, HOW MARTHA SWEET-TALKED HIM.
AND THEN SHE SAID...
OTHER PEOPLE LIKE IT.
JUST AS I MEDITATE ON THIS WHILE BREAKING DOWN THE SALAD STATION...
PEOPLE?

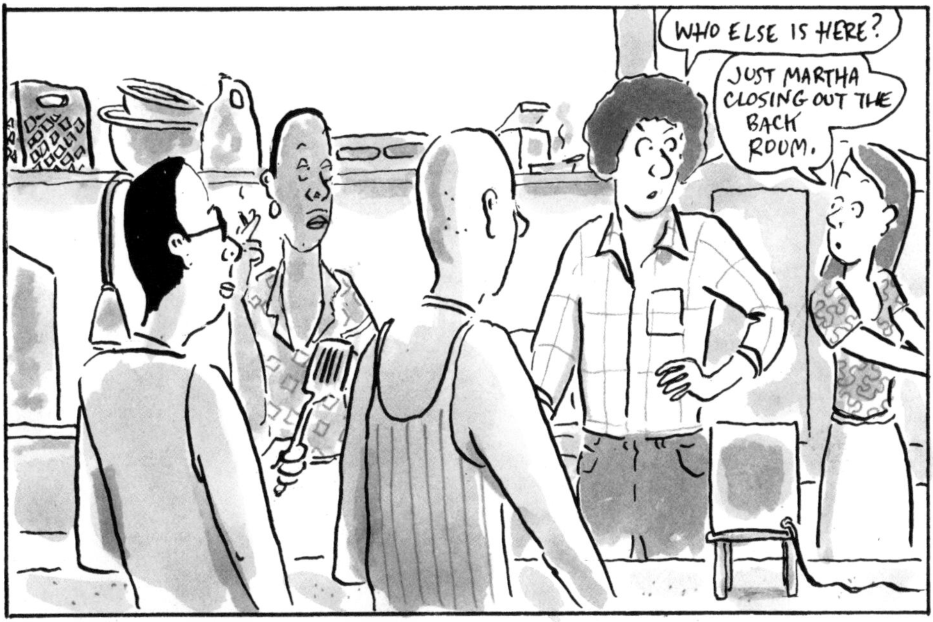
WHO ELSE IS HERE?
JUST MARTHA CLOSING OUT THE BACK ROOM.

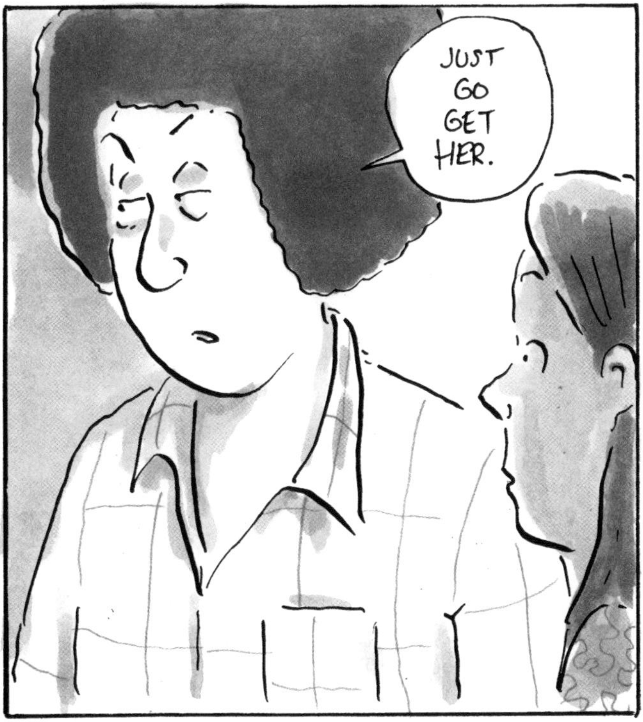
JUST GO GET HER.

SHELTERED BY A HOPELESSLY LONG-LIVED FAMILY, I HAVE NO INTIMACY WITH DEATH, NOT EVEN PRACTICE RUNS WITH GRANDPARENTS OR AUNTS OR COUSINS, PEOPLE ABOUT WHOM YOU COULD FEEL AT LEAST A DISTANT REGRET. EVEN DAISY'S DEATH, AWFUL AS IT WAS, WAS STILL ABSTRACT TO ME.

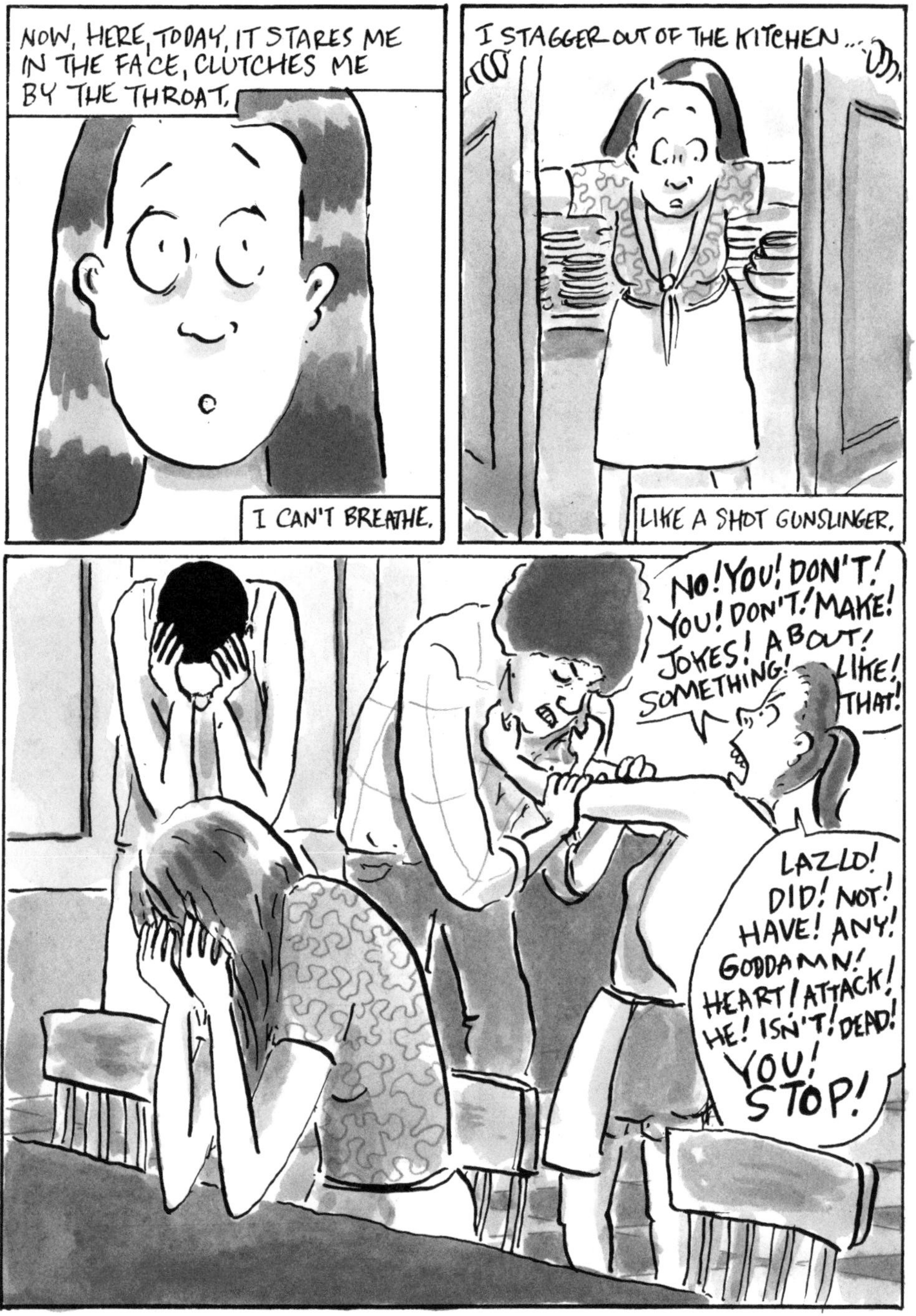

NOW, HERE, TODAY, IT STARES ME IN THE FACE, CLUTCHES ME BY THE THROAT.
I CAN'T BREATHE.
I STAGGER OUT OF THE KITCHEN...
LIKE A SHOT GUNSLINGER.
NO! YOU! DON'T! YOU! DON'T! MAKE! JOKES! ABOUT! SOMETHING! LIKE! THAT!
LAZLO! DID! NOT! HAVE! ANY! GODDAMN! HEART! ATTACK! HE! ISN'T! DEAD! YOU! STOP!

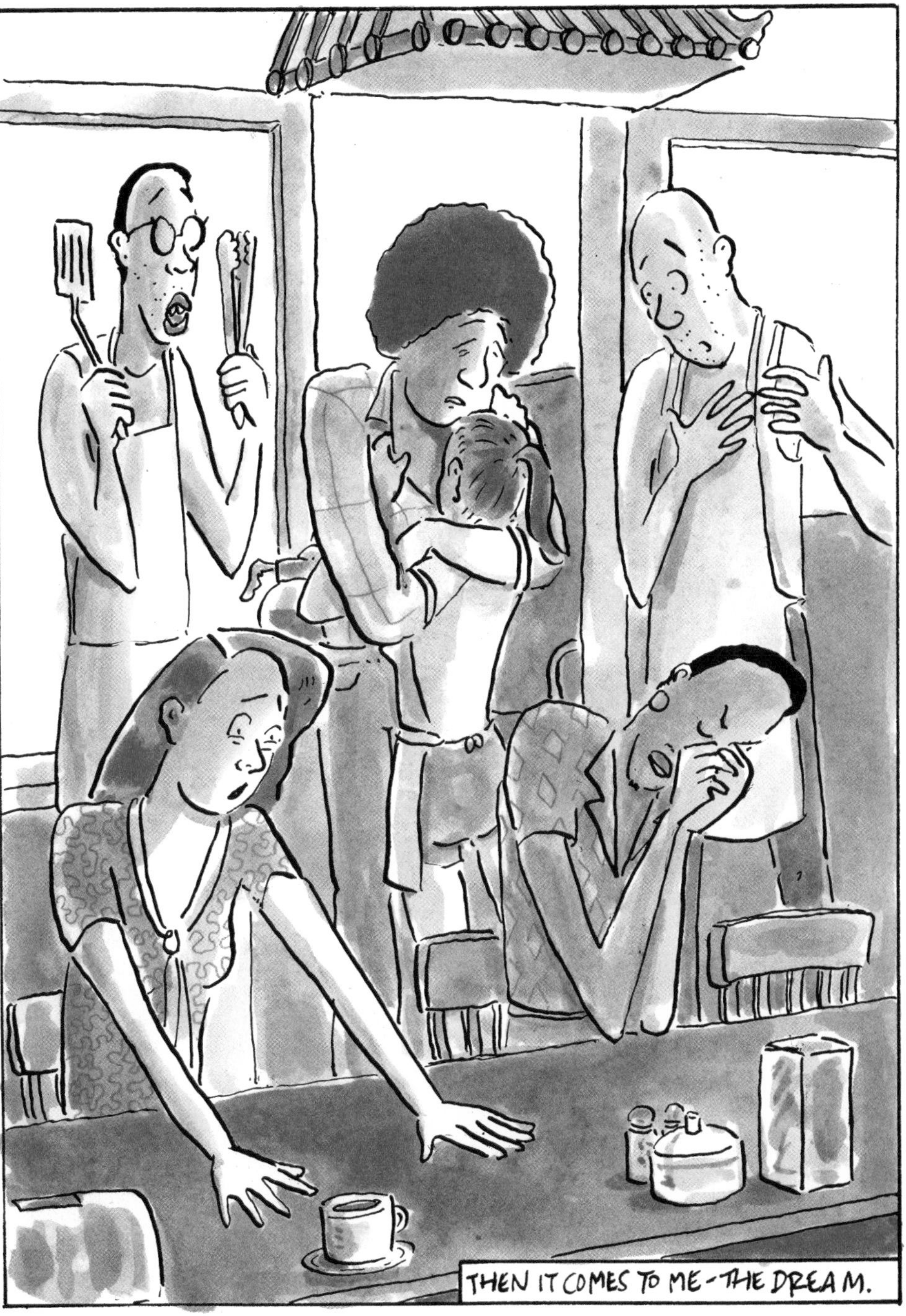
THEN IT COMES TO ME - THE DREAM.

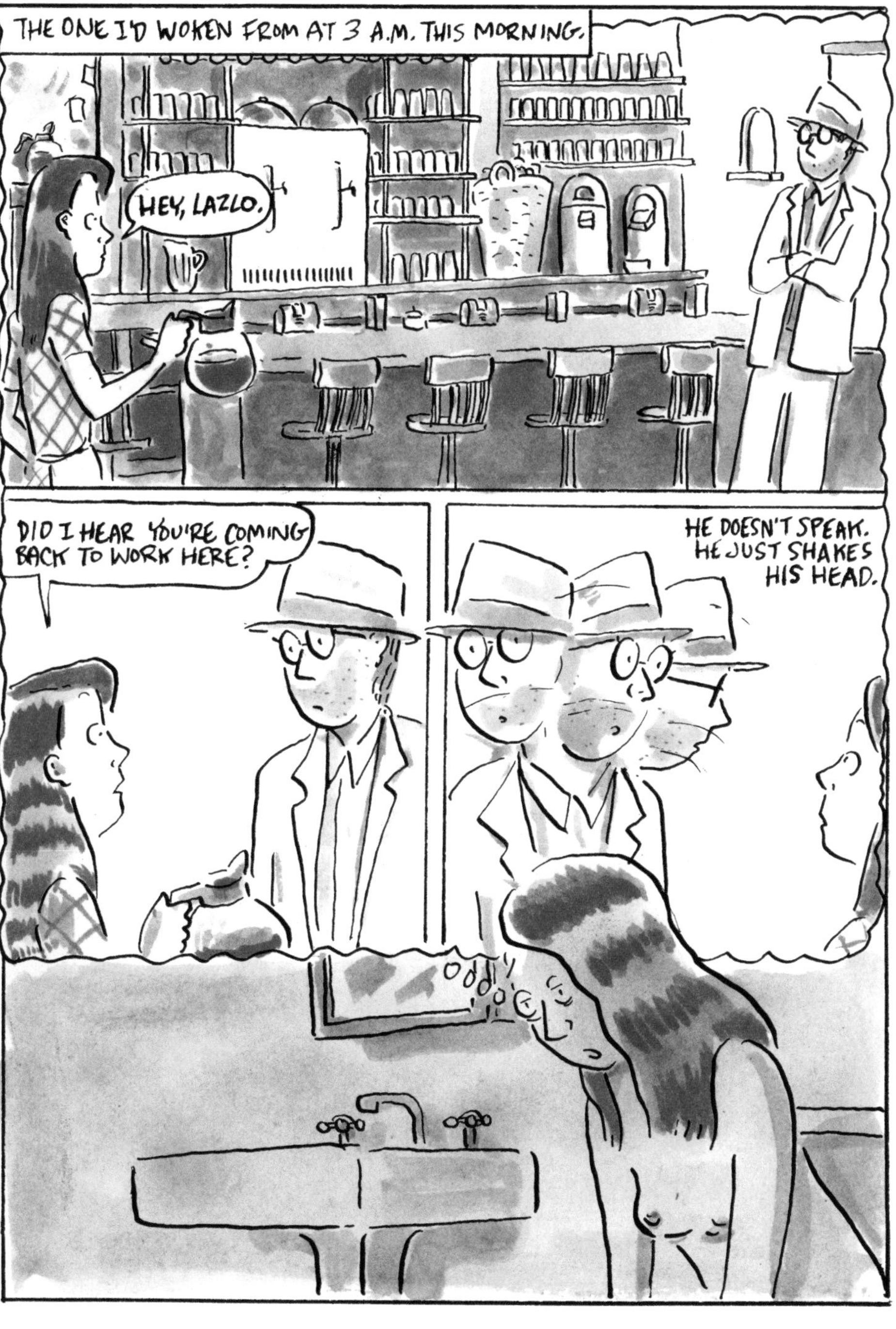
THE ONE I'D WOKEN FROM AT 3 A.M. THIS MORNING.
HEY, LAZLO.
DID I HEAR YOU'RE COMING BACK TO WORK HERE?
HE DOESN'T SPEAK. HE JUST SHAKES HIS HEAD.

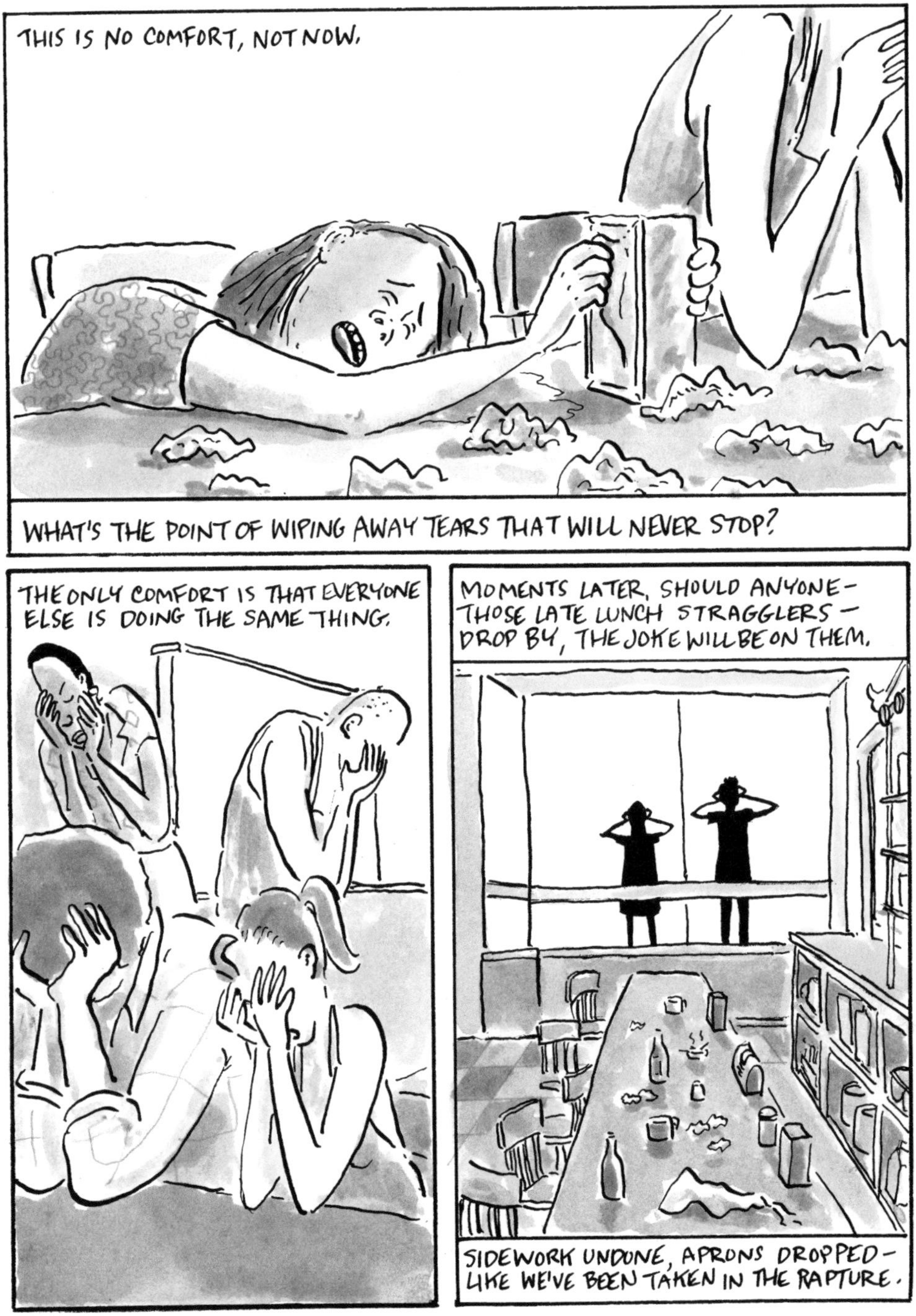
THIS IS NO COMFORT, NOT NOW.
WHAT'S THE POINT OF WIPING AWAY TEARS THAT WILL NEVER STOP?
THE ONLY COMFORT IS THAT EVERYONE ELSE IS DOING THE SAME THING.
MOMENTS LATER, SHOULD ANYONE- THOSE LATE LUNCH STRAGGLERS - DROP BY, THE JOKE WILL BE ON THEM.
SIDEWORK UNDONE, APRONS DROPPED - LIKE WE'VE BEEN TAKEN IN THE RAPTURE.

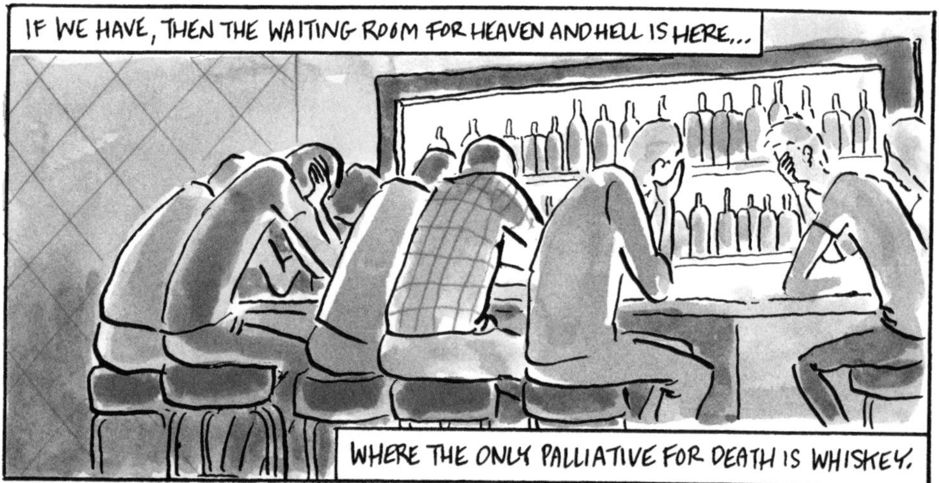
IF WE HAVE, THEN THE WAITING ROOM FOR HEAVEN AND HELL IS HERE...
WHERE THE ONLY PALLIATIVE FOR DEATH IS WHISKEY.

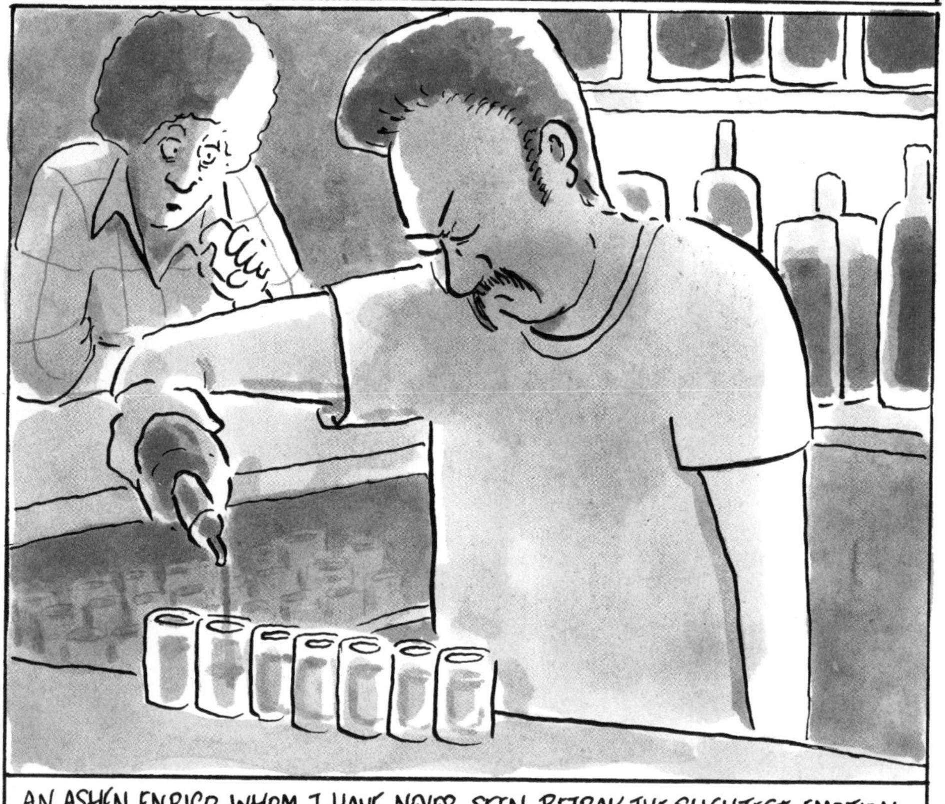
AN ASHEN ENRICO, WHOM I HAVE NEVER SEEN BETRAY THE SLIGHTEST EMOTION, POURS FREELY WITH A SHAKING HAND.

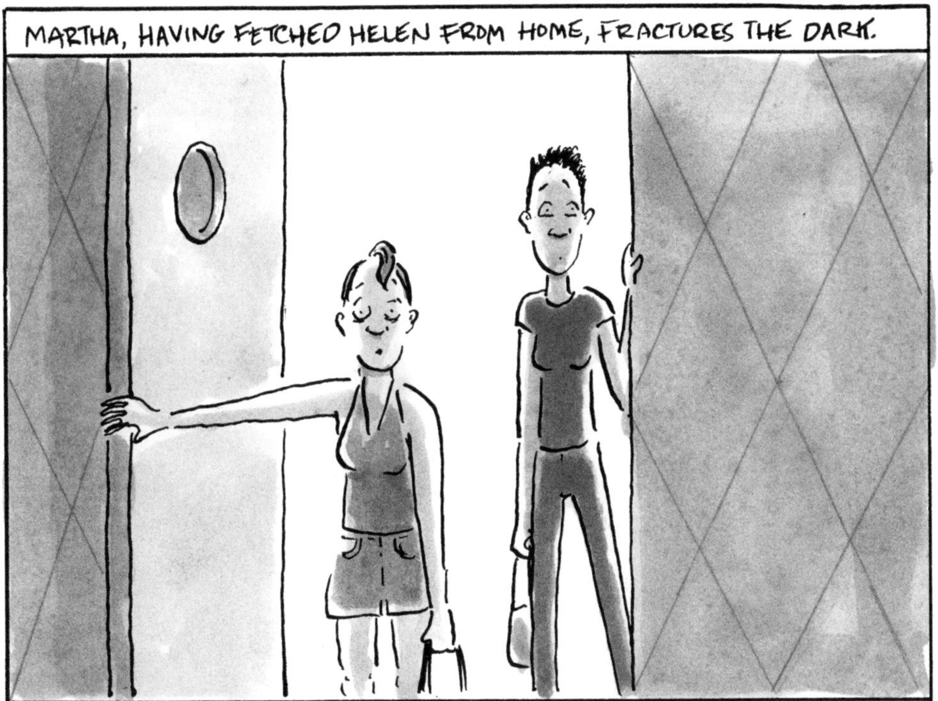
MARTHA, HAVING FETCHED HELEN FROM HOME, FRACTURES THE DARK.

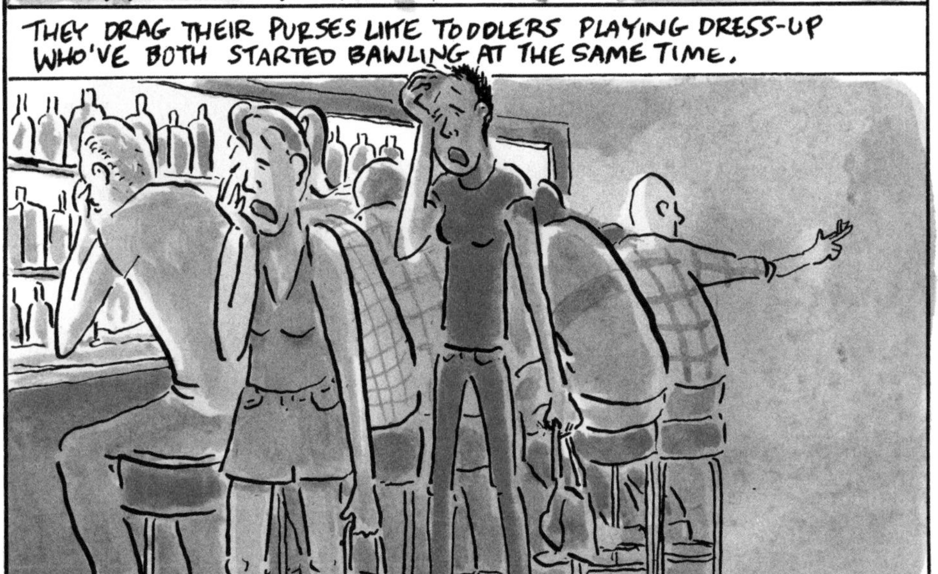
THEY DRAG THEIR PURSES LIKE TODDLERS PLAYING DRESS-UP WHO'VE BOTH STARTED BAWLING AT THE SAME TIME.

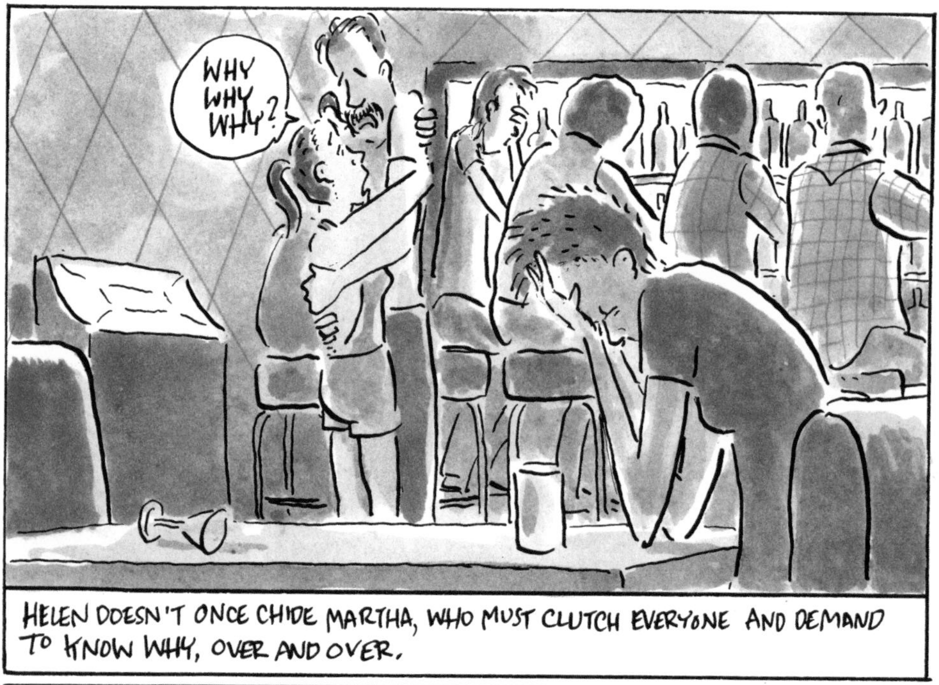
WHY WHY WHY?
HELEN DOESN'T ONCE CHIDE MARTHA, WHO MUST CLUTCH EVERYONE AND DEMAND TO KNOW WHY, OVER AND OVER.

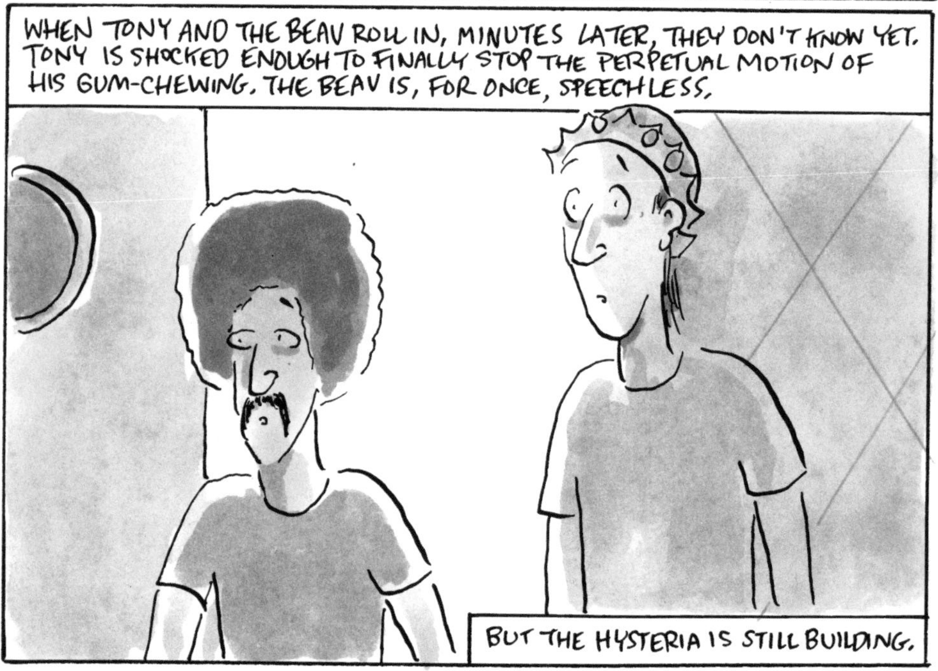
WHEN TONY AND THE BEAV ROLL IN, MINUTES LATER, THEY DON'T KNOW YET. TONY IS SHOCKED ENOUGH TO FINALLY STOP THE PERPETUAL MOTION OF HIS GUM-CHEWING. THE BEAV IS, FOR ONCE, SPEECHLESS.
BUT THE HYSTERIA IS STILL BUILDING.

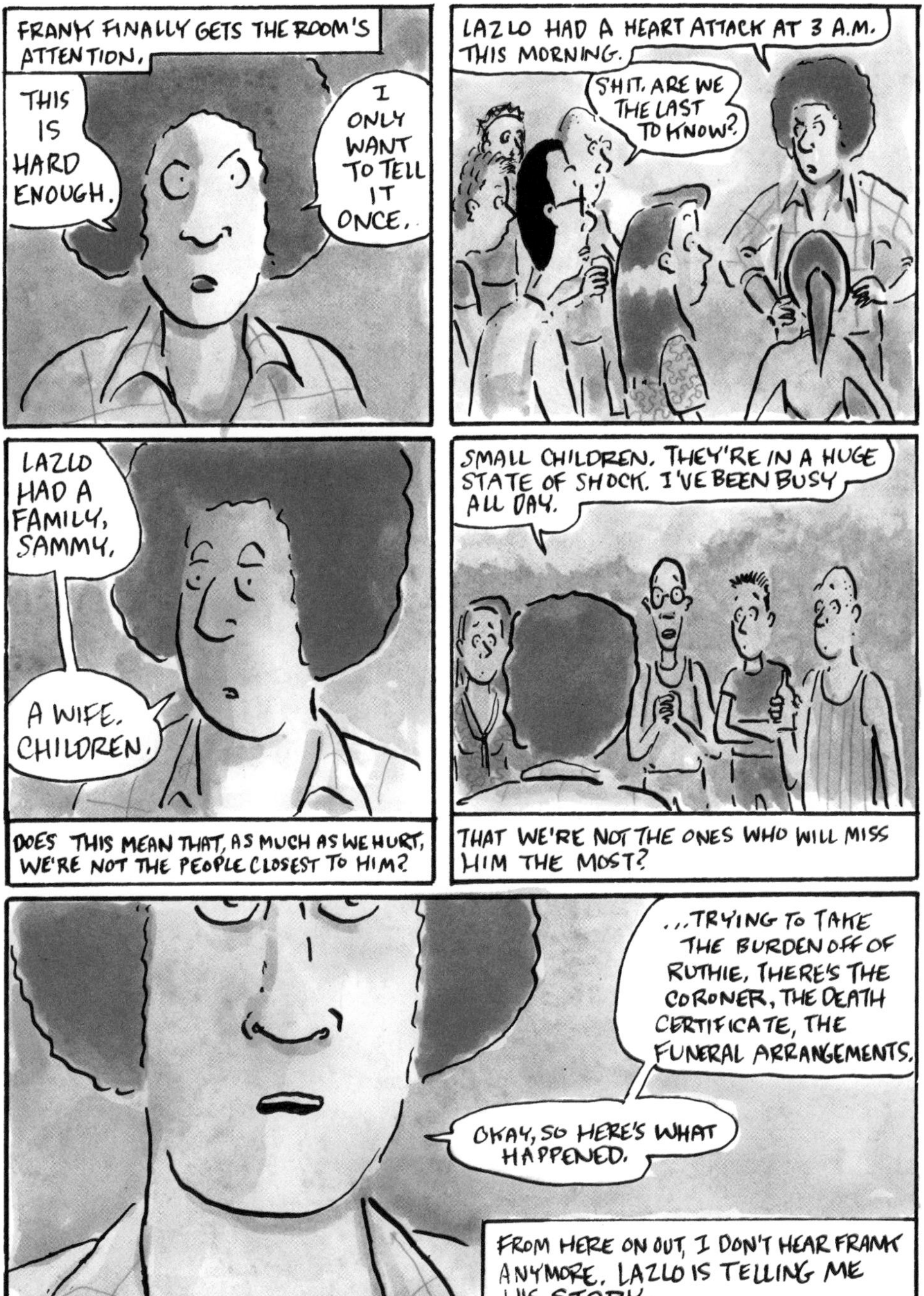
FRANK FINALLY GETS THE ROOM'S ATTENTION.
THIS IS HARD ENOUGH.
I ONLY WANT TO TELL IT ONCE.
LAZLO HAD A HEART ATTACK AT 3 A.M. THIS MORNING.
SHIT. ARE WE THE LAST TO KNOW?
LAZLO HAD A FAMILY, SAMMY.
A WIFE. CHILDREN.
DOES THIS MEAN THAT, AS MUCH AS WE HURT, WE'RE NOT THE PEOPLE CLOSEST TO HIM?
SMALL CHILDREN. THEY'RE IN A HUGE STATE OF SHOCK. I'VE BEEN BUSY ALL DAY.
THAT WE'RE NOT THE ONES WHO WILL MISS HIM THE MOST?
...TRYING TO TAKE THE BURDEN OFF OF RUTHIE. THERE'S THE CORONER, THE DEATH CERTIFICATE, THE FUNERAL ARRANGEMENTS.
OKAY, SO HERE'S WHAT HAPPENED.
FROM HERE ON OUT, I DON'T HEAR FRANK ANYMORE. LAZLO IS TELLING ME HIS STORY.

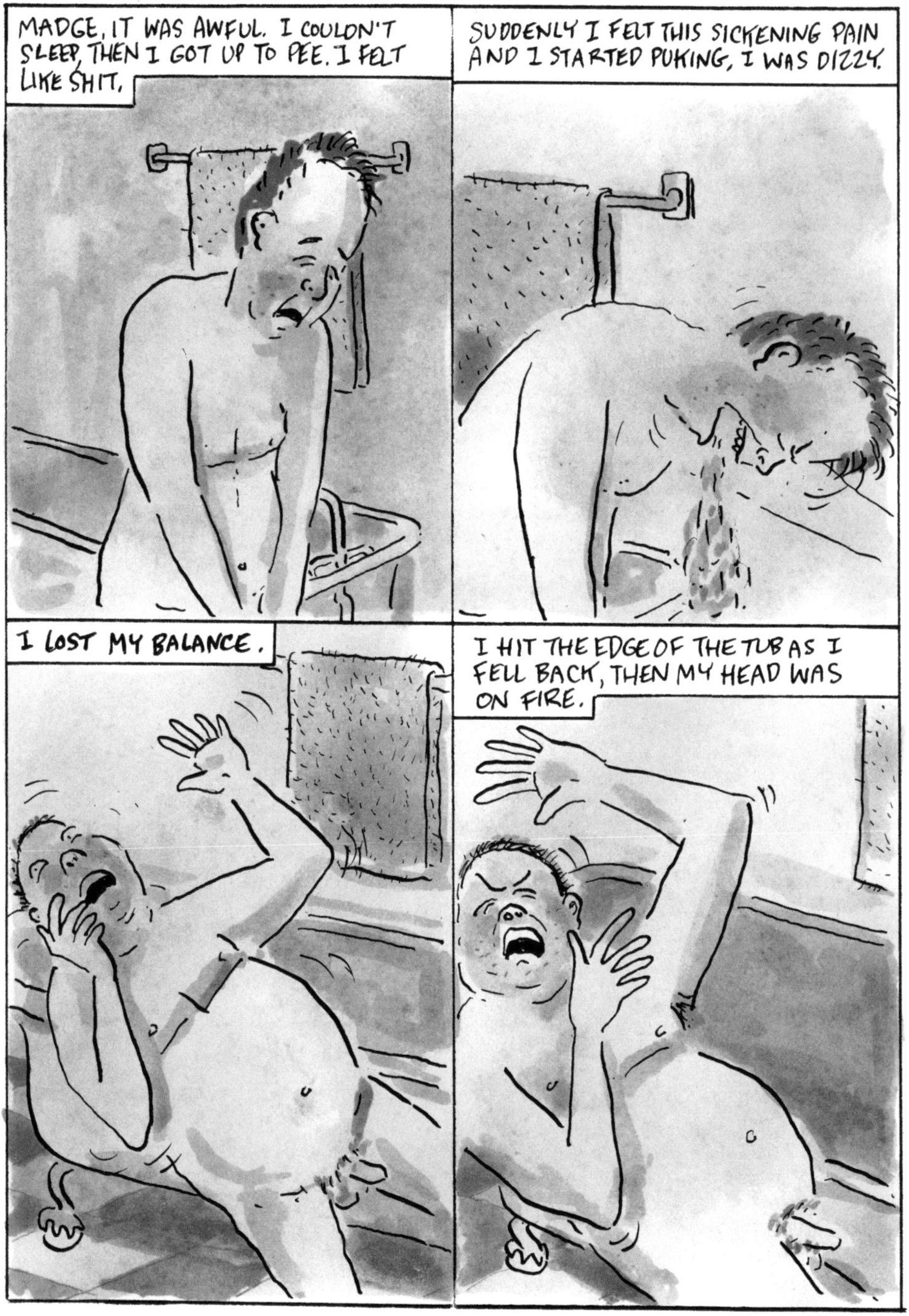
MADGE, IT WAS AWFUL. I COULDN'T SLEEP, THEN I GOT UP TO PEE. I FELT LIKE SHIT.
SUDDENLY I FELT THIS SICKENING PAIN AND I STARTED PUKING, I WAS DIZZY.
I LOST MY BALANCE.
I HIT THE EDGE OF THE TUB AS I FELL BACK, THEN MY HEAD WAS ON FIRE.

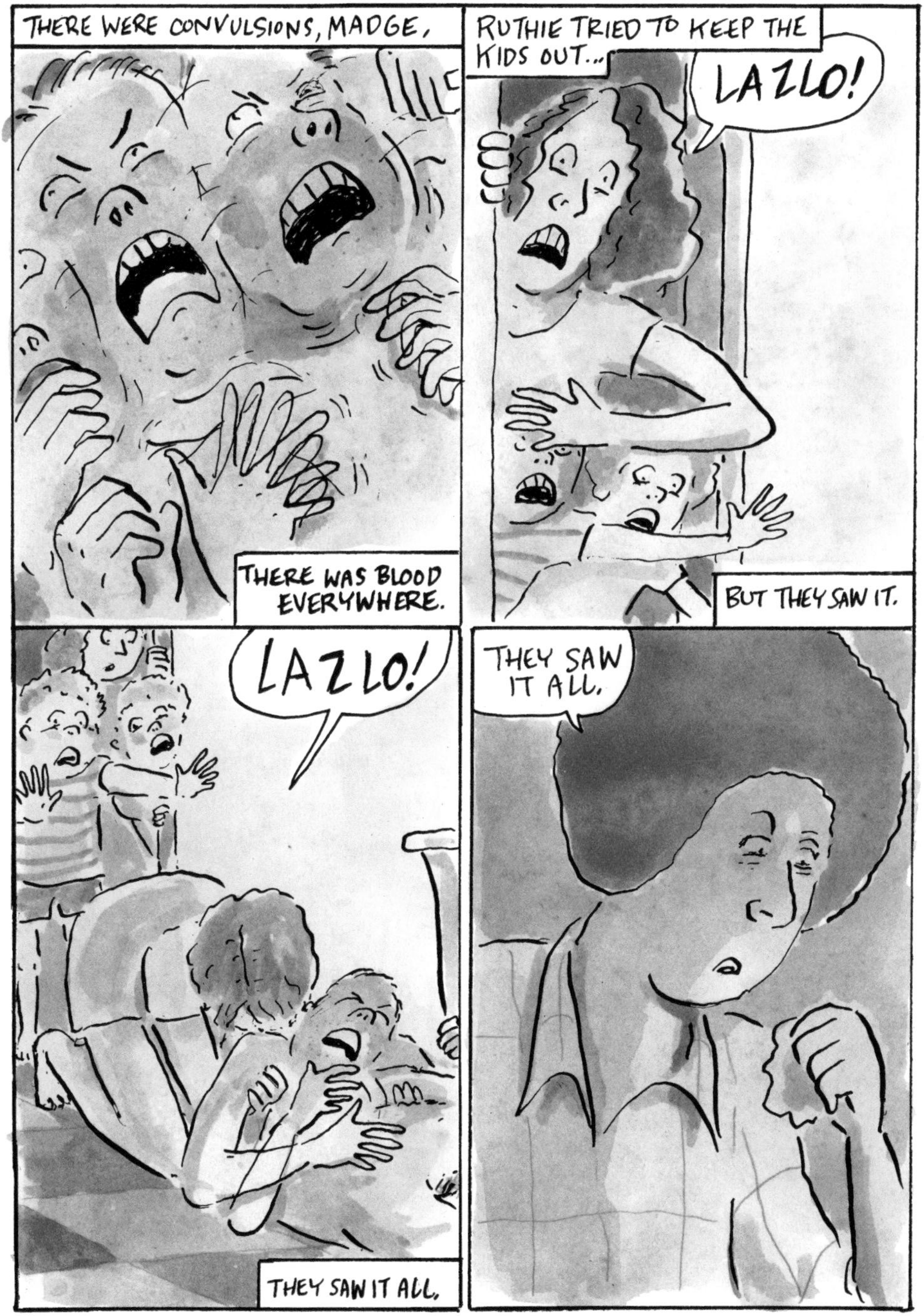
THERE WERE CONVULSIONS, MADGE,
THERE WAS BLOOD EVERYWHERE.
RUTHIE TRIED TO KEEP THE KIDS OUT...
LAZLO!
BUT THEY SAW IT.
LAZLO!
THEY SAW IT ALL.
THEY SAW IT ALL.

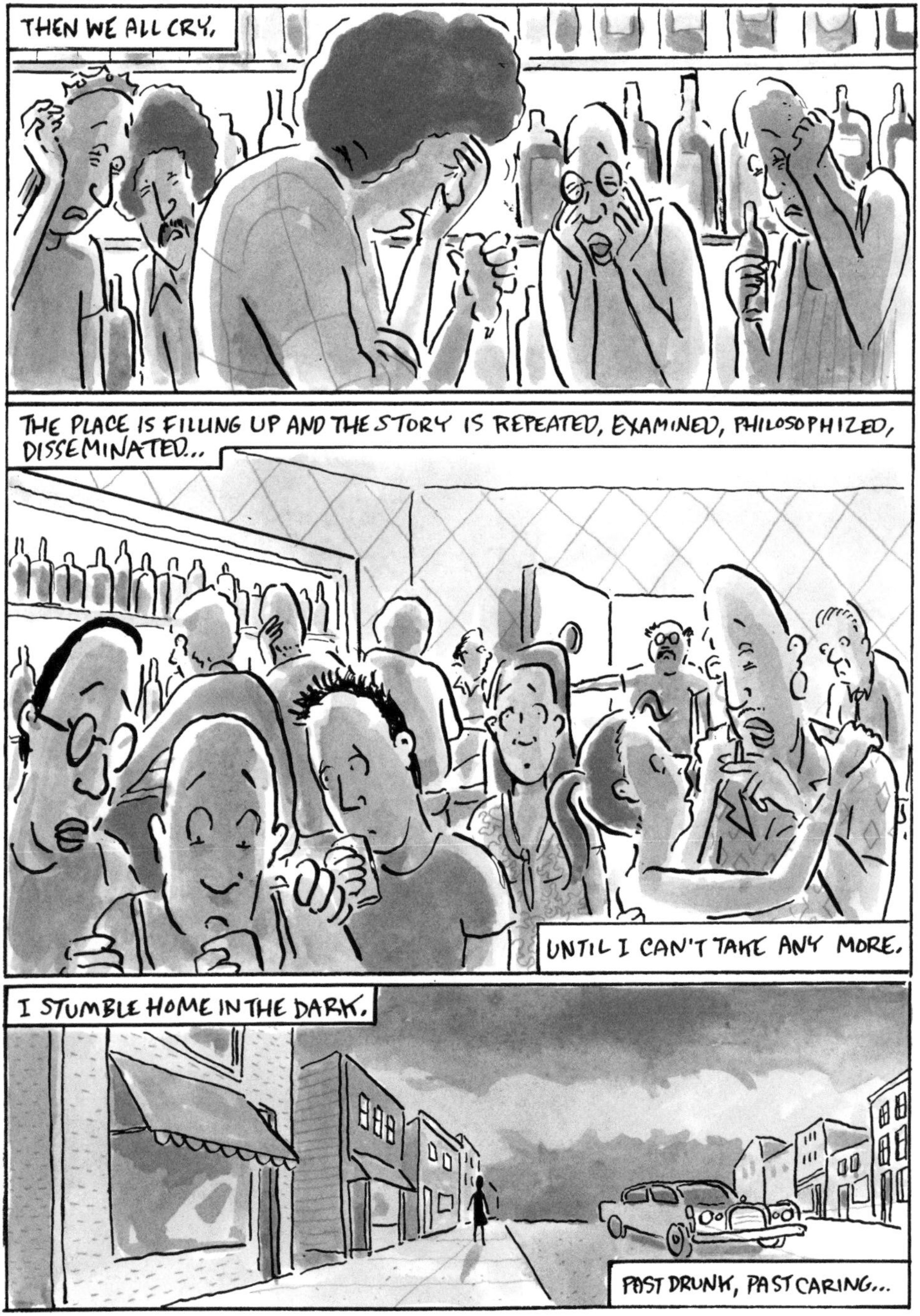
THEN WE ALL CRY.
THE PLACE IS FILLING UP AND THE STORY IS REPEATED, EXAMINED, PHILOSOPHIZED, DISSEMINATED...
UNTIL I CAN'T TAKE ANY MORE.
I STUMBLE HOME IN THE DARK.
PAST DRUNK, PAST CARING...

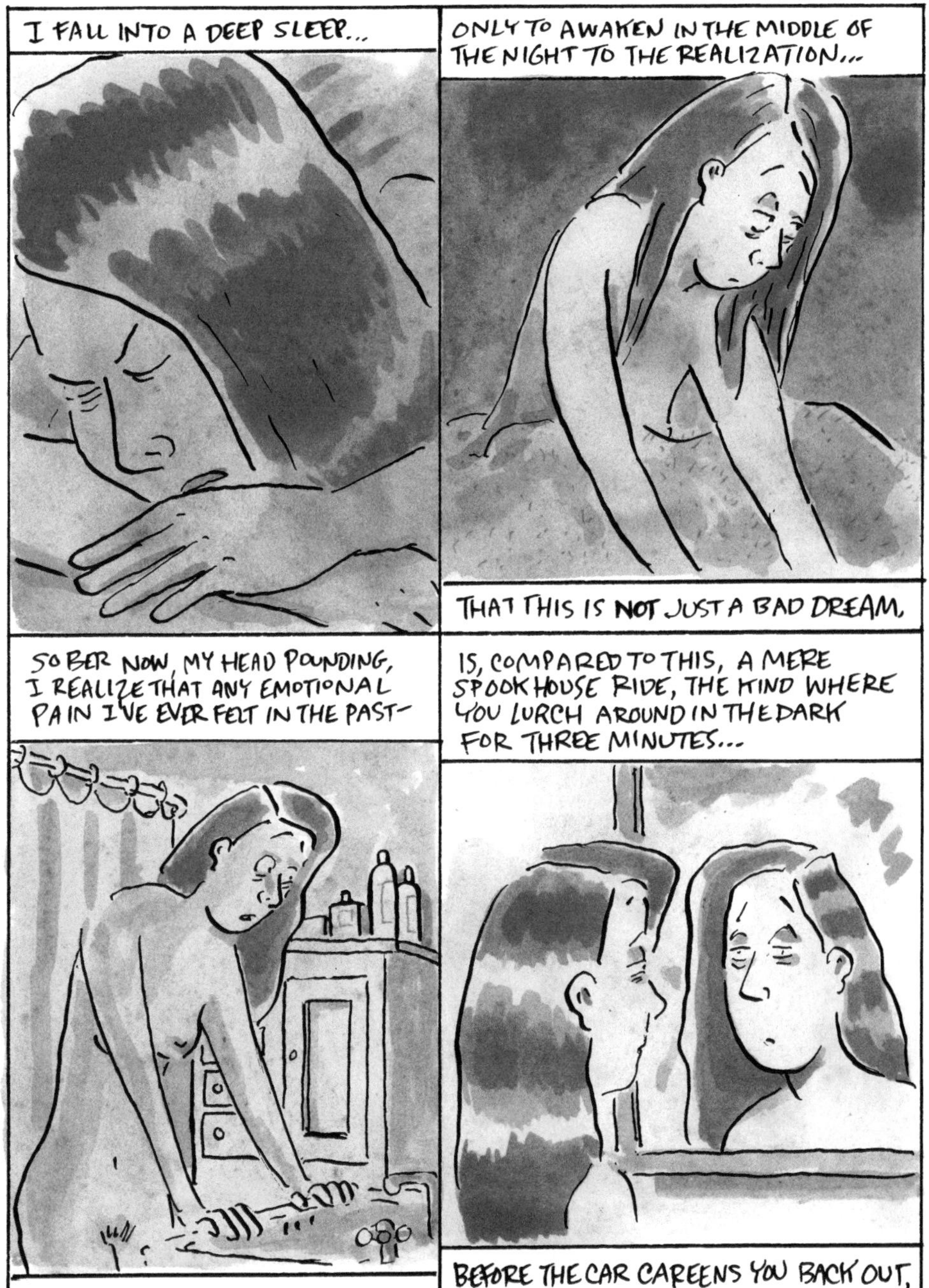
I FALL INTO A DEEP SLEEP...
ONLY TO AWAKEN IN THE MIDDLE OF THE NIGHT TO THE REALIZATION...
THAT THIS IS NOT JUST A BAD DREAM.
SOBER NOW, MY HEAD POUNDING, I REALIZE THAT ANY EMOTIONAL PAIN I'VE EVER FELT IN THE PAST-
BRYAN IMMEDIATELY COMES TO MIND-
IS, COMPARED TO THIS, A MERE SPOOK HOUSE RIDE, THE KIND WHERE YOU LURCH AROUND IN THE DARK FOR THREE MINUTES...
BEFORE THE CAR CAREENS YOU BACK OUT, LAUGHING, INTO THE CARNIVAL WORLD.

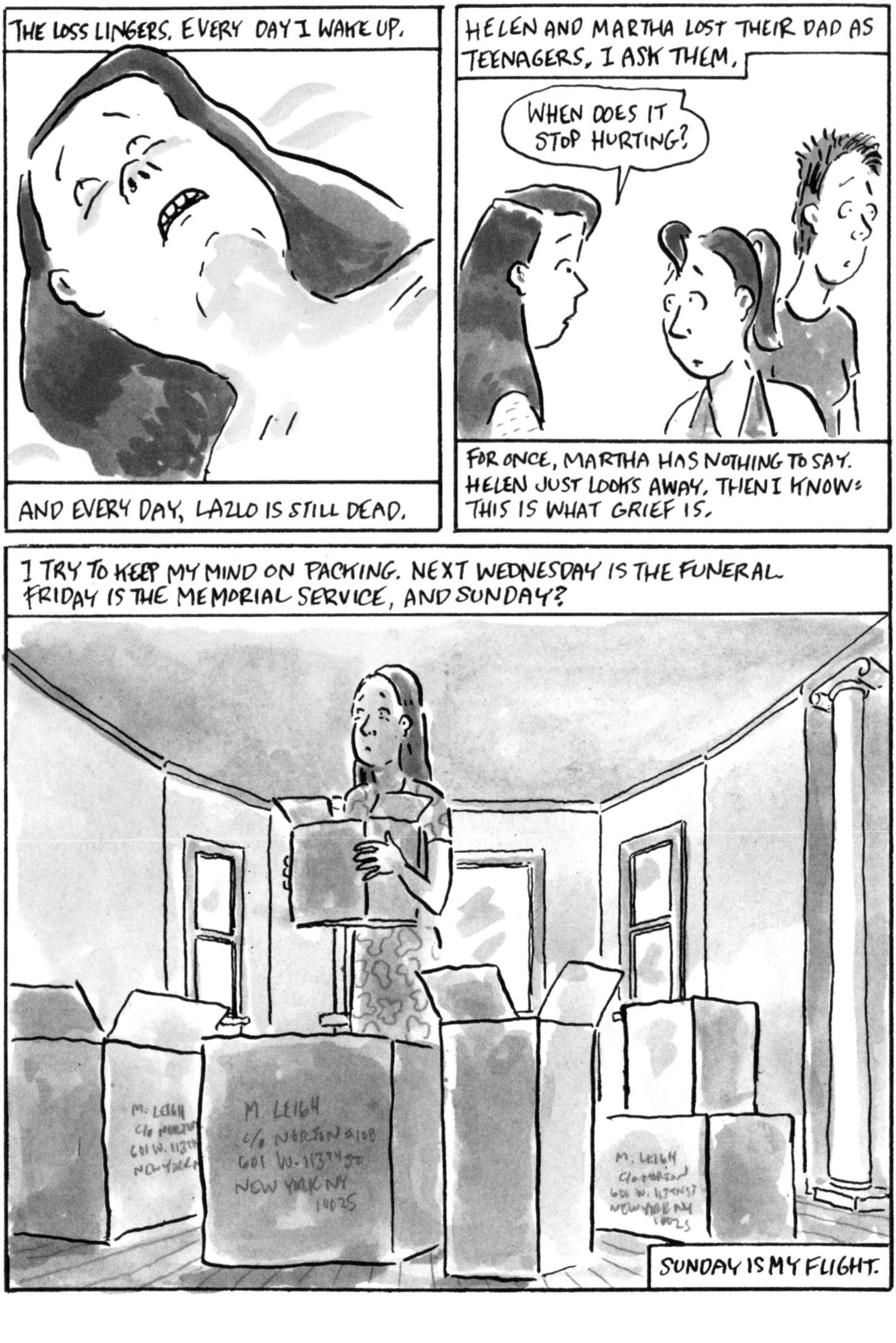
THE LOSS LINGERS. EVERY DAY I WAKE UP.
AND EVERY DAY, LAZLO IS STILL DEAD.
HELEN AND MARTHA LOST THEIR DAD AS TEENAGERS. I ASK THEM,
WHEN DOES IT STOP HURTING?
FOR ONCE, MARTHA HAS NOTHING TO SAY. HELEN JUST LOOKS AWAY. THEN I KNOW: THIS IS WHAT GRIEF IS.
I TRY TO KEEP MY MIND ON PACKING. NEXT WEDNESDAY IS THE FUNERAL. FRIDAY IS THE MEMORIAL SERVICE, AND SUNDAY?
SUNDAY IS MY FLIGHT.

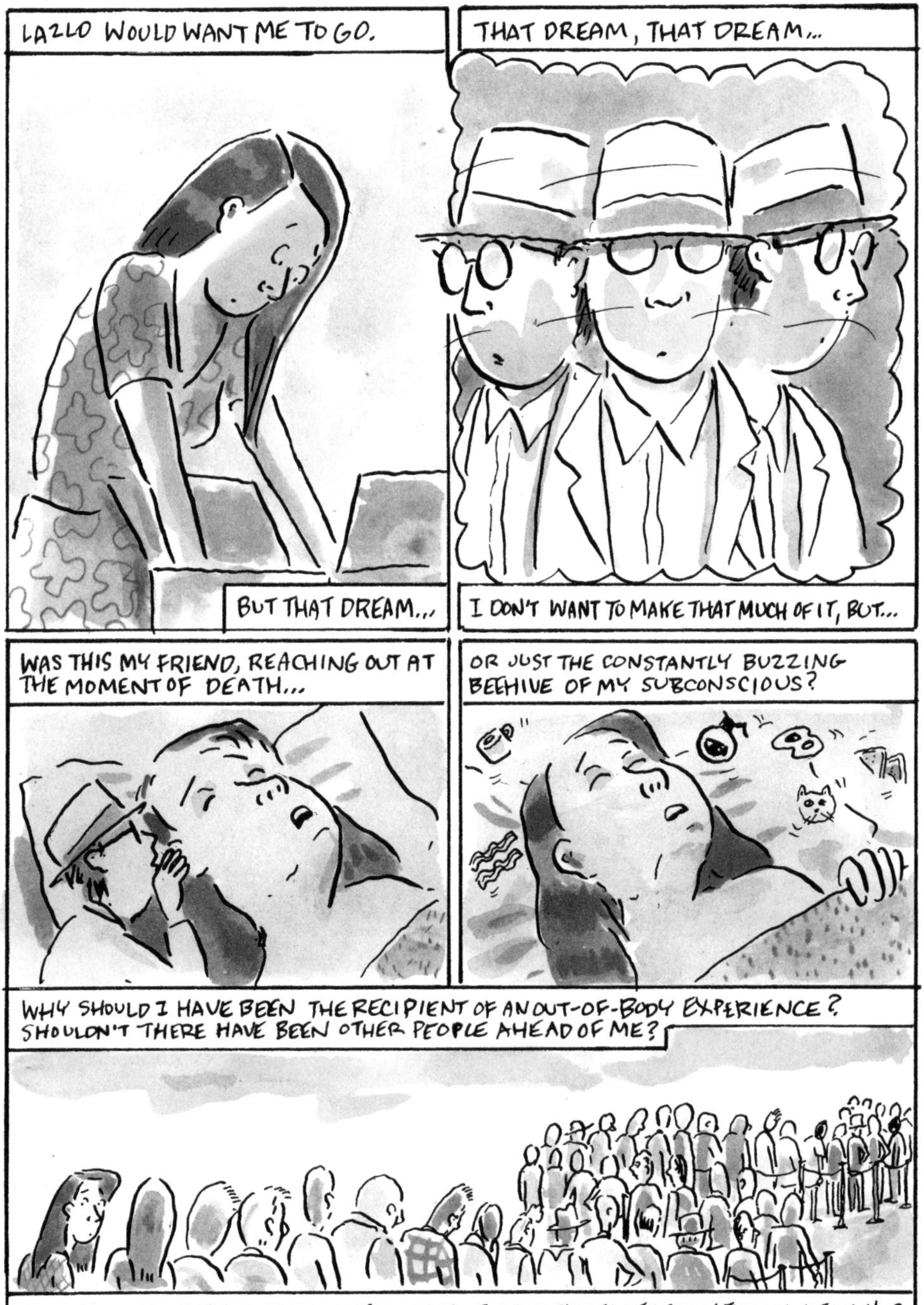

LAZLO WOULD WANT ME TO GO.
BUT THAT DREAM...
THAT DREAM, THAT DREAM...
I DON'T WANT TO MAKE THAT MUCH OF IT, BUT...
WAS THIS MY FRIEND, REACHING OUT AT THE MOMENT OF DEATH...
OR JUST THE CONSTANTLY BUZZING BEEHIVE OF MY SUBCONSCIOUS?
WHY SHOULD I HAVE BEEN THE RECIPIENT OF AN OUT-OF-BODY EXPERIENCE? SHOULDN'T THERE HAVE BEEN OTHER PEOPLE AHEAD OF ME?
ALL I KNOW FOR SURE IS LAZLO IS DEAD. HE HAD TO LEAVE THE PARTY EARLY. THIS IS WHAT DEATH IS.

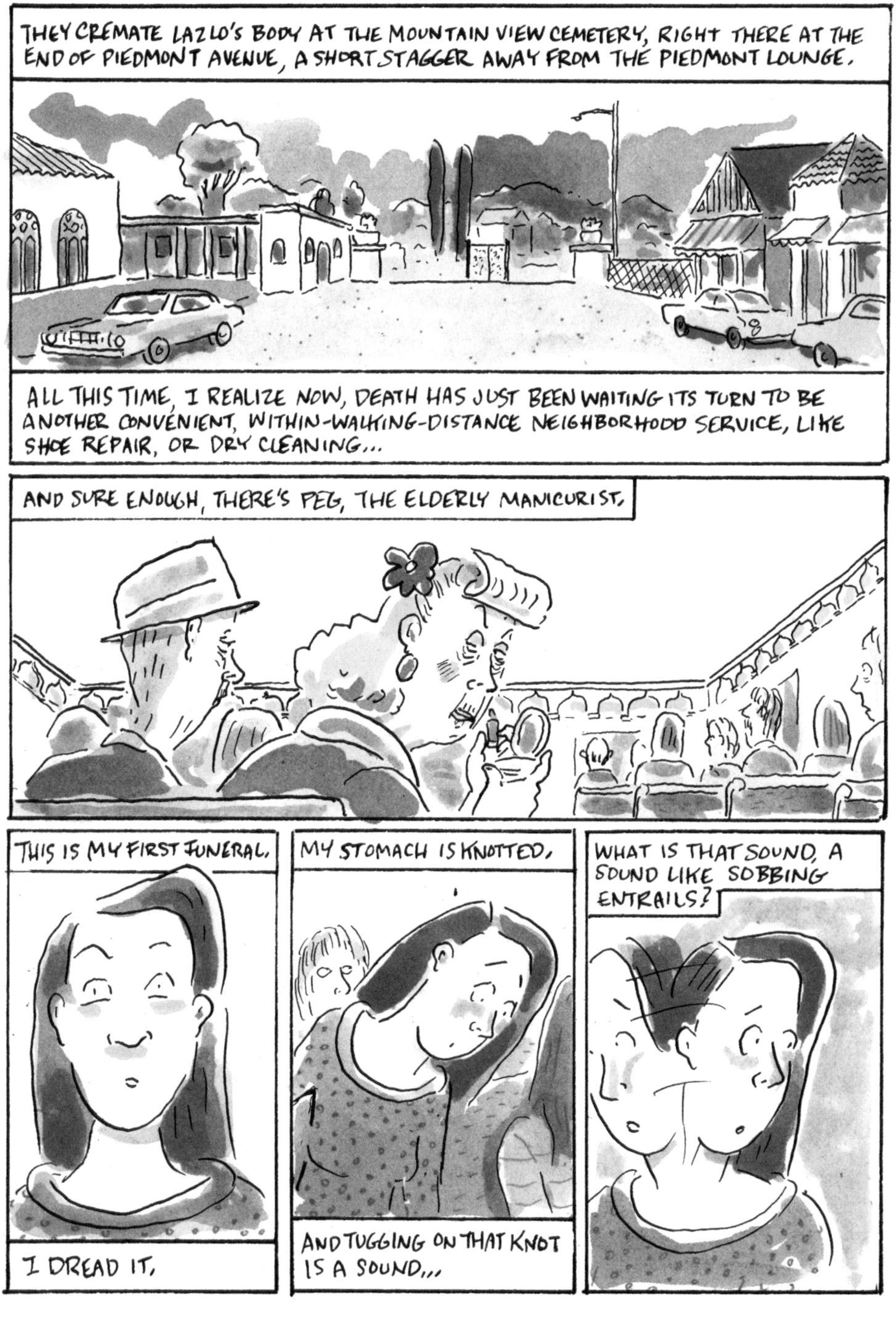
THEY CREMATE LAZLO'S BODY AT THE MOUNTAIN VIEW CEMETERY, RIGHT THERE AT THE END OF PIEDMONT AVENUE, A SHORT STAGGER AWAY FROM THE PIEDMONT LOUNGE.
ALL THIS TIME, I REALIZE NOW, DEATH HAS JUST BEEN WAITING ITS TURN TO BE ANOTHER CONVENIENT, WITHIN-WALKING-DISTANCE NEIGHBORHOOD SERVICE, LIKE SHOE REPAIR, OR DRY CLEANING...
AND SURE ENOUGH, THERE'S PEG, THE ELDERLY MANICURIST.
THIS IS MY FIRST FUNERAL.
I DREAD IT.
MY STOMACH IS KNOTTED.
AND TUGGING ON THAT KNOT IS A SOUND...
WHAT IS THAT SOUND, A SOUND LIKE SOBBING ENTRAILS?

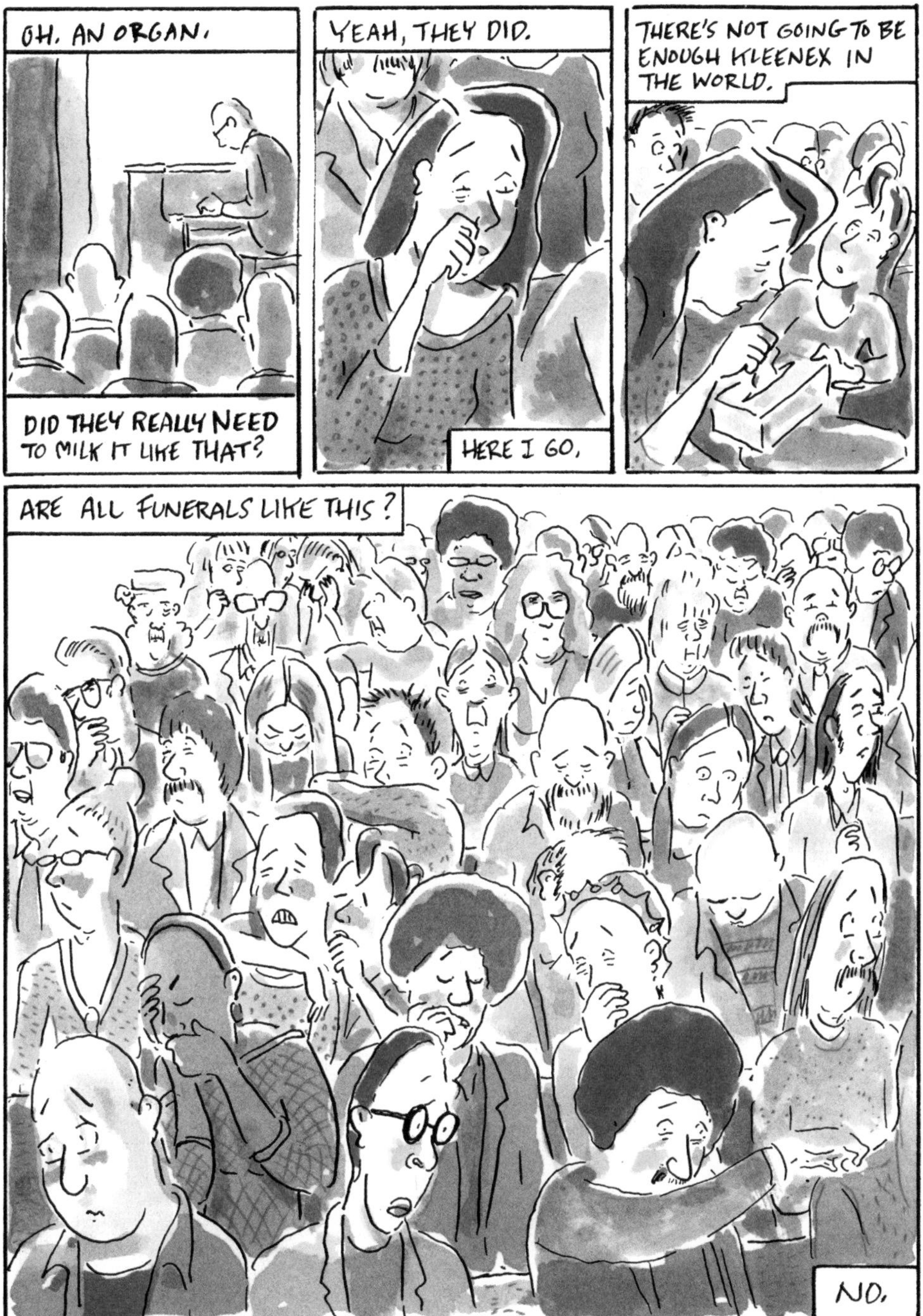
OH. AN ORGAN.
DID THEY REALLY NEED TO MILK IT LIKE THAT?
YEAH, THEY DID.
HERE I GO.
THERE'S NOT GOING TO BE ENOUGH KLEENEX IN THE WORLD.
ARE ALL FUNERALS LIKE THIS?
NO.

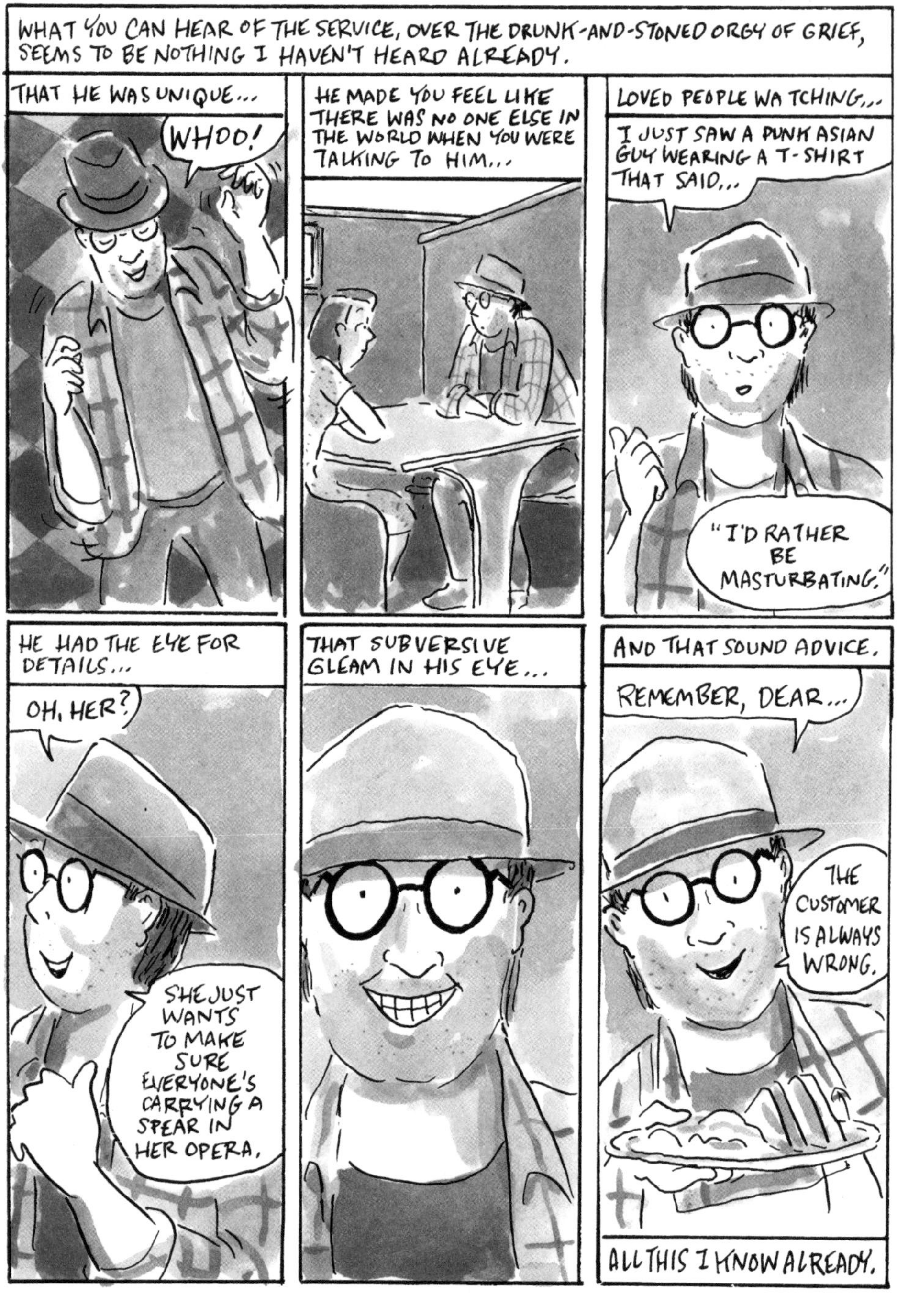
WHAT YOU CAN HEAR OF THE SERVICE, OVER THE DRUNK-AND-STONED ORGY OF GRIEF, SEEMS TO BE NOTHING I HAVEN'T HEARD ALREADY.
THAT HE WAS UNIQUE...
WHOO!
HE MADE YOU FEEL LIKE THERE WAS NO ONE ELSE IN THE WORLD WHEN YOU WERE TALKING TO HIM...
LOVED PEOPLE WATCHING...
I JUST SAW A PUNK ASIAN GUY WEARING A T-SHIRT THAT SAID...
"I'D RATHER BE MASTURBATING."
HE HAD THE EYE FOR DETAILS...
OH, HER?
SHE JUST WANTS TO MAKE SURE EVERYONE'S CARRYING A SPEAR IN HER OPERA.
THAT SUBVERSIVE GLEAM IN HIS EYE...
AND THAT SOUND ADVICE.
REMEMBER, DEAR...
THE CUSTOMER IS ALWAYS WRONG.
ALL THIS I KNOW ALREADY.

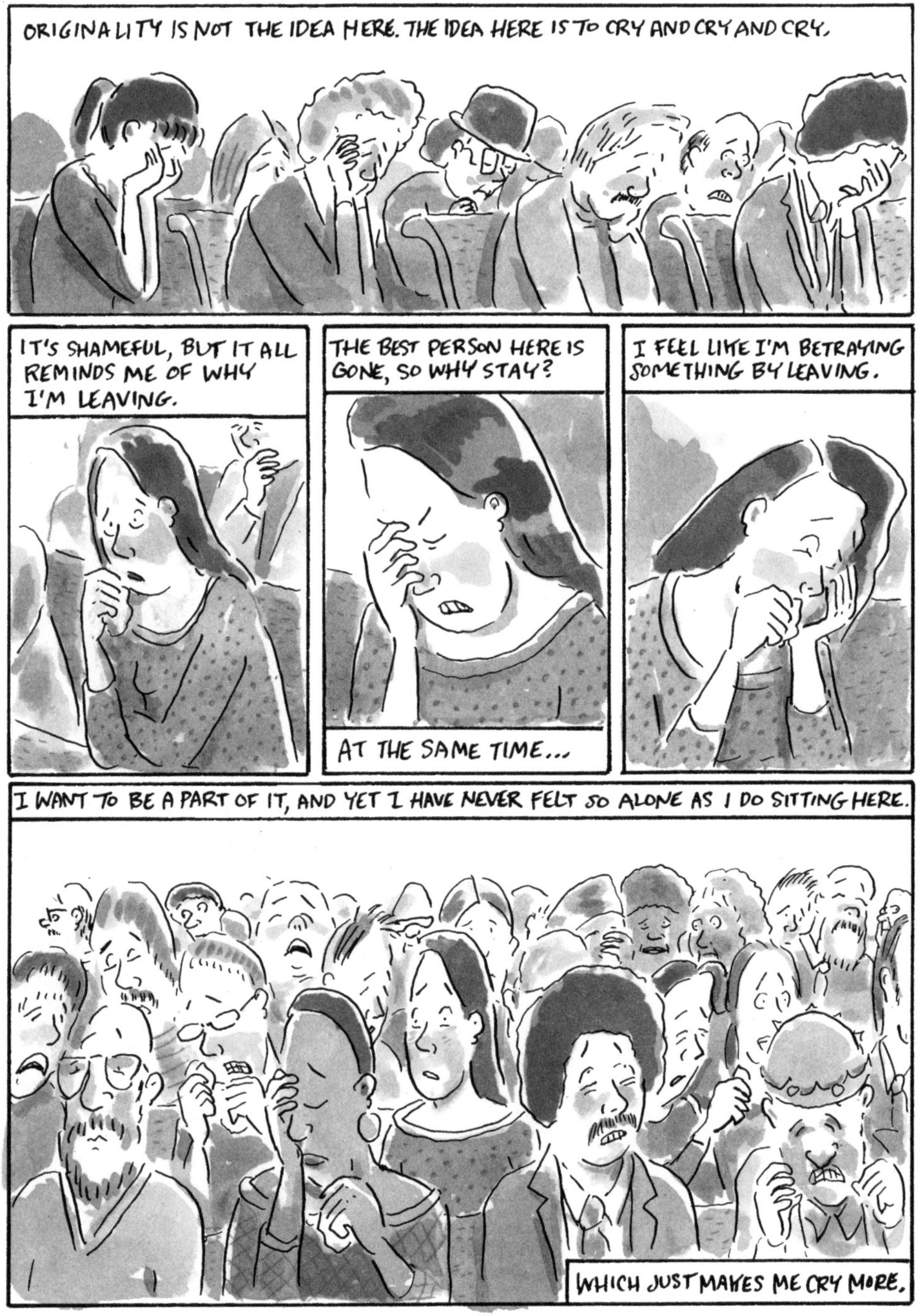
ORIGINALITY IS NOT THE IDEA HERE. THE IDEA HERE IS TO CRY AND CRY AND CRY.
IT'S SHAMEFUL, BUT IT ALL REMINDS ME OF WHY I'M LEAVING.
THE BEST PERSON HERE IS GONE, SO WHY STAY?
AT THE SAME TIME...
I FEEL LIKE I'M BETRAYING SOMETHING BY LEAVING.
I WANT TO BE A PART OF IT, AND YET I HAVE NEVER FELT SO ALONE AS I DO SITTING HERE.
WHICH JUST MAKES ME CRY MORE.

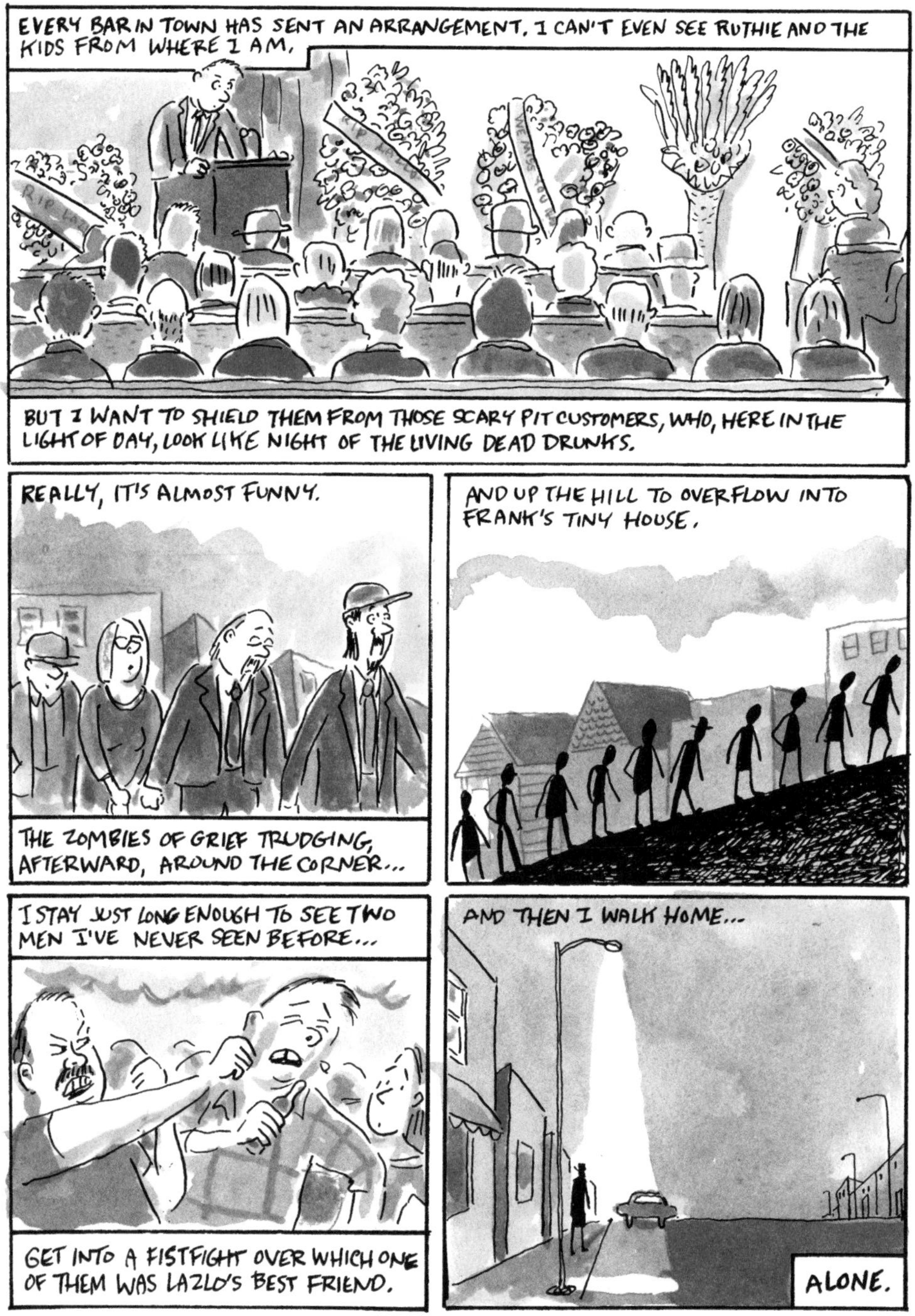
EVERY BAR IN TOWN HAS SENT AN ARRANGEMENT. I CAN'T EVEN SEE RUTHIE AND THE KIDS FROM WHERE I AM,
BUT I WANT TO SHIELD THEM FROM THOSE SCARY PIT CUSTOMERS, WHO, HERE IN THE LIGHT OF DAY, LOOK LIKE NIGHT OF THE LIVING DEAD DRUNKS.
REALLY, IT'S ALMOST FUNNY.
THE ZOMBIES OF GRIEF TRUDGING, AFTERWARD, AROUND THE CORNER...
AND UP THE HILL TO OVERFLOW INTO FRANK'S TINY HOUSE.
I STAY JUST LONG ENOUGH TO SEE TWO MEN I'VE NEVER SEEN BEFORE...
GET INTO A FISTFIGHT OVER WHICH ONE OF THEM WAS LAZLO'S BEST FRIEND.
AND THEN I WALK HOME...
ALONE.

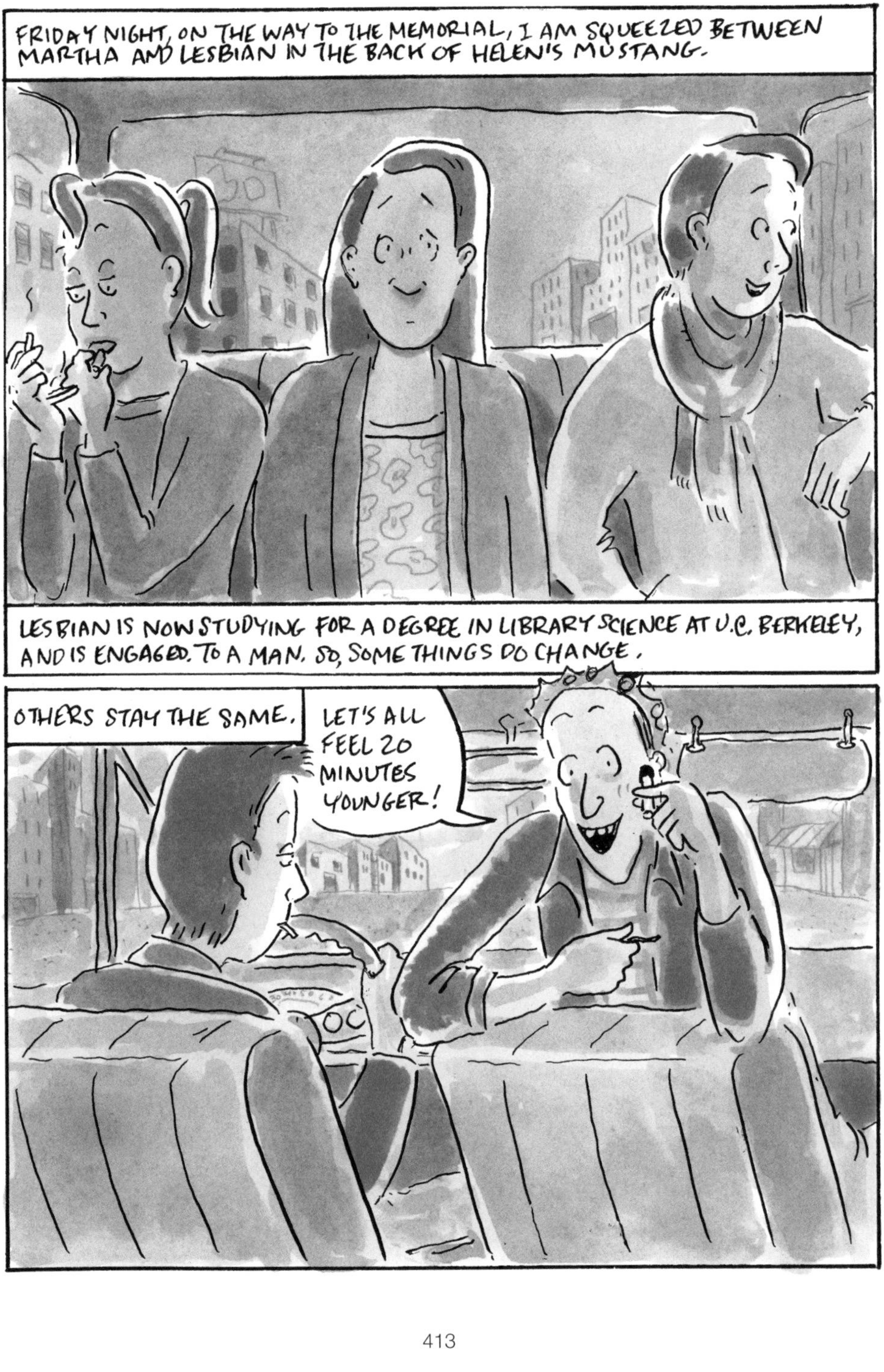
FRIDAY NIGHT, ON THE WAY TO THE MEMORIAL, I AM SQUEEZED BETWEEN MARTHA AND LESBIAN IN THE BACK OF HELEN'S MUSTANG.
LESBIAN IS NOW STUDYING FOR A DEGREE IN LIBRARY SCIENCE AT U.C. BERKELEY, AND IS ENGAGED. TO A MAN. SO, SOME THINGS DO CHANGE.
OTHERS STAY THE SAME.
LET'S ALL FEEL 20 MINUTES YOUNGER!

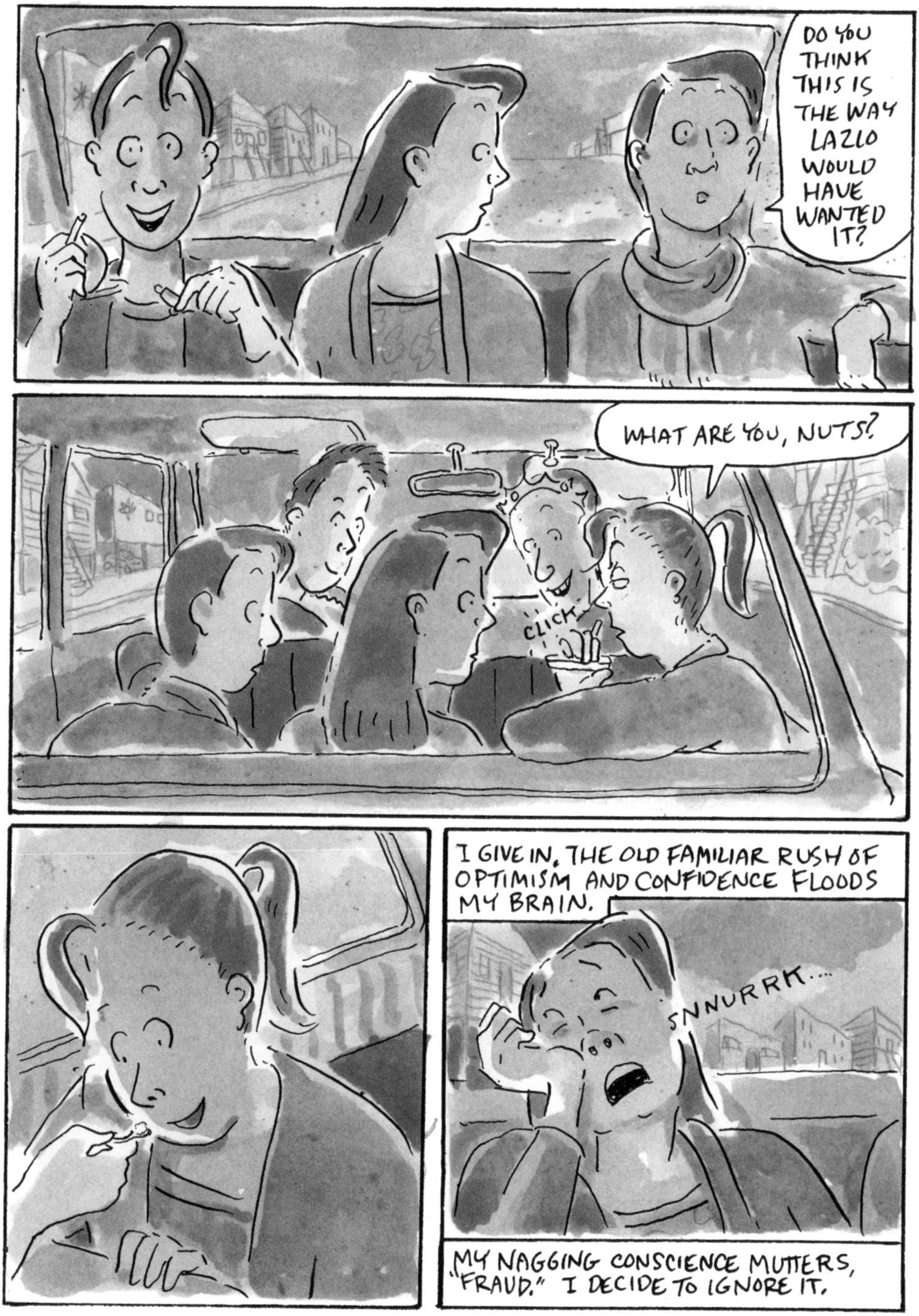
DO YOU THINK THIS IS THE WAY LAZLO WOULD HAVE WANTED IT?
WHAT ARE YOU, NUTS?
CLICK
I GIVE IN. THE OLD FAMILIAR RUSH OF OPTIMISM AND CONFIDENCE FLOODS MY BRAIN.
SNNURRK....
MY NAGGING CONSCIENCE MUTTERS, "FRAUD." I DECIDE TO IGNORE IT.

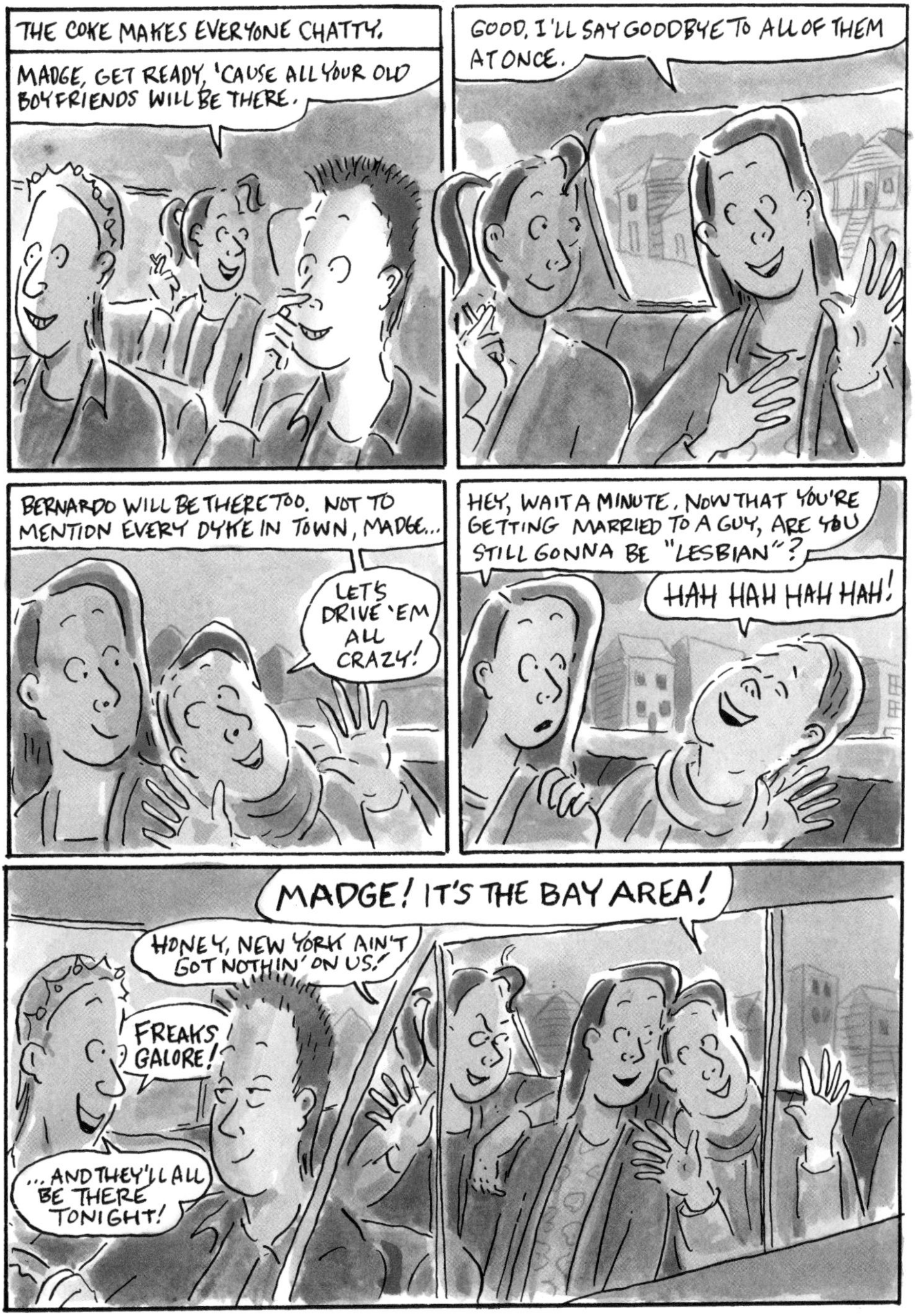
THE COKE MAKES EVERYONE CHATTY.
MADGE, GET READY, 'CAUSE ALL YOUR OLD BOYFRIENDS WILL BE THERE.
GOOD. I'LL SAY GOODBYE TO ALL OF THEM AT ONCE.
BERNARDO WILL BE THERE TOO. NOT TO MENTION EVERY DYKE IN TOWN, MADGE...
LET'S DRIVE 'EM ALL CRAZY!
HEY, WAIT A MINUTE. NOW THAT YOU'RE GETTING MARRIED TO A GUY, ARE YOU STILL GONNA BE "LESBIAN"?
HAH HAH HAH HAH!
MADGE! IT'S THE BAY AREA!
HONEY, NEW YORK AIN'T GOT NOTHIN' ON US!
FREAKS GALORE!
...AND THEY'LL ALL BE THERE TONIGHT!

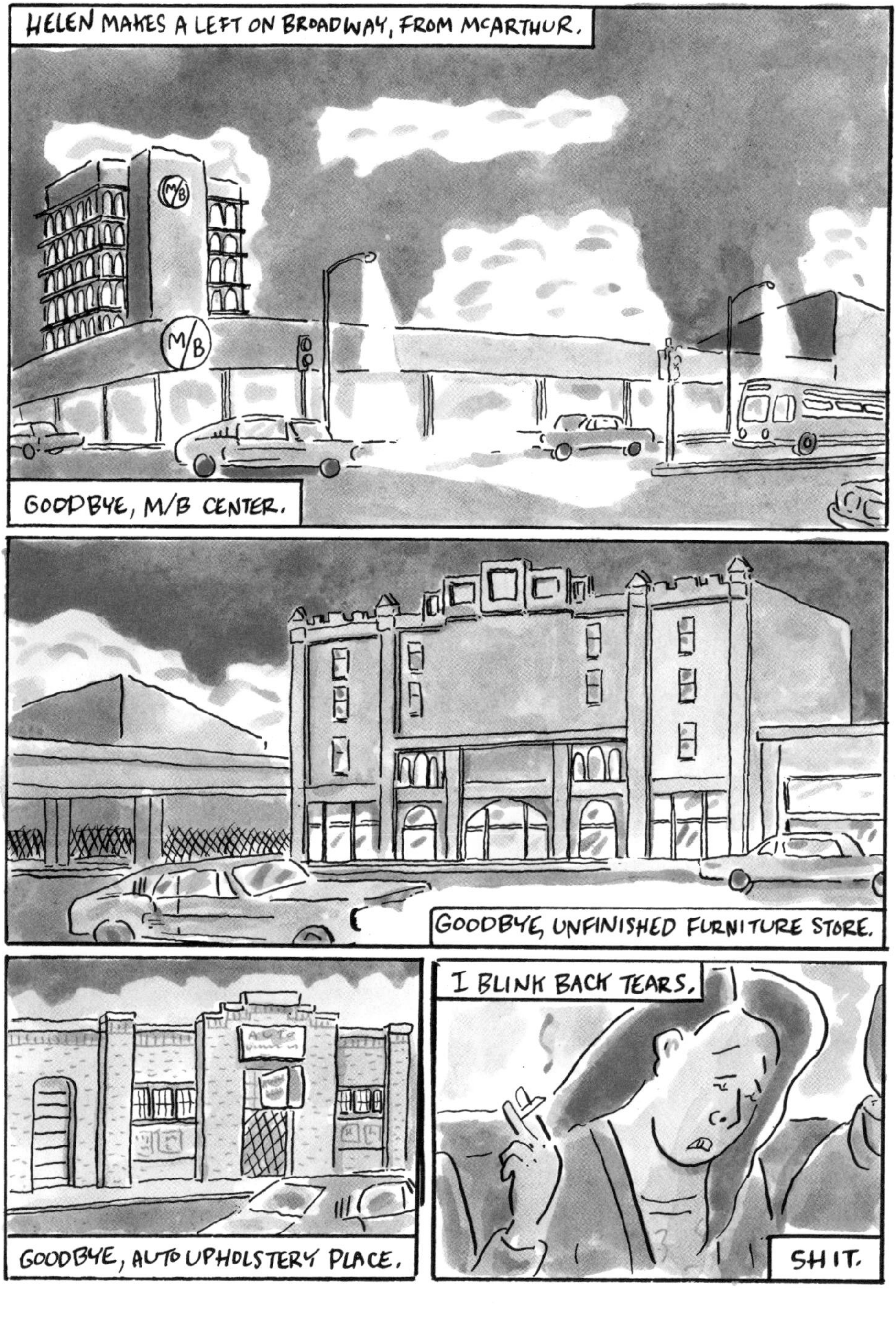
HELEN MAKES A LEFT ON BROADWAY, FROM MCARTHUR.
M/B
GOODBYE, M/B CENTER.
GOODBYE, UNFINISHED FURNITURE STORE.
GOODBYE, AUTO UPHOLSTERY PLACE.
I BLINK BACK TEARS.
SHIT.

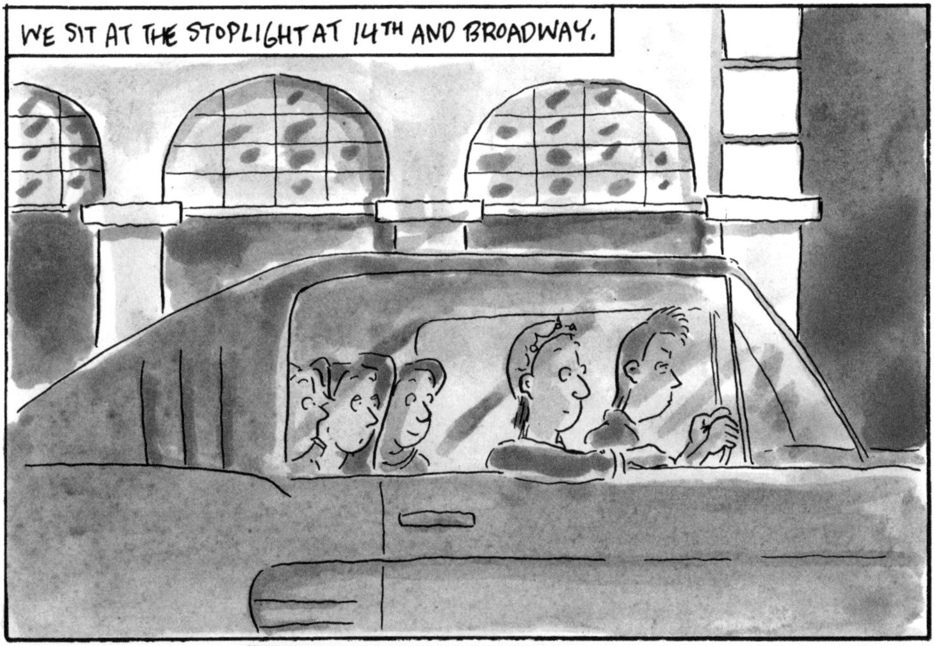
WE SIT AT THE STOPLIGHT AT 14TH AND BROADWAY.

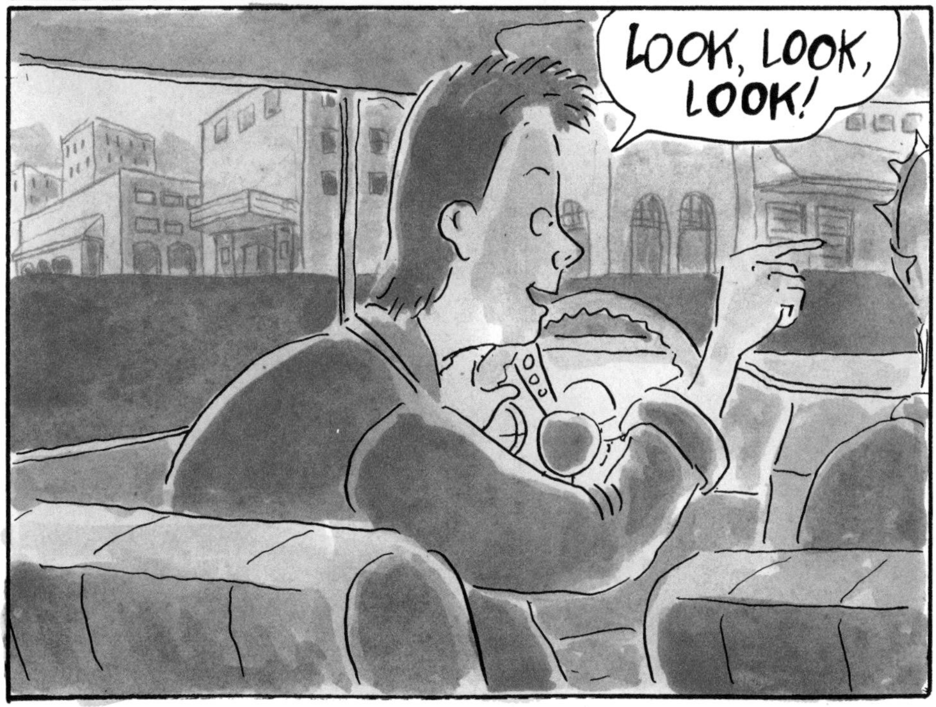
LOOK, LOOK, LOOK!

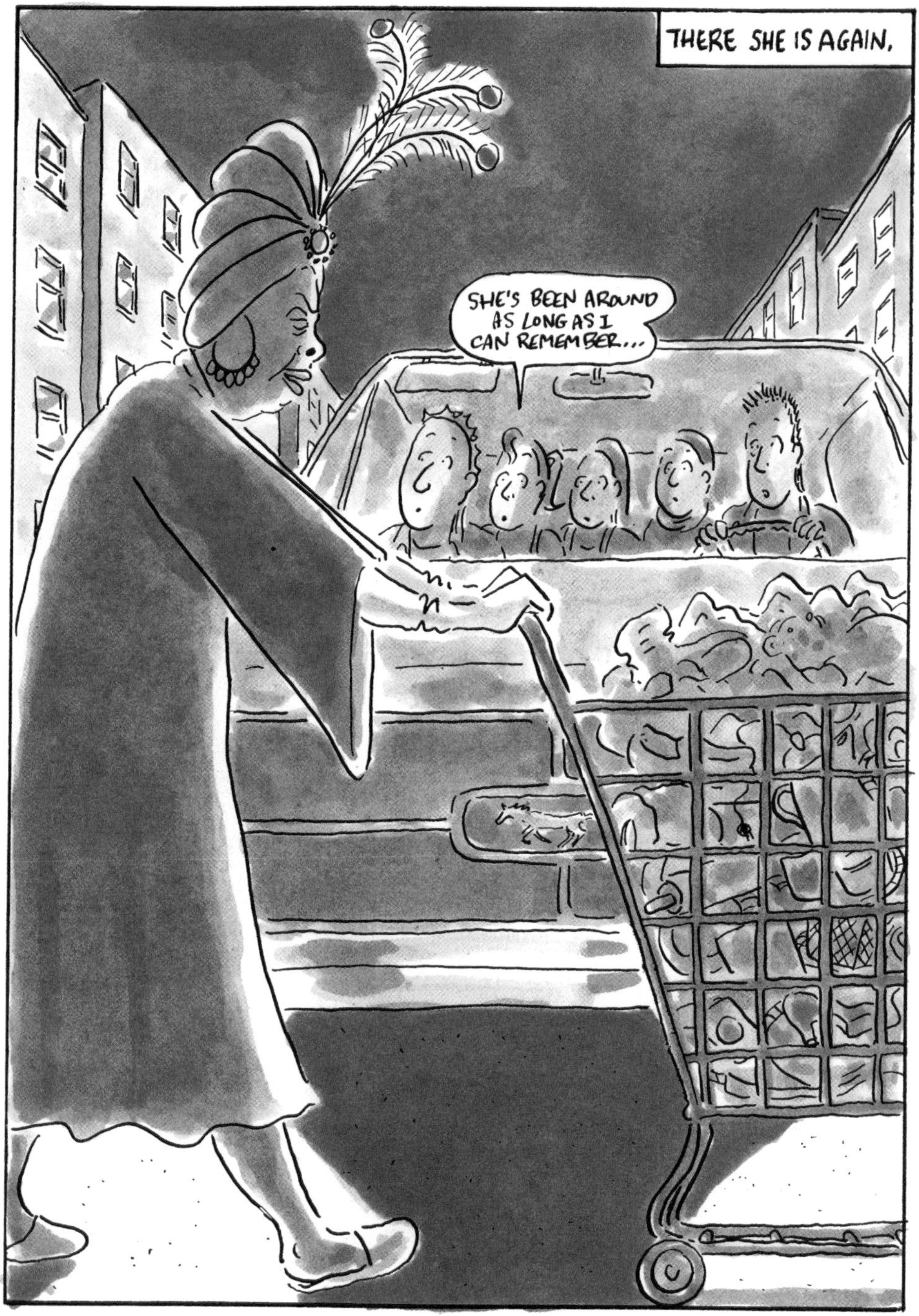
THERE SHE IS AGAIN.
SHE'S BEEN AROUND AS LONG AS I CAN REMEMBER...

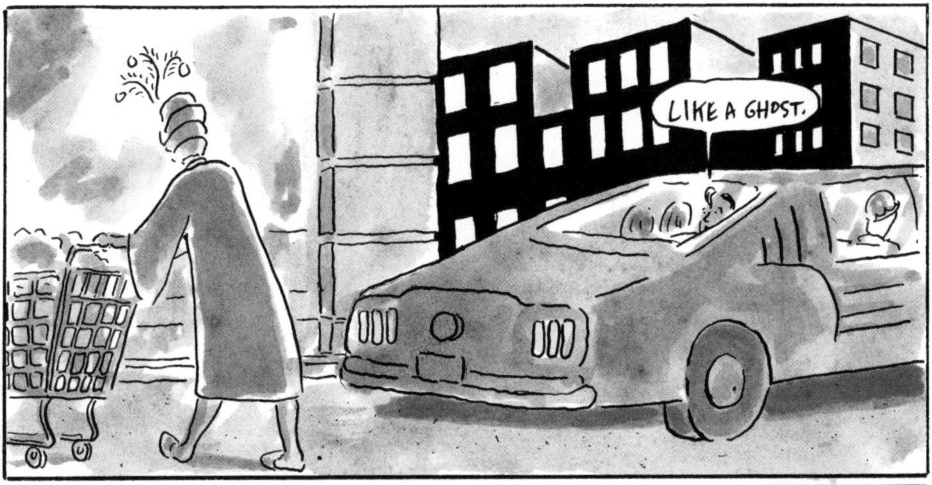
LIKE A GHOST.

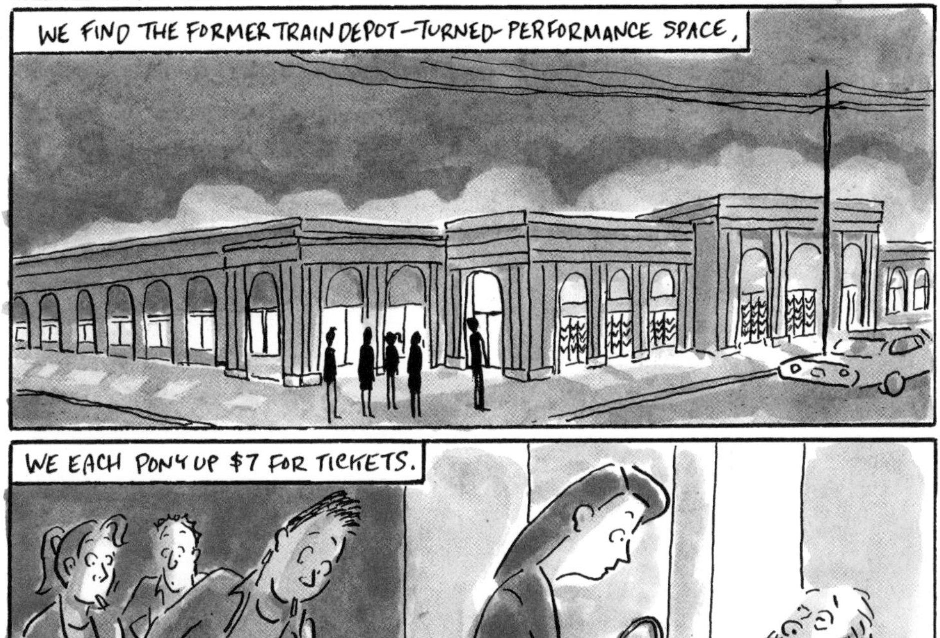
WE FIND THE FORMER TRAIN DEPOT—TURNED-PERFORMANCE SPACE,

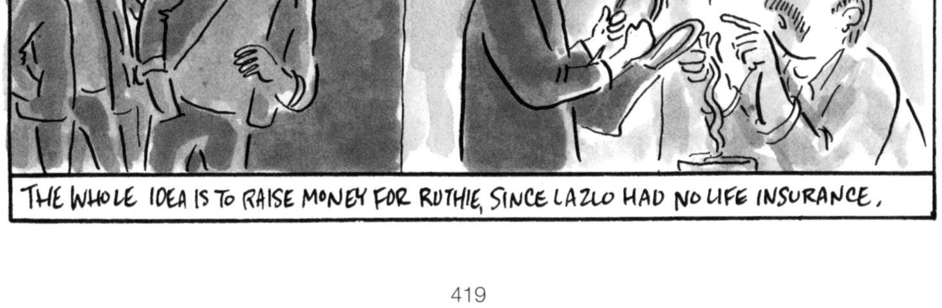
WE EACH PONY UP $7 FOR TICKETS.
THE WHOLE IDEA IS TO RAISE MONEY FOR RUTHIE, SINCE LAZLO HAD NO LIFE INSURANCE.

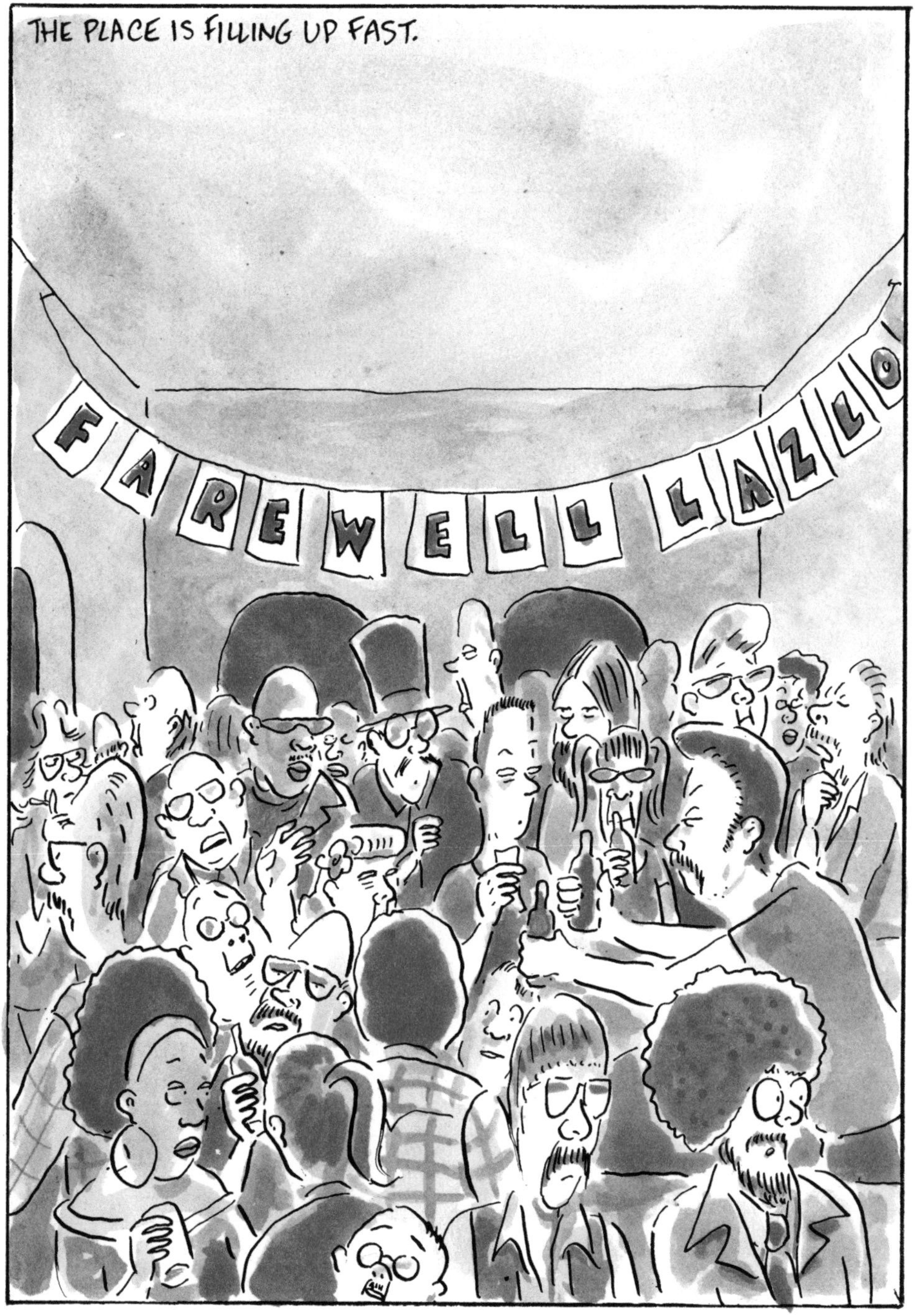

THE PLACE IS FILLING UP FAST.
FAREWELL LAZLO

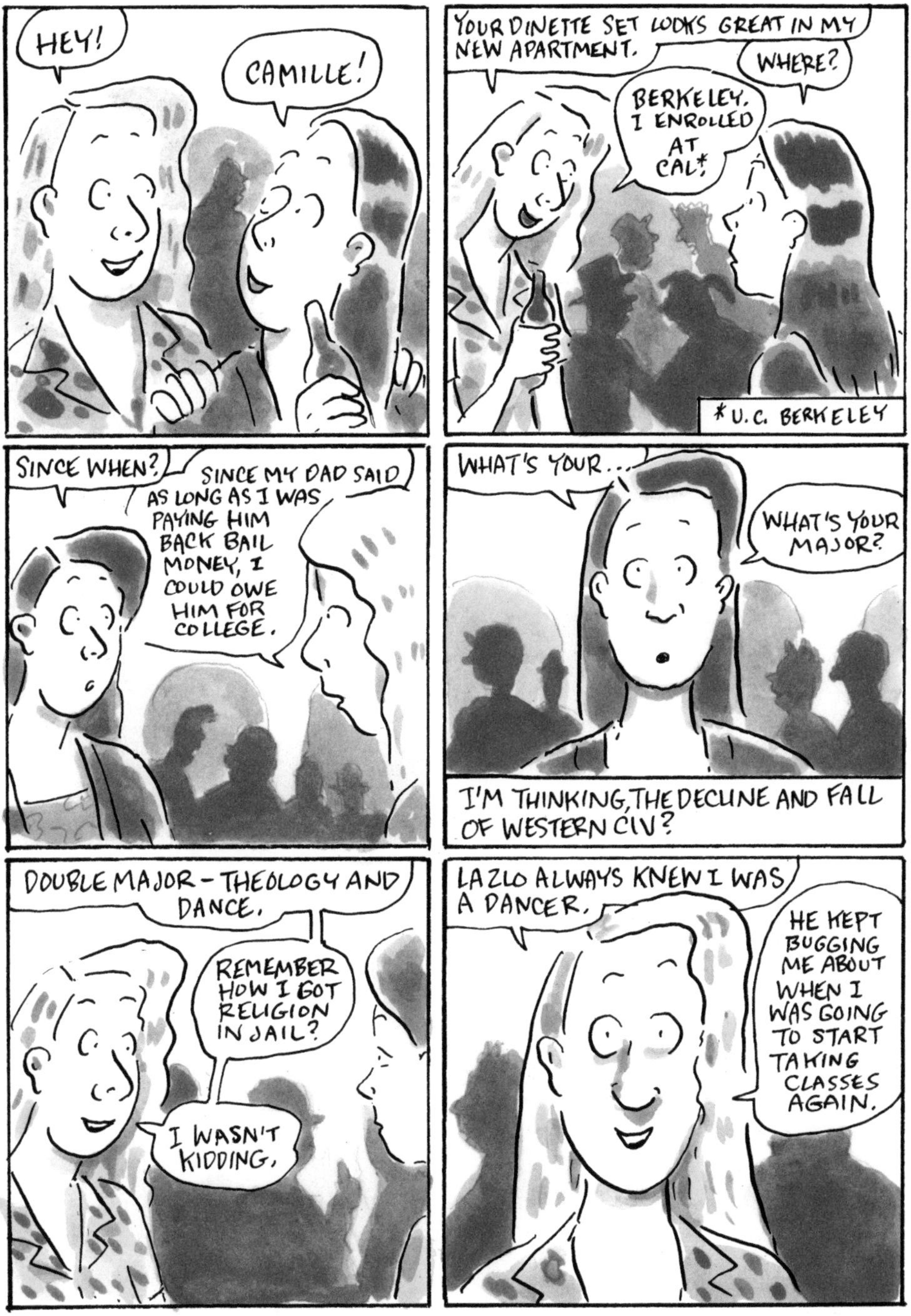
HEY!
CAMILLE!
YOUR DINETTE SET LOOKS GREAT IN MY NEW APARTMENT.
WHERE?
BERKELEY. I ENROLLED AT CAL.*
*U.C. BERKELEY
SINCE WHEN?
SINCE MY DAD SAID AS LONG AS I WAS PAYING HIM BACK BAIL MONEY, I COULD OWE HIM FOR COLLEGE.
WHAT'S YOUR...
WHAT'S YOUR MAJOR?
I'M THINKING, THE DECLINE AND FALL OF WESTERN CIV?
DOUBLE MAJOR - THEOLOGY AND DANCE.
REMEMBER HOW I GOT RELIGION IN JAIL?
I WASN'T KIDDING.
LAZLO ALWAYS KNEW I WAS A DANCER.
HE KEPT BUGGING ME ABOUT WHEN I WAS GOING TO START TAKING CLASSES AGAIN.

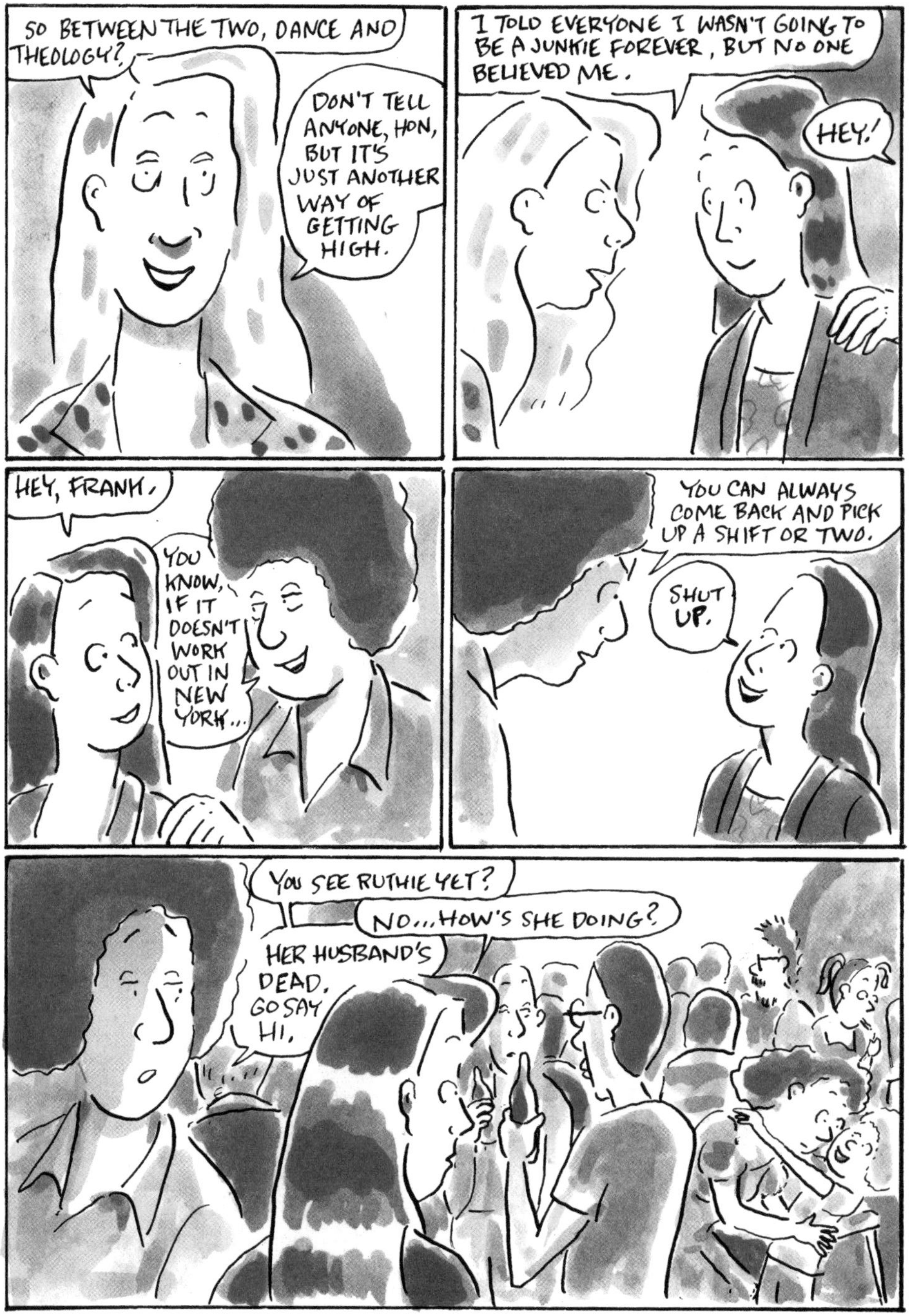
SO BETWEEN THE TWO, DANCE AND THEOLOGY?
DON'T TELL ANYONE, HON, BUT IT'S JUST ANOTHER WAY OF GETTING HIGH.
I TOLD EVERYONE I WASN'T GOING TO BE A JUNKIE FOREVER, BUT NO ONE BELIEVED ME.
HEY!
HEY, FRANK.
YOU KNOW, IF IT DOESN'T WORK OUT IN NEW YORK...
YOU CAN ALWAYS COME BACK AND PICK UP A SHIFT OR TWO.
SHUT UP.
YOU SEE RUTHIE YET?
NO... HOW'S SHE DOING?
HER HUSBAND'S DEAD. GO SAY HI.

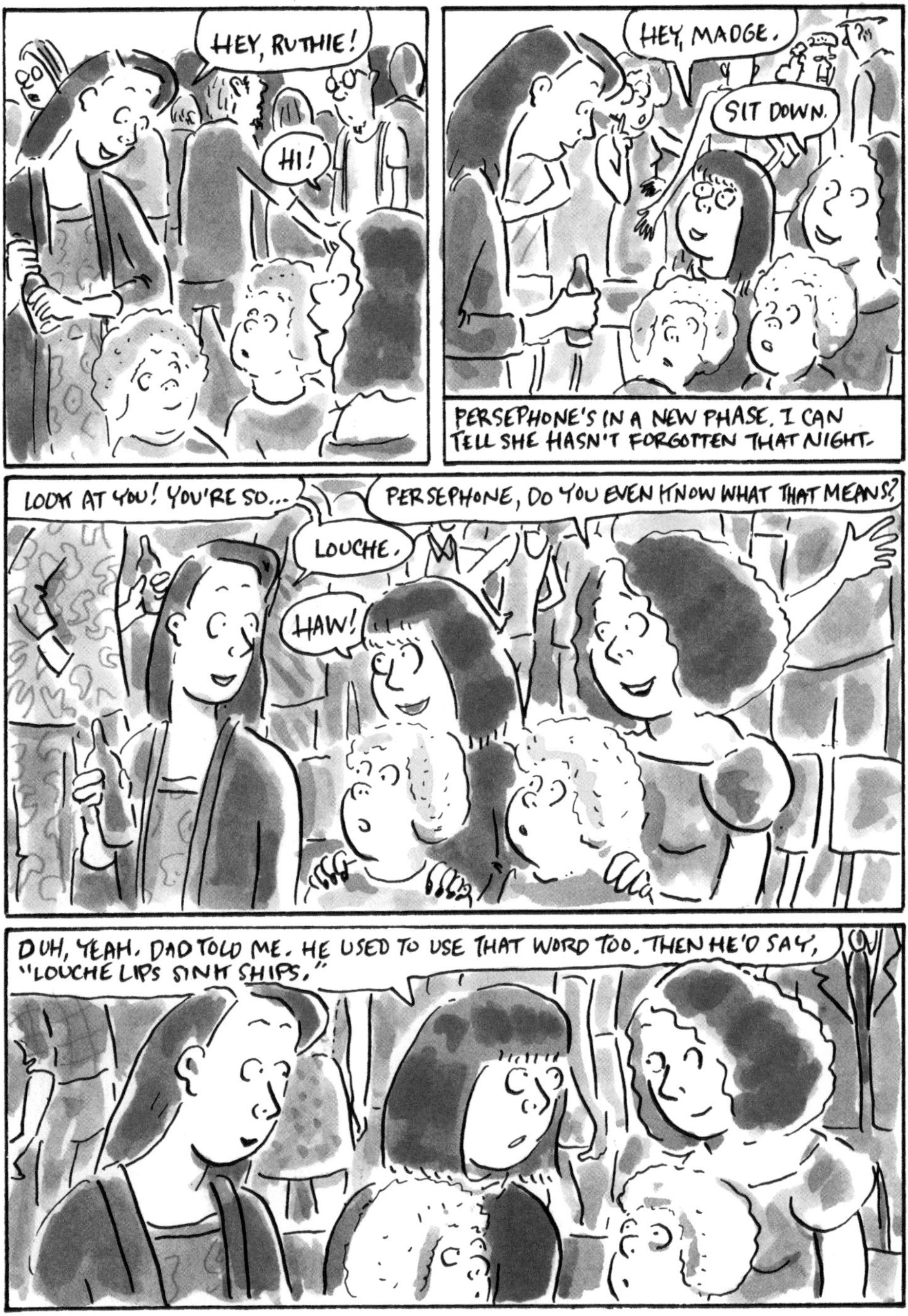
HEY, RUTHIE!
HI!
HEY, MADGE.
SIT DOWN.
PERSEPHONE'S IN A NEW PHASE. I CAN TELL SHE HASN'T FORGOTTEN THAT NIGHT.
LOOK AT YOU! YOU'RE SO...
LOUCHE.
HAW!
PERSEPHONE, DO YOU EVEN KNOW WHAT THAT MEANS?
DUH, YEAH. DAD TOLD ME. HE USED TO USE THAT WORD TOO. THEN HE'D SAY, "LOUCHE LIPS SINK SHIPS."

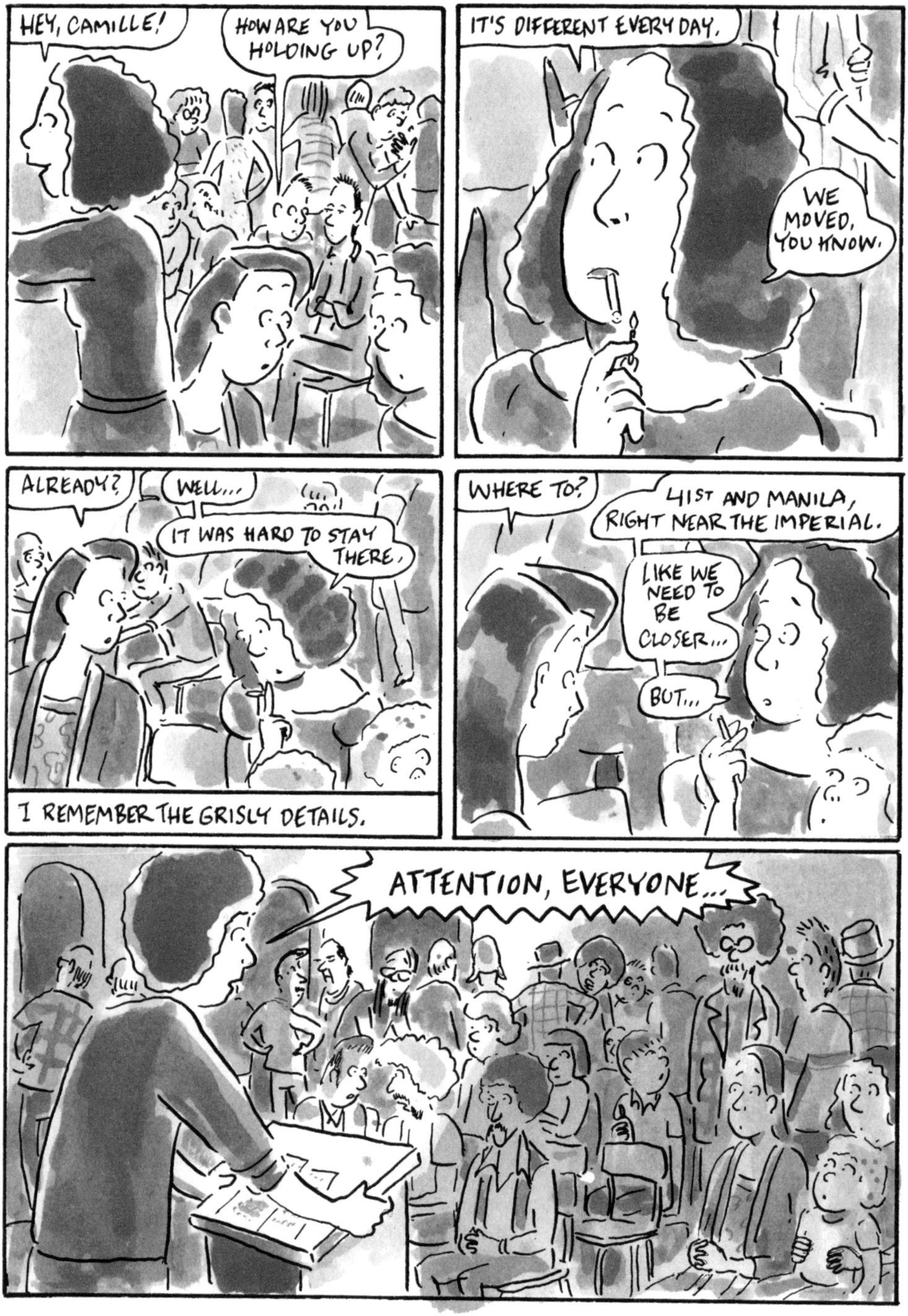
HEY, CAMILLE!
HOW ARE YOU HOLDING UP?
IT'S DIFFERENT EVERY DAY.
WE MOVED, YOU KNOW.
ALREADY?
WELL...
IT WAS HARD TO STAY THERE.
I REMEMBER THE GRISLY DETAILS.
WHERE TO?
41ST AND MANILA, RIGHT NEAR THE IMPERIAL.
LIKE WE NEED TO BE CLOSER...
BUT...
ATTENTION, EVERYONE...

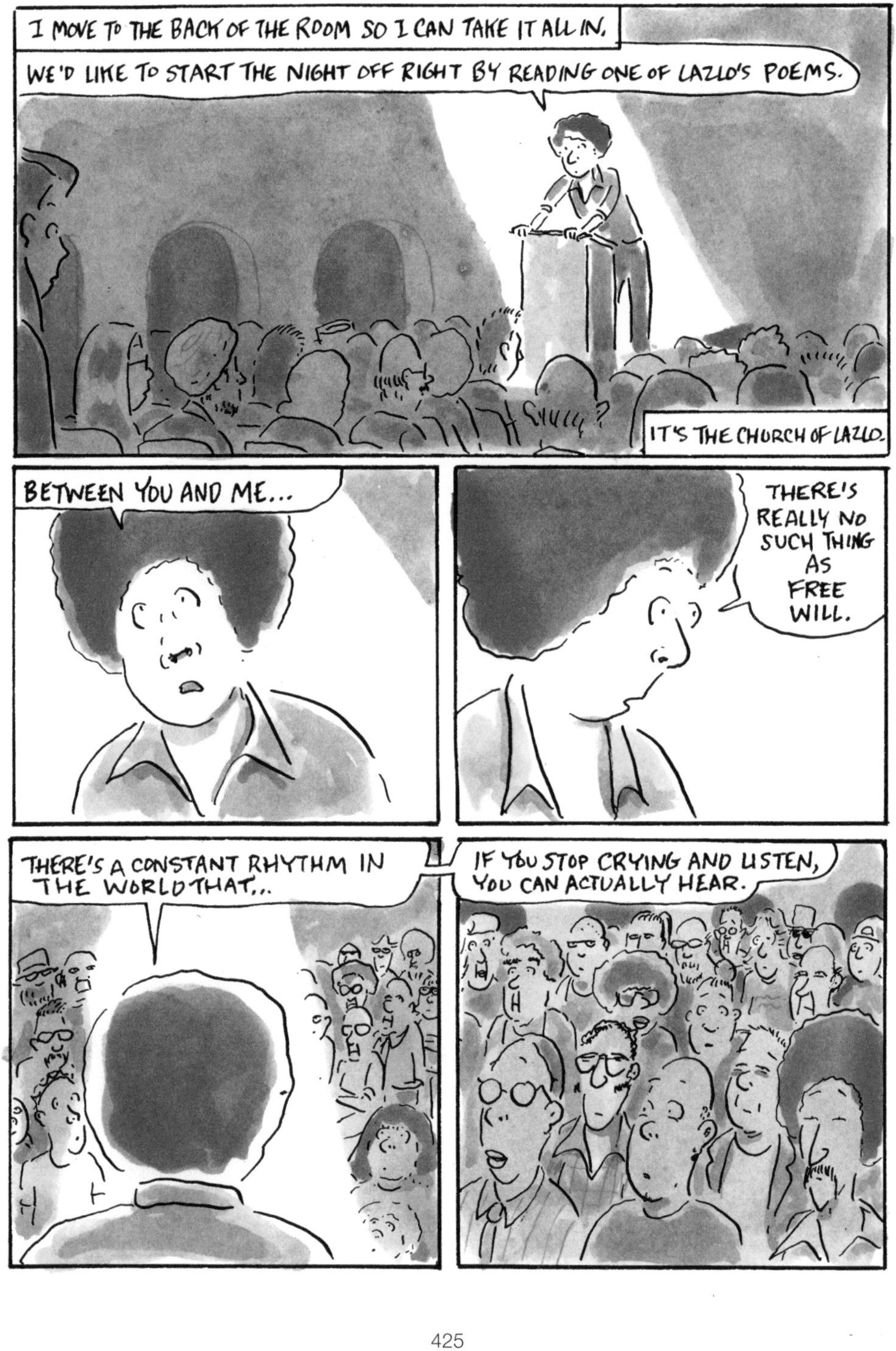
I MOVE TO THE BACK OF THE ROOM SO I CAN TAKE IT ALL IN.
WE'D LIKE TO START THE NIGHT OFF RIGHT BY READING ONE OF LAZLO'S POEMS.
IT'S THE CHURCH OF LAZLO.
BETWEEN YOU AND ME...
THERE'S REALLY NO SUCH THING AS FREE WILL.
THERE'S A CONSTANT RHYTHM IN THE WORLD THAT...
IF YOU STOP CRYING AND LISTEN, YOU CAN ACTUALLY HEAR.

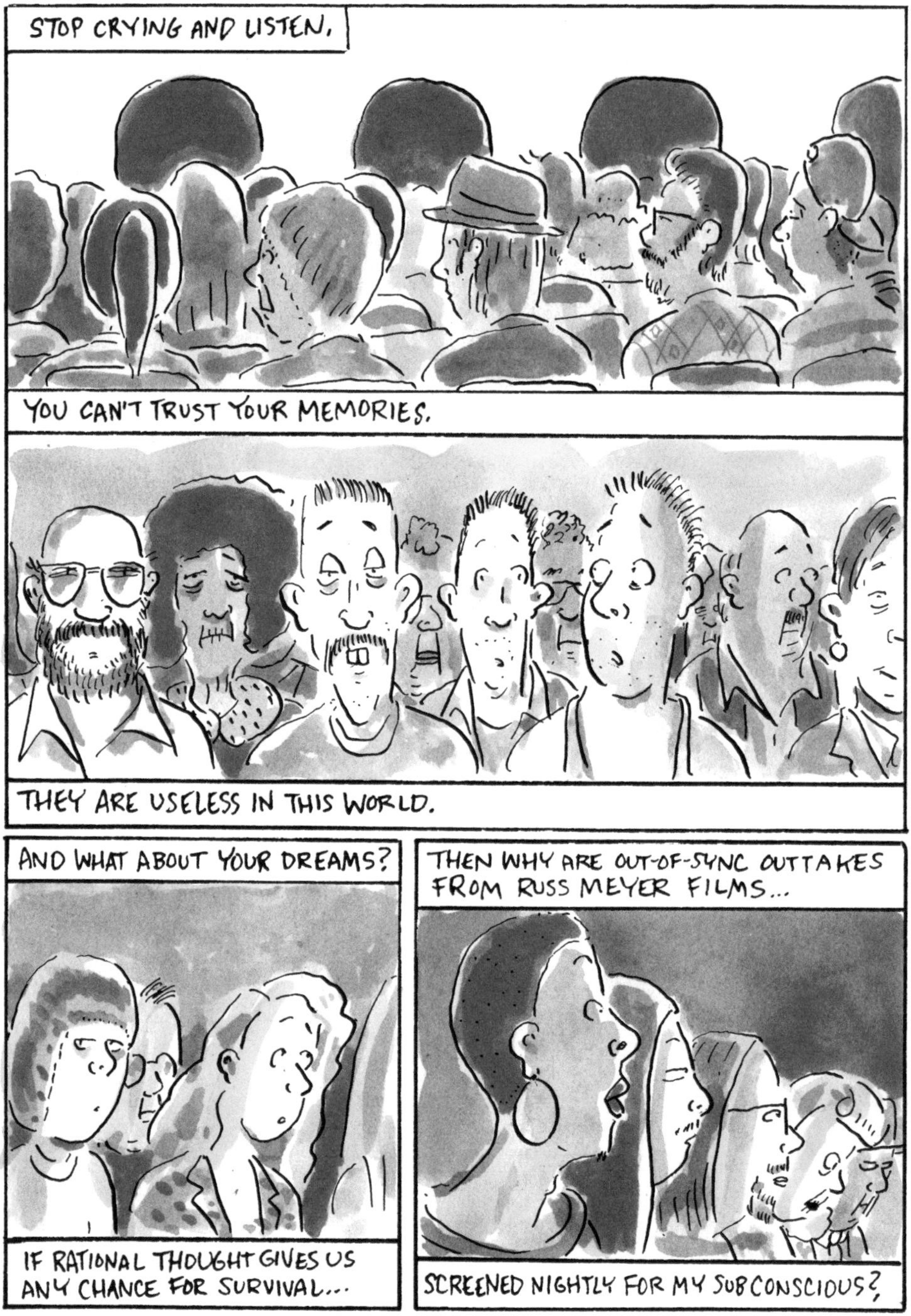
STOP CRYING AND LISTEN.
YOU CAN'T TRUST YOUR MEMORIES.
THEY ARE USELESS IN THIS WORLD.
AND WHAT ABOUT YOUR DREAMS?
IF RATIONAL THOUGHT GIVES US ANY CHANCE FOR SURVIVAL...
THEN WHY ARE OUT-OF-SYNC OUTTAKES FROM RUSS MEYER FILMS...
SCREENED NIGHTLY FOR MY SUBCONSCIOUS?

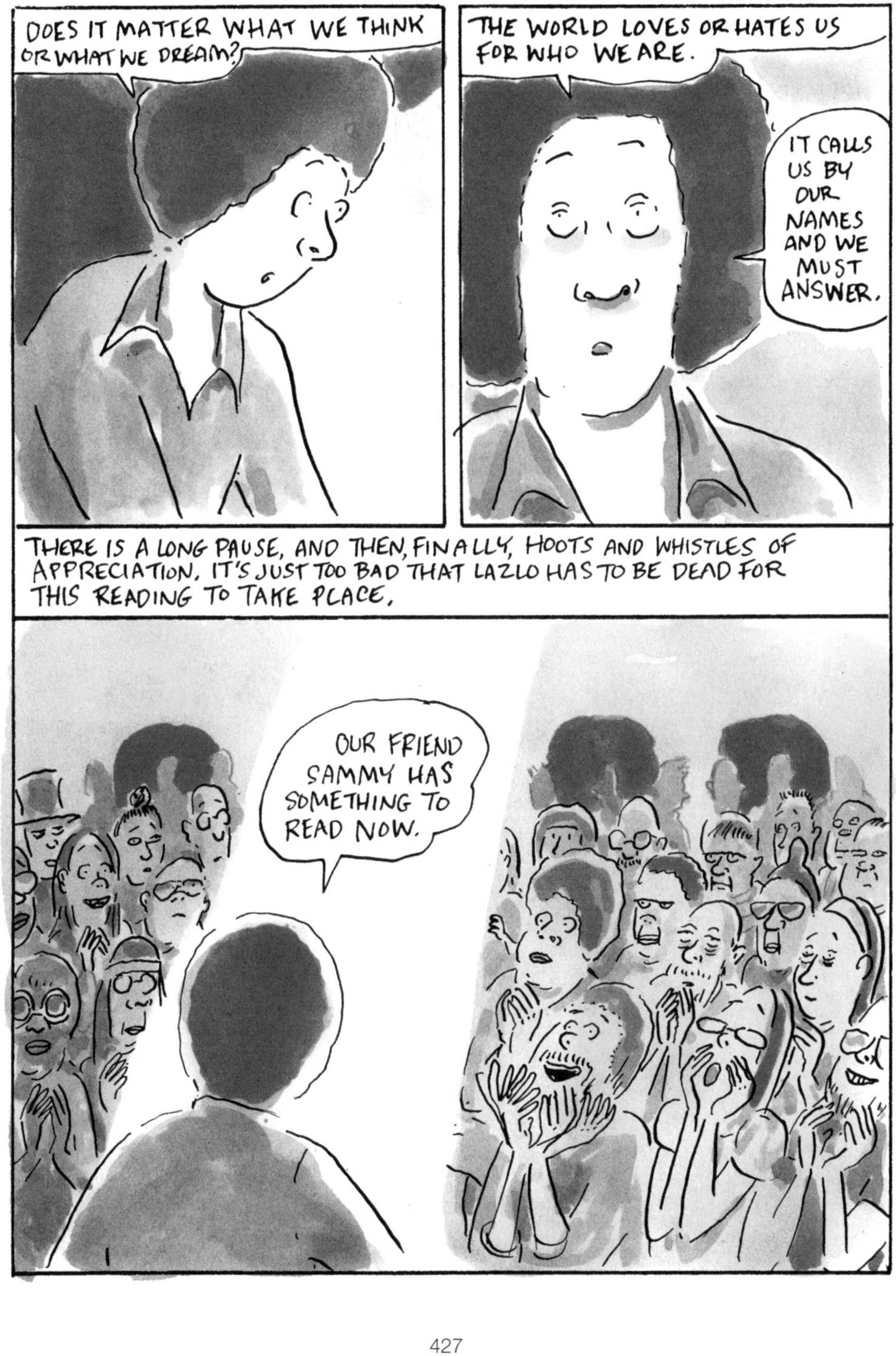
DOES IT MATTER WHAT WE THINK OR WHAT WE DREAM?
THE WORLD LOVES OR HATES US FOR WHO WE ARE.
IT CALLS US BY OUR NAMES AND WE MUST ANSWER.
THERE IS A LONG PAUSE, AND THEN, FINALLY, HOOTS AND WHISTLES OF APPRECIATION. IT'S JUST TOO BAD THAT LAZLO HAS TO BE DEAD FOR THIS READING TO TAKE PLACE.
OUR FRIEND SAMMY HAS SOMETHING TO READ NOW.

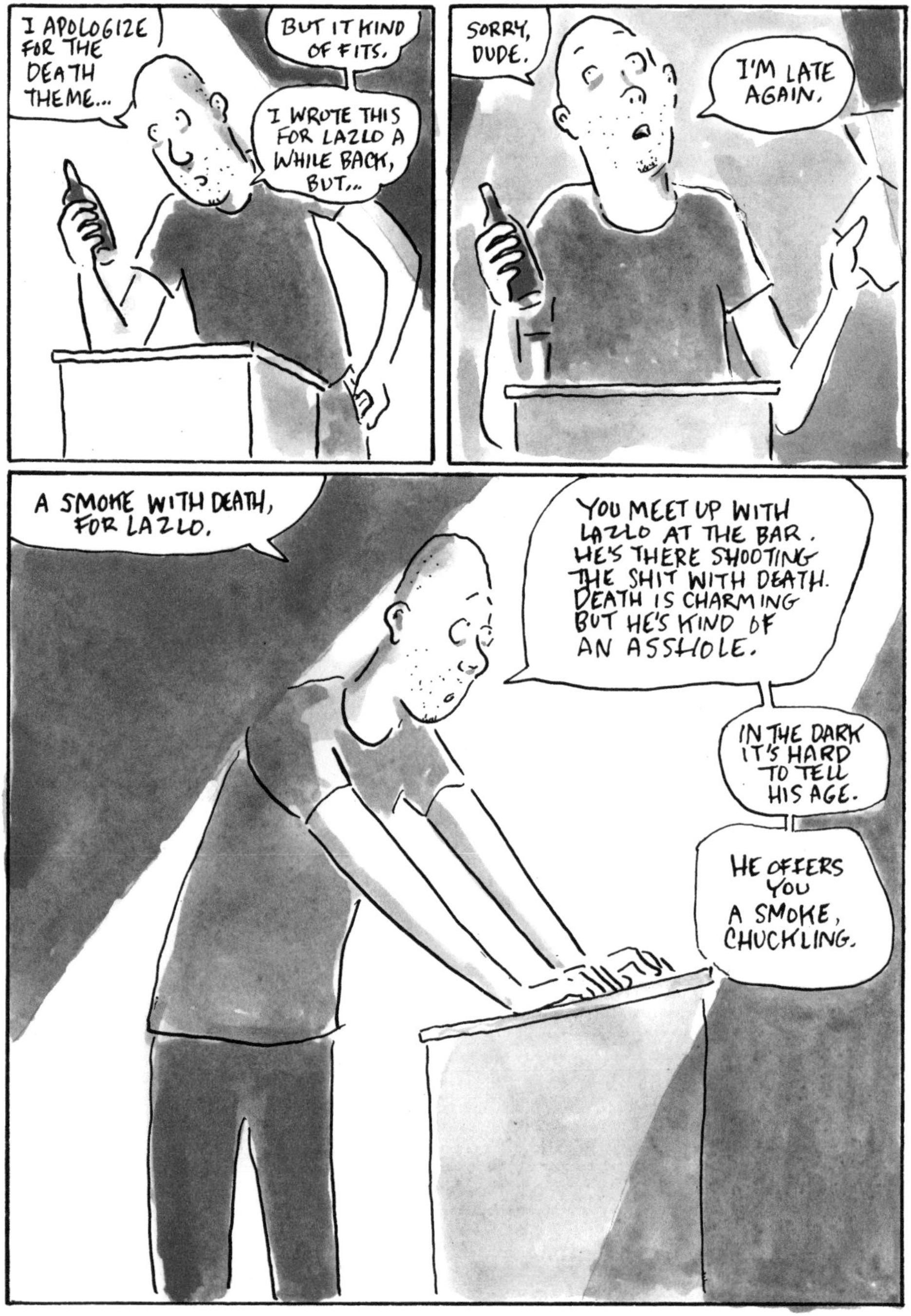
I APOLOGIZE FOR THE DEATH THEME...
BUT IT KIND OF FITS.
I WROTE THIS FOR LAZLO A WHILE BACK, BUT...
SORRY, DUDE.
I'M LATE AGAIN.
A SMOKE WITH DEATH, FOR LAZLO.
YOU MEET UP WITH LAZLO AT THE BAR. HE'S THERE SHOOTING THE SHIT WITH DEATH. DEATH IS CHARMING BUT HE'S KIND OF AN ASSHOLE.
IN THE DARK IT'S HARD TO TELL HIS AGE.
HE OFFERS YOU A SMOKE, CHUCKLING.

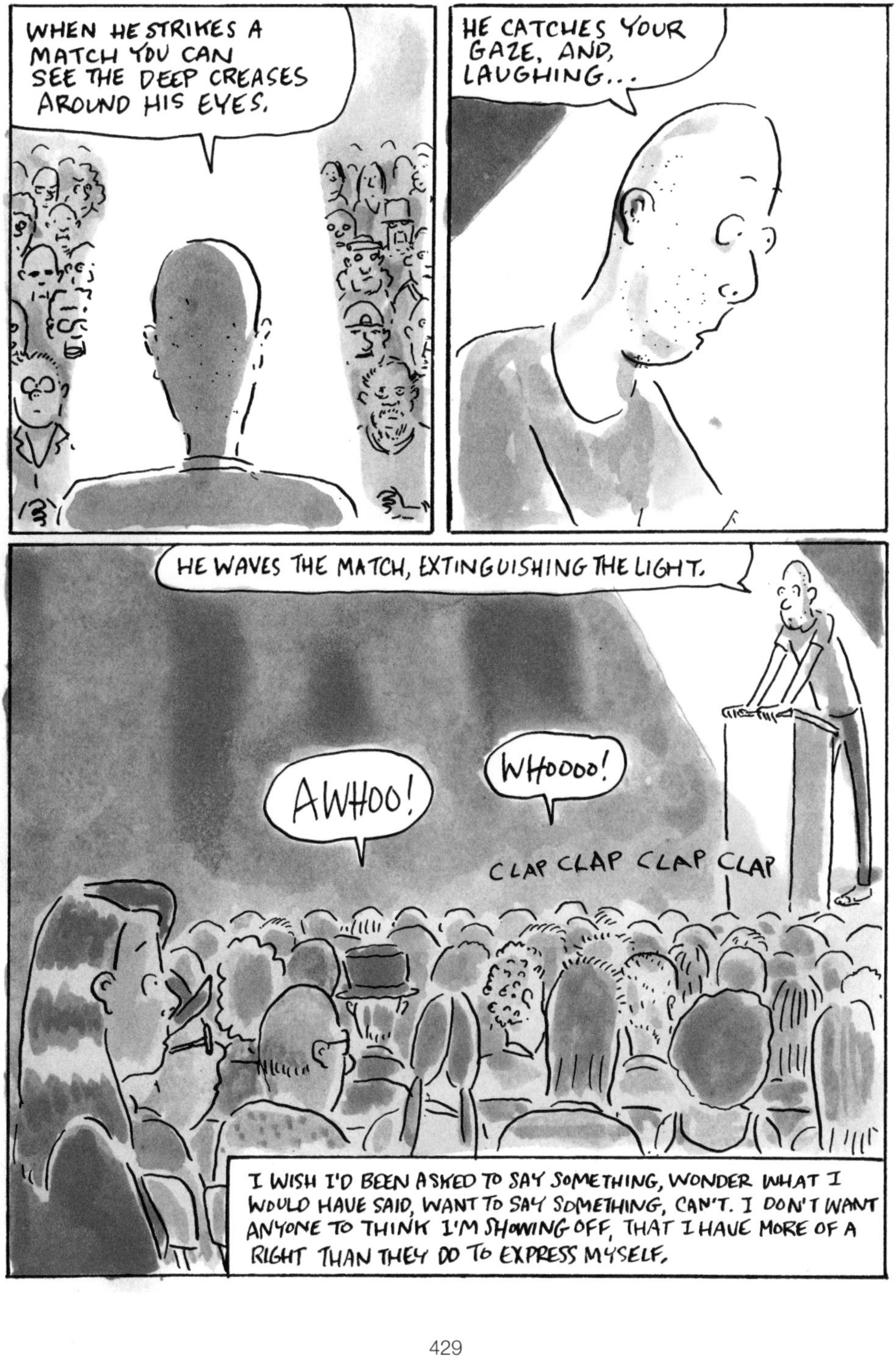
WHEN HE STRIKES A MATCH YOU CAN SEE THE DEEP CREASES AROUND HIS EYES.
HE CATCHES YOUR GAZE, AND, LAUGHING...
HE WAVES THE MATCH, EXTINGUISHING THE LIGHT.
AWHOO!
WHOOOO!
CLAP CLAP CLAP CLAP
I WISH I'D BEEN ASKED TO SAY SOMETHING, WONDER WHAT I WOULD HAVE SAID, WANT TO SAY SOMETHING, CAN'T. I DON'T WANT ANYONE TO THINK I'M SHOWING OFF, THAT I HAVE MORE OF A RIGHT THAN THEY DO TO EXPRESS MYSELF.

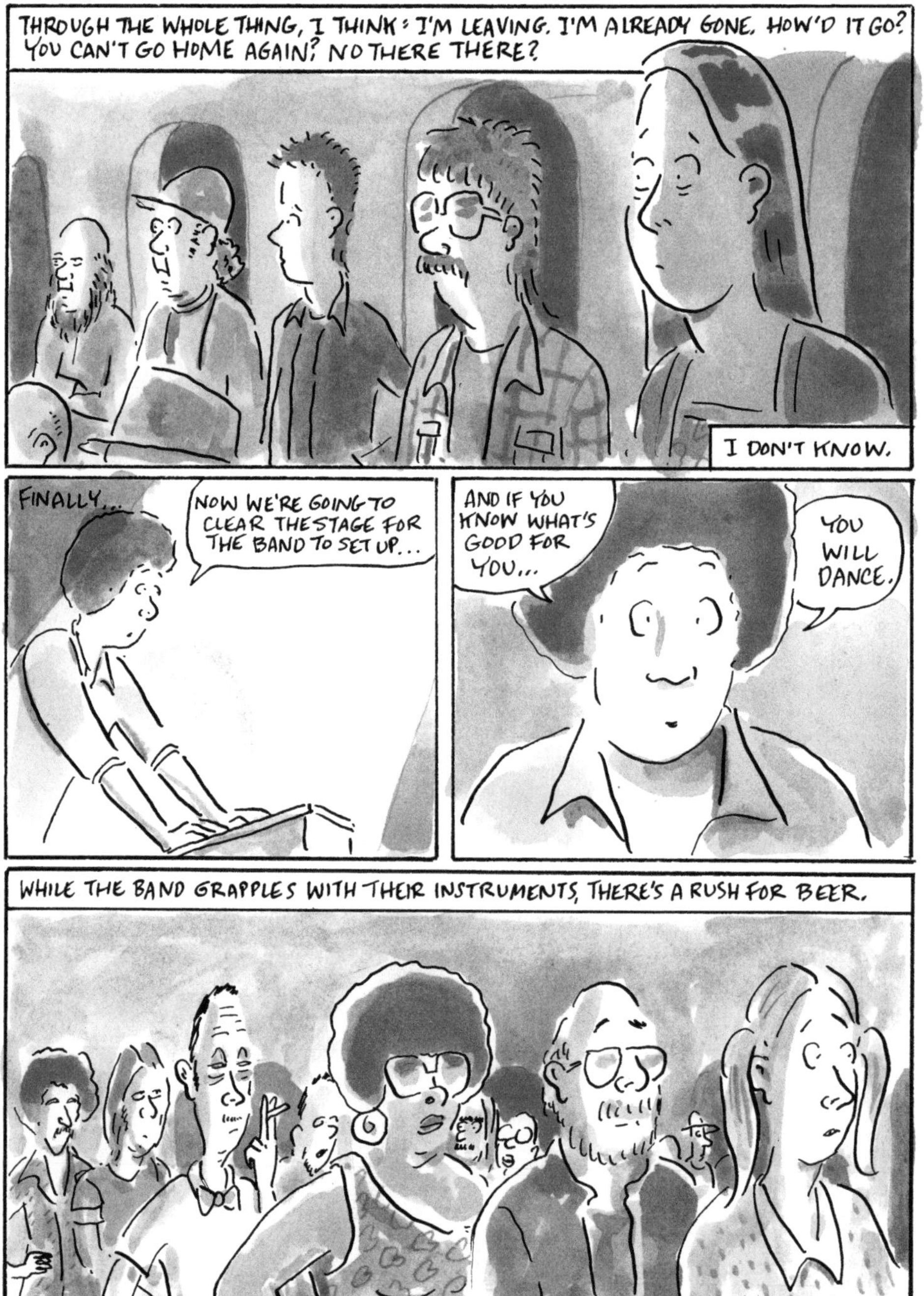
THROUGH THE WHOLE THING, I THINK: I'M LEAVING. I'M ALREADY GONE. HOW'D IT GO? YOU CAN'T GO HOME AGAIN? NO THERE THERE?
I DON'T KNOW.
FINALLY...
NOW WE'RE GOING TO CLEAR THE STAGE FOR THE BAND TO SET UP...
AND IF YOU KNOW WHAT'S GOOD FOR YOU...
YOU WILL DANCE.
WHILE THE BAND GRAPPLES WITH THEIR INSTRUMENTS, THERE'S A RUSH FOR BEER.

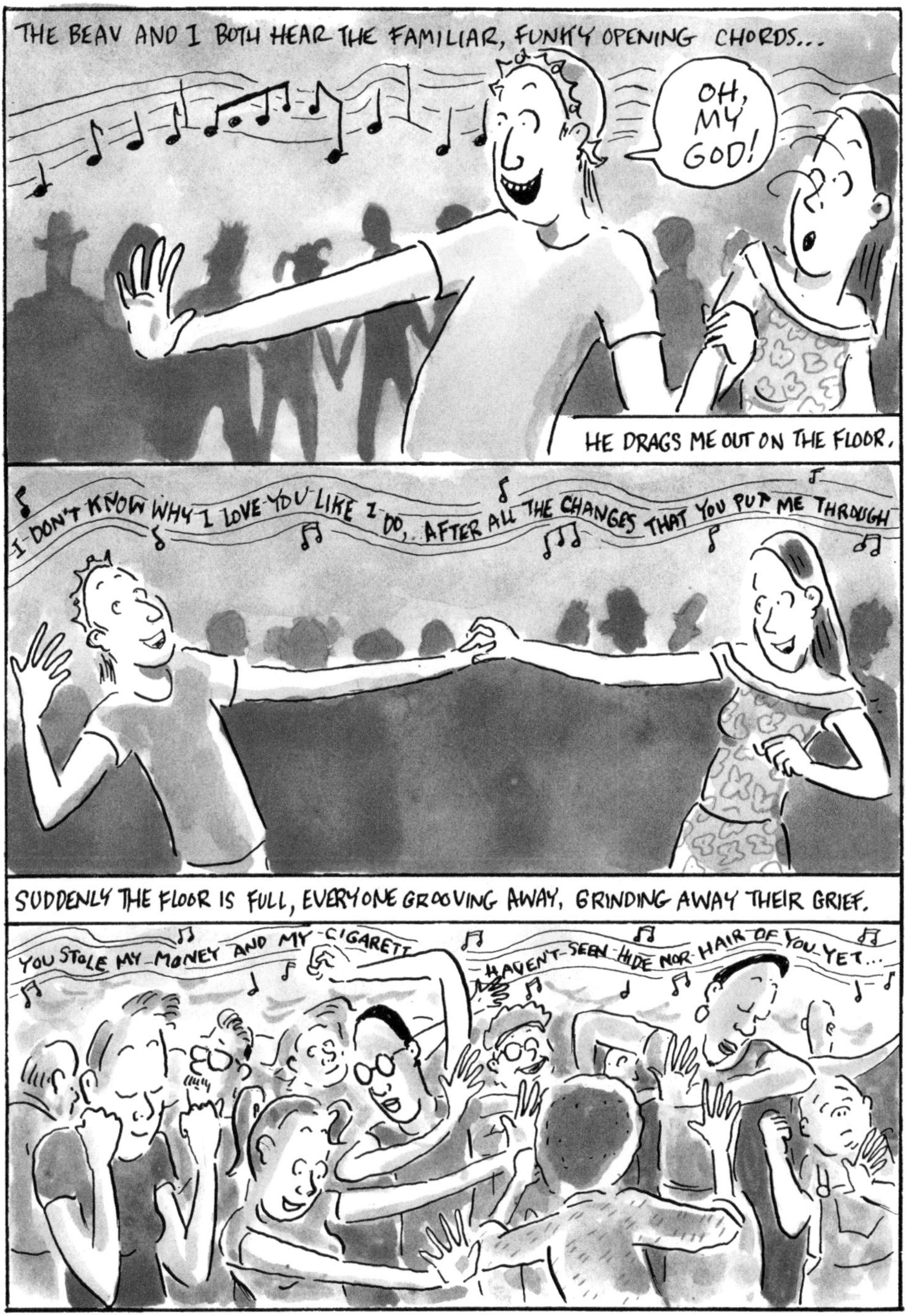
THE BEAV AND I BOTH HEAR THE FAMILIAR, FUNKY OPENING CHORDS...
OH, MY GOD!
HE DRAGS ME OUT ON THE FLOOR.
I DON'T KNOW WHY I LOVE YOU LIKE I DO, AFTER ALL THE CHANGES THAT YOU PUT ME THROUGH
SUDDENLY THE FLOOR IS FULL, EVERYONE GROOVING AWAY, GRINDING AWAY THEIR GRIEF.
YOU STOLE MY MONEY AND MY CIGARETT
HAVEN'T SEEN HIDE NOR HAIR OF YOU YET...

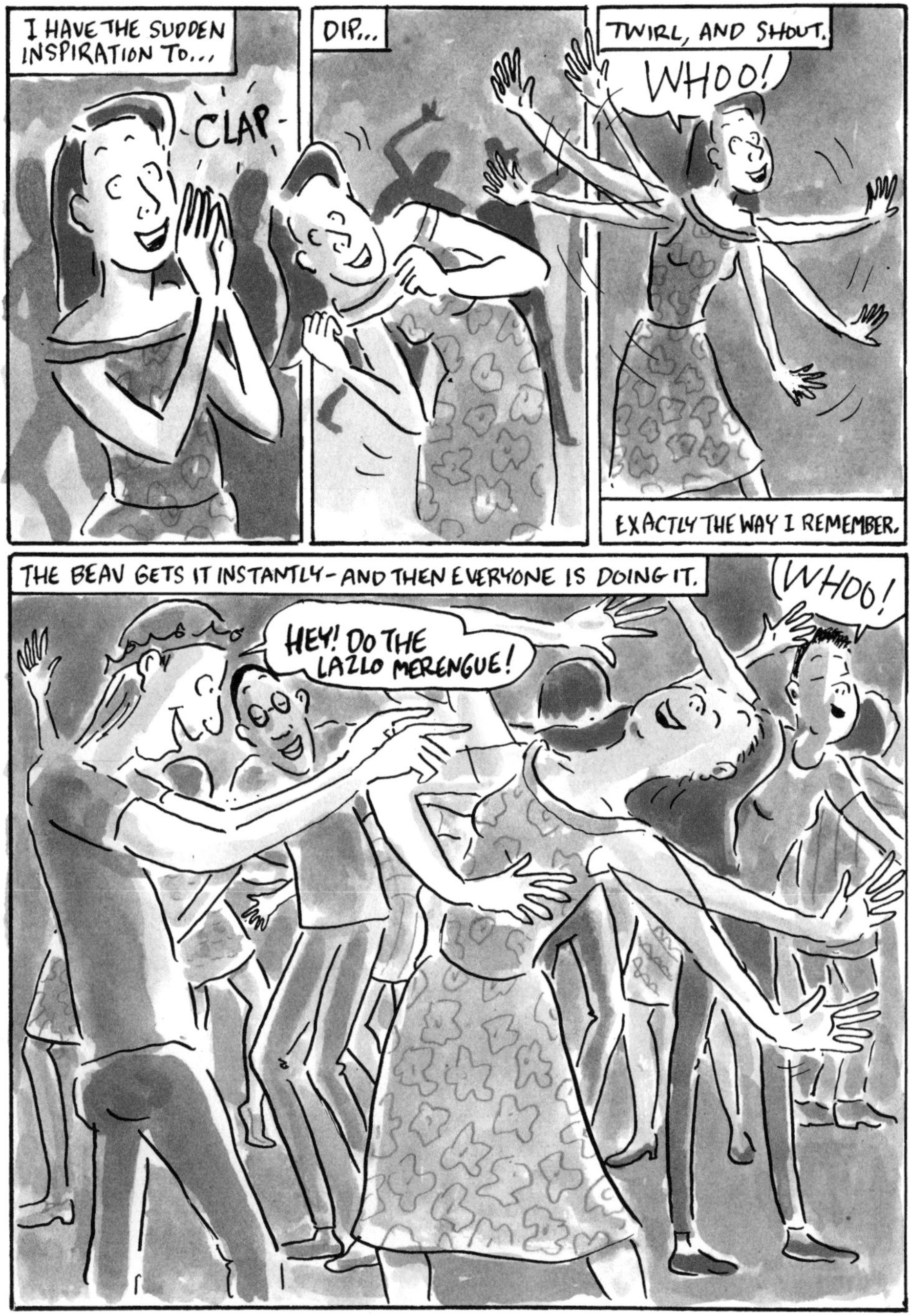
I HAVE THE SUDDEN INSPIRATION TO...
CLAP
DIP...
TWIRL, AND SHOUT.
WHOO!
EXACTLY THE WAY I REMEMBER.
THE BEAU GETS IT INSTANTLY- AND THEN EVERYONE IS DOING IT.
HEY! DO THE LAZLO MERENGUE!
WHOO!

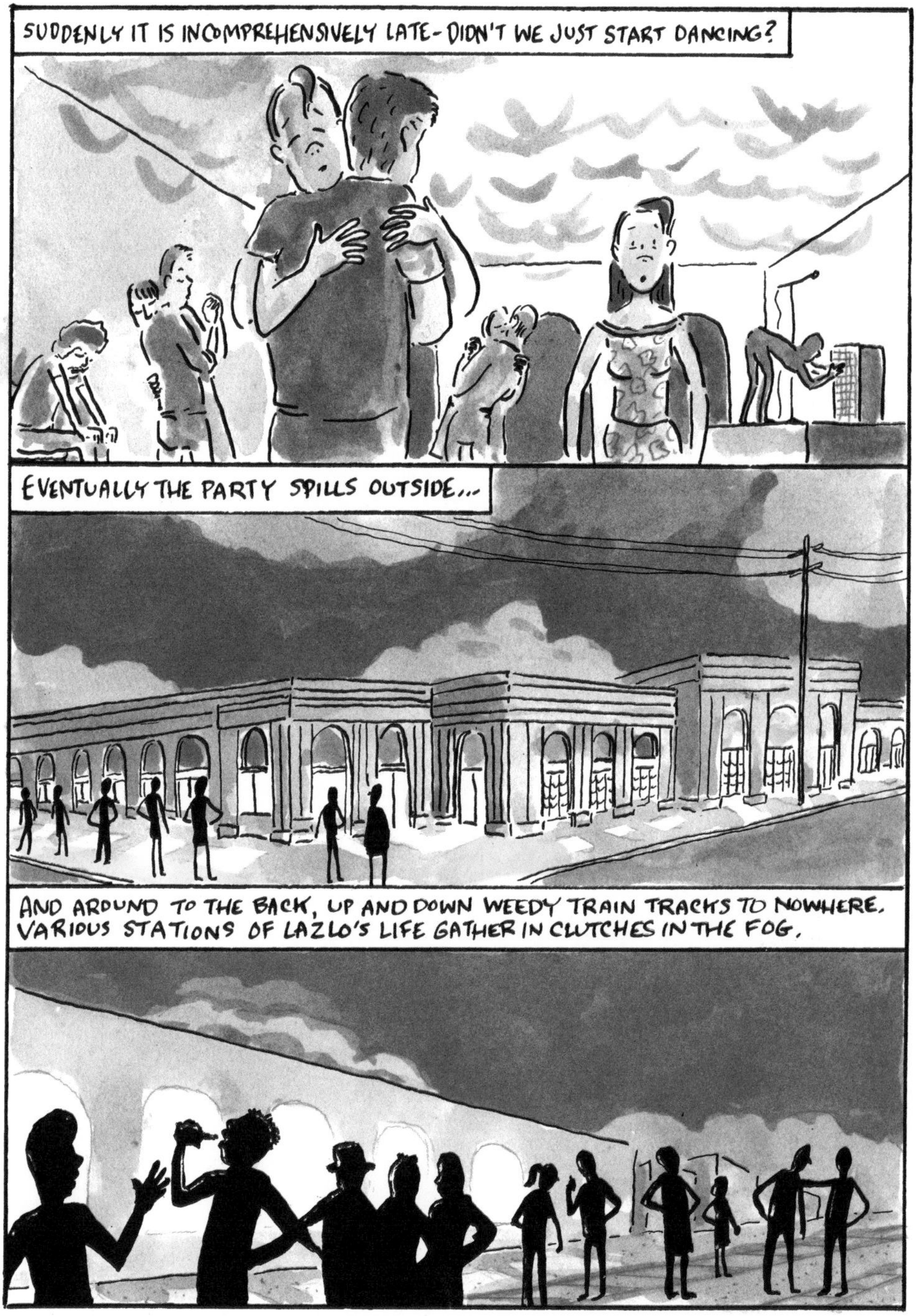
SUDDENLY IT IS INCOMPREHENSIVELY LATE- DIDN'T WE JUST START DANCING?
EVENTUALLY THE PARTY SPILLS OUTSIDE...
AND AROUND TO THE BACK, UP AND DOWN WEEDY TRAIN TRACKS TO NOWHERE. VARIOUS STATIONS OF LAZLO'S LIFE GATHER IN CLUTCHES IN THE FOG.

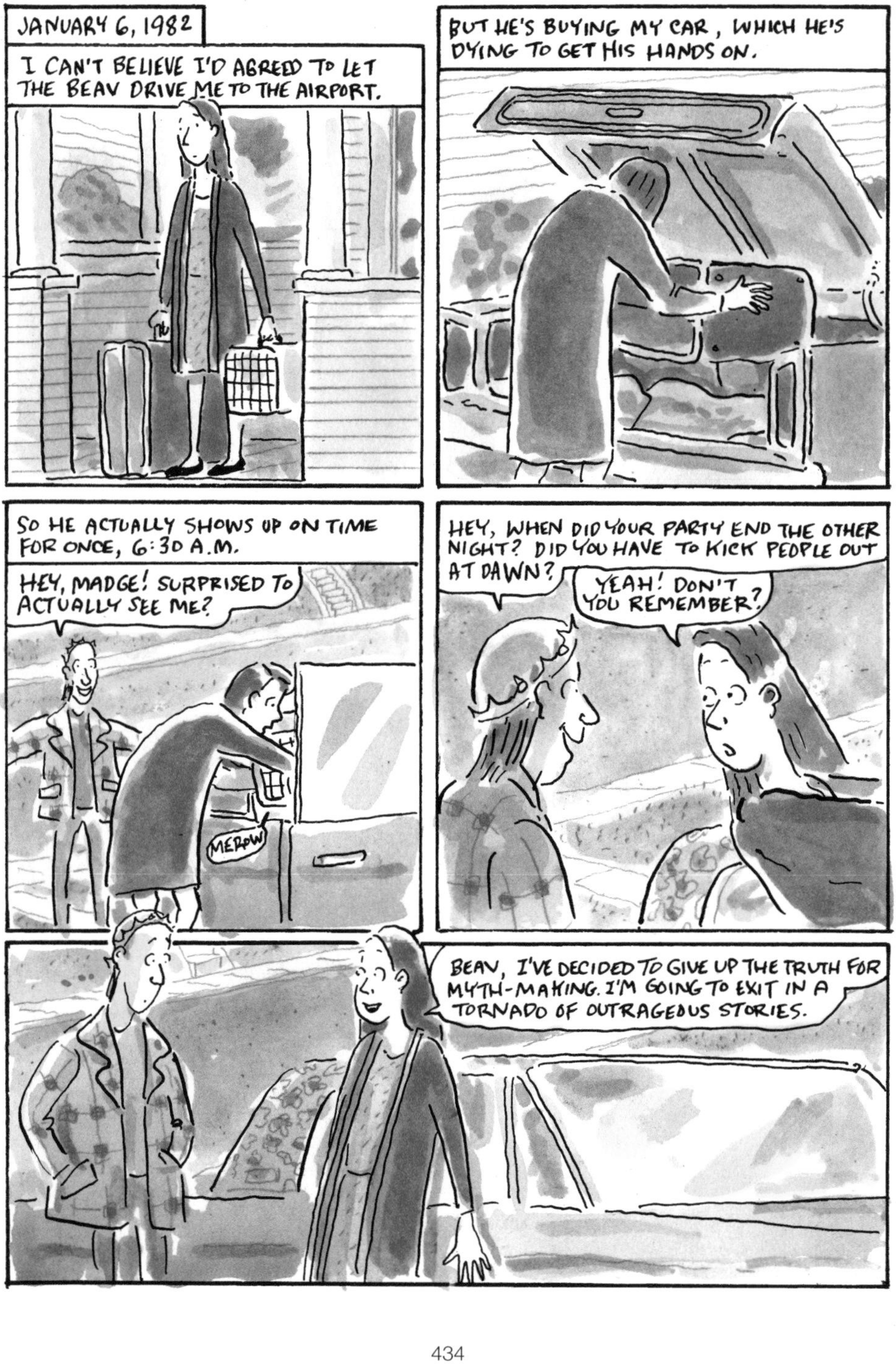
JANUARY 6, 1982
I CAN'T BELIEVE I'D AGREED TO LET THE BEAV DRIVE ME TO THE AIRPORT.
BUT HE'S BUYING MY CAR, WHICH HE'S DYING TO GET HIS HANDS ON.
SO HE ACTUALLY SHOWS UP ON TIME FOR ONCE, 6:30 A.M.
HEY, MADGE! SURPRISED TO ACTUALLY SEE ME?
MERROW
HEY, WHEN DID YOUR PARTY END THE OTHER NIGHT? DID YOU HAVE TO KICK PEOPLE OUT AT DAWN?
YEAH! DON'T YOU REMEMBER?
BEAV, I'VE DECIDED TO GIVE UP THE TRUTH FOR MYTH-MAKING. I'M GOING TO EXIT IN A TORNADO OF OUTRAGEOUS STORIES.

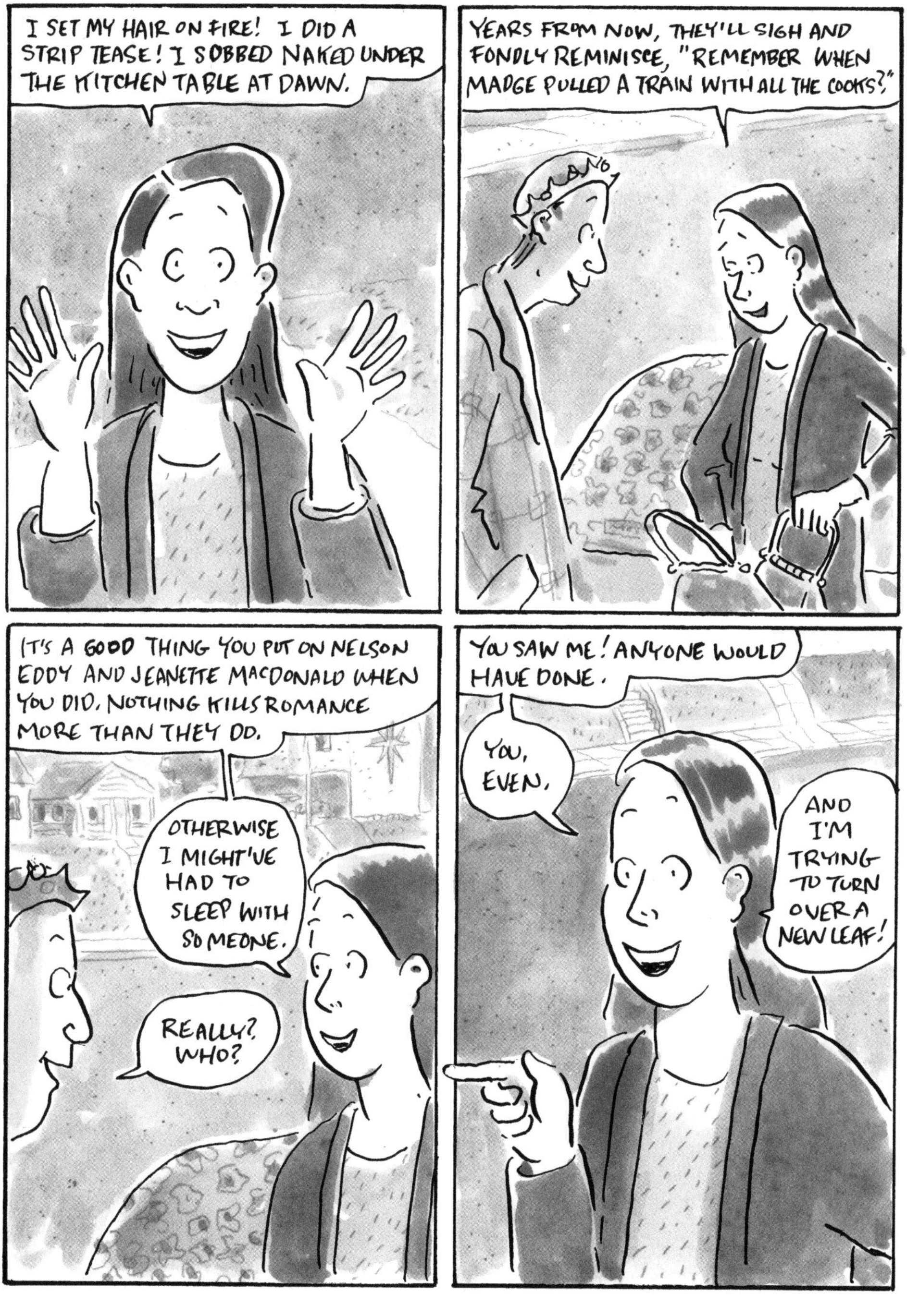
I SET MY HAIR ON FIRE! I DID A STRIP TEASE! I SOBBED NAKED UNDER THE KITCHEN TABLE AT DAWN.
YEARS FROM NOW, THEY'LL SIGH AND FONDLY REMINISCE, "REMEMBER WHEN MADGE PULLED A TRAIN WITH ALL THE COOKS?"
IT'S A GOOD THING YOU PUT ON NELSON EDDY AND JEANETTE MACDONALD WHEN YOU DID. NOTHING KILLS ROMANCE MORE THAN THEY DO.
OTHERWISE I MIGHT'VE HAD TO SLEEP WITH SOMEONE.
REALLY? WHO?
YOU SAW ME! ANYONE WOULD HAVE DONE.
YOU, EVEN.
AND I'M TRYING TO TURN OVER A NEW LEAF!

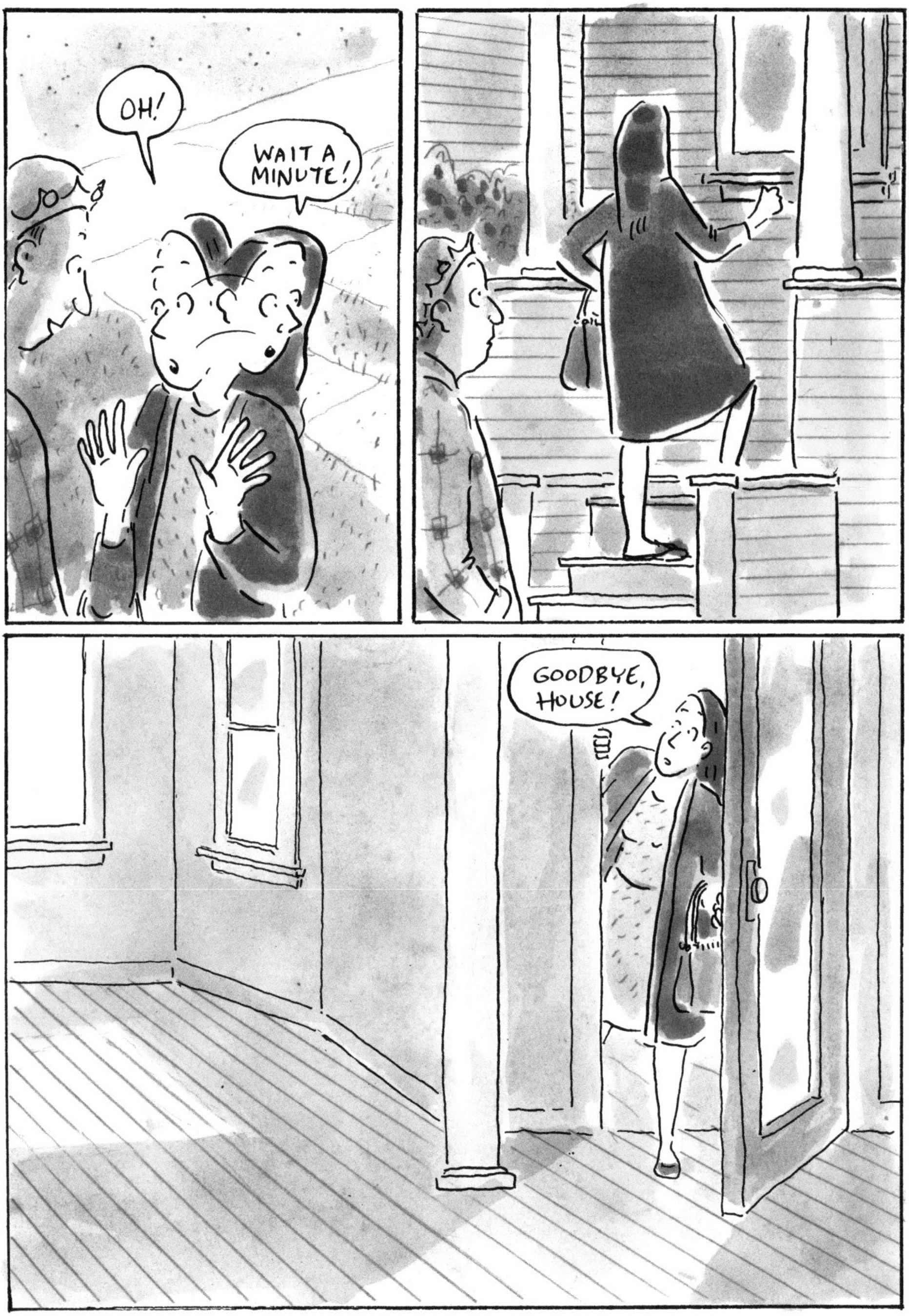
OH!
WAIT A MINUTE!
GOODBYE, HOUSE!

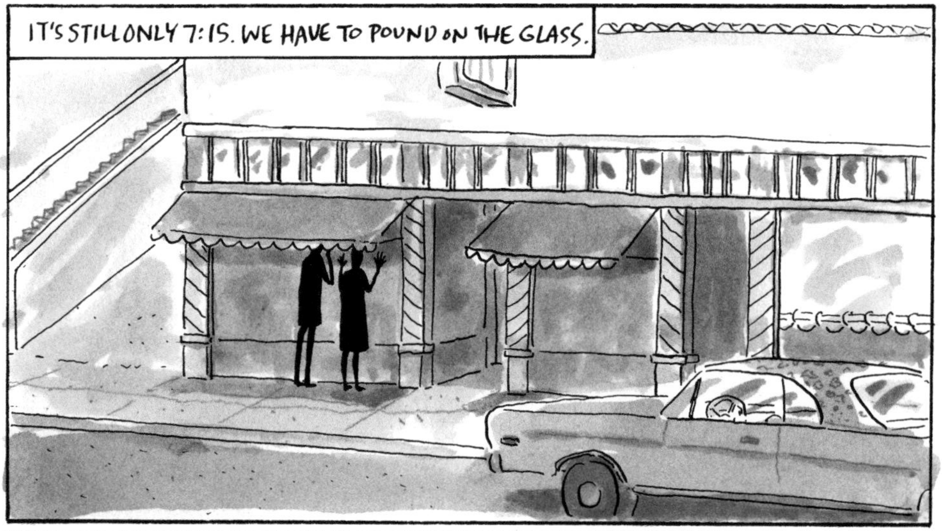
IT'S STILL ONLY 7:15. WE HAVE TO POUND ON THE GLASS.

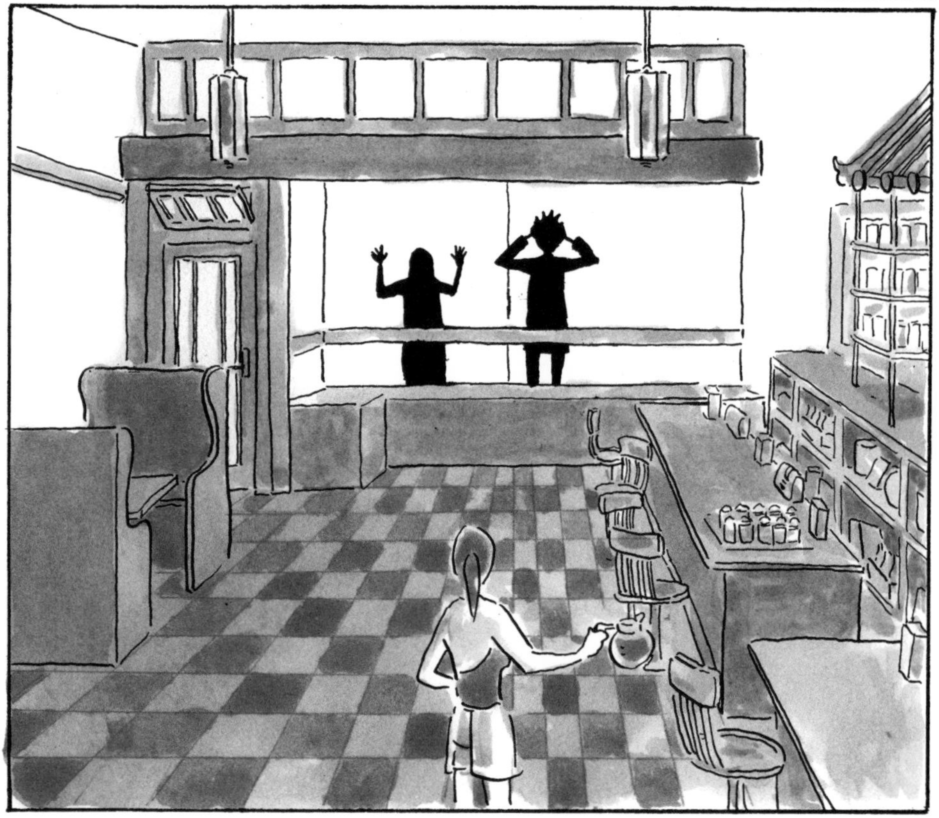

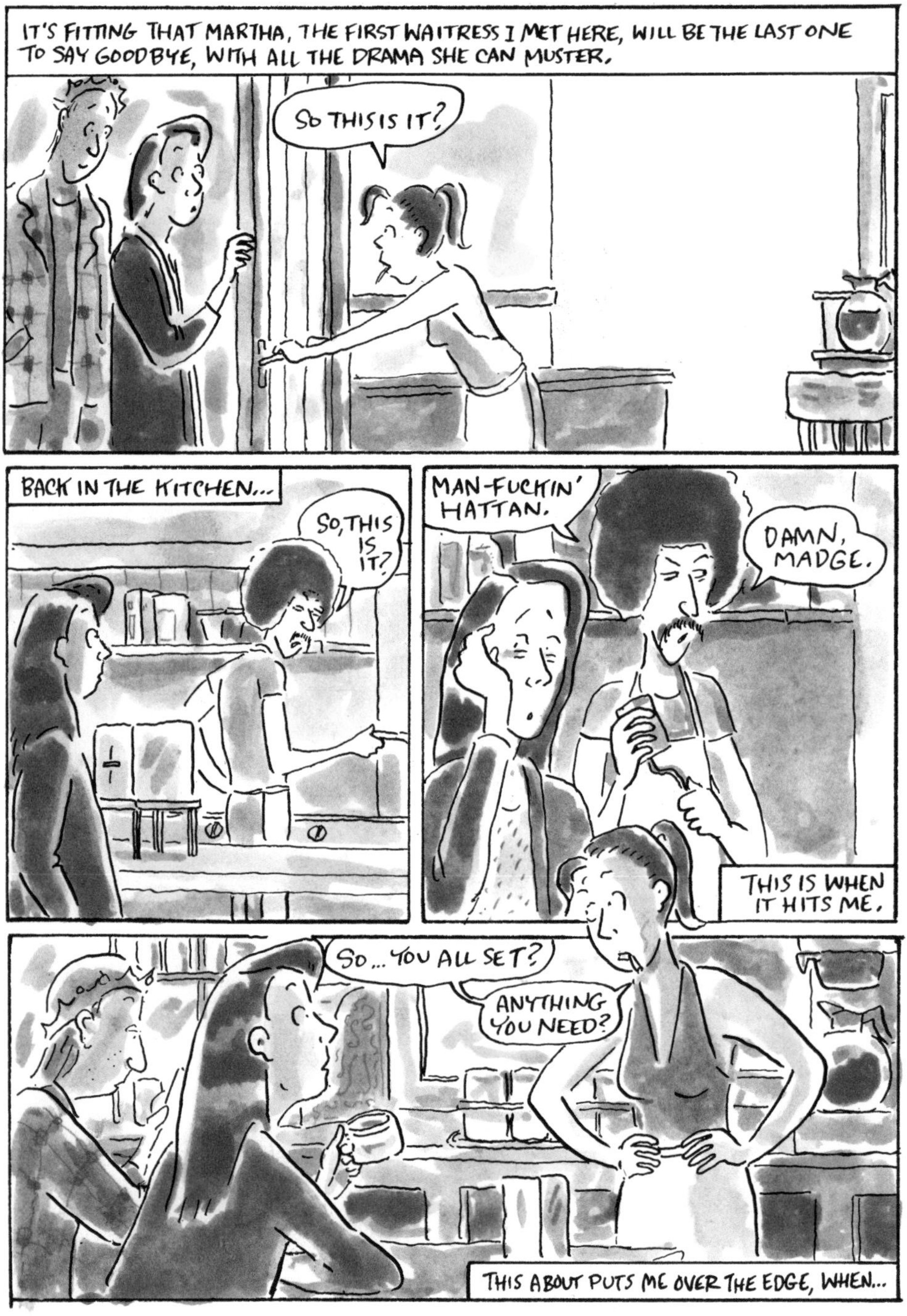
IT'S FITTING THAT MARTHA, THE FIRST WAITRESS I MET HERE, WILL BE THE LAST ONE TO SAY GOODBYE, WITH ALL THE DRAMA SHE CAN MUSTER.
SO THIS IS IT?
BACK IN THE KITCHEN...
SO, THIS IS IT?
MAN-FUCKIN' HATTAN.
DAMN, MADGE.
THIS IS WHEN IT HITS ME.
SO... YOU ALL SET?
ANYTHING YOU NEED?
THIS ABOUT PUTS ME OVER THE EDGE, WHEN...

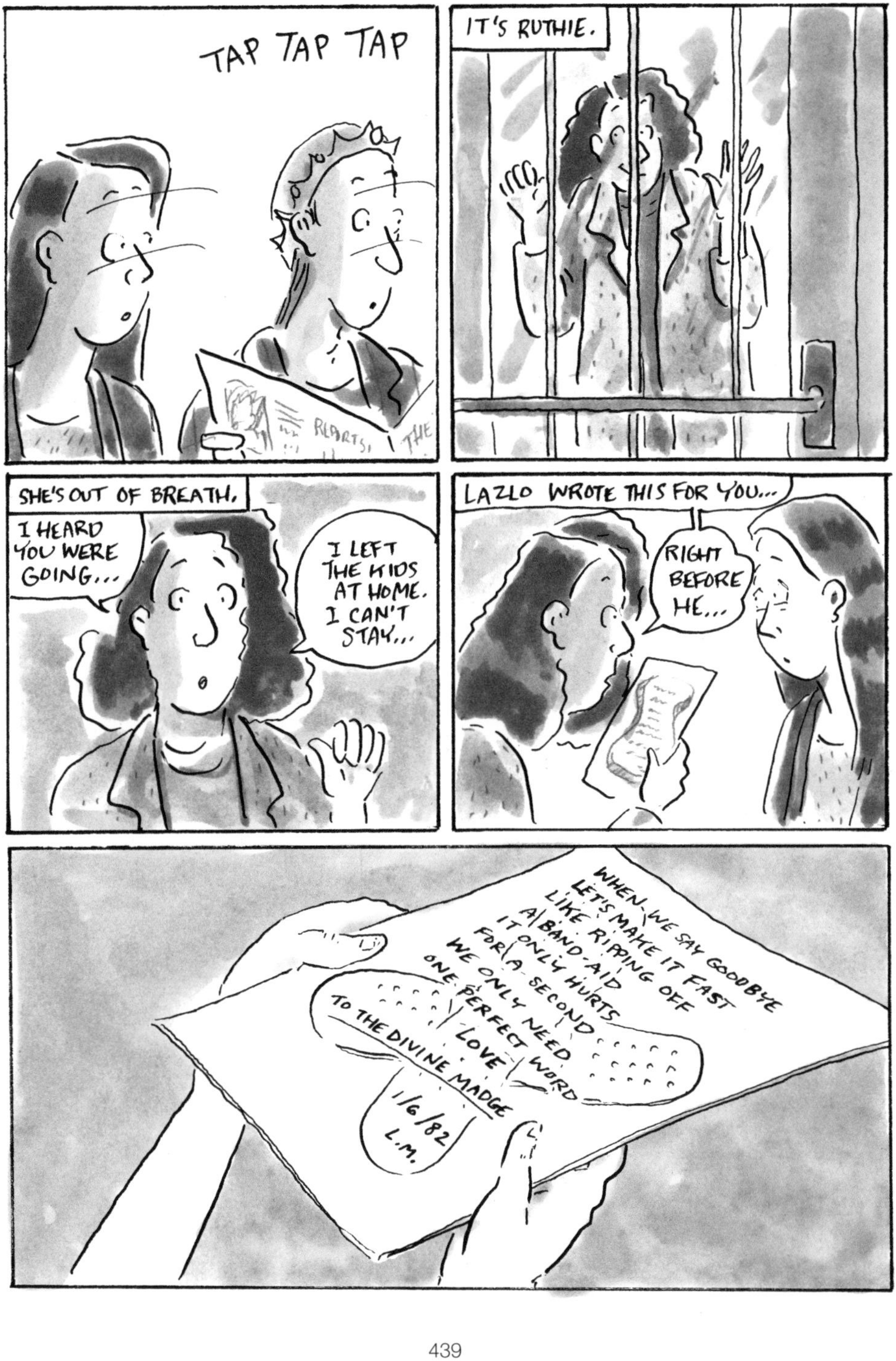
TAP TAP TAP
IT'S RUTHIE.
SHE'S OUT OF BREATH.
I HEARD YOU WERE GOING...
I LEFT THE KIDS AT HOME. I CAN'T STAY...
LAZLO WROTE THIS FOR YOU...
RIGHT BEFORE HE...
WHEN WE SAY GOODBYE
LET'S MAKE IT FAST
LIKE RIPPING OFF
A BAND-AID
IT ONLY HURTS
FOR A SECOND
WE ONLY NEED
ONE PERFECT WORD
LOVE
TO THE DIVINE MADGE
1/6/82
L.M.

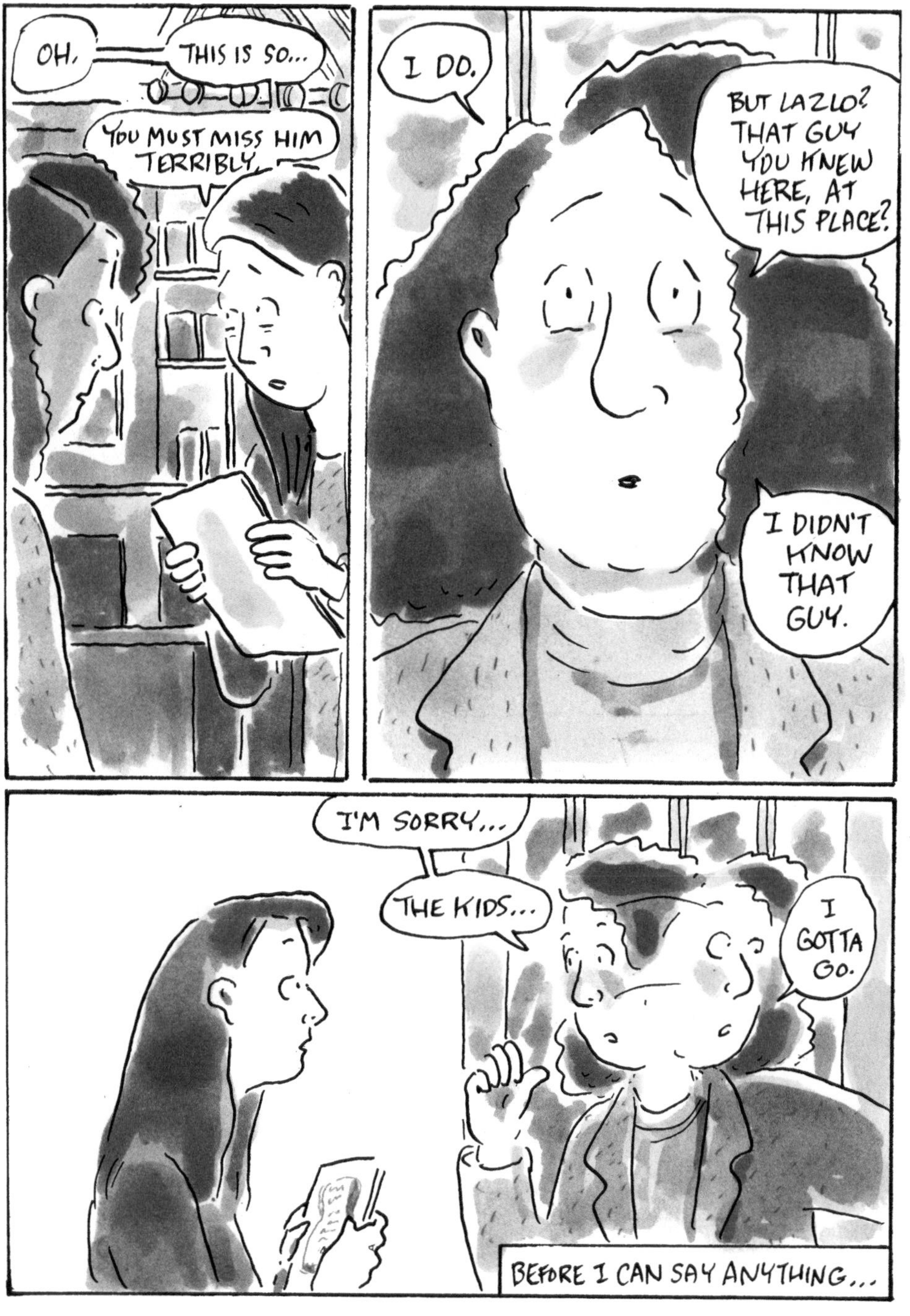
OH,
THIS IS SO...
YOU MUST MISS HIM TERRIBLY.
I DO.
BUT LAZLO? THAT GUY YOU KNEW HERE, AT THIS PLACE?
I DIDN'T KNOW THAT GUY.
I'M SORRY...
THE KIDS...
I GOTTA GO.
BEFORE I CAN SAY ANYTHING...